SMITHSON
BUREAU OF AN
BU

A DICTIONARY
OF THE CHOCTAW LANGUAGE

BY

CYRUS BYINGTON

EDITED BY

JOHN R. SWANTON AND HENRY S. HALBERT

WASHINGTON
GOVERNMENT PRINTING OFFICE
1915

CYRUS BYINGTON

LETTER OF TRANSMITTAL

Smithsonian Institution,
Bureau of American Ethnology,
Washington, D. C., April 22, 1909.

Sir: I have the honor to submit herewith for publication, with your approval, as a bulletin of this Bureau the manuscript of "A Dictionary of the Choctaw Language," by the late Cyrus Byington, under the editorship of Dr. John R. Swanton.[1]

Very respectfully, yours,

W. H. Holmes, *Chief.*

Dr. Charles D. Walcott,
Secretary of the Smithsonian Institution.

---

[1] Subsequently, as stated in Dr. Swanton's Introduction, Mr. Henry S. Halbert became associated with him in the editorship.

CONTENTS

	Page.
Introduction	VII
Phonetic key	X
Choctaw-English vocabulary	1
English-Choctaw index	379

ILLUSTRATION

PLATE 1. Cyrus Byington.. frontispiece

A DICTIONARY OF THE CHOCTAW LANGUAGE

By Cyrus Byington

EDITED BY

John R. Swanton and Henry S. Halbert

INTRODUCTION

By John R. Swanton

This dictionary represents a portion of the results of nearly fifty years of missionary service among the Choctaw Indians on the part of its compiler, Rev. Cyrus Byington. Mr. Byington was also the author of translations into Choctaw of several books of both the Old and the New Testament, Choctaw almanacs, a Choctaw definer, a grammar of the Choctaw language, and some minor writings. His grammar, edited by Dr. D. G. Brinton, was published in Philadelphia in 1871, in the *Proceedings of the American Philosophical Society* (vol. 11, pp. 317–367). In the introduction to this grammar Dr. Brinton gives the following account of the author's life:

This eminent scholar and missionary, whose name is inseparably connected with the later history of the Choctaw nation, was born at Stockbridge, Berkshire County, Mass., March 11, 1793. He was one of nine children, and his parents were in humble circumstances, but industrious and respected. His father was at one time a tanner, and subsequently a small farmer. Necessarily, therefore, his early education was limited.

When a well-grown lad he was taken into the family of Mr. Joseph Woodbridge, of his native town, from whom he received some instruction in Latin and Greek, and with whom he afterward read law. In 1814 he was admitted to the bar, and practiced a few years with success in Stockbridge and Sheffield, Mass.

His father though a moral was not a religious man, and it seems to have been only after he reached manhood that Mr. Byington became, as he expressed it, "a subject of divine grace." He then resolved to forsake the bar and devote himself to missionary life. With this object in view he entered the theological school at Andover, Mass., where he studied Hebrew and theology, and was licensed to preach, September, 1819. At this time he hoped to go to the Armenians in Turkey. But Providence had prepared for him another and an even more laborious field.

For about a year he preached in various churches in Massachusetts, awaiting some opportunity for missionary labor. Toward the close of the summer of 1819, a company of 20 or 25 persons left Hampshire County, Mass., under the direction of the American Board of Missions, to go by land to the Choctaw nation, then resident in Mississippi. They passed through Stockbridge, in September, and were provided with a letter from the Board, asking Mr. Byington to take charge of them, and pilot them to their destination. He was ready at a few hours' notice.

The company journeyed by land to Pittsburgh, where they procured flatboats, and floated down the Ohio and Mississippi to a point near the mouth of the Yalobusha River, whence a land journey of 200 miles brought them to their destination. . . .

Throughout his missionary life Mr. Byington appreciated the value which a knowledge of the language and traditions of the Choctaws would have to scholars. From his arrival among them, therefore, he devoted assiduous labor to their language with a view to comprehend its extremely difficult construction, and to render it available for the missionary and philological student. The first draft of his Grammar was completed in 1834. It was written and rewritten, until at the time of his death, which occurred at Belprè, Ohio, December 31st, 1868, he was at work upon the seventh revisal.

As left by Mr. Byington, the Choctaw dictionary consisted of five paper-bound folio volumes, having entries on both sides of the leaves; the whole work was modeled after the English or classical dictionary of the author's time. Separate entries were therefore made of the same word when used as noun, adjective, verb, etc., each followed by a letter indicating the proper part of speech. The phonetic system was constructed for the greater part by employing the English letter representing most closely the Indian sound. Only two innovations were introduced—the use of v (a true v sound not being present in the Choctaw language) for the obscure a, and of lines under the vowels to indicate nasalization. For these devices I have substituted the more commonly used a and ^{n}. I have also changed the aspirated l (hl) into l. The sh and ch have been allowed to stand, although it is now customary to represent these by c and tc, respectively. Furthermore, in many instances I have combined in one word syllables separated by Mr. Byington and later missionaries—as, for instance, the syllables indicating pronominal relations, the reflexive, the negative, and some of the tense signs—for it is evident that in these cases the syllables all constitute one complex. Undoubtedly absolute accuracy has not been attained in this particular, but the course followed is certainly a move in the right direction. With the exceptions just mentioned the material is reproduced substantially as recorded by the author. It would be fair neither to Mr. Byington nor to the editors, however, to present the dictionary as a finished work. In the quotation given above Doctor Brinton speaks of the great care which the missionary bestowed on the manuscript of his grammar when preparing it for the press; unfortunately he had opportunity to make only a beginning in the editing of his dictionary. Many entries consisted merely of brief notes to be elaborated later or of references to cases not observed elsewhere and to be explained by further investigations. But the plan which Mr. Byington had set before himself for his dictionary is one not now of much value to students of American languages, and to carry it to completion along those lines would involve an enormous amount of unprofitable labor.   Therefore the work is presented almost as he left it, as a source of valuable linguistic, and also ethnologic, information faithfully recorded by one of the most capable of the early missionaries at a time when many things were to be learned which are now doubtless entirely forgotten.   In order to increase the utility of the dictionary an English-Choctaw index has been compiled and appended, which will make it possible to find where information is to be had regarding the Choctaw equivalent of each English word or phrase given.   This part is in no sense a dictionary, nor is it to be regarded as such.

As might naturally have been expected, Mr. Byington's inspiring motive was his desire to translate the Biblical writings into Choctaw and to further the conversion of the Choctaw tribe to the Christian religion.   The present work contains therefore numerous references to early translations of the Biblical writings undertaken by him. From the changes incorporated into later editions it is evident that the exact shade of meaning was not always determined in those first efforts, but, in any event, perhaps it could only have been approximated, and no attempt has been made to alter the references except in a few cases where palpable errors had been made.   Nevertheless, these citations have been verified as far as possible and a few question marks inserted where no words resembling the ones under consideration could be found.   In other instances it will be noticed that Mr. Byington has ignored certain affixes of common occurrence which alter the exact form as it appears in the text.

Anciently there were several Choctaw dialects, but only one of these, that of the Sixtowns Indians living in the southern part of the old Choctaw country, differed to any considerable degree from the standard, or Longtown, dialect spoken in the western part of the Nation. Moreover, this difference seems to have been confined mainly to certain words, involving but very slightly the language as a whole.   A number of these Sixtowns words will be found interspersed throughout the present work.

It has been my good fortune to have enlisted as coeditor Mr. Henry S. Halbert, of the Department of Archives and History, Montgomery, Ala., who has spent many years of his life among the Choctaw Indians, is familiar with their language, and is an enthusiastic student of everything relating to the history and present culture of the tribe. While he has noted and corrected many errors, he has deemed it best to let certain doubtful words and sentences stand as in the original manuscript, with the idea that they may represent certain dialectic or archaic variations which have escaped him.

Acknowledgment is here made of the courtesy of Mrs. Eliza Innes, of Lockesburg, Ark., daughter of the Rev. Cyrus Byington, and of that of her son, Mr. E. S. Byington, of Broken Bow, Okla., in placing at the disposal of the Bureau the photograph from which the accompanying portrait of the author was reproduced; also his note-books for the years 1844–46 and 1861.

Abbreviations.—While a great many abbreviations have been used, most of these will be readily understood. C. B. or B. indicates the compiler, Cyrus Byington; J. R. S. and H. S. H., the editors, John R. Swanton, and Henry S. Halbert, respectively. Of the other abbreviations the principal are the following: a., adjective; adv., adverb; caus., causative; con., connective; dem., demonstrative; dim. or dimin., diminutive; fem. or f., feminine; freq., frequentative; imp., imperative; mas. or m., masculine; n., noun; nas. form or n. f., nasal form; per., personal; pl. or plu., plural; pro., pronoun, also prolonged; ref., reflexive; sing. or s., singular; v. a. i., active intransitive verb; v. i., intransitive verb; v. n., neuter verb; v. t., transitive verb. Besides these will be found the names and initials of various Choctaw Indians who are given as authorities for certain forms, and abbreviations of the names of other works in the Choctaw language.

The description of Choctaw phonetics which follows is taken from the first page of the manuscript dictionary, only such changes having been made as were necessitated by the innovations already referred to.

PHONETIC KEY

ALPHABET

Letters	Sounded
A a	as *a* in father.
Ạ ạ	as *u* in tub, and *a* in above, around.
B b	as in English.
Ch ch	as in church.
E e	as *e* in they, and short *e* as in met.
F f	as in English.
H h	as in English.
I i	as *i* in marine and short as *i* in pin.
K k	as in English.
L l	as in English.
Ł ł	as an aspirated *l*.
M m	as in English.
N n	as in English.
O o	as *o* in note, go.
P p	as in English.
S s	as in sir; never as *s* in his.
Sh sh	as in shall.
T t	as in English.
U u.	as *oo* in wool, *u* in full.
W w	as in war, we.
Y y	as in you.

DIPHTHONGS

Ai ai	as *i* in pine.
Au au	as *ow* in now, how.

NASALIZED VOWELS

A^n a^n
I^n i^n
O^n o^n
U^n u^n

These are pure nasals, and retain the vowel sounds, except before the letter k, in which case they are like the long *ang, ing, ong, ung.* The usual sound is softer than *ang*, and like that of the French vowel followed by n in the same syllable.

CONSONANTS AND VOWELS

Let it be remembered that each consonant has but one sound and that the sounds ascribed to the vowels are such as they have, respectively, in accented syllables; in unaccented syllables they have the sound of short vowels. English readers should remember not to give the English sound to the vowels, except as noted in the alphabet.

a^n, i^n, o^n, and u^n, or some of them, are used as separate words or final syllables. They are used also before the consonants and semivowels b, f, h, k, m, n, s, sh, w, and y. Before the consonant p, sometimes before b and the vowels, for the sake of euphony the letter m is added, or the nasal sound becomes m of necessity from the position of the organs of speech at that time, as *am, im, om, um.*

Before *ch, l, t,* and *l* the letter n is added, as *an, in, on, un,* and before the vowels in many words the letter n is added to the nasal. a^n is never used; a^n is used in its place. The vowel e is never used as a nasal, i^n being used in its place.

In making these remarks general rules are stated. It is not to be supposed that each and all of the nasals are thus used. There are exceptions, which the student must be ready to notice. An unwritten language has its anomalies and irregularities.

CHOCTAW—ENGLISH
VOCABULARY

a, the first letter of the alphabet, sounded as *a* in father.

a (when followed by a verb beginning with a consonant), adv. or locative particle or prefix, means there, in that place, at that time, at, from, on, in, of, by; when the verb begins with a vowel, *a* becomes *ai; achumpa,* to bury at; *aminti,* to come from; *aiilli,* to die at or in. *a* and *ai* are used where in English place is used; *nusi,* to sleep; *anusi,* a sleeping place; *aiimpa,* an eating place, a plate, dining room, table; *chikaiamiho,* repeated in Matt. 5: 35; of, in *chianukshopa,* he is afraid of you; *chiatoba,* he is begotten of you: by, in *aiokchaⁿya,* to live by, Matt. 4: 4: used as a sign of the future tense; *chi chia,* cf. John 1: 49; *achiⁿ, ahe, ahinla; atuk, ashke,* as *satoshbihashke; siakmat,* hymn 66, v. 2: prefixed to a verb often changes the verb to a noun, as *aminti,* a source; literally, to come from; *isht ahachia,* see John 15: 3; *aiatta,* a residence; lit., to stay at. *a* and *ai* are much used as prefixes in compounding words: prefixed to some cardinals the latter become ordinals, as *tuklo,* two; *atukla,* second; *atuchina,* third; and before a vowel *a* becomes *ai,* as *ushta,* four; *aiushta,* fourth: an intensive before consonants; *aputta, abillia, afehna:* used before *tuk* and *tok* and their compounds *a* partakes of the sense of a definite article or of a relative pronoun. *Sabannahatuk,* that which I wanted; "This is used when the person has some doubt as to obtaining the thing sought, while *sabannashke* indicates a certainty in the expectation."—J. Hudson.

a, ah, v. a. i., to say, to tell, to call; *ali,* I say; *alikamo,* I did say, and you know it; *imalikashkint,* I told him so before, or that is what I told him, and you heard it (*kashkint* implies previous knowledge on the part of the hearer as well as on that of the speaker); *alahe keyu,* I should not call, Acts, 10 : 28.

aⁿ [cf. *at*]. 1. A determinative particle in the objective case after nouns and meaning the; as, *wak aⁿ pisali,* I see the cow. Sometimes this article is pronounced *haⁿ* and *yaⁿ* [cf. *hat* and *yat*] for euphony. It is also a sign of, or with, the future tense, and is used as a particle of specification or emphasis after verbs in present, future, and past tenses; *iⁿnukhaⁿklotok aⁿ,* Luke 10: 37; *katimichilahe aⁿ,* future tense, Luke 18: 41; *hoponayolahe aⁿ,* Luke 18: 41. See Matt. 15: 31 for instances in the past tense; [also] *onaⁿshahatok,* Matt. 28: 2. *Cheluselem aⁿ,* Jerusalem it, Matt. 2: 1. 2. A relative pronoun in the objective case after verbs and adjectives and equivalent to the English relatives the which, the one which, that which, etc. It may also be translated by the personal pronouns him, her, it, them, as *Lakab aⁿ,* Rachab her, Matt. 1: 5. It is sometimes written *haⁿ* or *yaⁿ;* cf. *hat* and *yat.* The aspirated forms are *ah, hah,* and *yah.*

aⁿ, a dative pronoun first per. sing., my; to or for me; as, *aⁿholisso,* my book. Written also *am* and *an;* as *amisuba,* my horse, lit., horse to or for me; *aⁿholitopa,* Matt. 3: 17. When it stands before a verb, or a word where a verb is understood, it is generally translated by a preposition; as, for me, to me, of me, from me; *aⁿholissochi,* write for me, or to me; *aⁿpota,* lend me; *aⁿchumpa,* buy of me, or buy for me; written also *am,* as *amithana,* to learn of me. In the negative forms this pronoun is written *saⁿ* and *sam;* as *iksaⁿchumpo, iksamiksho,* I have none, or there is none by me; *chiksaⁿpeso,* you have not seen of mine, or for me.

abaha, n., a mortar for mixing meat and corn by beating or braying; a meat mortar.

abaiya, n., the side, as the side of a creek, swamp, or road.

abaiya, v. a. i., to be along the side of; to lie along the side of.

abaiyạchi, v. a. i., to go along the side of; to roam up and down; to range; to wind its way, as a bullet discharged and lodged in a deer, or a man going along on the side of a swamp.

abaiyạchi, n., a roamer; one that goes along the side of a creek, etc.

abaiyạchi, adv., lengthwise (of a field); ahekạchi (of cloth), q. v.

abaiyạka, n., the side of a swamp or creek.

abaiyạt, adv., alongside of, along; as abaiyạt aⁿya, two verbs connected by the letter t, meaning to be at the side of and go along; bok abaiyạt aⁿya, to go along the side of the creek; hina abaiyạt aⁿya, to go along the roadside.

abakli, v. a. i. pl., to split into large pieces, blocks, slabs, or bolts for shingles.

abakli, pass., split; split into bolts.

abakli, n., the place where the wood is split; a split.

abaklichi, v. t. caus., to split into large pieces; to score off large pieces when hewing logs.

abaklichi, n., a splitter; a scorer.

abaksacheka, n., a declivity; a side hill, or mountain side, 2 Sam. 16: 13.

ạbaksileka, n., a mountain side; the mountain side.

abaksha, ạbbaksha, n., the name of the serpent commonly called chicken snake.

ạbana, pass. of abạnni; aiitạbana, founded upon, Matt. 7: 25.

abanali, v. tr. or intr., to lay on the neck, or shoulder; hạshilabanali, Matt. 11: 29, 30; isht iabạnali, Luke 15: 5.

abani, v. t. (pass., ạlbạni), to cure by drying over a fire; "to barbecue;" wak nipi abani, to cure beef; takkon abani, to dry peaches over a fire.

abani, n., a curer; one who cures meat or fruit over a fire.

abasa, n. [from abạsli, to lay laths], lath; the ribs of a roof.

abasali, v. i., to sprout; to germinate; tanchi ạt abasali, the corn sprouts.

abasali, ạbasạlih, n., a sprout.

abasalichi, v. t. caus., to cause to sprout.

abạchechi, v. t. caus., to practice; to teach by practice.

abạchi, v. t., to teach, Matt. 15: 9; imabạchi, Matt. 5: 2; abahanchi, Matt. 13: 52, 54; holisso haⁿ imabạchi, to teach him the book or the letters. Passive ạlbạchi.

abạchi, v. a. i., to practice; to learn by practice; to exercise.

abạchi, n., a practicer.

abạchi, n., an exercise; a practice; nan isht imabạchi, his doctrine.

abạnkạchi, pl. pass., laid across; lying crosswise, as timbers at the corner of a house, or as rails in a worm fence.

abạnni, v. t. pl., to lay across, as the logs of a house; abana, pass. sing., laid across; itabana, pass., laid across one another, as house logs at the corners; itabạnni, to raise a log house; to lay across one another.

abạsli, v. t., to lay laths; to lath; to lay the ribs of a roof.

abạsli, n., he that lays laths.

abạslichi, v. t., to cause laths to lie.

abạsha, n., a sawpit; a place cut with a knife, a saw, or an ax; a gash.

abạsha, n., a place sawn; a cut with a knife; a wound; a gash made by a knife, scythe, sickle, or ax; harvest, Matt. 13: 30; abạsha, pp., sawed at.

abạsha, n., a mill; a sawmill.

abạshli, v. t., to cut at; to cut there or upon with a knife, scythe, or sickle, or an ax, except in cutting wood; to cut with a drawing motion; chanli is to cut with a striking motion.

abạshpoa, n., a place swept; paⁿshpoa, pass., swept, Matt. 12: 44; Luke 11: 25.

abeha, v. a. i. pl., to be in, Matt. 2: 11; to enter in; okhissa iskitinosi akoⁿ hạsh aiabehashke, enter ye in at the strait gate, Matt. 7: 13; to go in; ont ilabehaheakoⁿ, we go away into, Matt. 8: 31; also, Matt. 12: 45; 14: 22. Passive, ạlbeha, John 6: 22; 21: 3.

abeha, pass. pl., put in; put on; rammed in.

abeha, a., fraught; full.

abeha, n., those which are in or on.

abehkạchi, v. a. i. pl., to be clothed, Matt. 11: 8; Rev. 7: 9; na fohka hofaloha abehkạchi, Mark 12: 38.

abehma, a., farther up; higher up; abehma talalituk, he set up. See abema.

abehpa [from *abeha*], v. a. i. dual, to enter; to come in.

abeka, n., sickness; disease; malady; illness; a disorder; a distemper; an indisposition; *isht abeka*, infection, lit., sick with, or by means of; cause of sickness.

abeka, n., the sick; the person or persons affected with disease; *abeka imaⁿsha*, their sick, Matt. 14: 14.

abeka, a., sick; unwell; diseased; indisposed; out of health; disordered; ill; sickly; unsound; *isht abeka*, a., infected; sick with; neg., *ikabeko*, salubrious; not sickly. See Matt. 9: 2.

abeka, v. t., to be sick; to be unwell, diseased, or indisposed.

abeka, v. a. i., to sicken; *isht abeka*, sick of, Matt. 8: 6, 14; 9: 6.

abeka, pass., distempered.

abeka apistikeli, n., a nurse; a watcher.

abeka apistikeli, v. t., to watch the sick; to nurse; to tend the sick.

abeka chuhmi, a., poorly; sickly; somewhat sick.

abeka haleli, v. t., to take a disease by infection; to catch sickness.

abeka haleli, n., contagion; infection.

abeka haleli, a., contagious; infectious; catching.

abeka lakna, n., the yellow fever; jaundice; lit., yellow sickness.

abeka okpulo, n., a fatal or mortal sickness; applied to a pest; a pestilence; a plague; the cholera.

abeka shali, n., sickliness; a., sickly.

abeka shali, n., an invalid.

abeka yatuk, v. t., that were diseased, Matt. 14: 35.

abekachi, v. t. caus., to sicken; to make sick; to disease; to distemper; to indispose; *isht abekachi*, v. t., to infect; to sicken by means of; *ilabekachi*, 2 Sam. 13: 2, 5, 6.

abekoma, v. a. i., to be sickly, as *Timoli abekoma*, 1 Tim. 5 (heading).

abela (from *abili*), pp. poled; bushed.

abela, n., the place or thing poled or bushed.

abeli, v. t. pl. of *fohki*, to put in, Mark 12: 42; to put on; to ring, i. e., to fit with a ring, as the fingers; to stuff.

abeli, n., he who puts on or in.

abema, abehma (from *aba* and *ima*), v. i., to be half way; to be higher up.

abenili, abinili (from *a*, there, and *binili*, to sit), v. a. i., to sit down at; to settle at, as in making any place a home.

abenili, abinili, abenili, n., a settler; a colonist; the sitting down or meeting, as at a "cry;" a colony, see *okla wiha abinili*, Acts 16: 12.

abenilichi, abinilichi, v. t., to settle; to establish in business or in life, or at any place.

abenilichi, abinilichi, n., one that settles another in a place, or in business.

abeta, abita, passive of *abili*, poled.

abi, v. t., to kill, Gen. 37: 26. See *abi*, from which *abi* is derived by lengthening the first vowel; *abitok aⁿ*, which killed, Luke 13: 4.

abicha, abicheli, n., a tap hole; a bung-hole; a faucet; a spout.

abichakali, a., nineteen.

abichakaliha, adv., nineteen times; *abichakaliha pisali kamo*, I did see it nineteen times.

abicheli, see abicha.

abicheli isht akamassa, n., a spigot; a spile.

abichkachi, n. pl., tap holes.

abila, v. a. i., to thaw, as snow or ice; to thaw there; to melt at or there; pl., *abela; (taloa kat sachuⁿkash a abelah*— J. E.); *ikabilo*, or *ikabelo*, a., undissolved, where it does not melt.

abilia, adv., always, John 11: 42.

abila, pass. of *abili*, poled; bushed; pointed at.

abilepa, n., the place aimed at, or pointed at.

abilepa, a., seated round.

abilepa, v. a. i., to be seated round.

abili, v. t. pl., to set in by the ends; to stick; to pole; to bush; to furnish with poles or bushes, as peas or beans.

abilibli, v. t. sing., to point at a place or thing, some object.

abina, n., a camp; a lodging out of doors with or without a shelter overhead.

abina, v. i., to camp; to encamp; to lodge out of doors.

abinachi, n., an encampment.

abinanchi, n., a place where a camp is being made, Josh. 4: 8. [the ed. of 1852 has *abinachi*].

abinanchi, v. t., to be making a camp at.

abinạchi, v. t., to make a camp.

abinili, abenili (q. v.), v. i. sing., to sit at or on; to settle at.

abinili, pass., peopled.

abinili, n., a settler.

abinili, n., settlement; the place where one sits; a seat; a pew; *abinit* is contracted from *abinili*.

abinilichi, see *abenilichi*.

abinilit nan apesa, abinit nan apesa, n., a judgment seat.

abinołi, v. a. i. pl. of *abinili*.

abinołi, n. pl., settlers.

abinołi, n. pl., settlements.

abinołichi, v. t. pl., to settle; to establish at a place; to colonize; to cause to take seats, as children or visitors.

abinot maⁿya, to sit round.

abishlichi, n., a milk pail; any vessel to milk into.

abita, see *abeta*.

aboha, n., a house; a building; a dwelling; a residence; a cabin; a room; a dome; a domicile; a door, as *abohaⁿsha*, he is indoors; a fabric; a habitation; housing; a lodging; a mansion, Matt. 17: 25; Luke 15: 8; *ạmaboha yaⁿ*, under my roof, Matt. 8: 8.

aboha abạska, n., a gaming house; a gambling room.

aboha achạfa, n., one room; the other room; a single room.

aboha afoha, n., an inn; a house of rest.

aboha ahoponi, n., a kitchen; a cook room; a galley or caboose on shipboard.

aboha aiimpa, n., a dining room; an inn; a tavern; a refectory; an eating house.

aboha aioⁿholmo itiitikołi, n. pl., rafters of a house; sing., *aboha aioⁿholmo itiitikili*, a rafter.

aboha anusechi, v. t., to entertain; to lodge in a room.

aboha anusi, n., a bedroom; a lodging room; a dormitory; a bower; a chamber, 2 Sam. 13: 10.

aboha anutaka, n., the place under a house.

aboha anutaka kula, n., a cellar.

aboha apalạska, n., a bake house; a bakery.

aboha apisa, n., a glass window; a house window.

aboha apisa aiạlbiha, n., a window sash.

aboha apishia, n., a piazza; a veranda; a shed that extends quite round the house.

aboha aⁿshaka okhissạ, n., a back door; a door in the rear of a house.

aboha atampa, n., an adjoining room; a separate room; a spare room.

aboha ayupi, n., a bath room; a bathing house.

aboha chaha, n., a tower; a high house.

aboha chito, n., a hall; a large house.

aboha hanta, n., a white house; a house of peace; a senate house; a state house; a fane.

aboha hanta okla, n., Congress.

aboha holitopa, aboha holitompa (Matt. 26: 69), n., a palace; a temple; a sacred house; a costly house.

aboha hoshontika, aboha hoshintika, aboha iⁿhoshuntika, aboha impạta, n., a porch; a piazza; a portico; a veranda; a stoop; a gallery.

aboha inluksi, n., a house padlock.

aboha inpaiasha, n., a larder; a meat house.

aboha intula, n., the foundation of a house; the sill.

aboha iskitini, n., a cabin; a cot; a hut; a lodge; a small house.

aboha isht holmo, n., a roof; a shingle; a split board.

aboha isht holmoạli, n., eaves of a house; edge of the roof.

aboha isht okhilishta, n., a house door.

aboha itabana, pass., built, as a house.

aboha itabana, n., a building; a log house.

aboha itabạnni, v. t., to build a log house; to put up a house; to raise a log house.

aboha itabạnni, n., a house raiser; a house builder.

aboha itatapa, n., an apartment; an adjoining room; an additional room.

aboha itintakla, n., a hall; space way; the place between two or more houses.

aboha itipatạlhpo, n., a house floor.

aboha ititakla, n., the hall, entry, or passage; a space between the houses or the rooms.

aboha ḳạllo, n., a prison; a jail; a castle; a fortress; a strong room; a citadel; a dungeon; a prison house; a ward, Matt. 5: 25; 11: 2; 14: 3; 25: 36; Acts 16: 23; hold, Acts 4: 3.

aboha ḳạllo apistikeli, n., a jailer; the keeper of a prison.

aboha ḳạllo apistikeli, v. t., to keep a jail; to guard a prison.

aboha ḳạllo ạlhpinta, pl., the prisoners; see Acts 16: 25.

aboha ḳạllo chaha, n., a tower.

aboha ḳạllo foka, n., imprisonment; incarceration.

aboha ḳạllo foka, pp., imprisoned; confined in prison; confined; immured; incarcerated; prisoned.

aboha ḳạllo foka, v. i., to lie in jail; to be in prison.

aboha ḳạllo foka, n. sing., a prisoner; a jail bird.

aboha ḳạllo foki, v. t. sing., aboha ḳạllo apitta, pl., to put in jail; to confine; to immure; to incarcerate; to prison; to imprison; to cast into prison.

aboha ḳạllo foki, n., an imprisoner.

aboha kinạffi, v. t., to take down a house.

aboha kuchichi, v. t., to unhouse; to turn out of a house; to turn out of doors.

aboha mismiki, n., a house with a roof nailed on.

aboha nan aiachefa, n., a laundry; a wash room; the room where clothes are washed.

aboha nan chukushpa, n., household stuff; furniture; aboha iⁿnan chokushpa, its furniture.

aboha nana aiasha, n., a lumber room; a lumber house.

aboha pakna, n., roof of a house, Josh 2: 6, 8.

aboha toshbi, n., rubbish.

abohush ạtta, n., a cottager.

abohushi, n. (dimin.), lit., "son of a room," a closet, Matt. 6: 6; a cottage; a cot; a small room; a hut.

abohushi fohka, pp., closeted; put in a closet.

abohushi fohki, v. t., to closet.

abohushi foⁿka, a., being in a closet.

aboluktoli, v. t., to surround there.

aboli, n., a thicket; a brake; a hedge.

aboli, n., a place of deposit; place of laying down anything; a deposit, Mark 12: 41.

abolichi, v. t., to hit, as fạni iti oyiatuk aⁿ abolichi, hit the squirrel that was going up the tree; iti isht pạla abolichi, strike the wedge.

abonulli, v. t. sing., to roll up in; to fold up in; to infold; to inwrap; nan tạnna kashofa linen achukma hoⁿ abonulli, wrapped it in a clean linen cloth, Matt. 27: 59; linen aⁿ abonulli, wrapped him in the linen, Mark 15: 46; na lapushki linen oⁿ abonullit . . . fohkitok, wrapped it in linen and laid it in, Luke 2: 7; 23: 53; nalilati oⁿ abonulli, Acts 5: 6.

abonullichi, v. t. caus., to cause it to be rolled up in; to wrap it up.

abonunta, pass. sing., rolled up; being rolled up in; ulloⁿsi ạt nalilali oⁿ abonunta, the babe wrapped in swaddling clothes, Luke 2: 12.

abonunta, n., a wrapper.

abuⁿkachi, pass. pl., infolded; inwrapped; rolled up in; rolled up.

abukbo, n., down, the fine soft feathers of fowls, particularly water-fowls.

abunni, v. t. pl., to roll up; to double up.

achafa (from chạfa, to run), v. t. sing., ayilepa, pl. to run after; to run down; achafat ạbi, to run down and kill.

achaⁿfa, a. (nasal form, from achạfa one), being one out of a number.

achafoa, a., a few and scattering; here and there one; not many; rare; precious, 1 Sam. 3: 1; achafoa, pass., singled out.

achafoachi, v. t. caus., to select a few; to take a few; to cause a few to be taken.

achafoha, v. i., to be a few; achafoⁿha (nasal form), being a few.

achafolechi, ạchafolichi, v. t. caus., to select a few; to take here and there one; to single out, Matt. 25: 32.

achafoli, v. t., to select a few.

achaka, n., a continuation.

achaka, pass., spliced (from achakạli), continued; itạchaka, pass., joined together, reannexed, spliced, united, welded; ikitạchako, a., unconnected, not welded.

achaⁿka, a. (nasal form), succeeding, following, next; *itachaⁿka*, v. a. i., to join together.

achakalechi, v. t., to continue; to add.

achakachi, v. t., to cause to advance.

achakalechi, v. t. caus., to continue; to add on; to join to; *itachakalechi*, v. t., to reannex; *achakalinchi* (nasal form), to add; to continue; *achakalinchimat*, he added when, Luke 19: 11.

achakali, v. t. sing., to splice; to add to; to new lay an edge tool; applied to putting edge to an ax; to piece; to scarf; to subjoin; to unite; to weld; *itachakali*, to splice together; to couple; to join; to scarf; *hash ilachakali*, Matt. 6: 27.

achakali, achakallechi, n., one that splices, or new lays.

achakali, v. i. (*achakanli*, nasal form; *achakakanli* freq.), to advance, to continue; *aba chakali* Josh. 5: 13 and *akka-chakali*, are perhaps formed from this word.

achakli, v. t. pl. of *achakali*, to splice, etc.; *alhchaka*, pass. sing.; *alhchakoa*, pass. pl.; *itachakli* (Heb. 4: 12), "joints;" *itachakachi*, n., a joint; v. t., to splice and join together.

achakli, n., one that splices.

achaya, v. i., to be wont; to be accustomed to a place, as animals; *wak at achayat taha*, the cattle are wont; *ikachayo*, a., unwonted.

achaⁿya, n., a cutting block; a chopping block; place cut, or wounded; a gash made by an ax; pass., wounded at, or there; n., a wound.

achayachi, v. t. caus., to accustom a creature to a place so that it will stay there; to wont; to habituate to a place.

achaba, asalbash, asachap, asalhchap, hahchaba, n., a log foot-bridge; a log lying across a creek on which to pass over. [*ahchap* is the word for footlog in use among the Mississippi Choctaw.—H. S. H.]

achafa, achaffa, n., oneness; singleness; a unit; unity.

achafa, a., one; the other; another; a; an; certain; individual; particular; simple; single; sole; undivided, Matt. 8: 18; 12: 6; 17: 4; *salap achafa*, one; *nanashachi achafa*, Luke 15: 7; *hatak*

achafa, a man, a certain man, Luke 15: 11; *ninak achafa*, a night, or all night.

achafa, v. n., to be one; to be single; *achafa yoke*, it is one; *imachafa*, for him one, or, he has one; *ikachafo*, neg. form, not one; *ibaiachafa*, Matt. 5: 25; *achaⁿfa*, nasal form.

achafa, v. a. i., *ishachafa; isht ilachafa*, Gen. 1: 11; *achafali*, I make one; I do one; *achafa sia*, I am one.

achafa atampa, a., plural; more than one.

achafa yuka, a., dist. pro., each one; *achafa aiyukat kohchat ihiⁿya mat*, John 8: 9; *achafa aiyukali*, every one, Josh. 6: 5; *hatak achafaiyukali*, man by man, Josh. 7: 16.

achafahpi (from *achafa* and *ahpi*), v. a. i., to be the first one; the being the first one: *achafampi*, nasal form and a., neither; with a neg., *achafampi keyu; achafampi kia keyu*, not either; not even one; not the first one.

achafali, v. t., to give one; to do one; to single out one, Matt. 6: 24; Gen. 2: 21; *achafalichit aiiⁿhotofahiaⁿ alhpesahatok*, for of necessity he must release one, Luke 23: 17.

achafalichi, v. t., to select out one; to make one of all, Eph. 1: 10.

achafalit, adv., *achafalit ishi*, each one take; individually take; *achafalit iⁿ-nukkilli cha*, or individually, Luke 16: 13; *achafat*, an abbreviation; *achafat ofi at abi*, for *achafalit ofi at abi*, the dog singled out one and killed it.

achafoa (see *achafoa*), John 8: 9 [in the printed edition *achafa*].

achafona, a. (from *achafa* one, and *ona* to reach to), even one; as much as one; perhaps one, Matt. 5: 30; 6: 29, 10: 29; 18: 6, 10, 12.

achafonachi, v. t., to make one; to select out one, Luke 9: 36.

achakaya, n., an addition, piece spliced on.

achakaya, a., spliced at.

achanaiya, v. i., *siachanaiya hoka* (perhaps a misprint for *siahanaiya hoka*; see *ahinna*).

achapi, ahchapi, v. t., to play at a certain game of chance in vogue among the Choctaw. This is an ancient game, not in much use now; pass., *alhchapi*.

achapi, n., a player of the above; one that plays; the play.

achchukmali, v. t., intensive form, Matt. 17: 11; to improve; to repair; to make good; to ameliorate; to benefit; to better; to rectify; to regulate; to substantiate; *ilaiachukmali*, to justify himself, *yammak ashot ilaiachukmali banna kat*, he is willing to justify himself; Luke 10: 29.

acheba, a., mischievous; troublesome.

acheba, v. n., to be mischievous.

achebachi, v. a. i., to preserve; to hold out.

achefa, ahchifa (q. v.), v. t., to wash; to cleanse, Matt. 15: 2; pass., *ahchifa*, to be washed, Mark 7: 5; *ilaiachifa*, to wash one's self, John 2: 6; to purify; pass., *alhchefa*, John 13: 10; *ikahchifo*, unwashen, Matt. 15: 20; *alhchefa*, pp., washed.

achelita, see *achillita*.

achi, v. a. i., to say; to speak; to call; to assert; to declare; to answer; quoth (as quoth he; quoth I); to rehearse; to suggest; to utter; John 1: 21; 3: 1; 4: 25; 1 Sam. 9: 9. *aiachi* pro., *ahanchi*, freq., Matt. 7: 27, 28; *aiahanchi*, pro. and freq. *achi a*^{n}*sha*, to be said; this is an expression, not the passive form of *achi; achitok a*^{n} *a*^{n}*shashke*, Luke 4: 12; *ikacho*, not to say, the neg. form of *achi; ikacho*, a., undetermined; unsaid. *achishke*, they say, Matt. 11: 19. *achit*, adv., or a verb, to say and; when two verbs are thus united the first has an adverbial sense as in Heb., *achit anumpuli*, really to say; really to speak; to say what he means; lit., he says and speaks; *achit hochifo*, to call by name; lit., he says and names. *achit anoli*, v., to speak freely; without fear; lit., he says and declares.

achi, n., a maxim; a saying.

achi, n., a rehearser.

achi^n, chi^n, sign of the instant or immediate future of the indicative mood, but it does not mean purpose or intention; it simply expresses futurity as to time; shall, will.

achiba, a., slow, laborious, tedious, belated, hard, late, Mark 2: 9; occupying some time; see *ahchiba*.

achiba, v. n., to be slow, laborious, or tedious; *ahchieba*, pro. form of *ahchiba*.

achibachi, v. t. caus., to cause to be slow, tedious, or troublesome.

achibali, v. t., to render tedious; to protract; to draw out; *chiksamahchibalo kia*, "trouble me not," Luke 11: 7.

achifa, see *achefa*.

achik, fut. sign, will, shall; same as *chi*^{n}; as *ialachik*, I will go; *anumpulachik*, he will speak.

achike, adv., probably will be, and sign of imp. in a mild sense.

achiletali, v. t. caus., to make fierce.

achillita, n., eagerness.

achillita, achelita, achilita, v. n., to be fierce, zealous, engaged, resolute, or unflinching, Matt. 11: 11; *achillinta*, nasal form.

achillita, a., fierce; zealous; resolute; eager.

achillita, pass., rendered fierce; made resolute.

achillitachi, v. t. caus., to make fierce.

achilanlichi, see *chilanlichi*.

achini, adv., likely; probably; seemingly; apparently.

achini, v. n., to seem so; to appear. *ahchini*, to be certainly so; when not before known; to be certain after inquiry is made, Deut. 17: 4; *aka itulatuk achinitok*, unexpectedly, but so, 1 Sam. 5: 3, 4; see *chini*.

achinto, a., from *chito*, being large when others are small; *anumpa na yukpali achinto fehna*, "good tidings of great joy," Luke 2: 10.

achintok (a sign of tense), was to be, should have to be, compounded of remote past and instant future.

achintuk (tense sign), was to be, should have to be, as *ialachintuk*, I was to have gone.

achishi, v. t., to scent; to smell, as dogs.

achishi imponna, a., sagacious, as a dog in smelling.

achohmi, see *achuhmi*.

achokushpa, pass., to be accused, belied, or slandered.

achokushpa, a., slanderous.

achokushpachechi, v. t., to cause a person to be slandered.

achokushpalechi, v. t., to slander; to tattle.

achokushpalechi, n., a slanderer; a tattler.

achokushpali, v. t., to slander; to tattle; to backbite; to accuse.

achokushpali, n., a slanderer; a backbiter.

achokushpachi, pp., to be slandered.

achokushpachi, a., slandered.

achosha, pp., to be inserted, as an ax in wood or a plow in the earth.

achoshuli, v. t. sing., to insert; to set in endwise, as a cog or a spoke in the hub or nave of a wheel, or a linchpin; *achushli,* pl.

achoshunni, achoshoninchi, v. a. i., to grow, as a young peach.—Jackson.

achowa, v. t. to differ; to disagree; to dispute; to contend in conversation. *itachowa,* the reciprocal form is often used; to contend; to brangle; to dispute; to debate; to fall out; to jangle; to quarrel; to strive; to vary; to wrangle. *itachoa,* n., a broil; a dispute; a feud. *itachoa,* n., a disputant. *itachowachi,* to cause to differ. *itachoachi,* n., an incendiary; one who inflames a faction.

achuhmi, achohmi, v. i., to be thus, or so. *achiyuhmi, achoyuhmi.* pro. form.

achuka, v. a. i., to dwell at; to reside at; to keep house at; see Josh. 2: 15; *itinchuka,* reciprocal form; to dwell together; to keep house for each other as husband and wife; *itachuka,* v. a. i., to keep house together; *itinchuka,* n., a husband or a wife; *itinchukali,* my husband or my wife, as the case may be; generally used by the woman when speaking of her husband to others; *achoyuka,* pro. form of *achuka.*

achukbi, achukbika, place of a corner; *achukbeli,* pl., corners, Rev. 7: 1.

achukma, pass., improved; bettered; mended; rectified; redressed; refined; regulated; made good.

achukma, a., pl. *hochukma,* good; excellent; benevolent; kind; gracious; choice; sound; sterling; substantial; useful; valid; virtuous; well; acceptable; sound; wholesome; whole, Luke 6: 10; handsome; courteous; delicate; delicious; delightful; decent; elegant; esteemed; exquisite; fair; fine; finical; generous; genuine; gracious; healthful; healthy; honest; nice; perfect; pleasant; pretty; respectable; reputable; righteous; royal; salutary; sane; serviceable; *ikachukmo,* a. neg., not good; bad; degenerate; disastrous; evil; gross; injurious; offensive; preposterous; sinful; troublous; unapt; uncomely; uncomfortable; unfavorable; ungenial; unhealthy; unholy; unjust; unlawful; unlovely; unpleasant; unprofitable; unrighteous; unwholesome; unworthy; *ikimachukmo,* a., unacceptable.

achukma, n., goodness; excellence; excellency; fairness; good; pureness; purity; safety; soundness; virtue; weal; peace, 2 Kings 9: 17, 18, 19; *nana achukma,* n., grace; a good deed; *nana achukma kaⁿ,* Matt. 12: 11; *aiachukma,* n., Matt. 6: 34.

achukma, v. a. i., to act good; to do well, Matt. 6: 4; to be good, Matt. 6: 22; *ishachukma,* thou doest well.

achukma, v. n., to be good or excellent; *pimachukmashke,* Matt. 17: 4; *ikachukmo,* neg.; *achuⁿkma,* nasal form; *achohuⁿkma,* freq.; *achoyukma,* pro. form; *imachukma,* to be good for him; v. t., to love to delight, 2 Sam. 24: 3; *itinachukma,* to be good to each other.

achukma, adv., finely; soundly; *ikachukmo,* adv., ill.

achukma ahoba, a., specious; seemingly good.

achukma aiali, a., prime.

achukma aⁿsha, n., welfare; a., well.

achukma atapa, a., supereminent.

achukma fehna, a., very good; rare.

achukma iⁿshaht tali, a., best; first rate; in the superlative degree.

achukma iⁿshali, a., better; preferable; superfine; supereminent; transcendent.

achukma keyu, a., not good; unadvisable.

achukma moma, a., unimpaired.

achukmaⁿka, n., a good condition of health; the goodness (well, as to health.)

achukmaⁿka, v. n., to be well, or in health.

achukmalechi, v. t. caus., to make good; to repair; to heighten; to better; to improve; to mend; to redress; to refine; to make peace.

achukmalechi, n., a repairer.

achukmali, n., an improver; a repairer.

achukmalit, adv., diligently, Matt. 13: 36; 15: 15; Luke 15: 8; "in order," Josh. 2: 6; *achukmalit imaponoklotok*, inquired of them diligently, Matt. 2: 7.

achukmalit ashachi, v. t., to dispose; to lay away with.

achukmalit pisa, v. t., to scrutinize.

achukmat, adv., well; orderly; plainly; securely.

achukmat anoli, v. t., to depict.

achukmat apesa, v. t., to arrange.

achukmat alhpisa, pass., arranged; adjusted rightly.

achukmat boli, v. t., to hoard; to lay up well.

achukmat inshat isht ia, v. a. i., to improve.

achukoa, n., an entrance; an entry; a passage into.

achumpa, n., a market; a place for purchasing or buying; the place where bought.

achunanchi, v. a. i., to persevere; to continue; to make an effort; to endure; to persist; to plod; to strive; to weather; see Matt. 10: 22.

achunanchi, a., ardent; persevering; close; keen; pertinacious; sedulous; unwearied; *ikachunancho*, a., unconstant.

achunanchi, n., perseverance; resolution.

achunanchit pisa, a., studious.

achunli, v. t., to sew; to darn; to stitch; *itachunli*, reciprocal; to sew together; to list; to sew; to tack together.

achunli, n., sewing; stitching.

achunli, n., a sewer; a seamstress.

achunsha, v. n., pass. of *achoshuli*, to stand in, or hang by one end, as an arrow to a wounded deer, or as a linchpin.

achunsha, a., hanging in.

achushkanchi, v. n. pl., to stand on end, as spokes in the hub of a wheel.

achushkanchi, nasal form, being placed in.

achushkachi, pass., inserted; placed in.

achushli, pl., see *achoshuli*.

achushoa, pass. pl., inserted.

achushoa, v. n., to stand in.

achushoa, n. pl., those which stand in, as spokes, cogs, etc.

achunwa, ahchunwa, pp., sewed; a., sewed; united by stitches; seamed.

afabi, a., left; left handed.

afabi, n., a left-handed person.

afabi, v. i., to be left handed.

afacha, v. n., to be fast, close, tight, or shut; *itafacha*, v. a. i., to lock; to fasten it together.

afacha, afancha, pass., fastened; latched; *isht afacha*, fastened with; n., a latch; a hasp.

afachali, sing., *afashli* pl., *afashkachi* pass., to fasten; to latch; to hasp; *afasha*, pass. pl., latched; fastened.

afachali, n., a fastener; one that makes fast or firm.

afahama, v. t., to strike at or on.

afahama, n., the place smitten or struck.

afahata, v. a. i., to swing in, on, or at.

afahata, n., a swing; the place where the thing swings.

afalama, v. a. i., to turn at; to return, Luke 2: 43; to relapse; to return from; to turn back at.

afalama, n., a return; the place at which one turns back; a relapse.

afalamaka, n., the place or point of turning back; the return.

afalamichi, afalaminchi (nasal form), v. t., to answer; to reply; to make return, I Sam. 2: 16; Josh. 1: 16; 4: 7; Matt. 8: 8; 11: 4; 13: 14; 17: 11; John 3: 5; Gen. 40: 18; *afalaminchit ikmihokitok*, he answered nothing, Matt. 27: 12.

afalapoa, adv.; *afalapoat pisa*, to behold sideways; to look sidelong.

afalapoli, v. a. i., to look at a thing sideways; to ogle (in a woman).

afalapa, v. a. i., to be obscure or doubled over (applied to language).

afalapa, v. a. i., to place the head on the side of, as of a tree; to listen to a bell at a distance.

afama, v. a. i., v. t., to meet; to join; to come across, Matt. 8: 28, 34; Josh. 2: 16; 8: 5; 9: 11, 12; *siafama*, he met me; *itafama*, to meet with; to meet together; to meet each other; to encounter; to light upon; *itafamali*, I met with him; *aiitafama*, to meet with each other at; to meet together at, or there; *afamahe keyu*, a., will not meet.

afama, n., one that meets; also the name of a man, a meeter; *afamat abi*, to meet at and kill.

afana, pass., staked (as a fence).

afanalechi, afanalechi (from a stem *afanali*), v. t., to see into; to search; to make search; *afanalechititihana*, to search and know, Rev. 2: 23.

afanali, v. t., to direct; to guide.

afananchi, v. a. i., to look through a hole; to peep or peek; *afanantat hikikina*, v. a. i., to be peeping; to stand about and peep.

afanata, n., a helmsman; the man at the helm.

afancha, see *afacha*.

afataha, n., a place to swing in or at; a swing.

afataiya, v. a. i., to be crosswise—like *okfowata, okfoata,* or *okhoata* (q. v.).

afabeka, n., the left hand.

afabekimma, a., sinister; left handed.

afabekimma, adv., to the left hand; on the left hand; *alhfabeka*, is also used in Luke 23: 33.

afama (from *fammi*, to whip); n., a whaling; a whipping post.

afammaiyukali, adv., annually; yearly; each year.

afammi, n., a year; also a yearling, Josh. 5: 6, 12; *ilappat afammi atuchina makon,* "these three years," Luke 13: 7; *afammi pokoli untuchina akocha ushta,* 84 years, Luke 2: 37.

afammi, v. i., to be a year, as *ont afammi*.

afammi achafa, n., one year; a twelve-month; *afammi hosh afammikma,* "from year to year."

afammi hannali, a., sexennial.

afammi hannalikma, a., sexennial; when it is six years.

afammi iklanna, n., half a year.

afammi iklanna, a., semiannual.

afammi iklannakma, adv., semiannually.

afammi talepa achafa, n., a century.

afammi talepa achafakma, adv., every century; every hundred years.

afammi talepa sipokni achafa, n., a thousand years; the millennium.

afammi tuchinakma, a., triennial.

afammi untuklo, a., septennial.

afammi untuklokma, a., septennially.

afammikma, adv., yearly; annually; every year, Luke 2: 41.

afammikma ilhpeta, n., a pension; a yearly allowance or gift.

afammikma ilhpitachi, v. t., to pension.

afanalechi, see *afanalechi.*

afashkachi, pass. pl., fastened; latched; from *afashli.*

afashkachi, n. pl., cogs.

afashli, pl. of *afachali*, to fasten; to latch; *alhfasha* or *afashkachi,* pass.

afebli, v. t., to dent in deep, as into the skull, or anything hard like a gourd shell.

afehna, v. i., to be very; *mihma nukowakan afehna mat,* Luke 6: 11, 45. (These references are to the first translation of Luke.)

afehnichi, afehnachi, v. t., to praise; to extol; to make much of; to laud.

afekommi, v. i., to be mischievous; to be impatient.

afekommi, a., mischievous; impatient; *isht afekommi,* v. t., to tease with; to worry with.

afekommichi, v. t. caus., to make mischievous.

afena, v. a. i. sing., to come up; to rise when pried.

afena, pass. sing., pried up; raised up by prying.

afenali, v. t. pl., to pry up; (*afinni,* sing.; *afikachi,* pass. pl.).

afepa, v. i. and pass. of *afebli.*

afepoa, pl. of *afebli.*

afetapa, v. i., to be hurt by accident.

afetapa, n., an accidental injury.

afetibli, v. t. sing., to ensnare; to enchant; *afetipoli,* pl.

afetibli, n., an ensnarer; an enchanter.

afetipa, pp., enchanted; greatly interested; see *affetipa.*

afetipa, v. i., to be enchanted.

afetipa, n., enchantment.

afetipoa, pass. pl., enchanted.

afetipoa, v. i. pl., to be enchanted.

afetipoa, n., enchantings.

afetipoli, v. t. pl., to ensnare; to enchant.

afetipoli, n. pl., enchanters.

afinkachi, pass. pl. of *afenali*, to be pried up; pried.

afilema, v. a. i., to relapse; to backslide; to turn over back.

afilema, n., a relapse.

afilemoa, v. a. i. pl. of *afilema*.

afilemoa, n., relapses.

afilimmi, v. a. i. sing., to relapse; to turn back; to turn over; *afilammi* is to turn away to the right or left.

afilimmichi, v. t. caus., to cause a relapse or turning back.

afinni, v. t. sing., to pry; to turn the helm; to turn a boat by the helm; *afinnit aba isht ia*, to pry up; to pry and take up.

afinnit abishtia, v. t., to pry.

afisa, n. (from English "officer"), an officer, Gen. 39: 1.

afoa, v. t., to scuffle for; to contend; to resist; to force, 1 Sam. 2: 16; *itimafoa*, to scuffle together; to contend; to contest with each other; *ilafoa*, n., contumacy.

afoa, affoa (q. v.), pp., wound around; *nantapaski noshkobo isht afoatuk ato*, the napkin that was about his head, John 20: 7.

afoachi, n., a wrapper; an envelope.

afobli, afopli, v. a. i., to go round; to pass around; to encircle.

afoblichi, v. t. caus., to cause to wind or go round.

afoha, n., a rest; a place of rest; a harbor, Josh. 1: 13, 15; *afohahe aⁿ hash ahauchahimakoke*, "ye shall find rest," Matt. 11: 29.

afoha, v. i., to rest at, on, in, or there; *afohahe*, Matt. 12: 43.

afohachi, v. t. caus., to give rest at, on, in, or there.

afohka, afoka, n., a pocket; a case; a place into which a single thing is put.

afohka, afoka, pass., put in at; placed in there; *afoyuka*, "conceived in her," Matt. 1: 20.

afohka, v. i., to go in at; to go in there.

afohkachi, v. t. caus., to put in; to cause to go in.

afohkechi, afokkechi, v. t., to cause to go into a path or river.

afohki, v. t., to put in.

afohoma, n., a hem; a rim; a band; a welt.

afohoma, pp., hemmed, rimmed, lined, welted.

afohommi, v. t., to hem; to rim; to put on a rim or hoop at the border; to line; to welt a shoe; to rim a basket; *afoli*, pl., q. v.

afohommi, n., one who makes a hem or rim.

afoka, afohka, pp., put in; *afoⁿhka*, nasal form.

afoka, afohka, n., a case.

afolakto, v. i., to be forked at, as the limbs of a tree or as a road.

afolakto, n., a fork; the place where there is a fork.

afolakto, pass., forked.

afolaktochi, afolaktuchi, v. t. caus., to make a fork.

afolaktua, v. i. pl., to be forked.

afolaktua, n., forks.

afolaktua, pass., forked.

afolaktuli, v. t. pl., to make forks there or at.

afolokachi, see *fullokachi*.

afololichi, v. t. sing., to surround; to turn about at.

afolota, afoluta, afullota, v. a. i., to go round at; to take a circuit there or at; *afolotoa*, pl.

afolota, pass., taken round at; *afolotoa*, pl.

afolota, afullota, n., the circuit; the extent round; a range; *afolotoa*, n. pl. of *afolota*.

afolotachi, caus. sing., to compass, Josh. 6: 3, 7.

afolotolichi, v. t. pl. of *afolotichi*.

afolotowachi, v. t. caus. pl., to lead round; to take round.

afolubli, v. a. i., to encircle; to surround; to environ, Josh. 7: 9; *aiimpa yaⁿ afoluplit echiya*, was it to surround; *afolublit binohmaⁿyatok*, "sat about him," Mark 3: 32.

afolupa, pp., encircled; *afolumpa* (nasal form), as *afolumpa yakni moma kaⁿ*, "round about," Mark 1: 28.

afoluplichi, v. t. caus., to encircle; to surround; to cause others to surround.

afoluta, see *afolota*.

afoli, v. t. pl., to wind round; to roll round; to wrap round; to involve; to inwrap; to reel; to rim; to swathe; to twine; to wind; *alhfoa*, *affoa*, pass., *nantapaski yosh isht alhfoyukatok*, was bound about with a napkin, John 11: 44; *nantapaski noshkobo isht afoatuk ato*, the napkin that was about his head, John 20: 7.

afolichi, v. t. caus., to cause to be wound; to make them wind; to turn; to whirl; to furl.

afopa, v. a. i., to be around.

afotoha, n., an auger hole, the place where it is bored; a mill, the place where it is ground; a grist mill; *tanch afotoha*, a corn mill.

afotoha, pass., ground at; bored at.

afotoli, v. t., to bore at or there; to grind at or there. This word describes the motion round in grinding and boring, and *a* means place where.

afoyua, afoyuha, (pp. from *afoi*, to wind round; from *afoa* or *affoa*, pp.) lengthened form, wound round. See John 11: 44 (*alhfoyuha* in the last translation).

afulli, v. t., to stir a liquid and to thicken food while cooking, as mush, and *tanfula*, Indian hominy; *affula*, *alhfula*, pass. form.

afullichi, v. t. caus., to make or cause to stir.

afullota, see *afolota*.

ah, int., oh!, calling attention, like hark! listen!

anh, adv., yes, it is; one form of the verb to be and in the third person; *siah*, I am; *chiah*, thou art; *ah*, he is; it is; *hatuk*, it was; *anh* is nasalized to make it distinctive, or definite like *an+h*, the substantive verb being added.

ahabli, ahapli, n., a stirrup; a step; a stepping place; a degree; a pace; a treadle belonging to a loom, 1 Kings 10: 19.

ahabli, v. t., to tread there; to tread on; to trample; *ahali*, pl.

ahabli, pass., trodden on; *ahala*, pl.

ahablichi, v. t. sing., to tread into the ground; to make one tread on it; *ahalichi*, pl., Matt. 7: 6; Luke 10: 19; also Rev. 11: 2.

ahablichi, n., a treader; *ahalichi*, pl.

ahanh, n., a negative; a negation.

ahanh, adv., no; not so; a decided negative; nay; *aha*, 2 Sam. 13: 12.

ahah achi, v. a. i., to say no; to refuse; to deny; to negative.

ahah ahni, v. a. i., to take heed; to be cautious; to beware of; to be careful; to take care; to be watchful; to heed; to look; to see; *ahah hashimahnashke*,

Matt. 7: 15. *ahanh hashaiahni*, Matt. 16: 6, 11; also Matt. 6: 1; 8: 4; Mark 8: 15; *ahah ikahno*, v. a. i. neg. form, not to take heed.

ahah ahni, a., mindful; scrupulous; solicitous; vigilant; careful; cautious; wary; circumspect; considerate; *ahah ikahno*, *ahah ahni iksho*, a., careless; heedless; incautious; inconsiderate; reckless; unguarded; unmindful; unwary.

ahah ahni, adv., warily; carefully.

ahah ahni, n., a caution; care; heed.

ahah ahni iksho, a., heady; careless; supine. [This may be used also as a noun, meaning heedlessness, etc.— H. S. H.]

ahah ahni iksho, adv., loosely.

ahah ahni keyu, n., rashness.

ahah ahnit impa, n., regimen; or to eat with care.

ahah ikahno, n., mistrust.

ahah imahni, v. t., to take heed of him; to look out for him; to beware of him, Matt. 7: 15.

ahaklo, n., a hearing.

ahaksa hinla, a., pardonable.

ahaksi, v. n., v. t., to forget; not to notice; to neglect; to omit; *holisso han siahaksi*, I forgot the book.

ahaksi, n., an excuse.

ahaksi, pass., forgotten; overlooked; neglected; excused; pardoned.

ahaksichi, v. t., to overlook; to miss; to neglect; to excuse; to forgive; to omit, Matt. 23: 23; *achafa kamo ahaksicha hinla*, Luke 16: 13; *holisso han pisalahetuk osh ahaksichili*, the book which I should have studied I neglected.

ahaksichi, n., one that forgets, overlooks, neglects, misses; a forgiver; a pardoner.

ahaksichi shali, a., remiss; very forgetful.

ahaksit kania, n., oblivion.

ahalaia, v. a. i., to meddle; *ahalaiali keyu*, I have no interest, Luke 12: 9. (See below.)

ahalaia, n., a meddler.

ahalaia, ahalaya, v. a. i., to be interested; to have a care or concern, or interest; to pertain; Luke 15: 7; *nanta hon isht ishpiahalaia cho?* what hast thou to do with us? Matt. 8: 29; *ahalan-*

ya, Matt. 13: 11: 16: 23; *siahalaia keyu*, I am not interested; *ilahalaia keyu*, we are not interested; *amahalaia; isht ahalaia*, v. t., to care about; to have a concern or interest in; to have to do with, Luke 4: 34; to concern; to interest; *isht ikahalaio*, a., disinterested; *isht ahalaia keyu*, a., impertinent; v. n., to be impertinent.

ahalaia, a., interested; concerned; meddlesome; rightful; *ikahalaio, ahalaia, keyu*, a., neutral; uninterested; free Matt. 17: 26; *itimahalaia*, interested in each other; *itimahalaia*, n., intercourse; mutual interest.

ahalaia, n., a concern; an interest.

ahalalli, n., a shaft; a thill; a trigger; a handle; a bail; a button; a knob; a hilt.

ahalalli, v. t., to take hold of, or at, or there.

ahalupa, n., the edge; the place which is sharp; *iskifa ahalupa*, the edge of an ax.

ahalupa anukpilefa, n., a feather edge; an edge that is turned up.

ahalupa anukpilefa, a., feather edged.

ahalupa anukpilifi, v. t., to turn up the edge.

ahama, n., ointment; oil for the purpose of anointing; unction; *pansh ahama*, hair ointment, Matt. 26: 9, 12; *nan ahama*, ointment, Mark 14: 3; Luke 7: 37; John 12: 5.

ahama, n., anointing. 1 John 2: 27. See 1 John 2: 20, where unction is translated as a verb.

ahama, pass., anointed; oiled; smeared or rubbed over with oil; *wak nia ahama*, pass., tallowed; greased; ointed; *nan ahamat imalhtoka*, his anointed, 1 Sam. 2: 10.

ahauchi, ahayuchi, v. t., to find; to discover; to acquire; to furnish; to have, John 3: 36 [?]; to gain; to meet; to procure; to provide; *ikahayucho*, Matt. 12: 43; 16: 25; 18: 13; Josh. 2: 22; Luke 15: 4, 5, 6, 8, 9; Matt. 2: 8; 7: 7, 8; 10: 39; 13: 44; *imahauchi*, to furnish him; *ilahauchi*, to furnish or find himself (with provisions, tools, etc.); *isht ilahauchi*, v. t., to make (as money); to furnish himself by means of; *haiaka*, pass., found, Luke 15: 32; *isht ilahauchi*, pass., profited by means of.

ahauchi, n., a finder; a gainer; a procurer.

ahaya, a., v. n., sufficient to fill a hole; filling a place or hole; also *ikahayo*, neg. form and most used, not being large enough to fill, as *shapo an ikahayo*.

ahayu, v. t., to find; found in a man's name; *Ahayutabi*.

ahala, pp. pl. of *ahabli*, trodden down; trodden on; trampled.

ahali, v. t. pl., to tread on; to trample on.

ahali, see *ahabli*.

ahalichi, pl. of *ahablichi*, to tread into the ground; to make them tread on it, or them; to tread under foot.

ahalichi, n. pl., treaders; tramplers; *ahalinchi*, nasal form.

ahammi, v. t., to anoint; 2 Cor. 1: 21; Matt. 6: 17; Mark 14: 8; 16: 1; Luke 7: 46; Rev. 3: 18; to smear with grease or oil; to grease; to rub gently; to oil himself or another thing; to embrocate; to gum; to iron; to oil; to oint; *isht ahammi cha*, anointed with and, John 11: 2; *chinoshkobo ishahammi cha*, anoint thy head and, Matt. 6: 17; *ahammoli*, pl.; *tali hata isht ahammoli*, to wash over with melted silver.

ahammi, n., unction.

ahammichi, v. t. caus., to cause to anoint; to anoint another person; *isht ahammichitok*, he anointed him with, Acts 10: 38.

ahapi, ahe api, n., a potato vine.

anhatak, anhatak, n., my husband, or my man; *chinhatak*, thy husband; thy man. When the pronoun is prefixed, *hatak* has the meaning of husband. [From my experience and observation the word for "man" is always pronounced *hattak*, never *hatak*.—H. S. H.]

ahbichakali, v. n., to be nineteen.

ahbichakali, v. a. i., to make 19, as *ilahbichakali*, we make 19, or are 19.

ahbichakali, a., nineteen; XIX; 19.

ahbichakaliha, adv., nineteen times.

ahchapi, see *achapi*.

ahchiba, n., tediousness; irksomeness; a task.

ahchiba, achiba, (q. v.), a., tedious; slow; disadvantageous; tiresome; troublesome; difficult; irksome; laborious; wearisome, Matt. 9: 5.

ahchibali, v. t., to trouble; to weary; *chiksamahchibalokia*, "trouble me not," Luke 11: 7; also Mark 5: 35.

ahchifa, achefa, v. t., to wash; to lave; to rinse; *alhchefa*, pp.

ahchifa, n., a wash.

ahchihpo, akchihpo, n., a drift; a float.

ahchishi, v. a. i. and v. t., to scent; to smell the track; to follow by the scent; to wind.

ahchishi, n., scent.

ahchuⁿwa, see *achuⁿwa*.

ahe, ahi, he, sign of remote fut. tense of the indicative mood—shall, will; as *ahi oke*, and *ahe tuk*, should have; it means future *time* simply, and not purpose or intention.

ahe, n., a potato; a sweet potato; a yam.

aⁿhe, he, adv., almost, Acts 7: 17; *etalaⁿhe*, we have almost finished them or it; *ilonaⁿhe*, we have almost arrived there; *aⁿhusi* and *aⁿhesi* (q. v.) are diminutives of *aⁿhe*.

ahe aholokchi, n., a potato patch; a place where potatoes are planted.

ahe alhpusha, n., a roasted potato.

ahe api, n., a potato vine.

ahe bunto, ahe munto, n., a potato hill.

ahe buntuchi, ahe muntuchi, v. t., to make potato hills.

ahe hobi, v. t., to boil potatoes.

ahe holbi, n., a boiled potato; a steamed potato.

ahe ibish, n., a potato hill.

ahe inchuka, n., a potato house.

ahe kamassa, ahkamassa, n., a wild potato; a hard potato.

ahe kashaha, n., a yam; a potato which has a good relish.

ahe keyu, adv., shall not; can not; must not; will not.

ahe lumbo, n., a round potato; an Irish potato. *ahe hoba* and *iksahe*, a Six-towns word.

ahe pata okla, n., name of the Choctaws belonging to the northeast district of the Nation. The name is said to have been given them from the fact that at an early immigration they found a place where there were many wild potatoes—*pata* means spread out. But others explain this name in other ways.

ahe pehna, n., seed potatoes.

ahe shua, n., a rotten potato.

aheka, v. t., to owe; to be in debt; to get on trust; *imaheka*, to owe him; his debtor; *pimaheka*, Matt. 6: 12; *issamaheka*, or *aheka issamiⁿtakali*, you owe me; *chimahekali*, I owe you; *itimaheka*, to owe each other; *aheka amiⁿtakanli*, to be due me from him; see *ahecha* in *ilappa momaka nana issamahechishke*, all these things are against me, Gen. 42: 36; *aheka iⁿhoyo*, v. t., to dun; to look after a debt; to seek of him a due, that which he owes; *aheka itannali*, to collect debts. *aheka atobbahe keyu*, a., insolvent; unable to pay his debts. *aheka atobbahinla*, a., solvent.

aheka, n., Luke 7: 41; a debt; a due; an obligation; a charge; a duty; a score, Rom. 13: 8; Matt. 18: 24; *ilaheka*, our debts, Matt. 6: 12.

aheka, pass., v. n., trusted; owed; due; credited; obtained on credit.

aheka iksho, a., unindebted; out of debt.

aheka imasha, n., a debtor, Luke 16: 5.

aheka intakanli, v. t., to owe him, Matt. 18: 28; Luke 16: 5; Philem. 18; *aheka intakanlili*, I owe him; *aheka antakanli*, he owes me: a., indebted; *ahekat takali*, pass., charged.

aheka ishi, n., a creditor.

aheka takalichi, v. t., to score; to enter a debt; to charge with a debt.

aheka takanli, a., due.

aheka takanli, n., arrear; arrears; arrearage; balances remaining due; a due.

ahekachi, v. t., 1. to sell on credit; to trust; to get another in debt; to credit; to charge; *chiahekacheli*, I trust you; *issiahekachi*, you trust me; *itimahekachi*, to trust each other. 2. To buy on credit; "to run in debt;" to get on credit, as by purchase. *ahekachit holissochi*, v. t., to debit; to trust and write it.

ahekachi, n., a creditor; a seller on credit; a buyer on credit, *nan ahekachi*.

ahekachi, ahhekachi, ahheka, adv., lengthwise (of cloth); *abaiyachi*, lengthwise, of a field; n., the length.

aⁿhesi, aⁿhusi, adv., almost; very near; nearly; *tahaⁿhesi*, nearly done, or gone.

aheto, adv., will not; can not; shall not; *umbaheto*, it will not rain.

ahetok, sign of the remote fut. perf., would have; should have; would have been. *achukmahetok,* it would have been well.

ahetuk, sign of the recent fut. perf.; *mintahetuk,* he should have come. The first syllable *a* unites with the last syllable of the preceding word, which is according to the usage of the language, or, rather, the last syllable of the previous word is elided; thus—*chumpa,* to buy, *chumpahetuk; minti,* to come, *mintahetuk; haklo,* to hear, *haklahetuk.*

ahheka, n., the length, as of a piece of cloth; see *ahekachi.*

ahhekachi, n., the length. See *ahekachi.*

ahi, see *ahe.*

ahika, n., a station; a stand; a post; a degree.

ahika, v. i. sing., to stand at, or in; to stand there; *ahinka,* nasal form., standing in, or at, as a stick in a hole or an arrow in the side; *uski naki at issi ak on ahikia,* the arrow stands in the deer.

ahikia, n., a station; an estate; a footing.

ahikiat anumpuli, n., a pulpit; the place where anyone stands and talks.

ahikma, as *alhtahanhikma,* if it is nearly ready.

ahilechi, n., an establishment; a place where anything is set up.

ahila, n., a place where persons dance; from *hila,* to dance; and *a,* adv., at, there; *aboha ahila,* a ball room.

ahila, v. a. i., to dance at, or on.

ahinla, sign of the potential mood, present tense; can, may, shall (in a mild sense). The final syllable of the verb is elided before *ahinla. hashhominchahinla cho?* will ye season it, eh? cf. Mark 9: 50.

ahinlatok, past tense; could have, might have, may or can have.

ahinlatuk, recent past tense; could have, might have.

ahinna, ahina, v. t., v. a. i., to tend; to watch (as with the sick); to keep company; to be the companion of another person; to stay with, to guard. *ahinat apela hioka imikbilashke,* I will make an helpmeet for him; *chiahinnali,* I keep you company; *issiahinna,* you are company for me; you stay with

me; *itahinna,* to keep company or be pledged together; to consort together.

ahinna, pass., to be pawned; pawned; pledged.

ahinna, n., security; a pledge; company; a companion; surety; *itahina,* a companion; an escort; a watcher.

ahinnachi, v. t., to pawn; to pledge; to cause to be the companion of another.

ahinnia, ahiniya, v. i., to relish much; to be fond of.

ahkamassa, see *ahe kamassa.*

ahmpi, see *ahpi.*

ahni, ahli, v. a. i., v. t., to think; to expect; to fear; to hope; to wish; to presume; to calculate; to design; to desire, Matt. 16: 1; also, to seek, Matt. 16: 4; to aim at; to notice; to observe; to will; to care for; to contemplate; to count upon, Matt. 14: 5; to destine; to dispose; to entertain; to incline; to intend; to like; to mark; to mean; to notice; to purport; to purpose; to reckon; to remark; to see; to tend; *aba anumpa ahni,* to seek or desire the gospel, or religion; *chimahni,* to desire of thee; *chiahni,* to think or to wish thee; *alhpesa ahni,* to comply; *yohmi imahni,* v. t., to suspect concerning him; *yohmi ikimahno,* a., unsuspected; *nana okpulo imahni,* v. t., to execrate; to imprecate; to wish him something evil; *nana ahni iksho,* a., indifferent, or to care for nothing; to wish nothing; *ilap ahnit yamohmi,* himself wishes and does; *imahni;* to let him, Matt. 6: 3; to suffer, Matt. 8: 31; 17: 4; *aiahni,* pro. form, Matt. 18: 10; *hashaiahni,* Matt. 7: 12; *ikahno,* neg. form; *isht ikinahno,* to hate him; *isht ikiminahno,* to deride him, Luke 16: 14; *ahnituk keyu,* a., unpremeditated.

ahni, a., disposed; minded; optional; aware; designed; willing; *ikahno,* indisposed; unaware; undesigned; unmarked; unperceived; unthinking; unwilling; *ahnahe keyu,* a., undesirable; will not wish.

ahni, n., a will; a wish; a desire; a purpose; a disposition; an expectation; an inclination; an intent; a meaning; mind; motive; option; a plan; a purport; a volition; *ikahno,* n., indisposition; *ạlhpesa ahni*, to suffer; to permit; *ạlhpesa issạmahnashke*, suffer me, Matt. 8: 21.

ahni, n., a wisher; an expectant; an expecter.

ahnichi, v. t., to respect; to like; to applaud; to love; to approve; to esteem; *ahninchi*, nasal form, which is most used; to reckon; to regard; to receive, Matt. 18: 5; to savor, Matt. 16: 23; *ikahnincho*, to despise; to dislike, Matt. 12: 7; *ahnihinchi*, freq.; *ahniechi*, protracted form; *ilahninchi*, to respect himself; *ilahninchi*, n., self-esteem; *ileahninchi*, to trust in himself; *ikahnincho*, a., disliked; loathed; *ikahninchot isht anumpuli*, v. t., to remonstrate.

ahnit, adv. (*t* is sometimes used as a conjunction), purposely; *ahnit anukfilli*, to remember; *ahnit ishi*, v. t., to choose; to wish and take; *ahnit holitobli*, to observe, Josh. 1: 7, 8.

ahoba, n., an illusion; an appearance; a prospect.

ahoba, a., worthy; *ikahobo*, neg. form, worthless; unworthy; having no worth; stale; *isht ikahobo*, a., disgraced by it; v. n., to be disgraced by it; *isht ikimahobo*, a.

ahoba, v. i., v. n., to seem; to appear; to have worth; to look; to conjecture; to think, Matt. 6: 7; *siahoba keyu*, "I am not worthy," Luke 3: 16; *imahoba*, it seems to him, or he presumes; *nan ikimahobo*, a., unconcern; being nothing to him, etc.; *ikimahobo*, it does not seem to him, or it is of no worth to him; *ikahobo*, a., unuseful; unworthy; useless; vain; waste; of no worth; of no account; cheap; idle; inefficient; insignificant; jejune; mean; refuse [?]; *nana ạpaikahobo*, a., insipid; *ikchiahobo*, Matt. 5: 22; *isht iksạmahobo*, it is of no worth to me; it is nothing to me; *ahobachi*, v. t., to cause to seem; *ilehobachi*, to make like himself; *ahobali*, *ahobạlli*, which see for definitions; *ikahobalo*, neg. f., v. t., to mock; to despise; to disparage; to sneer; to make light of; to despise, 2 Sam. 1: 21; Matt. 9: 3; *ikahobalo pisamạt*, when he saw that he was mocked, Matt. 2: 16; *Chihowa ikahobalo*, v. t., to blaspheme Jehovah; *isht ikahobalo*, v. t., to blas-

pheme, Mark 3: 28, 29; *ikahobalot anumpuli*, to blaspheme, Mark 2: 7; Acts 26: 11; *ikahobalot nan ikmihacho*, not blaspheme, 1 Tim. 2: 20; *ikahobalot nana mihanchi*, "blaspheme," James 2: 7; *ikahobalot anumpuli*, to blaspheme, Matt. ¶2: 31; *ahomba*, v. a. i., to have, as *nipi chiahomba*.

ahobạchi, v. t., to represent; to instruct; to imitate.

ahobạlli, v. t., to represent; to cause to appear like; *ahobanli*, nasal form.

ahobi, see *ilahobbi*, to pretend.

ahochifochi, see *hochifochi*.

ahochukwa, a., chilly; cold (as a person, not a thing); aguish. This word is applied to the feeling or sensation of cold, and not to the weather or any object; *kapạssa* is applied to objects, *hochukwa* to a person's sensation.

ahochukwạ, v. i., to be cold; to feel the cold (as a person); *siahochukwa*, I am cold.

ahochukwa, n., chilliness; coldness; ague.

ahochukwạchi, a., chilly; coolish.

ahochukwạchi, v. i., to be chilly; *chiahochukwạchi*, you are chilly.

ahochukwạchi, n., chilliness; coldness. These words are applied to describe the sensation of cold which a person experiences; *kapạssa* is applied to objects, as weather, water, etc.; *kapạssa aiena hatukoka*, Acts 28: 2.

ahofahya, n., shame, reproach.

ahofalli, pass., hatched.

ahofanti, n., nourishment; the place or means of raising a being or a creature; nurture; nutriment; pabulum.

ahofạllechi, v. t., to hatch or multiply (as fowls), Gen. 1: 22.

ahofobi, n., a deep place; an abyss, Matt. 18: 6; *ikahofobo*, n., a shallow.

ahofobika, n., the deep place; the depth; the deep; an abyss; the abyss; *kohchạt ahofobika*, Luke 8: 31; *ahofobi fehnaka*, Rom. 10: 7.

ahofombika, n. (nasal form of above), the deep; the place where it is deep. *ahofombika pit takalichi cha*, "launch out into the deep," Luke 5: 4.

ahoiya, n., a strainer; a filter, or the place where liquid runs through it in drops or small streams.

ahokchi, v. t., to plant at.

ahokchichi, v. t., to plant with something else. See Matt. 13: 25.

ahokli, n., a handle; a haft; a place at which to seize or take hold; a gin; a hilt.

ahokofa, n. sing., ahokoli, pl., the end, or cessation; the place at which it is cut off; a decision; a termination; iti ahokofa, the place where the tree is cut off; a stump.

ahokofa, v. i. sing., to cease; to end; ont ahokofa wa, it will never cease or end; ahokoli, pl.

ahokofa, pass., cut off at, ended, concluded, decided, extinguished; ahokofa iksho, a., without end, ceaseless, endless; itahokofa, pass., unjointed; itahokofa, n., a gap; nanih itahokofa, a mountain gap.

ahokoffi, v. t. sing, to cut off at; to cease; to put an end to at; to decide; to destine; to discontinue; to set; imahokoffi, v. t., to silence him; to cut him off. itahokoffi, v. t., to unjoint; to cut asunder.

ahokoffi, n., one that cuts off.

ahokoffichi, v. t., to end; to finish; to conclude; to extinguish.

ahokoli, pl. of ahokofa (q. v.).

ahokolichechi, v. t. caus., pl. of ahokoffichi.

ahokolichi, v. t. caus., pl. of ahokoffi.

aholabechi, v. t., to procure false witnesses; to accuse falsely.

aholabechi, n., a false accuser.

aholabi, v. t., to bear false witness; to lie; to perjure, Luke 3: 14.

aholabi, n., a false swearer; a liar; a perjurer.

aholba, n., an image.

aholba, v. i., to resemble; ahoyulba, pro. form.

aholhpokunna, n., a dream, Gen. 42: 9.

aholhpokunna, v. i., to dream; aholhpokunnatukon, that which he had dreamed.

aholhtachi, see ahotachi.

aholhtapi, n., a string, a file, anything on which beads, meat, fish, and the like are strung; nani aholhtapi, a string of fish; shikala aholhtapi achafa, one string of beads.

aholhtina, n., the number; aholhtina iksho, without number.

aholhtina, v. i., to be numbered, to become; yakni aholhtina, to become earth; lukfi aholhtina, to become dust.

aholhtina iksho, a., innumerable, unnumbered, numberless, sumless.

aholhtufa, n., a reel.

aholihta, n., an inclosure.

aholisso, n., paper.

aholissochi, n., a desk, a writing table, a slate, a place to write on; aholissochi an hoyo cha, "he asked for a writing tablet and," Luke 1: 63.

aholitobli, v. t., to worship. isht aholitobli.

aholitopa, n., honor, John 4: 44; a sanctuary.

aholitopaka, n., glory, Luke 4: 6; John 11: 40.

aholitopanka, n., glory. See Matt. 25: 31; isht aholitopaka in last edition.

anhollo, v. t., he loves me; chinhollo, he loves thee; inhollo, he loves him; anhollo, dear to me; chinhollo, dear to thee; inhollo, dear to him. This verb and ima have the dative pronouns im, in, etc., inseparably united. sanhullo, chinhulloli, John 21: 15, 16, 17. See inhollo or inhullo, the later and more correct mode of spelling.

anhollo, v. n., with a pronoun in the dative case, dear to me; or it is rendered, I love it or him, her, or them; inhollo is also rendered, he is stingy, he loves it, he will not part with it, he is close. (See above.)

ahollohpi, ahollopi, n., a grave; a place of burial or interment; a graveyard, 2 Kings 9: 28; a tomb; a sepulcher; a vault, John 11: 31, 38, 44.

aholloka, aholloka, n., a sacred thing; hatak imilhfiopak at aholoka fehna hoke, the life of a man is very sacred.

ahollopi boli, v. t., to sepulcher; to lay in the grave; to entomb.

ahollopi kalli, n., a grave digger; a sexton.

ahollopi tali hikia, n., a grave stone; a tombstone.

aholokchi, n., ground planted; a place planted; ikaholokcho, n., fallow ground, ground not planted; a fallow.

aholuya, n., a filter; a leach tub.

ahonala, ahonala, pp. pl., nailed; nailed up or upon.

ahonaḷi, v. t. pl., to nail on; to nail up.

ahonaḷichi, v. t. pl. caus., to nail on; *itahonaḷichi*, to tack together.

ahonola, n., a spinning wheel.

ahonola isht talakchi, n., a wheel band.

ahonolushi, n. diminutive, a small spinning wheel.

ahopoka, n., refuse.

ahopoksa, a., wise.

ahopoksia, a., wise.

ahopoksinka, n., wisdom, Luke 2: 40 [?].

ahoponi, n., a kitchen; any place where cooking is performed; a cook-room.

ahopoyuksa, n., wisdom, Matt. 11: 19.

ahopoyuksa, v. i., pro. form, to be wise.

ahopoyuksaka, n., righteousness, Matt. 5: 6.

ahosi, n., a mortar; a place where corn, salt, and the like, are pounded fine.

ahosi, v. t., to beat there; to bray in; to pound there.

anhosi, Matt. 1: 11; see *anhusi*.

ahoshmi, n., altar; place where anything is burnt, Luke 1: 11. [*alta* in ed. of 1854.]

ahoshonti, n., a cloud.

ahoshontika, ahoshintika, n., a shade; a shadow of any inanimate object.

ahotachi, aholhtachi, n., warping bars.

ahotupa, n., a wound.

ahoyo, n., the place where a search has been made; as *tanchi ahoyo*, where the corn has been gathered; the harvest, his harvest, Matt. 9: 38.

ahoyo, v. t., to search at, there, or in.

ahpaḷli, v. t., to fondle; to fawn; to play with a living object.

ahpaḷli, n., a fondler.

ahpi, n, the commencement; the first.

ahpi, v. a. i., to be first; *aiahpi*, where it commences.

ahpi, ahmpi, a., first, as *aḷlahpi*, first child; *aṭtapi*, first born; *nitak ahpi*, first day. It is sometimes written as being part of another word, as *aḷlahpi* for *aḷla ahpi*; *aḷlanakni ishi ahpi*, Matt. 1: 25; *tofahpi*, spring, first of summer; *haṣhtolahpi*, fall, first of winter.

ahsakti, n., wild potato.

ahumba, v. i., to have; from *ahoba*, (q. v.).

ahumma, n., a tan vat.

ahummachi, n., a tan vat; a tan pit.

ahunsa achafa, n., a gunshot.

anhusi, anhosi, adv., most; almost; near; nearly. "Near," 1 Sam. 4: 19; *isht ianhosi*, Matt. 1: 11; derived from *anhe*, q. v.

ai, a diphthong having the sound of *i* in pine; mine.

ai, a "locative particle" or adverb before vowels, meaning at, from, in, on, place where, or in which, or time when, there, by means of, *aṭta, aiaṭta*, to stay at; born at, or born there; *ai imonatok*, went unto him there, Matt. 14: 36; when the verb begins with a consonant the adverb is *a* (q. v.). *peni anunkaka aiokchalinchitok;* before *y ai* is used, as *pit aiyilepa*, Josh. 8: 15. *ai* often changes the verb to which it is prefixed to a noun; as *aṭta*, to reside, *aiaṭta*, a residence; *ali*, true, *aiali*, the truth, or where it is true, the true place. *ai* is prefixed to some verbs in the intensive form; *anli, aianli; ahni, aiahni; yohmi, aiyohmi; yamohmi* [generally spelled *yammohmi*—H. S. H.], *aiyamohmi; aia* is a repetition of this adverb, as *chik aia miho*, Matt. 5: 35. NOTE.—In the intensive forms, made by doubling a consonant, where *y* occurs and is doubled, the letter *i* is used for the first *y; yakohmi aiyakohmi*, and not *ayyakohmi; hoyohoiyo*, not *hoyohoyyo*.

ai is used for the final *a* of some nouns; when the article *a* or *ya* is suffixed, as *chuka*, a house; *chukaiya* or *chukaia*, the house. The original vowel is changed for euphony's sake.

aia, ia (q. v.), v. a. i., to go.

aia, n., a going; one that goes.

aiabachi, n., doctrine; see Mark 12: 38.

aiabeka, a., unhealthy; *ikaiabeko*, salubrious.

aiabiha, n. pl., bins; receptacles; places filled up.

aiachafa, n., a kind.

aiachafa, v. a. i., to pertain to; *ibaiachafa*, to be one of, Josh. 5: 13.

aiachefa, n., a wash tub; a wash place.

aiachukma, n., a good place; *aiachunkma*, n., nasal form, being a good place.

aiachunkma, a., good; being good; John 1: 46 [?].

aiachukmaka, n., the good place; goodness; peace; Luke 2: 14; the state [of peace]; *aiachukmaⁿka*, n., nasal form, being the good place.

aiachuⁿwa, n., a seam.

aiafacha, n., a staple.

aiahalaia, v. a. i., to be of, or to belong to; to be interested in; 1 John 2: 16 [?]; *ishahalaia, chiahalaia, chimahalaia.*

aiahanta, n., capacity, state, or condition.

aiahni, n., will, John 1: 13; 4: 34; a point, a project, a sentiment; *nan aiahnika,* the will, Matt. 7: 21.

aiahni, v. a. i., to think of; to wish, Matt. 1: 19; to will, Luke 5: 12; 6: 31.

aiahni, v. t., as in *aba anumpa aiahnili,* I think about the gospel.

aiahninchi, v. t., to respect; to like; *isht aiahninchi,* n., favor, grace, Luke 2: 40.

aiahoba, v. a. i., to appear, 1 John 3: 2.

aiahpi, n., place or time of beginning; *Chihowa hokat atobat aiahpitok:* v. t., *ikimiksho hoke,* Child's Cat., p. 4, question 7.

aiaka, a., large, long, much, Luke 16: 10; *anumpa aiaka anumpuli imponna; anumpa ikaiako hachimanumpohonlila chiⁿ hoke (ikaiako*=not worthy—said by the speaker).

aiaka, v. n., to be large; to be long, Luke 16: 10.

aiakachi, v. t. caus., to make large or long; to lengthen; to enlarge.

aiakmi, n., a model.

aiakmo, n., a foundry.

aiakmochi, v. t., to solder; to cause it to adhere to; *itaiakmochi,* v. t., to solder; to solder together.

aiakostininchi, v. t., to know about, John 3: 8.

aialota, n., fullness; the place filled.

aialota, a., filled up.

aiaⁿli, v. a. i., to succeed; to prosper; to be true to; *akchimaiaⁿlot,* Josh. 1: 5.

aiaⁿli, v. n., to be successful.

aiaⁿli, adv., *lakafi aiaⁿlitok,* perfectly healed, Matt. 14: 36.

aiaⁿli, n., success; fulfillment; justice; might; a reality; a surety; thrift; truth; trueness; veracity; virtue; *isht aiaⁿli,* power, Mark 12: 24; *ikaiaⁿlo,* n., treachery; untruth.

aiaⁿli, a., successful; thrifty; just, Matt. 1: 19 [?]; loyal; open; peremptory; perfect; plain; pure; positive; real; sterling; substantial; *ikaiaⁿlo,* a., pending; unsuccessful.

aiaⁿli, v. a. i., to succeed.

aiaⁿli, pp., prospered; fulfilled; ratified.

aiaⁿli achukma, a., holy.

aiaⁿli fehna, a., prevalent.

aiaⁿli ikakostinincho, a., uncertain.

aiaⁿli ikithano, a., dubious.

aiaⁿli keyu, a., truthless.

aiaⁿlichi, v. t., to accomplish; to verify; to fulfill, Matt. 5: 17; to comply; to prosecute; to ratify; to substantiate; to support; to perform, Matt. 5: 33; *imaiaⁿlichi,* v. t., to sanction; *aiaⁿlichi,* n., probation.

aialika, n., power, Luke 4: 6; glory, John 2: 11.

aiaⁿlika, a., mighty, Luke 1: 49.

aialipa, n., a crown, a wreath, a turban, John 19: 2.

aiaⁿlishke, v. n., to be true; it is true, John 4: 37.

aiaⁿlit, adv., loyally.

aiamona, aiammona, n., the beginning; the commencement.

aianompisa, n., the sight of the gun.

aianowa, aiannowa, pp., to be called to; to be invited, to be told, John 2: 2.

aianoyuwa, n., pro. form, fame; the report.

aianta, nasal form of *aiatta,* to reside.

aianta, v. a. i., to stay at; to be staying at; *aiahanta,* freq. form.

aianta, n., an abode.

aianukcheto, v. t., to trust to; to commit unto, John 2: 24.

aianukcheto, n., trust; confidence; dependence; resource.

aianukpalli, n., temptation; place of excitement, interest, or desire; see the Lord's prayer.

aianukpallichi, v. t., to tempt with; to excite the feelings by means of.

aianukpallichi, n., a tempter.

aianukpallika, n., the place of temptation; the temptation.

aianumpuli, n., the place where any one speaks; a council; a desk; a pulpit; a stand (used in camp meetings).

aianumpulika, n., the place of speaking; the council ground.

aianumpuli aboha hanta, n., a chapel; a church; a meeting house; an oratory.

aianumpuli chuka, n., a council house; a house used as a place of public speaking, debate, or council.

aiapesa, n., a hall, common hall, place of judgment, Matt. 27:27; a place where anything is measured; establishment.

aiapoksia, n., an office (as the office of a priest), Luke 1: 8.

aiapushli, n., a place for broiling or roasting; an oven.

aiasittia, n., a hobby.

aiasha, v. a. i. pl. (sing., *aianta*), to sit; to tarry; to remain; to dwell; to be there; to occupy, Matt. 2: 5, 6; *aiasha*, are in, Matt. 11: 8; *aiashahe oke*, shall be, Matt. 13: 42, 43; 18: 10; used often for the plural of the verb to be (Luke 5: 2); see *a*ⁿ*sha*, the intensive form of *asha; aiasha* and *aianta* are in the prolonged form of *asha* and *anta*.

aiasha, n. pl., inhabitants; residents, Josh. 9: 3, 11.

aiasha, n. sing., "place," 1 Sam. 5: 3; throne, Matt. 5: 34; see also Matt. 17: 14.

aiasha, n. pl., seats; abodes; habitations; mansions, John 14: 2; *Chintail aiasha;* Matt. 10: 5; *aiaha*ⁿ*shwa*, freq., John 1: 39.

aiasha holitopa, n., a throne.

aiasha holitopa ombinili, pp., enthroned; seated on a throne; v. a. i., to sit on a throne.

aiasha holitopa ombinilichi, v. t., to enthrone.

aiashachi, v. t. pl., to lay them on; to lay them at, or there; *boli*, sing.; *pit aiashacha he*, cast them into, Matt. 13:42.

aiashachi, n., receptacle; a place where are laid or placed.

aiashạchi, v. t., to err at; to make a mistake at, or by means of; to sin about, or at; to overlook.

aiashạchi, n., a prisoner; a transgressor; one who makes mistakes.

aiashạchi, n., a mistake; an error; an oversight; a sin, John 1: 29; a fault, Matt. 18: 15.

aiashạchika, aiashạcheka, n., a sin; a mistake, Luke 3: 3–6; 5: 21; Mark 2: 7; Matt. 12: 31; *ilaiashạcheka*, n., our sins; *hạchimaiashạcheka*, Mark 11: 26.

aiataha, pp., qualified.

aiataia, n., a landing; a place to lean against or to rest upon.

aiatali, v. t., to qualify, to capacitate, to furnish.

aiatikonofa, n., a strait, 2 Sam. 24: 14.

aiatokko, aiatukko, n., a shelter, a protector, a refuge. See *atukko*.

aiatokowa, n., declaration; testimony, John 3: 11; witness, John 4: 44.

aiatokowali, v. t., to bear testimony.

aiaya, n., passage, route, place of going.

aiạlbi, or **aiạlli** (q. v.) n., reward, Luke 23: 41; price; cost; mark, Phil. 3: 14; see *aiilli* and *ạlbi*.

aiạlbichi, v. t., to price.

aiạlbiha, n., a vessel, Matt. 13: 48; Mark 11: 16; a winefat, Mark 12: 1.

aiạlbina, n., a camp; an encampment.

aiạlbinanchi, v. t. nasal form, to camp at; to make an encampment.

aiạlbo, n., the place soldered or glued together.

aiạlbo, v. a. i., to adhere; to stick on; to cement; to cleave to; *itaiạlbo*, to adhere to each other; *itaiạlbo*, pp., a., cemented together.

aiạlbo, pp., a., adhered; cemented; glued; sticky.

aiạlbuchi, v. t., to solder; to glue; to cause to adhere; to cement; *itaiạlbuchi*, to solder together; to glue together.

aiạlhchạpi, aialhchipi, n., a place for playing a Choctaw game; see *achạpi*.

aiạlhchuⁿ**wa**, n., a seam; the union of two edges of cloth by the needle; a stitch.

aiạlhpesa, n., a preparation; proper place or time; the nick (of time); the critical time; season; power, Matt. 7: 29; 9: 6.

aiạlhpesa, a., suitable; expedient; opportune; ordinary; rightful; *aiạlhpiesa keyu*, evil, Matt. 12:34; *nana ikaiạlhpeso*, folly, Josh. 7: 15.

aiạlhpi, aiuⁿ**lhpi**, n., a handle; a hasp.

aiạlhpiesa, v. n., prot. form, to fulfill; to be justified; *isht chiaiạlhpiesa*, Matt. 12: 37.

aiạlhpiesa, pp., fulfilled, Matt. 2: 17; *aiimaiạlhpiesa*, n., need, Matt. 9: 12; an intensive form doubled by the prefix *ai*.

aiạlhpiesa, n., an opportunity.

aiạlhpiesa, n., righteousness, Acts 10: 35; Matt. 3: 15; 5: 20; a., righteous; *hatak aiạlhpiesa*, Gen. 18: 23.

aiạlhpusha, n., an oven; a meat oven; a place or vessel used for roasting; a place where things are roasted; from *ạlhpusha*, roasted, and *ai*, place where.

aiạlhtaha, a., full; complete; plenary; pp., completed; made ready.

aiạlhtaha, n., fullness; completion; perfection; plenitude.

aiạlhto, n., a bin; a box; a canister; a receptacle; that in which dry articles and liquids are kept; a vat; a vessel, 1 Kings 10: 21, 25.

aiạlhto, v. a. i., to be in; to be inside; *aboha ilaiạlhto*, we are in the house; *aiaⁿlhto*, nasal form.

aiạlhtoba, n., a reward, Matt. 10: 41.

aiạlhtoba ikono kiⁿsha, a., undue; not due yet.

aiạlhtoka, n., lot; office; duty, Luke 1: 9.

aiạlhtokowa, pp., appointed; required; assigned as a duty, Luke 3: 13.

aiạlli, aiạlbi, n., price, 17th hymn, 3d verse; see *aiilli*.

aiạlwạsha, n., a frying pan.

aiạli, v. a. i., to start from; to commence from; to end at, Matt. 1: 17.

aiạli, n., the edge; end, Matt. 10: 22; limit; border; extent; bounds; the butt; compass; conclusion; the extremity; period; pitch; the reach; term; termination; the upshot; the sum total; as *yạmmakosh aiạli*, that is all or the whole; *yakni aiạli*, n., the coast; border, Josh. 1: 4; 15: 6; confine; the extreme; limitation.

aiạli, a., finite; last; utmost.

aiạli, adv., through.

aiạli, pp., limited; *ant imaiạli*, until, Matt. 11: 13; *ant aiạli*, unto, Josh. 5: 9.

aiạli, v. t., to reach.

aiạli, v. a. i., to be from; *aiạlit mihinti ma*, Matt. 4: 17.

aiạli iksho, a., unlimited; without limit; infinite.

aiạlichi, v. t., to terminate.

aiạlichi, v. t., to limit; to bound; to bring to an end or close.

aiạmmona, see *aiamona*.

aiạmo, v. t., to gather from or of, Luke 6: 44.

aiạmoma, see *aiimoma*.

aiạni, n., a funnel; a tunnel.

aiạnnowa, see *aianowa*.

aiạshwa, v. a. i. pl., to be there; to stay there.

aiạshwa, n., the place where they stay, sit, etc.

aiạtta, v. a. i., to reside at; to dwell; to inhabit.

aiạtta, n., a residence; an abode of any kind; the place of one's birth; a native place; a domicile; a habitation; a lodging; a mansion; a room, 1 Kings 10: 26.

aiạtta, n., an inhabitant; a lodger; a native; one born in any place.

aiạtta ikithano, a., unfixed.

aiạtta iksho, a., vagabond; being without a home; vagrant.

aiạttatok nitak, aiyạttatok nitak, n., a birthday, Gen. 40: 20; Matt. 14: 6.

aieha, pp., washed, as to the head.

aiehchi, ayehchi, aiyehchi, v. t. See *aiehchi*, 1 Sam. 19: 2; Josh. 8: 2.

aiehnạ!, aiyehnaⁿ! int. (used by females; not a manly word), Oh, ah, alas, O dear, an inter. of sorrow or regret; *aiyehnahe!* is a longer term.

aieli, v. t., to wash one's own head.

aielichi, v. t., to wash the head of another, or to cause it to be done.

aiemoma, a., always; see *aiimomachi*.

aiena, con. adv., and, together, withal; prep., with.

aiena, v. a. i., to be with; to be one with; to go with; Matt. 5: 6, *moma aiena kạt*, etc., Matt. 2: 3; Josh. 8: 5; *aienali keyu*, I am not with; I am not one of; *aienali kạt, ilaiena kạto*, Josh. 14: 11; Matt. 9: 14; *hạchimaienahe*, shall be added unto you, Matt. 6: 33; *ilaiena*, Gen. 47: 3; Josh. 5: 11; to be together with, Matt. 6: 33; 2 Sam. 24: 4; Matt. 12: 3, 4; *ohoyo ạlla aiena kạto aⁿsha hoⁿ*, beside women and children; *itaiena*, to be together with; *imitaiena*, used for a concubine, see 1 Kings 11: 3 (the word *tekchi* comes in before *imitaiena;* in Judges 19: 2, it appears without *tekchi*).

aiena, adv., also; likewise; and with a negative, neither, Matt. 6: 19; 18: 17; Josh. 7: 11; *ilaiena*, Matt. 9: 14.

aieninchi, v. t., to put with; to put along with; to include; *itaieninchi*, to put together with; to do both together, Matt. 10: 28; 13: 29; *aieninchit*, v. t. and conj., to put with and, or an adverbial expression; *aienint*, contracted from *aieninchit*, as *iḷappa aienint isht ia; itianint*, to go together; *itaieninchi*, v. t., to put together with; Luke 4: 40; *itaieninchi*, *itianinchi*, both, Luke 5: 7; with, Luke 5: 19 [?]; Matt. 6: 24.

aieshi, n., a handle; a haft.

aieshi, v. t., to take hold at; to take hold there.

aieta, see *akaieta* and *akaboⁿshc̣*.

aifoli, n., ivory, Rev. 18: 12.

aiibachaⁿfa, v. a. i., to be one with, from *iba* and *achạfa; anumpa hạt Chihowa yaⁿ aiibachaⁿfatok*, John 1: 1, 2.

aiibetạbli, n., an offense, Matt. 18: 7.

aiiⁿfalạmmi, n., a schism.

aiihchi, v. a. i., to lie in ambush; to lie in wait for, in order to catch or kill; to watch.

aiikhana, **aiithana**, n., knowledge; understanding; place of knowledge; seat of learning; *aiikhana ạli*, limit or scope of knowledge; as far as one remembers; see *aiithana ạli*.

aiikhạna, n., a place for learning; a school.

aiikhạnanchi (nasal form), n., a place of instruction; a place of teaching; a school.

aiiklạna, n., the middle; where the middle is; the half way; the center.

aiiklạnaka, n., the middle.

aiiklạnna, n., the half; where the half is, John 8: 3.

aiiklạnnaⁿka (nasal form), n., the middle place; the half; being the half; *yakni aiiklạnnaⁿka*.

aiiksiachi, see *aiiskiachi*.

aiiksho, v. a. i., "consumed," Josh. 5: 6.

aiilbạsha, n., wretchedness; poverty; misery; affliction; hell.

aiilbạsha imma, a., infernal; hellish.

aiilbạshaka, n., the place of sorrow; the state of sorrow; hell.

aiilekostininchi, n., repentance; place of reformation.

aiilhpeta, n., place where feed is given; a trough; a manger; a stall; a place of receiving a benefaction or annuity.

aiilli, n., place of death; a death bed; home, death, John 21: 19.

aiilli, v. t., to cost; to fetch.

aiilli, **aiạlli**, **aiạlbi**, n., price; worth; value; cost; an estimate; fare, 1 Kings 10: 28.

aiilli, pp., valued.

aiilli atạbli, **aiilli atable**, v. t., to overcharge.

aiilli atạpa, pp., overcharged; a., dear; too high.

aiilli atạpa, v. a. i., to be dear, or too high; to be too costly.

aiilli atạpa, n., an overcharge.

aiilli atạpa, a., overvalued; unvalued.

aiilli chaha, n., a high price.

aiilli chahạchi, v. t., to raise the price.

aiilli chito, a., dear; having a large price; costly; expensive; high.

aiilli chito, pp., priced high.

aiilli chitoli, v. t., to price high.

aiilli ikchito, a., cheap.

aiilli ikchitocho, **aiilli ikchitolo**, v. t., to price low.

aiilli iklauo, a., cheap; bearing a small price.

aiilli iksho, **aiilliksho**, a., without price; gratuitous; priceless.

aiilli iksho, n., cost free.

aiilli iskitini, a., cheap; bearing a small price.

aiilli iskitinichi, v. t., to reduce the price; to cheapen.

aiilli onanchi; *aiilli ikonancho*, v. t., to underrate; to undervalue.

aiilli onitula, pp., rated; priced.

aiilli onuchi, v. t., to rate; to price; to value.

aiilli onuchi, n., an appraiser; a rater; a prizer.

aiillichi, v. t., to set a price upon; to price; to value.

aiiłauạlli, n., a playground; a play; the stage.

aiiłauạlli, n., a scene.

aiiłauạlli chito, n., a scene.

aiiłauạlli chuka, n., a theater; a playhouse.

aiimaiyachi, v. t., to overcome; *yakni aⁿ aiimaiyachit talili hoke*, John 16: 33.

aiimạlhpesa, n., his disposition, custom, way, habit, humor, instinct, nature, style.

aiimạlhtaha, n., maintenance.

aiimmi, a., his; his kind; after his kind.

aiimmi ayukali, n., each one after his kind.

aiimmi biⁿka, a., alike in kind; *bashpo aiimi biⁿka ishishi athpesa*, you may take knives that are like each other; *aiimmi biⁿka ayuka*, a., every one after his kind.

aiimoma, aiamoma, a., adv., always so; natural; naturally small; *isuba aiimoma*, a horse that is naturally small; *hatak aiimoma*, a man of small stature; *abeka aiimoma*, always sick or feeble.

aiimoma, v. n., to be naturally small; to be thus always, 1 John 2: 17[?].

aiimomachi, v. a. i., to be accustomed; to be so naturally; to be habituated; *aiimomali*, I usually do so.

aiimomaka, n., a habit; a custom.

aiimomaka, aimomaka, a., habitual.

aiimomachi, n., a habit.

aiimomachi, v. t., to habituate; to reason.

aiimomachi, a., habitual; veteran.

aiimpa, n., lit., an eating place; any place where any creature eats, as a rack, a range, a manger, a plate, a table, a dish, Matt. 15: 27.

aiimpa, n., a boarder.

aiimpa, v. t., to eat at, or on; to eat there.

aiimpa foki, v. t., to stall [or to stake a horse out to grass; lit. "to put in an eating place."—H. S. H.]

aiimpa iskitini, n., a stand; a small table.

aiimpa iyi, n., a table leg.

aiimpa oⁿlipa, n., a table cloth.

aiimpa ona, n., meal time.

aiimpa umpatalhpo, n., a table cloth.

aiina, v. a. i., to become the wife of a man in company with another woman; to become a wife of inferior condition, there being another wife of the husband; *itaiina*, to marry a second wife, the first being alive and living with her husband.

aiina, aiena, n., a wife of inferior condition; the second wife; a concubine; *itaiina*, n. pl., wives together of one man; *itaiena*, 2 Sam. 5: 13.

aiinla, v. a. i., to alter; to change.

aiinla, pp., altered, Luke 9: 29.

aiinlachi, v. t., to alter; to change.

aiintakobi, a., tired out by means of or with it; wearied with.

aiintakobichi, v. t., to tire down with; to weary with.

aiiⁿnukkilli, n., anger (an attribute), 2 Sam. 24: 1.

aiisikkopa, aiissikkopa, n., wrath; place of torment, Luke 3: 7 [?].

aiiska, pp., fixed; regulated; put in order.

aiiskia, v. t., to fix; to regulate; to put in order; to repair.

aiiskia, n., a regulator; a repairer.

aiiskiachi, aiskiachi, v. t. caus., to fix; to repair; to put in order; to reconcile, 1 K. 11: 27; see *aiskiachi*.

aiiskiachi, aiskiachi, n., a repairer.

aiiskiali, v. t., to mend; to repair.

aiissa, n., a place deserted, abandoned, left, or forsaken; a ruin.

aiissa, v. t., to ravish, 2 Sam. 13: 12; *hokli cha aiissa*, to commit a rape, 2 Sam. 13: 14.

aiissachechi, v. t. caus., to end; to cause to end; to cause to abandon; to employ one to cause another to quit or abandon a plan or project.

aiissachi, pp., ended, Luke 4: 2.

aiissachi, v. t. and v. a. i., to desert; to leave off; to cause to quit; *pissachi*, he causes us to quit; *aiissacheli*, I quit, or I have quit it.

aiisso, v. t. sing, to beat; to smite at, there, or on; *itaiisso*, to smite each other at, on, etc.; to bunt; to strike together; pl., *aboli*.

aiisso, n., the blow; the place struck; a slam.

aiiⁿshali, a., extreme.

aiiⁿshali, n., the extremity.

aiishi, n., the handle; the haft.

aiishi, v. t., to take hold at; to seize it there, or at.

aiishko, n., a drinking place; a watering place; a drinking vessel, 1 K. 10: 21.

aiishko, v. t., to drink at; to drink from or out of.

aiisht ahalaia, n., right.

aiisht ahollo, n., a miracle, John 2: 11; a sign, John 2: 18[?]; a wonder.

aiisht ahollochi, v. t., to perform miracles or wonders.

aiisht aiokchaya, n., the vitals.

aiisht aiopi, n., the extreme; the last.

aiisht atiaka, n., a progenitor; a kinsman.

aiisht awechi, n., foundation; origin.

aiisht ia, v. a. i., to start from; *ilạppa isht ia*, to start from this.

aiisht ia, n., the beginning; the commencement; the start; the germ; the spring.

aiisht ia ạmmona, n., the beginning; the first commencement; the rise; the origin; the ground.

aiisht ilahauchi, n., profit; *nana aiisht ilahauchi achukma*, a., profitable.

aiisht ilaiyukpa, n., enjoyment.

aiisht ilapisa, a., profitable.

aiisht ilapisa, n., a benefit.

aiisht ilapisahe keyu, a., unprofitable.

aiisht illi, n., occasion of death; reason for death, Luke 23: 22.

aiisht inchakali, a., conceived in her by means of; pregnant by means of. Matt. 1: 20.

aiisht itintakla, n., a medium; that by means of which.

aiishwa, v. t., to smell of.

aiitachaka, pp., spliced at.

aiitachakạlli, v. t. sing., to splice it at or with; to add on at; to continue at; to weld at.

aiitachakli, v. t. pl., to splice them at or with.

aiitafama, v. t., to meet at.

aiitafama, n., a confluence; a meeting; the place where they meet; a junction.

aiitahoba, n., a place of meeting; a place of assembling; *tạli holisso aiitahoba yaⁿ*, the receipt of custom.

aiitahoba, v. a. i., to gather at; to assemble at.

aiitahobi, v. t., to assemble at.

aiitaiyokoma, n., a flutter; a puzzle.

aiitanowa, n., a road; a highway.

aiitatoba, n., a market; a trading place; a factory; a house of merchandise, John 2: 16; an emporium; a shop; a store.

aiitatoba chito, n., a fair.

aiitatoba chuka, n., a market house; a factory; a trading house; a storehouse.

aiitatobanowa, v. a. i., to shop.

aiitạchaka, n., a joint; a place spliced or welded.

aiitạchakịlli, n., a suture.

aiitạnaha, n., the place of meeting or assembling; a rendezvous; a resort.

aiitạnaha, v. a. i., to assemble at; to rendezvous.

aiitạnnali, v. t., to assemble at.

aiitạnowa, n., a street, Matt. 6: 2, 5.

aiitạpiⁿha, v. a. i. nasal form, to be with; to be associated with, Luke 23: 32.

aiithana n., a disciple; *nan aiithana ạleha*, Matt. 17: 10.

aiithana, n., knowledge; place of knowledge; or *aiikhana*, q. v.

aiithana ạli, n., memory; the extent of knowledge; see *aiikhana*.

aiithanaka misha, a., immemorial.

aiithạna, v. t., to learn at; to acquire knowledge at; *imaiithạna*, v. t., to learn of him; *imaiithạna*, n., a learner; his disciple.

aiithạna, n., a school; a place of learning; a seminary; *nana aiithạna*, n., a disciple; a scholar; *nan imaiithạna*, n., his disciples, Matt. 13: 10.

aiithạna chuka, n., a schoolhouse.

aiitibafoka, n., a junction; a peer.

aiitibbi, n., a field of battle; a place or scene of a battle, a battle ground; a field, 2 Sam. 18: 6; *aiitihimbi*, 2 Cor. 7: 5.

aiitiⁿbiliⁿka, n., propinquity; place near to each other.

aiitilaui, n., an equal; equality.

aiitintakla, con., through; by means of; adv., in the meanwhile, John 4: 31; between, Josh. 3: 4; during (the time of harvest), Josh. 3: 15.

aiitisetạli, n., junction (as the junction of one water course with another).

aiitishali, v. t., to ride three together on one horse; to ride treble.

aiitishali, n., a generation.

aiitisholi, v. t., to ride two together on one horse; to ride double.

aiititakla, con., among, Josh. 3: 5.

aika or eka, interjection of dislike.

aiksiachi, aiiksiachi, see *aiiskiachi*.

Ailish, n., Irish; the Irish.

Ailish, a., Irish.

Ailish hatak, n., an Irishman.

Ailish okla, n., the Irish; the Irish people or nation.

Ailish yakni, n., Ireland.

aimomaka, see *aiimomaka*.

aioa, aiyoa, aiowa, v. t. pl. of *ishi*, to pick up, Matt. 13: 29; to choose, *aioạt ilitahoba he aⁿ*, Matt. 13: 28; *aioạt . . . pit apitta*, Matt. 13: 48; *aiyua*, pp., picked up; *aiuwa*, pass., to be chosen; 2. Chron. 25: 5.

aioⁿbinili, aiombinili, aiomanili (q. v.), n., a seat; a chair.

aioⁿbinili api, n., a chair leg.

aioⁿbinili falaia, n., a bench.

aioⁿbinili hanta, n., a sacred seat.

aioⁿbinili holitopa, n., a holy seat; a sacred seat; a throne.

aiochi, see *aiuchi*.

aioⁿfaiokachi, n., a rocker, the curving piece of wood on which a cradle or chair rocks.

aioⁿhikia, n., a vestige.

aiohmi, v. n., to be so; *siaiohmi*, I am so.

aiohmichi, v. t., to cause; to make it so.

aioⁿholissochi, n., a writing table; a desk; a line.

aioholissochit achunli, n., a sampler.

aiokami, n., a wash basin; a wash bowl; a place for washing the face; a laver.

aiokami, v. t., to wash the face in or at.

aiokchaliⁿka, n., redemption; *isht aiokchaⁿya*, redemption, Luke 2: 38.

aiokchaⁿya, v. n., to live by, Luke 4: 4.

aiokchaⁿya, pp., to be saved, John 3: 17.

aiokchaⁿya, a., vital.

aiokchaⁿya, aiokchaya (Matt. 18: 8, 9), n., life; salvation; support; sustenance; vitality; see *aiokchaⁿya* in *aiokchaⁿya yaⁿ*, Matt. 7: 14.

aiokchaⁿya alhpisa, n., salvation, John 4: 22.

aiokchipelih, aiokchifelih, v. a. i., to gaze at.

aiokhaneli, see *aiyukhaneli*.

aiokhankachi; *itaiokhankachi*, corners, Matt. 6: 5.

aiokla, n., a settlement of persons.

aiokla, v. t., to settle at; to inhabit.

aiokla, pp., settled; inhabited; *ikaioklo*, a., uninhabited; wild.

aiokla achafa, n., a habitant; an inhabitant.

aiokla hinla, a., inhabitable; habitable.

aioklachechi, v. t., to populate; to furnish with inhabitants.

aioklachi, v. t., to settle others at a place; to cause to be inhabited.

aioklachi, n., one that settles others in a place.

aiokluha, a., all; *itaiokluⁿha*, all together, John 18: 1; 21: 2.

aiokluha, adv., heartily.

aiokluhali, v. t., to take all together.

aiokluhalinchi, v. t. caus., to cause all to be taken together; *aiitaiokluhalinchi*, Luke 23: 32.

aiokluhanchi, v. t., to take all together; to take also; to take together with.

aioklileka, n., darkness; the dark; the dark place; obscurity; obscureness; *kocha aioklileka*, outer darkness.

aioklili, n., darkness; where it is dark, or where the dark is.

aiokliliⁿka, n., nasal form, darkness, John 3: 19· a shade.

aiokliliⁿkaka, n., the darkness, John 12: 46; the dark place.

aiokpancha hinla, a., laudable.

aiokpanchi, a., thankful; courteous; grateful; heedful; officious; welcome; as *hatak aiokpanchi achukma; ikaiokpancho, ikaiokpacho*, a., ungrateful; unthankful; unwelcome.

aiokpanchi, n., thankfulness; saluting; greeting; applause; a benediction; a blessing; gratitude; notice; observance; a reception; respect; reverence; a welcome.

aiokpanchi, n., a saluter; an esteemer.

aiokpanchi, v. t., to celebrate; to applaud; to approbate; to thank; to receive well; to laud; to magnify.

aiokpanchi achukma, n., readiness.

aiokpanchi achukma, a., cheerful.

aiokpanchi keyu, a., unthankful, Luke 6: 35; inattentive; ungenerous; *iksamaiokpancho at*, he is not grateful for what he has of mine [?].

aiokpanchit anoli, v. t., to recommend.

aiokpachechi, aiyukpachi, v. t. caus., to amuse; to cause to greet; to make glad; to cheer; to delight. This word is a form of *yukpachi*.

aiokpachi, aiyukpachi, v. t. (from *yukpa*; properly *ayukpachi* instead of *aiokpachi*), to salute, Matt. 10: 12; to greet; to approve; to bless, Matt. 14: 19; to accept; to accost; to acknowledge; to worship, Matt. 4: 9; 8: 2; 14: 33; to receive well, Matt. 10: 40; to congratulate; to shake hands; to dignify; to fawn; to gratulate; to homage; to honor; to notice; to prosper; to regard; to respect, Matt. 12: 7; to revere; to reverence; to sanction; to thank; to glorify; to warrant; to welcome; to worship, Matt. 8: 2; Josh. 5: 14; *aiokpanchi, aiyukpanchi,* nasal form; *aiokpahanchi,* freq., Matt. 9: 8; 15: 9, 31; *aiokpaiyachi,* protracted form; *isht aiokpachi,* v. t., to treat; *ikaiokpacho,* to refuse; *isht aiokpachi,* n., gift, Matt. 8: 4; *ikaiokpacho,* pp., refused; unnoticed; unregarded; unrespected; repulsive.

aiokpachi, n., a greeter; a saluter; a worshiper.

aiokpachi, n., a compliment; eclat; gratitude; a valediction; *ikaiokpacho,* n., ingratitude; a slight.

aiokpachi, a., diligent; (*aiokpachi achukma,* industrious), attentive; *ikaiokpacho,* a., unconstant.

aiokpachi, n., diligence; (*aiokpachi achukma,* industry).

aiokpachi achukma, adv., readily.

aiokpachi alhpesa, a., worshipful.

aiokpulo, n., evil; guilt.

aiokpulo, n., a bad place; an evil place.

aiokpulo, v. a. i., to be bad.

aiokpulo iksho, n., innocence; innocency.

aiokpuloka, v. a. i., to be ruined.

aiokpuloka, n., the bad place; a bad place; hell, Matt. 10: 28; an abyss; the abyss; a furnace; perdition; tophet; destruction, Matt. 7: 13; a desolation, Josh. 8: 28.

aiokpuloka, a., evil, Luke 11: 13; vexed; *isht aiokpuloka,* vexed with, Luke 6: 18.

aiokpuloka chito, n., the great place of evil.

aiokpuloka chukoa, pp., damned.

aiokpuloka foka, pp., damned; put into hell; cast into hell.

aiokpuloka foki, v. t., to damn; to put into a bad place.

aiokpuloka iksho, n., soundness.

aiokpuloka iksho, a., unblemished.

aiokpuloka luak, n., hell fire; Matt. 5: 22; 18: 9.

aiokpulunka, n., perdition; *aiokpolunka ushi,* John 17: 12; a wreck; hell; *aiokpuloka,* Matt. 5: 22; 11: 23; 16: 18.

aiokshilinta, pp., nasal form, shut up; being shut up; Luke 4: 25.

aiomanili, n., a seat; a chair; bottom of a chair; a stool.

aiomanili api, n., a chair post; a chair leg.

aiomanili falaia, n., a bench; a form; a settle.

aiomanili iyi, n., a chair leg; a chair post; leg of a stool.

aiombinili, see *aionbinili* and *aiomanili.*

aiona, n. (from *ona* and *ai*), access; the place by which to go to.

aiona, n., time; season, Luke 2: 6; *ikaiono,* before the time; *ikaiono kinsha hon,* before the time, Matt. 8: 29; *ikaiono,* adv., untimely.

aiona, v. a. i., to go to; to betake to; to reach to or there; *aionashali,* v. t., v. a. i., to haunt; *ikaiono,* neg. form; *ikaiono,* a., immature; *ikaionocheli,* v. t., to bring forth before the proper time; to miscarry; *ikaiono ieshi,* v. t., to miscarry; n., an abortion; *ikaiono atta,* v. t., to bring forth before the proper time; *ikaiono atta,* n., an abortion.

aionasha, n., a seat; a chair; a cricket; room.

aionasha aiataya ansha, n., an elbow chair.

aionasha umpatalhpo, n., a cushion for a chair.

aionitola, n., a bier, Luke 7: 14; that which he lies on; a rest.

aiontalaia, n., a site.

aiontalat fulokachi, n., a pivot; a pin on which anything turns.

aionusha, n., a bed; a frame on which a man lies or sits. See Luke 5: 18.

aiopi; *ont aiisht imaiyopi,* Luke 11: 26.

aiopitama (pl., *aiopitamoa*), v. n., to lap over (as shingles on a roof); *itiaiopitama,* to pass each other.

aiopitama, pp., made to pass each other; passed.

aiopitammi (pl., *aiopitamoli*), v. t., to pass by one that is coming from the opposite quarter; *itiaiopitammi,* to pass each other, whether in sight or not, especially when going in opposite directions.

aionshobolichi, n., a kiln (as where boards are kiln dried).

aiowa, n., a long hunting expedition; a hunt after wild animals. See *aiba,* to pick; to select.

aiowa, v. a. i., to go out on a hunting expedition; to hunt wild animals.

aiowata, n., hunting ground.

aiskachi, pp., mended; fixed; repaired.

aiskia, aiiskia, v. a. i., to ameliorate; to improve, the second form is probably the correct one; *aiiskia keyu*, a., uncorrected.

aiskia, a., pp., fixed; repaired; regulated; amended; corrected; ameliorated; mended; redressed; refitted; relieved; renovated; trimmed; *ilaiskia*, ref. form.

aiskia hinla, a., reparable.

aiskiacha hinla, a., reparable.

aiskiachi, aiksiachi, v. t., to settle; to trim; to unclog; to wind; to fix; to repair; to regulate; to ameliorate; to better; to improve; to correct; to dress; to fit; to indemnify; to mend; to redress; to refit; to relieve; to remedy; to renovate; to ripen; *ilaiksiachi*, to reform himself; see *aiiskiachi*.

aiskiachi, n., a repairer; one that fixes; a mender; *aiskiali*, a second form (?).

aiskiahe keyu, a., irreparable.

aiuchi, aiochi, a place at a spring, well, branch, or pond, where water is dipped up or taken up by means of a bucket.

aiuh, int.

aiukleka, n., an embellishment; an ornament.

aiukli, n., a beauty; fineness; a form; grace.

aiukli, a., beautiful; handsome; comely; fine; pretty; *ikaioklo, ikaiuklo*, a., ill favored; ugly; not handsome; unhandsome.

aiukli, v. n., to be beautiful, pleasing, acceptable; neg., *ikaioklo*, not to be beautiful, pleasing, etc.

aiukli, pp., embellished; beautified; garnished.

aiukli keyu, a., homely.

aiuklichechi, v. t., to embellish.

aiuklichi, v. t.; to beautify; to adorn; to make handsome; to garnish, Matt. 23: 29.

aiukluhali, v. t., see *aiokluhali*.

aiulhkachi, n., a steeper.

aiulhpi, or aialhpi (q. v.), n., a handle; a haft; a hilt.

aiulhti, n., a fireplace; a district; a council fire; a state; a government.

aiunchololi, n., a tribe, Josh. 4: 2; 7: 14.

aiunchululi, v. a. i., to form a generation.

aiunchululli, n., the sprouts that grow up from the roots; a generation; a young generation; a race; a tribe, Josh. 3: 12; *itaiunchululi*, generations, see Matt. 1: 17; *itaiunchululi auahushta*, 14 generations.

aiuntalali, see *haiyantalali*.

aiushta, a., the fourth; *ont aiushta*, adv., fourthly.

aiushtaha, adv., fourth time; the fourth time.

aiya, v. a. i., to go along; see *anya*.

aiyabechi, aiyubechi, v. t., to aggravate, to make worse, especially when sick; to give a death blow or a finishing stroke to the dying; to heighten (as a fever); to impair.

aiyabechi, n., one that makes worse.

aiyaka, a., great; many: *aiyanka*, in *nan aiyanka*, "great things," Mark 3: 8.

aiyakohmi, ayakohmi, v. a. i., to do so, John 1: 28; 2: 12.

aiyakohmichi, ayakohmichi, v. t., to do thus or so.

aiyala, aiyala, pro. form of *ala*, to come at length or at last; to arrive at last; *aiyahanla*, freq., they come or keep coming.

aiyammi, pp., salted; sweetened; saturated.

aiyataia, see *ayataia*.

aiyabbi, aiyubi, a., pp., worse; made worse; heightened; impaired (as health); from *ai* and *abi*, to kill; *aiyambi*, nasal form.

aiyabbi isht inshali, a., worse (as when sick).

aiyammi, a., pp., sweetened with; salted with or in.

aiyammichi, v. t., to salt with or in; to sweeten with.

aiyamohmahe alhpesa, n., fatality; office.

aiyamohmi, n., a habit; manners; method; a mode; order; principle; a rite; a style; a trade; a vogue; a way.

aiyamohmi keyu, a., unfashionable.

aiyamohmi makali, n., vulgarity.

aiyatta tok nitak, see *aiatta tok nitak*.

aiyehchi, see *aiehchi*.

aiyehnan, see *aiehna*.

aiyichifichi, n., a hawk; a hen hawk; a pigeon hawk.

aiyimita, aiyinminta, v. n., to be bold, brave, or animated.

aiyimita, n., boldness; bravery; courage; eagerness; zeal.

aiyimita, a., bold; brave; animated; doughty; eager; valiant; *ikaiyiminto*, a., unanimated.

aiyimitachi, v. t. caus., to make bold; to embolden; to prompt; to provoke.

aiyimmika, n., faith; confidence, Luke 18: 42.

aiyoa, aioa (q. v.), ayoah, v. t. pl., to pick up; to cull; to garble; to sort; *aiyua*, pp.

aiyoba, aiyuba, a., good; excellent; selected; select; choice.

aiyoba, v. n., to be good; *aiyomba*, nasal form, good things mixed with bad, as good potatoes mixed with bad ones.

aiyobachi, aiyubachi, to do good to; to make good; see Matt. 18: 15.

aiyobaⁿka, n., a good place; being a good place.

aiyobali, v. t., to mix good things together; *aiyubali*, see Hymn 31, 4th verse.

aiyohmi, v. n., v. a. i., to be thus; to do so.

aiyokoma, imaiyokoma, v. a. i., to puzzle.

aiyokoma, aiyukoma, v. n., to be puzzled; to be at a loss; to be in doubt; to doubt; *amaiyokoma*, I am puzzled; it is a puzzle to me; *itaiyokoma*, pass., confused together; cluttered; confounded; deranged; discomposed; disordered; jumbled; tumbled.

aiyokoma, n., confusion; a nonplus; *itaiyokoma*, n., a clutter; disorder.

aiyokoma, a., *imaiyokoma*, pp., puzzled; *imanukfila aiyokoma*, pp., distracted.

aiyokomi, v. t., to puzzle; to perplex; *itaiyokommi*, v. t., to clutter; to disorder; to jumble; *itaiyokommit itannali*, v. t., to lumber.

aiyokomichi, v. t. caus., to cause to be puzzled; to puzzle; to derange; to nonplus; *imaiyokomichi*, v. t., to pother; to puzzle; to bewilder; *itaiyokomichi*, to confound or confuse each other; to derange; to discompose; *imanukfila imaiyukomichi*, or *imanukfila aiyukomichi*, to confuse the mind; to distract.

aiyopi, Luke 11: 26. See *aiopi*.

aiyopisa, n., a scene.

aiyoshoba, n., error; wandering; sin; place of wandering.

aiyoshoba iksho, a., holy; without error.

aiyoshoba iksho, n., holiness.

aiyua, aiyuah, pp. of *aiyoa* (q. v.), or *ayoah*, picked up; gathered; culled; garbled; chosen.

aiyua, a., picked up.

aiyua, n., that which is picked up.

aiyuba, see *aiyoba*.

aiyubachi, see *aiyobachi*.

aiyubechi, see *aiyabechi*.

aiyuka, adj. pro., every one, *asilha aiyuka*, Matt. 7: 8; *na holissochi aiyuka*, every scribe, Matt. 13: 52, *aⁿyuka* in *hapichuka aⁿyuka, aiyuka*, each; see *ilaiyuka; aiyuka*, is the root from which is formed *aiyukali, ilaiyukali, ilaiyuka*, etc., Matt. 4: 24; 12: 31.

aiyukali, a., each, Josh. 4: 5; 5: 8; 7: 14; *iskifa iⁿshi aiyukali*, each has an ax; *afammi aiyukali*, each year; yearly.

aiyukhaneli, v. a. i., to cross a row.

aiyukhana, v. a. i., to cross; *itaiyukhana*, v. a. i., to cross each other; to intersect; n., a cross; *itaiyukhannali*, v. t., to cross each other; to intersect.

aiyukhana, aiokhana, aiukhana, n., a cross; *itaiokhankachi*, corners, Matt. 6: 5.

aiyukhanni, v. t. pl., to cross; to intersect; *itaiyukhanni*, v. t., to cross each other; to intersect.

aiyukoma, see *aiyokoma*.

aiyukpa, n., joy; a happy place; a place of happiness.

aiyukpa, pp., made glad; profited, Matt. 15: 5; *aiisht ilaiyukpa*, to take joy to himself in.

aiyukpali, v. t., to make glad; to make glad with; to gladden.

aiyukpachi, v. t., to cheer. See *aiokpachi*.

aiyuma, a., pp., mixed; *itaiyuma, itaiuma*, pp., mixed together; blended; mixed; compounded; commingled; commixed; intermixed; mingled; shuffled; tumbled; *ikitaiyumo*, a., unmingled.

aiyuma, v. a. i., to mix; *itaiyuma*, v. a. i., to mingle; *ikitaiyumo*, not to mingle; *aiyumichi; itaiyumichi*, to temper; to blend; to mix; to tumble together.

aiyummi, v. t., to mix; to mingle; *itai-yummi*, to mix together; to commingle; to commix; to compound; to intermingle; to intermix; to mingle; to shuffle.

aiyupi, ayupi, n., a bath; any place for bathing or wallowing in the sand or mire; a laver.

aiyushkami, a., lecherous.

aiyushkammi, v. a. i., to lust.

aiyushkammi, n., lust.

ak, sign of the first per. sing. of negative verbs, as *mintili*, I come; *akminto*, I do not come.

ak, sign of the first per. sing. of one of the forms of the imp. mood, as *pisali*, I see; *akpisa*, let me see.

ak, a particle of frequent occurrence in the Choctaw language. It is found, together with its compounds, in some form after nouns, pronouns, adjectives, verbs, adverbs. The sense of this particle varies according to the part of speech it succeeds. It is sometimes *ak*, then *hak* or *yak* (perhaps *kak* should be added, from *k*, definite, and *ak*). It follows verbs. It is used as an article and a relative pronoun. It is a word often used for designation or distinction, not only of a thing, i. e., a noun, but also of action and herein it differs from the English, except when we render the verb as a noun. In *akoke*, Matt. 2: 6, it is distinctive and marks one object from all others. It is usually rendered by the, that, one singling out from others; *luak akkeyukma pilashpahe keyu*, if it were not for the fire, etc. Compounds of *ak* are: *akan, hakan, makan—akano—akat, akat*, not used, *akhet*, being substituted—*akatukan*, the, Matt. 16: 12—*akato, akato—akchoba—akcho?* 2 Sam. 24: 13; *akbano* and *akbato*, sign of optat. mood—*akbano*, adv., that only—*akbat*, adv., that only (*t* makes the word the subject of some verb) — *akhe, akhiⁿ—akheno*, in particular; especially that; and by way of disparagement—*akhet*, especially that one to his disadvantage—*akheto*, that in particular; contradistinctive, and disparaging (*ano akheto*, how much less I, if *you* can not (bid at an auction))—*akiⁿ*, contracted

from *akinli—akilla kia*, only the, Matt. 14: 36—*akinli*, adv., also; likewise; too (*ak*, that; *inli*, also); that again; *iⁿ yakni akinli*, Matt. 13: 57; *lakofi akinli*, he is well, that again—*akinli*, pro., self; selves—*akinlika*, the same, Matt. 18: 1—*akint*, a contraction from *akinlit—akkia* (*ak*, that; *kia*, let it go), even; even as; so much as, Matt. 11: 23; even the, Matt. 12: 8; also the, Matt. 13: 26; 15: 16; 17: 12—*akma*, sign of the sub. mood. The first word is changed when the verb ends with *i* or *o;* see *ikma* and *okma*. The real particle is *kma* and *kmat—akmako — akmakocha — akmakoka — akmakoke—akmakona—akmakosh—akmakot—akmakhet* (and -*heto*); see *akhet*, etc.—*kmakhe* (and -*heno*)—*akmano—akmat—akmato—akoⁿ*, the, it, Matt. 5: 24; 17: 4; *iⁿsinikak akoⁿ*, their synagogue, Matt. 12: 9; *haiyuⁿkpulo akoⁿ*, the tares; *aⁿkanchak akoⁿ*, my barn, Matt. 13: 30; *ilap akoⁿ*, him, Matt. 18: 6; *chuⁿkash akoⁿ aminti*, Matt. 15: 18; *ano akoⁿ*, me, Matt. 18: 5.—*akocha.—akoka.—akokano; onush akokano*, Matt. 13: 30.—*akoke; hatak ushi akoke*, Matt. 13: 37; *imalla akoke*, Matt. 13: 38; *Setan akoke, enchil aleha akoke*, Matt. 13: 39. — *akokano. — akokat. — akokato.—akokia.—akona.—akosh*, Matt. 17: 10; *ushi akosh*, who is the son, Matt. 11: 27.—*akot.*

aka, a particle, with *olbal*, as *olbal aka;* (also *anuⁿk aka* and *paknak aka, yakni paknak aka*), sometime; *olbal aka*, hindward, rearward.

aka itula, see *akka itula.*

akaboⁿsha, akabosha, pp., a., charred, burnt, or reduced to coal; reduced to a mass, like coals or rotten potatoes; same as *taha. akaieta* is a synonym of this word.

akabuⁿshli, v. t., to char; to burn or reduce to coal, as is the custom of the Choctaw with the dry bark in their hot houses; to burn to a coal.

akachakali (from *aka* and *achakali*), v. a. i., to lift up the head; to stand with the head up; to cock; to lift up the eyes.

akachakalichi, causative or compulsive, to lift up the head, etc., 2 Kings 9: 32.

akachuli, akachạli, n., edge of a door yard; border of a door yard, Luke 16: 20. [?].

akachunni, see akkachunni.

akaieta, synonymous with akaboⁿsha (q. v.) and same as taha.

akaieta, plu. of aiena? many; with all; ahe ạt shuạt akaieta; hatak illi akaieta; ilhkolitakaieta, ilhkolit atomafa, Matt. 3: 10 [?].

akaⁿk anusi, n., a hen roost; a roost.

akaⁿk ạbi, n., a hen hawk.

akaⁿk chaha, n., a tall hen; a tamé turkey.

akaⁿk chaka, n., the wattles of a hen.

akaⁿk hishi, n., hen feathers; a hen feather.

akaⁿk huⁿkupa, n., a poacher; one that steals fowls.

akaⁿk impạsha, n., the wattles of a hen.

akaⁿk inchuka, n., a henhouse; a hen-coop.

akaⁿk ishke, n., a hen that has had chickens; an old hen; a mother hen.

akaⁿk kofi, n., a guinea hen; a pintado.

akaⁿk nakni, n., a cock; a rooster.

akaⁿk nakni himmita, n., a cockerel.

akaⁿk nakni itibbi, n., a cock fight.

akaⁿk ola, n., cock crowing; the time at which cocks crow; early morning.

akaⁿk ola, v. a. i., to crow; to cry or make a noise, as a cock.

akaⁿk tek, n., a hen; the female of the common domestic fowl.

akaⁿk tek himmita, n., a pullet.

akaⁿk ushi, n., the young of the domestic hen; a chicken; a hen's egg; akaⁿk ushi peliechi, n., a brood of chickens.

akaⁿk ushi achạfa boⁿli, n., a nest egg.

akaⁿk ushi hakshup, n., a hen's egg shell.

akaⁿk ushi holba, a., oval; oblong; of the shape or figure of an egg.

akaⁿk ushi iⁿwạlaha, akak ushi wạlakạchi, n., albumen; the white of an egg.

akaⁿk ushi lakna, n., the yolk of a hen's egg.

akaⁿk ushi lobunchi, n., a hen's egg.

akaⁿk ushi lobunchi shua, n., a rotten egg.

akaⁿk ushi peliechi, n., a brood of chickens.

akaⁿk ushi wạlakạchi, n., glair; albumen; the white of an egg.

akaⁿka, n. of com. gen. and number, a hen; hens; name of a domestic fowl; a chick; a chicken; poultry.

akakoha, v. i. pl., to fall (as in battle), 2 Sam. 18: 7; see 1 Sam. 4: 2, 10; to fall down, chaⁿyạt akakoha, "hewn down," Matt. 7: 19.

akakoli, v. t., to fell, Deut. 20: 19.

akakolichi, v. t. caus., to cause to fall, 1 Sam. 4: 3.

akalampi, see kalampi.

akalạpechi, v. t. caus., to freeze; to cause to freeze; to congeal; akalampichi, nasal form; to congeal.

akalạpi, n., frost.

akalạpi, pp., frozen; akalampi, frozen; congealed.

akalạpi, v. n., to freeze; to congeal; akalampi, nasal form, and the one most used.

akalạpit taha, pp., frozen up.

akaⁿlusi, pp., humbled.

akaⁿlusi, a., v. n., to be low, grave (in music), or humble; akanlusi, nasal form (q. v.).

akaɫa, pp., broken and spilt, as an egg.

akaɫạlli, v. t., to break; to break open so that the contents run out; akaⁿk ushi aⁿ akalạlli, he breaks the egg.

akama, akạma, ạlhkạma, pp., shut up; stopped.

akamaɫoli, v. a. i. sing., to leer (as a horse).

akamaɫushli, v. a. i. pl., to leer.

akamạli, akamạlli, v. t. sing., to stop up; to cork; to close; see akamoli.

akamạssa, v. a. i., to harden.

akamạssa, n., atachi, Ex. 26: 6, and isht akamạssa in the same verse; itakamạssa, v. a. i., to settle.

akamạssa, pp. and a., fastened; buckled; buttoned; compacted; itakamạssa, fastened together; joined together strong (as the planks of a floor when well laid); clasped together; consolidated; strengthened; sealed; ikakamạsso, a., open; not fastened.

akamạssali, v. t., to fasten; to button; nạfoka akamạssali, to seal; to buckle; itakamạssali, to fasten together; to clasp; to compact; to consolidate.

akamolechi, v. t., to strangle; to stop up; see *akomolechi.*

akamoli, v. t. pl.; to stop up; to cork; to bung (applied to any hole or gap); *alhkamoa,* pl. pp., see *akamali.*

akanali, v. a. i., to approach; to approximate.

akanalichechi, v. t. caus., to approximate, to bring near.

akanalichi, v. t. caus., to move along; to remove from.

akanallechi, v. t. caus., to remove from.

akanalli, akanallih, v. a. i., to remove from; to go from; to move from.

akanimi, n., manner; fashion; means.

akanimi, a., after some fashion; somehow.

akanimi, v. a. i., to be after some manner.

akaniohmi, n., a deed; an action, John 3: 19; a dealing, John 4: 9; matter; circumstance; providence; *itimakaniohmi,* mutual dealings, John 4: 9; *hash akaniohmi,* your works, Matt. 5: 16 (here a verb is used for a noun).

akaniohmi, v. t., to do; to act; *imakaniohmi,* Josh. 2: 23; *itimakaniohmi,* to deal together.

akaniohmichi, v. t., to cause to do; to cause to be done.

akanli, a., low; humble.

akanli, v. n., to be low; v. t., to humble; to lower.

akanlusechi, akanlusichi, v. t. caus., to humble; to bring low; to lay low; to lower; to abase; *ileakanlusichi,* to humble himself, Matt. 18: 4; *imanukfila akalu*ⁿ*sichi,* to depress; to discourage.

akanlusi, a., very low; low down; abased; low (as tones in music).

akanlusi, v. n., to be very low; to be low down, Matt. 18, caption of chapter.

akanlusi, adv., low.

akanlusi, n., lowness.

akanlusichi, n., a humbler.

akanta, pp., pressed.

akantalechi, v. t., to press together; to press; *itakantalechi,* v. t., to press together.

akantali, v. a. i., to press, Mark 5: 31; *itakantali,* Mark 2: 4.

akantalichi, n., a press.

akaona, see *akkaona.*

akapassaka, n., a cold climate; a cold region.

akapoa, akopoa (q. v.), v. t., to overshadow.

akashofa, n., an erasure; a clean place or place cleansed.

akasholichi, n., a doorscraper.

akataiya, pp. pl.; patched; *alhkata,* sing.

akataiya, n. pl., patches, or places patched; *alhkata,* sing.

akatali, v. t. pl., to patch; *akalli,* sing.

akauwi, v. t. sing., to break and bend down.

akauwichi, v. t. pl., *iti shima ya*ⁿ *akauwichi; fuli a*ⁿ *akauwichi,* they break switches.

akawa, pp., broken and bent down, but not broken off (as limbs or twigs).

akalli, akkalli (q. v.), v. t., to mend.

akalli, n., a mender.

akallo, pass. voice, to be made strong or sure, as *akallashke,* Matt. 27: 64.

akallo, pp., a., made strong; sealed; bound to.

akallo, v. a. i., to harden; to grow hard there.

akallo, n., an establishment.

akallochi, v. t. caus., to make strong; to fix; to seal; to make sure, Matt. 27: 66.

akama, v. i., to fall, 1 Sam. 18: 25; 1 Kings 22: 20.

akama, see *akama.*

akammi, v. t. pl., to stop up; to close (a book), Luke 4: 20; to shut up, Matt. 6: 6; to bung; to spike; to shut, Josh. 2: 7; see *akamali,* sing; *akamoli,* pl., *itakammi,* to close together.

akammi, n., a stopper.

akania, v. n., to be exhausted by; *siakania,* John 2: 17 [?]; to be absorbed at; to sponge.

akania, pp., absorbed at; exhausted at; disappeared at.

Akas, n., August.

akashchukali, v. a. i. sing., to lift the head; to stand erect.

akashchunoli, v. a. i., to bow down the head.

akashtala, akishtala, n., the lower end; the butt end; the bottom; the root (of a tree), Luke 3: 9.

akat, adv., yes; to be sure; indeed; aye; from *ah,* it is, and *kat,* the definite article.

akchalhpi, hakchalpi, n., ross bark; the coarse outside bark of a tree. [*Chalhpi* is the form of this word used by the Choctaw of Mississippi.—H. S. H.]

akchihpo, ahchihpo, n., drift; driftwood.

akchupilhko, see *hakchupilhko*.

akeluachechi, v. t. caus., to cause the heartburn, or flatulency.

akeluachi, v. n., to have the heartburn, or flatulence; to belch.

akeluachi, n., the heartburn; flatulency.

akeluachi, a., flatulent.

a^nki, a^nke, my father; my sire. As a word of respect it is applied to all the brothers of the father and their male cousins by the children. This word is not found without the prefix pronoun; remove it and say *ki* or *ke* and no idea of father, etc., remains. *a^nki a^n ont hohpilahea^n*, I go and bury my father, Matt. 8: 21; 11: 26; 15: 13; Josh. 2: 13.

akintak, int. of resolution used by those who are ready to fight, etc.

akishtala, akashtala, n., the root; the butt end; the lower end, Matt. 3: 10.

akishtala kullit kinaffi, v. t., to sap; to undermine.

akka, aka, n., the place beneath, below, or down; the bottom (as of water). *aka*, 2 Kings 9: 33; *aka et pilatok*, the ground, 2 Sam. 24: 20.

akka, a., down; belonging to the earth; earthly; earthy.

akka, v. n., to be down; *akkachi, akachi*, v. t.; *akachit taiyali cha*, 2 Sam. 8: 2.

akka, pp., felled; thrown down.

akka, adv., prep., earthly.

akka a^nya, see *akkaya*.

akka ia, akkia, v. a. i., to go down; to sink; to decline; to descend; to lower; to pitch; to stoop; *akia*, to go down, Matt. 11:23.

akka iksho, a., without bottom; fathomless.

akka itanowa, v. a. i., to travel on foot, Matt. 14: 13.

akka itipatalhpo, n., a ground floor; a lower floor.

akka itula, akka itola, aka itula, akkitula, v. a. i., to fall down; to precipitate; to fall on the ground, Matt. 10: 29; *akka satula*, I fall down; *akka chitula*, thou fallest down; *akka itonla, akkitonla*,

nasal form, lying down; *akka itoyula*, pro. form, to be lying along; *akka ituyula*, to descend, Matt. 7: 27.

akkabata, n., a bat; a ball stick.

akkabilepa, n. pl., to be lying down.

akkabinoli, pl., to sit down, Matt. 13: 48; 15 :35; *aka hashuk aiombinoli*, Matt. 14: 19.

akkaboli, v. t., to lay down; to put down; to deposit; to throw down; to ground.

akkachunni, akachunni, v. a. i. pl., to bow the head; to throw the head up and down.

akkachunochunli, v. a. i. pl., to wag or wave the head.

akkachunoli, akachunoli, sing. v. a. i., to bow the head; to condescend; to crouch, 2 Sam. 24: 20; *imakkachunoli*, to bow the head to him; to render obeisance to him; to resign up to him; *akkachunohonli*, freq.

akkachunoli, n., a bow; an act of obeisance.

akkafehna, a., nethermost; lowest.

akkafohobli, v. t. pl., to spill much or many.

akkafohopa, pp., spilt; *akkafohompa*, nasal form, being spilt.

akkahika, v. a. i., to stand on the feet; to travel on foot; *akkahi^nka*, nasal form, to be standing on the feet.

akkahikat a^nya, v. a. i., to journey on foot; to travel on foot.

akkahikat a^nya, n., a pedestrian.

akkahoyo, v. t., to search for the bottom; to fathom; to sound.

akkahu^nkupa, n., a pad; a foot pad.

akkakaha, v. a. i. dual, to fall down; to lie down.

akkakaha, pp., laid down; *akkakaiyaha*, pro. form, to be lying down along; lain down at last.

akkakahat aiasha, v. a. i. pl., to lie down; a number lying down.

akkakahat ma^nya, v. a. i. pl., implying that three are lying down or have lain down; to lie down.

akkakali, v. t., to lay down.

akkakoha, akakoha, v. a. i., to fall down, Matt. 3: 10; to fall in battle, Josh. 8: 25.

akkakoha, pp., fallen; fallen down; smitten, 1 Sam. 4: 2.

akkakoli, akakoli, v. t., to cast down, Luke 1: 52; to slay; to cut down trees, Josh. 17: 15, 18.

akkakolichi,v. t. caus., to smite, 1 Sam. 4: 31.

akkaⁿlusi, akaⁿlusi (q. v.), a., low.

akkalali, v. t. pl., to spill and scatter (applied to corn, shot, and like objects).

akkalatapa, pp. sing., spilt; poured down.

akkalatapa, v. a. i., to spill; to pour out and scatter.

akkalatabli, v. t. sing., to spill and scatter; applied to milk, water, or any single object.

akkalaya, pp. pl., spilt and scattered; akkalaⁿya, nasal form, being spilt and scattered.

akkalaya, v. a. i. pl., to spill and scatter; to pour out; akkalaⁿya, nasal form.

akkalipeli, v. t., to spread down; to lay down with the face or upper side next to the ground; to lay bottom side up or upside down.

akkalipia, v. a. i. sing., to lie down on the face.

akkalipia, pp., to be down; laid down on the face or bottom side up.

akkalipkachi, v. a. i. pl., to lie down on the face; akkalipkaiyachi, pro. form.

akkama, akkama, akama, v. a. i., to fall down (spoken of living creatures); to fall; ikakamo, it fell not, Matt. 7: 25; akama, it fell, Matt. 7: 27.

akkama, akkama, pp., fallen down; demolished; prostrated; stopped.

akkamololi, v. a. i., to slink.

akkanowa, v. a. i., to walk; to travel on foot.

akkanowa, n., a pedestrian.

akkaona, akaona, v. a. i., to go down; to be abused, Luke 18: 14.

akkapila, adv., downward; downwards.

akkapila, v. t., to cast down; to throw down; to unhorse; akkasapela, to throw me down.

akkapushli, n., a stole; a pucker.

akkasiteli, v. t., to undergird.

akkasoli, n., name of a bush which grows at the edge of water, having a ball-like fruit. A decoction of the leaves is a good sudorific.

akkashalachi, n., a scraper.

akkashalallichit liteli, v. t., to draggle.

akkashaloli, v. a. i., to hold the ears forward (as a horse).

akkatala, v. a. i., to ground; to run aground.

akkatalla, a., duck-legged.

akkatalla, v. n., to be duck-legged.

akkaya, akka aⁿya, v. a. i., to go on foot, not on horseback; to travel on foot.

akkachi, v. t., to lower; to bring down; to demolish; to prostrate; to lay low; to disburden; to take down (as from a house); to fell; to raze; to suppress; to throw; akachi, Josh. 10: 27.

akkachi, n., a throw.

akkalli, akalli, v. t. sing., to patch; to mend with patches; to botch; to clout; to cobble; alhkata, pp., isht alhkata, n., a patch; shulush akkalli, to patch a shoe.

akkalli, n., a patcher.

akkama, see akkama.

akket (from akka and et), down this way, from above; aket hapihohoyoshke, 12th hymn, 4th verse, ed. 1844.

akkia, n., a descent; see akka ia.

akkitola, akkaitula (q. v.), to fall down.

akkitula, n., a fall.

akkitula, pp., fallen.

akkoa, akowa, v. a. i., to descend; to go down; to come down, Matt. 14: 29; to dismount; to get down; to alight; attat akowa, "come down," Matt. 8: 1; 17: 9; Josh. 2: 23; 15: 18, "to light off," Josh 15: 18.

akkoa, akowa, v. t., to dismount.

akkoli, v. t., to mold; to plate over (as silver or iron); to shape; isht akkoli, to plate; alhkoha, pp.; isht alhkoha, pp., plated.

akma, sign of sub. mood after verbs ending with a; see ak and its compounds.

akmichi, see akmochi.

akmo, hakmo pp., soldered; congealed; hardened or cold (as tallow); itakmo, soldered together; cemented; closed up.

akmo, v. a. i., to harden; to congeal; to stiffen.

akmochi, akmichi, v. t., to solder; to harden; to congeal; to found; to run; itakmochi, recip. form, to cement together; to cause to adhere; to close up; to press the sides of a wound and cause them to unite; itaiakmochi, v. t., to solder.

akmochi, n., a founder.

aknaⁿka, vile; bad; worthless. See John 9: 34.

akni, n., the eldest among a family of children, male or female; in a larger sense any one of the children who is older than others of the same family; the first born, Josh. 17: 1.

aknip, see *haknip*.

akobafa, n., a breach; the place broken.

akobafa, v. a. i., to break at, or by.

akobafa, pp., broken there, or at.

akocha (see *akucha*), and (used in counting); *pokoli chakali akocha chakale*, ninety and nine.

akochofa, pp., bent down (as cornstalks to preserve the ears from the weather and the birds); *akushli*, pl.

akochofa, v. a. i., to bend down; *akushli*, *akochulli*, pl.; *akochoha*, pp.

akochuffi, v. t., to break and bend down; *tanchạpi aⁿ akochuffi*, he bends down the cornstalk; *akushlichi*, pl.

akochuffichi, v. t. caus., to cause to break and bend down.

akohcha, see *akucha* and *kohcha*.

akohchawiha, see *akuchawiha*.

akolạs, n., a jar.

akolofa, n., the place where anything has been cut off, or broken off; a part left; a stump.

akolofa, v. a. i., to come off at.

akolofa, a., cut off at; severed at; *akoloⁿfa*, *akoluⁿfa*, nasal form, being cut off at.

akoluffi, v. t., to cut off at.

akomachi, v. a. i., to be sweet; to be pleasant to the taste.

akomolechi, v. t., to strangle; to stop by holding something on at the mouth, or nose; also *akamolechi* (q. v.).

akomuta, v. n., to dread; to fondle; *akomunta*, nasal form.

akonoli, n., a circle round the sun or moon; see *hạshi akonoli*.

akopoa, v. t., to overshadow, Matt. 17: 5; *oⁿhoshontikachi*, later edition; see *akapoa*.

akopulechi; *itakopulechi*, v. t., to press together; to close (as the sides of a wound).

akostinincha hinla, a., perceptible.

akostininchahe keyu, a., inscrutable; undistinguishable.

akostininchi, v. t., to know, Luke 2: 43; to be acquainted with; to find out,

Matt. 6: 3; 7: 20; to discern; to ascertain; to apprehend; to comprehend, John 1: 5; to see, Matt. 2: 16; to read, Matt. 16: 8; to perceive, Luke 5: 22; 1 Sam. 3: 8; to prove; to realize; to recollect; to remember; to understand; to consider, Matt. 7: 3; to have knowledge of, Matt. 14: 35; *hạshakostinincha chiⁿ kak oka*, that ye may know; Matt. 9: 6; also Matt. 12: 7, 15, 25; 15: 12, 16, 17; 17: 13; *ilekostininchi*, *ileakostininchi*, *ilakostininchi*, ref. form, to come to himself, to know himself, Luke 15: 17; to repent, Matt. 13: 15; 16: 12; *ikakostinincho*, neg. form, not to know, Josh. 8: 14; *ikakostinincho*, a., unconscious; undecided; undetermined; uninformed; *achukma ikakostinincho*, a., uncertain.

akosha, pp. pl., broken down; bent and broken down; see *akochofa*.

akosha, v. a. i., to break down; to bend and break down.

akowa, see *akkoa*.

akshish, hakshish, n., the sinews; roots; veins; arteries; a fiber; a nerve; a sinew; a source; *akshish chito*, the large sinews, roots, veins, arteries; the tap root.

akshish, a., sinewy.

akshish aⁿsha, a., sinewed.

akshish lakna chito, n., columbo [or calumba] a medicinal plant that grows in the woods.

akshish laua, a., stringy.

akshish toba, v. a. i., to root; to take root.

akshish toba, pp., rooted.

aksho, n., disuse; neglect; desuetude.

aksho, a., pp., neglected; forsaken; disused; obsolete; out of date; exploded; extinct; invalid; null; quashed; abandoned; deserted, like an old, untraveled road; abolished; annulled; repealed; vacated; *hina aksho, nafohka aksho*.

aksho, v. t., to neglect; to disuse.

akshot taha, a., obsolete; done away.

akshucha hinla, a., voidable.

akshuchi, v. t., to abolish; to annul; to repeal; to disannul; to explode; to fail; to null; to nullify; to quash; to vacate; to undo; and, in reference to closing the time of mourning for the dead, *aiakshuchi*, the time of doing so.

akshuchi, n., an abolisher.

akshuchi, n., an abolition; a vacation; nullification.

akshuki!, akshukehih!, oh dear!, said when cold and suffering.

akshupi!, akshupehih!, oh dear!, said when burnt.

akta, hakta, conj. or prep., therefore; as *hokạt, mih hakta isht ạlali kạt*, therefore I brought them.

Aktoba, Aktuba, n., October.

akucha, akocha, prep., over; and; used in counting between 20 and 30, and 30 and 40, etc., and on to 100, Luke 2: 37; 1 Kings 10: 14; to express over and above or more, as *pokoli tuklo akucha*, over 20; *akucha* is compounded of *a*, of, from, out of, and *kucha*, to go out.

akucha, akohcha, n., a pass; a ford; a ferry; a crossing place; the place where anything comes out; an extract; a landing.

akucha, adv., out of.

akucha, akohcha, v. a. i., to come out of; to proceed out of, Matt. 15: 18; Josh. 4: 16, 17, 18, 19; 5: 5; *akuncha*, nasal form; *akoyucha*, pro. form.

akucha, pp., taken from; brought out; extracted.

akuchaka, n., the place of appearing or coming out, applied to the rising of the sun; *hạshi akohchaka*, Matt. 2: 1, 9.

akuchaweli, v. t. pl., to take out from; to subtract.

akuchaweli, n., subtraction.

akuchawiha, akohchawiha, pp. pl., subtracted; taken from.

akuchawiha, v. a. i. pl., to come out of; *akohchawiha*, Josh. 8: 16.

akuchechi, v. t., to take out from, Gen. 2: 22; to cause to come out.

akuchi, v. t., to take out; to out; to oust; to bring out of; to extract from.

akuhish, n., a jug.

akuncha, adv., out.

akunti, n., growth of vegetables or a vegetable; a plant.

akushli, pp. of *akochofa*, bent and broken down.

akushlichi, v. t. pl., to bend and break down; *akochuffi*, sing.

ala, v. a. i., from *ạla*, to arrive at a place or point in sight, but not at the place where the speaker stands.

ala, n., an arrival.

alahki, v. a. i., to lie with the back to the fire; *luak iⁿfilạmmit itola* [lying turned from the fire].

alahkichi, v. t., to make him lie with his back to the fire, or to lay him, her, or it with the back to the fire.

alaka, alạka, n. sing.; edge; border; shore; the margin, John 21: 4, 8, 9; *ont alaka*, n., the coast; *peni alaka*, side of a boat.

alaka ikaiyu, v. i., not going one side, i. e., costive, a delicate mode of speaking.

alakali, pl., edges.

alakchakali, pl., edges of a field, water, prairies, or woods.

alakna, v. a. i., to ripen; to turn yellow; to rust; to be ripe.

alakna, a., ripe; yellow; rusty.

alakna, pp., ripened; rusted; turned yellow.

alaknạbi, v. t., to rust; to kill with rust (as grain).

alaknạchi, v. t., to ripen; to rust.

alaknạt ia, v. a. i., to begin to ripen.

alaksha, n., a hothouse.

alatichi, a., cunning; sly.

alama, pp., silenced; prevented; forbidden; see *alạmmi*.

alapalechi, v. t., to place at the side or on the side of something; to cause to adhere to the side; to give boot; to give interest; to charge interest.

alapali, v. a. i., to adhere to; to stick to the side; to be on the side; to cleave to.

alapali, n., the margin.

alapalika, n., the side.

alapanli, nasal form, being placed at the side.

alapanli, n., boot; interest.

alata, n., a lining; a facing; a covering; *nishkin alata*, spectacles.

alata, pp., a., lined; faced; sided; *italata*, pp., lined together or laid together, as two leaves in a book, side by side; *italanta*, *italantạt kaha*, *italatạt kaha*, Luke 19: 44; *italạtkạchi*, to lie like pieces of slate.

alata, v. a. i., to set; to incubate; to nestle; to sit.

alata, n., a sitting.

alatali, v. t., to line; to put on a lining; to ceil; to lap; to put on a facing; to face; to sheathe.

alatkạchi, v. a. i. pl., to lie on the side (as a facing or lining); *italatkạchi*, pl., to lie side by side (as several leaves in a book).

alauechi, v. t., to be equal to; to be adequate; neg., *ikalauecho*, Josh. 8: 15.

alaui, v. n., to be equal; to be adequate; *isht ikalauo*, Luke 3: 16.

alạlli, see *lạllichi*; *italạllit boli*, to pack (as meat).

alạllichi, v. t., to harden by pounding, as *wak hakshup alạllichi*; n., a lapstone.

alạmmi, alạmi (see *olạbbi*), v. t., to forbid; to prevent; to take from, applied to the taking of a man's wife from him by her relations (*ohoyo han imolạbit aiishi*); *imalạmmi*, to prevent him; to rebuke, Matt. 17: 18.

alạmmichi, alạmichi, v. t., to silence; to prevent; to forbid, Luke, 6: 29; *imạlạmminchi*, to rebuke him, Matt. 16: 22.

alạshpaka, n., a warm climate; a warm region.

alạtkạchi, a., lined, or laid on in several thicknesses.

ale, exclamation, to halloo (used in calling another person); hulloa or holla.

aleli, v. t., to weed; to plow among corn or other vegetables the first time; *leli* is to weed; the *a* prefixed probably denotes the place where.

aleli, n., a weeder; one that weeds or frees from anything noxious.

ali, ạlleh, exclamation, uttered by children when in pain; oh dear.

alia, pp., weeded, or the place weeded.

alikchi, ạllikchi, n., a doctor; a physician, Matt. 9: 12; an Indian doctor.

alikchi, v. t., to doctor; to practice as a physician; to administer medicine; to attend to the sick, as a physician; *imalikchi*, v. t., to doctor him. One mode of treating the rheumatism is thus described: The patient shuts himself up in a hot house, strips himself naked, makes a fire, and lies there and sweats freely. He then takes a fragment of a bottle and scarifies himself. After this he goes to a creek and bathes and anoints his body with oil.

alikchi ilahobi, n., a quack; an empiric.

alikti, v. a. i., to spring up, to grow.

alikti, pp., a., grown up.

alikti, n., the growth; the young growth.

aliktichi, v. t., caus., to cause it to grow.

aliktichi, n., young birds just fledged or feathering; a pin feather.

allạlluak, see *alolua*.

almuk, n., the almug tree, 1 Kings, 10: 11, 12.

aloah, see *alua*.

alohbi, allohbi, a., sultry; hot; warm, still, and without wind.

alohbi, v. n., to be sultry, hot, warm and still and without wind.

alohbi, n., the heat; warmth; sultriness.

alokoli, n., a cluster; a collection; *chuka alokoli*.

alolua, v. a. i. pl., to fill up; v. n., to be full; *alota*, sing.

alolua, ạllolua, allạlluak, a., pl., full.

alolua, pp., filled.

alolua, n., fullness.

aloḷichi, v. t., to cause to be sultry, hot, or warm.

aloshuma, v. n., to be finished off at.

aloshuma, n., the place where it is finished.

aloshuma, pp., finished off at.

aloshummi, v. t., to finish off at.

aloḷa, v. a. i., sing., to fill up; it fills up; *ạllota*, less than *alota*; a diminutive of *alota*; v. a. i., to fill up slowly.

alota, v. n., to be full.

alota, a., full; big, Luke 5: 7; fraught; high; replete; Matt. 14: 20; 15: 37; *alota-ma*, "when it was full," Matt. 13: 48.

alota, pp., filled; crowded; stuffed.

alota, n., fullness; a fill; plenitude.

alotoli, alotuli, sing. and pl., to fill, John 2: 7; to replenish; to stuff; to fill to the brim; full banks, Josh. 9: 13.

alotowa, alotoa, a. sing. and pl., passive and intransitive, very full; brimful; *alota*, simple form.

alotowa, v. a. i., intensive form, to fill up, Gen. 1: 28.

alotowa, v. n., to be full, Matt. 6: 22.

alotowa, pp., to be filled to the brim, Luke 1: 15.

alotowa, n., fullness; abundance; *chunkash an alotowakmakon*, Matt. 12: 34.

alta, n., an altar, 2 Sam. 24: 18, 21.

alua, n., a burn; a place burnt; a scald.

alua, aloah, a., pp., a burnt place; v. a. i., to burn at, or on; to burn there, as it burns there.

aluachi, v. t., to burn; to consume; *isht aluachi*, to burn with, Luke 3: 17.

aluhmi, v. t., to hide at or in; to conceal; to secrete.

aluhmi, v. a. i., to hide; to lie concealed; *kohchi aluhmi*, to hide in a thicket.

alukoli, see *lukoli*.

alulli, v. t. pl., to fill, Gen. 44: 1.

aluma, pp., hid or hidden at.

aluma, n., a hiding place; a place of concealment; concealment; a lurking place; obscureness; obscurity; a recess.

alumaⁿka, n., a secret; a secret place.

alumpoa, pp. pl., hid or hidden at; cf. *aluma*.

alumpoa, n. pl., secret places; hiding places.

alusa, n., a black place; a place made black; black.

alusachi, v. t., to blacken; to make black.

alusachi, a., dark colored.

alusachi, v. n., to be dark colored.

aḷabocha, n., a vessel for boiling food in; a pot; a boiler.

aḷacha, v. n., to fit in; to fill up; to stand in; to fit in, as a stick of timber is fitted for another; *aḷachaya*, pro. form; *aḷachkạchi*, pass. pl.

aḷachahạchi, v. t. pl., to set them in.

aḷachali, v. t. sing., to set a stick in.

aḷaⁿfa, n., a trace; a line; a mark.

aḷaka, n., the midriff; the diaphragm.

aḷakofahe keyu, a., inevitable; incurable.

aḷakofi, v. a. i., to escape at; to escape from; to heal; to recover from.

aḷakofi, n., a refuge; a place of escape; deliverance; salvation; a remedy; *isht alakofahe*, Luke 4: 18.

aḷakofi, n., a refugee.

aḷakofi, pass., healed; rescued; saved.

aḷakofichi, v. t. caus., to heal; to save; to rescue from.

aḷakofichi, n., a deliverer.

aḷanta, pass. nasal form of following, being mixed, as *uksakalanta*.

aḷatali, v. t., to mix; *aḷantali*, nasal form.

aḷạchaya, v. i., pro. form, from *alacha* (q. v.), to stand in; to fit in; to fill, Jer. 23:24.

aḷạchkạchi, v. n. pl., to fit in; to fill up, as to fit a tenon for the mortise.

aḷechi, v. t., to destroy; *isht imalechi*, his destruction, 2 Chron. 22: 4.

aḷeka, n., misery or distress brought on one by his own misconduct; danger; Matt. 5: 21, 22; 10: 15; 11: 22, 24.

aḷeka, a., distressed.

aḷeka, v. n., to be in distress, as *imaḷeka fehna*, he is in great misery; *imaḷeka*, to suffer pain from his own misconduct; *alekạchi*, v. t., as *imalekạchi;* *alekạchechi*, v. t. caus., as in *imaḷekạchechi*.

aḷeli, v. t., to scuffle; *towa yaⁿ itimaḷeli*, they scuffle with each other for the ball.

aḷeli, n., a scuffler.

aḷelichi, v. a., to roll up the sleeves, etc., above the elbows, and the pantaloons above the knees; *aliha*, pass., rolled up.

aḷepa, n., a drum; a fiddle; a common drum or fiddle; a harp; a stringed instrument of music; a lyre; an organ; a tabor.

aḷepa boli, v. t., to drum; to beat the drum; to play on the drum.

aḷepa boli, n., a drummer.

aḷepa chito, n., a large drum; a bass viol; a drum; a viol.

aḷepa chito boli, v. t., to drum; to beat the big drum.

aḷepa chito boli, n., a drummer.

aḷepa chito isht boli, n., a drumstick.

aḷepa chito isht olachi, n., the bow used in playing on the bass viol.

aḷepa chito olachi, v. t., to play on the bass viol.

aḷepa chito olachi, n., one that plays on the bass viol.

aḷepa olachi, v. t., to play on the fiddle or violin; to fiddle; to drum; to harp.

aḷepola, n., a march; a particular beat of the drum; the music of the drum.

aḷepolachi, n., a fiddler; a harper.

aḷepush ikbi, n., a fiddle maker.

aḷepush olachi, n., a fiddler; fiddling.

aḷepushi, n., a diminutive, a fiddle or violin smaller than the *aḷepa;* a hand organ.

aḷepushi isht olachi, n., a fiddlestick; a fiddle bow.

aḷepushi isht talakchi, n., a fiddle-string.

aḷepushi olachi, v. t., to fiddle; to play on the violin.

aⁿli, from ạli, limit, etc.; being the end of it.

aⁿli, a., true; faithful; correct; pure (1 K. 10: 21); fair; upright; just; certain; honest; valid; virgin (as virgin gold); great in the sense of real; (aiaⁿli, Matt. 7: 27); intrinsic; immaculate; legitimate; nice; open; proper; right; sheer; simple; sincere; single; solid; sound; stable; straight; strict; sure; trusty; unaffected; undoubted; unfeigned; unmingled; real; genuine; authentic; accurate; sure (during the age of an adult); conscientious; cordial; effectual; equitable; frank; good; nakni tạshka aⁿli, n., an able-bodied man or warrior; neg. form ikaⁿlo, a., uncandid; unjust; unsound; unstable; vain; unhandsome; false; not true; untrue; faithless; dishonest; erroneous; fallacious; groundless; hollowhearted; inaccurate; incorrect; indirect; ineffectual; insincere; perfidious; spurious; treacherous; unfair; unfaithful; ikaⁿlo kawa a., undesirable; not to be desired. ikaⁿlo achahe keyu, undeniable; he can not say it is false; imali, true of him; true to him; true for him; ikimaⁿlo, a., not true of him (i. e., the accusation); innocent.

aⁿli, n., truth; equity; execution; a fact; fairness; faithfulness; integrity; openness; right; simplicity; sincerity; singleness; trueness; verity; virtue; ikaⁿlo, n., a falsehood; an untruth; hollowness; treachery; vanity.

aⁿli, v. n., to be true, faithful, honest, etc., Matt. 17: 25; aⁿli makoⁿ, that is true, or true that is, Matt. 6: 2, 5; 8: 10; 13: 17; aiaⁿli, pro., Luke 16: 11, to be fulfilled, Matt. 1: 23; 2: 15; ont aiaⁿli-tok·makoke, was fulfilled, Matt. 12: 21; be established, Matt. 18: 16; ikaⁿlo achi v. a. i., to say it is false; to deny; to contradict; to gainsay. aⁿlishke, a sentence; it is true. See John 3: 3, 5, 11; shke is a particle of affirmation in the definite present tense. Verbs neuter may be rendered as sentences by adding shke to them (as kạlloshke, it is strong), and without this appendage merely by accenting the last syllable, as aⁿli′, it is true; kạllo′, it is strong.

aⁿli, pass., authenticated; attested; established; verified; fulfilled; Matt. 2: 17; 5: 18.

aⁿli, adv., truly; certainly; really; faithfully; heartily; nicely; richly; rightly; sincerely; strictly; surely; verily; ikaⁿlo, adv., falsely; untruly.

aⁿli, v. a. i., to act truly; to be true; to hold; to prove; ishaⁿli, you act truly; aⁿlili, I act truly.

aⁿli achit anoli, v. a. i., to affirm; to testify; lit., to speak and tell truly.

aⁿli achit miha, v. t., to assert; to avouch; to say and speak truly.

aⁿli fehna achit miha, to allege; to say and speak very truly.

aⁿli hoⁿ, adv., verily, Matt. 18: 3.

aⁿli makoⁿ, adv., verily, Matt. 8: 10; Matt. 10: 15, 23, 18: 13. John 3: 3. aⁿli makoⁿ chimachilishke, verily I say unto thee; aiaⁿli makoⁿ chimachilishke, in truth, to thee I do say, Luke 23: 43.

alia, v. t., to commit whoredom, i. e., for a plurality of men to humble one woman. See Judg. 19: 25.

aⁿlichi, v. t. caus., to make true; to establish the truth; to fulfill a promise; to attest; to ratify; to assure; to authenticate; to establish; to evidence; to evince; to execute; to prove; to strengthen; to verify; to warrant. Matt. 3: 15.

alifa, liⁿfa, pass. sing., stripped off.

aliⁿfa, v. a. i., to come off.

aliⁿfạchi, v. t. caus., to tie a running knot or noose.

aliⁿffi, v. t., to strip off.

aliⁿfichi, v. t. caus., to tie with a noose; to tie a running noose.

aliⁿkạchechi, v. t. caus., to strip off.

aliⁿkạchi, pass. pl. of aliⁿfa, stripped off.

alikạchi, v. a. i. pl., to come off.

alioa, lioa, v. t. pl., to take the track and follow, to pursue. See lioli.

alioli, v. t., to pursue.

alipa, v. n., to lie on the face; alipạt ishko, to lie down and drink; alipia, pro. form.

alipo, n., covering of a camp; roof of a little shed. ·

aⁿlit, adv., surely; truly; with truth; in truth. When the letter t is suffixed to a word it is connected with the next following word and often qualifies it if verb, as adverbs do.

a^nlit achi, v. a. i., to speak truly; or, to true and speak; or, he trues and speaks.

aliyuha, v. a. i., to pursue, Josh. 8: 16; neg. ikaliyuho, Josh. 8: 17.

alohbi, a., warm; hot.

alohbi, v. n., to be warm or hot; sialohbi, I am warm.

alohbi, pass., heated; burnt; warmed; tanchi at alohbi, the corn is burnt.

alohbichi, v. t. caus., to warm; to heat.

alopoli, n. pl., fords, passes.

alopoli, v. a. i. pl., to pass through at.

alopolichi, v. t. caus., to take through.

alopulli, n. sing., a ford; a pass; a ferry; a crossing.

alopulli, v. a. i., to pass through at.

alopullichi, v. t. caus., to take through at.

alopullichi, n., one that conducts through at.

alukafa, n., a perforation.

alukali, n. pl., perforations; or pp., perforated at.

alumpa, n., a perforation; place pierced; a puncture.

am, a prefixed pronoun; of the same meaning as a^n, an, and am; I, as amponna, I am skilled, I know; amahoba, I reckon, I presume, or it seems to me; me in the objective or dative case, as ampota, to lend to me; am is usually found before words beginning with p and b; am before vowels, amissuba; amia; go for me and sam after 2d person sing., and plural, issamithana, thou knowest me; hassamithana, ye know me.

ama; see kama, Acts, 24: 11 [?].

amakali, a., graceful.

amakali, v. n., to be graceful.

amakalichi, v. t., to render graceful.

amali, v. a. i., to turn there, on, or over.

amalichi, n., a floor or place for winnowing grain, Luke 3: 17.

amalichi, v. t., to winnow there, at, or by; to fan.

amashlichi, v. t., to fan.

amashlichi, n., a fan; a fanner.

amba, conj., but, John 1: 12; however; unless; amba is the nasal form of aba, and is derived from aba, being above or out of; or from a^n, and ba, an ad-

verb meaning really [merely]; amba, but, Matt. 6: 33; 18: 16; amba na holissochi, and, Matt. 7: 29; 10: 30; amba yammak okato, Matt. 13: 11, 48.

amia; Chihowa at amia tuchina, Hymn Book, page 206. II.

amih, see mih.

amih achafa, a., one; the same; tuchina iknanakia amih achafa hoke, 1 John 5: 7 [?].

amiha, n., a saying; a maxim; a remark; a subject of conversation.

amihachi, v. t., to accuse, Matt. 27: 12.

ami^nko, v. t., to reign, Luke 19: 15.

amilofa, n., a place which is filed; or, pp., filed there.

aminti, n., source; origin; the place whence anything comes; a fountain; a germ; the spring.

aminti, v. a. i., to come from.

amisho^nfa, sing. v. a. i., to rub on or against.

amisho^nfa, pp., a., rubbed.

amishoffi, v. t. sing., to rub against.

amishoha, pp. pl., rubbed.

amishohachi, v. t. pl., to rub against.

amishokachi, n., a rub.

ami^nshokachi, amoshokachi, amishokachi, v. a. i. pl., to rub; it rubs against.

amisholichi, v. t., to rub.

amisholichi, n., a rubber.

amo, art., the; the one which; the said; it is used in the nom. and obj. cases, Josh. 6: 22; amo, hamo, yamo, kamo, kamo, chamo may be classed with adverbs of past time, Matt. 22: 8; in nom. case, John 21: 21.

amochonli, v. t., to wink at.

amohsholechi, v. t. caus., to precipitate; to drive forward.

amokafa, v. t., to attack; to run upon, Luke 14: 31; to meet in battle, Matt. 24: 7.

amokafi, v. a., to rise; itamokafi, Matt. 24: 7; Luke 14: 31.

amona, ammona, hammona, adv. or n., the first; the beginning, amona ya^n, at first, John 1: 1.

amoshokachi, see ami^nshokachi.

amosholi, a., greedy; precipitous; resolute.

amosholi, see amoshuli.

amoshuli, amohsholi, v. t., v. a. i., to

run on; to venture on; to precipitate; to have courage, Josh. 1: 6, 7; to persevere, Josh. 10: 25; to rush; to venture.

amoshuli, n., precipitancy; prowess; a rush; an onset.

ampa, nasal form from *ạpa*, eating, to be eating; to eat meat, bread, and potatoes, dipped in gravy; *ahampa*, freq., to keep eating; to be often eating.

ampatoba, n., a pottery.

amphạta, n., a plate; a pan; pottery; crockery.

amphạta chito, n., a platter; "a charger," Matt. 14: 8, 11.

ampi, n., an ear (as *tanch ampi*, an ear of corn).

ampkoa, n., a potsherd; a piece or fragment of a broken pot; a piece of a broken earthen vessel; Job. 2: 8; a broken bowl; a piece of broken crockery; *ampkokoa*, pl.

ampmahaia, ampmaiha, n., a griddle; a broad, shallow pan for baking cakes.

ampmahaia apalạska, n., a griddle.

ampmalaha, n., a dish.

ampmalaspoa, n. pl., plates; platters.

ampmalaswa, n. pl., plates.

ampmalạssa, n., a plate.

ampmạlha, n., a dish.

ampo, n., a bowl; a pan; crockery; earthenware; pottery; a vessel.

ampo aiacheła, ampo aiokami, n., a wash bowl.

ampo atạla, n., a crockery shelf; a shelf for bowls.

ampo chito, n., a large bowl; a large dish.

ampo ikbi, ampo tạna, n., a potter.

ampo mahaia, n., a pan, 2 Sam. 13: 9.

amppatạssa, n., a large plate.

ampushi, n., a small bowl.

an, pro. pre. "my" used in this form before a noun which begins with *ch, l,* or *t,* as *anchuka,* my house; *antạshka,* my warrior; *anluak,* my fire; *anchitokaka,* my Lord, Luke 1: 43; before a verb, an adjective, and other parts of speech which begin with *ch, l,* or *t, an* means to me, of me, for me, etc; a preposition is understood. Before some words *an* is written *a,* and before others *am,* and sometimes *ạm.* Before nouns it is parsed with the nouns. Before verbs, etc., it is generally in the da-

tive case—sometimes rendered as in the nom. case, as *a^{n}hollo,* dear to me, or, I love it, and the like; *sa^n* or *san* occurs after the 2d person, and plural of the active pronouns; *issa^n, issan, hạssa^n, hạssan.*

anakfi, n., my brother, an appellation used only by females, Josh. 2: 13; *chinakfi,* thy brother, addressed to a female; *i^{n}nakfi,* her brother.

anakłopulli, v. a. i., to pass through; to prevail.

anaksi, n., the side.

anaksi, v. a. i., to turn the side.

anaksika, n., the side; outside.

anaksika, v. a. i., to go to the side.

anaksi^{n}ka, nasal form, going to one side.

anaksikachi, v. t. caus., to put to one side; to thrust into a corner.

anaksho^{n}fa, v. a. i., to scorch; to parch.

anaksho^{n}fa, anukshu^{n}fa, pp. sing., singed; scorched; burnt.

anaksho^{n}fa, v. n., to be singed; to be parched; *ikanakshufo,* a., unscorched.

anaksho^{n}ffi, v. t. sing., to singe; to burn; to parch; to parch up; to toast.

anaksholi, v. t. pl., to singe; to scorch; to burn; to parch up; to toast.

anaksholi, n., a singer; one who singes.

anakshua, anakshoha, pp. pl., singed; scorched; burnt; parched; toasted; *ikanaksho,* a., unscorched.

anakshua, v. a. i., to scorch; to parch.

anakshua, v. n., to be singed; to be burnt; to be scorched, Matt. 13: 6.

anaktibała, pp. sing., glanced.

anaktibała, v. a. i., to glance; it glances.

anaktibaloa, pp. pl., glanced.

anaktibaloa, v. a. i. pl., to glance; it glances.

anaktibaloli, v. t. pl., to make or cause to glance; *anaktibalolichi,* causative.

anaktibaffi, v. t. sing., to glance; to cause to glance; to stumble.

anaktibạlli, v. t. pl., to make them glance; to stumble.

anaktibạllichi, v. t. caus., to cause them to glance.

anaktiboa, pp. pl., glanced.

anaktiboa, v. a. i., to glance.

anạla, anała, unạla, pp., nailed on.

anạla, n., a wound.

anạli, v. t. sing., to nail; to nail on; to fasten with a nail; to wound; *ahonạli,* pl. (q. v.).

anạlichi, v. t. caus., to nail on; to nạil to; to fasten with a nail; ahonạlichi, pl. (q. v.); ahonala, pp.

anchaha, pp., a., painted; color laid on the face.

anchaḻi, v. a. i., to paint; to lay colors on the face; to rouge, 2 Kings 9: 30.

anchaḻi, n., a painter.

anchaḻichi, v. t., to paint another; to lay colors on the face of another; to rouge.

anchi, n., a cloak; a mantle; a robe; a shawl; a blanket; clothes; a coverlet; a scarf; a stole; raiment, Matt. 3: 4; a garment, Matt. 9: 16; imanchi, his garment, Matt. 14: 36; his raiment, Matt. 17: 2.

anchi, v. a. i., to put a cloak, etc., on one's self; to cloak; to robe.

anchi, pp., robed; see Mark 14: 51, nipi bano hosh linen anchi.

anchi holitopa, n., a pall.

anchichechi, v. t., to robe another person; to put a cloak and the like on to another person; to robe.

anchichi, v. t., to put a cloak, etc., on another person; to blanket another; to mantle; to robe another.

ani, v. t., from ạni, to pour in; anilish, I pour in, etc. (sh has the force of a conj.).

anihechi, anihichi, n., a threshing floor or threshing place, 2 Sam. 24: 16, 18, 21.

aninchi, v. t., to respect; see ahnichi.

aninchichechi, v. t., to cause to suppurate; to cause to maturate; to promote suppuration.

aninchichi, v. a. i., to suppurate; to maturate; to become ripe; to fester; to gather pus; to matter; to rankle.

aninchichi, n., matter; pus; suppuration; corruption.

aninchichi, a., mature; ripe.

anitaⁿki, n., light, Luke 16: 8.

annumpa, see anumpa.

ano, ạno, art., the obj. case of ạto, or ato. Sometimes the article in this case is written hano, and yano, for euphony's sake.

ano, ạno, rel. pro. in the obj. case, used after adj. and verb, subj. ato; the which; the one which; that which; see aⁿ. It differs from a rel. pro. It appears to be used to give more distinction of object and is more sonorous and appears often in solemn style; ano, hano, yano, kano are often heard in the speech of a Choctaw orator. The last syllable is accented.

anoa, annoa, ạnnoa, ạnnowa, pp., declared; described; designated; detailed; enunciated; famed; stated, Matt. 9: 26; told; related; reported; proclaimed; noised abroad, Luke 1: 65; rumored; informed; posted; mentioned; narrated; noised; published; reported; revealed; ikannoo, a., unpublished; untold; anohoⁿwa, pp. freq., often told; imanoa, pp., warned; notified; bidden; ikimannoo, a., unbidden; uncalled; uncommanded; undirected; uninvited.

anoa tạpa, a., ineffable.

anoa, annoa, anowa, n., a narration; a report; a rumor; fame, Josh. 9: 9; information; imanoa, a citation; a relation; renown; tidings, 1 Sam. 4: 19; isht annoa, fame of, Matt. 4: 24; annohoⁿwa, fame, Matt. 14: 1; see below.

anoa, annowa, ạnnoa, a., famous; noted; notable; illustrious; known, Matt. 10: 26.

anoa, annowa, v. n., to be famous; to be noted; to be well known; annohoⁿwa, freq., to be often told, Matt. 14: 1.

anoa, adv., again; once more.

anoachi, ạnnoachi, v. t. caus., to proclaim; to tell; to cause to be told; to promulgate; to promulge; to post; annowachi, Matt. 9: 31.

anoachi, n., a proclaimer; a promulgator.

anoli, v. t., v. a. i., to tell; to relate; to narrate; to publish; to declare; to rehearse; and to convey (news); to carry intelligence; to describe; to designate; to detail; to direct; to disclose; to divulge; to draw; to enunciate; to inform; to mention; to noise; to notify; to open; to preach; to predicate; to proclaim; to project; to promulgate; to promulge; to recite; to recount; to repeat; to report; to represent; to return; to reveal; to rumor; to show; to signify; to speak, Matt. 10: 27; to specify; to state; to story; to suggest; to tell; to touch; to unfold; to utter; to vent; to witness; imanoli, Josh. 2: 2;

Matt. 2: 8; 14: 12; *annonli*, nasal form, *anont*, contracted; *anont ia*, to go and tell or gone to tell; *anohonli*, freq., to say; to reiterate; *issamanoli*, tell me; Josh. 7: 19; *anoyuoli*, pro. form; *imanoli*, v. t., to tell him; to cite him; to warn him; to summon him; *isht anoli*, to tell about; to narrate concerning; *pit anoli*, to send word yonder or that way; *et anoli*, to send word here or this way; *nan anoli*, v. t., to blab; to tattle; *isht ilanoli*, Matt. 12: 36; *itanoli*, to confess; to acknowledge; to own; to speak of himself, John 1: 22; to render, Matt. 3: 6; *ilimanoli*, Josh. 7: 19; *ilanoli*, n., a confession; a concession; *ilanoli*, n., a confessor; *itimanoli*, to tell each other; *anolahe keyu*, a., unutterable; *ilanolahe keyu*, to disown; he will not confess; *nan anoli*, v. t., to tattle.

anoli, n., a teller; a relator; a narrator; an advertiser; a declarer; a director; an informer; an informant; a promulgator; a rehearser; a reporter; a representative; a story teller.

anoli, n., a murmur; a narration; a narrative; a publication; a recital; a relation.

anompisachi, anumpisachi, v. t., to take aim; to level. This is probably a compound word from *a* there, *on* on it, *pisachi*, to take sight.

anonowa achukma keyu, a., unpopular.

anonti, adv., again; once more; a second time; further; and, Matt. 12: 25; 11: 4; 17: 4; "again," Matt. 13: 44, 45; *anonti*, Mark 11: 27; Matt. 2: 8; 5: 33; conj. "and," Matt. 7: 22.

anonti, exclam. of surprise and regret.

anopoli, v. t., v. a. i., to speak; to talk; Luke 2: 33. This form of the word is rare; *anumpuli* is the most usual form (q. v.).

anowa, v. a. i., to wade; *anowat lopulli*, v. t., to wade through.

anowa, pp., trodden, traveled; *ikanowo*, a., untraveled, untrodden.

anowa, verbal, from *a* and *nowa*, a path; an alley; an avenue; a walk; a track; a small path; a footstep; a mall; a trace.

anowa, conj., similar to *anonti*, "used by the late Col. D. Folsom."

anowa, n., fame; or *anoa*, (q. v.).

ant, a "directive particle" indicating the direction of an action toward the speaker and usually rendered by "come." It is perhaps derived from *ala*, to come. It is used with verbs of motion, generally prefixed, and does not occur alone. See *anyat alat ant akim*, John 15: 22; *okla ant*, etc., Matt. 4: 11; Luke 5: 7; *ant pesa*, come and see; *ant aiokpachi*, Matt. 8: 2; *ant chumpa*, come and buy; *ant ia*, come and go, i. e., come on by. It is the opposite of *ont* (q. v.); *ont* may be contracted from *ona*, to go to; *ant ia*, to come by; to come past; to come on; *ont ia*, to go by; *ant apat tali tok*, came and devoured them up, Matt. 13: 4; *peni an ant alhtoma*, when they were come into the ship; *ant itimanumpuli*, Matt. 17: 3; *ahanta*, Matt. 13: 45, to be engaged in, Josh. 1: 5.

anta, antta, nasal form, of *atta*, to reside; to sojourn; to while.

anta, v. a. i., to stay; to reside; to abide; to live; to dwell; to inhabit; to rest; to tarry, Luke 2: 43; to remain; to harbor; to last (as a living creature); to lodge; to tabernacle; *isht anta*, v. t., to be busy about, etc.; to attend to, Matt. 4: 11; to wait on; to ply; to wait; to wage. This word *anta* is often used to supply the want of the verb to be, Matt 12: 6; *ilanta*, refl., to retire; to reside alone; *ilanta*, pp., retired; *ahanta*, freq. form; *ibaianta*, to stay with; to cohabit; *itibaianta*, to stay together with; *ikanta ahni*, v. t., to harbor; to wish him to remain; *ikanto*, a., unsettled; *aianta*, intensive form of *anta*, v. t., to occupy; to stay at; *aiahanta*, Matt. 6: 6; see *minko aiahanta*, Matt. 2: 1.

anta, n., a stay.

antek, my sister; Matt. 12: 50. An appellative proper only for a brother to use to his sister or concerning his sister. When *anmakfi* is proper for a woman in speaking to or of a brother, this is proper for a man in speaking to or of his sister; *chintek*, thy sister; *intek*, his sister.

antia, v. t., to obey; to conform; as *imantia*, to obey; from *atia* (q. v.); *antia*, the nasal form, is most used; *ikimantio,* v. t., to disobey him; *ikimantio,* a., disobedient; unduteous; undutiful.

antta, see *anta.*

anuⁿka, a., inner; interior.

anuⁿka, prep., within; in; *osapa anuⁿka,* in a field, Matt. 13: 44.

anuⁿka, v. n., to be within; to be inside.

anuⁿka, n., the inside.

anuⁿka alata, n., a lining.

anuⁿka hanta, n., same as *aboha hanta,* a white house; a senate house; state house; house of peace and friendship.

anuⁿka lashpa, n., a hot house; the winter house or sleeping room of the ancient Choctaw.

anuⁿkaka, n., the space or place within; the interior; the inside; the bowels, as *sinakak anuⁿkaka,* Matt. 6: 2; *aboha kallo anuⁿkaka yaⁿ,* in the prison; *yakni anuⁿkaka,* the bowels of the earth; *chuⁿkash anuⁿkaka,* in the heart; the inside of the heart; recesses of the heart, Mark 2: 6, 8; *anuⁿkaka yokato,* Matt. 7: 15; 14: 10, 33; Josh. 2: 19; 7: 21.

anuⁿkaka, a., internal; intestine; intrinsic; intrinsical; inward.

anuⁿkaka, adv., prep., within.

anuⁿkaka fehna, a., inmost; *aboha anuⁿkaka fehna ka,* 2 Kings 9: 2.

anukaⁿka iklanna, a., inner.

anuⁿkaka pisa, n., insight.

anukbaⁿkchi, n., the tenderloin.

anukbata, a., raging; mad.

anukbata, v. a. i., to rage; to rave.

anukbata, n., rage; madness.

anukbatachi, v. t., to enrage; to cause a raging.

anukbiafe, pass. sing., *anukbia,* pl., peeled off; *uski anukbia, kuⁿshak anukbia,* knives of cane bark peeled off.

anukbiaffi, v. t. sing., to peel off the bark of hickory or cane, etc., in strips; *anukbieli,* pl.; *anukbiafa,* pass. sing.

anukbikeli, v. n., to press or hang in the throat; or lie hard in the stomach, as food that adheres to the throat, or distresses the stomach.

anukbikeli, n., a stoppage; an obstruction in the throat.

anukbikelichi, v. t. caus., to cause a pressure or stoppage in the throat, or to cause food to lie hard in the stomach.

anukchaha, a., envious; ill natured.

anukchaha, v. n., to be envious; to be ill natured.

anukchaha, n., envy; ill nature.

anukchahachi, v. t., to cause envy or ill nature; to provoke.

anukcheta hinla, a., trusty.

anukcheto, v. t., to trust in; to depend upon; to serve; to wait upon; to confide; to resign; to stay; *anukchieto,* pro. form (and one much used), to trust, Matt. 12: 21; Mark 10: 24; *anukchinto,* nasal form, trusting; confiding; to rely; to repose.

anukcheto, n., a dependent; one who relies upon another for aid, etc.; *inla anukcheto keyu,* a., independent; not dependent on another.

anukcheto, n., confidence.

anukchilafa, v. a. i. sing., to prate; to talk impertinently.

anukchilafa, n., a prater.

anukchilali, n. pl., praters.

anukchilali, v. a. i. pl., to prate.

anukchito, v. a. i., to hesitate; to falter; *anukchinto,* nasal form.

anukfila, v. a i.; *imanukfila,* to be minded, Matt. 1: 19.

anukfila, n., thought; usually found with a prefixed pronoun, as *am, chim, im, pim.,* etc.; see *imanukfila,* 1 Tim. 6: 11; Articles of faith, sec. v.; *nan anukfila,* mind, Phil. 2: 5; *anukfila,* pp., considered.

anukfilema, v. a. i. sing., to turn inside out (as the inside comes out); *anukfilemoa,* pl.

anukfilema, pp., a., turned inside out; turned wrong side out.

anukfilema, n., the turning of the inside out.

anukfilemoa, v. a. i. pl., to turn inside out.

anukfilemoa, pp. pl., turned inside out; turned wrong side out.

anukfilemoli, v. t. pl., to turn the inside out.

anukfilimmi, v. t. pl., to turn inside out.

anukfilli, v. a. i., v. t., to deem; to digest; to entertain; to hammer; to heed; to imagine; to invent; to look; to muse; to ponder; to purpose; to reason; to reckon; to reflect; to regard; to remark; to repute; to resolve; to ruminate; to scheme; to speculate; to study; to view;

to weigh; to will; to wish; to think; to consider; to reflect; to judge; to meditate, Josh. 1: 8; to muse; to deliberate; to feel; to cogitate; to conceit; to conceive; to contemplate; to count upon; to debate, i. e., to consider; *anukfieli*, pro. form; *isht anukfieli*, to muse, Luke 3: 15; to ruminate; to run; *anukfihinli*, to think on, Matt. 1: 20; 6: 27; *isht anukfilli*, v. t., to thiuk about or concerning; *ilanukfilli*, to think within himself, Luke 16: 3; *nan isht ilaianukfihinli*, take thought for the things of itself, the reciprocal pro. applied to things; *ikanukfillo*, a., unstudied.

anukfilli, v. t., to think of; *chianukfillit binililishke*.

anukfilli, a., thoughtful; wishful; *ikanukfillo*, a., mindless; unfeeling; unmeditated; unstudied; unthinking.

anukfilli, n., meditation; study; thinking.

anukfilli, n., a thinker; a considerer; a contemplator; a speculator.

anukfillit hobachi, v. t., to image; to imagine.

anukfillit pisa; *ilanukfillit pisa*, v. ref., to examine one's self; *ilanukfillit pisa*, n., self-examination.

anukfillituk keyu, a., unpremeditated.

anukfohka, v. a. i., to understand; to know; to remember; to lodge; *anukfoⁿka*, nasal form, *hachi anukfokahi oka*, for ye shall know, Matt. 10: 19.

anukfohka, a., pp., enlightened; having knowledge of; having embraced; *anukfoⁿka*, nasal form; *isht anukfoka*, enlightened by means of, Luke 1: 41 and 67; *isht anukfohkat imalotowa*, being filled with, Luke 4: 1.

anukfohka, n., knowledge; understanding; knowledge received and embraced.

anukfohkachechi, v. t., to instruct or to persuade; to put it into their minds; *iⁿmiⁿko ikimantio ka chiⁿka anukfohkachichi*, sedition, Luke 23: 25.

anukfohki, v. t., to embrace; to acquire knowledge (used in regard to those who embrace the gospel); to believe; *ilanukfohki*, reflexive.

anukfohkichi, v. t. caus., to give knowledge; to enlighten; to impart knowledge; to impart a *believing* knowledge

of a subject; *anukfokinchi*, nasal form; *anukfokihinchi*, freq.

anukfokichi, n., an enlightener; an instructor; one that imparts knowledge.

anukhaⁿklo, n., a place of sorrow; an occasion of sorrow.

anukhammi, v. n., to be in pain; *sianukhammi*, I am in pain; *anukhaiyammi*, pro. form.

anukhammi, n., pain.

anukhammi, a., painful.

anukhammichi, v. t., to cause pain.

anukhobela, v. n., to be angry; to be wroth; *sianukhobela*, I am enraged; *anukhobiela*, pro. form, Matt. 2: 16.

anukhobela, n., fury; madness.

anukhobela, a., furious; mad.

anukhobela iksho, v. a. i., to be meek, or without wrath.

anukhobelachi, v. t., to enrage; to madden; to make mad.

anukkilli, v. a. i., to hate; to bear malice.

anukkilli, n., hatred.

anuklamampa, v. n., to feel surprise.

anuⁿklupatka, n., the peelings from the inside of the intestines in dysentery.

anuklakancha, v. a. i., to take fright; to fear; to marvel; to start.

anuklakancha, a., pp., frightened; amazed; surprised; astonished; *okla hat anuklakancha tok*, the people were astonished, Matt. 7: 28.

anuklakancha, v. n., to be frightened; to be amazed, John 3: 7.

anuklakancha, n., fright; amazement.

anuklakashli, v. t., to frighten; to amaze; to astound; to astonish; to surprise.

anuklamalli, v. a. i., to strangle; to choke.

anuklamalli, pp., strangled.

anuklamallichi, v. t., to strangle.

anuklamallichi, n., a strangler; strangulation.

anuktiⁿfa, v. a. i., to run or slip through a noose.

anuktiⁿfa, pp., drawn through.

anuktiⁿfa, n., a slipping through (perhaps a noose); a slipknot.

anuktiⁿffi, v. t., to draw through a noose or a loop; to make a slipknot.

anuktiffichi, v. t., to cause to draw through a noose.

anukłiha, pp. pl., drawn through a noose.

anukłiha, v. a. i. pl., to run through.

anukłilelichi, v. t. pl., to draw a rope through a noose, as in roping cattle.

anukpalli, v. n., to feel interest; to feel a temptation; to feel the influence of an object; *sianukpalli*, I am interested.

anukpalli, a., interested; excited; enticed; tempted.

anukpallichi, v. t., to interest; to excite the passions; to tempt; to allure.

anukpallichi, n., a tempter.

anukpallika, n., temptation, Matt. 6: 13; Luke 11: 4.

anukpilefa, pp. sing., turned inside out, or wrong side out; turned.

anukpiliffi, v. t., to turn; to turn inside out.

anukpiloa, pp. pl., turned; turned inside out.

anukpilołi, v. t. pl., to turn: to turn inside out.

anukpoali, v. a. i., to feel sick at the stomach; to nauseate.

anuksita, n., a gallows; a gibbet.

anuksita, v. a. i., to cleave to; to adhere with attachment; to hang to; *anuksitia*, pro. form, and the one most used.

anuksita, n., attachment.

anuksiteli, v. t., to hang by the neck; to execute by hanging.

anuksiteli, n., a gibbet; a gallows.

anuksitkachi, v. t. pl., to cleave to; to hang to; see *hatak anuksitkachi.*

anuksitkachi, n. pl., a hanging to.

anukshomota, v. a. i.; *anukshomunta,* nasal form v. n., to be in a rage; to rage; to be peevish; *sianukshomunta,* I am in a rage.

anukshomunta, a., raging; peevish; fierce; *anukshomunta fehna hatukon*, being exceeding fierce, Matt. 8: 28.

anukshomunta, n., rage; peevishness.

anukshunfa, see *anakshunfa.*

anukshumpa, v. a. i., to wish for more food or instruction, not having had enough.—P. Fisk.

anuktapa, v. n., to be greedy; to be insatiable.

anuktapa, a., greedy; insatiable.

anuktapli, anuktabli, v. a. i. pl., to go to excess.

anuktaptua, v. n., to be insatiable; to be greedy.

anuktaptua, a., pp., insatiable; greedy.

anuktaptuli, v. t. pl., to go to excess.

anuktiboha, anuktoboha, v. n., to be roiled, agitated, or disturbed, as roily water or water boiling up in a spring.

anuktobulli, v. a. i., to boil up; to rise up, as water in a spring.

anuktobullichi, v. t., to cause to boil up.

anuktuklichi, anuktuklochi, v. t., to hamper; to embarrass.

anuktuklo, n., a hesitation; an impediment; suspense.

anuktuklo, v. n., to be at a loss; to be in doubt; to doubt, Matt. 14: 31.

anuktuklo, v. a. i., to hesitate; to doubt; to stammer.

anuktuklo, a., pp., embarrassed, *ikanuktuklo*, a., pp., unembarrassed.

anuktuklo iksho, a., unhesitating.

anuktuklochechi, v. t., to embarrass.

anuktuklochi, v. t., to embarrass; to trouble, Gal. 5: 10.

anuktuklochi, adv., doubting; *chunkash mat anuktuklochi*, Mark 11: 23.

anukwanya, v. n., to be in haste; to be in a hurry; v. a. i., to hurry.

anukwanya, a., hasty; hurried; in haste.

anukwanyachi, v. t., to hasten; to hurry.

anukwia, v. n., to hesitate; to be timid, fearful, or doubtful; to be afraid; to dread; to be afraid to do or to venture (not to be afraid of any creature, but to be afraid of such things as trying to cross a stream, and the like); *innukwia*, afraid of him, *anukwia*, he is afraid of me; *sianukwia*, I am afraid; *ikchianukwiokashke*, fear not, Matt. 1: 20.

anukwia, a., timid; fearful; doubtful; afraid; reluctant.

anukwiachi, v. t., to render timid; to frighten.

anukyiminta, v. a. i., to be angry.

anukyohbi, v. a. i., to soften; to become moist and soft, as by the dew.

anukyohbi, pp., softened; moistened; soft; moist.

anukyohbichi, v. t., to soften; to moisten.

anump ikbi, v. t., to make a speech.

anump ikbi, n., a speechmaker.

anump iksho, a., speechless.

anump iⁿkucha achukma, n., fluency.

anump imeshi, n., his secretary; his aid; one that receives instructions from his superior; the combination *im* is a prefixed pronoun.

anump imeshi, v. t., to hear a message; to receive instructions.

anump isht ika, n., a haranguer.

anumpa, annumpa, pp., spoken; worded; uttered; pronounced; declared; talked; delivered; enunciated; expressed; mentioned; preached; pronounced; *aianuhumpa*, Matt. 3: 17; *isht imanuhumpashke*, Matt. 11: 5; *itimanumpa*, conversed together; spoken; *isht anumpa*, pp., debated; preached; *imanumpa*, pp., warned.

anumpa, a., oral; verbal.

anumpa, adv., orally; verbally.

anumpa, annumpa, n., a talk; a speech; a word; Josh. 1: 13; a communication; a message; a promise; advice; counsel; a language; a tongue; the voice; the mode of speaking; a sermon; a discourse; a sentence; an oration; a declamation; tidings, Luke 1: 10; a charge; chat; a declaration; a detail; a dialect; doctrine; elocution; enunciation; an errand; intelligence; a law; a lecture; a mandate; mention; nourishment or instruction; an observation; parlance; parley; a passage; a phrase; a proclamation; a proverb; a report; a saying; a sentence; a statement; style; a tale; tattle; a term; terms; testimony; a text; a theory; a topic; a tract; a treatise; a treaty; utterance; a verse; a voice; a vote; *amanumpa*, sayings of mine, Matt. 7: 24, 26; *isht anumpa*, word of, or about, Matt. 13: 19.

anumpa achafa, n., a paragraph; a sentence.

anumpa achukmalit chukashichi, v. t., to blandish; to flatter; lit. to talk with and take the heart.

anumpa afolotowa, n., an equivocation; lit. a roundabout talk.

anumpa afolotowachi, v. a. i., to equivocate.

anumpa aialhpisa, n., headquarters; the place where counsel is adopted.

anumpa annoa, n., tidings.

anumpa apakfokachi, v. a. i., to evade.

anumpa apakfopa, n., an evasion.

anumpa apesa, v. t., to dictate; to pass sentence; to fulminate.

anumpa apesa, n., a dictator, a lawgiver; a lawmaker.

anumpa asilhha, n., a prayer; a petition; a request.

anumpa asilhha holisso, n., a prayer book.

anumpa atatoa, n., a verse.

anumpa aⁿya, n., a message; a rumor.

anumpa alhpisa, n., a law; a sentence; an ordinance; a statute; an agreement; a covenant; a commandment; a rule; a precept; a judgment; "a determined or settled word;" a constitution; a decision; a decree; a dictate; a doom; an edict; a fiat; a government; an injunction; an institution; an interdict; an order; a resolution.

anumpa alhpisa, pp., legislated.

anumpa alhpisa holisso, n., a written law; a law book.

anumpa alhpisa ikbi, n., a legislator.

anumpa alhpisa ikbi, v. t., to legislate; to enact a law or laws.

anumpa alhpisa iksho, a., lawless; without law.

anumpa alhpisa isht atta, n., a scribe.

anumpa elhpisa keyu, a., lawless.

anumpa alhpisa onuchi, v. t., to fine.

anumpa alhpisa onuchi, n., a suitor.

anumpa alhpisa onutula, pp., fined.

anumpa alhpisa toba, v. a. i., to become a law.

anumpa alhtoshowa, see *anumpa toshoa*.

anumpa bachaya, n., a column; a division of a page; lit. "a row of words."

anumpa bachoha, n. pl., columns.

anumpa chokushpikbi, n., a libeler.

anumpa chuⁿkushnali, n., a sarcasm; a retort.

anumpa chukushpa, n., hearsay; a report; evil speaking; a libel.

anumpa chukushpa ikbi, n., a tale bearer.

anumpa chukushpa ikbi, v. t., to make tales or stories.

anumpa chukushpali, v. t., to slander; to backbite; to libel.

anumpa chukushpali, n., a slanderer; a gossiper.

anumpa chukushpashali, v. t., to carry news or slander; to gossip.

anumpa chukushpashali, n., a tale
bearer; a slanderer; a gossiper; a peace
breaker; a sycophant.

anumpa falama, n., an answer; a reply;
lit. the word returned.

anumpa falama, pp., answered.

anumpa falamoa, n. pl., answers; re-
plies.

anumpa falamolichi, v. t. pl., to answer;
to reply.

anumpa falammichi, v. t., to reply; to
answer; "to return a word;" *anumpa
falamminchi*, nasal form; *anumpa falam-
mihinchi*, freq.; *anumpa infalamminchi*,
v. t., to reply to him.

anumpa fimmi, n., a propagator.

anumpa himona, n., tidings.

anumpa hinla, a., speakable; utterable;
what can be expressed.

anumpa holabi, n., a fib.

anumpa holisso nowąt anya, n., an
epistle.

anumpa ikaiako, n., a short speech.

anumpa ikbi, n., a propagator of stories,
etc.

anumpa ilatomba, a., reserved.

anumpa ilatomba, v. n., to be reserved.

anumpa ilonuchi, v. ref., to assume an
obligation; to promise; to oblige himself.

anumpa inlaua, a., talkative; *anumpa
ikinlauo*, a., silent.

anumpa intuklo, n., a trimmer.

anumpa isht auehinchi, n., a tradition.

anumpa isht anya, v. t., to carry a message.

anumpa isht anya, n., a messenger; a
runner.

anumpa isht ąlhpisa, n., a parable.

anumpa isht hika, v. t., to deliver a
speech; to harangue; *anumpa isht ika*,
see Child's Cat., p. 10, q. 42.

anumpa isht hika, n., a speech; an
oration; a formal speech; a set speech;
a harangue; an address; oratory.

anumpa isht hika, anumpa isht ika,
n., an orator; a speaker; a declaimer;
a haranguer.

anumpa isht okchaya, n., the word of
life.

anumpa itimapesa, v. t., to bargain;
to covenant together.

anumpa itimapesa, n., a bargain; a
mutual covenant.

anumpa itimąlhpisa, pp., bargained;
covenanted.

anumpa itinlaua, n., an altercation; a
controversy.

anumpa itinlaua, v. a. i., to have an
altercation; to have many words between them.

anumpa itinlauachi, v. t., to altercate;
to dispute; to make many words between them.

anumpa kaniohmi, n., news; a word of
some sort.

anumpa kaniohmi keyu, n., nonsense;
a word of no sort.

anumpa kąllo, n., a strong talk; a law;
a rule; a command; a canon; an ordinance; testimony; an oath, Matt. 14:
7, 9; a league, Josh. 9: 6.

anumpa kąllo ikbi, n., a lawmaker; a
legislator.

anumpa kąllo ilonuchi, v. ref., to bind
himself; to lay himself under obligations; to swear.

anumpa kąllo ilonuchi cha ia, v. t.
ref., to abjure; to vow; to vouch.

anumpa kąllo ilonuchit anoli, v. t., to
depose; to bear testimony.

anumpa kąllo isht anumpuli, v. t., to
swear.

anumpa kąllo miha, v. t., to damn.

anumpa kąllo onitula, see *anumpa kąllo
onutula*.

anumpa kąllo onuchi, v. t., to sue; to
prosecute; to condemn; to sentence; to
command; to order; to curse; to damn;
to doom; to execrate; to indict.

anumpa kąllo onuchi, n., a prosecutor.

anumpa kąllo onuchit anoli, anumpa
kąllo onuchit miha, v. t., v. a. i., to
testify.

anumpa kąllo onutula, anumpa kąllo
onitula, anumpa kąllo onątula, pp.,
sued; prosecuted; condemned; sentenced; commanded; ordered; cursed.

anumpa kąllo onutula, n., a prosecution; a sentence; a curse; a vow.

anumpa keyu, n., nonsense.

anumpa kobafa, n., a transgression; a
broken law; a breach of the law; perfidy.

anumpa kobąffi, v. t., to transgress; to
break a law; to revolt.

anumpa kobąffi, n., a transgressor; a
criminal; a culprit; a lawbreaker; an
offender; a rebel.

anumpa kobaffi, n., a transgression; a crime.

anumpa kochanli, anumpa kuchanli, a verbal message; traditions, Matt. 15: caption, 2, 3, 6.

anumpa kochanli, v. a. i., to come along, or to be out, as a verbal message.

anumpa kololi, n., pl. short words; short speeches.

anumpa kolunfa, n., a short word; a short speech.

anumpa kolunfasi, n. dimin.; a very short talk; a shortish talk.

anumpa kuchanli, see anumpa kochanli.

anumpa laua, a., verbose; wordy.

anumpa lumiksho, n., frankness.

anumpa makali, n., scurrility.

anumpa nan anoli, n., a story.

anumpa nan alhpisa isht atta, n., a lawyer; an attorney.

anumpa nan isht alhpisa, n., an allegory; a parable.

anumpa nukoa, n., rant.

anumpa nushkobo, n., a summary; the heads of discourse; a head; topic of discourse; subject-matter of a speech; a text.

anumpa okpulo, n., bad language; vile talk; calumny; an invective; scandal.

anumpa okpulo onuchi, v. t., to calumniate; to slander.

anumpa okpulo onuchi, n., calumny; slander.

anumpa okpulo onuchi, n., a calumniator.

anumpa okpulo onutula, pp., calumniated.

anumpa onucha hinla, a., accusable; impeachable.

anumpa onuchi, anumponuchi, v. t., to accuse; to blame; to impeach; to indict; to charge; to condemn, Matt. 12: 7; to prosecute; to sentence.

anumpa onuchi, n., an accuser; an informer; a prosecutor.

anumpa onuchi, n., an impeachment.

anumpa onutula, anumponatula, pp., impeached; accused; blamed; condemned; sentenced to punishment; indicted; anumpa ikonitulo, a., uncondemned.

anumpa onutula, anumpa onatula, n., an inpeachment; an accusation; blame.

anumpa onutulahe keyu, a., excusable; irreproachable.

anumpa shali, v. t., to carry a message.

anumpa shali, n., a messenger; a runner; an ambassador, Josh. 9: 4.

anumpa shanaioa, n., a prevarication; imanumpa shanaioa, n., a prevaricator; imanumpa shanaioa, v. t., to prevaricate.

anumpa tikba, n., a summary.

anumpa tikbanli anoli, n., a prophecy.

anumpa tilofa, n. sing., a short address a short speech; the name often given by an orator in his introduction to the speech he is about to make.

anumpa tilofasi, a dim. n., a brief address; the si has nearly the force of sh in some English words, as short, shortish.

anumpa tiloli, n. pl., short speeches; short addresses.

anumpa toshoa, anumpa alhtoshowa, n., a translation; an interpretation; a speech translated; an explanation.

anumpa toshoa, pp., translated; interpreted; explained.

anumpa tosholi, v. t., to interpret; to translate; to construe.

anumpa tosholi, n., a translator; an interpreter; an expositor; a linguist.

anumpa tosholi ashachi, v. t., to misinterpret; to mistranslate.

anumpeshi, n., a presiding officer in a council; a secretary; a messenger, Matt. 11: 10; an aid-de-camp; a consul, a disciple, John 3: 22; a servant, Luke 2: 29; an apostle, Luke 6: 13; a legate; an officer; a representative; a resident.

anumpeshi atokulli, v. t., to officer.

anumpisachi, v. t., to take aim; to level; or anompisachi (q. v.).

anumponatula, see anumpa onutula.

anumponuchi,, see anumpa onuchi.

anumpulechi, v. t., to trouble; to pester to plague; to annoy; to worry; to disturb; to molest; to embarrass; to hector; to incommode; sianumpulechi fehna, he troubles me very much.

anumpulechi, n., a troubler; a hectorer; isht itimanumpuli, to hold a council against, Matt. 12: 14.

anumpuli, v. a. i., v. t., to talk; to speak, Joshua 1: 1; to utter; to say, Matt. 17: 4; to say a word; to pray, Matt. 6: 9;

to preach, Luke 3: 3; to chat; to declaim; to deliver; to discourse; to enunciate; to exhort; to express; to gab; to gabble; to harangue; to lecture; to mention; to observe; to phrase; to pronounce; to reason; to tattle; to word; *imanumpuli*, v. t., to talk to him; to counsel; to deal with; to exhort; to expostulate; to rebuke; to reprehend; to read, as *holisso imanumpuli; imanumpuli*, n., a reader; *isht anumpuli*, to talk about; to advocate; to comment; to descant; to preach; to plead; to praise; *ikanumpolo*, n. f., v. a. i., a., dumb; unsocial; *isht anumpuli*, to talk about, Matt. 7: 22; *yammakosh ahąchi anumpuląhi oka*, which shall speak in you, Matt. 10: 20; *aiitimanumpuli*, Matt. 12: 4; to read, Josh. 8: 35; *anumponli*, nasal form, v. a. i., and a.; *ąbanumpa isht anumpohonli*, preaching, Matt. 12: 41; *itimanumpuli*, to speak with him; *chitimanumpuli*, to speak with thee; *anumpohonli*, freq.; *isht imanumpohonli*, to speak to them by, Matt. 12: 46, 47; *anumpoyuli*, pro. form; *itimanumpuli*, v. t., to converse together; to talk together; to commune; to contest; to discuss; to negotiate; to parley; to reason, Matt. 16: 7, 8; *isht itimanumpuli*, v. t., to reason; *itimanumpuli*, n., a colloquy; a dialogue; a conference; a parley; *isht ishimanumpuli*, Matt. 13: 10; *itinnupolih* used for *itimanumpulih; imanumpuli*, v. t., to reprimand; to school; *ilanumpuli*, to talk to one's self; *isht ilanumpuli*, to talk about himself; *isht anumpuli*, v. t., to handle; to talk about; to intercede; to treat; to vindicate.

anumpuli, n., preaching; pronunciation; "voice," Gen. 4: 10.

anumpuli, n., a speaker; a counselor; a declaimer; a deliverer; a lecturer; a herald; a speechmaker; a talker; *ikanumpolo*, n., a mute; a dumb person, Matt. 12: 22; *ikanumpolo*, a., mute; silent.

anumpuli anuktuklo, v. a. i., to stammer; to stutter.

anumpuli ilahobi, v. a. i., to babble.

anumpuli ilahobi, n., a babbler.

anumpuli imponna, a., eloquent; fluent.

anumpuli imponna, v. n., to be eloquent.

anumpuli imponna, n., a linguist.

anumpuli itąlhpesa, v. t., to respond.

anumpuli keyu, a., mute; speechless; mum.

anumpuli shali, n., a talker; a great talker; a chatterbox; a prater.

anumpuli shali, v. a. i., to talk much; to prate.

anumpuli shali, a., flippant; loquacious; talkative; voluble.

anumpulit aⁿsha, v. a. i., to sit and talk; to be in session; to be engaged in any kind of speaking.

anumpulit aⁿsha, n., a session; a sitting; the actual presence of any body of men who have met for speaking, consulting, etc.

anumpulit chuⁿkąsh ishi, v. t., to persuade.

anusi, n., a bed; a bedroom; any place for sleeping; the place where any one or any creature sleeps; a couch; a dormitory; a harbor; an inn; a lodging.

anusi, v. n., v. a. i., to sleep at, in, or on; to sleep there; *asanusi, anuseli*, where I sleep.

anusi ona, n., bedtime; time for sleep.

anusi ona, v. a. i., to arrive (as bedtime); the time to go to bed has come.

anushkunna, n., a lover.

anushkunna, n., fancy; liking; passion.

anushkunna, v. a. i., v. t., to fancy; to like; to desire; to be fond of; to love, 1 Kings, 11: 1; to have a passion for another, a female, 2 Sam. 13: 1, 2 15; *aianushkunna*, Matt. 13: 22; to covet, Josh. 7: 21.

apa, v. a. i., from *ąpa*, to eat and in regard to eating a single article of food; *impa*, to eat, implies the eating of a number of things, or a common meal; *ishimpa hinla?* will you eat? *ahe ishpahinla*, will you eat a potato? See *ąpa*.

apahyah, pp., shouted at; called to.

apahyąchi, v. t., to shout at; to halloo.

apahyąchi, n., a shouter; one that halloos.

apakama, n., guile, John 1: 47.

apakąma, apakama, pp., deceived in any way; imposed upon.

apakąmmi, v. t., to deceive.

apakąmmi, n., a deceiver.

apakąmoa, pp. pl., deceived.

apakąmoli, v. t. pl., to deceive.

apakąmoli, n., deceivers.

apakchilofa, pp., tripped up.

apakchiloffi, v. t., to trip up.

apakchulli, v. a. i., v. t., to climb up; to cling; to wind round and ascend, as a man climbs a tree or a vine runs up a pole.

apakchulli, n., a climber.

apakfoa, pp. pl., banded; bound round; tied round; from apakfoli.

apakfoa, v. a. i., to go round; to reach round; to wind round.

apakfoa, v. n., to be round; to be wound round.

apakfobli, v. a. i. sing., to go round; to encircle; to surround; to wrap round; to environ; to inclose; as, it goes round, etc., Luke 13: 8; Mark 12: 1.

apakfoblichi, v. t., caus., to wind round; to cause to go round; to wrap round.

apakfokąchi, pp. pl., surrounded; encircled.

apakfokąchi, v. n., to be around.

apakfokąchi, v. a. i., to go round; to encircle; to avoid by going round; apakfokahanchi, freq., Rev. 20: 9.

apakfoli, v. t. pl., to surround; to wind round; to wrap round; ilapakfoli, v. ref., to bewrap; to wrap himself, Gen. 37: 34.

apakfopa, apakfoyupa (pro. f.), n., the circumference; the compass; a zone; apakfoyupa, prep., round.

apakfopa, apakfompa (nas. f.), pp., from apakfobli, wound round; wrapped round; circled; encircled; environed; inclosed; shunned; surrounded.

apakfopa, a., spiral.

apakfopa, v. a. i., to go round; to wind round; to circuit; to come round; to deviate; to encircle; to fly; to shun; to compass, Josh. 6: 3, 4; apakfompa, nasal form; apakfohompa, pro. form.

apakfopa, v. n., to be wound round; v. t., to compass; to double, as a cape; apakfoyupa, pro. form.

apakfopahe keyu, a., inevitable.

apakfoyupa, see apakfopa.

apakna, n., a plenty; an abundance; a fullness.

apakna, adv., freely.

apakna, a., plenteous; abundant; copious; exuberant.

apakna, v. n., to be plenteous; to abound; itimpakna, to compete together; kilitim-

pakna, let us compete, or try and see which will excel; see pakna.

apaknaⁿka, n., the top, Luke 23: 38.

apaknali, n., the surface; the face.

apaknali, a., superficial; being on the surface.

apaknali, v. n., to be superficial; to be on the surface.

apaknąchi, v. t., to cause an abundance; to make a plenty, 1 Kings 10: 27.

apakshanofa, v. a. i., to cling.

apakshąna, v. a. i., to cling to; to grip; itapakshąna, to strive together, Deut. 25: 11.

apakshąna, pp., twisted round; itapakshąna, pp., intwined; twisted together.

apakshąnni, v. t., to twist round; itapakshąnni, itapakshąnnichi, v. t., to intwine; to twist together.

apaląska, n., an oven; any place where anything is baked; a baking place.

apali, v. a. i., to lurk; to creep slyly in quest of prey or game, like a cat.

apanlichi, v. t., to encourage by shouts; to halloo.

apanta, a., nasal form, from apata, situated at the side; being on the side; sing. of pąlli; iⁿchukapanta, chuka iⁿpąlli.

apantali, nasal form, from apatąli.

apanukfila, n., a whirlwind.

apanukfila, v. a. i., to blow and rise, as a whirlwind; to be a whirlwind, or to whirlwind, making a verb of the noun.

apashia, n., a piazza; a porch; a portico; chukapashia, house porch.

apata, v. a. i., to lie at the side; apanta, nasal form; apataiya, pro. form, to lie along at the side.

apata, pp., laid at the side.

apatafa, n., a plowed place.

apatalechi, v. t., to spread a blanket so that one-half is under and the other over a person; see apolomichi.

apatąlhpo, n., a spread; a mattress; a seat; a cushion, John 19: 13. Perhaps this word is used for "seat" because in early times the Choctaw spread out some kind of skin as a seat for visitors and others.

apatąli, v. a. i., to grow at the side like corn suckers; itapatąli, recip.

apatąli, n., suckers; young sprouts at the side.

apaha, n., attendants; companions; fellows; *itapiha*, fellows.

apala, n., a frying pan or anything in which to carry a torch or a light; usually applied to a frying pan, because it was used to carry a light by those who hunted game in the night. The light was made of fat pine knots or wood cut and split fine.

apalli, apulli, pl. of *apotali*, v. a. i., to stand side and side; to lie side by side; *chuka apallit anya keyu*, not to eavesdrop.

apalichi, v. t., to hew wood.

apalichi, n., a hewer.

apeha, apiha, v. a. i. pl., many to join one; to go in company with; to be with others, 2 Sam. 18: 1; or being with, Matt. 12: 3; Josh. 7: 24; *apehat aiasha*, about him, i. e., multitudes, Matt. 8: 18; *apehat anya*, to go along with one; to accompany him, Matt. 12: 3, 4; Josh. 8: 5; *itapiha*, to join together; to accompany; to go together, John 3: 22; *aiitapiha*, to join together there, or at, Matt. 8: 11; here are plurals in both companies that united *apehkachi, itapekachi, aitapekachi, aiapinhat hieli*, Matt. 12: 41, to stand together with; *itapinhat hiohmanya*, Matt. 13: 30; *aiitapinhat attat ia*, Matt. 14: 13; *apinha*, to be with, Matt. 4: 21.

apehali; *aiapehalinchi*, pl., led with him, Luke 23: 32.

apehachi, v. t. caus., to cause to be or go together; to take part with.

apehpoa, see *apepoa*.

apela, n., a helper; an assistant; an ally; an auxiliary; an aid; a coadjutor; a help; a second; a subsidiary.

apela, a., subservient; *ikapelo*, a., unaided; unassisted; unhelped; unsupported.

apela, v. t., to help, Josh. 1: 14; to assist; to abet; to succor; to back; to second or strengthen by aid; to support; to favor; to further; to interpose; to second; to side; to stickle; to subserve; *siapela*, to help me; *chiapelali*, I help thee; *itapela*, to help each other; *itapela*, n., a help; a helper; a partner; an ally; an auxiliary; mutual helps, etc.; *apinla*, nasal form, helping; *apihinla*, freq. form, keep helping; *apiela*, pro. form,

to help at last; *apela ikimiksho*, a., helpless; without help.

apelachi, apelachi, v. t., to help another; to cause to help; to favor; to further; to patronize; to promote; to relieve; to succor, *siapelachi*, help me, Matt. 15: 25; *apelanchi*, nasal form; *apelahanchi*, freq. form; *apelaiyachi*, pro. form.

apelachi, n., a help; a remedy; succor.

apelachi, apelachi, n., a promoter; a succorer; a helper; an abettor; an ally; an assistant; an auxiliary; a coadjutor; a favorer; a paraclete; a patron; *itapelachi*, n., a copartner; mutual helpers.

apeli, n., a hurricane; a tempest; the place where a hurricane passed along and blew down the timber; a whirlwind.

apeli, v.a. i., to storm; to blow, as a hurricane.

apelua, pp., turned up.

apelulichi, v. a. i., to turn up sleeves or legs of pantaloons or leggings.

apeli, v. t., to bring, sweep, or scrape together; to rake up, as bears and hogs rake or bring together grass and leaves for a nest.

apeli, n., a raker; a nest maker.

apelichi, v. t., to push up the wood on a fire; to put the sticks or brands together; to hoe earth up around plants.

apelichi, v. t. pl., to rule at; to preside in; to govern there; *apelinchi*, nasal form; *apelihinchi*, freq.; *apeliechi*, pro. form.

apelichi, apeliechi, n., the course, class or term (of Abia), Luke 1: 5.

apelichi, n., the place ruled; a kingdom, Mark 11: 10; a tribe, 1 Kings 11: 31, 32; 2 Sam. 24: 2.

apelichi fullota, n., a territory; the extent of the place that is ruled.

apelichika, apeliechika, n., the place ruled, whether kingdom, province, town, district, plantation, bishopric, diocese, or a single house; or the place ruled by domestic animals; domain; dominion; a dukedom; an empire; a government; a kingdom; a monarchy; a province; a sphere; a tribe, 1 Kings 11: 13; *yakni apelichika moma*, Matt. 4: 8; 3: 2; 5: 3; 6: 13, 33; 12: 25, 26;

13: 19, 41, 43; 18: 1; *apelichika*, in Matt. 6: 10, used as a verb, having *ish*, thou, prefixed; or this *ish* is used as a poss. pronoun, similar to *ish* in *ishitibapishi*, thy brother, so here it is thy kingdom, 1 Kings 10: 20.

apelichika fullota, n., a precinct.

apeliechi achafa, n., a body; a number of men united by a common tie or form of government.

apeliechi, see *apelichi.*

apepoa, apehpoa, apepowa, v. t. pl., to help; to assist by counsel, not in labor; to advocate for; to plead for; to argue for; to stand up for; to fight for; *ilapipowa* to help himself.

apepoa, apepowa, n., helpers; advocates; allies; justifiers; *apipoat illi,* n., a martyr; *apipoat illi,* n., martyrdom.

apesa, apisa, v. t., to order; to appoint, Josh. 1: 7; to fix; to measure, Matt. 7: 2; to judge; to adjudge; to reconcile; to regulate; to resolve; to rule; to scale; to scheme; to set; to settle; to span; to square; to survey; to test; to time; to tolerate; to transact; to will; to destine; to devise; to direct; to dispose of; to doom; to enact; to engage; to establish; to estimate; to gauge; to instruct; to lay a plan; to legalize; to machinate; to manage; to marshal; to mediate; to mete; to methodize; to order; to maneuver; to plan; to prescribe; to project; to purpose; to adjudicate; to sanction; to command, Matt. 8: 4; 14: 9; to conclude; to decide; to decree; *imapesa*, to appoint for him; to allow him; to send him; to license; to restrict; to make for them, i. e., a feast, Luke 5: 29; to give them power, Matt. 10: 1; *nan isht apesa*, Matt. 13: 3; *ikimapeso*, v. t., to disallow him; *ikapeso*, a., undetermined; *isht apesa*, to measure with; to maneuver; to model; *isht apesatima*, v. t., to devote; *apihinsa*, Matt. 15: 4; *itimapesa*, to league; to agree together; to concert together; to contract; to covenant; *itimapesa*, n., an agreement; a concert; a contract; a league; *ilitibapesa*, we agree together; *ilapisa*, to measure for himself, Luke 12: 21; to make himself, John 5: 18; *itapesa*, to contract; to liken; *itapesalashke*, I will liken, Matt. 7: 24; also

Matt. 11: 16; *pitimapesa*, Josh. 9: 6; *alhpisa, alhpesa,* pp.

apesa, n., a judge; one that measures, appoints, etc.; a director; an enactor; an estimator; a manager; a measurer.

apesa, n., a measurement; mensuration.

apesachi, v. t., to oversee; to direct; to manage; to rule; to tend; *chiapesahanchi*, etc., Matt. 4: 6; *apesaiyachi*, pro. form.

apesachi, n., an overseer; a director; a manager; a curator; a tender; a keeper; *apesachi aleha hatuk at yilepat*, and they that kept them fled, Matt. 8: 33; *apesachi*, a shepherd, Matt. 9: 36; a keeper, Gen. 4: 9.

apiha, n. (see *apeli*, act.; *apiha* is pass.), a place brushed, raked, etc.; as *onush apiha*, where the oats have been raked away; *itapiha*, together with, John 21: 2; *itapehachi*, collected together; *aiitapiha*, with; together with; *apinha*, nasal form of *apeha*, pl., being with, John 11: 31; 21: 3; *apinhat anya kashon*, them that followed, Matt. 8: 10.

apinni v. t., to twist a stick into hair, as the mane.

apinnichi v. t., to break down the top limbs of bushes; like *akauwichi*.

apisa, n., a glass; a looking glass; a lesson in reading assigned to a pupil; a window; a light; a mirror; scenery; a speculum.

apinsa, n., a prospect; a study.

apisa achafa, n., a pane of glass; a pane.

apisa isht alhkama, n., a window; a window shutter.

apisa isht alhpolosa, n., putty.

apisa isht hoponkoyo, n., a telescope; a spy glass.

apisaka, n., a vision; that which is the object of sight; a view; a sight; a prospect.

apisahukmi, n., a burning glass.

apisaka ali, n., the horizon.

apisali, n., ken; view; reach of sight.

apissa, pp., straightened; made straight; dressed; unbent.

apissa, a., straight.

apissa, v. n., to be straight.

apissalechi, see *apissalechi.*

apissali, a., due; direct; straight; v. t., to choose, Luke 10: 42; *ikapissalo*, a., indirect; vague.

apissanli, a., nasal form of *apissalli*, or a form like *hinanli, kochanli*, etc. (q. v.) (Josh. 5: 5); express; direct; straight; being straight; true; erect; firm; unequivocal; genuine, as *hatak api humma apissanli*, a genuine redman, not a man of mixed blood; explicit, as in *anumpa apissanli achukma;* fair; genuine; honest; invariable; regular; right; upright.

apissanli, adv., regularly.

apissanli, n., fairness; frankness; integrity; probity; simplicity.

apissanli, v. n., to be straight; to be direct, genuine, etc.

apissanlit, apissant, adv., plainly; directly; in a direct course; the nearest way; downright; right; uprightly; as *apissant ishla*, did you come directly here?; *apissant hikia*, a., precipitous; perpendicular.

apissallechi, apissalechi, v. t. caus., to make straight; to direct; to dress; to straighten, Matt. 3: 3; *ilapissalechi*, John 11: 41 [?]; *uski naki apissalechi*.

apissalli, v. t., to straighten; to unbend.

apissat hikia, a., erect.

apistikeli, n., a watch; a spy; custody; an eyer; a guard; a guardian; a guarder; a manager; an overseer; a supervisor; a surveyor; a troubler; a vigil; a warder; a warden.

apistikeli, n., vigilance; watch; ward; a watcher.

apistikeli, a., troublesome; watchful.

apistikeli, v. a. i., v. t., to watch; to eye; to observe; to look out for with an evil intention; to embarrass; to guard; to look; to oversee; to ward; to be vigilant; to infest; to manage; to molest; to pester; to plague; to superintend; to supervise; to tend; to transact; to trouble.

apistikeli ahikia, n., a watchhouse.

apistikelichi, v. t., to cause to watch; to get one to watch.

apistiket, cont. from *apistikelit*, to watch, etc.

apitta, v. t. pl., to put in; *wak apitta*, to put in cattle; *tanchi apitta*, to put in corn; *okapaⁿkki apitta*, to put in a liquid, Matt. 9: 17; 13: 48; *alhpita*, pp.

apoa, apoba, v. t., to raise, as cattle or any domestic animals, or fruit trees; to have for the purpose of raising, or to let it grow; to domesticate; to tame; *alhpoba*, pp., *imapoa*, to ally; to betroth; to espouse; *itimapoa*, to espouse each other; *itimalhpoba*, pp., of above; *apoahanchi*, "to spare," 1 Sam. 15: 3; *chikapoancho*, Gen. 18: 24.

apoa, n., preemption; a refusal.

apoachi, or apobachi (q. v.) v. t., to raise; *alhpoba*, pp.

apoachi, n., one that betroths or bespeaks.

apoba, see *apoa*.

apoba, n., a saver; a preserver.

apobachi, v. t., to betroth; to bespeak; to speak for; to bargain for; to pet; to preengage; *alhpoba*, pp.

apohko, pp., protected; covered; *ikapohko*, a., exposed.

apohko, n., protection.

apohkochi, v. t., to protect; to cover; *ilapohkochi*, v. ref., she protects herself, or covers herself.

apohkolechi, v. t., to hold the hand and hide or hold something; to hold the flat hand over the ear to prevent hearing; *itapokolechi*, v. t., to put two flat things together.

apohota, n., the fringe; the flounce.

apohtuka, a., shut in so that the air does not circulate, as a house by a thicket.

apohtukachi, v. t., to shut in; to make close.

apohtukih, v. a. i., to be close or tight, as a room.

apokni, appokni, n., my grandmother. The same appellation belongs to all the sisters of the grandmother and to their mother also. When there is an occasion to express the real difference it can be easily done.

apokofa, v. a. i., to thrust against; to run against, Num. 22: 25.

apoksia, v. t., to prepare, John 14: 2, 3; 15: 2; to mend, Matt. 4: 21.

apoksia, n., a repair.

apoksia, pp., repaired; mended; reconciled; redressed; regulated; remedied.

apoksia, a., good; wise.

apoksiachi, v. t., to repair; to adjust; to dispose; to prepare, Luke 3: 4; Matt. 3: 3; 11: 10; to reconcile; to redress; to regulate; to shape; *ilapoksiachi*, to reform himself.

apoksiachi, n., a reformer; a repairer.

apoksiali, v. t., to arrange.

apokshiama, n., a flap; a clout, called a square; a diaper. The *apokshiama* is a garment worn by Choctaw men.

apokshiama, pp., clouted.

apokshiami, apokshiami, apokshiammi, v. t., to put the clout upon one's self; to clout one's self.

apokshiamichi, v. t., to put the clout upon another.

apokshiammi, see *apokshiami*.

apokshiammi, pp., clouted; having a flap put on.

apokta, n., a double.

apokta, pp., doubled; grown together, as two potatoes fastened together side by side.

apokta, a., double; as *ahe apokta, noti apokta*.

apokta, v. n., to be doubled.

Apokta chito, n., the name of a particular creek.

apoktachi, v. t., to double; to cause anything to be doubled.

apolichi, hopochi (q.v.) v. t., to hill corn; to work in the corn for the last time, Luke 13: 8.

apolukta; *itapolukta*, v. a. i., to coalesce.

apoluma, n., a conjurer at ball plays, called a ball play witch.

apolumi, v. t., to conjure; to act the ball play witch.

apolusa, n., a daubing; *apolusa achafa*, one coat of daubing.

apolusa, alhpolosa, pp., a., daubed; plastered; pitched.

apolusa, v. n., to be daubed.

apolusli, v. t., to daub; to plaster; to pitch; to smear.

apolusli, n., a dauber; a plasterer.

apolusli, n., a casing; the act or operation of plastering a house with mortar on the outside.

apoloma, n., a hem; a bend; a spring made by a bend.

apoloma, pp., hemmed; bent over double.

apolomachi, n., a hem of a garment.

apolomachi, pp., hemmed.

apolomachi, v. t., to hem; to bend over double.

apolomi, apolommi, v. t., to hem; to bend over; to go across a bend in a river or road; to lap.

apolomi, n., a hemmer.

apolomichi, v. t., to fold a blanket and sleep in it, one part under and the other part over a person.

apolomoa, pp. pl., hemmed.

apolomoa, n., hems; bends.

apolomolili, v. t., to hem; to bend over; to go across bends in a river or in a road.

aponaklo, v. a. i., v. t., to inquire; to query.

aponaklo, n., an inquirer.

aponaklo, n., an inquiry.

aponaklo shali, a., inquisitive.

aposhokachi, n., the border; the hem; *imanchi aposhokachi ya*[n] *pit potoli*, the hem of his garment; Matt. 9 20; Luke: 8: 44; *imanchi aposhokachi ak illa kia*, only the hem of his garment, Matt. 14: 36.

apota, v. a. i., to lie at the side; *itapota*, to lie together; *ikitapoto*, Matt. 1: 25; *chiapota*, 1 Kings 1: 2.

apota, n., the side; *Eli at hina apota ka*, 1 Sam. 4: 13.

apota, v. n., to be at the side; *apunta*, nasal form; *itapota*, v. a. i., to make snug; to lie sidewise.

apotaka, n., the side; a by-place; *apotaka ia*, to go one side to void, or to a by-place; an expression used to describe the going away to ease nature, etc.

apotaka itola, apotaka atta, v. n., to lie in a retired place; this expression is applied to describe the retirement of females. See Lev. 15: 19–28; *apotakachi*. The Choctaw women have a small camp near the house to which they retire at such seasons, and where they remain alone till they have their usual health.

apotali, v. a. i., to lie at the side.

apotoa, pl., *apotoat hielitok*, to stand beside; to be at the side, 1 Kings 10: 19.

apotoli, apotuli, sing. v. t., to place by the side of, 1 Sam. 5: 2; *apotulit hohpi*, Acts 5: 10; *itapotuli*, v. t., to accouple; to adjoin; to couple.

apoyua, v. t., to gather up; to pick up and carry away.

apuⁿfa, n., a forge, or the place where the mouth of the bellows acts upon the fire; the mouth of a bellows.

apuⁿfạchi, v. t., to blow with a bellows, mouth, pipe, etc.; to expire; to puff; *isht apuⁿfạchi*, n., a blow pipe, or v. t., to blow with.

apulli, v. t. pl., in *himakaⁿ apullit itikbo;* see *alulli.*

apulli, n., corn suckers.

apulli, apạlli, pl. of *apotali* (q. v.).

apullichi, v. t., to hill up (corn); to heap up around anything.

apunta, nasal form (from *apota*), v. n., being at the side to make an exchange equal.

apunta, prep., by; near, as at the side.

apunta, a., contiguous; *hohchifo apunta,* surname, Matt. 10: 3.

apuskiachi, v. t., to divine; to act as a priest. See Gen. 41: 45.

apushi (from *api* and *ushi*), n., a sprout, as *itapushi*, a sprout of a tree, (q. v.); a staddle; *kạti apushi*, Mark 12: 1.

apushi hika, n., a stake.

apushli, v. t., to roast, 1 Sam. 2: 15; to broil; to bake in the hot ashes, as potatoes (*ahe apushli*); *ạlhpusha*, pp.

apushli, n., a roaster; one that roasts.

aputa, a., from *puta*, all. See 1 John 3: 18.

aputkạchi, v. n. pl., to lie or stand side by side.

aputkạchi, a., pp., laid at the side; lying at the side.

asahnoyechi, a., old, aged; or *sahnoyechi* (q. v.).

asanali, see *asonali.*

asanali, n., the forefront of a rock; see 1 Sam. 14: 5; a jamb; the sidepiece of a fireplace.

asanalichi, v. a. i., *asạnni*, pl., to cause it to face; *ahe aⁿ hạshi aⁿ asanalichi*, to lay the potatoes in the sun; *itasạnali*, to face each other.

asananta, ạsananta, n., a large bee, resembling the bumble bee, that bores into wood, etc.

asanata, a., lazy.

asạlbạsh, achạba, asạlhchạp, n., a footbridge, made of a log or tree; *asilhchạp, asạhchạp*, Ch. Sp. Bk., page 50; *sạlbạch*, Ch. Sp. Bk., page 18.

asạlhchap, see above.

asạnni, pl. of *asonali*, to face; to front; to stem.

asạno, n., an adult; a grown person.

asạno, v. a. i., to grow up, a word of general signification; *ạlla ạt asạno*, Luke 1: 80; 2: 40; *itapushi ạt asạno, nusạpi ạt chahạt isht ia; asaiyano*, pro. form; *asạno*, n., an adult; *asạno ikono*, n., a minor; *asạno*, pp., a., grown; grown up; mature; adult; *asaiyano*, pro. form; *asạno, asạnno*, n., maturity; puberty; rankness; *asạnochi, asạnochika,*

asạnochi, n., an elder in a church.

asạnochika, n., the elders of an assembly.

asạnonchi, asanonchi, n., the elders; the aged; the fathers (by way of respect); an elder; a presbyter; *asạnonchi*, Josh. 8: 10, 33; 9: 11; *asạnochi*, Titus 2: 2, 3; *asạnhochi.*

asechip, asechạp, n., a footbridge; a log or tree lying across a creek or water course and used as a footbridge. See *asạlbạsh.*

asehta, pp., tied up; bound up; tied to a tree, as a horse; *asinta*, tied, Mark 11: 2.

asehta, n., a bundle; a sheaf.

aseta, v. t., to accept a wager; to bet against; *itaseta*, to bet against each other.

aseta, n., a rawhide rope or string; a rope; a cord; a strap; a string; a thong; *aseta isht takchi*, to tie with a cord; to cord.

aseta chạnaha, n., a coil of rope.

aseta falaia, n., a long rope; a long rawhide rope; a rope; a tedder.

aseta falaia isht takchi, v. t., to tedder.

aseta isht fạmmi, v. t., to strap.

aseta isht ochi, n., a well rope.

aseta pạna, n., a twisted rawhide; a hide rope made by plaiting two strands, John 2: 15.

aseta tanạffo, n., a plaited hide rope; a braided hide rope made of three or more strands.

asetikbi, n., a cord maker; a rope maker.

asetilechi, v. t., to make tie; *asetilechiⁿka*, n., junction of streams.

asetili, asetilli, v. a. i., *asetoli*, pl., to empty; to disembogue; to flow out at the mouth; to discharge into another stream.

asetili, n., *asetoli*, pl., the mouth of a stream.

asetilli, n., end of or uttermost part of (the Jordan), Josh. 15: 5.

asetoli, v. a. i. pl., to empty.

asilballi, v. a. i., to go to excess in eating or drinking; to gormandize.

asilballi, n., a gormandizer.

asilballichi, v. t. caus., to lead another into excesses.

asilhchap, n., a footlog over a creek.

asilhha, n., an invitation; an invocation; a petition; a request; a suit.

asilhha, v. t., to beg; to beseech, Matt. 14: 36; to entreat; to supplicate; to ask, Matt. 5: 42; 14:7; to implore; to importune; to request; to petition; to crave; to demand; to espouse, invite, invocate, invoke; to supplicate; to wish; to woo; *hashasilhhakma*, if or when ye ask, Matt. 7: 7. *echimasilhha*, we beg of thee; *anumpa ilbasha asilhha*, to present in supplication, as humble words, i. e., to pray; *achunanchit asilhha*, to importune; *imasilhha*, v. t., to beseech him, Matt. 8: 6; to pray, Matt. 6: 6; 9: 38.

asilhha, v. a. i., to beg; to entreat; to solicit.

asilhha, n., a beggar; a petitioner; a suppliant; a demander; an entreater; an implorer; a petitioner; a solicitor; a suitor.

asilhha, pp., entreated.

asilhha, a., suppliant; *ikasilhho*, unasked; unsolicited.

asilhha keyu, a., prayerless.

asilhhachi, v. t., to beg; to ask, Luke 3: 10; to implore; to petition; to entreat; to request; *asilhhanchi*, nasal form; *asilhhahanchi*, freq.

asilhhachi, v. a. i., to beg; to entreat.

asilhhachi, n., a beggar; an entreater; an implorer.

asilhhi, v. t.; John 5: 39; from *silhhi;* the *a* prefix is a locative.

asinta, v. t., to seize; to hold, as a dog holds his prey.

asishchab, n., a footbridge; a log lying across a stream which is used by foot passengers.

asitabi, v. t., to earn; to merit, or deserve by labor; to gain by labor, and not as a gift; to gain; Josh. 24: 13; *ikasitabo*, a., unearned; unmerited.

asitabi, n., the one who earns.

asitia, v. a. i., to cleave to, 1 Kings 11: 2, 4; to love; to feel an attachment; to hang to; to join; *itasitia*, to cleave to each other; to cohere.

asitilli, v. t., to tie to; to tie up, as to tie a horse, cow, or calf to a tree.

asitoha, asitoa, pp. pl., tied up; bound to.

asitoli, v. t. pl., to tie to, or to bind to (from *a* and *sitoli*), Matt. 13: 30.

asitopa, v. a. i., to persevere.

asonak, n., a brass kettle; a vessel made of brass or tin; a kettle.

asonak aholuyachi, n., a colander.

asonak atakali, n., a kettle bail; a crane; a pot hook; a trammel.

asonak atoba, n., a furnace.

asonak hata, n., a tin kettle; a tin pail.

asonak hata maiha, n., tin pan (*maiha*= wide).

asonak isht atta, n., a tinker.

asonak isht talakchi, n., pot hooks; the hooks used in lifting kettles, oven lids, etc.

asonak lakna, n., brass; a brass kettle.

asonak lakna atoba, a., brazen.

asonak lakna chito, n., a large brass pan.

asonak lakna chuhmi, a., brassy.

asonak lakna ikbi, n., a brazier.

asonak lakna isht akmi, pp., brazed; soldered with brass.

asonak lakna isht akmichi, v .t., to braze; to solder with brass.

asonak lakna isht akmichi, n., a brazier.

asonak malha, n., a tin pan.

asonak toba, n., tin.

asonali, asunali, asanali, v. a. i., v. t., to go against wind or tide; to ascend; to fly against the wind; to sail against the current; to face; to front; to stem; to confront; to thwart; to withstand, Ruth 1: 13; *asanni*, pl.

asunanta, n., the going against.

asunonchi, n., the elders; the aged; the fathers, by way of respect.

asunonchika, n., elders, Luke 22: 52.

ash (and its compounds), an article; the one, the said, the one which, referring to some particular object that had been the subject of conversation before; *peni ash,* the ship, Matt. 14: 29. The idea of past time in this article differentiates it from other articles and it may be called a past tense article, Matt. 5: 24. Compounds: *ashakosh, ashakot, ashakocha—ashano,* ob. case, the one which—*ashaṭo,* the one—*ashba, himmak ashba, nitak nana ash,* compounded of *ash,* the future, and *ba* (see below); *onnak mak ashba,* Ch. Sp. Book, p. 77—*ashiⁿ—ashinli,* the same; the one which also—*ashkia,* the one also, even that one—*ashoⁿ,* the one; the, Matt. 9: 6; *Chihowa ashoⁿ,* God, Matt. 9: 8; *yạmmak ashoⁿ,* the which, Matt. 13: 44; *osapa yạmmak ashoⁿ,* that field, Matt. 13: 44, *yạmmak ashoⁿ,* him, Matt. 13: 57—*ashocha,* nom. case, the one—*ashoka,* ob. case, the one—*ashokako,* ob· case, although the one or the said—*ashokakosh,* nom. case, although the said—*ashokạno,* ob. case, the one—*ashokạt,* nom. case, the said one which—*ashokạto,* the said one which—*ashoke—ashokia,* even that one—*ashona,* ob. case, the one—*ashosh,* nom. case, the said one; *Chisạs ashosh,* Matt. 14: 27; 15: 16; *tuk ashosh,* Matt. 14: 33; *okla ashosh,* Matt. 16: 4; *imi shilombish ashosh* (also *ilap shilombish ashosh*), his soul, Matt. 16:26—*ashot,* contracted, nom. case, the said one. This word is sometimes written *hash. kash, kạsh, kosh,* and *chash* are generally used after verbs, but have a similar use and meaning; *ash,* the, the said, Matt. 5: 24; *chuka yạmmak ash aiihiⁿso,* beat upon that said house; Matt. 7: 25, 27; *Lewi ushi ash keyu hoⁿ?* is not . . . the son of David? Matt. 12: 23; *ạno ash siahoke?* it is I, Matt. 14: 27; *chishno ash chiahokmạt,* if it be thou, Matt. 14: 28.

aⁿsha, sing., *asha,* pl., v. a. i., to sit; to reside; to continue; and often as a substitute for the verb to be; to be there, John 1: 48, 50; there is; he is; she is there, etc., Matt. 14: 13; 15: 37; 17: 4; to kennel; to abide, Matt. 12: 45; *ashạt toshowa,* to remove from, Josh. 3: 1, 3; *asht ia,* to remove from, Josh. 3: 14; *imaⁿsha,* to have, Matt. 18: 12; *isht aⁿsha,* v. t., to be busy about, Luke 5: 5; *iksho,* neg. form; *ikaⁿsho* is not used; but *iksho, iksaksho, iksạm-*

iksho are used; *aⁿsha,* nasal form, made by drawing out the nasal sound of the first vowel; having, Mark 11: 13; *aⁿsht,* contracted from *aⁿshạt,* Matt. 3: 5; *aⁿsht minti,* sing., *asht minti,* pl., Mark 11: 12; *aⁿsht akowạ,* Matt. 17: 9; *aiasha,* pl. and pro. form and also a compound of the adv. of place, *ai* before the verb, as *aiasha,* to sit there; *chintail aiasha* (see Matt. 10: 5); Josh. 5: 12; *imaⁿsha,* he has, Matt. 13: 44. This word *aⁿsha,* with the prefix pronouns *ạm, chim,* and *im,* etc., means to have; as *ạmasha,* I have, or there is of mine, John 4: 32; *ikimiksho,* neg. form, to have none; *aheka imashali,* I have a debt (see Matt. 3: 5).

aⁿsha, pp., entered.

aⁿsha, a., extant.

•**aⁿsha,** n., room; sitting.

aⁿsha kuchạt, to come out; John 4: 30.

ashabi, ạshahbi, n., the place to which the mourning poles were taken and thrown away. "Mourning poles" were several poles set at the grave or near the house on account of the death of some friend, beneath which friends sat and mourned the dead.

ashabi, a., mournful; lonesome; barren; stripped.

ashabi, v. n., to be mournful, lonesome, or barren.

ashabichi, v. t., to render mournful, lonesome, or barren.

ashachi, causative form of *asha,* v. t. pl., to put down; to lay them down; to deposit; to store; to leave, as a flock of sheep; Matt. 18: 12; Josh. 2: 6; 7: 23; 8: 2, 12; *aiashachi,* to lay them there, or in a receptacle; *hạchikashachokashke,* "neither cast ye," Matt. 7: 6; to gather into, Matt. 6: 26; to bestow in, 1 Kings 10: 26.

ashaⁿfi, n., the place where one shaves; also a shaving; what is shaved off.

aⁿshaka, prep., behind; in the rear; *imashaka yaⁿ,* "behind him," Matt. 9: 20; *ạmashaka yoⁿ,* behind me, Matt. 16: 23; *ạmaⁿshaⁿka,* behind me, Luke 4: 8; 2 Kings 9: 18, 19; Josh. 8: 2, 4; *chimaⁿshaka,* behind thee; *ashaⁿkaⁿya,* going along in the rear; *mish ashaⁿkaⁿya,* beyond and along behind; *amba apakfopạt aⁿshaka,* 2 Sam. 5: 23.

aⁿshaka, v. n., to be in the rear; to be behind.

aⁿshaka intạnnạp, n., the back side; the rear.

aⁿshakachi, v. t., to place in the rear; aⁿshakachit na mihachi, to backbite; aⁿshakachit na mihachi, n., a backbiter, Rom. 1: 30.

aⁿshakba, v. a. i., to have time, or be at leisure.

ashali, n., a vehicle.

ashaliⁿka, adv., in haste; with haste; hastily; quickly, Luke 2: 16; shortly; straight; immediately, Luke 4: 39; straightway, Matt. 14: 27, 31; Mark 12: 8; ashalika iⁿkashofatok, immediately he was cleansed of it, i. e., the leprosy, Matt. 8: 3; anon, Matt. 13: 20; suddenly, Josh. 10: 9.

ashaliⁿkạchi, v. t., to hasten; to hurry.

ashalinchi, v. t., to quicken.

ashalint, adv., in a short time (a contraction of ashalinchit).

aⁿshali, n., my master; my lord; rabbi, John 3: 2; sir, John 4: 11; chiⁿshali, thy master, 2 Sam. 24: 3.

ashana, pp., turned; twisted; locked.

ashana, v. a. i., to turn; to twist; as it turns.

ashatapa, pp., extended; stretched; spread, as the wings or arms.

ashatapoa, pp. pl., extended; stretched; spread.

ashatapoli, v. a. i. pl., to extend the arms or wings.

ashatạbli, v. a. i. sing., to extend the wings or arms; to spread the wings.

ashatạblichi, v. t., to cause to extend the arms or wings; to extend the arms or wings of another.

ashatạpa, n., a fathom; the wings spread; the arms extended.

ashatạpoa, n. pl., fathoms; wings or arms extended.

ashatạpolichi, v. t. caus. pl., to cause the arms or wings to be extended; to extend the arms or wings of another.

ashạchahe keyu, a., infallible.

ashạchechi, v. t., to cause to err; to lead astray.

ashạchi, v. a. i., to go astray; to mistake; to miss; to err; to sin, Josh. 7: 11, 20; 2 Sam. 24: 10; to deviate; to fail; to miscount; to offend; to do wrong; chim-

ashạchi, to trespass against thee, Matt. 18: 15; ashạchi, pp., missing; ashanchi, nasal form; ashahanchi, freq.; ashaiyachi, pro. form.

ashạchi, v. t., to mistake; to miss; to sin; to slip; to stumble.

ashạchi, a., amiss; sinful; mistaken; erring; inaccurate; ikashacho; ashạchi iksho, a., sinless; without sin.

ashạchi, n., a sinner; a mistaker; a blunderer; a stumbler; or nan ashạchi (q. v.).

ashạchi, n., a sin; a mistake; a blunder; a debt; harm; a lapse; an offense; in scripture, an error; a deviation; a fault; a miss; or aiashạchika (q. v.).

ashạchi keyu, a., guiltless; Matt. 12: 7; innocent (pl. in Greek testament).

ashạchit anoli, v. t., to misrepresent.

ashạchit anukfilli, v. t., to misjudge; to mistake.

ashạchit apesa, v. t., to misjudge.

ashạchit boli, v. t., to mislay.

ashạchit hochifo, v. t., to misname.

ashạchit ishi, v. t., to mistake.

ashạchit isht ạtta, v. t., to mismanage.

ashạchit tosholi, v. t., to misinterpret.

ashạkạchi, pp. pl., locked; turned; twisted.

ashạna, pp., fastened; locked.

ashạna, n., a spinning wheel; a spire.

ashạnatạli fabạssa, n., a spindle.

ashạnni, v. t., to spin on or twist on or at.

ashạnnichi, v. t. sing. and pl., to lock; to turn a key, or to cause it to lock or turn, 2 Sam. 13: 17, 18; to cause to spin or twist on.

ashạnnichi, n., a spinner; a turnkey.

asheha, pp. pl., bound; tied up at the ends and round the sides, as a packet of letters, or as the Choctaw bind dry skins; isht asheha yaⁿ shoeli, Gen. 24: 32.

ashehachi, sing., tied up; bound up; isht ashihachit taiyaha mạt, 2 Sam. 20: 8.

ashekonoa, ashekonowa, pp. pl., tied in single knots, as knots on a single string; itashekonoa, or itashekonowa, tied together, i. e., the two strings are tied together and pairs of them. See noshkobo hạt nosạpi ash isht ashekonowa, his head caught hold of the oak, 2 Sam. 18: 9.

ashekonoa, n., knots; itashekonoa, knots made by tying two strings together.

ashekonoachi; *itashekonoachi*, v. t., to snarl; to knot.

ashekonobli, ashikonobli, v. t. pl., to tie a hard knot with a single string or on a single string; to knot; *itashekonobli*, to tie two strings together; *ashekonombli*, nasal form.

ashekonopa, pp. sing., tied in a single knot; *itashekonopa*, tied together, as the two strings of a shoe; *ashekonumpa, itashekonumpa*, nasal forms.

ashekonopa, n., a knot; a noose; a tie; *itashekonopa*, a knot made by tying two strings together.

ashela, pp., thickened, as food; inspissated, as mush and food of that kind.

ashela, v. a. i., to thicken.

ashela, n., mush, hasty pudding, pudding; a poultice; a cataplasm; a sinapism; spawn.

ashela lapalechi, v. t., to poultice; to put on a poultice.

ashelachi, v. t., to thicken food; to make thick; to inspissate.

asheli, v. t., to fill up or stop up fissures, cracks, holes, etc.

ashelikbi, v. t., to make mush, etc.

ashelokchi, n., water gruel; the watery part of *ashela*.

ashelichi, v. t., to bind up; to tie up by winding round the sides and the ends.

ashepachechi, v. t., to boil down till nearly dry; to dry it.

ashepachi, pp., boiled down till nearly dry; dried away.

ashepachi, v. a. i., to dry away.

ashikonobli, see *ashekonobli*.

ashinla, n., a dry place in distinction from wet places, both existing at one time.

ashinli (from *asheli*), v. t., to fill up chinks, or small holes, cracks, or fissures, with something else; *kishi ashelili*, I fill the chinks of a basket.

ashippa, pp., stewed dry; dried up at; absorbed at.

ashippa, n., a dry place.

ashinya, pp., filled up; having the chinks filled up.

ashke, aux., will or shall; of the will; found at the end of a sentence, as *ialashke*, I will go. This form expresses a strong purpose having something of the optative; compounded of *ash* and *ke;* cf. *ashba* from *ash* and *ba; tekashke*, shall be female, Gen. 6: 19; *ilhpakashke*, it shall be food, Gen. 6: 21.

ashke, imp., sign of the imp., and found also at the end of an expression or sentence. *issanyimmashke*, do thou believe me! John 4: 21; *pinshali ma, ishimpashke*, "master eat" John 4: 31; used for may in 2 Sam. 24: 2; *ithanalashke*, I may know; *pisashke*, he may see, 2 Sam. 2: 43; let, Josh. 7: 3; *ikaiyokashke*, let them not go; assertive of the future known; *shke*, assertive of the present known; *ialishke*, I go, emphatic specification; *ashke*, emphatic and specific future tense; *ialashke*, I shall go.

ashoboli, ashobulli, n., a flue; a chimney; a funnel.

ashobolichukbi, n., a chimney corner.

ashobolinaksika, n., a chimney corner; the side of the chimney.

ashobolipaknaka, n., a chimney top.

asholi, n., a hod; any instrument for carrying on the shoulder.

asholichi, n., a rubstone.

ashua, n., a place that is rotten and smells foul.

ashuahchi, n., a grindstone; an instrument for sharpening edge tools; a whetstone.

ashuachi, see *ashuwachi*.

ashuchoha, v. i., to be tempted. See *shochoha*.

ashueli, n. pl., the places where they were taken off.

ashueli, v. t., to take them off from.

ashunfa, n., the place where it was taken off.

ashunfa, pp., taken off from.

ashunffi, v. t., to take it off from.

ashuma, v. a. i., to mix; to mingle.

ashuma, pp., mixed; *itashuma*, mingled together.

ashuma, n., a mixture; *itashuma*; a mixture.

ashumbala, n., the cottonwood tree.

ashummi, v. t., to mix; to guide; to mingle; *itashummi*, to mix together; to mingle.

ashummi, n., a mixer, a mingler.

ashuwachi, ashuachi, v. t., to cause rottenness or a foul smell; to cause anything (as meat) to smell bad; to taint.

ashwa, ashwa, aⁿshwa (nasal form), v. a. i. pl., to stay there, whether standing, sitting, or lying; dual, Matt. 4: 18; *tuklo hosh ashwat kuchat minti*, coming out of, Matt. 8: 28; *ahaⁿshwa*, freq., Luke 2: 6. The nasal in *aⁿshwa* expresses the idea of a continued act.

ashwanchi, ashwanchi, v. a. i., to be busy; to be engaged in some employment; *itashwanchi*, to be employed together or busy together; *isht ashwanchi*, n., employment or busy with something; *nanta isht ashwanchi?* what are they doing?

at, art., the.

at, rel. pro., as *iksamaiikpacho at*, he is the one who does not thank me; *lipat*.

atabli, v. t., to stop; to check (a diarrhea).

atabli, v. t. sing., to overdo; to overstock; to put on, lay down, bring, or collect more than is needed or can be disposed of; to exaggerate; to exceed; *bok sakti atabli*, to overflow the banks, Josh. 3: 15; 4: 18; *atambli*, nasal form; *atamblit apotuli*, v. t., to superadd.

atablichi, v. t. caus., to cause to overflow or superabound; to cause an overplus; *isht atablichi*, v. t., to aggravate by means of.

atablit abeli, v. t., to overcharge; to overload, as a gun; to surcharge.

atablit apa, v. a. i., to surfeit.

atablit shapulechi, v. t., to overload; to overpack.

atablit tikambichi, v. t., to overdo; to overtire.

ataha, pp., finished; completed; provided; done; tired; worn out; wearied; *ataiyaha*, pro. form, concluded, Matt. 2: 9 [?].

ataha, n., completion; end; the close; the termination.

ataha, v. n., to have an end, or completion; *nitak nana ont ataha himma keyu*, it will never have an end.

ataha hinla, a., that which can have an end.

ataha iksho, a., endless; immeasurable; immense; eternal; immortal; infinite; perennial; unbounded; everlasting, Matt. 18: 8.

ataha iksho, n., immensity; infinity; perpetuity.

atahahe iksho, a., that which will never end; sempiternal.

atahpali, v. t., to dress; to adorn; to dress extravagantly; *ilatahpali*, to dress himself, Luke 16: 19.

atahpalichi, v. t., to dress another with fine clothes.

atai, n., buckeye, name of a poisonous shrub or tree, used in killing fish; see *atai*. [In the Sixtowns dialect this is *ataii*.—H. S. H.]

ataioha, pp. pl., brought to the landing.

ataioha, v. a. i., to come to land; as they land or come to land, meaning the boats.

ataioha, n. pl., landings.

ataiohali, v. t., to bring to land, Luke 5: 11.

ataiya, ataia, ataya, v. a. i. sing., to lean against; to land; to come to land; to recline; to rest; to side; *itataya*, to lean toward each other, spoken of the legs of a horse that bend inward and come near each other.

ataiya, pp., landed.

ataiya, a., recumbent.

ataiya, n., a landing.

ataiyali, v. t., to bring to land; to lean or rest it against.

ataiyachi, v. t. caus., to lean it; to make it rest against.

ataiyuli, n. pl., sources, fountains, of a river or stream of water.

atak, hatak, adv., a colloquial word, not elegant nor used in solemn style; always so; usually; commonly; a., usual. It is perhaps compounded of *tak* with a *ha* or *ya* prefix, as in these examples: *takon at apaka yamohmi hatak, yohmi kia apa ka yohmi tak;* see *tak*.

atakafa, n., a dish.

atakalam iksho, a., undisturbed; unembarrassed; unresisted; *ikataklamo*, a., uninterrupted; unmolested; *isht ikataklamo*, a., untroubled.

atakalama, see *ataklama*.

atakali, n. sing., a peg; a hook; a pin; a nail; a gambrel (as *shukha atakali*); a stem; a hanger; a hinge; a loop; a thole.

atakali, pp., hung by; suspended from; hitched to; *atakanli*, Matt. 18: 6.

atakali, v. a. i., to hang by; to hang to.

atakali hilechi, v. t., to hinge; to hang.

atakalichi, v. t., to hang; to suspend; to fasten to some fixed object, Josh. 2: 15.

atakaffi, v. t. sing., to dip out of.

atakaffi, n., a dipper; one that dips from.

atakchechi, atakchichi, v. t., to tie on; to tie to another thing; to hitch; *itatak-chechi*, to tie together; to alligate; to hook.

atakchi, v. t., to tie at; to tie to; to tie on.

atakchichechi, v. t., to tie to anything else.

atakchichi, v. t., to lash on; to tie on; to tie it to something. This form is plainly explained by the word *ahokchi-chi* (see Matt. 13: 25), to plant with other seed or plants after they have been planted.

atakla; *ataklachi* (see Luke 22: 6), from *takla* (q. v.), I presume, made into a causative verb.

atakla, to be with, see John 4: 27.

ataklamma, v. a. i., to assent; Acts 24: 9.

ataklachi, in the meantime, or in the time of absence, Luke 22: 6.

ataklama, a., officious.

ataklama, atakalama, pp. sing., hindered; prevented; delayed; cumbered; detained; disturbed; interrupted; troubled.

ataklama, atakalama, v. n., to be hindered or perplexed.

ataklama, atakalama, n., a hindrance; a disturbance; an impediment; a let; *isht ataklama*, a hindrance; an interruption; a nuisance; an obstacle; a plague; a pother; trouble.

ataklammi, v. t., to hinder; to interrupt; to oppose; to perplex; to pother; to prevent; to trouble; to cumber; to delay; to discommode; to disturb; to impede; to incommode; to interfere.

ataklammi, n., a hinderer; an opposer.

ataklammi, n., a hindrance; an impediment; an interruption.

ataklammichi, v. t., to cause a hindrance; to hinder; *ilataklammichi*, to hinder or trouble one's self, Luke 10: 41; *issiataklammi chishke*, thou art an offense unto me, Matt. 16: 23.

ataklammichi, n., a hinderer; one that causes a hindrance.

ataklamoa, pp. pl., hindered; prevented; delayed.

ataklamoa, v. n., to be hindered, prevented, or delayed.

ataklamoli, v. t. pl., to hinder; to prevent; to trouble.

ataklamoli, n., hinderers; troublers; plagues.

ataklamolichi, v. t., to cause hindrances.

ataklamolichi, n., hinderers; troublers.

atakli, v. t. pl., to dip out of; to dip in; to dip from; to dip into.

ataklokami, v. t., to hinder.

atakoli, n. pl., pins; pegs; stems; nails; hooks; gambrels.

atakoli, pp. pl., hung up.

atakoli, v. a. i., to hang on; to hang to.

atakolichi, v. t. pl., to hang them upon.

atalaia, pp. sing., placed on; set on.

atalaia, n., a shelf.

atalakchi, n., a knot.

atalakchi, pp., tied at; tied on or to; hitched; *ittatalakchi*, pp., tied together; tied to each other.

atalali, v. t., to place on.

ataloa, n., a hymn; a psalm; a song; a canticle; a carol; an anthem; a lay; a music book; a note in music; an ode; a singing book.

ataloa ikbi, n., a bard; a poet.

ataloha, pp. pl., placed on; set on; standing on.

ataloha, n. pl., shelves; a safe.

atalohmaya, n., shelves.

ataloht maya, v. a. i. pl., to sit round.

atali, v. t., to do; to provide for; to make ready; to complete; to conclude; to appoint for, 1 Kings 11: 18; to execute; to find; to furnish; to finish; to fit; to gird; to perfect; to perform; to prepare; to prosecute; to provide; to purvey; to ripen; to settle; *aiatali*, to lay up there, Matt. 6: 19, 20; *ilatali*, v. t. ref., to provide for one's self; *ilatali*, n., providence for himself; *imatali*, v. t., to purvey; to qualify; to recruit; to satisfy; to support; to provide for him; to enable him; *atanli*, nas. form, Luke 22: 8; *ataanli*, freq.; *ataiyali*, pro. form.

atali, n., a provider; one that does or makes ready; a preparer; a purveyor.

atali, n., provision; purveyance.

atampa, n., leavings; offal; orts; over- plus; refuse; remains; remainder; a remnant; a residue.

atampa, a., odd, as an odd one left or remaining after any specified number; spare; more, Matt. 5: 37; 15: 37; 2 Sam. 13: 15.

atampa, nasal form of *atapa* (q. v.).

atampa, n., a yearling.

atapa, pp., blocked up; *itatapa,* blocked up and separated from each other; *itatampa,* nas. form.

atapa, n., a stoppage; the place at which anything has been separated or cut in two.

atapachi, v. t., to block up; to obstruct; to hinder; to fasten; *isht atapachi,* v. t., to stop with; to button; *isht atapachi,* n., a button; a hasp; *isht atapachi ikbi,* v. t., to make a barb; to barb; *itatapachi,* to clasp together; to fasten together; *itatapachi,* n., a clasp; see *atapachi.*

atapachi, n., a fastener; one that makes fast.

atapoa, n. pl., stoppages; places at which things are separated.

atapoli, v. t. pl. of *atabli; atahpoli,* a va- riant.

ataya, isht ataya, n., descendants; pro- geny; also *isht atia* and *isht aiunchuloli,* Matt. 1: 1.

atanya, v. a. i., to come, Luke 3: 4; John 1: 23; to go, Josh. 10: 10.

atanya, n., a way, Luke 3: 4; John 1: 23; a conduit; *atanya yatuk an,* Josh. 4: 18; applied to a new way, one first used, John 1: 23.

atabli, v. t., sing., to separate at; to sun- der at; to break off at; *ataptuli,* pl.

atala, sing., a shelf; *ataloha,* pl.

atalhpi, n., a frame in which the Choc- taw formerly laid their young infants and there confined them for days in order to flatten their heads.

atalwa, n., a song; a death song sung at funerals, pole pullings, etc.

atalwachi, n., a song; a war song sung by the women when the men were go- ing out to war, and in which they were often exhorted to depend upon the sun and fire for success.

atana, n., a loom.

atapa, n., an overplus; an exaggeration; excess; lateness, as to time set; the rest; a surplus.

atapa, v. n., to be an overplus; to overgo; to superabound; what is remaining; *atampa,* nasal form; *atampat anshaka,* Matt. 14, 20; *ataiyapa,* pro. form; *atai- yampa,* pro. nasal form.

atapa, v. a. i., to act as an austere man, Luke 19: 22; to take more than is proper or right; *atampa,* nasal form, Luke 16: 24; Matt. 14: 20.

atapa, pp., overstocked; overdone; ex- aggerated.

atapa, a., belated; later than the proper time; excessive; exorbitant; immoder- ate; inordinate; intemperate; intense; intolerable; intolerant.

atapa, adv., far; immoderately; too; unduly.

atapa fehna, a., insufferable; late; over- much; redundant; superfluous.

atapa ont ia, adv., late.

ataptua, n. pl., places at which things are sundered; pieces.

ataptua, v. a. i. pl., to separate at; to break at; to come in two at.

ataptuli, v. t. pl., to separate at; to break at; to sunder at.

atashi, n., a club; a bludgeon; a cudgel. The stick called *atashi* by the Choctaw has a part of the root at the heavy end and is from two to three feet long; used by boys as a throwing club.

atebli, v. a. i., to press on.

ateblichi, v. t. caus., to press on; to make it press; to jamb; to press; to screw; to squeeze.

ateblichi, n., a presser; one that presses.

atechi, see *atelichi.*

ateli, n. sing., source; fountain; rise; head of a stream; *ataiyali, ataioli,* pl., sources, heads.

atela, see *atila.*

atelachi, pp., hewed on both sides; *iti atelachi,* hewed on two or four sides.

ateli, v. t., to compact.

atelichi, atelichi, atechi, v. t., to com- pact; to ram down; to ram in; to push in; to ram; to compress; to cram; to crowd; to squeeze; *attia,* pp., squeezed; *atinlichi,* nasal form; *atelichi,* n., com- pression; *atehkaohi,* pass.

atelifa, atilifa, v. a. i., to crowd; to press, Luke 5: 1; to stand in a crowd, as a multitude of people.

atelifa, pp., crowded; pressed; neg. Mark 3: 9.

atelifichi, v. t., to throng; to crowd, Luke 8: 45.

atepa, pp., screwed.

atepa, n., a tent.

atepuli, v. t., to make a camp with a shelter or covering, whether made of bark, wood, cloth, or grass; to tent.

atia, n., a way; an alley; an avenue; a passage; a track; a row; an access; an exit; an orbit; a pathway; a road.

atia, v. a. i., to travel a road for the first time; hashatia keyu chatuk, Josh. 2: 16; hashatia hetuk, Josh. 3: 4; to go up, Josh. 12: 7; see atanya.

atia, v. t., to obey; to follow; to serve, Josh. 5: 6; antia, nasal form and the one most used, with a prefixed pro. am, chim, im, etc.; imantia, to obey him; ishimantia, you obey him; iksamantioshke, he does not obey me; isht atia, v. a. i., to rise from; to descend from, as a race of beings; isht atiaka, n., seed; progeny, 1 Kings 11: 14.

atiballi, a., greedy; gluttonous.

atiballi, v. n., to be greedy; to be gluttonous.

atiha, n., a place that has been plucked, or where anything has been pulled up by the roots.

atikeli, n., a rack.

atikkonofa, v. a. i., to be near to; to approach, Josh. 3: 4; 8: 5; to be narrow, Josh. 17: 15.

atila, atela, n., a place hewed or blazed; a mark on a tree made by hewing off the bark.

atila, pp., cut; hewed.

atilichi, v. t., to hew; iti an atilichi, to hew the wood; to cut the wood.

atilichi, n., a hewer.

atilifa, see atelifa.

atiwa, atua, n., an opening; a gap; an aperture; a breach; a break.

ato, art., the one, as for the; the sign of the distinctive article pronoun in the conjunctive form, as ano is of the disjunctive form. This form is more distinctive than at and at. It is also written hato, yato, ato, hato, and yato (q. v.).

ato, rel. pro., used after verbs, the one which or who, as for the one which.

atoba, v. a. i., to make of or from; to be begotten of; Chisas at atobat attatuk, Matt. 1: 16; chiatoba, Matt. 2: 5, 6; isht atoba, to increase by means of.

atoba, n., the place where anything was made, formed, grew, ripened, or came into being; a germ. The word has a general meaning and is formed from a, place where, and toba, to be made, to become.

atobachi, atobachi, v. t., to raise up at; to make; to cause to become; to cause to supply the place of another; to cause to fill the place of another, Luke 20: 28; itatobachi, v. t., to commute; to fill each other's places.

atobahpi, n., beginning; first formation; ahpi first, toba made, a at.

atobba hinla, a., responsible; rewardable.

atobbi, v. t., to pay, Matt. 5: 26; to recompense; to reward, Matt. 6: 4, 18; to atone; to avenge; to revenge; to retaliate; to liquidate; to render an equivalent; to compensate; to defray; to disburse; to expiate; to fee; to give; to quit; to redress; to remunerate; to repay; to requite; to respond; to retribute; to return; to satisfy; to toll; isht atobba hinla, to give in exchange for, Matt. 16: 26; isht imatobbi, to reward him, Matt. 16, 27; alhtoba, pp., paid; akchialhtoba, v. a. i., let me take your place; ilatobbi, v. ref., to revenge himself; ilatomba, to save for himself.

atobbi, n., a payer; a rewarder; a revenger; an avenger; a defrayer; a paymaster.

atobbi, n., a payment; remuneration.

atobbichi, v. t., to change; to replace; to cause to pay; to exact; to put in place of, Josh. 5: 7; to place instead of; itatobbichi, v. t., to reverse; to invert; to exchange.

atobbichi, n., an exactor.

atobbichi hilechi, v. t., to pawn.

atobbit foka, v. t., to shift a garment; to change, as clothes.

atohchi, n., a shot bag; a shot pouch; a pouch.

atohni, v. t., to watch; see atoni.

atohnichi, v. t., to set on; to halloo, as in setting on the dogs; to cause to bay.

atohno, atonho, v. t., to hire; to employ; to engage; to warn, Matt. 2: 22; to send; to give charge of, Matt. 4: 6; *atoho*ⁿ*nokma,* when he sends forth, Matt. 13: 41; *pit atohno,* to send, *ilhtono,* pp. By some *atohno* is pronounced *atolo,* and they say *atolohinchi,* used for parents to urge them to send their children to school.

atohno, n., a hirer.

atohnuchi, atohnochi, v. t. caus., to authorize another to act; to engage another; to prompt; to put up to; *atohnohonchi,* freq., Matt. 26: 19; *pit atohnochi,* v. t., to refer.

atohnuchi, n., an employer; a prompter.

atohwakali, n., the firmament.

atohwali, n., an opening.

atohwiḳaliⁿka, n., the place of light.

atohwikeli, n., light. See *tohwikeli.*

atohwiḳinli, nasal form, light, John 3: 19, 20.

atok, often written *tok;* sign of the remote past tense, and may be rendered so as to correspond with the preterit tenses in English, was, has, had. The *a* before *tok* may be a word by itself. See *a.* But by entering the word *atok* here some assistance may be obtained on the subject. *Atok* and *atuk* follow *he* sometimes. *Chi*ⁿ *mak atok oke,* that is what it was to be, Matt. 9: 13. Compounds:—*atoka*ⁿ, 1 Kings 11: 4, 6—*atokako*ⁿ—*atokakosh*—*atokano* —*atokato*—*atokinli*—*atokkia*—*atokma*— *atokmako;* *ano pulla hatukmako*ⁿ, "for my sake," Matt. 10: 18—*atokmakocha*— *atokmakona*—*atokmakosh*—*atokmakot*— *atokmano*—*atokmạt*—*atokmạto*—*atokoa*- *ka*—*atokoka*—*atokoke*—*atokokia*—*atok*- *okạno*—*atokokạt*—*atokokạto*—*atokona*— *atokosh*—*atokot*—*atokạt*—*atokạto.*

atokko, see *atukko.*

atokoa, a., definite.

atokoa, atokowa, v. t., to testify; to declare; to take out; to select, Josh. 3: 12.

atokolechi, v. t., to choose; to select, John 6: 70; to bear testimony, Mat. 10: 18.

atokoli, atokuli, atokkoli, v. t., to point out; to state; to particularize; to appoint; to authorize; to empower; to choose, 2 Sam. 24: 12; Luke 6: 13; 1 Kings 11: 13; to commission; to define; to delegate; to depute; to elect; to nominate; to ordain; to send; to vote; to warrant; to take out of, Josh. 3: 12; 4: 2; 8: 3; *mihio atokoli,* to identify; *atokonli* nasal form; *ilatokoli,* to choose for himself, Josh. 20: 2.

atokoli, n., one that points; a testifier; a chooser; an elector; a voter.

atokoli, n., a choice; an ordination.

atokolit halạlli, v. t., to anoint; to do, Luke 4: 18.

atokot pisa, v. t., to eye; *ạlhtuka,* pp.

atokowa, see *atokoa.*

atokowa, pp., pointed out; proved; fastened, as the eyes on an object, Luke 4: 20; *itatokoa,* Gen. 45: 15; delegated; deputed; sent; nominated; ordained; *mihio atokowa,* identified.

atokowa, n., a declaration.

atoksạla hinla, a., tillable.

atoksạli, n., work, John 4: 38; employment; a field; a shop; *ikatoksalo,* a., uncultivated.

atoksạli chuka, n., a workhouse; a working house; a workshop.

atokuli, see *atokoli.*

atokulit aiyua, v. t., to choose; to pick out.

atokulit ishi, v. t., to choose; to pick; to select; *mi*ⁿ*ko atokuli,* to choose a chief.

atoli, n., a ball ground.

atoma, atuma, adv. of doubt, in interrogations; *okcha*ⁿ*ya chatuk atuma,* Deut. 5: 26.

atonho, atohno, v. t., to hire; to engage.

atonho, n., a hirer.

atonhuchi, atohnuchi, v. t., to authorize another; to empower; to engage another.

atoni, atohni, v. t., to watch; to guard; to keep in safety, Josh. 10: 18; 1 Sam. 2: 9; Gen. 2: 15; to attend the bride or groom at weddings, 2 Kings 9: 14; *ohoyo atoni, hatak atoni.*

atoni, n., a watch; a guard; a sentinel.

atoni hikia, n., a sentinel.

atoni hioli, n. pl., sentinels.

atonli, nasal form; from *atulli,* to hop.

atonli, n., a hop.

atonli, n., a hopper.

atonoli, v. a. i., to roll in.

atonolichi, atononchi, v. t., to roll in.

atosh, see *hatosh.*

atoshafa, n., the place where anything has been cut off or sliced off, as meat or bread.

atoshba, adv., not; written also *hatoshba* (q. v.) and *yatoshba.*

atoshke, adv., probably; see *hatoshke.*

attia, pp., compacted; pressed down in; compressed. ,

atua, atiwa, n., a gap; an opening; an entrance through an enclosure, fence, etc.

atuchina, a., third; the ordinal of three; *ont atuchina,* adv., thirdly; *nitak ont atuchinakma,* the third day; Matt. 16: 21.

atuchina, v. n., to be the third.

atuchinaha, adv., three times; thrice.

atuchinanchi, v. t., to repeat three times; to do anything the third time; *atuchinanchit.*

atuk, sign of the immediate past tense, did; was; has; had; has been; had been; sometimes written *hatuk* and *yatuk;* see *atok.* This is a compound word from the particle *a* and *tuk,* "which was and is still"; the *a* is the definite article, *tuk* sign of the past tense, "was the." Compounds: *atuka,* them that, John 2: 16—*atukako — atukakocha — atuka-kona — atukakosh — atukakot — atuk-ano—atukash,* Judges 7: 15—*atukato—atukạt; ikanumpolo atukạt,* the dumb; *atuk* means state of, have been and are; *hanali okpulo atukạt,* the lame, i. e., their state, condition—*atukato—atukin-li—atukkia—atukma,* the, when that is the state of (any thing), when it has become thus, which was and is then; *ma,* then, Matt. 18: 17; as a conj., Judg. 7: 14.—*atukmak, atukmakhe, atukmak-het, atukmakheno, atukmakheto,* especially, in particular that one, those, etc.; this is a comparative particle, and to the disadvantage of the person or thing compared with another—*atuk-makoⁿ, hatukmakoⁿ,* for, Matt. 14: 9—*atukmakosh — atukmakot — atukmano — atukmạt; yạmmak atukmạt,* he, Matt. 18: 17—*atukmạto, atukoⁿ,* then in past

time, which having been (*a* which, *oⁿ* having, *tuk* been and brought), Matt. 1: 2; *atukoⁿ yakohmi,* and then it came to pass, Matt. 7: 28. This is used as a contradistinctive conjunction — *atuko-cha — atukoka — atukokạno — atukokạt—atukokạto — atukoke — atukokia — atuk-ona—atukosh,* then, John 2: 10; then in past time; when he; and he, Matt. 7: 1 [?]; *atuk osh Chisạs ạt,* Matt. 8: 5; *Saimon atukosh?* Simon who is, etc., Matt. 10: 2; *osh* is contradistinctive, the Simon who has been and is called Peter; this distinguishes him from other men named Simon, Matt. 17: 27; 18: 13—*atukot.*

atukko, atokko, v. a. i., v. t., to take refuge; to shelter; to take shelter; to harbor; v. t., to protect; *chuka atukko, iti atukko; atokko achukma keyu,* a., insecure.

atukko, n., a haven; a retreat; protection.

atukkochechi, v. t., to screen; to shelter.

atukkuchi, v. t., to shelter; to protect others; to shield.

atukkuchi, n., a screen.

atukla, a., second; next.

atukla, adv., next; *ont atukla,* adv., secondly.

atukla, v. n., to be the second; to be a second; *nanta hosh atukla wa.*

atuⁿkla, pp. nasal form, repeated.

atuklaha, adv., twice.

atuklanchi, v. t., to repeat; to do again; to react; *atuklahanchi,* freq.; *atukla-hanchit.*

atuklanchi, n., a repetition.

atuklant, adv., second time; again.

atuklant achi, v. a. i., to speak again; to repeat.

atuklant aiskia, pp., revised; corrected again.

atuklant aiskiachi, v. t., to revise.

atuklant akmi, pp., recast; molded anew.

atuklant akmichi, v. t., to recast; to mold anew.

atuklant aⁿlichi, v. t., to reassure.

atuklant anoli, v. t., to tell it again; to repeat.

atuklant anukfilli, v. t., to reconsider.

atuklant apesa, v. t., to revoke; to recall.

atuklant atokoli, v. t., to reappoint; to rechoose; to choose a second time; to reelect.

atuklant alhtuka, pp., rechosen.

atuklant chukoa, v. a. i., to reenter; to enter anew, or a second time.

atuklant fimmi, v. t., to resow.

atuklant haiaka, v. a. i., to reappear.

atuklant haiaka, pp., found again; discovered a second time.

atuklant haklo, v. t., to rehear; to hear a second time.

atuklant hilechi, v. t., to reestablish.

atuklant hobachi, v. a. i., to reecho.

atuklant hokli, v. t., to reseize.

atuklant hoyo, v. t., to recall; to call a second time.

atuklant ikbi, v. t., to rebuild; to remake; to re-edify; to regenerate; to renew; to reorganize.

atuklant ikbi, n., regeneration.

atuklant imatali, v. t., to recruit.

atuklant imalhtaha, pp., recruited.

atuklant ishi, v. t., to reassume; to retake; to regain.

atuklant isht ia, v. t., to recommence; to resume; to begin again; to renew.

atuklant isht ilaiyukpa, v. t., to reenjoy; to enjoy a second time.

atuklant itauaya, pp., remarried.

atuklant itauaya, v. t., to remarry, as the parties marry each other.

atuklant itauayachi, v. t., to remarry, as an officer marries others.

atuklant itannaha, v. a. i., to reassemble.

atuklant itannaha, pp., reassembled.

atuklant itannali, v. t., to reassemble; to re-collect; to rally.

atuklant lopuli, v. a. i., v. t., to repass.

atuklant miha, v. t., to rehearse; to repeat.

atuklant oia, v. a. i., to reascend.

atuklant okchaya, v. n., to relive; to live again.

atuklant oti, v. t., to rekindle.

atuklant pila, v. t., to recast; to resend.

atuklant pisa, v. t., to reexamine; to revise.

atuklant poloma, pp., redoubled; doubled a second time.

atuklant polomi, v. t., to redouble; to double a second time.

atuklant toba, pp., a regenerate; regenerated; made again; renewed.

atuklant ulhti, pp., rekindled.

atuklant yammichi, v. t., to react.

atuklant yammiht pisa, n., to reattempt.

atuklonchi, and; see Matt. 2: 13.

atuklakafa, v. a. i., to jest; to joke.

atuklakafa, a., jocose.

atuklakafa, n., a joke; idle talk.

atuko, adv., not; also spoken *hatuko*, *yatuko*.

atukonofa, atikkonofa, v. a. i., to approach near on both sides, Luke 22: 47. Possibly this is a compound word.

atukonofa, pp., pressed on both sides.

atukosh, adv., not, not to.

atulli, v. a. i., to hop.

atuma, see *atoma*.

atush, hatush, yatush. *Sinti yatush*, Satan, Scrip. Biog., p. 31.

atushali, pl., to hew, Josh. 8: 31; applied to stones; see *tushali*.

atu^{n}shpa, pp., hastened; hurried.

atu^{n}shpa, v. a. i., to hurry; to hasten.

atu^{n}shpalechi, v. t., to press; *atushpalihinchilitok*, "I compelled them," Acts 26: 11.

atushpachi, v. t., to hasten; to hurry.

atuya, n., a ladder; stairs; a flight of stairs; steps; 1 Kings, 10: 19; a style; a rundle; Samson's post; a scale; a stair; a stepping stone.

au, a diphthong, having the sound of *ow* in now.

aua, auah, a word used in counting the numbers between ten and nineteen, having the sense of and, or with, as ten and one, 11; ten and two, 12; *pokoli auahchafa*, ten and one, eleven, but the word *pokoli* is usually omitted.

auah achafa, a., eleven, 11, xi.

auah achafa, v. n., to be eleven, as *auah achafa yoke*, there are eleven.

auah achafa, v. a. i., to be eleven, or to make 11; as *hashauah achafa*, you make eleven; you are eleven.

auah hannali, a., sixteen, 16, xvi.

auah hannali, v. n., to be sixteen.

auah hannali, v. a. i., to make sixteen, as *ilauah hannali*.

auah huntuchina, a., eighteen, 18, xviii.

auah huntuchina, v. n., to be eighteen.

auah huntuchina, v. a. i., to make eighteen.

auah huntuklo, a., seventeen, 17, xvii.

auah huntuklo, v. n., to be seventeen.

auah huntuklo, v. a. i., to make seventeen; as *ilauah huntuklo.*

auah hushta, auahushta, n., fourteen, 14, xiv, Matt. 1: 17.

auah hushta, v. n., to be fourteen.

auah hushta, auahushta, v. a. i., to make fourteen; as *ilauahhushta,* Josh. 5: 10.

auah tałapi, a., fifteen, 15, xv.

auah tałapi, v. n., to be fifteen.

auah tałapi, v. a. i., to make fifteen; as *ilawahtałapi.*

auah tuchina, a., thirteen, 13, xiii.

auah tuchina, v. n., to be thirteen.

auah tuchina, v. a. i., to be thirteen, or to make thirteen; *ilauah tuchina.*

auah tuklo, a., twelve, 12, xii, a dozen, Matt. 14: 20; Josh. 4: 2.

auah tuklo, n., a dozen.

auah tuklo, v. n., to be twelve.

auah tuklo, v. a. i., to be twelve; to make twelve.

auah tuklo bat auah tuklo, n., a gross, 144; lit. twelve times twelve.

auahsholichi, v. t., to make one dream.

auahushta, see *auah hushta.*

auanapa, pp. sing., passed over; put over; gone over or by.

auanapoa, pp. pl., passed over; put over; gone over or by.

auanapoli, auanopoli, v. a. i. pl., to pass over; to go over; *auanạbli,* sing.; see *tanapoli.*

auanapolichi, v. t. pl., to put over; to throw over; to cause to go over; *auanạblichi,* sing.

auanạbli, v. a. i., to pass over; see *tanạbli, ạbanạbli.*

auanạblichi, v. t., to put over.

auant, see *awant.*

auaⁿsa, v. a. i., to chew a cud; or *hopaⁿsa, howaⁿsa* (q. v.).

auasholechi, v. t. caus. (an old word), to make one dream.

auata, v. a. i., to appear; to come out; to expand; to spread; to extend; *ilauata,* to spread out one's self; to be proud.

auata, a., wide; broad.

auata, pp., expanded; extended.

auata, n., breadth; width; extent, Ex. 26: 2.

auatali, v. a. i., to stand crooked, as in a half moon or circle.

auatali, n., a bent line, like the appearance of the new moon.

auataya, comp. verb, to be spread and stretched out over something wide as well as long, hence applied to the firmament; [earlier and less correct meanings obtained] to go along with, to accompany; *Shutik ạt ạba moma ka auataⁿyakma,* Sp. Book, page 18, 5th edition. See *auata.*

auatạchi, v. t., to expand; to spread; to extend.

auatạlli, v. t., to extend in a line.

auaya, v. t. (a compound word from *auah* and *aⁿya*), to have in marriage; to wed; to marry, fem. gen. This word is used when it is said that a woman marries, but *itauaya* when a man marries, or when it is the act of both; *ikitauayo,* neg., not married; single.

auaya, pp., a., married, fem. gen., Mark 10: 12.

auaya, n., a woman that marries; the marriage state; *ikauayo,* n., celibacy; *ikauayo,* a., unmarried.

auaya, v. t., v. a. i., to marry (fem. gen.); *itauaya nitak,* n., a wedding day; *itauaya,* pp., married; matched; mated; espoused; *ikitauayo,* a., unmarried; single; *itauayạchi,* v. t., to marry; to mate; to settle; *itauaya,* n., matrimony; nuptials; a match; a settlement; wedlock; *itauaya ahalaia,* a., nuptial; *itauaya ipetạchi,* n., a wedding feast; *itauaya,* v. a. i., v. t., to cohabit; to marry, Matt. 5: 32; to couple; to have each other, or to have her; to settle; to wed, Matt. 14: 4; to join; *itauaya,* a., pp., married, mas. gen. and com. gen.; wedded; *itauaya ona,* a., pp., marriageable.

auaya ạlhpesa, a., marriageable.

auaya ona, a., marriageable.

auayạchi, v. t. caus., to marry a woman to a man; to join; *itauayạchi,* v. t., to marry; to cause to marry, the act of an officer or minister, etc.; to join in wedlock.

auạshli, v. t., to fry; to cook in a frying pan, as meat is cooked; to parch; to burn, as coffee is burnt for grinding and use; to poach; to toast; *alwasha*, pass., *aialwasha*, a place for frying, 2 Sam. 13: 9.

auechi, v. t. caus., (see *echi*); to send it this way; to send it toward the speaker by the hand of another; to cause it to come this way—not to the speaker but toward him; to transmit toward (the speaker); *isht auechi*, v. t., to send this way; to bring this way; *isht auehinchi*, freq.; *auehinchi*, freq., John 5: 23.

aueli; *ilaueli*, to take along with him, Matt. 4: 8.

auet, a "directive particle" before verbs indicating the direction of an action toward the speaker; *auet a^{n}hopakishke*, is far from me; *auet i^{n}hopaki*, a good way off, Matt. 8: 30.

auet, awet (cont. of *auechit*), adv., this way; toward—but always toward the speaker, never from; *pit* means the opposite of *auet*, Matt. 3: 17; 10: 40; 17: 5; Rev. 14: 13; Josh. 4: 16, 17, 18, 19. *et* (q. v.) and *auet* have different meanings. *et* means toward the speaker; *auet*, quite to him, as *haksobish et weli cha imanumpa auet haklo; auet* is the prolonged form; *t* is a connective as with other words.

aume, exclam., well! indeed! O!

auola, v. a. i., to refrain; to stop; to hold up; to cease, as the rain ceases, holds up, stops, etc.

auola, n., a cessation; a holding up.

auolachi, v. t. caus., to cause the rain to cease.

au^{n}s, ou^{n}s, n., an ounce; *ou^{n}s awahtuklokmat weki achafa*, troy weight; *ou^{n}s awah hanalikmat weki achafa*, avoirdupois weight.

awa, wa, adv., can not; shall not; will not; John 2: 4 [?].

awalakachechi, awalakachechi, v. t., to plait; to pucker; to ruffle.

awalakachechi, n., a plaiter.

awalakachi, awalakachi, n., a frill; a fringe; a plait; a pucker; a ruffle; gathers.

awalakachi, awalakachi, pp., a., ruffled; plaited; puckered.

awalalli, n., a boiler.

awalalli iskitini, n., a saucepan; a small boiler.

awant, auant, awat (from *au+aya*), prep., with; along with; to go with; to accompany, Josh. 1: 5, 9; 3: 7; 7: 12; Luke 1: 56; Matt. 5: 41.

awashoha, n., a scene; a place for play; a playground.

awat, see *awant*.

awaya, n., product; crop.

awaya achukma, a., rich; fertile.

awaya achukma, n., richness; fertility.

awaya fehna, a., productive; fruitful.

awet, see *auet*.

awiachi, v. a. i., to hover over to get food; to swarm; *sheki at isubilli awiachi*, to hover in swarms over the dead horse; *foebilishke at awiachi; foebilishke at tansh hinak awiachi*, the bees come round the corn tassels in quest of something to eat.

awiachi, n., a swarm.

awiha, n., a deserted place; a place from which persons have removed.

awokokonlichi, n., a place rooted up by swine.

awokokonlichi, v. t. pl., to root, as swine.

a^{n}ya, aiya, v. a. i., to go; to travel; to go along ; to move along; to pace; to pass; to shoot, as an arrow; to stir; to strike; to sweep; to tend; to waft; to depart; Luke 2: 29; Matt. 5: 17; 10: 34; 11: 18; Josh 1: 5; 3: 7; to come, John 1: 31; to pass in any manner (Josh. 3: 4) or to any end, as to fly, to sail, etc.; *imaya* (from *im* and *a^{n}ya* united) also *imayachi, imaiya*, and *imaiyachi* (the spelling varies), Matt. 10: 24; *isht a^{n}ya*, v. t., to take along; to carry; to conduct; to drive; to lead, Luke 4: 1; to govern; to sail; to treat; to fare; to fly; to run; *shat a^{n}ya*, to convey; *achukmat isha^{n}yashke*, farewell.

a^{n}ya, pp., passing; *chisht a^{n}ya*, Matt. 4: 6.

a^{n}ya, n., a mover, sojourner, traveler, or one that moves along; a passenger; a stirrer; *kanima yo^n chik a^{n}ya kia*, whithersoever thou goest, Matt. 8: 19; *ima^{n}ya*, v. t., to visit him, her, 1 Sam. 2: 21.

a^{n}ya, n., a going; a motion; a passage; a pace; a sailing.

a^{n}ya, n., a flock; a herd; *chukfalhpoa a^{n}ya kaniohmi, micha wak a^{n}ya kaniohmi,* 1 Sam. 30: 20.

a^{n}ya achafa, n., a flock; a company, 2 Kings 9: 17; a herd.

aⁿya hinla, a., passable.

ayaiya, n., lamentation, Matt. 2: 18; place of weeping.

ayaka, a., many; *ikaiako*, not many; not much.

ayakohmi, aiyakohmi, n., a deed; something done, or things done, John 1: 28; 2: 12.

ayakohmi, aiyakohmi, v. n., to take place or transpire at.

ayakohmichi, v. t., to do something.

ayamaska, n., a kneading trough.

ayamasli, v. t., to knead in; to mix in; to make mortar there or in.

ayanalli, n., a channel for water to flow in; a tube; a pipe.

ayataia, aiyataia, n., a landing place; a resting place; a landing.

ayamihchi, v. t., to do, John 2: 11; 3: 2.

ayehchi, see *aiehchi*.

ayimmi, v. t., to believe in, John 1: 7.

ayoah, see *aiyoa*.

ayofanichih, v. t., to make motions—in trying to commit sodomy.

ayuka, pro., each.

ayukali, aiyukali, pro., each one; *aiyukali*, adv., apiece.

ayukpa, a., pleased; *isht ayukpa*, v. n., to be pleased with.

ayukpa, n., joy, Acts 8: 8.

ayupi, aiyupi, n., a bath; a place in which to bathe or wallow, whether in sand or mud, by man, beast, or fowl; a pool.

a, a locative particle preceding words; *akanalli, atakchichi, akallo, akallih, ahpota; a* is often used with such words; *a* means place; *a*, at, to, in.

aba, a., high; heavenly; divine; celestial.

aba, v. n., to be up; to be heavenly; *amba*, etc.

aba, adv., up; on high; aloft; heavenly, John 3: 14.

aba, n., the upper regions; heaven, Luke 3: 21; John 3: 27; Matt. 5: 3; 23: 22; *aba akoⁿ*, the air; *aba hushi puta kat*, the birds of the air, Matt. 8: 20; *aba apelichika*, kingdom of heaven, Matt. 13: 44.

aba aholitopa, n., heaven above, Josh. 2: 11.

aba aiachukmaka, n., heaven; the happy place above.

aba aianumpuli, n., a preaching place; a pulpit.

aba anumpa, abanumpa, n., the gospel, Matt. 11: 5; the Scriptures; the word from heaven; Christianity; religion; faith, i. e., the object of faith; light; revelation; theology.

aba anumpa ahalaia keyu, a., unchristian.

aba anumpa ahni, v. t., to desire the gospel; to be anxious on the subject of religion.

aba anumpa ahni, n., a serious person.

aba anumpa aiisht atta, n., a meeting house; a preaching place.

aba anumpa anumpa, n., a sermon.

aba anumpa apiha at illi, n., martyrdom.

aba anumpa iⁿflammi, n., apostasy.

aba anumpa ikhana, n., Christians; Christianity.

aba anumpa ikithano, n., heathens; heathenism.

aba anumpa ikyimmo, n., infidelity.

aba anumpa ikyimmo, n., a deist; an infidel.

aba anumpa issa, v. a. i., to apostatize; to fall away.

aba anumpa issa, n., an apostate.

aba anumpa issat falama, v. a. i., to backslide.

aba anumpa issat falama, n., a backslider.

aba anumpa isht aianumpuli, n., a tabernacle.

aba anumpa isht anumpuli, aba anumpa isht holissochi, v. t., to sermonize; to preach; n., a preacher; a sermonizer.

aba anumpa isht atta, n., to preach the gospel; to serve in the gospel.

aba anumpa isht atta, n., a preacher; a clergyman; a clerk; a divine; an evangelist; a priest.

aba anumpa isht atta aliha, n., the clergy; the ministers of religion.

aba anumpa isht atta imalhtayak, aba anumpa isht atta aliha, n., priesthood.

aba anumpa isht ika, n., a homily.

aba anumpa ithana, n., a theologian.

aba anumpa ithananchi, v. t., to gospel; to make the gospel known; to evangelize.

ạba anumpa nukfoka, a., serious; devout; religious.

ạba anumpa nukfoka, v. n., to be serious, devout, etc.

ạba anumpa nukfoka aiaⁿli, a., pious; truly pious.

ạba anumpa nukfokichi, v. t., to evangelize.

ạba anumpa taloa, n., church music; sacred music.

ạba anumpa tosholi, n., an evangelist.

ạba anumpa yimmi, v. t., to believe the gospel.

ạba anumpa yimmi, n., a professor of or a believer in the gospel.

ạba anumpa yimmi, a., orthodox; religious; ạba anumpa ikyimmo, n., an infidel; scepticism.

ạba anumpa yimmi aiali, a., pious.

ạba anumpa yimmi keyu, a., irreligious; not orthodox; heterodox.

ạba anumpeshi, ạbanumpeshi, ạbanumpeshi ạmmona, n., an apostle.

ạba anumpuli, v. t., to preach; to pray; to talk up; to talk about religion.

ạba anumpuli, ạbanumpuli, n., a preacher; a praying person; a Christian; a professor of religion; a missionary; a chaplain; a minister.

ạba anumpuli aiaⁿli, a., godly.

ạba anumpuli aⁿli, n., a true Christian.

ạba anumpuli apistikeli, n., a pastor; a bishop.

ạba anumpuli ạliha, n., the church; all Christians; the church in general.

ạba anumpuli ibafoka, v. a. i., to join a church; to profess religion.

ạba anumpuli ibafoka, pp., united to the church.

ạba anumpuli ibafoki, v. t., to give up to the church; to join to the church.

ạba anumpuli ikbi, v. t., to christianize; to make Christians; to convert.

ạba anumpuli iksa, n., a church; the church; a Christian sect or denomination.

ạba anumpuli iksa ibafoka, n., a church member.

ạba anumpuli iksa kucha, v. a. i., to leave a church.

ạba anumpuli iksa kucha, pp., excommunicated.

ạba anumpuli iksa kuchi, v. t., to excommunicate; to unchurch.

ạba anumpulí iksa nana isht imạshwa ạliha, n., Presbytery.

ạba anumpuli iksa nana isht imạtta, n., a Presbyter.

ạba anumpuli ilahobbi, n., a professed Christian; a pretended Christian; a hypocrite.

ạba anumpuli kobafa, n., an apostate; a broken Christian.

ạba anumpuli kucha, n., an excommunicated person.

ạba anumpuli pelicheka ạlhtoka, n., a parson.

ạba anumpuli toba, n., a convert.

ạba anumpuli toba, v. a. i., to become a Christian.

ạba anumpuli toba, n., conversion.

ạba apelichika, n., the kingdom of heaven, Matt. 8: 11; 11: 11, 12; 16: 19.

ạba aⁿya, v. a. i., to waft.

ạba chakali, v. a. i. (from ạba and achakali), to lift up the head; to lift up the eyes, John 4: 35; Matt.17: 8; Luke 19: 5; Josh. 5: 13; ạba pit ạba chakalimạt, when he had looked up to heaven, Matt. 14: 19.

ạba hatak, n., an angel; an inhabitant of heaven; a seraph.

ạba holitopa, n., a holy one.

ạba ia, ạbia, v. a. i., to ascend; to go up; to rise; to go to heaven.

Ạba iⁿki, n., God.

Ạba iⁿki imantia, a., godly; one who obeys God.

Ạba iⁿki imasilhha shạli, a., prayerful.

ạba imma, ạbema, adv., upward; high.

ạba isht aholitobli, v. t., to worship, John 4: 20, 24.

ạba isht aianumpa chuka, n., a synagogue, Matt. 10: 17.

ạba isht aiokpạchi, n., sacrifice, Matt. 9: 13; 12: 7; a gift, Matt. 15: 5; tribute for the service of the temple, Matt. 17: 24.

ạba isht anumpa, n., a sermon; a religious discourse; a lecture; a discourse.

ạba isht anumpuli, v. t., to preach; to pray for, Matt. 5: 44.

ạba isht anumpuli, n., a preacher.

ạba isht aⁿya, v. t., to waft.

ạba isht holitobli, n., a worshiper.

ạba isht ia, v. t., to hoist; to lift; to mount; to raise; to carry up; to rear; to weigh.

ạba isht ikahobalo, v. t., to blaspheme.

ạba isht ikahobalo, n., a blasphemer.

ạba isht ona, v. t., to take on high; to carry to heaven.

ạba iti patạlhpo, n., a chamber.

ạba miⁿko, n., the king of heaven; the heavenly king.

ạba minti, v. a. i., to descend from heaven.

ạba patạlhpo, n., an upper floor; a chamber floor.

Aba piⁿki, n., God; our Father in heaven; Providence; Divine Providence.

ạba pila, v. t., to heave; to throw up; to toss.

ạba pila, n., a toss; a heaver.

ạba pila, adv., upward.

ạba pilla, adv., upward; on high; away up; far up; heavenward; to heaven; in heaven.

ạba pit anumpuli, v. t., to pray; to speak toward heaven, Matt. 17: 21.

ạba shilombish, n., an angel; a spirit of heaven.

ạba shutik, n., heaven, Matt. 5: 34; 1 Sam. 2: 10.

ạba takali, v. a. i., to hang up; to depend.

ạba takali, pp., hung up; suspended; lifted up; a., dependent.

ạba takalichi, v. t., to heave; to hang up; to lift up, John 3: 14; to uplift.

ạba taloa, n., a hymn; a psalm; a sacred song.

ạba tạla, n., a mantel piece; a shelf; a scaffold; a scaffolding; see tạla, from talali, to set or place.

ạba tạla boli, v. t., to scaffold; to put on a scaffold.

ạba tạla ikbi, v. t., to scaffold; to make a scaffold.

ạba topa, n., an altar.

ạba yakni, n., heaven, Matt. 6: 20; 18: 10.

ạba yakni aholitopa, ạba yakni nan isht ilaiyukpa, n., glory; the felicity of heaven prepared for the children of God.

ạba yakni pila, adv., heavenward.

ạbai anumpuli chuka, n., a temple, Luke 2: 27; a church; a meeting house.

ạbana, v. a. i., to lie across; to rise; ạbanaya, ạbanaiya, pro. form.

ạbana, pp., laid across.

ạbana, n., that which lies across.

ạbanali, ạbanoli, v. t. sing., to lay across; to lay over or on; to put on, as a yoke; bahta yaⁿ ạbanoli, to lay a bag on.

ạbanapoa, pp. pl., passed over; put over.

ạbanapolechi, v. t., to put over; to cause to go over, or pass over.

ạbanapoli, v. a. i., to pass over.

ạbanạbli, auanạbli, tanạbli, v. t. sing., to pass over; to leap over; to go over; to run over; to get over; to overreach; to superabound; to go past the time; to jump; to leap; to overflow; to overgo; to overrun; to pass; to surmount; to transcend; to transgress.

ạbanạblichi, v. t., to cause to go over; to put over; to defer; to adjourn; to prorogue; to delay; to overreach; to postpone; to procrastinate; to reprieve; to respite.

ạbanạblit ont ia, n., the Passover, Josh. 5:10, 11.

ạbanạpa, pp. sing., passed over; put over; delayed; postponed; reprieved; respited; from ạbanạbli, v. a. i.

ạbanạpa, n., a respite.

ạbanạpa, v. a. i., to delay; to procrastinate; siạbanạpa, I procrastinate; nitak hollo achạfa siạbanạpa keyukma, if I do not delay a week.

ạbanoli, see ạbanali.

ạbanopoli, pl., to go over; to walk over, Luke 11: 44; ạbanobli, sing.

ạbanumpa, see ạba anumpa.

ạbanumpeshi, see ạba anumpeshi.

ạbanumpeshi ạmmona, see ạba anumpeshi.

ạbaona, pp., raised.

ạbbaksha, see abaksha.

ạbema, see ạba imma.

ạbenili, see abenili.

ạbi, abi, v. t., to kill, Matt. 10: 28; to slay; to destroy, Matt. 2: 13; to butcher; to deprive of life; to dispatch; to slaughter; to martyr; to win at a game of chance; to murder; ahhabi, to kill quickly (ahbi, aiabi, ahambi, ambi); imạbi to win from him or to beat him; he wins from him; to put to death, Matt. 14: 5; aiạbi, to smite of, Josh. 7: 5; ạbeli, ishbi, ạbi, ebi, ilohạbi, hạshbi, ạbi; akbo, chikbo, ikbo, kebo, kilohabo, hạchikbo, iksabo, ikpebo, etc.; itimabi, to kill each other; ilebi, to kill himself; to commit suicide, John 8: 22; ilebi, n., self-murder; suicide; ahambi, freq., Josh. 10: 10.

ạbi, n., a killer; a slayer; a murderer.

ạbi, n., slaughter; the killing; destruction.

ạbi, v. n., to be sick with certain diseases, generally cutaneous, or to have the disease, etc.; as *chiliswa ạbi*, to have the measles; *chilakwa ạbi*, to have the smallpox; *chinak ạbi*, to have the pleurisy; *wạshkạbi*, to have the itch; *wakcha ạbi*, to have the venereal disease; *palsi ạbi*, Luke 5: 24.

ạbia, ạba ia, v. a. i., to mount; to ascend.

ạbichi, v. t., "to smite," 1 Sam. 5: 12.

ạbit ạpa, v. t., to prey upon; to kill and eat.

ạbit ạpa shạli, a., rapacious.

ạbit tạli, v. t., to destroy; to kill all; to cut off.

ạbitampa, n., a male fairy; a hobgoblin; one who kills.

ạboa, v. t., to strike against; to fall against; to knock; to bunt; *wak ạt yilepa mạt itaboa; hatak ạt itulat ia cha chuka yaⁿ ạboa; chukfi itibik mạt itaboa hoka.*

ạbonumpuli, see *ạba anumpuli.*

ạchafoa, a., a few and scattering; not many.

ạchafoa, v. n., to be few and scattering; *ạchafoⁿha,* nasal form.

ạchafoachi, v. t., to cause a few; to select or take a few; to cause a few to be taken, etc.

ạchafolechi, v. t. caus., to select a few; to single out.

ạchafoli, v. t., to take a few.

ạffekoma; *osapa ạffekoma,* n., a large field.

ạffekomi, a., mischievous; impatient; exceeding; superabounding; large; see *afekommi.*

ạffekomi, v. n., to be mischievous; *chito kạt ạffekomi fehna* and *chito kạt atampa fehna* mean the same.

ạffetạbli, v. t. sing., to ensnare; to enchant to his ruin or death.

ạffetipa, afetipa (q. v.), a., enchanted; greatly interested; captivated.

ạffetipoa, a. pl., ensnared; enchanted to his ruin or death.

ạffetipoa, v. n., to be ensnared.

ạffetipoli, v. t. pl., to ensnare; to enchant.

ạffoa, afoa, v. a. i., to wind round.

ạffoa, ạfoha, pp., wound round, John 20: 7; furled; see *afoa.*

ạffula, pp., stirred; thickened while cooking; *aiạlit maⁿya kakoⁿ,* from that (time) forth; see *afulli.*

ạhokuⁿfa, n., piece cut off.

ạholloka, see *aholloka.*

ạhoyo, see *ohoyo.*

ạla, v. a. i., to arrive at, when coming toward the speaker or place spoken of; as *ona,* to arrive at in going from the speaker; to touch; to come; to come to; to get there; to get here; to get to; to attain, Matt. 8: 2, 11, 25; 11: 14; 17: 7, 10; *ahanlat,* Josh. 7: 14; *aiạla,* pl. and intensive; *hạchimaiạla,* come to you, Matt. 7: 15; *alali, ishla, ạla, ela, ilohạla, hạshla, ạla; aiyala, aiyạla,* and *aiyahanla; itạlachi,* for two to arrive together; *isht ạla,* v. t., to fetch; to reduce; to bring, Matt. 12: 22; to take it and come; *ont isht ạla,* to go and bring; to go and take it and come.

ạla, n., an arrival; a pass.

ạla, n., one who arrives or comes; a comer; *himo ạla,* one who has just come; a new comer.

ạlachi; *itạlachi,* to arrive together (dual).

ạlba, n., vegetation; herbs; plants; weeds.

ạlbạchi, v. a. i., to practice; to make experiments; to be instructed, Matt. 13: 52.

ạlbạla, pp., gleaned.

ạlbạlli, v. t., to glean; to gather up the remnants or fragments.

ạlbạlli, n., a gleaner; a gleaning.

ạlbạna, v. a. i., to lie across; see *ạbanali.*

ạlbạna, pp. pl., laid across; *abạnni,* v. t. pl.

ạlbạni, v. a. i., to cure over a fire; *abani,* v. t.

ạlbạni, pp., cured; *isi nipi ạt ạlbạni;* takkon ạt ạlbạni; abani, v. t.

ạlbạni, n., that which is cured.

ạlbạnkạchi, pl.; *hina ạt ạlbạnkạchi.*

ạlbạsa, n., lath.

ạlbạska, n., lath.

ạlbạska, pp., lathed; ribbed, as a roof; *abạsli,* v. t.

ạlbehkạchi, v. a. i. pl., to repeat; *itạlbehkạchi,* Phil. 2: 27.

ạlbehpo, n., a sack of some kind, Matt. 2: 11.

ạlbi, aiạlbi, aiilli, aiạlli, n., cost; price; a price, 2 Sam. 24: 24; *tanchi ạlbi.*

ạlbi, pp., valued; perhaps from ạbi.

ạlbichi, v. t., to price; to set a price; to value, John 12: 5.

ạlbiha, pp., charged; stuffed.

ạlbiha, n., a charge; a load.

ạlbiha atạpa, n., an overcharge; an overload.

ạlbihkạchi, pp. pl., put in; put on, as garments.

ạlbilli, v. t. pl., to repeat; to add; to put on another thickness; it ạlbilli, Matt. 6: 7; itishima ạlbillit umpohomo; na foka ạlbillit foka; shukbo ạlbillit patali.

ạlbina, n., a camp, Josh. 6: 11; an encampment; a host, Josh. 3: 2.

ạlbinachi, ạlbinanchi, v. t., to camp; to encamp; to pitch a camp.

ạlbita, pp., repeated; done twice; tanchi ạt ạlbitạt holokchi; ạlbitạt holisso, copied; anumpa hạt hituklaha ạlbitạt anumpuli.

ạlbita, n., a repetition, Rev. 18: 6; v. a. i., to be double.

ạlbitạt holisso, pp., copied; rewritten.

ạlbitạt holisso, n., a copy.

ạlbitạt holokchi, pp., replanted.

ạlbiteli, v. t., to repeat; to double; to iterate.

ạlbiteli, n., an iteration.

ạlbitelichi, v. t., to double; to make double, Rev. 18: 6.

ạlbitet anoli, v. t., to repeat the story; to relate a second time; to recapitulate.

ạlbitet hokchi, v. t., to replant.

ạlbitet holissochi, v. t., to copy; to write over again; to transcribe.

ạlbitet ikbi, v. t., to renew.

ạlbitet pisa, v. t., to review.

ạlbitet shạnni, v. t., to double and twist.

ạlbitet yạmmichi, v. t., to redouble.

ạlbitkạchi, pp. pl., repeated; having other covers or coats; itạlbitkạchi, John 1: 16; ạlbilli v. t.

ạlbo, v. a. i., to adhere; to stick, as glue or mud; lukfi ạt ashoboli yạⁿ ạlbo; itiạlbo v. a. i., to cohere; itiạlbot ọffo, v. a. i., to coalesce.

ạlbo, pp., soldered; made to stick or adhere; glued; itiạlbo, glued together.

ạlbochi, v. t. sing., to solder; to cause to adhere; to set with putty; to glue; to stick; isht ishko aⁿ ạlbochi, to solder a cup; itạlbochi, to solder together; to glue.

ạlbokạchi, v. t. pl., to solder; to fasten in with putty; itạlbokạchi, to solder together.

ạlbonli, ạlmoli, v. i., to catch; to take infection; itạlbonli; itạlmoli.

ạlhchakaya, n., an addition; a piece spliced on.

ạlhchakaya, a., additional; something added; anumpa ạlhchakaya.

ạlhchạba, n., a log lying across a creek used as a foot bridge.

ạlhchạka, pp. sing., spliced; new set; new laid or welded, as an iron tool; welded.

ạlhchạkoa, pp. pl., spliced; welded.

ạlhchefa, pp., washed (from achefa, to wash).

ạlhchiba, a., tedious; tiresome; requiring or consuming time; slow in accomplishment; ạlhchieba, Gen. 40: 4.

ạlhchiba, v. n., to be tedious, tiresome, or slow.

ạlhchifa, pp., washed, John 13: 10.

ạlhchilofa, pp., paid; liquidated; ikạlhchilofo, a., unpaid.

ạlhchowa, see ạlhchuⁿwa.

ạlhchunna, a., cheap; low.

ạlhchunna, v. n., to be cheap.

ạlhchunnạchi, v. t., to cheapen; to lower; to sink.

ạlhchuⁿwa, ạlhchowa, pp., sewn; stitched; sewed; itạlhchuⁿwạ, sewn together; sewed.

ạlhchuⁿwa, n., that which is sewn.

ạlhfạbek imma, adv., on the left hand; toward the left.

ạlhfạbeka, n., the left, Luke 23: 33; Matt. 6: 3.

ạlhfạsha, pp., fastened; latched; okhissat ạlhfạsha; afashli, v. t.

ạlhfoa, n., a ligature; a bandage.

ạlhfoa, pp., wound round; bound round; reeled; hooped; afoli, v. t.

ạlhfula, pp., stirred, as a liquid with a stick; afulli, v. t.

ạlhfullinchi, v. a. i., ạlhfullihinchi, to compass, Matt. 23: 15.

ạlhkaha, pp., laid down.

ạlhkạma, pp., sing. stopped up; fastened up; calked; barred; aboha ạlhkạma; okhissa yạt ạlhkạma, Josh. 2: 5; shut up, Josh. 6: 1; see akama.

ạlhkạma, a., fast.

ạlhkạniạ, a., gone; forgotten; pass. of kạnia of the form ạlhtaha.

ạlhkạniạ, v. n., to forget; chimạlhkạnia, you have forgotten it.

ạlhkạta, pp., patched; botched; mended; clouted; akkạlli, v. t.

ạlhkạta, n., a patch; a botch; a clout; isht ạlhkạta, a patch.

ạlhkoha, pp., molded, as pottery; shaped; plated, as metals with silver; shuti ạt ạlhkoha; ampo ạt ạlhkoha; lukfi nuna yạt ạlhkoha; tạli holisso lakna isht ạlhkoha, plated with gold; akkọli, v. t.

ạlhkomo, v. a. i., to dissolve; to melt, as salt, sugar, etc.

ạlhkomo, pp., dissolved, as sugar in water; ikạlhkomo, a., undissolved; unmelted; okomo, v. t.

ạlhkomoa, pp. pl., stopped up; calked; barred; aboha ạlhkomoa; haksobish ạlhkomoa.

ạlhkucha, n., the balance; the remainder; an odd one, Num. 3: 48; shulush ạlhkucha, an odd shoe; waktoksạli ạlhkucha, an odd steer.

ạlhkuna, n., a gown; a dress for a lady; cf. the alconand of French writers.

ạlhkuna falaia, n., a long gown; a frock; a slip.

ạlhkuna kolofa, n., a petticoat.

ạlhpạtak, n., a fan made of a wing.

ạlhpesa, n., convenience; decency; sufficiency; an execution; fairness; fitness; reason.

ạlhpesa, ạlhpisa, a., proper; suitable; enough; sufficient, Matt. 6: 34; lawful, Matt. 12: 2; 14: 4; right, Matt. 11: 26; Luke 6: 2; straight, Luke 3: 5; John, 4: 17; necessary; worthy, Matt. 10: 11, 13; John 1: 27; comely; commodious; compatible; competent; consistent; convenient; correct; decent; decorous; due; eligible; fair; fit; honest; just; justifiable; lawful, Matt. 12: 12; legal; meet, Matt. 15: 26; moderate; passable; reasonable; scrupulous; seemly; staple; timely; profitable, Matt. 5: 29; ạlhpiⁿsa, tolerable, Matt. 11: 22, 24; ikạlhpeso, wicked, Matt. 12: 45; disagreeable; ill; erroneous; unadvisable; imạlhpisa, John 1: 14 [?]; itạlhpesa, responding; agreeing together.

ạlhpesa, v. n., to be proper, etc., Matt. 5: 5; it is enough, 2 Sam. 24: 16.

ạlhpesa, ạlhpisa, pp., measured; determined; agreed; appointed; accomplished; concluded; corrected; decided; decreed; effected; enacted; established; suited; surveyed; estimated; executed; filled; fulfilled; gaged; gauged; judged; justified; ordered; passed, as a law; reconciled; regulated; resolved; settled; stipulated; nitak ạlhpisa, an appointed day; ikạlhpeso, evil, Matt. 12: 35; idle, Matt. 12: 36; imạlhpisa, pp., judged; imạlhpesa, a., contented; agreeable to him; ont ạlhpesa, pp., passed; ikimạlhpeso, a., dissatisfied; unallowed; uncommanded; ikimạlhpesochi, ikimạlhpesacho, to dissatisfy; ikạlhpeso, a., illegal; illicit; improper; inadmissible; incorrect; unapproved; unapt; unbecoming; undignified; undue; unfit; ungenteel; unmeasured; unreasonable; unseasonable; unseemly; unsuitable; unsuited; wrong; wrongful; ạlhpisahe keyu, a., immeasurable; ikạlhpeso, n., an impropriety; a wrong; ikạlhpeso, adv., unduly; ạlhpiesa keyu, n., injustice; itimạlhpesahe keyu, a., irreconcilable; ạlhpiesa, adv., justly; imạlhpesa, to please; to feel pleased; ikimạlhpeso, v. a. i., to repine; ikimạlhpeso, n., a repiner.

ạlhpesa, v. a. i., to become, Matt. 3: 15; to behoove, Luke 4: 43; to eventuate; itạlhpisa, to respond; to suit; to be likened to, Matt. 7: 26.

ạlhpesa, adv., well; very well; comely; fairly; rightly; well done.

ạlhpesa, v. a. i., to do or be right; ishạlhpesa, Acts 10: 33.

ạlhpesa achi, v. a. i., to approve; to approbate (rather, to express approbation), as red men do when they approve of a talk.

ạlhpesa ahni, ạlhpiesa ahni, v. a. i., to acquiesce; to comply; to consent; to be willing; to feel contented; ạlhpesa ishahnihokmạt, if thou wilt, Matt. 8: 2; ạlhpesa ahnilishke, I will, Matt. 8: 3.

ạlhpesa miha, v. a. i., to assent.

ạlhpesali, v. a. i; see ikạlhpesalo, fraud, James 5: 4; to be true or virtuous, Mark 10: 11; ohoyo ạlhpesali, a virtuous woman.

ạlhpesashke, even so, Matt. 11: 26.

ạlhpesạchi, v. t., to correct; to humor; to justify; imạlhpiesạchi, to right; ikitim-

alhpesacho, Matt. 10: 35; *ikimalhpesochi*, to grieve.

alhpesachi, n., a justifier.

alhpi, n., a wooden spoon; a horn spoon; *nakalhpi*, a pewter spoon.

alhpichik, n., a nest; a bird's nest; applied to birds, squirrels, hogs, and bears, *alhpichik at imasha hoke*, have nests, Matt. 8: 20.

alhpichik ikbi, v. t., to nest; to make a nest.

alhpiesa, v. a. i., to fay; to suit exactly; *aialhpesa*, suitable, Matt. 6: 11; worthy; *sialhpesa keyu hoke*, I am not worthy, Matt. 8: 8.

alhpiesa, a., deliberate; exact; nice; pat; precise; respectable; strict; *alhpiesashke*, John 1: 12 [?] *italhpisashke*, shall be likened; Matt. 7: 26; *ikimalhpieso*, offended, Matt. 15: 12; Luke 3: 14.

alhpiⁿkachi, n., a pile of corn piled like cord wood.

alhpisa, pass. of *apesa*, to be judged, Matt. 7: 2; measured, Josh. 3: 4.

alhpisa, n., a decision; an estimate; a fulfillment; an institution; a judgment; a justification; a measure; an ordinance; a plot; a scheme; a standard; a stint; a stipulation; a measure, Matt. 13: 33.

alhpishechichi, v. t., to prepare a pillow for another, 1 Sam. 19: 13.

alhpishi, n., a pillow.

alhpishi, v. a. i., to pillow; *alhpishi hosh itonla tok*, 1 Sam. 19: 16. ·

alhpishi afoka, n., a pillow case; a pillow-bier.

alhpishi falaia, n., a bolster; a long pillow.

alhpishi iⁿshukcha, n., a pillow case; a pillow-bier.

alhpitta, pp., loaded; charged; put in, Matt. 6: 30; *alhpinta* (nas. form).

alhpitta, n., a load; a charge; *isht alhpitta*, n., wadding; some say *naki impatalhpo*.

alhpoa, alhpoba, alhpowa, n., domestic animals; fruit trees, such as are cultivated; produce; cattle; stock; live stock; a pet.

alhpoa, pp., espoused, Matt. 1: 18; bespoken for; domesticated; raised; saved, as a tree or plant; tamed; *itimalhpoba*, espoused to each other.

alhpoa aiimpa, n., a pasture.

alhpoa apistikeli, n., a pastor; a herdsman.

alhpoa foni, n., a rack; the frame of bones of an animal.

alhpoa ilhpita, pp., foddered.

alhpoa imilhpak, n., fodder; forage.

alhpoa imilhpak itannali, v. t., to forage.

alhpoa ipeta, v. t., to fodder.

alhpoachi, alhpolachi, v. t., to heap up dirt or ashes around anything.

alhpoba, see *alhpoa*.

alhpoba, a., exotic; tame.

alhpoba hinla, a., tamable. .

alhpohomo, v. a. i., to be laid on or covered:

alhpolachi, see *alhpoachi*.

alhpolosa, pp., daubed; plastered; pitched; smeared *apolusli* v. t.

alhpowa, see *alhpoa*.

alhpoyak, n., goods; wares; merchandise; a commodity; manufactures; stuff; *alhpoyak oklushinla aiisht ala*, v. t., to import goods, Matt. 17: 25.

alhpoyak aiasha, n., a store; a store room; a store house.

alhpoyak holisso, n., an inventory.

alhpoyak ikbi, n., a manufacturer.

alhpoyak shali, n., a peddler; one who carries goods.

alhpoyak toba, pp., manufactured.

alhpuⁿfa, pp., blown into; blowed; breathed in; inspired; puffed.

alhpuⁿfa chuhmi, a., puffy.

alhpusha, pp., roasted; broiled; toasted; *ahe alhpusha; nipi alhpusha*.

alhpusha, n., a roast.

alhtaha, v. a. i., to ripen; *hachimalhtaha*, prepare you, Josh. 1: 11.

alhtaha, a., pp., ready; prepared; done; finished; completed; complete; consummated; expert; fitted; forward; furnished; matured; ripened; *aiimalhtaha*, Matt. 13: 54, 56; thorough, Josh. 1: 14; 8: 4; *ikalhtaho*, a., imperfect; undone; unexecuted; incomplete; unfinished; *imalhtaha*, pp., qualified; *ikimalhtaho*, a., unprepared; unready; unsupplied.

alhtaha, v. n., to be ready; to end; to finish; to get through or to be so; *chimalhtaha*, you are ready; *anumpuli chimalhtaha*, have you done talking?

ạlhtaha, n., accomplishment; readiness; a consummation; fullness; maturity; preparation; ripeness.

ạlhtaha hinla, a., handy.

ạlhtakla, a., bereaved; without friends, kindred, parents, etc.; forlorn; *ohoyo ạlhtakla*, a widow; a bereaved woman; *ạlla ạlhtakla*, an orphan child.

ạlhtakla, v. n., to be bereaved.

ạlhtakla, n., bereavement; orphanage; an orphan.

ạlhtaklạchi, v. t., to bereave.

ạlhtaloa, n., a song; a hymn.

ạlhtaloak, n., a song; see Rev. 15: 3, *Moses imạlhtaloak.*

ạlhtampa, n., overplus; surplus; balance; remainder.

ạlhtanafo, n., the rim of a cane basket.

ạlhtayak, n., character; profession; calling; nature; *imạlhtayak*, his calling.

ạlhtạlwa, pp., sung; *ikạlhtạlwo*, a., unsung.

ạlhtạlwak, ilhtạlwak, n., a song; a ditty; a hymn; note, 2 Chron. 29: 27.

ạlhtạnnafo, pp., woven; plaited; braided.

ạlhtekạchi, v. t., to press down, Luke 6: 38.

ạlhtipo, n., a tent; a pavilion; a booth; a lodge; a tilt; a tabernacle, 1 Sam. 2: 22; Josh. 7: 21, 22; 2 Cor. 5: 1.

ạlhtipo, a., tented; *ạlhtipo asha*, tented.

ạlhto, v. a. i. pl., to be in; to stand in, Matt. 2: 12; from *ạni*, v. t., *ibạlhto*, Matt. 13: 49; Josh. 10: 1; *peni ạlhto*, Matt. 14: 13; *ilaiạlhto*, we are in here; *anlhto*, nasal form, being in, John 21: 8; Matt. 4: 21. Cf. also Matt. 14: 32.

ạlhto, v. t., to hold; to contain.

ạlhto, pp., poured in; put in; from *ạni*, v. t., to pour in; *ibạlhto*, mixed, Matt. 13: 49; *itibạlhto*, mixed together.

ạlhto, n., lading.

ạlhtoba, v. a. i., to be in the place of another; to be in the stead of; to succeed; to be sold, Matt. 10: 29; *akchiạlhtoba*, let me take your place; *imạlhtomba*, have their reward Matt. 6: 2, 5, 16.

ạlhtoba, adv., instead.

ạlhtoba, a., vicarious; expiatory.

ạlhtoba, n., pay; wages; hire; price, Matt. 13: 46; reward, Matt. 5: 12; recompense; postage; a charge; ferriage;

pilotage; carriage; freight, etc.; compensation; damages; a disbursement; expense; a fee; fees; a fine; a lien; meed; merit; payment; a premium; a prize; remuneration; a render; a reward; room or stead; salary; salvage; satisfaction; a stipend; toll; value; see *isht ạlhtoba.*

ạlhtoba, n., atonement.

ạlhtoba, n., a deputy; a proxy; a substitute; a succeeder; a successor.

ạlhtoba, pp., refunded; remunerated; rewarded; paid; recompensed; avenged; revenged; atoned; compensated; defrayed; exchanged; expiated; liquidated; *itạlhtoba*, exchanged; *ikạlhtobo*, a., unpaid; unrepaid; unrewarded.

ạlhtoba chito, n., highness; dearness; high price.

ạlhtoba hinla, a., expiable; expiatory; *imạlhtoba hinla*, a., rewardable.

ạlhtoba hosh ishi, v. t., to supplant.

ạlhtobạt ạtta, n., a vicegerent.

ạlhtoboa, v. a. i. pl., to take the place of; to take turns with; *itạlhtoboa sholit isht anya*, to take turns in carrying it; *itạlhtoboa*, to exchange with each other; to reciprocate; *itạlhtoboa*, n., rotation; *itạlhtoboạchi*, v. t., to transpose.

ạlhtohno, ilhtohno, pp., hired; engaged; employed; *hatak ilhtohno*, a hired man.

ạlhtohno, ilhtohno, n., a hireling.

ạlhtoka, ạlhtuka, pp., pointed out; set apart; sent, John 3: 28; authorized; appointed; delegated; deputed; elected; selected; nominated; ordained; voted; to be taken, Josh. 7: 16, 17, 18; *hatak ạlhtoka*, a committee; *atokuli*, v. t.

ạlhtoka, n., authority; appointment; a delegate; elect; the Messiah; the anointed; Jesus Christ; an ordination.

ạlhtokoa, ạlhtokowa, pp., pointed out; set, Luke 2: 34; commissioned.

ạlhtoshoa, ạlhtoshowa, pp., removed from one place to another; translated; construed; rendered into; interpreted, Matt. 1: 23; explained.

ạlhtosholi, v. t., to transfer; to remove; to translate; to interpret; to construe; to render into.

ạlhtosholi, n., a translator.

ạlhtuka, see *ạlhtoka.*

alhtuka keyu, a., unengaged.

alla, n., a child; children, Matt. 14: 21; a brat (a low word); a papoose; *hachim-alla*, your children, Matt. 7: 11; *alla yosh*, children, Matt. 11: 16.

alla, v. a. i., to be a child; *sialla*, I am a child; *chialla*, thou art a child; *sialla ma*, when I was a child; nasal form *a^{n}la*.

alla aiimpa, alla aiishko, n., a porringer; a basin for a child.

alla anusi, n., a child's bed; a cradle; a crib.

alla anusi foki, v. t., to cradle.

alla apistikeli, v. t., to watch or nurse children; to nurse.

alla apistikeli, n., a nurse.

alla ayupi, n., a bathing place for children.

alla alhtakla, n., an orphan; a bereaved child without father or mother.

alla chipunta, n., young children; small children.

alla chuhmi, a., child like; puerile.

alla eshachi^n i^{n}palammi, v. a. i., to labor; to travail.

alla eshi, alleshi, v. t., to bear children; to bring forth a child; to have a child; "to be confined."

alla eshi, n., childbearing.

alla haksi, n., "a sauce box;" a tomboy; an urchin.

alla himmita, n., a stripling.

alla holisso pisa, n., a pupil; pupilage; a schoolboy.

alla i^{n}foka, v. a. i., to conceive; to become pregnant.

alla i^{n}ki iksho, a., base born; illegitimate.

alla i^{n}ki iksho, n., a bastard; an illegitimate.

alla ikimiksho, a., childless; barren, Luke 23: 29.

alla ilahobbi, allilahobbi, a., acting like a child; pretending to be a child; puerile; childish.

alla isht aiopi, n., the youngest child; the last child.

alla isht illi, v. a. i., to die in childbed.

alla nakni, n., a boy; a male child; a chap; a lad; a shaver; a son; a male infant; see Matt. 1: 21, 22; Luke 1: 13, where *alla nakni* is the translation of son.

alla oka isht imokissa, n., pedo-baptism; infant baptism (the old form of expression).

alla pishechi, v. t., to suckle a child.

alla sholi, v. t., to bring forth a child; to dandle.

alla sholi, n., a nurse.

alla tek, n., a girl; a female child; a lass.

alla tek haksi, n., a romp; a rude girl.

alla tek holisso pisa, n., a school maid.

alla toba, n., adoption.

alla tomba, n., childhood.

alla tomba, v. n., to be in the state of a child; *alla satombama illitok*.

alla yakni pataffi, n., a plow boy.

allahe! interjection of displeasure, used by the ancients in scolding children.

allachi, causative form; *ilallachi*, to make himself a child.

alleh, ali, hale, exclam. of distress, uttered by children when in pain; oh! oh, dear!

alleshi, see *alla eshi*.

allikchi, alikchi (q. v.), n., a doctor; a physician; a curer.

allilahobbi, see *alla ilahobbi*.

alloluat, see *alolua*.

allo^{n}sabi, n., infanticide.

allota, see *alota*.

allu^{n}si, allo^{n}si, alosi, n., an infant; a babe; a baby; a papoose; a suckling, Matt. 2: 8, 11; Luke 18: 15; *alosi puta ha^n*, Matt. 11: 25.

almachi, n., a fan.

almo, pp. pl., trimmed; cut; picked; pulled; mown; reaped; clipped; cropped; sheared; shorn.

almo, n., that which is picked, etc.

almochi, n., cream; scum.

almoli, see *albonli*.

alosi, see *allu^{n}si*.

alwasha, v. a. i., to fry; to parch, as coffee.

alwasha, pp., fried; parched; poached; toasted, Josh. 5: 11; *nipi at alwasha; kafi at alwasha*.

aleha, see *aliha*.

ali, v. a. i., to end; *ont aiali* and *il-aiali; ikali*, to verge; *ontali*, to eventuate; to terminate.

ali, n., the edge, end, limit, boundary, line, borne or bourne; the extent; the margin; the mete; the verge; a wing; a border, Josh. 4: 19; *yammat imali*;

yammokosh imạli; yammak osh ạli, etc.; *isht imạtekashkeh*, take him to the edge or verge of, Matt. 5: 21, 22.

ạlichi, v. t., to end; *ont aiạlichi*, Josh. 5: 3.

ạliha, ạleha, n. pl., all; the whole; the whole company; each one and all of, Luke 6: 17; Matt. 5: 1; 12: 2, 46; 13: 49; 17: 6, 10; it differs from "all" in that it directs the mind to each one; *tạshka ạlihama*, the body of warriors. This word is added to nouns to indicate plurality of persons and sometimes of things. See Matt. 2: 1, 4, 5, 6, 7, 16, 17, 18, 23; (of wolves), *nashoba isikopa ạleha*, see Matt. 7: 15; *ạleha hạt* is distributive; *ạleha yạt* is collective.

ạlipila, adv., toward the end.

ạlipilla, at the end; away to the end; outmost.

ạm, my, pre. pos. pro. 1st per. sing. in the nom. case before a noun beginning with a vowel, as *ạmisuba*, my horse, Matt. 2: 6; John 2: 2.

ạm, pre. per. pro. 1st per. sing. in the dative case before verbs beginning with a vowel or diphthong, and to be rendered often with a prep. in Eng. as of me, to me, for me; *ạmia, ạmanumpuli, ạmanoli, ạmaiạⁿli, ạmachi*, "saith unto me," Matt. 7: 21.

ạm, I, per. pro. 1st per. sing. before a neuter verb formed from an adj., as *ạmokpulo*, I am mad; "to me evil;" see *chim*, John 1: 33.

ạm, used before verbs when removed from the noun, as *isubat ạmilli, ạllat ạmilli*, instead of *ạmạllat illi*.

ạma, to give me; from *ima*, to give or to give him; *chiksamo*, neg. form; *ikemo*, he did not give him; *issiaiạmashke*, give thou me, Matt. 14: 8.

ạmafo, n., my grandfather and his brothers, including their father, grandfathers, etc., male cousins and their paternal ancestors; my father-in-law, i. e., the father of a woman's husband, the proper appellation for a woman to use in speaking to her husband's father; *chimafo, imafo, pimafo*, etc.

ạmalak, n., my sister's husband; my brother-in-law.

ạmalak usi, n., my wife's brother; my brother-in-law.

ạmalak usi ohoyo, n., my wife's sister; my sister-in-law.

ạmạnni, n., my brother, and one older than the brother who speaks; my brother who is older than myself.

ạmạnni, n., my sister, and one older than the sister who speaks; my sister who is older than myself (always both persons are of the same gender).

ạmiffi, a., equal in size and age.

ạmiffi, v. n., to be equal in size and age.

ạmintạfi v. t., to open; to cut open, as the carcass of a hog; *ạmintafa*, pp; see *mitạffi*, from which these are derived. *ạmintoli*, pl.

ạmishoa, v. a. i. sing., to rub against.

ạmishofa, pp., rubbed; rubbed ạgainst.

ạmishoffi, v. t., to cause to rub against and pass by; to cause to graze; *iti chanạlli ạt iti aⁿ ạmishoⁿfa*, the wagon was rubbed against the tree.

ạmishokạchi, pp. pl., rubbed off; *shapo ạt ạmishokạchit hishi taha*.

ạmisholichi, v. t. pl., to rub against; *suba hạt shukcha yaⁿ iti aⁿ ạmisholichit okpạni fehna*.

ạmmi, a., my; mine.

ạmmi, v. n., to be mine, Matt. 10: 37.

ạmmi keyu achi, v. t., to disclaim; to disown.

ạmmi toba, v. a. i., to become mine, Luke 4: 6.

ạmmona, a., incipient.

ạmmona, n., the beginning; the dawn; the commencement; *ạmmona ataha aiena kạt iksho*, a., eternal; n., eternity.

ạmmona, adv., first, Matt. 12: 45; Josh. 8: 5; *ạmmona kano*, Matt. 8: 21.

ạmmona isht ia, v. a. i., to rise.

ạmo, v. t. pl., (*tabli*, sing), to pick; to pull; to trim; to mow; to reap, Matt. 6: 26; to cut; to clip; to gather, Luke 6: 44; to cut off; to crop; to rid; to shear; to slip; *paⁿki aⁿ aiạmo*, gather grapes of, Matt. 7: 16; *shumạti akoⁿ aiạmo*, gather of thistles.

ạmo, n., a gatherer; a picker; a shearer.

ạmohmi, v. i., to do anything entirely, utterly, and absolutely, Matt. 5: 34; *ikshok ạmohmi; ikshoka ạmohmi* (for *ikshokạmohmi*, as often heard) there is none at all; *ạmohmichi, ạmohminchi*, caus., 1 Sam. 15: 3; Josh. 10: 1; 11: 11, 12, 20, 21.

ạmohoyo, n., my woman; my wife.
ạmombạlaha, n., my brother-in-law,
i. e., my husband's brother, his uncles
and nephews (language of a woman).
ạmoshi, ạmoshshi, n., my uncle, i. e.,
my mother's brother or brothers and
male cousins.
anaⁿkosh, pro., I the one who.
ạni, v. a. i., to bear fruit; to yield fruit;
. to bring forth fruit, Matt. 7: 17; ạna-
he keyukma, when it can not bear fruit,
Matt. 7: 18; ạni chatuk; ạnikmạt, Matt.
13: 23; ahani, Ps. 1: 3.
ạni, n., fruit of the berry kind; a berry;
a nut; fruit in general, Matt. 7: 16.
ạni, v. t., to pour into a vessel; to infuse;
ilani, in yourselves, Mark 9:50; pass.
ạlhto.
ạni chilofa, n., a windfall.
ạnit waⁿya, v. t., to bring forth fruit,
Luke 3: 9; Matt. 13: 8.
ạnnoa, annoa, anoa, (q. v.), n., fame.
ạnnoa, anoa (q. v.), pp., noised.
ạnnoachi, see anoachi.
ạnnonto, pro., as for me.
ạno, I, me, mine, Matt. 5: 11; ạno ạto,
Matt. 5: 22, 32, 34, 39, 44; 17: 27;
ạno aⁿ, me, Matt. 11: 6; ạno ạkinli,
myself; compounds: ạnoⁿkosh; .ạnnon-
to; ạnonto; see ano.
ạpa, v. t., to mouth.
ạpa, v. a. i., v. t., to eat; generally used
when speaking of a single article of
food; when a meal or several articles
is spoken of, the word impa is used;
to fare; to feed; to pick, Matt. 15: 32;
onush ạpa, onush ạlwasha ạpa, Josh. 5:
11, 12; ạpạt isht ia, began to eat, Matt.
12: 1; Josh. 5: 11; ikpo, Matt. 15: 32;
ampa, ahampa, ahampahi oke, shall be
gnashing, Matt. 8: 12; noti ahampa,
Matt. 13:42,50; ạpa is an irreg. verb, like
ạbi and ạla; conj.: ạpali, ishpa, ạpa, epa
(Matt. 6: 31); ilohạpa, hạshpa, ạpa, akpo,
chikpo, ikpo, kepo, kilohapo, hạchikpo,
ikpo; sạpa, eat me, John 6: 57;
okapaⁿki pạska isht ạlhpisa ạpa, to
commune; ạpạt tali, v. t., to devour;
ạpạt pisa, v. t., to taste; ạpạt ikpeso, a.,
untasted.
ạpa, n., food.
ạpa, n., an eater.
ạpa kitinisi, n., a morsel.
ạpanukfila, n., a whirlwind.

ạpanukfila, v. a. i., to blow, as a whirlwind.
ạpạt tali, v. t., to devour; to consume.
ạpi, n., the stalk; a vine; a handle; a tree;
a cob; a helve; a haft; a trunk; a body;
a leg; a blade, Matt. 13: 26; a straw;
a spire; the warp or chain of cloth as
woven; a staff; a stock; ahạpi, a potato
vine; aiomanili ạpi, a chair leg; bihi
ạpi, a mulberry tree; chahạpi, a hoe
handle; hạshuk ạpi, a spear or blade of
grass; iskifạpi, an ax helve; nusạpi,
an oak tree; the trunk of an oak; the
body of an oak; onushạpi, a blade of
wheat; wheat straw; a stalk of wheat;
tanchạpi, a cornstalk; a corncob.
ạpi aiishi, n., a thole.
ạpi isht ạla, n., the lower end.
ạpiha, see apeha.
ạpishia, n., a piazza; aboha ạpishia, a
piazza that extends all round an old-
fashioned house.
ạpohtuki, v. a. i., to be close and light,
as a room.
ạppokni, apokni, n., my grandmother;
my granddam.
ạsananta, see asananta.
ạskufa, v. t., to put a petticoat upon
one's self (feminine gender).
ạskufa, pp., girded; belted; begirt (feminine gender).
ạskufa, n., a petticoat (doubtful).
ạskufa tạpa, n., a coat; a petticoat.
ạskufạchechi, v. t., to put a petticoat or
belt upon another person; to begird
another person; to gird; ilaiạskofạche-
chi, to gird himself, John 21: 18.
Perhaps there is a mistake and it
should be ilaiạskofạchi, as in John
21: 7.
ạskufạchi, pp., girded.
ạskufạchi, v. t., to gird one's self; to
put a belt on; to begird; ila isht ạsko-
fạchi, to gird himself, John 13: 4; to
gird the loins, 2 Kings 9: 1.
ạsseta, v. a. i., to cleave to; to love.
ạshke, see ishke.
ạshwa, ashwa (q. v.), v. a. i. pl. and
dual, to sit; to be there; chuka ilạshwa.
ạshwanchi, ạswanchi, ashwanchi, v.
a. i., to be engaged about something;
to be active or busy; ittạshwanchi, to
keep at work (at it), singular.—J. E.

ạt, art. (see *hạt* and *yạt*), the; the one;
Chekob ạt, Jacob he, Matt. 1: 2; *iti okpulo ạt*, a corrupt tree, Matt. 7: 18; *iti
ạt*, a tree, Matt. 7: 19; *ạt*, rel. pro., who;
the one who; the which.

ạta, adv. particle, as *ishlạta*, have you
come (when not expected)?

ạtai, atai, n., buckeye (accent on last
syllable; unusual in this respect and
unusual in ending with a diphthong).

ạtaiya, v. a. i., to lean on or touch at;
ạtayạli, tr. sing., to cause to lean
against or to touch at, as a boat or ship;
· *ạtayoli*, pl.

ạtakapulechi, see *itakopulechi*.

ạtanapoa, v. t., to jump over; *iti aⁿ
itanapoa*, to jump over a log.

ạtanapolechi, v. t., to cause to jump
over.

ạtanapoli, v. t., to jump over.

ạtanạbli, v. t., to lay on the second
strata of leaves, etc.

ạtanạbli, n., underbrush; undergrowth;
the second layer of leaves in woods.

ạtanạpa; *wak ạtanạpa*, a yearling.

ạtapa, pp., scotched.

ạtapạchi, ạtapạchi, v. t., to hasp; to
fasten.

ạtaya, v. a. i., to lean; *pit atayạt*, John
21: 20; 2 Kings 9: 30; see *ataiya*.

ạto, ato, art., the one; as for the (by
way of contrast to others); *ạno ạto*, I,
in distinction from them of old time,
Matt. 5: 22, 32, 34, 39, 44; *aiishi ạto*, he
that received, Matt. 13: 23; *hatak ạto*,
men, Matt. 16: 13.

ạto, ato, rel. pro., the one who, as for
the one who, etc.

ạtta, v. a. i., to be born; to come into
the world; to stay; to live; to reside;
ạmạtta, aiạttatok, Matt. 14: 6; *anta*,
nasal form, to abide; to dwell; to
inhabit; *isht ạtta*, v. t., to use; to employ; to be busy with or about.

ạtta, v. a. i., to heal; to cicatrize; *ikạto*,
not healed; *lachowa ikạto*, a chronic
ulcer.

ạtta, v. t., to occupy; *isht ạtta*, to occupy;
isht imạtta, ministered unto him, Matt.
8: 15.

ạtta, n., a birth; *nitak aiạtta*, a birthday.

ạtta, n., an occupant; a resident.

ạtta, pp., born; healed; cured; cicatrized; remedied; *ạtạtta* or *itatonli* (old

style), healed up or united and healed;
ikạtto, a., unborn.

ạtta ạmmona, n., infancy; an infant;
primogeniture.

ạtta ạmmona, a., primogenial.

ạtta hinla, a., healable; curable.

ạttahe keyu, a., incurable.

ạttahpi, n., birth, Matt. 1: 18; primogeniture; the first born, Josh. 17: 1.

ạttapạchi, v. t., to hasp; to fasten.

ạttạchi, n., a healer; a curer.

ạttạchi, v. t., to heal a sore or wound;
to cicatrize.

ạttạt akowa, v. a. i., to come down,
Matt. 8: 1.

ạttạt aⁿya, Matt. 15: 22.

ạttạt falama, v. a. i., to return from,
Luke 4: 1.

ạttạt hofanti, pp., educated; raised;
brought up.

ạttạt hofantichi, v. t., to raise; to educate; to bring up.

ạttạt ia, v. a. i., to start from; to depart
from, Matt. 12: 9; 15: 22; to go from,
Luke 3: 4 [?]; to go on from, Matt. 4:
21; to pass forth from, Matt. 9: 9.

ạttạt isht ia, v. a. i., to rise; to begin to
heal, etc.; to take a start.

ạttạt minti, v. a. i., to come from;
ashwat minti, pl. (*antạt minti* and *aⁿshwạt
minti*, nasal forms, can not be used
because they include the idea of con-
tinuance).

ạttepuli, v. t., to make a pavilion; to
pavilion; to tent.

ba, adv., nothing; merely; certainly;
surely; *ia li ba*, I merely go; I just go;
I will just go, and meaning that nothing
shall prevent; a word used chiefly by
children.

ba is compounded with, and forms the
termination of, several words; *amba,
kamba, chumba, yoba, hioba, chikimba,
tokba, nahba, kbato, okbato, kbano,
okbano*.

bachali, n. sing., *bacholi*, pl., a row; a
course; a stick of timber lying straight,
as a joist; *sabaiyi bachali wia*, my
nephews; lit., my row of nephews;
tanchi iⁿhina bachali, rows of corn, i. e.,
the furrows and not the standing corn;
(*tanchi baiilh*, a row of standing corn;
takkon ạpi ạt baiilli, a row of peach
trees).

bachali, v. t. sing., to make a furrow for planting corn; to lay in a straight line; *iti tilit bachali,* to blaze trees in a line for a road.

bachaya, a., prostrate, and lying in a row so as to touch all the way.

bachaya, v. a. i. sing., to lie connected in a line or row; *tanchi inhina at bachanya,* the corn rows are laid off; *iti at bachaya,* the tree or the timber is laid; *ahchaba at bok anbachanya,* a foot log lies across the creek.

bachaya, v. pass., laid in a line; laid off; *lusa at bachaya,* the black (line) is laid, i. e., on a stick of timber for hewing; *hina at bachaya,* the road is laid off, or the road is marked off.

bachaya, n., a row; a line; a course; a vein; *hina bachaya,* line of a road, Josh. 2: 19.

bachoha, v. a. i. pl., to lie in courses; *hina at bachoha,* to lie in lines; *issuba ai-itintimia yat bachoha,* the race paths for horses are laid off, or are there.

bachoha, n. pl., rows; ranks; courses.

bachoha, pp. pass., laid in lines or courses.

bachohat manya, v. a. i., to lie in rows or lines; *hina at bachohat manya hoka ishpisa chin,* as the roads are laid off, you will see them.

bachohmanya, n., a noun derived from the foregoing verb.

bacholi, v. t., to lay in rows or lines; to make rows, lines or furrows for rows.

bacholi, n. pl., rows.

bacholi, n. pl., those that lay off in rows.

bafaha, v. a. i., to grow, as a bush; *osapa at bafahat kania,* the field is grown over with bushes.

bafaha, n., a bush; a green bush; a thicket; *bafaha* and *bafalli* are both used for bush and bushes; *bafaha chanli,* cut a bush; *bafalli chanli,* cut the bushes; but *bafaha anunka* and *bafalli anunka,* in the bushes, is proper.

bafalli, n. pl., bushes; a thicket; green brush.

bafalli, v. a. i., to grow, as bushes; *osapa yat bafallit kania,* the field is grown over with bushes.

bafalli, a., shrubby; bushy.

bafalli foka, a., bushy; grown up with bushes (applied to a large place).

bafalli talaia, n., a clump; a tuft; a small thicket (applied to a small place).

baha, pass., gored, stabbed, jabbed, by being struck with a straight forward blow; pricked; pierced; *uski osh baha,* the cane jabbed him, *iti osh baha,* the wood jabbed him, and *bashpo yosh baha,* the knife jabbed him, are transitive forms.

baha, n., a jab; a stab; *banshpo baha,* a knife stab; *uski baha,* a cane stab.

banhachi, n., baa, the cry of a sheep; *chukfi at banhachi,* the sheep says *banh* or *bananh.*

bahafa, pass., gored, stabbed, or jabbed by being struck with a blow that comes up, as cows do when they hook; *alla nakni at bahafa,* the boy is gored.

bahaffi, v. t. sing., to gore; to stab; to jab; to pierce; to stick; to thrust with an upward motion, as hogs with their tusks and cattle with horns, and to thrust a man with a knife with the point up.

bahaffi, n., a stabber; a gorer.

bahpo, bappo, n., a kind of nut pudding made of corn and peanuts.

bahpo, pass. of *bahpuli* (q. v.), made into a nut pudding; *bahpot alhtaha,* it is beaten and ready.

bahpuli, v. t., to beat up parched corn and parched peanuts for *bahpo;* to pound corn and peanuts for *bahpo.* The corn and peanuts are both parched and then beaten or pounded together. The meat of hickory nuts is sometimes used.

bahta, n., a bag; a pack; a budget; a knapsack; a scrip; a wallet, Matt. 10: 10, *bahta at iksho,* no scrip, Mark 6: 8. This word differs but little from *shukcha* (q. v.); *hapi shukcha,* salt sack, *kafi shukcha,* coffee sack, are used, but not *bahta.*

bahta chito, n., a bale; a big bag.

bahta chito abeli, v. t., to bale, or to put up in a bale or big bag; *tanchi an bahta chito yon abeli,* to put up corn in a big bag.

bahta chito abiha, pass., baled; put up in a bale.

bahta chito hoshiⁿsh aiạlhto, n., a tick; a bed tick; lit., a big bag holding feathers.

bahta shinuk aiạlhto, n., a sandbag; a bag having sand in it.

bahtushi, n., a pouch; a small bag; a satchel; a scrip; a wallet.

baiạlli, v. a. i., to stand in files or rows; or *baiilli* (q. v.).

baiạllit aⁿya, v. a. i., to move in a single file.

baiạllit ạla, v. a. i., to arrive in a row.

baiạllit heli, v. a. i. pl., to stand in ranks.

baiạllit hika, v. a. i. sing., to stand in a row or single file.

baiạllit maⁿya, v. a. i., to advance in file.

baiạllit minti, v. a. i., to come in a row.

baiet biⁿya, bait biⁿya, v. a. i. pl., to move in ranks as soldiers, not abreast but one following another.

baieta, v. a. i. sing., to stand or go in a row, one after another, as men or animals in a single road; caus., *baietạchi* or *baietạt hinli*, to stand in a row; *baietạt aⁿya*, to go along in a row; to stand in a row, as planted corn or trees when set out.

baieta, n., a row of corn, trees, men, or animals.

baii, baiyi, n., white oak; name of an oak tree and its fruit; a white-oak acorn; *baii laua*, plenty of white-oak acorns.

baii toba, a., oaken; made of white oak.

baiilli, baiạlli (pl. of *baieta*), pass., ranked; placed in rows or ranges; *abaiạli*, 2 Kings 11: 8.

baiilli, baiạlli (pl. of *baieta*), v. a. i., to stand in files or rows; to rank; to follow in order one after another.

baiillichi, v. t., to cause to follow in ranks; to march; to place in ranks.

baiillit nowa, v. a. i., to march in single ranks, but not abreast. It differs from *auatali*, v. a. i., to march abreast.

baiillit nowa, n., a march.

bait biⁿya, see *baiet biⁿya*.

baiyana, v. n., to want. See *bạnna*, from which it is derived.

baiyi, see *baii*.

bakafa, v. a. i. sing., to split off; and pp., split off.

bakaha, pl., *bakalichi* sing., v. t., to cane; to baste; to strike with a cane or stick; to maul; *ofi yoⁿ bakahali*, I beat the dog.

bakaha, n., a caning.

bakali, pp. pl., split; blocked; slabbed; *bakali ushta*, split in quarters.

bakali, v. a. i., to split; to block; to slab into several, i. e., more than two, pieces.

bakalichi, v. t., to split into large blocks; to slab; to block; to split puncheons for a floor.

bakalichi, n., a splitter.

bakapa, pass. sing. of *bakạbli* (q. v.); halved or divided into two equal parts; cleft; riven.

bakapa, v. a. i., to divide into two equal parts; to cleave; to split; to divide once in the middle; *iti ạt bakapa*, the tree divides or opens in the middle.

bakapa, n., a half when split in two; a cleft; *shuka nipi bakapa*, half of a hog.

bakastoa, pass. pl., split in two; divided into two equal parts.

bakastoa, v. a. i. pl., to split in two; to divide.

bakastoa, n. pl., halves; when things have been split open.

bakastuli, v. t. pl., to split in two; to halve them; to rob; *holisso haⁿ bakastuli*; same as *wehpuli*, say M. Dyer and Thompson.

bakạbli, v. t. sing., to split in two; to halve.

bakạbli, n., a splitter; a divider.

bakạsto, bakạstuli, pass., finished; completed; all takèn, as when a robbery is committed, or grain in a field is destroyed.

bakạstuli, v. t., to get all; to take all; to finish.

bakạstuli, n., a finisher; one that takes all.

bakbak, n., a large red-headed woodpecker, smaller than the *tiⁿkti*. *bakbak ạt paⁿki akbano hoⁿ ạpa*, the *bakbak* eats grapes only.

bakli, v. t. pl., to split into large blocks, whether halves, fourths, or eighths; *bakali*, pass. (q. v.), *nusạ pi aⁿ baklili*, I split the black oak into blocks.

baklichi, v. t., to score.

bakna, n.; *imbakna*, the rennet (or runnet) or stomach of cows or deer.

bakoa, bakowa, a., spotted; pied; large check; brinded; tabby brinded; tabby; dapple; dappled; *wak at bakoa*, the cow is spotted; *nan tanna at bakoa*, the cloth has large checks; *abaksha hat bakoa*, the chicken snake is pied.

bakoa, v. n., to be spotted, pied, etc.

bakoachi, bakowachi, v. t., to make spotted, pied, etc.; to dapple.

bakokoa, n. pl., spots.

bakoko^{n}a, a. pl., spotted; pied; large check.

bakoko^{n}a, v. n. pl., to be spotted.

bakoku^{n}kachi, n. pl., large white and red spots.

bakoku^{n}kachi, bakoku^{n}kachi, a. pl., spotted; *sintulo at bakoku^{n}kachi*, the rattlesnake is spotted.

bakoku^{n}kachi, v. n. pl., to be spotted.

bakowa, see *bakoa*.

bakowachi, see *bakoachi*.

balakli, v. a. i. sing., to leap up; like *halakli*.

balakli, balakli (the best forms) bilakli, v. a. i., to wilt; *iti hishi at bilakli*, the leaves wilt.

balakli, pass., wilted; see *bilakli*.

balaklichi, v. t., to wilt; to make it wilt.

balali, v. a. i., to creep, as a child; to crawl; to grovel; *alla yat balali*, the child creeps.

balali, n., a creeper; a crawler; a groveler; *alla balali*, a child creeper.

balama, a., fragrant; odoriferous; ambrosial; balmy; sweet; odorous; redolent—used with reference to the smell of objects only.

balama, v. n., to be fragrant.

balama, n., a sweet odor; savor; flavor; scent; smell, as of a rose; *na balama*, n., incense, Luke 1: 10; Rev. 5: 8. *nan isht balama*, 2 Cor. 2: 15; a savor; Eph. 5: 2.

balama, pass, perfumed.

balamachechi, v. t., to perfume another person or thing; to incense another person or thing; to cause one to perfume another.

balamachi, balamachi, v. t., to make it fragrant, balmy, sweet; to scent well; *pa^{n}shi a^n balamachi*, to make the hair *balama*; *na foka ya^n balamachi*, to make the garments *balama*.

balalli, v. a. i., to creep, as a vine; to run, as a vine; to scramble.

balalli, n., a creeper; a scrambler; a vine.

baleli, maleli, v. a. i. sing., to run, as an animal or a man, 1 Cor. 9: 24; Gal. 5: 7; *emallihinlashke*, Heb. 12: 1; *maleli* is the more common word: *tilaya* dual (q. v.); *tilaha^{n}ya*, *tilaha^{n}yatok* "did run," Matt. 28: 8: *yilepa*, pl., Mark 9: 15.

baleli, n., a runner.

baluhchi, n., the hickory bark which is used in making ropes.

balup, n., slippery elm; also the linden, or lind tree; the teil tree.

bali, v. t., to stab; to gore; to hook and jab; to strike straight forward; to jab; to beat up the materials for making *bahpo;* to dagger; to dirk; to pick; to prick; to push; to spur; to stick; to beat, as meat in a mortar; to thrust; to pierce, John 19: 34; Rev. 1: 7; *iti^{n}bali*, to gore each other; *issi nipi ya^n bali*, beat the venison; *tu^{n}shpat bali ho^n*, or *tushpat bali ho^n*, make haste and beat it!

bali, n., a stabber; one that gores or hooks; a thruster; a beater.

bali, n., a push; a stab; a thrust.

balichi, v. t., to make anything stab, gore, etc.

bam, balam, n., balm, Gen. 37: 25; *bam* is the Choctaw pronunciation of balm.

bambaki, bamboki, a., not even; rough; bulbous; rolling, as land having swells.

bambakichi, v. t., to make uneven.

bamboki, v. n., to be uneven.

bamppoa, pass., shot with a blow gun; discharged from a blow gun, whether the arrow has hit the object shot at or not.

bamppoa, n., a discharge; a shoot.

bamppulli, v. t., to shoot with a blow gun.

bamppulli, n., a shooter; one that shoots with a blow gun.

banatboa, banatboha, v. a. i. pl., to wave; to billow.

banatboa, banatboha, n. pl., waves; willows.

banatbohachi, v. t., to cause the waves to rise; to cause the water to wave.

banatha, n., a wave; a billow; a rolling; a surge; a heave, James 1: 6; Matt. 8: 24; *oka banatha*, Matt. 14: 24.

banatha, v. a. i., to wave; to billow; to roll; to heave.

banąthąchi, v. t., to make it wave, billow, or roll; banątkąchi, pl.

bano, adv., only; altogether; perfectly; completely; all; merely; simply; totally; utterly; wholly; entirely; ishibano, Matt. 7: 8; receives entirely, Josh. 1: 16, 17; yammakbano, that only; yakbano hon, Matt. 4: 4.

bano, a., mere; naked; simple; only; iyi bano, barefoot; nipi bano, naked.

bano, a., alone; entire; stark; ilap bano, himself alone; Matt. 14: 23; hatak bano, man alone; bano preceded by k is used for the sign of the optative mood; mintikbano, only that he comes.

bano, v. n., to be alone; to be entire; banokmąt, 2 Sam. 18: 25; banot, Matt. 11: 21.

banochi, banuchi, v. t., to make it entire; to make solitary or alone; ilap banochit hassanfiląmmachinka, ye shall leave me alone, John 16: 32.

baptismo, n., baptism, Matt. 20: 23; 21: 25.

baptismo, pass., baptized, Matt. 20: 23; 1 Cor. 10: 2; baptismo used with active prep.

baptismochi, v. t., to baptize, Matt. 3: 11; baptismohonchi, freq. Mark 1: 4; Matt. 28: 19; baptismochechi.

baptismochi, n., a baptist; one who administers baptism; a baptizer.

baptist, n., a baptist; John the Baptist, Matt. 3: 1; 11: 11.

basaboa, pass. pl., sparks made.

basacha; basancha, in luak basancha, a spark of fire.

basachi, see basalichi.

basaha, v. a. i. sing., to pop or snap, as burning wood.

basaha, n., a pop; a snap.

basahąchi, v. t. sing., to cause it to pop or to snap; to make sparks.

basahkąchi, v. a. i. pl., to pop; to snap.

basahkąchi, n. pl., a popping; a snapping.

basak, bąsak, n. sing., a pop; a snapping noise; snap of a stick, of clay thrown against a wall, or of the fist in giving a blow.

basakachi, v. a. i., lit. to say basak; to snap; to pop.

basali, v. a. i. pl., to snap; to pop; to explode, as burning wood.

basali, n. pl., a popping; a snapping.

basalichi, basachi, v. t. pl., to cause a snapping or popping.

basasunkąchi, n. pl., a popping; a snapping.

basasunkąchi, a., brindled; striped; scarred.

basasunkąchi, bąsąsunkąchi, v. n., to be brindled or striped.

basisakąchi, v. a. i. pl., to snap; to crack; to pop.

basoa, v. n., to be striped; to be brindled; to be brinded; to be checked and tabby; bąsąsoah.

basoa, a., striped; brindled; brinded; tabby.

basoa, pass., streaked.

basoa, n., stripes; spots of different colors; a streak; a stripe; bąsąsoah.

basoachi, basoąchi, v. t., to stripe; to make brindled; to streak.

basali, v. t. pl., to stripe.

basali, n. pl., stripes.

basalichi, v. t. caus., to make striped work, as cloth.

basosunkąchi, bąsąsunkąchi, n. pl., scars; marks; small checks; small stripes.

banspoah, n., slabs, or slats of paling.

basunląsh, n., the gall; the bile; basunląsh homi, gall of bitterness, or bitter gall, Acts 8: 23.

basunląsh aiątto or aiąlhto, n., the gall bladder.

basunląsh okchi, n., the gall; the matter secreted in the liver, Matt. 27: 34.

bashankchi, n., elder, name of a shrub.

banshka, n., a good nature; a gentle disposition.

banshka, a., good natured.

banshka, v. n., to be good natured.

banshka achukma, a., friendly.

banshkiksho, a., sullen; irritable; cross; morose; perverse; rugged; unpeaceable.

banshkiksho, v. n., to be sullen.

bashukcha, n., the sumac which bears the purple bud. The other kind is called bąti (q. v.).

bat, adv., only; each; contracted from bano or bano hosh; tuklo bat ia, two and two go, or two in each company go.

bat, times, as tuklo bat tuchinakmąt hanali, twice 3 is 6.

batammi, watammi, v. t., to trip up another in wrestling.

bato, conjunctive form of bano. See kbato and kbano.

bachalusha, n., sleet.

bachalusha, v. a. i., to sleet.

bachalushachi, v. t., to cause the sleet to fall.

bahcha, bachcha, n., a ridge of land.

bahcha ikbi, v. t., to ridge; to make ridges.

bahcha pissa, n., a straight ridge.

bahcha tabokaka, n., the top of the ridge.

bakokunkachi, bakokunkachi (q. v.), a., spotted; having many colors, as Joseph's coat, Gen. 37: 3.

bala, n., a bean; the name of one kind of bean which is large.

bala hakshup, n., a bean pod; skin of a bean.

bala hobbi, n., boiled beans.

bala okchi, n., bean porridge.

balakachi, v. a. i., to gulp; to swallow in large drafts.

balbaha, v. a. i., to talk in a foreign or unknown language; to prattle, as an infant.

balbaha, n., one that talks in a foreign language.

balbaha toba, v. a. i., to become one that talks in a foreign language.

Balbancha (from balbaha + ansha), n., New Orleans; a place of foreign languages.

balli, v. t., to cut up underbrush; to clear land by cutting off the undergrowth.

bali, v. a. i., to hit.

banaha, n., boiled corn bread wrapped in leaves, in which boiled beans are mixed; a roll, as of bread or butter.

banaiya, n., a ridge, as a corn ridge, etc.; banaboa, pl.

banaiyachechi, v. t., to ridge; to ruffle.

banaiyachi, n., a ridge, such as is made in a field where corn is planted.

banakachechi, v. t., to cause to fluctuate or ripple.

banakachi, v. a. i., to fluctuate; to roll, as the waves; to ripple; to ruffle; to undulate.

banakachi, n., a sea; a wave.

banakachi, a., rough, as troubled water.

banakachi, pass., ruffled.

banna, v. a. i., to want; to desire; to wish, Matt. 5; 42; to crave; to seek, Luke 6, 19; to will, Matt. 14: 5; to gape; to long; to need; to pant; to strive; to water, as the mouth waters; ikbanno, n. f. ikchibannokashke, thou shalt not wish; baiyana, pro. form. abanna, to want of or for; in want of, Matt. 6: 8; to need, Matt. 6: 32; ikbaiyanno, a., not willing; ikbanno, a., averse; loath; reluctant; unwilling; v. n., to be averse.

banna, a., minded; prone; wishful; ikbanno, a., reluctant.

banna, n., a longing; a wish; a need; a wanting.

banna, n., a wisher; one who wants.

banna fehna, v. t., v. a. i., to covet; to hanker; to wish intently.

banna fehna, a., covetous, greedy.

bappo, see bahpo.

basa, n., the name of the fish called pike.

basak, see basak.

basasunkachi, see basasunkachi and basosunkachi.

baska, basto, v. a. i., to game; to gamble; to play with cards or marbles; to card.

baska, basto, n., a gambler; hatak baska, a gambler.

basha (from bashli, v. t.), pass., sawn; cut; carved; mown; mowed; reaped; clipped; gashed; gelded; marked; plowed; sheared; shorn; ikbasho, a., unmarked; unwounded.

basha, n., a gash; an incision; a mark; a cut with a saw or knife.

basha hinla, a., perishable.

bashat holisso, bashat holisso, pp., graved; engraved; cut and written.

bashat holisso, n., an engraving.

bashechi, v. t., to wilt; to blast; to wither; to shrink.

bashi, bashshi, pass., wilted; blasted; blighted; contracted; faded; withered.

bashi, bashshi, v. a. i., to wither, Matt. 13: 6; to wilt; to blast; to contract; to fade; to flag; to languish; to perish; bashi chatuk, John 15: 6; bashit tahatok, withered away, Matt. 13: 6; 21: 19.

bashi, n., a languisher.

bashkachi, pass. pl., laid in rows; laid side by side, as sleepers under a floor; bachaya, sing.

bashkachi, a. pl., lying in rows, as rows of timber; *hina bashkachi puta,* the rows of roads; *bok ushi bashkachi puta,* the branches running in one direction, side by side, as if in rows.

bashkachi, v. n., to lie in rows; to be in rows.

bashkachi, n., rows.

bashli, v. t., to saw; to cut with a drawing motion, as with a knife, sword, scythe, or sickle, and therefore also meaning to mow and to reap; to clip; to castrate; to emasculate; to gash; to geld; to hurt; to mark; to nick; to reap; to shear; to slash; see Matt. 5: 30, *bashlit taplit ishkanchashke; ilebashli,* to cut himself.

bashli, n., a cutter; a sawyer; a mower; a reaper; a marker; a shearer.

bashli, n., an incision; a cut.

bashlit holissochi, v. t., to engrave.

bashlit holissochi, n., an engraver.

Bashokla, or Paskokla, n., Pascagoula; bread people, or cutting people [almost certainly "bread people."—EDS.].

bashpapi, n., a knife handle—a compound word from *bashpo* knife, and *api,* handle, stem, or stalk.

bashpo, n., a knife; a knife blade; a blade; Josh. 5: 2, 3.

bashpo chito, n., a large knife; *bashpo chito inshukcha,* n., a scabbard; a sheath.

bashpo falaia, n., a long knife; a sword, Josh. 5: 13; the blade of a sword; a rapier; a dirk; a bilbo; a dagger, Matt. 26: 51, 52; 10: 34; *Turk inbashpo falaia,* a Turk's sword, i. e., a scimiter.

bashpo falaia aiulhpi, n., a hilt; the hilt of a sword.

bashpo falaia atakali askufachi, n., a sword belt.

bashpo falaia halupa, n., a sword blade.

bashpo falaia inshukcha, bashpo falaia afohka, n., a scabbard for a sword, Matt. 26: 52.

bashpo falaia inshukcha fohki, v. t., to scabbard.

bashpo falaia patha, n., a broadsword.

bashpo ibbak pishinli, n., a table knife; a case knife.

bashpo isht impa, n., a table knife; a case knife, lit. a knife to eat with.

bashpo isht itibi, n., a dirk; a rapier; a stiletto, lit., a knife to fight with.

bashpo italankla halupa, n., a two-edged knife; a knife sharpened on both sides.

bashpo poloma, n., a clasp knife; a pocketknife.

bashpo wishakchi, n., the point of a knife.

bashpuli, v. t., to sweep; to remove; to obviate, as to prepare a path.

bashpuli, n., a sweeper.

bashpushi, n., a small knife; a penknife; from *bashpo,* knife, *ushi,* son.

bashshi, see *bashi.*

basht, cut and; this is a contraction from *bashlit,* to cut and.

basht pisa, v. t., to cut and see.

basht tapli, v. t., to cut off.

basht tapli, n., excision; *basht tapa,* pass., cut off.

basht tapli, v. t., to amputate; to cut off; to mutilate.

basht tushaffi, v. t., to cut off; to slice off.

bashto, n., the overcup oak tree.

bati, n., the high sumac.

beka, a., alone; mere; stark; *bieka,* the prolonged form of *beka.*

beka, v. n., to be alone; *bieka* in *ano sabieka hosh hikialachin hoke,* John 16: 32, in an old translation; *ishbieka,* Deut. 28: 13.

beka, bieka, adv., always; commonly; usually; only; merely; simply; totally; hitherto, Acts 23: 1; Luke 20: 20; *yohmi beka,* he does so always; *yammak beka,* that one only; *beka* is used in speaking of the customary actions of one who is dead, while *chatuk* is used in speaking of such actions of one who is yet alive; *chatuk* connects a past act with present time, *beka* does not.

beli, v. t., to breast, as a suckling calf or lamb.

biakak, biyankak, n., a hawk; a chicken hawk.

bicha, pass., drawn; taken from a cask.

bicha, v. a. i., to spout, as water.

bichataha, pp., racked; drawn off.

bicheli, v. t., to draw liquor; to take from a cask; to cause a liquid to run out; to draw; *Inta! ho bicheli cha,* "Draw out now!" John 2: 8.

bicheli, n., a tapster; a drawer.

bicheli, v. t., to draw a small quantity of liquid from a cask.

bichet tali, v. t., to rack; to draw off from the lees; to draw the liquor all off·

bichillahe keyu, a., waterproof; (lit.)' it will not leak.

bichilli, pichilli, v. a. i. pl., to leak out; to ooze; to percolate; to run out gently; *oka hạt sakti apichilli*, the water drips from the bank; *italhfo aiyạt bichilli*, the keg leaks.

bichillichi, pichelichi, v. t. pl., to cause to ooze out; to burst them; to break them so that the liquid will flow out gently.

bichokạchi, pp. pl., bent; sprung; *iti ạt bichokạchi*, the wood is bent.

bichokạchi, v. a. i. pl., to bend; to spring.

bicholi, v. t. pl., to bend.

bicholi, n. pl., benders.

bicholichi, v. t. pl. caus., to bend; to make them bend.

bichota, pass., bent; sprung.

bichota, v. a. i., to bend; to spring.

bichotakạchi, v. a. i., to spring a single time.

bichubli, bochubli, v. t. sing., to squeeze in the hand.

bichuⁿko, n., the brisket.

bichulli, v. t. sing., to bend; to spring; *bichunli*, nasal form, bending.

bichulli, n., a bender.

bichullichi, v. t. caus., to bend.

bichupa, bochopa, pass., squeezed in the hand; from *bichubli*, v. t. (q. v.).

bieka, from *beka* (q. v.), a., mere, John 16: 32.

bieka, adv., merely; only.

bifisha, n., a cluster of little bushes.

bihi, n., a mulberry; the fruit of the mulberry tree.

bihi ạpi, bihạpi, n., a mulberry tree.

bihi chito, n., a large mulberry; a fig, John 1: 48; Luke 13: 6 (changed to *fik* in the last edition).

bihi chito hishi, n., a fig leaf.

bihi holba, n., a sycamore, 1 Kings 10: 27.

bihi talaia, n., a mulberry grove.

bihạpi, see *bihi ạpi*.

bihkạchi, pl., to be rent and worn out, as cloth. This may be a contraction of the genuine word.

biⁿka, miⁿka, a., each; both; like; resembling; of the same kind or species; *chaha kạt kubit pokoli biⁿka*, each ten cubits high, 1 Kings 6: 23; *ilabiⁿka*, each himself; both; Gen. 40: 5.

biⁿka, n., a fellow; *tishu pibiⁿka*, our fellow-servant, Col. 1: 7; *ilap biⁿka*, their fellows, Matt. 11: 16.

biⁿka, v. n., to be like, or of the same kind; *hatak sabiⁿka*, a man who is like me; *na hollo chibiⁿka*, a white man who is like you.

biⁿka, v. a. i. sing., to whine, as a puppy; to yelp.

biⁿkbia, v. a. i. pl., to whine; to yelp.

biⁿkbia, n., a whine.

biⁿkbia, n., a whiner.

bikbina, n., a knop, Ex. 37: 17; 25: 23; see *kibikshi*.

bikeli, v. t., to touch; to press up against with a point or the end of anything; to touch the side with a pointed object; to flow in or over, as the tide; *okhạta chito ạt bikeli; mikma wishakchi okạt shutik tabokaka bikelashke*, and whose top shall reach heaven, Gen. 2: 4.

bikeli, n., a stick or anything that touches or reaches to something else; a support; a supporter.

bikelichi, v. t., to cause to reach up to; to strike against an object overhead; *shutik hạkakkia bikelichi bạnnạt ahaⁿshuatok*, they desired to cause it to reach up to the sky.

bikobli, bokobli, v. a. i., to bud; to put forth buds; to shoot; *takon ạpi ạt bikobli*, the peach tree buds.

bikobli, pass., budded; put forth in buds.

bikobli, n., a bud; buds; a germ; the shoot of a plant.

bikoblichi, v. t., to cause to bud.

bikoha., v. a. i. pl., to bend.

bikoha, pp. pl., bent; *bikota*, sing.

bikoha, n., bends.

bikokạchi, pass. pl., bent.

bikokạchi, v. a. i. pl., to bend.

bikoli, v. t. pl., to bend without breaking.

bikoli, n. pl., the persons who bend; benders.

bikolichi, v. t. caus., to bend; to make them bend.

bikota, pass. sing., of *bikulli*, bent.

bikota, v. a. i., to bend; to crouch; to sag; to sway.

bikota, n., a bend; the bend.

bikota hinla, a., flexible.

bikota keyu, a., unyielding.

bikotahe keyu, a., inflexible; *imanuk-fila bikotahe keyu* (his mind bend will not), inflexible in purpose.

bikotakạchi, v. a. i. sing., to bend once.

bikulli, v. t. sing., to bend; to incurvate; to sag; *bikunli*, nasal form, to be bending.

bikulli, n., a bender.

bikullichi, v. t., to bend; to cause to bend; to make it bend.

bikuttokạchi, v. a. i., to cower; to squat; to courtesy (as a lady); to bow or bend down; *isi ạt bikuttokạchi* (the deer bends down), *koi ạt* (the tiger); or *ạba hushi ạt bikuttokạchi* (air, fowl of, it squats).

bila, n., oil; fat; gravy; grease; *nita bila*, bear's oil; *shukha bila*, hog's fat.

bila, v. a. i., to melt; to dissolve; to fuse; to thaw; to resolve; *bihinla*, Josh. 2: 9, 11; to melt or faint, Josh. 7: 5.

bila, a., unctuous; greasy.

bila, pass., melted; dissolved; fused; thawed; liquefied; resolved; *ikbilo*, a., unmelted, unthawed; *ikabilo*, a., undissolved.

bila bieka, a., oily; only oil; oil entirely.

bila hinla, a., fusible; dissolvable, (lit.) melt can.

bila chạpka, nạni chạpka, nia chạpka, n., a cockroach.

bila oⁿlaha, pass., basted; moistened with fat.

bila oⁿlali, v. t., to baste; to drip fat upon meat; to moisten with fat.

bila pạla, n., a lamp; an oil lamp.

bilahama, pass., oiled; anointed; anointed with oil.

bilahạmmi, v. t., to anoint with oil; i. e., him or herself.

bilahạmmichi, v. t., to anoint another with oil.

bilahe keyu, a., indissoluble, (lit.) melt will not.

bilakli, balakli (q. v.), v. a. i., to wilt; to droop; to wither.

bilakli, pass., wilted; a., flaccid; pp., withered.

bilaⁿkli, n., a small round and long hill.

bilaklichi, v. t., to wilt; to wither.

bileli, v. t., to melt; to fuse; to thaw; to dissolve; to colliquate; to liquefy; to resolve; to run; "to make melt," Josh. 14: 8; *bilet*, contracted form with *t* conjunctive.

bileli, n., a melter.

bilelichi, v. t., to melt; to cause to melt.

bilhkạchi, pl. of *binili*.

bilia, adv., always, Matt. 18: 10; perpetually; forever; continually; eternally; regularly; off, Josh. 4: 7, 24; away; *iạt bilia*, gone away, gone off, Heb. 13: 8; *hikia biliạt peh biliạshke*, stands forever and ever, Heb. 1: 8.

bilia, a., continual; eternal, John 3: 15; ever; e'er; everlasting, John 3: 16; incessant; lasting; perennial; permanent; perpetual; unbegotten; unceasing; unintermitted; unremitted; *aiissikkopa bilia* and *aiokchayạt bilia*, Matt. 25: 46.

bilia, v. a. i., to be or do always; to continue, *ạno yokạt hạchiapehạt ayạt biliali*, Matt. 28: 20 (old translation).

bilia, v. n., to be always; to be forever; to be continual; to continue evermore; *okchaⁿya na biliahe*, John 6: 51; *hạchi-yukpa na biliashke*, rejoice ye evermore, 1 Thess. 5: 16; *abilia*, adv., forever, Matt. 6: 13; where it is always; to eternity.

biliachechi, v. t., to perpetuate.

biliachi, v. t., to make perpetual or continual.

biliⁿka, adv., just; nigh; close by; at hand; *Chihowa aiibiliⁿka*, nigh to God, James 4: 8.

biliⁿka, n., nearness; vicinage; vicinity; *biliⁿka ạlatok*, 2 Sam. 18: 25; *abiliⁿka*, a suburb; a neighborhood, Josh. 20: 5; *iⁿbilika*, n., propinquity to it, him, or her; *iⁿbiliⁿka*, a., snug.

biliⁿka, a., near; close by; close; *bilika fehna*, too close; contiguous; adjacent; imminent; nigh; proximate, Matt. 3: 5; *itiⁿbiliⁿka*, a., thickset; near to each other; *biliⁿkakmak bạno pisa*, a., near-sighted; to see that only which is near.

biliⁿka, v. t., to come near; to near; to approach; *itiⁿbiliⁿka*, to come near each other; *itiⁿbilika fehna*, to be too near each other.

biliⁿka, v. n., to be near; to be close by, Matt. 15: 29; *biliⁿkạt ibataklạt*, Scrip. Biog., Abraham and Lot, p. 20; *itiⁿbil-*

iⁿka, to be near each other; itibiliⁿka aⁿsha, n., a neighborhood; a proximity to each other; nearness to each other.

biliⁿkasi, a. dim., very near; not far off; quite near, Matt. 15: 8.

biliⁿkasi, v. n., to be very near; isht in-biliⁿkasi ilonashke, "let us draw near," Heb. 10: 22.

biliⁿkatta, v. a. i., to reside near.

biliⁿkạchi, v. t., to bring near; to draw near; to fetch near; to approximate; ilabiliⁿkạchi, Luke 9: 47.

biliⁿkạtta, n., a neighbor; one that dwells near.

bilinchi, v. a. i., v. t., to draw near; to come near; to make near; to draw nigh; to near; ishpiⁿbilinchashke, do you come near to us; ilap mạt hạchiⁿbilinchachiⁿ hoke, he will draw nigh to you, James 4: 8.

bilinchi, a., near.

bilinchi, adv., nearly.

bilinchi kạt iⁿshaht tali, a., nearest.

[biliⁿsbi, n., the name of a bird.—H. S. H.]

biliⁿsbili, n., a very young turkey, just beginning to cry.

biła, pass. pl. of bili, perforated; wounded; hurt; pricked.

biła, a., wounded; hurt.

biłepa, sing., łipia, pl., to lie on the face; to lie low; to sit with a downcast eye; bilimpa, nasal form.

biłepa, pl. of binili.—N. Gardner.

bili, v. t., to bunt, as a calf bunts the bag to make the mother's milk come, i. e., to work at the bag by pushing, bunting, etc. This word is applied to the rubbing of deer skins with a stick flattened and sharp at one end to make the skin soft and pliant.—J. Hudson.

bili, v. t. pl., to point at; to prick; to wound; to hurt; to injure the feelings; to spur; chuⁿkạsh bili, to wound the heart; itiⁿbili, to point at each other, etc.; abili, to perforate at, i. e., to set up bushes or poles for peas, beans, etc.; nipi isht bili, n., a flesh hook, 1 Sam. 2: 13.

bili, n. pl., wounders; those that wound, hurt, point, etc.; or one that wounds, etc., more times than once.

biłibli, v. t. sing., to point at; to prick; to point out; bili is the plural form

(q. v.); cf. bilihimbli in okchalinchi yaⁿ chiⁿbilihimbli kạt kạllo keyu.

biłibli, n., a pointer.

bim, n., sound of a tree falling through the air; a roaring.

bimihạchechi, v. t., to make a roaring.

bimihạchi, v. a. i., to roar, as fire in dry grass, or as a flock of birds when on the wing; to crash; to mumble; to murmur; to peal.

bimihạchi n., the roar; the roaring; a peal.

bimimpa, v. a. i., to crash; to roar.

bina, n., a camp; a lodging place out of doors and without shelter; a camping ground; an encampment; a tabernacle; a tent, Josh. 3: 14; a host, Josh. 1: 11; binah, 1 Sam. 4: 6; bina wihat kucha, v. t., to decamp; to move out of camp.

bina aⁿsha, pass., tented; camped.

bina awiha, n., a deserted camp.

bina awiha, v. t., to move from a camp.

bina hilechi, v. t., to pitch a camp.

bina talali, v. t., to tent; to set a tent.

binachi, v. t., to camp; to encamp; 1 Sam. 4: 1; Josh. 8: 9; binanchi, nasal form, to be camping; Josh. 4: 19; 5: 10; 10: 5.

binachi, n., one that camps.

binanchi, n., a camping; the act of encamping.

binili, v. a. i., to sit; to take a seat; to settle; ont binilima "when he was set," Matt. 5: 1; 13: 1; to fix one's habitation or residence; to abide, John 1: 32; to sit down, Luke 4: 20; to encamp; to light; to nestle; binint; ilebinili, to seat himself; to sit; to perch; to rest on the feet, as fowls; ilabinili, to retire; to sit alone; ilabinili, n., a retreat; a retirement; ombinili, v. t., to sit on; to incubate; to ride; taⁿkla binili, v. a. i., to intrude; to sit among.

binili, n., a sitter; a setter; one that settles; wihat binili, a colony; apeliechi ka yạt wihat binili, Col. Folsom's colony; oklat wihat binili, a colony of people.

binili, n., a sitting; taⁿkla binili, n., an intruder; binili hoⁿ ont pisatok, Matt. 9: 9; taⁿkla binili, n., an intrusion.

binili, pp., seated; settled; located; kanạllit binili, colonized; ikbinilo, a., unseated; achukmat ikbinilo, a., unsettled; binili bilia, a., sedentary.

binilichi, v. t., to seat; to place on a seat; to establish one in a habitation or place; to cause to sit down; to settle him or her at a place, as on new land; *kanąllichit binilichi*, v. t., to colonize; to install; to locate; to set; to settle.

bininili, v. a. i. freq., to sit here and there; to be sitting here and there; moving about from seat to seat.

bininli, v. t., nas. form, to be sitting, Gen. 18: 1; 19: 1; John 4: 6; plural *chinya; binihinli*, frequentative; *binininli, onbinininli*, iterative.

binnilechi, v. t., to cause to sit a long time.

binnili, v. a. i., to sit down a long time; to abide, 2 Kings 1: 9; to be there, Matt. 6: 9; 15: 13; 16: 17; 18: 10.

binohmaya, n., a sitting round.

binoht, cont. from *binoli; binoht taiyaha ma* or *binolit taha ma*, and were set down together, Luke 22: 55.

binoht aiasha, v. a. i., to sit around.

binoht aiasha, pass., seated around, John 6: 11.

binoht maya, v. a. i. pl., to sit round; to sit by; *yąmma binohmanyatuk*, "sitting by," Luke 5: 17; *ąlla yosh binohmanya*, Matt. 11: 16.

binoli, v. a. i. pl., to lodge, Matt. 13: 32; to sit; to take a seat; to settle; to sit down; *okla laua yąt aka hashuk aiombinolachi*, Matt. 14: 19; *onbinolit manya*, "which sat," Rev. 12: 16; *yąmma ombinilihatukma*, "him that sitteth thereon," Matt. 23: 22; *binolahe oke*, shall sit down, Matt. 8: 11.

binoli, n., sitters; those who take seats or settle; *abinoli*, seats. See Matt. 21: 12.

binoli, pass., seated; settled.

binolichi, v. t. caus., to seat; to place on a seat; to colonize; to settle them.

binolichi, n. pl., one who colonizes or settles others; one that seats others or those who colonize.

bint, in *mih bint achukma*.

bisakchakinna, bisukchakinna, n., a bramble; a green wild vine having briars and bearing berries, growing in swamps and low grounds, and called the bamboo brier.

bisakchakinna foka, a., brambly; thorny; *foka*, about, etc.

bisakchula, n., the name of a weed resembling *nita inpisa;* the leaves are long and tough.

bisali, bisinli, n., a sprout; a twig; *uksakąpi bisinli*, a hickory withe.

bisali, v. a. i., to sprout; to shoot forth, as young leaves; to germinate; *bisanli*, nasal form; *bisali, bisanli*, pp., sprouted.

bisanli, n., a sprout.

bisanlichi, v. t. caus., nasal form, to sprout; to cause it to sprout and grow.

bisanlih, n., a crack; a chap in the skin of the hands or face; a small crack.— J. G.

[biskantak, n., a bird of the tomtit family.—H. S. H.]

biskinak, biskinik, n., a small speckled woodpecker, called by some a sapsucker.

bislichi, v. t., to milk.

bissa, n., a blackberry.

bissalunkani, n., the seed of the weed spoken of below.

bissalunko, n., a weed, the vulgar name of which is beggars' lice.

bissąpi, n., a blackberry brier; a bramble bush; a bramble; *bissąpi akon panki an aiąmo*, Luke 6: 44.

bissąpi foka, a., brambly.

bissukchanaki, bissalukko, n., thorns, Luke 8: 7, 14; thorns is rendered *kąti* in the last translation.

bissuntalali, haiuntalali, n., a dewberry.

bisukchakinna, see *bisakchakinna*.

bishahchi, pass., milked; *ikbishacho*, a., unmilked; not milked.

bishahchi, wishahchi, a., milch; giving milk.

bishbeli, bishbeli, v. i., to ooze out.

bishkoko, bishkokok, n., a robin; robin redbreast.

bishkoni, n., name of an oak; the acorns are long and yellow, bark yellowish.

bishkumak, n., a red bird.

bishlichi, wishlichi, v. t., to milk; *wak an bishlichi*, he milks the cow.

bishlichi, n., one that milks; a milker.

bita, n., a turban or tire; a frontal; a frontlet; a head band; a band for the head. Choctaw men wear a silver band on the head called *tąli hąta bita*, a silver head band.

bita, pass., turbaned; having on a frontal or head band.

bitanli, n., a crack; a small crack; a chap; a crevice; a flaw; *yakni bitanli*, a crack in the ground, and cracked ground; a large crack.

bitanli, v. a. i., to crack open slightly; to chap.

bitanli, pass., cracked open; *yakni bitanli*.

bitanlichi, v. t., to crack open; to chap; to flaw.

bitataⁿya, v. a. i. pl., to crack open.

biteli, v. t., to put a frontlet or turban called a *bita* on one's self; to put on a silver headband.

bitelichi, v. t., to put a turban or head band on another person; to crown, Ps. 8: 5.

bitema, a., fetid; having a disagreeable smell, like that of old bones; *foni at bitema*, the bones are fetid.

bitema, v. a. i., to smell bad; to be fetid; to stink.

bitema, n., fetid; a stench like that of old bones.

bitemachi, v. t., to cause a fetid smell.

bitepa, v. t. sing., to put the hands on; to press on with the hands; *ibbak at . . . umbitepa*, Luke 4: 40; to rest upon, while leaning on the hands; *ombitepa*, *umbitepa*, or *oⁿbitepa* are usual expressions for "laying on."

bitka, v. t. pl., to bear on with the hands.

bitonoa, botonoa, pass., bent.

bitonoa, botonoa, v. a. i., to bend.

bitonoli, botonoli, v. t., to bend.

biuⁿko, n., a strawberry; *biuⁿko at nuna*, the strawberries are ripe.

biuⁿko api, n., a strawberry vine.

biuntalali, see *haiyantalali*.

biyaⁿkak, biaⁿkak, n., a hawk; a large chicken hawk.

boa, pass., beaten; beat; hammered; pounded; drubbed; see *boli*.

boafa, see *boyafa*.

boat pilefa, pass., riveted; beaten and turned down on; *botpiliffi* v. t., to rivet.

boaffi, see *boyaffi*.

bochokachi, pass. pl., squeezed in the hand.

bocholi, v. t. pl., to squeeze in the hand.

bochopa, bichupa, pass. sing., squeezed in the hand.

bochubli, bichubli, v. t., sing., to squeeze in the hand; to hold fast as a trap holds game.

bochunoa, pass., squeezed up.

bochunoli, v. t. pl., to squeeze them up.

bochupha, v. a. i., to contract; draw up and sink in like the breast of a child with sickness in the breast.

bochusa, v. a. i., to warp; to curl up; to twist; *itishima at bochusa*, the shingle warps.

bochusa, pass., warped; bent; twisted.

bochusachi, v. t., to warp; to twist; to curl; to cause it to warp.

boha; *oka itiboha*, water mixed and rendered dirty or roily; *kafi itiboha*, roily or muddy coffee.

bohokachi, v. t., to churn.

bohpoa, pass. of *bohpuli*, thrown; slung.

bohpuli, v. t. pl., *boli*, sing., to send; to throw; to sling; *isht bohpulit foki*, v. t., to inject; *isht bohpulli*, to take and throw; *isht bohpulit oka itokachi* (from *it* and *okachi*), to douse.

bohpuli, n., a sender; a thrower.

bok, n., a brook; a creek; a natural stream of water less than a river; a river, as *Bok humma*, Red river; *Mississippi Bok*, Mississippi river.

bok aiitisetili, n., a junction of creeks; a place where the creeks meet and run together.

bok aiyanalli, n., the channel of the creek; the place where the creek flows.

bok anuⁿka, n., a swamp on the sides of a creek; (lit.) within the *bok*.

bok anuⁿka, a., swampy.

bok asetili, n., the mouth of a creek.

bok chulaffi, n. sing., a single division of the creek; a branch of a creek; the word branch as used in the South means a small brook, a rivulet.

bok chuli, n. pl., the branches of water courses belonging to one creek; the head branches which mingle and form the creek.

bok falaia, n., long creek; the name also of a particular creek, Long creek; *Bok falaia akoⁿ mintili*, I came from Long creek.

bok falakto, n., the fork of a creek.

bok intannap, n., the side of the creek; the other side of the creek; the opposite side of the creek.

bok itạhnoli, n., junction of creeks.

bok itipatạlhpo, n., a bridge made over a creek, or a crossway made in the swamp near the creek.

bok mishtạnnạp, n., the farther side of a creek; the other side of a creek.

bok ola intạnnạp, n., this side of the creek; the side of the creek this way. Four words are here compounded, *bok* creek, *ola* this way, *in* to it, *tạnnạp*, side.

bok ola tạnnạp, n., this side of the creek.

bok sakti, n., banks of a river, Josh. 3: 15.

bok ushi, n., (a diminutive from *bok*, a river, and *ushi*, son, lit., the son of a river); a rivulet; a brook; a branch (a word in use in the South, meaning the same as brook); a rill.

bok wiheka, top of a side of a creek.

bok wishahchi, n., the fountain; the head of a creek.

bokafa, pass. sing., broken open; burst; cracked; *bokạffi*, v. t.

bokafa, v. a. i., to break open; to crack; to burst; to open; to explode.

bokafa, n., a crack; an eruption.

bokakạⁿkạchi, v. a. i., to break open; to burst open.

bokạli, pass. pl., broken open.

bokạlichi, v. a. i. pl., to break open; *bokạnli*, nasal form, being cracked open; *na pakạnli bokạnli putaka,* "open flowers," 1 Kings 6: 18.

bokạlichi, v. t. pl., to crack them open; to burst; to cause them to open.

bokạnli, n., a bud.

bokạnli, v. a. i., to bud.

bokạnli, pass., budded.

bokạnlichi, v. t., to cause it to bud.

boⁿkạchi, pass. pl., doubled up; rolled up; wrapped up; folded up; pass. of *bunni* (q. v.), v. t., to double up.

boⁿkạchi, v. a. i., to roll up.

boⁿkạchi, n. pl., bundles; rolls.

bokạffi, v. t. sing., to break open; *bokafa,* pass.

bokboki, a., roan; *isuba bokboki,* a roan horse; moldy, as bread, Josh. 9: 5.

bokboki, v. n., to be roan.

bokbokichi, v. t., to make of a roan color.

bokko, v. a. i., to be a hill; *boⁿkko,* nasal, being hilly; *boⁿkko ilaⁿya,* we go among the hills.

bokko, n., a hillock; a knoll; a hummock; a bank; a mound; a mount; a swell; anything round (see Josh. 5: 3), or like a cup; the top of the head.

bokko, pass., banked.

bokkuchi, v. t., to make a bank or hill; to bank, 2 Kings 19: 32.

bokkushi, n. (a dim.), a small hillock; from *bokko* and *ushi.*

bokobli, see *bikobli,* v. a. i., to bud.

bokokakạchi, bokokaⁿkạchi, pass., broken open, as the pod of certain fruits, etc.

bokonnoa, pass., pressed against.

bokonoli, v. t., to press up; to bend up; to raise up, as the seed which grows underground presses against the earth, and makes it crack open.

bokota, bikota, v. a. i., to bend.

bokota, bikota (q. v.), pass., bent; a., crooked.

bokulli, bikulli (q. v.), v. t., to bend.

bokupli, bikobli (q. v.), v. a. i., to bud.

bokusa, v. a. i., to warp; to crisp; to draw up; to turn up.

bokusa, pass., warped; crisped; drawn up.

bokusạchi, v. t., to warp; to cause to bend up at the sides or at the ends.

bolbokechi, v. t. pl., to make circles or squares.

bolboki, a. pl., circular; square.

bolboki, n. pl., circles; squares.

boli, v. t. pl., *isso* sing., to strike; to beat; to bang; to hammer; to pound; to batter; to pelt, Acts 7: 57; to hit or strike once; to bastinade; to smite; to forge; to lay on, as blows; to maul; to pelt; to thrash; *boa* (q. v.), pass., beaten; shaken; *bonli,* nasal form; *bohonli,* freq.; *boyuli,* pro. form; *ileboli,* to smite himself; *itiboli,* to strike each other; to fight.

boli, n., a striker; a hammerer; one who works with a hammer; a pelter; a thrasher; as *tạli boli,* a blacksmith or ironsmith.

bolkạchechi, v. t., to make circles or squares.

bolkạchi, a. pl., *bolukta* sing., circular.

bolkạchi, n., circles; squares.

bolunkboa, v. a. i., to make a cry like that of a person who has the nightmare.

bolukta, n. sing., a circle; a square; orbed; a quadrangle; roundness; *bolbuki*, pl. This word is used for both because there are no distinct words.

bolukta, pass., orbed; squared; rounded.

bolukta, a., square; circular; round; four square; quadrangular; *nantapaski bolukta*, a square pocket handkerchief.

bolukta, v. n., to be square or circular; to be round.

boluktali, v. t., to go round; to take round.

boluktachi, v. t., to make a square or a circle; to round.

boli, v. t., to stock; to store; to stow; *kanima aboli*, where to lay; Matt. 8: 20; to send, Matt. 10: 34; 25: 27; to lay, Luke 6: 48; to lay down; to deposit; to lay up; to put; to give; 2 Kings 6: 28, 29; Josh. 7: 11; to put out a proclamation, 2 Chron. 30: 5; to bestow; to lay up in store; to offer; to couch; to dispose; to pack; to pawn; to pledge; to stake; *boyuli*, pro. f., *italallit boli*, to pack together; *itaboli*, to lay up for himself; *ishilaboli*, you lay it by itself; *itinboli*, to lay down against each other, as a wager; *ikboto*, a., unstored; unlaid.

boli, n., one that lays down, deposits, etc.; an offerer; a pawner.

boli, n., a pawn; a pledge; a wager.

bombaki, bambaki (q. v.), a., rough; uneven.

bonna, a., rolled up.

bonuha, v. a. i. sing., to roll up.

bonuha, pass., rolled up; from *bonulli* (q. v.).

bonuha, n., a roll.

bonulli, v. t. sing., to double up; to roll up; to bundle up; to wrap up.

bonulli, n., a wrapper; one that wraps.

bonunta, pp., rolled up; doubled up.

bonunta, v. a. i., to roll; to double; to curl.

bonunta, n., a roll; a bundle; a pack; a parcel.

boppoa, pp., sent.

boshulli, v. a. i., to crumble; to break in pieces.

boshulli, pass., crumbled; broken in fragments; mashed.

boshulli, pl., crumbs; bits; fragments; small pieces; *imaiimpa yon boshulli*, crumbs of his table, Luke 16: 21; fragments, Matt. 14: 20; 15: 27, 37.

boshullichi, v. t., to crumble; to break in pieces; to mash.

bot, contracted form of *boli; bot abi*, to kill by blows; *isht bot kanchi*, to strike with and kill.

bot apelifichi, v. t., to rivet.

bot apiliffi, v. t., to rivet.

bot shebli, v. t., to malleate; to draw into a plate or leaf by beating.

bot shepa, pp., malleated.

bota, pass., pounded; pulverized; powdered.

bota, v. a. i., to become flour.

bota, n., flour made of parched corn by pounding it; powder.

bota hata, bota tohbi, n., wheat flour.

bota kapassa, n., cold flour made of parched corn.

bota lakchansha, bota lakchi ansha, n., coarse meal.

bota lashpa, n., flour made of parched corn.

bota onfima, pass., powdered.

bota tanshpa, n., corn flour made of corn parched without being boiled.

bota tohbi, bota hata, n., wheat flour; white flour.

bota tohbi isht onfimmi, v. t., to powder with wheat flour.

botoli, v. t., to pulverize; to pound fine; to reduce to a fine powder by pounding in the mortar.

botolichi, botullichi, v. t., to rub fine; to pulverize (not quite fine); to powder.

botona; *uski botona*, a cane bent for tongs.

botonoa, see *bitonoa*.

botonoli, see *bitonoli*.

botosha, buttoshah, v. a. i., to dazzle; to be overpowered by light; to be enfeebled; *nishkin botosha*, applied to the eyes of the aged; *iyi at botosha*, the leg is feeble.

botulli, n., filings; dust; small pieces; powder.

botullichi, see *botolichi*.

boyafa, boafa, pass., rubbed off, as the hair is rubbed from a hide; molted; *ikboafo*, a., unshed.

boyafa, v. a. i., to shed the hair, feathers, or coat; to molt; see *boyaffi*, trans. verb.

boyafa, n., the shedding of the hair.

boyali, pass. pl., rubbed off.

boyali, v. a. i. pl., to shed the hair.

boyali, n., the shedding of the hair.

boyalichi, v. t. pl., to rub the hair off from skins.

boyaffi, boaffi, v. t. sing., to rub the hair from a skin, as tanners dress hides when taking off the hair; to molt; *ileboaffi*, to shed his own hair or coat and horns, as a deer.

boyaffi, n., one who rubs the hair from a skin.

bufboli, v. a. i., to pant for breath, as a man in a fever.

buna, pass. pl., rolled up; doubled up.

buna, v. a. i., to roll up.

buna, n., rolls; bundles.

bunni, v. t. pl., to double up; to roll up; to fold up; *alhbona*, pass., doubled up.

bunto, n., a hill; a small hill; a barrow; a mound; a potato hill.

bunto, pass., made into a hill.

buntochi, v. t., to make hills for potatoes; to hill up the ground.

busha, pass., squeezed; wrung out; expressed; extracted.

busha hinla, a., expressible, i. e., can be squeezed out.

bushli, v. t., to squeeze out a liquid; to wring out water, as from wet clothes after being washed; to express; to extract; to press; to wring.

bushli, n., a wringer.

bushto, n., name of an oak which bears a large acorn.

bushul, n., a bushel.

bushul iklanna, n., a half bushel.

bushul iklanna iklanna, n., a peck, i. e., half of a half bushel.

buttoshah, see *botosha*.

butummi, n., fine drizzle; fine rain.

ch, see *chi*.

cha, conj., and, usually connects two verbs which have the same nominative; *itih han wakammi cha*, opened his mouth and, Matt. 5: 2; if the second verb has a different nom. from the first, *na* is often used. *Cha* is also used at the close of some questions, as John 1:50; Matt. 2:7, 8, 13, 14, 16; *haklo*

cha, Matt. 7: 24; *mali cha*, Matt. 7: 25; *haklo cha*, Matt. 7: 26; 17: 27; *chiyimmi hacha?* It seems to refer at times to something not looked for or expected; *fik api at bashit taha chá*, the fig tree is withered away, Matt. 21: 20. See *hacha*.

chachachi, v. i., to hop and flit like a bird.

chaha, n., height; altitude; grandeur; growth; loftiness; rankness; stature; a steep; steepness; sublimity; *hachi chaha*, your stature, Matt. 6: 27; *achahaka*, n., a high place, 1 Kings, 11: 7.

chaha, a., pp., high; lofty; tall; sublime; elevated; steep; eminent; grand; high, as to musical key; *sakti chaha*, a steep bluff, Matt. 5: 1; *nanih chaha yon*, a high hill.

chaha, v. n., to be high or lofty.

chaha, v. a. i., to tower.

chaha, chahat, adv., aloft; on high; stately.

chaha, pass., heightened; elevated; exalted; raised higher; raised.

chaha inshaht tali, a., uppermost; highest.

chaha inshali, a., upper; higher, Luke 14: 10.

chaha inshali nanih, n., an eminence; a mountain higher than (others).

chaha moma inshali, a., the highest, Luke 2: 14.

chahachi, v. t., to elevate; to raise up; to heighten; to enhance; to ennoble; to exalt; to raise; to sublimate; to sublime; to cause it to be higher.

chahachi, n., a raiser.

chahachi, n., a raising.

chahapi, chahe api, n., a hoe handle.

chahe, n., a hoe.

chahe aialhpi, chahe aiulhpi, n., a hoe handle.

chahe iskifa, n., a mattock; lit., a hoe ax.

chahikcheli, v. a. i., to limp.

chahikcheli, n., a limper.

chahikli, v. a. i., to limp.

chahikli, n., a limper.

Chahta, n., a Choctaw; Choctaw (pl.).

Chahta, a., Choctaw; *Chahta yakni*, Choctaw nation; *Chahta anumpa*, Choctaw language.

Chahta, v. n., to be a Choctaw.

Chahta anumpa, n., the Choctaw language; a Choctaw speech or word; the Choctaw tongue.

Chahta ạlla, Chahtạlla, a Choctaw child; Choctaw children.

Chahta hatak, n., a Choctaw man; Choctaw men.

Chahta iⁿkowi, n., a Choctaw mile.

Chahta imanumpa, n., the language of the Choctaw; the words of a Choctaw.

Chahta imisuba, n., the horse of a Choctaw.

Chahta isuba, n., a Choctaw horse; a Choctaw pony.

Chahta isht atia, v. n., to be descended from the Choctaw; to be of the Choctaw race.

Chahta isht ia, n., the Choctaw race; Choctaw descent; Choctaw origin; Choctaw blood.

Chahta ohoyo, n., a Choctaw woman.

Chahta okla, n., the Choctaw; Choctaw; the Choctaw nation; the Choctaw tribe; the Choctaw people.

Chahta yakni, n., Choctaw land; Choctaw nation; Choctaw country; Choctaw soil; Choctaw ground.

Chahtạlla, see *Chahta ạlla.*

chahto, n., a drought; dryness; want of rain.

chahto, a., dry; droughty; wanting in rain.

chahto, v. n., to be dry; to be droughty.

chahtochi, v. t., to cause a drought.

chahtoshba, a., never.

chaka, n., a comb; a gill; gills; the flaps that hang below the beak of a fowl; *inchaka,* his comb; his gills.

chakali, chakkạli, a., nine, 9, ix (numeral), Matt. 18: 12; 2 Sam. 24: 8; *hạshi chakkali,* nine months.

chakali, v. n., to be nine.

chakali, v. a. i., to make nine; as *echakali,* we make nine; *chakali bat chakali,* nine times nine.

chakali, chạkali, a., pregnant; gravid; great; bịg.

chakali, chạkali, v. n., to be pregnant; to be with child, Matt. 1: 23; v. a. i., to teem.

chakali, n., pregnancy.

chakaliha, adv., nine times.

chakapa, n., vile language; reviling; profaneness; the language made use of in the place of common swearing as in use among the lowest classes of white and black people.

chakapa, a., vile; low; vulgar; indecent; reproachful; filthy.

chakapa, v. a. i., v. t., to revile; to utter filthy language; to blackguard; to inveigh; to vilify.

chakapa, n., a reviler; one who utters foul language in contempt and reproach; a blackguard.

chakiffa, n., a gizzard; the gizzard.

chakkạli, see *chakali.*

chakla, n., an oyster.

chakli, n., a cup (authority, Nelson McCoy's mother, May 15, 1855); a vessel used for boiling coffee; a coffee pot; a tin coffee pot.

chakoa, pass., notched.

chakoa, n. pl., notches.

chakofa, pass., notched.

chakofa, n., a notch.

chakoffi, v. t. sing., to notch; to cut a notch.

chakoffi, n., a notcher.

chakoli, v. t., to string, as to string venison for drying.

chakoli, v. t. pl., to notch; to cut notches; *chakonli,* nasal form.

chakolichi, v. t. caus., to cut notches; to make notches; *chakonlichi,* see 1 Kings 6: 18; Exodus 31: 5.

chakowa, pass., strung up and dried; *isi nipi chakowa,* venison strung up and dried; *chakoⁿwa,* see 1 Kings 6: 29.

chakpa, a., being part way; not midway; *iti chakpa; nitak iⁿchakpa.*

chakpa, v. n., to be part way; to be not midway.

chakpaka, n., side, as of a well or cup.

chakpatali, n., the foot of a hill; the base of a hill; *chakpatali ka,* Luke 8: 33; Judg. 19: 1.

chakpatalika, n., the place at the foot of the hill; the foot of the hill.

chakwa, n., soreness in the throat; an ulcer in the throat; bronchitis.

chakwạbi, chakwaạbi, v. n., to have such a soreness.

chalaⁿka, v. a. i., to scream.

chalaⁿka, n., a scream.

chalakbi, see *chilakbi*.

chalakwa, see *chilakwa*.

chalantak, see *chilantak*.

Chalakki, n., a Cherokee; the Cherokee.

Chalakki, a., Cherokee.

Chalakki hatak, n., a Cherokee man; a Cherokee.

Chalakki okla, the Cherokee people; the Cherokee nation; the Cherokee.

chalak, n., a snap; the noise made by snapping a gunlock.

chalakachi, v. a. i., to snap; to say *chalak*.

chalakwa, chalakba, n., a copperhead snake.

cha^{n}lchaha; *aka^{n}ka at cha^{n}chaha*, the cackling of a hen after laying an egg.

chalek, a., possible, and known to both speaker and hearer; *chalek*, recent past time; -*k* is contracted from *kamo*; it may have been, Gen. 3: 1; it might have been; perhaps it was, and you and I knew it; *chi^{n}chuka onali chalek?* did I not go to your house (and you knew it)?

chali, v. n., to be possible, and something known to both speaker and hearer.

chali, v. a. i., to stride; to walk fast.

chali, a., fast; swift.

chali, n., a fast walker.

chalichi, v. t. caus., to cause to walk fast; to make him walk fast.

chalik, adv., possibly; perhaps; surely, and known (*chalek*, Gen. 3: 1, old translation; *hachimachi chalek*).

chalin, adv., possibly; probably; same as *chalek*, but referring to a more remote past time.

chamak, n., a clink.

chamakachi, chama^{n}kachi, v. a. i., to clink; to say *chamak*.

chamo, a., past, gone by and remotely; *kamo* and *kamo* express a time that is recent. These words can be translated by was, were, have been. *chamo* is used for renewed mention and indicates something seen or well known to the speaker; *yohmi chamo*, it was so. There is another mode of expressing the same idea, viz., *yohmin*, it was so, and I saw it; *lakoffi^{n}n*, he has recovered to my personal knowledge.

chamo, v. n., to be past.

chamo, adv., used after verbs, and not only qualifies them, but also indicates the remote past tense and that the thing spoken of was seen or well known to the speaker, as though he were an eye or ear witness; still *tok* is used by some speakers before *chamo*. See *kamo* and *kamo*.

champko, n., the shin.

champulachi, v. t., to sweeten; to honey.

champuli, n., sweetness; honey.

champuli, a., sweet; grateful to the taste; grateful to the heart; dulcet; luscious; saccharine.

champuli, v. n., to be sweet.

champuli, pp., sweetened.

champuli, n., sweetness; honey.

chanahachi, v. t. pl., to turn them around; to roll them over; to cause them to run around.

chanaia; *itachanaia*, v. a. i., to be two together alone, like an old man and woman at home alone.

chanakbi, v. n., to be crooked; see *chinakbi*.

chanakbichi, see *chinakbichi*.

chanashik, n., a large yellow wasp.

chanalli, v. a. i., to roll over; to move or run on wheels, as a wagon; to run; to roll; to turn; to turn over, as a wheel, not as a log (*tonoli*, to roll over as a log); *itachanalli*, to roll together.

chanalli, n. pl., a wheel; a circle.

chanalli, n., a rotation.

chanallichi, v. t., to roll; to turn it over; to wheel; *itachanallichi*, to roll them together.

chanichi, v. t. sing., to roll; to turn around; to cause to run round, as a wheel.

chanla, a., dry, as corn and hickory meats; dry and tough; cured.

chanli, v. t., to chop; to cut with an ax or hoe by striking; to gash; *chali*, subpositive, to peck; to hew; to strike with the teeth, as a venomous serpent; to chop (modern); to hurt; to pick; to slash; *cha^{n}heli*; *chanlit tablitok*, cut off, Mark 14: 47; *ilechanli*, to cut himself; *itinchanli*, to peck or to chop each other.

chanli, n., one who chops; a pecker; "a hewer," Josh. 9: 21.

chanlichi, v. t., to cause to chop.

chant, contracted from *chanlit*; the *t* has the force of the conj. and.

chant akkachi, v. t., to cut down or to chop and bring down; *chanlit akachi,* cut it down; Luke 13: 7.

chant kinaffi, v. t., to cut down; or to chop and fell.

chant lakot bakli, v. t., to score.

chant tapli, v. t., to cut off; to chop and sever; *chanlit tabli,* Mark 14: 47.

chant tushtuli, v. t., to hack, or to chop and cut up fine.

Chanueli, n., January.

chansa, chans, n., a sound in the ear; a tingle, 1 Sam. 8: 11; 2 Kings 21: 12.

chansa, a., shrill.

chansa, v. n., to be shrill.

chansa, v. a. i., to shrill; to utter an acute, piercing sound; to shriek; to tingle, as the ear. See 1 Sam. 3: 11.

chasaloha, v. n., to be crooked.

chasaloha, n., crooks; bends.

chasaloha, chassaloha, a., pl. of *chasola,* crooked; bent; having hollows or bends; pass., warped; *ikchasaloho,* unwarped.

chasalohachi, v. t. pl., to make them crooked, or to make crooks; to warp.

chasala, a., crooked; bent; having a hollow or bend; *wak nali chasala,* a crooked-back cow.

chasala, pass., warped; bent; *ikchasalo,* a., unwarped; unbent.

chasala, v. a. i., to warp; to bend; *itibasha at chasala,* the plank warps.

chasala, n., a bend; a crook; a warp.

chasalachi, v. t., to crook; to bend; to make crooked; to warp; *hashi at itibasha yan ontomi kat chasalachi,* the sun which shines on the plank warps it.

chasalla, v. n., to be crooked or bent.

chasalli, v. a. i., to glance off.

chasallichi, v. t., to turn it; to glance off.

chash, the said; the same, known to both speaker and hearer, and in remote past time; *chash* and its compounds are used as simple or compound relative pronouns in relation to subjects that are past; it may be called a personal pronoun in the remote past tense; *kash* and *kash* (q. v.) refer to the immediate past tense; *chash* signifies the same which; the said; late, known to both speaker and hearer; a renewed mention particle; *oh chash,* it is the said; being "the said"; used in calling

the dead to mind; or in speaking of them, instead of mentioning their names. Compounds: *chashinli,* the same also which was; compounded of *chash* and *inli,* same, also—*chashket* the same that was; that which; *alichashket,* that is what I said but recently, and you know it; it is in the nom. case; *ket* may be formed from *kat* or it may be from *ke* and *t,* like *kesh* from *ke* and *sh*—*chashkia,* even the same which was, and you knew it—*chashkint,* the same which was, but more remote than *chash ket,* in the nom. case—*chashon,* the same which; the said one (in the obj. case); see grammar for these particles or article pronouns — *chashocha* — *chashoka*—*chashokako* — *chashokakosh* — *chashokano* —*chashokat* — *chashokato* — *chashoke* — *chashokia*—*chashoma*—*chashona*—*chashosh*—*chashot.*

chasha, chasha, n.; *inchasha,* his rattles; *sintulo inchasha,* the rattles of the rattle snake.

chashahachechi, v. t., to make him rattle; to rattle.

chansha, v. a. i., to rattle, like a rattlesnake.

chashahachi, v. t. pl., to rustle; to rattle, as the rattlesnake; *sintulo at chashahachi,* the rattlesnake rattles.

chashaiyi, v. a. i., to be round and elevated, as a mound.

chashak, n., a rustling; a rattling—a single motion.

chashakachi, v. a. i. sing., to rustle once; it says *chashak.*

chashakachi, n., a rattling; a rustling.

chashampik, n., a grindstone (called also *tal ashuahchi* and *tashika*).

chashana, v. a. i., to hang over and own as the skirts of a common coat.

chashana, a., having skirts that hang down; hanging over and down, as *na foka chashana,* a coat.

chashanachi, v. t., to cause to hang over.

chashap, n., a variety of grasshopper.

chashlichi, v. t., to rattle; to make a rustling noise.

chanshpo (a Sixtowns word), a., former; ancient; of things, or time: *nitak chanshpo,* a former day; future, like *tikba;* first in order.

chaⁿshpo, v. n., to be ancient, or of former times.

chaⁿshpo, adv., formerly; anciently; before; former time; in ancient times; "before time," Josh. 11: 10; 14: 15.

chato, chatoh, adv.; in *okishko chatoh.*

chatok, adv., commonly; usually; always; ever. This form implies also the remote past tense. The particles which are used after *tok* are used after *chatok*, generally. In the past tense *chatok* may be rendered, has been usually, always has been, etc.; *chatuk* and *chatok* are often used with verbs to express general truths or common usage, custom, etc., and when used in reference to persons it is implied that they are alive. For the dead, *bekatok* is used instead of *chatok; ishla chatoko?* did you ever come here? *alali chatok keyu*, I never came here.

chatok, v. n., to have been always so; to have been usually so; was so always; *tok* is the sign of the remote past tense and not connected with the present.

chatoshba, adv., never.

chatoshba, v. n., never to be so.

chatoshke, in *hash yamohmi chatoshke*, page 130, Chahta Holisso Atukla.

chatuk, adv., usually has been and still is, etc.; commonly; usually. This word differs from the other, *chatok*, only in the last syllable and means the immediate past tense and up to the present time, John 2: 10; Matt. 5: 21; 6: 2, 5; 17: 25; *ehahaklo chatukokat*, Josh. 2: 10. "*bilia*" is used for always— Matt. 3: 10; 12: 4, 33; 18: 12; *chatukatok*, Matt. 27: 15. *chatuk keyu*, adv., never has been; never was; never has; ne'er; Josh. 3: 4.

chauala, a., slim; tall and slender, applied to the figure of a horse; *issuba hat chauala*, the horse is tall and slender.

chawana, a., crooked.

chawana, v. n., to be crooked.

chawana, n., a crook; a hook.

chaⁿya, pass., cut; chopped; gashed; pecked, Matt. 3: 10; *ikchayo*, a., unwounded; unchopped.

chaⁿya, n., a gash.

chaⁿyat pashaⁿfa, n., a gash made by an ax.

chabbi, v. t., to dip into oil, honey, or grease.

chabiha, a., a few; some; scarce.

chabiha, v. n., to be a few, some, scarce; *chabiha keyu*, not scarce.

chabiha, n., a scarcity.

chabiha keyu, n., no want; no scarcity.

chabihachi, v. t., to render scarce; to make a few or a small number.

chabihasi, dim. a., a very few; a few.

chabihasi, v. n., to be a very few.

chabli, n., dry bark.

chach, n., a church, Matt. 18: 17.

chafa, v. a. i. sing., to run; to flee; *chaⁿfa, chahaⁿfa, chaiyafa; chahaⁿfa*, 2 Sam. 24: 13.

chafa, pp., fled; banished; chased away; exiled; expelled.

chafa, n., a runner; an exile; a flier.

chafa, n., a flight.

chafali (from *achafa*), v. t., to make one; to do one; to one; *kana kia ikimikshokma inchafalashke*, if there is any one who has none, give one to him, Luke 3: 11.

chafichi, chaffichi, v. t., caus. (from *chafa*), to send off, Matt. 11: 10; 15: 23; to cause to flee; to drive off; to banish; to exile; to expatriate; to expel; to rouse; to run; to rid; to spring, Mark, 12: 3, 4, 5, 6; to send men, Josh. 2: 1; *achaffichi*, to send from, Josh. 14: 7.

chafichi, n., a sender; a driver.

chakali, chakali (q. v.), a., pregnant.

chakbi, n., a projection beyond surrounding objects; an overplus; a continuation; *chakchubi*, pl.

chakchak, n., a small speckled woodpecker with a red head.

chalhchakachechi, v. t., to cause them to shine, sparkle, twinkle, etc.

chalhchakachi, v. a. i. pl., to shine; to glisten; to sparkle, as particles of oil on the surface of warm water; to twinkle as the stars; to scintillate.

chalhchakachi, n., a twinkling; a shining.

chalhchaki, v. a. i. sing., to sparkle.

chalhchaki, n., a spark, a sparkling.

chalhpi, see *akchalhpi.*

chalabakko, n., name of a fish of the sucker genus.

chalakachi, v. a. i., to rattle.

chalakchi, n., a rattling.

chamakachi, v. a. i., to clank; to rattle; to ring; *asonak at chamakachi*, the kettle rattles or rings.

chamakachi, n., clank; ringing; din; noise; clangor.

chamalichi, v. t., to clank; to make din or clangor.

champoa, see *chimpoa*.

chanafila, shanafila, n., black haw; a haw.

chanaha, v. a. i., to turn round; to roll over; to coil; to curl; to roll, as the wheel of a carriage; to round; to wheel.

chanaha, n., a wheel; a circle; a coil; a felly; a ring; a round; roundness; *aseta chanaha*, a coil of rope.

chanaha, v. t., to coil up, as a serpent; to querl; to turn.

chanaha, a., rotund; coiled up; round; being in a circle; orbed; pass., rolled; *ikchanaho*, a., uncoiled.

chanaha folota achafa, n., a square; a circuit.

chanaha holitopa, n., a hack.

chanaha iklanna, n., a semicircle.

chanahachi, v. t., to coil; to roll; to round.

chanal, n., a general (from the English).

channi, pp. sing., probably from *chanichi*, (q. v.).

channichi, v. t., to roll a wheel.

chassaloha, see *chasaloha*.

chassalohachi, see *chasalohachi*.

chasha, chasha (q. v.), n., *inchasha*, his rattles; those of the rattlesnake.

chashanoha, v. a. i., to be long tailed, like some coats.

chashwa, n., sinews of the loins; *inchashwa*, his sinews of the loins.

chashwa nipi, n., the flesh of the loins; the loin; the tenderloin; *inchashwa*, his sinews of the loins; *inchashwa nipi*, n., his loin.

chechik, adv., probably; likely; perhaps.

chechik, v. n., to be likely, or probable.

chechike, adv., probably; spoken by way of inquiry and in modesty.

chechike, v. n., to be probable.

chechuk, adv., probably; expressing a supposition.

cheki, a., speedy; quick; near; late; recent.

cheki, v. n., to be near, etc.

cheki, adv., soon; immediately; newly; quickly; recently; *chekikma*, in a short time, i. e., when it is soon, from *cheki* and *kma*.

chekichi, v. t., to cause it to be soon; to hurry.

chekikash, adv., lately. See *kash*, late, recently.

chekikash, v. n., to be lately, in reference to things past.

chekusi, a., very near; immediate; soon; used in reference to the future; a diminutive formed from *cheki* and *usi* or *ushi*.

chekusi, v. n., to be very near in time, or soon.

chekusi, adv., very soon, immediately; forthwith; quickly, Josh. 2:5; straight; shortly; straightway; thereupon.

chekusi fehna, adv., quickly, Josh. 8:19.

chekusi kania, a., transitory; passing away very soon.

chekusi ont ia, a., transient; passing by very soon.

chekusikash, adv., latterly; recently.

chekusikma, v. n. sub. mood, when it shall have been a short time.

chekusikma, adv., in a short time; after a short time.

chelahpi, n., the animal which has young for the first time, as heifers, etc.

chelahpi, n., the firstling; the first produce or offspring, Gen. 4:4; from *cheli* and *ahpi*, the first, as *tofahpi*, spring, lit. the first of summer; *tikba attahpi*, the first born, Rom. 8:29.

cheli, v. t., to bear; to bring forth young, applied to animals and some plants and not to the human species; to cub; to foal; to teem; to whelp; to lay; to calve; to pig; to spawn; to kid; to breed; to blow; to deposit eggs, as flies; to bear, as vines; *okchaⁿk at cheli*, the muskmelon bears; *shukshi at cheli*, the watermelon bears; *isito at cheli*, the pumpkin bears; to draw interest, as money lent out; *tali holisso at cheli*, the money bears interest.

cheli, v. a. i., to propagate; *oncheli*, v. t., to prime a gun; to lay on the powder; pass., *onchiⁿya*.

cheli, n., parturition.

cheli, n., a breeder; the female that breeds or produces.

cheli imponna, a., prolific; skilled in bearing.

chelichi, v. t., to cause to bear or breed; to cause to bring interest; to put out on interest; *achelichi hosh akhoyo cho?* Luke 19: 23. See also Matt. 25: 27, where *ushi* is used for interest or usury.

Chelusalim, Chilusalim, n., Jerusalem.

chepulechi, v. t., to make a feast, banquet, festival; to dance; to feast; *impa chito ikbi* is used in the New Testament translation.

chepulli, n., a feast; a great feast; a banquet; a frolic; a great dance; an Indian feast or a heathen feast.

chepulli, v. a. i., to attend a feast; to feast and to dance; to frolic.

chepullit aⁿsha, v. a. i., to have a feast; to be at a feast.

chetoma, adv., for *chintoma*, in the future; see *tuma*.

chi, ch, pro., thou, nom. case 2d per. sing. of neuter verbs. *chinukshopa na*, Luke 1: 13; *chilbasha*, thou art poor; *chilli*, thou diest.

chi, ch, thou, nom. case 2d per. sing. of passive verbs, as *chinala*, thou art wounded.

chi, ch, thee in the obj. case before active transitive verbs; *chipesali*, I see thee; *chithanali*, I know thee; cf. *chitikba*, before thee, Matt. 11: 10.

chi, is prefixed to nouns of near relation or family interest; *chitekchi*, Matt. 1: 20. It is applied to the family dog, *chipaf*.

chi, ch, poss. pro., thy; prefixed (with a few exceptions) to the names of the body and most of its members, as *chichuⁿkash*, thy heart; *chibbak*, thy hand.

chi, a diminutive, in *kapasachi*, coolish; *hochukwachi*, chilly.

chi, sign of the causal form, meaning to cause, to make, to render; as *minti*, to come; *mintichi*, to cause to come, etc. *chi* is also suffixed to adjectives, etc., as *kallo*, a., strong, hard; *kallochi*, to make it hard or strong; to harden; *Saimon Ba Chona chia hat na chiyukpashke*, Blessed art thou Simon Bar-Jonah, Matt. 16: 17. *chi* is also suffixed to adjectives, verbs, and adverbs to make v. t. in the caus. form. *chumpa*, *chumpachi*; *kallo*, *kallochi*; *fehna*, *fehna-*

chi. It is a "particle of form" or the causative form of verbs.

chi, a suffix to verbs, which take the locatives *a* or *ai;* others make a new form of verbs, where one thing is made to act on or with another; *onush ash haiyuⁿkpolo yoⁿ ant ahokchichi tok*, Matt. 13: 25; Judg. 16: 13.

chiⁿ, thy and thine, prefixed poss. pro., meaning "thy," prefixed to nouns that do not begin with a vowel or the consonants *p*, *ch*, *l*, *t*. See *chim* and *chin*. *chiⁿholisso*, thy book; *chiⁿhatak*, thy husband; *chiⁿhina*, thy way, Matt. 11: 10.

chiⁿ, prefixed per. pro. in the dative case before verbs, and usually translated with a prep., as, of thee, to thee, for thee, from thee, against thee. It is found before verbs which do not begin with a vowel or *p*, *ch*, *l*, or *t*. See *chim*, which is written before vowels and diphthongs.

chiⁿ, 2d per. sing., poss., thine, thy, removed from the noun in the nom. and placed before the verb, as *tali holisso chiⁿhotina*, he has counted your money, instead of *chintali holisso hotina*.

chiⁿ, achiⁿ, sign of the immediate future tense of the indicative mood, shall, will; *achiⁿ* is the true form; the final vowel of the verb is dropped when *achiⁿ* is suffixed, as *chumpa*, *chumpachiⁿ*, he shall buy; *minti*, *mintachiⁿ*, he shall come; *haklo*, *haklachiⁿ*, he shall hear.

chia, sub. pro., 2d per. sing.; thou; thee; *chia ma*, Matt. 1: 20; *chia hokₐ*, Matt. 5: 22; 7: 5; *Kapenaam chia*, thou Capernaum, Matt. 11: 23; *chia hoⁿ*, thou art, Matt. 16: 14; *Pita chia*, thou art Peter, Matt. 16: 18; *chia ma*, O thou, Matt. 14: 31; *chia hoⁿ*, Matt. 14: 33; *chiama*, Matt. 15: 22; *chishno akosh saso aⁿholitopa chia hoke*, Luke 3: 22; *chishno akoⁿ nan isht achia saiyukpa makoke*, Luke, 3: 22; *na hollo chiahoke*, thou art a white man. It is now called a substantive personal pronoun, as the verb *to be* is used in translating it, thus *chia*, thou art, *sia*, I am. *Lewi ushi chia ma;* Matt. 1: 20; *Chihowa ushi chia hokmat*, Matt. 4: 3; *chiashke*, from *chia*, thou art, John 1: 49; *Chihowa ushi chiashke*, thou art the Son of God.

chiashke, see *chiⁿshki*.

chibak, chibuk, n., a noise, such as is
made by the falling of a stone into
water.

chibakachi, chibukachi, v. a. i., to
make a noise; to say *chibak.*

chibaⁿko, n., the shin.—J. E.

chibokachi, v. a. i., to work, as a liquid;
to ferment, etc.

chibolichi, see *chobolichi.*

chiⁿchint, adv., will not; can not.

chichoⁿli, v. a. i., to be coarse grained or
gritted, like a grindstone.

chiffoko, see Josh. 8: 28; 10: 27; *chiffon-
kot,* a heap of rubbish; *chiffokohonchi,*
2 Kings 19: 25.

chihakli, see *chilukli.*

Chihowa, n., Jehovah; the Scripture
name of the Supreme Being; Deity;
God; Judge; the Supreme Being; *Chi-
howa achafa kia tuchina, Iⁿki, Ushi, Shilombish holitopa,* n., the Trinity.

Chihowa aiasha, n., the throne of Jehovah; the dwelling place of Jehovah.

Chihowa aiokpachi, v. t., to worship
Jehovah; *nanakia abit Chihowa isht aiokpachi,* v. t., to immolate.

Chihowa aiokpachi, n., a worshiper of
Jehovah.

Chihowa aiokpachi, n., the worship of
Jehovah.

Chihowa apiliechika, n., the kingdom
of Jehovah.

Chihowa abanumpa, n., divinity; theology; the revelation from God.

Chihowa chitokaka, n., the Lord God,
or the God Jehovah.

Chihowa hobachi, n., an idol; an image
of God used in idol worship.

Chihowa hobachit ikbi, v. t., to deify;
to make an image of God.

Chihowa hobachit ikbit aiokpachi, n.,
an idolater.

Chihowa ikimantio, n., impiety; ungodliness.

Chihowa ikimantio, a., impious; ungodly.

Chihowa imantia, v. t., to obey Jehovah.

Chihowa imanumpa alhpisa pokoli, n.,
the decalogue; the ten commandments
of Jehovah.

Chihowa inchukfalhpo yushi, n., the
Lamb of God, John 1: 29.

Chihowa iⁿyimmi keyu, n., impiety.

Chihowa pallammi, Chihowa palammi, the Almighty God.

Chihowa ushi, n., the Son of God.

chiishke, chishke, v. n., to be likely;
to be probable; *onatok chishke:* Ch. Sk.,
p. 12, sec. 6.

chik, likely to be so, as *iala chik,* probably
I shall go.

chik, used for *ish; chiksiataklammi hoh
kia,* Judg. 13: 15; *chik aⁿya kia,* Luke
9: 57; Matt. 8: 19.

chik, thou, pro. 2d per. sing. of the neg.
verbal form, as *chikono,* thou dost not
go to it.

chiⁿka, v. a. i., to squeal; *shukha yat
chiⁿka,* the hog squeals.

chiⁿka, n., a squealer.

chikchik, n., a small species of wren;
a small wren; *okchiloha* is the name of
the common wren.

chikchikechi, v. t., to make spotted or
speckled.

chikchiki, pass., speckled; spotted with
small spots; freckled.

chikchiki, n., small spots; small check;
a freckle; freckles.

chike, v. n., to be hereafter; as, it will
be so; it may be so; *kucha kapassa chiⁿ-
ke,* there will be cold weather.

chiⁿke, n., thy father, Matt. 15: 4.

chikfikowa, see *itukfikowa.*

chikiⁿha, v. t., to jog with the hand,
elbow, or foot; to peck like a hen.

chikiⁿha, n., a jog; a slight blow.

chikihah, v. a. i., to be thick and close
together, like corn or piles of manure.

chikimba, v. n., not to be so; to be mistaken; it is a mistake.

chikimba, adv., no; not.

chikinoha, see *kinoha.*

chikisana, a., bent; twisted; having a
twisted neck, or one bent sideways.

chikisana, v. n., to be bent or twisted;
to have a twisted neck.

chikisanali, a., bent; twisted; crooked;
having a twisted or crooked neck.

chikisanali, v. n., to be bent, twisted, or
crooked.

chikki (an old word), a., old; past; gone
by; middling old; partly worn.

chikki, v. n., to be old.

chikkichi, v. t. caus., to make old.

chiksanakli, sing., to dodge, or bend the body suddenly; see *halakli, kanakli, shalakli.*

chiksanali, a., bent; inclined to one side, like a crooked neck.

chiksanalli, v. a. i., to bend one's self; to incline.

chila^nk, n., a scream.

chila^nkachi, v. a. i., to scream.

chilakbi, chalakbi, a., hard; dry and stiff, as a dry hide.

chilakbi, v. n., to be dry; to be stiff, as a hide or leather.

chilakbi, v. a. i., to stiffen.

chilakbi, pass., dried; stiffened; starched.

chilakbi, n., stiffness.

chilakbichi, v. t., to stiffen; to harden; to dry; to starch; to size thread.

chilakchawa, n., a common wart.

chilakto, chulakto, a., forked; split; cloven; *iyi chilakto,* a forked foot; a cloven foot.

chilakto, v. n., to be forked; to be cloven.

chilaktochi, v. t., to split; to cleave; to make forked.

chilakwa, chalakwa n., the smallpox; a pock; *hashtap inchilakwa,* chicken pox.

chilakwa abi, a., sick with the smallpox.

chilakwa abi, v. n., to be attacked by the smallpox; to have the smallpox; *chilakwa sabi,* I have the smallpox; n., cancer.

chilantak, chalantak, n., the small red-headed woodpecker.

chilantakoba, n., the pelican, or a bird resembling the *chilantak.*

chila^nwa, halanchilawa, n., a lizard.

chiletalli, chilitalli, v. t., to inflame; to animate.

chilhpatha, chilhpata api, n., the Spanish oak.

chililli, v. a. 1., to provoke.

chiliswa, n., the measles.

chiliswa abi, a., sick with the measles; attacked with the measles.

chiliswa abi, v. n., to be attacked with the measles; to have the measles; to be sick with the measles.

chilita, n., keenness; resolution; spunk.

chilita, a., fierce; ardent; zealous; resolute; brave; animated; doughty; intent; keen; masculine; rude; sharp; spirited; strenuous; urgent, Josh. 1:14.

chilita, v. n., to be fierce, zealous, ardent, brave.

chilita, pass., inflamed; animated; provoked.

chilitachi, v. t., to animate; to inflame; to make zealous; to provoke.

chilitalli, see *chiletalli.*

chilofa, chiloffi (q. v.), v. t., to pay; to liquidate.

chilofa, n., payment.

chilofa, v. a. i., to fall; to drop, as leaves from a tree, or as crumbs, Matt. 15:27.

chilofa, pass., fallen; paid, as a debt; *ikchilofo,* a., unpaid; unliquidated.

chilofa, n., the falling; a falling.

chilofachi, v. t., to cause to fall; to cause to pay.

chiloffi, v. t., to pay; to recompense; see *chilofa.*

chiloha (see *okchiloha*), n., a wren.

chilosa, chulosa, a., still; quiet; calmed; calm.

chilosa, chulusa, v. n., to be still, quiet, calm; *chulusat talaiatok,* Luke 8:24.

chilosa, chulosa, n., a calm; a quiet.

chilosachi, v. t., to make a calm; to quiet; to calm.

chilpitha, n., name of a tree.

chiluk, chuluk, n. sing., a hole; a cavity; a hollow; a pit; an eye, as the eye of a needle; a chasm; a chink; hollowness; a leak; an orifice; a vent; it is usually applied to a cavity or hollow and not to a hole through anything, for which other words are used, as *lukafa, lu^na, lumpa* (q. v.).

chiluk, a., hollow; having a hole, as *iti chiluk,* a hollow tree; *chula puta kat chiluk at ima^nsha,* foxes have holes; *aboha chiluk,* an empty house.

chiluk chukoa, v. a. i., to hole; to enter a hole.

chiluk ikbi, v. t., to hole; to make a hole.

chiluk iksho, a., tight.

chiluk toba, v. t., to chink; to open and form a fissure.

chilukka, chiluka, v. t., to shell, as corn.

chilukka, pass., shelled.

chilukoa, pl., having holes; hollow; broken.

chilukoa, n. pl., holes; pits.

Chilusalim, Chelusalim, n., Jerusalem, Matt. 2:1; 3:5.

Chilusalim hatak, n., a man of Jerusalem; a Jerusalemite.

Chilusalim okla, n., the people of Jerusalem; *Chelusalem okla moma aiena*, all Jerusalem with him, Matt. 2: 3.

chilafa, v. a. i., to peel up, as the skin of boiled potatoes; *nishkin at chilafa*, to open the eyes wildly, like sick people; applied also to the eye of an untamed horse.

chilakba, chilakwa, chalakwa, chalakba, n., the name of a serpent called a copperhead. The best form is *chilakba*, in the Oklafalaia dialect.

chilanli, n., the scrofula; the king's evil; struma.

chilanli, v. a. i., to have the king's evil; scrofula.

chilanlichi, achilanlichi, v. t. caus., to cause the king's evil; to cause a hard swelling.

chilichi, in *luak isht chilichi*, to make fire sparkle.

chilina, n. sing., a bruise of the flesh; numbness from pain.

chilina, pass., bruised in the flesh.

chilinanchi, v. t., to make the cords swell.

chilinoha, n. pl., great numbness or pain.

chilukli, chihakli, v. a. i., to limp; see *chahikli*.

chim, dative pro., 2d per. sing. in the dat. case before a noun beginning with a vowel, as *chimisuba*, your horse, or, a horse for you; *chimanumpa han imalituk oke*, I have given them thy word, John 17: 14; Luke 7: 44. See *chin* and *chin*, thy.

chim, dative per. pro., 2d per. sing. before verbs beginning with a vowel, and to be rendered with a prep., as, of thee, for thee, to thee, from thee, as *chimia*, *chimona*, he goes for you or to you; *chimanoli*, he tells you; *ano at chimanyali makoke*, I come to thee, John 17: 11; *chimaiyamohmashke*, be it unto thee, Matt. 15: 28.

chim, dative pro., 2d per. sing., before a neuter verb formed from an adjective and one which begins with a vowel, as *chimokpulo*, thou art angry, or there is bad to thee, or there is evil with thee; this mode of expression is like "thou;" *inhollo*, he loves it; it is dear to him;

or he is stingy; *inholitopa*, he loves it, or it is sacred to him, etc.

chim, dative pro., used before neuter verbs and where the pro. is not found with the noun, as *allat chimilli*, your child is dead; the child for thee is dead.

chimmi, pro. a. and pass. pro., thine; thy.

chimmi, v. n., to be thine, as *chimmi*, it is thine; *chimmi hokma*, when it is for thee, Matt. 17: 4; John 17: 10.

chimmitoba, v. a. i., to become thine; *chimmihashke* in last translation, Luke 4: 7.

chimpoa, champoa, v. a. i. pl., to be small.

chin, thy; thine; dative pro., 2d per. sing., before nouns beginning with the letters *ch*, *l*, and *t*, as *chinchuka*, thy house; *chintakkon*, thy peach; see *chin* and *chim*.

chin, dative pro., before words beginning with the letters *ch*, *l*, *t;* it is 2d per. sing. and is usually to be rendered with a prep. as of thee, for thee, to thee, from thee; as *chinchumpa*, to buy of thee, or for thee, or from thee; *apat chintali*, they have eaten it all up for thee.

chin, thine; poss. pro., found before some verbs, chiefly neuter, when not before the noun in the nom. case, as *tanchi at chintaha* instead of *chintanchi at taha*.

chin, see *chint*.

chinachubi, pl., *chinakbi*, sing., a., hooked; crooked.

chinachubi, v. n., to be hooked; to be crooked.

chinachubi, n. pl., hooks; crooks.

chinachubichi, v. t., to make them crooked.

chinakbi, chanakbi, a. sing., hooked; crooked.

chinakbi, v. n., to be crooked.

chinakbi, n., a crook; a hook; Ex. 27: 11; hooks.

chinakbichi, chanakbichi, v. t., to make it crooked; to make a hook or crook; to hook.

chini, achini, v. n., to seem so; to appear so (when not before known).

chini, adv., apparently; seemingly; *iksho chini; achini* (q. v.) has a different meaning.

chinifa, chenafa, n., a small piece; a bit.

chini{}^{n}ffa, pass., pinched; chinowa, p. pl.

chiniffi, v. t. sing., to pinch with the fingers, but not with any instrument; to pick; chinoli, pl.

chiniffi, n., a pincher; one who pinches.

chiniffi, n., a pinch.

chinisa, a., brindled; striped.

chinisa, v. n., to be brindled or striped.

chinisa, n., a small ground squirrel; a chipmunk.

chinoli, v. t. pl., to pinch; to nibble; to pick.

chinowa, pass. pl., pinched.

chinowa, n., a pinching.

chint, chin, adv., not; okpanachi{}^{n} chint, he will not destroy it; a{}^{n}li chint, hope it is not true.

Chintail, n., a Gentile; Gentiles, Luke 2: 32; oklushi taloha puta, all nations.

Chintail, a., Gentile, Matt. 18: 17.

Chintail hatak, n., a Gentile, Matt. 18: 17.

Chintail okla, n., Gentiles.

chintok (more remote in time), should have been; should be; was about to be; about to have been.

chintuk (less remote in time), should have been; was about to be; about to have been.

chinuko, see chunoko.

chipinta, chipunta, a. pl., very small; very fine; fine; naku{}^{n}shi chipinta, very fine shot.

chipinta, v. n., to be very small.

chipinta, chipunta, n., small ones; chipunta ilappa, Luke 17: 2.

chipintasi, n., particles.

chipintasi, a. dim., quite small; from chipinta and asi.

chipintasi, v. n., to be quite small.

chipintachi, v. t. caus. pl., to render them quite small.

chipota, n. pl., young children; little ones, Matt. 10: 42; 18: 10, 14; children (of Ammon), Josh. 12: 2; anchipota aliha ma, oh, my young children.

chipota, a., small.

chipunta, nasal form, being small; hushi chipunta, sparrows, Matt. 10: 29; alla chipunta, children, Matt. 2: 16; alla chipunta, little children, Mark 10: 14; nani chipunta, little, Matt. 15: 34; 18: 3

chisa, n., name of a tree; perhaps it should be written chisha, and is thus a post oak.

chi{}^{n}sa, n., name of a small bird, one kind of sparrow.

Chisas, Jesus, Matt. 7: 28; Chisas ashosh, Matt. 8: 20.

Chisas Kilaist, Chisas Klaist, n., the name of our Saviour, Mark 1: 1.

Chisas Kilaist imanumpeshi, n., an apostle of Jesus Christ.

Chisas Kilaist inanisht alhpisa, n., a sacrament; an ordinance of Jesus Christ.

Chisas Kilaist isht anumpuli, n., an evangelist.

chisbi, v. a. i. sing., to extend; to stretch; to be continued in length.

chisbi, pass., stretched out; extended in a line.

chisbichi, v. t., to extend; to stretch; to draw out in length.

chisemo, v. a. i. sing., to stretch the limbs, or the body; to yawn.

chisemo, pass., stretched out.

chisemoa, v. a. i. pl., to stretch the limbs or the body.

chisemoa, pass., stretched; extended.

chisemochi, v. t., to extend; to stretch another; to cause to stretch; chibbak a{}^{n} chisemochi, stretch forth thine hand! Matt. 12: 13; chisemochi, stretch forth thine hand, Mark 3: 5.

chisemoli, v. t. pl., to stretch.

chiskilik, n., a blackjack, name of a variety of oak.

chiso, n., thy son, from iso, son; chiso ilappat, this thy son, Luke 15: 30; saso, my son, Luke 15: 31.

chisoha, chusoha, v. a. i., to rattle; to make a noise; tali yosh chisoha yoke, the iron rattles.

chisoha, n., a rattling.

chisohachi, chusohachi, v. t., to rattle; to make it rattle.

chisohachi, n., a rattler.

chisha, n., a post-oak tree and its acorn.

chishaiyi, n., a grasshopper that sings in the night.

chishakko (see itichishakko), n., an arbor; a bush arbor; also see ahoshontika.

chishba, v. n., to be doubtful; kaniohmachi{}^{n} chishba, it is doubtful how it will be. This is often translated "I don't know," and is used in that sense.

chishba, a., doubtful; unknown; uncertain; perhaps.

chishba, adv., possibly and possibly not; perhaps so, and perhaps not so.

chishinto, v. a. i., to be round and elevated, like a mound. See *chashaiyi*.

chinshka, n., an infant girl; a babe; a baby.

chinshka keyu, n., an infant boy. This expression and the above were used in the southern part of the nation.

chishke, n., thy mother, Matt. 15: 4.

chishke, see *chiishke*.

chinshki, chiashki, v. n., to be probable; used at the end of another verb, as *yohmi chishke*, it is probable that it was so; *keyu chishke*, Matt. 12: 7; *okpula chishke*, it will be foul, Matt. 16: 23.

chinshki, adv., probably, will be.

chishno, pro., 2d per. sing., thou, Josh. 1: 2; *chishno ato*, Luke 7: 45, 46; thou, Matt. 6: 17; *chishno akosh*, Matt. 14: 33; *chishno at*, thou, Matt. 16: 18; *chishno, akon chimmi*, for thee. *chishno*, ob. c., thee; *chishno an*, Matt. 3: 14; *chishno chinishkin*, thy eye, Matt. 7: 4; 17:27; *chishno*, poss. pro., thine, thy; *chishno akinli*, thyself; yourself; *chishno yokan*, thine, in the obj. case; *chishno yokat*, thine, in the nom. case.

chito (subpos. forms, *chito, chitto, chehto, chinto*); *hochito*, pl., n., size; greatness; enlargement; the extent; fullness; grandeur; growth; largeness; loudness; magnitude; majesty; scope; splendor; sublimity; *chito fehna*, n., vastness.

chito (subpos. forms, *chitto, chehto*), a., great, Matt. 13: 50; large; big; huge; immense; heavy; capacious; august; egregious; enormous; extensive; gigantic; grand; grievous; gross; handsome; heavy; high, as a price; immense; lusty; majestic; massive; mighty; noble; profuse (as *laksha chito*); prominent; protuberant; signal; capacious; splendid; stocky; stout; sublime; superb; *chitto*; a diminutive of *chito*, less than *chito*, in music, low, base, grave; *chieto*, pro. form of a.; *chito fehna*, a., herculean; prodigious; thick, as hair, cane, etc.; tremendous; unwieldy; vast; *ikchito*, a., scant; not great.

chito, v. n., to be large, *chinhohchifo chinto ka*, thy great name, Josh 7: 9; *chinto*, nasal form *na chiyimmi kat chintoshke* (thy path) excels or is great (greater than others), Matt. 15: 20; *okla chinto*, Matt. 4: 25; 5: 1; *yammat chinto*, Matt. 6: 23; of great, Matt. 13: 46; *chintoshke*, great is, Matt. 15: 28; *chihinto*, freq.; *chieto*, pro. form.

chito, pass., made large; enlarged; distended; *chinto*, nasal form, being made large; the large one; cf., Matt. 2: 17, 18.

chito, adv., largely; profusely; thickly.

chitochi, v. t., to enlarge.

chitokaka, n., a prince; a great one.

chitokaka, n., a lord; sir; God, Luke 1: 25; John 4: 1; majesty; excellency; honor; the great one, Matt. 7: 21 (*chitokaka ma*, Lord); 11: 25; 14: 28.

chitoli, a., loud; hard; large; stentorian.

chitoli, v. a. i., to swell; to enlarge; to increase, as a storm of rain.

chitoli, v. t., to enlarge; to make louder or larger; to do on a large scale; to dilate; to distend; to elevate; to rage; to stretch; to swell, Josh. 6: 5; pl. *hochetoli*.

chitolichi, v. t., to enhance; to enlarge; to magnify.

chitolit, adv., hard; loudly; as *chitolit umba*, it rains hard.

chitolit fiopa, v. a. i., to sigh; to breathe loud.

chitolit fiopa, n., a sigh; also, a sigher.

chitot (a contraction of *chitolit*), adv., greatly; nobly.

chitot anumpuli, v. a. i., to rant.

chitot anumpuli, n., a ranter.

chitot fiopa, v. a. i., to heave; to sigh; to puff; to wheeze.

chitot ia, v. a. i., to grow large; to enlarge; to rise; to thrive.

chitot ishko, chitot nalli, v. t., to swig, to drink largely; to swallow largely.

chitot nanabli, v. t., to quaff.

chitot nanabli, n., a quaffer.

chitot ola, chitot ola hinla, a., sonorous.

chiya, chiyya, v. a. i. pl. pass., from *cheli*, v. t. (q. v.). It is applied to persons and things and signifies to sit; to lie. Some say that *chiya* is strictly dual, but it is not always thus used. It implies that the sitting is for a time, like seated on a bench, as a court; to stop and sit down, not expecting to leave soon; *itachiya, to sit together; chi*ⁿ*ya*, nasal form, Josh. 3: 2; 7: 21; *pinchiyashke*, Luke 9: 13; *chihįⁿya*, freq.; *chieya, chiyeya*, pro. form.

chiya, v. n., to be seated.

chiyuhmi, see *chohmi*.

chiyuhmichi, see *chohmichi*.

cho, ha; sign of a question and having an adverbial meaning also, like eh! in English, Matt. 2: 2; 18: 1; Luke 3: 12; *cho* implies ignorance in those who inquire. It implies a question and a demand for an answer. It is a strong interrogative word; *impa cho?* Matt. 9: 11; compounds are *yakohmichicho?* John 2: 18; *akcho? akchuba?* or *akchu?* (which last is said to be a contracted form of (*ak*)*chuba*), see Luke 7: 19, 20; *hassiachi cho?* Luke 6: 46. *akchu*ⁿ*? nanta chi*ⁿ *cho?* Matt. 11: 3; *akcho* is used in disjunctive forms of interrogation, or, Matt. 11: 3; 1 Kings 20: 15; 2 Sam. 24: 13; *choba, chuba*, or *chomba*, is the perfect form of the word; it is used in asking questions where there is an alternative.

chobilhkạn, chobilhkạsh, n., chips.

chobohạchi, v. a. i., to ripple; to roar, as the running water of a stream.

chobohạchi, n., a roaring of water.

chobokạchi, chibokạchi, v. a. i., to bubble, as water.

chobokạchi, chibokạchi, n., the bubbling of water.

chobolichi, chibolichi, v. t., to rinse; to shake up; to shake, as water is shaken in a keg or cream in a churn when producing butter.

chohmi, chuhmi, a., like; similar; somewhat; such; tolerable; *choyuhmi, chiyuhmi*, Luke 6: 10.

chohmi, v. n., to be like; to be similar; to be as, Matt. 5: 16; 6: 29; *chohmitok*, it was like, Matt. 12: 13; *chohmi hoke*, is like Matt. 13: 44, 46; to be so, Matt. 3: 17; *yạmmakinli ho*ⁿ *chohmit*, even so, Matt. 7: 17; *choyuhmi, chiyuhmi*, pro.; *chiyuhmashke*, Matt. 5: 48; *hạshchiyuhmi*, Matt. 10: 16; *chiyuhmi hoke*, Luke 6: 48, 49; *chiyuhmi ma*, Matt. 17: 2; 18: 3, 4.

chohmi, chiyuhmi, choyuhmi, v. a. i., to do like; to act like; *chiyuhmi*, to become as, Josh. 7: 5; Matt. 10: 16.

chohmi, adv., somewhat; in some degree; measurably; moderately; in a limited degree; to some extent; partly; partially; hardly; like; pretty; scarcely; tolerably; *achukma chohmi, kapạssa chohmi*.

chohmichi, choyuhmichi, chiyuhmichi, v. t., caus., to make it like; to cause it to resemble in some respects; to do as, 1 Kings 10: 27; Josh. 1: 15; *ilechoyuhmichi, ilechohmichi*, to make yourself like, Luke 10: 27; to make as if or to feign, Josh. 8: 15.

chohpa, n., the meat provided for a pole pulling or Choctaw funeral which is observed at the end of the days of mourning; meat cured and dried; venison dried.

chokạmo (for *kạmo*, see under letter *k*), adv., always; usually; connected with verbs when general customs, habits, truths are expressed, see *chatok; hakloli chokạmo*, I always have heard it.

chokạmo, a., usual; wont; the said; the definite known one; *cho* has the sense of *cha* in *chatuk*.

chokạsh, a. and rel. pro., in past tense; the said who was always, John 6: 42; *Ilạppạt a*ⁿ*shat nana asihi*ⁿ*ła chokạsh mako*ⁿ *keyu?* "Is not this he that sat and begged?" John 9: 8; *hạshachi chokạsh ohcho?* who ye say was, John 9: 19; *chokạsh o*ⁿ, Luke 7: 32 [?]; *ikchokạsh osh* 2 Sam. 7: 6.

chokạshosh, etc., see *kash*.

choⁿ**ki, chu**ⁿ**ki**, n., martin, a bird of a particular kind.

chomi, a., such; like; and so on; and so forth, or others of the kind; like the et cetera taken from Latin in use among the English.

chopa, v. a. i., to roar, as falling water at a cascade.

chopilhkạsh, chupilhkạsh, n., chips; trash; a dunghill, 1 Sam. 2: 8; dung, Phil. 3: 8.

chopiłak, chupiłak, n., a swallow; a chimney swallow.

chowa, a., displeased; offended; see *achowa; itachowa*, 1 Tim. 3: 3.

chowa, v. n., to be displeased; to be of- fended, Luke 7: 23.

chowa, v. a. i., to differ, as *itachowa*, to dispute; to differ with each other.

choyuhmi, see *chohmi.*

choyuhmichi, see *chohmi.*

Chu, n., a Jew, the Jews.

Chu, a., Jewish.

Chu chepuli chito, n., the Passover, the great Jewish feast; a great Jewish feast.

Chu hatak, n., a Jew; a Hebrew; an Israelite.

Chu ohoyo, n., a Jewess.

Chu okla, n., the Jewish nation; the Jewish people; Jews; *Chu okla i^{n}mi^{n}ko,* King of the Jews, Matt. 2: 2.

Chu okla imabohahanta, n., a Jewish synagogue; a Jewish temple.

Chu yakni, n., Judea; Palestine; the Jewish country.

chuala, n., a cedar.

chubuk, n., sound of a bell.

chufak, n., a nail; a spike; an awl; a rowel; the little wheel of a spur; a fork.

chufak ahokli, chufak aholhpi, chu- fak aiulhpi, n., an awl haft; an awl handle.

chufak chipinta, n. pl., tacks; brads; small nails.

chufak chito, n., a spike; a large nail.

chufak chito isht ahonạla, pp., spiked; nailed with big nails.

chufak chito isht ahonạlichi, v. t., to spike.

chufak falakto, n., a forked nail; an iron fork; a fork.

chufak ikbi, n., a nailer.

chufak isht ahonạla, n., a hammer; a nail hammer.

chufak isht bili, chufak isht impa, n., a table fork. The common name is *chufak.*—Capt. Shoni.

chufak iyạlhfoa, chufak iyafoa, n., a spur.

chufak nan isht achunli, n., a needle; a sewing needle.

chufak nishkin, n., the eye of a needle; a needle's eye.

chufak nishkin a^{n}sha, chufak ushi nishkin a^{n}sha, n., a needle; the son of a nail that has an eye.

chufak nishkin lopulli achạfa, n., a needleful.

chufak nushkobo chito, n., a hob nail.

chufak ush ikbi, n., a pin maker; a needle maker.

chufak ushi, n., a pin; son of a nail; a tack; a pin; a needle; a small nail; a brad.

chufak ushi ashamoli, chufakush a- shamoli, n., a pin cushion.

chufak ushi shuekạchi, pp., unpinned.

chufak ushi shueli, v. t., to unpin.

chufak wishakchi, n., the point of a needle.

chufak wushạla, n., the tine of a fork.

chufak yushkoboli, n., a pin with a head, such as are used by females for fastening their clothes.

chufak yushkololi, n., a tack; a short nail; *chufak yushkolushi,* n. pl., tacks.

chuhmi, see *chohmi.*

chuk, sign of future imp. tense.

chuka, chukka, n., a house; a building; a dwelling; a domicile; a cabin; an abode; a residence; a seat; a home, Matt. 8: 6; a nest; a den; the hole or the abode of animals; a dome; an edi- fice; a habitation; housing; a mansion; a mansion house; a structure; a tene- ment; *chi^{n}chuka,* thy house, Matt. 9: 6; *chuka yo^n,* an house, Matt. 10: 12; 7: 24, 25, 26, 27; *inchuka kak illa hoh chatuk oke,* Matt. 13: 57; *itinchuka,* v. t., to keep house together; *itinchukali,* n., my husband, or my housemate, but usually uttered by the woman.

chuka, v. a. i., to house or live; *achukạt ahanta,* Josh. 2: 15.

chuka abaiya, chukabaiya, n., a vaga- bond; a vagrant; one that wanders from house to house.

chuka abaiya, a., vagrant.

chuka abaiya, v. n., to be vagrant; to wander or go from house to house.

chuka abaiyạchi, v. t., to act as a vaga- bond; to go from house to house; *chuka abaiyạchit hạchikitanowokashke,* go not from house to house! Luke 10: 7.

chuka abaiyạt nowa, v. a. i., to gad abou

chuka abaiyạt nowa, n., a gadder; a gadabout.

chuka abili^{n}ka, n., a neighbor, Josh. 9: 16; 20: 5.

chuka achạfa ahalaia, a., domestic, per- taining to a family.

chuka achąfa, chukachąfa, n., a family; a household; a house, Luke 1: 27.

chuka afoha, n., an inn; a tavern; a hotel; a house of rest.

chuka afoha hatak, n., a host; an innkeeper.

chuka afoha iⁿhikia, chuka afoha intalaia, n., a taverner; an innholder; one to whom stands a house of rest.

chuka aholitopa, n., a sanctuary, or a sacred house.

chuka aiitola, n., the site of a house; the foundation of a house.

chuka aiontąla, n., the foundation of a house; the underpinning.

chuka akinli ashąna, a., homespun; spun in the house itself.

chuka akinli atoba, a., home made; made in the house itself.

chuka anusi, n., a hotel; an inn; a house of sleep, or where they sleep.

chuka apanta, n., a neighbor; an adjoining house; chuka panta hatak, John 9; 8; Matt. 5: 43.

chuka apanta aⁿsha, n., neighbors, Luke 1: 58.

chuka apantali, n., an adjoining house; a neighbor.

chuka apąlli, chukapąlli, pl., in iⁿchukapąlli, his neighbors.

chuⁿka aⁿsha, a., homebred.

chuka aⁿsha, v. a. i., to be at home; to sit at home.

chuka chaha, n., a tower; a high house.

chuka chukoa, v. a. i., to enter a house; to house.

chuka foka, pass., housed; inchuka foka, cooped; put in his house.

chuka foki, v. t., to house; inchuka foki, to coop; to put in his house.

chuka hanta, n., a council house; a state house; a senate house; a house of peace and friendship; a white house; the capitol; a temple.

chuka hukmi, v. t., to burn a house; inla inchuka hukmi, v. t., to burn the house of another; n., an incendiary.

chuka ikbi, n., a carpenter, Matt. 13: 55; see chukikbi.

chuka impalata, a., homesick; longing for home.

chuka impalata, v. n., to be homesick, or he is homesick; chuka ampalata, I am homesick.

chuka impalata, n., homesickness.

chuka ishi kanchąk, n., a witch; a hobgoblin.

chuka isht ąlhpolosa, n., mortar for a house; daubing for a house.

chuka isht holmo, n., the roof of a house; shingles for a house; covering for a house.

chuka isht holmo ąli, n., the eaves.

chuka isht holmo ibitahaka, n., the eaves.

chuka itabana, n., the sides of a house.

chuka itabana, n., a log house.

chuka itabąnni, n., a house raising.

chuka itontąla, n., a story in a building.

chuka ituksita, n., a dooryard.

chuka lukonli, n., a number of houses near each other; a neighborhood; a settlement.

chuka limishki, n., a framed house.

chuka na chokushpa, n., the furniture of a house; household furniture.

chuka naksika, n., the side of the house.

chuka osapa, n., homestead; the house field.

chuka patali, v. t., to massacre.

chuka pąllit aⁿya, chuka pulalit aⁿya, v. a. i., to saunter; to act the vagabond.

chuka pila, adv., homeward; homewards; toward the house.

chuka pulalit aⁿya, chuka pulalit nowa, n., a saunterer; a vagabond.

chukabaiya, see chuka abaiya.

chukachąfa, n., a family; a house; a household; lit. one house, Matt. 10: 6; 15: 24; Josh. 7: 14; see chuka achąfa.

chukachąfa abinili, n., a few; a seat for a single family.

chukachąfa isht atia, n., a house lineage, Luke 1: 27, 33.

chukachąfa nan isht ątta, n., a steward.

chukachąfa pelicheka, n., a householder; the ruler of a house; a housekeeper.

chukachąfa pelichi, n., a housekeeper, a householder, Matt. 13: 27.

chukafa, pp., plucked out; pulled out.

chukafoha ohoyo, n., a hostess; a woman who keeps an inn.

chukah, in *tahchukah*, indeed; something unlooked for by the speaker; from *tah*, an adverb in the recent past tense; *ishtatahchukah* or *tohchukah*, same but in the remote past tense.

chukalaha, n., the present made in food to a visitor.

chukalahachi, v. t., to go in search of a present in food; to obtain food as a present.

chukalahachi, n., a visitor who comes for food.

chukali, chukli, v. t., pp., pl., plucked out; pulled out, as grass or hair; to pluck out, etc.; see *chukaffi*.

chukalichi, v. t. caus., to make him pull out, or to pull out from another.

chukanakbila, see *hachukbilankbila*.

chukani, n., the common house fly; the green-headed fly that blows meat, etc.

chukanicheli, v. t., to fly blow.

chukanushi, n., a fly-blow; a maggot.

chukanushi ansha, pp., fly-blown.

chukanushi laua, a., maggoty.

chukapanta, chuka apanta (q. v.), n., a neighbor; *chuka palli*, pl.

chukapalli, see *chuka apalli*.

chukapishia, n., an old-fashioned house built with upright logs, and having a shed all around it; a porch, Matt. 26:71.

chukashana, n., a houselock.

chukashaya, v. a. i., not to come out even, in folding a handkerchief; *itachukashaya*, to cross each other, as bridle reins when crossed.

chukachi, a., mad.

chukaffi, v. t. sing., to pluck out; to pull out; *chukli*, pl.

chukaffi, n., a plucker.

chukalbaska, n., the ribs of a house, or roof.

chunkash, n., the heart; the center; the stomach; the feelings; the affections; spirits; conscience; pluck; the reins; spirit; temper; disposition; a grain; *chunkash akon aminti*, Matt. 15: 18, 19; *chunkash yohbi*, *chunkash akanlosi*, the person; himself, Matt. 11: 29; *chunkash anunkaka okla ahnitok*, think or say within themselves, Matt. 9: 3; *yakni chunkash*, heart of the earth, Matt. 12:

40; *okla ilappa chunkash*, this people's heart; *chunkash okato*, their heart, Matt. 15: 8; *inchunkash*, his or her heart; *imichunkash* (I once heard this form used.—Byington).

chunkash achukma, n., a good heart; grace.

chunkash akkanlusechi, v. t., to daunt; to sink the spirits; to depress; to humble.

chunkash akkanlusi, n., melancholy; a depressed heart or spirits; humility.

chunkash akkanlusi, v. a. i., to despond.

chunkash akkanlusi, pass., daunted; spirits sunk; depressed; humbled.

chunkash akkanlusi, a., lowly, Matt. 11: 29.

chunkash akkanlusi keyu, a., unhumbled.

chunkash anli, n., a pure heart; a true heart; a sincere heart; an honest heart; sincerity.

chunkash apa, n., animalculæ from which mosquitoes grow, called wiggletails.

chunkash banna, v. a. i., to wish for with the heart; the heart desires.

chunkash bila, pp., piqued.

chunkash bili, v. t., to pique.

chunkash chaha, a., high minded; high hearted.

chunkash chaha, v. a. i., to be high minded.

chunkash chumpa, v. t., to bribe; to buy the heart.

chunkash halupa, a., high tempered; angry; having quick feelings.

chunkash halupa, v. n., to be high tempered.

chunkash himmona, n., a renewed heart; a new heart; regeneration.

chunkash himmona, pp., regenerated; having the heart renewed.

chunkash himmona, a., regenerate; having a new heart.

chunkash himmonachi, v. t., to renew the heart; to regenerate.

chunkash homi, n., a bitter heart; bitterness of heart; a venomous temper; fire; gall.

chunkash homi, a., fervent; fiery.

chunkash hominchi, v. t., to envenom; to embitter the heart.

chunkash hutupa, n., a wounded heart; an offended spirit.

chu^{n}kash hutupa, pp., insulted; offended.

chu^{n}kash hutupali, v. t., to affront; to wound the feelings; to insult; to offend.

chu^{n}kash hutupali, n., an offender.

chu^{n}kash ia, v. a. i., to desire; the heart goes; to wish for.

chu^{n}kash ikhotopo, a., unwounded; unoffended.

chu^{n}kash iknakno, n., a hypochondriac; a dispirited person.

chu^{n}kash illi, a., disheartened.

chu^{n}kash illichi, v. t., to dishearten.

chu^{n}kash imanukfila, n., the affections of the heart; the thoughts of the heart.

chu^{n}kash imanukfila achukma, n., charity.

chu^{n}kash imanukfila nukoa, n., resentment.

chu^{n}kash inla, a., alienated; another heart, generally used in a bad sense; iti^{n}chu^{n}kash inlah, shaken in mind.

chu^{n}kash inla, v. n., to be alienated.

chu^{n}kash inlachi, v. t., to shake the purpose; to change the mind or the affections.

chu^{n}kash ishahinla, a., impressive; can take the heart.

chu^{n}kash ishi, v. t., to seize the heart; to captivate; to overcome; to rap; to touch the feelings; to charm; to steal the affections; to gain or get the affections; to fascinate.

chu^{n}kash ishi, n., rapture; a spell.

chu^{n}kash kapassa, a., cold-hearted; insensible.

chu^{n}kash kallo, a., flint-hearted; hard-hearted; headstrong; obstinate.

chu^{n}kash kallo, n., hardness of heart; obstinacy; sangfroid.

chu^{n}kash lua, v. a. i., to burn; to be inflamed with passion.

chu^{n}kash lua, n., heartburn.

chu^{n}kash nakni, n., hardihood; bravery; boldness of spirit.

chu^{n}kash nala, n., a wounded heart.

chu^{n}kash nala, pp., piqued; offended.

chu^{n}kash nali, v. t., to pique; to offend.

chu^{n}kash okpani, v. t., to demoralize; to injure the heart.

chu^{n}kash okpulo, n., a bad heart.

chu^{n}kash okpulo, pp., demoralized; ruined in heart.

chu^{n}kash shanaiachi, v. t., to wean the affections; to pervert the heart.

chu^{n}kash tuklo, n., a double dealer.

chu^{n}kash tuklo, a., double-hearted.

chu^{n}kash walwaki, a., tender-hearted.

chu^{n}kash weki, n., gravity.

chu^{n}kash weki, a., grave-minded.

chu^{n}kash yiminta, a.; hearty; zealous; fierce-minded.

chu^{n}kash yohbi, n., a serene heart; a subdued heart; a sanctified mind; clemency; meekness; righteousness.

chu^{n}kash yohbi, a., clement; as hatak chu^{n}kash yohbi, a clement man, or a man of clemency; clever; familiar; holy; meek, Matt. 11: 29.

chu^{n}kash yohbichi, v. t., to subdue the heart; to sanctify the heart.

chu^{n}kash yukachi, v. t., to fascinate; to captivate the heart.

chu^{n}kash yukpa, n., cheer; a joyful heart; consolation.

chu^{n}kash yukpa atapa, n., ecstasy; overgladness of heart.

chu^{n}kash yukpali, v. t., to console; to feast; to rejoice the heart.

chukbaiyachi, v. t., to act the vagabond.

chukbaiyachi, n., a vagabond; a vagrant.

chukbi, n., the corner; the inside corner; the lee; chukbeli, pl., corners, Rev. 7: 1.

chukbika, n., the corner; the place occupied as a corner, Mark 12: 10, 11; corner of a sea, Josh. 18: 14.

chukbilaklak, see chukkilakbila.

chu^{n}kcho, n., a fishhawk.

chukchu n., a maple; a soft maple, the most common kind among the Choctaw.

chukchu chito, chukchu imoshi, n., hard maple or big maple.

chukchu hapi champuli, n., maple sugar.

chukchua, pass., tickled.

chukchua, n., a tickling.

chukchuki, v. a. i., to be spotted, like cattle; see chikchiki.

chukchulli, v. t., to tickle.

chukchulli, n., a tickler.

chukfaluma, n., a cony burrow.

chukfalhpoba (Matt. 7: 15; 15: 24; 18: 12), chukfi alhpoba (John 10: 1, 3, 7; Matt. 12: 11, 12) chukfalhpowa, chukfi alhpowa, n., a sheep; lit. a domesticated rabbit. This form of expression is used sometimes for the sake of distinguishing the sheep from the rabbit; *chukfi ạlhpoba yoⁿ*, the sheep, Matt. 10: 16.

chukfạlhpowa apistikeli, chukfạlhpoba apesạchi, n., a shepherd, John 10: 11.

chukfạlhpowa hishi, n., wool.

chukfạlhpowa iⁿhollihta, n., a sheepfold, John 10: 1.

chukfạlhpowa nakni, n., a ram; a buck.

chukfạlhpowa nipi, n., mutton; the flesh of sheep.

chukfạlhpowa tek, n., a ewe.

chukfạlhpoyushi, chukfi ạlhpowaushi, chukfushi, n., a lamb.

chukfi, n., a sheep, or a rabbit which is the first definition as sheep have not been long known among the Choctaw; a cony.

chukfi aiasha, n., a sheepfold.

chukfi apesạchi, n., a shepherd.

chukfi apistikeli, n., a shepherd.

chukfi ạlhpowaushi, see *chukfạlhpoyushi*.

chukfi hakshup, n., a sheepskin.

chukfi hishi, n., wool; sheep wool.

chukfi hishi ạlmo, n., a fleece.

chukfi hishi ạlmo, pp., fleeced.

chukfi hishi ạmo, v. t., to fleece; to shear off wool; to shear sheep.

chukfi hishi ạmo, n., a shearer; a sheep shearer, Acts 8: 32.

chukfi hishi itapana achạfa, n., one hank of woolen yarn.

chukfi hishi nan tạnna, n., flannel; woolen cloth; cloth made of wool.

chukfi hishi nan tạnna aiskiachi, n., a clothier.

chukfi hishi shạna, n., woolen yarn.

chukfi hishi shạpo, n., a felt; a hat made of wool; a wool hat.

chukfi hishi tạnna, n., flannel; woolen cloth; woven wool.

chukfi imaseta, n., the vine which grows and adheres to the bark of trees, having a trumpet-shaped blossom. It is said to be good in dysentery.

chukfi isht abeka, n., the rot; a disease among sheep; a fatal distemper incident to sheep.

chukfi luma, n., a rabbit.

chukfi nakni, n., a ram; a buck; the male of the sheep; Joshua 6: 4, 5, 6, 8, 13.

chukfi nishkin, n., a painful, obstinate ulcer which comes on the foot or leg; stone bruise on the thick muscles.

chukfi pạttakạta nakni, n., a buck; the male of the hare.

chukfi pạttakita, chukfi pạttakạta, n., a hare.

chukfi tek, n., a ewe.

chukfi yoba, n., the cramp in the hand.

chukfikoa, nukfichoa (q. v.), n., the hiccough or hickup.

chukfikoa, v. a. i., to have the hiccough; to hiccough.

chukfikoli, v. t., to cause the hiccough.

chukfikolichi, v. t., to make him hiccough.

chukfikpelo, n., the northeast.

chukfikpelo, a., northeast.

chukfitohtoloḥ, n., a viper; "a ground rattlesnake."

chukfoba, a. (from *chukfi* and *holba*, like), sheepish; like a sheep.

chukfoba, v. n., to be sheepish.

chukfoloha, a., dizzy; drunk; giddy.

chukfoloha, v. n., to be dizzy; to be drunk.

chukfoloha, v. a. i., to stagger; to reel; to swim in the head.

chukfoloha, n., dizziness; the vertigo; giddiness; the staggers.

chukfulli, chukfolli, chukfolulli, v. t., to stagger; to make dizzy; to cause to swim; to cause to reel.

chukfulli, a., dizzy; drunk.

chukfushi, n., a lamb; a young rabbit.

chukfushi holba, a., lamblike.

chukfushicheli, v. t., to lamb; to bring forth a lamb.

chuⁿki, see *choⁿki*.

chukikbi, n., a house maker; a house wright; a joiner.

chukillissa, n., a deserted house; an empty house; a vacant house; solitude.

chukillissa, a., desert; vacant; empty, as a house that stands vacant; desolate; waste; *hạchinchuka yạt hạchinchukillissạt taiyaha*, Matt. 23: 38.

chukillissa, chukilissa (from *chuka* and *ilissa*), v. t., to desert a house or houses that are their own; *ikchukillissa*, Acts 1: 20.

chukillissa, n., those who desert their house.

chukillissa, pp., desolated.

chukillissachi, v. t., to cause to desert the house; to make another leave his house; to desolate; to depopulate.

chukillissachi, n., a destroyer; one who causes others to leave their homes.

chukimma, adv., homeward, homewards.

chukimpata, n., a piazza.

chukka, see chuka.

chukkilakbila, chukkilakpila, chukkila^npila, hachukbila^nkbila (q. v.), chukbilaklak (Ch. Sp. Book, p. 55), n., the whip-poor-will.

chukli, v. t. pl., to pluck out; to pull up, as hair or grass, with the hands; chukali, pp.; chukoffi, sing; see chukali.

chukli, n., a plucker; one that plucks.

chukłampulli, hachukłampuli (q. v.), tukłampuli, n., a cobweb; an air thread; a spider's web; a spider's nest.

chukma, a., good; well; healthy. This is usually written achukma.

chukma, v. n., to be good, well, healthy, agreeable; iksanchukmo, I am not well; ikinchukmo, he is not well, Matt. 4: 23; haknip ikinchukmo; inchukma, he is well.

chukoa, chukowa, v. t., to enter; to go in; to come in; to thrust, Matt. 5: 20; 7: 21; 8: 5; 12: 4, 9; 13: 2; 17: 25; 18: 3, 8, 9; Josh. 1: 11; 8: 19; Luke 2: 27; 4: 16; ikchukoo ahni, v. t., to admit; to permit to enter; isht chukoa, v. t., to carry in, Luke 4: 1; to take into; to obtrude; ant chukowa, to come under, Matt. 8: 8; to come in, Josh. 6: 1; chukoyua, pro form; ibachukoa, v. t., to invade; to enter with another; v. a. i., to obtrude; achukowa, n., an entrance, Josh. 8: 29.

chukoa, n., an entrance.

chukoa, n., an enterer; one who enters.

chukokhisa, n., a house door.

chukowa hinla, a., penetrable.

chukowahe keyu, a., impenetrable.

chukpalali, v. a. i., to shine dimly, as on a cloudy day.

chukpalantak, hachukpalantak, n., a tree toad.

chukulbi, n., a nook or point of land lying in the bend of a creek or in a fork between two creeks; bok chukulbi, the fork of creeks; achukulbi, united; companionship; communications, 1 Cor. 15: 33.

chukushi, n., a small house; a cot; a cottage; a hut.

chukushi abeli, v. t., to hut.

chukushmi, n., a desert; chukushmi foka ya^n, John 6: 31.

chukushmi, a., sandy, sandish; yakni chukushmi, sandy land.

chukushpa, a., small; i^nna chukushpa, "their stuff;" Josh. 7: 11.

chukushpa a., slanderous.

chukushpali, v. t., to amuse.

chukyiweta, chukyuata, v. a. i., to loathe; to feel sick at the stomach.

chukyiweta, chukyuata, a., loathsome.

chula, n.; a fox; chula puta kat, the foxes, Matt. 8: 20.

chula aiabi, n., a fox trap.

chula hishi, n., fox fur; fox hair.

chula holilabi, n., a mad fox; a rabid fox.

chula isht abeka, n., a diarrhea; a looseness; a more modest way of speaking than ikfia.

chula nakni, n., the male fox.

chula tasembo, n., a mad fox; a rabid fox; a raving fox.

chula tek, n., the female fox.

chula ushi, chulushi, n., a young fox; a cub.

chulahtu^nsh, n., a small variety of mushroom.

Chulai, n., July.

chulakto, chilakto (q. v.), a., forked; cloven.

chulaktochi, v. t., to fork; to cleave.

chulabi, n., a fox hunter.

chulhah, v. a. i., to say chulh; to rumble, as the bowels.

chulhkan, n., a spider.

chulhkan inchuka, n., a spider's nest; a spider's web.

chulosa, chilosa, a., calm; quiet; still; hush; mum; peaceful; quiescent.

chulosa, v. n., to be calm; to be quiet; to be still.

chulosa, v. a. i., to become calm, quiet, still, silent; 1 Sam. 2: 9; to assuage; to calm; to lull; to moderate; to subside; chulusat talaiatok, Luke 8: 24.

chulosa, pass., becalmed; allayed; quieted; appeased; hushed; lulled; moderated; stilled; unruffled.

chulosa, n., moderation; peace; quiet; quietness; silence.

chulosachi, v. t., to quiet; to still; to allay; to appease; to hush; to lull; to moderate; to silence.

chulosachi, n., a calmer; a quieter; a luller.

chuluk, chiluk (q. v.), n., a hole; a pit; a cavity.

chulushi, see chula ushi.

chula, v. a. i. pl., to split; to shiver.

chula, pass., split; riven; slit; cut; marked; surveyed, as land; laid off; shivered.

chula, n., that which is split; strands.

chulafa, v. a. i. sing., to split off a piece; to rive.

chulafa, pass., split; riven.

chulafa, n., that which is split; a piece split off; a splinter; a shiver; a slit.

chulali, v. a. i. pl., to splinter; to shiver.

chulata, v. a. i. sing., to split; to scantle.

chulata, pp., split; slit; rived; riven; split off from another piece; chulanta, nasal form, being slit or rived.

chulata, n., a slit; a piece that is split off; a shred; a slip; a strand; a slit in the ear.

chulaffi, v. t. sing., to split off a piece; to splinter; to cut off a piece (not to tear it off).

chulaffi, n., a splitter.

chulalli, v. t., to split off a piece; to slit; to shred.

chulalli, n., a splitter.

chuli, v. t. pl., to rive; to slit; to cut out, as cloth when a garment is cut; to shred; to subdivide; to lay off land into sections or smaller portions; to survey; yakni achuli, to survey the land; iti aⁿ chuli, to slit up the wood; nantanna yaⁿ chuli, to cut up the cloth.

chuli, n., a splitter; a river; a slitter, etc.; shivering.

chuloli, chulullih, to drip; chulohonli; chulohonlit aba yakni.

chulotah, v. a. i., to fly, as a spark.

chumaⁿko, n., the shin.

chumba, choba, adv., consequently, said in anger by a child; chumba ialachiⁿ, so I will be off; see cho.

chumpa, v. t., to buy and pay with cash at the time and not with a promise of cash; to purchase; to redeem; to shop; to negotiate; to ransom; he buyeth, Matt. 13: 44, 46; ilimpa chumpat tamaha ilhkoli, John 4: 8; okla achumpashke, they shall buy there, Matt. 14: 15; isht chumpa, to buy with, Rev. 5: 9, 10; chumpat pifalaminchi, Gal. 3: 13; chuhpa, subpositive form; chuhopa, immediate future form, to buy now; ilechumpa, to buy himself; to redeem himself; chohumpa, freq.; choyumpa, pro.; ikchumpo, a., unbought.

chumpa, n., a buyer; a purchaser; a redeemer.

chumpa, n., a purchase.

chumpa hinla, a., purchasable.

chumpa hinla, a., venal.

chumpahe keyu, a., irredeemable.

chumpachi, v. t., to cause to buy; to make him buy.

chunasha, n., a moccasin snake.

chuncho, n., a bird of some kind.

Chuni, n., June.

chunna, a., lean; poor; spare; low in flesh; meager; raw-boned.

chunna, pass., emaciated.

chunna, v. n., to be lean, poor, etc.

chunna, v. a. i., to emaciate; to fall away.

chunna, n., leanness; poorness.

chunnachi, v. t., to make lean, poor, etc.

chunnat ia, v. a. i., to waste; to wither.

chunukabi, n., the pleurisy.

chunukabi, a., sick with the pleurisy.

chunukabi, v. n., to be sick with the pleurisy; to have the pleurisy; chunuko sabi, I have the pleurisy; chinuko chibi, thou hast the pleurisy.

chunuko, chunoko, chinuko, n., the side below the armpit; the pleura; chinuko foka akoⁿ, Rev. 1: 13.

chunuko takchi, v. t., to lace the chest; isht takchi hosh hikiatok, Rev. 1: 13.

chunuko talakchi, pass., strait-laced.

chunuli, a., bowed down; bowed together.

chunuli, v. n., to be bowed; to be bent double, Luke 13 :11; chunohonli, freq.

chupilhkash, chopilhkash (q. v.), n., chips; trash; sweepings.

chupilhkash isht piha, n., a rake; a chip rake.

chupilak, chopilak (q. v.), n., a chimney swallow.

chuⁿsa, chiⁿsa, n., a sparrow.

chuⁿsa, n., neck of a junk bottle.

chuⁿsa, v. a. i., to be pointed or tapering; smaller at one end than at the other.

chusoha, chisoha (q. v.), v. a. i., to rattle.

chusoha, chisoha, n., a rattling.

chusohạchi, chisohạchi (q. v.), to rattle; to make it rattle; to purl.

chusokạchi, v. a. i., to chink.

chusolichi, v. t., to chink.

chusopa, v. a. i., to rattle, as chains.

chusopa, n., a rattling.

chusopa, a., rattling; tạli chusopa, rattling iron; a trace chain.

chusopạchi, v. t., to cause it to rattle.

chushak, n., the back side of the neck next to the shoulders.

chushak hishi, n., the mane.

chushak hishi aⁿsha, a., maned; having a mane.

chushak hishi kạllo, n., bristles.

chuⁿshkiksho, a., peevish.

chushukli, iachushukli, v. a. i., to be lame.

chushukli, a.', lame.

e prefixed per. pro. 1st per. pl. of active verbs beginning with consonants, as chanli, to chop; echanli, we chop; ehạchimolachi, ehạchiⁿyaiya, Matt. 11: 17.

ebi, we kill; 1st per. pl. irreg., from ạbi.

echi, v. t., used only in the imp., hand; give; put this way into the hand; see auechi; isht echi, v. a. i., to begin, Luke 24: 27.

eha, ehah, int., oh dear! heigh! heigh ho!

ehehe, int., la; alas.

eho, prefixed, per. pro. 1st per. inclusive, pl. of active verbs, beginning with consonants, as ehochanli, we all chop; ehofokachiⁿ cho? shall we put on? Matt. 6: 31.

eka; in yakni paknak eka; see aika.

ela, we come (from ạla to arrive), 1st per. pl. irreg.

elefant, n., elephant; elefant noti, n., ivory, 1 Kings 10: 18.

elli, a., grievous; from illi.

ema, we give; 1st per. pl. irreg., from ima, to give (q. v.).

emo, we pick; we trim; 1st per. pl. irreg., from ạmo, to pick, to trim.

enchil, n., angel; the English word written in Choctaw; yạmmakoka imenchil, their angels, Matt. 18: 10; enchil okla, angels, Luke 2: 15.

epa, we eat, 1st per. pl. irreg., from ạpa, to eat.

Eplil, Epilil, n., April.

eshi, v. t., to take, from ishi (q. v.); eshitok, 1 Sam. 2: 21. This is nothing more than an intensive of ishi, requiring more time for the action: ishi, to take; eshi, to hold.

eshi, n., parturition.

eshichi, caus., to cause to take; ạla eshi, to travail, "to have a child," 1 Sam. 4: 19.

et, adv. this way, i. e., toward or in the direction of the speaker, but not up to him; auet. (q. v.) means quite to the speaker.

fabaspoa, a. pl., long and slender.

fabaspoa, v. n., to be long and slender.

fabạsfoa, a. pl., long and slender; slim.

fabạssa, fobạssa, a. sing., long and slender; slim.

fabạssa, v. n., to be long and slender; to be slim.

fabạssạchi, v. t., to make it long and slender.

fabạssạt itonla, v. a. i., to lie prostrate.

fabạssoa, a. pl., long and slender; slim.

fabạssoa, v. n., to be long and slender.

fachachi, v. t. pl., to throw with a stick, which is done by holding a stick and pressing the lower end of it against an object on the ground and then making the stick spring suddenly, whereby the object is thrown; fachali, v. t. sing.; facholi, pl.

fachama, pp. sing., thrown by a stick, as described under fachachi.

fachamoa, pp. pl., thrown by a stick, etc.

fachamoli, v. t. pl., to throw by springing a stick, as above.

fachanli, fichanli (q. v.), fạchanli, v. a. i., to peel up, as bark on a tree, or to scale; to open; to crack open; to burst open, as a bur or pod; to scale, Deut. 28: 27.

fachanli, n., peeling up; the act of peeling; a crack; lachowa fachanli, Deut. 28: 27.

fachanlichi, v. t., to cause to peel; to scale.

fach**a**mmi, fichammi, v. t. sing., to throw by springing a stick; cf. *fachachi*, pl.

fach**a**mmi, n., one who throws by springing.

facho**n**wa, v. n., to be scaly; to have scales, Deut. 14: 9.

faha, pp., waved.

fahakachechi v. t. caus., to swing; to cause to vibrate; to vibrate.

fahak**a**chi, v. a. i. pl., to swing slowly and heavily, as a bag filled and laid across a horse swings as he walks along; to seesaw; to swingle; to vibrate; to wave; to undulate; frequently, to swing or wave, as a leaf in the wind; to vibrate, as the pendulum of a clock; *takant faha-k**a**chi*, v. a. i., to dangle; *fahakanchi*, nasal form; *fahakahanchi*, freq. form.

fahak**a**chi, fahakachi, pp., swung; made to vibrate; vibrated; waved; whirled.

fahak**a**chi, n., a vibration; a whirling.

fahali, fahali, v. a. i. pl., to swing; to vibrate; to wave.

fahali, pp., swung; vibrated; shaken; waved; single act like *shalakli*.

fahalichi, v. t. caus., to swing; to vibrate; to shake; to wave.

fahalichi, n., a swinger.

fahama, v. t. sing., to beat; to smite; to strike.

fahama, pp., hurt.

fahama, n., a stripe; a lick; a blow; a lash.

fahata, v. a. i. pl., to swing; to vibrate a long distance, as a long rope or grapevine, when suspended from a tree; to oscillate.

fahata, pp.; swung; vibrated.

fahata, n., a swinging; a vibration.

fahat**a**chi, v. t. pl., to swing; to vibrate; to cause to swing.

fah**a**mmi, v. t., to sling; to throw sideways with a whirling motion; to scourge, Matt. 10: 17; *fahamm**a**t pila*, to swing and throw; to hurl; to supplant; to thrust a sickle, Rev. 14: 19.

fah**a**mmi, n., a hurler.

fahattak**a**chi, n., a swing; a swinging.

fahattak**a**chi, fahattak**a**chi, v. a. i. sing., to swing; to turn; *fah**a**tk**a**chi*, v. t. pl., to swing; also passive; *fah**a**tkahan-chi*, pp., keep turning, Gen. 3: 24; to turn every way, Gen. 3: 24.

fahfoa, v. a. i. pl., to move in various directions; to whirl about.

fahfoa, pp., brandished; whirled about.

fahfuli, v. t. pl., to brandish; to move about in various directions; to turn, as to turn a grindstone; to move about a sword, the arms, the feet (as a child), or the tail (as a cow).

fahko, a. sing., long and slender; thin; *oski fahko*; *iti fahko*; see *fabaspoa*.

fahko, v. n., to be long and slender; to be thin.

fahkochi, v. t., to make long and slender.

fahpo, fappo (q. v.), n., magic.

faiok**a**chi, v. a. i., to stagger; to reel; to shake; to wave, as growing grain in the wind; to nod; to rock; to roll, as a boat; to totter; to vacillate.

faiok**a**chi, pp., rocked; shaken, Matt. 11: 7; *faiokanchi*, nasal form, reeling; waving; *faiokahanchi*, freq., to reel; to keep reeling.

faiok**a**chi, n., a vacillation.

faioli, v. t. pl., to shake; to make them reel; to make them wave.

faiolichi, v. t., to vibrate; to shake; to cause to vibrate; to rock.

faiolichi, n., a rocker.

faiotlak**a**chi, v. a. i. sing., to swing; to shake.

faiotlak**a**chi, n., a nod; a shake.

faiu**n**kli, v. a. i., to reel; to stagger; same as *chukfulli*, to reel (q. v.).

fakit, n., a turkey, whether domestic or wild—named from one of its notes, which sounds like this name; other fowls have received names in the same way.

fakit homatti, n., a male turkey; a gobbler; a turkey cock.

fakit inchahe, n., a turkey's spur.

fakit ishke, n., a hen turkey that has raised a brood.

fakit kucha**n**kak, n., a young male turkey, not a year old.

fakit nakni, n., a male turkey; a turkey cock.

fakit salakoba, n., lit., like the liver of a turkey; the name of a plant, called by some hart leaf.

fakit tek, n., a hen turkey.

fakit ushi, n., a young turkey; a turkey's egg.

fankkulih, see fankulli.

fako, n., a tree without limbs.

fakobli, see fakopli.

fakoha, v. a. i. pl., to peel off; to scale off; to drop off; to come off; lukfi at fakoha, the dirt peels off.

fakoha, pp. pl., peeled off; dropped off; scaled off.

fakoha, n., the peelings; scalings; pieces that come off.

fakoli, v. a. i. pl., to peel off; to strip off; to come off; to scale off; to slough.

fakoli, n., a peeling; a stripping.

fakoli, pp., peeled off.

fakolichi, v. t., to cause them to be stripped off.

fakolichi, n., a peeler; a stripper.

fakopa, v. a. i. sing., to peel off; to scale off; to drop off; to come off; to shell.

fakopa, pp., peeled off, etc.; shelled.

fakopa, n., the peeling, or piece that comes off.

fakopli, fakobli, v. t. sing., falli or fakoli pl., to peel; to scale; to strip; to tear off, or up, as to peel off bark, or tear up a floor.

fakopli, n., a peeler; a stripper.

fakoplichi, v. t. caus., to cause to strip, to peel, etc.

fakowa, pp., peeled; scaled; stripped; torn up.

fakowa, v. a. i. pl., to scale off, etc.

fankulli, fankkulih, v. t., to throw mud, etc., with a stick.

falaia, a., long; tall; lengthy; livelong; prolix, drawn, as wire; ikfalaio, a., short.

falaia, pp., elongated; lengthened; prolonged; protracted.

falaia, v. n., to be long or tall.

falaia, n., length; tallness; height; longitude; a strip.

falaia alhpesa, a., ample; long enough.

falaia inshali, a. comparative degree, longer; thus falaia, long; falaia inshali, longer; falaia inshat tali, longest.

falaia inshat tali, a., sup. degree, longest.

falaiachi, v. t., to lengthen; to elongate; to prolong; to protract; to spin out; to make long, Josh. 6: 5.

falaiakat auataka inshali, n., oblong, the length is longer than the width.

falaiat ia, v. a. i., to grow long; to lengthen.

falankna (by metathesis), properly fanankla n., a large yellow squirrel.

falakto, n., a crotch; a fork.

falakto, a., forked; crotched.

falakto, v. n., to be forked.

falakto, v. a. i., to fork; to divide into two prongs.

falaktuchi, v. t., to make a fork; to cause it to fork; lapish falaktuchi, to make the horn fork.

falaktuli, v. t., to make a fork or crotch; to fork.

falama, v. a. i., to return; to turn back; to turn about; to backslide; to turn; to recede; to fall back; to react; to recoil; to revert; to revolve; falamat achukmat tcha, restored whole, Matt. 10:13; 12:13; 17:9; Josh. 4:18; 7: 3; falamat ialashke, I will return, Matt. 12:44; infalama, v. t., to return to him; infalamahe keyu, a., irrecoverable; he will not return to him; falahama, freq.

falama, pp., returned; turned back; reduced; refunded; reverted.

falama, falama, n., a return; a turning back; a backslider or turncoat (?); a recess; a defection; a regress; infalama, a recovery; a render.

falamaka, n., the return; the turning back; afalamaka, the place of turning back.

falamakachi, falamakachi, v. a. i., to recoil; to start back suddenly.

falamat, adv., again, as falamat anya, he comes back again.

falamat abeka, v. a. i., to relapse; to become sick again.

falamat anya, v. a. i., to return along; to come back again.

falamat anya, n., the return.

falamat anya, n., a returner.

falamat ala, v. a. i., to return; to return and arrive; to come again.

falamat alhtoba, pp., refunded; repaid; also n., repayment.

falamat chumpa, v. t., to redeem; to return and buy.

falamat ia, v. a. i., to go back; to return; to retrograde.

falamat ia, a., retrograde.

falamạt minti, v. a. i., to start back.

falamạt okcha, v. a. i., to revive; to come to.

falamạt okcha^{n}ya, v. a. i., to revive; to rise as from the dead.

falamạt okcha^{n}ya, pp., resuscitated; revived; n., a revival.

falamạt ona, v. a. i., to return.

falamạt tani, v. a. i., to rise again, John 2: 22; Matt. 16: 21; 17: 23.

falamichi, falạmmichi, v. t., to return; to cause to go back; to send back; to bring back; see *afalaminchi*, to answer; Matt. 11: 4; *falaminchi*, v. t., to restore, Matt. 17: 11.

falamoa, v. a. i. pl., to return; to oscillate; see *falama*; *falamohoa*, freq.

falamoa, pp., returned; turned back; a., elastic.

falamoa, n. pl., returns; turnings back; backsliders.

falamoaka, n., the returns.

falamoa, v. a. i. pl., to go backwards and forwards; to go and return more than once.

falamolichi, v. t. pl., to cause to go backward; to cause to turn from or return; to cause them to go and return; *itifalamolichi*, 1 Sam. 18: 7.

falamolichi, n., a returner; returners.

falạm isht ikhạna, n., a compass, an instrument used in surveying land; "an instrument to learn where the north is."

falạma, see *falama*.

falạma, n., a relapse.

falạmakachi, falamakachi, v. a. i., to recoil; to start back suddenly.

falạmakạchi, n., a recoil; a recoiling.

falạmmi, n., the north.

falạmmi, a., north.

falạmmi, v. n., to be north; *i^{n}falạmmi*, it is north of it.

falạmmi chohmi, northerly; northern.

falạmmi fichik, n., the north star; the north polar star.

falạmmi hạshi aiokatula itintakla, n., northwest; between the west and north.

falạmmi imma, falạmimma, a., adv., northern; northerly; northward; northwards.

falạmmi mali, n., the north wind; Boreas.

falạmmi minti, a., northern, i. e., come from the north.

falạmmi pila, adv., northwards; toward the north; northerly, but not in the north.

falạmmi pilla, adv., at the north; to the north; away to the north; northern; in the north.

falạmmi pilla, a., arctic; polar.

falạmmichechi, v. t., to reclaim; to cause to return.

falạmmichi, v. t. sing., to return; to bring back; to give back; to back; to cause to retreat or recede; to avert; to defend; to recall; to reduce; to reflect; to refund; to remit; to render; to repel; to replace; to repulse; to restore; to retaliate; to retribute; to revert, 2 Sam. 24: 13; *iti^{n}falạmmichi*, to swap back; to return to each other; *falạmolichi*, pl.; *ilefalạmmichi*, v. ref., to return himself; *falạmminchi*, nasal form, *i^{n}falạmminchi*, v. t., to recompense him; to re-cede; to return to him; see *falamichi*.

falạmmichi, i^{n}falạmmichi, n., a returner; a restorer; a return; *i^{n}falạmmichi*, n., a restitution.

falạmmichit anumpuli, v. t., to retort; to answer again.

falạmmichit ishi, v. t., to recapture; to retake.

falạmmichit miha, v. t., to respond.

falạmmichit pila, v. t., to retort; to cast back.

falạmmichit pila, n., a return.

falạmmint, contracted form of *falạmmichi*.

falạmmint atobbi, v. t., to reimburse; to repay; to refund.

falạmmint ạlhtoba, a., repaid; *falạmmint ikạlhtobo*, a., unrepaid.

falạmmint boli, v. t., to replace.

falạmmint chumpa, v. t., to redeem; to buy back; to repurchase.

falạmmint chumpa, n., a redeemer; a repurchaser.

falạmmint chumpa, n., redemption; a repurchase.

falạmmint chumpa hinla, a., redeemable; can buy and return it.

falạmmint fohki, v. t., to reinstate; to return and place in.

falạmmint heliche, v. t., to reinstate; to return and set it up.

falammint hoyo, falammint ihoyo, to reclaim; to return and look after.

falammint inkanchi, falammint kanchi, v. t., to re-cede; to reconvey; to sell back to him.

falammint ima, falammint ibbak fohki, v. t., to render; to restore; to give back; to redeliver; to return and place in his hands.

falammint ishi, v. t., to recover; to get again; to resume; to retake.

falammint ishi, n., a recovery.

falammint isht ia, v. t., to carry back.

falammint isht ona, v. t., to reconvoy.

falammint nanabli, v. t., to regorge.

Falisi, n., a Pharisee.

fali, v. t. sing., to brandish; to wave the hand, as to beckon with the hand; to flirt; to sweep; to vacillate; to wave; to whirl; to whisk.

fali, n., a brandisher; a whirler.

fali, n., a whirl.

fanankla, see falankla.

fapa, fopa (q. v.), v. a. i., to roar, as wind.

fappo, fahpo, n., magic; tricks; enchantment; witchcraft; conjuration; a charm.

fappo, pass., charmed.

fappo onuchi, v. t., to practice magic or tricks upon; to charm.

fappo onuchi, n., a charmer; an enchanter.

fappo onuttula, pp., practiced upon with tricks.

fappuli, v. t., to charm; isht infappuli, v. t., to reprove.

fappuli, n., a magician.

fappuli imponna, n., a skillful magician.

fataha, a., waving in the wind; sita fataha, a ribbon.

fatali, v. a. i., to swing; to wave.

fatalichi, v. t., to cause to swing or to wave.

fatema, v. a. i., to open the eyes like an infant.

fatohachi, v. a. i., to swing round; fatohanchi, nasal form; fatohahanchi, freq.

fatoma, fatuma, pp., opened, as a clasp knife, or the eye; nishkin at infatumat oklatok, Matt. 9: 30; ikfatomo, a., unopened.

fatummi, fitammi, v. t., to open his own eyes; to unclose; to open (a knife); to untwine.

fatummi, n., an opener.

fatummichi, v. t., to cause to open, i.e., the eyes of another; to make him open.

fatummichi, n., an opener.

fachanli, v. a. i.; see fichanli, and fachanli, to crack open, as chestnut burs, pea pods, etc.

fala, pp. pl. of fakopa, scaled off; oksak falla, shagbark hickory; pecan (?)

fala, n., a crow.

fala atoni, n., a scarecrow; one that watches the crows.

fala atoni, v. t., to watch crows.

fala chito, n., a raven.

fala imisito, n., a May apple; a mandrake.

fala intanchi, falaknimushi, n., a mandrake.

falakna, see fanakla.

falla, v. a. i. pl., to peel off.

falli, pl. of fakopli, v. t., to scale off; to peel; hashi at itihakshup an falli, the sun peels off the bark of the tree; isito an falli, peel the pumpkin.

falushi, n., a crow's egg; a young crow.

fama, n., a whipping.

fama, pp., whipped; flogged; chastised; scourged; lashed; punished; chastened; ikfamo, a., unpunished; unchastised; not whipped.

fammi, v. t., to whip; to flog; to chastise; to scourge; to lash; to castigate; to chasten; to correct; to discipline; to leather; to punish; to lick.

fammi, n., a whipper; a castigator; a chastiser; a chastener; a lasher; a scourger.

fammi, n., a whipping.

fanakla, falakna, a fox squirrel—fannakla and not fallakna—J. E.

fani, n., a squirrel.

fani hasimbish holba, n., yarrow or wild tansy.

fani imalakusi, n., a lizard that changes his color; a chameleon.

fani lusa, n., a black squirrel, rarely seen in the Choctaw Nation.

fani okchako, n., a gray squirrel.

fani shapha, n., mistletoe.

fani ushi, n., a young squirrel.

fanikoyo, n., a sycamore tree—lit. "the squirrel does not climb it" (Sixtowns word).

fanitasho, n., a gray squirrel.

fappo, see *fappo.*

fatokachi, v. a. i., to wiggle; to shake loosely, as the loose blade of a knife.

fattahachi, v. a. i., to shake, as a leaf; to swing back and forth quickly as leaves shaken by the wind and with noise, or as a loose penknife blade.

fehna, fena, fehnha, v. a. i., to do intensely, or considerably; to effect a good deal; *itafehna*, to fight, 2 Sam. 14: 6.

fehna, fiena, a., much; very; real; own, John 1: 41; self; exceeding; excessive; exorbitant; intense; intimate; intrinsic; mighty; particular; passing, as passing strange; peculiar; quite.

fehna, fiena, v., n., to be much, very, real; *ikfehno*, Matt. 7: 11.

fehna, adv., well, Matt. 17: 5; John 2: 10; much, Matt. 6: 7; very; often; extremely; far; freely; heartily; maturely; mightily; mighty; most; much; oft; richly; rapidly; terribly; grievously, Matt. 8: 6.

fehna keyu, adv., seldom; little, Matt. 6: 30.

fehnakma, in *nitak yamma fehnakma*, in that very day, Matt. 7: 22.

fehnachi, v. t., to make much of; to effect much; *ilefehnachi*, v. ref., to think much of himself, Matt. 13: 22 [?]; to make much of one's self; to praise one's self; to boast; to make much of himself; *fienachi*, pro. form; *ilefehnachit nowa*, to stalk; to strut; to walk proudly; *ilefehnachi*, a., proud; vain; arrogant; consequential; self-important; *ilefehnachi*, v. n., to be proud; *ilefehnachechi*, v. t., to make proud; *ilefehnachi*, n., pride; vanity.

felami, filammi, n., a branch or a limb, of a tree or of a river; *itinaksish filammi*, Gen. 40: 12; *bok ushi filammi*, prong of a stream of water.

felamichi, n., a branch; a limb, Gen. 40: 10.

Fibueli, n., February.

fichak, fichak, n., the dew, or water (from any cause), as the rain standing in drops like the dew on the grass or elsewhere; dew drops.

fichak champuli, n., a honey dew; a sweet dew; a mildew.

fichak chito, n., a heavy dew; a great dew.

fichak kashanha, n., a honey dew; a mildew; a sweet dew.

fichak toba, v. a. i., to fall, as dew; to become dew.

fichama, v. a. i., to spring; to spring open, as a door when pushed; to fly open.

fichama, pass., sprung open; sprung and thrown.

fichamoa, v. a. i. pl., to spring and fly.

fichamoa, pp. pl., sprung open.

fichamoli, fichammi (q.v.), pl., to spring them; to throw them by springing.

fichanli, fachanli (q. v.), v. a. i., to open; to crack open, as pods, bean pods, etc.

fichanli, pp., a., cracked open; opened.

fichanli, n., a cracking open.

fichapa, v. a. i., to fork; to divide into two parts.

fichapa, pp., a., forked, as a road.

fichapa, n., a fork.

fichapoa, v. a. i. pl., to fork.

fichapoa, pp. pl., forked.

fichapoa, n., forks.

fichapoli, v. t. pl., to fork; to turn off, as to turn off from a road.

fichapolichi, v. t. pl., to cause to fork.

fichabli, v. a. i. sing., *fichapa*, pp. (q. v.), to fork; to turn off, Matt. 2: 22.

fichablichi, v. t., to cause him to turn off.

fichammi, fachammi, (q. v.), v. t., to spring and throw; to spring open by pushing against.

fichik, fochik, n., a star; stars; planets; a planet, Matt. 2: 2, 7.

fichik ansha, a., starry.

fichik atia, n., the orbit of a planet.

fichik asha, v. a. i., to have amaurosis; *anfichik asha*, I have amaurosis; *chinfichik asha*, thou hast amaurosis.

fichik baieta, n., the yard stars.

fichik chito, n., a large star; a planet that appears to be large, as Venus and Jupiter; Lucifer; Saturn; Venus; Vesper.

fichik heli, n. pl., shooting stars; meteors; flying stars.

fichik hika, n. sing., a shooting star; a meteor.

fichik homma, n. a red star; Mars.

fichik isi nạła silhhi, n., the yard stars; the ell stars; lit., the stars that track the wounded deer.

fichik issuba, n., the stars called the pointers, or dipper, or butcher case, that point toward the North Star; lit., the horse star.

fichik laua, a., starry.

fichik luak, n., a blazing star.

fichik lukoli, n., a constellation.

fichik połoli, n., a blazing star; a comet.

fichik shobota, fochik shubota, fichik shobulli, n., a comet.

fichik tohwikeli, n., starlight.

fichik watạlhpi, n., the seven stars, pleiads, or pleiades.

fichonli, fochonli, v. a. i., to scale off.

fichonli, pp., scabbed off; scaled off.

fichonlichi, v. t., to scale off; to cause it to scale off.

fichukbi, n., a den; a hole in the ground.

fihobli, v. t., to satisfy; to gratify by treatment, as in feeding, paying, or treating well; to cloy; to slake; to suffice.

fihobli, n., a satisfier.

fihobli, a., satisfactory.

fihoblichi, v. t., to make satisfied; to satisfy the mind.

fihoblichi, n., a satisfier.

fihopa, v. a. i., to stalk.

fihopa, pp., satisfied; gratified; cloyed; sufficed; ikfihopo, a., unsatisfied.

fihopa, n., satisfaction; gratification; satiety.

fihopahe keyu, a., insatiate; insatiable.

fik, n., a fig, Matt. 7: 16.

fikomi, see isht afikomi.

filaⁿkiⁿsin, n., frankincense.

filama, pp., turned away; hạshiⁿfilahaⁿmashke, Peter 2: 11; filammi, v. t., itiⁿfilama, pp., separated from each other; disunited; parted.

filamoa, pp. pl., turned away from; turned from; itiⁿfilamoa, turned from each other.

filamołechi, v. t., to turn them away from it or them; to separate from and turn away; to part them from each other; mikmạt itiⁿfilamołechikmạt, and when he separated them from each other, Matt. 25: 32; late edition, itiⁿfilamolichi.

filamołechi, n., a separator; a divider.

filamoli, v. a. i. pl., to turn away; to branch, as the limb on a tree; itiⁿfilamoli, to turn from each other; to part; itifilamoli, pp., separated from each other.

Filanchi, n., French.

Filanchi anumpa, n., French, or the French language.

Filanchi hatak, n., a Frenchman.

Filanchi okla, n., the French people, or nation; Frenchmen.

Filanchi yakni, n., France; French country.

filạmmi, felạmi (q. v.), a branch of a tree or stream.

filạmmi, v. a. i., to turn away; to turn from, Matt. 2: 12; Josh. 1: 7, 8; to leave; to depart from, Matt. 4: 11; Luke 4: 13; Chihowa yaⁿ iⁿfilạmmi; 1 Kings 11: 9; aⁿfilạmmit, depart from me, Matt. 7: 23; itiⁿfilạmmi, to turn away from each other; to part; iⁿfilạmmi, to leave him; to turn from him; aiiⁿfilạmmi, to turn away from at. This differs from filạmmi, to depart out of.

filạmmi, n., obliquity; iⁿfilạmmi, n., a turncoat; one that turns away from him.

filạmmichi, v. t., to cause to turn away from; to lead off from, Josh. 5: 9; to cause to go from; to cause to branch off from; itiⁿfilạmmichi, v. t., to turn from each other; to separate them; to disunite.

filạmminchi, v. a. i., nasal form, to branch; to shoot or spread in branches.

filạmminchi, n., a branch, of the limb of a tree or a water course; a fork; a knag; a prong; a bay, Josh. 15: 2; 18: 19; bok filạmminchi, branch of a creek; naksish filạmminchi, branch of a limb; naksish filamoli, pl., branches of a limb.

filehkạchi, v. a. i. pl., to turn back and forth; nashuka yạt filehkạchi, their faces turn back and forth; itihishi ạt filehkạchi, the leaves of the tree turn, etc.

filekạchi, n., a turning.

filema, v. a. i. sing., to turn the person, i. e., one's own person; to turn round; to turn over; to turn, as in looking back; filemạt chikpsokashke, to veer; Chisas ash ot pit filema, "Jesus turning unto them," Luke 23: 28; to turn about, Matt. 7: 6; 9: 22; to turn, Josh. 8: 20, 21.

filema, pp., turned round; turned back.

filemachi, v. t., to turn; to veer.

filemat itola, v. a. i., to turn over; to fall over; to capsize.

filemoa, v. a. i. pl., to turn over and over, or backwards and forwards; to veer; to turn this way and that way; *filemoat pisa*, to look around, Mark 11: 11.

filemoa, pp. pl., turned over; turned.

filemolechi, v. t., to cause to turn away; to sever from, Matt. 13: 49; see *filamolechi*.

filemoli, v. t. pl., to turn over; Mark 11: 15.

filetakachi, v. a. i., to turn once suddenly.

filinka, filinko, adv., very; *achukma filinko*, very good, used by some persons.

filimmi, v. t. sing., to turn it over; to come about; to upset; to turn away, 1 Kings 11: 2, 3, 4; *holisso han filimmi*, to turn the book over; *filihinmi*, Josh. 7: 8; *mali hat filimmi*, v. a. i., the wind turns.

filimmichi, v. t. caus., to turn it over or round.

filimmikachi, v. t., to turn.

fima, pp., scattered; sowed; sown; strewed; disseminated; dissipated; sprinkled; *onfima*, pp., sprinkled on; *ikfimmo*, a., unsowed; seed not sown; *osapa ikafimmo*, a field unsown (the *a* is locative.)

fima, v. n., to be scattered; to be dissipated.

fima, v. a. i., to scatter; to dissipate.

fimibli, v. t. pl., to sow; to scatter; to strew; to disperse; to dissipate, but not liquids; to spread; see *latabli*, to spill; *itafimibli*, v. t., to dispel; to disperse; to shatter.

fimibli, n., a sower; a scatterer; a spreader.

fimibli, n., a spreading.

fimiblichi, v. t., to scatter; to sputter; to cause to scatter.

fimimpa, a., sparse.

fimimpa, adv., thinly.

fimimpa, pp., scattered; dispersed; strewn; dissipated; diffused; littered; sowed; sown; spattered; sprinkled, 2 Kings 9: 33; *ikfimimpo*, a., neg. form,

unscattered; *itafimimpa*, dispelled; scattered from each other, John 10: 12; dispersed; *itafimimpa*, pp., interspersed; scattered with; scattered abroad; Matt. 9: 36; *onfimimpa*, pp., spattered on; sowed on, as seed.

fimimpa, v. a. i., to dissipate; to scatter; to disperse; *itafimimpa*, to scatter about; to scatter apart from each other; *wak at fimimpa*, the cattle disperse; *hoshonti at fimimpa*, the clouds disperse; *itafimimpa*, to scatter or disperse from each other; to straggle away from each other.

fimimpa, n., a dispersion; the state of being scattered; litter; *itafimimpa*, n., a dispersion, James 1: 1.

fimmi, v. t., to sow; to scatter; to disperse; to dissipate; to issue; *na fimmi*, to sow something; to diffuse; to disseminate; to seminate; to spatter; to sprinkle; *fihimmi*, Matt. 12: 20; *ibafimmi*, v. t., to intersperse; to sow with; *onfimmi*, v. t., to splash on; to sprinkle on; to sow on.

fimmi, n., a sower; a scatterer; a disseminator.

fimmichi, v. t., to scatter; to sprinkle; to cause to scatter.

fimmichi, n., a scatterer.

fimpkachi, pp., sowed; sprinkled, as when water is sprinkled on the ground by shaking a garment.

fimpkachi, v. a. i., to scatter; to sprinkle.

fiopa, n., breath; expiration; respiration; a whiff; wind; a blast, Josh. 6: 5; *safiopa*, my breath.

fiopa, v. a. i., to breathe; *fiopali*, I breathe; *fiopa*, to draw a breath; v. t., to expire; to respire; to whiff; *onfiopat foyuki*, to breathe into, Gen. 2: 7; *ilafiopa*, to inhale; to snuff up; to inspire; to snuff; to draw in the breath.

fiopa ikfalaio, a., short-breathed; breath not long.

fiopa imokpulo, n., the asthma; breath bad for him, or breathing bad for him.

fiopa isht aiopi, v. a. i., to expire; to breathe the last time.

fiopa kobafa, n., broken wind; short breath.

fiopa kobafa, a., short-winded; short-breathed.

fiopa taha, a., broken-winded; breathless; breath exhausted; short-breathed.

fiopa tali, v. t., to exhaust the breath.

fiopa tapa, a., dead; breath-sundered.

fiopa tapli, v. t., to destroy life, Luke 6: 9; *fiopa intapli*, to separate the breath.

fiopat taha, v. a. i., to pant.

fiopat taha, n., broken wind; short breath.

fiopachi, v. t., to cause to breathe; to give breath; to bring back the breath; to save.

fitekachi, v. a. i., to veer about; to whirl, as a top.

fitekachi, n., a whirling.

fitekachi, pp., whirled.

fitelichi, v. t., to whirl quickly; to cause to fly and whirl as a handkerchief or a flag when suspended and shaken by the wind.

fitelichi, n., one that whirls.

fitiha, v. a. i., to whirl about; to veer about; to shift about.

fitihachi, v. t. caus., to whirl about.

fitilema, pp., turned over, i. e., from being under another person or thing to bring it on top; *hatak at fitilema*.

fitilimmi, v. t., to turn over, from being underneath; to bring on top as may be seen when two men wrestle and one is thrown, but he gets the ascendancy of his antagonist.

fititekachi, pl. of *fitekachi*, pp., whirled.

fititekachi, v. a. i., to whirl; to veer.

fitukhak, n., name of a bird often called the yellow hammer, or yellow woodcock.

fo, adv., may be; perchance; as *katima iafo*, where may he have gone.

fobassa, see *fabassa*.

fochi, see *foechi*.

fochik, see *fichik*.

fochik shubota, see *fichik shobota*.

fochonli, see *fichonli*.

foe, n., honey.

foe akmo, n., beeswax; bee bread.

foe bila, foi bila (Josh. 5: 6), n., honey or "bee oil"; melted honey or honey oil.

foe bila hakshup, n., honeycomb.

foe bila iti ansha, n., wild honey; woodland honey; honey in the woods.

foe bilishke, foishke, n., honey bee or honey bees; those which collect the honey; the mother of the honey; *foe bilishke hocheto*, n., big bees.

foe bilishke inminko, n., the queen bee.

foe bilishke inchuka, a bee hive; a bee gum.

foe bilishke inchuka fohki, v. t., to hive bees.

foe bilishke inchuka foka, pp., hived.

foe bilishke inchuka inhoshontika, n., an apiary; a bee house or shelter.

foe bilishke inpokni, n., the drones or grandmother bees.

foe hakmi, n., wax; beeswax.

foe inlakna, n., bee bread; wax.

foe nia, n., honeycomb filled with honey.

foechi, fochi, fohchi (M. Dyer); *on foechi*, 1. Cor. 3, caption; to sprinkle on water, salt, etc.

foeli, fulli, v. t., to pick out; to take out.

foha, v. a. i., to rest; to take ease; to ease; to harbor; to recruit; to repose; to respire.

foha, n., rest; respite; cessation; ease; an intermission; recreation; a vacation.

fohachi, v. t., to give rest; to cause to rest; to rest another; to ease; to harbor; to recreate; to repose; to unburden. *ilefohachi*, v. ref., to rest himself; *hachifohachilashke*, I will give you rest, Matt. 11: 28.

fohchi, see *foechi*.

fohka, foka, v. t., to put in; to put on; as to put garments upon one's self; to clothe one's self; to dress one's self; to ornament; *albikachi*, v. t. pl., *ilalbikachi*, we dress ourselves (by putting on more garments).

fohka, foka, v. a. i., to enter, Matt. 15: 17; to go into, John 3: 4; *chinfoyuka*, to be in, Matt. 6: 23; to conceive, Luke 2: 21; *alla infoka*, to conceive, Luke 1: 24; *alla infoyuka*, to be with child, Matt. 1: 18; *ilefohka*, to put on himself; hence, *ilefohka* or *ilefoka*, n., a garment, a shirt; *itibafoka*, n., a coalition; *fonhka, fonka*, nas. form, *foyuka, afoyuka* (Josh. 3: 3, 6; 4: 18), pro. form.

fohka, foka, sing., (cf. *fohki*), *albikachi*, pp. pl.; put on, as garments; dressed; clothed, Matt. 11: 8; clad; girded; inclosed; put in, as a horse is put into a stable or a field; invested; laded; loaded; lodged; shut; vested; *itibafoka*, pp., combined; *sabafohka*, Matt. 12: 30; *foⁿhka, foⁿka*, nasal form, being in; being on, Josh. 2: 11, 19; possessed, Matt. 4: 24; *aiiⁿfoⁿka*, Matt. 12: 22; *afoⁿka*, "is in," Matt. 7: 3; *foⁿka kano*, that is in, Matt. 7: 3; *aiiⁿfoⁿka*, possessed with, Matt. 8: 16; 12: 40; 17: 27.

fohka, foka, n., a lading; a passage; that which is put on; found in compound words, as *na fohka*, a garment or dress; *fohka achąfa*, a suit of clothes; *foyuka*, Matt. 12: 40.

foⁿhka, foⁿkka, v. a. i., to roar, as the wind; to murmur; cf. John 3: 8.

foⁿhka, n., the sound or roaring of wind, John 3: 8.

fohkachechi, v. t., to array another in a garment; to gird; to girdle; *na fohka tohbi holitompa hoⁿ fohkachechi cha*, arrayed him in a gorgeous robe, etc. Luke 23:11; some say this word means putting several garments upon another; *ąlla yaⁿ fokachechili*, I dress the children; *fohkąchichi mąt*, Matt. 27: 28, 31.

fohkąchi, v. t., to dress; to put garments upon another person; to clothe another; to furnish another with clothes; to invest; to indue; to ornament; to vest.

fohkąt aⁿya, n., a passage; a passenger.

fohki, foki, to put in, Matt. 14: 3; I Kings 10: 24; to fall into, 2 Sam. 24: 14; to inclose; to inject; to lade; to load; to lodge; to put; to shut; to tuck; to deliver to, Matt. 5: 25; 11: 27; *ibafohki*, to combine; to hide in, Matt. 13: 33; Josh. 2: 24; 6: 2; 7: 7; *itibafohki*, to combine together; *fohkihchih, fohkichi*, v. t., to anoint; to grease; *fohoⁿki*, freq.; *foyuhki*, pro. form; *itifohki*, v. t., to put in together; to unite; to set, as a bone; *itifohkit ikbi*, to frame; *itifohkit itabana*, framed, p.

fohkul, pohkul, n., a hornet; see below.

fohkul inchuka, n., a hornet's nest.

fohobli, fohopli, v. t., to take out; to unload; to take and spill; to pour out; to shed forth; *oⁿfohomplilahi oke*, Acts 2: 17; to put on, Josh. 7: 6; *fohombli*, nasal form.

fohobli, n., an unloader.

fohoblichi, v. t., to cause to take out.

fohopa, v. a. i., to pour out largely; to fall down, Josh. 6: 5; *hohtak oka fohopąt illit taha tok*, Luke 8: 33; *fohompa*,

nasal form, being poured out; *fohompa*, n., a bunch; a pile; a collection; *fohohumpa*, freq.; *foyupa*, pro.

fohopa, pp., spilled; unloaded; poured out.

fohopa, n., that which is poured out; an effusion.

fohopli, see *fohobli*.

fohukfunli, see *fotukfunli*.

fohukli, v. a. i., to pant or puff, like a laboring ox; to blow.

foi bila, see *foe bila*.

foishke, foe bilishke (q. v.), n., a honey bee.

foiya, see *hoiya*.

foka, see *fohka*.

foka, n., rate.

foka, adv., about, as to time, place, degree, quality, etc., *nitak yąmma fokama*, about that time, Acts 12: 1; *fokama*, Matt. 1: 11; *nitak yąmma fokama*, at that time, Matt. 12: 1; *katiohmi foka*, how long? Matt. 17: 17; *fokatok*, were about, Matt. 14: 21; *fokama*, Josh. 2: 5; 9: 1; in, i. e., in one place; *aiasha*, for plurality of places.

foka, fuka, n., a place; a residence; *miⁿko foka iatuk*, he has gone to the king's or about the king's; *ishke foka iatuk*, he has gone to his mother's, or about his mother's; *iti fuka*, about or in the woods.

fokahota, adv., perhaps.

fokakash, adv. of past time, ago; about that time, at or in that time; agone.

fokali, v. i., see 1 Sam. 4: 20; *atuk osh illi fokalima*, when she made about to die, or went about to die, *yąmma fokalika*, at that time, 2 Kings, 16: 6; *fokalechi*, with *himak*, 1 Tim. 5: 22; see *yąmmakfokalechi*.

fokąchi, n., a dresser.

foki, see *fohki*.

fokichi, v. t., to cause to go in; to put in; *fokinchi*, nasal form; *fokihinchi* freq.; *fokiechi*, pro. form.

folokąchi; see *fullokąchi*.

fololi, folulli, v. t., to go round; to take round; *iⁿfolulli*, v. t., to edge it; to go round it.

fololichi, folullichi, v. t., cause to turn round, as to turn a horse round at the end of a row of corn; to curb; to rein; to guide; to turn; 2 Kings 9: 23; to cause it to go round; *iⁿfolololichit achunli*, to sew on a border; to border; to skirt; *iⁿfolullichi*, to skirt; to face.

folota, fullota, n., a circuit; action or performance in a circle; a round; a zone; the region; the part; an excursion; a period; a wandering; *iⁿfolota*, its edge; lace; edging; *folotoa*, pl. circuits; rounds.

folota, n., a stroller; a wanderer.

folota, a., crooked; roundabout; going round; circuitous.

folota, fullota, v. n., to be circuitous, Matt. 2: 22; *fullotạt Kalile iⁿkaniohmi hoⁿ onatok;* *fullota* is a diminutive of *folota*, to go about slowly; round about, Matt. 14: 35; to come about, 2 Sam. 24: 6; all round, Josh. 13: 2.

folota, fullota, v. a. i., to go round; to deviate; to straggle; to stray; to stroll; to swim; to wanton; to wheel.

folota, pp., taken round; put round; *iⁿfolota*, edged; skirted; faced.

folota, adv., round.

folota, a., crooked; roundabout; circuitous.

folotạt ạla, n., a revolution.

folotoa, v. n., to be crooked.

folotoa, pp., taken round; put round; *iⁿfolotoa*, edged; skirted.

folotoa, v. a. i., to go round; to take circuits.

folotolichi, v. t. caus., pl.; to turn them round; to cause them to go round.

folotolichi, v. t. pl., to put them round.

folotowạchi, v. t., to take round; to cause to wave backward and forward.

folulli, see *fololi.*

folullichi, see *fololichi.*

folumpa, round about, Mark 1: 28; see *afolumpa*, from *afolubli.*

folichi, v. t., to pour; *oⁿfolichi*, to pour on, as water on a plant; *foholihinchi*, Ps. 40: 2 [?].

fomohạchi, v. a. i., to roar, as the wind in the top of a tree; *mali hạt fomohạchi.*

fomohạchi, n., a roaring.

fomoli, v. a. i., to weary; *itafomoli*, Gen. 19: 2.

fomosa, a., slender; slim; without a border; naked; without hair.

foni, n., a bone; stone, as of a peach, etc.; shell, of a hickory nut, etc.; a nut shell.

foni bano, a., bareboned; bony; full of bones; nothing but bones; raw; rawboned.

foni bano, n., raw bones.

foni falạmmint itifohka, pass., set or replaced, as bones after a dislocation.

foni falạmmint itifohki, v. t., to replace bones; to set bones; to reduce from a dislocation.

foni falạmmint itifohki, n., a bone setter.

foni hotupa, n., bone-ache; pain in the bones; rheumatism.

foni ikbi, v. t., to ossify; to form bone.

foni iksho, a., boneless.

foni kommichi, n., bone-ache.

foni kommichi, v. a. i., to ache in the bones; the bones ache.

foni laua, a., bony; full of bones; having many bones.

foni lupi, n., marrow; marrow of the bones.

foni toba, v. a. i., to ossify; to become bone; to form into bone.

foni toba, pp., ossified.

foni toshbi, n., a rotten bone; rottenness of the bone; caries; an ulcerated bone.

foni toshbi, a., carious.

foni toshbichi, v. t., to cause the bone to rot; to render carious.

fopa, fapa, v. a. i., to bellow; to roar as wind in the top of a pine, or as water falling at a distance in a shower; to estuate; to murmur.

fopa, n., a roaring; a roar; a rapid; rapids; a sound; *fopa hosh mintit ạla cha.* Acts 2: 2.

fopạchi, v. t., to cause to roar.

fota, adv., perhaps.

fotoha, n., a bore; a turn; a grinding; motion of a mill.

fotoha, v. a. i., to run, as a mill; to grind; to move, as a grindstone.

fotoha, pp., etc., ground; bored; *taⁿsh fotoha*, ground corn, or corn meal.

fotokạchi, v. a. i., to shake as a scythe when not tightly fastened to the snath; *fotokahanchi*, pro. form.

fotoli, v. t., v. a. i., to grind; to wind; to bore; to mill; to turn; *isht fotoli*, to bore with; *isht fotolit lumbli*, v. t., to mill.

fotoli, n., a borer; one who bores; a miller; a grinder; a turner.

fotoli, n., a turn.

fotukfunli, fohukfunli, v. a. i., to be out of breath; to pant hard like a running horse.

fuka, see *foka.*

fuli, n., a switch; a rod; a twig; a slip; a sprig; a wattle; a wand.

fuli atoba, a., wicker, made of a switch.

fuli isht fama, pp., switched; whipped with a switch.

fuli isht fama, n., a switching; a whipping with a switch.

fuli isht fammi, v. t., to switch; to strike with a small twig or rod.

fuli isht fammi, n., a whipper; one who whips with a switch.

fuli kaua, n., broken twigs; a name applied to the broken sticks or small split pieces of cane made use of in notifying of any public meeting. They are made and sent by the headmen to others at the time when the appointment is made, and one is thrown away every morning, and on the last morning the last is thrown away, and at night the assembly takes place.

fulli, v. t., to gouge; to pick out; to take out; *nishkin fulli,* to gouge or to pick out the eye; *foeli,* pro. form.

fullichi, v. t. caus., to cause to gouge or to pick out the eye of another.

fullokachi, afolokachi, v. a. i. pl., to wander; Josh. 14: 10, to rove; to keep moving about; to shuffle; to go round; to circle; to sinuate; *folota,* sing; *fullokahanchi,* freq., to move round, as a horse in a mill; to roam; to wander; *fullokahanchi,* a., serpentine.

fullokachi, n., a rover; a shuffler; *fullokahanchi,* n., a roamer; a trollop.

fullokachi, pp., taken round.

fullokachi, n. pl., circuits; rounds.

fullokachit anumpuli, v. t., to ramble in speaking.

fullokachit aⁿya, v. t., to ramble; to rove about.

fullota, see *folota.*

fullottokachi, v. a. i. sing., to part; to move suddenly, as if by a twitch.

fullottokachi, n., a start.

fulomoli, a., devious; crooked.

fulomoli, v. n., to be devious.

fulumi; in *asht itafulumit yakni yamma itanowa chatukoⁿ,* sermon: Duties to children, page 13.

fulup, n., the shoulder down as far as the elbow.

fulup foni, n., the shoulder bone.

fulush, n., a clam (a shell).

fulush hakshup, n., a clamshell.

fulush isht impa, n., a shell spoon.

h, an aspirate, at the end of words after a vowel, to indicate a verb or an assertion, etc.; see *oⁿ, a, i.*—Note: I think it is the verb to be; *siah,* I am, etc. (Byington).

ha is used before *tok* and *tuk* and their compounds, in some sense as a definite article, to make definite the action; *hatok, hatuk,* it was; as, *sabannahatok,* that which I want, it was; the want I have; *aⁿyalihatok okat,* Luke 4: 43; *ammihahetuk ash,* the, Luke 15: 12; *ushi atok,* Luke 3: 23; *kilik hatak atok,* Acts 16, 1.

ha, adv., time or times, used after ordinals; *atuklaha,* second time; twice; *hituchinaha,* three times, thrice; *hayak oⁿ,* after that, 2 Sam. 24: 10; Acts 1: 3; *hayokmato,* John 21: 18; *haya,* Matt. 5: 32; 12: 29; *a, ha,* or *ya* is considered as a *locative* of time, as in *acheki, abilia, atuk, achiⁿ,* etc.

ha, adv., after verbs, meaning after or before next; *minti ha,* after he comes; *ibbak achifa hayoⁿ keyukmat,* if they had not first washed their hands (hands wash after it is so, if not) they do not eat, Mark 7: 3; *alla aleha akosh tiⁿkba kaiya ha yoⁿ,* Mark 7: 27; *pima hama,* after, when he has given us, Josh. 1: 1; 2: 14; 7: 2.

haⁿ, a definite particle, in the obj. case, used after verbs, etc.; subj. case, *hat,* the which; the one which; *tamaha haⁿ,* town it, or town the, Matt. 2: 1; *ishia haⁿ,* are you the one that goes? *haⁿ* is found after verbs and verbal nouns, derived from verbs more frequently than *aⁿ* or *yaⁿ,* that which, but *holisso haⁿ, issuba haⁿ, imanukfila haⁿ, chula haⁿ,* are exceptions. This *h* may be the aspirate of the verb, which in speaking is carried over, like *ilohia,* spoken *ilo hia.* See *a,* particle.

haⁿ, ahaⁿh (q. v.), adv., no; not so; a word of denial; *haⁿ keyu*, no, it is not so.

habali, v. a. i., to tassel, as corn; *tanchi at habali; habanli,* nasal form.

habali, n., a tassel; *tanchi habali,* a young corn tassel.

habali, pp., tasseled.

habalichi, v. t., to cause to tassel.

habani, a., being ready to tassel.

habani, v. n., to be ready to tassel.

habefa, pp. sing., a., dented; *habefoa,* pl.

habefa, n. sing., a dent; *habefoa,* pl., dents.

habefoli, v. t. pl., to make dents.

habena, v. t., to receive a favor gratuitously; to receive a present; to receive, Matt. 10: 8; to obtain a favor, applied to receiving money or goods as an annuity; *habena sabanna,* I wish for a favor. It differs a little from *asilhha,* to beg, being a little more honorable in its meaning.

habena, n., a present; a gift; an annuity received; a boon.

habena, pp., received as a present; obtained as a present; presented.

habenachi, v. t., to make a gift; to make a present; to present; to give, Matt. 6: 2; to do alms, Acts 10: 2.

habenachi, na habenachi, n., a benefactor.

habenachi, n., a gift; a boon; a bribe, 1 Sam. 8: 3.

habenat aⁿya, habint aⁿya, v. a. i., to go in quest of a favor.

habenat aⁿya, habint aⁿya, n., one that goes to seek gifts; a beggar, but not in the worst sense; one that solicits charity.

habiffi, v. t. sing., to dent.

habiffi, n., one that dents.

habifkachi, pp. pl., dented.

habifkachi, n., dents.

habifli, v. t. pl., to dent.

habiⁿshak, n., a large grasshopper.

habishko, habishko (q. v.), v. a. i., to sneeze.

habli, n., a treader; a kicker.

habli, n., a tread; a step; the space passed by the foot in walking or running; a pace; the space between the two feet in walking; a kick.

habli, v. a. i. sing., to tread; to step; to stamp; to kick; to foot; *isht habli,* v. t., to kick; to spurn; to trample; to winch, 1 Sam. 2: 29.

hablichi, v. t., *halichi,* pl., to cause him to tread on it.

habofa, v. a. i., to cease; to subside; to abate, as a swelling; to go down.

habofa, pp., abated; subsided; gone down; *shatali at habofa,* the swelling has abated.

habofa, n., abatement.

habofachi, to disrupt; to scatter a swelling.

haboffi, v. t., to reduce; to abate; to diminish; to remove; to cause a swelling to abate.

haboli, pl., *habofa,* sing., v. a. i., to cease; to subside; to go down.

haboli, n. pl., abatement of swellings, etc.

haboli, pp. pl., abated; subsided.

habolichi, v. t. pl., to cause swellings to abate; to remove swellings; to scatter them.

hacha, adv., perhaps; how? what? in relation to something that was not looked for, 1 Sam. 20: 18; John 1: 50; *chiyimmi hacha? ishachi hacha,* do you say then, Mark 5: 31.

hachiⁿ, will; shall, Josh. 1: 6.

haⁿchi, see *hanahchi.*

hacho, a., a Creek word meaning "mad." It is found only as part of the war names of men, viz., Tashka hacho, Hopaii hacho (David Folsom), Ishtanaki hacho (Mr. Dyer's grandfather), and has an honorable meaning among Choctaw.

hachofaktapi, n., the chinquapin tree.

hachofakti, n., a chinquapin; the dwarf chestnut.

hachoⁿmalhmokki, v. a. i., to swim with the face under water.

hachotakni, n., a large turtle, called by some the loggerhead turtle; a tortoise; *hachotakni hakshup,* turtle shell.

hachotakni okhata aⁿsha, n., a sea turtle.

hachowanashi, v. a. i. sing., to fall heels over head.

hachowanashi, n., a somerset.

hachowanashi, adv., head first; headlong.

hachowanashichi, v. t. sing., to throw another heels over head.

hachowani, v. a. i. pl., to fall heels over head.

hachowani, n., a somerset performed by a number of persons, or a number of times by the same man; somersets.

hachowanichi, v. t., to throw others heels over head.

hachukbilankbila, chukbilankbila, chukkilakbila (q. v.), chukanakbila, n., name of a bird, the whip-poor-will.

hachukbilhka, v. a. i. pl., to kneel; to couch.

hachukbilhkachi, v. t. pl., to kneel; to make them kneel.

hachukbilepa, v. a. i. sing., to kneel; to fall on the knees; to bend the knee, Matt. 17: 14.

hachukbilepa, n., a kneeler; hachukbilhka, pl.

hachukkashaha, n., sorrel; name of a weed; see pichi or pihchi.

hachukłampulechi, v. t., to spin, as a spider; to make a web.

hachukłampulechi, n., a spinner; a spider which spins.

hachukłampuli, chukłampulli (q. v.), n., a cobweb; a spider's web; an air thread.

hachukpalantak, chukpalantak, n., a tree toad.

hachumbilhka, v. a. i. pl., to kneel, Matt. 27: 29.

hachunchuba, n., an alligator.

hachunchuba, a., being without hair, as an elephant.

hachunchuba, pp., deprived of hair.

hachunchubachi, v. t., to deprive of hair; to cause to be without hair.

hafakbi, n., a dent.

hah, ha, adv., perhaps; likely; shilup on episa ha, perhaps we saw a spirit.

hahchabah, n., a footlog for a bridge; see achaba.

hahe, uksak hahe, n., a walnut.

hahe api, n., a walnut tree.

hahka, hakka, hakha, v. a. i., to loll; to pant from fatigue or from heat or from overexertion; wak at hahka, the cow lolls; ofi at hahka, the dog lolls; akanka yat hahka; fakit at hahka; akanka yat hahka the hen lolls.

hahka, v. t., to loll; to thrust out, as the tongue.

hahkachi, v. t., to cause to loll.

hahta, hahwash (Sixtowns word), n., an adder.

hahwa, see hawa.

hahwash, see hawash.

haiaka, v. a. i., to appear, Matt. 1: 20; to come out; to occur; to peep; to show; to transpire; haiaka hinla, a., ostensible.

haiaka, pp., exhibited; presented; undissembled; unequivocal; unfolded; manifested; made manifest, John 1: 31; appeared, Matt. 2: 7; found, Luke 15: 32; discovered; developed; divulged; elucidated; exposed; illustrated; manifested; revealed; haianka, nasal form; ikhaiako, neg. form, not found; undetected; inhaiaka, pp., undeceived.

haiaka, n., appearance; an opening; an open place, Josh. 3: 4; an exposure; nakedness; ostentation; a peep; ikhaiako, n., a secret; something not known, or not made known.

haiaka, a., visible; in sight; that may be seen; audible; plain; conspicuous; discernible; evident; expressed; frank; full; legible; lucid; manifest; naked; notorious; obvious; open; ostensible; overt; palpable; perspicuous; prominent; undissembling. ikhaiak o, a., latent; secret; shadowy; unexposed; unfound; unpublished; vague.

haiaka, adv., abroad; out; haiaka pinusi, clearly; legibly.

haiakachechi, v. t., to simplify; to make plain.

haiakachi, haiakechi, v. t., to cause to appear; to make known; to publish; to show, Josh. 5: 6; Luke 4: 5; to manifest, John 2: 11; to develop; to disclose; to discover; to divulge; to elucidate; to exhibit; to expose; to illustrate; to indicate; to manifest; to present; to represent; to reveal; to solve; to tell; to unfold; to unmask; to unravel; haiak-aiyachi, pro. form; ilehaiakachi, to make himself known, Gen. 45: 1; 1 Sam. 3: 21; inhaiakachi, v. t., to undeceive; to show it to him; ishilehaiakachi, show thyself, Matt. 8: 4.

haiakachi, n., one that manifests; an exposer.

haiakạt, adv., openly; clearly; manifestly; plainly; simply. This and other adverbs ending with *t* precede verbs, as *haiakạt anoli, haiakạt hikia.*

haiakạt anoli, v. t., to unbosom; to tell plainly or openly.

Haiaketạbi, a man's name, derivation uncertain.

haieli, v. t., to scuffle; *towa yaⁿ itiⁿhaieli,* to scuffle against each other for the ball.

haieli, n., a scuffler.

haiemo, a., miry; soft, as mud when filled with water.

haiemo, v. n., to be miry.

haiemuchi, v. t., to make it miry.

haili, v. a. i., to get away from him in a scuffle, as *towa yaⁿ iⁿhaili,* to snatch away.

haiochi, see *haiuchi.*

haiochichechi, v.t., to tear, Luke 9: 39, 42.

haiochichi, see *haiuchichi.*

haioli, hioli, v. a. i. pl., to stand up, and sometimes *hieli,* pl., to stand up erect.

haioli, pp., set; placed erect; made to stand up.

haioli, n., standers; those who stand.

haiolichi, v. t. pl., to set up; to cause to stand; to erect.

haiolichi, n., one that sets up; an erecter.

haiombish, n., the navel string; the placenta.

haiowạni, see *haiyowạni.*

haiuchi, haiochi, n., a fit; a convulsion; the fits which are incident to hydrophobia; epilepsy; pp., convulsed.

haiuchi, haiochi, v. a. i., to shake; to convulse, Matt. 17: 15.

haiuchichi, haiochechi, haiochichi, v. t., to cause a shaking with fits; to shake with fits; to convulse.

haiuchichi, n., a fit; a spasm; hydrophobia.

haiyantalali, biuntalali, bisuntalali, aiuntalali, iuntalali, n., a dewberry, or running blackberry.

haiyichichi, n., a fit; spasms.

haiyiⁿhchi, haiyiⁿkchi, n., the kidney or kidneys; the reins.

haiyiⁿhchi hotupa, n., pain in the kidneys; inflammation of the kidneys.

haiyiⁿhchi nia, n., suet; the fat about the kidneys.

haiyiⁿhchi nipi, n., the kidney meat.

haiyiⁿko, haiyinto, n., soft mud; mire, whether in a swamp, plowed land, or elsewhere.

haiyiⁿko, a., miry; mellow.

haiyiⁿko, v. n., to be miry.

haiyiⁿko, v. a. i., to mellow.

haiyiⁿko, pp., made miry.

haiyiⁿkuchi, v. t., to make *haiyiⁿko,* mire or soft mud; to mellow.

haiyip, n., a pond; a lake; a puddle.

haiyip ikbi, v. t., to pond; to make a pond.

haiyowạni, haiowạni, n., a worm called the cutworm.

haiyuⁿkpulo, n., a weed; an herb, Matt. 13: 32; a plant; a tare, Matt. 13: 25, 26; a vegetable; herbage; a hollyhock; thoroughwort; any weed for which there is no particular name is called by this general name.

haiyuⁿkpulo awalạlli, n., a saucepan.

haiyuⁿkpulo holokchi, n., a plant; a planted herb.

haiyuⁿkpulo ilhpak, n., sauce; vegetable food.

haiyuⁿkpulo ishkot hoita, n., a vegetable emetic, such as ipecacuanha.

haiyuⁿkpulo nihi, n., the seed of plants.

haiyuⁿkpulo nihi aiạlhto, n., the capsule.

haiyuⁿkpulo nihi hakshup, n., the capsule or pod for the seed.

haiyuⁿkpulo pakanli humma, n., a pink; a weed with a red blossom, particularly the Carolina pink.

haiyup, n., a twin; twins.

haiyup ạtta, a., twin born; born at the same birth.

hak, the, and its compounds. See *ak,* etc.; but as the compounds of the two differ in some instances, it is best to insert those of *hak* here at length, that necessary comments may be made regarding such particles as require them, having in mind also the different senses of the same word after different parts of speech. Compounds: *haka—hakano—hakat* or *hakạt — hakato* or *hakạto —hakbano — hakbano,* adv., that only— *hakcho — hakbanot — hakbat — hak choʔ* a form of inquiry used in anger—*hakhe,* etc., probably not used—*hakiⁿ—hakinli,* adv., also; likewise—*hakinli a,* pronoun, meaning self—*hakint—hakkia—hakma*, probably not used — *hako*, a particle — *hakocha—hakoka—hakokano —hakokat — hakokato —hakoke — hakokia—hakona—hakosh—hakot.*

hakbona, a., moldy; *tansh hakbona*, moldy corn.

hakbona, v. n., to be moldy.

hakbona, n., mold.

hakbonachi, v. t., to mold; to cause mold.

hakchalhpi, akchalhpi, n., the coarse outer bark of a tree.

hakchalhpi shila, n., ross; dry outside bark.

hakchihpo, n., driftwood.

hakchipilhko, see *hakchupilhko.*

hakchulhkapi, see *hakchupilhko api.*

hakchuma, hakchumak, n., tobacco.

hakchuma ashunka, hakchuma shunka, n., a pipe; a tobacco pipe; a calumet.

hakchuma alhfoa, n., a roll of tobacco bound up with bark.

hakchuma bota, n., snuff.

hakchuma bota aialhto, n., a snuff box.

hakchuma hishi, n., a tobacco leaf.

hakchuma holba, n., mullein; resembling tobacco.

hakchuma inshunshi, n., a tobacco worm.

hakchuma palaska, n., a brand of tobacco.

hakchuma shana, hakchumak shana, n., a twist of tobacco; a cigar.

hakchuma shunka, v. t., to smoke tobacco.

hakchuma shuti, n., an earthen tobacco pipe; a tobacco pipe of any kind; a calumet; the pipe used among the aboriginals of America.

hakchupilhko, hakchipilhko, akchupilhko, hakchupilhkash, n., dogwood.

hakchupilhko ani, n., dogwood berries.

hakchupilhko api, hakchupilhkapi, hakchulhkapi, n., the dogwood tree.

hakha, hahka, hakka, v. a. i., to loll.

hankha, n., a wild goose.

Hankhaiola, n., place where the goose cries; the name of a creek.

hankhobak, hankhoba, n., a large, wild water duck called a mallard, resembling a wild goose.

haklo, v. a. i., to hear; to listen; to assent; to comply; to yield; to attend; to hearken; to heed; to mark; to mind; to notice; to receive; Josh. 5: 1; Matt. 7: 24; 13: 15, 16; 15: 10; 17: 6; *ikhaklo*, not to hear; to dissent; to grudge; to refuse; to abnegate; to deny; to decline; to object; *ikhaklo*, a., deaf; listless; *hanklo*, nasal form, Matt. 5: 27; *hahanklo*, freq., Josh. 2: 10; *haiyaklo*, prolonged form; *ilehaklo*, to hear himself; John 3: 20 [?]; to listen to himself; *ilahaklo*, to hear of himself, what is said of him; *nana hash hanklo ka*, things which ye hear, Matt. 13: 17, 43; *haiyaklo*, intensive form, Matt. 2: 17, 18; 12: 19.

haklo, n., a hearer; a listener.

haklo, a., mindful; *ikhaklo*, a., mindless; deaf; reluctant; unheard; unwilling.

haklo, n., a hearing; heed; *ikhaklo*, n., a refusal; tardiness.

haklochi, v. t., to cause to hear; to make to hear; to inform; to notify; to signify; *haklonchi*, nasal form; *haklohonchi*, freq., made to hear; *sahaklohonchi tok*, made me to hear, John 15: 15.

haklochi, n., one that makes others hear; an informant.

haklotokosh anoli, n., an ear witness; he who heard it told.

haklopish, haklobish, n., ross, as *iti haklopish*, the ross of a tree; chaff; bran; shorts; fish scales; scales, Acts 9: 18.

hakmo, akmo, v. a. i., to congeal; to cool; to harden, as tallow when it cools.

hakmo, pp., a., congealed; hardened; cooled; cast; run; molded, as in a furnace.

hakmo, n., congelation.

hakmuchi, v. t., to cool; to cause to harden; to congeal; to found; to cast.

hakmuchi, n., a caster; a founder.

haknip, aknip, n., the body, trunk, chest, or frame; the thorax, Matt. 5: 29; 6: 22; 14: 12; *siaknip*, my body.

haknip achukma, n., health.

haknip achukma, a., healthy; healthful.

haknip bano, a., naked; nothing but the body.

haknip foni, n., the thorax; the bones of the trunk or chest.

haknip ikbi, v. t., to embody; to make a body.

haknip iksho, n., bodiless; incorporeal; without a body; disembodied.

haknip illi, pp., a., palsied.

haknip illi ạbi, n., the palsy.

haknip illichi, v. t., to palsy.

haknip inla, n., a monster; a strange body; another body.

haknip kota, n., feebleness; a feeble body.

haknip toba, n., incarnation.

haknip toba, a., incarnate.

hakonlo, n., name of a weed.

haksa hinla, a., fallible; capable of doing wrong; knavish.

haksi, a., deaf; drunk; tippled; intoxicated; inebriated; boozy; besotted; cunning; wicked; vile; stubborn; obstinate; abominable; arrant; bewitched; felonious; roguish; drunken; sinful; deceitful; disguised; double faced; evil; flagitious; fraudulent; fuddled; groggy; guileful; guilty; hollow; immoral; impure; insidious; lascivious; lewd; licentious; mellow; naughty; profligate; roguish; saucy; subtle; tipsy; turbulent; unfair; unprincipled; unruly; venal; vicious; villainous; wanton; wicked; wily; *nashuka haksi*, applied to an old man.

haksi, pass., seduced; stunned; swindled; deceived; cheated; cozened; defrauded; deluded; duped; fooled; gulled; muddled; overreached; *ilehaksi*, self deceived; *ilehaiyaksi*, Matt. 13: 22; *iⁿhaksi*, pp., tricked, or he is tricked.

haksi, v. n., to be vile, deaf, drunk, sinful, etc.

haksi, v. a. i., to act vilely, as *ishhaksi*, you act wickedly; to inebriate; to get drunk; to wanton.

haksi, n., drunkenness; deafness; deceit; deception; guile; a gull; hollowness; inebriation; inebriety; intoxication; lewdness; roguery; a shift; a sleight.

haksi, adv., rascally.

haksi chohmi, a., boozy; partly drunk; merry with liquor.

haksi keyu, a., guileless; guiltless; not *haksi*.

haksicha hinla, a., fallible; liable to be deceived.

haksichi, v. t., to beguile, Josh. 9: 22; to cheat; to deceive; to bewitch; to bilk; to impose upon; to mislead; to overreach; to delude; to befool; to abuse; to cajole; to coax; to surprise; to make drunk; to get drunk; to intoxicate; to cozen; to bribe; to lead astray; to deafen; to debauch; to decoy; to defraud; to delude; to disguise; to dishonor; to dupe; to fascinate; to fool; to fuddle; to gull; to inebriate; to juggle; to lure; to muddle; to overreach; to palm; to reach; to reduce; to sharp; to sponge; to stun; to swindle; to tantalize; to trick; *isht haksichi*, v. t., to cheat with; to bribe; *ilehaksichi*, to deceive himself, Gal. 6: 3; *haksinchi*, nasal form, *haksihinchi*, freq., v. t.

haksichi, n., a cheater; a deceiver; a rogue; a villain; a rascal; a cheat; a cozener; a defrauder; a deluder; a double dealer; a juggler; a seducer; a sharper; a swindler.

haksichi, n., chicane; a fallacy; a fraud; an intrigue; knavery; a lure; a stratagem; a trick; treachery, 2 Kings, 9: 23.

haksichi shali, a., tricky; knavish.

haksiepi, see *haksipi*.

haksinchi, a., unexpected.

haksinchit, adv., by surprise; or it may be rendered as a verb transitive with a consonant, as to cheat, etc.; *haksinchit anta*, he deceives and stays.

haksinchit ạbi, v. t., to assassinate.

haksinchit ạbi, n., an assassin.

haksint, contracted from *haksinchit*, adv., unexpectedly; by surprise; suddenly; *haksint ạla*, to arrive unexpectedly.

haksint ạla, v. a. i., to arrive unexpectedly.

haksint ishi, v. t., to take by surprise; to surprise.

haksint ishi, n., a surprise.

haksipi, haksiepi, n., rascality.

haksit illi, a., dead drunk.

haksit okpulot taha, pp., debauched.

haksobachi, see *haksubachi*.

haksobish, n., an ear; the skirts, as of a saddle; ears, Matt. 13: 9, 15, 16, 43; Luke 4: 21.

haksobish anli, n., a large flying insect, called by some a mosquito hawk or spindle. [Perhaps really *haksobish nuli*.—H. S. H.]

haksobish awiachi, n., an earring.

haksobish ạlmo, n. pl., cropped-ears.

haksobish ạlmo, a., cropped-eared.

haksobish bạsha, n., a marked ear; a cut ear; a cropped ear; an ear mark.

haksobish bạshli, v. t., to ear mark; to cut the ears; to mark the ears.

haksobish chaⁿsa, n., a sharp sound in the ear.

haksobish chiluk, n., the hole of the ear.

haksobish chuła, n., slit ears.

haksobish chułafa, n., a slit ear.

haksobish chułali, n. pl., slit ears.

haksobish hokofa, n., a cropped ear; an ear cut off.

haksobish hokołi, n. pl., cropped-ears.

haksobish hokołi, a., cropped-eared.

haksobish hotupa, n., the earache.

haksobish ibakchufanli, n., a foxed ear; an ear cut in the shape of a fox's ear.

haksobish ibakchufaⁿshli, n. pl.,foxed ears.

haksobish iksho, a., earless; without ears.

haksobish itakchulali, n. sing., a forked ear.

haksobish itakchulaⁿshli, n. pl., forked ears.

haksobish łitilli, n., the wax of the ear; ear wax.

haksobish takali, n., an ear ring; a pendant; jewelry; a jewel.

haksobish takalikbi, n., a jeweler; one who makes pendants.

haksobish takołi, n. pl., pendants; earrings.

haksobish tạpa, n., a cropped ear.

haksobish tạptua, n. pl., cropped ears.

haksobish walobi, n., the lobe; the lower and soft part of the ear.

haksuba, a., harsh; deafening.

haksuba, pp., stunned with noise; confused; deafened.

haksuba, n., confusion.

haksubachi, haksobachi, v. t., to confuse; to stun with noise; to deafen; to deafen with noise.

haksulba, a., simple; foolish; somewhat deaf.

haksulba, v. n., to be simple, foolish, somewhat deaf.

haksulba, n., foolishness; folly; deafness.

haksulbachi, v. t., to deafen; to make somewhat deaf.

haksun, n., a priming pan.

haksun aionchiya, n., the priming pan.

haksun chiluk, n., the vent of firearms; the touchhole.

haksun chiluk isht shinli, n., the priming wire.

haksun hishi, n., the earlock.

haksun oncheli, v. t., to prime.

haksun onchiya, pp., primed.

haksun tapaiyi, n., the temple; the part where the head slopes from the top.

haksun tapaiyi hishi, n., the earlock.

hakshish, akshish, n., the veins; sinews; arteries; cords; root, Matt. 13: 6, 21.

hakshish chito, n , an artery; a big vein; a large cord.

hakshup, n., skin; hide; shell; pod; comb; bark; scales; bur; husk; crust; rind; chaff of grain; integument; coat; cuticle; a film; a hull; a peel; peelings; the scarfskin; a tegument.

hakshup akuchichi, v. t., to shell.

hakshup aⁿsha, a., scaled.

hakshup fachowa, n., scales of a fish, Deut. 14: 9.

hakshup hish aⁿsha, n., a pelt; a rawhide; the skin of a beast with the hair on it.

hakshup ikbi, v. t., to crust; to make a crust; to incrust.

hakshup laua, a., scaly.

hakshup lufa, n., a paring.

hakshup lufa, n. pl., parings.

hakshup tạbli, v. t., to circumcise; *hakshup tạptuli*, v. t. pl., Josh., 5: 2, 3, 5, 7, 8.

hakshup tạpa, pp., circumcised.

hakshup tạpa, n., circumcision, or having circumcision.

hakshup tạptua, pp. pl., circumcised, Josh. 5: 5, 7.

hakshup toba, v. a. i., to produce pods; to form, as skin; to pod.

hakta, akta (q. v.), therefore; because.

haktampi, n., the armpit, and the spot or place just behind the forelegs of animals, on the chest.

halabushli, v. i., to begin to ripen, as corn, as *alaknat ia*, to turn yellow.

halaia, ahalaia, v. n., to feel an interest in; to be interested in.

halaiya, a., interested, concerned.

halaiya, n., interest; concern.

halakli, halalli, v. t. sing. (see *halalli*), to hold once; to jerk by seizing; see *shalakli, kannakli, chiksanakli*.

halalua, v. a. i., to be smooth.

halalunkachi, v. a. i., to shine.

halalunkachi, a., bright.

halalunkachi, n., brightness.

halalunkachi, pp., made bright.

halalunlichi, v. t., to brighten; to make bright.

halali, hallali, v. t. pl., to hold; to draw; to touse; to twitch; to jerk; to work a pump handle; *halalli*, sing (q. v.).

halali, v. a. i., to have the nerves affected.

halali, a., nervous.

halali, n. pl., a drawing; an affection of the nerves; a jerk; a twitch.

halali, n., a jerker.

halalichi, v. t. caus., to employ others to draw; to make them draw; to cause the nerves to be affected; *itahalalichi*, to make them draw together.

halambia, n., a scorpion.

halambisha, n., a bat.

halampa, hallampa (q. v.), n., a ringworm; a tetter.

halanchilanwa, n., a lizard.

halanchilanwa chito, n., a horned frog.

halanli, n., a hold; a restraint; a stay; see *halalli*.

halanli, n., a holder.

halat, hallat, adv., a contraction from *halalli*.

halat akkachi, v. t., to pull down; to pull and down it.

halat isht anya, hallat isht anya, v. t., to tow; to draw and take along; to tug.

halat kuchi, v. t., to pull out.

halata, v. a. i., to abate; to subside; to assuage; to remit.

halata, pp., assuaged; abated; *oka falama chito yokat halatatokoke*, the waters of the deluge abated.

halata kallo, a., headstrong.

halatali, v. t., to assuage; to abate.

halatat taha, a., low; entirely abated; gone down.

halalli, v. a. i., to draw.

halalli, n., a drawer; a holder; a hauler; an occupier; a puller; a supporter; an upholder.

halalli, a., tenacious.

halalli, halakli, v. t. sing., to keep; to occupy; to own; to preserve; to pull, Matt. 5: 29; to support; to treat; to tug; to cleave to; to draw, Matt. 13: 48; to hold; to sustain; to uphold; to lead; to conduct; to haul; to cling to; to drag; to grapple; to hale; to hand; to have; to jerk; to withhold; to catch, Matt. 14: 31; *itihalalli*, to draw together; to cleave together; to join; *itinhalalli*, to draw against each other; to pull against each other; *itihalalli*, pp., joined in marriage; *halanli*, to bear up, Luke 4: 11; to be holding; to hang or to hold on; to restrain; to retain; to stay; to steady; to suffer; *pit halanli*, to hold to, Matt. 6: 24.

halalli, n., a draw; a gripe; a haul; a pull; a support; a tug.

halallichi, v. t., to make him draw; *itihalallichi*, to cause them to unite or embrace, as in wedlock; to marry; to join; *ohoyo itihalallichi* (or *itahalallichi*), to marry him to a woman.

halappa, see *halupa*.

halasbi, halusbi, a., slippery; glib; smooth; shining; *halalua* and *halalunkachi*, pl.

halasbi, v. n., to be slippery.

halasbichi, halusbichi, to make slippery; to glib; to lubricate.

halatkachi, v. a. i. pl., to abate; *halata*, sing.

halatkachi, pp., assuaged; abated.

halatkachi, n., the state of being assuaged or abated.

hale! or alleh!, exclamation of children, uttered in time of distress.

haleli, v. t., to touch, but not with the hands; to affect with disease; *sahaleli*, it affects me, or I am affected with; to catch, as a disease.

haleli, n., a contagion.

halelili, v. t., to have caught; to graze.

halluns, see *haluns*.

haloka n., son-in-law; father-in-law; an appellation proper only for those who sustain this marriage relation, and not even used by others in speaking of them; a man who sustains the relation of uncle calls his niece's husband *haloka*, and the latter calls this uncle *haloka* in return.

haloka, a., sacred; beloved; dear.

halonlabi, halunlabi, halunlawi, n., the largest kind of bullfrog. [The word is to be found in Halunlawaⁿsha, "Bullfrogs are there," or, more concisely, "Bullfrog place," the name of a village which stood on the site of the present Philadelphia, Neshoba County, Mississippi, and is recorded on Bernard Romans' map of 1775 as Alloon Loanshaw.—H. S. H.]

halupa, haluppa, halappa, a., sharp; acute; keen; fine; piked; poignant; rough; rude; rugged; shrill; *ikhalupo*, a., dull; not sharp; obtuse.

halupa, v. n., to be sharp, acute, keen.

halupa, pp., sharpened; filed, as a saw; pointed; whetted.

halupa, n., sharpness; keenness; edge; an edge tool; point; roughness; *tanap aⁿya iⁿna halupa*, armor, 1 Kings, 10: 25.

halupa, ·adv., sharply.

halupa tuklo, a., double-edged; two-edged.

halupoa, v. n. pl., to be sharp.

halupoa, a., sharp; keen; acute.

halupoa, pp. pl., sharpened.

haluppa, see *halupa*.

haluppachi, v. t. sing., to sharpen; to edge; to file a saw to sharpen it; to point; to tip; to whet.

haluppachi, n., a whetter.

haluppalli, v. t. pl., to sharpen.

haluⁿs, yaluⁿs, halluⁿs, n., the leech; a bloodsucker.

haluⁿs chito, n., the horse leech.

halusbi, see *halasbi*.

halusbichi, see *halasbichi*.

halussi, see *holussi*.

halushki, n., lubricity; sleekness.

halushki, a., smooth; sleek; glib.

halushki, v. n., to be smooth; to be sleek or glib.

halushki, pp., smoothed; sleeked; lubricated; planed.

halushkichi, v. t., to make it smooth or sleek; to plane; to glib; to sleek; *itibasha yaⁿ halushkichi*, to plane a plank; to make smooth the sawed wood.

hala, n., name of a serpent.

halaⁿ, n., a large blackbird.

hali; in *alla nakni siahalili*, I am a boy; perhaps it should be *alili*, from which comes *ahnili*.

[**hamintini,** n., the june-bug.—H. S. H.]

hamo, adv.; in *imaiïthana aleha hamo*, John 4: 8; see *amo* and *yamo*.

hanahchi, haⁿchi, v. a. i., to hop on foot.

hanahchi, n., a hopper; a hop.

hanaiya, a., triangular; three cornered; *nantapaski hanaiya*, a three-cornered handkerchief.·

hanaiya, n., a triangle; the shape made by splitting a square handkerchief diagonally.

hanaiyachi, v. t., to make a triangle.

hanali, n., a limb of the body, or a quarter; one limb of a quadruped with the adjoining parts; a member; *hanali okpulo*, lame, Matt. 15: 30; halt, Matt. 18: 8.

hanalushta, n., the four limbs; the four quarters of any animal.

hanaweli, v. t., to double a handkerchief diagonally, tie it over one shoulder, and around the body under the other arm, and wear it.

hanaweli, n., one who wears a handkerchief thus.

hanannuⁿki, v. n., to be dizzy.

hananukichi, v. t., causative, to cause dizziness.

hanchi, v. t., to shell, as to shell off the outer shell of hickory nuts.

hanla, haⁿya, pp., shelled.

hanlichi, v. t., to shell or shuck hickory nuts.

hannali, hannali, n., six; 6; VI; the number six.

hannali, a., six.

hannali, v. n., to be six; *hannali hoke*, there are six; see below.

hannali, v. a. i., to make six; as *ehannali*, we make 6; *hannalashke*, Josh. 6: 3.

hannalichi, v. caus., to make six; *hannalet abelih*, I killed off six, or took six and killed; *lichi* is contracted to *let*.

hano, part., as for the; *antishu hano*, Matt. 12: 17, 18.

hanta, a., nas. form, from *hata* (q. v.), pale; white; bright; clear; ripe, as grain ready for the harvest, John 4: 35; wan; peaceable; *anumpa hanta*, Matt. 4: 23.

hanta, v. n., to be pale, white, bright, clear, wan.

hanta, n., wanness; righteousness; peace.

hantąchi, v. t., to make white, clear, bright.

hap, n., a harp, 1 Kings 10: 12.

hapąlak, n., a weevil; an insect which destroys ripe grain in the crib.

haponaklo, v. a. i., to listen; to attend; to give attention; to lend an ear, Josh. 1: 17; to give ear; to hear; to hearken; to hark, Matt. 11: 5; 17:5; isht haponaklo, to hear with, Matt. 13: 9, 43; 18: 15, 16: ikhaponaklo, neg. sing., not to hear; ikhaponaklo, a., deaf; surd, Matt. 11: 5; halhpanaklo, pp., to be heard.

haponaklo, n., a hearer; an auditor; a hearkener; a listener; sahaponaklo, my hearer (distinguish between this word and aponaklo, to inquire of).

haponaklo, n., a hearing; an audience.

haponaklo achukma, a., heedful.

haponaklochi, v. t., to cause to hear or attend.

hapukbo, n., down; the fine soft feathers of fowls.

hapullo, n., the seat of a man; the rump or the protuberant part behind; the buttocks.

hasimbish, n., the tail; a skirt.

hasimbish fali, v. t., to whisk; to flirt the tail.

hasimbish foka, n., a crupper.

hasimbish hishi, n., the hair of the tail.

hasimbish humma, hasimbichomak, n., a large red-tailed hawk.

hasimbish tąpa, n., a cropped tail; a bobtail; a short tail; a dock.

hasimbish tąpa, v. n., to be bobtailed; to have the hair cut short.

hasun, n., a bug that lives on the surface of water.

hash, renewed mention particle and its compounds; the said; the same; see ash and its compounds. The meaning of hash is nearly the same as ash, but as it occurs in a different connection, and chiefly for euphony's sake, I shall enter the word separately. Usually hash follows verbs, ash and yash nouns. nan imaiithąna ąleha hash, his disciples, Matt. 16: 20. hashke, let it be, Matt. 17: 4; see ashke. Compounds: hashano—hashąto — hashin — hashinli— hashkia—

hashon, the said, John 4: 42—hashocha, obj. case—hashoka, obj. case—hashoka-kon—hashokakocha—hashokakosh—hash-okano—hashokąt—hashokąto —hashoke—hashokia—hashona—hashosh, the said, John 4: 33; Luke 6: 2; ohoyo hashosh, Josh. 2: 4; nan imaiithąna ąleha hashosh, the disciples—hashot, the; the said, John 4: 11, 25, 40.

hashaya, see hąshaya.

hashinka, n., a pallet made of bearskin or buffalo skin.

hashinko, n., name of a plant, the leaves good for food mixed with tanfula (Indian hominy).

hashintak, see shalintak.

hashonti, v. a. i., to be puny, like liposhi; hashontichi, caus. form.

hat, adv., in akostininchili hat, ahni ąlhpesa.

hatachi, v. a. i., to ripen; to grow white; takkon ąt hatachi, the peaches ripen.

hatachi, a., ripe; white.

hatachi, n., ripeness.

hatanfo, n., hail; a hailstone, Josh. 10: 11.

hatanfo, v. a. i., to hail.

hatanfochi, v. t., to cause it to hail.

hatafottula, v. a. i., to hail; to fall, as hail.

hatak, see atak.

hatak, hątąk, n., a man; Matt. 9: 2; 18: 12; a person; a husband (hatak ąt ikimiksho, she has no husband); a being in some senses, but not in all; a human being; mankind; folk; folks; a mortal; mortals; a subject; an inhabitant; Kenan hatak, Matt. 10: 4; a red man; a native; an Indian, being used to distinguish the red men from the whites; hatak ąt ikbi, a red man made it; hatak an, a man, Matt. 15: 11. This word implies nationality; a man of the nation to which the speaker or the hearer belongs. hatak inkoi, an Indian mile; na hollo inkoi, an English mile. Kalili hatak, an inhabitant of Gallilee. hatak is a Jew with Jews, see Luke 10: 30; inhatak, n., a husband; a consort; a lord; her lord; her man.

hatak abeka, n., a patient; a sick man.

hatak achąfa, n., one man; an individual.

hatak afoha, n., a tavern.

hatak ahalaia, a., personal; pertaining to a man.

hatak aholopi, n., a graveyard; a burying ground; a cemetery; a tomb; a sepulcher; a place of burial; a catacomb; a churchyard.

hatak aianumpuli, n., a council ground; a place where men talk.

hatak aianumpuli chuka, n., a council house.

hatak aiattahe keyu, a., uninhabitable.

hatak aiyimita, n., a zealot.

hatak anuksita, n., a gallows.

hatak anuksiteli, n., the hangman.

hatak anuksiteli, v. t., to hang a man there or on.

hatak anuksitkạchi, n. pl., the gallows.

hatak anumpa isht aⁿya, n., an express; a messenger.

hatak anumponli, n., a speaker; a councilor; a counselor.

hatak anumpuli, n., a talking man; a pleader; *hatak ikanumpolo*, a mute; a dumb man.

hatak asahnonchi, hatak asonunchi, n. sing., an elderly man; a presbyter; *hatak asahnonchika*, pl., elderly men; elders.

hatak ashosh, the men, *hatak ashosh okla nukłakancha*, they marvelled, Matt. 8: 27.

hatak awaya, n., a married man; married by a woman, i. e., she has married him.

hatak ạbi, v. t., to murder; *hatak biⁿka ạbi* is the usual expression, to kill a fellow-man.

hatak ạbi, hatak biⁿka ạbi, n., a murderer; a man slayer; a homicide; a man killer; see Rev. 21: 8.

hatak ạbi, n., murder; manslaughter.

hatak ạbi, a., tragical; murderous.

hatak ạbi, pp., murdered.

hatak ạbit tałi, v. t., to murder or kill all the men.

hatak ạbit tałi, n., a murderer of men; a man killer.

hatak ạfikommi, n., a barefaced man; an impudent man.

hatak ạlhpesa, n., a gentleman; a fair man; a moral man.

hatak ạlhtoka, n., a committee man; a man that has some appointment; a commissioner; a delegation; a deputation; a legation; an official man; an officer.

hatak ạpa, n., a cannibal; an anthropophagite; a man eater.

hatak ạpi humma, n., a red man; a man of a red trunk or stalk; an Indian; a native of America; aborigines of America; aboriginals of America.

hatak ạpi humma iⁿmiⁿko, hatak ạpi humma miⁿko, n., a sachem; a sagamore; a miⁿko or mingo.

hatak ạpi humma inchuka, n., a wigwam; an Indian cabin.

hatak ạt, n., a man, Matt. 9: 9.

hatak baleli, n., a runaway.

hatak bạska, n., a gambler; a gamester.

hatak biⁿka ạbi, n., murders, Matt. 15: 19.

hatak chakapa, n., a blackguard.

hatak chaⁿshpo, n., the ancients; an ancient man.

hatak chạfa, n., a runaway.

hatak chilita, n., a blade; a bold, forward man.

hatak chito, n., a giant; a great man.

hatak chitokaka, n., a great man; a ruler; a lord; a noble; *hatak hochitokaka*, pl., the great men; rulers and magnates.

hatak chuka achạfa, n., a family; a household; a house; men of one house.

hatak chuⁿkash ạpa, n., animalculæ from which musquitoes grow, called by some wiggle tails.

hatak chuⁿkash kạllo, n., a hard-hearted man.

hatak chunna, n., a bare bones; a very lean person; a skeleton.

hatak fappo, hatak fạppo, n., a magician; a conjurer; a soothsayer (Balaam), Josh. 13: 22.

hatak fappoli, n., a magician, Gen. 41: 8.

hatak haiaka keyu, n., a recluse; a hermit.

hatak haksi, n., a bad man; a rogue; a villain; a caitiff; a rascal; a scoundrel; the wicked, Matt. 13: 49; 16: 4; a man given to crimes of any kind; a drunken man; a culprit; a debauchee; an evil doer; an evil worker; a knave; a profligate.

hatak haksi atapa, n., a ruffian.

hatak haksi okpulo, n., a renegade.

hatak haksichi, n., an impostor; a sharper; a cheat.

hatak halalli, n., the old-fashioned manager of funerals, who picked the bones of the dead and buried them and pulled up the red poles at graves.

hatak hikia puta, n., all men; all men in general; all standing men.

hatak hilechi, v. t., to man; to set men; to place men; to furnish with men.

hatak himaka, n., the moderns.

hatak himmita, n., a young man; a chap; a lad; a shaver; a swain; a youth.

hatak himmitaiyachi, n., a young man.

hatak himmitacheka, pl., young men.

hatak himmithoa, pl., young men.

hatak himona ohoyo itauaya, n., a groom.

hatak hobachi, n., an effigy.

hatak hobak, n., a poltroon; a coward; lit., a castrated man; a castrato.

hatak hochitoka, n. pl., the great men; senators; rulers; lords; elders, Mark 11: 27.

hatak hochitoka itanaha, n., a senate; the council of great men; elders, Matt. 16: 21.

hatak hofahya, n., a shamed man; a guilty man.

hatak hofahya iksho, hatak hofah-yiksho, n., a barefaced man; a shameless man.

hatak holba, n., an image or shape of a man; a picture of a man; the resemblance of a man; a statue.

hatak holba isht washoha, n., a puppet; an image of a man for a toy.

hatak holhkunna, n., a witch; a wizard; a dreamer; a necromancer.

hatak holhpa, pp., nettled.

hatak holhpa, n., a stinging worm; a nettle; one kind of caterpillar.

hatak holhpalli, v. t., to nettle.

hatak holhpalli, n., a caterpillar whose hairs are poisonous.

hatak holhpalli holba, n., a caterpillar resembling the one above named.

hatak holhtina, n., a census of the inhabitants; men numbered.

hatak holissochi, n., a scribe; a secretary; a writer.

hatak holissochi imponna, n., a penman; a skillful writer.

hatak holitompa, n., a nobleman, John 4: 46; a rich man; a gentleman.

hatak holitopa, n., a gentleman; a respected man; a beloved man; a rich man; a worthy man.

hatak holitopa banna, n., an ambitious man.

hatak hopi, n., a funeral; a burial; an interment.

hatak hopoksia, n., a wise man.

hatak hopoyuksa, n., a wise man; the magi, Matt. 2: 1; a sage; *hatak hopoyuksa yosh*, a wise man, Matt. 7: 24; *hatak ikhopoyukso yosh*, a foolish man, Matt. 7: 26.

hatak hotina, n., a capitation.

hatak hunkupa, v. t., to kidnap.

hatak hunkupa, n., a thief; a kidnaper; a man-stealer.

hatak hunkupa peni fokat anya, n., a privateer.

hatak hullo, n., a priest; the name also of one of the officers of government in ancient times; a sacred man (almost obsolete).

hatak hulloka, n., an enchanter.

hatak inhaklo, v. a. i., to listen to a man, i. e., to a seducer; to commit adultery (by a woman); n., a fornication.

hatak inhaklo, n., an adulteress; a fornicatress; a man listener.

hatak inhaklo, n., adultery, as committed by a woman.

Hatak inholahta, n., name of one of the great Choctaw families, the laws of which affect marriages, one of which is that any person may not marry another belonging to the same family.

hatak inkana, n., humanity; kindness to men.

hatak inkana achukma, n., a hospitable man.

hatak inkanohmi, n., a relation; kindred; a man's relations.

hatak ikhana, hatak ithana, n., an acquaintance; a friend; lit., a known man.

hatak ikhananchi, n., a tutor; a teacher.

hatak iksitopo, n., a cripple.

hatak ilakshema shali, n., a spark; a blade; a fop; a coxcomb.

hatak ilawata, n., a brag; a braggadocio; a boaster.

hatak ilbasha, n., a poor man.

hatak ilbạsha inla anukcheto, n., a pauper.

hatak illi, n., a dead man; a corpse; a corse; relics; remains.

hatak illi achopa, hatak illi chopa, n., the hunters for a funeral or pole-pulling who furnish venison, etc., for the company on that occasion.

hatak illi aiasha, n., tombs, Matt. 8: 28.

hatak illi ashali, n., a hearse.

hatak illi asholi, n., a bier.

hatak illi foni aiasha, n., an ossuary; a charnel house.

hatak illi isht afoli, n., a shroud.

hatak illi isht afoli, v. t., to shroud.

hatak illi isht anumpa, n., an obituary.

hatak illi shilombish aiasha, n., the place of departed spirits, sometimes identified with hell.

hatak illichi, v. t., to murder; to cause death.

hatak illichi, n., a murderer.

hatak imabạchi, n., a teacher; an instructor.

hatak imanukfila, n., the mind of man; the understanding of man; the thoughts of man.

hatak imanukfila achukma, n., a man of good mind, or good affections.

hatak imanukfila apissanli achukma, n., a candid man.

hatak imanukfila aⁿsha, n., a man of mind.

hatak imanukfila holitopa, n., a saint; a holy-minded man.

hatak imanukfila ikkạllo, a., feeble-minded.

hatak imanukfila iksho, n., a blockhead; a fool; a dunce.

hatak imanukfila shanaioa [or shanaia—H. S. H.], n., a capricious man.

hatak imanukfila tuⁿshpa, n., a wit; a ready-minded man.

hatak iⁿmiⁿko, n., an undertaker; the manager of a funeral, or for the disposal of the dead, as practiced in former times. He presided over the ceremonies, especially at the feast.

hatak iⁿmoma, n., a dwarf; a pigmy.

hatak impashali, n., an epicure.

hatak imponna, n., a proficient; a learned man.

hatak inla, n., a stranger; a foreigner; another man, Matt. 17: 25, 26.

hatak inlaua, n., polyandry on the part of the woman; lit., having many men.

hatak intakobi, n., a sluggard; a lazy man; an idler.

hatak intiⁿkba, n., an ancestor; his ancestors (and by his mother's side, or of her family; but see hatak tiⁿkba).

hatak iⁿnukkilli, n., a man hater.

hatak isikopa, n., an epicure; a glutton, Matt. 11: 19.

hatak isht ahalaia, a., human; pertaining to man or mankind.

hatak isht ahollo, n., a wizard.

hatak isht atia, n., the human race; generation of man; the human species.

hatak isht atia, a., descended from man; belonging to the human race.

hatak isht atia, v. n., to be descended from man.

hatak isht ạfekommi, n., a prig.

hatak isht ilawata, hatak nan isht ilawata, n., a braggadocio; a brag; a braggart.

hatak isht unchololi, n., the descendants of man; progeny.

hatak itahoba, n., an assembly of men; a collection; a gathering; a congregation of men.

hatak itakhapuli shali, n., a hector; a rioter; a rowdy.

hatak itạchowạchi, n., a peacebreaker; a breeder of dispute or quarrels.

hatak itạnaha, n., an assembly of men; a collection; a congregation; a multitude; a convention; a council.

hatak itạnaha pelichika, n., a moderator.

hatak ithana, see hatak ikhana.

hatak itiⁿkana, n., friends; mutual friends.

hatak itiⁿmiko, n. pl., the managers of a funeral or pole pulling.

hatak itiⁿnanaiyachi, n., a peacemaker.

hatak itishali, n., a boxer; a man who carries a club.

hatak kamạssa, n., a strong man; a firm man.

hatak kamạssạlleka, n. pl., aged men; men advanced in years.

hatak kamạssạlli, n., an aged man; a firm man.

hatak kanomona (from hatak kanohmi ona), n., a crew; a gang; a number of men.

hatak kauasha, n., a man somewhat past middle age and low in stature.

hatak kauashachi, n., approaching old age; being past middle age.

hatak kania, n., an exile; a straggler.

hatak keyu, n., no man; a worthless man.

hatak kostini, n., a wise man; a sensible man; a civil man; a moral man.

hatak lakna, n., a yellow man; a mulatto.

hatak laua, n., a crowd; a multitude.

hatak laua itanaha, n., a mob; a mass.

hatak laua yahapa shali, n., a rout.

hatak lauat anya, n., a caravan; a multitude of travelers.

hatak litiha okpulo, n., a sloven; a dirty man.

hatak luma, n., a recluse; a silent man.

hatak lumbo, n., an individual; one man.

hatak lusa, n., a black man; a black moor; a negro.

hatak lusa haui, n., a wench; a black woman who is a strumpet.

hatak lusa iklanna, n., a mulatto; a half black man.

hatak lusa isht atiaka, n., a zambo; a descendant of an African.

hatak lusa inyakni, n., Africa; the land of negroes.

hatak lusa inyannash, n., an elephant or African buffalo.

hatak lusa inyannash noti isht itibbi, n., ivory; the tusk of an elephant; lit., the fighting tooth of an African buffalo.

hatak lusa lakna, n., a mulatto; a yellow negro.

hatak lusa nipi humma, n., a mulatto.

hatak lusa ohoyo, n., a black woman; a negress.

hatak lusa ushi, n., a zambo; a son of an African.

hatak makali, n., a groveler; a scrub; a wretch.

hatak moma, n., the world; all mankind.

hatak moma okchalinchi, n., the savior of the world, or of all men.

hatak na pilesa, n., a laborer; a workingman; a hireling.

hatak nakni, n., a male (opposite to the female, who is *hatak ohoyo*); a man; a brave man.

hatak nan achefa, n., a launderer; a laundryman.

hatak nan anoli, n., an informer; a newsman; a notifier; a tale bearer.

hatak nan apesa, hatak nana apesa, n., a committee; a court; a senator; a judge.

hatak nan apistikeli alhtuka, n., a trustee.

hatak nan chumpa, n., a merchant man, Matt. 13: 45.

hatak nan inholitopa, n., an avaricious man; a hard-fisted man; a hunks; a scrimp.

hatak nan inhollo, n., a niggard; a miser.

hatak nan ikhana, n., a doctor, i. e., one qualified to teach.

hatak nan ikithano, n., a savage; a heathen; an ignorant man.

hatak nan inlaua, n., a rich man; a man of wealth or property.

hatak nan ithana, n., a learned man; a man of learning or knowledge; a statesman.

hatak nan ithana ilahobbi, n., a pedant.

hatak nan olabechi, n., a hinderer; a peacemaker; a mediator.

hatak nana yoshoba isht nukhanklo, n., a penitent man; a penitent.

hatak nanumachi, hatak nanumanchi, v. t., to backbite; to defame.

hatak nanumachi, n., a backbiter; a defamer.

hatak nanumachi shali, n., a great backbiter.

hatak nipi achukma, a., hale; healthy; n., a healthy man.

hatak nipi tohbi, n., a white man; the white man.

hatak nipi tohbika, n. pl., white men; the whites.

hatak nowat anya, n., a pilgrim; a wayfarer; a traveler; a lodger.

hatak nukoa shali, n., a churl; a hot-brained man; a hotspur; a madcap.

hatak nuksiteli, n., a death man; a hangman; an executioner.

hatak nusilhha shali, n., a blunderhead; a booby; a sleepy fellow; a dunce.

hatak ohoyo, n., a woman; a female.

hatak ohoyo ikimiksho, n., a bachelor; a single man; an unmarried man.

hatak okishko, n., a sot; a bibber; a tippler; a drinker.

hatak okishko atapa, a., intemperate; drunken.

hatak okishko shali, n., a hard drinker; a great drunkard; a bacchanalian.

hatak okla, n., humanity; mankind.

hatak okpulo, n.,a monster; a profligate; a wretch.

hatak ona, n., manhood.

hatak osapa toⁿksali, n., a farmer; a planter; an agriculturist.

hatak owatta, n., a huntsman.

hatak palammi, n., a potentate.

hatak paⁿsh amo, n., a barber.

hatak paⁿshi, n., man's hair; a scalp.

hatak paⁿya, n., a crier.

hatak pelichi, n., a ruler; a headman; a leader; a leading man.

hatak pelichika, n. pl., rulers; headmen; grandees.

hatak peni isht aⁿya, n., a pilot.

hatak pishukchikanchi, n., a milkman; a dairy man.

hatak puta holhtina, n., a census of all the people; the number of the men.

hatak sipokni, n., a graybeard; an old man; an elder.

hatak shaui, n., an ape, 1 Kings 10: 22; a monkey.

hatak shema shali, n., a fop; a coxcomb; a dandy; a man excessively fond of dress.

hatak takchi, n., a constable; a sheriff; "a man tier."

hatak tasembo, n., an insane person; a lunatic; a maniac; a rake.

hatak tasembo aiasha, n., a madhouse; a lunatic asylum.

hatak tamaha pelichi, n., a mayor.

hatak tanap aⁿya, n., men of war, Josh. 6: 3; 8: 3.

hatak tekchi imantia, a., henpecked; n., a henpecked husband.

hatak tiⁿkba, n., a man's uncles; a forefather; elders, Matt. 15: 2; antiⁿkba, my living uncles.

hatak tiⁿkba, n., an ancestor or antecessor; an ancient; the ancients; antiquity.

hatak tiⁿkba aliha, n., all antiquity.

hatak toba, n., manhood.

hatak toⁿksali, n., a laborer; a hireling; a working man; a workman, Matt. 10: 10.

Hatak Ushi, n., the Son of Man; Jesus Christ, John 3: 13, 14; Matt. 8: 20; *Hatak Ushi okato*, the Son of Man; *Hatak Ushi yat*, Matt. 10: 23; *Hatak Ushi at*, Matt. 18: 11.

hatak wishakchi, n., the tip end men; remnants of men; the last, or least among men.

hatak yahapa laua, n., a rabble.

hatak yopisa, n., a spectator; a looker-on.

hatak yopula, n., a jester; a joker; a humorist; a wag.

hatak yopula shali, n., a great joker; one addicted to joking.

hatak yoshoba, n., a lost man; a man who has wandered out of the way; a fallen man; a sinful man; a sinner; a malefactor; a wretch.

hatak yoshubli, n., a snail.

hatak yuka, n., a bondman; a prisoner; a captive.

hatak yuka atoksali, n., a penitentiary; a state prison, where prisoners labor.

hatak yuka keyu, n., a freeman.

hatak yukpali, n., a man pleaser.

hatak yushpakama, n., a bewitched man.

hatak yushpakammi, v. t., to bewitch a person.

hatak yushpakammi, n., a witch; a bewitcher; *ikhiⁿsh isht yushpakammi*, Rev. 21: 8.

hataklipush, n., a hen hawk.

hatakwa, a., like wood beginning to rot.

hatambish, n., the navel; the navel string; the umbilicus; see *haiombish.*

hatapofokchi, hatapofukchi, ibafakchi, hatabafakchi. n., a prairie hawk.

hatapushik, hashtapushik, hatapashi, hatapushik, hashtampushik, n., a butterfly.

hataffo, n., a grasshopper.

hato, hatoh, adv. of certainty. See *toshke. Weke hato?* heavy indeed, when not thought to be so; *chi banna hato? hatoh chikeh, hachi moma hato?* are ye also yet? Matt. 15: 16. *kahato*, old style of *kaheto.*—N. Graham.

hatoⁿfalaha, n., an eschalot; an onion; a leek; a scullion; *shachuna* is a name in use among the Sixtowns Choctaw for an onion.

hatoⁿf̱alaha chito, n., an onion; a large onion or eschalot.

hatok, hatuk, ẖattok, sign of the remote past tense, with *ha* prefixed. See *ha* and *atok*. These words pertain to the grammar as "particles;" cf. Matt. 13:13; *aⁿyali hatuk keyu*, I am not come, Matt. 9: 13; *atok*, Matt. 9: 13—Compounds: *hatoka—hatokako—hatokakocha—hatokakona—hatokakosh; hatokàkot—hatokano—hatokato—hatoḵat—hatoḵato—hatokinli—hatokkia—hatokma—hatukma; nan isht ạlhpisa hetukma*, the parable, Matt. 13: 18—*hatokmako; hatukmakoⁿ*, the sake of, Matt. 16: 25—*hatokmakocha—hatokmakona—hatokmakosh—hatokmakot—hatokmano—hatokm̱at—hatokm̱ato—hatukoⁿ*, for, Matt. 14: 4—*hatokocha—hatokoka; hatukoka*, because, Matt. 14: 5—*hatokoḵano—hatokoḵat—hatokoḵato—hatokoke—hatokokia—hatokona—hatokosh; hatukosh* in *hohchạfo hatukosh*, Matt. 12: 1; *hatukosh*, for, Matt. 13: 44—*hatokot; iknạlokahato* expresses a wish as well as certainty; as, he will not fail to be wounded.

hatokbi, a., pale; whitish.

hatokbi, v. n., to be pale; *hatak nashuka y̱at hatokbi*, the man's face is pale.

hatokbichi, v. t., to make pale; to bleach or whiten.

hatombạlaha, hatomạlaha, n., a beech; a beech tree.

hatombạlaha ạni, n., a beech nut.

hatomma, see *hatuma*.

haton lakna, a., brown colored.

haton lakna, v. n., to be brown colored.

haton lakna, n., brown color.

haton laknạchi, v. t., to color ḇrown; to brown.

hatonchi, v. a. i., to jump; to leap, as a man or a hobbled horse; *hatak ạt hatonchi*, the man jumps.

hatonchi, n., a jumper; a leaper.

hatonli, nasal form pl. of *hatulli* (q. v.); to jump.

hatonli, n., a jumper.

hatosh, atosh, yatosh, the compound particle made of *ạt* and *osh*, a strong contradistinctive of the simple definite *a; ạlat osh aⁿsha.*

hatosh, adv., not; not so; said when a person corrects his own statements; similar to *chikimba*.

hatoshba, atoshba, yatoshba, adv., can not; never can. *Holisso haⁿ* (Book it) *pisali* (see I) *keyu ḵat* (not who) *itẖanala* (learn I) *hatoshba* (never can); *issạmanoli* (thou me tell) *keyukma* (if not) *itẖanala* (learn I) *hatoshba* (never can).

hatoshke, adv., truly, John 4: 19[?]; certainly; spoken as an inference from facts which took place without the knowledge of the speaker; see *toshke* and *hato*.

hattaui, v. a. i., to prance.

hattauichi, v. t., to cause to prance.

hattauichi, v. a. i., to ride ostentatiously.

hattauichi, n., a prancer.

hatuk, ẖattuk, see *atuk* and *hatok*, Matt. 4: 24; those which were; those which had been, implying continued state of, or condition in; the immediate past tense; with the particles *a, ha, ya*, did; was; has; had; has been; had been; *chinchuka ialihatuk*, I was on my way to your house; *hatuk*, have, Matt. 2: 2; *sabạnnahatuk*, I have wanted and want now; *imaⁿyalihatok keyu*, I came not to them, past tense completed. Compounds: *hatukaⁿ*, the; *intishu hatuk aⁿ*, who sustained the relation of servant to Moses, and although Moses was dead, retained the name; had been and was the servant of Moses, Josh. 1: 1.—*hatukakoⁿ—hatukakocha—hatukakoka—hatukakoḵat—hatukakona—hatukakosh—hatukakot—hatukano—̇ hatukato—hatuḵat; intishu hatuḵat*, Matt. 8: 13—*hatuḵato—hatukinli—hatukkia—hatukma*, Matt. 7: 24—*hatukmakoⁿ*, for the sake of, Matt. 18: 5—*hatukmakocha—hatukmakona—hatukmakosh—hatukmakot—hatukmano—hatukm̱at; umba hatukm̱at*, the rain, Matt. 7: 25, 27; *ha*, which; *tuk*, was and is; *m̱at*, also, *t*, con. in nom. case; *antishu hatukm̱at*, Matt. 8: 8—*hatukm̱ato—hatukoⁿ*, by reason of, Josh. 9: 13—*hatukocha—hatukoka—hatukokakoⁿ, ilạppat hatak katiohmi hatukokakoⁿ*, what manner of man is this? Matt. 8: 27—*hatukoḵano—hatukoḵat*, for; because, Matt. 13: 5, 6; Josh. 1: 3; *tali paknạka* *yo^n aiitabana hatukòkạt*, rock on there founded for, Matt. 7: 25—*hatukokạto— hatukoke—hatukokia—hatukona—hatuk-osh—hatukot.*

hatukchaya, see *hạtukchaya.*

hatuko, adv., not (see *atuko*); *hina* (road) *yạt* (the) *aiyamba* (well chosen) *hatuko^n* (not) *a^nyalahe keyu* (go along I can not).

hatukosh, adv., not; *nahullo sia nanta hatukosh*, as I am not a white man.

hatulli, v. a. i. pl., to jump, as a hobbled horse; to canter; *hatonli*, nasal form, jumping; *isuba hạt hatonli.*

hatulli, n., a jumper.

hatullichi, v. t., to cause to jump; to canter.

hatuma, hotuma, hatomma, adv., evidently; *Mạshkoki ishittibitoko^n? Na katihmi hatomma; akbokitok.*

hatush, see *atush.*

hauachikchik, n., name of one kind of grasshopper.

haua^nsa, hopa^nsa, v. a. i., to champ; to chew; to chaw.

hauashko, hauwashko, a., sour; acid; tart; acetous; frowsy; hard; rancid.

hauashko, v. n., to be sour.

hauashko, v. a. i., to prick; to become acid; to quail, i. e., to curdle, as milk.

hauashko, n., sourness.

hauashko, pp., soured.

hauashko chohmi, a., subacid.

hauashkochi, v. t., to sour; to make anything sour; to turn sour, etc.

haui, v. t., to act the harlot; applied to females not to men, though in the New Testament this word is used in the masculine gender.

haui, n., a harlot; a whore; a strumpet; a fornicatress; an adulteress, Matt. 5: 32; Rev. 21: 8.

haui, n., lewdness; whoredom; *ahaui*, whoredom; 2 Kings 9: 22.

haui, a., lewd; lascivious; given to lewdness, as an abandoned female; wanton; adulterous, Matt. 12: 39; 16: 4.

haui, v. n., to be lewd (a female).

haui anukfoyuka, a., wanton; given to lewdness.

haui ikbi, v. t., to debauch.

haui ikbi, n., a whoremaster.

haui itimalhpisa, v. t., to commit adultery, Luke 16: 18 old translation.

haui pelichit nowa, v. t., to act the whoremonger; to pander.

haui toba, v. a. i.. to become a harlot; to prostitute one's self or herself.

haui toba, n., fornication, Matt. 15: 19.

haui tobạt nowa, v. a. i., to act the harlot.

hauk, huk, exclamation, oh, dear; alas; a man says *hauk* when a woman says *aiehna.*

hauwashko, hauwashkochi, see *hauạshko* above.

hawa, hahwa, v. a. i., to gape; to yawn.

hawa, n., a gaper.

ha^nwa, n., a locust; the small kind of locust; *washa* is the large kind.

hawạchi, v. t., to cause to gape.

hawạsh, hahwạsh, n., an adder.

haya, adv. of time, after. The particles are suffixed to it. The final syllable *ya* is changed in some respects for sound's sake, when some of the particles are suffixed; *ha* is the true word; *ya, yạt, yosh*, and *yo* are art. pronouns. In Matt. 1: 12 we have *ha* after *ya^n*, the; also cf. *hayokmakosh*, Luke 6: 42; *hayashke*, Matt. 17: 9.

ha^nya, pp., shelled or shucked, as hickory nuts.

hạbishko, n., a sneeze.

hạbishko, habishko v. a. i., to sneeze.

hạbishkuchi, v. t., to make one sneeze.

hạbishkuchi, n., snuff; maccaboy.

hạcha, n., a river; the name of Pearl River.

hạchi, hạch, per. pro., n. case of neuter, and passive verbs, 2 per. plu., you; ye or you; *hạchinusi*, you are asleep; *hạchilli*, ye die; *hạchinukshopa na*, Luke 2: 10; *hạchitalakchi*, you are tied; *hạchiachukma*, you are good, Matt. 5: 48.

hạchi, hạch, per. pro., in the obj. case before active trans. verbs, meaning "you;" *hạchianoli*, Matt. 15: 7; *hạchipisali*, I see you; *hạchipi^nsa chi^n ka;* Matt. 6: 1; *hạchikhanali*, I know you; *hạchikanimachi*, to despise or slight you; Matt. 5: 44, *hạchilbạshachi*, to persecute you, Matt. 5: 44.

hạchi, hạch, pos. pro. prefixed to nouns which are the names of the body and its members or personal qualities; your; *hạchinushkobo*, your heads; *hạchinish-*

kin, your eyes, Matt. 13; 16; *hachibbak*, your hands; *hachitekchi*, your wives, Josh. 1: 14.

hachiⁿ, pos. pro. prefixed to nouns which do not begin with a vowel or with p, ch, l, t, meaning your, as *hachiⁿholisso*, your books; *hachiⁿki*, your father; *hachiⁿ nan alhpoa*, your cattle, Josh. 1: 14; see *hachim, hachin, chiⁿ*, etc.

hachiⁿ, per. pro., in the dative case, prefixed to verbs, and usually translated with a preposition, as, of you, to you, from you, for you, and the like. This form of pronoun for the sake of sound precedes the same letters as described above; *hachiⁿhullo*, Matt. 5: 46; *hachiⁿnukkilli*, Matt. 5: 44.

hachia, per. pro., 2d per. plu., ye or you; *na hollo hachiahoke*, Matt. 5: 13, 14, 45; see *chia;* *hachiama*, Matt. 12: 34; ye, Matt. 15: 7; 16: 3; *hachia hokato*, ye, Josh. 1: 14; *hachia kat*, Matt. 12: 34.

hachik, n., a small bag; a satchel, such as are made by the Choctaw women.

hachik, 2d per. pl., neg. form, ye or you; *hachikminto*, ye do not come; *hachik chohmokashke*, Matt. 6: 2; *hachikayamihchokashke*, Matt. 6: 1.

hachim, prefix ed, pos. pro., 2d per. pl. in the obj. case before nouns beginning, with a vowel, as *hachimisuba*, your, horses; *hachimalhtoba*, n., your reward, Matt. 6: 1; *hachimalla*, your little ones Josh. 1: 14. See *hachiⁿ, hachin*.

hachim, prefixed, per. pro., 2d per. pl., in the dative case, before verbs beginning with a vowel and to be rendered with a prep., as, of you, for you, to you, from you, and the like, *hachimanoli, hachimanumpuli, hachimachilishke*, Matt. 5: 20; *hachimalhtoba*, Matt. 5: 46; *hachimanukfillit*, Matt. 5: 44. In Matt. 7: 2; *hachishnomat* and *hachim* stand in apposition; one is considered to be in the nominative and the other in the dative case.

hachim, nom. case before some neuter verbs beginning with a vowel, as *hachim okpulo*, you are angry, or there is evil in you. See *chim*.

hachimmi, adj. pro., your.

hachimmi, v. n., to be your.

hachimmi toba, v. a. i., to become your.

hachin, pre. per. pro., 2d per. pl., in the nom. case before nouns beginning with ch, l, and t, as *hachinchuka*, your houses; *hachintanap*, Matt. 5: 44; but *hachinmiha*, command you, Josh. 1: 13. See *hachiⁿ, hachim*.

hachin, pre. per. pro., 2d per. pl., in the dative case before verbs beginning with *ch, l,* and *t,* and is usually rendered with a prep., as, of you, for you, from you, to you, and the like.

hachin, pre. pro., your, found before some verbs when not before the noun in the nom. case, as *tanchi at hachintaha* instead of *hachintanchi at taha*.

hachishno, pro. pl., ye or you; *hachishno aⁿ*, Matt. 7: 1; *hachishnoma*, you also; *hachishnomat*, ye also.

hachishno, obj. case, you, Matt. 5: 46; 11: 21; *hachishno ashoⁿ*, you; *hachishno ashoⁿ hachiokpani*, rend you, Matt. 7: 6; *hachishno akint*, yourselves; your own; *hachishno akinli*, yourselves; your own; *hachishno yoka*, a., your; *hachishno yokat*, your; *hachishno yokato*, Matt. 13: 11.

hachishno, pos. pro., yours; your.

hafikbi, v. a. i., to sink, as land.

halapoli, v. a. i., to lap over; *nitak itoⁿhalapoli;* see *walapolih*.

halba, n., a glow worm; a lightning bug; the matter discharged from sore eyes.

Halbamo, n., Alabama.

Halbamo okhina, n., the Alabama River.

halbaⁿsha iksho, n., ill nature; ill will; see *halhpaⁿsha iksho*.

halbabi, v. n., from *halba* and *abi*, to have sore eyes, as *halba sabi*, I have sore eyes.

halbabi, n., sore eyes.

halbina, n., a present; a donation; a gift; a gratuity; *na halbina*, a present, 1 Kings 10: 25.

halbina, pp., presented; given as a present.

halhpaⁿsha, v. n., to be amiable, peaceable, kind, etc., Gen. 33: 10.

halhpaⁿsha, n., peace; kindness.

halhpaⁿsha, a., amiable; peaceable; kind; peaceful.

halhpaⁿsha iksho, halbaⁿsha iksho, a., unkind; cruel; ill natured,

halhpaⁿshi, adv., peaceably, Gen. 37: 4;
v. a. i., to be pleased, Gen. 33: 10.

hallali, see *halali.*

hallampa, halampa, n., a ringworm; a
tetter; herpes.

hallampabi, v. n., to have a ringworm or
tetter.

halwa, n., a soft-shelled turtle.

hala, pp. pl., kicked; trodden.

hali, v. t. pl., to kick; to tread; to step;
to stamp, to trample; *habli,* sing.

hali, n., treaders; steps.

halichi, v. t., to cause to tread on; to
trample; *isht ahalichi,* Matt. 7: 6.

hama, pp., rubbed; stroked.

hammi, v. t., to rub gently with the
hand; to stroke.

hammi, n., a stroker.

hammoli, v. t.; in *anumpa alhpisa ya hatak
okat kobahafitokoka* (or *okat*) *achukmalit
hammolit imantia cha, alhtobat illi tok cha.*

hanawia, n., suspenders.

hanan, hannan, n., a bird called a small
eagle, or a hawk; a swift bird of prey.

hannali, see *hannali.*

hannanuki, v. i., to turn round; to be
giddy.

hannaweli; hanaweli, n., one strap of
a suspender; a handkerchief hung over
the shoulders like a sword belt; a sling
by which to carry things.

hannaweli, v. t., to carry, as a gun,
with a sling that comes over the breast
and under one arm, the gun being behind.

hapi, n., salt, Matt. 5: 13.

hapi, a., salt.

hapi, v. n., to be salt.

hapi, hap, per. pro. we, nom. case, 1st
per., social pl. of neuter verbs, as *hapi-
nusi,* we sleep, i. e., we all sleep; *hapi-
taⁿkla,* all with us, Matt. 13: 56.

hapi, hap, per. pro. we, nom. case, 1st
per., social pl. of passive verbs, as *hapi-
talakchi,* we are bound, i. e., we are all
bound.

hapi, per. pro. us, ob. case, 1st per., social
pl., before active transitive verbs, as
hapipesa, he sees us, i. e., all of us;
hapiakaiya, to follow us, Matt. 15: 23.

hapi, hap, pos. pro. our, in the nom.
case, prefixed to nouns which are the
names of the body and its members,
as *hapichuⁿkash,* our hearts.

hapi aialhto, n., a saltcellar; a salt-bin,
basin, etc.

hapi aiikbi, n., a salt-work.

hapi atoba, n., a saline; a salt-work.

hapi champuli, n., sugar.

hapi champuli aialhto, n., a sugar bowl,
barrel, box, etc.

hapi champuli api, n., sugar cane.

hapi champuli okchi, n., molasses; the
sirup of sugar.

hapi champuli tohbi, n., white sugar,
called loaf and lump sugar.

hapi champuli yammi, pp., sweetened
with sugar.

hapi champuli yammichi, v. t., to
sweeten with sugar; to sugar.

hapi holba, n., salts; resembling salt;
saline.

hapi kanchi, n., a salter.

hapi kapassa, n., saltpeter; niter.

hapi kali, kali hapi oka, n., a salt
spring; a saline.

hapi lakchi, n., coarse salt; alum salt;
hominy salt.

hapi lakchi chito, hapi lakchi hochito,
n., rock salt.

hapi oka, n., salt water.

hapi okchi, n., brine.

hapi okhata, n., salt sea, Josh. 3: 16.

hapi pushi, n., fine or blown salt.

hapi yammi, pp., salted; seasoned with
salt; *hapi ikyammo,* a., fresh; not salted;
unsalted; unseasoned.

hapi yammichi, v. t., to salt; to corn.

hapi yammichi, n., a salter.

hapiⁿ, pre. pos. pro., our, prefixed to
nouns that do not begin with a vowel
or with *p, ch, l, t.; hapiⁿholisso,* our
book, or our books.

hapiⁿ, per. pro., us, 1st per. pl. in the dat.
case before verbs, and usually translated with a prep., as of us, to us, for
us, from us. This word is found written *hapiⁿ* before the same sounds as the
above.

hapiⁿ, 1st per. pl. social, our; the pro. is
removed from the noun in the nom.
and placed before the verb, as *nakni
tashka hapiⁿhotina,* he has counted our
warriors.

hapia, per. pro. nom. case, we, as *hatak
api humma hapia hoke,* we are all red
men.

hapim, pre. pos. pro., our, 1st per. social pl., prefixed to nouns which begin with a vowel and sometimes *p*, as *hapimisuba*, our horses.

hapim, per. pro., us, 1st per. social pl. in the dative case before verbs that begin with a vowel and usually translated with a prep., as *to, for, of*, etc., as *hapimanoli*, he told us; *hapimanumpuli*, he spake to us.

hapim, 1st per. social pl., our; the pro. is removed from the noun in the nom. and placed before the verb, as *isubat hapimilli* instead of *hapimisuba hat illi.*

hapimmi, a., our.

hapimmi, v. n., tu be our, or ours, Mark 12: 7.

hapimmi toba, v. a. i., to become our.

hapin, pre. pos. pro., our, 1st per. social pl. in the nom. case, before nouns beginning with *ch, l*, and *t*, as *hapinchuka*, our house.

hapin, per. pro., us, 1st per. pl., dat. case, before verbs beginning with *ch, l*, and *t*, and usually rendered with a prep., as *of, for, to, from.*

hapin, pos. pro., our.

hapishno, per. pro., we, 1st per. social pl., nom. case, i. e., you and I; you and we, etc.; all of us.

hapishno, obj. case, us.

hapishno, per. pro., our, 1st per. pl.; *hapishno akinli*, ourselves.

has, per. pro., ye or you, as *hassathana*, ye know me; *hassiachi*, ye say of me, Matt. 16: 15; *hassamashke*, Josh. 2: 13.

hash, per. pro., ye or you, 2d per. pl., nom. case, before active verbs, as *hashia*, Matt. 5: 44, 47, 48; 6: 1, 2; 13: 14.

hash isht ikhana, see *hashi isht ikhana.*

hashaⁿya, hashaⁿya, v. a. i., to get mad; to become mad, bristled or vexed; to pout.

hashaⁿya, v. n., to pout; to be cross or angry; *ilehashaya*, to be angry with himself, Gen. 45: 5.

hashaⁿya, a., cross; fretful; sulky; surly.

hashaⁿyachi, v. t., to fret; to make a person mad, cross, or fretful.

hashcha, n., an offense.

hashi, n., the sun; a luminary; a light, Josh. 10: 12; *hashi at kohchama*, when the sun was up, Matt. 13: 6; *hashi akoⁿ*, the sun, Matt. 13: 43; 17: 2.

hashi, n., a sunflower.

hashi, n., a moon; a lunar month; a month, Josh. 4: 19; 5: 10.

[Mr. Byington says of the Choctaw months: "But very few Choctaws know all the names or know when the months come in or go out." At first he inserted a list of month names in alphabetical order without stating whether they were obtained from one person or from several. Later he obtained and recorded two others, one October 23, 1854, from Ilapintabi, and the other December 31, 1856, from Iyapali. Ilapintabi told him that the year began in the latter part of September, while, according to Iyapali, it was in the latter part of March. Both of these statements are reconciled by a subsequent note to the effect that the year was divided into two series of six months each, a summer series and a winter series. From the time when these are said to have begun, September 21 and March 21, it is evident that the autumnal and vernal equinoxes were taken as starting points. The list of months obtained from Iyapali is in almost complete agreement with the earliest list recorded by Byington, and therefore is probably more correct than that of Ilapintabi. It is as follows:

March–April,	*chafo chito* (from *hohchafo chito*, "big famine")
April–May,	*hash koiⁿchush.*
May–June,	*hash koichito.*
June–July,	*hash mali.*
July–August,	*hash watullak.*
August–September,	*tek iⁿhashi.*
September–October,	*hash bihi.*
October–November,	*hash bissa.*
November–December,	*hash kaf.*
December–January,	*hash takkon.*
January–February,	*hash hoponi.*
February–March,	*chafiskono* (from *hohchafo iskitini*, "little famine").

Besides some inconsequential differences the earliest list has *hash watonlak* instead of *hash watullak.* No May–June month occurs in this list unless it is represented by "*luak mosholi*," the specific application of which is not given, and which appears to have been questioned by Mr. Byington's later informants. Since, however, a year of twelve strictly lunar months must be corrected at intervals to agree with the solar year, the editor suggests that *luak mosholi*, which means "fire extinguished," may have applied to an intercalary month or period at the time of the annual festival when the year began anew. Ilapintabi's list differs from that given only in inverting *hash koiⁿchush* and *hash koichito*, and *hash mali* and *hash watullak*, the first being made to fall in May–June, the second in April–May, the third in July–August, and the fourth in June–July.—J. R. S.]

hashi achafa, n., a month; one month; one moon.

hashi achafakma, adv., monthly.

hashi ahalaia, a., solar; pertaining to the sun.

hashi aiitolaka, n., the west.

hashi aiokatula, n., the west.

hashi aiokatula, a., west; occidental; western; westward.

hashi aiokatula imma, adv., occidental; westward, Josh. 1: 4; 8: 9.

hashi aiokatula mali, n., a zephyr.

hashi aiokatula pila, adv., occidental; westward; toward the west.

hashi aiokatula pilla, adv., to the west; at the west; away to the west; a., western.

hashi akochaka, hashi akuchaka, n., the east, Matt. 2: 1, 9.

hashi akonoli, n., a circle around the sun or moon.

hashi akuchaka, hash akuchaka, n., the east, Matt. 8: 11; orient; a., oriental.

hashi akuchaka imma, hash akuchaka imma, adv., eastward; easterly; toward the rising sun, Josh. 1: 15; 4: 19.

hashi akuchaka okla, n., the eastern people; the orientals.

hashi akuchaka pilla, adv., at the east; to the east; in the east.

hashi akuchapila, adv., toward the east; eastward.

hashi aopiaka, n., the west, Matt. 8: 11.

hashi atomi, n., the sunshine; the place where the sun shines.

hashi alhpisa, n., terms; the monthly course of females; menses.

hashi bolukta, v. a. i., to full, as the moon.

hashi bolukta, n., the full moon.

hashi himmona, n., the new moon.

hashi himmona talali, v. a. i., to change, as the moon; to pass the sun, as the moon in its orbit.

hashi himmona talali, n., the new moon.

hashi himo auata, v. a. i., to change, as the moon; to appear, as the new moon.

hashi himo auata, n., the new moon.

hashi holba, a., sunlike.

hashi inni, v. t., to bask; to warm by the sun.

hashi isht ikhana, hash isht ikhana, n., a watch; a timepiece; a chronometer; a dial; a timekeeper.

hashi isht ikhana iⁿshukcha, n., a fob; a watch pocket.

hashi isht ithana chito, n., a clock.

hashi isht ithana ikbi, n., a watch maker; a clock maker.

hashi kanalli, n., an hour, John 1: 39.

hashi kanalli alhpisa, n., an hour, Matt. 8: 13; 10: 19; 15: 28; 17: 18.

hashi kanalli isht alhpisa, n., an hour.

hashi kania, v. a. i., to go; to disappear, as the sun when eclipsed.

hashi kania, n., an eclipse of the sun or moon.

hashi kucha, n., sunrise.

hashi kuchaka, n., the east.

hashi libisha, v. t., to bask in the sun; to get warm by the sun.

hashi loshuma, n., the old of the moon.

hashi lua, a., sunburnt.

hashi lua, v. n., to be sunburnt.

hashi luhmi, v. t., to hide the sun, i. e., to eclipse the sun.

hashi luma, pp., eclipsed or hid, as the sun.

hashi moma, adv., monthly.

hashi ninak aⁿya, n., the moon, Josh. 10: 12.

hashi nitak isht ikhana, n., a calendar; an almanac.

hashi okatula, n., sunset; sundown.

hashi talali, n., the new moon, Ch. Sp. Book, p. 95.

hashi tohwikeli, n., daylight.

hashi tuchinakma, adv., quarterly.

hashilabi, ushelabi, n., a sty; a disease of the eyelid.

hashilli, v. a. i., to change, as the moon; this refers to the old of the moon.

hashilli, n., the change or death of the moon.

hashintak, n., a comb.

hashintak yauaha, n., a coarse comb.

haship, n., the breast of a fowl.

hashitombi, see *hashtomi*.

hashki, n., my mother, Josh. 2: 13; Matt. 12: 48, 49, 50; mam, or mamma; *chishke*, thy mother.

hashninak a^{n}ya, n., the moon; a luminary; a light.

hashninak a^{n}ya isht alhpisa, n., lunar measurement or calculation.

hashninak a^{n}ya tohwikeli, n., moonlight; moonshine.

hashontombichi, v. t., to sun.

Hashtali, n., the Great Spirit; the governor of the world, whose eye is the sun.

hashtampushik, hashtapushik, see *hatapushik*.

hashtapola, n., the bull nettle.

hashtap, hashtip, n., fallen leaves; dead leaves.

hashtap inchilakwa, n., chicken pox.

hashtap mali shali, n., drift.

hashtap yuloli, hashtap yoluli, n., a salamander; a small lizard.

hashtomi, hashtombi, hashitombi, n., a sunbeam; sunshine.

hashtula, n., winter; the winter season.

hashtula anta na lopulli, v. a. i., to winter.

hashtula chohmi, a., wintry.

hashtula iklana, n., midwinter.

hashtula tashka chipota aiasha, n., winter quarters for an army.

hashtulahpi, n., the fall; autumn; the fall season.

hashtulammona, n., the early part of winter.

hashuk, n., grass; herbage; sward, Matt. 6: 30; 14: 19.

hashuk abasha, n., a place mowed; where grass has been cut; a meadow.

hashuk aiamo, n., a meadow.

hashuk ashachi, v. t., to mow; to put away hay or grass.

hashuk ba^{n}si, n., a wild grass of which hand brooms are made.

hashuk basha, pp., mowed; mown.

hashuk basha shila, n., hay; mowed grass.

hashuk bashli, v. t., to mow; to cut grass.

hashuk bashli, n., a mower.

hashuk cha^{n}shlichi, n., a large green grasshopper which sings loud and in the morning.

hashuk chito, n., great grass; stout grass; thick and heavy grass.

hashuk foka, a., grassy.

hashuk hata, n., a bird having a small body and long legs, often seen around water and muddy places.

hashuk impa, v. a. i., to pasture.

hashuk impachi, v. t., to pasture; to graze.

hashuk ipeta, v. t., to graze.

hashuk isht bashli, n., a hook.

hashuk isht holmo, n., a thatch.

hashuk isht homo, v. t., to thatch.

hashuk isht itannali, n., a rake.

hashuk itanaha, n., a haycock; a pile of hay; a rick of hay; a mow; a swath of grass.

hashuk itannali, v. t., to collect hay; to rake hay.

hashuk lohammichi, v. t., to trail the grass.

hashuk malli, v. a. i., to lighten; to flash, as lightning (lit., grass leaps, or to leap over grass).

hashuk malli, n., lightning; a thunder bolt; electricity; a flash of lightning.

hashuk pancha, n., a flag; a blue flag; a "cattail" flag.

hashuk patalhpo, n., a grass bed; a straw bed.

hashuk pata, n., crab grass; crop grass.

hashuk shila, n., hay; cured grass.

hashuk shileli, v. t., to hay; to cure grass.

hashuk shileli, n., a haymaker.

hashuk umpoholmo, n., thatch.

hashuk umpoholmo, pp., thatched.

hashuk umpohomo, v. t., to thatch.

hashwish, hashwash, n., worms; those of a small kind that affect children as a disease.

hat, art., the, nom. case, suffixed to nouns; *aleha hat*, they; Matt. 2: 1. Sometimes written *at* and *yat* as well as *ha*, *a*, and *ya* (q. v.).

hat, rel. pro., when suffixed to verbs.

hat, used before *tok* and *tuk*.

hąta, an adv. in recent past tense, expressing surprise.

hąta, n., paleness.

hąta, a., pale; white; cadaverous; pallid; sallow.

hąta, v. n., to be pale; *hanta*, nasal form (q. v.).

hąta, n., a gleet; gleets.

hąta lakna, n., a yellow white; an orange color.

hąta lakna, a., having a yellow-white color.

hąta laknąchi, v. t., to color a yellow white.

hąta ont ia, v. a. i., to have the gleets; to gleet.

hąta ont ia, n., the whites.

hątabafakchi, see *hatapofokchi.*

hątachi, v. a. i., to turn white; to become pale; to ripen, as peaches. See *hatachi.*

hątachi, n., a light color.

hątakbi, a., white, like a man's tongue in fever.

hątapakli, v. a. i., to gallop.

hątapaklichi, v. t., to gallop.

hątapofukchi, n., a prairie hawk.

hątapusha, n., the bull nettle.

hątapushik, hatapushik, n., a butterfly.

hątąk, see *hatak.*

hątąt kąnia, a., very pale.

hątąt kąnia, v. n., to be very pale; v. a. i., to become very pale.

hątip, n., the rump; the croup or crop.

hątto^n, adv.; *ishwiha hątto^n?*

hąttoK, see *hatok.*

hątukchaya, hatukchaya, n., a great witch; an imaginary being who makes Choctaw doctors.

he, art., see *ak.*

he, heh, ahe (q. v.), adv., almost; well nigh; *etala he,* we have almost finished it; nearly, Luke 8: 42; cf. *hikma.*

he, hi, sign of the remote future of the indicative mood; shall; will. Compounds: *hea—heakano—heakat—heakato— heakąt— heaki^n — heakinli — heakint — heakkia — heakma — heakmako— heakmakocha — heakmakona—heakmakosh—heakmakot—heakmano—heakmąt—heakmąto—heako—heakocha—heakoka—heakokąno— heakokąt— heakoke — heakokia—heakona—heakosh—heakot—heatok, heatuk, hiatuk,* etc., should have—

hekak, etc., see *kak,* and its compounds—*hekako^n,* but; for—*hemak—hemaka—hemakano—hemaki^n — hemakinli — hemakint — hemakkia — hemako —hemakocha—hemakoka — hemakokat — hemakoke — hemakona — hemakosh — hemakot — heo^n,* Matt. 6: 1—*heoka—heokama—heokąt—heoke, hioke; laua hioke,* many will there be, Matt. 7: 22; *achilahioke,* say I will; Matt. 7: 23—*heokmano—heokmąt—heokmąto—hetok,* should have been; would have been; might have been; remote—*hetuk,* recent past tense, might have been; ought; *hąshata^nyahetuk ąt,* Josh. 2: 16; 3: 4.

he keyu, adv., can not; shall not: will not.

heahni, see *hiahni.*

heąlhpesa, n., an occasion.

hehi, v. a. i., fem. gen., to sing.

hehi, n., fem. gen., a singer.

hehio, hehyo, n., the name of a wild root.

hehka, v. a. i., to start; to recoil; to startle; to wince.

hehka, n., a starter; a wincer.

hehkąchi, v. t., to startle.

hehkąt anumpuli, v. t., to extemporize.

hehkąt anumpuli, n., an extemporizer.

hekąno, n., the last speech of a dying man.

heli, v. a. i. pl., to fly; to go in haste, Matt. 28: 8; *hika,* singular.

heli, n., fliers.

heli, a., flying; volant.

helichi, v. t., to cause to fly; to scare away, as birds; to make them fly.

heląchi, see *hiląchi.*

heno, art. in the obj. case, from *heto.*

hepulla, a., apt; liable; obnoxious; probable; subject.

hepulla, n., danger.

hepulla, v. n., to be surely; surely to be.

het, art. in nom. case; *hi^n,* oblique case; see *akhet.*

het, adv.; see Acts 7: 17; *nitak ąt aiona^n het maha^nyama; het* is a sign of the future with the connective *t.* The word is *a^nheh,* near; a diminution of which is *a^nhusi;* the final *h* is elided by the substitution of *t* copula.

heto, art., see *akheto; hato* obsolete style for *heto; iklokahato, ikaiyohkaato.*

heto, adv. of neg., can not; will not; shall not; impossible; when this follows a verb in the neg. form it becomes an affirmative, as *iklokaheto*, he will not not come, i. e., he will surely come.

heto, a., impossible.

heto, v. n., to be impossible.

hetuk, ought, Matt. 18: 6.

hi, ahi, sign of indic. fut.; see *he* (properly *ahe*).

hiⁿ, int., pshaw, meaning dislike or contempt.

hiahni, heahni, v. a. i., to love; to esteem, *heishahni, hiahnili, heilahni*.

hiahni, v. t., to caress; to love; to dote upon; irreg. v., *tali holisso hiahni*, he loves money; *hiahnili*, I love; *hiishahni*, thou lovest; *hiahni*, he loves; *hiilahni, hiiloahni, hehachahnili*, I love you (pl.).

hiahni, n., a lover.

hiahni, a., merciful.

hiahni iksho, n., apathy; fell.

hiahni iksho, a., without love.

hiahni iksho, v. n., to be without love.

hiasinti, see *iasinti*.

hichali, a., spiteful; brave; *iⁿhichanlitok*.

hichali, v. n., to be spiteful.

hichali, n., spite.

hichi, n., a boil; a tubercle; a wild turnip.

hichuk, n., the name of a root, of which the Choctaw have made bread in a time of scarcity; see *kifash*.

hichukbi, hochukbi, n., a natural pit or hole in the ground, or one that runs under ground, as a chasm; a pit; a hole; a cave; a cavern; a den, Josh. 10: 17, 18, 27; 2 Sam. 18: 17; cave of Machpelah, Gen. 23: 9; see *tali chiluk*.

hichukbi chito, n., a cavern.

hichukbi foⁿka, v. a. i., to den; to dwell, as in a den.

hichushi, n., a tubercle; small boils.

hieli, v. a. i. pl., to stand, Josh. 3: 14, 17; 6: 4, 13; 7: 12; 8: 10; *itikba hieli*, to stand before; *hikia*, sing.; *hinli*, nasal form.

hieli, pp., set up; placed.

hieli, n., those which stand; those who stand.

hielichi, hiolichi, v. t., to erect; to set up; to cause to stand.

hiⁿha, v. a. i., to groan.

hiⁿha, n., a groan.

hiho, int., ah.

hika, pp., pawned; pitched; placed; set; cocked; *ikhehko*, a., uncocked; *iⁿhika*, n., a pillar.

hika, v. a. i. sing., to fly; to flit; to wing; to soar; to. touch with the feet; *aioⁿhikahe* or *hikiahe*, to stand on (*ai*, there or where); to tread on, Josh. 1: 3; to rest in, Josh., 3: 11, 13, 15; 4: 18; *heli*, pl.

hika, a., volant; volatile; flying.

hika, n., a flier; a line.

hika, n., a stand.

hika, n., a tree called sweet gum, and the gum or wax.

hiⁿka; *aka hiⁿka*, a footman; *oka hiⁿka*, to be in the water.

hika nia, n., the gum of the sweet gum tree.

hikachi, v. t., to cause to fly; to scare away a bird; to make it fly.

hikat aⁿya, v. a. i., to soar.

hikbat, adv.; *ayukpa hikbat*, can not be joyful.

hiket aⁿya, v. a. i., to be with, Luke 9: 41.

hiket ia, v. a. i., to start; to begin, as in running a road or lines.

hikia, v. a. i. sing., to stand, Josh. 3: 13; 5: 13; to go; to get, Luke 4: 8; to be or stand, as a well or spring, Josh. 4: 6; to hold; to look, as *pit hikia, et hikia*, to look toward; *hikiⁿa*, nasal form, to sit, as fowls on their roost; to stop, Matt. 11: 11; *hikia*, for to be, to stand; *hikiashke*, for the verb to be; Matt. 16: 23; *hikiatok*, Matt. 17: 2; *iⁿhikia*, to have; *tanampo iⁿhikia*, he has a gun; *hikint; oⁿhikia*, to stand on; to perch; *hieli* pl.

hikia, n., that which stands; a stand.

hikia, a., standing, as *hatak hikia*.

hikia, pp., erected; set up; established; installed; pitched; placed.

hikia toba, v. a. i., to get able to stand or walk.

hikiat ia, prep., from, Josh. 1: 4.

hikikia, v. a. i., to go, as one looking for a lost object, Matt. 18: 12.

hikikiⁿa, v. a. i., to stand about; to walk about; to attend to some little business; a frequentative after the example of *bininiⁿli* and *yananaⁿli;* see Matt. 18: 12. *Chisas at . . . hikikiⁿatok*, John 10: 23 *nowat hikikiⁿa*, Mark 11: 27; *binili*, to sit, *bininiⁿli; kanalli*, to move, *kananaⁿli; yanalli*, to run, *yananali*.

hikikiⁿa, n., one that walks about.

hikma, from *he*, almost or well-nigh, and *ikma*.

hilechi, v. t., to set, Matt. 18: 2; Josh. 7: 26; to set up; to put up; to take up, as a stray; *isuba haⁿ aioⁿhilechi*, to set on; *ikbit hilechi*, to rear, Matt. 16: 18; 2 Sam. 24: 18; to rear up, John 2: 20; to check; to cock, as a gun; to erect; to establish; to fill, i. e., to supply a place with an incumbent; to ground; to fix; to inaugurate; to install; to instate; to institute; to invest; to ordain; to pawn; to place; to pledge; to present; to raise; to seat; to settle; to station; to stick.

hilechi, n., a setter up; an institutor; a pawner; a placer.

hilechi, n., an installation.

hiⁿlhhiⁿlhachi, v. a. i., to quack; *okfochush at hiⁿlhhiⁿlhachi;* the duck says *hiⁿlhhiⁿlh.*

hiloha, v. t., v. a. i., to thunder; to fulminate; to intonate, 1 Sam. 2: 10.

hiloha, n., thunder; a peal of thunder; a clap of lightning; a thunder clap.

hiloha, a., thunder, as a thunder storm.

hiloha abi, hilohabi, pp., killed by lightning.

hiloha abi, hilohabi, v. t., to kill by thunder; to strike with lightning; to thunder strike.

hiloha hoshintika, n., a thunder cloud.

hiloha tassa, hiloha bassa, n., a sharp peal of thunder.

hiloha umba chito, n., a thunder shower.

hilohachi, v. t., to cause it to thunder.

hilohachi, n., a thunderer.

hila, v. a. i., to dance; to frolic; to gambol; to hop, Matt. 14: 6; *hachikheloshke*, ye have not danced, Mat. 11: 17; *ishit hila*, v. t., to triumph over by means of, 2 Sam. 1: 20.

hila, n., a dance; a ball; a frolic; a minuet; *nakni hila*, a male dance, in which none but men are engaged; *nashoba hila*, n., a wolf dance; *paⁿshi isht hila*, n., a war dance, or a hair dance or scalp dance.

hila, n., a dancer; a frolicker.

hilachi, helachi, hilachi, v. t., to cause to dance; to make others dance; to dance.

hima, may be the root of the following words: *himma, himak, himmak; hima.*

himak, a., instant; current; present; modern; this; *himak at*, this is, Luke 1: 36.

himak, adv., now; at this time, 2 Sam. 24: 2; *himakashke*, v. i., Matt. 11: 12.

himak, n., now; the present time, moment, or instant.

himak afammi, n. or adv., this year; the present year.

himak ano, adv. or n., now; as for the present time.

himak foka, n. or adv., about this time; *palashash himak foka, pilashash himak foka*, yesterday about this time.

himak fokalechi, a., presumptuous; hazardous; wandering.

himak fokalechi, v. a. i., to act at random; to run a hazard; to act rashly; *himak fokalechit anumpuli*, v. t., to chatter; *himak fokalechit aⁿya*, to wander.

himak fokali, v. a. i., to go or act at random or at hazard.

himak fokali, n., random.

himak fokalit, adv., with hazard or carelessly; headlong; head first.

himak fokalit anumpuli, v. a. i., to babble; to prate; to talk at random; to quibble.

himak fokalit anumpuli, n., a quibbler.

himak fokalit aⁿya, v. a. i., to go along at random without a guide or road; to wander.

himak fokalit hochefo, v. t., to nickname.

himak fokalit hohchifo, n., a nickname.

himak fokalit holissochi, v. t., to scrawl; n., a scrawler.

himak fokalit miha, v. a. i., to guess; to conjecture.

himak hashi, n., this month.

himak ninak, n., adv., this night; tonight.

himak nitak, n., this day; adv., today; the present day, or time, Matt. 6: 11; 11: 23; this day, Josh. 5: 9; now, Matt. 15: 2.

himaka, adv., n., now; the time now; the present time, Josh. 1: 2; Matt. 14: 15.

himakma, a., more; moreover.

himma, adv., aux. (from *he*, future gen., and *imma*, toward; direction of), shall hereafter; shall toward; will; with *keyu*, not ever; never; *lakofa himma keyu*, he will never recover; toward recovery he never will.

himma, v. n., to be hereafter, as *chihimmali*, I, after you.

himma keyu, adv., never; ne'er.

himma keyu, v. n., never to be.

himmak, a., subsequent; following; unborn; future; younger; intensive form of *himak*, as *pilla* is the intensive form of *pila;* see *ilappak, yammak*, words of a similar character.

himmak, v. n., to be subsequent; *inhimmak*, to be after him; *sahimmak*, to be after me, John 1: 27.

himmak, adv., hereafter; afterward; after; at last; *himmak ishanya*, at last, you are along.

himmak foka, adv., hereafter; about this time.

himmak pila, n., the coming time; adv., henceforth; henceforward; hereafter.

himmak pilla, n., the time that is to come; the future time; the future.

himmak pillama, adv. or n., hereafter; from henceforth; for the future time; henceforward.

himmakma, v. n., in the sub. mood; lit., when it shall be hereafter, but it is usually rendered as an adverb, hereafter; at a future time; by and by; furthermore; next, Matt. 5: 13; then, Matt. 18: 16; any more, Josh. 5: 1, 12.

himmita, v. n., to be young.

himmita, a., young; fresh; sappy; youthful.

himmita, n., the young; youth; the flower; a youngster.

himmita aliha, n., the youth.

himmita chohmi, a., youngish.

himmitasi, a., young, Luke 2: 36; green.

himmitasi, v. n., to be young.

himmitacheka, a. pl., young.

himmitachi, v. t., to make young; to rejuvenate; to renew; *himmitaiyachi*, pro. form.

himmithoa, a. pl., young; *wak himmit hoa*, young cattle, but not very young.

himmithoa, v. n. pl., to be young.

himmithoa, n. pl., those who are young; the youth; the young ones; the flower.

himmitushi, a. (dim.), young.

himmona, n., newness; a novelty; once, Matt. 9: 33; with a negative, never.

himmona, himona, a., new, Matt. 13: 52; brandnew; present; fresh; novel; recent; virgin; young.

himmona, pp., renewed; renovated.

himmona, v. n., to be new.

himmona aioklachi, v. t., to repeople.

himmona chuhmi, a., newish.

himmona iktobo, a., unrenewed; unregenerate.

himmona isht atta, n., a novice.

himmona toba, pp., renovated.

himmonacha hinla, a., renewable.

himo, adv., now; just now, John 2: 9; *himo ela*, we have just arrived.

himona, n., now; the present time.

himona, adv., now; just; afresh.

himona achafanlit kanima anta, n., ubiquity.

himona hofanti, v. a. i., to be growing up now.

himona hofanti, n., present generation.

himona hofanti, a., pp., just raised; just grown.

himonachi, himonachi, v. t., to make new; to renew; to renovate; *ilehimonachi*, to renew himself.

himonali, v. n., to be at once or in a moment; *himonanli*, nasal form.

himonali, v. a. i., to do at once.

himonali, adv., at once; all at once; instantly; forthwith.

himonanli, adv., forthwith.

himonasi, v. n., to be instantly.

himonasi, n., now; just now; this moment, Matt. 9: 18; 17: 12.

himonasi, adv., immediately; instantly.

himonasi achafa, n., one minute.

himonna, n., a single instance.

himonna, adv., once; Luke, 5: 1; Josh. 6: 3.

himonna, v. n., to be once or a single time.

himonnan, v. n., to be often; to be frequently or repeatedly; Matt. 17: 15.

himonna achafa, v. n., to be at one time.

himonna achafa, adv., at the same time; *himonna achafa mont ikanumpuli*, let all speak at once.

himonna achafa halalli, n., a single haul.

himonna achafanli, adv., once.

himonna isht atta, n., a novice.

himonna tapli, v. t., to sunder once; to clip off once; n., a single clip.

himonnaha, adv., once; one time.

hina, n., a road; a path; a street, a way, Josh. 2: 19; Matt. 7: 13; a furrow; a pass; a pathway, Luke 3: 4; a route; a row; a track; a trace; an alley; an avenue; a walk; *Nachi inhina*, the Natchez Trace.

hina apesa, v. t., to run a road; to lay out a road.

hina abanabli, v. t., to cross another road; to go over the road.

hina abanabli, n., a crossroad; crossroads.

hina bashpuli, n., a scavenger.

hina chito, n., a large road; a highway; a broad way; a large path; a wagon road.

hina falakto, n., a fork in a road.

hina hanta, n., a bright path; the way of peace; the gospel path; the narrow way of life.

hina ikbi, hinikbi, v. t., to make a road, or a row; to furrow; to lay off furrows for planting; to path.

hina ikbi, hinikbi, n., a road maker; one who makes roads or furrows; a way maker.

hina ikpatho, n., a lane; a narrow way.

hina kucha, n., a ford; a pass.

hina onhanabli, v. t., to cross over another road.

hina onhanabli, n., a crossroad; crossroads.

hina patha, n., a broad road; a wagon road; a highway; a street.

hina takla kahat hunkupa, n., a high wayman.

hinak, okhinak, n., a corn tassel, or the flower of corn on the top of the stalk; also v. a. i.

hinak bitepuli, hinak atepuli, hinak batepuli, n., the rainbow; the bow of promise; Iris.

hinak bitepuli, v. a. i., to form or become a rainbow; lit., to rainbow.

hinak kucha, n., the appearance or coming out of the corn tassel.

hinak toba, v. a. i., to become a corn tassel; to tassel, as corn.

hinak toba, pp., made as corn tassels; tasselled.

hinakfoata, n., a crossroad.

hinakfoata, v. a. i., to cross another road.

hinakshu, n., an old deserted road; an unused road.

hinanli, a., along the road.

hinanli, v. n., to be along the road.

hinikbi, see *hina ikbi*.

hinla, a., liable; likely; obnoxious.

hinla, ahinla, sign of the potential mood, can; may; shall; will, Matt. 6: 7, 21; 12: 29; Luke 5: 7; *katiohmihahinla*, Luke 8: 9; *hahinla*, Luke 4: 7, 38; Matt. 2: 4, 13; John 4: 40, 47; *hinlashke*, would, Matt. 12: 38.

hinla, can be, or the English ending -ble, as in fusible.

hinlatok, could; could have; would.

hinlatuk, could; could have; might; might have; should; would.

hinli, nasal form, from *hieli; haksobish at inhinlikmat*, Matt. 11: 15; *aiapinhat hieli*, Matt. 12: 41.

hinli, pl., i. e., from two to four; to be standing; *haksobish at inhinlikmat*, if he have ears, Matt. 13: 9.

hinluk, n., a small green-headed wild duck; a wood duck.

hiohmanya, n., a standing round.

hiohmanya, v. a. i., to stand around, Matt. 6: 5; 13: 2, 30; *hiohmanyashke*, Matt. 12: 47.

hioht, adv., contracted from *hioli*.

hioht ansha, v. a. i., to sit around; to stand.

hioht manya, hiohmanya, v. a. i., to stand around.

hokm a, see *hokma*.

hioli, hiyoli, haioli (q. v.), v. a. i. pl., to stand.

hioli, a., pp., set up; erected.

hioli, n., those which stand; those which are set up.

hiolichi, hiolechi, v. t., to set up; to to erect; to put up; to raise up, Luke 3: 8; to team; to set on the feet; *aka pit hiolichi*, Josh. 2: 15; 5: 7; see *hielichi*.

hiolichi, n., a teamster.

hionshakeli, n., a grasshopper of the largest kind.

hish ansha, a., haired; having hair; hairy.

hish ansha, v. n., to be haired.

hishi, n., hair, except that of the head, which is *pa*ⁿ*shi;* fur; feathers; wool; leaves; a blade; a coat (*hishi boafa*, to shed his coat); a leaf; a spire; a fleece.

hishi aialhto, n., a woolsack.

hishi alikti, n., a pin feather.

hishi atoba, a., woolen.

hishi chito, a., hairy; having much hair; shaggy; leafy.

hishi chito, v. n., to be hairy.

hishi chito, n., a shag; a shag lock.

hishi chito aⁿsha, a., shagged.

hishi homi, tishi homi (q. v.), n., pepper.

hishi homi ani, n., a pepper corn.

hishi homi humma, n., red pepper; cayenne pepper; capsicum; see *tishi humma*.

hishi iksho, a., naked; destitute of hair, except on the head; bare.

hishi laua, a., leafy.

hishi lapishta, n., short, fine hair; fuzz.

hishi toba, a., fledged; feathered.

hishi toba, pp., leafed; having leaves; leaved.

hishi toba, v. a. i., to fledge; to grow, as feathers; to become feathers; to leaf.

hishi tobat taha, pp., feathered entirely; leafed out.

hishi wanuksho, n., short fine hair; fuzz.

hishi lukchi, see *pishilukchi.*

hishunluk, see *hoshunluk.*

hitoka, hotoka, n., a ball ground.

hituchina, a., third.

hituchina, v. n., to be the third.

hituchinaha, adv., thrice; three times, Acts 10: 16.

hituchinanchi, v. t., to do it three times, or the third time.

hituk, hittuk, n., powder; gunpowder; Choctaw pearlash, or potash.

hituk aialhpisa, n., that in which powder is measured, especially a single charge, and called a charger.

hituk aialhto, n., a powderhorn or flask; a keg, or canister of powder.

hituk aiikbi, n., a powdermill.

hituk aionchiya, n., a pan; a priming pan.

hituk atoba, n., a powdermill.

hituk bofota, n., dust; flying dust.

hituk chubi, hituk chubbi, n., ashes; dry dust; dust; wood ashes, Matt. 11: 21.

hituk chubi ahoiya, n., a lye leach; an ash leach; *hoiya* is the active verb.

hituk chubi aholuya, n., an ash leach; a leach; *holuya* is the passive of *hoiya.*

hituk chubi aialhto, n., an ash box, bin, or tub.

hituk chubi holuya, n., lye.

hituk chubi inchuka, n., an ash house.

hituk chubi isht peli falaia, n., a peel; a large fire shovel.

hituk chubi isht piha, n., an ash shovel; a fire shovel.

hituk haksun onchiya, n., a priming; the powder lying on the priming pan.

hituk hoiya, n., lye.

hituk isht alhpisa, n., a powder charger; the measure of a load.

hituk lakna, n., brimstone; sulphur.

hituk lakna bota, n., the flour of sulphur or of brimstone.

hituk laya bachaⁿya, n., a train of powder.

hituk shibota, n., flying dust; smoke of powder.

hituk tohbi, n., flying dust; dust, Matt. 10: 14; pearlash; potash, such as is manufactured by Americans.

hituk yanha, n., embers; hot ashes.

hitukla, hotukla, a., second.

hitukla, v. n., to be second.

hituklaha, adv., twice; second time.

hituklanchi, v. t., to do it twice, or a second time, or again.

hiyoli, see *hioli.*

ho, 2d per. pl. imp. mood, when the word begins with a consonant, and *oh* when with a vowel; *hominti*, come ye; *ohia*, go ye.

ho, oh, the "marriage pronoun," a syllable thrown into the verb, or placed at the beginning of a verb which indicates certain relations by marriage, such as son-in-law, daughter-in-law, or father-in-law and mother-in-law; used only by those who sustain this relation, and called "shame talk."

ho, an exclamation.

ho?, interrogative. See John 6: 29.

ho, hoⁿ, an art. used after a noun, usually rendered as a or an, the indefinite article; as *nana ho pisali*, I see a thing, or something. As the art. *a*ⁿ is written *a*ⁿ, *ha*ⁿ, and *ya*ⁿ, so this has three ways, *o*ⁿ, *ho*ⁿ, *yo*ⁿ, and chiefly for the sake of euphony, yet *hon* usually follows a verb, *yon* a noun, and *on* a word which ends with a consonant, as *wak on*, *hatak on*. But the sense and the idiom of the Choctaw will not always admit of rendering *hon*, *on*, and *yon* by the article a or an; nor will that of the English admit it wherever the Choctaw language does. It is also a relative pronoun, simple and compound, when compounded having different senses and used after different parts of speech; *ho*, *hon*, *hoh* (see *o*, *on*, *oh*), have the sense of the verb to be in the 3d person, or of the auxiliary; also to do; *hachibaptismochilishke*, I do indeed baptize you, Matt. 3: 11. Compounds: *hocha — hoka*, because, since, Matt. 5: 22—*hokaka—hokakano—hokakant—hokakanto*, Luke 1: 37; *Chihowa hokakanto — hokakat* (I have heard this particle used)—*hokakato—hokakhe—hokakheno—hokakhet — hokakheto—hokakkia; mali, micha okhata aiena hokakkia*, even the winds and the sea, Matt. 8: 27—*hokakon—hokakocha—hokakona—hokakosh; ishpisa hokakosh*, thou seest, Matt. 7: 3; *chiahokakosh*, thou art, John 3: 10; *pinsa hokakosh*, they seeing, Matt. 13: 13; *hahanklo hokakosh*, hearing, Matt. 13: 13; *hashasha yokakosh*, "ye dwell," Josh. 9: 22—*hakakot—hokamo (ho* and *kama); mintilihokamo, — hokano (from ho* and *kano); na holissochi aleha hokano*, the scribes, Matt. 7: 29; *itihhokano*, their mouth, Matt. 15: 8; *keyu hokano*, which not, Matt. 15: 13; *isht impa hokano* to eat with, Matt. 15:20—*hokano, hokano,* Josh. 1: 3, Matt. 16: 3; *hahanklo hokano*, by hearing, Matt. 13: 13; *pihinsa hokano*, seeing—*hokat*, he who does, Matt. 5: 21—*hokato*, Matt. 5: 19, the one who does (distinctive by way of comparison), Matt. 5: 19; *imachi hokato*, Matt. 5: 22; *atampa hokato*, Matt. 5: 37, *ishanumpulachinhokato*, Matt· 6: 6; *ani keyu hokato*, that bringeth not forth fruit, Matt. 7: 19; they that, Matt. 11: 8; *chunkash okato*, their heart, Matt. 15: 8; *banna hokato*, Matt. 16: 25; *abit iktalo hokato*, Josh. 8: 26; *hoke*, final word; *lauahoke*, are many, Matt. 7: 13; *ahauchihoke*, do find Matt. 7: 14; *isht imaholitopahoke*,

Matt. 11: 19, *alhpesahoke* it is lawful, Matt. 12: 12; *saiyukpa fehnahoke*, Matt. 17: 5—*hokia—hokon*, the, Matt. 17: 2—*hona—hosh—hot.*

hoansa, v. t., to chew; to chaw; to champ; to masticate; see *hopansa*.

hobachahe keyu, a., inimitable.

hobachi, v. t., to imitate; to liken; to assimilate; to ape; to mimic; to echo; to conform; to depict; to pattern; to jeer; to mock; to reverberate; to shape; to simulate; *isht ahobachi*, to pattern by means of it; to figure; *itihobachi*, to cause to resemble each other or to make them alike; *itiobachi*, to compare; *sahobachi*, to imitate me; *ilahobachi*, v. t., to make like himself, Gen. 1: 26, 27.

hobachi, v. a. i., to echo; to pattern; to resound; to reverberate.

hobachi, n., an echo; a mock; mockery.

hobachi, n., an imitator; a mimic.

hobachi, a., mock.

hobachi, n., the act of imitation.

hobachit, adv. or the v. and conj., same as to imitate, etc.

hobachit anumpuli, v. t., to mock; to mimic; to talk like another.

hobachit anumpuli, n., a mocker; a mimicker.

hobachit holissochi, v. t., to copy; to write like another; to imitate the writing of another.

hobachit holissochi, n., a copyist.

hobachit ikbi, v. t., to make after a pattern; to make a likeness; to copy; to assimilate.

hobachit ikbi, n., one that makes after a pattern; an imitator.

hobachit miha, v. t., to rehearse.

hobachit nowa, v. t., to walk like another.

hobak, n., a coward; a poltroon; a dastard; a eunuch; a gelding; a recreant (a word of peculiar reproach and offense).

hobak, a., pp., castrated; altered; cut; gelded; cowardly.

hobak chohmi, adv., cowardly.

hobak ikbi, v. t., to castrate; to geld; to cut; to alter.

hobak toba, pp., become a gelding, coward, etc.; castrated; gelded.

hobak toba, a., faint hearted; unmanly.

hobak tobachi, v. t., to unman.

hobechi, v. t., to steam; to make a steam; to sweat in order to cure disease as was often done by the Choctaw doctors after this manner: herbs and roots were collected and boiled in an iron pot, a hole was dug in the ground large and deep enough to admit the pot, which having been done, a cover of wicker work was laid over it. The patient lay down over this pot, covered himself with blankets, and took the steam. *ilehobechi*, v. ref., to steam oneself.

hobechi, n., one who applies steam; one who steams.

hobechi, n., a steaming.

hobi, v. t. (pp., *holbi*), to boil whole, as eggs with the shell on, potatoes, chestnuts, corn on the ear, beans in the pod; to foment.

hochąffo, v. a. i., to starve; to hunger.

hochąffo, hohchąffo, a., hungry; *hohchąffo fehna*, very hungry.

hochąffo, hohchąfo (Matt. 12: 1), hochaⁿffo, v. n., to be hungry; *hochaiyafo*.

hochąffo, n., hunger; *hohchąfo*, famine, 2 Sam. 24: 13.

hochąffo, v. a. i., to hunger.

hochąffo, pp., starved.

hochąffochi, v. t., to starve; to distress by famine.

hochąffochi, n., one that distresses by famine; one that starves others.

hochąffochit ąbi, v. t., to starve; to kill with hunger; *hochąffochit ąbit tali*, to starve all to death.

hochąffot illi, v. a. i., to die with hunger; to starve to death.

hochąffot illi, pp., dead with hunger; starved to death.

hocheto, hochito, a. pl., large; big; great; huge; vast; immense; stupendous.

hocheto, v. n., to be large.

hocheto, n. pl., greatness; great ones.

hochetochi, v. t., to cause to be large.

hochetochi, n., an enlarger.

hochetoli, v. t., to make large, loud, or great; to enlarge; to increase.

hochetoli, n., an enlarger; enlargers; those who make large.

hochifo, hochefo, hohchifo, v. t., to name; to call; to denominate; to entitle; to specify; to style; to term;

hochinfo, hochihinfo, hochiefo, Matt. 1: 21, 22, 23; 10: 25; John 1: 42.

hochifo, n., a name, Matt. 6: 9; a denomination; a character; a label; a style; a title; *hohchifo ash illi, ilap ąt illi keyu*, this character is dead, he is not dead; *yamma hohchifo hoⁿ*, his name, Matt. 12: 21.

hochifo, hohchifo, pp., named, Matt. 9: 9; called; denominated; entitled; labeled; styled; termed, John, 3: 1; *iti hochifo*, named after another person.

hochifo, hochefo, n., a namer; a denominator.

hochifo bieka, a., nominal.

hochifo holisso takali, pp., enrolled.

hochifo holisso takalichi, v. t., to enroll; n., a signer.

hochifo iksho, a., unnamed; without name; nameless; anonymous.

hochifo iktakalo, a., anonymous; not labeled.

hochifo ishi, v. t., to list.

hochifo okpulo, n., a by-name; a nickname; a bad name.

hochifo takali, n., a signature.

hochifo takali, pp., labeled; having the name entered; named; signed; listed.

hochifo takali, v. a. i., to list.

hochifo takalichi, v. t., to label; to enter the name; to sign the name; to subscribe.

hochifo takalichi, n., a subscriber.

hochifochi, ahochifochi, v. t., to cause to name; to name, Josh. 19: 47.

hochito, see *hocheto*.

hochitolit holissochi, v. t., to engross.

hochitot holisso, pp., engrossed.

hochuⁿaⁿlhto, see *hoshuⁿaialhto*.

hochukbi, hichukbi, n., a natural pit; a hole; a cave; a cavern.

hochukma, a. pl., good; excellent; pleasant; agreeable, Josh. 5: 2; *achukma*, sing., which see, Matt. 5: 16; 6: 28; 13: 45; *na hochukma*, good things, Matt. 7: 11; *hochuⁿkma*, the good, Matt. 13: 45.

hochukma, hochuⁿkma, v. n., to be good; *hochuyukma*, pro. form.

hochukma, v. a. i., to do well; to do good; to act good, as *hashhochukma*.

hochukma, n., goodness; excellencies.

hochukmalechi, v. t. pl., to repair them; to make them good.

hochukmąlechi, n. pl., repairers.

hochukmali, v. t. pl., to improve them; to repair; to better, etc.

hochukmali, n., repairers.

hochukmat, adv., well; in a good manner or state.

hochukwa, a., cold; chilly; this word describes the sensation of cold; aguish; hochukwat illi, very cold.

hochukwa, v. n., to be cold or chilly; aguish; sahochukwa, I am cold; not sakapassa.

hochukwa, v. a. i., to freeze.

hochukwa, n., a cold; chilliness; ague; a chill; an ague fit.

hochukwa yanha, n., the fever and ague.

hochukwat yanha, v. t., to have the fever and ague; to be sick with the fever and ague.

hochukwachi, a., aguish; chilly; somewhat cold.

hochukwachi, v. n., to be aguish, chilly, etc.

hochukwoba (from hochukwa and holba) a., aguish; shivering.

hochukwoba, v. n., to be aguish; to be shivering.

hoeta, v. a. i., v. t., to puke; to vomit; to discharge; to gulp; to regorge; to spew.

hoeta, n., a puke; a vomiting; a vomit.

hoeta banna, v. t., to gag; v. a. i., to retch.

hoeta banna, n., nausea; a qualm.

hoeta banna, a., qualmish; queasy.

hoetachi, v. t., to cause to puke or vomit.

hoetachi, n., an emetic; a puke; a vomit.

hoetachi banna, a., sickish.

hoetat pisa, v. t., to heave; v. a. i., to retch; to gag.

hofah iksho, hofahyiksho, a., immodest; impudent; shameless; unblushing; ikhofahyo, not ashamed; unblushing; unshamed.

hofahya, a., ashamed; abashed; chagrined; mortified; scandalous; hofaya (subpositive), shameful; sheepish.

hofahya, v. n., to be ashamed.

hofahya, n., shame; dishonor; mortification; scandal; ishtahofahya, reproach, Josh. 5: 9.

hofahya, pp., mortified; ashamed.

hofahyachi, v. t., to shame; to abash; to expose to shame; to mortify.

hofahyachi, n., a shamer.

hofahyat, adv., shamefully.

hofaloha, a. pl., long; tall; lengthy, as in uski hofaloha; falaia, sing.

hofaloha, v. n., to be long, or tall.

hofaloha, n., length; tallness.

hofalohachi, v. t., to make them long; to lengthen.

hofaloli, v. t., to make long, Matt. 23: 5.

hofanti, v. n., to grow up; to advance in stature, as animate or inanimate objects, children, cattle, etc., 1 Sam. 2: 21; siahofanti, raised up by me or with me; katimako chiahofanti hon?

hofanti, pp., grown, Matt. 8: 32 [?]; reared; raised; brought up; cherished; nourished; protected.

hofanti, n., a growth; that which is raised or reared.

hofantichi, v. t., to raise; to rear; to bring up; to cherish; to foster; to nourish; to nurture; to protect; hofantinchi, nasal form; hofantihinchi, freq., Luke 7: 28.

hofantichi, n., a raiser; the person who raises, educates, or brings up; a nourisher.

hofantit taha, pp., grown up; fully grown.

hofayali, hofayali, v. t., to shame; to abash; to expose to shame; to humble; am anumpa isht hofayaliletuk, I shamed him by my words; isht hofali, persecution, Matt. 13: 21; isht hofayali, v. t., to stigmatize; ilehofayali, to disgrace himself.

hofayali, n., a shamer.

hofayalichi, v. t., to put to shame, Luke 18: 32; Mark 12: 4.

hofayalit, adv., shamefully.

hofalli, v. a. i., to hatch; to come out of the shell, as birds, fowls, turtles, and any creature that is formed in a shell; to grow, as the young who thus come into being.

hofalli, n., a growth; a hatch; the act of exclusion from the egg.

hofalli, pp., hatched; grown; raised.

hofallichi, v. t., to hatch; to raise; to cause to raise or to hatch; ikhofallecho, a., unhatched.

hofallichi, n., a raiser of poultry; a breeder.

hofobi, a., deep; profound; ikhofo, a., shallow.

hofobi, hofombi, v. n., to be deep.

hofobi, n., depth; deepness; thickness; *ikhofobo*, n., shallowness; a shoal.

hofobi, pp., made deep; deepened.

hofobi, adv., thick; thickly.

hofobichi, v. t., to deepen.

hofobichit hilechi, v. t., to radicate; to set deep.

hofobichit hokchi, v. t., to root.

hofobika, n., the depth.

hofobit ia, v. a. i., to deepen; to become more deep.

hofombika, n., the deep.

hoh, a distinctive emphatic particle, which perhaps should be regarded as a pronoun; it; that; see Luke 2: 44; *hachimachi hohkia*, Mark 13: 21; *ishla hohcho?* art thou come? Matt. 8: 29; *imaleka hohkia*, Matt. 11: 22.

hohchaffo, see *hochaffo*.

hohchifo, pass. of *hochifo*; *ahohchifo*, called in, Matt. 5: 19.

hohchifo, n., a name; his name, Matt. 1: 21; *chinhohchifo*, thy name; Matt. 7: 22; sign, Acts 28: 11; *anhohchifo*, my name, Matt. 18: 5; 2 Sam. 14: 7.

hohchifo, pp., named, Josh. 2: 1; called, Josh. 5: 9.

hohoeta, pl., or freq., *hoeta*, sing., to puke continually; to vomit continually; *hoihinta*, freq.

hohoeta, n., a puke; a vomiting.

hohoetachi, v. t. pl., to puke; to vomit; to cause to puke.

hohpi, see *hopi*.

hohpi, hopi, hoppi, v. t., to bury; to inter; to commit the dead to the ground or grave; to inhume; to entomb; to sepulcher; *hohpili*, I bury, Matt. 8: 21; *hohpashke*, let them bury, Matt. 8: 22; 14: 12; 1 Kings 11: 15; *hohpit iatok*, they went to bury her, 2 Kings 9: 35.

hohpi, n., an interment; a burial; obsequies; sepulture.

hohpi, n., a grave digger; a sexton; *hohpi at ikshokahioke*, 2 Kings 9: 10.

hohtak, n., a pond; a beaver pond; a lake, Luke 5: 1.

hohtak ushi, n., a small pond; also name of a creek.

hoiya, foiya, v. a. i., to drip; to leak; to strain; to filter; *hohoniya*, 1 Sam. 14: 26, spoken of honey.

hoiya, pp., strained; filtered.

hoiya, n., a leak; a drop.

hoiyachi, v. t., to strain; to filter; to percolate.

hoiyachi, n., one who strains, filters, etc.; a straining.

hok, sign of past tense, having also an adverbial meaning, as *mintili hok;* same as *tukoke*, a contracted expression.

hokak, etc.; see *ho* and its compounds.

hokama, hokamba, conj., because.

hokbali, v. t., to warm over again, as *kafi hokbali, tanfula hokbali; hokba*, pp.

hokbano, okbano, yokbano, sign of optative mood; *anya hokbano, ilahnishke*, only be along, Josh. 1: 17; oh, that it might be; *hokbano ahni*, 2 Tim. 1: 4; *hokbano* is used without *ahni* in 2 Tim. 1: 16, 18; 2: 7; *kbato, okbato*, nom. case; *kbano, okbano*, obj. case.

hokbato, sign of optative mood, Luke 19: 42.

hokchi, v. t., to plant; to sow; to lay; to set; as, *onush hokchi; tanchi hokchi; ilahokchi*, to plant anything by itself, separated from others; *ahokchichi*, v. t., to sow among other grain; *ant ahokchichi*, and some other sort, Matt. 13: 25; see *atanachi*, Judg. 16: 13; where Samson's seven locks were woven with the web, i. e., two different things are woven together.

hokchi, n., a planter; a sower.

hoke, a final particle of assertion from *ho* and *ke;* an affirmative particle.

hokli, v. t., v. a. i., to catch; to seize; to lay hold of, Matt. 14: 3; to take; to clasp; to entrap; to fasten; to gin; to have; to ensnare; to noose, to trammel; to trap; *itinhokli*, Mark 12: 3; *hohonkli*, nasal form; *hoyukli*, pro. form; *ikhoklo*, a., untaken.

hokli, n., a catcher; a seizer; a taker.

hokli, n., a seizure.

hoklichi, v. t., to cause to catch; to employ to catch.

hoklit aiissa, v. t., to ravish; to force; to commit a rape; to violate, 2 Sam. 13: 12.

hoklit aiissa, n., a ravisher; a violator.

hoklit aiissa, n., a rape.

hokma, hiokma, if it shall (from *ho* and *kma, ho*, is, *kma*, then, that), Matt. 11: 14; 12: 27; if, Matt. 18: 8, 9; if shall, Matt. 18: 15; *hiokma* is in the future,

from *he* and *okma; nana hokma,* what
it be, Matt. 9: 13; *ỵammakosh,* that;
nana hokma, that, Matt. 10: 13; *achi
hokma,* when they ask, Josh. 4: 6; *hokmá,* or, Matt. 10: 14, Josh. 1: 7; *tamaha
hokmá,* that house, or that city, *nana
iskitini hokmá, chito hokmá nana kia,*
1 Sam. 30; *hokmá* as here used is
similar to the Latin suspensives.
Compounds: *hokmak; hokmakbanoho-
ka* those that be, Matt. 16: 23—*hok-
maka*—*hokmakano*—*hokmakato*—*hok-
makhe*—*hokmakheno*—*hokmakhet*—*hok-
maketo*—*hokmako,* then, Josh. 1: 15—
hokmakocha—*hokmakoka*—*hokmakokano*
—*hokmakokạt*—*hokmakokạto*—*hokmak-
oke*—*hokmakokia*—*hokmakona*—*hokmakosh; ona hokmakosh,* he were, Matt. 10:
22; 18: 6, 9; for then, Joshua 1: 8—
hokmakot—*hokmano, hokmạno; keyu hokmạno,* Matt. 10: 13; *yohmihokmạno,* so
if then; then, Matt. 12: 28; 18: 16—
hokmạt, if, Luke 4: 3; John 4: 10; *chiahokmạt,* if thou art; Matt. 4: 3; shall,
Matt. 5: 19; when, Matt. 6: 3; *bạnna-
hokmạt,* if he will, Matt. 16: 24; shall,
Matt. 18: 5; *ishpikochawelihokmạt,* if
thou cast us out, Matt. 8: 31—*hokmạto.*

hokofa, v. a. i. sing., to end; to close; to
come up, as in tow; to rest; to stanch;
to fail, Josh. 3: 16; *itahokofa,* to come
apart, Josh. 3: 13; *ont ahokofa,* v. a. i.,
to terminate.

hokofa, pp., ended, Josh. 4: 7; closed;
cut off; shut; stanched; terminated, *itahokofa,* sundered; cut in two; unjointed.

hokofa, n., the end; the close.

hokoffi, v. t., to cut off, Matt. 18: 8; to
end; to rebuke, as a fever, in Luke 4:
39; to dock; to shut; to stanch; to terminate; *itahokofi,* to sunder; to cut in
two; to unjoint; *imahokofi* v. t., to silence; see *ahokoffi.*

hokoffi, n., one that cuts off, ends, etc.

hokola, adv., also; of the same sort or
species; just like the other; used in
speaking of two sons-in-law.

hokola, v. n., to be like the other.

hokoli, v. a. i. pl., to end; to come off;
to close.

hokoli, pp. pl., cut off; severed; ended;
cut in pieces; cut up; *itahokoli,* cut
apart.

hokolichi, v. t., to sever; to cut off, as
logs; to cut up, as a tree; *itahokolichi,*
to sever them from each other; to
shorten, Mark 13: 20.

hokolichi, n. pl., those who cut off, or
sever.

hokulbi, a., moist; pliable; succulent;
wet, as land.

hokulbi, v. n., to be moist; to soften, as
a dry hide in water; *wak hakshup ạt
hokulbi.*

hokulbichi, v. t., to moisten; to render
pliable.

holabi, v. a. i., to lie; to utter a falsehood;
to tell a lie; to belie; to fib; *itinholabi,*
to lie to each other.

holabi, a., lying; false; counterfeit; sham;
untrue; *itinholabi,* false to each other.

holabi, v. n., to be false, or counterfeit;
to fable; to falsify.

holabi, n., a lie; a falsehood; a fable; a
fabrication; a falsity; a fib; untruth; a
liar; a falsifier; a fibber; a recreant.

holabi, adv., untruly; falsely.

holabichi, v. t., to belie; to make a person lie; to procure a liar; to falsify; to
suborn.

holabichi, n., a suborner.

holabit anoli, v. t., to misrepresent.

holabit anumpa kạllo ilonuchi, v. t.,
to perjure; n., a perjurer.

holakshi, v. t., to lick.

holakshi, n., a licker.

holạshki, v. a. i., to be thickened like
soap, etc., when made; applied to
honey and horehound boiled together.

holba, a., like; resembling; similar; alike;
itioba, a., similar; *ttiholba,* like each
other; similar; *ikitiholbo,* differing from
each other; dissimilar; unlike; *ikitiholbo,* v. a. i., to differ.

holba, v. n., to be like, or similar; to
appear, Matt. 6: 8; 13: 24, 31; *inholba,*
to appear to them, Matt. 6: 18; *itiholba,*
to be like each other; v. a. i., to match;
ikitiholbo, to differ; *itiholba,* v. a. i., to
harmonize.

holba, v. a. i., to savor; to span.

holba, n., an appearance; a shape; a likeness; resemblance; imitation; *itioba,*
n., a comparison; a figure; a form; an
image; a picture; seeming; semblance;
itiholba, n., harmony; similitude; *itiholba keyu,* n., odds.

holba, pp., imitated; made to resemble; likened; compared together; resembled; *itiholba* or *itioba*, a., made like each other; kindred.

holba, adv., like.

holbachi, holbąchi, v. t., to imitate; to savor; see *hobachi; itiholbąchi*, to harmonize; to resemble.

holbąt toba, v. a. i., to become alike.

holbąt toba, pp., made alike.

holbi, pp., boiled in the pod, skin, etc.; *hobi*, v. t.

holbi, n., that which is boiled.

holbichi, v. t., to cause to boil, or to be boiled.

holhkunna, hulhkunna, n., a witch; witchcraft.

holhpa, n., a burn; a scald; small blisters.

holhpa, pp., scalded; burnt; nettled; see *hatak holhpą.*

holhpąlli, holhpąli, v. t., to burn; to nettle; see *hatak holhpąlli.*

holhpela, pp., distributed; divided; dispensed; *hopela*, v. t.

holhpela, n., a distribution; a division; a portion, 1 Sam. 1: 5.

holhpena, holhpina, pp., counted; enumerated; numbered; *hopena*, v. t.

holhpena, n., enumeration; number; count.

holhpokunna, holhpokna, yulhpokona, v. a. i., to dream; to see visions; *holhpokuna*, Matt. 1: 20.

holhpokunna, holhpokna, n., a dream.

holhpokunna, holhpokna, n., a dreamer.

holhpokunnąchi, v. t., to cause to dream.

holhponayo, v. a. i., to see; to exercise the power of seeing and not to look at single objects.

holhponayo, n., eyesight.

holhponayochi, holhponayuchi, v. t., to give eyesight; to cause to see, Luke 4: 18.

holhponi, pp., cooked.

holhponi, n., victuals; commonly a dish of boiled corn and beans; samp.

holhpusi, pp., pounded; brayed in a mortar.

holhpusi, n., that which is brayed.

holhta, pp., separated from; taken out; robbed, as bees are robbed; *foe ąt holhta, chukfi ąt holhta*, etc.; *hota*, v. t.

holhta, n., that which is thus taken.

holhtampi, n., a file or string; from *holhtąpi.*

holhtąpi, pp., strung; filed; put on a line or stick, as beads, birds, or fish, etc.; *hotampi*, v. t., *shikąla holhtąpi; holhtampi*, nasal form, being strung; *holhtampi*, n., see above.

holhtena (from *hotina*), pp., numbered, Matt. 10: 30; enumerated; counted; computed; estimated; liquidated; reckoned; summed; valued; *ikholhteno*, pp., excluded; exempted; a., uncounted; unnumbered.

holhtina, n., the number; the enumeration; the census; the tale; the number reckoned; figures; 2 Sam. 24: 2; Josh. 4: 8; *holhtina tonksąli*, to work figures, to cipher; an estimation; a computation.

holhtina, v. a. i., to become; to be reckoned as one of a multitude.

holhtina atąpa, a., unnumbered.

holhtina hinla, a., numerable.

holhtinahe keyu, a., incalculable; inestimable; innumerable.

holihta or hollihta, pp., fenced; inclosed by a fence; inclosed; *ikaholihto*, a., unfenced.

holihta, n., a fence; a yard; a barricade; a lot; a court; a pen; *wak inholihta*, a cow yard or lot; an inclosure.

holihta abeli, v. t. pl., to put into a lot, yard, etc.

holihta apotaka, n., fence side; the side of a fence.

holihta atiwa, n., an opening in a fence; a gap in a fence.

holihta ąlbiha, pp., pent; put up in a yard.

holihta ąlhpoa ąlbiha, n., a pasture.

holihta fohka, pp., penned; put in a pen; *holihta fonhka*, nasal form.

holihta fohki, v. t., to pen; to shut in a pen; to confine in a small inclosure.

holihta halupa, pp., paled.

holihta halupa, n., a paling or picket fence; a picket; a pallisade.

holihta halupa ikbi, v. t., to pale; to picket; to make a pale or picket; to pallisade.

holihta iksho, a., fenceless.

holihta isht ąlhkąma, n., a gate; a gate belonging to a fence.

holihta itafena, pp., staked, as a fence.

holihta itafena, n., a staked fence.

holihta itafenali, v. t., to stake a fence.

holihta itintakla, n., a lane between fences.

holihta kạllo, n., a fort; a pallisade; a palisado; a bulwark; a fortification; a fortress; a rampart; a fastness; a garrison; a parapet; a stockade; a ward; a stronghold, 2 Sam. 24: 7.

holihta kạllo ikbi, v. t., to fortify; to make a fort.

holihta kạllo isht okpạni, n., a battering ram.

holihta okhisa, n., a gate; the opening through a fence for passing in and out, Josh. 2: 7.

holihta okhisa achushkạchi, n., the bars of a gate, or such as are used instead of a gate.

holihta okhisa aiachushkạchi, n., bar holes in a post.

holihta okhowataka, holihta okfoataka, n., the side of a fence, lot, yard, etc.

holihta okpạni, v. t., to unfence; to destroy a fence.

holihta pạla, n., rails; fencing stuff.

holihta yiⁿyiki, n., a worm fence; a Virginia fence; a crooked fence.

holihtạchi, v. t., to fence; to make a fence; to put up a fence; to empale; to immure; to inclose; to rail, Mark 12: 1.

holihtạchi, n., one that makes a fence.

holihtạlhto, pp., folded; penned.

holihtạni, v. t., to fold; to pen.

holihtạni, n., a folder; one that folds.

holihtushi, n., a small pen; a small lot.

holilạbi, a., rabid; mad.

holilạbi, v. n., to be rabid, etc.

holilạbi, n., hydrophobia; frenzy.

holillạbi, a., gluttonous; greedy.

holissa hinla, a., expressible.

holissichi, see holissochi.

holissikbi, see holisso ikbi.

holisso, pp., written; recorded; entered in a book; composed; expressed; indited; lettered; marked; minuted; narrated; noted; penned; printed; holihiⁿso, freq.; aholihiⁿso, Josh. 1: 8, written therein; oⁿholisso, engraved; inscribed; written on; ikholisso, a., unwritten.

holisso, n., a book; a writing; a letter; a paper; a volume; a brief; the Bible; Scripture, Luke 4: 21; a character; a letter or figure used to form words; a composition; an essay; a dissertation; a gazette; handwriting; an instrument; a ledger; a manuscript; a mark to shoot at made of paper; a note; oⁿholisso, an inscription; a minute; a magazine; a pamphlet; a pass; a passport; a permit; a piece; a print; a receipt; a record; a remark; a roll; a safe conduct; a schedule; Scripture; a suffrage; a table; a title; a tome; a transcript; a treatise; a volume; a vote; a warrant; a work; isht holisso, of whom it is written, Matt. 11: 10.

holisso ahikia, n., a book shelf.

holisso aiasha, n., a library; book shelves; a place for books.

holisso aiạlbiha shukcha, n., a pocketbook

holisso aiạlhto, n., a bookcase; a book basket, box, etc.; a mail; a letter bag; a satchel.

holisso aiikbi, n., a printing office; a paper mill.

holisso aiitatoba, n., a book store.

holisso aiithana, n., a place of learning; a seat of learning, or knowledge.

holisso aiithạna, n., a school; a place in which persons are instructed in learning; an institution; a lyceum.

holisso aiithạna chito, n., a college; an academy.

holisso aiithạna (or aiikhạna) chuka, n., a schoolhouse; an academy.

holisso aiithạnanchi, n., a place of instruction in books.

holisso aiitimanumpuli, v. t., to read a book; to talk with a book; Matt. 12: 4, 5.

holisso akaha, n., a book shelf.

holisso alapalachi, v. t., to paper, as a room.

holisso alapali, pp., papered.

holisso anumpa atakali, n., a register.

holisso apisa, n., a study; a school; a lyceum; a school room; a schoolhouse.

holisso apisa akucha, n., vacation.

holisso apisa chito, n., a large school; a college.

holisso apisa chuka, n., a schoolhouse; an academy.

holisso asilhha, n., a written request; a petition.

holisso atakali, n., a record.

holisso atakalichi, v. t., to schedule.

holisso atalaia, n., a book shelf.

holisso ataloa, n., a hymn book; a psalm book.

holisso ataloha, n., book shelves.

holisso atoba, n., a paper mill; a type.

holisso ạlhtoba, n., postage; price of a letter, book, etc.

holisso ạlhtoba iksho, n., a frank.

holisso bahta chito fohki, v. t., to mail a letter.

holisso hakshup iksho, n., a pamphlet.

holisso hochifot itimanumpuli, v. t., to spell.

holisso holitopa, n., a sacred book or writing; the Bible; often applied also to treaties and communications from the government; Scripture; the Testament.

holisso holitopa holissochi, n., an evangelist; a sacred writer; a sacred penman.

holisso holitopa takali, a., scriptural.

holisso ibapisa, n., a book mate; a classmate; a fellow student; a schoolmate.

holisso ikaholisso, n., a blank; a void space on paper.

holisso ikbi, v. t., to print; to make a book; to write; to publish.

holisso ikbi, holissikbi, n., book making; the author of a book; one who makes a book; a printer; an editor; a paper maker; a bookman.

holisso ikhana, holisso ithana, n., a scholar; scholarship.

holisso ikhana, pp., educated.

holisso ikithano, a., uneducated; unread; unschooled.

holisso imanumpuli, v. t., to read; to read aloud from a book, Luke 4: 16.

holisso imanumpuli, n., a reader.

holisso imponna, n., a scholar; one skilled in books.

holisso intạnnạp achạfa, n., a page.

holisso iskitini, n., a small letter; a line; a manual; a note.

holisso isht akamạssa, n., a water; sealing wax.

holisso isht akạllo, n., a wafer; sealing wax.

holisso isht anumpuli, v. t., to talk about a book, writing, a letter, etc.

holisso isht ashana, n., a wafer; sealing wax.

holisso isht ạlhkạma, n., a wafer.

holisso isht bạska, n., a card used in games.

holisso isht kashoffi, n., rubber; India rubber.

holisso isht laⁿfa, n., a ruler; an instrument by which lines are drawn on paper.

holisso iⁿshukcha, n., a pocket book; a letter bag.

holisso iⁿshuⁿshi, n., a book worm.

holisso ithana, holisso ikhana, v. t., to understand a book.

holisso ithana, pp., taught; learned; *holisso ikithano*, pp., untaught; unlearned; a., illiterate.

holisso ithạna, v. t., to learn; "to learn the book."

holisso ithạna, n., a learner; a student; a scholar.

holisso ithạnanchi, v. t., to teach a knowledge of books; to teach; to school.

holisso ithạnanchi, holisso ithananchi, n., a teacher; a school teacher; an institutor; an instructor; a professor.

holisso ithạnanchi, n., schooling.

holisso itibapisa, v. t., to study together.

holisso itibapisa, n., a fellow-student; a fellow-scholar.

holisso itimanumpuli, v. t., to read; to read a book; to spell.

holisso itimanumpuli, n., a reader.

holisso kanchi, v. t., to sell a book or books.

holisso kanchi, n., a book seller; a stationer.

holisso kạllo, n., a writ.

holisso lapalichi, v. t., to enlist; to record.

holisso lapushki, n., a bank bill; a bank note; paper money.

holisso lapushki ikbi, n., a cashier.

holisso lapushki ikbi, v. t., to make bank bills.

holisso lapushki okpulo, n., a counterfeit note.

holisso lapushki okpulo ikbi, v. t., to counterfeit paper money.

holisso lilafa, n., a piece of torn paper; a slip of paper; a bit of paper; a ticket; a butt, used as a mark; a certificate, because written on a small piece of paper.

holisso nan anoli, n., a story; a story book.

holisso nowąt aⁿya, n., a newspaper.

holisso nowąt aⁿya ąlhtoba, n., postage.

holisso nowąt aⁿya inchuka, n., a post-office.

holisso nowąt aⁿya ishi, n., a postmaster.

holisso okpulo, n., a bad book; waste paper; a scrawl.

holisso oⁿłipa, n., a book cover.

holisso oⁿłipa ikbi, n., a bookbinder.

holisso pąta, n., a spread paper; a paper spread out.

holisso pąta achąfa, n., a page in a book.

holisso pisa, v. t., to study a book; to study; to attend school; to read.

holisso pisa, n., a scholar; a pupil; a student; a book man.

holisso pisa ąlhtoba, n., schooling.

holisso pisa imponna, a., book learned.

holisso pisa shali, n., a book worm.

holisso pisa shali, a., bookish; given to learning.

holisso pisachi, v. t., to teach; to keep a school; to show the books.

holisso pisachi, n., a teacher; an instructor; a schoolmaster; a pedant; an usher.

holisso puła, n., a scroll; a sheet of paper.

holisso puła pokoli tuklo akucha ushta, n., a ream of paper.

holisso shali, n., a postman.

holisso shali fohki, v. t., to mail.

holisso shali foka, pp., mailed.

holisso shali inchuka, n., a post-office.

holisso takali, pp., recorded; entered in a book; booked; slated.

holisso takalichi, v. t., to slate; to record; to enter in a book; to book; to register; n., a recorder.

holisso talakchi achąfa, n., a ream of paper.

holisso tohbi, n., white paper; writing paper.

holisso umpątha, n., a book cover.

holissochi, holissichi, v. t., to write; to compose; to draft; to draw; to express; to indite; to letter; to limn; to mark; to narrate; to note; to pen; to pencil; to print; to scrawl; to scribble; to sign; to table; to take; to value; to venerate; *hollisonchi*, nas. form, *holissohonchi*, freq., Matt. 2: 5; John 1: 45; *itiⁿholissochi*, to correspond; *oⁿholissochi*, v. t., to inscribe.

holissochi, n., an amanuensis; a writer; a scribe; a clerk; a scrivener; a chirographer; a composer; a copier; a penman; handwriting, as *B. holissochioka* B's handwriting; a marker; a penner; a printer; a recorder; a secretary; *na holissochi*, a scribe, Matt. 7: 29.

holissochi ikhananchi, n., a writing master.

holissochit anoli, v. t., to certify; to communicate by letter.

holishki, v. a. i., to be thick, glutinous, like dried oil, or like paste or mush.

holitobli, v. t., v. a. i., to love; to reverence; to respect; to bless; to worship, John 4: 21; to honor, Matt. 15: 4, 5; to keep holy; to magnify; to observe; to regard; to revere; to serve, Matt. 6: 24; to keep, Josh. 5: 10, 11; to keep a birthday, Matt. 14: 6; to fear, Josh. 4: 14, 24; *holittobli*, intensive form; *ileholitobli*, to respect one's self; *itiⁿholitobli*, to love each other; *iⁿholitobli*, to make sacred before him, so that he may not profane it, like the tree of life in Eden.

holitobli, n., a lover; a worshiper; love; an honorer; a magnifier; *ileholitobli*, self-respect; self-esteem.

holitobli keyu, a , unvalued.

holitoblichi, v. t. caus., to set apart as sacred; to celebrate; to consecrate; to dedicate; to dignify; to ennoble; to enrich; to esteem; to exalt; to glorify; to grace; to hallow; to illustrate; to prefer; to sanctify; to solemnize; to sublime; to magnify, Josh. 3: 7; 4: 14; to give glory to, Josh. 7: 19.

holitoblichi, n., a sanctifier.

holitoblichit isht anumpuli, v. t., to eulogize; to extol.

holitoblit aiaⁿłichi, v. t., to serve, Luke 4: 8.

holitoblit aiokpąchi, v. t., to worship, Luke 4: 7; to glorify, Luke 5: 25; to homage.

holitoblit hofantichi, v. t., to cherish.

holitoblit isht anumpa, n., an eulogy; a panegyric.

holitoblit isht anumpuli, v. t., to celebrate; to panegyrize; to praise.

holitoblit isht anumpuli, n., a celebration.

holitompa, n., eminence; a high rank;
a prince; a noble; *okla han inholitompa,*
Josh. 9: 15.

holitompa, a., reputable; holy, *nana kat
holitompa kano,* that which is holy, Matt.
7: 6; *na holitompa isht ansha,* a priest,
Matt. 8: 4.

holitopa, pp., a., dear; valuable; estimable; excellent; glorious; holy; honorable; illustrious; magnificent; near; precious; reverend; royal; sacred; solemn;
splendid; sublime; sumptuous; venerable; worthy; Matt. 10: 31; Matt. 12:
12; sacred; beloved, Matt. 17: 5; holy,
Josh. 5: 15; rich; august; hallowed;
Matt. 6: 9; good, Matt. 6: 26; choice;
honored; blessed; consecrated; darling;
ennobled; enriched; esteemed; exalted; graced; glorified; illustrated;
respected; revered; sainted; sanctified;
valued; venerated; *ikholitopo,* honorless; unhallowed; unholy; unhonored;
unwealthy; *isht aholitopa, nan isht imaholitopa,* glory of them, Matt. 4: 8; *na
holitopa,* n., a pearl, Matt. 7: 6; *holittopa,*
intensive form; *itinholitopa,* dear to each
other or to love each other; *inholitopa,*
n., his saints, 1 Sam. 2: 9; *inholitopa,*
dear to him, or to love him; to reverence; *inholitopa,* n., his dear friend;
holitompa, nas. form; *holitohompa,* freq.
form; *holitoyupa,* pro. form.

holitopa, n., riches; glory; that which is
sacred; credit; honor; dearness; dignity; exaltation; grandeur; highness;
holiness; love; magnitude; majesty;
merit; reputation; repute; sanctity;
splendor; sublimity; value; worship;
worth; worthiness.

holitopa atapa, a., inestimable; invaluable; unvalued.

holitopa banna, n., cupidity.

holitopachi, v. t. caus., to glorify, John
12: 28; *ilaholitopachi,* to glorify himself,
John 12: 28.

holitopat, adv., sacredly; solemnly;
worthily.

holitopat annoa, n., glory.

holitopat hofanti, pp., cherished.

holitopat isht anumpa, pp., celebrated;
eulogized.

holiya, see *holuya.*

hollihta, see *holihta.*

hollo, pp., drawn on; put on, as shoes,
boots, stockings; *holo,* v. t. (q. v.).

hollo, n., a pair, or that which is drawn
on, as stockings upon the feet; *shulush
hollo achafa.*

hollo, hullo, v. n., to have the monthly
flow or discharge, as a female.

hollo, n., menses; the monthly flow of
females.

hollohpi, pp., entombed, *hollopili,* I entomb; *ahollohpi,* n., a grave.

hollokmi, holukmi, pp., burnt; fired;
scalded; *luak isht hollokmi,* burned in
the fire, Matt. 13: 40; *ikholokmo,* a.,
unburnt.

hollopi, holohpi, pp., buried; interred;
entombed; *ikhollopo,* a., unburied; not
interred.

holmo, pp., covered; roofed; housed;
shingled.

holmo, n., a roof; a covering.

holo, v. t., to draw on; to put on (oneself), as shoes, boots, moccasins, stockings, pantaloons; *hoyolo,* Josh. 9: 5.

holochi, v. t., to put shoes, etc., upon
another. See Luke 15: 22.

holohpi, see *hollopi.*

holokchi, pp., planted; sown; *nana im-
aholokchitukash,* Matt. 13: 19; *na holokchi,* n., a plant.

holopi, pp., stocked; hafted; helved.

holoti, holotti, pp., wound, as feathers
on the small end of an arrow; *holoti,* n.

holufka, pp., sunned; dried; aired; *ik-
holufko;* a., unsunned.

holufka, n., that which is sunned.

holukmi, n., a burn; a conflagration; see
hollokmi.

holunsi, holussi, a., brown, dark brown;
turning black; *isi at holunsi.*

holunsi, v. n., to be brown; *aholunsi,* v. t.,
to blacken; to color black.

holussi, halussi, pp., pounded; brayed;
beaten.

holussi, n., that which is beaten.

holushmi, pp., burnt; fired.

holushmi, n., that which is burnt; a
burning; a conflagration.

holuya, holiya, v. a. i., to drip; to leak; to filtrate; to run through; to distill; to drain; to dribble; to filter; to percolate.

holuya, n., a dripping.

holuya, pp., distilled; filtrated; strained; filtered; percolated; *ikholuyo*, a., unstrained.

holuyachi, v. t., to drain; to leach; to filtrate; to percolate; to strain.

holi, n., a wedge or bar (of metal); see Josh. 7: 21, 24.

homaiyi, n., carnation; red; purple.

homaiyi, hummaiyi, a., reddish; red; fallow, as a deer; purple.

homaiyi, v. n., to be reddish or red.

homaiyichi, v. t., to make reddish; to color red; to purple; to empurple.

homakbi, n. pl., a purple.

homakbi, a. pl., reddish; purple; brown.

homakbichi, v. t., to make purple; to color purple.

homechi, v. t., to season, Mark 9: 50; to embitter; to make bitter or strong, as a liquid, etc.; to turn sour, etc.; to sour; to make sour, acrid, bitter, etc.; *hominichi*, nasal form; *ikhomecho*, neg. form; to dilute; to weaken; to reduce.

homechi, a., sour; somewhat sour or bitter; sourish; frowy; harsh.

homi, pp., soused; made bitter; embittered; turned; *ikhomo*, pp., reduced; diluted, as spirits; a., weak; *ikhomokitaha*, a., vapid.

homi, a., bitter; sour; acrid; strong; smart; acetous; ardent; fiery; astringent; brackish; hard; poignant; pungent; racy; sharp; tart.

homi, v. a. i., to prick; to become acid; to sour.

homi, v. n., to be bitter, etc.

homi, n., bitterness; pungency; sharpness; tartness.

homi chohmi, a., somewhat bitter; sourish.

homi chohmi, v. n., to be somewhat bitter, etc.

homi fehna, a., virulent.

homilhha, a., sourish, like a bad taste in in the mouth from indigestion.

homma, see *humma*.

homo, v. t., to cover; to shingle; to roof; to house.

homo, n., one who roofs, shingles, etc.

honala, pp. pl., nailed; strung; pierced; *anala*, sing.

honayo, honnayoh, a., wild; untamed; shy; *ikhonayo*, tame; not wild.

honayo, v. n., to be wild, etc.; *ikhonayo*, neg. form.

honayo, n., shyness, wildness; *ikhonayo*, gentleness; tameness; mansuetude.

honali, v. t. pl., to pierce; to sting; *nali*, sing.

honalichi, v. t., to nail; *analichi*, sing.; *itahonalichi*, to tack together.

honammona, v. t., to parboil.

honi, honni, v. t., to cook; to seethe; to prepare food for the table; to boil; to prepare for use; to brew; to decoct; to distill; to extract; to stew.

honi, n., a cook; a boiler; a person who boils.

honichi, v. t., caus., to make her cook.

honnayoh, see *honayo*.

honni, pp., cooked; boiled; seethed; brewed; distilled; extracted; stewed; sodden; 1 Sam. 2: 15; *ikhonno*, a., unboiled.

honni, n., food; victuals; that which has been cooked, boiled, etc.; a stew.

honola, v. t., to twist.

honola, n., a twister.

hononammona, pp., parboiled.

honula, pp., twisted.

honula, v. a. i., to twist (it twists).

honula, honnula, n., a twist; *pala inhonnula lua*, the wick of a candle, Matt. 12: 20; "smoking flax."

hopahki, subpositive form; farish; somewhat far.

hopaii, n., a prophet; a priest; a military leader or captain; a captain-general; a general; a war chief; a war prophet; a major-general; a seer; an augur; Matt. 1: 22; 10: 41; 11: 9; 12: 17–18; 14: 5.

hopaii puta, n., the prophets, Matt. 7: 12.

hopakachi, see *hopakichi*.

hopaki, n., a distance; a length of time; a remove; a while, Matt. 13: 21; *ikhopako*, n., a spell; a short time.

hopaki, a., distant as to time or place; remote; far away; far off; far; Josh. 8: 4; a long way; a long time; old, Matt. 13: 52; removed.

hopaki, v. n., to be distant; *inhopaki*, to be far from it; *hopakishke*, Matt. 15: 8.

hopaki, adv., for a long time; for a long way; far; late; long; remotely; wide; widely; *hopaki tahachi*[n], it will last a long time.

hopaki achạfa, n., a minute; one minute.

hopaki fehna, adv., farthest.

hopaki i[n]shaḷi, a., farther; longer as to time; farthest.

hopaki kash, adv., long ago, Matt. 11: 21.

hopakichechi, v. t., to cause to go far off, or to delay a long time.

hopakichi, hopakạchi, v. a. i., to make off to a distance, said of horses that stray—said of water, Josh. 3: 16; v. t., to make it a long time; to delay; *himak foka hopakichit tali; hopakinchi*, v. t.; *hopakint*, Gen. 37: 18.

hopakichit, adv., widely.

hopakichit habli, v. a. i., to stride.

hopakikma, v. n., in the sub. mood, but rendered adverbially by and by, after a while, in a short time.

hopakikmako, v. n., sub. mood, when it shall be a time; adv., in a short time; after a while; by and by.

hopa[n]sa, hoa[n]sa, hua[n]sa, howa[n]sa, haua[n]sa, v. t., to chew; to champ; to chaw; to grind; to masticate; v. a.i., to ruminate; *isht hopa[n]sa*, v. t., to ruminate.

hopa[n]sa, n., a cud; a chaw.

hopatuloa, n., a war whoop.

hopạlhka, a. pl., wide.

hopạtka, a. pl., *pạtha*, sing., wide; broad.

hopạtka, v. n. pl., to be wide; to be broad.

hopạtka, n., breadth; width.

hopạtkạlli, v. t., to make broad, Matt. 23: 5.

hopela, v. t., to distribute; to divide; to deal; to lot; to give alms, Acts 10: 4, 31; *iti[n]hopela*, v. t., to divide among them; to dispense; *hoyupela*, pro. form; *iti[n]hoyupela*.

hopela, n., a distributer; a divider.

hopena, v. t., to count; to number; to enumerate; to appoint the time for a meeting by counting the previous days; to numerate.

hopena, n., a counter; an appointer; a numerator.

hopena, n., numeration.

hopi, hohpi, ohpi, v. t., to stock; to haft; to helve, etc.; to put a handle upon any edge tool; to put woodwork to iron or steel tools or instruments; *ulhpi, olhpi*, pp.

hopi, hohpi (q. v.), v. t., to bury, etc.; to sepulcher.

hopoa, hopoba, a., hungry.

hopoa, v. n., to be hungry; v. a. i., to hunger; to starve.

hopoa, hopoba, n., famine; hunger; starvation; impotency.

hopochi, v. t., to hoe corn for the last time; to hill corn; "to lay it by;" *hopochichi; yakni a[n] isht hopochichi*, to hoe up small hills; see *apolichi*.

hopochi, v. a. i., to arrive at a middle state, as corn; to grow to the size when corn is "laid by" by farmers.

hopochi, n., corn at that age; the state of corn at that time.

hopohka, v. t., to graze; to pick food with the mouth, as horses and cattle or fowls; or as a man picks meat from a bone with his mouth.

hopohka, n., a picker; one that picks or grazes.

hopohkạchi, v. t., to graze; to feed on grass; to cause another to pick.

hopoiksa, see *hopoksia*.

hopo[n]koyo, v. a. i., to see; to behold; to look; to view; to watch, as a wild beast, Matt. 11: 5; 2 Sam. 24: 20; Josh. 5:13. The difference between *hopo[n]koyo* and *pisa* may be this: *hopo[n]koyo* is to look, in general, or to see, but *pisa* is a more definite use of the eye, as can you see (generally)? and can you see it (particularly)?

hopo[n]koyo, n., sight; eyesight; a lookout.

hopo[n]koyo ikimachukmo, a., dim; not having good eyesight.

hopo[n]koyo shaḷi, a., watchful.

hopoksa, a., wise.

hopoksa, v. n., to be wise.

hopoksa, n., wisdom; discretion; morality; rectitude; sapience.

hopoksia, hopoiksa, hopoyuksa, a., wise; prudent; good; well-disposed; chaste; civil; coy; considerate; continent; discreet; judicious; humble; moral; righteous; sage; witty, *ohoyo* hopoyuksa, a chaste woman; *ikhopoyu-kso*, a., ill-bred; impolite; impolitic; imprudent; indiscreet; injudicious; uncivilized.

hopoksia, hopoiksa, hopoyuksa, v. a. i., to behave well; *ikhopoyukso*, v. a. i., to misbehave; v. n., to be wise or prudent; *ikhopoyukso*, to be ill-bred; *hopoksiali; hopoyuksali* in *ilehopoyuksali*, 1 Sam. 18: 14, 30.

hopoⁿksia, hopoiⁿksa, hopoyuⁿksa, nasal form; the righteous; those who are righteous.

hopoksiachi, v. t. caus., to make wise; to civilize; to make good; to cause him to conduct well; to moralize.

hopoksiachi, n., a reformer.

hopoła, a., quiet; peaceable; good natured; tranquil; peaceful; *ikhopolo*, a., unconsoled; unreconciled.

hopoła, v. n., to be quiet, peaceful, or tranquil.

hopoła, v. a. i., to become tranquil; to become quiet or good-natured; to subside.

hopoła, pass, to be quieted, allayed, soothed, assuaged, comforted, composed, conciliated, healed, solaced, Matt. 2: 17, 18; 5: 4.

hopoła, n., a comfort; a solace.

hopołahe keyu, a., irreconcilable.

hopołachi, v. t., to comfort; to quiet; to pacify; to tranquilize; to allay; to appease; to soothe; to assuage; to compose; to propitiate.

hopołachi, n., a comforter, etc.; a propitiator.

hopołalli, v. t., to tranquilize; to comfort, etc.; to quiet; to conciliate; to console; to heal; to nourish; to pacify; to propitiate; to silence; to solace.

hopołalli, n., a comforter.

hoponi, v. t., to cook.

hoponi, n., a cook.

hoponti, v. a. i., to blow smoke through the nose.

hopoyuksa, pp., reclaimed; *ikhopoyukso*, a., unreformed; untamed; unwise; wild; see *hopoksia*.

hopoyuksa, adv., wisely.

hopoyuksa, n., chastity; *ohoyo hopoyuksa*, a woman of chastity; *ikhopoyukso*, n., ill-breeding; imprudence; wildness;

hopoyuksaka, in *Solomon imisht ahopoyuksaka*, wisdom of Solomon, Matt. 12: 42; the righteous, Matt 13: 43; the just, Matt. 13: 49; wisdom, 1 Kings 10: 23, 24.

hopoyuksa keyu, a., uncivil; unmannerly.

hopoyuksahe keyu, a., untamable.

hopoyuksalechi, v. t., to reclaim.

hopoyuksalli, v. t., to civilize; to convert.

hopoyuksalli, n., a civilizer.

hoppi, see *hohpi*.

hopulbona, n., a priest's sacred bag.

hopumpoyo, v. a. i. pl., to see; to look about; to exercise the power of seeing, Luke 18: 41.

hopunayo, v. a. i. sing., to see; to look about; to take one look; *ikhoponayo*, blind, Matt. 15: 30.

hopuⁿsi, v. t., to bray; to pound.

hopuⁿsi, n., one that brays or pounds.

hosh, a particle used to connect words, and having the meaning of the verb to be in the 3d person (see *osh* in *hoshkin*) *ilap banna hoshkin*.

hoshiⁿko, see *hoshuⁿka*.

hoshila, hoshela, n., a sty.

hoshilabi, v. i., to have a sty; *hoshilasabi*, I have a sty.

hoshinti, see *hoshonti*

hoshintika, see *hoshontika*.

hoshiⁿshi, n., a quill; a feather.

hoshiⁿshi patałhpo, n., a feather bed; a feather pallet.

hoshiⁿshi patałhpo topa, n., a feather bed.

hoshiⁿshi topa, n., a feather bed.

hoshontakapi, see *hoshontikiyi*.

hoshonti, v. a. i., to cloud.

hoshonti, pp., clouded.

hoshonti, hoshinti, n., a cloud, Matt. 17: 5; a shade; a shadow of an inanimate thing; *hatak laua hoshonti chiyuhmi; aiilli aioⁿhoshonti*, shadow of death, Luke 1: 79

hoshonti, a., cloudy.

hoshonti pit tikeli, hoshonti pit bikeli, v. t., to reach the clouds.

hoshonti pit tikeli, a., cloud capped.

hoshonti toba, v. a. i., to cloud up; to become cloudy.

hoshonti toba, pp., clouded.

hoshonti yabata, n., flying clouds.

hoshontichi, v. t., to becloud; to cause a shade or clouds to appear; to cloud; to darken, Matt. 16: 3.

hoshontichi, v. n., it is cloudy.

hoshontika, hoshintika, n., the shade of inanimate objects, Matt. 17: 5; a cloud; a piazza; a canopy; an arbor; a bower; a gallery; a hood; a porch; a shade; a shed; a shadow, of a thing, not an animal; umbrage.

hoshontika, a., shady; umbrageous.

hoshontika, pp.; onhoshontika, shaded; ikhoshontiko, a., uncloudy; unshaded.

hoshontika, v. a. i., to shade.

hoshontika ashachi, v. t., to embower.

hoshontika laua, a., shady; having much shade.

hoshontikachi, v. t., to make a shade; to shade; ili onhoshontikachi, to make a shade over himself; isht hoshontikachi, to screen with; onhoshontikachi, v. t., to overshadow, Matt. 17: 5; to shade.

hoshontikilhkiki, n., broken, thin cloud; "mackerel" clouds.

hoshontikiyi, hoshontạkạpi, n., a piazza post; a rafter.

hoshontoba, n., a scud.

hoshun aiạlhto, hochun anlhto, n., the bladder; see imokạto.

hoshunka, hoshinko, n., the beard of grain, or the matter on some weeds which irritates the flesh if it lodges in the shirt, etc.

hoshunluk, hishunluk, n., bran; na hishunluk, a mote, Matt. 7: 3, 4.

hoshunwa, v. a. i., to state; to discharge urine; to void water; to urinate; to water; to "make water."

hoshunwa, n., urine; the liquor secreted in the bladder; chamber lye.

hoshunwa aminti, n., the urethra.

hoshunwa shalı, n., the diabetes.

hota, adv., probably; it may be; it seems so; ilap akinli hota?

hota, v. t., to separate; to take away, as bran from the meal by the hand; to take honey from the bees by the hand; foe hota; chukfi hota.

hotachi; see ponola ahotachi.

hotampi (see holhtạpi, pp.), v. t., to string; to file; to put on a string, as beads, birds, fish, etc.

hotampi, n., a filing.

hotampi, n., one who files, strings, etc.

hotạpi, v. t., to string beads or fish; hotampi, nas. form; holhtạpi pass.

hotepa, imp. pl., go ahead; start off; go first; go on; mia, imp. sing.; hotimpa, nasal form.

hotilhko, v. n., to cough; to have a cough or cold.

hotilhko, n., a cough; a cold.

hotilhko finka, n., the whooping cough.

hotilhko finka, v. n., to have the whooping cough.

hotilhkot tofa, v. t., to expectorate.

hotina, hotehna (Rev. 7: 9), hotihna, hotinna, v. t., to count; to number; to enumerate; to cast up; to reckon up; to compute; to calculate; to take a census; to account; to cipher; to estimate; to foot; to liquidate; to rate; to settle; to tell; to value; to number, 2 Sam. 24: 2; Josh. 8: 10; holhtina, pp.; ikhoteno, v. t., to exclude; to exempt; ibahotina; itibahotina, v. a. i., to enlist; hotihinna, freq.; hotiena, pro. form.

hotina, n., a counter; a calculator; a computer; a caster; a teller; an arithmetician; a numerator.

hotina, n., numeration; a reckoning.

hoton, adv., in nan tiht koa hoton?

hotofi, hotuffi, v. t. sing., to untie; to unbind; to unwind; to loose, Matt. 16: 19; Mark 11: 2, 4; holhtufa, pp.

hotofi, n., one that enters.

hotoka, see hitoka.

hotokbi, hotukbi, a., moist; damp; being not quite dry; not so wet as hokolbi; pp., damped.

hotokbi, v. n., to be moist, damp; nipi ạt hotokbi, from a gentle perspiration.

hotokbichi, hotukbichi (J. E.), v. t., to moisten; to dampen.

hotokohmi, see hotukohmi.

hotokok, see hotukok.

hotolı, pp. pl., untied; unbound, etc.

hotolichi, v. t. pl., to untie; to unbind.

hotonti, n., a frost.

hotonti, a., frosty.

hotonti, v. n., to be frosty; to have a frost; there is a frost.

hotontichi, v. t., to cause a frost.

hotonsi, hotonsichi, v. t., to prepare a bait for beaver.

hotonsichi, n., a baiter for beaver.

hotti, v. t., to wind or bind feathers on the end of an arrow; *holoti*, pp. (q. v.).

hotuk; *chithanalihotukokeh*, I reckon I should know you; *mihahotuk*, he says what he should not say; *mihahotuk* for *mihahotukohmi*.

hotuk, hotok, a Chickasaw word.

hotukbi, see *hotokbi*.

hotukla, hitukla (q. v.), a., second.

hotukohmi, hotokohmi, adv., probably, John 20: 16; Luke 22: 41; Gen. 21: 16.

hotukok, hotokok, adv., probably.

hotuma, (compounded of the particle *ho* or *hoh* and *tuma*), adv. of doubt, Luke 2: 49; *ishpimabachi hotuma*, John 10: 34; Matt. 17: 26; *hotumashke*, see *tuma*, here it is a word of certainty; 1 Sam. 30: 24; Acts 11: 18; Deut. 4: 7, 8; see *hatuma*.

hotupa, hutupa, huttupa, v. n., v. a. i., to ache; to be in pain; to throe; to travail; to twinge.

hotupa, n., a hurt; a pain; an offense; a pang; persecution; smart; a sore; a throe; torture; travail.

hotupa, pp., hurt; wounded; injured; harmed; persecuted.

hotupa, a., sore; painful; *ikhotupo*, unhurt.

hotupachi, v. t., to hurt; to wound; to injure.

hotupali, v. t., to hurt; to wound; to abuse; to give pain; to inflict an injury; to injure; to harm; to outrage; to pain; to persecute; to torture; to twinge; *chukash hotupali*, to wound the feelings; to affront; to insult.

hotupali, n., a hurter; a persecutor; a wounder.

hotupali, n., persecution; a wounding.

howaⁿsa, see *hopaⁿsa*.

hoyapa, a., not strong; sleazy; not woven strong, as *shukbo at hoyapa*.

hoyapa, v. n., to be sleazy.

hoyabli, v. n., to be weary; Matt. 9: 36; *ahoyabli*, Matt 6: 28; to be faint; *sahoyabli*, I am weary.

hoyabli, a., weary.

hoyabli, pp., wearied.

hoyablichi, v. t., to tire; to weary; to make weary.

hoyo, v. t., to look after; to hunt; to search for; to seek; to inquire after; to ask for; to expect; to await; to wait for; to course; to demand; to invite; to quest; to summon; *imahoyo*, to take or demand of, Matt. 17: 25; to seek, Matt. 18: 12; 13: 45; to seek to call, Matt. 2: 13; 6 : 32, 33; 7: 7; 15: 32; Luke 2: 25; *hot*, cont., as *hot ia*, imp., go and look after it; go in quest of; *hot ala*, imp., go and bring it; come after or for; *ikhoyo*, a., unsought.

hoyo, v. t., to harvest; to gather fruits, John 4: 35; to pry; to scan; to search; to seek; to watch; to look for, *ehoyokma*, or do we look for, Matt. 11: 3.

hoyo, n., a search; a hunt; a quest.

hoyo, n., a seeker; a gatherer; an inquirer; a demander; an expectant; an expecter; a hunter; a searcher; *na hoyo*, the harvest; *ahoyo*, the place of seeking; a harvest ground, etc.; see Matt. 9: 38.

hoyo fehna, v. t., to re-search.

hoyochi, v. t. caus., to cause to look after; to make search; *hoyohonchi*; *chihoyohonchishke*.

hoyopa, a., brave; warlike.

Hoyopa humma, n., a man's name.

hoyopa taloa, n., a brave death song; a few words of one of these run as follows: *we kanihe shap iⁿwali weh kanihe*.

hoyot anta, v. a. i., to wait.

huaⁿsa, see *hopaⁿsa*.

hufka, ufka, v. t., to sun; to air; to dry; *holufka*, pp.

huk, hauk, an int., Oh; O dear; alas; ah me.

hukma hinla, a., scalding hot.

hukmi, v. t., to set on fire; to fire; to burn; to scald, Matt. 13: 30; Josh. 7: 25; 8: 19; same as *hushmi*.

hukmi, n., a firer; an incendiary; a consumer.

huksoh, v. a. i., to discharge wind; to break wind.

huⁿkupa, v. t., to steal; to purloin; to commit larceny; to depredate; to filch; to peculate; to pilfer; to plunder; to rob; to shark; to thieve; *ahuⁿkopa*, Matt. 6: 19, 20.

huⁿkupa, v. a. i., to prey.

huⁿkupa, huⁿkopa, n., a thief, Matt. 6: 19, 20; a felon; a filcher; a pad; a prig; a purloiner; a rover; a stealer.

hunkupa, n., a theft; larceny; depredation; stealth; *hulkunpa*, Matt. 15: 19.

hunkupa, pp. and a., stolen; felonious; thievish.

hunkupa akka nowa, n., a footpad.

hunkupa shali, a., thievish.

hunkupat itanowa, v. a. i., to maraud.

hulbona, pp. pl., doubled; rolled up; see *bunni*.

hulbona, n., bundles; rolls.

hulhkachi, see *ulhkachi*.

hulhki, n., the calf of the leg.

hulhki foni, n., the leg bone.

hulhkupa, hulhkopa, pp., stolen.

hullo, see *hollo*.

hullochi, v. t., to sanctify; to set apart to a sacred use; to fast, Matt. 6: 16; *holitoblit hullochi*, Gen. 2: 3; *hash ilehullochashke*, Josh. 3: 5; 7: 13.

hullochi, v. a. i., to abstain from; to diet one's self, as in taking medicine; to fast, Matt. 9: 14; to sanctify (one's self and others) for the Lord; *ilehullochi*, Josh. 7: 13. See v. t., above.

hulloka, n., a sacred thing.

humma, n., red; crimson; redness; rouge; scarlet.

humma, homma, a., red; angry; inflamed, as a sore; flagrant; florid; fresh; roseate; ruby; ruddy; sanguinary; scarlet; tawny, Matt. 16: 2, 3.

humma, v. n., to be red; v. a. i., to flush; to glow; to redden.

humma, pp., reddened; tanned red; made red; *ikhummo*, pp., not tanned; raw, as a hide.

humma, adv., redly.

humma, an addition to a man's name which gives him some distinction, calling on him for courage and honor. The "*na humma*" may not run or turn the back on the field of battle.

humma talaia, n., a red spot.

humma taloha, n. pl., red spots.

humma tishepa, n., very red; a bright bay; scarlet.

hummaiyi, homaiyi (q. v.), a., reddish.

hummachi, v. t., to color red; to dye red; to tan; to paint red; to make red; to redden; *siaihummachi*, to redden for me and mine,—applied to the red poles of graves.

hummachi, v. a. i., to blush; to become red; to redden, as the countenance.

hummachi, pp., reddened.

hummalhha, v. a. i., to be reddish.

humpah, v. a. i., to say "humph", the report of a gun; to whoop, as a drinking man.

hunssa, v. t., to shoot; to fire; to discharge a gun; to shoot an arrow; *uski naki an isht hunssa*.

hunssa, n., a shoot.

hunssa, n., a shooter.

hunssa, n., a shooting.

hunssa, pp., shot; discharged.

hunssa imponna, n., a marksman; a sharpshooter.

hussi, v. t., to beat; to pound; to bray.

hush, exclamation, oh; alas.

hush abi, v. t., to fowl; to kill birds.

hush abi, n., a fowler.

hush apa, iti ani, n., the black gum. So named, I think, because birds eat the berries.—C. B.

hushi, n., a bird; a fowl; a screamer, Matt. 6: 26; *hushi puta kat*, the fowls, Matt. 13: 4; *aba hushi puta kat*, the fowls of the air.

hushi aialhpita, n., a bird cage.

hushi balbaha, hush balbaha, n., a mocking bird.

hushi chipunta, n., sparrows, Matt. 10: 29, 31.

hushi hishi, n., bird feathers; a feather.

hushi humma, n., a red bird.

hushi imalhpichik, n., a bird's nest.

hushi inchuka, n., a bird cage; a house for birds.

hushi inchuka fohka, pp., caged, as a bird.

hushi inchuka fohki, v. t., to cage.

hushi isht albi, n., a bird trap.

hushi isht hokli, n., a bird snare.

hushi iti chanli, n., a pecker; a woodpecker.

hushi iyakchush, n., a pounce; a bird's claw; a talon.

hushlokussa, n., a bird; the name of some that flock or huddle together. The English name is unknown to me.— C. B.

hushmi, v. t., to burn; to fire; to set on fire; to ruin. Same as *hukmi; holushmi*, pp., *holahushmi*, fiery, Eph. 6: 16.

hushmi, n., a burner.

hushmi, n., a conflagration; a burning.

hushpa, pp., burnt.

hushpali, v. t., to burn.

hushshiho, n., the feeling of chaff in the clothes; v. a. i., to prickle from this cause.

hushushi, n., a young bird; a nestling.

huttupa, hutupa, see *hotupa.*

hunwa, v. t., to scent; to smell; to snuff.

i has the sound of *e* in me or *i* in pique and of short *i* in pin. The letter *i* is used for *y* in words where *y* is doubled in sound. The letter *a* often precedes *i*, thus making a diphthong Thus *yukpa, yukpạchi, aiyukpa, aiyukpạchi,* and not *ayyukpa, ayyukpạchi.* The consonant is doubled to express intensity.

i, prep., meaning at, in, place where, as *iiksho. iiksho* belongs to the intensive form, but *i* occurs before other words, *ichapaka, imoma, itikba.*

i, adv., there, used as above. It rarely occurs except before the word *iksho* and has the same use as *a* and *ai* before verbs. [Mr. Byington says, however, in a note: "This needs correction."]

in, pre. poss. pro. in the nom. case, 3d per., prefixed to nouns that do not begin with a vowel or with *p, ch, l,* or *t.* The noun is often in the poss. case, as *miko inholisso,* the king's book. It may be in the nom. or obj. case, but the pronoun in Choctaw should be parsed as *an, chin, in, pin; anholisso,* my book; *inhaiaka,* visible to him; Matt. 1: 20. See *im* and *in.*

in, pre. per. pro. in the dative case before verbs and usually translated with a prep., *s,* of him, for him, etc.

in, his, their, 3d per. sing. and pl., removed from the noun in the nom. and placed before the verb, as *tạli holisso inhotina,* he has counted his money, etc., or he has counted the money for him. See *chin, hạchin, hạpin.*

in, of it; from it, etc. There are a few instances in which *in, in,* etc., seem to have the use of a prep. rather than a pronoun. These have the neuter gender. See Gen. 2: 17, *ishpakmạt innitak mihinli ho chillahioke; infalạmmi,* to the north of it, north of it; *inhopaki,* far from it; *inmisha,* two days from it (every other day, *inmishakma*).

in, contraction for *inli,* or *in; makin, akin* (for *akinli*).

in, oblique case of *lish, ialish, ialin.*

in, inh, adv., yes.

ia, v. a. i., to go; to move; to depart; to stir; to pass; to proceed; to resort; to sail; to start; to set; to get away, Matt. 4: 10; 13: 44 (he goeth); *hạshiashke,* go, Matt. 8: 32; to grow; to increase, as *kapạssạt ia,* it grows cold; *ilhkoli,* pl., *ikaiyu, ikaiyo,* sing., not to go; *iha* in *ont iha,* a little past; *ihinya* in *ont ihinyama,* Luke18: 36; *ikia ahni,* v. t., to let go; to permit to go; to wish to go; *isht ia,* v. a. i., to commence; to begin; to found; to originate; *isht ia,* v. t., to carry; to begin; to start with; to take; to commence; to institute; to tote; to transfer; to undertake; to transport, John 2: 16; *kapạssạt isht ia; ikaiyo,* not to go, Luke 4: 42; Matt. 14: 16; *ont ia,* v. a. i., to exceed; to go by; to found; to outgo; to pass; to touch; to transcend; *isht ont ia,* to carry by; *imia, itimia, itintimia,* to run against each other in a race; *ia talali,* v. t., to carry on the head.

ia, n., a goer; one who goes.

ia, n., a going; a proceeding.

iabạnnali, iabanali, v. t., to lay on the shoulders, Luke 15: 5. See *ilabạnnali,* Matt. 11: 29, 30; Gen. 21: 14.

iabạnnalichi, v. t., to lay upon the shoulders of another.

iachi, v. t. caus., to send; to cause to go; to impel; *itiachi,* dual, they go together, Luke 2:45.

iachi, n., a stirrer.

iachikchik, n., a grasshopper, i. e., one species, as each species has a distinct name.

iachuka, n., a turban; a cap; a headdress; a handkerchief or shawl worn on the head; a fillet; *minko imiachuka,* a crown; a coronet.

iachuka, pp., turbaned.

iachuka, v. t., to wear a turban.

iachukolechi, v. t., to put a turban, handkerchief, or headdress on the head of another person.

iachukoli, iachokoli, v. t., to put a turban, handkerchief, or any headdress upon one's own head.

iachuna, n., the nape; the back of the neck; the withers of a horse; some say *yauạska* and some *inkoi.*

iachunahika, n., the collar of a garment.

iachushak, n., the back side of the head; the upper part of the neck on the back side; the nape.

iachushukli, v. a. i., to limp. See *chushukli*.

iahiⁿsht ia, to follow in haste; to chase after or run after; from *ishi*, *iⁿshi*, *ihiⁿshi*, *iahisht ia*, went to take him.

iakaiya, iakaya, iyakaya, v. t., v. a. i., to follow; to come after; to pursue, Josh. 2: 5, 7; to dog; to second; to trace; *siakaiya*, he follows me; *issiakaiyashke*, do you follow me, Matt. 8: 22; 9: 9; 10: 38; 14: 13; 16: 24; *chiakaiyalachiⁿ*, I will follow thee; *hachiakaiya*, Josh. 2: 16; *hassiakaiyashke*, Matt. 4: 19; *iakaiyat okla*, dual number, Matt. 4: 20, 21; 8: 1; Josh. 6: 8; 8: 6; *iakat*, cont., *iakant*, John 13: 37; *iakat ia*, go and follow, Gen. 44: 4; *itiakaiya*, v. a. i., to go after each other in a single rank; to defile; to pursue.

iakaiya, a., second; subsequent.

iakaiya, n., a follower; a disciple; a pursuer; a succeeder; a successor.

iakaiya, n., a pursuit; a sequel; a train.

iakaiyachi, iakaiyachi, sing., to cause to follow; to send after or behind, Luke 19: 14.

iakaiyachit pisa, v. t., to follow; to endeavor to obtain.

iakaiyoha, v. a. i. pl., to follow.

iakaiyoha, n. pl., followers.

iakaiyohachi, v. t. pl., to cause to follow; to make them follow.

iakaya, see *iakaiya*.

ialipa, n., a cap; a turban; a bonnet; a cover; a lid; a coif; a hood.

ialipa, pp., turbaned; dressed with a cap, etc.; covered; hooded; wreathed.

ialipa, v. t., to wear a turban.

ialipa hashtap toba, n., a wreath; a garland.

ialipeli, v. t., to put on a turban, cap, bonnet; to put his turban on, i. e., on his own head; to coif; to hood; to wreathe.

ialipelichi, v. t., to put a turban or cap upon the head of another; to put on a lid or cover; to hood another.

iasinti, yasinte, hiasinti, n., an eel.

ialli, a., worth.

ialli, v. n., to be worth; *itialli*, to be worth against each other.

ialli, n., the worth; the value; the price; *aialli*, *aialbi*, *aiilli*.

ialli chito, a., dear.

iallichi, v. t., to price; to set a value upon; to rate; *itiallichi*, v. t., to price against each other.

iba, v. a. i., to be with, among, amidst, Josh. 7: 11; *itiba*; *itibai*, Matt. 9: 11.

iba, ibai, prep., with; in company with; along with; together with. It is compounded with many verbs and written *iba* before a verb beginning with a consonant and *ibai* before a verb beginning with a vowel. When a personal pronoun is prefixed in the obj. case it is not prefixed to the verb but to the preposition; as *ibaianta*, to stay with; *sabaianta*, to stay with me. *itiba*, double reference, together, etc., together with, John 4: 36; Luke 1: 58; *ibachukowa*, *ibaiimpa*, Acts 11: 3. A number of compounded verbs follow, to serve as specimens as well as to define the verbs.

ibabinili, v. t., to sit with; to settle in company with; *ibabinoli*, pl.

ibabinili, pp., seated with; settled in company with; *ibabinoli*, pl.

ibabinili, n., a fellow; a seat mate; a fellow settler; *ibabinoli*, pl.

ibabinilichi, v. t., to seat with; to cause to settle with; *ibabinolichi*, pl.

ibabukbo, ibbabukbo (q. v.), n., a double handful; a handful.

ibachaⁿfa, n., a companion; an equal.

ibachafa, ibachaⁿfa (nasal form), v. a. i., to be one with; from *iba* and *achafa*, John 1: 1.

ibachukoa, ibachukowa, v. t., to invade; to enter into and be with; to penetrate.

ibachukoa, v. a. i., to obtrude.

ibachukoa, pp., invaded.

ibachukoa, n., an invader.

ibachukoa, n., an invasion; an irruption.

ibafakchi, see *hatapofokchi*.

ibafohki, see *ibafoka*.

ibafoka, v. a. i., to join, as to join the church; to obtrude; to sort with; to unite with, to follow, as *sabafokashke*, John 1: 43; Luke 5: 11; to be in, Matt. 18: 1, 4; *itibafoka*, to join together; to put together; *imanukfila itibafoka*, to agree; to company; to consociate; to associate. See *foka*.

ibafoka, pp., united; joined with; combined; leagued; mixed; consociated; *ibafoⁿka*, nasal form, *ibafoyuka*, prop., *ibafoyuka*, with, 2 Sam. 24:2.; *itibafoka*, pp., conjoined; joined; *ikitibafoko*, a., uncompounded.

ibafoka, n., a union; membership; combination; consociation; unity; a contribution; *imbafoka*, n., increase; income.

ibafoka, n., a member; a follower; a communicant; a fellow; *itibafoka*, n., a companion; a contribution; a partaker; *itibafoka*, n., a joint.

ibafokat, adv., or v. a. i. with conj. *t*, to be with, etc.

ibafokat aⁿya, v. a. i., to go with, or in company with; to follow.

ibafokat hochifot takalichi, v. t., to enlist.

ibafoki, ibafohki, v. t., to join with; to contribute; to enter in; to put in with; to mix; to add to; to unite to; to combine; to insert; to involve; to obtrude, 2 Sam. 24: 3; to put among; Matt. 13: 33; Josh. 7: 11, *itibafoki*, to conjoin; to consociate; to identify; to join; *aⁿbafohki*, Gal. 2: 6. See *fohki*.

ibafoki, n., a mixer; one who joins, unites, or puts in; a contributor.

ibafokichi, v. t., to cause another to join, or unite with; to combine.

ibai, see *iba*.

ibaianta, v. a. i., to stay with; to cohabit; to dwell with.

ibaianta, n. sing., a companion; a mate; a fellow.

ibaiaⁿsha, v. a. i. pl., to sit with; to dwell with.

ibaiaⁿsha, n., companions.

ibaiaⁿya, v. a. i., to go with; to journey with.

ibaiaⁿya, n., a fellow traveler.

ibaiatta, a., twinborn.

ibaiatta, n., an inmate.

ibaiłauạlli, v. t., to play together.

ibaiłauạlli, n., a playmate; a play-fellow.

ibaiimpa, v. t., to eat with; to eat in company with; *itibaiimpa*, to eat together.

ibaiimpa, n., a messmate.

ibaiishko, v. t., to drink with.

ibaiishko, n., a companion in drink; a little companion.

ibaiyi, n., a nephew; *sabaiyi*, my nephew; my sister's sons and their male cousins by their mother's side, and not my brother's sons, which are called sons.

ibakaha, v. a. i., to mix together; to flock. *ibakaha*, pp., mixed; multiplied; *itibakaha*, amalgamated; confounded; see *ibạlhkaha*; *ikitibakaho*, a., unmingled; unmixed; *ibakaha*, n., a mixture; *itibakaha*, n., a contribution; a putting together.

ibakahachi, v. t., to cause to be mixed.

ibakali, v. t. pl., to mix them; to add; to put them together; to confound; to confuse.

ibakali, n., a mixer.

ibakchifanli, see *ibakchufanli*.

ibakchishinli, v. a. i. sing., to bend and turn up the nose and lips, as a fox when he smells. See *ibakpishinli*.

ibakchishinli, pp., bent and turned up.

ibakchishinlichi, v. t., to cause to turn up, as the nose.

ibakchufanli, ibakchifanli, v. a. i., to taper.

ibakchufanli, a., peaked; pointed; slender pointed; tapering; tapered.

ibakchufanli, v. n., to be peaked.

ibakchufanlichi, ibakshakanli, v. t., to taper; to sharpen, as to a point; to make sharp pointed like a wooden pin or a spade.

ibakchufaⁿshli, v. a. i. pl., to taper.

ibakchufaⁿshli, a., taper; peaked; pointed.

ibakchufaⁿshli, v. n., to be peaked or pointed.

ibakchufaⁿshlichi, v. t., to taper; to sharpen as to the point.

ibakchushli, pl., *ibakchishinli*, sing., v. a. i., to bend and turn up, as a fox turns up her nose, etc.

ibakchushli, pp., bent; turned up.

ibakchushlichi, v. t. pl., to bend them up; to turn them up.

ibakhatanli, n., a bald face.

ibakhatanli, a., baldfaced; palefaced, like a sickly man.

ibakhatanli, v. n., to be baldfaced.

ibakhataⁿshli, n. pl., baldfaces.

ibakhataⁿshli, a., bald faced.

ibakhataⁿshli, v. n., to be baldfaced.

ibaklipinli, ibaktokonli, v. n., to be short- or blunt-faced.

ibaklalanli, v. a. i., to be half laughing.

ibaklatinli, v. a. i., to run at the nose.

ibaklatinli, n., a running at the nose; a dirty nose.

ibaklatinlichi, v. t., to cause the nose to run.

ibaklololi, v. i., to run at the nose.

ibakoli, v. t., to search for in a hole.

ibakpishanli, a., round and pointed.

ibakpishanli, v. n., to be round and pointed.

ibakpishanlichi, v. t., to make it round and pointed.

ibakpisha^{n}shli, a. pl., round and pointed.

ibakpisha^{n}shli, v. n., to be round and pointed.

ibakpisha^{n}shlichi, v. t. pl., to make them round and pointed.

ibakpishinli, v. a. i., to turn noses and lips; see *ibakchishinli*.

ibaksuku^{n}lichi, v. a. i., to pout, Ps. 22: 7.

ibakshakanli, a., straight and tapering, like a spade, not hollowed or dishing; see *ibakchufanli*.

ibakshulanli, a., having white face and feet, as a horse; white-faced and -footed.

ibakshulanli, v. n., to have white face and feet; or to spread the nose like a horse out of breath.

ibakshula^{n}shli, a. pl., having white faces and feet; white-faced and -footed.

ibakshula^{n}shli, v. n., to be white-faced and -footed.

ibaktabanli, v. a. i., to be broad-nosed.

ibaktasanli, a., having a star in the forehead.

ibaktasanli, ibaktasanli bolukta, n., a star in the forehead.

ibaktasa^{n}shli, n. pl., stars in the forehead.

ibaktasa^{n}shli, a., having stars in the forehead.

ibaktokonli, a., blunt, as an old ax; short faced.

ibaktokonli, v. n., to be blunt.

ibaktokonli, pp., made blunt; blunted.

ibaktokonlichi, v. t., to blunt.

ibaktoko^{n}shli, ibaktoka^{n}shli, a. pl., blunt.

ibaktoko^{n}shli, v. n., to be blunt.

ibaktokoshlichi, ibaktoka^{n}shlichi, v. t., to blunt; to make them blunt.

ibani, (from *iba* and *ani*), to pour in with; to put in with; to add to; to mix; to eke; *itibani*, to mix together, applied to liquids; *nana kia itibanit okpani*, to adulterate by mixing.

ibani, n., a mixer.

ibanowa, v. a. i., to walk with; to travel with.

ibanowa, n., a traveling companion.

ibanowachi, v. t., to cause to walk with.

ibanukha^{n}klo, v. a. i., to condole; to mourn with; to lament with; to sympathize with.

ibanukha^{n}klo, n., a companion in sorrow; a sympathizer.

ibanusi, v. n. or v. a. i., to sleep with.

ibanusi, n., a bedfellow.

ibata^{n}kla, v. a. i., to partake with, Matt. 23: 30; to be among, Josh. 3: 10.

ibata^{n}kla, n., a partaker; a spy, 2 Sam. 15: 10.

ibata^{n}kla ishi, v. t., to share with.

ibata^{n}kla ishi, n., a sharer.

ibatepa, v. a. i., to injure himself; *imbatepa*, he is hurt; *ibatepa*, a second hurt; *ibatabli*, v. t., two words, from *iba* and *tabli*.

ibatoksalechi, v. t., to work him with.

ibato^{n}ksali, v. t., to work with; to labor with.

ibato^{n}ksali, n., a fellow laborer; a work fellow.

ibawichi, v. t., to aspire to help; to try to do; to attempt; *na hollo imanumpa anumpuli ibawichi*; *ibawinchi*, nas. form.

ibawichi, n., a help. See *ibalhkaha*, etc., for other verbs compounded with *iba*.

ibachifa, v. t., to wash the hands, Matt. 27: 24. See *ibbak achefa*.

ibalhkaha (from *iba* and *alhkaha*), v. a. i. pl., to mix together; to join. See *kali*.

ibalhkaha, pp., mixed; added together; *itibalhkaha*, mixed together.

ibalhkaha, n., an addition; addition; the name of a rule in arithmetic; a union.

ibalhto, v. a. i., to mingle with; to get among, as *wak at ibalhto*; from *iba alhto*, pp. of *ani* or *ibani*; *itibalhto*; *itibalhtot yanalli*, a., confluent.

ibalhto, pp., mixed; poured in.

ibalhto, n., a mixture.

ibbabukbo, ibbapukko, n., a double handful.

ibbabukbo achafa, n., a single double handful.

ibbak, ibbak, n., the hand; the arm as far up as the elbow; the paw; *sabbak*, my hand; *chibbak*, thy hand, Matt. 6: 3; 12: 13; 18: 8; *ibbak*, his hand (*Chisas at ibbakaⁿpit weli*, Matt. 8: 3); Matt. 14:31; *ibbak*, her hand, Matt. 8: 15.

ibbak abeha, n. pl., gloves; mittens.

ibbak achefa, v. t., to wash the hands; *ibachifa*, contr., Matt. 27: 24.

ibbak alibishli, n., a muff.

ibbak alota, n., a handful.

ibbak alhfabek imma, adv., toward the left hand; at the left hand.

ibbak alhfabeka, n., the left hand.

ibbak alhto, n., a handful.

ibbak aska, n., the wrist.

ibbak bonuht isht isso, v. t., to fist.

ibbak bonunta, n., the fist; the doubled hand.

ibbak chush, ibbakchus, n., the finger nail, or finger nails.

ibbak fahfulli, v. t., to gesticulate; to wave the hand about.

ibbak fohka, pp., given; committed; put into the hand; delivered; intrusted.

ibbak fohka, v. a. i., to come to hand.

ibbak fohki, v. t., to give; to commit; to deliver; to put into the hand; to consign; to grant; to intrust; to leave; to resign.

ibbak fohki, n., a giving; a resignation.

ibbak foka, n. sing., a glove; a mitten.

ibbak foka, pp., committed; received; placed in the hand; delivered.

ibbak foni, n., the hand bone; the arm bone.

ibbak iⁿlumpat ikhiⁿsh foka, pp., inoculated.

ibbak iⁿlumplit ikhiⁿsh foki, v. t., to inoculate.

ibbak ishki, n., the thumb.

ibbak ishki patta achafa, n., an inch; the breadth of the ball of the thumb.

ibbak isht impak imma, n., the right hand.

ibbak isht impak imma, adv., to the right hand.

ibbak isht impaka, n., the right hand.

ibbak isht itibbi, n., a pugilist.

ibbak isht kasholichi, n., a napkin.

ibbak isht talakchi, n., a handcuff; a manacle.

ibbak isht toⁿksali, n., a manual.

ibbak iⁿshuⁿkani, shakba iⁿshuⁿkani, n., the elbow; the point of the elbow joint.

ibbak itachakalli, n., the wrist joint.

ibbak onuchi, n., imposition.

ibbak paknaka, n., the back of the hand; lit., the top of the hand.

ibbak pata, n., the palm of the hand; lit., the spread hand; *ibbak patha*, palms of her hands, 2 Kings 9: 35.

ibbak takchi, v. t., to manacle; to bind the hands; to pinion.

ibbak talakchi, pp., manacled; handcuffed; pinioned.

ibbak tilokachi, n., the wrist joint; a joint that bends any way.

ibbak tilokachi abiha, n. pl., wristbands, such as are used by the Choctaw. They are made of silver and worn over the sleeves.

ibbak tilokachi afohoma, n., a wristband; a cuff.

ibbak tokonli, a., blunt; dull, as an ax.

ibbak umbitepa achafa, n., a span.

ibbak ush ali, n., the little finger.

ibbak ushi, n., a finger.

ibbak ushi abiha, n. pl., finger rings.

ibbak ushi foka, n., a finger ring; a cot; a thimble.

ibbak ushi isht pasholi, v. t., to finger.

ibbak ushi itachakalli, n., a finger joint; a knuckle.

ibbak ushi olachi, n., a fillip.

ibbak ushi tikba, n., the forefinger.

ibbak ushi wishakchi, n., the finger end.

ibbak wattachi, v. t., to unclinch the hand.

ibbapukko, n., a double handful.

ibbak, see *ibbak*.

ibetabli, v. a. i., to stumble; to dash the foot against, Luke 4: 11; to stub; to stump; to trip; to be offended; *ibetablit satula kamo*, I stumbled and fell; *iksiaiibetablokmat*, Matt. 11: 6; *isht aiibetabli tok*, they were offended in him, Matt. 13: 21, 57.

ibetabli, n., a stumbler.

ibetabli, n., a stumble.

ibetablichi, v. t. caus., to make him stumble or stub, Matt. 5: 29; to offend, Matt. 18: 8, 9; *kil ibitablecho*, we not offend, Matt. 17: 27.

ibetạp, n., the fountain; the source; the head, as of a water course; the part of a water course between you and the fountain, as *sokbish* is the other part; the upstream part of a river, Josh. 3: 13, 16; 15: 19.

ibetạp iⁿbok, n., the head of the creek; the name of a creek that runs into the Yalobusha from the south.

ibetạp pilla, adv., toward the head.

ibetạp pilla, adv., at the head; from the fountain.

ibiạli, n., the end of anything, as a table, plank, or rail.

ibichilu, n., the nose; the nostrils; the neb.

ibichilu foka, n., a halter; what is put on over the nose.

ibichilu foka foka, v. t., to halter; to put on a halter.

ibichilu patạssa, a., flat-nosed.

ibikoa, v. n., to bleed at the nose; *sabikoa*, I bleed at the nose.

ibikoa, n., the nose-bleed.

ibikoạchi, v. t., to make the nose bleed.

ibilhkạn, n., phlegm; rheum.

ibilhkạn chito, a., phlegmatic; abounding in phlegm.

ibilhkạn kucha, v. a. i., to snivel.

ibiłatampa, n., the combs or crest of a turkey.

ibish, n., a rise; a swell; a hill of earth where corn, etc., is planted; the bow and the stern of a boat; the round end; the end, as of a cask; a pommel; a prow; a saddlebow; the part of a junk bottle next to the neck; the nipple; the teat.

ibish ikbi, v. t., to hill; to make a hill about corn, etc.

ibish isht ạlhkạma, n., the head of a cask.

ibishakni, n., the nose; the snout; the bill; the beak of a bird; the trunk of an elephant; the proboscis; the neb.

ibishakni chiluk, n., a nostril; the nostrils.

ibishakni foka, n., a muzzle.

ibishakni patạssa, a., flat-nosed.

ibishạchi, n., the foretop.

ibishạno, v. n., to have a cold.

ibishạno, n., a cold, i. e., the disease well known to all.

ibitakla, n., the forehead, Rev. 7: 3.

ibitakla paⁿshi, n., the foretop; the front.

ibitek, n., a niece, his niece, her niece; sisters' daughters, and their female cousins; *sạbitek*, my niece.

ichabli, ichạbli, v. t., to mate; to match; to put together; to yoke together; *itichabli*, to pair; *ichapoli*, pl.

ichabli, n., one who mates.

ichapa, v. t., to resist.

ichapa, v. a. i., to match; to mate with; to go at the side of.

ichapa, pp., mated; matched; *itichapa*, mated together; paired, as *wak itichapa*, *itichampa*, both, 1 Sam. 3: 11; *shulush itichapa; itichapa*, v. t., to fellow.

ichapa, n., a mate; a fellow; a yokefellow; an adversary, 1 Sam. 1: 6; *itichapa*, n., an antagonist; a pair; a brace; a span; a match.

ichapa, n., a reverse; a contrary; an opposite.

ichapa, a., impudent; answering again; opposite; repugnant.

ichapa, v. n., v. t., to be impudent; to oppose; to contradict; *ạllat iⁿki aⁿ ichapat shali*, the child is very disrespectful to his father; *aiitachapoa* or *aiitichapoa*, to strive together, Luke 22: 24.

ichapaka, a., opposite; standing over against, Matt. 27: 61; Mark 11: 2; 12: 41; right against, Josh. 3: 16; 5: 13; beside, Josh. 7: 2; 8: 33; 12: 9.

ichapaka, v. n., to be opposite; to stand over against.

ichapoa, v. a. i. pl., to mate with; to go at the side of.

ichapoa, pp., mated; matched; mated together; sing., *itichampo*.

ichapoa, n., mates; fellows; cf. *wak toⁿksạli itichapoa talapi; itichapoa*, n., a yoke; a pair; a span.

ichapoa, a. pl., impudent; answering again.

ichapoa, v. n., to be impudent.

ichapoli, pl., *ichabli*, sing. v. t., to mate; to match.

ichạbli, see *ichabli*.

ieshi, v. t., from *ishi* (q. v.); to bring forth; to bear, i. e., young.

iⁿfalammichi, see *falạmmichi*.

iffuka, ikfuka, n., the abdomen; the belly; the bowels; the core of a watermelon; the inwards; the waist.

iffuka apakfopa, n., a waist band.

iffuka hotupa, n., the colic.

iffuka kashofa, pp., evacuated.

iffuka kashoffi, v. t., to evacuate the bowels.

iffuka kucha, pp., emboweled; eviscerated.

iffuka kuchi, v. t., to embowel; to eviscerate.

iffuka sita, pp., surcingled.

infolota, infulota, n., from folota (q. v.); lace or its edge.

infolota, pp., laced; bound on at the edge.

infolota ikbi, v. t., to lace.

inhaiya, ihaiya (J. E.), n., his brother's wife; his uncle's wife, etc.; his sister-in-law.

inhatak, n., her husband; her man; her lord.

inhatak illi, n., a widow, Luke 2: 37.

inhin, an interjection in talking to gain time, or to show that the speaker is at a loss; used by some old women.

inhika, n., a pillar.

inhikia, n., a keeper; a possessor.

inhimmak, n., a junior; his junior.

inhimmak, a., after it, him, her, or them; later; inhimmak on, a., latter.

inhimmak, v. n., to be after it, him, etc.

inhiya, pp., scolded.

inhiyachi, v. t., to scold.

inhiyachi, n., a scold; a scolder.

inhoa, inhowa, v. t., to call him, her, it, or them; to hail; to halloo; cf chinhatak ont inhowat ala, John 4: 16; isht inhoa, to call with; pit inhoa, to call for; to send for, Matt. 4: 21. See 1 Sam. 3: 4, 5, 6; ikinhoo, a., uncalled; inhowa, to call, Matt. 18: 2; Josh. 4: 4.

inhoa, n., a caller.

inholitopa, n., a favorite; a fancy; his fancy; his saint, 1 Sam. 2: 9.

inholitopa, a., dear to him; loved by him; stingy.

inholitopa, v. n., to be dear to him; sometimes inholitopa is rendered as a transitive verb; as, he loves him, it, her, or them; see John 3: 35.

inholitopaka, n., a friend; his friend; one loved by him.

inhollo, n., a favorite; one that is loved.

inhollo, n., tenderness; stinginess.

inhollo, v. t., to love him, her, or it; to fancy; to spare; as, ishinhollo, thou lovest him, Matt. 5: 43, 44; issanhollo, thou lovest me; chiminholloli, I save it for thee; I value it for thee; inhohonlo, freq.; inhoyullo, pro.; itinhollo, to love each other.

inhollo, n., a lover; itinhollo, mutual lovers.

inhollo, a., dear to him; loved by him; stingy; close; tight; illiberal.

inhollo, v. n., to be dear to him, etc.

inhollohe keyu, a., unlovely.

inhollot issa, v. t., to cease to love; to alienate the affections.

inhowa, see inhoa.

inhukni, n., his aunt; the sister of his father and her female cousins.

iiksho, v. n., to be without; to be none there, John 1: 47; for explanation of i prefixed to iksho, see a and ai.

ik, 3d per. sing. and pl. of active verbs in all the tenses except imp. in the neg. form, as ala, to arrive, iklo, not to arrive; sometimes found in the imp., as iklokia, do not let him come.

ik, a syllable prefixed to neuter and passive verbs in all persons of the neg. form; as, iksabanno, ikchibanno, ikbanno, ikpibanno, ikhapibanno, ikhachibanno, iksatalakcho, ikchitalakcho, etc.; ik is also prefixed to verbs in the negative form where there is a prefix pronoun in the accusative or dative cases, as iksachumpo, ikchichumpo, ikhachichumpo, etc.; iksankancho, ikchinkancho, ikinkancho, etc.

ik, sign of the 3d per. sing. and pl., imp. mood; ikminti, let him come.

ik, conj., although, or although let it be. See John 3: 19; iklakia, John 4: 4.

ika (in isht ika); anumpa isht ika, a speech delivered standing.

inkania, n., a loser.

inkania, n., a loss.

ikbano, sign of the opta. mood, Oh!; Oh that! Where the final vowel of the verb is i the opt. mood is suffixed as above; still one of the vowels is dropped, as is often the case where two come together in this way. After a and o the opt. form is akbano or okbano, sometimes hokbano, etc. (q. v.). Perhaps kibano

is the best representative of the opt.
mood; *kbano* and *hokbano* are most used.

ikbato, one sign of opt. mood, but this
is an elliptical expression. See Luke
19: 42, *ishithaiyanatokokbato*, "if thou
hadst known," then thou wouldst
have prepared thyself; *chumpakbato* is
said to request persons to buy something and then go away, or to buy and
furnish themselves and not trouble
others. It is used in the second and
third persons of both numbers; *kbato*
is a form that connects two predicates
with one subject, "oh that he would
buy and have it, or be off," etc.

ikbi, v. t., to make; to create; to raise;
to form; to manufacture; to build,
Matt. 16: 18; to construct; to erect; to
produce; to engender; to beget; to procreate; to constitute; to fabricate; to
fashion; to figure; to found; to frame;
to generate; to get; to grow; to manufacture; to originate; to seminate; to
shape; to work; *inkbi*, nasal form;
ihinkbi, freq.; *ilikbi*, to make himself;
ilimikbi, to make for himself, Gen. 7: 14;
aiikbi, Matt. 17: 4; *ikikbo*, a., unbegotten.

ikbi, n., a maker; a creator; a manufacturer; an author; a fabricator; a father;
a founder; a framer; a generator; a procreator; a raiser; a source.

ikbi, n., make; work.

ikbi, n., making; *aiikbichi*, to accuse,
Acts 24: 8.

ikbichi, v. t., to cause to make or do,
Matt. 5: 32.

ikfeksa, n., the side of a man or beast
between the hip bone and the rib.

ikfełichi, v. i., to be swollen in the
bowels.

ikfetap, ikfitukhak, n., the upper end
of the breast bone.

ikfia, n., a diarrhœa; a looseness; a relax;
a lax (a coarse word; *ulbal ont ia* is
better).

ikfia, v. n., v. a. i., to have a diarrhœa;
to purge; to relax; to scour.

ikfia, pp., purged; relaxed.

ikfiachi, v. t., to purge; to evacuate the
bowels; to drench; to relax; to scour.

ikfiachi, n., a purgative; a laxative;
physic; a purging.

ikfichukbi, ikfinksa, n., the side of a
man or beast between the hip bone and
the rib; the flank. See *ikfeksa*.

ikfihechi, n., a lax; a laxative; laxity;
laxness.

ikfitukhak, see *ikfetap*.

ikfuka, ikfoka, n., the abdomen; the
bowels; the belly, Matt. 12: 40; see
iffuka, ilhfoka.

ikfuka hotupa, n., the colic; pain in the
bowels; the bellyache.

ikfuka hotupali, v. t., to gripe; to distress the bowels.

ikfuka isht talakchi, n., a girth; a surcingle; a bellyband.

ikfuka katapa, n., the colic.

ikfukasita, iffukisita, n., a girth; a surcingle.

ikhana, ithana, v. a. i., v. t., to know,
Matt. 6: 8; Josh. 3: 4; to acknowledge;
to understand; to have acquaintance
with; to discern; to fathom; to feel; to
note; to observe; to perceive; to recollect; to recur; to remember; to take;
to wit (v. t., to witness); to wot; *ikha-
hana, ithahana*, freq.; *ileithana*, to know
himself; *ikhaiyana, ithaiyana*, pro.
form, to remember; to bear in mind; to
occur; to recollect, Josh. 1: 13; 4: 24.

ikhana, n., a knower; an observer.

ikhana, n., knowledge; intelligence; lore;
notice; recollection; regard; remembrance; science; cognition; understanding; erudition; experience; feeling; information; instruction; learning; light; wit; *ileikhana*, self-knowledge; *ikithano*, n., inexperience; ignorance; rawness.

ikhana, a., knowing; conscious; mindful;
notorious; scientific; aware; known;
expert; familiar; intelligent; learned;
literate; *hatak ikhana*, a known man, or
an acquaintance; *ikithano*, artless; ignorant; awkward; unacquainted; inexperienced; insensible; unconscious; uninformed; unknown; unmanaged; unperceived; unpracticed; unremembered;
untaught; *itikhana*, known to each
other; *itikhana*, n., acquaintance, Luke
23: 49; *itikhananka*, n., acquaintance,
Luke 2: 44.

ikhana, v. n., to be known, conscious,
etc.

ikhana, pp., taught; instructed; enlightened; indoctrinated; informed; learned; noted; regarded; *ikithano*, neg. form.

ikhana achukma, a., eminent; noted; well known.

ikhana ạlhpesa, a., memorable; notable.

ikhana fehna, a., memorable.

ikhana hinla, a., perceptible.

ikhananchi, v. t., to teach, Matt. 15: 9; to instruct; to inform; to educate; to bring up; to breed, Luke 5: 17; 6: 6; to civilize; to convey or communicate intelligence; to disciple; to drill; to edify; to enlighten; to familiarize; to indoctrinate; to introduce; to lighten; to nourish; to rear; to remind; to tell; to train; *ileithananchi*, to make himself known, Gen., 42: 7.

ikhananchi, n., a teacher; an instructor; as *Chahta ikhananchi*, the Choctaw instructor; a doctor; an enlightener; a preceptor; a remembrancer.

ikhananchi, n., tuition; instruction.

ikhananchit pelichi, v. t., to discipline.

ikhạna, ithạna, v. a. i., v. t., to learn; to acquire knowledge; to acquaint oneself; to embrace; to find; to get; to hear; to improve; to see; *ikithano*, neg. form; *ikhayana*, to remember, Matt. 5: 23; to understand, Matt. 15: 10; *ile-ithạna*, to teach himself.

ikhạna, pp., known.

ikhạna, n., a learner; *nan ithạna*, a disciple, Matt. 17: 6.

ikhạna, n., edification; improvement.

ikhạna hinla, a., teachable; capable of learning; intelligible.

ikhạnahe keyu, a., incomprehensible; inscrutable; unapt; unteachable.

ikhạnahe pulla, a., teachable.

ikhạnanchi, v. t. caus., to cause to learn; to teach; to acquaint; to instruct, Matt. 15: 9; Josh. 4: 22; or *ikhananchi* (q. v.).

ikhạnanchi, ikhananchi, n., a teacher.

ikhinsh, ithinsh, ishhinsh, ikhinsh, okhinsh, n., medicine; physic; a drug; the general word for anything used for the sick, as medicine, or applied to sores, as salve, or to the flesh, as ointments; a medicament.

ikhinsh ahama, n., opodeldoc.

ikhinsh akmo, n., salve.

ikhinsh apesa, v. t., to prescribe medicine.

ikhinsh balam, n., camphor; any fragrant medicine; an elixir.

ikhinsh bota, n., medicine prepared in powder.

ikhinsh bota ishkot hoita, n., tartar emetic.

ikhinsh bota ishkot ikfia, n., calomel.

ikhinsh chunkash libishli, n., a cordial.

ikhinsh hạpi holba, n., salts; Epsom salts; Glauber salts; sulphate of soda; sulphate of magnesia.

ikhinsh homi, n., bitters.

ikhinsh ipeta, v. t., to drug; to administer medicine.

ikhinsh ishkot hoita, n., a puke; a vomit.

ikhinsh ishkot ikfia, n., a cathartic.

ikhinsh ishkot nusechi, n., laudanum.

ikhinsh ishkot ontiachi, n., a cathartic.

ikhinsh isht apunfạchi, n., a syringe.

ikhinsh kanchi, n., a druggist; an apothecary.

ikhinsh lakshạchi, n., a sudorific.

ikhinsh luma, n., a nostrum.

ikhinsh lumbo, n., a pill; pills; medicine in pills.

ikhinsh lumboa, n. pl., pills.

ikhinsh nipi kạllochi, n., a tonic.

ikhinsh nusechi, n., opium; an opiate; an anodyne; laudanum.

ikhinsh okchalechi, n., a tonic; a stimulant.

ikhinsh patạssa, ikhinsh patạssapi, n., prickly ash.

ikhinsh shakba fohka, pp., vaccinated.

ikhinsh shakba fohki, v. t., to vaccinate.

ikhinsh shunsh isht ạbi, n., a vermifuge.

inki, n., his father (Matt. 15: 5); her father; father; sire; fatherhood; papa; a procreator; abba; *Inki*, the Father, Matt. 11: 27; 16: 27; *Inki on*, Father, Rom. 8: 15; *Chihowa akosh inki yon*, Jehovah was a father to him, John 5: 18; *hạchiinki*, Matt. 18: 14; Josh. 1: 6.

inki aiokla, n., paternal ancestors.

inki ansha, a., legitimate; born in wedlock.

Inki ạba, n., his Father in Heaven; God; *Pinki ạba*, our Heavenly Father.

Inki Chihowa, God Jehovah; Jehovah Father; his Father Jehovah.

iⁿki chohmi, n., fatherhood.

iⁿki ichapa, n., the firstborn; the child next to the father; the oldest son.

iⁿki iksho, a:, illegitimate; bastard; base born; fatherless.

iⁿki iksho, n., a bastard.

iⁿki ilikbi, v. t., to father.

iⁿki ishki ạbi, n., a parricide.

iⁿki ishki itatuklo, n., parents; father and mother.

iⁿki toba, n., a stepfather; his stepfather; her stepfather.

iⁿki toba, pp., fathered.

ikikki, int. of regret; O; alas; ah; oh; *ikikkeh*, alas, Josh. 7: 7.

Iⁿkilish imanumpa, n., the English language.

Iⁿkilish okla, n., Englishmen; English nation; the English; see *Miⁿkilish.*

ikimiksho, v. t., to lack; *ikshokahe nantahatuko;* pp., unfurnished.

ikistạp, n., tough meat of the neck.

ikithano, adv., unwittingly; ignorantly.

ikkishi, n., the brisket; the breast generally, not the paps, but the fore part of the thorax; the withers.

ikkishi foni, n., the breast bone; the sternum.

iklạnna, n., the middle; the center; midway, 1 Kings 10: 7; half the depth; the dead, as "in the dead of winter," etc.; half way; the heart; the interior; mean; midst; a moiety. Acts 1: 15; Josh. 4: 5, 8; midst of, Josh. 8: 33.

iklạnna, a., semi; half (Matt. 10: 29), as used in compound words; half pay; half pint, etc.; middling; mid, as found in compound words; midday, etc.; full, as the moon; mean; middle; mongrel.

iklạnna, v. n., to be middling, half or mid, etc.

iklạnna, pp., centered; divided in the middle.

iklạnna atampa, n., a majority; more than half.

iklạnnaka, n., the midst; the middle place; *aiiklạnnaka,* John 8: 3; the mean; the middle.

iklạnnaka iklạnna, n., a quarter.

iklạnnạchi, iklạnnachi, v. t., to center; to divide in the middle, Luke 19: 8.

Iⁿklisha, a., English; see *Miⁿkilish.*

Iⁿklisha, n., English.

ikma, sign of sub. mood, when the verb ends with *i;* see *ak* and *okma,* if, when; this particle begins with *k, kma,* when that. Compounds: *ikmako—ikmakocha—ikmakona—ikmakosh—ikmakot—ikmano, ikmạno—ikmạt,* if, when— *ikmạto.*

iⁿkoi, n, the withers of a hare or a buffalo.

iⁿkolumpi, see *kolumpi,* n., the throat.

ikonla, n., the neck; the throat.

ikonla afohoma, n., the collar; the part of a garment which surrounds the neck.

ikonla afohoma ishi, v. t., to collar; to seize by the collar.

ikonla awalakạchi, n., a ruffle; a ruff.

ikonla bana, see *ikonlabana.*

ikonla bekạt aⁿya, a., barenecked.

ikonla bekạt aⁿya, v. a. i., to go barenecked.

ikonla inuchi, n., a collar; something worn round the neck; a part of a harness for the neck of a horse or other beast used in draught; hames; the part of a yoke which embraces the neck.

ikonla shatali, n., a swelled neck; a swelled throat; the mumps (a disease); the quinsy.

ikonla umpạtta, n., a Vandyke.

ikonlabana, ikonla abana, n., a yoke, Matt. 11: 29; pp., yoked.

ikonlabana imaiishi, v. t., to unyoke.

ikonlabanali, v. t., to yoke.

iksa, n., a clan; a class; a denomination; a sect; a society; applied to the marriage clans, as *hatakiⁿholahta, kạshapokla.*

iksa, v. a. i., to be of a class, sect, or clan; as, *itimiksali bano kakoⁿ.*

iksa achạfa, n., one clan; the same clan or class.

iksa apistikeli, n., a bishop; one who has the watch of a class, clan, etc.

iksa asonunchi ạlhtoka, n., a deacon; an elder.

iksa ibafoka, v. t., to unite with a class, clan, denomination.

iksa inla, iksinla, n., another clan; a different clan; the other clan.

iksa issa, v. t., to desert a clan; to apostatize.

iksa issa, n., an apostate; apostasy.

iksa issạchi, v. t., to cause to apostatize.

iksa keyu, a., unrelated.

iksạmiksho, v. t., I have none, or there is none for me, or there is none of mine.

iksiachi, v. t., to fix; to repair; *aiksiachi.*

iksita, n., a hearth; *luak iksita,* Gen. 18: 6.

iksitopa; *nan isht ikaiiksitopa,* infirmities, Matt. 8: 17. See John 5: 5; 1st per. *iksaksitopa;* imperative forms, *ikchiksitopa, ikpiksitopa.*

iksho, v. n., to be absent; to be gone; to be none; not to be; *iiksho,* intensive form, Matt. 2: 17, 18; *ikimiiksho,* hath not, Matt. 8: 20; *aⁿsha* (q. v.), pro. form; *iksaksho, ikchiksho, iksho, ikpiksho,* etc.; *ikchimiksholih, akchimiksho.*

iksho, v. a. i., to want; *ikaiiksho,* as *oka ikaiiksho,* dry places, Matt. 12: 43.

iksho, a., absent; none; not any; destitute; devoid; wanting; missing; no; vacant; void.

iksho, n., a dearth; a privation; a wantage; wanting.

iksho, prep., without.

iksho, with a poss. pro. *sam, chim, im,* etc., to have none; the neg. of *amasha, chimasha,* etc., v. t., to want.

ikshokechi, v. t., to bring to nought; to destroy, 1 Cor. 6: 13.

il, a prefix per. pro., 1st per. pl. of active verbs beginning with a vowel, as *ia,* to go; John 4: 42; *ilia,* we go; *ithana,* to know; *ilithana,* we know. See *e.*

ila, to itself; by itself, as *ishilaboli,* you lay it by itself, from *ile,* reflexive, and *a,* locative.

ila, to himself, as *ilahalalli,* to draw it to himself; before a vowel, *ilai,* as *ilaieshi,* to take to himself. See Luke 12: 37; 17: 8; John 21: 18; *imokla ilahashia,* his peculiar people, Deut. 26: 18.

ilabannali, v. t., to shoulder; see *iabannali.*

ilabiⁿka, ilamiⁿka, a., different; various; separate.

ilabiⁿka, v. n., to be different.

ilabiⁿka, adv., separately.

ilafaya, ilafia, a., handsome, as *isuba ilafia,* a good-looking horse.

ilafia, v. n., to be handsome; to look well, as a horse.

ilafiopa, n., inspiration.

ilafoa, n., contumacy.

ilafoa, a., headstrong; obstinate; unyielding; unwilling.

ilafoa, v. n., to be headstrong.

ilafoa, v. a. i., to refuse; to struggle.

ilahninchi, n., self-esteem.

ilahobbi, v. a. i., to pretend; to profess; to attempt; to make a vain effort; to dissemble; to feign; to make as if, Josh. 9: 4.

ilahobbi, n., an attempt; a pretense; a feint; hypocrisy.

ilahobbi, n., a pretender; a professor; a seemer; a hypocrite, Matt. 6: 16; *nan ilahobbichiahoka,* thou hypocrite, Matt. 7: 5.

ilahobbi, a., pretended; professed; *hopaii ilahobbi,* Matt. 7: 15.

ilahobbi, adv., vainly.

ilahtali, n., providence.

ilai, dative reflexive particle before vowels; *ilaieshi,* Josh. 8: 1.

ilaiukha, n., recompense; retaliation; vow of revenge.

ilaiukha, n., a revenger.

ilaiyuka, ilayuka, a., various; diversified; all; each; divers, Luke 4: 40; every; different; several; sundry, Matt. 4: 24; *hatak ilaiyuka,* each man; *abeka ilaiyuka puta,* all manner of sickness; *yakni ilaiyuka, pinimpatok, haknip ikinchukmo ilaiyuka moma,* all manner of disease; see *aiyuka.*

ilaiyuka, v. n., to be various.

ilaiyuka, v. a. i., to shift.

ilaiyuka, n., a diversity; a variety; *ilaiyuka puta,* every kind, Matt. 13: 47.

ilaiyuka hinla, a., versatile.

ilaiyuka takoli shali, a., unsteady; variable.

ilaiyukachi, v. t., to make various; to cause a diversity; to vary.

ilaiyukali, n., division.

ilaiyukali, a., various; divers.

ilaiyukali, v. n., to be various.

ilaiyukali laua, a., manifold.

ilaiyukalichechi, v. t., to diversify.

ilakhata, v. a. i., to dress up; to put on ornaments; *ilakhatat antali,* I am dressing.

ilakshema, v. t., to dress himself; to vest; see *shema.*

ilalechia, a., proud.

ilamiⁿka, a., different and separate; see *ilabiⁿka.*

ilanoli, v. a. i., to confess, Matt. 3: 6.

ilanoli, n., a concession; a confession.

ilanoli, n., a confessor.

ilanukfillit pisa, n., self-examination.

ilap, pro., his; her; hers, Josh. 2: 19; its; this; theirs; own; himself; herself; itself; self; he, Josh. 3: 1; Matt. 9: 1; *ilap at*, he himself, Matt. 12: 4; *ilap ani*, their fruit, Matt. 7: 16; *ilap ani*, his fruit, Matt. 12: 33; *minko ilap*, this is the chief's; *ilap hochifo*, his name. The particles are suffixed to this word.

ilap, ilapa, self; him, Mark 1: 34; Matt. 10: 32, 33; 12: 16; *salap achafa*, I alone; I myself alone; I only, *salap*, *chilap*, *ilap*.

ilap achafa, adv., singly.

ilap achafa, a., unattended.

ilap ahni, v. t., to determine himself; to volunteer; *ilapanli*, a., selfish; *ilap ahni*.

ilap ahni, n., self-determination; his wish; his will.

ilap ahni, a., voluntary.

ilap ahni bieka, a., willful.

ilap ahni ilekanchi, a., self-devoted.

ilap ahni keyu, a., involuntary.

ilap ahni yamohmi, a., spontaneous; voluntary.

ilap aiahni, n., self-will.

ilap aiahni, adv., freely.

ilap akinli, himself; herself; itself; self; *ilap akinli hosh*, Matt. 8: 17.

ilap anukfilli, v. a. i., to think himself; to determine himself.

ilap anukfilli, n., self-determination.

ilap ali hikia, a., free—to stand by himself.

ilap bano, a., alone; himself alone; single; he alone; lone; unattended, Matt. 17: 1; them alone.

ilap bano, a., lone.

ilap bano, adv., lonely; singly.

ilap banot anta, v. a. i., to live alone, or to be the only one that stays.

ilap bieka, a., alone; solitary.

ilap biekat kanima atta, n., a hermit.

ilap binka, adv., by or among themselves, John 4: 33; Luke 4: 36; separately, Matt. 12: 25; 16: 7.

ilap fena, a., himself; himself indeed; himself in person.

ilap fena, adv., personally; in person.

ilap im, their own, Matt. 17: 25.

ilap immi, a., his own; her own; private; proper, Josh. 8: 27.

ilap immi, n., a proprietary.

ilap in, Matt. 9: 1; his own, Matt: 10: 36; 13: 57.

ilapakpuna, ilapakpunwa, a., selfish; self-conceited; self-willed; haughty.

ilapakpuna, v. n., to be selfish.

ilapakpuachi, ilapakpuwachi, v. t., to make selfish.

ilapakpunla, a., selfish; haughty; from *ilapak pulla*, surely himself he.

ilapakpunla, v. n., to be selfish.

ilapat, obj. case, pro., he; himself, Matt. 14: 22; 16: 21.

ilapinli, a., himself; herself, Matt. 6: 4; *ilapint*, obj. case.

ilapisa, see *ilapissa*.

ilapisa, v. t., to make; this word is perhaps from *apesa*, and is a reflexive verb.

ilapissa, from *ilap* and *issa* or *il* and *apissa*, to give himself up.

ilapissa, see Gen. 43: 32; *mihma ilapissa intallalimat*, etc., by themselves; by himself.

ilapissa, a., downcast; dull; pensive; sad; weak and trembling from sickness.

ilapissa, pp., saddened; disfigured; *nashuka ilapissa*, Matt. 6: 16.

ilapissa, adv., sadly.

ilapissachi, ilapissachi, ilapissachi, v. t., to depress himself; to disfigure, Matt. 6: 16.

ilapo, a., his, himself; *ilapo haknip akinli kakon*, John 2: 21; *ilapo fena yat*, John 4: 54.

ilapo inli, pro., itself, Matt. 6: 34; 12: 26.

ilapoma, pro. ob., him; *ilapoma ishin yamohmi*, Luke 6: 31.

ilaposh, pro., he; himself; obj. case.

ilapuna, a., selfish; self-willed; haughty; from *apoa*, to raise; to sow for raising.

ilapuna, v. n., to be selfish.

ilapunla, n., haughtiness; independence; selfishness; stiffness; from *ila* and *pulla*, surely himself, or to himself, or from *ilap* and *pulla*.

ilapunla, a., selfish; haughty; high minded; independent; insolent; lordly; stiff necked; stubborn; supercilious; wayward; presumptuous; rash; heady; from *ilap* and *pulla* (nasalized), surely himself.

ilapunla, v. n., to be selfish, etc.

ilapunla, v. a. i., to stiffen.

ilatoba, v. a. i., to spare; from *toba*, to become; *ikilatobo*, a., unreserved.

ilatomba, v. t., to save; to economize; to preserve for future use; to husband; to reserve; to spare; made by prefixing the particles *ile* reflexive and *a* locative to *toba; anumpa ilatomba fehna.*

ilatomba, a., saving; prudent; economical; reserved; frugal.

ilatomba, n., economy; prudence; reserve; saving.

ilatomba, n., an economist; a saver.

ilatomba atapa, a., penurious.

ilatomba keyu, a., unsparing.

ilauata, ilauata, v. a. i., to boast; to brag; to crow; *imilauata*, to crow over him; *isht ilauata*, to boast about; to vapor; to vaunt; from *auata* and the pronoun *ile.*

ilauata, n., a boaster; a brag; a vaporer; a vaunter.

ilauata, n., a boast; a brag; a prank.

ilaueli, ilauweli, v. t. sing., to lead along; to conduct; to rule; to govern; to lead, Matt. 15:14; to take, Matt. 16: 22; Luke 4: 5; to guide; to take a wife, Matt. 1: 24; 4: 5; this is a reflexive form from *aue, auechi, auet,* etc.; *pelichi,* pl.

ilaueli, n., a leader of one; a conductor; a guide; a guider; *wakushi ilauinli,* a cow that is the leader of a calf, i. e., a cow and calf, Matt. 18: 24.

ilauet, cont. of above, John 1: 42.

ilauet anya, v. t. sing., to rule; to lead; to conduct; to govern.

ilauet anya, n., a ruler; a leader; a husband.

ilanyak, imilayak, n., goods, Matt. 12: 29; wares; merchandise; riches, 1 Kings 10: 23; treasure, Matt. 6: 19; his goods; *imilayak chokushpa,* chattel; chattels; concern; riches; *imilayak isht yupomo;* v. t., to dissipate.

ilayuka, see *ilaiyuka.*

ilallachi, a., childish.

ilallachi (from *ile* and *alla*), v. t., to make himself a child.

ilapisa, v. t., to look on himself; to deem himself.

ilapissa, ilapisa, a., sad; of a sad countenance; depressed.

ilapissa, v. n., to be sad; to have a fallen countenance, Gen. 4: 6.

ilapissachi, ilapissachi, v. t., to depress.

ilappa, pro., this; these, Matt. 1: 20; 2: 3; 4: 9; *ilappa yakohmichi,* do this,

Matt. 8: 9; a demonstrative of person, thing, and place; this; here; *ilappa* refers to the nearest objects, *yamma* to the most distant; hither, Josh. 3: 9; *ilappa ishla hohcho?* art thou come hither? Matt. 8: 29.

ilappa, adv., here, Matt. 14: 17; hither, Josh. 2: 2; thence, Luke 4: 9; *ilappa fehnaka,* herein; here; John 4: 37; Matt. 12: 6; this place.

ilappa, demon. pro. in the obj. case or in any case, this; these; this person or thing; used instead of the third person of the per. pro. he, she, it, they, Luke 1: 6 [?] (*ilappa* is here in the n. case); *ilappa fenaka,* in this or herein, John 4: 37; Matt. 6: 29; the; these, Matt. 6: 32; 18: 14; this, Josh. 1: 2, 4.

ilappa foka, adv., hereabout.

ilappa pila, adv., in this direction; toward this place; *ilappa pila iali,* I am going in this direction.

ilappa pilla, adv., away here, pointing at the same time to the place with the finger or lips, meaning quite to or at the place, and not merely toward.

ilappak, adv., here; right here; *ilappak atukma,* this, Matt. 8: 9; *ilappak fehna,* here, Matt. 14: 8; *ilappakinli,* adv., here in this place; right here; *ilappako,* adv., in this place; at this place; hither, Matt. 17: 17; *ilappak oka,* here is the place which; *ilappak okat,* v. n., here is the place which; *ilappak okato,* that very one; *ilappakosh,* here is the place; this is, Matt. 11: 10.

ilappak, this, Matt. 3: 17; a simple word, like *himak, himmak, yammak; ilappak ash,* the, Luke 3: 15; *ilappakinli,* this; himself, itself, etc., Matt. 13: 22; *ilappakma,* this also; this too; *ilappakon,* in this; of this; from this; hither, Matt. 14: 18; Josh. 1: 4; in whom, Matt. 3: 17.

ilappak oka, adv., this the one which.

ilappak okat, nom. case, this is the one which.

ilappak osh, nom. case, this is the one, Matt. 17: 5.

ilappasi, adv., here.

ilappano, obj. case, this is the one.

ilappat, nom. case, this; *okla ilappat,* Matt. 15: 8.

ilappąto, nom. case, def., this is the one which.

ilappimma, adv., hither, this way, Josh. 8: 20.

ilappimma pilla, adv., thitherward.

ilbąsha, a., poor; wretched; miserable; destitute; calamitous; cheerless; contrite; deplorable; desolate; devoid; grievous; heavy; humble; indigent; lean; low; meager; necessitous; needy; piteous; rigorous; rueful; submissive; pp., degraded; troubled; depressed; distressed.

ilbąsha, adv., unhappily; miserably.

ilbąsha, v. n., to be poor, etc.; ilbąⁿsha; ilbaiyasha.

ilbąsha, v. a. i., to mourn; to ruin; to smart; to suffer; to undergo; isht ilbąsha, v. t., to mourn.

ilbąsha, v. t., with a pro. in the dative case; imilbąsha, to pray to him, Luke 5: 12; to importune of him; to supplicate; echimilbąsha, we pray to thee; we are humble before thee, Josh. 2: 12; ilbąⁿsha; ilbaiyasha.

ilbąsha, pp., distressed; impoverished; reduced to want; afflicted; persecuted; cursed; humbled; oppressed; racked; ruined; screwed; stripped; tormented; wronged, Matt. 6: 25; ililbąsha, pp., self-abased; ishpilbąshachi, thou tormentest us, Matt. 8: 29; ilbaiyasha.

ilbąsha, n., poverty; misery; a calamity; affliction; persecution; distress; the heartache; illness; impotency; indigence; need; necessity; oppression; penury; plaint; a privation; punishment; a strait; a stripe; suffering; torment; trouble; woe; wretchedness.

ilbąsha, n., the poor; a sufferer, Matt. 11: 5; ilbąsha atąpa, n., extremity; extreme distress.

ilbąshachi, v. t., to torment; to wring; to wrong; to depress; to oppress; to screw; to shave; to sterilize; to straiten; to strip; to distress; to impoverish; to afflict; to persecute, Matt. 5: 44; to deject; ililbąshachi, to distress himself.

ilbąshachi, n., an oppressor; a distresser; a tormentor; a wrongdoer; a wronger.

ilbąshahe ąlhpesa, a., damnable; tragical; unhappy; woful; wretched; wrongful; ikilbąsho, neg. a.

ilbąshalechi, v. t., to impoverish; to cause distress or poverty; to oppress.

ilbąshali, v. t., to distress; to afflict; to oppress; to persecute; to curse; to grind; to gripe; to pinch; to ruin; to destroy, Matt. 10: 28; Josh. 7: 25, to trouble; ililbąshali, to distress himself.

ilbąshali, n., oppression; persecution.

ilbąshali, n., an oppressor; a persecutor; v. t., to beggar; to condemn, John 3: 17.

ilbąshali, a., murderous.

ilbąshalit ąbi, a., murderous.

ile, sign of the reflexive form of active verbs beginning with a vowel, as anta, to stay; ilanta, to stay by himself or alone; akostininchi, to understand; ontilakostininchi, to understand himself; to come to himself, Luke, 15: 17; ilekostininchi, to repent.

ile, sign of the reflexive pronominal form before verbs beginning with a consonant; before a vowel one vowel is often dropped, especially the vowels i and a, as ilebi, to commit suicide; to kill one's self.

ilebi, n., self-homicide; self-murder; suicide.

ilefehnąchechi, v. t., to fan pride; to render proud; to elevate; to exalt; to lift.

ilefehnąchi, v. t., to pride.

ilefehnąchi, ilifehnąchi, (two long vowels, e and e, do not come together or follow each other.—later note by B.); a., ostentatious; pompous; self-sufficient; supercilious; proud; vain; arrogant; consequential; haughty; lofty; pp., elevated; high minded; insolent; lordly; magisterial; puffed; see fehna.

ilefehnąchi, adv., loftily.

ilefehnąchi, v. n., to be proud; to be vain.

ilefehnąchi, v. a. i., to crow; to boast; to prink; to swagger; to swell.

ilefehnąchi, n., a swaggerer.

ilefehnąchi, n., pride; vanity; hauteur; loftiness; pomp; self-conceit.

ilefehnąchit nowa, v. a. i., to stalk; to strut.

ilefoka, n., a garment; a coat, Matt. 5: 40; apparel; an undergarment; a tunic, Luke 6: 29; a dress; clothes.

ilefoka, v. t. ref., to put clothes on himself, herself, one's self.

ilefoka awalakạchi, n., the ruffle of a
shirt.

ilefoka chito, n., a cloak; a surtout; a
great coat.

ilefoka foka, v. t., to attire himself; to
dress himself; to clothe himself.

ilefoka foka, pp., clothed; dressed, by
himself or others.

ilefoka fokạchi, v. t., to clothe another;
to dress another.

ilefoka halushkichi, n., a flatiron; a
sadiron; a heater.

ilefoka isht boa, n., a pounder used in
washing clothes.

ilefoka isht kashokạchi, ilefoka isht
kasholichi, n., a clothes brush.

ilefoka isht shema, n., a dress.

ilefoka kolofa, n., a roundabout; a
short coat; a spencer.

ilefoka koloti, n. pl. of above.

ilefoka lumbo, n., a shirt; a coat, Matt.
10: 10.

ilefoka patafa, n., a hunting frock; a
garment that is open in front.

ilefoka shakba afohoma, n., a cuff; a
wristband.

ilefoka shukcha, n., a pocket in a garment.

ilefoka walaha, n., a ruffled shirt.

ilefoka yushkololi, n., a vest; a jacket;
a waistcoat; a short garment.

ilehaksi, a., self-deceived.

ileholitobli, n., self-love.

ileissikkopali, n., a self-tormentor.

ilepushpuli, v. i., to be cross.

ileyimmi, n., self-confidence.

ileyukpali, a., self-pleasing.

ilhfiopa, n., breath.

ilhfiopa okchaya, n., breath of life.

ilhfiopak, n., wind; breath; life, Matt.
6: 25; 10: 39; 16: 25; Josh. 9: 24; *imilhfiopak ishituk*, he took his life, Matt. 2:
19, 20; *imilhfiopak fohki*, to give life; to
animate; *pimilhfiopak*, our life, Josh.
2: 14; *imilhfiopak ikfalaio*, a., short
winded.

ilhfoka, n., the abdomen; see *ikfuka*.

ilhkola hinla, a., excitable.

ilhkolechi, ilhkolichi, v. t. caus. pl., to
move; to stir, as *shakba ilhkolechi;* to
move the arms; to cause them to move;
to bestir; to excite.

ilhkolechi, ilhkolichi, n., one that causes
a moving.

ilhkoli (ia, sing.), v. a. i. pl., to move; to
go, Matt. 8: 33; to leap, Luke 1: 41; to
budge; to start off; to take leave, Matt.
14: 22; to circulate; to pace; to stir; to
come, Matt. 8: 34; 2: 12; 11: 7; Josh. 7:
4; *aiilhkoli*, Matt. 11: 13; *ilhkola hinla
ka*, to depart, Matt. 14: 13; *ilhkot*, cont.;
ilhkonli, nas.; *ilhkohonli*, freq.; *ilhkoyuli*,
pro.

ilhkoli, n., those who move; movers.

ilhkoli, n., action.

ilhkoli, n., a motion; a movement; *ik-
ilhkolecho*, a., unshaken.

ilhkoli keyu, n., inaction.

ilhkolichi, v. t., to move; to circulate;
to set in motion; to start; to stir; to
shake; to work.

ilhkolichi, ilhkolechi, n., a stirrer.

ilhpa, n., food; provisions; cooked provisions; food prepared; an eatable.

ilhpak, n., food; provisions; bread, Matt.
6: 11, 25; Mark 3: 20; victuals, Matt.
14: 15; 1 Kings, 11: 18; cooked provisions; aliment; board; diet; entertainment; an esculent; fare; meat; nurture; nutriment; pabulum; subsistence;
sustenance; a viand.

ilhpak akanchi, n., a market, Matt. 11:
16; 23: 7.

ilhpak atali, v. t., to board; to furnish
with food; *ilhpak imatali*, to subsist.

ilhpak atali, n., a provider.

ilhpak imataha, pp., furnished with
food; boarded.

ilhpak tola achạfa, n., a mess.

ilhpapa, n., the hunters for a funeral, or
pole pulling.

ilhpapa, v. t., to hunt for the same.

ilhpansh, v. n., to be friendly, Gen. 40: 7.

ilhpita, n., a gift; a donation; "meat"
as a gratuity, or a ration, Matt. 10: 10.

ilhpita, v. t., to receive as a gift; *hatak
at ạlhpoyak ilhpita*, the men who receive
goods as a present.

ilhpita, ilhpitta, pp., given; put in; fed;
charged; nourished; *isuba hạt ilhpita*.

ilhpita achạfa, n., a charge; a load for a
gun.

ilhpitachi, v. t., to give; to keep.

ilhpitachi, n., a giver; a donor.

ilhtalowak, ilhtạlwak, n., song, Ex.
15: 2; a note in music; songs, Gen.
31: 27; see *ạlhtạlwak*.

ilhtohno, ạlhtohno, n., a servant, John 4: 51; a domestic; a help; a hireling; a mercenary; an undertaker.

ilhtohno, pp., hired; employed; instigated; engaged; from *tohno*, v. t., or *itohnochi*, to instigate.

ilhtohno keyu, a., unengaged.

ilifehnạchi, see *ilefehnạchi*.

ililli, n., pestilence, 2 Sam. 24: 13.

ilimpa, illimpak, n., food; victuals; meat; *ạmilimpa*, John 4: 34; nourishment; nurture; nutriment; pabulum; table; a viand; also sig., we eat.

ilissa, v. t. ref. (from *issa*), to surrender; to capitulate; to give himself up.

ilissa, n., a surrender; a capitulation.

ilissa, n., one who surrenders or gives himself up.

ilissạchi, v. t., to cause to surrender himself; to conquer.

ilissạchi, n., a conqueror.

illa, a., odd; singular, as *nakni illa siahoke*, I am a singular man.

illa, v. n., to be odd or singular.

illa, adv., oddly.

illa, v. a. i., to be only; *illạshke*, Mark 12: 32; *ushi akilla*, save the son, Matt. 11: 27; *illạt*, Matt. 14: 23.

illa, adv., only; barely; merely, John 4: 23[?]; *anumpa illa ho*, the word only, Matt. 4: 10; 8: 8; 10: 42; but, Matt. 14: 17, adj., a single word.

illa hinla, a., mortal; expirable; perishable.

illa husi, a., half dead; nearly dead; almost dead.

illahe imma, a., mortal.

illahe keyu, a., immortal; deathless.

illahe keyu ikbi, v. t., to make immortal; to immortalize.

illechi, a. (from *illi*), grievous.

illi, a., pp., dead, Matt. 11: 5; deceased; departed this life; lost at a game of chance; defunct; numb from cold; lifeless; benumbed; torpid; vapid; *ikillo kia ạba ia*, to go to heaven without dying; to be translated.

illi, v. t., to die, Matt. 17: 9; Josh. 1: 1; Matt. 15: 4; *imillilikạt*, Gal. 2: 19.

illi, v. n., to die; to perish, John 3: 16; to lose at a game of chance; to expire; to decease; to depart this life; to fail; to faint; to go; to pass; to perish; to rest; *ạlla isht illi*, to die in childbed;

pillimakoke, we perish, Matt. 8: 24; *imilli*, he lost; *illi, ili, ihili, inli, ihinli, ielli, ikello*, Josh. 1: 9; 8: 1; *inli*, nasal form, dying, John 4: 49; *hạshi ạt illi*, to change, as the moon; *ihinli*, freq., *iyilli*, pro. *ikiello*, neg.; Josh. 8: 1; *imilli*, v.t., to lose; *imilli*, n., a loser.

illi, n., death, Matt. 10: 21; the dead; *illi akosh*, the dead, Matt. 8: 22; deadness; decease; a departure; destruction; dissolution; an end; numbness; quiet; rest; torpor; *nan illi* is used for death in Rom. 6: 23.

illi, used as an intensive, as *sanukhaklot sạlli*, I am very sorry; lit., I sorrow and I die; *nusit illi*, fast asleep.

illi atukla, n., death; the second death; destruction.

illi biⁿka, dead like themselves, a fellow mortal, Matt. 8: 22.

illi cha ạtta, n., still born.

illichi, v. t., to kill; to put to death; to slay; to deaden; to dazzle; to numb; to end; to benumb; to obtund; to palsy; to paralyze, Matt. 10: 28; 16: 21; *itillichi*, to kill each other; *hạshi ạt nishkin aⁿ illichi*, the sun dazzles the eye.

illiissa, v. t., to proscribe; to offer to death; to give up to die, Matt. 10: 21; *illiimissa*, v. t., to betray, or give him to death, Matt. 27: 3.

illiissa anumpa, n., a proscription.

illilli, n., a disease, Luke 4: 40; a distemper, such as the smallpox; pleurisy; a malady; pestilence, 2 Sam. 24: 13.

illilli okpulo, n., a deadly distemper; a disease; a leprosy.

illilli okpulo, n., a leper.

illinaha, a., in the past tense, half dead; near dead; was well-nigh dead.

illit akosh falamạt tani, v. a. i., to rise from the dead; n., a resurrection.

illit okcha, n., one who has been resuscitated.

illuhmi, illohmi, a., deathlike.

ilo, iloh, per. pro., 1st per, pl., before active verbs beginning with a vowel; *ia*, to go; *ilia*, we go; *ilohia*, we all go; *ilohishko*, Matt. 6: 31.

ilokpạni, n., self-abuse.

ilolạbbi, n., self-denial.

iⁿlachi, n., a large green-headed duck.

iⁿlapa, n., caul or fat of the paunch (Billy Thomas, informant).

iłapa, n., the milt or spleen; some say it is the midriff, diaphragm, or caul, the milt being takạshi.

iłauạlli, iłoạlli, v. a. i., v. t., to play; to frolic; to parade; to revel; to romp; to sport; to toy; to trifle; to wanton, 2 Sam. 2: 14.

iłauạlli, n., a play; a diversion; a frolic; fun; a pastime; sport.

iłauạlli, n., a player; a frolicker; a reveler; a tumbler.

iłauạllichi, v. t., to make others play; to parade soldiers; to drill; itinhowa, to call each other, Matt. 11: 16.

im, pre. pos. pro., 3d per. sing. and pl. in the n. case, before nouns beginning with a vowel; as imisuba, his, her, or their horse. See chim, in, etc. imi, before shilombish, as ạmi, chimi, imishilombish, etc., with nouns of place; tạmaha holihta imisht impak imma, right side of the city; Chuta yan imoka mali pilla, to the south of Judah, 2 Sam. 24: 5, 7.

im, pre. per. pro., 3d per. sing. and pl., in the dative case before verbs beginning with a vowel, and to be rendered with a prep., as of him, for him, to him, etc.; to it, as a tree; see Mark 11: 23, imachi; imanoli, to relate to him; ima, of him; from him, Matt. 6: 1; ima, of them, Matt. 6: 2.

im, per. pro., 3d per. sing. and pl., in the nom. case before some neuter verbs, as okpulo, bad; imokpulo, he is angry, or there is evil with him; see chim.

im, pos. pro., removed from the noun and placed before the verb, as ạllat imilli, instead of imạllat illi. Many words have the pronouns im, etc., inseparably united. It is necessary to write them as they are used; imi, before the word shilombish, as imishilombish, Matt. 10: 20.

ima, ema, v. t., to give, Matt. 14: 7, 9; to sell; to cede; to send, John 3: 17; to impart; to bestow; to bear to, John 2: 8; to let one have; to accommodate with; to deliver to, Luke 4: 17; to communicate; to title, hạchimahe, Matt. 7: 7; imatok, had given, Matt. 9: 8; 14: 19; ima, to give him; chima, to give thee; ạma, to give me; anumpa ima; et ima, pit ima; ihinma, freq., iksamo, neg.,

ikchemo, ikemo, ikpemo, etc.; issạma, to give me; issahama, John 17: 8.

ima, v. t., to confer; to consign; to convey; to deal; to dispose of; to grant; to hand; to invest; to leave; to let; to offer; to present; to render; to resign; to transfer; chimali, Matt. 4: 9; aiyama, intensive form; isht ima, to take and give, Matt. 7: 9, 10; ạmaiyama, to give me much.

ima, n., a giver; a donor.

ima, n., a gift; a largess; a donation; a cession; a sale; a dedication; a legacy; a render.

ima, see imma.

ima hinla, a., that can be given.

ima keyu, a., ungranted.

imabachi, n., a teacher.

imabạchi, v. t., to teach or to teach him; to instruct; to show him how; to indoctrinate; to inform; imạlbạchi, pp., imabanchi, nasal form; imabahanchi, freq.

imachạnho, a., better, after being sick.

imafo, imạfo, n., 1, a grandfather, his grandfather, her grandfather, or her father-in-law, i. e., the father of her husband, while like other words denoting kindred, others are embraced, as imafo embraces all the brothers of the grandfather; a grandsire; 2, also great-grandfather.

imahaksahe keyu, a., unpardonable.

imahaksi, a., mindless; forgetful; ungrateful, unmindful.

imahaksi, pp., unlearned; forgotten; pardoned; unremembered; weaned; ikimahakso, a., unpardoned.

imahaksi, imihaksi, v. t., to forget; to forgive; to misremember; to miss; to omit; to overlook; to pardon; to pass; to remit; to unlearn; ạmahaksi, chimahaksi.

imahaksi, n., forgetfulness, remission.

imahaksicha hinla, a., pardonable; ishpimahaksichi, itimahaksichi.

imahaksichi, v. t., to cause it to be forgotten or forgiven; to forget; to pardon.

imahaksichi, n., forgiveness.

imahoba, v. t. (see ahoba), to suspect; to guess; to reckon; to figure; to presume; to suppose; to surmise.

imahoba, n., a guess; a presumption; a supposition; a surmise.

imaiąłechi, n., a lesson; a stint; his
lesson.

imaiya, a., superior to; better; surpassing.

imaiya, imaⁿya, (see aⁿya); v. t., v. n.,
to overthrow; to overtop; to prevail; to
surmount; to surpass, Matt. 10: 24; to
exceed; to conquer, 2 Sam. 24: 4; to
defeat; to master; to outdo; to outgo;
to outgrow; to outlast; to outlive; to
outwalk; to overcome; to overgo; to
overpower; ąmaiya, to be greater to
me; itintimaiya, v. a. i., to run a race;
to compete; to refute; to repress; to
revolt; to vie; to rival; to transcend; to
triumph; to win; itintimiya, n., a race;
itintimiya, n., a racer; a rival, Matt. 11:
9, 11; 12: 6, 41.

imaiya, n., excess; a conquest; a defeat;
a subjection; a triumph; vantage; a
victory; a winning.

imaiya; imaiyahe keyu, a., triumphant;
victorious; unconquerable.

imaiya, n., a conqueror; his conqueror;
a victor; a winner.

imaiya, pp., subdued; taken; ikimaiyo,
a., unsubdued; unconquered.

imaiya hinla, a., vincible.

imaiyahe keyu, a., invincible.

imaiyąchi, v. t., to exceed; to conquer;
to beat; to excel; to surpass; to defeat;
to humble; to master; to outdo; to overcome; to overpower; to overthrow; to
subdue; to subject; to suppress; to surmount; to take; to vanquish; to prevail against, Matt. 16: 18.

imaiyąchi, n., a conqueror; a subduer;
a vanquisher.

imaiyąchi, n., a subjection.

imaiyąmohmi, n., luck.

imaiyąt faląmmint ishi, v. t., to reconquer.

imaiyokoma, a., perplexed; bewildered;
at a loss.

imaiyokoma, v. n., to be perplexed or
bewildered; to be at a loss; imaiyokomi,
he is bothered.

imaiyokomichi, v. t., to bewilder; to
cause perplexity; to maze.

imaiyopik, n., a relative by marriage;
the brothers, uncles, and nephews of
her husband are thus called by a
woman. It is now obsolete.

imaⁿka, imąka, a., natural; proper; suitable; acceptable.

imaⁿka, v. n., to be natural; ikimaⁿko,
neg., to be unnatural or unsuitable.

imalak, n., a brother-in-law; his
brother-in-law; a man's sister's husband, and brothers.

imalakusi, n., a brother-in-law; his
brother-in-law; his wife's brothers, and
cousins.

imalakusi ohoyo, n., his sister-in-law,
i. e., his wife's sister.

imaląma, a., guarded; kept.

imaląma, v. n., to be guarded; he is
guarded or kept.

imaląmi, v. t., to hinder; to oppose; to
object.

imaląmmi, n., an objector.

imaląmmichi, v. t., to cause objections;
to cause to hinder.

imałaka, n., the midriff.

imałechi, v. t., to maim.

imałeka, v. a. i., to suffer pain from
his own misconduct; to smart.

imałeka, pp., distressed; pained;
maimed.

imałeka, a., unfortunate; unlucky.

imałeka, n., a doom; misfortune.

imałeka hinla, a., unsafe.

imałeka shaȟ, a., hapless.

imałekahe keyu, a., safe.

imałekahe keyu, n., safety.

imałekąchechi, v. t., to cause pain.

imałekąchi, v. t., to cause pain.

imantąnanchi, n., the breastbone.

imantia, n., an obeyer.

imantia, a., obedient; dutiful; submissive.

imantia, n., duty; obedience; observance; observation.

imantia, v. t., to heed; to obey; to mind;
to observe; to serve, Matt. 4: 10; see
antia.

imantia achukma, a., obsequious.

imantiahe keyu, a., ungovernable.

imanukfela, a., sad; sorrowful; imanuk-
fiela.

imanukfela, v. n., to be sad, Gen. 40: 6.

imanukfeląchi, v. t., caus., to sadden; to
to make sad; imanukfieląchi.

imanukfila, a., ideal; mental; thoughtful.

imanukfila, n., his thought; their
thoughts, Matt. 9: 4; his mind; thought;
mind; an opinion; reflection; understanding; brain; intellect; judgment;

sentiment; conceit; conscience; consideration; contemplation; counsel; discernment; eye of the mind; a faculty; the faculties; a fancy; a phantasm; a phantom; feeling; heart; an idea; an imagination; an impression; an intent; a meditation; memory; mettle; a notion; a project; reason; sense; sentiment; a speculation; spirit; temper; a tenet; a theory; a thought; unanimity; a view; a voice; a judgment; will; wit, Mark 2: 8.

imanukfila, v. a. i., to think; to reason; v. t., to intend; *imanukfila fehna,* Luke 4: 22 [?]; *imanukfilachi.*

imanukfila achafa, a., like-minded; of one mind; unanimous.

imanukfila achafa, n., resolution; a resolve; "one accord," Josh. 9: 2.

imanukfila achafa, v. n., to be like minded; to agree; *imanukfila ikachafo,* to dissent.

imanukfila achafa, n., concord.

imanukfila achafa keyu, a., unprincipled; unstaid; wavering.

imanukfila ahalaia, a., mental; spiritual.

imanukfila aiimma, a., intellectual.

imanukfila akanlusi, a., dampened, as to the feelings; discouraged.

imanukfila anli achukma, a., conscientious.

imanukfila apissanli, a., stable-minded.

imanukfila apissanli keyu, a., unstable.

imanukfila ansha, a., rational; reasonable; sensible.

imanukfila alhpesa, a., unprejudiced.

imanukfila chaha, a., magnanimous; high-minded; *imanukfila chaha,* v. n.

imanukfila chito, n., magnanimity; a reverie; sconce; strength.

imanukfila chito, a., having a large mind; magnanimous.

imanukfila fehna, a., meditative; thoughtful.

imanukfila hopoyuksa, a., magnanimous.

imanukfila ikkallo, a., happy.

imanukfila iksho, n., idiocy; shallowness; stupor; dotage.

imanukfila iksho, a., foolish; senseless; without mind; idiotic; ignorant; irrational; shallow - brained; silly; simple; sottish; stupid; thoughtless.

imanukfila iksho, n., a fool, Matt. 5: 22; 23: 17; a natural; raca (Heb.); a simpleton; a sot; a witling, an idiot; an ignoramus; a dotard; dotage.

imanukfila iksho, v. n., to be foolish; to know nothing.

imanukfila iksho aiimoma, n., an idiot; a natural fool.

imanukfila ilaiyuka, v. a. i., to vacillate; a., whimsical.

imanukfila ilbasha, n., gloom; gloomy thoughts.

imanukfila inla minka, v. t., to disagree.

imanukfila ishi, v. t. to seize the mind; to interest the mind; to captivate.

imanukfila itibafoka, v. t., to agree in opinion; to concur.

imanukfila itiholba, a., like-minded; resembling each other in sentiment.

imanukfila itiholba, v. n., to be like-minded.

imanukfila kapassa, n., insensibility.

imanukfila kapassa, a., insensible.

imanukfila kallo, a., unfeeling; hardhearted.

imanukfila kallo, n., comprehension; genius; harshness.

imanukfila komunta a., anxious; distressed; uneasy in mind.

imanukfila komunta, v. n., to be anxious.

imanukfila komunta, n., anxiety.

imanukfila laua, n., maze; perturbation.

imanukfila laua, a., fickle; changeable; fanciful; fertile; fluctuating; indecisive; notional.

imanukfila nukhanklo, n., melancholy; mercy.

imanukfila nuktanla, n., modesty.

imanukfila okpani, v. t., to delude.

imanukfila okpulo, a., evil-minded; malevolent.

imanukfila okpulo, n., malevolence; malignity.

imanukfila onuchi, v. t., to apply the mind.

imanukfila shanaia, a., perverted in opinion.

imanukfila shanaioa, v. a. i., to whiffle.

imanukfila shanaioa, a., fickle; feverish; light-minded; whiffling.

imanukfila shanaioa, n., lightness.

imanukfila shananchi, v. t., to persuade; to pervert the mind; to incline; to prejudice; to prepossess.

imanukfila tohwikelichi, v. t., to illume; to illumine; to illuminate.

imanukfila tuklo, a., double-minded.

imanukfila tuklo, v. a. i., to trim.

imanukfila tunshpa, a., eagle-eyed; quick-minded; witty.

imanukfila yohbi, n., meekness.

imanumpeshi, n., a lieutenant; a vice-agent; a second in command; a minister.

imansha, v. t., to have; to keep; see ansha.

imansha, n., a keeper; a possessor.

imashaka, n., the rear.

imatali, n., a maintainer; a supporter.

imatali, v. t., to maintain; to minister; to satisfy; to store; to supply.

imatananchi, imantananchi, n., his breast.

imafo, imafo, n., her father-in-law, 1 Sam. 4: 19; see imafo.

imaka, see imanka.

imalhpisa, n., a license; a ration.

imalhtaha, pp. (from atali), maintained; ministered; satisfied; prepared; stored; supplied; sustained; ikimalhtaho, a., unprepared; unprovided; unqualified; unready; unsupplied; ikimalhtaho, n., unreadiness.

imalhtayak, n., a vocation.

imallunsak, issimallunsak, n., the name of a weed called in vulgar parlance the devil's shoestring. It is used to intoxicate fish in water ponds and to break up fever and ague.

imala, v. n., to be timid, or wild; isi at imala, allat imala.

imala, a., timid; wild; fortunate.

imanni, n., his older brother, i. e., any one, or all, older than himself, as nakfish means any one or all younger than himself. This expression by brothers only expresses their relation. Sisters do not call their older brothers by the same epithet.

imanni, n., her older sister. Sisters speak of older and younger sisters as brothers do of brothers. A sister calls her brother nakfi, annakfi, my brother, etc. A brother calls his sister antek, my sister.

imbakna, n., the rennet, see bakna.

imi, his, Matt. 16: 26; 1 Sam. 2: 9.

inmiha, n., a mandate; a nod; a reproof.

inmiha, n., a monitor.

imihaksi, v. a. i., to forget, Matt. 16: 5; see imahaksi.

imikfetukhak, imikfetuphak, n., the upper end of the breastbone.

imilayak, n., substance; goods; wares; merchandise; an estate; mammon; property.

imilayak chito, a., wealthy.

imilayak iklauo, a., unwealthy.

imilayak isht yopomo, a., extravagant.

imilbik, n., prey; booty; good fortune.

imilhfitukhak, n., the hole or notch in the breastbone under the windpipe; his, etc.

imilhlah, v. a. i., to be low-spirited.

imilli, n., a loser at a game.

imilli, n., a loss.

imiskauata, imiskatukli (inf., Judah Dana), n., the collarbone; his collarbone.

imissa, v. t., to offer him; to promise him; to give, Mark 12: 9; Josh. 1: 6; to tender; to bid at an auction; to offer; to proffer; to propound, John 3: 16 [?]; to will, i. e., to devise; ilimissa, to offer himself; to dedicate himself.

imissa, n., an offerer; one who makes an offer; a profferer; a propounder; a testator; an offering; a proffer; a proposal; a testament; a will; ilimissa n., self-dedication.

imitaklish, n., the breastbone; his breastbone.

imma, ima, adv., toward, Matt. 12: 49; hashi akuchaka imma, Matt. 2: 1, 9; the way to, Josh. 2: 7. Compounded with other words, as abema, upward; ilappimma, this way; akema, downward; mishema, abroad; beyond; yammimma, that way; olema, this way; yamma immaka, that way, Matt. 13: 28 [?]; pila imma, Acts 28: 14; imma, v. a. i.

imma, prep., concerning; of; about; Chihowa apeliechika imma ya, Luke 4: 43; paska imma, concerning bread, Matt. 16: 11; isht imanumpohonlilahe; okhata imma nana inla hachimanolila hinla.

immachi, v. t., 1 John 2: 26.

immi, pos. pro. or adj. pro., his; her; hers; its; their; theirs; his own; *itimmi*, his and hers; belonging to each other.

immi, n., a title; inheritance, Mark 12: 7.

immi, v. n., to possess, Josh. 13: 1; to be his, hers, etc.; to own, Mark 12: 17; Matt. 17: 4; *immichi*, v. caus., and *itimmi; kąna immi keyu*, a., unowned.

immi, n., an owner; an heir, Mark 12: 7; lord of, Mark 12: 9.

immi, n., right; property in.

immi ikbi, v. t., to entitle.

immi toba, v. a. i., to become his.

immi toba, pp., made his; entitled.

immoshi, see *imoshi*.

imokąto, hoshuⁿ aiąlhto, n., the bladder.

imoklaya, a., kind; gentle.

imokpulo, n., an injury to him; a loss to him; *imomokpulo*, an injury for or to him; a lameness, etc.

imoksini, n., pudenda mulieris; the clitoris.

imoksini, see *imosini*.

imola, a., lucky; favored; fortunate.

imola, v. n., to be lucky; to have good luck.

imola, n., good luck; good fortune.

imoma, a., customarily or naturally small; *ofi imoma*, a naturally small dog; *hatak imoma*. a small man; a dwarf; see *aiimoma*.

imoma, pp., inured.

imoma, v. n., to be naturally small.

imoma, v. a. i., to dure, Matt. 13: 21.

imoma, v. a. i., to do thus; *asi momali*, I still do so.

imoma, n., a runt; a dwarf.

imomaka, n., an experiment; experience.

imomaka pisa, v. t., to tempt, Matt. 16: 1.

imomaka pisa, n., a tempter, Matt. 4: 3.

imomaka pisa, v. t., to make a trial; to have a trial; to tempt, Matt. 4: 1; 16: 1; 19: 3.

imomakachi, v. t., to make an experiment.

imomakąt pisa keyu, n., inexperience.

imomąchi, imomachi, v. t. caus., to cause it to be naturally small; to exercise; to inure.

imomąchi, n., a custom.

imomąchi, a., old.

imombąlaha, n., her brother-in-law; i. e., her husband's brother.

imomokpulo, a., lame; halt; deformed naturally; misshapen, Luke 14: 21; Matt. 11: 5; 15: 30; maimed, Matt. 18: 8. Perhaps from *imoma okpulo*, which would be a natural injury. See below.

imomokpulo, v. n., to be lame; from *imoma* and *okpulo*, a long-continued or natural deformity of the limbs.

imomokpulo, n., the lame; the halt; a deformity; impotency; a monster.

imomokpulo aiasha, n., a lazaretto.

imosana, n., the forehead; the eyebrow; the brow of the eye.

imosana hishi, n., the foretop; the eyebrow.

imosini, imossini, imoksini, n., a bumblebee or humblebee.

imoshątto, imushątto, imoshąto, n., the womb; her womb, John 3: 4.

imoshi, immoshi, n., uncle; his uncle; her uncle; the brother of the mother.

impa, v. t., to eat sundry articles of food (*ąpa*, to eat one article); to take food; to take a meal; to board; to feast; to feed; to diet; to mess; to regale; to take; *ibaiimpa*, to eat with; *itibaiimpa*, to eat together with; *impa chiⁿka*, to eat, Matt. 14: 16, 20; 15: 37, 38; to feed; *shukha laua kąt impa hosh*, Matt. 8: 30; *ihimpa*, eating, Matt. 11: 19; *ikimpo*, v. a. i., to fast; *ikimpo hosh*, Matt. 4: 2; *ikimpo*, Matt. 11: 18.

impa, n., an eater; a feaster; *itibaiimpa*, n., a messmate.

impa, n., food; victuals; board; entertainment.

impa, n., a meal; a feed; a ration; *impa achąfa*, one feed; one meal; one ration; a repast.

impa aiyimita, a., voracious.

impa atabli, n., a surfeit.

impa chito, n., a feast; a banquet; a carnival; a festival.

impa fena, a., voracious.

impa fena, v. n., to be voracious.

impa fena keyu, a., abstemious.

impa fena keyu, v. n., to be abstemious.

impa iskitini, n., a collation; a snack; a bite; a luncheon; a lunch.

impachi, impąchi, v. t., to feed; to make one eat; to cause to eat; to diet; to entertain; to feast; to foster.

impachi, impạchi, n., a feeder; a feaster.

impafakchi, n., the crop of a fowl.

impakti, n., the gills of a fowl, or his gills.

impashia, impashaia, n., the brim of a hat.

impạchi, n., a feast, Gen. 19: 3; 21: 8.

impạchi, v. a. i., to feed, Mark 5: 14.

impạsha, impạshi, n., a gill of a fowl; his gill or gills; a cock's comb; a crest.

imponaklo, v. t.; see ponaklo.

imponna, n., skill; craft; cunning; wit; understanding; faculty; handiness; improvement; ingenuity; a knack; workmanship.

imponna, n., a master hand; a skillful person; hạchimponna, ye know how, Matt. 7: 11.

imponna, a., pp., skillful; adroit; dexterous; ingenious; capable; versed; taught; skilled; clever; crafty; cunning; expert; exquisite; fine; gifted; handy; happy; improved; ripe; sagacious; scientific; shrewd; sly; smart; talented; ikimponno, a., inexpert; crude; raw; rude; unexpert; inexperienced; unskilled; unhandy; unpracticed.

imponna, v. n., to be skillful; to know how; to understand; anumpuli chimponna, you know how to speak; or, you are a skillful speaker.

imponna, v. a. i., to excel.

imponna, n., an adept.

imponna, adv., well.

imponna taha, a., perfect.

imponnat, adv., masterly; shrewdly.

imponnạchi, v. t., to teach; to instruct.

imponnạchi, n., a teacher.

imposhot infullolichi, v. t., to fringe.

imposhota, n., a fringe.

impota, v. t., to lend; to lend him; to loan; to farm; to let; to rent; to lease; sapota, I lend.

impota, n., a lender; a renter.

impota, n., a lending; a loan.

impota hinla, a., lendable.

[impunsa, v. t., to kiss.—H. S. H.]

impusnakni, n., a woman's relation to her husband's brothers, uncles, and nephews.

impunspoa, impunspoa, to kiss him. This is the Choctaw word and is better than insunksowa.—Thomas Jefferson. [impunsa, H. S. H.]

impushnayo, n., the master of an animal; see pushnayo.

impushnayo iksho, a., unowned.

imuksak, n., the ankle; his ankle.

imuksak foni, n., the ankle bone.

imushạtto, see imoshạtto.

in, pos. per. pro., 3d per. sing. and pl. in the n. case before nouns beginning with ch, l, t, as inchuka, his house; see im.

in, pre. per pro., 3d per. sing. and pl. in the dative case before verbs beginning with ch, l, or t, and generally rendered with a prep. to or for, etc.; inchumpa, to buy of him, or from him.

in, per. pro., 3d per. sing. and pl. in the nom. case before some neuter verbs; imokpulo, he is angry; ạlla chintalapi, you have 5 children; see im.

in, pos. pro., removed from the noun and placed before the verb, as tanchi chinlaua or chintanchi ạt laua.

innakfi, n., her brother.

innakfish, her younger sister; see imạnni.

innakfish, n., his younger brother; see nakfish.

innaki, n., his sting; fohkul innaki, nakishwana innaki.

innalạpi, n., the gullet; his gullet; the gorge; the throat.

innasobaksobish, n., muscles near the groin.

inchahe, n., a spur, the hard-pointed projection on a cock's leg; his spur; akank inchahe, the spur of a rooster; fakit inchahe, the spur of a turkey.

inchaka, n., the gills or the comb of domestic fowls.

inchạsha, n., rattles; his rattles; sintullo inchạsha.

inchạshwa, n., small of the back, or the sinews of the small of the back.

inchạshwa nipi, n., the loin.

inchuka, n., his house; his home; see chuka.

inchunli, inchonli, v. t., to brand, as men brand cattle or rogues; to stamp; to embroider; to impress; to imprint; to seal; to stigmatize; to tattoo, Matt. 27: 66; Rev. 7: 3.

inchunwa, pp., branded; stamped; sealed; tattooed, stamped or printed, as calico; nan tạnna inchunwa, calico, Rev. 7: 4.

inchuⁿwa, n., a brand; the mark made in branding; an impress; an impression; a stigma; a tattoo; *isht inchuⁿwa*, n., a brand, the instrument used in branding; a seal, Rev. 7: 2.

inla, a. pro., other; another; else; new, Matt. 7: 1; *inla tohnot*, to send others, Matt. 14: 35.

inla, adv., oddly.

inla, a., strange, Luke 5: 26; queer; foreign; different; other; any other; some other; contrary; dissimilar; unwonted; wrong, as *hina inla*, the wrong road; *inla yoⁿ*, another; Matt. 10: 23; *inla hoⁿ*, another place, Acts 12: 17; marvelous; odd; quaint; singular; uncouth; *inlaka yạto*, other; Matt. 13: 8, *hatak inla*, John 4: 38.

inla, n., a change; an innovation; an oddity; the rest; strangeness.

inla, v. n., to be strange, etc.

inla, v. a. i., to alter; to change; to vary, as, it alters, it changes, etc.; *aiinlạt ia keyu hoke*, Ch. Sp. Book, p. 36; *aiinla*, Matt. 17: 2.

inla, pp., changed; altered; *inlat taha*, entirely changed.

inla anukcheto keyu, a., independent.

inla fehna, a., marvelous; monstrous.

inla hinla, a., mutable; variable.

inla ikbi, v. t., to transform.

inla ikholbo, v. a. i., to differ.

inla ilahobbi, v. t., to personate.

inla immi, a., another's.

inla immi kia ahalaia, a., impertinent.

inla shali, a., changeable; addicted to change; unsteady.

inla toba, v. n., to be converted, etc.

inla toba, n., variance; a variation.

inlahe keyu, a., unalterable; unchangeable.

inlat toba, pp., converted, Matt. 18: 3; changed; made different; modified; *aiinla toba*, transfigured, Matt. 17: 2; *inlat iktobo*, a., unconverted.

inlat toba, n., conversion.

inlạchi, v. t., to alter; to change; to make a change or difference; to convert; to innovate; to modify; to shift; to vary; *inlanchi*, nasal form.

inlạchi, n., one who alters or changes; a changer; an innovator.

inlạt, adv., strangely..

inli, a., self; as *ạno inli*, I myself; *ilap inli, yạmmak inli*, etc.

inli, adv., also, generally used with *ak*, as *akinli*, that also, again, Matt. 4: 7; *akinli*, that again; also, Matt. 6: 21.

inluhmi, a., fold, the same quantity added; double, 2 Sam. 24: 3; from *inli* and *ohmi; inluhmi tuklo*, a., twofold, or double; *inluhmi tuchina*, a., threefold; treble; triple; *inluhmi tuchinạchi*, v. t., to treble; *inluhmi ushta*, a., fourfold; *inluhmi talạpi*, a., fivefold; *inluhmi hanali*, a., sixfold; *inluhmi untuklo*, a., sevenfold; *inluhmi untuchina*, a., eightfold; *inluhmi chakali*, a., ninefold; *inluhmi pokoli*, a., tenfold; and so of other numbers, which therefore need not all be written out.

innuchi, pp., put round the neck, as beads, necklace, etc.

innuchi, inuchi (q. v.), n., a neckcloth, etc.

iⁿnosishboya, n., the joint of the neck; vertebra.

iⁿnowa, v. t., to visit; to visit him.

iⁿnowa, n., a visitor.

iⁿnowa, n., a visit.

inta, exclamation, come; well; now; behold, Matt. 10: 16; 13: 3.

intakạshi, n., his melt. This is one of a few common nouns that take dative pronouns, viz., *imiskauata foni*, his collar bone; *iⁿwalwa*, pit of his stomach; *iⁿkolupi*, his windpipe.

intakobi, v. a. i., to lounge.

intakobi, a., lazy; indolent; slothful; dull, Matt. 13: 15; tired; wearied; idle; languid; slothful; supine; truant. This is one of a few words that are now used only with the dative pronoun, viz., *iⁿhullo, ima, iⁿsanali, imponna, iⁿshali, imaⁿya*.

intakobi, v. n., to be lazy; v. a. i., to saunter.

intakobi, pp., harassed.

intakobi, n., laziness; sloth; slothfulness; idleness; indolence; languidness.

intakobi, n., a lounger; a truant.

intakobi, adv., lazily.

intakobichi, intakobechi, v. t., to make lazy; to tire; to weary; to harass, Luke 18: 5.

intạnnạp, n., the other; the other side, Luke 6: 29; the reverse.

intạnnạp, a., off; most distant, as the offside or off horse.

intek, n., his sister; language proper for a man. If a woman should say *antekma* it would imply that she was a man. See Matt. 13: 56.

intek ạtiha, n., the sisterhood.

intek toba, n., his stepsister.

intikba, n., his or her maternal ancestors; a patriarch.

intikba heka, n., a pilot.

intoksạli, n., service.

intola, intula, v. t., to have; to have something lying by him.

intolahpi, n., a foundation, 1 Tim. 6: 19.

intula, n., a foundation; underpinning.

intula boli, v. t., to underpin.

inuchechi, v. t., to put a neckcloth, etc., upon another.

inuchi, v. t., to put a neckcloth, cravat, etc., upon one's self; *inunchi*, nasal form; see *innuchi*.

inuchi, innuchi, n., a neckcloth; a necklace; a shawl; a cravat; a stock; a string of beads, or anything worn round the neck, even a strap or collar; a tucker.

inuchi, n., a pawner.

inuchi chinakbi, n., a gorget; a semicircular breastplate, or a silver neck covering, such as Choctaw wear.

inuchi foki, v. t., to collar; to put on a collar.

inuchi lusa, n., a black neckcloth; a black cravat; a black silk handkerchief.

iⁿnukhaⁿklo, n., charity; mercy; compassion.

iⁿnukkilli, see *nukkilli*.

iⁿnukoa, n., a railer.

inunchi lusa, n., a black stock.

ipạf, n., a dog of any kind; *sapạf*, my dog; *chipạf*, thy dog; usually spoken of dogs as belonging to some person; see *ofi*.

ipeta, v. t., to minister; to nourish; to nurture; to serve; to administer, as medicine; to give; to feed; to present; to bestow; to foster; to furnish; to impart, Matt. 6: 11; 10: 42; 14: 19; 15: 26; *hạshipetashke*, Matt. 14: 16; *sapeta*, give me; *issapeta*, you give me; *ilhpita*, pp.; *ilimpa ipeta*, v. t., to treat; *ipehinta*, Matt. 6: 26.

ipeta, n., a giver; a feeder; a nourisher.

ipeta atabli, v. t., to surfeit.

ipetạchi, v. t., to give; to marry a woman, as many things are given as presents; *ohoyo ipetạchi*, to feed.

ipiⁿshik, pishik, n., the teat; the breast; the nipple; the bag; the dug; the pap; an udder, Luke 23: 29.

ipo, n., her sister-in-law, i. e., her husband's sister; his son's wife.

ipochi, n., his father-in-law; *sappochi*, my father-in-law.

ipochi halloka, n., his father-in-law, the father of his wife; *halloka* is an appellative proper only for the son-in-law and the father-in-law to use; see *haloka*.

ipochi itimạpa, n., a coachwhip snake.

ipochi ohoyo, n., his mother-in-law, the mother of his wife.

ipokni, n., his grandmother; his great-grandmother; her mother-in-law; *sahpokni* or *hapokni*, my grandmother.

ippok, v. n., to be a son-in-law; *ont ippok taiyaha*, Luke 20: 31 [?].

ippok, ipok, n., a son-in-law; a daughter-in-law, Matt. 10: 35; a grandchild.

ippok nakni, n., a grandson.

ippok tek, n., a granddaughter.

ippokni, n., grandmother, or his, her, or their grandmother; a granddam; a mother-in-law, Matt. 10: 35; *ạppokni*, my grandmother.

iⁿpuⁿspoa, see *impuⁿspoa*, and *iⁿsuⁿksowa*.

is, changed from *ish*, pro. 2d per. sing., before active verbs, thou; *is* appears before another pronoun, as *issanhollo*, *issạpihiⁿsạshke*, Luke 1: 38; *issapesa*, *issathana*, etc.; *issaiokpạchi*, Matt. 4: 9; 8: 21; *issaiạmashke*, give me, Matt. 14: 8.

isakshup, isi hakshup, n., a deerskin.

isapuntak, ishapuntak, n., a mosquito or muskito.

isapuntak inchuka, n., mosquito bars; bed curtains.

iⁿsạnnih, to meet with; to come against on a road, as a hunter meets a deer; *iⁿsạnnali; iⁿsạnnant aⁿya*.

isi, issi, n., a deer.

isi anowa, n., a deer's track.

isi ạbi, isạbi, n., one who kills venison; a hunter.

isi chito, n., an elk.

isi chito nakni, n., a hart.

isi chufakni, n., a spike buck; a buck about two years of age.

isi folaktuli, n., a forked-horn deer, more than two years old.

isi hakshup, see, isakshup.

isi humma tek, n., a hind.

isi intakkonlushi, n., a species of wild plum.

isi kosoma, n., a goat; a fetid deer; a chamois.

isi kosoma nakni, n., a he-goat; a buck.

isi kosoma nukshopa, n., the ibex.

isi kosoma tek, n., the female goat; a she-goat.

isi kosomushi, n., a kid.

isi kosomushicheli, v. t., to kid.

isi lahpitta, n., a stag; a full-horned buck.

isi lapish filamminchi, n., trochings; the small branches on the top of a deer's head.

isi nakni, n., a buck.

isi nakni afammi tuchina, n., a sorrel; a buck of the third year.

isi nakni hakshup, n., a buck's skin.

isi nakni humma, n., a stag.

isi nakni lapish falaktuchi, n., a pricket; a buck in his second year.

isi nia, n., deer's tallow.

isi nia pichelichi, n., name of a bird called the whistling plover.

isi nipi, n., venison.

isi tek, n., a doe.

isi ushi, isushi, n., a fawn; a young deer.

isi ushi cheli, v. t., to fawn.

isikkopa, issikkopa, n., torment; distress; misery.

isikkopa, issikkopa, pp., tormented; accursed; cursed; punished; racked, Matt. 4: 24; 8: 6; 15: 22.

isikkopa, a., miserable.

isikkopalechi, v. t. and caus., to torment; to cause torment.

isikkopalechi, n., a tormentor.

isikkopali, v. t., to distress; to torment to chasten; to chastise; to curse; to punish; to rack; to persecute, Matt. 10: 23; isht issikkopali, tribulation, Matt. 13: 21; ilisikkopali, to torment oneself.

isikkopali, n., a tormentor; torment; ilisikkopali, a self-tormentor; self-torment.

isikkopalit abi, v. t., to massacre.

isikkopalit abi, n., a massacre.

isikkopalit pelichi, v. t., to tyrannize.

isikopa, v. t., v. a. i., to cram; to gluttonize.

isikopa, n., a glutton; debauchery.

isikopa, a., gluttonous; v. n., to be gluttonous.

isikopa shali, a., gluttonous to excess.

isikopa shali, n., a great glutton; a voluptuary.

isikopali, v. t., to raven.

isikopali, a., ravenous.

isiminlusak, n., the devil's shoestring (a plant).

isito, n., a pumpkin; a squash; a pompion.

isito api, n., a pumpkin vine.

isito holba, n., a squash.

isito honni, n., cooked pumpkin; stewed pumpkin.

isito ibish, n., the end of the pumpkin where the stem grows.

isito ikfuka, n., the meat part of the pumpkin.

isito lakna, n., a yellow pumpkin; a ripe pumpkin.

isito sala, n., a hard-shelled pumpkin.

iskali, n. (from escalin), a dime; a ninepence; a bit; a 12½-cent piece of money; a drachm; a penny, Mark 12: 15.

iskali achafa, n., a ninepence; one bit.

iskatani, a., small.

iskatani, v. n., to be small.

iskatanichi, v. t. caus., to make small; to lessen; to retrench.

iskatanusi, a., very small; quite small.

iskatanusi, v. n., to be very small.

iskatinosi, adj., smallish, Matt. 7: 13; na hishunluk iskatinosi, a mote, Matt. 7: 3, 4.

iskifa, iskinfa (Longtown form), n., an ax.

iskifa ahalupa, n., the edge of an ax.

iskifa chiluk, n., the eye of an ax.

iskifa chushak, n., the head of an ax.

iskifa halupa, n., a sharp ax.

iskifa nishkin, n., the eye of an ax.

iskifa nushkobo, n., the head of an ax.

iskifa patha, n., a broad ax; a carpenter's ax.

iskifa ulhpi, iskifaiulhpi, n., an ax helve.

iskifa wishakchi, n., the bit of an ax.

iskifapi, n., an ax helve.

iskifushi, n., a hatchet; a tomahawk.

iskifushi isht chanli, v. t., to tomahawk.

iskitini, iskitani, a. sing., small; little, Matt. 18: 2; diminutive; paltry; petty; puny; scanty; acute or high as to sound; fine, in music; *chipunta* pl. Some Choctaw use the word *chaha*.

iskitini, v. n., to be small, Matt. 13: 32.

iskitini, pp., lessened; made small; diminished; extenuated; reduced.

iskitini, n., smallness; littleness; a high key; little; a small quantity.

iskitini, adv., little.

iskitini chohmi, a., smallish.

iskitinichi, v. t., to lessen; to make small; to pitch too high, as a sound in music; to diminish; to extenuate; to narrow; to reduce; to scrimp. Some say *chaḥachi*.

iskitinisi, iskitinesi, iskitinusi, a., small; smallish, John 2: 15 [?]; quite small; also adv., *chiskitinesi*, 1 Sam. 15: 71.

iskitinisi, iskitinusi, v. n., to be small.

iskitinisi, iskitinusi, n., a jot; a small quantity; a particle; a whit.

iskuna, n., the bowels; the entrails; the intestines; the guts; the inwards; the core; the heart; the pith; tripe; viscera; the heart of a tree in distinction from the bark and sap.

iskuna kucha, pp., emboweled; gutted; ruptured; eviscerated.

iskuna kucha, n., a rupture.

iskuna kuchi, v. t., to embowel; to gut; to rupture; to viscerate; to eviscerate.

iskuna laua, a., pithy.

iso, n., offspring; son; a child; *saso*, my son; a son, Mark 12: 6; Matt. 3: 17; *ushi* is the word most in use for son, etc., in the 3d person, *saso ma*, my son, Matt. 9: 2.

iso nakni, n., a son; a male child; see *alla nakni*.

iso tek, n., a daughter; see *oshetik*.

issa, v. t., v. a. i., to quit; to leave; to forsake; to renounce; to abandon; to stop, Luke 5: 4; to abdicate; to cede; to end, Luke 4: 13; to cease; to come off; to depart; to desert; to discontinue; to expire; to fail; to flinch; to forego; to give; to halt; to hush; to knuckle; to part; to pause; to recant; to reject; to release; to relinquish; to remit; to resign; to rest; to revolt; to secede; to stanch; to vacate; to void to; waive; to yield; *sassa*, to leave me; *iesa*, pro. form.

issa, exclam., hush; quit, etc.

issa, n., a forsaker; one who quits; a leaver; a turncoat.

issa, n., a cessation; a desertion; a quitting; abdication; a departure; a release; a remission; a render; a resignation; a stop.

issa, pp., deserted; forsaken; abolished; abdicated; stanched; vacated; yielded.

issa, a., extinct; quit.

issaⁿ, thou-me; *issaⁿkashofahinlashke*, Matt. 8: 2; *issaⁿmihashke*, bid me, Matt. 14: 28; *haklot issa*, Matt. 15: 12; *issat ia*, to leave me, Matt. 16: 4; Josh. 6: 8.

issa hinla, a., expirable.

issahe keyu ikbi, v. t., to immortalize.

issachechi, v. t., caus., to cause to abolish.

issachi, v. t., to abolish; to arrest; to cease; to discharge; to dismiss; to abandon; to cause to quit, etc.; to check; to decide; to discharge; to free; to discontinue; to intermit; to stanch; to stifle; to still; to stop; to suppress; to stay, 2 Sam. 24: 16.

issachi, n., an abolisher, etc.; one who discharges, dismisses, etc.; a check; a stopper.

issap, n., a louse; lice.

issap isht albi, n., a louse trap; a fine comb; an ivory comb.

issap laua, issap inlaua, a., lousy; swarming with lice; or he is lousy.

issap laua, issap inlaua, v. n., to be lousy.

issap likeli, a., lousy.

issap nihi, n., a nit; the seed of a louse.

issi, see *isi*.

issi, thou-me, Matt. 14: 8.

issi okla issa, n., a traitor.

issikkopa, see *isikkopa*; tormented, Matt. 8: 6; to suffer, Matt. 17: 12, 15.

issimalluⁿsak, see *imalluⁿsak*.

issish, n., blood; gore, Matt. 16: 17; *imissish*, his blood, Josh. 2: 19.

issish akshish, n., veins; blood vessels; arteries.

issish bano, a., bloody; all blood; sanguinary.

issish bano, v. n., to be bloody; *issish banochi*, to make all bloody; to bloody.

issish bieka, a., bloody.

issish hanta, n., sacred blood.

issish hoeta, v. n., to puke blood; to vomit blood.

issish hoeta, n., a vomiting of blood.

issish iⁿhina, n., a blood vessel; a vein; an artery.

issish iⁿhina chito ikonla bachaya, n., the jugular vein.

issish iⁿhina łumpli, v. t., to bleed.

issish iⁿhina łumpli, n., venesection.

issish ikfia, n., a dysentery.

issish ikfia, a., sick with the dysentery.

issish ikfia, v. n., to be sick with the dysentery.

issish iklanna, n., half blood.

issish iⁿkucha, pp., bled; blood taken from him.

issish iⁿkuchi, v. t., to take blood; to let blood; to bleed him; to take out his blood.

issish iⁿkuchi, n., one who bleeds.

issish iⁿkuchi, n., venesection.

issish inchito, a., plethoric; full of blood; lit., his blood is large.

issish inchito, v. n., to be plethoric.

issish inchito, n., plethora.

issish inlaua, v. n., to be plethoric.

issish inlaua, n., plethora.

issish isht kuchi, n., a fleam; a lancet.

issish isht okchaya, n., lifeblood.

issish kucha, v. a. i., to bleed.

issish laksha, n., a bloody sweat.

issish laksha, v. n., to sweat blood.

issish laua, a., sanguinary; sanguine.

issish minti, v. a. i., to bleed.

issish mitafa, v. a. i., to bleed.

issish mitafa, n., a bleeding; a hemorrhage.

issish mitaffi, v. t., to press out blood; to bleed; to cause to bleed.

issish walakachi, n., a clot of blood; clotted blood.

isso, v. t., sing., to smite; to strike; to beat; to bunt; to bump; to cuff; to hit; to jostle; to knock; to lay, as to lay on a blow; to pelt; to pound; to touch; *aiihiⁿso*, beat upon, Matt. 7: 25; *issot kanchi*, Josh. 8: 22; *chik aiisso*, Matt. 4: 6; *sasso*, to strike me, or he strikes me; *aiisso*, v. t., to hit; *itaiisso*, to smite

each other; to clash; to collide; to hit each other; to hitch; to interfere, as a horse; *isht aiisso*, v. t., to stand.

isso, n., a striker; a smiter; a knocker; a pelter.

isso, n., a blow; a stroke; a beat; a bump; a lick; a dent; a hit; a slam; a touch; a trip; *itaiisso*, n., a clash; a collision.

issochi, v. t., to cause to strike; *itaiissochi*, to cause to strike each other; to clash; to overreach, as a horse.

issot falama, v. a. i., to rebound.

issot kanchi, v. t., to destroy, 2 Sam. 24: 16.

isuba, issuba, n., derived from *isi holba*, as some say; a horse; a steed; a nag; a courser; a pony; a hobby.

isuba ahalalli, n., a swingtree; a swingletree; a whippletree; a whiffletree.

isuba aiimpa, n., a horse range; a horse pasture; any place for feeding horses; a stall.

isuba aiimpa foki, v. t., to stall.

isuba aiimpa peni, n., a manger; a horse-trough; a crib, Luke 2: 7.

isuba aiitanowa, n., a horse range; the place where horses ramble.

isuba aiitintimiya, n., the turf; a race ground.

isuba aiomanili itanowa, n., a spurway.

isuba akucha, n., a horse ford; a horse pass.

isuba ałopulli, n., a horse ford; a horse pass.

isuba apa, n., oats.

isuba basoa, n., a zebra.

isuba bokboki, n., a roan horse.

isuba fochunli, n., the dandruff of a horse.

isuba foka sita, isuba iffuka, n., a surcingle.

isuba haksobish falaia, n., a mule; an ass; a donkey, 1 Kings 10: 25.

isuba haksobish falaia nakni, n., a jackass; a male donkey.

isuba halalli, n., a draft horse.

isuba hioli achafa, n., a horse team.

isuba hishi, n., horsehair; the short hair of a horse.

isuba hobak, n., a gelding.

isuba huⁿkupa, n., a horsethief.

isuba iⁿhina, n., a horse way; a bridle path; a spurway.

isuba ikonla isht talakchi, n., a throat-latch; a martingale.

isuba ilafia, n., a handsome horse.

isuba imalikchi, n., a farrier; one who professes to cure the diseases of horses.

isuba imbita, n., the headband or strap of a bridle; the ear band of a bridle.

isuba imilhpak, n., feed; horse feed.

isuba imponolo, n., a long halter; a long horse rope.

isuba inchahe, n., a plow.

isuba inchuka, n., a stable.

isuba inchuka fohki, v. t., to stable; to put into a stable.

isuba intintimia, n., a racehorse; one that races.

isuba inuchi, n., a horse bell; a bell collar; a horse collar.

isuba inuchi anunkaka takali, n., a clapper.

isuba inuchi ikbi, n., a bell founder; a bell maker.

isuba inpeni, n., a ferryboat for horses.

isuba iskitini, n., a small horse; a pony; a nag.

isuba ishke, n., a breeding mare; an old mare; lit., a mother horse.

isuba isht fama, isuba ishit fama, n., a horsewhip.

isuba isht fullota, n., a leading line; a long rein used in guiding a plow horse.

isuba isht halalli, n., the gear of a horse; the tackle of a horse.

isuba isht halalli fohki, v. t., to gear; to put the gears on a horse.

isuba isht inshilli, n., a currycomb.

isuba isht pilesa, n., the gear of a horse; horse gear; horse tackling; harness.

isuba isht shali, n., traces for a horse.

isuba isht toksali, n., harness for a horse; gear for a horse.

isuba inshulush, n., a horseshoe.

isuba itatoba, n., a jockey; a horse jockey; a horse trader.

isuba itichapa, n., a span of horses.

isuba itikapali, n., the bit of a bridle.

isuba itintimia, n., a horserace.

isuba itintimia, v. a. i., to run in a race, as horses; to race.

isuba iyakchush, n., the hoof of a horse.

isuba iyakchush isht bashli, n., a buttress.

isuba iyi hishi, n., the fetlock.

isuba iyi isht talakchi, isubiyi isht intalakchi, n., a horse fetter; a horse hobble; a hobble, a name in use in the Southwest.

isuba iyi tali iyi lapalichi, n., a farrier; a horseshoer.

isuba iyi tali lapali, n., a horseshoe.

isuba iyi tali lapalichi, v. t., to shoe a horse.

isuba kanchi, n., a horse dealer.

isuba kapali, n., a bridle.

isuba kapali isht talakchi, n., bridle reins.

isuba kapali kapalichi, v. t., to bridle a horse.

isuba kostininchi, n., a horse-breaker.

isuba liposhi, n., a jade.

isuba nakni, n., a male horse; a stallion; a stone horse; a seed horse; a studhorse.

isuba nashoba, n., an ass; a mule; a donkey.

isuba nashoba nakni, n., a jackass.

isuba nali, n., horseback; the back of a horse.

isuba omanili, isuba ombinili, n., horseback; a horseman; a rider, 1 Kings 10: 26.

isuba omanili tashka, n., a light-horse man; a dragoon; a hussar; light horse; a trooper.

isuba omanili tashka aliha, n., cavalry; a company of light-horse men.

isuba ontala tashka, n., a light-horse man; a dragoon.

isuba shali achafa, n., a horse load.

isuba shapo shali, n., a sumpter; a baggage horse; a pack horse.

isuba shapulechi, v. t., to pack a horse; to load a horse.

isuba shapuli, n., a led horse; a sumpter; a baggage horse; a pack horse.

isuba shinimpa, n., a courser.

isuba tanchi fotoli, n., a horse mill.

isuba tansh fotoli, n., a mill horse.

isuba tek, n., a mare.

isuba tek himmita, n., a filly.

isuba tikba heli, n., the fore horse.

isuba toksali, n., a draft horse; a hackney.

isuba umpatalhpo, n., a saddle.

isuba umpatalhpo akama, pp., unsaddled.

isuba umpatạlhpo alata, n., a saddle pad.

isuba umpatạlhpo ashapuli, n., a pack saddle.

isuba umpatạlhpo falakto, n., a side saddle.

isuba umpatạlhpo haksobish, n., a saddle skirt.

isuba umpatạlhpo ikbi, n., a saddler; a saddle maker.

isuba umpatạlhpo nushkobo, n., the pommel of a saddle.

isuba umpatạlhpo oⁿlipa nan tạnna, n., housing.

isuba umpatạlhpo patali, v. t., to saddle.

isubiyi isht intalakchi, see *isuba iyi isht talakchi.*

isubushi, n., a colt; a foal.

isubushi cheli, v. t., to foal; to colt.

iⁿsuⁿksowa, iⁿpuⁿspoa, v. t., to kiss him.

isunlạsh, n., the tongue; the instrument of taste and the chief instrument of .speech; a neap or the pole of a cart.

isunlạsh chulata, a., double-tongued; false.

isunlạsh illi, a., tongue-tied.

isunlạsh illi, v. n., to be tongue-tied.

isunlạsh illi, v. a. i., to stutter; to lisp.

isunlạsh illi, n., a stutterer.

isunlạsh tuklo, a., double-tongued; false; two-tongued.

isunlạsh ushi, n., the palate.

isushi, n., a fawn; a young deer. It is said by old hunters that dogs can not smell the track of a young fawn while it remains spotted; see *isi ushi.*

ish, per. pro., pre. to active verbs, thou, nom. case, as *ishia,* thou goest; *is* before *sạm* and *saⁿ,* thou-me, thou for me or to me; *issạma,* thou give me; *issaⁿnukhaklo,* thou pity me; thou, Matt. 17: 27. Used also, as a possessive, thy, thine; thy prayers, etc. Acts 10: 4.

ish, a conj., used with *li,* I; as *ialish,* I go and; also cf. *akithanokish;* one vowel is dropped, as is common where two thus come together; cf. *sh* and *cha.*

ishahe keyu, a., inadmissible; unattainable.

ishahpi (from *ishi* and *ahpi*), n., first born; see Matt. 1: 25.

iⁿshaht ia, v. a. i., to grow; to increase; to enlarge; to rise; to wax.

iⁿshaht isht ia, v. t., to increase; to swell.

iⁿshaht taha, pp., made greatest; rendered greatest, etc.

iⁿshaht tali, a., greatest; largest; highest; sign of the sup. deg. of comp.; superlative.

iⁿshaht tali, v. n., to be greatest.

iⁿshalakli, a., being a little more; a little larger.

iⁿshalechi, see *ishalichi.*

iⁿshalechichi, v. t. caus., to cause to exceed; to dominate; to enhance.

iⁿshali, a., superior; better; surpassing; sign of the comparative degree of comp.; above; greater; *iⁿshali fehna,* extreme; dominant; main; major; more; predominant; prevalent; principal; sovereign; supereminent; greater, John. 1: 50.

iⁿshali, v. n., to be superior; to be greater; to exceed, Josh. 4: 24; Matt. 5: 20; 6: 25; 11: 22, 24; *iminⁿshali,* to prefer; *chiminⁿshali,* better for thee; *iⁿshashuli,* pl., *iⁿshaiyali,* pro., in *iminⁿshaiyali;* isht *iⁿshali* v. a. i., to increase, John 3: 30, Matt. 12: 12, to outgo; *nanta isht iⁿshala heto; isht iⁿshalechi,* v. t., to cause to increase; to aggravate; to increase; *isht iⁿshat isht ia,* v. a. i., to increase; to thrive; pp., increased; *isht iⁿshat mahaya,* v. a. i., to progress.

iⁿshali, v. a. i., to exceed; to be greater; John 4: 12; to prevail; to wax; *iminⁿshali,* v. t., to prefer.

iⁿshali, n., a superior; a lord; the main body; a majority; a master, Matt. 6: 24; sir; rabbi.

iⁿshali, adv., mainly; more; supremely.

iⁿshali bano, a., paramount.

iⁿshali bạnna, a., emulous; wishing to excel.

iⁿshali bạnna, v. n., to be emulous.

iⁿshali bạnna, v. t., to emulate.

iⁿshali bạnna, n., an emulator.

iⁿshali hatak, n., a principal; a chief man.

iⁿshali imanumpa, n., an embasssy; embassage.

iⁿshali imanumpa isht aⁿya, n., an express.

iⁿshali imanumpeshi, n., an ambassador; an envoy.

iⁿshali nan isht imatta, n., a minister; a servant.

ishalichi, iⁿshalihchi, iⁿshalechi, v. t., to exceed; to surpass; to cause to exceed; to excel; to master; to outdo; to predominate; to subdue; to top; to do much more, Matt. 7: 11.

iⁿshalihchi, see ishalichi.

iⁿshalit okpulo, v. a. i., to be made worse, Matt. 9: 16.

ishapuntak, see isapuntak.

ishbi, v. t. irreg., 2d per. sing., from abi, thou killest. The first vowel of the verb abi is dropped, and so of apa, ala, amo.

ishhiⁿsh, see ikhiⁿsh.

ishi, eshi, v. t., to take; to hold; to get; to seize; to apprehend; to draft; to draw; to embrace; to entertain; to gain; to grab; to grasp; to harbor; to cover, as the floor; to bear children, as a woman, 1 Sam. 2: 21; covered the hills, Ch. W., p. 18, to assume; to attach; to come by; to receive, Matt. 10: 41; 14: 20; ishwa, pl. of ishi; iⁿshi, iⁿhiⁿshi, having, holding, etc.; isht holisso haⁿ iⁿshili, I am holding the pen; ieshi, pro., to keep, 1 Sam. 7: 1; Matt. 5: 23; chinshachi, shall hold thee, Luke 4: 10; ieshi, to draw (the sword), 2 Sam. 24: 9; saⁿshi, John 6: 56; ieshichi, to make; to inherit, 1 Sam. 2: 8; itishi, to take together; to take each other; to wrestle; ilaitiⁿshi, to take unto himself, as to take an evil spirit, John 8: 48, 52; ilaieshi, to have, Matt. 11: 18; 15: 30; 16: 27; eshi, to travail, 1 Sam. 4: 19; imaiishi, to dispossess him; to unfurnish him; iⁿshi, to keep back; imishi, to wrest; hatak imishi, v. t., to unman: aiishi, to unhinge; to take off as a saddle; to unsaddle; to divest; to take away, Matt. 5: 40; 7: 4; 13: 20, 22, 23; to imbibe; to include; to keep; to maintain; to obtain; to partake; to preserve; to procure; to receive; to touch; to twine; to vest.

ishi, iⁿshi, n., a taker; a seizer; a holder; a maintainer; an obtainer; a partaker; a receiver; a winner.

ishi, n., a grasp; a hold; a holding; an occupation; a possession; a receipt; reception; a taking; a touch; a winning.

ishi, a., engaging; captivating.

iⁿshi, v. t., to have; to hold; to occupy; to keep; to own; to provide; to reserve; to restrain; to retain; to steady; to win; to have, Matt. 13: 12; 15: 34; Acts 5: 2, 3; ikesho, to refuse; ikesho, a., unaccepted; not taken; uncollected; unreceived; untaken; ihiⁿshi, Matt. 11: 12; iⁿhiⁿsht ia, to go to catch or take.

iⁿshi, n., a reservation; a reserve.

iⁿshi, n., an occupier; an owner.

iⁿshikalla, see shikalla.

ishit, see isht.

ishit fohki, v. t., to take and put in; to betray, Matt. 17: 22; ishahe keyu, a., unrecoverable.

ishit tiwa, see isht tiwa.

ishkanapa, isht kanapa, a., casual; accidental, Luke 10: 36.

ishkanapa, v. n., to be casual or accidental; to happen, as an injury; sashkanapa, I met with an accident.

ishkanapa, n., an accident; a casualty; a disaster; an ill.

ishkanapachi, v. t., to jeopard, 2 Sam. 23: 17.

ishke, shke, oshke, ashke, a particle used at the end of sentences and suffixed to the last word to give a little more strength and dignity to the style, being much used in solemn style. It may be regarded as an intensive having the force of do in English, but is a more dignified expression than do. Generally suffixed to verbs or to words where a verb is understood, or an adverb, as it closes a sentence or a period, which requires a verb to compose it. The final vowel of the verb is generally retained, except that a becomes a and e is changed to i before shke.

ishki, n., a mother; a dam; also his mother, her mother, their mother. The sisters of a mother are called ishki also. Matt. 2: 11, 13, 14, 19, 20, 21; 8: 14; 10: 35; 12: 46; 13: 55; hashke, my mother, Matt. 12: 48, 49, 50.

ishki ahalaia, a., maternal.

ishki abi, n., a matricide.

ishki imanumpa, n., mother tongue; his mother's language.

ishki toba, n., a stepmother; also an aunt who is sister to the mother; a step dame.

ishkiⁿsh, ikhiⁿsh (q. v.), ithiⁿsh,ok-
hiⁿsh, ishhiⁿsh; n., medicine; *ikhiⁿsh*
is the most common word.

ishkitini, n., an owl; a large night owl;
the horned owl.

ishko, v. t., v. a. i., to drink, Matt. 6: 31;
to imbibe; to partake; to sup; to take,
ikishko, Matt. 11: 18; *ihiⁿshko,* drinking,
Matt. 11:´19.

ishko, n., drink; a draft; a potation.

ishko, n., ʼa drinker; a partaker.

ishko achafa, n., a dram; a drink; one
draft; aˈdose; a drench; a potion.

ishko achafa ikbit itakashkuli, v. t.,
to dose; to prepare doses.

ishko chito, n., a large draft; a swig.

ishko fena, v. t., to booze; to drink
deeply.

ishko fena, n., a hardˈdrinker.

ishko fena keyu, a., abstemious.

ishko hinla, a., potable.

ishko shali, n., a great drinker, Matt.
11: 19.

ishkochechi, v. t., to drench; to give
drink; to cause to drink; to dose, to
administer liquid medicines; *oka ish-
kochechitok,* 1 Sam. 30: 11.

ishkochechit nusechi, n., an opiate
administered.

ishkot hoeta, n., an emetic.

ishkot ikfia, n., a cathartic.

ishkot ikpeso, a., untasted.

ishkot nusi, n., an opiate.

ishkot pisa, v. t., to taste; to try to drink.

ishkot tali, v. t., v. a. i., to drink up; to
drink it all; to drink off.

ishla, v. t. irreg., 2d per. sing., from *ala;*
thou arrivest.

ishmo, v. t. irreg., 2d per sing., from
amo, thou pickest.

ishpa, v. t. irreg., 2d per. sing., from
apa, thou eatest.

Ishpani, a., Spanish; n., Spain.

Ishpani hatak, n., a Spaniard.

Ishpani okla, n., Spaniards; Spanish
people.

Ishpani yakni, n., the Spanish country;
Spain.

isht, ishit, formed from *ishi* and *t,* to take
and *iⁿsht iat,* Matt. 8: 4, from *iⁿsht,* take
and *iat,* go. This is an abbreviated
mode of speaking. This word is much
used: (1) as a preposition, with, for,
on account of, concerning, and in this
way indicates the cause, manner, or
instrument by which some action
takes place, as *isht chanli,* to chop
with; *isht abeka,* to be sick with; *isht
anumpuli,* to talk about; *isht hachiⁿ-
mihachahe,* shall condemn you with,
Matt. 7: 2; *isht hachimalhpisahe; ishit
saholitobli,* to honor me with; *isht
imaholitopa,* Matt. 11: 19, 20; *nan
isht amihachi,* to upbraid ·for; *isht a,* of;
by; therewith; thereby; by means of;
by whom, Matt. 18: 7, 13; *isht ai,* Matt.
18: 16: (2) when combined with a verb
it gives it a new form, and indeed makes
it a compound word, as *minti,* to come;
isht minti, to bring, or take it and start
or come; *ia,* to go; *isht ia,* to carry, or
take it and go; *aba,* to arrive; *isht ala,*
to bring or take it and come: (3) it is
used to make verbal nouns, i. e., nouns
derived from verbs, as *ishko,* to drink;
isht ishko, a cup; *talakchi,* to be tied; *isht
talakchi,* a string; a tether: (4) it is used
to express all the ordinal numbers except the first four, 1, 2, 3, 4; *isht talapi,*
the fifth; *isht hanali,* the sixth; *isht
aiushta,* fourth, is also used: (5) used
with a v. a. i. it makes it v. t.; *yaiya,* to
cry; *isht yaiya,* to cry about it or him
(this may be classed also under sec. 1):
(6) means, cause, or instrument; with;
by means of, etc.; thereby; therewith;
thereat; therein; *isht a,* means and
source; by means of; *isht aholitopa,* become rich by means of.

isht abahchakli, n., a spoon (old name);
isht impa is a better word.

isht abeka, n., infection; cause of sickness.

isht abeka, v. n., to be sick with.

isht abekachi, v. t., to infect by means
of it; to make sick with it.

isht abiha, n., the string or cord used in
stretching hides when hung up to dry.

isht aboli, n., a small ball playground
for practice.

isht achunli, n., a needle; a sewing
needle; an awl; any sewing instrument.

isht afacha, n., a latch; a button to a
door; a fastener; a hasp.

isht afana, n., a pry; a lever; a handspike.

isht afekomi, see *isht afekommi.*

isht afikomi (see *isht afekommi*); pro. form, *isht afekoyumi*.

isht afinni, n., a lever.

isht afoli, v. t., to shroud; to wrap round with it.

isht ahabli, n., the strap used by shoemakers to bind the shoe to their knees, etc.

isht ahalaia, n., a care; a concern; an interest.

isht ahalaia, a., responsible.

isht ahama, n., ointment; unction; unguent.

isht ahauchi, n., avails; profits.

isht ahbichakali, a., nineteenth.

isht ahbichakaliha, adv., nineteenth time.

isht ahchifa, n., soap; a lotion.

isht ahchifa apokpokechi, n., a lather box.

isht ahchifa balama, n., castile soap; scented soap.

isht ahchifa kạllo, n., bar soap; hard soap.

isht ahchifa nashuka ahạmmi, n., lather for shaving the beard.

isht ahchifa oⁿtali, v. t., to soap.

isht ahchifa pokpoki, n., soapsuds; suds.

isht ahobachi, n., a pattern.

isht ahofahya, n., reproach, Josh. 5: 9.

isht aholitopa, n., the glory, Matt. 6: 13; 16: 27.

isht ahollo, v. t., to perform a miracle, John 4: 54; to witch.

isht ahollo, a., magnificent; majestic.

isht ahollo, n., one who performs miracles; a wonderful being; a witch; a demoniac; a sorcerer.

isht ahollo, n., a miracle, John 2: 11; see *aiisht ahollo*, conjuration; witchcraft.

isht ahollo ilahobi, isht ahullo ilahobbi, v. a. i., to juggle; to conjure; to pretend to witchcraft.

isht ahollo ilahobi, n., a juggler.

isht ahullochika, a., clean; ceremoniously clean or religiously clean; see Gen. 8: 20.

isht aiaⁿli, n., evidence.

isht ạiạlhpisa, n., a sign, Matt. 16: 3.

isht aiilbạsha, n., adversity.

isht aiiⁿpalạmmi, n., a cursing; a curse, Josh. 8: 34.

isht aiokpạchi, n., an oblation; an offering; a salute; a sacrifice or gift, Matt. 23: 19; a treater.

isht aiopi, a., the last; the youngest; the least, Matt. 2: 6; extreme; final; ultimate; *ont isht aiopi*, finally, Matt. 5: 26.

isht aiopi, isht aiyopi, v. n., to be the last, Matt. 12: 45; *ont imisht aiyopikmạt*, in the end of, Matt. 13: 40, 49.

isht aiopi, n., the last one; the one who is last; conclusion; finis; the hindmost; the rear; the upshot; utmost.

isht aiopi, adv., last; ultimately; uttermost.

isht aiopi aiokpạchi, n., a valediction.

isht aiopi aⁿya, n., rearward.

isht aiopichi, v. t. caus., to make it last; to close; to make an end.

isht aiukli, n., an ornament; an embellishment; garniture.

isht aiuklichi, v. t., to ornament with.

isht aiunchululli, n., a generation, Luke 3: 7; Matt. 1: 1; a tribe, Rev. 7: 4.

isht aiushta, a., fourth, Matt. 14: 25.

isht aiushta, v. n., to be the fourth.

isht aiyopi, see *isht aiopi*.

isht akama, n., a stopple.

isht akamạssa, n., a buckle; a button; a brooch; paste; putty; a seal; sealing wax; a tache, Ex. 26: 6.

isht akamạssạchi, n., a latch; a button; a buckle.

isht akamạssạlli, n., a buckle; a button; a fastener.

isht akanohmechi, v. t., to cause mischief; to seduce, 1 John 2: 26.

isht akanohmi, a., mischievous; compounded of *isht*, a., and *kanohmi* or *kaniohmi*, to do somehow.

isht akanohmi, v. n., to be mischievous.

isht akashofa, n., a remission.

isht akmo, n., solder.

isht akostininchi, n., sense.

isht ałampko, n., strength.

isht ałepulli, isht ạłopulli, n., a brooch; a breastpin.

isht ałopulli, see *isht ạłopulli*.

isht amałichi, n., a fan, Luke 3: 17.

isht amiha, n., an excuse; a put off.

isht amiha iksho, a., groundless; without excuse.

isht anchaha, n., paint.

isht aniwilạli, n., a sty; a sore on the eyelid. [I do not recognize this word.—H. S. H.]

isht anoli, n., record, John 1: 19.

isht anowa, isht anonowa, cause of fame; means or occasion of fame.

isht anta, v. t., to do; to be busy with; to be employed about; *nan isht anta*, n., employment.

isht anta, n., occupation.

isht anukfokạt alota, a., filled with, Luke 4: 1.

isht anukhaⁿklo, n., adversity; cause of sorrow.

isht anumpa, n., a description; an account of; a narrative; a dissertation; praise: also, about (lit., a word about it); a commentary; an intercession.

isht anumpuli, n., a lauder; a praiser; a treater; a commentator; a commentary; a debater; an intercessor; an encomium; an intercession.

isht anumpulit holissochi, isht anumpạt holisso, n., a memoir.

isht apakfoa, n., a bandage.

isht apesa, n., a compass; a gage.

isht apuⁿfạchi, n., a blowpipe.

isht ashana, n., a screw; a lock; a stock lock.

isht atakalạma chito, n., vexatious.

isht ataklạma, n., a hindrance; a cause of delay; a disadvantage; a restraint.

isht atapachi, see *isht ạtatetpạchi*.

isht ataya, n., posterity; *chisht atayaka, yakni ilạppa chimalikma*, Gen. 48: 4.

isht atia, n., a race; a descent; a breed; a stock; an extraction.

isht atiaka, n., a clan; fruit; a house; lineage; pedigree; progeny; a stock; offspring; *pisht atiaka*, our offspring; generation, Matt. 3: 7; tribe, Josh. 1: 12; 3: 12; 4: 12; 7: 16, 17.

isht atiaka, a., cognate (a descendant).

isht atiaka keyu, a., unrelated.

isht atokowa, n., a sign, Matt. 24: 3; John 4: 48.

isht auahchạfa, a., the 11th; *isht auahtuklo*, a., the 12th; *isht auahtuchina*, a., the 13th, and so of other numbers up to 18th; *isht auahuntuchina*, a., eighteenth; 18th; *isht auahchạfahaha*, adv., eleventh time; *isht auahtukloha*, adv., twelfth time, etc.; *isht auahtalapiha*, fifteenth time, and so of other numbers.

isht auechi, n., a sender; one who sends.

isht aⁿya, n., a driver; a carrier; a conductor; a teamster.

isht aⁿya, n., a conveyance.

isht aⁿya shali, n., a carrier; "to take and carry along."

isht ạfekommi, n., mischief; obstinacy.

isht ạfekommi, isht afekomi, isht ạfekoma, a., troublesome; baleful; forward; mischievous; peevish; pestilent; petulant; plaguy; refractory; restive; impudent; troublous; unruly.

isht ạfekommi, v. n., to be troublesome.

isht ạla, v. t., to bring, Matt. 9: 2; to draw near, Matt. 15: 8.

isht ạla, n., a bringer; an introducer.

isht ạla, n., an introduction.

isht ạlbi, n., a witch ball; a bait; a trap; a snare; a net; a springe.

isht ạlbi intakalichi, v. t., to bait him.

isht ạlbi isht hokli, v. t., to snare.

isht ạlbi nạla, pp., shot with a witch ball.

isht ạlbi nạli, v. t., to shoot with a witch ball.

isht ạlbi talali, v. t., to trap; to set a trap.

isht ạlbiha, n., stuffing.

isht ạlhchefa, n., soap.

isht ạlhfoa, n., a garter; a binder.

isht ạlhkạma, n., a stopple; a cork; a plug; a tap; a wad.

isht ạlhkạta, n., a patch.

isht ạlhkoha, n., varnishing; gilding.

isht ạlhpisa, a., figurative.

isht ạlhpisa, n., a measure; a yard; a bushel; a gallon; a mile; any measure; a badge; an ensign; an emblem; a degree; a figure; a gauge; insignia; a metaphor; a model; a note; an omen; a picture; a plan; a rule; a sample; a scale; a sign; a specimen; a square; a symbol; a symptom; a simile; a test; a token; a type; *ninak isht ạlhpisa*, n., watch of the night, Matt. 14: 25.

isht ạlhpisa tuklo, n., a fathom; two yards; two measures.

isht ạlhpolosa, n., mortar; daubing; plaster.

isht ạlhtoba, n., a ransom, Matt. 17: 27; payment; price paid.

isht almo, n., a scythe; a sickle; any cutting instrument of the knife kind; a reaping hook.

isht alopulli, isht alopulli, n., a broach; a breastpin.

isht askufachi, n., a belt; a sash; a cincture; a girdle.

isht atapachi, isht atapachi, n., a button; a barb; a hasp.

isht atapachi ikbi, v. t., to barb; to make a barb.

isht atta, v. t., to follow.

isht atta, n., business; employment; a function; an occupation; an office; use.

isht atta, n., an agent or attorney; an administrator, an actor; any person having any particular business; a doer; a factor; a functionary; a manager; a practicer; a practitioner.

isht attacha hinla, a., sanative.

isht baha, isht bali, isht bahaffi, n., a piercer; a spear.

isht baska, n., a card used in games; a pack of cards; a pack.

isht basto, n., a marble.

isht basha, n., a saw.

isht basha chito, n., a crosscut saw.

isht bashpoa, isht panshpoa, isht pashpoa, n., a broom.

isht bicheli, n., a tap; a spout; a faucet; a brass cock; a funnel; a tunnel.

isht boa, n., a hammer; a maul; a mallet; a beetle.

isht boa api, n., a broomstick.

isht boa chito, n., a large maul; a commander; a heavy beetle.

isht boli, n., a flail.

isht bopuli, n., a sling.

isht chakali, a., ninth; 9th.

isht chakaliha, adv., ninth time.

isht chanli, n., a pickax.

isht chanya, n., an addice; an adz; an ax; any edge tool used for chopping.

isht chumpa, n., funds; purchase money; means of making a purchase.

isht fali, n., a crank.

isht fama, n., a whip; a scourge, John 2: 15; a lash.

isht fiopa, n., the windpipe.

isht fotoha, n., an auger; a borer.

isht fotoha iskitini, n., a gimlet; a small auger.

isht fotoha ulhpi, n., an auger handle.

isht fotoha wishakchi, n., the bit of an auger; the point of an auger.

isht fotohushi, n., a gimlet.

isht fotoli, n., a winch.

isht fotolit lumbli, v. t., to drill.

isht haksichi, n., a wile; a means of cheating; a trick; a bribe; hush money; a train.

isht haksichi, n., a briber.

isht halalli, n., a bail; a long oar; harness; a trace; a tug.

isht halupalli, n., a hone; a whetstone; a strap.

isht hanali, isht hannali, a., sixth; 6th.

isht hanaliha, adv., sixth time.

isht hashanya, n., the cause or occasion of fretfulness.

isht hofahya, n., shame; cause of shame.

isht hokli, n., a net; a trap.

isht holissochi, isht holissichi, n., a pen; a pencil; ink.

isht holissochi aialhto, n., an inkstand; an ink bottle; an ink horn.

isht holissochi humma, n., red ink.

isht holissochi ikbi, n.., an ink maker; a pencil maker; a pen maker.

isht holissochi lusa, n., black ink; ink.

isht holissochi onlatapa, n., a blot.

isht holissochi onlatapa, pp., blotted.

isht holissochi onlatabli, v. t., to blot; to spill ink on it.

isht holitabli, n., a worshiper, John 4: 23.

isht holmo, n., a roof; a shingle.

isht hopunkoyo, n., the eyesight.

isht hopunkoyo imachukma, a., sharp-sighted.

isht hopunayo, n., the eyesight.

isht hoshintikachi, n., a screen; a shade.

isht hummachi, n., a red dye; tan.

isht hunsa, n., ammunition; a dart; any instrument with which to prick.

isht ia, v. t., to carry, Matt. 1: 11; to lead, Matt., 4: 1; to begin, Matt. 11: 7, 20; 16: 21, 22; Josh. 3: 7.

isht ia, n., a beginner; a beginning; a conveyer; a founder.

isht ia ammona, n., the first beginning; the commencement, Josh. 4: 19.

isht ika (from isht and hika); anumpa isht ika); an ovation.

isht ikahobalo, n., a blasphemer; see ahobali.

isht ikalauo, a., not equal.

isht ikalauo, v. n., not to be equal, Luke 3: 16.

isht inkạma, n., a lid.

isht ikhana, n., memory; a memorial; a monumental record; a remembrance; a remembrancer, Josh. 4: 7.

isht ikhạna, n., the means of learning, whether books or anything else.

isht ikhạnanchi, n., means of teaching.

isht ikinahno (from ahni), v. t., to hate him; to abhor him; to dislike him; to abominate him; to despise; to disdain.

isht ikinahno, a., pp., contemptible; despised; indignant.

isht ikinahno, n., a hater; contempt; despite.

isht ikinahnochechi, v. t., to disaffect; to cause to hate.

isht ikinahnochi, v. t., to cause to hate.

isht ikinyukpo (from yukpa), v. t., to dislike him; to hate him; to despise, Mark 10: 41.

isht ikinyukpo, n., a hater.

isht ikono, n., inability.

isht ilahauchi, n., the things furnished by one's self; proceeds.

isht ilaiyukpa (from yukpa), n., advantage; happiness; means of his own happiness.

isht ilakshema, n., dress; ornaments; see isht shema.

isht ilakshema shali, a., tawdry; dressy; addicted to dress.

isht ilakshema shali, v. n., to be tawdry.

isht ilamalichi, n., a fan; an instrument with which to blow toward one's self.

isht ilaneli, n., a crutch; a prop; means by which to sustain one's self.

isht ilanumpuli, n., self-praise.

isht ilaueli, n., a coward.

isht ilaueli, a., cowardly; alla isht ilaueli, a cowardly child; a child that cries for nothing.

isht ilawata, n., an occasion of boasting; pomp.

isht ilaweha, n., a desertion.

isht ileanumpuli shali, n., egotism; an egotist.

isht ilehoshontikachi, n., an umbrella.

isht illa hinla, a., fatal; mortal,

isht illi, n., poison; bane; occasion of death; cause of death; death; venom; virus.

isht illi fohki, v. t., to poison; to empoison; to put in poison.

isht illi foka, pp., poisoned.

isht illi ipeta, v. t., to poison; to give poison; to empoison; to envenom; to venom; to administer poison.

isht illi okpulo, a., virulent.

isht illi yạmmichi, v. t., to empoison; to mix poison.

isht imaiokpulo, n., peril; his peril.

isht impa, n., a spoon; an instrument used at table for dipping liquids, etc., and as this was the chief utensil employed by the Choctaw, it is called the eating instrument; it was made of wood or of the horns of buffalo and later of those of cattle.

isht impa alota, n., a spoonful.

isht impak imma, adv., toward the right; to the right hand, Matt. 5: 29; 6: 3; the right side of, 2 Sam. 24: 5.

isht impak imma ibbak, n., the right hand.

isht impaka, n., the right; being on the same side as the right hand.

isht impạtta, n., a wadding.

isht impushi, n., a small spoon; a teaspoon; "the son of isht impa."

isht inchunli, n., a brand iron; a branding instrument; a seal.

isht inchunwa, n., a brand iron; a seal; a stamp; a type; as wak isht inchunwa.

isht intalakchi, pp., fettered.

isht ishi, n., a holder.

isht ishko, n., a cup; a chalice; a mug; a tankard, Matt. 10: 42.

isht ishko chaha, n., a pitcher; a mug.

isht ishko chupak, n., a quart measure; a cup or pot with a spout.

isht ishko latạssa, n., a tin cup.

isht ishko latạssa achạfa, n., a pint.

isht ishko patạla tuklo, n., a quart.

isht ishko patạssa, n., a basin.

isht ishkushi, n., a small cup; a teacup; a small mug.

isht itibbi, n., a weapon; an instrument for fighting; a bayonet; a dog tooth; a tusk; the eyetooth; a fang; a javelin; munition; a poniard.

isht itibbi ansha, a., fanged.

isht itihalạlli, n., a bond.

isht ittulá, int. of anger, used in scolding children (N. Graham, informant).

isht kachaya (from *ishit* and *kachaya*, the pass. of *kạhchi*), n., shears; scissors.

isht kachaya chito, n., large shears.

isht kachayushi, n., scissors.

isht kalasha, n., shears; a pair of shears.

isht kalashushi, n., scissors; a pair of scissors.

isht kanạpa, see *ishkanạpa*.

isht kashofa, n., an offset.

isht kashokạchi, n., a brush; a wiper.

isht kasholichi, n., a brush; a wiper.

isht kạfa, n., a ladle; a dipper; a gourd.

isht kạllochi, n., stiffening.

isht kiselichi, n., a clamp; a vise; pincers or pinchers.

isht kula, n., a pick; a pickax; an instrument used in digging.

isht laknạchi, n., a yellow dye.

isht luli, n., an instrument for paring; a parer.

isht lusachi, n., a black dye; blacking.

isht laⁿfa, n., a ruler.

isht laⁿfi, n., a compass; a gage.

isht lakoffi, n., a remedy.

isht lopulli, n., a cathartic.

isht lukata, n., a lash; a whip lash.

isht lukạffi, n., a perforator.

isht lumpa, n., a lancet; a punch; a fleam; a drill; a puncher.

isht lumpli, n., a perforator.

isht miha, n., a reason.

isht milofa, n., a file; a rasp; a rubber.

isht milofa chito, n., a large file; a rasp.

isht minti, n., a bringer.

isht misholichi, n., a rubber.

isht moeli, n., a skimmer; a short paddle.

isht moⁿfa atapạchi, n., a rowlock.

isht mofi, isht moⁿffi, n., a skimmer; an oar; a paddle.

isht nanạbli, n. sing., the swallow.

isht nạlli, pl., swallows.

isht nạli, n., a sting.

isht nukhaⁿklo, n., a lamenter.

isht nukhaⁿklo, n., cause of sorrow; an affliction.

isht nukhobela, n., wrath, Josh. 7: 1.

isht nukoa, n., vexation.

isht nukpạllichi, n., an enticement.

isht nukshobli, n., a scarecrow.

isht ochi, isht ohchi, n., a bucket; a pail; a water pail; a can; a piggin; any vessel or instrument used in taking up water from a well, spring, pond, etc.; a flagon; a water pot.

isht ochi alota, n., a pailful.

isht okchila, n., a riddle.

isht oklushi, v. a. i., to make fun of; to deride; to joke.

isht okpeha, n., a skimmer.

isht okshilita, isht ukshilita, n., a barrier; an obstruction; a shutter; something that closes a passage; the door; the gate of a house; a gate; a stopple.

isht oktạpa, n., a barrier; an obstruction; a dam; a shutter; a stopper; a a wad; a wear.

isht okyoli, n., a fin.

isht ona, v. t., to carry to; to bring to, Matt. 1: 12.

isht paⁿshpoa, see *isht bạshpoa*.

isht pashpoa iskitini, n., a whisk.

isht pạla, n., a glut; a wedge.

isht pạshpoa, *isht bạshpoa*.

isht piⁿfi, n., a swimmer.

isht piha, n., a shovel; a scoop.

isht pila, n., a sting.

isht pisa, n., sight.

isht pokoli, a., tenth; 10th, Josh. 4: 19; *isht pokoli tuklo*, a., twentieth; 20th; *isht pokoli tuchina*, a., thirtieth; 30th; *isht pokoli ushta*, a., fortieth; 40th; *isht pokoli talapi*, a., fiftieth; 50th; *isht pokoli hanali*, a., sixtieth; 60th; *isht pokoli untuklo*, *isht pokoluntuklo*, a., seventieth; 70th; *isht pokoli untuchina*, a., eightieth; 80th; *isht pokoli chakali*, a., ninetieth; 90th.

isht pokoli, n., a tithe.

isht puⁿfa, n., a trumpet; a pipe; a horn; a bugle; a bugle horn; a trump, Matt. 6: 2; Josh. 6: 4, 5, 6, 8.

isht puⁿfolachi, n., a horner; one who blows a trumpet; a trumpeter.

isht shaⁿfa, n., a drawing knife; a drawshave; *itiisht shaⁿfa*.

isht shaⁿfi, n., a plane; *itiisht shafi*.

isht shạffi, n., a scraper used in scraping up dirt, ashes, etc.

isht shạnni, n., a winch.

isht shema, isht ilakshema, n., ornaments; attire; finery; fine clothes; a decoration; a dress; garb; garniture; a guise; habiliment; a rig; rigging.

isht shiahchi, n., cards used in carding cotton.

isht shilli, n., a comb.

isht shima, n., a power.

isht shuahchi, n., an instrument for sharpening; a whetstone; a hone; a rubstone; a rubber.

isht tabeli, ishtabeli, n., a cane; a staff; a crutch.

isht tahpala, n., a cry.

isht taka, n. pl., dippers.

isht takafa, n., a dipper.

isht takali, n., a stem; a hinge; that by which anything hangs; *isito isht takali*, a pumpkin stem.

isht takaffi, n., dippers.

isht takli, n., dippers.

isht takoli, pl., stems; hinges.

isht talakchi, n., a string; a tether; a band; a bond; a hamper; a lace; a leash; a ligament; a shackle.

isht talapi, a., fifth; 5th; *ont isht talapi*, adv., fifthly.

isht talepa, a., a hundredth; 100th; *isht talepa achafa*, one hundredth.

isht talepa sipokni, a., a thousandth.

isht tana, n., a shuttle, i. e., a weaver's shuttle.

isht tanna, n., the woof; the filling (in weaving cloth).

isht tikili, n., a prop; a brace or stick used in stretching hides.

isht tikoli, pl., props; braces; tenters.

isht tiwa, ishit tiwa, n., a key, Matt. 16:19.

isht tiwa chiluk, n., a keyhole.

isht tobli, n., a setting pole; a pushing pole; any instrument for pushing.

isht tonksali, n., a tool; a utensil; an implement; an instrument.

isht tonolichi, n., a lever; a handspike; a crowbar; any instrument used in rolling logs and the like.

isht ukfoata, isht ukhoata, n., the side; the ribs of a man or animal.

isht ukhatapa, n., a blind; a shutter, as for a window.

isht uklakafa, v. t., to mock; to jest; to deride, John 19: 3 [?].

isht ukshilita, see *isht okshilita*.

isht umpoholmo, n., a covering.

isht untuchina, a., eighth; 8th.

isht untuchinaha, adv., eighth time.

isht untuklo, a., seventh; 7th; *ont isht untuklo*, Josh. 6:4.

isht untukloha, adv., seventh time.

isht wakeli, n., a lever; a pry.

isht washoha, n., a toy; a plaything; a trinket.

isht weki, n., a poise.

isht wekichi, n., steelyards; scales; balances.—Ch. Sp. Book, p. 66.

isht yaiya, n., a lamenter; a lamenting.

isht yammichi, n., an instrument.

isht yopomo, n., a waster; a lavisher.

isht yopomo, v. t., to waste, as *imilayak isht yopomo;* to lavish; to spend; to squander.

isht yopomo, pp., wasted; lavished.

isht yopomo shali, a., wasteful; lavish.

isht yopula, n., a joker; a maligner; a scoffer; a trifler.

isht yopula, n., a game.

isht yopula, v. a. i., v. t., to flout; to fool; to fleer; to gibe; to jeer; to scandal; to scandalize; to scoff; to traduce; to trifle; to vilify.

isht yopula, a., prodigal; profane; wasteful.

isht yopulat, adv., prodigally; profanely.

isht yopulat isht anumpuli, v. t., to ridicule.

isht yuha, n., a sieve; a sifter; a bolter; a bolt.

isht yupomo, n., waste.

isht yupomo, n., a spendthrift; a waster.

isht yuwala, n., odium.

ishtilema, see *shittilema*.

ishto, a., great; big; large; huge; immense. This is the Chickasaw equivalent for *chito* (q. v.).

ishto, v. n., to be great.

ishtokaka, n., the great one; a lord; a ruler; same as *chitokaka*.

ishwa, v. t., to smell; see *aiishwa*.

ishwa, v. t. pl., to take, i. e., a number; *ishi*, v. t. sing.

it, iti, reciprocal pronouns, sign of the doubly reflective form, a mutual or reciprocal verb; *abeli, itabeli*, v. t., to put them together; *boa, itaboa*, to hunt each other; *pisa, itipesa*, to see each other; also cf. *itapissali, itiakaiya, itichapa*, 1 Kings 7: 5.

ita, adv., together, as *itatuklo, itanowa, itafama*, etc. *ita* and *iti* are different words.

itabana, p. of *itabani*, v. t., to put logs together as in making a log house; to fit to each other.

itabani, v. t., to put together, Josh. 4: 20.

itabanni, n., a raising; see *abanni*.

itabi, v. a. i., to howl, as a wolf; same as *shakapa*.

itabiha, n., a mixture.

itachoa, itachowa, n., a broil; a dispute; a variance.

itahina, n., a companion; a consort; see *ahinna*.

itahoba (from *ita* and *ahoba*), v. a. i., to assemble; to congregate; to come together; to collect; to convene; to gather; to huddle; to shoal; *ant imaiitahoba*, Matt. 13: 2. The main form (*ahoba*) of this word in the sense of meeting is not used; *itahomba, itahohomba*.

itahoba, pp., assembled; gathered together, Matt. 13: 40; collected; a., collective; convened; gathered.

itahoba, n., an assembly; an association; a collection; a concourse; a convention; a gathering; a mass; a shoal.

itahobi, v. t., to assemble; to amass; to collect together; to collect; to congregate; to convene; to gather, Matt. 10: 1; 13: 28, 29, 30; 15: 10; John 11: 47; 1 Kings, 10: 26; Josh. 4: 4; 7: 16, 17, 18.

itahobi, n., one who assembles; an assembler; a gatherer.

itahobli, v. t., to assemble; to collect; to congregate; to convene; to gather.

itahobli, n., an assembler; a convener; a gatherer.

itaiena, n., the wives of one man; *imitaiena*, his concubine, Judg. 19: 1.

itaiisso, n., a clashing; a concussion; a shock.

itaiunchululi, n., generations, Matt. 1: 17.

itaiyokoma, n., a puzzle.

itaiyokommi, n., a puzzler.

itaiyukhana, n., a cross, +; corners of streets; see *aiokhaneli*.

itaiyukhankachi; *aiitaiokhankachi*, Matt. 6: 5.

itaiyuma, n., a mixture.

itaiyumi, n., a mixer.

itakaiyat ia, n., a procession.

itakamassalli, n., a pinner.

itakantali, v. a. i., to be close together, Mark 2: 4; from *akantali* (q. v.).

itakapuli, see *itakopuli*.

itakashkoa, n., separation.

itakashkuli, n., separation; a separator.

itakashkulit, adv., separately.

itakchulakto, a., forked, as the roots of a tree that is turned up.

itakchulakto, v. n., to be forked.

itakchulakto, n., a tree that is turned up by the roots.

itakchulali, a., forked, as the ear of an animal when marked.

itakchulali, v. n., to be forked.

itakchulalichi, v. t., to fork.

itakchulashli, a. pl., forked.

itakchulashli, v. n., to be forked.

itakchulashlichi, v. t., to fork them.

itakha, see *itakha*.

itakhapuli, a., troublesome; *hatak itakhapuli shali*, n., a heeler.

itakhapuli, v. n., to be troublesome.

itakhapuli shali, v. a. i., to riot.

itakhapuli shali, a., riotous; waggish.

itakhapuli shali, n., a zany.

itakhapulichi, v. t. caus., to cause to be troublesome.

itakhauali, a., having the lips open a little.

itakhauali, v. n., to have the lips open a little.

itakkomulih, v. n., to close the lips tight.

itaklalashli, v. a. i., to be moist in the mouth; to drivel from the use of alum.

itakmacheli, n., thin lips.

itakmofoli, a., having the lips closed tight or firm.

itakmofoli, v. n., to be open, as the mouth of another.

itakommuchi, v. a. i., to shut the mouth.

itakomoli, v. a. i., to place in a fold, i. e., two sides of a cloth or paper; to fold together.

itakonofa; *itatikkonofa*, v. a. i., to stand near each other.

itakopulechi, atakapulechi, v. t., to close; to press together, as the sides of a wound.

itakopuli, itakapuli, v. a. i., to close together; to come together.

itakowa, itakoa, n., fire wood.

itakowa intula, n., andirons; firedogs.

itakpashakli, itąkpashakli, v. a. i., to gasp.

itakpashakli, n., a gasp.

itakpashali, v. a. i., to open the mouth.

itakpąshpąli, v. a. i., to gape.

itakpąshpąli, n., a gaping.

itakpisheli, a., shaped like the snout of a hog or the rim of a vial or a bell, smallest at the upper end and opening wide.

itakpofonli, v. a. i., to open the mouth, as another's mouth.

itakshish, n., the root of a tree; a grub; a snag.

itakshish isht chaⁿya, itakshish isht kuchi, itakshishi isht kula, itakshish isht ąlmo, n., a mattock; a grubbing hoe; a grub ax.

itakshish kulli, v. t. to grub; to dig up roots; to stub.

itakshish kulli, n., a grubber.

itakwacholi, n., high chin.

itakyuinli, v. a. i., to grin; itakyueli, to grin.—J. E.

italaⁿkla, a., both ways at the same time; in opposite directions at once.

italaⁿkla, v. n., to be both ways.

italaⁿkla halupa, a., two-edged; double-edged.

italaⁿkla hotupa, v. n., to pain on both sides or quite through, as when the head aches on both sides.

italaⁿkla ont ia, n., a puking and purging at the same time; cholera morbus.

italaⁿkla ont ia, v. n., to be sick with puking and purging, or cholera morbus.

italaklaka, talalaⁿka, n., on both sides, 1 Kings 11: 31.

itamoa, a. pl., lost; gone off; kąnia, pp. sing., lost.

itamoa, v. n., to wander off; to be lost; antamoa, mine are lost.

itampikbi, n., a cooper.

itampo, n., a pail; a wooden bowl; a tray; a trencher.

itampo chito, n., a tub.

itampushi, n., a small wooden bowl.

itanali, itąnnali, v. t., to collect together; to assemble.

itanowa, v. t. pl. (from ita and nowa), to travel, Josh. 2: 16; to travel together, Matt. 2: 2; to troop.

itanowa, n., travelers; an expedition; na hąllo itanowa, traveling white men.

itapela, n., a partner; see itąpela.

itapelachi, n., a copartnership; a firm.

itapushi, n., a sprout without leaves, used as a switch; a staddle.

itasitia, n., a coherence; those who cleave together.

itashali, itishali, n., a generation.

itashekonompa, n., a knot made by two strings together.

itashekonopa, n., a knot where two strings are tied together; itashekonopa, p.; see Acts 10: 11, wishakchi uⁿshtąt itashekonopa.

itashekonopli, v. t., to tie in a knot.

itashekonowa, n. pl., knots.

itashuma, n., a mixture.

itatakąli, ititakąli, n., a chain; a link; a concatenation.

itatiapa, n., a schism.

itatoba, v. t., v. a. i., itatoboli, pl., to trade; to swap; to exchange; to barter; to traffic; to shop; to commerce; to commute; to contract; to deal; to interchange; to market; to speculate; to swap; to truck.

itatoba, n. (from toba plus the reciprocal particle iti and the locative a), a customer (at a store); a dealer; an exchanger; a trader; a swapper; a trafficker; a contractor; a merchant.

itatoba, n., a trade; trade; commerce; a commutation; an exchange; an interchange; merchandise; a speculation; a swap; a traffic; a truck.

itatoba holisso, n., an account book or a book account.

itatoba kąllo, a., close; hard, when trading.

itatoba kąllo, n., a shaver.

itatobąchi, v. t., to commute.

itatobąt aⁿya, v. t., to peddle.

itatobąt aⁿya, n., a peddler.

itatobąt tąli holisso ishi, v. t., to cash; to swap and take the money.

itatuklo, a., both together, or two together; along with; see tuklo; also used for a conj., and; see Gen. 1: 1; Matt. 18: 15.

itatuklo, v. n., to be two together; to unite.

itatuklo, adv., together.

itatuklo, v. a. i., to make the second, or to go with, as itatukloli; to be a partner where there are only two, as in marriage; *ittatukloli*, I unite with him, John 10: 30.

itauaya, v. t., mas. gen., to marry a woman; to couple; *auaya*, fem. gen.

itauaya, n., a marriage; a couple; a partner; a partnership; a spouse.

itauaya, n., a married man; a married woman.

itauayąchi, v. t., to solemnize a marriage.

itauayąchi, n., the one who solemnizes a marriage.

itąchaka, n., a joint.

itąchakąchi, n., a joint.

itąchanaia, dual, to be two together by themselves, like an old man and his wife when their children are all gone.

itąchi, v. t., to throw anything upon a fire; to cast into the fire, Acts 28: 5.

itąchoa, n., a quarreler; a stickler; a wrangler.

itąchoa, n., a broil; a dispute; a wrangle; a contention; a jangle; a quarrel; a strife.

itąchoa shali, a., quarrelsome; wranglesome.

itąffoa, see *itąlhfoa*.

itąkha, itakha, n., the mouth; the inside of the mouth; the gills of a fish; the voice; Matt. 17: 27; *nąni itąkha*, fish's mouth.

itąkha, a., vocal.

itąkha achąfa, n., a mouthful.

itąkha akkąmi, v.t., to gag; to stop the mouth.

itąkha ąlhkąma, pp., gagged.

itąkha chinto, a., hoarse.

itąkha isht ąlhkąma, n., a gag.

itąkha litoli, v. t., to make the mouth sore.

itąkha litowa, v. a. i., to canker; to become sore in the mouth.

itąkha litowa, pp., mouth sore; cankered mouth.

itąkha litowa, n., the sore mouth; canker in the mouth; the thrush.

itąkpashakli, itakpashakli (q. v.), v. a. i., to gasp.

itąlbaⁿsa, n., petrifaction.

itąlhfoa, itąffoa, n., a keg.

itąlhfoa chito, n., a barrel; a hogshead; a cask; a puncheon; a tierce or terce; a pipe; a tun.

itąlhfoa chito abeha, pp., barreled.

itąlhfoa chito abeli, v. t., to barrel.

itąlhfoa chito fohki, v. t., to barrel; to put into a barrel.

itąlhfoa chito foka, n., barreled.

itąlhfoa chito ibish, n., the chine of a barrel.

itąlhfoa chito ikbi, n., a cooper.

itąlhfoa ikbi, n., a cooper; a hooper.

itąlhfoa isht ąlhkąma, n., a bung.

itąlhfoa isht talakchi, n., a hoop.

itąlhfoa takchi, v. t., to hoop.

itąlhfoa takchi, n., a hooper.

itąlhfoa talakchi, pp., hooped.

itąlhfoa tikpi, n., the bilge of a cask.

itąlhfoushi, n., a keg; a small keg.

itąlhkątta, n., patchwork, such as a bed quilt made of pieces.

itąlhpali, n., the forearm.

itąlhtoboa, n., rotation; see *ąlhtoboa*.

itąlikchi, n., a cherry tree.

itąlikchi ąni, n., a cherry.

itąlląt akkąchit kaha, pp., packed, as meat.

itąmintąfa, itąmintąfi, n., a chasm or split like the opening made by butchers when they open a hog.

itąnaha, v. a. i., a verb reciprocal and locative—*iti* and *a* united, used in this way only—to assemble; to collect; to come together; to congregate; to convene; to flock; to herd; to huddle; to embody; to parade; to rally; to shoal; to troop.

itąnaha, pp., assembled; collected; accumulated; piled up; collective; congregated; contributed; convened; convoked; embodied; amassed; gathered; heaped; levied; lumped; raked; piled; stacked.

itąnaha, n., an assembly; a collection; a concourse; a congregation; a contribution; a convention; a convocation; an accumulation; a gathering; a huddle; a levy; a mass; a pile; a shoal; a stack; a throng.

itąnaha laua, v. a. i., to throng.

itąnahachi, v. t., to cause to assemble; to congregate; to herd.

itąnahachi, v. a. i., to heap together, Josh. 3: 13, 16.

itąnahachi, ittanahahchi, n., a pile; as *iti itąnahachi*, a pile, or cord of wood piled, Josh. 8: 29; Ps. 33: 7.

itąnaho, a., uncollected.

itạnnali, itạnaḷi, v. t., to accumulate; to lump; to assemble; to collect; to bring together; to congregate; to contribute; to convene; to convoke; to cumulate; to embody; to gather; to heap; to herd; to levy; to muster; to parade, as soldiers; to pile; to raise; to rake; to stack; to trump.

itạnnali, n., an assembler; a collector; a convener; a gatherer; a heaper.

itạnnali, n., a rally.

itạnnalichi, v. t., to heap; to collect; to pile; to assemble; to make a pile.

itạpaiyali, n., a huddler.

itạpaiyali, v. t., to huddle.

itạpaiyata, n., a huddle.

itạpela, itapela, n., a help; a helper; a partner; an ally; a colleague; mutual helps, Luke 5: 7.

itạpiha, n., a colleague; an attendant.

itạshi, n., a club; a cudgel; a bludgeon; a small stick having the root for one end.

itạshiha, n., a snarl; a tangle.

itạtakạli, n., a link; a chain.

itạtonla, to lie together, John 21: 9.

ithaiyana, see ikhana.

ithana, ithạna, to learn; see ikhana, ikhạna.

ithiⁿsh, see ikhiⁿsh.

iti, each other; see it; a reciprocal pronoun.

itiⁿ, to each other; from each other, etc. This form differs from the others as it requires a prep. to be used before the pro. iti is in the accus. case; itiⁿ is in the dative case; see after iti, wood, and its compounds. It is sometimes written itim as before vowels, and itin before ch, l and t, itiⁿ before the other letters of the alphabet.

iti, itih, n., the mouth; the front part of the mouth; itạkha, the inner part, Matt. 4: 4; 15: 8, 11, 17, 18; 18: 16; Josh. 1: 8; 9: 14.

iti, n., wood; timber; a tree.

iti abạsha, n., a sawpit; a sawmill.

iti achushkạchi, n., a peg; a wooden peg.

iti ahulạlli, n., a whiffletree.

iti akishtạla, n., the root of a tree; the foot of a tree.

iti alua, n., burnt wood; burnt woods.

iti ana, n., a rib pole.

iti anuⁿka, a., woody; being in the woods; sylvan.

iti anuⁿka, v. n., to be in the woods.

iti anuⁿka, n., the woods; a forest; a wilderness.

iti anuⁿkaka, a., wild.

iti aⁿsha, pp., timbered.

iti ashaⁿfa, n., a joiner's bench; a joiner's horse.

iti ashaⁿfa botulli, n., shavings.

iti ashaⁿfi, n., a wood-shaver.

iti atikoa, n., a stud; a well-known piece of timber used in a frame house.

iti atoba, a., wooden; made of wood.

iti ạlbạsa, n., lathing; ribbing.

iti ạlbạsto, n., a litter for the sick to ride on.

iti ạlhpoa, n., a shade tree; a domesticated tree.

iti ạni, itạni, n., a black gum.

iti bachoha, iti bạchoha, n., beams; joists; sleepers, or any pieces of timber lying parallel (horizontal?).

iti baka, n., a block.

iti bakapa, n., the half of a tree split.

iti bakli, v. t., to split wood into large pieces; to block out; to bolt wood.

iti bạsha, n., a plank; a sawed board; sawed timber; lumber; a scantling; a slab.

iti bạsha ahonạla, n., clapboards.

iti bạsha ashila, n., a board kiln.

iti bạsha patali, v. t., to plank.

iti bạsha sukko, n., a plank.

iti bạshkạchi, n., timbers lying parallel.

iti bạshli, n., a sawyer; a cutter.

iti boli, n., an imaginary being said to kill birds; a phantasm.

iti boshulli, n., fragments of wood.

iti botulli, n., the dust of wood, made by a saw or worms.

iti chakbi, n., a wooden peg.

iti chanạlli, n., a wagon; a cart; a carriage; a dray; tạnạp iti chanạlli, a war chariot, 1 Kings 10: 26; a chariot, 2 Kings 9: 21, 24, 25.

iti chanạlli achosha, n., an axletree.

iti chanạlli ashali, v. t., to wagon; to cart.

iti chanạlli haknip, n., a wagon body; a wagon box or bed.

iti chanạlli iⁿhina, n., a wagon road.

iti chanạlli iskitini pạlhki, n., a chariot; a gig; a chaise; a sulky; a cabriolet.

iti chanạllushi, n., a small wagon; a
hand wagon; a wheelbarrow; a child's
wagon.

iti chanli, n., a chopper; a hewer of
wood; a cutter; a pecker.

iti chant ạbi, n., to girdle trees; to kill
timber.

iti chant tushalichi, v. t., to chip; to
hack.

iti chauạna, iti chauạnaya, n., a
notched stick; having a notch, as in
the rafters of some log houses, or the
pommel of a Spanish saddle.

iti chạkpa, n., the side of a tree some
distance from the ground.

iti chạnaha, n., a wooden wheel; a
wagon; a cart; a carriage; a car; the
wheels of a wagon, etc.; a roller; a
water wheel.

iti chạnaha afacha, n., a linchpin.

iti chạnaha alota, n., a wagonful; a
wagon load; a loaded wagon.

iti chạnaha anowa, n., a wagon rut;
a cart rut; a rut.

iti chạnaha ashali, see iti chạnaha isht
shali.

iti chạnaha holisso shali, n., a mail
coach.

iti chạnaha holitopa, n., a coach; a
hack.

iti chạnaha holitopa aiomanili, n.,
a coach box.

iti chạnaha holitopa ikbi, n., a coach
maker.

iti chạnaha iⁿhina, n., a wagon road.

iti chạnaha ikbi, n., a wagon maker;
a cartwright; a wheelwright.

iti chạnaha iklạnna, n., the nave of
a wheel.

iti chạnaha iskitini, n., a wheelbarrow;
a barrow; a little wagon.

iti chạnaha isht aⁿya, v. t., to wagon.

iti chạnaha isht aⁿya, n., a wagoner;
a carter; a carman; a teamster.

iti chạnaha isht halạlli, n., a wagon
harness; tackling.

iti chạnaha isht shali, iti chạnaha
ashali, v. a. i., to wagon.

iti chạnaha isht talakchi, n., a wagon
tire; a tire.

iti chạnaha pạlhki, n., a chaise; a chair;
a chariot; a hack; a stage; a sulky.

iti chạnaha umpoholmo, n., a wagon
cover.

iti chạnaha ushi, n., a wheelbarrow;
a little wagon.

iti chinisa, n., the laurel tree.

iti chishakko, n., brush cut for a bower;
a brush bower.

iti chishaⁿkko, n., a bush put up for
shade.

iti chishaⁿkko hoshontika, n., a bush
arbor; a bower made of bushes; a
booth; chishaⁿka, Neh. 9: 14.

iti chito, n., a large tree; a beam, Matt.
7: 3.

iti chito tạpa, n., a log.

iti chufak, n., a pin.

iti fabạssa, n., a pole; a slender tree; a
perch.

iti fabạssoa, iti fabaspoa, iti fabạsfoa,
iti fahko, n. pl., poles.

iti haklupish, n. pl., the ross of a tree;
the outer dry pieces of bark.

iti hakshup, n., the bark of a tree.

iti hạta, n., whitewood.

iti hika, n., a stake; a post.

iti hikia, n., a standing tree.

iti hishi, n., leaves of a tree; tree leaves;
leaf of a tree.

iti hishi halupa, n., the holly tree, the
leaves of which have small thorns on
them.

iti honni aiạlhto, n., a fat or vat.

iti hoyo, v. a. i., to wood.

iti humma, n., a red pole; a pole stained
red; such poles as are erected as a sign
of mourning for the dead.

iti illi, n., a dead tree.

iti iskuna, n., the heart of a tree; the
center of a tree.

iti iskuna paknaka, n., the sap of a tree.

iti ishi, v. a. i., to wood.

iti isht ahonạla, n., a peg; a pin, used
to fasten timbers together.

iti isht ạlhpisa, n., a yardstick.

iti isht bạsha, n., a saw.

iti isht bạsha chito, n., a pit saw; a sawmill saw.

iti isht bạsha falaia, n., a whipsaw.

iti isht boa, n., a maul or a mall; a
beetle; a wooden hammer.

iti isht boa chito, n., a large maul; a
commander.

iti isht boa iskitini, n., a mallet.

iti isht boa ushi, n., a mallet.

iti isht fotoha, n., an auger; a borer.

iti isht fotohushi, n., a gimlet.

iti isht halạlli, n., a swingletree; a whiffletree; a hame.

iti isht honni aiạlhto, n., a fat or vat.

iti isht ishko, n., a noggin.

iti isht kula, n., a chisel.

iti isht kula kofusa, n., a gouge.

iti isht miłofa, n., a rasp.

iti isht pạla, n., a wooden wedge; a glut; a wedge; *iti isht pạla alạlichi*, to wedge.

iti isht shaⁿfa, n., a drawing knife; a drawshave.

iti isht shaⁿfiⁿ, n., a plane.

iti isht shaⁿfit haluskichi, n., a plane.

iti isht shima, n., a power.

iti isht tonolichi, n., a handspike; a lever; a wooden pry.

iti itikeli, n. sing., a rafter.

iti ititakạlli, n., an evener; a swingletree; a doubletree.

iti ititekili, n. pl., rafters.

iti kạfi, n., sassafras.

iti kạlaha, n., a wooden roller; a spool; a truck; a roll; a roller; a wheel.

iti kạlaha chanạlli, n., a truck wheel.

iti kinafa, n., a fallen tree.

iti kinałi, n. pl., fallen trees.

iti kolofa, n., a stump; a stub; wood cut off, applied to a half bushel, a tub, etc.

iti kosoma, n., sour wood.

iti kula, n., a trough; a canoe; a boat; a tray.

iti kula aiimpa, n., a trencher.

iti kula falaia, n., a long trough.

iti kula peni, n., a canoe; a pirogue.

iti kusha yaiya, n., a crane.

iti laua, a., woody.

iti lukoli, n., a grove.

iti lumbo, n., a roll; a wooden globe.

iti litilli, n., tree gum; the gum of a tree.

iti łoli, v. t., to gall (a tree); to peel a tree.

iti naksish, n., a limb; a bough; a branch of a tree; a knot (on a tree).

iti naksish filạmminchi, n., the arm of a tree.

iti naksish laua toba, v. a. i., to ramify.

iti naksish tạpa, n., brush; a limb broken off.

iti nipa, n., a club.

iti oiya, v. t., to climb a tree.

iti oka aiyanạlli, n., a water trough; an eave trough.

iti okchaⁿki, n., green wood, not dry or seasoned.

iti okchako, n., an evergreen tree; green wood.

iti okchamali, n., green wood.

iti okchi, n., sap of wood.

iti osh toba, a., ligneous; made of wood; wooden.

iti pałanta, n., split wood; split boards.

iti patali, v. t., to floor.

iti patapo, n., a floor; a bridge; wood spread out; a wooden causeway.

iti patạlhpo, n., a floor; a bridge; a causeway; a wooden crossway; a platform; a stage.

iti patạlhpo ạlhtoba ahoyo, n., a toll bridge.

iti patạlhpo ikbi, v. t., to bridge; to make a bridge.

iti patạlhpo ikbi, n., one who makes bridges; a bridge maker.

iti patạlhpo umpatạlhpo, n., a carpet; a floor carpet; a floor cloth.

iti pạla, n., split wood; rails; rail stuff.

iti pạla patạlhpo, n., a puncheon used in making floors.

iti peni, n., a canoe; a manger; a trough.

iti połoma, n., a hoop; a wooden spring.

iti pushi, itapushi (q. v.), n., a sapling; a sprout without the leaves on.

iti shaⁿfa, n., a shaved board; a planed board.

iti shaⁿfi, n., a joiner; a carpenter; a planer.

iti shalạlli, n., a sled; a runner; the support of a sleigh or sled; a sleigh.

iti shalạlli isht aⁿya, v. t., to sled.

iti shạna, n., a screw; a wooden screw.

iti shibafa, n., a splinter; a sliver, thin, flat, and small.

iti shibałi, n. pl., splinters.

iti shila, n., a dry tree; dry wood; dry timber; seasoned wood.

iti shima, n., a shingle; a split wood; shingles; a stave.

iti shima halupa, n., a pale.

iti shimafa, n., a splinter; a sliver: a splint.

iti shimafa shaⁿfa, n., a ferule.

iti shimałi, n. pl., splinters; slivers.

iti shukafa, n., a chip.

iti shukali, n., chips.

iti shumo, n., moss of trees; Spanish moss.

iti shumo laua, a., mossy.

iti taiyukhana, n., a cross; a wooden cross, Luke 23: 21; Matt. 10: 38; 16: 24; Mark 10: 21; see *aiyukhana.*

iti taiyukhana ahonalichi, v. t., to crucify; to nail to the cross.

iti talaia, n., a clump (of trees).

iti tanampo, n., a bow; a wooden gun, 2 Kings 9: 24; 2 Sam. 1: 18.

iti tanampo isht a^{n}ya, n., an archer; a bowman.

iti tanampo isht talakchi, n., a bow-string.

iti tapena, n., a cudgel; a bludgeon; a war club.

iti tapokachi, v. a. i., to be 4 square; wood shaped like a box.

iti tala, n., a wooden pin.

iti tapa, n., a stick of wood; a block; a club; a chunk; a billet of wood.

iti tapa ahabbi talapi, n., a perch.

iti tapa lua, n., a brand; a firebrand.

iti tapa tonoli, n., a roller.

iti taptua, n. pl., sticks of wood; clubs, etc.

iti taptua isht nowa, n., crutches.

iti tikpi, n., a large round knot on a tree.

iti tilofa, n., a billet of wood; a chunk of wood.

iti tiloli, n. pl., billets of wood.

iti tila, n., a blazed tree; a marked tree; a butt; a mark; a target; a way mark.

iti tila bachaya, n., a line; a line of blazed trees; a row of blazed trees.

iti tili, v. t., to blaze a tree; to set a white mark on a tree by shaving off the bark.

iti tili, n., one who marks trees.

iti toshbi, n., touchwood.

iti tushafa, n., a chip.

iti tushali, n. pl., chips.

iti ulhti, iti olulhti, n., fire wood.

iti unchuloli, n., the sprouts of a tree.

iti waiya, n., a leaning tree.

iti wa^{n}ya, n., a stool; a seat; a cricket.

iti wishakchi, n., the top of a tree.

iti yileha, fallen trees.

itiachi, v. a. i., two to go together, Matt. 9: 31; 11: 7; Josh. 2: 1.

itiachi, n., two fellow-travelers.

itiakaya, n., a file; a single rank.

itialbi, n., the lip; a lip; lips, Matt. 15: 8.

itialbi, n., the price.

itialbi abi, v. t., to revenge.

itialbi abi, n., the revenger of blood.

itialli, n., the price; see *ialli.*

itiammi, n., temper.

itibafoka, n., a comrade; fellowship; a companion; a contribution.

itibafoka, n., a mixture; a junction; a partnership.

itibaiimpa, n., a messmate.

itibanowa, n., a fellow-traveler.

itibanusi, n., a bedfellow.

itibapisa, n., a classmate; a class in a school, Matt. 10: 21; 12: 46; brethren, Matt. 13: 55; 14: 3.

itibapishi, (*iti* each other; *iba*, with; *pishi*, to suck) n. com. gen., a brother or sister; a friend; those who drew the breast together; a fraternity; brethren; *itibapishili*, my brother; I sucked with him, her, or them, Matt. 12: 48; *ishitibapishi*, your brother; you sucked with him; Matt. 5: 23; 7: 3; 18: 15; or *chitibapishi*, he sucked with thee; *hachitibapishi*, Josh. 1: 14.

itibapishi aliha n., brothers; brother-hood; fraternity.

itibapishi fehna, n., a real brother.

itibapishi o^n, a., fraternal.

itibapishi toba, n., a cousin; half blood; a stepbrother.

itibalhkaha, n., a mixture; an addition.

itibalhto, n., a mixture.

itibbi, n., a fight; a battle; a contest; a combat; a conflict; a duel; an engagement; a fray; a match; a rencounter; a skirmish; a storm.

itibbi, a., militant.

itibechi, v. t., to cause to fight or combat.

itibechi, n., one that causes fighting; an instigator of quarrels, fights, etc.

itibi, v. t. (from *abi*, to kill;) to fight; to combat; to kill each other; to conflict; to contend; to defend; to engage; to fence; to rencounter; to skirmish.

itibi, itibbi, n., a fighter; a combatant; a duelist; a fencer.

itibili^{n}ka a^{n}sha, n., a neighborhood.

itiboshali, n., a wry mouth.

itichabli, n., a mate; a pair.

itichakbi, n., a wooden peg or pin.

itichapa, n., mates; a pair; a mate; a fellow; a partner; a partnership.

itichapat ia, n., a procession.

itichunkash paknaka, n., the sap of a tree.

itinha; *ant pimitinhahilah* (J. C.); *amahobah.*

itihaklo, n., mutual hearing.

itihoba, itioba, n., an equality; a resemblance.

itiholba, n., a resemblance; a similarity.

itinhollo, n., mutual friends; friendship; mutual lovers.

itihpila, v. a. i. (compounded of *itih* and *pila*), to fall; *itihpelat akiat*, Acts 1: 18.

itihpilachi, v. t., to cast headlong; *itehpelat*, Luke 4: 29.

itihtakchi, v. t., to muzzle; to bind the mouth.

itinkana, n., peace.

itinkana, n., mutual friends.

itinkana, a., happy; friendly; harmonious; kind-hearted.

itinkanomi, n., kin; kindred; kinsfolk; relations; a relative.

itikba, n., the van.

itikba, adv., prep., before, Matt. 2: 9; 5: 24; 10: 18; 14: 6; 2 Sam. 24: 4. Possibly a compound of *i* and *tikba.*

itikba hakshup, n., the foreskin.

itilauahe keyu, a., irreconcilable.

itilaui, adv.; *imitilaui*, adv.; *ikitilauo*, adv., unequally.

itilaui, a., even; equal; level; smooth, Luke 3: 5; coequal; commensurate, Mark 12: 31, 33; tantamount; *ikitilauo*, unequal; uneven; unsmooth.

itilaui, pp., evened; leveled; smoothed, etc.; matched.

itilaui, n., equality; evenness; an equivalent; a level; a par; harmony; *ikitilauo*, n., disparity; imparity; inequality.

itilaui, v. a. i., to square with; to tally.

itilaui, n., an equal; a peer.

itilaui achafa, a., harmonious; n., order; harmony.

itilaui fulota, a., harmonious.

itilaui iksho, a., irregular; unequal; rugged.

itilaui keyu, a., odd.

itilaui keyu, n., the odds; *isht ikitilauo*, n., odds.

itilauichi, v. t., to harmonize; to match; to smooth; to tally.

itilauichi, v. n., to even; to make equal, level, smooth, etc.; to equal.

itilauichi, n., a leveler.

itilauichit takolichi, v. t., to tally.

itilauit, adv., orderly; evenly.

itilauit hika, v. a. i., to range; pp., ranged.

itilauit hilechi, v. t., to range.

itim, from each other; form before vowels; one to another, Luke 2: 15; 4: 35.

itimafoa (from *afoa*) n., contention; a contest.

itimahalaia, itimakaniohmi, n., intercourse.

itimanumpa, n., a pact.

itimanumpuli, n., a conversation; a dialogue; a colloquy; a conference; a debate; a contest; reading.

itimapesa, n., a contract; a league.

itimalhpisa, n., a pact; a reconciliation.

itimolabbi, n., contention.

itimpakna, n., a striver; a rival; a competitor.

itimpakna, n., a competition; a race; see *pakna.*

itimponaklot ansha, n., mutual inquiry.

itin, from each other; to each other, etc., a form used before *ch*, *l* and *t;* to one another, John 4: 33; see *itin.*

itinchuka, n., housekeepers; man and wife; a spouse.

itinchukali, n., my husband.

itinlumanka, n., fornication, Matt. 15:19.

itinnan aiya, n., peace; reconciliation.

itinnan aiyachechi, itinnan aiyachi, n., a peacemaker; a daysman; a mediator; *pitinnan aiyachi*, our mediator.

itinnukoa, n., contention; a fracas; odds.

itinnukoa, n., a quarreler.

itinnukoa shali, a., quarrelsome.

itintakla, n., an intervention; a while.

itintakla, adv., while; whilst; among, Matt. 11: 11.

itintakla, v. a. i., to intervene.

itintakla, n., a partition; presence, as before anyone.

itintakla, adv., since; thence.

itintakla atia, n., a pass; a narrow place; a narrows.

itintanampi, n., hostility.

itintimiya, n., a race.

itintimiya, v. t., to run a race; to race.

itioba, see *itihoba*.

itipesa, n., an interview.

itisukpi, itisuppi, itisopi, n., the cheek, Matt. 5: 39.

itisukpi foni, itisuppi foni, n., the cheek bone.

itishali, see *itashali*.

itishi, n., a wrestler.

itishi, n., a match; a scuffle; a squabble; a strife; a struggle; a wrestling; see *ishi*.

itishi, v. t., to wrestle; to conflict; to strive together; to scuffle; to squabble; to strive.

itishi, n., a scuffler; a stickler; a striver.

itishi imponna, n., a wrestler.

ititakạli, see *itatakạli*.

ititakla, v. n., to be between; adv., while; so long as.

ititakla, n., an interval.

ititapa, n., a separation from each other into parts.

ito; this word is compounded with others where fire is mentioned; it is a locative signifying for fire, in fire, with fire, etc.; a reciprocal with fire.

itoashachi, v. t., to cast into a fire, Matt. 13: 50.

itobila, v. a. i., to melt; to fuse in the fire; to burn, as wood on the fire; to coal.

itobila, pp., melted; fused.

itobila, n., a fusion; a melting.

itohnichi, n., an instigation.

itohnichi, n., an instigator.

itohnichi, v. t., to instigate.

itokaha, pp., cast into the fire; Matt. 7: 19.

itokanchi, v. t., to throw them into fire.

itokạnia, v. a. i., to go away; to be cast away; see Matt. 18: 8, 9.

itola, itula, v. a. i. sing., to fall; to couch; to remain; to reside; to rest; to lie or to be, Matt. 6: 21; 13: 44; *itoyula*, Matt. 2: 2; Josh. 1: 4, *itoitola*, Matt. 17: 15[?]; *itonla*, falling; *itonlạshke*, he lies, Matt. 8: 6; *itonla*, lying, Matt. 9: 2; *intonla*, to have; *itohonla*, Matt. 17: 15; *itonla*, v. a. i., to reside.

itola, n., a fall; prostration.

itola, a., recumbent.

itolaⁿkạbi, a., brown; tanned in the sun.

itoloⁿkạbi, a., brown.

itoma, ituma, a., near; nigh; *iyi ituma*, at his feet, Matt. 15: 30.

itoma, v. n., to be near.

itoma, n., a short distance; nearness.

itomasi, itumasi, a., very near; a diminutive of the above; also v. n.

itombi, n., a box; a chest; a trunk; a bin; a coffer; a case; a coffin; a drawer; a shrine.

itombi abeha, pp., cased; coffered; put into a trunk; boxed up.

itombi abeli, v. t., to case; to coffer up; to put into a trunk; to box up.

itombi aiạlhto, n., a vat.

itombi aiimpa chuhmi ikbi, n., a cabinetmaker.

itombi alota, n., a boxful.

itombi alota achạfa, n., a box; what one box contains.

itombi fohka, pp., boxed; put into a trunk; incased.

itombi fohki, v. t., to box up; to chest; to coffin; to put in a coffin; to incase; to case.

itombi holitopa, n., the ark, Josh. 3: 3, 6, 13; 4: 16; 6: 4, 6; 8: 33.

itombi ikbi, n., a trunk-maker; a coffin-maker. It is said that the river Tombigbee was called so from the fact that a trunk-maker or box-maker lived on one of its branches.

itombi oⁿlipa, n., the lid of a box or trunk; the cover of a box; a drawer.

itombushi, n., a small box; a small drawer; a caddy; a casket; a case; an ark such as that of the Jews, etc.; a drawer.

itomushi, n., prickly heat.

itonachi, v. a. i. dual, to go there together, 1 Sam. 2: 20; Josh. 2: 1.

itopa, ittopa (*ito topa*, a bed of fire?), the mouth of a crater; the hole; the aperture; the muzzle, as of a gun; a crater; the mouth of a bottle.

itopihinla, to throw on the fire, 2 Kings 19: 18.

itot aⁿya, v. a. i., to march or travel, as an army; to burn; to ravage by fire; *itotit aya*.

itot ia, v. a. i., to go from, Luke 24: 47 (old edition).

itoti, v. a. i., to fight; to be at war.

itoti, n., war.

itotonla, v. a. i., to lie on fire, John 21: 9; *itatohonla*, Matt. 17: 15.

itowulhkạchi, v. t., to blister; *luak o*ⁿ
isht itowulhkạchi, Rev. 16: 8; see *towulh-
kạchi*.

itowulhko, v. a. i., to blister; to burn
and blister.

itowulhko, pp., scorched; blistered.

ittạnahahchi, see *itạnahạchi*.

ittopa, see *itopa*.

ittula, v. a. i., to fall.

itukawiloha, itukahiloha, n., the name
of a tree, called iron wood.

itukchabạchi, v. a. i., to feel sick at
the stomach, so as to discharge water,
etc., from the mouth.

itukchi, n., saliva; spit; spittle; slaver.

itukchi ikbi, n., to salivate; to make
saliva.

itukchi ikbi, n., salivation.

itukchuba, v. a. i., to slobber, as a young
child; to discharge saliva, etc., from the
stomach when in pain; to be sick at the
stomach.—J. Hudson, May, 1857.

itukchuba, n., a slobberer.

itukfikowa, nukfichowa; chikfikowa,
n., the hiccough.

itukfikowa, v. n., to be affected with
the hiccough.

itukholaya, v. a. i., to slobber; to discharge saliva, rheum, etc.; to drool; to
slaver.

itukholaya, n., rheum; slobber.

ituklipaya, ituklupaya, v. a. i., to drool.

ituklipaya, n., rheum; saliva; drooling
from the mouth.

ituklua, v. a. i., to be very thirsty; to
burn inwardly, as in a fever.

itukłakafa, v. a. i., to joke.

itukłakafa, n., joking; jocose.

itukłakafa, n., a joker.

itukłikali, v. a. i., to drool from the
mouth.

itukpiława, v. a. i., to discharge saliva;
to emit thick saliva.

itukpiława, n., thick saliva.

itukpokpoki, v. a. i., to froth at the
mouth, Mark 9: 18; *itukpokpokihinchi*,
Luke 9: 39.

itukpokpoki, n., froth formed by the
mouth.

ituksita, n., the edge of a fireplace;
luak iksita, Gen. 18: 6.

itukshibeli, v. a. i., to swell the lips.

itukshibeli, n., thick lips.

itukshila, a., dry; thirsty; a thirst;
hoarse; droughty.

itukshila, v. n., to be dry; *satukshila*, I
am thirsty, or, I thirst; v. a. i., to thirst.

itukshila, n., thirsty; drouth.

itukwạlahạchi, v. t., to gargle the
mouth.

itukwạtichi, v. t., to rinse the mouth;
to gargle the mouth.

itukwesoli, v. a. i., to affect the mouth,
as sugar and spirits.

itukwisli, a., astringent; having power
to pucker the mouth, as astringents; or,
like alcohol, to heat or burn in the
mouth.

itukwisli, v. n., to be astringent.

itukwislichi, v. t., to cause the mouth
to pucker; to produce an astringent
effect.

itukwołolichi, v. t., to gargle the mouth;
to rinse the mouth.

itula, itola, v. a. i., to lie; to lie down;
ittola, intensive form; *itoyula, ittoyula*,
pro. (Acts 28: 8).

ituma, see *itoma*.

itumasi, see *itomasi*.

itunla, itonla, nasal form, to lie, 2 Kings
9: 16.

iuntalali, see *haiyantalali*.

iⁿwạlwa, n., the lower part of his breast
bone; the midriff; the hollow of the
body at the stomach; the pit of the
stomach.

iyabiha, n., leggings.

iyafoa, iyạlhfoa, n., a garter.

iyafoli, v. t., to garter.

iyakaya, see *iakaiya*.

iyakchush, iyakchus, n., a toe nail; a
claw; a talon; talons; a hoof; clutches;
a fang.

iyakchush aⁿsha, pp., fanged; having
nails, claws, etc.

iyanạbi, n., ironwood; witch-hazel; name
of a creek.

iyasha, n., an iron pot that has legs.

iyasha ahalạlli, n., the ears of a pot; the
bail of a pot.

iyasha chito, n., a large pot.

iyasha isht talakchi, n., pothooks,
such as are used in removing a pot
from the fire.

iyasha oⁿłipa, n., a pot lid.

iyashushi, n., a small pot; a kettle.

iyatoboka, n., top of the head.

iyạbbiha, see *iyubiha*.

iyạbi huski, see *iyubi huski*.

iyạlhfoa, iyafoa (q. v.), a garter.

iyapi, n., leg below the knee.

iyapi champko, n.,shinbone.

iyi, n., the foot; the paw; the fin (naniyi); a hoof; a footstep; the feet, Matt. 10: 14; chiyi, Matt. 18: 8; kanchak iyi, a post; aiimpa iyi, a table leg; iyi anowa, a footstep; a track; a foottrack; a sole; a vestige.

iyi api, iyapi, n., the leg.

iyi bano, a., barefoot.

iyi bano, n., a naked foot.

iyi bano, v. n., to be barefooted.

iyi beka, a., barefooted.

iyi beka, n., naked feet.

iyi bekat anya, v. a. i., to go barefooted.

iyi bitanli, n., a chapped foot.

iyi champko, see iyinchampko.

iyi chilakto, iyi chulakto, n., a cloven foot; a cloven hoof.

iyi falakto, n., a cloven foot; a cloven hoof; a forked foot.

iyi hotupa, a., lame.

iyi hotupa, n., lameness.

iyi hotupa chohmi, adv., lamely.

iyi hotupali, v. t., to lame.

iyi hulhki, iyulhki, n., the calf of the leg.

iyi imuksak, iyi imonssak, n., the ankle.

iyi imuksak itachakalli, n., the ankle joint.

iyi intakchi, iyintakchi, v. t., to fetter.

iyi isht abeka, a., foundered; sick in the feet, as a horse.

iyi isht intalakchi, n., a fetter; a hobble.

iyi isht intalakchi, pp., fettered.

iyi itabanali, v. a. i., to cross the legs.

iyi itabanali, a., having the legs crossed; cross legged.

iyin kalankshish, iyin kolankshish (Josh. 11: 6, 9), the hamstring; the hock; from iyinkalaha and akshish.

iyin kalankshish tabli, v. t., to hock.

iyin kalaha, iyi kalaha, n., the knee; the kneepan, Luke 5: 8.

iyin kalaha ali, n., knee deep; knee high.

iyin kalaha itachakalli, n., the knee-joint.

iyin kalaha wishakchi, n., the kneepan; the point of the knee; the whirl bone; the patella; the kneecap.

iyi kallo, n., the stiff leg (a disease).

iyi kinafa, a., hipped, as a horse.

iyi kinafa, n., a hipped leg.

iyin kinali, n. pl., hipped legs.

iyin kolankshish, see iyin kalankshish.

iyin kotoba, n., the heel.

iyi linfa, n., a cramped foot; a cramp in the foot.

iyi paknaka, n., the instep; the top of the foot.

iyi pata, iyi patha, n., the sole of the foot; lit., the spread foot, or the foot spread, Josh. 1: 3; 3: 13; 4: 18; Acts 7: 5; iyi pata is the correct spelling of this word; "the spread-out foot," not "the broad foot."

iyi pata boli, v. t., to bastinade.

iyi pata paknaka, n., the instep.

iyi patha, n., a wide foot; the width of the foot.

iyi ponkshi, a., club-footed; n., a club foot.

iyin shilukwa, n., the calf of the leg.

iyi taha, a., tender-footed; having the feet worn out.

iyi taha, v. n., to be tender-footed.

iyi tanakbi, n., a crooked leg; a bent leg; a bow leg; bow shins; a., bowlegged.

iyi tanalla, n. pl., crooked legs.

iyi tikba, n., a forefoot.

iyi tilokachi, n., the foot joint; the ankle joint.

iyi tuklo, n., a biped; two feet.

iyi ushta, iyushta, n., a quadruped.

iyimmi, a., fiducial.

iyimmi, n., fiduciary.

iyinchampko, iyi champko, n., the shin; the marrow bone; the shank.

iyinchampko foni, n., the shinbone; the hock.

iyintakchi, iyi intakchi, v. t., to hobble; to fetter.

iyintalakchi, pp., hobbled; fettered.

iyinuta, a., under foot.

iyishke, n., the great toe.

iyubbachosha, n., the hip.

iyubi, iyobi, obi, n., a ham; the thigh; a hock.

iyubi achoshoa, n. pl., the hips; the hip joints.

iyubi achoshuli, n. sing., the hip; the hip joint.

iyubi huski, iyabi huski, n., a stocking; hose; hosiery.

iyubi huski isht alhfoa, n., a garter.

iyubi huski kanchi, n., a hosier; one who deals in stockings and socks.

iyubi huski kolofa, n., a sock.

iyubi huski kololi, n. pl., socks.

iyubi pakna, n., the lap.

iyubiha, iyabbiha n. pl. (from *iyi* and *abeha*), leggings; a legging; spatter-dashes.

iyubiha isht alhfoa, n., garters for leggings.

iyukbal, n., the gambrel; the hind leg of a horse.

iyukbal iti atakali, n., a gambrel; a crooked stick used by butchers.

iyukhana, n., a cross; where four corners meet.

iyukhanna, pp., crossed.

iyukhannali, v. t., to cross; to make a cross.

iyulhki, see *iyi hulhki.*

iyulhki foni, n., the leg bone.

iyup, n., a son-in-law; *chiyup*, your son-in-law.

iyupi, v. a. i.; cf. *nanta hatuk oⁿ miⁿko yaⁿ iyupi la hinla cho?* 1 Sam. 18: 18, 21, 22.

iyush ali, n., the little toe; the end toe.

iyush tikba, n., the long toe; the toe next to the large toe.

iyushi, n., the little toe; the small toes, but *iyishke* is a toe.

iyushi wishakchi, n., tiptoe.

iyushta, see *iyi ushta.*

k, a limiting particle and suffix; *k* is compounded with *at*, *aⁿ*, and *ah;* *k* has reference to the preceding word; *at* is nom. and agrees; *aⁿ* is obj. and is governed by *k;* *iak fehna*, Mark 13: 1; *katiohmik*, Matt. 13: 4; *anumpulik fehna*, Matt. 9: 18, a demonstrative or a definite article, the. The examples show this, and that it is not a contraction; *antak fehna; talapik*, Luke 3: 1; *nunak fehna, ahashwak fehna*, Luke 3: 2[?]. *Ilappa, ilappak; nanta, nantak; yamma, yammak; achik fena akoⁿ*, John 4: 27[?]. *k* is the sign of the demonstrative and definite article pronouns, as *ak, hak, yak, kak, mak.* It follows verbs and nouns also, *k* being suffixed to the preceding word.

k, sign of the past tense, as *chumpak*, which may be a contraction from *chumpa tuk*, he bought; he did buy; here *k* limits the act of buying. It is thus like don't in English. *k* is a contracted form of the adv. *kamo*, as in *ialek*, I went (for *iali kamo*). *k* is here a demonstrative of action, in the past tense, indefinite, or aorist; used in the nasal form, *lakoⁿffik.*

ka, art. and rel. pro., in the accus. case or dative case, the which; the one which; that which, John 4: 14, 29. *puta ka*, these, in the ob. case, Matt. 1: 20; 2: 3; *k* is distinctive; *a*, objective.

ka, kah, adv., perhaps; *ishla ka*, Luke 4: 34[?]; spoken by way of inquiry. The interrogative tone makes it adverbial.

ka, euphonic, for sound's sake, in the neg. forms of verbs, future tense, etc.; *akpesokachi, akpesokahe, akpesoka hinla, akpesoka wa, akpesoka heto;* the *k* is suffixed to the verb. Perhaps this *k* has a designating sense, as *ke* and *ki*, in the neg. form; *akpeso ketuk, akpesoketuk, akpesakitok, akpesokitok.*

kabak, n., a noise made by a single blow; a blow; a knock.

kabakachi, v. a. i., to make a noise.

kabakachi, n., pl., knocks; blows.

kabakachi, v. a. i., to ring; to sound when knocked.

kabuk, n., a blow; a rap; a knock, made on a hollow thing, as a hollow tree.

kabukachi, v. a. i., to ring.

kachakachechi, v. t., to cause to squeak.

kachaⁿya, pp., cut with shears.

kacheli, v. t. sing., to cut with shears or scissors; *kacholi*, pl.

kacheli, n., one who cuts with shears; a shearer.

kachiⁿ, sign of first future indic., neg. form, as *iklokachiⁿ*, he will not come.

kachoa, kachowa, a., having an edge or border like saw teeth or yam leaves; see *kalaskachi.*

kachombi, kachumbi, kochombi, a., hard, as a swelling; swelled; caked.

kachombi, v. n., to be hard, etc.; *hichi at kachombi; ofosik ikonla yat shatalit kachomba*, the puppy's neck is swollen hard.

kachombi, n., a hard swelling; a cake in the flesh; a bunch; a cancer; a cancerous swelling; a scirrhus; a tumor.

kachombi toba, v. a. i., to swell; to become swollen.

kachowa, see *kachoa.*

kachumbi, see *kachombi*, and *kochombi.*

kafakbi, n., a dent; a dint.

kafakbi, a., concave.

kafakbi, v. n., to be concave.

kafakbi, pp., made concave; rendered concave; dented; excavated.

kafakbichi, v. t., to make it concave; to dent; to dint; to excavate.

kafali, pp., put into a crack or fork.

kafalichi, v. t. sing., to put into a crack; to crowd into a place between two logs; *holisso kia, chufak kia aboha ititakla kafalichi.*

kafanli, n. f., a gore of land or in a garment.

kafoli, pp. pl., put into a crack; laid up in a crack; *kafonli,* n. f.

kafolichi, v. t., to put up in a crack.

kaha, v. a. i. pl., to fall down; to lie down; to fall, Matt. 13: 4, 7, 8 (seeds fell); 15: 14; 17: 6; *kaiyaha, ibakaha, alhkaha.*

kaha, pp., fallen down; laid down; staked; wagered; *holisso hat kaha; kaiyaha; itibakaha,* confounded together; put together; *itibalhkaha,* summed up.

kaha, n., a fall; a bet; that which is laid down; a lay; a wager.

kahama, pp., trodden down; *hashuk at kahama; kahammi,* v. t.

kahama, n., a trail; that which is trodden down.

kahat manya, kahat manya, v. n., to be down; to lie about, as on the ground.

kahato; in *nana kia ikkanihmo kahato ikahno hosh.* Sermon: Duties to Children, p. 5.

kahammi, v. t., to tread down; to bend down; to trample down, as grass.

kahammi, n., a trampler; one that treads down.

kahammichi, v. t., to cause to trample down.

kahe, sign of 2d per. indic. mood, neg. form, as *iklokahe,* he will not come.

kaheto, sign of 2d per. indic. mood, double neg. form; as *iklokaheto,* he will not not come—i. e., he will surely come.

kahinla, sign of neg. pot. mood, *iklo ka hinla.*

kahioke, sign of 2d per. indic. mood, neg. form, with a word that terminates a sentence, meaning, to give a little more strength and dignity, or fullness, of expression, to a sentence.

kahkahachi, v. a. i., to caw, as a crow.

kahpuli, kapuli, v. t. pl., to lay them down; to put them away or out, as horses to feed; to set, Josh. 4: 8; 8: 13; 10: 27; *isuba kahpulli ashachi* is used for many; *ilakapuli,* to put by themselves.

kaiakachi, v. a. i., to waddle; *kaiakahanchit anya,* to waddle along.

kaialli, n., a pacer; a pace; a racking pace; *kaiallichi,* v. t., to make (a horse) pace.

kaiilli, kaialli, v. a. i., to pace; to rack (local).

kaiolichi, v. t., to affect the mouth, as in eating peaches with the fuzz on; to set on edge, as teeth.

kaiya, v. a. i., to englut.

kaiya, a., full; well fed; filled; pregnant, as an animal; having young; before birth, Matt. 14: 20.

kaiya, v. n., to be full; to be well fed; to be pregnant, applied to animals; to be with young; to teem; *sakaiya,* I am full, Matt. 15: 33, 37.

kaiya, n., a bellyful.

kaiyachi, v. t., to fill; to feed well.

kak (see *ak, hak,* and their compounds), the; used chiefly after verbs. It is found also after nouns; *umba kakosh,* it rains that is it (*kocha yan kapassachi*). Compounds: *kaka; koi hannali kak ahinla,* six miles that may be (the distance)—*kakahe,* Matt. 13: 39; *ont imisht-aiyopi kakahe—kakano—kakat—kakato kakanto,* nasal form—*kakat — kakato— kakbano—kakbat—kakbato—kakhe—kak-heno—kakheto—kaki—kakilla,* but the, Matt. 16: 4—*kakinli,* adv.—*kakinli,* p r o.— *kakint — kakkia; aiishikakkia,* Matt. 13: 22—*kakon; yohmi kakon,* Matt. 13: 13; 14: 5, *lakofichila hinlakakon,* I should heal them, Matt. 13: 15, *chumpa kakon,* Matt. 13: 44, 46, 48—*kakocha— kakoka; paska kileshokakoka,* it is because we have taken no bread, Matt. 16: 7—*kakoke; ishikakoke,* Matt. 13: 20; *haklo kakoke, ikanotoba kakoke,* Matt. 13: 22; *akostininchi kakoke,* Matt. 13: 23; *moma kakoke,* Matt. 13: 28; *anki aba binili kakoke,* my Father which is in Heaven, Matt. 16: 17—*kakokano—kak-okat—kakokato—kakokia— kakona—kak-osh,* John 4: 26; *yohmi kakosh,* Matt. 14:

7; 15: 11, 20; 18: 8—*kakoshba*, John 4: 18 [?]—*kakot.*

kakaachi, v. a. i., to caw, as a crow.

kakaachi, n., a caw.

Kaⁿkish, Kaⁿkilish, n., Congress.

kalafa, pp., scratched; marked; *iyi ąt kalafa; aiimpa yąt kalafa.*

kalafa, n. sing., a scratch.

kalakbi, n., see *kolokbi.*

kalaki, kalahki, n., a lizard; a long slender lizard.

kalakshi, a., despised; disgraced; ruined, as to character; without credit; broken; abject; degraded; cashiered.

kalakshi, pp., debased; decried; depreciated; exploded; reduced; cursed, 2 Kings, 9: 34.

kalakshi, v. n., to be despised; to be cursed, Josh. 9: 23.

kalakshi, n., a disgrace; a curse.

kalakshichi, v. t., to disgrace; to degrade; to cashier; to debase; to decry; to deface; to depreciate; to dishonor; to explode; to reduce; to slur; to curse.

kalakshichi, n., one who degrades, etc.; an exploder.

kalampi, akalampi, v. a. i., to freeze.

kalampi, a., frozen; congealed; frost bitten.

kalampi, v. n., to be frozen; *iyi ąt kalampi; oka yąt kalampi.*

kalampi, pp., frozen; congealed; *ikkalampo,* a., uncongealed.

kalampichi, v. t., to freeze.

kalancha, a., rancid; brackish.

kalancha, v. n., to be rancid; to be brackish; *nipi ąt kalancha; oka yąt kalancha.*

kalancha, n., rancidity; brackishness.

kalaⁿska, n., a small frog; a name of one kind of frog; other frogs have other names, as *halonląbi; kiba; shuⁿkątti,* etc.

kalaskąchi, kachoa, a., having a border like saw teeth.

kalasha, pp., cut with shears, *isht kalasha,* n., shears.

kalasha, n., that which is cut with shears.

kalaffi, v. t., to scratch.

kalaffi, n., a scratcher.

kalan, n., a gallon.

kalan tuklo, n., a peck; two gallons.

kalashli, v. t., to cut with shears.

kaⁿlhkuha, v. a. i., to cackle; to cluck.

kaⁿlhkuha, n., a cackler; a cackling.

kalochi, see *kąllochi.*

kaloⁿshi, n., the windpipe of a fowl.

kalowa, pp., notched; v. t., to notch.

kalowa, n., a notch.

kalush, n., a cabbage; a collard.

kalushąpa, n., a cabbage eater; a cabbage worm.

kalaⁿfa, n., phlegm.

kałahąchechi, v. t., to cause a rustling.

kałahąchi, v. a. i., to rustle, as leaves; *hąshtąp ąt kałahąchi.*

kałahąchi, n., a rustling.

kałali, kąłali, v. t. sing., to break open, as an egg; to contuse; to crash; to crush; to open; *kąla,* pp.

kałama, a., strong; rancid; musty.

kałama, v. n., to be strong or rancid.

kałama, n., rancidity; must; a sour smell, taste, etc.

kałamąchi, v. t., to make it rancid.

kali, v. t., to bet; to wager; to lay down, Josh. 2: 14; to stake, as a wager; to lay; to venture; *isuba kali,* v. t., to bet a horse; to stake a horse; *iⁿkali,* to bet with him, or against him; to wage; *itiⁿkali,* to bet against each other; *ilekali,* to lay himself down, as an offering; *echim ilekalishke,* Josh. 2: 14; *ibakali,* to put with; *itibakali,* to mix with; to confound together; *itibakalit hotina,* v. t., to spurn.

kali, n., one who bets.

kali, n., a wager; a stake; a lay; a bet.

kałoha, v. a. i. pl., to burst open and spill.

kałoha, pp., burst open; *itąlhfoa yąt kałoha.*

kałoha, n. pl., the bursting open; those which are burst open.

kałoli, v. t. pl., to burst them open, as eggs, kegs, etc.; to break them; to crack them; *akaⁿkushi aⁿ kałoli;* see *kałali.*

kama, conj. but; adv.; *nafohka achukma kąt pimasha kama; ishithaiyanahinla kama,* because that thou mayest understand, see Acts 24: 11; probably this *kama* is composed of *k* and *ama.*

kamak ąt kąnia; *masheli kamak ąt kąnia,* entirely fair weather; *ninak oklili kamak ąt kąnia,* Egyptian darkness.

kamali, v. t., to stop; to bung; *iⁿkamali,* to bung it; to plug; to preclude.

kamąssa, a., strong; firm; hard; brave; hearty; aged; ripe in years; mature; callous; inveterate; permanent; resolute; rigid; vigorous; solid; stable; steadfast; stiff; straitlaced; tough; unpliant; unshaken; *nakni kamąssa piahoke*, we are brave men; *ikkamąsso*, unhardened.

kamąssa, v. n., to be strong.

kamąssa, v. a. i., to stiffen; *itakamąssa*, to settle.

kamąssa, pp., strengthened; confirmed; hardened; stiffened; *itakamąssa*, pressed together; strengthened by each other; pinned; *akamąssa*, sealed; *ikakamąsso*, a., unsealed.

kamąssa, n., strength; firmness; hardness; rigidity; rigor; solidity; steadiness; stiffness.

kamąssa, adv., rigidly; stiffly.

kamąssalli, v. t., to strengthen; to confirm; to harden; to stiffen; to toughen; *itakamąssalli*, to press them together, as planks on a floor; to paste; to pin.

kamąssalli, n., a strengthener; a supporter; a hardener.

kamąssalli, a., strong; ripe in years; *nakni kamąssalli*.

kamąssalli, v. n., to be strong.

kamba, adv., conj., because.

kamil, n., a camel.

kamil hishi, n., camel hair.

kamo, kąmo, adv., signifying also the immediate past tense; formed from *k* and *amo; alikamo*, I said so; when *li* or the last syllable before *kamo* is accented, *a* is changed to *ą*, as *pisalikąmo*, I saw it. See *chamo*. It implies that the speaker has knowledge of what he speaks and not the hearer; *kąmo* is sometimes contracted to *k; chumpak, ialek;* for *kamo*, in the nom. case, see 2 Sam. 18: 9; *kamo ont iatok*.

kamomi, adv., (derived from *ka* and *ąmohmi iksho ka ąmohmi*, in full), in the least degree; in the smallest amount; used with neg. verbs as *iksho kamomi*, none at all; *ikachukmo kamomi*, good for nothing at all.

kampila, v. t. pl., to send; to throw; to cast away; to reject, Matt. 8: 12; 13: 40. Perhaps this is derived from *kanchi* and *pila. kanchi*, sing., means to sell, but *kampila* does not.

kana, n., an intimate, Matt. 11: 19; a friend; usually written with a prefix pronoun, as *aⁿkana*, my friend; *iⁿkana*, his friend; friendship; grace; kindness; *iⁿkana*, v. t., to befriend him; to show kindness; *hąchiⁿkanali, hąshiⁿkanahe*, Josh. 2: 12; *ikiⁿkano*, a., inimical; v. n., to be inimical; unkind; n., unkindness; *itiⁿkana*, to befriend each other; to favor each other; to harmonize; *itiⁿkanąt aⁿsha*, a., peaceable; *itiⁿkana*, n., mutual friends; friends; *itiⁿkana*, n., amity; friendship; harmony; peace; *itiⁿkanali*, n., my friend; the one whom I befriend; *iⁿkana*, a., friendly; humane; kind; officious; propitious; *iⁿkana iksho*, a., unfriended; *iⁿkana keyu*, adv., unfriendly.

kanakli, kannakli, v. a. i., to dodge; to move out of the way; a single motion like *halakli;* (1 Sam. 19: 10).

kanaktakli, v. a. i., to toss the head.

kanali, kanąlli, v. a. i., to move; to step one side; to remove; to go; to shift; to come away or to go away; to depart; to hitch; *kanąlli*, imp., move; get out of the way.

kanali, pp., moved; see *kanąlli*.

kanali, n., a mover; a moving; see *kanąlli*.

kanalichi, kanąllichi, v. t., to move; to remove; to take out of the way.

kananali, kąnanali, v. a. i. freq., to keep moving about at or near one place.

kananant aⁿya, v. a. i., to be moving about.

kanąlla hinla, a., movable.

kanąllahe keyu, a., immovable; immutable; stationary.

kanąlli, pp., removed; *ikkanąllo*, a., unmoved; unremoved; see *kanali*.

kanąlli, see *kanali*.

kanąlli, n., a moving; a mover; a departure; a shift; see *kanali*.

kanąllichahe keyu, a., immovable; immutable.

kanąllichi, v. t., to remove; to displace; to move; to translate; to obviate; to take away; to transfer; to unsettle; 2 Sam. 24: 10; see *kanalichi*.

kanąllichi, n., a shifter.

kanąllichit binilichi, v. t., to remove and settle; to colonize.

kanạllit aⁿya, v. a. i., to move along, and, as an adverb, gradually.

kanạllit binili, v. a. i., to move and settle.

kanạli, v. a. i., not to go far.

kanạpa, n., an injury in some mysterious witchcraft-like way; *isht kanạpa.*—J. Hudson.

kancha hinla, a., salable; vendible.

kanchahe keyu, a., unsalable.

kanchạk, n., a corn crib; a corn house; a barn; a corn loft; a crib; a garner; a granary, Matt. 6: 26.

kanchạk fohki, v. t., to harvest; to put up in the crib.

kanchạk foka, pp., harvested; put up in the crib.

kanchi, v. t. sing., to sell; Matt. 13: 44, 46; to cede; to grant; to transfer; to alienate; to convey; to dispose of; to part with; to bargain away; to deal; to deliver; to discard; to dispose of; to eject; to fling; to forsake; to leave; to put away, Matt. 5: 31; to reject; to throw away; to renounce; to cast away, Matt. 18: 8, 9; to hurl; to pass; to repudiate; to shift; to spend; to transfer; to vend; to waste; to wane; *isht kanchi,* v. t., to take away; *ạbit kanchi,* to do the uttermost; *kaiyanchi,* Matt. 5: 26; *ilekanchi,* to throw himself away; to deny himself, Matt. 16: 24; to give himself; *ilekaiyanchi; itiⁿkanchi,* to sell to each other, or for each other; *ilap imanumpa kanchi,* v. t., to throw away his own word, or, v. a. i., to recant; *imokla kanchi,* n., a traitor to his own people; *isht tahpạtạt kanchi,* n., a vendue; an auction.

kanchi, n., an alienation; a sale; a cession; a transfer; a rejection; a throw; a vent.

kanchi, n., a seller; a caster; a rejecter; a thrower; a vender.

kanchi, a., sale; unaccepted.

kanchi keyu, a., unsold; ungranted; unceded.

kanchichi, v. t., to cause to sell.

kanichi, kạnihchi, v. t., to do with, Luke 4: 34; Matt. 27: 19; *nana kanihchi,* to chasten; to chastise, Luke 6: 11.

kanih, a contraction for *kanihma,* as *kanih pilla pit kaiyanchahe aⁿ imabahanchi; kani,* the root (like *katih, nantih, nanih,* and *mih*) and *h.*

kanihma, see *kanima.*

kanihmi, a., convalescent; better; improved in health; less affected with disease. *kanihmit ia,* v. a. i., to mend; to improve in health; *kanihmit taha,* pp., mended, etc.; *iⁿkanihmi,* he is better.

kanihmi, v. n., to be convalescent or better; to get better; to improve; see Luke 13: 24, to be able; to effect; *nan iⁿkanihmi,* v. t., to ail him; to trouble him; to affect him with something that produces uneasiness; see *nan iⁿkanihmi; iⁿkanihmi,* he is better, or it is better for him.

kanihmichi, v. t., to cause to get better.

kanihmit ia, v. a. i., to mend; to get better.

kanihmit taha, pp., mended; recovered.

kaniⁿlau iksho, a., brave; not to be conquered.

kanima, a., some, as to place or persons; any, Matt. 18: 8.   In Josh. 7: 3; 8: 17, used for "or," as in Ai or Bethel. *kanimakia,* some one; any one; either; with a neg. verb, none, none of them; *kanimako; kanimashinli.*

kanima, v. n., to be some.

kanima, v. a. i.; *nan ashạchi kạt kanima hatukma,* 1 Sam. 14: 38; *kanimaia,* imp., hence; go off.

kanima, kanihma, adv., somewhere; a while; some time; hence, Matt. 4: 10; whither, Josh. 2: 5; where; for a season; *kanimaia,* Luke 4: 13 [?]; *kanima minti;* where, Matt. 2: 4; 6: 21; *kanima aboli,* Matt. 8: 20; where to lay, Josh. 1: 7.

kanima inla kia, adv., elsewhere.

kanima kia, adv., anywhere; somewhere; or, whencesoever; wheresoever; wherever; with a neg. verb, nowhere.

kanima kia, pro., anyone.

kanima kia keyu, adv., nowhere; in no place; no way; no ways.

kanima moma, adv., everywhere; every place; all about, Luke 4: 37 [?].

kanimachi, kanimanchi, a., partial; *ikkanimancho,* a., impartial; pp., unbiased; *ikkanimancho,* n., impartiality; *kanimanchi keyu,* pp., unbiased; "is no respecter," Acts 10: 34.

kanimachi, kanimali, v. a. i., v. n., to be partial; to despise, Matt. 5: 44; 18: 10; to act partially; *kanimanchi,* n. f., to act with partiality; *kanimachilahe keyu*, to despise; *kanimanchi*, nasal form, Matt. 6: 24.

kanimampo, a., which of two; either of two; whichsoever; *kanimampo hon; kanimampo hokia; kanimampo hosh; kanimampo hot.*

kanimampo keyu, a., neuter; neutral; neither.

kanimampo kia, adv., either.

kanimash inli, adv., sometimes.

kanimash inli kia, adv., whenever.

kanimi, v. a. i., to be some; it is definite, and *kaniohmi*, distinctive.

kanimi, kanimi, a., some; somebody; certain, Luke 6:.2; Mark 2: 6; 12: 5; 13: 4, 5, 7, 8; some (seeds); *kanimi kat ansha, kanimimat ia; kanimi hosh abeka; kanimi hon chumpa sabanna*, I wish to buy some one; *na kanimi keyu*, a., sound; "nothing the matter;" *nan ikinkanihmo ka hioke*, "he shall be free," Matt. 15: 5.

kanimichi, v. t. (definite), to do it somehow or in any way; *kanimihchi*, v. t., Mark 11: 18; Matt. 10: 19; 12: 14; *kanimiechi, kaniemichi*, pro. form; *kanimichit ikbit chibannakmat ikbi; kanimihinchi*, v. t., Acts 10: 39.

kanimusi, see *kaniohmusi*.

kaniohmi, n. (distinctive), matter; a measure; manner; fashion; an occasion; an occurrence; parts of; *Kalili inkaniohmi*, Matt. 2: 22; face; appearance, Matt. 16: 3; *pinkaniohmi*, our business, Josh. 2: 14, 20.

kaniohmi (see *akaniohmi*), a., any, as *nitak kaniohmi*, any day, Matt. 4: 6; being of some sort or of some kind; in some way or time, Luke 13: 25; some; certain, Matt. 9: 3; 12: 38; some, i, e., a part, Josh. 8: 22; *wak kaniohmi chimalachin*, I will give you a cow of some kind.

kaniohmi, v. t., to do; *Chisas at akaniohmitokan*, John 21: 25; Acts 1: 1; Matt. 6: 3.

kaniohmi, v. n., to be of some sort, Matt. 5: 20; to be in some way or time, etc., Luke 5: 19; Matt. 26: 24; 10: 42; *kaniohmi*, is the responding form of *katiohmi*, or *katiohmi* is transitive and *kaniohmi* intransitive; *kaniohmahe ikithano*, a., dubious, Luke 18: 17; *kaniohmit offo*,

how they grow, Matt. 6: 28; *kaniohmi tokba; kanioht*, a contracted form.

kaniohmi, v. a. i., to do somehow; *kaniohmilahe keyu.*

kaniohmi, n., a sort; a kind; a fact, *okfa kaniohmi moma*, valleys of every kind, i. e., all valleys, Luke 3: 5.

kaniohmi chishba, a., uncertain; in a way unknown.

kaniohmi chishba, v. n., to be uncertain; to be in a way unknown.

kaniohmi foka hon, adv., when, Josh. 2: 18; 3: 3.

kaniohmi kash, adv., when, in time past.

kaniohmi kia, adv., somehow; in any way whatever; of any kind; however, Matt. 18: 7.

kaniohmichi, v. t., to cause it to be somehow or of some fashion; to do to, Josh. 8: 2; 9: 3; to do unto; to do as a custom, 1 Sam. 2: 13, 22; to do, Ps. 37: 8; to improve opportunity, Matt. 26: 16.

kaniohmiho, adv., somehow.

kaniohmikma, a., occasional; some time; sometimes.

kaniohmusi, kanimusi, n., a particle; diminutive of *kaniohmi.*

kanliksho, n., tenderness.

kanliksho, a. (from *kallo* and *iksho*), tender; not strong; not hard; not tough; fragile.

kanliksho, v. n., to be tender.

kannakli, a form of *halakli, shabakli, chiksanakli*; see 1 Sam. 19: 10.

kanni, see *kani.*

kano, art., the, the which, a distinctive art. pro. indicating contrast; the letter *k* is definite with *ano*, distinctive; also a rel. pro., *hatak puta kano*, Matt. 6: 18.

kanon, adv., here and there; used in the sing; *kanon pit ishchaffichashke*, send her away to another place, Matt. 15: 23; for pl. see Acts 5: 40; *kanon pit hika*, to stagger; *kanont kanchi; kanon pit kampila*, to throw them away; *kanon pit tileli*, to send them off. This is sometimes written *kanompit*, Matt. 13: 36; 15: 23.

kanon, n., different places, or another place; *kanon* may be a contraction of *kaniohmi*, like *katio* of *katiohmi.*

kanoha, art., rel. pro., the, the which.

kanohmi, a., how many, Matt. 16: 9; some; several, Luke 5: 18; various, used to make the plural number, as *hatak kanohmi*, men, Josh. 7: 2; *hatak kanohmi hosh minti.*

kanohmi, v. n., to be some.

kanohmi kia, howsoever.

kanomi, n., relations; kindred; used with prefix pronouns, as *akanomi, chi^nkanomi, i^nkanomi,* etc.; *iti^nkanomi,* kinsfolk; mutual relations.

kanomi, a., related; *i^nkanomi,* related to him; *iti^nkanomi,* related to each other.

kanomi, v. n., to be related; *ha̱shiti^nkanomi,* you are related to each other.

kanomona, a. (from *kanomi* and *ona*), several; many, John 2: 12; some; sundry.

kanomona, v. n., to be numerous or many; to amount to several.

kanomona, n., a number; a parcel; a quantity.

kanompit, Matt. 13: 36; see *kano^n* for the correct orthography of *kanompit.*

kanomusi, kanimusi, a., very few; very little; a few; a little, Josh. 7: 3.

kanomusi, v. n., to be small, little, etc.

kanomusi, n., a small quantity; a small number; a pittance, Matt. 15: 34.

kantak, n., the kind of brier from which bread is made; a smilax.

kantak a̱pi, n., a bramble; a brier.

kantak pa̱ska, n., kantak bread; brier-root bread.

kantali, v. a. i., to press; to crowd, like the houses in a city, or people, Mark 5: 27, 31; see *akantali.*

kanumpa, n., name of a weed which grows in low grounds.

kapali, v. t., to hold in the mouth; to put into one's own mouth; *hakchuma kapali,* he holds tobacco in his mouth.

kapali, pp., put in the mouth.

kapali, n., that which is put in the mouth, as a bridle bit.

kapali isht talakchi, n., bridle reins; a rein; see *isuba kapali,* etc.

kapali isht talakchi nushkobo foka, n., headstall.

kapalichi, v. t., to put into the mouth of another; pl. *kapa.*

kapassa, a., cold; icy; frosty; fresh; frigid; gelid; phlegmatic; raw; repulsive; rigorous; wintry; *lukfi kapassa chohmi,* clay cold.

kapassa, v. n., to be cold. This does not mean the sensation of cold; *hochukwa* means to feel cold, to experience cold, as a sensation.

kapassa, n., coldness; a cold; frigidity; iciness; strangeness.

kapassa, pp., cooled; damped; refreshed; *ta̱li a̱t kapassa̱t taha.*

kapassa, v. a. i., to cool.

kapassa fehna, a., hard; very cold.

kapassachi, a., cool; *kucha kapassachi,* cool weather.

kapassachi, v. n., to be cool.

kapassachi, v. t., to cool; to make cool; to refrigerate; to shadow; to shade, or to refresh by shade.

kapassalli, v. t., to cool; to refresh; to refrigerate; *umba kakosh kucha ya^n kapassachi,* the rain cools the weather.

kapash, n.; *uski kapash,* cane tongs; a large cane is bent double; *luak isht kapash,* fire tongs (not used).

kapko, n., a large hickory nut.

kapucha, n., ball sticks, such as the Choctaw use at ball plays.

kapulhachi, v. a. i., to crunch.

kapuli, see *kahpuli.*

kapuli, v. a. i., to champ.

kapuli, n., a champer.

kapulichi, v. a. i., to champ.

kapun, n., a shagbark hickory nut.

kapun a̱pi, n., a shagbark hickory.

kasali, kasalichi, v. t., to strike with a stick.

kasmo, kosmo, n., a turkey-feather shawl or robe worn by the ancient Choctaw.

kasolichi, v. t. sing., to thump; *alla nushkobo ya^n kasolichi,* to thump the child's head with the thumb and finger.

kasuha, pl., to thump.

kash, ka̱sh, immediate past tense article and rel. pro.; see *ash, hash, chash,* (which is remote past tense,) etc., adv., last; late; lately, Matt. 2: 21; *puta kash,* the said, i. e., plural, Matt. 8: 16; 11: 20; Compounds: *kashano— kasha̱to— kashi^n— kashinli,* Matt. 5: 25—*kashke— kashket,* rel. pro., that which; the same that; as *ali kashket,* that is what I said; this form is not much used; it is called a hard expression, — *kashkia—kashki^n, kashkint*, rel. pro., nasal form, being the same; that which—*kasho^n; nani tuklo aiena kasho^n*, the two fishes also, Matt. 14: 19; *nana kasho^n*, whatsoever, Matt. 15: 5—*kashocha—kashoka—kashokako^n — kashokakocha — kashokakosh— kashokano—kashoke—kashokia—kashokat—kashokato—kashona—kashosh*; *amintili kashosh*, Matt. 12: 44; Josh. 2: 5; 6: 8—*kashot*.

kashapa, v. a. i., to divide.

kashapa, pp., divided, as a part, in two; parted; subtracted; *itakashapa*, divided into two; halved; separated; sundered; divided against itself, Matt. 12: 25; *ikkashapo*, a., undivided.

kashapa, n., a half; a part; a division; a proportion; a share; a snack.

kashapa ishi, v. a. i., to share.

kashabli, v. t. sing., to divide; to separate; to part; to subtract; *itakashabli*, v. t., to half; to separate from each other into two parts; to sunder.

kashablit ishi, v. a. i., to share.

kasheho, a. fem. gender, old; aged.

kasheho, v. n., to be old or aged; *ohoyo hat kasheho; isuba hat kasheho*.

kasheho, n., age; anility; old age.

ka^nshi, n., a bird which eats poke berries and black-gum berries.

ka^nshka lusa, n., the name of a fish.

ka^nshkachi, v. a. i., to squeak; to grate, as the hinges of a door.

ka^nshkachi, n., a squeaking; a grating.

kashke, neg. form of *ashke; as ialashke*, let me go, or I will go; *akaiyukashke*, let me not go; I will not go.

kashkoa, kashkoa, pl. of *kashapa*, v. a. i., to divide; to separate; *kashkoli*, v. t., to divide.

kashkoa, pp., divided; separated; *itakashkoa*.

kashkoa, n., divisions; parts; portions.

kashofa, a., tidy; unspotted; clean; cleanly; immaculate; pure; neat; null; *ikkashofo*, a., impure; unclean; uncleansed; unfaded; unpardoned; unrepealed; unwashed.

kashofa, v. n., to be clean.

kashofa, v. a. i., to fade.

kashofa, pp., faded; cleansed; forgiven; erased; blotted out; clarified; cleared; effaced; expunged; expurgated; fined;

freed; fulled, as cloth; justified; obliterated; pardoned, Luke 5: 20; purgated; purified; quashed; razed; refined; vacated; wiped; *chi^nkashofahoke*, Matt. 9: 2; 12: 31; *i^nkashofo*, remitted to him.

kashofa, n., a cleansing; a pardon; a justification; a purgation; a purification; cleanness; fairness; fineness; refinement; tidiness; *ikkashofo*, impurity; *iki^nkashofo*, a., unremitted.

kashofa hinla, a., pardonable, venial.

kashofahe keyu, a., unfading; unpardonable.

kashofat, adv., neatly.

kashoffi, (*kasholi*, pl.,) v. t., to clean; Matt. 8: 2; to cleanse; to wash clean; to erase; to cross out; to forgive; Matt. 6: 12, Luke 5: 21; to cancel; to clarify; to efface; to expunge; to expurgate; to fade; to fine; to free; to justify; to null; to obliterate; to pardon; to purge; to purify; to quash; *isht kashoffi*, to offset.

kashoffi, n., a cleanser; a justifier.

kashoffi, n., a purgation; a purification; a rasure; a refinement.

kashoffichi, v. t., to make clean; to clean another; to bleach; to blanch; to cleanse; to crop; to erase; to expunge; to expurgate; to full or scour cloth; to obliterate; to purify; to rase; to refine; to repeal; to try; to vacate.

kashoffichi, n., a refiner.

kashoffichit kanchi, v. t., to cancel; to forgive; to blot out; to wipe out; to erase.

kashokachi, v. a. i., to rub against.

kashokachi, pp., wiped; rubbed; brushed; scoured.

kasholichi, v. t., to wipe; to brush; to scour; to rub; to dust; to mop; to scrub; to swab; from *kasholi*.

kasholichi, n., a scourer; a wiper, etc.; one who wipes; *kasholihinchi*, freq., Luke 7: 44.

katali, v. a. i., to gird; to pinch; *isht ilakatali*, they girded themselves with, Gen. 3: 7; *katanli*, nasal form; *ilakatali*, to gird one's self.

katanli, n., a girding; strictness.

katanli, a., girded; drawn tight, as a ligature; bound tight; close; strict; tight.

katanli, adv., tightly.

katanlichi, v. t., to draw tight round another person; to bind tight; to brace; to pinch; to squeeze; to straighten; to tighten; *kataya*, pp.

katapa, v. a. i., to divide; to separate; to break.

katapa, pp., divided; cut off; intercepted; headed, as cattle separated; stemmed; withheld; precluded; *inkatapa*, he is cut off, or to cut him off.

katapa, n., a division.

katapoa, v. a. i. pl., to divide.

katapoa, pp., divided; *ikatapoa*.

katapoli, v. t. pl., to cut them off; to intercept; to head; *inkatapoli*, to cut them off; to head them.

kataya, pp., squeezed; see *katanli*.

katabli, v. t., to divide; to separate; to intercept; to fend; to withhold; *wak inkatabli*, head the cow; stop the cow; *inkatabli*, to preclude; to shed; to stop; to trammel.

katablichi, v. t., to cause to head, or intercept, or to do it, i. e., to head by another.

kati, kati, a word used in compound words; *katiohmi, katihmi;* see *kani*.

katichi, see *katihchi*.

katiffi, v. t., to cut off; sing. *katoli*.

katih, why; *nanta katih; kanih, kati,* or *katih* is used in compounding words.

katih (from *kani*), *katit hashmanyah?*, what are you about? Similar verb to *mih;* also cf. *nantih* from *nanih*.

katihchi, katichi, katichi, v. t., to do with; *nanta ishtishkatichachin?* what will you do with it?

katihmi (from *katih* and *mih*); *nan katih-miho?* why? Mark 2: 7.

katima, katima (from *kati* and *ma*), adv., where; anywhere; whence; whither; also pro., which, *katima kakosh,* Mark 12: 28; *hachi katima,* what of ye, Matt. 12: 11.

katimafoka, adv., whereabout.

katimaho, where; which; *hash katima kakosh,* which of you, Matt. 6: 27.

katimahosh, where; which.

katimaian, which; *hatak katimaia,* which man?

katimakakosh, what, Matt. 7: 9; *hatak hash katimakakosh.*

    atimakakosh, whether of two, Mark 2: 9; *katimampokakosh,* Matt. 9: 5.

katimakon, where; whence, John 1: 48; which; whence, Matt. 2: 2; 13: 54; 15: 33; *katimak,* from *katima* and *k,* definite.

katimampo, which of two; whether, Luke 5: 23; whichsoever.

katimampo aiyukali kakosh, which of all, Luke 6: 9 [?].

katimampo ho, which; whom, in objective case.

katimampo ka, which; *tanampo katima-mampo ka,* which of the two guns.

katimampo kakon, which.

katimampo kakosh, which one is it of the two, Matt. 9: 5; *hash katimampo kakosh hashiachi; katimampo kakosh ahchiba kat iklauwo cho?* "whether (of two) is easier," Matt. 9: 5; *katimampo kat; katimimampo kat.*

katimi; *katima heto,* it will come to nothing; *katima wa,* it will not be.

katimichi, katihmichi, v. t., to do in some way; *katimichit ishhokchi,* how did you plant it? Luke 19: 15 [?]; *katiminchi,* nas. form.

katiohmi, katiohmi, v. t., to do, Luke 3: 10; to do somehow; how? Matt. 18: 12; *katiohmili,* Luke 18: 18; *nanta katiohmi han?* why.

katiohmi, what, Matt. 17: 25.

katiohmi, a., pp., done in some way; after some manner; of some kind.

katiohmi, v. n., to be done in some way; to be after some manner, or, how is it; *katiohmi hokakosh ilappat yamohma hinla cho?* after what manner is it that this can be done? John 3: 9; *katiohmit hachiyimma wa,* it is no way that ye will believe, John 3: 12; *katiohmi hosh yammichi.*

katiohmi, adv., how; in what manner; of what kind; *katiohmit ishiachin,* how will you go? *chikatiohmi cho,* how d'ye, or, how do you do—*katohmi fohka,* adv., when; in what manner is it; about what time is it—*katiohmi foka kash,* about what time was it; when was it—*katiohmi foka kashon,* when was it—*katiohmi foka mako,* when—*katiohmi foka makosh,* when—*katiohmi hon,* how; wherefore; how is it, Matt. 16: 11—*katiohmi hosh,* how—*katiohmi ka—katiohmi kakon,* how is it—*katiohmi kakosh,* how is it—*katohmi kash,* when was it?

katiohmi kash ishla?—*katiohmi kasho,* when was it; at what time was it—*katiohmikma,* when; *katiohmikma ishiachin?* when will you go?—*katiohmikmakon,* when—*katiohmit,* how; whence.

katiohmi hon, why, Matt. 7: 4; 17: 10, 19; *katiohmi hon?* how is it? 2 Sam. 14: 2 [?].

katiohmichi, v. t., to do it in some way, Matt. 10: 25; 1 Sam. 5: 8; Josh. 7: 9.

katioht, cont. of *katiohmi; chishno akosh katioht issanlakofahinla chimahoba.*

kato, kato, hatoha, the; that which; who.

katoba, see *kotoba.*

katohmi, a., how many.

katohmi, katomi, adv., how many, Matt. 15: 34; what number, John 4: 53 [?]; *katohmi,* a.; *katohmi,* v. n; *katohmi ho; katohmia; katomona; katomola,* etc.

katohmona, a. (from *katohmi* and *ona*), several; sufficient number; coming to some.

katohmona (from *katohmi* and *ona*), v. n., to come to, or amount to several; *katomonahatukosh iktalo,* because there was not a sufficient number they did not finish it.

katola, pp., cut up, as *ahe katola,* potatoes cut for planting.

katoli, v. a. i. pl., to cut off, as *ahe katoli,* to cut potatoes; *katiffi,* sing., to cut in two, as firewood, ribs, etc.

katomi, see *katohmi.*

kaua, see *kauwa.*

kauasha, a., aged; middle aged; *hatak kauasha,* a middle-aged man.

kauasha, v. n., to be middle aged.

kauashachi, a., near to middle age; somewhat advanced in years.

kauashachi, v. n., to be somewhat advanced in years.

kauehto, kauihto, n., glue; size; the name of a wild vine.

kauwa, kaua, a., broken; *fulli kauwa,* broken twigs.

kauwa, v. n., to be broken.

kauwa, v. a. i., to break.

kauwi, v. t. sing., to break.

kauwichi, v. t. pl., to break; to break down; to cause them to break.

kawa, sign of double neg.; *ikminto kawa,* Luke 18: 7 [?].

kawa, pp., broken; *kauwichi,* v. t.

kawa, v. a. i., to break.

kanwa, kawa, v. a. i., to bark, as a fox; to sing, as insects on trees.

kanwa, n., a fox which barks.

kabaha, kapaha, v. t. pl., to beat; to pound; to hammer; to drub.

kabaha, n., a beater; a hammerer.

kabahachi, v. a. i., to rumble, as a wagon in motion on hard ground.

kabalichi, v. t. sing., to beat; to strike.

kachakachechi, v. t., to make it creak, as a door hinge.

kachakachi, v. a. i., to creak; to squeak.

kachakachi, n., a creaking; a creak; a squeak.

kachi, pl. termination of passives, Ch. Sp. Bk., Table 31.

kafa, pp., dipped; *isht kafa,* dipped out with; n., a ladle.

kafabicha, n., a coffee-pot spout.

kafafotoha, n., a coffee mill.

kafahonni, n., a coffee boiler; a coffee pot.

kafaialhto, n., a coffee pot (used on the table); a coffee sack, bin, box, etc.

kafaiishko, n., a coffee cup; a coffee saucer.

kafaiishko aiontala, n., a salver.

kafaiishko ataloha, n., a waiter.

kafaiontala, n., a salver; a waiter.

kaffi, v. t., to dip out; to take out with a ladle; *isht kaffi,* to dip out with.

kafi, n., sassafras; but *iti kafi* is also sassafras or sassafras tree.

kafi, n., coffee, being an imitation of the English name.

kafi auashli, v. t., to parch coffee; to brown coffee.

kafi homi, n., strong coffee.

kafi honi, v. t., to boil coffee.

kafi honni, n., boiled coffee.

kafi lakchi, n., coffee grounds.

kafi nihi, n., a coffee berry or seed; a coffee kernel.

kafi okchimali, n., green coffee; West India coffee.

kafi tohbi, n., white coffee; Java coffee.

kahchi, v. t., to cut with shears; pass., *kachaya.*

kala (from *kalli*), pp., scratched.

kalaha, a., round, as a wheel or log; *iti kalaha,* a truck wheel.

kalaha, v. n., to be round.

kalaha, n., a wheel; a round; a rundle.

kạlakachi, v. a. i., to gulp; also a noise made in the throat by swallowing; see *kolak*.

kạlanchah, v. a. i., to be hoarse.

kạli, n., a spring of water; a fountain; a font; a fount; a well.

kạli aholihta, n., the curb of a well above ground; a well curb.

kạli hạpi oka, n., a salt spring; a brine spring; a saline.

kạli hofobi, n., a well; a deep well; a deep spring.

kạli kula, n., a dug spring.

kạli oka, n., well water; spring water.

kạlli, v. t., to scratch; to claw.

kạlli, n., a scratch.

kạllo, a., strong; athletic; powerful; mighty; brawny; cogent; firm; hard; tough; stiff; callous; acute, as a disease; severe; bony; braced; able; energetic; forcible; furious; hardy; harsh; hearty; heavy; high; inveterate; lusty; masculine; nervous; obdurate; pithy; potent; powerful; profound; resistless; rigid; solid; vigorous; violent; boisterous, Matt. 14: 30; robust; rough; sinewed; sinewy; stable; steadfast; steady; stern; stout; straightlaced; strict; stubborn; sturdy; substantial; tense; tight; trusty; tyrannical; unrelenting; unshaken; valiant; valid; *itinkạllo*, mutually strengthened; strong against each other; *ikkạllo*, a., enervate; faint; flat; flimsy; soft; stale; unfirm; infirm; unhardened; unseasoned; unsolid; unsound; unstable; weak; weakly.

kạllo, adv., rigidly; stiffly; straitly, Josh. 6: 1; *ikkạllo*, adv., weakly.

kạllo, v. n., to be strong, etc.

kạllo, v. a. i., to act with strength; to harden; to indurate; to rage; to stiffen; *ishkạllashke*, you must act with vigor.

kạllo, pp., made strong; strengthened; hardened; confirmed; consolidated; enforced; established; fixed; indurated; invigorated; ratified; seared; set; tempered; *ikkạllo*, enervated; softened.

kạllo, n., strength; vigor; power; hardness; energy; firmness; force; harshness; intensity; might; nerve; pith; potency; rigidity; severity; sinew; solidity; steadiness; stiffness; stress;

strictness; valor; violence; virtue; *ikkạllo*, feebleness; weakness.

kạllo ạlhpesa, strong enough.

kạllo iⁿshaht tạli, a., strongest.

kạllo iⁿshaht tạli, v. n., to be strongest.

kạllo iⁿshạli, a., stronger.

kạllo iⁿshạli, v. n., to be stronger.

kạllo keyu, n., inability.

kạllo keyu, adv., loosely.

kạllo keyu, a., powerless; without strength.

kạllochi, kalochi, v. t., to straighten; to temper; to toughen, Matt. 9: 30; 12: 16; 16: 20; to harden; to strengthen; to make strong, as coffee, rum, etc.; to confirm; to consolidate; to corroborate; to enforce; to establish; to indurate; to invigorate; to ratify; to sear; to season; to stiffen; *ikkạllocho*, v. t., to dilute; to weaken; to enervate; *ikkạllochochi*, v. t., to enervate.

kạllochi, n., a hardener; a strengthener; an enforcer; a ratifier.

kạllochit hilechi, v. t., to fix.

kạllot, adv., with hardness; severely; strongly.

kạllot flopa, v. a. i., to heave; to breathe hard.

kạllot hika, pp., rooted.

kạllot ia, v. a. i., to strengthen; to toughen.

kạllot ishi, v. t., to engrasp.

kạllot ishi, a., tenacious.

kạllot isht ia, v. a. i., to rankle.

kạla, v. a. i. sing., to burst open, as an egg; to open.

kạla, pp., burst open; contused; crushed; opened; *kalali*, v. t.

kạla, n., a bursting open; a breaking; a contusion; see *kula*.

kạlahạchechi, v. t., to cause to clatter; to make a rattling; to clatter.

kạlahạchi, v. a. i., to clatter; to rattle.

kạlahạchi, n., a rattling; a clattering.

kạlali, v. t., to burst; to open.

kạma, pp., stopped; *iⁿkama*, precluded; *isht iⁿkạmakạchi*, v. t., to uncork.

kạmahạchechi, v. t., to cause to tinkle.

kạmahạchi, v. a. i., to tinkle, as a bell.

kạmahạchi, n., the tinkling of a bell.

kạmakạchi; komahạchi, komakạchi, n., pl., knocks; raps; blows on a bell.

kạmakạchi, v. a. i., to ring, as a bell.

kₐmmi, v. t. pl., to stop up; to plug; *iⁿkₐmmi*, to plug them up.

kₐmo, kamo (q. v.), adv., having the sense of the immediate past tense; *kₐmo* is distinctive of a known object and implies immediate past time. See *chamo* for the remote; was so, did, etc., John 4: 54; *hakₐmo, chokₐmo*.

kₐmomi, kamomi (q. v.), **kₐmmohmi**, adv., at all; in the least degree; in the smallest amount, Luke 4: 2. This word is compounded from the art. pro. *ka* and the verb *ₐmohmi; iksho ka ₐmohmi*.

kₐna, n., a person.

kₐna, a., anyone.

kₐna, v. n., to be anyone.

kₐna iksho, a., vacant; no one present.

kₐna keyu, pro., no one; nobody.

kₐna kia, pro., anyone, Matt. 13: 19; somebody; anybody; whosoever, John 3:16;2:25;whoever; whomsoever, Matt. 5: 41; 10: 14; *kₐna imma kia*, towards whomsoever; *kₐnaimmi kia*, whosoever; to whomsoever, etc.

kₐnaho, pro., who so; he that; to whom, Matt. 11: 27.

kₐnaho kia, pro., anyone whatever.

kₐnahosh, pro., anyone; who, Matt. 10: 11; he that, Matt. 10: 22; 13: 9; whosoever; he that, Josh. 2: 19; John 3: 18; 4: 36; Matt. 5: 31, 32; he; whosoever, Matt. 7: 8; 18: 4; 7: 24; 10: 32, 33, 37, 38; 18: 4; whoso, Matt. 18: 5, 6.

kₐnalichi, kanₐllichi, kanalichi (q. v.), v. t., to remove.

kₐnanali, kₐnanli, kₐnananli, kananali (q. v.), v. a. i. freq., to keep moving about.

kₐnapₐchi, v. t., to catch, Mark 12: 13

kₐni, kanni, contracted, I presume, from *kanima*, anywhere, somewhere; see John 6: 67. See *kₐti*. Acts 14: 18; *kₐnichi*, causative form.

kₐnia, a., pp., gone; lost; strayed; departed; dead; obviated; removed; translated; *kₐninihya*, went away swiftly, Luke 24: 31; *kₐnnia*, intensive form. This word makes its changes of form like *yanₐlli, binili, yanananli, binininli, kanananli, kaninihya*, instead of *yanohanli*, etc.

kₐnia, (the sing. number of *tₐmoa* or *tₐmmoa*), v. n., to be gone or lost; to stray away, Matt. 18: 12; *kₐninihya*, to go

away suddenly, Luke 24: 31; *iⁿkₐnia*, v. t., to lose, Matt. 10: 39; he loses or it is lost to him, Matt. 16: 25; *iⁿkₐnia*, n., a loser.

kₐnia, v. a. i., to go away, Matt. 13: 25; to disappear; to elope; to pass; to escape; to spend; to stray; to vanish; to wag; *itakₐnia*, to go away from each other or together, as to offset accounts; *itiⁿkₐnia*, to leave each other, as man and wife when they part, Matt. 5: 31; *itiⁿkₐnia*, to go off together, as in runaway or clandestine matches; *kₐniₐt ia*, to dwindle; *itakₐnia*, v. t., to offset; to go away together.

kₐnia, n., a departure; a loss; the one who goes away; expense; a fugitive; a stray.

kₐnia, pp., exiled; taken away; expended; *kanₐlli*, v. a. i., to move one's self; *kanₐllichi*, v. t., to remove it, them, etc.

kₐnia, adv., entirely; *alotₐt kₐnia*, entirely full; *okshilintₐt kₐnia*, Luke 4: 25; 5: 1 [?].

kₐniachi, v. t., to lead astray; to cause to be lost, gone, etc.

kₐnichi, see *kanichi*.

kₐnimi, see *kanimi*.

kₐnnakli, kannakli, v. a. i. sing., to move quickly once; see 1 Sam. 19: 10.

kₐno, kano (q. v.), the which; that which; see *ka, kₐt*, and *kₐto*.

kₐpa, pl. of *kapalichi*.

kₐpaha, see *kₐbaha*.

kₐpbₐt, n. (Eng.), a cupboard.

kₐpitₐni, kₐpotₐni, n.(Span.), a captain, Josh. 5: 14; a centurion; *tₐshkachipota iⁿkₐpetₐni*, a military captain; a captain among the Choctaw is a civil as well as military officer or ruler.

kₐpitₐni iakaiya, n., a vicegerent.

kₐpitₐni imanumpeshi,n., a lieutenant.

kₐs, n., a noise made by striking on the head.

kₐsachi, v. a. i., to sound, or say *kₐs; noti kₐsanchi*, to chatter, as the teeth, with cold.

kₐsahₐchi, v. a. i., to patter; v. t., to ring.

kₐsbi, n., a dooryard; any place made smooth and hard; a court.

kₐsbi, pp., trod hard and made smooth.

kₐsbichi, v. t., to make a *kₐsbi*.

kaskaha, a., sour; acid; tart; acetous.

kaskaha, v. n., to be sour or acid; v. a. i., to turn sour; to become sour; to sour.

kaskaha, n., sourness.

kaskahachi, v. t., to make it sour; to sour.

kassa, v. a. i., to ring; to tinkle.

kassaha, v. a. i. pl., to ring; to tinkle.

kassahachi, v. a. i., to tinkle; to patter.

kassahachi, n., a tinkling.

kash, see kash.

kashaha, n., a relish; a savor; zest.

kashaha, a., sweet; palatable; pleasant to the taste; dulcet; nice.

kashaha, pp., seasoned; ikkashaho, unpalatable; unseasoned.

kashaha, v. n., to be pleasant to the taste.

kashaha, v. a. i., to relish; to savor; inkashaha, v. t., to relish; to love; ikinkashaho, to disrelish.

kashahachi, v. t., to season; to render pleasant to the taste; to cause to relish; to give a relish; to relish; to zest.

kasheho, n., an old woman, applied to a man's wife when aged.

kashin, see kash.

kashka, n., name of a fish; the catfish.

kashke, neg. form in the indic., as akpesokashke, I do not see.

kashkoa, pl., kashapa sing., divided; itakashkoa, divided into parts; Josh. 11: 23; allotted; dispensed; parted; shared.

kashkoa, v. a. i. pl., to divide into parts; itakashkoah, to divide among themselves or with each other; see kashkoa.

kashkoa, n., a division; a partition; itakashkoa, n., a partition.

kashkoachi, v. t., to divide; itakashkoachi, to divide for others, Luke 18: 22

kashkoli, pl., kashabli, sing., v. t., to divide them; to deal; to dispense; itakashkoli, to divide among others, Josh. 1: 6; 13: 6, 7; itakashkoli, to divide them into parts; to allot; to dispense; to disperse; to lot; to part; to proportion; to separate; to share; itinkashkuli, to share out among them.

kashkolit kampila, v. t., to retail.

kashkolit kampila, n., a retailer.

kashti, n., a flea.

kashti akobli, n., flea bites.

kashti akopoli, n., a flea bite.

kat, art., the; made by prefixing k demonstrative to at, Matt. 18: 14.

kat, art. and rel. pro., the; which; that which; what; n. case; kat is used in the place of at when at is removed from a noun and placed after an adjective agreeing with it, as hatak at, hatak achukma kat, and hatak ohoyo aiena kat; chula hat chito kat ofi an, the fox in size is greater than a dog; used here for specification; if less would be iklauo hoke.

kata, interrog. pro., who, John 1: 19, 22; 2 Kings 9: 32; kata chia hon? who art thou? Compounds: kata han, obj. case, whom—kata hakon, obj. case, whom; to whom; for whom; by whom, Matt. 12: 27—kata hakosh [?], nom. case, who is it; who, John 4: 33—kata hat—kata hon, obj. case, to whom; for whom; what one of some kind; whom, Matt. 16: 13, 15—kata hokako—kata hokakosh, Luke 5: 21—kata hosh, kata hosh mintahe keyu, no person will come; who, Matt. 18: 1—kata ilapon, whose.

kata, pro., any one; kata hosh anola heto, any one shall not tell, or no one shall tell.

katanih, v. a. i., to breathe hard; "of hard breathing."

katelichi, v. t., to clip off.

kati, n., a thorn; a locust tree; a honey locust; a locust.

kati, see kati.

kati ancho, n., a wild rose.

kati chito, a., thorny.

kati holba, n., a thorn.

kati laua, a., thorny.

katichi, see katihchi.

katihmichi, see katimichi.

katima, see katima.

katiohmi, see katiohmi.

kato, art. and rel. pro., the one; that which; the one which; kanimi kato, some, Matt. 16: 14.

kattit; nanta kattit ilapela hinla.

kbano, ikbano (q. v.), okbano (q. v.), oh that!, sign of optative mood; O, int. This is a compound word from k demonstrative, and bano, all; only; the all; the only. This is the disjunctive form, while kbato is the conjunctive; yohmikbato, he wants to try it; let him try, being his own wish and act. This statement helps to explain these expressions; *kbano*, what others may wish, not of themselves, but of another; *kbato*, what one wishes to be or to have himself; and when others use it concerning a man, it is rather a reproachful expression. But see *okbato*, Luke 19: 42.

kbato, ikbato, okbato, oh that! See above.

ke, first per. pl., per. pro., before verbs in neg. form, which begin with a consonant, *eminti, keminto; ela, kelo; echanli, kechanlo.*

ke, per. pro., first per. pl., imp. mood, of verbs which begin with a consonant, as *keminti, kechanli* (let us chop), and in the neg. form imp., as *keminto kia, kechanlo kia.*

ke, adv., usually; commonly, as *kanche ke, isht anumpule ki,* John 3: 34; Luke 4: 27.

ke, a euphonic word, before *tuk, mạli,* etc., in the neg. form of verbs, as *akpeso ke tuk, akpeso kemạli;* it has the power of designation also.

kebibi, n., the noise of two talking.

keh, ke, final syllable of some particle pronouns, etc., as *oke, achiⁿke, yakeh, toshke, shke, omishkeh, ikikkeh,* calling attention and asserting.

kehepa, n., noise of many voices; see *kihepa.*

keho, per. pro., first per. social pl., before verbs in neg. form beginning with a consonant; *kehominto, kehochanlo.*

keho, per. pro., first per. social pl., imp. mood, of verbs beginning with a consonant, as *kehominti, kehochanli, kehotisheli,* (let us disperse), and in the neg. form imp., as *kehochanlokia, kehomintokia.*

kesh, kạsh, and; with neg. verb, neither, John 4: 15; see *ket* and *kish.*

ket (for *kesh,* above), rel. pro., who, Luke 18: 32 [?]; in Luke 1: 7; *ạlla yạt ikimiksho ket, okla hosh,* etc.; the *t* of *ket* is conjunctive and puts *okla* in the dual number; *keto, ketoⁿ; ketoma,* adv., *lashpa ketoma,* always and known.

ketoshke, adv.; *episahe keyu ketoshke.*

keyoh. This differs from *keyu* in some way.

keyu, adv., no; nay, Matt. 5: 37; not.

keyu, v. n., Mark 9: 28; *keyuketuk.*

keyu, n., a negative, a negation; a nay, as the "nays."

keyu, a., no; not any; as *hatak keyu,* no man.

keyu, v. n., to be no; to be not any; *keyut,* Gal. 6: 4; *keyu hoke,* Matt. 6: 1; 2 Tim. 3: 5; Matt. 6, 23, 24; Josh. 5: 14.

keyuachi, v. t., to contradict; to deny; to say no; to refuse; to negative.

keyuchi, to cause no, or not to do or to be, Matt. 22: 34.

keyuchohmi, a., rare.

keyuhokmạt, if it is not so; or except, John 3: 5, 27.

keyukechi, v. t., to set at naught; see *yạmmakashoⁿ na keyukechi,* set him at naught, Luke 23: 11.

keyukma, or; if not; unless; otherwise; without; lest, Matt. 5: 25; 6: 1; 7: 6, 10; 13: 35; 9: 17; 17: 21.

keyukmạt, a disjunctive conjunction, Matt. 18: 16; Luke 13: 15; 14: 5; Josh. 5: 13; rather, Matt. 18: 8; "or else," Matt. 12: 29, 33; except, Matt. 12: 29.

keyushke, does not, Matt. 17: 21.

keyut; *nana ạlhpesa keyut,* in vain, Matt. 15: 9.

ki, a euphonic word, before *tok,* as *akpeso-kitok,* or a determinative or limiting *k* to be suffixed to the previous word.

kiⁿ, adv. (contraction of *kiⁿsha*), yet; with a negative verb, not yet; as *akapeso kiⁿ,* I had not yet seen.

kia, kiah, an obsolete verb, or used only in the imperfect; a concessive.

kia, from *ia; ikia* imp., let him go; let it go; let it be so; *ikminto kia,* he does not come; let it go; let it be so; i. e., do not let him come; *tanchi kia, wak kia,* corn let it be; cattle be it so.

kia, even; also; any; although; but; or; though; hold; never mind; nevertheless; notwithstanding; no; a word of dissent; *kiah ahnili,* no I think; *yohmi kia,* "but;" lit., so let it go, Matt. 1: 20, 6: 26; *kanchak kia,* a crib let it be; a crib even, or although; Matt. 6: 26; *ishanumpuli kia,* but speak thou; thou speak; *kia,* let it be, Matt. 8: 8.

kia, nor; with a neg.

kiba, n., a small frog.

kibikshi, tibikshi; *noshkobo kibikshi*, "chapiters," 1 Kings 7: 20, 41, 42; Ex. 37: 22; *bik bina*, Ex. 37: 17.

kichali, v. a. i., to crack; to have the scratches.

kichanli, a., cracked; chapped, as the skin of the hands, feet, face, or lips; reddened in cold water, or by the action of cold winds when the part is wet.

kichanli, v. n., to be cracked or chapped; v. a. i., to crack; to chap; *iyi ąt kichanli*.

kichanli, n., a crack; a chap.

kichanlichi, v. t., to crack; to chap; to cause to crack.

kichaya, a., cracked, as the skin of the hands.

kichaya, v. n., to be cracked; *ibbak ąt kichaya*.

kichaya, v. a. i., to crack; to chap.

kichaya, n., a crack.

kichayąchi, v. t., to crack; to make it crack.

kifaha, v. a. i., to groan; to grunt; *hatak abeka kąt kifaha*, to pule; to whine; to moan, as a sick child, Ex. 2: 23.

kifaha, n., a groan.

kifanali, v. t., to hold under the arm.

kifanli, v. a. i., to groan; to grunt.

kifąsh, n., name of a plant with erect stalk. The root resembles that of the Irish potato; formerly used for food, when the root, called *hichuk*, was used, in times, too, of famine.

kifehąchi, v. a. i., Ps. 42: 7.

kifeta, n., steam.

kifeta, pp., steamed; *oⁿkifeta*, steamed.

kifeta, v. a. i., to steam.

kifetąchi, v. t., to steam.

kifilli, v. a. i., to vapor; to steam; *oka yąt kifilli*.

kifilli, n., steam.

kifillichi, v. t., to cause it to steam.

kihepa, v. a. i., to fall, as water.

kihepa, kehepa, n., a waterfall; a cascade; a cataract.

kil, per. pro., 1st per. pl. of verbs in the neg. form beginning with a vowel; *kilaiyu; kilithano*.

kil, per. pro., 1st per. pl., imp. mood, as *kilia*, let us go; negative form also, as *kilaiyu kia*, let us not go.

Kilaist, n., Christ; The Anointed; an appellation given to the Saviour of the world, and synonymous with the Hebrew word Messiah.

kileha, v. a. i., to growl; to snarl; to roar, as a wild beast; to purr; to whinny, as a horse; *ofi ąt kileha, koi ąt kileha, wak nakni ąt kileha; kilihiⁿha*, freq.

kileha, n., a growl; a purr; a roar.

kileha, n., a roarer; a growler.

kilhkiki, a., stony; hilly; broken like thin clouds.

kiliⁿkki, n., a species of parrot; a parrakeet.

kiliⁿkoba, a., green; green colored; a color resembling the *kiliⁿkki*.

kilimpi, a., strong; stout; athletic; powerful; mighty; forcible; hardy; cogent; lusty; potent; robust.

kilimpi, v. n., to be strong; *ilekilimpi*, to be strong in himself; to exert himself.

kilimpi, n., strength; force; might; power; vigor.

kilimpichi, v. t., to strengthen.

kiloh, per. pro., 1st per., social pl. before verbs beginning with a vowel; *kilohaiyu*, let us all not go; *kilohimpo*, let us all not eat.

kiloh, per. pro., 1st per. pl., imp., etc.; *kilǫhia*, let us all go; *kilohimpa*, let us all eat; also in the negative, as *kilohaiyu kia, kilohimpo kia*.

kila, pp., gnawed; *foni ąt kila*.

kilaⁿfa, v. a. i., to hawk.

kili, v. t., to gnaw; to nibble; to pick; *kihiⁿli*.

kili, n., a gnawer; a nibbler.

kilihachi, v. a. i., to make a noise, such as is produced by rolling rocks or a mill or wagon in motion.

kilihachi, n., the noise made as above; a din; a rumbling, as that of a wagon.

kinafa, v. a. i., to fall; to break down; to overset; to topple; to tumble; to yield; *chuka yąt kinafa, iti ąt kinafa*, to fall, as the palate; *oⁿkinafat okpulo*.

kinafa, pp., fallen; broken down; demolished; overthrown; prostrate; subverted; *ikkinafo*, a., undemolished.

kinafa, n., a fall; an overthrow; a ruin.

kinafa hinla, a., ticklish; liable to fall.

kinafąt itula, n., a downfall.

kinakkali, kinąfkali, kinafkali, v. a. i., to limp.

kinakkali, n., a limper.

kinakli, v. a. i., to limp.

kinakli, n., a limper.

kinali, v. a. i. pl., to fall; to break down; to lodge.

kinali, pp., fallen; broken down; lying down; thrown down; lodged; prostrated; subverted, 1 Kings 11: 27.

kinalichi, v. t., to fell; to throw down; to break down; to prostrate; to subvert, Mark 11: 15; *mali at iti aⁿ kinalichi*, the wind prostrates the trees.

kinalichi, n., a seller.

kinaffi, v. t. sing., to fell; to throw down; to break down; to overthrow; to demolish; to overset; to subvert; to unsettle; to upset, John 2: 15; *chant kinaffi*, to chop down; *isht oktapa kinaffi*, to undam; *iloⁿkinaffi*, to throw himself on; *itakinaffi*, to divide; to cause to fall from each other, as the waters of the Red Sea; to separate; *oⁿkinaffit okpani*, to overwhelm.

kinaffi, n., a feller; a demolisher; a subverter.

kinafha, v. a. i. sing., to be lame; to limp with one foot.

kinafkali, v. a. i. pl., to limp; to be lame in more than one foot; see *kinakkali*.

kinafkali, n., a limper.

kinafkali, a., lame; *hatak kinafkali*, a lame man; a cripple.

kinihahanohi, n., a rattling; rattle.

kinihachi, kinnihachi, v. a. i., to make an indistinct noise, such as persons make when they converse in an adjoining room or at a distance; to hum, as bees; *kinihahanchi*, freq., to make a rattling.

kinihachi, n., the din of words indistinctly heard; a hum.

kininiachi, v. a. i., to make a din by conversing; *kininiahanchi*, freq.

kininiachi, n., the din or noise made in conversation.

kinint iksho, a., silent; calm; *kucha kinint iksho*.

kinni, v. t., to rake open a fire.

kinnihachi, see *kinihachi*.

kinoha, chikinoha, v. i., to be in pain.

kinta, n., a beaver.

kinta hishi, n., beaver fur; beaver.

kinta hishi shapo, n., a beaver hat; a fur hat.

kinta iⁿkasoma, n., beaver bait.

kinta isht albi, n., a beaver trap.

kinta oktabli, n., a beaver dam.

kintushi, n., a young beaver.

kisaha, v. a. i. pl., to crack; *iti at kisaha*, the trees crack; *tali iyasha yat kisaha*, the iron pot is cracked.

kisaha, pp., cracked.

kisaha, n., cracks.

kisali, v. a. i., to crack; *amphata, aiimpa yat kisali*.

kisali, pp., cracked.

kisali, n., cracks.

kisalichi, v. t., to crack.

kisaⁿya, v. a. i., to crack but a little.

kisaⁿya, pp., cracked a little.

kisaⁿya, n., a small crack.

kisayachi, v. t., to crack.

kiseli, v. t. sing., to bite; to clinch with the teeth or with the jaws of an instrument; *itikiseli*, v. a. i., to bite or gnash the teeth so that the teeth or instrument come together; to gnash.

kiseli, n., a biter.

kiselichi, v. t., to gnaw; to bite; to gnash; *itikiselichi*, to gnash the teeth against each other; to clamp; to pinch.

kiselichi, n., a biter.

kisli, v. t. pl., to bite; to mangle.

kisli, v. a. i., to gnaw, as when one bites a wild turnip.

kish, kesh, and, Gen. 3: 3; *hachikpotolo kish; k* belongs to *potolo*.

kiⁿsha, adv., not yet; before, Matt. 6: 8; John 1: 48; quite, 1 Sam. 3: 3, 7; *akpeso kiⁿsha; iklo kiⁿsha; iknuso kiⁿsha ho; ikaiono kiⁿsha hoⁿ*, before the time, Matt. 8: 29; "till," Matt. 10: 23.

kiⁿsha, v. n.; *akpeso kiⁿshakma*.

kishi, n., a basket; a hamper, Matt. 14: 20; 15: 37; 16: 9, 10; *kishi alota*.

kishi afohoma, n., the rim of a basket.

kishi yancho, n., a very large basket used as a bin.

kit, a particle used instead of *kat*, Matt. 2: 16; in *iklauwokit ia*, to decrease.

kitafa, v. a. i., to crack open and make a large crack; *iti at kitafa*, a tree cracked open; *yakni at kitafa*, ground cracked open.

kitafa, pp., cracked.

kitafa, n., a large crack.

kitaia, v. a. i., to be well on fire; to burn.

kitak, n., a worm, called a sawyer, that eats wood and has a flat head; the apple-tree borer.

kitali, v. a. i., to cave off, as the sides of a well or the banks of a river.— J. Taylor.

kitanli, pl., kitafa, sing., v. a. i., to crack.

kitanli, pp., a., cracked.

kitanli, n., large cracks or fissures.

kitanlichi, v. t., to crack; to produce cracks.

kitaffi, v. t., to crack; to produce a crack; kitafa, pp.

kitapi, a pestle.

kitiffi, v. t., to cut open, or rupture a blood-vessel.

kitihachi, v. a. i., to rattle and make a noise, as a wagon in motion; kitihahanchi; itichanahat kitihahanchi ehaklo mali.

kitihachi, n., a rattling noise; a tumult.

kitik, n., the noise made by a step or by striking with the end of a stick.

kitikachi, v. a. i.; lit., to say kitik; to sound; to make the noise kitik.

kitikachi, pl., kitik, sing., n., the noise made by stepping; kitikahanchi, 2 Kings 6: 32.

kitikachi, kitikshi, v. a. i., to make a noise by stepping; isuba nowa kat kitikachi.

kitikshi, a., stubbed, as hatak kitikshi, a thickset man.

kitinisi, n., a morsel; a spark.

kitinisi, kitinusi, a., very small; little.

kitinisi, v. n., to be very small.

kitti, n., a mortar.

kitush, kittush, n., a pestle; a pounder.

kitush api, n., a pestle handle.

kma, sign of subjunctive mood, if; when, John 2: 19; see below; when that; imachilikma, to him say I; that when, achilikma, Matt. 8: 9; kmano, kmano, if the; when the; after the; kmat, kmato, if the; when the; after the.

The above are signs of the subjunctive mood, composed of k demonstrative and the article pronoun ma and its changes. But cf. akma; akmano; akmat; akmato; ikma; ikmano; ikmat; ikmato; okma; okmano; okmat; okmato.

kon, a part. in the obj. case derived from akon, but contracted, or the first vowel of ako is merged in the last vowel of the word to which it is suffixed, as nanta kon, what is it; katima kon, where is it; see kosh.

kon; here are two words, k the demonstrative article pronoun and on the auxiliary verb.

koa, v. a. i., to break; to crack, as glass, earthenware, etc.

koa, pp., cracked; broken; fractured; flawed; koli, v. t. sing.

koa, n., a crack; a fracture.

koafabi, n., a yellow-striped wasp.

koat, n., a quart.

koat iklanna, n., a pint.

koat ushta, n., a gallon.

kobafa, v. a. i., to break; to fall; to snap.

kobafa, pp., broken; abolished; annulled; cashiered; removed from office; fractured; frustrated; infringed; invalidated; nullified; profaned; ruptured; deposed, as minko at kobafa, iti at kobafa; ikkobafo, a., unbroken; unviolated.

kobafa, a., broken; contrite; null.

kobafa, n., a breach; a dissolution; a fracture; a nullity; a rupture.

kobafahe keyu, a., stationary.

kobak, n., a knock; a rap on a tree or fence; the report of a knock, etc.

kobakuchi, v. a. i. sing., to sound like a knock, rap, etc.

kobali, v. a. i. pl., to break.

kobali, pp., broken; hanali akosh kobali, John 19: 31; 1 Sam. 2: 4, 10.

kobali, n., pieces broken.

kobalichi, v. t., to break; to cause to break, John 19: 32.

kobaffi, sing., kobbi, pl., v. t., to break, Matt. 5: 19; to destroy; to abolish; to annul; to cashier; to erase; to transgress, Matt. 15: 2, 3; to violate; to depose, as minko an kobaffi; to disannul; to dissolve; to fracture; to frustrate; to humble; to infringe; to invalidate; to null; to nullify; to profane; to remove, i. e., from office; to rupture; to snap; kobahanfi, to profane, Matt. 12: 5; Josh. 7: 4 [?].

kobaffi, n., a breaker; a violator; a humbler; a nullifier; a profaner.

kobaffi, n., a removal; a rupture.

kobaffichi, v. t., to cause to break.

kobbi, pl. of kobaffi (q. v.).

kobilhchạp, kobilhpash, n., chips.

kobish, n., the rectum.

kobli, n., a glass tumbler.

kobli, kopli, v. t. pl., to bite, to knab; ofi ạt kobli; koplit tạpuli, v. t. pl., to nip.

kobli, n., a biter.

koboha, pl., to knock any thing large that is hollow so as to make a noise; to make that particular noise which is heard when a hollow tree, for instance, is knocked; to drum.

kobohạchi, v. a. i., to ring, as a large bell, drum, or barrel when beaten.

kobohạchi, n., a ringing; a sounding; a din.

kobokạchi, pp. pl., pass. of koboha, made to ring; knocked; beaten.

kobokạchi, n., knocks; raps; kobak, sing.

kobokshi, a., bent up; the bowing side up; nạli kobonkshi.

kobolichi, sing., koboha, pl., v. t., to knock a large hollow vessel or thing, as a tree, barrel, drum, large bell.

kobolichi, n., a rapper; the one who knocks any large hollow thing.

kobuk, n., a knock or blow on a hollow vessel; the sound thus produced.

kobulli, v. a. i., to break in pieces.

kobulli, n., pieces; fragments.

kobullichi, v. t., to break in pieces; to dash to pieces.

kobuna, a., humpbacked; having a hump; isuba nạli kobuna, a humpbacked horse.

kobuna, v. n., to be humpbacked.

kobuna, n., a hump.

kobunoa, a. pl., having humps.

kobunoa, v. n., to have humps.

kobunoa, n., humps.

kocha, n., weather, Matt. 16: 2, 3.

kocha, see kucha.

kochanli, a., being out along; out.

kochanli, v. a. i., to be out along.

kochofa, pp., bent; broken, Luke 13: 11; 2 Kings 18: 21; itakochofa, broken asunder.

kochofa, v. a. i., to bend; to break, as a cornstalk, Luke 13: 11; itakochofa, to break asunder, as a wooden chimney; to fold together as a blanket.

kocholi, kochonli, v. t., pl. of kochuffi, to bend down; kochoha, pp., bent down.

kochombi, kachumbi (q v.), n., a hard bunch in the flesh; a hard swelling.

kochuffi, v. t. sing, to break; to bend; tanchạpi an kochuffi.

kochuffi, n., a breaker.

kofanto, a., lean; spare.

kofi, n., a quail, called by some at the south a partridge, where the partridge of the north is not known; a partridge.

kofi chito, n., a guinea hen; a pintado; a partridge.

kofkokạchi, v. a. i. pl., to steam, as boiling water; kofota, sing.

kofkokạchi, n., steam.

kofkoli, v. a. i., pl. of kofulli, to steam.

kofoha, v. a. i., to roar.

kofohạchi, v. a. i., to roar, as the wind; mali ạt kofohạchi.

kofohạchi, n., roaring of wind.

kofokạchi, v. a. i., to rumble, as the wheels of a wagon in passing over a bridge.

kofokạchi, n., a rumbling.

kofota, v. a. i., to steam, as boiling water.

kofota, pp., steamed; onkofota.

kofota, n., steam of boiling water.

kofulli, v. a. i., to steam; oka yạt kofulli, the water steams.

kofulli, n., steam.

kofullichi, v. t., to steam; hatak an onkofullichi, to steam a man.

kofuna, a., having a hump; crooked; bent; humpbacked; see kobuna.

kofuna, v. n., to be humped.

kofuna, n., a hump; a humpback; a hunch.

kofunoha, a. pl., having a hump; crooked.

kofunoha, n., crooks; humps.

kofunoha, v. n., to be crooked; kofunohạchi, v. t.

kofusa, pp., hollowed.

kofusa, a., hollow.

kofussa, sing., kofussoa, pl., v. n., to be hollowed.

kofussa, n., a hollow; an excavation; kofussoa n. pl., hollows.

kofussa, a., having a hollow like that of a trough; concave; scooped; hollowed; kofussoa, pl.

kofussạchi, sing., kofussoachi, pl., v. t., to scoop; to excavate; to make hollow.

kofushi, n., a young quail; a quail's egg.

kohcha; akohcha, v. a. i., to come out of, Josh. 4: 16; akohchạt ia, Josh. 6: 1; see kucha.

kohchi, n., a thicket.

kohchi, v. t., to take out, Matt. 5: 29; *akkohchi*, let me pull out, Matt. 7: 4; *ishakohchashke*, do thou cast out of, imp. mood, Matt. 7:5; *ishakohchahinla*, thou shalt cast out of, Matt. 7: 5; see *kuchi*.

kohchichi, see *kuchichi*.

kohta, n., a pole; a flagstaff; a mast, 1 Kings 10: 11.

kohuⁿachi, n., a warwhoop; a whoop.

koi, n., a mile.

koi, n., a tiger; a panther; a catamount; a jaguar.

koi chikchiki, n., a leopard; a spotted tiger.

koi chito, n., a lion; a large tiger.

koi chito inchuka, n., a lion's den; a lion's cage.

koi chito tek, n., a lioness.

koi isht ikhạna, n., a milestone; a milepost.

koi nakni, n., a male tiger; a tiger.

koi tek, n., a tigress.

koichup, n., chips of the door yard.

kokoa, kokua, pl., *koa*, sing., v. a. i., to break; to crack, as earthenware.

kokoa, pp., broken; cracked, as glass, an earthenware pot, metal, etc.; *itakokoa*, fractured.

kokoa, n., fragments.

kokuli, v. t. pl., *koli*, sing., to break; to crack, as glass or things like glass, as earthenware pots and metal; to fracture.

kokuli, n., a breaker.

kolak, n., the noise made by swallowing.

kolakachi, v. a. i., to swallow loudly; to make a noise in swallowing, as when swallowing a large draft.

kolhkobeka, kolokobi, n. pl., deep ravines.

kolhkoki, a., short; *iti shima kolhkoki*, short shingles.

koli, v. t. sing., to break, to crack glass and such like things; to fracture; to flaw; to stave.

koli, n., a breaker.

kolofa, v. a. i., to come off; to come in two; to break in two.

kolofa, pp., cut off; severed; truncated.

kolofa, n., a cut; a piece cut off; *itekoluffa, ittakoluffa*, n., a notch; cut asunder; *nạnih itikoluffa*, a mountain gap.

kolokbi, kalakbi (Sixtowns form), n., a gulf; a deep valley; an abyss; a ravine; a hollow; a valley; a vale; a hole, as on the bottom of a river; a gully; hollowness; *kolokbi bachaya*, a gully; *kolokbi bachoha*, gullies.

kolokbi, pp., made into a gulf; excavated.

kolokbichi, v. t., to make a gulf; to excavate; to hollow.

kolokobi, kolhkobeka, n. pl., gulfs; holes; deep valleys; *nạnih kolokobi*.

kolokobi, pp., made into gulfs; hollowed.

kolokshi, a., short, as *na foka kolokshi*, a vest; a roundabout.

kolokshi, v. n., to be short.

kolokshichi, v. t., to make it short.

kololi, v. a. i. pl., to come off; i. e., square off.

kololi, pp., cut off; severed.

kololi, n., those which are cut off.

kololichi, v. t., to cut off; to sever them, as logs, by the ax or fire, etc.

kolombish, n., the throat.

koluffi, sing., to cut off; to sever, by cutting square off, or nearly so; to truncate; *kolukoⁿpi*, pl.

kolumpi, iⁿkolumpi, kolupi, n., the windpipe; the swallow; *iⁿkolupi*, her windpipe, and usually found with a pro. prefixed.

kolaha, n., a rattling, as the leaves of trees when they strike each other.

kolaha, n., the bay tree; the magnolia.

kolahạchechi, v. t., to rattle; to cause to rattle.

kolahạchi, v. a. i., to rattle; to rustle, as the leaves of trees.

kolahạchi, n., a rattling.

komahạchi, komakạchi, see *kạmakạchi*.

komak, n., a single rap on a bell, or the sound thus produced.

komakachi, v. a. i., to sound once.

kommichechi, v. t., to inflict pain; to cause pain; to pain.

kommichi, v. a. i., to pain; to ache; to be in pain.

kommichi, a., painful; aching.

kommichi, v. n., to be painful.

kommichi, n., pain; misery.

komo, past, *ahaⁿya komo*, like *kamo*.

komoha, v. t. pl., to make heavy, grum noises by striking something hollow; to knock; to rap, as a door; *itiakomoha*, to bunt each other.

komohạchi, v. a. i., to hum as bees; *foebilishke ạt komohạchi*.

komok, n. sing., a noise made by rapping something hollow.

komokachi, v. a. i., to ring; to sound.

komokạchi, n., raps; knocks, etc.

komokạchi, v. a. i., to ring; to sound.

komolichi, sing., *komoha*, pl., v. t., to rap; to knock; to give a blow or rap; *okhissa yaⁿ komolichi*, to knock the door.

komolichi, n., a knock.

komota, **komuta**, a., pp., *komunta*, nasal form, restless; tedious; uneasy; wearied; unhappy; vexed; vexatious; tiresome; troublesome; discontented; distressed; *aⁿkomunta*.

komuk, n., the noise of a log falling on other logs.

komukah, v. a. i., to make the above noise.

komunta, v. n., to be uneasy, unhappy, wearied, troubled, Matt. 2: 3; 14: 26; see above.

komunta, v. a. i., to dread; to struggle; *iⁿkomuntali*.

komunta, n., uneasiness; distress; dread; an exigency; terror; weariness.

komuntạchi, v. t., to render uneasy; to distress, Josh. 10: 10.

komuntạt paⁿya, n., an outcry.

konamisli, v. a. i., to move the head and neck, as a fowl in swallowing a kernel of corn.

koni, n., a polecat; a skunk.

kopipia, a., lean; poor.

kopoli, v. t. sing., to bite; to pinch with an instrument, as a pair of tongs; to nab.

kopoli, n., a bite.

kopoli, n., a biter.

kopoli achạfa, n., a mouthful; one bite.

kopoli bạnna, v. t., to snap; a., snappish.

kopolichi, **kopoⱡichi**, v. a. i., to champ.

kosmo, see *kasmo*.

kosoma, a., fetid; having a foul smell, as a goat or musk; rancid.

kosoma, v. n., to be fetid; to smell strong.

kosoma, n., a fetid or a bad smell; a stench.

kosomạchi, v. t., to cause a fetid smell.

kostina hinla, a., tractable.

kostinahe keyu, a., untamable; implacable; incorrigible; ungovernable; unmanageable.

kostini, a., pp., humbled; mortified; reclaimed; sobered; softened; trained; sensible; moral; wise, Matt. 10: 16; civilized; subdued; disciplined; broken; chaste; modest; having one's senses; broken, as an animal to the harness; civil; continent; decent; decorous; gentle; honest; sagacious; sage; sane; sober; subtle; tender; tractable; vestal; virgin; virtuous; *ohoyo kostini*, a chaste woman; *kostini iksho*, a., immodest; *ikkosteno*, a., ungentle; ungoverned; unbroken; undisciplined; rude; unsubdued; *ikkostenot*, adv., rudely; *ikkosteno*, a., unmanaged; unreformed; untoward; unwise; wild.

kostini, v. n., to be sensible, moral, wise; to be subdued, gentle, tame; to have the senses.

kostini, v. a. i., to reform; to soften; to act wilily, Josh. 9: 4.

kostini, n., sense; understanding; chastity; mansuetude; probity; purity; reform; sanity; sobriety; *ohoyo kostini*, decorum; *kostinit kạnia*, the senses are gone; *ikkosteno*, wildness.

kostininchi, v. t., to reform; to sober; to soften; to train; to teach; to subdue; to break; to discipline; to civilize; to make *kostini;* to reclaim; to humble; to manage; to mortify; *ilekostininchi*, to repent; to reform himself, Matt. 3: 2; 11: 20, 21; 12: 41; *ikilekostinincho*, Matt. 11, caption.

kostininchi, n., a teacher; a subduer; a reformer.

kostinit, adv., [wisely.—H. S. H.]; *ikkostenot*, rudely; wildly.

kostinit kạnia, n., stupor.

kosh (see *ko*), art.; the; the which; that which; *nantakosh ikbi*.

koshiba, n., poke weed.

koshu (from Fr. *cochon*), n., a hog (obsolete).

koshuna, a., crooked; humpbacked; bent up, as the back of an angry cat; *koshunoa*, pl.

koshuna, v. n., to be crookèd; *koshunoa*, pl.

koshunạchi, sing., *koshunoachi*, pl., v. t., to make crooked.

kota, a., weak; languid; exhausted; faint; out of breath; enervated; feeble; frail; imbecile; slender.

kota, v. n., to be weak or languid.

kota, v. a. i., to faint; to flag; to relax.

kota, n., weakness; debility; faintness; languidness; languor; lassitude.

kota, pp., weakened; debilitated; enervated; relaxed; unnerved.

kota, n., a languisher.

kotachi, kotahchi, v. t., to render weak; to exhaust; to debilitate; to weaken; to palsy; to enervate; to stupefy; to unnerve.

kotafa, v. a. i., to break off; to get out of joint; to separate; *iti at kotafat itola*, the [limb] breaks off and falls.

kotafa, pp., dislocated; *iyi at kotafa*.

kotafa, n., a dislocation.

kotaha, pl., *kolak* sing., n., the noise made by swallowing.

kotahchi, see *kotachi*.

kotali, v. a. i., to break off; to get out of joint.

kotali, pp., dislocated; put out of joint.

kotalichi, v. t., to dislocate; to break off; to put out of joint; *tanchapi kotalichi*.

kotaffi, v. t. sing., to break off; to dislocate; to put out of joint, Ex. 13: 13.

kotoba, katoba, n., a bottle; a box for oil, 2 Kings 9: 1.

kotoba abeha, pp., bottled; embottled.

kotoba abeli, v. t., to bottle; to embottle.

kotoba aloli, kotoba alulli, v. t., to fill bottles.

kotoba alolua, pp., filled; bottled.

kotoba alota achafa, n., a bottle, as a bottle of wine.

kotoba bolukta, n., a canteen.

kotoba isht alhkama, n., a bottle cork; a cork.

kotoba ittopa, n., the muzzle of a bottle; the mouth of a jug.

kotoba okchimali, n., a common chunk bottle.

kotoba patassa, kotoba takassa, n., a flask; a flat bottle.

kotoba shohkalali, n., a decanter; a glass bottle.

kotobushi, n., a vial; a phial; a caster used on the table.

kotobushi bolukta, n., a canteen; a small canteen.

kotoma, a., fetid; rancid; stinking, as a dead horse or old dirty rags; having an ill savor.

kotoma, v. n., to be fetid or rancid; *isuba illi at kotoma*.

kotoma, n., fetor; stench.

kotomachi, v. t., to cause fetor or stench.

kotonli, n., dandruff.

kowi, konwi, n., the woods; unburnt woods; a desert.

konwi anunka, n., a wilderness, John 3: 14.

konwi anunka, a., being in the woods; situated in the woods.

konwi anunka, v. n., to be in the woods.

konwi anunkasha, n., a fairy; a woodland deity; a nymph; a dryad; a satyr; a wood nymph.

konwi chito, n., a forest; a wilderness.

konwi haiaka, n., a wilderness, Luke 3: 4.

konwi hochito, n. pl., the forests; the great forests.

konwi shabi, n., a howling wilderness.

koyofa, pp., divided; halved crosswise; see *sinti koyufa tohbi*, a coachwhip snake; *koyufa tohbi*, half white; *yakni koyofa*, "quarters," Acts 16: 3.

koyofa, n., a half.

koyofa, v. a. i., to divide; to come apart.

koyoffi, v. t. sing., to halve crosswise; to take part away; to cut off.

koyoha, pp., rubbed in pieces.

koyoli, koyuli, v. t., to rub in the hands, as the heads of grain, Luke 6: 1; to rub the eyes; *koyuhonli*, to break in pieces; "*chunkash an koyuhonli*," (death of friends causes such sorrow.)

koyolichi, v. t., to cause to rub to pieces.

kubit, n., a cubit, Josh. 3: 4; the length of a man's arm from the elbow to the extremity of the middle finger.

kucha, kohcha, kocha, adv., out; abroad; forth; out of; outward; outwards, Matt. 17: 5; *akohcha*, to depart out of, Matt. 17: 18; *kucha hikia: kucha pila*, v. t., to emit; to throw out.

kucha, prep., without.

kucha, a., out; being out; visible; exterior; external; extrinsic; free.

kucha, kohcha, v. n., to be out; to be visible; to go forth, Matt. 14: 14; *pit kucha*, to go out, Mark 11: 11; Matt. 10: 14; to come out, 2 Kings 9: 11; *kohchat kania*, Matt. 12: 15.

kucha, pp., taken out; brought out; cashiered; put out; dislodged; ejected; evacuated; excluded; expelled; extracted; extricated; ferreted; freed; landed; ousted; released; risen; secluded; unloaded; voided; *kucha ia* Matt. 3: 16; *kohchạt iatok;* Matt. 13: 53; *kucha wiha*, pl., John 5: 28. The letter *t* is not used to connect the two words.

kucha, v. a. i., v. t., to come out, Matt. 5: 26; to appear as a cloud; to proceed out, Luke 4: 22; to withdraw; to go out, as the sun; to issue; to land; to rise, as the sun; to come out into another place; *kuncha*, nasal, *kohuncha*, freq., *koyucha*, pro., *Chahta yakni akucha tok; kuchato*, dual, Acts 12: 10 [?]; *akucha*, v. a. i. (from *a* and *kucha*), to abdicate; to depart; to emanate; to emerge; to resign; to retire; to retreat; to come forth; to come out of or from, Matt. 8: 34; *kuchạt kạnia*, v. a. i., to go away; to leave and go out; *akuhcha*, time of going out, Josh. 2: 7; *kunchut oⁿwaka*, to go out and rise; applied to land that rises, as a bluff on a river; *kuchạt oⁿyilepa*, v. a. i., to sally forth; *kuchạt oⁿyilepa*, n., a sally; *kochạt aⁿyakmạt*, Matt. 13: 49; *kunchạt aⁿya*, v. a. i., to go openly, not shut up, as in a boat; *kunchạt hikia*, v. a. i., to stand out.

kucha, n., a departure; an eruption; an exit; an extrication; an issue; the outside; a release; a resignation; retirement; a vent.

kucha, n., an outcast.

kucha, n., weather; *kucha achukma; kucha okpulo, kucha lạshpạ*, etc.

kucha aianumpuli, v. t., to preach in the open air.

kucha aianumpuli, n., a field preacher.

kucha aⁿsha, v. a. i., to sit out.

kucha fehna, a., outer.

kucha fiopa, v. a. i., to respire.

kucha hikia, a., prominent.

kucha pila, v. t., to emit; to cast out.

kucha pit hikia, v. a. i., to project.

kucha takanli, v. a. i., to jut; to project out.

kucha umba, n., wet weather.

kucha weheli, v. t., to take them out; to move them out.

kucha weli, v. t., to cast out; *isht kocha weli*, Matt. 7: 22; 8: 16, 31; *akocha weli*, Matt. 12: 24; *isht kocha welili*, I by . . . cast out, Matt. 12: 27.

kucha wiha, v. a. i. pl., to move out, Matt. 9: 25.

kucha wiha, pp., taken out; moved out.

kuchapisa imponna, a., weatherwise.

kuchasha, n., name of a small rabbit.

kuchat ia, pl., to go out, Acts 12: 10.—J. Cogswell.

kuchạt, adv., see above.

kuchi, kohchi, v. t., to bring forth, Josh. 2: 3; to take out, Matt. 18: 9; to extract; to take away; to bring out, Matt. 13: 52; to bring in or send in, as *okchito yoⁿ iⁿkuchitokoke;* to discharge; to draw; to eject; to expel; to issue; to pull out; to unload; to unship; to vent; to void; to cast out, Matt. 17: 19.

kuchichi, kohchichi, v. t. caus., to cause to go out; to turn out; to draw out; to dislodge; to enfranchise; to evacuate; to exclude; to extricate; to ferret; to land; to oust; to out; to seclude, Luke 16: 3, 4; Josh. 8: 6; *kuchihinchi*, freq.

kuchimma, adv., outward.

kula, pp., dug; grooved; grubbed; *kulat apakfopa*, entrenched; dug around.

kula, n., that which is dug; a digging; a groove.

kulat apakfopa, pp., entrenched.

kulat holisso, pp., graved.

kulha, pp., dug, as *chant kulha*, Prov. 13: 17.

kulli, v. t., to dig; to excavate; to gouge; to groove; to grub; to hew; to trench.

kulli, n., a digger; a hewer; *lukfi kulli*, one who digs the earth.

kullit apakfobli, v. t., to entrench; to dig round.

kullit holissochi, v. t., to grave.

kullit holissochi, n., a graver.

kula, kạla, n., eruption.

kumpachi, v. a. i., to whoop, as a drunken man.

kunchoⁿwaka, n., a high bluff at the water edge or side.

kuni, n., young cane.

kunta, v. a. i., to whistle with the lips; *iⁿkunta*, v. t., to whistle.

kunta, n., a whistler.

kunta, n., a whistling.

kunti, v. a. i., to grow spontaneously without planting, as potatoes that are left in the ground and grow up.—Mantabi.

kusha, pp., broken; bent down; broken and bent down; or cracked and curled up, as the upper leather of an old shoe; *kushli*, v. t.

kusha, v. a. i., to break and bend.

kusha, n., that which is broken and bent.

Kunsha, n., the *Kunshaws*; the name of one part of the Choctaw.

kunshak, n., a reed, Matt. 11: 7; 12: 20.

kunshak ahe, n., a wild potato.

kunshak ansha, n., a moor.

kunshak chito, a., reedy; n., a large reed.

kunshak patakchi, n., a low reed.

kushikanchak, n., a female fairy.

kushkachi, pp., broken and bent.

kushkachi, v. a. i., to break and bend.

kushkoa, pp. pl., bent and broken; bruised; *kunshak kushkoa*, a bruised reed, Matt. 12: 20.

kushkoa, v. a. i., to bend and break.

kushkoa, n., that which is bent and broken; bruised.

kushkuli, v. t. pl., to break and bend down.

kushli, v. t. sing., to break and bend.

kushlichi, v. t., to break and bend or cause it to be done.

kushotah, v. a. i., to bow, like a wall, Ps. 62: 3.

la, apparent form of the per. pro., 1st per. sing., I, me, found after active verbs; before *chi, he, hinla, wa, heto*, etc. It is derived from *li*, and is pronounced *la* for the sake of euphony or, more probably, because a first vowel of the above words, *a*, is merged in *la*.

lahba, a., warm; tepid; lukewarm, applied to liquids, water, milk, etc.; pp., warmed; heated.

lahba, v. n., to be warm or tepid.

lahba, n., warmth.

lahbachi, v. t., to warm; to heat; to make lukewarm.

lakabli, v. t., to notch deep.

lakapa, v. a. i., to be notched; *ite at lakampat kania;* pl. *lakapoa;* v. a. i., pl., *lakapoli,* v. t. pl.

lakchi, n., dregs; grounds; feces; grains; lees; papulæ; pimples on the skin; sediment.

lakna, a., yellow; russet; saffron; ripe; *iklakno*, a., unripe, as pumpkins; *lakna*, v. n., to be yellow.

lakna, pp., dyed yellow; rusted; turned yellow; colored yellow; painted yellow.

lakna, n., yellow.

lakna, v. a. i., to rust.

lakna, n., rust; bile; the poison of venomous serpents; choler or bile; the yolk.

lakna ansha, a., rusty; bilious.

lakna inchito, a., bilious; having a redundancy of bile.

lakna inchito, v. n., to be bilious.

laknabi, a., rusty; ripened or yellow, as fruit turned yellow.

laknabi, v. n., to be rusty; to rust, as wheat; to turn yellow.

laknachi, v. t., to rust; to turn it yellow; to color yellow; to dye yellow; to paint yellow; to saffron.

laknachi, n., one who dyes yellow; a painter who paints yellow.

laknoba (from *lakna holba*), a., drab; drab colored; rusty; yellowish.

lakofa, pp., notched; indented; scored.

lakofa, n., a notch; a deep notch; a hack; an indent; a score.

lakoffi, v. t. sing., to notch; to cut a notch; to score; *aboha itabana lakoffi*, house log notches.

lakoli, n., notches; indents.

lakoli, v. t. pl., to notch; to jag; to score; *lakonli*, nasal form, to jag.

lakoli, pp., indented.

lakolichi, v. t., to notch; to cut notches; to make notches; to indent; *lakonlichi*, to jag.

lakowa, pp., notched; jagged; scored; prepared for hewing; *lakonwa*, nasal form.

lakowa, a., serrate; serrated.

lakonwa, n. pl., notches, such as are made on steelyards; jags; scores.

laksha, a., sweaty.

laksha, v. n., to be sweaty.

laksha, v. a. i., to sweat; to perspire; *salaksha*, I sweat or I am sweaty; *lanksha; laiyaksha*.

laksha, n., sweat; perspiration.

laksha akucha, n., a pore.

laksha chito, n., a profuse sweat.

lakshạchi, v. t., to sweat; to produce perspiration; to cause to sweat.

lampa, v. a. i., to have a place worn in, as in the inside of a ring used on a neckyoke; notched in wood or iron; *lampoa*, pl.

lanla, n., name of some insect; or (according to another informant) a small bird.

lanlakechi, v. t., to indent.

lanlaki, pp., indented.

lanlaki, a., scraggy.

lanlaki, n., a dent; a notch.

lapali, a., lateral.

lapali, n., the side; "by," Josh. 5: 13; *lapoli*, pl.

lapali, v. n., to stay on the side; to be the side; *lapoli*, pl.

lapali, pp., a., being on the side; placed on the side; plated, Matt. 9: 16; *lapoli*, pl.

lapali, adv., slightly.

lapalichi, v. t., to place on the side or bottom, as in setting a horseshoe, or in plating metal, or in sewing on a piece of cloth, Matt. 9: 16; *lapolechi*, pl.

lapalichi, n., one who sets or places on the side; *lapolichi*, pl.

lapalika, n., the side, Matt. 13: 1; the border, Matt. 4: 13; the edge, Luke 5: 1.

lapalit tosholi, v. t., to translate slightly.

lapisa, v. t., to make.

lapish, see *lạpish*.

lapitta, n., a buck with full-grown horns; a stag.

laⁿpli, v. t. sing., to make a notch in wood or iron; *laⁿpoli*, v. pl., to make notches.

laponli, Gen. 30: 35.

lapushki, a., mellow; soft, Matt. 11: 8, as flour or dry ashes; supple; fine; impalpable; pliable, as dressed skin; lank; silken; *iklapushko*, not fine; coarse.

lapushki, v. n., to be mellow, soft, or pliable.

lapushki, v. a. i., to soften.

lapushki, n., mellowness; softness.

lapushki, pp., mellowed; softened; triturated.

lapushki, adv., finely.

lapushkichi, v. t., to soften; to supple; to triturate.

alⁿsa, n., a scar.

lasimo, v. a. i., to curl or rrizzle up like hair or wool.

lasun, n., a leech; a blood sucker.

lashke, imp. mood, 1st per. sing., let me; also of future tense, indicative mood, 1st per. sing., I shall; I will; see *lakofichilashke*, Matt. 8: 7.

latasa, a., flat.

latasa, v. n., to be flat.

latasa, n., flatness.

latasạlli, v. t. sing., to flatten; *naki aⁿ latasạlli*, to flatten the bullet.

latastua, a. pl., flat.

latastua, v. n., to be flat.

latastuli, v. t., to flatten them.

lataswa, a. pl., flat; pp., flattened.

lataswa, v. n., to be flat.

lataswa, n., flat ones.

latạssa, a., flat.

latạssa, v. n., to be flat.

latạssa, pp., flattened.

latạssachi, v. t., to flatten.

laua, v. t.; *hahaⁿkloka laua hatukosh*, Luke 23: 8. [This should read *lauaka hahaⁿklo hatukosh*.—H. S. H.]

laua, a., many; plenteous; numerous; abundant; copious; dense, Matt. 7: 22; 10: 31; full; manifold; much; plentiful; sufficient; unmeasured, Matt. 13: 17; Luke 2: 34; large, as *itạnaha laua*, a large meeting; *laⁿwa*, nas. form; *iklauo*, few; insufficient; minor; scanty; scarce; short; thin; younger, Matt. 7: 14.

laua, v. a. i., to suffice; to superabound.

laua, v. n., to be many; to abound; *laua-li*, I abound; *laⁿwa*, nasal form, many, Matt. 7: 22; *laiyawa; iklauo*, v. a. i., to lack; to want; *lauạt ia*, to increase; *iklauot ia*, v. a. i., to fail; to remit; to wane; *lauạt isht ia*, v. a. i, to thrive; to increase.

laua, adv., freely; much; *laua fehna*, much more; profusely.

laua, n., a plenty; a number; an abundance; a multitude; a throng; a supply; a sufficiency; a crowd; a flood; a host; a legion; a mass; a myriad; richness; a shoal; a swarm.

laua ạlhpesa, n., a supply.

laua ạlhpiesa, a., ample; quite enough.

laua chuhmi, a., considerable; a good deal.

laua fehna, a., overmuch; redundant.

laua fehna, adv., many times.

laua iⁿshali, a., main; most.

laua kạt kaniohmi, as many, Matt. 14: 36.

lauachi, v. t., to multiply; to do many or much, Matt. 13: 58; to increase the number or supply; to amplify; to propagate; *lauachit anumpuli*, to amplify in discourse; *lauachit ishi*, to receive much; to hold a great deal; *lauachit*, adv., very much.

lauat taha, pp., redoubled.

laue, lauwi, a., equal; adequate; able; *chimaiitilauashke*, be to thee as, Matt., 18: 17; *itilaui*, Matt. 10: 16; 17: 2; *hạsh itilauashke; itilauishke*, it is like, Matt. 11: 17; *iklauo*, unequal; inferior; pp., decreased; *ikalauwo*, least, Matt. 5: 19.

laue, v. n., to be equal, or adequate; *iklauo*, to be unequal; *iklauot ia*, v. a. i., to decay; to decrease; to lessen.

lauechi, v. t., to equal, to do as much, or to do as well; *chiklauecho*, you do not do as much or as well as he; *lauinchi*, nasal form; *iklauecho*, a., not to equal; inadequate; unequal; unable; *iklauechokechi*, v. t., to decrease; to diminish; to lessen; to palliate.

lauechi kạt ikono, n., inability.

laya, n., a lawyer (an imitation of the English word); an attorney at law.

lạbaha, lạbbaha, n., jabber.

lạbaha, n., a jabberer.

lạbahahanchi, v. a. i., to keep jabbering.

lạbahahanchi, n., a rattle; a rattling.

lạbahạchi, v. a. i., to jabber; *lạbahanchi*.

lạbbi, oklạbbi, v. a. i., v. t., to touch with the tongue; to eat with the fingers, as honey or grease, first dipping the forefinger into the honey, etc.

lạbbi, v. t., to sop.

lạbbi, n., sop.

lạbli, a., choked up; stopped up, as the throat or a pipe; closed up, as the ears or heart, in a figurative sense.

lạbli, v. n., to be choked up.

lạbli, v. a. i., to choke up; to fill up, as a pipe.

lạblichi, v. t., to choke it up; to stop up; to obstruct, Gen. 19: 11; *nishkin aⁿ lạblichi*.

lạcha, a., wet; moist; damp; soggy.

lạcha, v. n., to be wet, damp, or moist.

lạcha, v. a. i., to relent; to give.

lạcha, pp., wetted; moistened; drenched; imbrued; irrigated.

lạcha, n., wetness.

lạchali, v. t., to wet; to moisten; to drench; to imbrue; to irrigate; to water.

lạlli, v. t., to beat, as gold; *tạli holisso lakna lạlli*, 1 Kings 10: 16; *lạlla*, pass., *tạli holisso lakna lạlla*, beaten gold, 1 Kings 10: 17.

lạllichi, v. t., to crack, as nuts; *oksak aⁿ lạllichi*, to beat; *lạllichi*, pp.

lạpa, a., blind, Matt. 9: 27, 28; 11: 5; 12: 22; 15: 14.

lạpa, v. n., to be blind; *lạpli; lạplichi*, v. t., to make blind; to blind, Gen. 19: 11.

lạpa, n., blindness; ablepsy.

lạpa iⁿmoma, a., born blind, John 9: 1.

lạpa iⁿmoma, n., natural blindness.

lạpchu, n., a worm; an earthworm, such as are used as bait for fish; also one species of those that are generated in the human body, the long round worm, a belly worm which sometimes occasions sickness.

lạpchu ạbi, n., a vermifuge.

lạpish, lapish n., a horn; a trumpet, 1 Sam. 2: 10; Josh. 6: 4, 5, 6, 8, 13.

lạpish filạmminchi, n., an antler; a start or branch of a horn.

lạpish hituk aiạlhto, n., a powder horn.

lạpish iⁿfilạmmi, n., an antler.

lạpish intakalichi, v. t., to cup with a horn.

lạpish isht impa, n., a horn spoon.

lạpish kobafa, n., a pollard; a stag that has cast his horns.

lạsaha, v. t. pl., to strike with the palm of the hand; to slap; to spank; to thump.

lạsaha, n., a striker; a spanking.

lạsalichi, v. t. sing., to strike once with the palm of the hand; to spank; to slap; to thump.

lạsalichi, n., a thumper; a trip.

lạsalichit akkạchi, v. t., to trip.

Lạshe, n., Russia.

Lạshe iⁿmiⁿko, n., the autocrat of Russia.

Lạshi yakni, n., the Russian empire.

lạshpa, a., hot; warm; sultry; burning; inflamed; ardent; fervent; fiery; torrid.

lạshpa, v. n., to be hot; *itinlạshpa*, to be warm against each other, as in debate.

lạshpa, pp., heated; warmed.

lạshpa, v. a. i., to glow.

lạshpa, n., heat, fervor; hotness; warmth.

lạshpa ạmmona, n., mild heat.

lạshpa fehna, a., scalding hot.

lạshpa isht akostininchi, n., a thermometer.

lạshpạchi, v. t., to heat; to warm.

lạshpạli, v. t., to heat; to warm.

lạshpạli, n., a heater.

lạshpạt humma, a., red-hot.

lạshpạt humma, v. n., to be red-hot.

lạshpạt hummạchi, v. t., to heat red-hot.

le, per. pro., 1st per. sing., I, found after active verbs before *tuk, kạmo, kạno,* etc. It is derived from *li,* and is pronounced *le* for the sake of euphony; see *la;* examples: *ialek, chumpaletuk, mintilekạmo, pisalekano.*

lek, part., similar to *kạmo; ont iliahlek;* some say *nek.*

leli, v. t., to hoe; to weed plants; to destroy the weeds; to plow among corn and similar vegetables the first time; see *aleli* [Byington has *lele*].

leli, n., a weeder.

leplosi, n. (Eng. word), leprosy.

leplosi ạbi, n., a leper, Matt. 8: 2.

li, per. pro. 1st per. sing. I, found after all active verbs, except where *la* and *le* occur, which are indeed the same word, being varied in pronunciation for the sake of euphony.

liⁿ, for *lina,* I, or I till, I while, Matt. 17: 17; Acts 24: 12.

lia, pp., weeded; hoed.

liahpo, n., a sore; an ulcer.

liahpo ạbi isht illi, n., a leper, Luke 4: 27.

liahpo ạbi isht illi, n., leprosy.

liahpo hakshup, n., a scab.

liạbli, v. t., to rend; to tear a skin.

libbachih, v. a. i., to burn and make a noise like burning sulphur.—J. E.

libbi, pp., inflamed; to be kindled, as wrath, Josh. 7: 1.

libbi, n., a blaze; a flame.

libbi, v. a. i., to blaze; to flame; to burn; *limbi,* nas. form; *lihimbi,* pro. form.

libbichi, v. t., to cause it to blaze; to make a blaze; to flame; to inflame.

libbika, n., the flame; the flames.

libbikạchi, a., feverish; *libbikahanchi,* continued burning from a fever.

libesha, a., warm; sanguine; tepid; n., warmth.

libesha, v. n., to be warm.

libisha, libbisha. v. a. i., to warm; to become moderately heated.

libisha, pp., warmed; heated; moderately heated; *libbisha,* a degree less, like *chitto* from *chito.*

libishli, v. t., to heat; to warm.

libishli, n., a heater.

lihpibichi, v. t., to make fine, as dust; Deut. 9: 21.

likefa, n., a dint.

likefa, pp., dinted.

likema, v. t., to warm one's self by the fire.

likema, v. a. i., to be warm; applied to water; *oka yat likema.*

likemạchi, v. t., to warm another by the fire.

likiffi, v. t., to dint.

likimmi, v. t., to warm.

lilli, n., a lily.

lin, I; as *ạpalin,* I may not eat; *lin* is from *li* and *na.*

lint, the *n* and *t* are united with *li,* I; the *n* has a neg. meaning; the *t* is a connective; see *n.*

lip, n., a sudden motion.

lipa, lipachi, lipat, v. a. i., to move suddenly, as *chukạsh ạt lipachi,* the heart moves quickly, is excited; *lipat kucha,* to go out quickly; *lipat lopulli,* to dart; *lipat ont ia,* to go past quickly.

lipeha, a., fine and soft, as thread or silk.

lipeha, v. n., to be fine and soft.

lipehạchi, v. t., to make fine and soft.

lipemo, a., fine and soft, as down or cotton.

lipemo, v. n., to be fine and soft.

lipemochi, v. t., to make fine and soft.

lipihbi, a., fine; *bota lipihbi,* fine flour, 2 Kings 7: 1.

lipiⁿka; *lipipiⁿkạchi,* a., soft, as raiment spoken of, Luke 7: 25; *lipiⁿkạchi,* a., soft and fine, as cloth.

lipinto, a., fine and soft.

lipisto, lipishto, a., fine and soft, as thread; *hishi lipishto.*

lipisto, v. n., to be fine.

lipistochi, v. t., to make fine and soft.

lipkạchi, v. a. i., to flare; to throb, as an inflammation; probably derived from *lip* or *libbi.*

lipko, a., swift; *lipki*, obsolete.

lipli, v. a. i., to flare.

liplichi, v. t., to cause it to flare.

liplosi, n., leprosy.

liplosi ạbi, n., a leper, Matt. 11: 5.

liⁿsa, v. a. i., to troat; to cry, as a buck in rutting time.

lisepa, a., fine, as cloth.

lisisiⁿkạchi, a., very fine and soft, as small threads.

lisisiⁿkạchi, v. n., to be very fine and soft.

lish, I, etc., from *li* and *cha*, the *ch* changed to *sh* for sound's sake, I presume, as in all the other persons the conj. is *cha*, Matt. 2: 8; *ialish*, I will go, etc., Matt. 8: 7; cf. *onalish pisalachiⁿ, ishona cha ishpisachiⁿ.*

lishke, per. pro. 1st per. sing. after active verbs at the end of a sentence; *ialishke*, I go; I do go; I am going; see *ishke.*

lishoa, v. a. i., to come to pieces; to rub to pieces; to crumble; to break in pieces.

lishoa, pp., rubbed to pieces; bruised to pieces; broken to pieces; mashed; *pạska yạt lishoat taha.*

lishoa, n., pieces; crumbs; orts.

lisholichi, v. t., to mash.

lisholili, v. t., to rub to pieces; to crumble; to mash.

litafa, v. a. i. sing., to break, as a thread or rope; to sever; to snap; to come in two.

litafa, pp. sing., broken, as thread; severed; *ponola yạt litafa*, sundered.

litafa, n., a breach; that which is broken.

litali, pl., *litaffi*, sing., v. a. i., to break, as thread.

litali, pp., broken, as cords.

litali, n., the things which are broken.

litalichi, v. t., to break; to snap them, as cords.

litạffi, v. t. sing., to break, as a cord; to sunder; to snap it off; to sever.

litạffii, n., a breaker; one who breaks a cord, thread, etc.

litạk, n., the snap of a rope.

liteha, a., pp., dirty; smeared; soiled; greased; besmeared; greasy; impure; defiled; dirtied; polluted; sordid; squalid; stained; sullied; turbid.

liteha, v. n., to be dirty, greasy, or muddy.

liteha, n.; dirt; smut and grease; impurity; pollution; a stain.

litehạchi, v. t., to besmear; to dirty; to grease; to make foul.

liteli, liteli, v. t., to besmear; to dirty; to defile; to foul; to mud; to muddy; to pollute; to stain; to sully.

litelichi, v. t., to strike with a stick.

litetuk, n., tramping of horses.

litiⁿha, pl. v. t., to strike with sticks, or to beat with sticks.

litiⁿha, n., a striker.

litikfo, n., grease.

litikfo, a., pp., greasy; greased; oiled.

litikfo, v. n., to be greasy.

litikfo, pp., greased.

litikfochi, v. t., to grease; to begrease.

litilakạchi, pp. pl., cracked, as dry ground.

litituⁿkạchi, a., shabby.

litituⁿkạchi, v. n., to be shabby.

litoa, litowa, v. a. i., to shatter; to digest, as food in the stomach.

litoa, litowa, pp., a., mashed; bruised; rent; contused; pommeled; shattered; trodden soft, like mud in a road; sore, as a sore mouth; contrite; crushed; quashed; *itialbi ạt litowa*, the lips are sore; *iklitowo*, a., unbroken.

litoa, n., contusion; shatters.

litoli, v. t., to mash; to bruise; to rend; to make sore, as the mouth; to contuse; to crash; to crush; to pommel; to quash; to smash; to squash. [I have always heard this *litoli.*—H. S. H.]

liwạli, luwali, v. a. i., to be sore, as the gums when diseased with scurvy.— *Hiletạbi*, informant.

liweli, v. a. i. pl., to fall; to drop off, as leaves or fruit.

liweli, n., a fall; a dropping.

liweli, v. a. i., to crumble off and drop like earth on a bluff, or the sides of a wall.

liwelichi, v. t., to cause to fall; to shake off fruit, leaves, etc.

lobafa, v. a. i., to turn up by the roots, as a tree ⸬hat falls down; to be plucked up; Luke 17: 6.

lobafa, ρp., turned up by the roots; eradicated; *iti ạt lobafa*, plucked up by the roots.

lobafa, n., roots turned up; that which is plucked up.

lobali, lubali, v. a. i. pl., to turn up by the roots.

lobali, pp., turned up by the roots; eradicated.

lobali, n. pl., the trees, etc., plucked up by the roots.

lobaffi, v. t. sing., to pluck up by the roots; to turn up by the roots; to eradicate.

lobbi, v. t. sing., to pluck up; to turn up by the roots, Matt. 13: 29; see *lubbi*.

lobli, see *lubbi*.

loboa, a., plump; round.

loboa, v. n., to be plump.

lobobumkạchi, a., plump.

lobobumkạchi, v. n., to be plump.

lobuhbo, pl., *lumbo* sing., a., round; globular.

lobuhbo, v. n., to be round.

lobuhbochi, lohbobochi, v. t., to make them round; *chakonlichit lohbobochi*, 1 Kings 6: 18.

lobuna, n., purslane, called pusley, a weed growing in gardens; *labuna, labaⁿla*.—James Wall.

lochussa, v. a. i., to be near each other and stand straight up like some cow's horn; *wak lạpish lochussa*.

lohboạchi, n., knops, 1 Kings 7: 24.

lohmạt taloa, v. a. i., to hum.

lohto, n., a cluster; *paⁿkki lohto*, a cluster of grapes.

lohto, a., being full of branches; clustered.

lohto, v. n., to be full of branches, or to be in a cluster, or clustered.

lokoli, see *lukoli*.

lokussa, v. a. i., to huddle.

lokussa, pp., huddled.

lokussa, n., a huddle.

lokussạlli, v. t., to huddle.

lokush, n., a dipper; a water-gourd; a ladle.

loma, adv., lightly; see *luma*, softly, as a wind, Acts 27: 13.

lopa, v. a. i., to turn up by the roots.

lopa, luba, pp., plucked up by the roots; exterminated.

lopa, n., that which is plucked up.

loshuma, lushoma (q. v.), pp., finished.

loshummi, lushomi (q. v.), v. t., to finish; to complete; to achieve; *lushummi*, 1 Sam. 3: 18.

lotohạchi, v. a. i., to trickle down like drops of sweat; to drop fast, as sweat

or blood, etc.; *laksha kạt lotohahanchi, issuba hạt lotohạchi*, a horse sweats when he runs.

lotuski, a., short and thick; *shukha lotuski*.

lotuski, v. n., to be short and thick.

lotuskichi, v. t., to make short and thick.

lua, v. a. i., to burn; to ignite; to fire; to take fire; to rage, as a fever; *italua*, to burn together; to consume; to kindle.

lua, pp., a., burnt, Josh. 7: 15; fired; cauterized; inflamed; burned; enkindled; fervid; fiery; ignited; kindled; scalded; scorched; torrid; *ikluo*, a., unburnt.

lua, n., a burn; a burning; a conflagration; fuel [?]; ignition.

lua taha, pp., consumed.

luachi, vt., to burn; to set on fire; to cause to burn; to inflame; to ignite; to cauterize; to enkindle; to fire; to scald; to scorch.

luachi, n., a burner.

luachi, n., ignition.

luahe keyu, a., incombustible.

luak, n., fire; *luak itokaha*, "cast into the fire," Matt. 7: 19; Josh. 7: 15; *luak ak keyukma pilạshpahe keyu*.

luak aiulhti, n., a fire-hearth; a hearth.

luak apạla, n., a fire-pan; a torch-pan.

luak ashoboli, n., a chimney; a flue; a fireplace; a hearth.

luak ataha iksho, n., everlasting fire, Matt. 18: 8.

luak atoba, n., a fire place.

luak chito, n., a great fire; the great fire, Matt. 13: 50; a conflagration; the place of future torment; hell.

luak ikbi, n., a fire man; a man who makes fires.

luak iksita, n., the hearth or fireplace, Gen. 18: 6.

luak ipokni, n., light white ashes, just after they are made by the fire.

luak isht apuⁿfạchi, n., a fire bellows; bellows.

luak isht chilichi, n., a fire-poker.

luak isht ikbi, n., a match.

luak isht kiseli, n., fire-tongs.

luak isht puⁿfa, n., a bellows.

luak isht shạfa, n., a fire-shovel.

luak isht shạffi, n., a fire-shovel.

luak ituksita, n., a fire-hearth; a hearth; a fireplace.

luak mosholi, v. a. i., to die or go out, as fire.

luak mosholi, pp., extinguished fire.

luak mosholichi, v. t., to extinguish fire; to put out fire.

luak mosholichi, n., a fireman; a man whose business is to extinguish fires.

luak palali, n., the ignis fatuus.

luak shali, n., the venereal disease (a proper name; lit., to carry fire).

luak toba, n., fuel; *luak toba nana kia isht ala.*

luak tobaksi, n., a coal of fire.

luak tobaksi mosholi, n., charcoal; blacksmith's coal; carbon.

luạt humma, a., red-hot.

luạt humma, v. n., to be red-hot.

luạt hummachi, v. t., to heat red-hot.

luba, lopa, pp., exterminated; *lubạt taha,* extirpated.

lubbi, lobbi, v. t. pl., to root up, Matt. 13: 29; to pluck up by the roots; to exterminate; *lobli,* sing.

lubbit tali, v. t., to extirpate.

luboa, see Child's Book on the Soul, pp. 5, 12.

lubona, pp., boiled in the kernel; *tanchi lubona.*

lubona, v. a. i., to boil in the kernel; *tanchi ạt lubona.*

luboni, v. t., to boil in the kernel; to cook in the kernel; *tanchi aⁿ luboni;* see *hobi.*

luehạchi, v. a. i., to shed hair.

lufa, pp., peeled; stripped; pared; shelled; husked; *tanchi ạt lufa, tobi ạt lufa, takkon ạt lufa.*

lufa, n., a husk.

luffi, v. t., to husk; to shell; to peel; to pare; to skin; to strip.

luffi, n., a husker; a parer.

luha, pp. pl., husked; pared; shelled; peeled.

luhmi, v. t., v. a. i., to hide; to secrete; to conceal; to cloak; to closet; to couch, Matt. 11: 25; 13: 44; Josh. 2: 4, 6; to abscond; to envelop; to shut, as a book; to skulk; to stifle; to suppress; to veil; *ikinluhmo,* 1 Sam. 3: 18; to cover; *ileluhmi,* to hide himself; to hide herself, Luke 1: 24; *itinluhmi,* to hide from each other.

luhmi, n., a hider; *ileluhmi,* an absconder.

luhmi keyu, a., unreserved.

luhminchi, v. t., to hide; to cause to hide; *ilaluhminchi,* to hide himself, John 1: 20 [?].

luhmit nana apesa, v. t., to conspire; to plan something secretly.

lukchuk, n., mud; mire; slush.

lukchuk aⁿsha, a., muddy.

lukchuk bano, a., muddy; all mud; pp., muddied.

lukchuk banuchi, v. t., to muddy; to soil with mud.

lukchuk chito, n., deep mud; a slough.

lukchuk chito, a., very muddy; heavy; miry; muddy.

lukchuk okakạnia, v. a. i., to stall; to mire down.

lukchuk yalạllahạ, n., a quagmire.

lukfanta, n., whitewash.

lukfanuna, n., a brick kiln.

lukfạpa, n., a lick or a saline place; a place where cattle and beasts of the forest—deer and buffalo—eat the dirt and lick for salt.

lukfi, n., dirt; clay; earth; soil; ground, dust; argil.

lukfi atoba, a., earthen; made of earth.

lukfi hạta, lukfạta, n., chalk; white clay.

lukfi humma, lukfomma, n., red dirt; vermilion; red paint; rouge.

lukfi isht kula, n., a spade.

lukfi isht patasạlli, n., a trowel.

lukfi isht piha, n., a shovel.

lukfi kotoba, n., a jug; a jar.

lukfi lumbo, n., a clod; a lump of clay.

lukfi nuna, n., a brick.

lukfi nuna boli, n., a bricklayer.

lukfi nuna ikbi, n., a brickmaker.

lukfi nuna isht ạtta, n., a mason; a brick mason.

lukfi nuna patali, v. t., to pave.

lukfi nuna pilesa, n., a mason.

lukfi nuna tushafa, n., a brickbat.

lukfi yamạska, v. t., to make mortar.

lukfi yạmmạska, n., mortar.

lukfomma, see *lukfi humma.*

lukluki, pl. of *lukoli,* Ch. Sp. Book, p. 77.

lukoli, lokoli, v. a. i., to collect; to flock; to cluster; to huddle, Josh. 4: 18; *italukoli,* to flock together; *lukonli,* n. f.; *italukonli,* being collected together.

lukoli, alukoli, n., a drove; a herd; a bunch; a cluster; a flock; a group; a tuft; *chuka alokoli*, a village.

lukoli, pp., collected; huddled; clustered; grouped.

lukolichi, v. t., to bring together in herds; to bunch; to cluster; to group.

luksi, n., a terrapin; a tortoise; also, a padlock; a lock; *luksabashka; luksinbiya; luksikonih; luksipatoni; luksishawi.*

luksi bashka, n., a striped-headed turtle.

luksi chito, n., a tortoise.

luksi fulup, n., the cock of a gun lock.

luksi konih, n., a gopher.

luksupa foli, n., a night hawk.

luli, v. t. pl., to husk; to peel; to shell; to pare.

luli, n., a parer.

luma, pp., hidden; secreted; out of sight; occult; concealed; covered; enveloped; retired; shut, as a book; suppressed.

luma, n., quietness; a retreat; a secret.

luma, a., occult; unseen; out of sight; clandestine; close; dim; dormant; disguised; latent; privy; quiescent; recluse; recondite; tacit; underhand; unexposed; unsearchable; Matt. 5: 14, hid; Matt. 10: 26; 13: 44; Josh. 7: 21; *iklumo*, a., naked; undisguised.

luma, v. n., to be occult.

luma, v. a. i., to disappear; to lurk; *ila-luma.*

luma, loma, adv., softly; secretly; privily; easily; obscurely; slyly; *loma* means in a less degree than *luma.*

luma keyu, a., undissembled.

lumanka, a., hidden.

lumanka, v. n., to be hidden; *isht inlumanka*, Matt. 5: 28; *anlumankashke*, be in secret; *itinlumanka*, to be hidden together; to fornicate; to commit fornication, Matt. 5: 32; to be guilty of lewdness or adultery, Matt. 5: 27.

lumanka, n., secrecy; *alumanka*, n., in secret; the secret place, Matt. 6: 4; *aialumanka*, n., in secret, Matt. 6: 18.

lumanamihachi, v. t., to murmur, Luke 5: 30.

lumasi, a., secret; easy; slight; unstrained.

lumasi, adv., secretly; easily; obscurely; quietly; softly; stilly.

lumasit, adv., secretly.

lumat ansha, imp., hush; keep still.

lumat ikhana, n., privity.

lumat taloa, v. a. i., to hum.

lumat, adv., silently; secretly, Matt. 1:19; Josh. 2: 1.

lumat anumpa, n., a whisper.

lumat anumpuli, v. t., v. a. i., to whisper.

lumat anumpuli, n., a whisperer.

lumat chinya, v. a. i., to sit in secret; to wait in secret for any object.

lumat fohki, v. t., to slip in.

lumat ishko, v. t., to sip; to drink a little.

lumat kania, v. a. i., to sneak off.

lumbo, a. sing., round; globular; spherical; convex; orbed; oval; rotund; *hatak lumbo*, an individual.

lumbo, v. n., to be round.

lumbo, pp., made round; rounded; rolled.

lumbo, n., a ball; a globe; a lump; a packet; a roll; roundness.

lumboa, lumpoa, pp. pl., hid; hidden; concealed; secreted, Josh. 10: 27; *luma*, sing.

lumbochi, v. t., to make round; to round; to roll; to make a ball.

lumiksho, a., ingenuous; without disguise; plain; self-evident.

lumpoa, a., occult.

lumpoa, v. n., to be occult.

lumpuli, v. t. pl., to hide; to secrete; to conceal.

lunatik, n., lunatic; an imitation of the English word.

lupaha, v. a. i., to discharge saliva; *itukchi lupaha.*

lupi, n., brains; marrow; brain; pulp.

lupi aialhto, n., the brain pan.

lusa, a., black; dark; jet; dull; sable; smutty; swarthy.

lusa, n., black; smut; a blemish; blackness; a blot; a blur; soil.

lusa, v. n., to be black.

lusa, pp., blacked; dyed black; colored black; soiled; blurred; blotted; tarnished; *ikluso*, a., unsoiled; unspotted; unsullied.

lunsa, n., a swamp; a fen.

lunsa aiali, n., the edge of a swamp; the end of a swamp; the limits of a swamp.

lunsa chito, n., a large swamp; Big Black, the name of a river in the old nation.

luⁿsa foka, a., swampy.

lusa iksho, a., unblemished.

luⁿsa shahbi, n., an open swamp, being without underbrush.

lusa talaia, n., a dot; a blot; a black spot or place.

lusa taloha, n. pl., black spots.

luⁿsa tikpi, n., a large round swamp, or the projection of a swamp.

lusachi, v. t., to black; to blacken; to color black; to soil; to dye black; to blot; to blur; to crock; to darken; to slur; to smut; to speck; to spot; to sully; to tarnish; to thumb; to make black, Matt. 5: 36.

lusachi, n., a blackener; one who dyes black.

lusachikchiki, a., dotted; n., dots.

lusachit talali, v. t., to dot.

lusakbi, n., brown; dun.

lusakbi, v. n., to be brown.

lusakbichi, v. t., to brown; to color brown.

lusbi, a., being of a dark-brown color; auburn; chestnut; dingy.

lusbi, v. n., be of a dark-brown color.

lusbi, n., a dark-brown color.

lusbichi, v. t., to color a dark-brown; to embrown.

luⁿslo, n., a mushroom.

lusluki, a., dark colored; dark-brown, Ch. Sp. Book, p. 94; also v. n. and n.; *luslukichi*, v. t.

lushka, v. a. i. (a Chickasaw word), to lie; to joke; to jest; to speak falsely in sport; *iklushko*, a., undeniable.

lushka, n., a liar; a joker.

lushka, n., a lie; a joke; a falsehood; a fetch; a hoax.

lushkachi, v. t., to cause to lie; to joke.

lushoma, loshuma, pp., finished; completed; see *aloshuma*.

lushomi, lushummi, loshummi, v. t., to finish; to complete; to achieve, Josh. 10: 39; *ileloshomi*, to complete one's self; with all one's self, Luke 10: 27.

luwali, liwali, v. a. i., to be sore, as the gums, when a person has the scurvy; to drool from a sore mouth.

łabaⁿka, v. a. i., to snore, as a person in troubled sleep.

łabaⁿka, n., a snorer.

łabaⁿka, n., a snoring.

łabeta, a., boggy; miry; muddy; marshy.

łabeta, v. n., to be miry.

łabeta, n., mire; soft mud; slush.

łabeta foka, a., marshy.

łabetąchi, v. t., to make it miry or muddy.

łabinta, nasal form, being miry, or a mire.

łabishko, n., mire.

łabishko, a., miry.

łabocha, v. a. i., to boil, as food in water.

łabocha, pp., boiled; done; dressed or cooked in boiling water; seethed; sodden.

łabocha, n., boiled food; victuals; hominy and boiled meat; pottage.

łaboshli, v. t., to cook; to boil; to dress or cook food in boiling water; to seethe.

łaboshli, n., a cook; one who boils, etc.

łaboshlichi, v. t., to cause one to boil food; to employ one to boil.

łachąnko, a., muddy.

łachąk, n., a single noise of a certain kind.

łachąkachi, v. a. i., to say *łachąk*.

łachąkat ishi, v. t., to snatch; to catch; to twitch.

łachiⁿko, a., muddy.

łachiⁿko, n., mud.

łachiⁿkochi, v. t., to make it muddy.

łacholi, v. t., to make a sore, or sores.

łachopa, a., soft; miry, as mud; boiled until it is soft.

łachopa., v. n., to be soft or miry.

łachopąchi, v. t., to make soft or tender.

łachowa, v. a. i., to become sore; to ulcerate.

łachowa, a., sore.

łachowa, pp., ulcerated.

łachowa, v. n., to be sore.

łachowa, n., a sore; sores; a humor; soreness; a pit; a pock; the scratches; an ulcer.

łachowa chito, a., scabby; scabbed.

łachowa hakshup, n., the scab of a sore; a scab.

łachowa imikhiⁿsh, n., salve.

łachowa laua, a., ulcerous; full of sores.

łachowąchi, v. t., to ulcerate.

łaⁿfa, pp., marked; ruled; written; scarified; delineated; described; gauged; scored; streaked; traced; *iklaⁿfo*, a., unmarked; unwritten.

laⁿfa, n., a line; a long mark, made by a carpenter's line on timber or by a pencil, etc.; a crease; a streak.

lafeha, n., mud; mire.

lafeha, a., muddy; miry.

lafeha, lafiⁿha, v. n., to be muddy.

lafehachi, v. t., to make it muddy.

lafeta, n., mud; mire.

lafeta, a., miry; muddy.

lafeta, v. n., to be miry; *lafinta* nasal form.

lafetachi, v. t., to make it miry.

laⁿfi, v. t , to make a mark; to mark; to rule; to write; to draw a line on something; to scarify; to crease; to delineate; to describe; to design; to draft; to draw; to project; to scar; to designate; to score; to streak; to trace; *holisso laⁿfi*, to write a book.

laⁿfi, n., a marker; a writer.

lafiⁿha, see *lafeha*.

lafintini, lafintini, lafintoni, n., a bird called a snowbird.

laⁿfit hobachi, v. t., to picture; to draw lines and imitate.

laha, pp., rubbed off; sucked by the doctors; cupped by their mouths; scarified.

laha, n., a scarification; marks.

lahkachi, laha, pp. pl., marked; marked with gullies, as a bluff bank by the water that has run down its sides.

lahkachi, n., marks.

lakoffa hinla, a., curable; extricable; healable; sanable.

lakoffahe keyu, a., cureless; incurable; irredeemable; remediless; unrecoverable.

lakoffi, v. n., to recover; to escape disease; to heal; *chilakofi*, you have recovered; *iⁿlakofi*, to lose, Matt. 10: 42.

lakoffi, n., a recovery; an escape; a cleaning; a cure; a come off; an extrication; a restoration; salvation.

lakoffi, a., whole.

lakoffi, pp., recovered; cured; escaped; delivered; healed, Matt. 15; 28; saved; missed; shielded; ransomed; redeemed; redressed; released; relieved; remedied; restored; extricated; freed; *chilakofi*, you are cured, Luke 5: 14 [?]; Josh. 5: 8; Matt. 8: 13; *lakofit intaha*, were whole; *lakoⁿffi* having escaped; missing; *lakoffik*, past tense; *iklakofo*, a., unransomed;

unrecovered; unredeemed; uncured; unrelieved.

lakoffi, lakofi, v. a. i., to escape, 2 Kings, 9: 15; to come off; to get well; to recover from sickness; to elude; to evade; to miss; to slip; to flee from; Luke 3: 7; *lakofolih*, pl.

lakoⁿffi, n., an escaping; a cure; a recovery; a release.

lakoffichi, v. t., to ransom; to redeem; to redress; to release; to relieve; to remedy; to rescue; to restore; to shield, Josh. 2: 13; to recover; to save; to deliver; to heal, Luke 5: 12; to cure, Matt. 1: 21; 8: 16; 17: 16; *ilelakoffichi*, to cure himself, Luke 4: 23; to cleanse of a leprosy, Matt. 12: 10; 14: 14; 15: 30; Luke 4: 27; 2 Kings 9: 15; *iⁿlakoffichi*, v. t., to beat him out; to defeat him, etc.; to free; *iklakofecho*, neg., Josh. 8: 22; *lakofihinchi, lakafihinchi*, freq. used for pl., Luke 5: 17; 9: 2; Matt. 4: 23; 9: 35; to deliver from; Matt. 6: 13; *lakofoa*, pl.

lakoffichi, n., a deliverer; a saver; a savior; a curer; a healer; a ransomer; a redeemer; a restorer.

lakoffichi, n., redemption.

lakoffiⁿk is in past time; nasal form of *lakoffek*, like *chumpak, nuselek*.

lakoffit isht ia, v. a. i., to begin to recover.

lakoffit isht ia, a., convalescent.

lakofi, see *lakoffi*.

lakofoat taha, pp., healed, Luke 17: 14.

lakofoht taha, pp. pl., healed; had been healed, Luke 8: 2.

lakofolichi, v. t. pl., to heal, Matt. 4: 24.

lali, v. t. pl., *latabli*, sing., to pour; to sprinkle; to scatter; *oⁿlali*, to scatter on; to shower; to splash; *laⁿya, oⁿlaya*, pp., splashed on, n., splash.

lali, n., a scatterer; a pourer.

lalichi, v. t., to cause to pour.

lali, v. t. pl., to mark; to scarify one's self; to cup with the mouth, as the Choctaw doctors are wont to do; to sprinkle; *lahnli*, nasal form, to rule.

lali, n., a scarifier; a cupper.

lalichi, v. t., to cause to be scarified; to scarify another; to mark.

lalinchi, v. t., nasal form, to sprinkle.

lampko, limpko, a., strong; plump; stout; athletic; lusty; robust; valid;

mighty; *hatak lampko;* mighty men, Matt. 12: 29; Josh. 1: 14; 6: 2; 8: 3.

łampko, v. n., to be strong.

łampko, n., strength; force; virtue, 1 Sam. 2: 10.

łampko, pp., strengthened; braced.

łampkuchi, łimpkuchi, v. t., to strengthen; to make strong; to brace; to corroborate; *isht lumpkuchi,* n., a strengthener.

łapa, v. a. i., to spread, as a flock of birds; to extend; *pachi at lapat aⁿya,* the pigeons spread as they fly.

łapa, pp., spread; extended; stretched.

łapa, n., extension; spreading; *iⁿlapa,* caul of the bowels.

łapat, adv., widely; to a wide extent.

łapuchi, v. t., to extend; to spread; to cause them to spread.

łatapa, v. a. i., to spill; to be suffered to fall; to pour; *latahampa,* freq.; *lataiyapa,* pro.

łatapa, pp., spilt; spilled; *latampa,* nasal form; *latahampa,* freq. form; *iklatapo,* a., unshed; unspilt.

łatapa, n., that which is spilt; an effusion; a drop, Luke 22: 44.

łatąbli, n., a spiller.

łatąbli, v. t., to pour; to shed (tears), Luke 23: 28; *oⁿlatąbli,* to shed on; to pour on, 2 Kings 9: 3, 6.

łatiⁿko, a., miry; muddy.

łatiⁿko, v. n., to be miry.

łatiⁿko, n., mire.

łatiⁿkuchi, v. t., to make it miry.

łatimo, łatemo, a., miry; boggy; soft.

łatimo, v. n., to be miry.

łatimo, n., mire; a bog.

łatimuchi, v. t., to make it miry.

łaya, see *tali.*

łaⁿya, pp., nasal form, scattered; split, Matt. 5: 13; 9: 17.

łafintini, see *lafintini.*

łeli, v. t., to scatter, as to scatter beads, shots, etc., on the floor; *liha,* pp.

łeli, n., a scatterer.

łeli, łili, v. t. pl. of *liffi,* to strip off; *linli,* nas. form; to pluck off heads of wheat, Mark 2: 23; *onush aⁿ łeli,* Matt. 12: 1; *lehha,* pp.

łepa, v. a. i., to lie or fall on the face, Luke 17: 16; Matt. 17: 6; *lipia,* pro. form.

łia, pp., scattered; *liⁿya,* nasal form.

łia, n., that which is scattered.

łibanta, łibanto, a., narrow, as a strip of land.

łibata, n., a leather string; a thong; a string.

łibli, see *lipli.*

łiⁿfa, pp., unraveled; pulled out; drawn out, raveled; stripped; *fuli at liⁿfa,* the switch is stripped of leaves; *lihaⁿfakachi,* to strain the cords or sinews.

łiⁿfa, v. a. i., to unravel; to ravel; to come out; to cramp; *iyi at liⁿfa,* the leg cramps.

łiⁿfa, n., that which is unraveled; the raveling; cramp; *iyi liⁿfa,* cramp in the foot.

łifelichi, v. t. sing., to pierce; to stab; *shuka yaⁿ lifelichi,* to pierce the hog; *lifiⁿha,* pl.

łifelichi, n., a stabber.

łiffi, v. t. sing., to strip; to pull off; to strip off; *iti hishi liffi,* to strip off the leaves; *paⁿki aⁿ liffi,* to strip off the grapes; *liⁿfi* nasal form; *lihiⁿfa,* freq.

łiffi, łiⁿfi, n., a stripper.

łiffichi, v. t. caus., to make him strip, etc.

łifiⁿha, pl., to stab; to pierce; *lifelichi,* sing; *lifoli,* also pl.

łifiⁿha, n., a stabber; or stabbers.

łiha, pp. pl., stripped off; *linfa,* sing.

łiⁿka, v. a. i., to blow the nose.

łikaha, a., slimy; ropy; stringy, like slippery elm bark when soaked in water; sizy; viscid.

łikaha, v. n., to be slimy, ropy, or sizy; *likaⁿha,* nasal form.

łikaha, n., ropiness; stringiness; mother (in vinegar); a thick, slimy substance concreted in liquors, particularly in vinegar.

łikahąchi, v. t., to render ropy or sizy.

łikancha, a., slimy.

łikancha, v. n., to be slimy.

łikancha, n., sliminess.

łikanchachi, v. t., to render slimy.

łikanli, a., slimy; soft; slippery, like soaked slippery-elm bark.

łikanli, v. n., to be slimy.

łikanli, n., sliminess.

łikanlichi, v. t., to render slimy.

łikaⁿsha, a., stringy; ropy.

łikaⁿsha, v. n., to be stringy.

łikaⁿsha, n., stringiness.

łikąshbi, v. a. i., to be slimy, or ropy; like *ilikaha* and *shinąshbi*.

łikiⁿhąchi, łikihąchi, n., the sound of a consumptive person's breath.

łikoa, łikoha, a., slimy; ropy, as soaked slippery-elm bark.

łikoa, v. n., to be slimy.

łikoa, n., sliminess.

łikohichi, v. t., to render slimy.

łikokoa, a., filthy, as unwashed eyes; smutty.

łikokoa, v. n., to be filthy.

łikokoa, n., filthy.

łikokoachi, v. t., to render filthy.

łikowa, n., a pumpkin color; a mixed color.

łikowa, a., having a pumpkin color; *is-suba likowa*, a pumpkin-colored horse.

łikuⁿklo, n., a small bird, called a humming bird.

łilafa, v. a. i. sing., to come apart, as cloth; to tear, as it tears; *italilafa*, to tear asunder from each other, Luke 23: 45.

łilafa, pp., torn; rent; lacerated; mangled; *italilafa*, rent in twain, Luke 23: 45; *italilaffi*, to tear asunder, Matt. 6: 65; Josh. 7: 6 (to rend clothes).

łilafa, n., a rent; the thing torn; a gap; a laceration.

łilalaⁿkąchi, łilallaⁿkąchi, pp. pl., torn, tattered; rent; ragged; shabby; *shukbo ąt lilalaⁿkąchi*, the blanket is torn to pieces.

łilalaⁿkąchi, n., rags; things rent, torn, etc.

łilali, pp. pl., torn; rent; mangled, Josh. 9: 4.

łilali, n., rents; things torn.

łilalichi, v. t., to tear; to rend; to mangle.

łilalichi, n., a tearer; a mangler.

łiląffi, v. t. sing., to tear; to rend; to lacerate; to sever, Matt. 9: 16.

łiląffi, n., a tearer; a render.

łiląffi, n., a laceration.

łilechi, łillichi, v. t. pl., to tear; to rend, to mangle.

łilechi, łillichi, n., a tearer; a render.

łilli, v. t. pl., to tear; to rend.

łilli, pass., rent; applied to salt kettles when old and scaling off.

łili, łeli, v. t. pl., to strip off (leaves or seed from a stalk); *linli*, nasal form.

łimimpa, a., smooth; sleek and hard, as flint corn.

łimimpa, v. n., to be smooth, sleek, and hard.

łimimpa, n., sleekness; smoothness; hardness.

łimimpąchi, v. t., to render sleek; to sleek.

łimishko, a., sleek, smooth, and shining, like flint corn or the hair of a well-fed horse.

łimishko, v. n., to be sleek or smooth; *shapo ąt limishko*, the hat is sleek; *tanchi ąt limishko*, the corn is smooth or sleek.

łimishkuchi, v. t., to sleek; to render smooth.

łimpko, see *lampko*.

łimpkuchi, see *lampkuchi*.

łinli, v. t., to rub in the hands, as ears of wheat, Mark 2: 23.

łioa, ałioa, v. a. i. pl., to pursue; to chase; to follow.

łioli, v. t., to pursue; to chase, 2 Sam. 24: 13; *itilioli*, to pursue each other; to rut, as animals.

łioli, n., a pursuer; a chaser.

łioli, n., a chase; a pursuit.

łipa, a., old; having been long used; threadbare; trite, Josh. 9: 4.

łipa, pp., worn out; worn; inverted; *lipli*, v. t.

łipa, n., that which is worn out.

łipachi, v. t. caus., to wear out; to cause to wear out.

łipeli, v. t., to turn over; to turn bottom side up; to lay anything with the face toward the earth; to invert; to overthrow; to reverse.

łipia (from *lepa*), v. a. i., to fall or lie with the face toward the earth, *aka lipia*, Matt. 4: 9; 2 Sam. 24: 20; Josh. 5: 14; 7: 10; to lie on the face; to fall down, as a man in an act of worship; see Luke 5: 8 (to lie low).

łipia, pp., turned over; laid on the face; inverted; overthrown; reversed.

łipia, a., prone.

łipia, n., that which is turned over; a lying on the face; proneness; attitude of worship; a humble posture; prostration.

łipiąt itola, v. a. i., to fall down, Matt. 2: 11; Luke 5: 12.

lipiạt itola, n., a worshiper; one that has fallen down; one that lies on his face.

lipkạchi, pl. of *lipia*, pp., turned over; lying on the face, Mark 3: 11.

lipkạchi, v. a. i., to turn over on the face; to fall down; to lie on the face; to take a humble posture for the worship of God; to lie low, Matt. 2: 11; Josh. 7: 6; *lipkanchi*, nasal form; *lipkaiyachi*, pro. form.

lipkạchi, n., those who lie on their faces; those who act as worshipers.

lipli, libli, v. t., to wear; to wear out, as a garment.

lipoli, v. t. pl., to turn over; to lay on the face, or bottom upward; *lipeli* sing.

liposhi, v. a. i., to pine away; to emaciate.

liposhi, pp., a., pined away; jaded; cheerless; emaciated; macerated; stunted.

liposhi, a., frail; imbecile; infirm or unfirm; languid; low; low-spirited; meager; morbid.

liposhi, n., the state of one who has pined away; infirmity; languor.

liposhi, n., an invalid.

liposhichi, v. t., to jade; to pine; to wear out; to make to languish; to macerate; to stunt.

lipulli, lopulli (q. v.), v. t., to go through; to pass through.

litiⁿka, v. a. i., to breathe with difficulty on account of some obstruction in the nose.

litilli, n., wax; gum; resin, as the wax of the ear.

litilli, v. a. i., to exude, as gum; to cause the gum to exude, as worms do that eat the bark; *litillichi*, v. caus.

litoa, v. a. i. pl., to untie, as it unties.

litoa, pp., loosed.

litoa, a., loose.

litofa, v. a. i. sing., to untie; to loosen; to get loose; to unwind.

litofa, pp., untied; unloosed; loosened; unwound; disengaged; disentangled; freed; loosed; *inlitofa*, pp., unfettered.

litoffi, v. t., to untie; to unloose; to loosen; to loose; to unwind; to unbind; to disengage; to disentangle; to unbuckle; to undo; to unfetter; to unshackle; to unstring; *inlitoffi*, to free him.

litoffichi, v. t. caus., to cause to untie, etc.

litofkạchi, v. a. i. pl., to untie; to loosen.

litofkạchi, pp. pl., untied; unloosed; loosed; unwound.

litoha, a., untied.

litoha, v. a. i., to unwind.

litoli, pl., *litoffi* sing., to untie; to unwind; to unloose, Luke 3: 16; to unbind; to unlink; see *hotofi*.

litoli, n., one who unties, unwinds, etc., more than once, or they who untie. Plural verbs are used where there is a plurality of action, and there may or may not be a plurality of agents.

litolichi, v. t., to cause to untie.

lobboa, a., round; plump.

lobboa, v. n., to be round and plump.

lobboa, n., a thing which is round.

lobboạchi, v. t., to round; to make it round.

loboboa, a. pl., round and plump.

loboboa, v. n. pl., to be round and plump.

lobocha, n., boiled food of all kinds.

lobohạchi, v. t., to clap; to clap the wings; to make a noise by flying.

lobonto, a., round.

lobukachi, v. a. i., to make a noise, as when anything falls into water; *oka lobukachi*, to douse; to fall into the water.

lobukta, a., short and round.

lobukta, v. n., to be short and round.

lobuktạchi, v. t., to render short and round.

lofa, a., raw, as the flesh where the skin has been removed.

loⁿfa, luⁿfa, pp., peeled; skinned; stripped, as corn leaves from a cornstalk; flayed.

loⁿfa, v. a. i., to peel off; to come off.

loⁿffi, luⁿffi, v. t. sing., to skin; to flay; to peel; to strip off (*wak aⁿ loffi; fạni aⁿ loffi*); *ileluⁿffi*, to molt, as a snake; to skin himself.

loⁿffi, n., a skinner; a flayer; a peeler.

loha, pp. pl., *loⁿfa*, sing., peeled; skinned; flayed; barked; stripped off, as fodder from the stalks; scaled; shelled; stripped.

loha, v. a. i., to peel off; to come off, as skin; to shell.

loha, n. pl., that which is taken off, as skins, etc.

łohama, łuhama, pp., beaten down; trodden down, as grass; trailed. See *kahama*.

łohama, a., underfoot; stretched out like an iron ring (Sixtowns meaning).

łohama, n., grass beaten down; a trail.

łohạmmi, v. t., to tread down.

łohạmmichi, v. t., to cause to tread down; to overrun.

łokaffi, see *lukaffi*.

łoli, v. t. pl., to skin; to peel; to flay; to strip off skin, etc.; to scale; *iti aⁿ loli*, to peel trees.

łoli, n. pl., peelers; skinners.

łołichi, v. t., to cause to peel.

łopish, n., dust.

łopohạchi, v. a. i., v. t., to flop the wings; to flop; to flutter; to hover, Deut. 32: 2.

łopoli, v. a. i., to pass through slowly, as in reading a book through; *alopulli*, Josh. 3: 16.

łopoli, n., those who pass through.

łopoli, pp., put through; passed through; pierced through.

łopołichi, v. t. pl., to cause to go through; to put through; to pierce; to perforate; to make holes through; to run through.

łopotoli, v. t. pl., to go through; to pass through; to pass; *lopohnli*, nasal form; *lopulli*, sing.

łopulla hinla, a., sing., passable.

łopullahe keyu, a., impassable; unpassable.

łopulli, łipulli, v. t., v. a. i., sing., to pass through; to go through, Matt. 4: 24; to come over; to penetrate; to stand; to endure, as trials, etc.; to traverse; to undergo; to weather; to cross; to go across: to cut across; to pervade; to run; to look through; to go over; Matt. 14: 34, to walk through; to go through; Matt. 10: 23; 12: 43; 2 Sam. 24: 2, 5; (to pass over) Luke 4: 30; *isht lopulli*, v. t., to take through; to carry through; to take and go through; *loponli*, nasal form.

łopulli, n., one who passes through.

łopulli, a., through.

łopulli, pp., perforated; ratified; passed; passed a house of legislation.

łopulli, v. a. i., to come through.

łopullichi, v. t., to penetrate; to cause to go through; to thrid; to put through, Josh. 2: 15.

łopullit ona, v. t., to reach.

łopushki, a., soft, as a dressed skin; pp., softened.

łopushki, v. n., to be soft.

łopushkichi, v. t., to soften.

łotama, łotamạchi, v. a. i., to pitch down, or to lower one end of anything long, as a plow beam.

łotạmmi, v. t., to give a pitch down, in hauling rails, etc.

łotuⁿka, v. a. i., to snort, as a frightened horse or a high-spirited horse in play; to sniff.

łotuⁿka, n., a snorter; a snorting.

łuⁿa, pp., perforated; *lunli*, v. t., to perforate.

łuⁿa, v. a. i., to pierce through.

łuⁿa, n., holes.

łuⁿfa, see *lonfa*.

łuⁿffi, see *lonffi*.

łuhama, łohama (q. v.), pp., trodden down, as grass; fallen down, as grass or grain; see *lukama*.

łuhạmmi, v. t., to tread down; to throw down, as grass.

łuⁿka, v. a. i., to grunt; to murmur like a hog.

łuⁿka, n., a grunter.

łuⁿka, n., a grunting.

łukafa, pp. sing., *lukali*, pp. pl., pierced through; worn through; bored through; punctured through; gone through; perforated; punched; *iklukafo* a., unperforated.

łukafa, v. a. i., to pierce; to make a hole through; to burst through.

łukafa, n., a hole.

łukaha, v. t. pl., to scourge with a whip that has a lash; to lash.

łukaha, n., a scourging; a lashing.

łukaha, n., a scourger; one that uses the lash.

łukalichi, v. t. sing., to lash; to snap a whip; *lukaha*, pl.; *lukalihinchi*, freq.

łukalichi, n., a pop; the quick sound of a whip, as a cow whip; a stripe.

łukali, pp., pierced; bored; perforated; punched; *lukanli*, nasal form; *shukbo ạt lukanli*, the blanket is pierced or full of holes; *iklukalo*, a., unperforated.

łukali, n. pl., holes.

łukali, v. a. i. pl., to break through; to work through.

łukałichi, v. t. pl., to perforate; to make holes which extend through, as through cloth, tin, etc.; to hole; to punch.

łukałichi, n., one that makes holes, or they who make holes.

łukałichi, n., a lasher.

łukama, n., that which is trodden down; (should be luhama (q. v.), I think.— B).

łukata, n., a whip.

łukata wishakchi, n., a whip-lash; a snapper.

łukatąpi, n., a whip stock; a whip-handle.

łukatola, v. a. i., to snap.

łukatola, n., the snapping of a whip.

łukatolachi, v. t., to snap a whip; to crack a whip.

łukatolachi, n., one that cracks a whip.

łu^{n}kąchi, pp., bored; worm eaten, as old garments by insects; filled with holes, as corn eaten by weevils; tanch łu^{n}kąchi, weevil-eaten corn.

łu^{n}kąchi, pp. pl., to eat holes, as worms eat garments.

łu^{n}kąchi, n., holes; perforations.

łukaffi, v. t. sing., to make a hole; to perforate; to hole; to punch; wak hakshup a^n lukaffi, he makes a hole in the cowhide; shu^{n}shi ąt holisso ha^n ąpąt lukaffi, the worms eat holes in the book; nan tąnna ya^n lukaffi; tąli a^n lukaffi, to stave.

łukaffi, n., one who makes a hole.

łu^{n}kłua, v. a. i. pl., to grunt; to murmur, as a hog.

łu^{n}kłua, n., grunters.

łu^{n}kłua, n., a grunting.

łumpa, v. a. i., to pierce; to penetrate.

łumpa, pp., pierced; penetrated; perforated; bled; lanced; punctured; shakba i^{n}łumpa, he is bled; ikłumpo, a., unperforated.

łumpa, n., the place pierced; the hole.

łumpli, v. t., to perforate; to penetrate; to pierce; to bleed; to lance; to open; to puncture; to tap; to thrill; i^{n}łumpli, to bleed him.

łumpli, n., one who pierces; a piercer.

łumpli, n., a perforation; a puncture; see ałumpa.

łunli, v. t. pl., to perforate; łu^{n}a, pp.

łunlichi, pl., to cause holes to be made; to perforate; to tear to shivers; hushi ąt tanchi a^n łunlichi, the birds peck the corn (when in the ear and on the stalk).

łunlichi, n., a puncher.

m, a post-positive particle, successive; simultaneous; compellative.

ma, exclam., strange, O, used by persons when they find they have misunderstood what was said.

ma, exclam., like O, in the voc., as mi^{n}ko ma, O king. It is often heard in personal salutations, but where in English there is no corresponding word. It is not an exclamation so much as an acknowledgment. It partakes also of a verb which asserts that the thing is so. Pi^{n}shali ma, Luke 3: 12. Chosef Lewi ushi chia ma, thou who art David's Son Joseph, Matt. 1: 20. Pi^{n}ki ąba ishbinili ma, Matt. 6: 9; chitokaka ma, Matt. 14: 28; Josh. 7: 19.

ma, art. and rel. pro. in the obj. case, the; which; that which; hatak ma pisaletuk, I saw the man, Luke 5: 10 [?].

ma, the also; used after the second or third noun and the last of all, when one or more come together; see Matt. 18: 18, where ma occurs after the second noun in each instance; ątta ma, when born, Matt. 2: 1.

ma, adv., when, expressing past time; mintilima, a^{n}sha impąt ila^{n}shama ąlatuk, Luke 4: 17 [?]; okchitot ąla ma, Matt. 7: 25, 27, when the floods came; chuka yąmmakash aiihi^{n}soma, when it beat upon that said house; hokchima, when he sowed, Matt. 13: 4; hąshi ąt kohchama, when the sun was up, Matt. 13: 6.

mabi, adj., high and open; conspicuous, as a hilltop; nąnih mabi.—P. Fisk.

mabli, v. a. i., to stretch; to extend; see 2 Cor. 10: 14.

Macha, n., March.

mah!, hark! listen! an interjection calling attention.

mahaia, a., bowing; bent up; curved, like the brim of a hat; asonak mahaia, a pan, 1 Sam. 2: 14; shuti mahaia, a kettle, 1 Sam. 2: 14.

mahaia, v. n., to be bowing or curved.

mahaia, v. a. i., to curve; to verge.

mahaia, n., a curve.

mahaiyakachi, v. a. i., to sail slowly up and down in curves, as a buzzard.

mahaiyakachi, n., a sailing in airy circles.

mahaiyạt aⁿya, v. a. i., to sail, as a bird; to float in the air; to skim.

mahaiyạt aⁿya, n., a sailing; one who sails, as a bird.

maia, v. t., to thrust in, as the hand.

maiachi, v. t., to put (the hand) in; to thrust in; John 20: 25.

maiha, a., wide.

maiya, v. a. i., to go forward; to be on the way going forward; this differs from maⁿya.

maⁿiya, n., those who move onward; a process; a progression.

mak, the; that; which, John 1: 21; mak I think is ma and ak united, or a contraction of yạmmak, and is a demonstrative; see Matt. 5: 17, 18; yukpamakoke, Matt. 3: 17; nashoba . . . mak oka, wolves, that is what they are, Matt. 7: 15; makikkokahato, if he would speak it would be good (an old word); makikaiyukahato, modern manner. Compounds: maka; makahi oke, that shall, Matt. 7: 21; mak is demonstrative—makano—makat—makato—makatuk aⁿ; Chisạs Kilaist makatuk aⁿ, that he was Jesus the Christ; Matt. 16: 20—makạt—makạto—makbano—makbat—makbato—makhemakheno—makhet—makheto, if haply, 1 Sam. 14: 30—makiⁿ—makinli—makinliho, as soon as, Josh. 2: 7, 11; 3: 13; 4: 18; and as, Josh. 3: 15—makinlikia—makint—makkia; okla ikaiyomakkia, they need not depart, Matt. 14: 16; sachuⁿkạsh makkia, my heart that also—makkiaba—makma—makoⁿ, that the; aiokpuloka makoⁿ, Matt. 11: 23; pulla makoⁿ, Matt. 14: 3; illi makoⁿ illashke, let him die the death, Matt. 15: 4; achạfona makoⁿ, Matt. 16: 14—makocha—makoka—makoke; ilạppạt Chan Baptist makoke, this is John the Baptist, Matt. 14: 2; Klaist chia makoke, thou art the Christ; 16: 16; 18: 7; makokakosh, Rev. 2: 9—makokạno—makokạt—makokạto—makokia—makona—makosh—makoshba—makot.

maka, v. a. i., to say; to say that; to say so; to call, John 1: 41; makahaⁿya, freq.

makachi, v. a. i., to say that, John 1: 37; 20: 22; peh makachi, he merely said so.

makali, a., mean; worthless; abject; base; contemptible; degenerate; ignoble; ignominious; insignificant; low; nig-

gardly; paltry; poor; scabbed; scandalous; scurrilous; sordid; underhand; unmanly; vulgar; pp., degraded.

makali, v. n., to be mean or worthless; v. a. i., to grovel; to degenerate; to grow mean; shulush ạt makali, shapo ạt makali, hatak ạt makali, makalit isht ia, to be mean and take and go.

makali, adv., meanly.

makali, n., baseness; lowness; a scandal; vulgarity.

makalichi, v. t., to render mean or worthless; to degrade.

makhaloka, yạmmakhaloka, an interjection of contempt.

maki, imp., take it! It is heard only in this form, like mia, go ahead!

maⁿko, see maⁿshko.

malancha, a., smooth; glossy; dazzling; bright; shining; hạshi ạt malancha, tạli hạta yạt malancha.

malancha, v. n., to be smooth or glossy; v. a. i., to shine.

malancha, n., brightness.

malanchạchi, v. t., to make it shine.

malanta, a., nasal form, bright; glossy.

malanta, v. n., nasal form, to be bright or glossy; tạli hạta yạt malanta; tạli or haksi ạt malanta.

malantạchi, v. t., to brighten; to make glossy; to glow.

malantkạchi, v. a. i., to shine.

malantkạchi, pp., brightened; made glossy.

malaspoa, a. pl., flat; as amp malaspoa, flat crockery, i. e., plates or platters.

malaspoa, v. n., to be flat.

malaspoạchi, v. t., to make flat; to flatten them.

malaswa, a. pl., flat.

malaswa, pl., malạssa, sing. v. n., to be flat.

malaswa, n., flat ones.

malaswạchi, v. t., to flatten them.

malata, a., bright, etc.

malạssa, a., flat and smooth; as amp malạssa, a plate.

malạssa, v. n., to be flat; malaswa, pl.

malạssạchi, v. t., to flatten; to make flat.

malạtha, a., glistening; shining.

malạtha, v. n., to be glistening.

malạtha, n., light; the lightning; brightness, Matt. 24: 27, malạttakạchi, v. a. i., to reflect light, as the rays of the sun; *apisa yạt malạttakạchi.*

malạttakạchi, n., a reflection of light; a thunderbolt.

maleli, baleli, v. a. i. sing., to run; to flee, as an animal; to course; to fly; to scamper; to scud; to scuddle; to streak; i^n*maleli*, to flee from, 1 Kings 11: 23; o^n*maleli*, to run after; *pit maleli*, to run off.

maleli, n., a runner; a flier; a fugitive.

maleli, n., a run.

maleli achạfa, n., a heat.

malelichi, v. t., to run; to make him run; to cause to run; to course.

malelichi, n., a runner; one that makes another run.

malelit kạnia, mạlit kạnia, v. a. i., to run away; to desert; *mạllet kucha*, to run out, Gen. 39: 12.

malelit kạnia, n., a runaway; a deserter.

maḷali, maḷạlli, a., afraid; pp., frightened; scared.

maḷali, v. n., to be afraid; *samaḷali*, I am afraid, or I am scared.

maḷalichi, v. t., to frighten; to scare.

maḷata, pp., scared; frightened; *malanta*, n. f., Luke 3: 14; i^n*malanta*, v. t., to force from him by fear.

maḷạlli, v. t., to scare.

maḷi, v. a. i., to blow, as the wind; to move, as air; to flow, Matt. 11: 7; *malicha*, blew and, Matt. 7: 25.

maḷi, n., the air; the atmosphere; the wind, Matt. 14: 24, 30, 32; a blow; a wind; a current of air; a flaw; a flurry; a gale; a gust; a squall; *mali hạt*, the winds, Matt. 7: 25; *mali ạt kucha*, the wind rises.

maḷi achạfa, n., a blast of wind; a single wind or blow.

maḷi chito, n., a great wind; a gale; a storm; a tempest; a tornado.

maḷi chito, v. a. i., to storm.

maḷi chito laua, a., stormy.

maḷi iskitini, n., a breeze.

maḷi isht ikhạna, n., a weathercock; a vane.

maḷi kạllo, n., a strong wind; a violent wind; a gale; a tempest; *mali kạllo fehna kạt*, a great tempest, Matt. 8: 24.

maḷi lạshpa, n., a hot wind; the sirocco.

maḷi okpulo, n., a bad wind; a dangerous wind.

maḷi pila, a., windward.

maḷi shaḷi, a., squally; very windy.

maḷi shaḷi, v. n., to be squally.

maḷi tanch afotoha, n., a windmill.

maḷichi, v. t., to blow; to ventilate.

mampa, v. a. i., to stretch in length, as a man (*hatak ạt mampa*); to extend in length.

mampa, pp., stretched; extended.

mampli, mambli, v. t., to stretch out; to extend; to draw out beyond the natural length (applied usually to animals); *sinti a^n mampli, fani a^n mampli.*

mampli, n., a stretcher.

mampoa, v. a. i. pl., to stretch; to reach forward, as in running a race.

mampoa, pp., stretched; extended.

mampoḷi, v. t. pl., to stretch them.

mano, art., the; rel. pro , which.

mano, adv., when; the time when.

masali, masa, a., healed; recovered from sickness.

masali, v. n., to be healed; v. a. i., to get well; *masa*, contracted form.

masali, pp., remedied.

masalichi, v. t., to cure; to heal; to restore to health.

masu^{n}fa, misu^{n}fa, used thus; *takon masu^{n}fa*, an apple.

masheli, v. a. i., to clear off and become good weather; to pass away, as clouds; *kuchat masheli.*

masheli, pp., cleared off; a., clear; fair; serene; unclouded; *masheli kamạk ạt kạnia*, entirely fair.

masheli, n., a fair sky; fair weather; serenity.

mashelichi, v. t., to clear away the clouds; to make fair weather.

mashko, adv., already, Matt. 5: 28.

ma^{n}shko, ma^{n}ko, adv., already; now; at this time, John 3: 18; Matt. 17: 12; *Chu okla hạt aiitiba achafat taha mashko hatuk o^n*, for the Jews had agreed already, John 9: 22; *mashkoshke*, 1 Cor. 5: 3. This may be one form of the renewed mention art. pronoun, now become obsolete, thus: *ash, hash, yash, kash, chash, mash.*

matali, a., level; pp., leveled; *yakni matali*, level land.

matali, v. n., to be level.

matalichi, v. t., to level.

maⁿya, v. a. i., to do thus: to be employed; to be; to continue; to fare; to go; to keep on; to proceed; to verge; *chinchuka yaⁿ maⁿiyalachiⁿtuk; hilạt maⁿya; itichanlit maⁿya, oklat abeka iksho hosh maⁿya; ishi maya,* v. t., to continue; to take ahead; *isht mahaⁿya,* freq. form; *mahaⁿya,* to progress, Matt. 10: 22; *maiya,* to go forward; to be there; *tạli yak maⁿya kạt,* Matt. 4: 3; 5: 25; 13: 25; *ant ikmaⁿya,* let them alone; Matt. 15: 14; to abide, Matt. 17: 22; *Chutia maⁿyatuk,* were in Judea, Acts 11: 1; to come, Matt. 9: 20.

mạfkạchi, a., feverish.

mạfkạchi, see *mufkạchi.*

mạlha, mạlhha, n., a tin pan.

mạlhmạkki, v. a. i., to swim with the face in the water, so that the person can not breathe.—J. Hudson; *hachoⁿ mạlhmạkki.*

mạli, n., myrrh.

mạlit kạnia, see *malelit kạnia.*

mạlkạchi, v. a. i. pl., to glisten.

mạlkạchi, a. pl., glistening.

mạlkạchi, n., a flash of light, as that of lightning.

mạllahtakạchi, v. a. i., to flash as lightning (a single act).

mạllahtakạchi, n. sing., a flash of lightning.

mạlli, v. a. i., to leap, as a frog, deer, or man; to jump.

mạlli, n., a jump; a leap; a long jump.

mạlli, n., a jumper; a leaper.

mạlmakạchechi, v. t., to varnish.

mạlmakạchi, pl., *malata,* sing., v. a. i., to shine.

mạlmakạchi, a., bright; shining.

mạlmakạchi, v. n., to be bright.

mạli, adv., indeed; truly; really, Josh. 2: 4; doubtless, 1 Cor. 9: 2; Matt. 13: 32; 17: 11; *mạli tuⁿ?*

mạli, v. n., to be so indeed; to be truly so.

mạno, the, *misha pila mạno,* Matt. 4: 2.

mạno, when; *yohmimạno,* "then," Josh. 2: 15.

mạssaha, v. t. pl., to whip with a switch.

mạssalichi, v. t. sing., to strike with a switch.

mạstạt, n., mustard.

mạstạt ạpi, n., a mustard stalk.

mạstạt nihi, n., mustard seed.

mạshahchi, moshahchi, pp., fanned; winnowed.

mạshlichi, mushlichi, v. t., to winnow; *mishahichi,* pp.

mạt, the; that; which, Matt. 2: 2; Luke 3: 9; 4: 18; *putamạt,* the also, Matt. 18: 16.

mạt, when, John 2: 15; Matt. 2: 1, 3, 8, 9, 10; *fonka na haklomạt,* Matt. 4: 12, where *na* and *mạt* both occur; *nuklakanchamạt,* when he marveled, Matt. 8: 10; *ạttạt iamạt,* when he was departed, Matt. 12: 9; *haklomạt,* when they heard, Matt. 12: 24, *ia mạt,* and *luhmimạt,* Matt. 13: 44; *anumpulimạt,* Matt. 17: 4; and, 2 Sam. 24: 5; when that, Josh. 9: 1.

mạto, the; which; the one; as for the one, Matt. 2: 2.

mạto, where; *hatak chimaboha chukoatuk mạto,* where is the, etc.

Me, n., May, name of one of the months.

mia, sing. imp., go ahead! start off first! *hotepa,* pl. These words are used only in this way and form.

michik, n., the name of a noise or motion of some kind; *michikachi,* v. a. i.

michikli, v. a. i., to throb: to beat, as the pulse; *ibbạk ạt michikli.*

michikminli, v. a. i. freq., to beat, as the pulse, continually.

michila, a., plethoric; having a fullness of the blood vessels.

michila, v. n., to be plethoric.

michila, n., fullness of the blood vessels.

michilhha, n., the pulse.

michilhha, v. a. i., plural of *mitikli,* to beat.

mih, mihi, v. a. i., to be the same (but it never takes any of the pronouns). *mihi atuk moma,* he is the same he was; *mih siamakokeh,* I am he, John 18: 5; used as a pronoun in the third person—*mih,* a., same; it; he; *mih sia keyu,* John 1: 21; *mih nitak,* same day; *mih ninak,* 1 Chron. 17: 3. Derivatives are: *mih achạfa,* n., one place; the same one, as to time or place; same kind, species, sort—*mih achạfa bieka,* a. uniform—*mih achạfa bilia,* a., equable; being always one and the same—*mih achạfanli,* a., simultaneous—*mih achạfanli,* v. n., to be simultaneous—*mihakta,* therefore;

because of that—*mihash*, the same; the said one—*mihashinli*, the selfsame; the same indeed; ditto—*mihashoa*, obj. case, that said same—*mihashocha*, nom. case, the same; that same— *mihashoka*, that same—*mihashosh*, nom. case, the same (*ash* and its compounds might all be inserted)—*mihayuka*, *mihaiyuka*, in different places, as where manure is dropped about in a garden—*mihcha*, and, Matt. 5: 33; 15: 1; 17: 27. This is an adjunctive rather than a conjunctive word—*mihfoka*, about then; at hand, John 2: 13—*mihhakta*, *mihakta*, because of that; therefore; see *hakta*—*mihhoka*, *mihhokato*, *mihkokat*—*mihi*, 1 John 3: 3 MSS., *mihiatuka*, Mark 10: 30—*mihiashinli*, a., identical; same; selfsame, n., synonymous—*mihiashinli*, n., sameness—*mihiocha*, nom. case, the same one; he—*mihioke*, it is the same—*mihiona*, the same—*mihiosh*, the same—*mihiyosh*, Matt. 5: 19; 11: 10; 18: 4; Mark 10: 30—*mihiot*, the same—*mihinli*, the same also; *Helot at mihinlituk*, Herod he the same was, Luke 23: 15—*mihinluhmi*, a. (from *mihinli* and *ohmi*) much the same as; double—*mihinluhmi*, v. n., to be much the same as—*mihinluhmichi*, *mihinliohmichi*, v. t., to make it much the same manner, John 13: 34 — *mihinluminchi*, nasal form—*mihinlu*—*mihinluhmi kat iksho*, there is none such; n., a nonesuch—*mihinluhmit toba*, v. a. i., to double—*mihio*, *mihiyo*, a., the same one; he; *mihion siahoke*, John 4: 26; Matt. 6: 21; to him, Matt. 13: 12—*mihio ashinli*, a., identical; n., the selfsame one—*mihka*, in that case; *mihka katiohma chinho — mihkakon — mihkakosh—mihkat*, but if—*mikato*, but if; then, John 1: 21—*mihhokato—mihma*, and, Luke 1: 38; Matt. 7: 24, 26; then, John 1: 22; so, John 4: 54; at the same time; then when; *mih*, same; *ma*, when, equivalent to and; *mat* and *ma* are used for the past tense, *kmat* and *kma* for the future—*mihmak*, he the same, John 13: 26—*mihmak ahioke*, the same, that it will be—*mihmakinli*, in the same place; immediately, Matt. 4: 22; the same; that also; selfsame, Matt. 8: 13—*mihmakinli hon*, straightway, Matt. 14: 22; that very, Matt. 17: 18—*mihmakinliho*

illitok — mihmakinli kia, even in the same place, or at the same time—*mihmakon*, this; the same, by way of inquiry; is this it? John 1: 21, 23; Matt. 17: 12; *mihmakon hashaiinyamohmi*, do ye even so to them, Matt. 7: 12 — *mihmakocha—mihmakoke*, it is the same, John 1: 30; Matt. 11: 10—*mihmakosh*, this; that; the same—*mihmano*, when; and when—*mihmat*, and, Luke 1: 28; Matt. 3: 2—*mihmato*, and the—*mihna*, and then; and therefore; therefore—*mihyanio*, the same; the said; see *miya*.

miha, v. a. i., v. t., to utter; to say; to bid; to warn; to promise; to direct; to command; to order; to give charge over; to reprove; to denounce; to enjoin; to announce; to import; to instruct; to mean; to profess; to protest; to repeat; to threaten; to twit; *inmiha*, to admonish him; to charge him; to menace; *inmiha imanumpuli*, to advise him; *inmiha*, v. t., to rate; to reprimand; to reproach; to reprove; to upbraid; to constrain; *ilemiha*, *ilamiha*, to say of himself, *issanmiha*, "bid me;" *isht ilemiha*, to excuse himself; *isht ilemihachi*, to excuse himself, *ilemiha iksho*, a., facile; easy; having nothing to object; *itinmiha*, v. t., to promise each other; *isht amiha*, to speak by means of or on account of; to swear by; *inmiha*, n., a monitor; a counselor; *mihahatuk*; *hachinmihalishke*, I say unto you: Matt. 4: 3; 34, 35, 36; 6: 16; 10: 15; 11: 7; 13: 17; 14: 7, 8, 22, 28; 16: 12, 14, 20; Josh. 4: 16, 17; 7: 8; 8: 4; Luke 3: 7, 19; 14: 18; 2 Sam. 15: 12; 24: 13.

miha, n., a meaning, a menace; a profession; a promise; tenor; a threat.

miha, n., a promiser; a rehearser.

mihachi, v. a. i., to talk; to talk about; to upbraid; to scold; to dictate; to revile. Matt. 11: 20; *mihahanchi*, Matt., 5: 11; to judge, Matt. 7: 1, 2; *isht ilemihachi*, to excuse himself by means of it; *isht mihachi*, v. t., to palliate.

mihachi, n., a talker; a reviler; a threatener.

mihachi, n., obloquy.

minka, **binka** (q. v.), each; both; like; of the same kind or species; *ikitihaklo minka;* they can not hear each other, *itinkana minka.*

miⁿka, v. n., to be like or of the same kind.

Miⁿkilish, Iⁿkilish (q. v.), n., English; the English.

Miⁿkilish, a., English.

Miⁿkilish hatak, n., an Englishman.

Miⁿkilish imanumpa, n., the English language.

mikma (this has a future and definite meaning, and is formed from *mih*, *k*, and *ma*), and; *John mikma*, *mikmat*, etc., are composed of these words, *mih*, verb "to be the same;" *k*, the demonstrative article, and *ma*, the common article, which, with a verb, means when. See *mih*, *ma*. This word is hard to render into English—*mikmano*, and the—*mikmat*, and, John 1: 1; Matt. 5: 38—*mikmato*, and the.

miⁿko, v. a. i., to reign; Matt. 2: 22; *Chihu at mikoshke*, 2 Kings 9: 13; to rule, Josh. 12: 2.

miⁿko, n., a chief; a sachem; a sagamore, among red men; a president; a governor; a prince; a duke; a monarch; a king; an emperor; a czar; an autocrat; a pasha, etc. among other nations; "his excellency;" "his honor;" a colonel; a commander; a captain-general; a dominator; the executive; his majesty; a potentate; power; a sovereign, etc., Matt. 2: 1, 9; 14: 1; 12: 24.

miⁿko, pp., enthroned; crowned.

miⁿko ahalaia, a., royal; regal; kingly.

miⁿko aiokpạchi, n., coronation.

miⁿko apełechika afullota, n., the circuit of a king's dominions; a kingdom; a realm; an empire.

miⁿko apełichi, miⁿko apełiechi, n., a realm; a kingdom; an empire, Luke 4: 5; the dominion of a king; the king's dominions.

miⁿko apełiechika, n., a kingdom; the place over which a king rules.

miⁿko chohmi, a., kingly.

miⁿko iakaiya, n., a major.

miⁿko ikbi, v. t., to crown; to make a king.

miⁿko ikimiksho, a., kingless.

miⁿko imanumpeshi, n., a consul; an ambassador; a king's chief secretary or aid.

miⁿko imiacbuka, miⁿko imiałipa, n., a crown; a miter; a king's turban; a diadem; a royal fillet or headdress.

miⁿko imma, a., royal.

miⁿko imohoyo, n., the king's wife; a queen; an empress; a chieftainess.

miⁿko inchuka, n., a palace; a royal dwelling; a king's house, Matt. 11: 8.

miⁿko intạbi, n., a scepter; the king's staff.

miⁿko iⁿpeni, n., a yacht; a royal yacht.

miⁿko kobafa, n., a dethroned king; dethroned.

miⁿko kobạffi, v. t., to dethrone a king.

miⁿko kobạffi, n., one who dethrones a king.

miⁿko tekchi, n., the king's wife; a queen.

miⁿko toba, v. a. i., to reign, Matt. 2: 22; to become a king.

miⁿko toba, pp., crowned king; made a king.

miⁿkochi, v. t., to make a king; to enthrone.

miⁿkochi, n., a coronation.

Miliki, n., America; the United States, in the view of a Choctaw, and not all North and South America.

Miliki, a., American.

Miliki hatak, n., an American; a Yankee.

Miliki okla, n., the Americans; American people; the people of the United States.

Miliki yakni, n., America; the United States.

millinta, v. a. i., to polish; to wear bright.

millinta, pp., polished.

millinta, n., a polish.

millintạchi, v. t., to polish.

millintạchi, n., a polisher.

miłofa, pp., filed; rasped.

miłoffi, sing., to file; to rasp.

miłoffi, n., a filer.

miłoha, v. t. pl., to file; to rasp.

miłohạchi, v. t., to file; pp., rasped.

miłohạchi, pp. pl., filed; rasped.

miłoli, pp. pl., filed; rasped.

miłolichi, v. t. pl., to file; to rasp them.

mintahpi, v. a. i., to begin to come.

mintahpi, n., that which or he who came first.

minti, v. a. i., to come; to start; to start this way; to approach; *iⁿminti*, to come to him; John 1: 29; *ạba minti*, to come from above; to descend, John 1: 32;

Matt. 8: 9; 14: 29; 15: 1, *aminti*, to come from, Josh. 2: 2, 4; 3: 9; *minti*, nasal form; *mihinti*, freq., Matt. 12: 32; *takla mihinti*, to approach; be approaching, Josh. 5: 7; *mienti, aminti*, to come from, Matt. 8: 11; to originate at; to come of, Matt 5: 37.

minti, n., a coming; a comer.

minti, from, Matt. 4: 25.

mintichi, v. t., to cause to come; to start off; to make him come; *mintinchi*, nas. form; *mintihinchi*, freq. form.

mintit ạla; *mintit imạla*, Matt. 8: 5, came unto him.

minsa, pp., scarred.

minsa, n., a scar; a stripe; a cicatrix.

misisunkạchi, pp. pl., scarred; striped; spotted white.

misisunkạchi, n.pl., scars; short stripes; whitish spots.

mismiki, a., fine; beautiful; as *aboha mismiki*, a fine house.

mismiki, v. n., to be fine.

mismikichi, v. t., to make fine.

misunfa, see *masunfa*.

misha, adv., beyond; further; off, as *mishaia*, go off; *mishia cha*, go off (and do not come back); *Chatan misha*, beyond Jordan, Matt. 4: 15, 25; *mish*, contracted; *mishtạnnạp*, the other side, Mark 5: 1; *misha ohia*, beyond go ye, Matt. 7: 23.

misha, a., ulterior; utter.

misha, v. n., to be beyond; to be further.

misha, n., place or time beyond (a later note says "*misha*, place; *mishsha*, time"); *misha pila*, Matt. 3: 2; *misha intạnnạp*, Matt. 8: 28, the other side, Matt. 16: 5; *misha tạnnạp*, Matt. 14: 22.

misha, n., the place beyond; the one beyond the other; *mishsha*, n., time beyond.—J. C.

misha, mishsha, adv., day before yesterday; day after to-morrow; *inmisha*, adv., tertian; day after to-morrow.

mishahchi, pp., winnowed; *mạshlichi*, v. t.

mishakash, the day before yesterday; two days ago.

mishakashon, on the day before yesterday.

mishapilla, adv., farther; further.

mishapilla, a., ultimate.

mishash, the day before yesterday.

mishema (from *misha* and *imma*), adv., beyond; farther; further.

mishema, v. n., to be beyond; to be farther off; *chinmishemashke*, be it far from thee, Matt. 16: 22.

mishema, pp., put beyond; delayed; removed.

mishema fullota, adv., abroad, Luke 2: 17.

mishemanchit apesa, v. t., to postpone.

mishemạchi, v. t., to put farther off; to remove along; *mishemanchi*, nasal form.

mishemạt ạlhpisa, pp., postponed.

mishofa, sing., to rub off.

mishofa, pp., rubbed off.

mishoha, pp. pl., rubbed.

mishohạchi, v. t., to rub.

mishokạchi, v. a. i. pl., to rub off; it rubs.

mishokạchi, pp., rubbed; rubbed off.

mishokạchi, n., a rubbing; the noise made by filing a saw.

misholi, pp. pl., rubbed.

misholi, v. a. i., to rub.

mishotichi, v. t. pl., to make them rub; to rub; *mishofli*, sing.

mishsha, see *misha*.

mishshakma, adv., on the day after to-morrow; when it shall be day after to-morrow; *inmishakma siabeka*, after to-morrow.

mishtạnnạp, n., the other side, Josh. 1: 2; over; beyond, Josh. 9: 10.

mishuk, n., a single noise made by filing a saw.

mishukachi, v. a. i., to make the noise; to ring, as a saw that is filed.

mitafa, v. a. i. sing., to burst open; to gush; to break open; to rupture; *tanampo ạt mitafa, hichi ạt mitafa*.

mitafa, pp., burst open; ruptured; opened.

mitafa, n., a break; a breach; a disruption; an eruption; a ruption.

mitali, v. a. i. pl., to burst open; to break open; to chap; to rupture; *yakni ạt mitali; shukcha yạt mitali*, the leathern bottles burst, Matt. 9: 17.

mitali, pp., burst open.

mitali, n., breaches; breaks.

mitaɫichi, v. t. pl., to break them open; to cause them to burst; to chap; to rupture.

mitạffi, v. t., to burst open; to break open; to gush; to open; to rupture; to wound, Mark 12: 4.

mitefa, v. a. i., to get loose; to unloose; to untie.

mitefa, pp., untied; ripped.

mitefa, n., a rip.

mitelichi, v. t., to strike with a switch.

mitelichi, n., a cut; a single stroke.

miteɫi, n., a rip.

miteɫi, v. a. i. pl., to get loose.

miteɫi, pp., untied; loose; ripped.

miteɫichi, v. t., to unloose; to untie; to rip; to unravel; to unseal.

mitibli, v. a. i., to swell, as corn or acorns when moistened; *tanchi ạt mitibli, nusi ạt mitibli, ahe ạt mitibli.*

mitibli, pp., swelled.

mitiblichi, v. t., to cause to swell; to swell.

mitiffi, sing., to unloose; to untie; to ungird; to unseal; to unstring.

mitifmiya, see *mitikminli.*

mitiⁿha, v. t. pl., to whip with a switch; to flog.

mitihachi, v. t., to strike with the wings; to flutter, as a bird; *ạba hushi ạt mitihạchi.*

mitihạchi, n., a flutterer.

mitikli, v. a. i. sing., to beat; to throb; to palpitate.

mitikli, n. sing., a beating; a throbbing; a pulsation.

mitiklichi, v. t., to cause to throb; to make it beat.

mitikmiⁿkli, v. a. i., to throb, as a sore.

mitikminli, mitikmiya, mitifmiya, v. a. i. pl., to beat; to throb; to pulsate; to palpitate.

mitikminli, n., a beating; a throbbing; a palpitation; the pulse.

mitikminlichi, v. t., to make it throb.

mitilhmiya, n., the pulse; a slow pulsation.

mitilhmiya, v. a. i., to pulsate slowly.

miya, miha, v. a. i., to be the same, 1 John, 2: 17; see *mih.*

moa, pp., skimmed.

moaha, a., thin, like soft mush.

moạshki, a., mushy or mushlike.

mocholi, v. a. i., to close the eye; to wink.

mocholi achạfa, n., a wink.

mochukli, v. a. i. sing., to wink.

mochukli, n., a wink.

moeli, v. t. pl., to skim; *pishukchi nia moeli; bila moeli.* [As a plural verb of action it means not only to skim, but to row, to paddle, to scull; it is used to denote the paddling of boats or canoes. There is reason to believe that in this word we have the tribal name, Maubila or Mauilla. Mobile is called by the modern Choctaw Moilla, a form resembling both *moeli* and Mauilla.—H. S. H.]

moⁿfa, pp., rubbed off; paddled; peeled off; skinned off; rowed; *peni ạt moⁿfa.*

moⁿfa, v. a. i., to peel off; to skin off; to rub; to rub off hair; *nipi ạt lua cha moⁿfa,* to shed hair.

moⁿffi, v. t., to rub off; to brush off; to scrape off; to peel off; to oar; to row; to paddle; to scull; to shoot and take off the hair only.

moⁿffi, n., a rower; a paddler.

moⁿffit isht ia, v. t., to oar; to begin to row; to take along by rowing.

mofi, v. t., to paddle; to row.

moⁿfkạchi, v. a. i., to rub against.

moⁿfkạchi, pp., rubbed; peeled off.

moha, pl., skimmed; peeled off.

mokafa, v. t., to strike and knock off with the hand or paw; *itamokạfa,* to conflict; to strike against each other; *mali hạt sioⁿmokạfa.*

mokạfa; *itamokạfahe,* to rise up against each other, Matt. 24: 7; to meet in battle.

mokofa, v. a. i., to slip out; to come out, Luke 4: 35; 13: 12; to withdraw, Luke. 5: 16; to be quit of, Josh. 2: 20; *isuba hạt mokofa,* the horse is loose.

mokoffi, v. t., to slack or slip out the hand, Josh. 10: 6.

mokofi, v. t. (cf. *mokofa*), to rend from; to rend away, 1 Kings 11: 11, 13.

mokoɫi, v. t. pl., Acts 12: 7.

moɫi, v. t., to skim; to peel off; to paddle; *peni moɫi.*

moma, a., all, Matt. 6: 32; whole, John 1: 3 [?]; every, Matt. 15: 13; entire; full; total; universal; *amoma,* Matt. 11, caption, 1st line; *moma iklauo,* a., least;

lowest; *moma iklauo* adv., least, Josh. 8:4; *moyuma*, every; *anumpa moyuma kat*, every word, Matt. 4: 4; *emoyuma kat*, every one of us, Judg. 16: 5; *hash moma*, Josh. 1: 2, 17.

moma, v. a. i., to all; *emoma*, we all; *momat*, they all, Luke 23: 1; *momat hussamaiala*, come unto me ye all, Matt. 11: 28; *momat shatummi*, Matt. 13: 33; *momat aiimonatok*, Matt. 14: 35; *momat okla impa*, Matt. 15: 37.

moma, v. n., to be all; *moyuma; ilappa moyuma*, Matt. 6: 33. In this instance *moyuma* becomes an intensive plurality and totality, every one, Josh. 1: 14.

moma, adv., more; throughout; so; yet; Matt. 16: 9; still; entirely; *abeka moma*, still sick.

moma, v. n., to be so yet; to continue, Matt. 17: 5; Josh. 4: 18; *samoma*, I am so.

moma, v. a. i., to be all, Matt. 6: 22.

moma, v. a. i., to do so yet; to continue; as *momali*, I still do so.

moma, n., a continuation; a full; the sum, 2 Sam. 24: 9; amount; total; totality; the whole.

moma chuhmi, a., general.

moma chuhmi, n., generality.

moma chuhmi, adv., generally; mainly.

moma iklauo, a., least, Matt. 11: 11.

moma inshali, a., over all; greater than all; highest, Luke 6: 35; Matt. 18: 1; greatest, Matt. 18: 4.

momaka ikpeso, a., untried.

momaka pisa, v. t., to try.

momaka pisa, n., a trial.

momaka pisa, n., a trier.

momat, mont (contracted), all (nom. case); *mont ia*, all are going.

mominchi, v. t., to go to all or over all; to affect all; to take all; *mominchit anya*, Matt. 4: 23; *mominchit lakofichi*, to cure all, Matt. 8: 16; 12: 15; *mominchit anoli*, "told everything," Matt. 8: 33; to sweep the whole, John 2: 15; Luke 6: 10; Matt. 13: 44, 46; 14: 35; *mominchit pisa*, to see all; *aiilamominchi*, to take the whole to himself, Matt. 16: 26; *ilemominchi*, v. t., to engross.

mominchi, adv., wholly.

mominchi, a., unreserved.

mominchit, adv., throughout.

momint, contracted from *mominchi;* adv., uttermost; utterly; *tanchi amomint luffi*, husk all the corn.

mont, see *momat*.

moshli, see *mushli*.

mosholahe keyu, a., inexcusable.

mosholahe keyu, a., unquenchable; inextinguishable.

mosholi, v. a. i., to go out, as fire; to expire; to pass; to go out, as a lamp; to vanish, 1 Sam. 3: 3.

mosholi, pp., extinguished; gone out; quenched; stifled.

mosholi, a., extinct.

mosholi, n., extinction.

mosholicha hinla, a., quenchable; extinguishable.

mosholichi, v. t., to extinguish fire; to quench, Matt. 12: 20; to stifle; to destroy, Josh. 7: 7; 10: 4.

motohki, a., without a tail, as a fowl; or short, as a short coat.

mototunkli, v. a. i. pl., to throb.

mototunkli, n., a throbbing.

motukli, sing., to throb, as a sore; to pulsate; to beat, as the pulse.

moyayankachi, a. pl., of the consistence of mush; or *halushki*, as said by a Natchitoches man, Aug. 29, 1854.

mufka, v. n., to be painful; to ache, as the flesh after being burnt.

mufka, a., painful.

mufkachi, mafkachi, v. t., to put in pain; to pain.

mushli, moshli, sing., *mushmoli*, pl., v. a. i., to wink; to wink hard and long.

mushli, n., a winker.

mushmushli, v. a. i., to wink.

muyaha, applied to some kinds of faces.

n, contracted from *na*, not, must not and made the final letter of verbs when it occurs, as *apalin, apali na*, I may not eat; *ishpan, ishpa na*, thou must not eat.

na, adv., not; must not; do not let (this form is aspirated, *nah* being verbal); *ishpa na, ishia na; akpoki na, chik aiyuki na, chinukshopa na*, Luke 1: 30; *yoba na*, do not possibly; lest possibly; *chifammi na*, do not let him whip you.

na, may; can; *ala yoba na*, perhaps he may come.

na, a particle; classed with conjunctions in its use in the second and third persons; in the first singular, objective case, it is simply a nasal, thus *pisalin;* *onalin,* cf. 1 Kings 9: 3; *aiolabbit ishi na ikano,* Matt. 7, 5; 13: 22.

na, by means of; because; that; so that; to the end that, 2 Sam. 24: 2; *iskali isht hassamala na pisalashke,* Mark 12:15; here the object is expressed by *na,* so that; *sinti at kopoli na illetok,* because the serpents bit them they died; *ant amanoli na akostininchiletuk, oka yan hachinshileli nan hashanyatok,* Josh. 2: 10; here the result in the mind of Rahab is expressed, but in the mind of Moses the object of God in drying up the waters would be expressed by *na; yohmi na,* when, Matt. 3: 16, see Matt. 4: 12, where *na* and *mat* both are used.

na, till, Matt. 2: 15; long; *chihaksi na,* 1 Sam. 1: 14; *na* used before "time how long," Acts 19: 8, 10, 22; time future, *anta na shohbi,* to stay till night; *ihinshi na,* Matt. 11: 12; *anta na bilia,* to remain forever; *anta na himaku,* to stay till this time; time past up to the present, *inhullo na bilia hatukosh,* 1 Kings 10: 9.

na, nah, adv., and; and then; that, Matt. 2: 8; *ont kehopesa na,* let us go and see it and then, etc. (we shall know); *ont kehopesa na ia; hot akla na,* let me look for and come then. The verb next after *na* has a different nom. from the one before it. When both verbs have the same nom. *cha* is used, as *ant impa cha,* come and eat and (go to work—as the case may be); *ant issa cha,* quit and (do not trouble me again), etc.; *ima na,* Matt. 15: 36; used in the oblique case, Josh. 7: 21; *iyinkalaha ombinili na tabokolimat illitok,* 2 Kings 4: 20; *mahyah nah,* scolding a dog a second time; i. e., again, over again; *kehotisheli nah,* let us now disperse, having been together a while.

na, n., a thing; an actor; an agent; an article, John 4: 38[?]; contracted from *nana;* before *b, m,* and *p,* usually written *nam;* before the vowels and *ch, l,* and *t* written *nan,* for euphony's sake; it is prefixed to verbs to form a noun;

name of an agent or thing; *nan okpani,* a criminal; *nan okpulo,* a vile thing.

na, lest; *maiyah na,* go off lest (I whip you).

na balama, n., incense; a fragrant thing; an odor; a perfume; a scent; spices; spicery, 1 Kings 10: 2, 15.

na balama ahushmi, n., an altar of incense, Luke 1: 11.

na balama alua, n., an altar of incense.

na banna, n., appetite; desire.

na banna, a., needy.

na bashli, n., a reaper, Matt. 13: 30, 39.

na bila, n., oil, Luke 16: 6; fat; grease; gravy; a greasy thing in a melted state; melted fat.

na bili, n., a pointer.

na boli, n., a striker.

na bolukta, n., an orb.

na buna, n., a bundle; a roll; a parcel.

na fammi, n., a whipper; a chastiser; a castigator.

na fehna, v. a. i., to matter, Mark 12: 10, 11; to be possible, Matt. 17: 20.

na fehna, n., something; a real thing; a reality; a feat; a wonderful work, Matt. 7: 22; wonders, Josh. 3, 5; mighty work, Matt. 11: 20, 21; 13: 54.

na fehna, a., material; notable; remarkable; stupendous; superb; wonderful; wondrous.

na fehna keyu, a., unimportant.

na fehna keyu, n., nothing; a nihility.

na fehna keyu, a., ordinary; immaterial.

na fehnachi, v. t., to make something of it, Luke 5: 26[?]; *na fienachi.*

na fehnachi, n., the one who makes something of it.

na fohka, na foka, n., a garment of any kind; a shirt; a coat; apparel; clothes, Josh. 7: 6; attire; clothing, Matt. 7: 15; habiliment; a habit; raiment; a vestment; a vesture; a wardrobe, Matt. 11: 8; Josh. 7: 21, 24; 9: 5, 13.

na foka abohushi, n., a press; a clothes press.

na foka afohoma, n., a hem.

na foka afohomi, v. t., to hem a garment; to hem in.

na foka afoli, v. t., to swaddle.

na foka aiasha, n., a wardrobe.

na foka aiitatoba, n., a slop-shop; a shop where ready-made clothes are sold.

na foka alhfoa, pp., swaddled.

na foka chashana, n., a long coat; a straight-bodied coat.

na foka chashana falaia, n., a surtout.

na foka chito, n., a great coat; a large garment; a cloak.

na foka chito fohka, v. t., to cloak.

na foka foka, v. t., to dress one's person; to attire; to dress up; to put on a garment; to clothe; to habit.

na foka foka, pp., dressed; clothed; appareled; habited.

na foka fokachechi, na foka fokachi, v. t., to dress another person; to clothe; to apparel; to furnish another person with clothes.

na foka ikbi, n., a tailor.

na foka ikbi, v. t., to tailor.

na foka iksho, a., naked; without clothes.

na foka iksho, v. n., to be naked; to be destitute of clothes.

na foka ilumpatali, n., a cape; a vandyke.

na foka intikba takali, n., an apron.

na foka isht kasholichi, n., a clothesbrush.

na foka kolukshi, n., a vest; a waistcoat; a jacket; a jerkin; a roundabout.

na foka kolukshi shakba ansha, n., a spencer.

na foka lumbo, n., a shirt; linen; an undergarment.

na foka lumbo falaia, n., a frock.

na foka lumbo foka, v. t., to shirt; to put on a shirt.

na foka lumbo foka, pp., shirted; clothed with a shirt.

na foka lumbo fokachi, v. t., to shirt another (as a child).

na foka patafa, n., a hunting-shirt; lit., a split garment.

na foka umpatta, n., a vandyke.

na foni, n., bones; a skeleton.

na fotoli, n., a grinder; a borer; a miller.

na fuli halali, n., a lot; lots, Luke 23: 34.

na habena, n., one who receives a present or favor; a beneficiary.

na habenachi, n., a benefactor.

na haklo, n., a hearer; an auditor; a listener.

na haksi, n., a criminal; a rogue; a villain; a cheat.

na haksichi, n., a rogue.

na hakshup, n., leather; peltry.

na hakshup kanchi, n., a skinner; one that deals in skins.

na halupa, n., a weapon made of iron or steel; arms; a lance; a pike; a pin: a spear, Josh. 1: 14; *Tusk in nahalupa; Tusk inna halupa*, a scimiter.

na halupa aiasha, na halupa aiitola, an armory; a deposit for arms; a magazine.

na halupa boli, v. t., to surrender; to lay down arms.

na halupa ilatali, v. a. i., to arm; to arm himself; to equip himself.

na halupa imatali, v. t., to arm; to furnish with arms; to equip.

na halupa imalhtaha, pp., armed; furnished with arms; equipped; prepared for war, Josh. 1: 14; 4: 12, 13.

na halupa isht bali, v. t., to spear.

na hashofichi, see *na kashofichi*.

na halbina, n., a present; a benefit; a benefaction; a donation; a gift.

na hata, n., a white cloth; a banner; a flag of truce; an ensign; a flag; a pendant; a pennant; a sail; a veil.

na hata alhtipo, n., a tent; a cloth tent; a pavilion.

na hata ikbi, n., a sailmaker.

na hata lilafa, n., a white rag.

na hika, n., a flier; one that flies.

na hila, n., a dancer; a top; a toy for children.

na himmonna, n., a novelty; a new thing.

na hobuna, n., a bundle.

na hochifo, n., a namer.

na hokchi, n., a planter; a sower, John 4: 36; Matt. 13: 3.

na hokchi, v. t., to sow; *na hokchit ia tok*, Matt. 13: 3.

na hokli, n., a catcher; a seizer.

na holba, n., a picture; a resemblance; an imitation; a statue.

na holhponi, n., food; victuals prepared for the table.

na holhtina, n., arithmetic; a calculation; mathematics.

na holhtina holisso, n., arithmetic; a book upon mathematics.

na holipafi, n., a mastiff; an English dog.

na holissochi, n., a writer; a scribe; a clerk, Luke 5: 21; Matt. 5: 20; 8: 19; 9: 3; 12: 38; 15: 1; 16: 21.

na holitompa, n., treasure, Matt. 13: 44.

na holitompa isht aⁿsha, n. pl., priests, Matt. 12: 4; 16: 21; Josh. 3: 3, 6; 6: 4, 6, 8.

na holitompa isht atta, n., sing., a priest, Matt. 2: 4; 1 Sam. 2: 11, 13.

na holitopa, n., a sacred thing; a treasure.

na holitopa aialhto, n., a shrine.

na hollo, n., a supernatural being; one that creates fear and reverence; an inhabitant of the invisible world. This name was thus anciently used, but when the whites first visited the Indians this name was given to them.

na hollo, n., a white man; white men of all nations. The name of man when applied to white people, as *hatak* means man when red people are spoken of; a master, as the master of slaves.

na hollo, a., pertaining to a white man.

na hollo hochitoka, n., the great white men; Congress; commissioners of the Government.

na hollo holitopa, n., a beloved or sacred white man; an agent of the United States Government; the Indian agent is often thus called.

na hollo inbissa, n., a raspberry.

na hollo inkowi, n., an English mile.

na hollo imahe, n., an Irish potato; Irish potatoes; English potatoes.

na hollo imanumpa, n., the word of a white man; the language of white men; the English language, as English are most known to the Choctaw among white people.

na hollo imalla, n., a white man's child.

na hollo imohoyo, n., a white man's wife.

na hollo imokchaⁿk, n., a cucumber.

na hollo intakkon, n., an apple.

na hollo itanowa, n., a traveler.

na hollo miⁿko, n., a royal white man; lit., a white man king, applied to the United States agent.

na hollo ohoyo, n., a white woman.

na hollo takchi, n., a sheriff; a constable.

na hollo tekchi, n., a white man's wife; the word *tekchi* after the pos. case has no pro. before it, of the third person.

na hollo toⁿksali, n., a laborer; a laboring white man.

na hollo yakni, n., the land or country of the white men, applied to the United States in distinction from the land of the Indians.

na hollochi, na hullochi, v. a. i., to abstain from certain food and drink; to fast, Luke 2: 37; Matt. 6: 18; to keep sacred; *na hullochit anta liⁿ*, Acts 10: 30.

na hollochi, n., one who fasts, abstains, etc.; a priest.

na hollochi iksa, n., a priest; the order of priests.

na hollochi iksa pelichi, n., a high priest.

na hollofi, n., an English dog; a bulldog.

na holloka, n., a sacred thing; a consecrated object.

na hollushi, n., a quadroon; the child or descendant of a white man by a red woman.

na holokchi, n., a plant; a vegetable that is cultivated, Matt. 15: 13.

na homi, n., alcohol; ardent spirits; whisky; liquor; any bitter thing.

na honni okchi, n., a decoction.

na hopoa, n., a beast; *na hopoa puta*, every beast, Gen. 1: 30.

na hoponi, n., a cook.

na hopuⁿkoyo, n., a spy.

na hotina, n., a counter.

na hotupa, n., a pain; *na hotupa hosh anlaua*.

na hoyo, n., a seeker; a hunter; a summoner.

na hoyo, n., harvest, John 4: 35; Matt. 9: 37; *nan ahoyo*, n., the harvest place.

na huⁿkupa, na hulhkupa, n., a thief.

na hullochi, v. a. i., to fast, Matt. 6: 16; 17: 21; see *na hollochi*, and *nan hullochi*.

na humma, n., the red warriors; the name of certain warriors, implying bravery, honor, etc., as *na humma aliha ona*.

na humma, n., red strand; red blanketing.

na humma, n., rouge; vermilion; red paint.

na humma chulata, n., a strip of red stroud.

na hummachi, n., a tanner; one that dyes red; one that colors red.

na huⁿssa, n., a gunner; a sportsman.

na imahaksi, n., a pardoner; a forgetter; one who forgets.

na kanchi, n., a seller; a trader; a merchant; a dealer; a negotiator; a shopkeeper.

na kanimi, n., the object.

na kanimi keyu, a., sound; not having anything out of order.

na kanimi keyu, v. n., to be sound and in order.

na kaniohmi keyu, a., safe; being without any disturbance; safely.

na kashofichi, na hashofichi, n., a pardoner.

na katimi, pro., why; wherefore; for what; what for.

na katimiho, pro., what is the matter; what is the reason; wherefore; why; *na katimiho hachinukshopa cho*, why are ye fearful? Matt. 8: 26; why, Matt. 16: 8; *na katima heto*, it will come to nothing; *na katimi kako*ⁿ.

na katiohmi, adv., why; wherefore.

na kallo, n., power; strength, Luke 5: 7.

na kallo, n., linen cloth; hemp cloth.

na kostini, n., the wise, Matt. 11: 25.

na kulli, n., a digger.

na lakna, n., rust, Matt. 6: 19, 20.

na luma, n., secrets, Matt. 13: 35.

na lumbo, see *nan lumbo*.

na lafa, n., something that is marked; a mark.

na laⁿfi, n., a marker.

na lakofi, n., a person that is cured, John 5: 10; an escape; one that escapes.

na lakofichi, v. t., to cure, Luke 6: 7; Matt. 12: 10.

na lakofichi, n., a healer; a curer; a restorer; a savior.

na lilafa, n., a rag; a clout.

na lilali, n., rags.

na litilli, n., a gum; a resinous substance.

na maleli, n., a runner.

na miha, n., a saying; a maxim; an adage.

na miha iksho, nan ikmiho, n., a silent person; a reserved person.

na miha shali, a., querulous; complaining.

na miha shali, v. n., to be querulous; v. t., to find fault.

na miha shali, n., a complainer.

na mihachi, v. t., to slander; to backbite; *na mihachit anumpuli*, to speak against, Matt. 12: 32; to curse, Matt. 15: 4.

na mihachi, n., a slanderer; a backbiter.

na mihachi shali, n., a noted slanderer; a whisperer.

na mihiksho, n., patience; silence.

na nihi, n., seeds, Matt. 13:4, 19, 20, 22, 23.

na nukhaⁿklo, v. a. i., to mourn, Matt. 5: 4.

na nukhamachi, n., pain.

na nuktalali, n., a comforter, John 14: 16.

na pakanli, see *nam pakanli*.

na palammi, n., a curse; a woe, 1 Sam. 14: 24, 28; see *nam palammi*.

na pelichi, n., a guide, Matt. 23: 24; a ruler, Matt. 9: 18; a governor, Matt. 10: 18.

na pisa, see *nam pisa*.

na piⁿsa, n., an eyewitness; a beholder; a seer, 2 Sam. 24: 11.

na pisat aⁿya, v. t., to spy, Josh. 2: 1.

na shali, n., a bearer; a carrier; *alhpoyak shali*, a peddler.

na shanaiya, a., perverse.

na shanni, n., a spinner.

na shilombish, n., a spirit; *na shilombish okpulo*, an unclean spirit, Luke 6: 18.

na shimmi, n., a river; a board-maker.

na shoeli, v. t., to draw lots, Josh. 15: 1; Matt. 27: 35.

na shoeli, n., a drawing lots; a lot, Josh. 13: 6; 14: 2.

na shoelichi, v. t. caus., to cast lots, Josh. 18: 6, 8, 10.

na shoelit ishi, n., a lot, Josh. 17: 14; 19: 1, 10, 17, 24, 32, 40.

na sholi, n., a bearer; a carrier.

na shua, n., filth; stench; offal; scent.

na tikbanli anoli, v. t., to prophesy; to foretell, Matt. 11: 13.

na waya, n., fruit, John 4: 36; a crop; mast.

na waya hoyo, v. t., to harvest.

na waya hoyo, na waya ishi, n., a harvester; a harvestman.

na waya ishi, v. t., to reap.

na waya kanchakfoki, v. t., to harvest; to put the fruits of the earth in a granary.

na wehpoa, n., pillage; plunder; prey; booty; a trophy, 1 Sam. 14: 30.

na wehpuli, n., a robber; a plunderer.

na weki, n., a burden; a weight; a heavy thing.

na yakohmi, n., this thing, Luke 2: 19; Matt. 16: 22.

na yimmi, n., a believer.

na yimmi, n., faith; *na yimmi chinto,* great faith, Matt. 8: 10; *na yimmi fehna keyu hachiama,* O, ye of little faith, Matt. 8: 26; 14: 31; 16: 8; 17: 20; *okla na yimmika,* their faith, Matt. 9: 2; *na yimmi iksho,* faithless; Matt. 17: 17, *nan ikyimmo,* unbelief, Matt. 17: 20.

na yopisa, n., a spectator.

na yoshoba, n., sin, 1 John 2: 12.

na yuka, n., a captive; spoil.

na yukachi, n., a captor.

na yukpa, n., joy; a joyful man; pleasure; rejoicing; peace, Matt. 10: 13; 13: 44.

na yukpa, v. a. i., to rejoice, Matt. 2: 10; to be blessed, Matt. 5: 3–10.

na yukpali, n., joy, Luke 2: 10.

nachofa, pp. sing., cut off; lopped; see *nachuffi.*

nachofa, n., that which is cut off.

nachoha, pp. pl., lopped.

nacholi, v. t. pl., to strip off leaves or cut off limbs; to lop.

nacholichi, v. t. pl., to strip off leaves or limbs; *iti naksisha na cholichi.*

nacholichi, n., one who strips or cuts off leaves or limbs; a lopper.

nachuffi, v. t. sing., to lop off; *iti naksish iloppa nachuffi,* cut off this limb.

nachuffi, n., a lopper.

naffi, v. t. sing., to pluck an ear of corn; pass., *nafa; nalichi,* v. t. pl., to pluck ears of corn; pass., *nahhachi.*

nafimmi, n., a sower; a scatterer, Matt. 13: 3.

nah, see *na.*

naha, v. a. i.; *ish naha.*

naha, adv., well nigh; for a time; almost; nearly; hardly; nigh; scarcely; *illinaha; hikikia naha.*

naha, pp., trimmed; picked off; cut off; *nalichi* v. t.

nahchaba, n., the backbone.

Nahchi, n., Natchez.

nahishi (Sixtowns word), n., rheumatic pains, also *shumantabi.*

na^{n}ka, a., having no worth; worthless, John 6: 27.

na^{n}ka, v. n., to be worthless; *yakni yammak na^{n}ka,* that land is of no value; see *ish atta tok ak na^{n}ka,* John 9: 34.

nakabila, n., a ladle used in melting lead; any place where lead is melted; a ladle.

nakachosha, n., a pile; the head of an arrow.

nakahakmo, nakaiakmo, n., a bullet-mold.

nakampo, n., a pewter basin.

nakfi, n., the brother of a woman; an appellation proper only for a sister to use; *a^{n}nakfi,* my brother.

nakfish, n., a junior; a junior brother, Matt. 4: 21; my brother, who is younger than the one speaking or the one spoken of; a younger brother, used to show this relation between two brothers or two cousins; a younger sister, used to show this relation between two sisters; a brother may not call his sister *sanakfish,* nor a sister call her brother *sanakfish,* my brother.

naki, n., lead; a dart; *i^{n}naki,* his sting.

naki fabassa, n., a pig of lead.

naki humma, n., red lead.

naki impatalhpo, n., wadding; some say *isht alhpitta.*

naki kallo, n., pewter.

naki kallo aiimpa, n., a pewter plate.

naki lumbo, n., a bullet; round lead.

naki lusa, n., black lead.

naki palalka, n., a pig of lead.

naki pila, v. t., to dart; to throw an arrow or dart.

naki tapuski, n., sheet lead.

naki yalhki, n., the dross of lead.

nakishtalali, n., a catfish; a bullhead.

nakishwana, n., a catfish; a bullhead.

nakni, n., the male sex of all creatures, where the distinction of sex is known; a man; a brave; a blade, used to denote a man of pith and spirit; manliness; a warrior.

nakni, a., brave; courageous; manful; manly; manlike; male; martial; masculine; valiant; *iknakno,* a hypochondriac; *naha^{n}kni.*

nakni, v. n., to be brave, courageous, manful, or resolute; *sanakni, chinakni; na^{n}ha^{n}kni.*

nakni hila, n., the name of a dance, at which none but men dance.

nakni tashka, n., a warrior; a subject; a male inhabitant.

naknichi, v. t., to render brave, bold, stout, manlike; *ilenaknichi,* to make a man of himself or to make himself bold; to rouse up one's courage or resolution when in trouble, distress, or danger.

naksakawa, n., corn bread made of green corn boiled, and wrapped in corn leaves; same as *tanch hiloha palaska* and *tanch hotokbi palaska*.

naksi, n., the side; the rib; *aboha naksi*, the side or the ribs of a house.

naksi, v. a. i., to turn on the side; to lean sideways, as a post; *naksit aⁿsha*, to turn and sit or to sit sideways; *naksit itola*, to lie on the side or to turn and lie.

naksi foni, n., a rib bone; a spare rib.

naksika, a., solitary.

naksika, n., a side; a corner; a by-place.

naksiⁿka, n., a corner, Luke 18: 13 [?].

naksika binili, pp., insulated.

naksika binili, v. a. i., to sit in a solitary place, as a corner; to retire.

naksika binilichi, v. t., to insulate.

naksika boli, v. t., to obviate; to lay one side.

naksika hilechi, v. t., to isolate.

naksikachi, v. t., to put in a corner or by-place; to put out of the way; to isolate; to slant.

naksikaia, v. a. i., to wander.

naksish, n., a limb; a knot; a joint, as in cane, reed, etc.; a branch, Matt. 13: 32. a bush; *iti naksish, uski naksish, kuⁿshak naksish, tanchapi naksish*.

naksish filamoli, n. pl., branches; limbs.

naksish filamminchi, n., a branch; a limb.

naksish iⁿfilammi, n., the branch of a limb.

naksish laua, a., knotty; full of limbs or joints; knurled.

naksish naha, pp., trimmed; having the limbs cut off.

naksish naha, n., a pollard; a tree lopped.

naksish nahachit taha, pp., pruned.

naksish nalichi, v. t., to poll; to cut off the limbs; to prune.

naksish nalichi, n., a pruner.

naksish taptuli, v. t., to poll.

nakshilup, n., tall wild grass, with a tassel.

nakshobi, naksobi, a., having the smell of fish when first taken from the water.

nakshobi, n., the smell of fish just caught.

nakshobi, v. n., to smell as newly caught fish; to stink, as fish.

nakshobichi, naksobichi, v. t., to cause to smell, as fish newly caught.

nakuⁿshi, n., shot; *pachi nakuⁿshi*, pigeon shot; *fani nakuⁿshi*, squirrel shot; *isi nakuⁿshi*, buckshot.

nalapi, n., the gorge; the throat; see *iⁿnalapi*.

nalichi, v. t., to pluck off ears of corn.

nalichi, v. t., pl. to trim off; to pick; to cut off; to lop; *tanchampi aⁿ nalichi; iti naksish aⁿ nalichi;* pass., *nahhachi, tanchi laua hosh nahhachi.*

nalichi, n., a lopper.

nalit illi apat nusi, n., opium.

nam, n., a thing, contracted from *nana*, and written *nam* before *p* for euphony's sake.

nam pakanli, na pakanli (Matt. 6: 28) n., a flower; a blossom; a bloom; a blow.

nam palammi, na palammi, n., a curse, 1 Sam. 14: 24, 28.

nam paⁿshi tanna, n., sackcloth; cloth made of hair.

nam pelichi, n., a ruler; a governor, Matt. 10: 18.

nam piheta, n., a lady's gown or frock; the old name is *alhkonapihita* (cf. *alconand*).

nam pilesa, n., a laborer; a workman; a hireling.

nam pisa, na pisa, n., a spectator; a looker; a looker on; a speculator; a spectacle.

nam poa, n., game; wild beasts

nam poa anusi, n., a lair.

nam poa hakshup, n., peltry.

nam poa inchuka, n., a kennel; a den.

nam poheta, n., a gown (not common); see *pohota*.

nam ponaklo, n., an inquirer.

nam pota, n., a borrower; a hirer.

nam potoni, n., a guard; a watch.

nan, n., a thing; contracted from *nana;* see *na* and *nam*.

nan abeka, n., sickness; a fever, Luke 4: 39.

nan achafa, n., an individual; one thing.

nan achefa, n., a washwoman; a laundress; a launderer; one who washes.

nan achefa ohoyo, n., a woman who washes; a laundress.

nan achunli, n., a tailor; a seamster; a tailoress; a seamstress; when a woman is intended, *ohoyo*, may be added as above.

nan aheka, n., a debtor; one who owes another money, goods, or services.

nan ahekạchi, n., a creditor; a truster.

nan ahoyo, n., the harvest; the harvest place; *nan imahoyo*, his harvest, Matt. 9: 38.

nan aiachefa, n., a washtub.

nan aiahni, n., the will, Matt. 12: 50.

nan aiapistikeli, n., a guard; prison, Gen. 40: 4.

nan aiashạcheka, n., sin; *na chimaiashạcheka*, thy sins, Matt. 9: 2, 6.

nan aiisht imałeka, n., peril.

nan aiithạna, n., a disciple; a learner; *nan imaiithạna*, his disciple, Matt. 8: 21, 23; *na chimaiithạna*, thy disciples, Matt. 9: 14.

nan aiokchaya, n., salvation, Luke 2: 30.

nan aiya, v. a. i., to act for peace, 1 Kings 2: 13.

nan aiya, n., peace; *itinnanaiya*, a peace between them, Josh. 9: 15; *nanaiya yoⁿ*, peace, Matt. 10: 34.

nan aiya, a., peaceful; living at peace; *itinnanaiya*, pp., conciliated; mutually reconciled, Matt. 5: 24; to make peace with, Josh. 10: 1, 4; *itin nanaiyahe keyu*, a., irreconcilable.

nan aiyạchi, v. t., to make peace; to cause peace; to mediate; *itinnan aiyạchi*, to cause them to be at peace; to mediate between them; to conciliate; *isht itiⁿnan aiyạchi*, Josh. 8:31.

nan aiyạchi, n., a peacemaker; a mediator; *itinnan aiyạchi*, a peacemaker; one who causes people to be at peace, Matt. 5:9; *pitinnan aiyạchi*, our mediator; *itinnan aiyạchechi*, v. t., to make peace between them; *itinnan aiyạchechi*, n., a peacemaker.

nan aiyukhạna, n., a cross, Luke 9: 23.

nan anoli, n., a newsman; a newsmonger; one who makes known the mind or counsel of a head man; a notifier; an informer; a crier; a herald; a publisher; a reporter; a talebearer; a tattler; a telltale; a witness, Matt. 18: 16; *na chimanoli*, your informant.

nan anoli shạli, n., a telltale; an officious informer; a blabber.

nan anusi, nan nusi, yanusi (from *yaiya* and *nusi*), n., a cry for the dead; a mourning for the dead; the place where the friends of the dead assemble at the end of the days of mourning to cry and bewail; and it is so called because they assemble about sundown and remain over night.

nan apela, n., a helper; an aid; an ally; an auxiliary; an assistant; a help.

nan apelạchi, n., a help; an aid, etc.

nan apesa, n., a judge; an arbiter; a ruler; a decider; a herald; an institutor; a magistrate, Matt. 5: 25; Josh. 8: 33; a manager; a marshal; a pretor; a schemer; *nam pimapesa bạnna hotuma*, it appears that he would be a judge over us; *na hạchimapesa*, your judges, Matt. 12: 27.

nan apesa abinili, n., a tribunal.

nan apesa ạleha, n., councils, Matt. 10: 17.

nan apesạchi, n., an overseer; a superintendent.

nan apistikeli, n., a guard, Gen. 40: 3.

nan apitta, n., a loader; one who puts on a load; one who charges a gun.

nan apoba, nanapoa, n., domestic animals, vegetables, trees, or fruits.

nan apoluma, n., a witch.

nan apuskiachi, n., a priest; a heathen priest, Gen. 41: 45.

nan ashạcheka, n., a mistake; applied also to our sins, in which sense it is much used by those who have come to know the nature of sin; a sin.

nan ashạchi, n., sin, 2 Sam. 24: 10; see *ashạchi*.

nan ashạchi, n., a sinner, Matt. 11: 19; *hatak nana ashạchi siahoke*, I am a man who is a sinner, Luke 5: 8.

nan atokowa anoli, n., a witness.

nan ạbanạblit ont ia, n., Passover; a thing that passes over.

nan ạbi, n., a killer; a slayer; a butcher; a murderer.

nan ạlhpisa, n., a custom, Luke 2: 27; a commandment, Matt. 5: 19; Josh. 1: 7, 8, 18; a law, Matt. 5: 17; 7: 12; *nan ạlhpisa pokoli*, the Ten Commandments; judgment, Matt. 5: 21.

nan ạlhpisa chinto, n., judgment, Matt. 11: 22.

nan ạlhpisa holisso, n., a book of the law; a law book, Josh. 8: 34.

nan ạlhpisa nitak, n., the day of judgment, Matt. 12: 36.

nan ąlhpisa onuchi, v. t., to accuse, Matt. 12: 10.

nan ąlhpoa, nan ąlhpoba, n., domestic animals; trees; fruits; plants; stock; anything raised by cultivation and care; see *nan apoba*.

nan ąlhpoba imatali, v. t., to stock.

nan ąlhpoyak, n., goods, wares, and merchandise.

nan ąlhtaha, n., things prepared; things in readiness.

nan ąlhtoba, n., wages, Luke 3: 14; Matt. 10: 42.

nan ąlhtoka, n., one who is appointed or elected; an official; an elect; a minister, Luke 4: 20; a servant, John 2: 5; an officer, Matt. 5: 25.

nan ąlhtokowa, n., testimony; things testified of, John 4: 39.

nan ąmo, n., a reaper; a picker, John 4: 36.

nan ąni, n., fruit, such as grows on trees; berries, etc.

nan ąpa, n., food; aliment; nutriment; an eatable; something to eat; meat.

nan ąpa okchaki, n., a salad.

nan ąpawaya, n., grain.

nan ąpawaya ahoyo, n., harvest, John 4: 35.

nan chąnaha, n., an orb; a sphere; a round thing.

nan chokushpa, n., trumpery.

nan chokushpa hunkupa, v. t., to pilfer.

nan chokushpa hunkupa, n., a pilferer.

nan chokushpa itatoba, n., a huckster.

nan chufichi, n., a sender; a driver; one who sends or drives another.

nan chumpa, n., a buyer; a trader; a merchant, Matt. 13: 45; a purchaser; a contractor; a storekeeper; a dealer; a negotiator.

nan chumpa kobafa, n., a bankrupt; a broken merchant.

nan hullochi, na hullochi, v. a i., to fast, Matt. 9: 14; 6: 16.

nan ihma heto, a., impossible.

nan ihmahe keyu, a., fruitless.

nan ihmi, nanahmi (from *nana* and *mih*), a., effectual; availing.

nan ihmi, n., cause; occasion; reason; *nan ihmi fehna keyu*.

nan ihmi, v. n., to be effectual; to avail; *nan ihmahe keyu*, it will avail nothing.

nan ihmi keyu, v. n., to avail nothing; to be ineffectual.

nan ihmichi, v. t., to cause to avail; to render effectual.

nan inhoa, n., a crier; a caller.

nan inholissochi, n., a scribe, Matt. 2: 4.

nan inholitopa, a., close; tight; ungenerous; avaricious; stingy.

nan inholitopa, v. n., to be close, tight, or stingy.

nan inholitopa, n., a thing loved by him; the object that is dear to him.

nan inhollo, a., close; tight; stingy.

nan inhollo, v. n., to be close.

nan inhollo, n., the thing or object of love.

nan inhoyąt anya, v. t., to wait.

nan inhullochi, n., the accursed thing, Josh. 7: 1, 11, 12.

nan ikahno, n., sangfroid.

nan ikahobo, n., nothing; a thing of no value.

nan ikaiąlhpeso, n., evil, Matt. 7: 11.

nan inkanimi, a., having some difficulty; disease.

nan inkanimi, v. n., to have some difficulty, or something is the matter with him.

nan inkanimi, n., an ailment; a trouble; a difficulty.

nan ikąlhpeso, n., iniquity, Matt. 7: 23.

nan ikbi, n., a mechanic; a manufacturer; a maker.

nan ikhana, nan ithana, n., a man of information or knowledge; a philosopher; a prophet; a seer; *nan ikithano*, an ignorant person; an ignoramus.

nan ikhana, pp., instructed; educated.

nan ikhana, a., erudite.

nan ikhana ilahobbi, n., a quack; a pedant.

nan ikhananchi, v. t., to educate.

nan ikhananchi, n., a teacher; an instructor; a preceptor; a tutor.

nan ikhąna, n., a learner; a pupil; a scholar; a disciple.

nan ikhąna, n., education.

nan ikhąnahe keyu, a., indocile.

nan ikimahobo, a., unconcern.

nan ikithano, n., an ignoramus.

nan ikithano, a., ignorant; unlearned.

nan ikmiho, a., uncomplaining; see *na miha iksho*.

nan ilachifa, n., purification of one's self.

nan ilahanchi, n., lucre.

nan ilahobbi, n., a hypocrite, Matt. 6: 2; 15: 7; 16: 3; a pretender, Luke 6: 42; hypocrisy, Mark 12: 15.

nan ilayak, n., treasure, Matt. 6: 19, 20.

nan ilhpak, n., food; victuals; meat, John 4: 32.

nan ilhpita, n., a benefaction; a present; the annuity received from the United States.

nan ilimpa, n., food; victuals; sustenance; aliment.

nan illasha, n., lamentation, Matt. 2: 18.

nan illi, n., a corpse; a dead body; a carcass; any dead creature; carrion; the relics; the remains of one dead; death, Rom. 6: 23.

nan imabachi, n., a teacher; an instructor.

nan imahombiksho, adv., easily.

nan imaianli, a., true to him; righteous before him, Luke 1: 6.

nan inmiha, v. t., to caution; to advise.

nan inmiha, n., an adviser; a cautioner.

nan inmihachi, v. t., to backbite him.

nan inmihachi, n., a backbiter.

nan inmiya, n., a councilor, Ezra 7: 14, 28.

nan imokpulo, n., adversity; harm.

nan imokpulot ilbasha, n., a calamity.

nan impa, n., food; an eater.

nan impota, n., a lender.

nan inla, n., a mystery; a vision; a strange thing.

nan inlaua, a., rich; affluent; wealthy; forehanded; opulent; strong.

nan inlaua, v. t., to have an abundance.

nan inlaua, n., affluence; the rich; the affluent; a fortune; a fullness; opulence; riches, Matt. 13: 22; wealth.

nan inlauachi, v. t., to enrich; to increase his substance.

nan innukhanklo, n., mercy, Matt. 9: 13; 12: 7.

nan ipetachi, n., a feast, Luke 2: 41.

nan isso, n., a striker; a smiter.

nan ishko, n., drink.

nan ishko, n., a drinker.

nan isht ahalaia, n., object of care, interest, concern.

nan isht ahoditopa, n., glory, Matt. 6: 29.

nan isht ahollo, nan isht ahullo, n., a witch; a spirit; an invisible being; a a supernatural being; a mammoth.

nan isht ahollo okpulo, nan isht ahullo okpulo, n., Satan; the devil; the prince of darkness; the old serpent; Abaddon; Apollyon; Luke 4: 41; Matt. 4: 24; 7: 22; 8: 16; 11: 18; 12: 24; 17: 18.

nan isht aianli, n., power, Matt. 6: 13; 9: 8.

nan isht aialhpesa, n., authority, Mark 11: 28, 29, 33.

nan isht aiibitabli, n., offences, Matt. 18: 7.

nan isht aiithananchi, n., doctrine, Matt. 16: 12.

nan isht aiokpachi, n., a present; a gift, Matt. 5: 23; a token of respect; a means of showing respect.

nan isht aiyukpa, n., a blessing, Josh. 8: 34.

nan isht aiyukpahe keyu, n., variety.

nan isht amiha, n., an apology; an excuse; a cavil; a pretext.

nan isht amiha inlaua, a., captious.

nan isht amiha inlaua, v. n., to be captious; to have excuses.

nan isht amihahe iksho, a., inexcusable.

nan isht anta, n., business; employment; occupation.

nan isht anukhanklo, n., grief; cause of sorrow.

nan isht apesa, n., a measure; a rule; a yard; that with which anything is measured.

nan isht apesa imponna, n., an artificer; an artisan.

nan isht atokowa, n., a sign, Matt. 12: 38, 39; 16: 1, 4; Josh. 4: 6; a testimony, Josh. 4: 16.

nan isht alhpisa, n., a rule; a carpenter's square; a measure; a yard; a yardstick; a parable, Mark 12: 1; 13: 10, 53; 15: 15.

nan isht alhtokowa, n., a testimony, Luke 5: 14.

nan isht atta, n., an agent; a transactor; an actor; any one that is intrusted with a particular business or employment; nan isht imatta, his agent.

nan isht atta, n., business; employment; object of labor or care; a transaction; nan isht imatta, his business.

nan isht atta ikimiksho, n., leisure.

nan isht atta imasha, a., busy.

nan isht atta inlaua, v. n., to have much business; to be busy.

nan isht ạtta inlauachi, v. t., to busy; to furnish with much business.

nan isht boa, n., a maul; a pounder.

nan isht fahạmmi, n., a sling.

nan isht fakuli, n., a wooden sling.

nan isht halạlli, n., harness; gears; nanatạnna isht halạlli; itichanạlli isht halạlli.

nan isht hummạchi, n., madder; red dyestuff.

nan isht huⁿsa, n., ammunition.

nan isht ikhana, n., a monument; a token, Josh. 2: 12.

nan isht ilaiyukpa, n., entertainment; a feast; a feasting; ilap nan isht ilaiyukpa, n., self-interest.

nan isht ilakostininchi, n., conscience, 2 Cor. 1: 12; Rom. 2: 15.

nan isht itatoba, n., a trader; an exchanger; changers of money, John 2:14.

nan isht itibbi, n., a weapon.

nan isht kasholichi, n., a mop; a wiper; a brush.

nan isht kula, n., any instrument used in digging; iti isht kula, a chisel; lukfi isht kula, a spade.

nan isht laknạchi, n., copperas; yellow dyestuff.

nan isht lusachi, n., black dyestuff.

nan isht łaⁿfi, n., a pencil; any instrument for drawing lines or making marks.

nan isht miha, v. a. i., to murmur; n., a murmurer.

nan isht nukpạllichi, n., an incitement.

nan isht okchakuchi, n., indigo; blue dyestuff.

nan isht okchalechi, n., a stimulus.

nan isht okchamalichi, n., indigo; blue dyestuff; green dyestuff.

nan isht piha, nan isht pełi, n., a shovel; a scoop.

nan isht pila, n., a sling; any instrument by which things are thrown.

nan isht shatạmmichi, n., yeast.

nan isht shema, n., ornaments; accoutrements; decoration.

nan isht takalamiksho, n., ease.

nan isht takalạma, n., a hindrance; an impediment; an obstruction; a difficulty.

nan isht talakchi, n., a string; a band; a bond; a tether.

nan isht tạli, n., any instrument for sharpening the end of a piece of wood.

nan isht tạna, n., a shuttle.

nan isht toⁿksạli, n., a tool; an implement of work.

nan isht weki, n., a steelyard; a scale; a balance, but generally used in the plural number, as steelyards, etc., except in the case of balance.

nan isht wekichi, n., a steelyard; a scale; a balance.

nan itạlhkạtta, n., a thing patched together; a pieced bed quilt; a quilt.

nan itạlhkạtta ikbi, v. t., to quilt.

nan ithana, n., knowledge; wisdom, Matt. 13: 54.

nan ithana, nan ikhana (q. v.), n., a man of information; a prophet, John 4: 8; the prudent, Matt. 11: 25; a prognosticator; nan ikithano, n., a stock.

nan ithana ilahobbi, n., a quack; a pedant.

nan ithạna, n., a disciple, Matt. 10: 24, 25; see aiithạna.

nan ithạnachi, n., a teacher, John 3: 2; a master, Matt. 10: 24, 25; master, Matt. 12: 38.

nan ithạnanchi, n., a master; a teacher, John 1: 38.

nan itimapesa, n., a covenant, Josh. 3: 3.

nan ittatoba, n., a trader; an exchanger; a speculator; a storekeeper.

nan ittatoba kobafa, n., a bankrupt.

nan luma, n., a mystery; a secret.

nan lumbo, na lumbo, n., an orb; a sphere.

nan lusa, n., black cloth; black stroud.

nan lusa chito, n., a bugbear; the name of an imaginary being that is an object of terror.

nan lusa isht tabashi, n., a weed; mourning.

nan lusachi, n., blacking.

nan lushka, n., a joker.

nan mihiksho, adv., tamely.

nan nihi, n., seed, Matt. 13: 37.

nan nukhaⁿklo, n., a man of sorrow.

nan nukpạlli, n., lust; temptation.

nan nukshopa, n., wild creatures; wild beasts.

nan nusi, nan anusi (q. v.), a cry; the last cry for the dead.

nan offo, n., vegetation.

nan okchako, n., blue stroud; blue blanketing. ·

nan okchalinchi, n., a deliverer; a savior; *na piokchalinchi*, our savior.

nan okchaya, n., a living creature; a creature.

nan okchaya keyu, a., inanimate.

nan okluha, n., all things, Luke 15: 31.

nan okpạna hinla, a., harmful.

nan okpạnahe keyu, a., harmless.

nan okpạni, n., a destroyer.

nan okpulo, n., a bad thing; a bad creature; destruction; a detriment; a pest; violence; an injury; evil, Matt. 6: 13; 9: 4.

nan okpulo anno, a., infamous.

nan tasembo, n., a wicked one, 1 John 3: 12.

nan tạnna, n., a weaver; a clothier; a knitter.

nan tạnna, n., cloth, Matt. 9: 16; domestic cloth; drapery; a fabric; stuff; a web.

nan tạnna aiapesa, n., a counter; a merchant's table.

nan tạnna akashofichi, nan tạnna asukkochi, n., a fulling mill.

nan tạnna ạba takali, n., a curtain.

nan tạnna bahta atoba, n., ticking.

nan tạnna bakoa, n., large checked cloth.

nan tạnna basoa, n., checked cloth; striped cloth.

nan tạnna bonunta, n., a roll of cloth; a bolt of cloth.

ñan tạnna holisso, n., checked cloth.

nan tạnna isht ạlhpisa, n., a yardstick; a measure for cloth.

nan tạnna kanchi, n., a draper; one who sells cloth.

nan tạnna kạllo, n., linen cloth; hemp cloth.

nan tạnna na kạllo, n., canvas; coarse cloth.

nan tạnna sukko, n., thick cloth; fulled cloth; duck; osnaburg.

nan tạnna sukko, pp., fulled.

nan tạnna sukkuchi, v. t., to full cloth.

nan tạnna sukkuchi, n., a fuller of cloth.

nan tạnna shauiya, n., striped cloth.

nan tạnna shukbo, n., duffel.

nan tạnna tohbi, n., shirting; sheeting; white cloth.

nan tiłeli, n., a driver; a drover (of a number, of more than one).

nan tiłi, n., a hewer; a marker of trees.

nan tishepa, red broadcloth; red stroud.

nan toba, pp., begotten, 1 John 5: 1.

nan tobachi, n., the maker; the one who begets; see 1 John 5: 1.

nan tohbi, n., white stroud; white blanketing.

nan tohno, n., a hirer; a contractor; an instigator; *nan pitohno*, our hirer, John 1: 22.

nan tohnochi, n., an instigator; one that excites a quarrel.

nan toksạli, n., work; labor; employment; *nan toksạli chimasha?* have you any work?

nan toksạli chipinta, n., chores.

nan toshbi, n., goods that perish; perishable things; rubbish; rotten things.

nan uha, a., all; everyone.

nan uⁿha (from *nan* and *uha*); v. n., to be all.

nan umachi, v. t., to defame; to slander; to talk about absent persons.

nan umachi, n., a defamer; a slanderer.

nan umachi, a., slanderous.

nan umanchi, n. f., as; *isht nan umachi*, v. t., to slander.

nan umanchi (compounded of *nan, om*, and *achi*, to say things on anyone), n., defamation.

nana, v. a. i., *nanakmạt*, Acts 5: 8; *nana kạt*, Scrip. Biog. Abraham and Lot, p. 29; *nanạt* and *nana cha filemạt*, she did something and turned; *iknano ka hi aⁿ*, Matt. 24: 20; *enana*, 1 Cor. 15: 11.

nana, rel. pro.; *nana ka*, what, Matt. 10: 27; whichever; *nana pelinchi*, them; *nana hoⁿ itih*, Matt. 18: 16; *nana akanchi*, "them that sold," Matt. 21: 12.

nana, n., a thing; a matter; a concern; a case; a cause; a fact; a subject; a substance; an affair; an article; stuff; materials; an event; an object; substance; a topic; *nạnna*, intensive form; *nana ho*, a thing; anything; something; *nana hoⁿ*, what, Matt 10: 19; 12: 7; 15: 4. *nana hosh*, anything in general; whatever; but *nana kosh* is definite; *nana kakosh*, demonstrative; *nana makosh*, which of the things; *nana*, used as intensive, as *hatak nana hosh*; see *hatak nana hosh Chihowa nitak nan ash*, John 1: 18.

nana, n., stroud; coarse woolen broadcloth.

nana achukma; *nana ikachukmo*, n., a vice.

nana ahaksichi, n., a pardoner.

nana aiaⁿli, n., a reality.

nana aiasha, n., a lumber room.

nana aiibetạbli, n., an offence, Matt. 18: 7.

nana aiikhạna, n., a school; a place of obtaining knowledge.

nana aiisht ilaiyukpa, n., pleasure.

nana aiisht imałeka, n., peril.

nana aiithạna, n., a scholar; a pupil; *nana imaiithạna*, his disciples, John 2: 2; 4: 8.

nana aiittatoba, n., a trading-house; a storehouse; a market.

nana aiyimmika, n., religion.

nana akaniohmi, n., conduct; see *nana kaniohmi*.

nana atoba, n., a manufactory.

nana ạlhpisa, n., a covenant; an agreement; a thing agreed upon; a commandment, Matt. 15: 6, 9; a tradition, Matt. 15: 6; *nan ạlhpisa*, Matt. 15: 3.

nana ạlhto keyu, n., emptiness.

nana ạlhto keyu, a., empty.

nana fehna, a., important.

nana fehna, n., a reality; the very thing; the thing itself; importance; stress.

nana fehna keyu, a., immaterial.

nana haleli, n., infection.

nana hạt, that which, Matt. 15: 11.

nana hoⁿ, whatsoever, Matt. 16: 19; that; *hatak nana hoⁿ*, that man, Matt. 18: 7.

nana holhtina, n., mathematics; things enumerated.

nana hosh, anything, Matt. 17: 20.

nana huⁿwa, n., a smell; a scent.

nana ikachukmo, n., an evil thing.

nana iⁿkaniohmi chito, okla nana iⁿkaniohmi chito, n., a revolution.

nana iksho, a., vacant.

nana imabạchi, n., a teacher; an instructor.

nana imilaⁿyak, n., goods; treasures, Matt. 2: 11.

nana inla yimmi, n., a proselyte.

nana inla yimmihechi, v. t., to proselyte.

nana iskitinusi, n., a mite; a mote; a trifle.

nana isht apesa, n., a rule; a parable, Luke 6: 39.

nana isht ạtta, n., employ; employment.

nana isht ilaiyukpa, n., consolation.

nana isht miha shali, n., a repiner.

nana itaiyuma, n., a mixture.

nana itatoba, n., a salesman.

nana ithạna, n., a disciple, Luke 6: 40.

nana ka, n., a thing, John 4: 22.

nana kanihchi, v. t., to do something with; to treat; to use; to manage; to punish.

nana kanihmi, n., an occurrence; an event.

nana kaniohmi, pp., punished.

nana kaniohmi, nana akaniohmi, n., a ceremony; conduct; a deed; news; performance.

nana kaniohmi iksho, a., unharmed.

nana kashofa, nana kashoffi, n., a., pardon.

nana keyu, n., nothing; not anything; vanity.

nana kia, n., anything; something; even a thing; whatsoever thing; whatever; whatsoever; nothing, with a neg. verb, Luke 4: 34; 5: 5; *hatak nana kia*, any man, Matt. 11: 27; 16: 20; *iknana kia*, although it may be so; even let it be so; *nana kạt*, a thing, Matt. 10: 26; 15: 11; Josh. 1: 8.

nana lua hinla, n., a combustible; something that will burn.

nana luma, a., private.

nana moma, n., all things; everything; nature; all nature.

nana moma iⁿshali, a., highest; superior to all things.

nana moma iⁿshali, v. n., to be highest.

nana moma iⁿshali, n., the highest, Luke 2: 14; The Most High.

nana okchaⁿya, n., a living thing; a living creature; life, John 1: 4.

nana piⁿsa, n., a witness; an evidence; an eyewitness.

nana silhha, n., a beggar; a supplicant; an applicant; a petitioner; a suppliant; a vagrant.

nana tạnna, n., a loom.

nana toba, n., a fabric.

nana toba puta, n., the universe; all created things.

nana waya, n., fruit, Josh. 5: 12.

nana wehpoa, n., plunder; articles taken by violence, as booty, spoils, etc.

nana yąmohmi, n., an instance.

nana yoshoba isht nukhaklo, a., repentant.

nana yuhmahe ąlhpesa, a., essential.

nana yukpa, n., life; happiness, in a theological sense.

nana yuwala, n., obscenity.

nanak, to say the thing.

nanąbli, v. a. i., v. t., to swallow; to englut; to engorge; to glut; to gobble; to gorge; to sup; to take.

nanąbli, n., a swallow; as much as is swallowed at once; a glut.

nanąbli, n., deglutition; the act of swallowing.

nanąbli achąfa, n., a draught; a single swallow; a dram.

nanąbli ikląnna, n., half a swallow; half a dram.

nanąblichi, v. t., to cause to swallow; to make another swallow; to drench.

nanąblichi, n., a drencher.

nanih; see *nantih, katih,* and *kanih;* similar to *h* and *mih;* he, she, or it is; *nantih, nanih,* are used of things.

nanta, any one; any thing; *nanta hosh anumpula wa.*

nanta, n., a thing; what; who; which— *nanta fehna ikachukmo kąt iląppa chiyuh-ma wa; nanta akoⁿ,* Matt. 16: 26—*nanta chiⁿ cho?* what shall it be? Matt. 11: 3— *nanta hako—nanta hakosh—nanta hoⁿ,* what? Matt. 11: 7, 8—*nanta hocha— nanta hona—nanta hosh, nantash,* what; Ch. Bk., p. 120, sec. 8—*nanta hot—nanta katimi—nanta katimiho,* how is it, John 4: 9; what, why, Luke 5: 22; 6: 41— *nanta katiohmi—nanta katiohmiho,* why then; why, John 1: 25; Matt. 7: 3; 14: 31; 15: 2; 2 Sam. 24: 3; wherefore, Josh. 7: 7—*nanta katiohmiho ahni,* v. a. i., to wonder, John 4: 27—*nanta kaheto— nanta kawa,* v. a. i., it can not be otherwise; to be without any alternative, *nantak,* from *nanta+k,* what the, Matt. 6: 31. *nantak oⁿ,* what is it, in the obj. case; whereunto, Matt. 11: 16. *nanta kocha—nanta kona—nanta kosh,* what is it, in the nom. case—*nanta makoⁿ,* wherewith—*nanta makocha—nanta ma-kona—nanta makosh.*

nantapąski, n., a handkerchief; thin cloth; calico. [This is probably from *nantąnna tapąski* meaning thin cloth, *nantąnna* itself being compounded of *nana,* something, and *tąnna,* woven.— H. S. H.]

nantapąski anchi, n., a shawl.

nantapąski chito, n., a shawl.

nantapąski iałipa, n., a kerchief; a turban.

nantapąski inuchi, n., a cravat.

nantąmi, nantihmi, (from *nanta* and *mih*), why, Luke 6: 2; what for; what?

nantih, see *nanih.*

nantih maheto, a., impossible.

nantih maheto, v. n., to be impossible.

nantihmi, nantahmi (from *nanta* and *mih*), v. a. i., v. n., how is it? Luke 2:49.

nantihmi, what?

nantimiho, wherefore.

nantukachi, (from *nanta, ka* and *achi*), v. t., to say, see Child's Catechism, question 11, *nantukachi hoⁿ?* see John 7: 26, *nanok ikimachoshke.*

nanuka, nanakaⁿ, nanoka, v. a. i., to say; to advise; to speak something designed for good; *chiⁿnanuka sabąnna; nanok ikimachoshke,* see John 7: 26; *nantukachi,* derived from *nana* thing, *ka* which, and *a,* to say.

nanukachi (from *nana, ka,* and *achi*), v. a. i., to say things; to counsel; to advise; to rail, 2 Chron. 32: 17; *nan ukahan-chi,* John 9: 22; *nan imokahanchi,* Rev. 3: 13.

naⁿpaⁿfi, see *paⁿfi.*

nashoba, n., a wolf; *nashoba isikopa,* ravening wolves, Matt. 7: 15.

nashoba hiła, n., the name of a dance.

nashoba ikląnna, n., a demiwolf; a half wolf; a wolf dog.

nashoba inchuka, n., a pen or trap made for catching wolves.

nashoba nakni, n., a he wolf.

nashoba tek, n., a she wolf; a bitch.

nashobushi, n., a young wolf; a whelp.

nasholichi, v. t., to destroy, 2 Sam. 22: 38.

nashuka, n., the face, Matt. 6: 16, 17; 17: 2; countenance; aspect; the visage; the looks; the head; *Aⁿki ąba binili ka nashuka yaⁿ,* the face of my Father which is in heaven, Matt. 18: 10.

nashuka bieka, a., barefaced; having a naked face.

nashuka bieka, v. n., to be barefaced.

nashuka hata, a., palefaced.

nashuka hita, v. n., to be palefaced.

nashuka humma, n., a red face.

nashuka hummat ont taha, v. a. i., to blush.

nashuka isht kasholichi, n., a towel.

nashuka isht umpoholmo, n., a veil, Gen. 24: 65.

nashuka okpulo, n., a grimace.

nashuka tuklo, a., doublefaced.

nalap, n., the swallow.

nali, n., the back, Josh. 7: 8; hatak nali, bashpo nali, holisso nali.

nali foni, n., the backbone; the chine; the spine.

nali foni aiitachaka, n., the vertebræ.

nali foni lupi, n., the spinal marrow.

nali hishi, n., a bristle; bristles.

nali nipi, n., a sirloin.

nalli, v. a. i. pl., to swallow; to booze; to gulp; to guzzle.

nalli, n. pl., swallows; drams.

nalli, n., deglutition.

nallichi, v. t. pl., to make others swallow; to drench.

nala, pp., wounded; shot; stung; iknalo, a., unshot; unwounded.

nala hinla, a., vulnerable.

nali, v. t., to wound; to sting; to shoot; to smite, as the heart, 2 Sam. 24: 10.

nali, n., a sting.

nali, n., a wounder.

nalichi, v. t., to cause to wound; to wound.

nan aiokweli, n., a fishery; a fishing-place.

nan isht albi, nani isht albi, n., a fish-hook, Matt. 17: 27; a seine.

nan isht okwia, n., a fishhook; a seine.

nan okweli, v. t., to angle; to fish.

nan okweli, n., an angler; a fisher; a fisherman.

nan okweli, n., a fishery.

nan ushi, n., the spawn of fish; young fish.

nanabi, n., a fisher; a fisherman, Luke 5: 2.

nanalbi, n., a fish trap.

nanapa, n., a watersnake; a fish eater.

nani, n., a fish, Matt. 14: 17; 17: 27; nani yon, a fish; Matt. 7: 10.

nani basa, n., a perch.

nani chapka, n., a cockroach.

nani chito, n., a great fish; a whale, Matt. 12: 40; a shark.

nani hakshup, n., a fish scale; fish scales.

nani hokli, v. t., to angle; to catch fish.

nani hokli, n., an angler; a fisherman, Matt. 4: 18.

nani humma, n., a red fish.

nani intali hata, n., the white shining part of the belly of a fish.

nani isht hokli, nan isht hokli, n., a fish net, Matt. 4: 18; 13: 47; a fish trap; a fish pot; a fish basket; a seine; a fishhook.

nani itakha, n., fish gills.

nani kallo, n., the garfish; a haniger.

nani patassa, n., a flat fish.

nani shupik, n., a kind of trout.

nanih, n., (nani, a fish), a hill; an eminence; a mount; a height; a mound; a mountain, Josh. 2: 16, 22; 8: 30.

nanih aiali, n., the brow of a hill; the edge of a hill, Luke 4: 29.

nanih akkia, n., the pitch of a hill; the descent of a hill.

nanih bunto, n., a round hill; a mound; a mount.

nanih chaha, n., a high hill; a mountain; a mount, Matt. 5: 1; Matt. 14: 23; nanih chaha yan, the mountain, Matt. 8: 1; 15: 29; Luke 4: 5; nanih chaha puta ka, mountains, Luke 23: 30; nanih chipunta yan, hills.

nanih chakpaka, n., down hill; a hill-side.

nanih chakpataka, n., the side of a hill.

nanih chakpatalika, n., the side of a hill.

nanih foka, a., hilly; into the mountains, Matt. 18: 12.

nanih foka, n., hills; highland; upland.

nanih lua, n., a burning mountain.

nanih paknaka, n., the top of a hill; the crown of a hill.

nanih tashaiyi, n., an island.

naniyi, n., the fins of a fish; a fin.

nek, part., like kamo; see lek.

nia, a., fat; adipose; corpulent; fleshy; gross; fatty; full; pudgy; squab; unctuous; *lukfi nia*, unctuous clay.

nia, pp., fattened; fleshed; larded; tallowed.

nia, v. n., to be fat; *niạt taiyaha*, waxed fat, Matt. 13: 15.

nia, v. a. i., to fat.

nia, n., fatness; the fat; the hard fat of animals; grossness.

nia chạpka, n., a cockroach; see *bila chạpka.*

niachi, v. t., to fat; to fatten; to batten; to feed; to lard; to tallow; *hạshileniachi,* 1 Sam. 2: 29.

niachi, n., a fattener.

niashmo, a., adhesive; v. n., to be adhesive.

niat isht ia, v. a. i., to fat; to fatten; to batten; to grow fat.

nibli, v. t. pl., to take off the limbs of a tree or of a body; to dismember; to dissect; to joint; to limb.

nibli, n., one who severs limbs from the main trunk.

nietak, see *nitak.*

niha, nihi (q. v.), pp., thrashed; ginned (seed taken from the stalk, etc.).

niheli, nihelichi, nihechi, v. t., to thrash out seed; to pick out seed; to gin; to thrash; *onush a^n nihelichi*, to thresh wheat; *ponola ya^n nihelichi,* to gin cotton.

nihelichi, n., a thrasher.

nihi, n., seed, Matt. 17: 20; a kernel; a grain; a nit, as *isạp nihi*; a bore, caliber; the core; a corn; the head of *onush; na nihi*, seeds, Matt. 13: 4.

nihi, pp., thrashed; shelled; ginned; *niheli*, v. t.

nihi aholokchi aiona, n., seedtime.

nihi chitofa, v. a. i, to seed; to shed the seed.

nihi fimmi, v. t., to seed.

nihi laua, a., seedy.

nihi toba, v. a. i., to seed; to grow to maturity so as to produce seed.

ninak, n., night.

ninak aiạtta, n., a birth night.

ninak ash, n., yesternight.

ninak ạba pit anumpuli, n., a vigil.

ninak foka, a., nocturnal; in the night.

ninak foka, v. n., to be nocturnal.

ninak iatipa, n., a nightcap.

ninak iklạnna, n., midnight; half of the night.

ninak impa, n., supper.

ninak impa impa, v. a. i., to sup.

ninak luak, n., night fire.

ninak oktili, n., night darkness; *ninak oktili kamạkạt kạnia,* Egyptian darkness.

ninak palali, n., night fire.

ninak tasembo, n., a night walker; night craziness.

nip illit shua, v. a. i., to mortify.

nip illit shua, pp., mortified.

nip illit shua, n., mortification.

nip illit shuachi, v. t., to mortify; to cause mortification.

nipa, pp. pl., stripped of limbs; dismembered; dissected; *ninipaha*, to rend in pieces, Gen. 37: 33.—this should be *nipa*, pass. of *nibli; nibli,* v. t.

nipa, n., limbs stripped off or cut off; jointed.

nipafa, pp. sing., stripped of limbs; cut off; jointed; *nipạffi*, v. t.

nipafa, n., a limb cut off.

nipaiạlhpusha, n., a gridiron; the place where meat is roasted or broiled.

nipati, pp. pl., stripped off; taken off; jointed; *nipafkạchi,* pp. pl.

nipatichi, v. t. pl., to take off; to strip off; to cut off limbs from a tree or a body.

nipauạshli, v. t., to fricassee; to fry meat.

nipạffi, v. t. sing., to take off a limb; to joint.

nipalwạsha, see *nipi ạlwạsha.*

nipạsha, n., a roasting ear; as *tanch nipạsha.*

nipạshi, v. a. i., to become a roasting ear; to grow to the state of roasting ears.

nipi, n., meat; flesh; a kernel; lean; leanness; pulp, Matt. 16: 17.

nipi abạshli, n., a meat bench.

nipi achukma, n., hardy; healthy; hearty; hale.

nipi ahoni, n., a vessel used for cooking meat.

nipi aiạlhto, n., a meat barrel; a meat trough or bin, or any place of deposit for meat.

nipi aiittatoba, n., the shambles; a flesh market.

nipi ạlhpusha, n., broiled meat; roasted meat.

nipi ạlwạsha, nipạlwạsha, n., fried meat; a fricassee.

nipi baha, pp., meat beaten up in a mortar.

nipi baha shila, n., sausage meat.

nipi bałi, v. t., to beat up meat in a mortar; to beat up sausage meat.

nipi bano, a., naked; naked flesh.

nipi bano, v. n., to be naked.

nipi banuchi, v. t., to strip naked.

nipi bạshli, n., a butcher.

nipi honni, n., cooked meat; stewed meat; boiled meat.

nipi humma, n., a mulatto.

nipi ikinchukmo, a., unwell.

nipi illi, nipilli, n., dead flesh; gangrene.

nipi isht chaⁿya, n., a chopping knife; a meat knife or ax.

nipi isht kapạsh, n., flesh tongs made of cane.

nipi isht kạfa, n., flesh tongs.

nipi kạllo, a., able bodied; athletic.

nipi kạllo, v. n., to be able bodied.

nipi lua, a., having the flesh burnt.

nipi lua, v. n., to have the flesh burnt; to burn, as a fever.

nipi lua, n., burning flesh; a fever.

nipi łabocha, n., boiled meat; meat cooked in boiling water.

nipi okchaⁿki, n., fresh meat.

nipi okchaⁿki tushałi, n., a steak; slices of fresh meat.

nipi shila, n., dried meat; cured meat; dry flesh.

nipi shua, n., carrion; putrid flesh; rotten meat; mortification; gangrene.

nipi shua, pp., mortified.

nipi shulla, n., perished flesh; withered flesh; dried flesh, applied to describe diseases in the flesh.

nipi tushafa, n. sing., a piece of meat; a slice of meat; a rasher.

nipi tushafa pạsa, n., a rasher.

nipi tushałi, n. pl., slices of meat.

nipi wạnnichi, n., horror.

nipinchuka, n., a meat house.

nishkin, n., the eye, Matt. 18: 9; the eyeball; the core of a boil; the sight; view; *ishitibapishi nishkin*, and *chinishkin*, Matt. 6: 22; 7: 3, 4; 13: 15; *chinishkin* Matt. 18: 9.

nishkin achạfa, a., one-eyed.

nishkin aheli chiluk, n. pl., sockets of the eye.

nishkin ahika chiluk, n. sing., a socket of the eye.

nishkin alata, n., spectacles.

nishkin alata aⁿsha, pp., spectacled.

nishkin ạłi, n., the corner of the eye; the edges of the eye.

nishkin hakshup, n., the eyelid.

nishkin halupa, a., eagle-eyed; quick-sighted; sharp-sighted.

nishkin halupa, n., a keen eye; a sharp eye.

nishkin hạta, n., a light-colored eye.

nishkin ikhalupo, a., short-sighted.

nishkin imalikchi, n., an oculist.

nishkin imikhiⁿsh, n., eye salve; eye water.

nishkin itasunali, n., cross-eyes; a., cross-eyed; goggle-eyed.

nishkin itiopitama, n., cross-eyes; a., cross-eyed.

nishkin kạła, n., a perished eye.

nishkin kạnia, a., sightless.

nishkin kucha, pp., gouged.

nishkin kuchi, v. t., to gouge.

nishkin lạpa, n., blindness; a blind eye.

nishkin lạpa, a., blind.

nishkin lạpa, v. n., to be blind.

nishkin lạpa ạmmona, a., purblind; partially blind.

nishkin lạpachi, v. t., to blind; to make blind.

nishkin lạpạt kạnia, a., stone-blind; entirely blind.

nishkin luhmi, v. t., to blindfold.

nishkin luma, pp., blindfolded.

nishkin lusa, n., a black eye; a., black eyed.

nishkin mochukli, n., the winking of the eye; the winking of an eye.

nishkin nihi, n., the pupil of the eye; the sight of the eye; eyesight.

nishkin nukbilaⁿkchi, n., the flesh in the corner of the eye.

nishkin okchi, n., a tear; tears.

nishkin okchi, v. a. i., to weep; to shed tears.

nishkin okchi minti, v. a. i., to weep (lit., the tears come).

nishkin okchiyanạlli, n., a weeping.

nishkin okchiyanạlli, v. a. i., to flow, as tears; the tears flow.

nishkin okhaiyanli, n., cross-eyes.

nishkin okpạni, v. t., to destroy the eye; to blind; to deprive of sight.

nishkin okpulo, n., a bad eye; a ruined eye.

nishkin oktalonli, n., a blear eye.

nishkin oktalonli, a., blear-eyed; wall-eyed; blind eyed.

nishkin okwalonli, a., wall-eyed.

nishkin shamba, n., a perished eye.

nishkin shanaiya, a., cross-eyed; squint-eyed.

nishkin shanaiya, n., cross-eyes.

nishkin shili^{n}hchi, nishkin shili^{n}kchi, n., the eyelash.

nishkin shili^{n}hchi hakshup, n., the eyelid.

nishkin tamoa, a., blind; having a blindness in both eyes.

nishkin tamoa, v. n., to be blind in both eyes.

nishkin tanla, n., an eye covered with a film, but not destroyed.

nishkin tạlhha, n., a cataract; a film over the pupil of the eye.

nishkin tạmp, n., an evil eye.

nishkin toba, n., a bubble.

nishkin toba, v. a. i., to bubble; to form a bubble.

nishkin tohbi, n., a dim eye; dimness of eyesight; *Isaac nishkin ạt tohbit taha hatokosh ushi a^n achukmạt ikithanokitok.*

nishkin tohbichi, v. t., to make the eye dim.

nishkin wishakchi, n., the corner of the eye.

nishkoba, see *nushkoba.*

nita, n., a bear.

nita bila, n., bear's oil.

nita hakshup, nitakshup, n., a bear-skin; a bear's hide.

nita i^{n}pisa, n., name of a strong, tough, green grass, similar to *bisakchula.*

nita nia, n., bear's fat; bear fat.

nita nipi, n., bear meat.

nita peli, n., a bear's nest.

nita tohbi, n., a white bear.

nitak, nittak, nietak, n., a day; day, Matt. 7: 22; 11: 23, 24, 25; Josh. 5: 11; light; from sunrise to sundown; day-time; a time, Matt. 3: 1; a season; a date, Matt. 12: 1; a term; *na pehna holokchi nitak,* seedtime.

nitak, a., temporal.

nitak achạfa ninak achạfa, n., one day of twenty-four hours.

nitak achạfa to^{n}ksạli, n., a day's work.

nitak aiạlhtoba, nitak aiạlhtoba hinla, n., pay day.

nitak aiạtta, n., a birthday.

nitak aiitauaya, n., a wedding day.

nitak atukma, adv., daily.

nitak atukma, a., diurnal.

nitak ạlhpisa, n., a period; measured or appointed days.

nitak chakpa, midst of days.

nitak echi, v. a. i., to begin, as a day; the day begins.

nitak echi, n., the commencement of the day; the forepart of the day; the name of a chief in Pushimataha district who died in the old nation.

nitak himmak pilla ma, n., futurity.

nitak holhtina takali, pp., dated.

nitak holhtina takalichi, v. t., to date.

nitak holhtina to^{n}ksạli, n., day's labor.

nitak holisso pisa, n., a school day.

nitak hollo, n., the Sabbath day; also a holy day; a week; Sunday, Matt. 12: 8.

nitak hollo achạfakma, adv., weekly.

nitak hollo chito, n., Christmas; the great holy day.

nitak hollo ikimiksho, a., sabbathless.

nitak hollo kobạffi, n., a Sabbath breaker.

nitak hollo nakfish, n., Saturday.

nitak hollo nitak, n., the Sabbath day; *nitak hullo nitak a^n,* the Sabbath days; *nitak hullo nitak o^n,* the Sabbath day, Luke 4: 16; Matt. 12: 1, 10, 11, 12.

nitak hollo tuklo, n., a fortnight; two weeks; two Sabbaths.

nitak hollotuk i^{n}misha, n., Tuesday.

nitak hollotuk onna, n., Monday.

nitak i^{n}falaia, a., longlived.

nitak iki^{n}falaio, a., shortlived.

nitak iklạnna, n., midday; half a day.

nitak iłauạlli, n., a holy day; a play day.

nitak inla, n., a week day.

nitak isht yopomo, v. t., to while; to waste time.

nitak kaniohmi kia, any day; any time, Matt. 13: 15; Josh. 6: 10.

nitak moma, a., every day; n., all days; ever.

nitak moma, adv., daily.

nitak moma holisso, n., a journal.

nitak nana, any day, Matt. 7: 23; with a neg., never; no day; *nitak nana tahq himma keyu.*

nitak nana ạlhpisa chito, n., doomsday; judgment day; the day of judgment.

nitak nanta, never; *nitak nanta fena akon ont hokofa wa.*

nitak omi, n., moonlight; moonshine.

nitak taha, v. a. i., to expire.

nitak tinkba, a., ancient; of old; adv., anciently; primitive; of old time, Matt. 5: 21.

nitak tinkba, v. n., to be ancient.

nitak tinkba, n., antiquity; ancient days; former days or times.

nitak tinkba minti, n., the future.

nitak tinkbahe, hereafter (day that will be first).

nitak tohwikeli, n., dawn; daylight.

nitak tonksạli, n., a working day.

nitak untuklo, n., seven night.

nitanki, a., mild; pleasant; good; seasonable; adv., timely.

nitanki, v. n., to be mild.

nitanki, adv., in time; in season; while it is day; *nitanki ona sabạnna* or *ikopiako ona sabạnna.*

nitanki, n., light, John 1: 5.

nitakshup, see *nita hakshup.*

nittak, see *nitak.*

nitushi, n., a young bear; a cub.

no, a rel. pro., or part. cont. from *ano* (q. v.); *nan aiokchayano,* Luke 2: 30.

no, art. cont. from *ano;* often suffixed to *ka, hoka,* etc.

Nofimba, n., November.

noḷichi, v. t. pl., to trim off small limbs or leaves.

noshkobo, see *nushkobo.*

noshkoboka, n., head of, Josh. 11: 10; see *nushkobo.*

nota, see *nuta.*

noti, n., a tooth; a grinder; teeth; a tusk; *noti ma,* teeth also, Matt. 8: 12; *noti ahampa,* gnashing of teeth, Matt. 13: 42, 50.

noti bolukta, noti polukta, n., a double tooth.

noti chukbi, n., a corner tooth; a grinder.

noti hotupa, n., toothache.

noti ibish, n., a foretooth; a front tooth.

noti isht impa, n., a grinder.

noti isht itibi, n., a fang; a tusk; the eyetooth; the dogtooth; the cheek tooth.

noti isht kasholichi, n., a toothbrush.

noti isht shinli, n., a toothpick.

noti itabalakchi, n., the gum of the teeth.

noti itạlbakchi, n., the gum of the teeth.

noti itạlbakchi chito, n., the lampas.

noti itikiselichi, v. t., to grind the teeth; to grate the teeth; to gnash the teeth together.

noti nukbalankchi, n., the gum of the teeth.

noti offo, v. a. i., to teethe.

noti pokta, n., a double tooth; a grinder.

noti polukta, noti bolukta, n., a double tooth.

noti shakaya, n., a tooth edge.

noti tikba, n., a foretooth; a front tooth.

nowa, v. a. i., to walk; to travel, Josh. 9: 13; to go; to journey; to move; to pace; to stalk; to tramp; to tread; *anowa,* Matt. 14: 29; *itanowa,* to travel together, Matt. 2: 2; 6: 26; 10: 7; *innowa,* to visit him, her, or them; to see him, etc.; *ohoyo innowa,* to visit a lady, i. e., to court; to pay attention to a lady; *akka nowa,* to travel on foot; *innowa* n., a visit; *iknowo* a., untraveled; *anowa,* n., the place to walk.

nowa, n., a walk; a walker; a traveler; a gait; a journey; a march; a pace; a ramble; a travel; a tread; a walking.

nowa pạlhki, v. a. i., to trip.

nowa shaḷi, n., a rambler; a., restless.

nowạchi, v. t., to walk; to cause to walk.

nowạt anya, v. a. i., to travel; to jaunt; to journey; to be walking, *anowạt anya,* Matt. 14: 25; *anohonwạt anya,* Matt. 14: 26; *anowạt manyạt,* Matt. 14: 28.

nowạt anya, n., a journey; a pilgrimage.

nowạt anya, a., wayfaring.

nowạt anya, n., a traveler; a guest; a passenger.

nowạt falama, n., a jaunt.

nowạt fullokahanchi, v. t., to itinerate.

nowạt fullokahanchi, n., an itinerant.

nowạt fullota, v. a. i., to jaunt; to travel about.

nowạt fullota, n., a jaunt; the person who jaunts; a tourist; a tour.

nowạt itạnaha, n., a levee.

nuchi, n., milk weed; flax; *nuchi ạpi,* Josh. 2: 6.

nukbepa, a., breathless.

nukbepa, pp., stunned by a blow on the trunk or chest.

nukbepa, n., the state of one stunned.

nukbepli, v. t. sing., to stun; to strike the breast, or chest, so as to deprive of breath for a season.

nukbeplichi, v. t., to cause to stun.

nukbepoa, a. pl., breathless.

nukbepoa, pp., stunned.

nukbepuli, v. t. pl., to stun; to smite the chest, so as to deprive of breath for a season.

nukbikili, v. a. i., to stifle; to lodge and press, in the throat, as some kinds of food.

nukbimikachi, v. a. i., to palpitate.

nukbimikachi, n., a palpitation.

nukbimimkachi, v. a. i., to palpitate.

nukchinto, v. a. i., to keep silence, Luke 4: 35; 18: 39; to forbear; *nukchintoli,* I keep silence.

nukchinto, a., silent.

nukfichoa, chukfikoa, n., hiccough; hickup.

nukfichoa, nukfichowa, v. a. i., to hickup.

nukficholi, v. a. i., to hickup.

nukficholi, n., the hickups; hiccough or hickup.

nukficholichi, v. t., to cause one to hickup.

nukfoka, v. a. i., v. t., to embrace; to comprehend; to understand or to be imbued with knowledge; to hear; to imbibe; to occur; to receive; to have, as faith, Matt. 17: 20; *chimanumpa hasanukfokat tahashke, chinukfoka himma keyu,* said to an obstinate child; *nukfonka,* nas. form; *nukfoyuka,* pro. form.

nukfoka, a., pp., instructed; made to understand; inspired; principled; received; *nukfoyuko,* pro. form.

nukfokachi, v. t., to instruct; to cause to understand.

nukfokechi, nukfokichi, v. t., to give knowledge; to cause to be established in the knowledge of anything; to inspire; to principle; prolonged form, *nukfokihinchi; aba anumpa han ishpinukfokihinchashke,* wilt thou establish us in the gospel?

nukfoki, v. t., to give knowledge; to establish in the knowledge of anything; *aba anumpa nukfoki,* to establish in the knowledge of the gospel; to inspire; to put into the mind; to move one to do or say, Josh. 15: 18.

nukfoki, n., a teacher.

nukfokichi, n., one who instructs or imparts knowledge; a teacher.

nukfokichi, n., inspiration.

nukhanklo, n., a deplorer; a dump.

nukhanklo, n., sorrow; grief; bowels, as used in the scriptures; compassion; dolor; gloom; lamentation; lenity; melancholy; plaint; regret; remorse; tenderness; pity; *isht innukhanklo,* n., his mercies, 2 Sam. 24: 14.

nukhanklo, pp., deplored; grieved; humbled; melted, as the heart with sorrow or compassion; *ikinnukhanklo,* a., unpitied.

nukhanklo, a., sorry; sorrowful; pitiful; merciful; broken in heart, Luke 4: 18; contrite; aggrieved; afflicted; compassionate; dull; doleful; dolorous; grievous; heavy; humane; humble; merciful; pitiful; plaintive; propitious; repentant; rueful; sad; spleeny; tender; tragical; *innukhaklahe alhpesa,* lamentable; pitiable; *iknukhanklo,* a., unrepentant.

nukhanklo, v. n., to be sorry or sorrowful; to be aggrieved, Matt. 17: 23.

nukhanklo, v. a. i., v. t., to feel sorrow; to exercise compassion; to commiserate; to sorrow; to spare; to yearn; to be sorry, Matt. 14: 9; to bewail; to lament; to mourn; to compassionate; to deplore; to moan; to repent; to wail; *isht nukhanklo,* v. t., to lament; to regret; to weep; to sigh; to mourn for; *innukhankloli, insanukhanklo; itinnukhanklo,* to pity each other; *innukhanklo,* to pity; to be moved with compassion, Matt. 14: 14; *ibanukhanklo,* v. a. i., to sympathize with; to sympathize; *ibanukhanklo,* a., sympathetic; *ibanukhanklo,* n., sympathy.

nukhanklo atopa, n., heart-break; overmuch sorrow.

nukhanklo chito, a., woful.

nukhanklo iksho, a., hard hearted; without pity; merciless; ruthless; savage; unrelenting; unsparing; *innukhanklo iksho,* a., unmerciful.

nukhanklochi, v. t., to grieve; to afflict; to deject; to depress; to humble;

to melt, as the heart; *chuⁿkạsh nuk-hạⁿklochi*, to sadden; to touch.

nukhaⁿklot naⁿhullochi, v. a. i., to fast religiously, Matt. 9: 14, 15.

nukhạma, v. a. i., to be in pain.

nukhạmạchi, v. t. caus., to cause pain.

nukhạmmi, a., painful; aching; severe; sharp.

nukhạmmi, v. n., to be painful; to ache; v. a. i., to struggle; to throe; *sanuk-hạmmi*, I am pained, *nukhahạmmi*, to have bitterness of spirit, 1 Sam. 1: 10.

nukhạmmi, nukhạmi, n., pain; misery; distress; agony; a throe; torture; uneasiness; "her pains," 1 Sam. 4: 19; 1 Thess. 4: 3 [?].

nukhạmmichi, v. t., to inflict pain; to cause pain or agony; to distress; to pain; to torture.

nukhobela, a., pp., angry; mad; furious; infuriated; passionate; enraged; irritated; agitated; excited.

nukhobela, v. n., to be mad or angry; to become mad (fixed or settled madness).

nukhobela, n., anger; wrath; excitement; fire.

nukhobelạchi, v. t., to enrage; to irritate; to anger; to provoke; to make mad; to fire; to infuriate.

nukhomechi, v. t., to render pungent; acrimonious, or strong, as whiskey, pepper, or peach leaves when taken into the mouth.

nukhomi, a., pungent to the taste.

nukhomi, n., pungency.

nukhushpa, Ch. Sp. Book, p. 44.

nukkilli, n., hatred; ill will; indignation; malice; spite; *iⁿnukkilli*, n., enmity; wrath; *aiiⁿnukkilli*, anger, 2 Sam. 24: 1; anger, an attribute, Josh. 7: 12, 26.

nukkilli, a., envious; indignant; invidious; malicious; malign; malignant; spiteful.

nukkilli, v. n., to hate, John 3: 20; to abhor; *iⁿnukkilli*, v. t., to hate him, Matt. 5: 22; 6: 24; to despite; to envy; to spite; *itinnukkilli*, to hate each other.

nukkilli, iⁿnukkilli, n., a hater.

nukkilli keyu, a., unenvied.

nukkillichechi, v. t., to cause to hate; to disaffect.

nukkillichi, v. t., to cause to hate.

nukkitekạchi, n., palpitation of the heart; pulsation of the heart, caused by fever as some say; *chuⁿkạsh nukkite-kạchi.*

nukkitekạchi, v. a. i., to palpitate; to flutter, .as in the stomach.

nukkiteli, n., burning in the stomach when very acid.

nuklibekạchi, v. a. i., to start quick, as the blood.

nuklibekạchi, n., a quick motion of the blood; heartburn; heart rising.

nuklibeshạchi, v. t., to enkindle; see below.

nuklibisha, a., pp., heated; warmed with passion; hot; enkindled.

nuklibisha, v. n., to be heated; to be in a passion.

nuklibisha, v. a. i., to glow; to warm; to get warm with passion.

nuklibisha, n., temper; warmth.

nuklibishakachi, a., heated suddenly with passion; impassionate; impassioned.

nuklibishakachi, v. n., to be heated; to be warmed with passion.

nuklibishạchi, v. t., to enkindle.

nuklibishli, v. t., to warm the flesh or person.

nuklibishlikạchi, n., passion.

nuklibishlikạchi, v. a. i., to fly into a passion.

nukłakancha, n., a fright; terror; destruction, 1 Sam. 5: 11.

nukłakancha, v. a. i., to start flesh trembling.

nukłakancha, pp., frightened; scared; surprised; affrighted; amazed; shocked; terrified; marveled, Matt. 8: 10, 27; 9: 8; Luke 4: 36, Matt. 12: 23; astonished, Matt. 13: 54; wondered, Matt. 15: 31.

nukłakanchichi, v. t., to startle; to affright; to affray; to start.

nukłakạshli, nukłakaⁿshli (n. f.), v. t. pl., to frighten; to startle; to scare; to shock; to terrify; to destroy, 1 Sam. 5: 9.

nukłamạlli, v. a. i., to choke or suffocate.

nukłamoli, nukłamonli (n. f.), v. a. i. pl., to strangle; to choke by taking food, etc., into the windpipe; to strangle by being under water too long.

nukłamoli, pp., strangled; choked.

nukłamolichi, v. t., to cause to strangle; to strangle another.

nukłamolli, v. a. i. sing., to strangle; to choke with food or drink.

nukłamolli, pp., strangled; choked.

nukłamollichi, v. t., to strangle; to strangle another.

nukłiⁿfa, v. a. i., to suffocate.

nukłiⁿfa, pp., suffocated.

nukłiⁿffi, v. t., to suffocate.

nukoa, nokoa, a., angry; mad; cross; fierce; fiery; frantic; furious; huffy; ill; ill natured; indignant; infuriate; invidious; malicious; malign; malignant; morose; offensive; outrageous; rabid; snappish; spiteful; spleeny; sulky; sullen; surly; unpeaceable; vexed; vindictive.

nukoa, nukowa, v. n., to be angry or mad.

nukoa, v. a. i., to inflame; to leer; to madden; to rage; to rankle; to stomach; to storm; to tear; to vex.

nukoa, pp., maddened; chagrinned; enraged; exasperated; fretted; incensed; inflamed; offended; piqued; ruffled; scandalized; provoked; iknukoo, a., unoffended; unprovoked.

nukoa, v. t. with a pro. prefixed, as iⁿnukoa, to drive him; isuba iⁿnukoa, to rein a horse; akaⁿka yaⁿ iⁿnukoa, to drive away the fowls; innukoa, iⁿnukoa, to be angry at him; to jaw; to rail; to rate; to resent; to scold; to spite; to bicker; to brawl; to quarrel; itinnukoa, to be angry at each other; itinnukoa shali, a., quarrelsome; iⁿnukoa, n., a scolder.

nukoa, n., a teaser; a mad man.

nukoa, n., anger; madness; wrath; choler; spite; malice; dudgeon; fierceness; fire; frenzy; fretfulness; fury; gall; a grudge; heat; ill nature; ill will; indignation; ire; mania; moroseness; offense; passion; a pet; a pique; rabidness; rage; scandal; spite; spleen; spunk; stomach; vengeance; vexation; wrath.

nukoa atapa, n., rancor.

nukoa atapa, a., rancorous.

nukoa banna, a., resentful.

nukoa fehna, a., wroth.

nukoa hinla, a., irritable.

nukoa keyu, a., wrathless.

nukoa okpulo, n., touchiness.

nukoa shali, a., choleric; very angry; often angry; irascible; irritable; passionate; perverse; pugnacious; refractory; ticklish; touchy; vindictive; waspish; wrathful.

nukoa shali, v. n., to be choleric.

nukoa shali, n., a madman; a madcap.

nukoachi, v. t., to madden; to make mad; to chagrin; to anger; to disgust; to displease; to enrage; to exasperate; to fire; to fret; to incense; to inflame; to infuriate; to irritate; to move, i. e., to irritate; to offend; to pique; to provoke; to ruffle; to scandalize; to trouble; to vex.

nukoachi, n., an offender; a provoker.

nukoachi, n., a provocation; vexation.

nukoat anumpuli, v. t., to grumble; to talk madly; to chide; to rant.

nukoat anumpuli, n., a grumbler.

nukowa, see nukoa.

nukpaualli, a., nauseous.

nukpalli, n., excitement.

nukpalli, a., pp., interested; excited; tempted; engaged; incited; enticed.

nukpalli, v. n., to be interested, excited, or tempted; to lust after; iⁿnukpalli, to lust after her, Matt. 5: 28.

nukpallichechi, v. t., to entice; to seduce.

nukpallichechi, n., an enticer.

nukpallichi, v. t., to excite; to interest; to tempt; to allure; to invite; to draw; to entice; to lure.

nukpallichi, n., a provocation; temptation.

nukpallichi, n., a tempter; a lure.

nukpoalli, v. a. i., to feel nausea; nukpoallichi, causing nausea.

nukpoallichi, v. t. causative.

nuksakki, v. a. i., to be choked, strangled in water, or drowned, Luke 8: 33.

nuksita, a., pp., hung by the neck with a cord; suffocated; hanged.

nuksita, v. a. i., to hang by the neck.

nuksiteli, v. t., to hang; to suffocate; to choke with a cord; to hang by the neck, Josh. 8: 29; ont ilenuksiteli, went and hanged himself, Matt. 27: 5.

nuksiteli, n., a hangman; a hanger.

nuksitiⁿfa, pp., hung.

nuksitiffi, v. t., to hang by the neck, Gen. 40: 19.

nuksitoha, pp. pl., or *nuksita*, sing., hung.

nuksitoha, v. a. i. pl., to hang by the neck.

nuksitoli, v. t. pl., to hang by the neck.

nukshachaiyakachi, v. a. i., to thrill.

nukshammi, nukshammi, a., hoarse; affected with a cold; having a cold.

nukshammi, v. a. i., to be hoarse; to have a cough.

nukshammichi, v. t. caus., to cause hoarseness.

nukshiah [?]; *itanukshinya* [?], being knotted or gnarled like tough wood.

nukshichaiakachi, v. a. i., to start and tremble from fear.

nukshinfi, v. t., to hang by the neck, Matt. 27: 5; *ilenukshinfi*, to hang himself, Matt. 27: 5; see *nukshiniffi*.

nukshikanli, a., pp., strangled with any hot and pungent drink, as a decoction of pepper; hot; suffocating.

nukshikanli, v. a. i., to tingle.

nukshikanli, v. n., to be hot and suffocating; to smart in the throat; *nukshikashli*, pl.

nukshikanlichi, v. t., to strangle; to choke; to cause the sensation above described; *nukshikanshlichi*, pl.

nukshikanshli, pp. pl., strangled; *nukshikanli*, sing.

nukshikiffi, a., hoarse.

nukshikiffi, n., hoarseness.

nukshila, a., dry; thirsty; having a dry throat; a thirst; hoarse.

nukshila, v. n., to be dry, thirsty, etc.; to be hoarse.

nukshila, n., thirst.

nukshilachi, v. t., to cause hoarseness or thirst; v. i., to have the throat stopped with a cold.

nukshinifa, v. a. i., to hang by the neck.

nukshininfa, pp., hung by the neck; having the breath stopped.

nukshininfa, n., asthma; phthisis.

nukshiniffi, nukshinfi, v. t., to hang by the neck; to choke; to afflict with the asthma.

nukshitilimmi, v. a. i., to satisfy (similar to *fihopa*).

nukshiwichi, n., a throat filled up from a cold.

nukshobba hinla, a., formidable.

nukshobli, v. t., to frighten; to scare; to cow; to daunt; to dismay; to terrify; to intimidate; *ilenukshobli*, to frighten himself.

nukshobli, n., a frightener.

nukshoblichi, v. t. caus., to frighten; to scare; to produce fear; to start; to startle.

nukshompiksho, a., undaunted.

nukshompiksho, adv., fearlessly.

nukshopa, a., coy; afraid; scared; chicken-hearted; dismayed; fearful; pusillanimous; shy; skittish; timid; timorous; wild; *hachinukshopa cho?* Matt. 8: 26; *iknukshopo*, fearless; unfeared; unappalled.

nukshopa, v. n., to be afraid, Matt. 10: 26; 14: 5, 26, 27, 30; *hachinukshopa na*, Luke 12: 4; v. a. i., to fear; to shrink; to shudder; to shy, *nukshumpa*, Luke 1: 65; *itinnukshopa*, to be afraid of each other, or to fear each other.

nukshopa, pp., frightened; cowed; daunted; intimidated; startled; terrified; appalled; afraid, Matt. 17: 6, 7.

nukshopa, adv., wildly.

nukshopa, n., fear; a fright; dread; pusillanimity; shyness; coyness; terror; *isht anukshopa*, terror, Josh. 2: 9.

nukshopat illi, n., horror.

nukshopat wannichi, v. a. i., to quake; to quake from fear.

nukshulla, a., having a wasting disease; having the vitals destroyed.

nukshulla, n., a consumption; a pulmonary disease.

nuktaiyala, v. n., to be easy; to be quiet.

nuktakali, v. a. i., to choke; to have something lodged in the throat; to throttle; *nuktakoli*, pl.

nuktakali, sing., *nuktakoli*, pl. n., a choking.

nuktakali, sing., *nuktakoli*, pl., pp., choked; strangled.

nuktakali, v. t., v. a. i., to choke; to strangle.

nuktakalichi, sing., *nuktakolichi*, pl., v. t., to choke; to strangle.

nuktakat illi, v. a. i., to choke to death.

nuktakba, v. a. i., to pucker up, as the mouth after eating unripe persimmons.

nuktalachi, v. t., to quiet; to calm; to comfort; to heal the heart, Luke 4: 18.

nuktalali, v. t., to quiet; to appease; to allay; to sober; to calm; to soothe; to assuage; to becalm; to compose; to cool (the temper); to ease; to lull; to mitigate; to moderate; to modify; to mollify; to pacify; to propitiate; to silence; to solace; to still; to suppress; to temper; to tranquilize.

nuktalali, n., a comforter; a quieter; a soother; a moderator; a pacifier.

nuktalalichi, nuktalaḷlichi, v. t., to cause quietness, etc.; to lay; to allay; to soothe.

nuktalalichi, n., a soother.

nuktaloḻi, v. t. pl., to quiet, etc.

nuktaloḻichi, v. t., to cause quietness.

nuktaḻali, v. t., to excite jealousy, Deut. 32: 21.

nuktanla, pp., tempered.

nuktanla, a., coy; dispassionate; grave; modest; patient; peaceable; placid; tender; serious; sober; tranquil; urbane; see nuktạla.

nuktanla, v. a. i., to be cheerful, Matt. 14: 27.

nuktanla, n., patience; sobriety; temperance; "peace," Acts 10: 36.

nuktanla iksho, a., impatient.

nuktanlạt, adv., tranquilly.

nuktạla, v. n., to be quiet.

nuktạla, n., sedateness, softness, stillness, quietness; a calm; contentment; patience; a mitigation; moderation; relief; iknuktalo, n., impatience.

nuktạla, nuktala, v. a. i., to become quiet, peaceful, sober (hạsh ilenuktanlashke), to cool; to lull; to moderate; to relax; to soften; nuktanla, n. f.; v. a. i., to pause; to subside; to be cheerful, Matt. 14: 27; nuktaiyala; ilenuktạla.

nuktạla, a., unruffled; harmless; quiet; sober; patient; calm; considerate; contented; cool, as to mind or feelings; pacific; sedate; pp., allayed; quieted; sobered; calmed; becalmed; subdued; composed; conciliated; cooled; lulled; mitigated; moderated; pacified; relaxed; solaced; soothed; stayed; stilled; unrelieved; nuktaiyala, Matt. 10: 16; iknuktalo, a., impatient.

nuktạlahe keyu, a., implacable.

nuktạllachi, n., relief.

nuktạla, a., jealous; suspicious; prejudiced.

nuktạla, v. n., to be jealous; v. a. i., to mistrust.

nuktạla, n., jealousy.

nuktạla; iⁿnuktaⁿla, to beware of, Matt. 16: 6.

nuktạla keyu, a., unprejudiced.

nuktik ahchi, n., some noise described by nutik.

nuktiḻefa, v. a. i., to choke.

nuktiḻefa, pp., choked.

nuktiḻiffi, v. t., to choke, Matt. 18: 28.

nuktimekạchi, nuktimikạchi, v. a. i., to beat; to pulsate, as the heart or pulse.

nuktimekạchi, n., a pulsation.

nuktimichi, v. a. i., to palpitate quickly; chuⁿkạsh ạt nuktimichi.

nukwai iksho, see nukwia iksho.

nukwaya, v. a. i., to shun, Acts 20: 27.

nukwạmakachi, sense of internal heat.

nukwạnnichi, v. a. i., to tremble through fear.

nukwạnnichi, n., a trembling.

nukwi iksho, see nukwia iksho.

nukwia, n., diffidence; mistrust; pusillanimity; scruple.

nukwia, a., diffident; pusillanimous; shy; timid; timorous; afraid to venture; afraid to do something; fearful.

nukwia, v. n., v. a. i., to be afraid; to be timid; to doubt, Matt. 1: 20; to misgive; to mistrust; to scruple; to shrink; to stagger; iⁿnukwia, to be afraid of him; to be timid before him.

nukwia, n., a shrinker; a starter.

nukwia iksho, nukwai iksho, nukwi iksho, a., courageous; hardy; intrepid; resolute; undaunted; unembarrassed; valiant; valorous.

nukwia iksho, n., hardihood; hardiness; temerity; valor.

nukwia iksho, nukwai iksho, v. n., to be without fear; to be courageous; to dare; to venture, Josh. 1: 6, 9, 18.

nukwia iksho, a., audacious; bold; brave; undaunted.

nukwia iksho, n., boldness.

nukwiachi, v. t., to render timid; to produce fear; to stagger.

nukwiloha, v. n., to be sad, sorrowful, just ready to weep.—J. E. Dwight.

nukwimekạchi, v. a. i., to shake or tremble; to palpitate, as after an effort at running.

nukwimekachi, n., a palpitation; an agitation of the heart, after violent running.

nuna, v. a. i., to cook; to bake; to ripen; to mellow.

nuna, a., mature; ripe; mellow.

nuna, pp., cooked in boiling water; baked; roasted; done; boiled; matured; *iknuno*, a., not cooked; unripe; immature; crude; heavy; not well baked.

nuna, n., maturity; ripeness.

nuna atapa, a., overdone.

nunachechi, v. t., to cause to ripen, or bake, etc.

nunachi, v. t., to cook; to ripen; to bake; to enripen; to mellow.

nusachaya, from *nusi* and *achaya*, a., sleepy; wanting to sleep.

nusapi, nusasapi (pl.), n., an oak; a black-oak tree; a red oak.

nusechi, v. t., to cause sleep; to throw into a sleep; to bring on sleep.

nusechi, n., a soporific.

nuseka, n., a dreamer; a fortune teller.

nusi, v. a. i., to sleep; to doze; to repose; to kennel; to drowse; to rest; to roost; to slumber; *sanusi, nuseli,* I sleep; *anusi,* to sleep at or there, Josh. 2: 1; *nusitukosh okcha,* to awake from sleep; *nusi hosh itonlatok,* he was asleep, Matt. 8: 24.

nusi, n., an acorn; a black-oak acorn; mast; *nusi hata, nusi lakna, nusi noti; nusushi, nusinoti, nusi shauiya,* water oak resembling *chilhpatha.*

nusi, n., a sleeper; a slumberer.

nusi, n., sleep; rest; repose; refreshment; a slumber; *iknuso,* n., a watch; forbearance of sleep.

nusi, n., a sleep; a measure of time, being one day or 24 hours.

nusi, a., dormant; *iknuso,* restless; without sleep.

nusi, adv., asleep.

nusi banna, a., somnolent; sleepy.

nusi fehna, n., lethargy.

nusi iskitini, n., a nap; *iskitini nusi,* v. a. i., to nap.

nusilhha, n., stupor; drowsiness; torpor.

nusilhha, a., sleepy; drowsy; dull; lethargic; somnolent; torpid.

nusilhha, v. n., to be sleepy or drowsy.

nusilhha, v. a. i., to doze; to drowse.

nusilhhachi, v. t., to drowse; to make one sleepy.

nusilhhachi, n., a soporific; an anodyne.

nusit illi, a., fast asleep; v. n., to be fast asleep.

nusolba, a., sleepy; adv., sleepily.

nushkobo, noshkobo, nishkobo, n., a head; the head; the pate; a poll; the top; the vertex; *yamma noshkobo,* his head, Matt. 14: 11; Josh. 2: 19; Matt. 6: 17; 10: 30; 14: 8, 10; *noshkobo yan,* his head; Matt. 8: 20; the pommel (of a saddle), Josh. 11: 10.

nushkobo atobbi, n., a capitation; a poll tax; a tax; a tribute, Josh. 16: 10.

nushkobo atobbi onuchi, v. t., to tax; to lay a poll tax.

nushkobo atobbichi, v. t., to put to tribute, Josh. 17: 13.

nushkobo beka, a., bareheaded.

nushkobo beka, v. n., to be bareheaded.

nushkobo chumpa, n., tribute; a poll tax; a per capita, Matt. 17: 25.

nushkobo fochonli, nushkobo fachonli, n., dandruff.

nushkobo foka, n., a headstall.

nushkobo foni, n., the skull; the cranium.

nushkobo foni aiitachakalli, n., a suture, the seam or joint which unites the bones of the skull.

nushkobo hakshup, n., the pate.

nushkobo hotupa, n., the headache.

nushkobo hotupa ahammi, n., camphor.

nushkobo ikbi, v. t., to make a head; to head.

nushkobo ikbi, n., a header.

nushkobo isht chumpa, n., tribute, Mark 12: 14.

nushkobo isht shema, n., a headdress; an ornament for the head.

nushkobo isht talakchi, n., a head band.

nushkobo iyafunfo, n., the crown of the head; the place where the hair grows in a circle on the top of the head.

nuskobo lachowa, n., scald head.

nushkobo tabokaka, n., the pan; the top of the head; the pate.

nushkobo tabli, v. t., to behead; to decapitate; to head.

nushkobo tabli, n., one who beheads.

nushkobo tapa, pp., beheaded; decapitated; decollated.

nushkobo tapa, n., a head severed from the body.

nushkoboka, n.; the head, Josh. 11: 10; 14: 1; *noshkobonhunka.*

nuta, nota, adv., under; below; beneath. See 1 Tim. 6: 1; *aboha nuta,* under the room. ·

nuta, v. n., to be below, under; *aiimpa nuta, aboha nunta, ilaiasha nani nuta; nunta* in *Klit akon nunta,* under Crete. Acts 27: 7; *nuta, nota,* n.

nutachanha, n., a large centipede.

nutaka, n., the space below; a state of subjection; the under side, Mark 12: 10, 11; Josh. 7: 21; beneath, Josh. 2: 11; in subjection, Matt. 8: 9.

nutaka, v. a. i., to be subdued, Josh. 18: 1; *ishnutakahe keyu,* Deut. 28: 13.

nutaka, a., nether; under foot; prep., under; adv., underneath; below.

nutaka ansha, a., subject; being under.

nutaka ansha, n., subjection.

nutaka boli, v. t., to underlay.

nutaka fehna, a., undermost.

nutaka ia, n., subjection.

nutaka ia, v. t., to submit; to come under; to go beneath.

nutaka ia, v. a i., to quail; to succumb; to surrender; to truckle; to yield.

nutaka ia, n., submission.

nutaka iahe keyu, a., uncontrollable; unyielding.

nutaka yakni kulli, v. t., to undermine.

nutakachi, nutakachi, v. t., to cause to go under; to put beneath, Josh. 17: 13; *aiimpa yan nutakachit boli.*

nutakbalankchi, n., gums; the hard fleshy substance of the jaws which invests the teeth.

nutakbalankchi offo, n., the lampas.

nutakfa, n., the chin; the jaw; the chap; the jowl.

nutakfa foni, n., the jawbone; the chin bone.

nutakfa isht atapachi, n., a curb chain; a curb strap.

nutakfa isht talakchi, n., a throat-latch.

nutakhish, n., the beard; a whisker.

nutakhish isht shafa, nutakhisht shanfa, n., a razor.

nutakhisht shanfa ahalapuchi, n., a razor strop; a razor hone.

nutakhisht shanfa ashuahchi, n., a razor hone; a hone.

o is a longer vowel than *u,* and when the sound is contracted *u* is heard; as *haklo, haklot, haklut; haponaklo, haponaklot, haponaklut.*

o, oh, on; this is used as the verb "to be" in the 3d person, or as an impersonal verb; *oh* is a stronger form of expression, as *iksho hohmali; katima ishia hoh cho?;* this word has puzzled many interpreters; *o,* to be; *oh,* it is; *on,* being; *o* is often added to some of the particles to make them more distinctive, as *hokat, hokato.* The forms of particles beginning with *o* are here inserted so that the law of euphony may be learned: *ocha— oka — okaka —okakano— okakant —okakanto—okakat—okakato—okakhe—okakheno—okakhet—okakheto—okakkia—okako,* Matt. 8: 27; *hatak katiohmi hatuk okako,* what manner of man?—*okakocha—okakona—okakosh—okakot—okano, okano—okat—okato—oke—okia—okomo,* a particle used at the end of a sentence, meaning it was so; remote past tense—*okono,* same as; it is so; it was, but recently—*ona—osh—ot.*

on, an auxiliary verb; *chukowaheon keyushke,* enter shall is not, Matt. 7: 21; or it may designate the act *chukowa,* enter shall that not.

on, a particle, in the obj. case, cf. *osh* and *ot,* whom, which, that.

on, an art., meaning a or an usually and used indefinitely; *peni on,* a ship, Matt. 9: 1; see *ho.*

on, on; after; *aionhikia,* to stand on, upon; *onhikia,* Matt. 10: 30; *onhilechi,* to set on, Matt. 4: 5.

obala, n., the breech; the hind legs; the buttock; the fundament.

obala, a., behind.

obala foka, n., a pantaloon; pantaloons; breeches; trousers; drawers; overalls; hose.

obala foka isht halalli, obala foka isht talakchi, n., suspenders; braces.

obachoshuli, n., the hip joint where the thigh bone enters the socket of the hip bone.

obalaka, adv., behind; *olbalaka,* Luke 2: 43.

obalh kanali, v. a. i., to move backward.

obalhpela, adv., backward; behind.

obi, iyubi, n., the thigh; a ham.

ochi, ohchih, v. t., to draw water; to dip up water with a bucket at a well, spring, stream, or pond; to draw, Josh. 9: 21; *ushtia*, to go after water; *usht alla*, to bring water; *polanka oyochi*, she has gone after water at length; *ohunchi*, freq.; *oyochi*, pro.

ochi, n., a drawer of water.

oe, int., pshaw.

ofanusi, n., a kennel for dogs.

offo, v. a. i., v. t., to spring up, Matt. 13: 26; to grow; to sprout; to chick; to grow, in the early stages of growing; to come up; to germinate; to rise; to shoot; to spire; to sprout; to vegetate; to spring; also in later stages, thus, *tanchi at chahat taha, iti at chitot isht ia.*

offo, n., a growth; the growing; a chit; a scion; a shoot; a springing; a sprout.

offochi, v. t., to cause to grow; *umba kat tanchi an offochi, aba pinki at nana putaka offochi chatok; offohonchi*, freq.

ofi, n., a dog; a cur; a spaniel.

ofi chuk atta, n., a house dog.

ofi haksobish falaia, n., a hound.

ofi hasimbish inhina, ofi hasimbish tapa inhina, n., the milky way; the galaxy.

ofi hata kolofa, n., the milky way; the galaxy.

ofi holba, a., canine; doglike; like a dog; doggish.

ofi holba, v. n., to be canine.

ofi holilabi, n., a mad dog.

ofi inchuka, ofinchuka, n., a kennel.

[ofi inhoshuwa, n., the nightshade.— H. S. H.]

ofi isht lioli, v. t., to hound; to chase with dogs.

ofi nakni, n., a male dog; a dog.

ofi palhki, n., a grayhound; a spry dog.

ofi puta, n., the dogs, Matt. 7: 6.

ofi tasembo, n., a mad dog; a rabid dog.

ofi tek, n., a female dog; a bitch; a slut.

ofi tohbi inhina, n., the milky way.

ofunlo, n., a screech owl.

ofunsik, n., a puppy; a whelp.

ofunsikcheli, v. t., to pup; to puppy.

ofushi, n., a puppy; a whelp.

oh, see *ho.*

oh, auxiliary verb; *chatuk oh cho?* Matt. 7: 16; *ak oh kia*, Matt. 8: 10.

oh, imp. mood, 2d per. pl. before vowels, as *ohia*, go ye, Matt. 2: 8.

oh, part., *Islael okla ak oh kia*, Matt. 8: 10; *tuk oh cho?* Matt. 14: 31.

ohchih, see *ochi.*

ohhoh, interjection of surprise at something new, oh!

ohmi, a., like; resembling.

ohmi, v. n., to be like or resembling, Josh. 7: 21.

ohmi, n., likeness.

ohmichi, ohmihchi, v. t., to make a likeness; to cause it to resemble.

onholisso, n., an inscription.

ohoyo, ahoyo, n., a woman; a dame; a lady; a female, Matt. 5: 28; a wife; a handmaid, Luke 1: 38; pl., women; *ohoyo hon*, women, Matt. 11: 11; 14: 21; *ohoyo ma*, Matt. 15: 28.

ohoyo aiomanili, n., a pillion; a woman's seat; a cushion for a woman to ride on behind a person on horseback.

ohoyo asanonchi, n., a matron.

ohoyo alla eshi apistikeli, n., a midwife.

ohoyo bishlichi, n., a milkmaid.

ohoyo chito, n., a large woman; a virago.

ohoyo chuka petichi, n., a housewife; a mistress.

ohoyo haksi, n., a hussy.

ohoyo haloka, n., a mother-in-law; see *haloka.*

ohoyo hatak ikhalelo, n., a virgin.

ohoyo haui, n., a lewd woman; a harlot, Josh. 2: 1; a strumpet; a prostitute; a wench; a whore.

ohoyo haui aiasha, n., a bawdy house; a brothel; a bad house.

ohoyo himmita, n., a young woman; a young lady; a lass; a damsel; a virgin, Luke 1: 27; a girl; a maid; a maiden.

ohoyo himmita okpani, v. t., to deflower.

ohoyo himmitasi, n., a young girl; a very young woman; *himmitasi* means of an age younger than *himmita*.

ohoyo himmithoa, n. pl., young women.

ohoyo himmitushi, n., a very young woman, under ten years of age.

ohoyo hokli, n., a rape.

ohoyo holba, a., effeminate; like a woman; womanish.

ohoyo holisso ithananchi, n., an instructress.

ohoyo holisso pisachi, n., a mistress; a school mistress; a school dame.

ohoyo hoponi, n., a kitchen maid.

ohoyo iⁿhatak, n., a husband; lit., a woman's man.

ohoyo iⁿhatak illi, n., a widow, Luke 4: 25.

ohoyo ikhananchi, n., a tutoress.

ohoyo imaⱡia, n., a whore master; a whoremonger.

ohoyo imissa, n., a testatrix.

ohoyo imisht iloⁿhoshontikachi, n., a parasol; a lady's parasol.

ohoyo iⁿna foka, n., a lady's garment; a mantua.

ohoyo iⁿna foka ikbi, n., a mantua maker.

ohoyo iⁿna foka lumbo, n., a chemise; a shift.

ohoyo ipetạchi, v. t., to celebrate a marriage; to salute a bride; to marry.

ohoyo ipetạchi, n., a marriage, John 2: 2; nuptials; a wedding.

ohoyo ipiⁿshik, n., a woman's breast; a pap.

ohoyo iⁿshạpo, n., a lady's bonnet; a calash.

ohoyo iⁿshạpo ikbit kanchi, n., a milliner.

ohoyo isht ahollo, n., a hag; a shrew; a witch.

ohoyo isht atiaka, n., womankind.

ohoyo itihalạllichi, n., a wedding.

ohoyo kasheho, n., an aged woman; an aged female; an old wife.

ohoyo keyu chohmi, a., unwomanly.

ohoyo litiha, n., a slattern; a slut.

ohoyo makali, n., a jade; a despised woman.

ohoyo miⁿko, n., a princess; a queen; an empress, Matt. 12: 42; 1 Kings 11: 19.

ohoyo na foka ikbi, n., a tailoress.

ohoyo nan achefa, n., a washerwoman; a laundress.

ohoyo nan achunli, n., a seamstress; a tailoress.

ohoyo nan apesa, n., a directress.

ohoyo nan iⁿhoyo, n., a waiting maid.

ohoyo nukoa, n., a mad woman· a termagant; a shrew; a scold.

ohoyo owạtta, n., a huntress.

ohoyo pisa aiukli, n., a fair; a fair woman; the female sex.

ohoyo sipokni, n., an old lady.

ohoyo tạshka, n., a warrioress.

ohoyo toⁿksạli, n., a laboring woman; a maid servant; a serving maid.

ohoyo yuka, n., a bond woman; a bond maid; a female captive; a female prisoner.

ohoyohmi, a., feminine.

ohpi, see *hopi* and *opi*.

ohulmo, pp., covered; sheltered.

ohulmochi, v. t., to cover; to cause to be covered; *tanchi aⁿ ohulmochi, aboha yaⁿ ohulmochi.*

oiya, oia, v. t., to ascend; to go up; to mount; to back (a horse); to climb, Matt. 5: 1; 14: 23; 15: 29; 17: 1; Josh. 6: 5; to run up; to scale; to get on; to arise; to rise; *hatak ạt nạni haⁿ oiya; shaui ạt iti aⁿ oiya; isht oiya,* to take up, Matt. 4: 8.

oiya, n., ascent; a mounter; one who ascends; a climber; a rise; a rising.

oiyạchi, v. t., to cause to ascend; to tree; *fạni yaⁿ iti oiyạchi,* or *fạni yaⁿ iti ạboiyạchi,* to compel a squirrel to ascend a tree.

ok, from *oh*, the verbal *o*, and *k*, determinative. See *hok* and compounds. Compounds are: *okakanto*, art. pro., the, Matt. 18: 7, distinctive from other objects — *akakaⁿ* (Ishmayạbi used this form)—*okma*, used for whether; lit., if so, or then if so, see Mark 2: 9; Matt. 15: 4, 5; derived from *o*, the auxiliary verb, affirmative, *k*, the demonstrative art. pro., and *ma*, the additional definite; when that is then, if that is then—*okạno*, distinctive article in the obj. case, showing a contrast or comparison; *ilạppak okạno*, Matt. 11: 16; *nitak okạno*, Matt. 5: 43; 11: 22; 18: 7; nom. case, *okạto*, Matt. 6: 2; 12: 31, 32; Josh. 2: 4; *okmak ohmak — okmaka — okmakano — okmakato — okmakhe — okmakheno — okmakhet*, especially that, by way of a disparaging comparison — *okmakheto — okmakoⁿ — okmakocha — okmakoka — okmakokano — okmakokạt — okmakokạto — okmakoke — okmakokia — okmakona — okmakosh—okmakot—okmano, okmạno—okmạt—okmạto.*

oka, n., water; aqua; liquor; a liquid; whisky; wet; ardent spirits; *oka ya*ⁿ, the water, Matt. 14: 28; *oka ishko*, to drink liquor; *oka kapassa ishko*, to drink cold water.

oka abicha, n., a tap hole; a tunnel; a funnel; a faucet; a waterspout; a spout for water.

oka abicha isht alhkama, n., a spigot; a tap; a spile; a cork; a stopple.

oka abicha isht shana, n., a tap that is put in with a screw or that has a screw on one end.

oka abicheli, n., a cock; a brass cock; a conduit.

oka aialaka, n., a shore; a coast; *haiyip oka aialaka; okhata oka aialaka; okhina oka aialaka.*

oka aiabi, oka aiillichi, v. t., to drown.

oka aialhto, n., a tub; a water-trough; a cistern; a vat; a water-piggin; a pitcher.

oka aialhto chito, n., a tank.

oka aiilli, v. a. i., to drown.

oka aiishko, n ., a tippling house; a grocery [groggery?].

oka aiyanalli, n., a channel; a water channel.

oka akanchi, n., a tap house.

oka alaka, n., a shore; a coast, Luke 5: 3; *haiyip alaka; okhina alaka.*

oka aⁿlhto, n., a piggin.

oka alibisha, n., a skillet.

oka atalaia, n., a pool; a reservoir.

oka ayanalli, n., a sluice; a water furrow.

oka alhto, n., a water-pot; a water-vessel, John 2: 6.

oka ali, okali, n., the water-edge; shore, Matt. 13: 2.

oka banapa, v. a. i., to overflow.

oka banapa, pp., overflowed.

oka banatha, n., a surge; a wave; a billow; a swell; *oka banatha kat*, the waves, Matt. 8: 24.

oka banathat aⁿya, v. a. i., to surge; to wave.

oka banaⁿya, n. pl., waves; surges; billows.

oka bicheli, n., a butler, Gen. 40: 1; a tapster.

oka bikeli, v. a. i., to flow, as tide water.

oka bikeli, pp., deluged; overflowed.

oka bikeli, n., back water; tide water; an inundation; a deluge.

oka bikeli, v. a. i., to ebb.

oka bikelichi, v. t., to deluge; to overflow.

oka bikelichi, v. t., to cause the water to flow in or set back.

oka chopa, n., a cascade.

oka falama, pp., deluged; overflowed.

oka falama, n., back water; a deluge; the deluge; a flood; the flood.

oka falama chito, n., the deluge, Gen. 7: 6.

oka fohopa, n., a fall.

oka foyuha, n., a whirlpool.

oka foyuha, okfoyulli, v. a. i., to whirl, as water; *okfoyullit oklobushlichi*, to draw into a whirlpool; to suck in.

oka foyulli, okfoyulli, n., a whirlpool; an eddy; a vortex.

oka foyulli, v. a. i., to whirl, as water.

oka fulush, n., a fresh-water clam; a clam.

oka fulush hakshup, n., a clamshell.

oka hafeta, v. a. i., to cave in, as the bank of a water course.

oka haksi, a., drunk; drunken; inebriated; intoxicated.

oka haksi, v. n., to be drunk.

oka haksi, n., drunkenness; ebriety; inebriation; intoxication.

oka hauashko, n., vinegar; wine; sour water; cider.

oka hapi, hapi oka, n., salt water; brine.

oka hapi yammi, n., a pickle.

oka hapi yammi fohki, v. t., to pickle.

oka hiⁿka, v. a. i., to be in water.

oka holba, a., watery.

oka homahonni, n., a distillery.

oka homatoba, oka homi atoba, n., a distillery.

oka homi, okhomi, oke homi, n., liquor; spirit; ardent spirits; distilled liquor of all kinds, called rum, gin, brandy, whisky, alcohol; high wines; aqua vitæ; bitter water; acrid water.

oka homi ahalaia, a., spirituous.

oka homi bikobli, n., a rum bud.

oka homi ikbi, v. t., to distill spirits; to manufacture ardent spirits; to still.

oka homi ikbi, n., a distiller.

oka homi nanabli achafa, n., a dram; a swallow of spirits.

oka homi oka ibalhto, n., grog.

oka humma, n., red water; Red river.

oka hushi, n., waterfowl.

oka iⁿhina, n., a water furrow.

oka illi, v. a. i., to drown; see *oka aiille, aioka illi,* Matt. 18: 6.

oka ipeta, v. t., to water.

oka isht ạlhpisa, n., a measure; a liquid measure; a gallon.

oka isht bicha, n., a tap; a brass cock.

oka isht bicheli, n., a brass cock; a tap hole; a spout for water; a tunnel; a funnel; a faucet.

oka isht ochi, n., a water-bucket; a piggin; a can; a water-pot.

oka isht okissa, pp., baptized with water.

oka isht okissa, n., baptism.

oka isht okissạchi, v. t., to baptize.

oka isht taka, n., a scoop.

oka kaha, v. a. i., to lie in water, Matt. 8: 32.

oka kaiya, okaiya, v. a. i., to fill with water, as the ground receives water.

oka kaiya, pp., filled with water; softened by water, as the earth.

oka kaiyạchi, v. t., to soften with water; to fill with water.

oka kapạssa, n., cold water; fresh water; cool water.

oka kạnia, v. a. i., to mire; to drown; to sink, Matt. 14: 30.

oka kạniachi, v. t., to mire.

oka lahba, n., lukewarm water; tepid water.

oka lapalika, n., the waterside.

oka laua, a., sloshy.

oka lạshpa, n., hot water; *oka lạshpa on-latạbli,* v. t., to scald; *oka lạshpa onlatapa,* pp., scalded.

oka libesha, n., warm water.

oka luak, oke luak, n., ardent spirits; lit., fire water, an early name for spirits.

Oka lusa, Oke lusa, n., name of a creek; name of a Roman Catholic priest.

oka lanya, n., a slop; spilt water; slosh.

oka lobukachi, v. a. i., to douse.

oka mali, n., the south; lit., the water wind, Matt. 12: 42.

oka mali, a., south.

oka mali, v. n., to be south.

oka mali hashi aiokạtula itintakla, a., southwest.

oka mali hashi akuchaka itintakla, a., southeast.

oka mali imma, adv., southward; southerly.

oka mali mali, n., the south wind.

oka mali pila, adv., southward; southerly; toward the south; southern.

oka mali pilla, adv., at the south; in the south.

oka nowa, okokanowa, v. a. i., to wade in the water; to walk in the water.

oka nowa, n., a wading.

oka ont alaka, n., the shore; the coast; a beach; a strand; the water-edge.

oka panki, oka pankki, n., wine; grape water, Matt. 9: 17; 11: 19; *oka panki pạska nan isht ạlhpisa ạpa,* to commune at the Lord's table.

oka panki aiạlhto, n., a wine cask.

oka panki aiishko, n., a wine glass.

oka panki humma, n., red wine; port wine; claret wine.

oka panki ishko shali, n., a wine bibber.

oka panki kanchi, n., a wine merchant.

oka piakạchi, v. a. i., to run in waves; to wave, as water in large waves; *wisakạchi* (q. v.), to run in small waves.

oka piakạchi, pp., made to wave; agitated, as water.

oka pit afohopa, v. a. i., to fall, as water; to roar, as falling water.

oka pit afohopa, n., a cascade; a waterfall.

oka pit akinafa, n., a cascade; a waterfall.

oka pit akinifa, v. a. i., to fall, as water.

oka poakạchi, v. a. i., to run in large waves; to wave.

oka poakạchi, pp., made to run in large waves.

oka pokafa, v. t., to dash water.

oka pokpokechi, to cause the water to foam.

oka pokpoki, v. a. i., to foam.

oka pokpoki, n., foam; surf.

oka sita, n., the edge of the water; the water-edge.

oka takba, n., astringent water; bitter water.

oka talaia, n., a puddle; standing water.

oka talali, v. t., to settle a liquid; to cause to sink or go down in a liquid.

oka tanch afotoha, n., a water mill.

oka tạla, v. a. i., to subside, as water; to settle, as a liquid; to fall to the bottom of liquor.

oka tạla, pp., settled.

oka toba, v. a. i., to water.

oka toba, a., watery.

oka tobli, v. t., to launch; to push into the water.

oka tobli, n., a launch.

oka umba, okumba, n., rainwater.

oka wisakạchi, v. a. i., to wave in small waves; *sinti ạt ayakma oka yat wisakạchi.*

oka wisakạchi, pp., made to wave.

oka yanạllipạlhki, n., a rapid; rapids; a torrent.

Okahpa, n., the name of a tribe called Quapaw.

Okahpa okhina, n., the Arkansas River.

okaiya, see *oka kaiya.*

okak, n., a swan.

okak ushi, n., a young swan; a cygnet; a swan's egg.

okałoli, v. t., to twist and break bushes, as a bull with his horns.

okami, v. t., to wash the face, i. e., one's own face; *okamali,* I wash my face.

okamichi, v. t., to wash the face of another; *ạlla yaⁿ okamichili,* I wash the child's face.

okashalayi; *oka shalali,* v. t., to wallow; to besmear, 2 Sam. 20: 12.

[okataktak, n., the shitepoke; the American green heron.—H. S. H.]

okatonoli, v. a. i., to welter.

okatula, v. a. i., to settle; to sink to the bottom in a fluid; to fall in water; to set; to go down, as the sun.

okạchi, v. t., to water; to let into the water, John 20: 6 [?]; pass., *ulhkạchi,* to be watered or soaked; from *oka,* John 21: 6; Matt. 4: 18; 13: 47; cast into (the sea); Matt. 17: 27; see *okkạchi.*

okạtaha, v. a. i., to descend, Josh. 7: 5; Gen. 24: 45; *okạttahha,* afternoon; *okạtahaka,* descent, Deut. 9: 21; see John 6: 16.

okạtanowa, v. a. i., to descend, Luke 19: 37.

okạttula, v. t., v. a. i., to fall into the water; to plunge into water or any liquid; *pinti ạt bila kia pishukchi kia okạttula chatuk*; to set, as the sun, Josh. 10: 27; see *okatula.*

okạttula, n., a plunge; a fall into a liquid; one who falls.

okbano, would God, Josh. 7: 7; see *hokbano.*

okbạl, adv., in the rear; behind; backwards; hind; hinder; see *ukbạl* and *ulbạl; obạlaka,* rearward.

okbạl, n., the rear.

okbilhha, v. i., to sink in water like a boat ready to fill, Luke 5: 7.

okbililli, a., in water swimming deep.

okbillichi, v. t., to make it swimming deep.

okbiłeli, v. a. i., the eyes stand out, Ps. 73: 7.

okbusha, pp., wrung out; water wrung out.

okbushli, v. t., to wring out water; *nafoka okbushli; nafohka aiokbusha.*

okcha, v. a. i., to wake; to awake; v. n., to be awake; to cheer; to rouse; to watch; *nusi tuk osh okcha.*

okcha, a., pp., awake; aroused; awaked; enlivened; excited; flush; incited; inspirited; refreshed; roused; stimulated; vigilant; vivid; vivacious; volatile; wakeful; wakened *ikokcho,* a, unawaked.

okcha, n., wakefulness; recreation; refreshment; vigilance; vivacity; watch.

okchachi, v. t., to awaken, John 11: 11.

okchaha, pp., hoed; broken up, as land; cut up, as grass, with a hoe.

okchaha, n., the ground thus hoed.

okchaⁿk, n., a muskmelon.

okchaⁿk balama, n., a muskmelon.

okchaⁿk holba, n., a cucumber.

okchakạlbi, a., blue; purple; greenish; *okchakolba,* probably from *okchako* and *holba.*

okchaⁿki, a., green, as newly cut wood, not as a color; raw, 1 Sam. 2: 15; fresh; rare; crude; alive, as a tree; unripe, as fruit; live; *nipi okchaⁿki, iti okchaⁿki, shukshi ạt okchaⁿki, takkon ạt okchaⁿki; iti ạt okchaⁿki oⁿ,* Luke 23: 31. In 2 Sam. 18: 14 *okchaⁿki* is applied to Absalom, as a man alive, but it is usually applied to things, as *iti okchaⁿki, nipi okchaⁿki.*

okchaⁿki, v. n., to be green, raw, fresh, unripe; *okchaⁿki,* v. a. i. to live, as a tree; *okchaⁿki,* n., rawness.

okchakkuchi, v. n., to be green, or greenish, like an unripe peach.

okchako, n., blue.

okchako, a., blue.

okchako, okchakko. v. n., to be blue.

okchako, pp., dyed blue; colored blue.

okchakochi, v. t., to blue; to color blue; to dye blue.

okchalechi, v. t., to stimulate; to stir; to vivificate; to cause to awake; to enliven; to prompt; to reanimate; to vivify; *alla yat saiokchalechi; tanampo tukaffi cha saiokchalechi.*

okchalechi, n., a stimulant.

okchali, v. t., to excite.

okchaliⁿka, n., salvation, Luke 3: 6.

okchalinchi, v. t., to save; to rescue; to deliver from danger, sickness, death, punishment, etc.; to conserve; to preserve; to protect; *ilokchalinchi,* to save himself, Luke 23: 35; *ishpiokchalinchashke,* do thou save us, Matt. 8: 25; *siokchalinchi,* save me, Matt. 14: 30; 18: 11; Josh. 2: 13; 8: 22.

okchalinchi, n, a savior; a deliverer; a saver.

okchalinchi, n., salvation.

okchali, v. t., to break up ground for planting with a hoe (as some poor families do); to hoe.

okchali, n., one who breaks up land with a hoe; a hoer.

okchalichi, v. t., to cause one to break up land with a hoe.

okchamali, n., green; blue; gray; greenness; the rust on copper called verdigris; verdure; *okchamashli,* pl.

okchamali, a., green; blue; gray; verdant; *okchamashli,* pl.

okchamali, v. n., to be green or blue; *okchamashli,* pl.

okchamali, v. a. i., to rust, as copper; to turn green.

okchamali, pp., dyed green; colored green; *okchamashli,* pl.

okchamali bilia, a., evergreen.

okchamali bilia, n., an evergreen.

okchamalichi, v. t., to color green or blue; to corrode, as copper; *okchamashlichi,* pl.

okchanawisha, n., an icicle.

okchanlush, n., a small blue bird.

okchanlush chito, n., a peacock, 1 Kings 10: 22.

okchanlush chito hoshiⁿshi, n., a peacock feather.

okchapassi, okchapaⁿsi, n., a shoal.

okchauabi, a., sizy, like thick soap.

okchauwi, okshauwi, v. a. i., to be watery, like *tanfula.*

okchawaha, n., a shoal, or watery, like *tanfula* before it is thickened.

okchaⁿya, a., alive; living; animate; live; *Chihowa okchaⁿya,* living God, Matt. 16: 16; John 4: 10; Josh. 3: 10; 8: 23.

okchaⁿya, v. n., to be alive; to live.

okchaⁿya, v. a. i., to live; to quicken; to quick; to subsist; *chiokchaⁿya,* Josh. 1: 5; *aiokchaⁿya,* to live by, Matt. 4: 4; *aiokchaⁿya,* life, Matt. 7: 14.

okchaⁿya, pp., made alive; saved alive; delivered; protected; quickened; resuscitated; saved; *hatak moma okchaⁿyahe achi,* n., a universalist.

okchaⁿya, n., life; time; *aiokchaⁿya,* life; *hachiaiokchaⁿya,* your life, Matt. 6: 25.

okchaⁿya hinla, a., salvable.

okchaⁿya takla, n., life; time.

okchaⁿyachi, v. t., to cause to live; to quicken; to raise, as from the dead; to resuscitate; to revive. .

okchaⁿyachi, n., a preserver of life; a quickener.

okchaⁿyachi, n., a raising.

okchalabi, v. n., to be thick like soap.

okchali, okchalli, v. t., to awake, Matt. 8: 25; to waken; to wake; to inspirit; to incite; to excite; to re-create; to refresh; to rouse; differs from *okchali* or *okchalili,* to dig up ground for planting.

okchali, n., a waker; a wakener.

okchala, n., the small blackbird with a red spot on his wings; *halan,* the large blackbird.

okchala chito, n., a large carnivorous bird; the loon.

okchi, n., broth; juice; sap; water; ooze.

okchilabi, v. a. i., to thrust out the tongue.

okchilabi, n., one who thrusts out the tongue.

okchilaklali, v. a. i. pl., to thrust out the tongue.

okchilaklali, n., those who thrust out their tongues, or the acts in so doing.

okchilaua, a., sappy; juicy.

okchiloha, n., a wren; name of a small bird; see *chiloha.*

okchila, see *isht okchila,* n., a riddle.

okchilali, n., a large gazing eye.

okchilanli, v. a. i., to gaze about; to stare at; to gaze at.

okchilaⁿshli, v. a. i. pl., to gaze about; to stare at.

okchilaⁿshli, n., large rolling eyes.

okchilunli, v. a. i., to gaze at; to stare at.

okchilunli, n., large eyes; goggled eyes; sharp eyes.

okchito (from *oka* and *chito*), n., high water; an inundation; a flood; a freshet; a deluge; a land flood; a water flood; *okchitot ala*, floods came, Matt. 7: 25, 27.

okchito, v. a. i., to rise, as water; to become a flood.

okchito, pp., deluged; floated; flooded; inundated.

okchito aiali, n., high-water mark.

okchitochi, v. t., to make a flood; to flow; to overflow; to inundate; to deluge; to flood.

okchitoli (from *oka* and *chitoli*), v. t., to flow; to make a flood; to deluge; to inundate.

okchuⁿs, n., the name of a bird; the killdee.

okchushba, v. a. i., to ooze and run out; to form matter and run, as an old sore; applied to wounded trees and plants when the sap oozes out; *okchohushba*, Luke 16: 21.

okchushba, n., the matter which runs from an old sore; a running sore; an old ulcer; serous matter; virus; water.

okchushbachi, v. t., to cause a sore to discharge a watery matter.

oke, part., it is, from *o* and *ke; ke* is final; *akoke*, it is the, Matt. 2: 5, 6; *shilup oke*, it is a spirit, Matt. 14: 26.

oke homi, oka homi (q. v.); ardent spirits.

oke luak, oka luak (q. v.), ardent spirits.

Oke lusa, see *Oka lusa*.

okfa (sing.), okfali (pl.), n., a valley; a vale; a dale; a glen; a ravine; 1 Kings 10: 27; Josh. 10: 12.

okfa maiha, n., a wide valley.

okfa pattasachi, n., low flat land; low land; a meadow; bottom land.

okfaha, pp., shown by argument.

okfali, v. t., to exhibit or show by argument.

okfaⁿya, ufkaⁿya, v. i., to stick or run a piece of wood, etc., into one's own flesh; *saiokfaⁿya*, etc.

okfichoha, n., a small round hill.

okfoata, see *okhoata*.

okfoalli, see *okhoalli*.

okfochush, n., a duck. This is the common name for ducks, both tame and wild. The different species of wild ducks are distinguished by different names, as *oklubbi, hinluk, haⁿkhoba*.

okfochush nakni, n., a drake.

okfochush tek, n., a duck; a female duck.

okfochushushi, n., a young duck; a duck's egg.

okfulli; *okfoyullit oklobushlichi*, v. t., to suck.

okha, ukha, v. t., to take back; to get satisfaction; to revenge; to win back what has been lost at a game; *okhat isso; okhat ishi; okhat imabi; ilaiokha banna*, he wants to avenge himself; *ilaiukha*, to revenge himself; to take pay; to recompense himself; to retaliate; to revenge; to take vengeance, 1 Sam. 14: 24; *ilaiokhali*, I avenge myself, 2 Kings 9: 7; *ilaiokha*, n., an avenger, Josh. 10: 13; 20: 2.

okha, n., an avenger.

okha, n., recapture; satisfaction; vengeance.

okhaiyanli, a., cross-eyed.

okhaiyanli, v. n., to be cross-eyed.

okhaiyanli, n., cross-eyes.

okhapayabi, a., cloudy; hazy clouds.

okhatali, a., pale.

okhatapa, v. t., to obstruct.

okhatabli, v. t., to fend, as fire.

okhawi, v. t., to catch; to hook up; *isht okhawi*, a flesh hook, Num. 4: 14.

okhapaioha, n., thin clouds.

okhapaioli, v. i., to form thin clouds.

okhata n., a lake, Josh. 1: 4; a large pond; a bay; a gulf; an arm of the sea; the water; a sea; *okhata haⁿ*, the sea, Matt. 8: 24; *okhata*, sea, Matt. 13: 1, 47; 14: 24, 25, 26; 15: 29; 17: 27; 18: 6.

okhata aiabeka, n., seasickness; seasick.

okhata aiahalaia, a., maritime.

okhata aialhtaha, a., marine.

okhata aⁿya, n., a seaman.

okhata bikeli, n., the tide.

okhata chito, n., an ocean, Josh. 1: 4; a sea; the deep; the great sea; the profound.

okhata chito aⁿya, n., a voyage at sea.

okhata chito aⁿya, n., a voyager.

okhąta chito lapalika, n., the sea coast; the seaside.

okhąta filąmminchi, n., an arm of the sea or of a lake.

okhąta imma, a., maritime; of or concerning the sea.

okhąta lapalika, n., sea coast, Matt. 4: 13; Luke 6: 17; "by the sea," Josh. 5: 1.

okhąta oka, n., sea water.

okhąta ont alaka, n., the sea bank, seaboard, sea coast, seashore; the strand.

okhątushi, n., a pond.

okhilishta, pp., shut; closed.

okhina, n., a river, 2 Sam. 24: 5; Josh. 1: 4; 12: 2; a water course; a ford; a stream.

okhina akka nowąt łopulli, v. t., to ford a river; to wade a river.

okhina akucha, n., a ford, Josh. 2: 7.

okhina ikbi, v. t., to make a canal.

okhina ikbi, n., a canal.

okhina oka, n., river water.

okhina ontalaka, n., the brink of a river, Josh. 3: 8; 12: 2.

okhina takchąka, n., the margin of a river; a river's side.

okhinak, hinak, v. a. i., to tassel, as corn.

okhinak, n., a corn tassel.

okhisa, okhissa, n., a door, Matt. 6: 6; the aperture or the gate of the house, 2 Kings 9: 3, 10, an entrance; an entry; a gate; light; a threshold; a vestibule, Matt. 7: 13; 16: 18; Josh. 2: 5; 8: 29.

okhisa aiafacha, n., a door latch.

okhisa apistikeli, n., a janitor; a door-keeper; a porter.

okhisa ąlhtoba ahoyo, n., a tollgate.

okhisa imokhoata, n., a door bar.

okhisa isht afacha, n., a door latch.

okhisa isht ąlhkąma, n., the door which fills the aperture.

okhisa isht takali, n., a door hinge.

okhisushi, n., a window, 2 Kings 9: 30; Josh. 2: 15.

okhisushi isht ąlhkąma, n., a window blind; a window shutter.

okhinsh, see ikhinsh, and ishkinsh.

okhishta, v. t., to shut a door; to close, 1 Sam. 1: 6; to close the eyes, Matt. 13: 15; see ukhishta.

okhitta, v. t., to shut; imokhitta, shut him up.

okho, int., nay, chiaiyąmohmi foka inokhoachi.

okhoata, adv., sideways.

okhoata, okfoata, okhowata, a., crosswise; across; athwart.

okhoata, v. n., to be across or crosswise; v. a. i., to lie across; ąlla yąt topa yan okhoata hosh onitonla.

okhoata, pp., laid across.

okhoata foni, n., a rib bone.

okhoataka, okhowataka, n., the side or sides; a crosspiece; ąbaiya is the length or the height; but the breadth of cloth is okhoataka, 1 Kings 6: 31.

okhoatakachi, a., crosswise.

okhoatakachi, v. n. pl., to be crosswise; to run or lie crosswise; nan tąnna yan okhoatakachit ikbi, work up the cloth crosswise, so that the long seams will run round the person.

okhoatali, okfoatali, v. t. sing., to lay it across or crosswise; to cross; to thwart; iti an ishokhoatali, do you lay the stick crosswise.

okhoatąchi, v. t., to cause it to lie across; okhoatakąchi, pl., see 1 Kings 7: 2, 3; 2 Kings 1: 2.

okhoatkąchi, n., a slat; a crosspiece; a crossbar; a round.

okhoąlli, okfoąlli, v. t. pl., to lay them crosswise, as the rounds of a ladder.

okhomi, see oka homi.

okhowata, see okhoata.

okhowataka, see okhoataka.

okinta, int., well, try again; a word of daring, used in renewing fights and after losses.

okissa, v. t., to purify ceremoniously; to fast; a dog is said to okissa when he eats green grass and vomits; okilissa, to purify one's self; okilissa, her purification, Luke 2: 22.

okissa, n., a ceremonious purification; a fast (observed after going to war, etc.); an old heathenish rite.

okissa nitak, a fast day; a purification day.

okissąchi, v. t., to purify another; to cause to purify; oka hanta isht okissachit hochifo, to christen; oka hanta isht okissat hochifo, pp., christened.

okishko, v. t., to tipple; to drink ardent spirits; v. a. i., to soak.

okishko, a., sottish.

okishko, n., a drunkard; a tippler; a bibber.

okishko, n., intemperance; drunkenness.

okishko fehna, v. t., to carouse.

okishko laua, n., a row.

okishko maⁿya, n., a carousal; a row; a drunken frolic.

okishko maⁿya, v. t., to have a drunken frolic.

okishko shali, n., a sot; a great drunkard; an habitual drunkard; a bibber; a tippler; a soaker; a toper.

okisht alhpisa, n., a gallon.

okkachi, okachi, v. t., to wet; to soak; to set down into water, Luke 5: 4; to soften; to steep, 1 Sam. 14: 27; okahanchi freq.; pass. ulhkachi.

okkachi, n., a soaker.

okkattaha, v. a. i., to descend; to go down, Josh. 10: 11; hashi at okkattaha, the sun descends, as at 2 p. m.; hashi at okkattahat akkia, the sun descends and goes down, as at 4 p. m.; okkattahakat ia, the descent goes.

okkattahaka, n., the side of a hill; the foot of a hill; under a hill; the slope; okkattahaka hikia na abeli, I killed him when standing at, etc.

okkattahakaia, n., a declivity.

okkattahakachi, v. t., to slope.

okko, int. of surprise, sorrow, and regret.

okkohonlih, v. a. i., to have a Roman nose.

okla, n., a people; a tribe; a nation; citizens; folks; persons; men; population, 2 Sam. 24: 2; a tongue; a multitude, Matt. 8: 1; inhabitants; they, i. e., mankind, animals, and things, John 1: 37 (when employed in this manner as a pronoun the particle pronoun t is omitted); a community; a party; a region; applied to boats, as isht iat okla, Luke 5: 7; Spani okla, Spanish people; people of Spain; Spaniards; Miliki okla, American people; people of America; Americans. In this way it corresponds to national adjectives, as French, etc.; Pask okla, Bread people, Pascagolians [Pascagoula]; Chahta okla talaia, the one nation, or the single tribe of Choctaw; hatak api humma, okla taloha puta, all Indian tribes; hatak toli okla, a ballplaying people; okla ibbak, their hands, Matt. 15: 2; imokla iⁿholitopa, a., patri-

otic; okla, following a verb, is dual, as anumpulit oklatok, preceding a verb it is plural; see John 9: 23, 24; oklaachi, they say, i. e., people say; Matt. 11: 18; oklat achi, all the people say, i. e., the people say; hatak ashosh okla nuklakancha, Matt. 8: 27; okla, they, often thus used before verbs; okla abi tukma, Matt. 17: 23; okla, n., the relatives of a man's wife, and his sister's husband; amoklama, my people (pl.); my countryman (sing.); of my wife's family, it is used in the singular number; okla, in the dual number, of persons and things and animals; achit oklatok, they two said, Matt. 8, 29; neg. form, tashkit ikoklo kiⁿsha hoⁿ, Josh. 2: 8.

okla achafa itibi, n., a civil war; imokla achafa intanampi, n., an insurrection.

okla achafa itibi, v. t., to have a civil war.

okla ahalaia, a., national; pertaining to a people.

okla anumpa kobaffi, n., sedition.

okla chafa, n., one people; a single tribe; countrymen; a fellow citizen.

okla chito, okla chinto, n., a multitude, Matt. 5: 1; the multitude, Matt. 9: 8; a great people, Luke 3, 7 [?]; many; great multitudes, Matt. 8: 1.

okla chito, a., populous.

okla iksho, a., without inhabitants; desolated.

okla ilappakoⁿ, in them, Matt. 13: 15.

okla imanukfila, n., their thoughts, Matt. 12: 25.

okla inla, n., a foreign people; foreigners.

okla laua, n., a multitude, Matt. 13: 2; 14: 5, 14, 15, 19, 22, 23.

okla laua, a., populous.

okla makali, n., the vulgar.

okla moma, n., the public; all people; a republic.

okla moma, a., public.

okla moma immi, a., belonging to the public.

okla nan ikithano, n., gentiles; heathen, Matt. 6: 32.

okla nana iⁿkaniohmi chito, see nana iⁿkaniohmi chito.

okla pelichi, n., officers, Josh. 8: 33.

okla talaia, n., one people; one nation, Matt. 1: 21; *imokla talaia*, his people.

oklạbbi, v. a. i., to lap, as a dog; see *lạbbi*; pp., lapping.

oklạbbi, n., a lapper.

oklobushli, v. a. i. sing., to dive; to dip; to plunge; to go under water; to duck; to sink; to submerge; *isht ochi ạt oklobushli*.

oklobushli, pp., plunged; immersed; ducked; submerged; whelmed.

oklobushli, n., a diver; a plunger.

oklobushli, n., immersion.

oklobushlichi, v. t., to dip; to immerse; to put under water; to duck; to plunge under water; to immerge; to merge; to sink; to souse; to submerge; to whelm.

oklobushlichi, n., immersion.

oklubbi, v. a. i. pl., to dive; to dip; to plunge; to duck; to submerge; *kiloklubbi*, let us dive in.

oklubbi, pp., ducked; immersed; whelmed.

oklubbi, n., the name of a duck; a diver.

oklubbichi, v. t., to dip; to immerse them; to duck; to beduck; to souse; to submerge; to whelm.

okluha, a., all; the whole, 2 Kings 9: 8; everyone; universal; *hatak oklunha*, all men; *nan oklunha*, all things, Matt. 7: 12; 11: 27; 17: 11.

oklunha, v. n., to be all; *oklulunha*, a frequentative, Josh. 14: 9.

okluhanchi, v. t., to extend to all; *okluhanchit ipetalahinla?* Shall I feed all? *okluhanchit ithaiyana*, he knows all things.

okluhant, cont., as *okluhant anoli*, relate the whole.

okluhant ishi, v. t., to take the whole.

oklunhachi, v. t., to make or cause all, 2 Kings 9: 24.

oklunhạli, v. a. i., to make very much.

oklunhạlinchi, v. t., to cause to reach to all; *oklahạlinchit haklo*, to hear all, Luke 2: 20.

oklusbi, n., dusk; dark; darkish; see *okpolusbi*.

oklush inla, n., a foreign tribe or nation; strangers; foreigners.

oklush inla, a., foreign.

oklush inla hatak, n., a foreigner; a foreign man.

oklushi, n., a small tribe; a small people; a family; a nation; *hatak ạpi humma oklushi taloha puta ka ishinnukhanklashke*.

oklushi ahalaia, a., national.

oklushi ạbanumpa ikithano, n., gentiles; pagans; a heathen nation.

oklushi nan ikithano, n., heathen, Matt. 6: 7.

okłachanko, a., muddy; miry.

okłachanko, v. n., to be muddy or miry.

okłachankochi, v. t., to make it muddy.

okłachinko, a., muddy; miry.

okłachinko, v. n., to be muddy.

okłachinkochi, v. t., to render it muddy.

okłafạshli, n., the end of a house log after it is put up.

okłafạshlichi, v. a. i., to put the log out too far.

okłanshko, n., a fen.

okłanshko, a., wet and miry; fenny.

okłanshko, v. n., to be wet and miry.

okłanshko, n., a moor; a fen.

okłanshkochi, v. t., to make it wet and miry.

okłauinli, a., striped.

okłauinli, v. n., to be striped; *kofi ạt okłauinli; nantạnna yạt okłauinli*.

okłauinlichi, v. t., to make stripes.

okłichanli, a., having dirty eyes; dirty-eyed, produced either by a sore or neglect.

okłichanli, v. n., to be dirty-eyed.

okłichanli, n., a dirty eye.

okłichoshli, okłichanshli, a. pl., having dirty eyes.

okłichoshli, v. n., to be dirty-eyed.

okłilahpi, n., the first darkness; evening; vespers.

okłilampi, n., evening.

okłilechi, v. t., to produce darkness; to darken; to becloud; to bedim; to cloud; to dim; *aboha yan okłilechi*, to darken the room; to embrown; *onokłilechi*, to bring darkness on him; to benight one; to shadow; to obscure.

okłileka, n., the dark; darkness, John 1: 5; a dark place; the place of darkness; *tạli chiluk anuka kat okłileka fehna*.

okłili, a., dark; dismal; gloomy; melancholy; obscure; opaque; rayless; shadowy; sombre; umbrageous; pp., darkened; shaded; *onokłili*, benighted; dark on him; n., opacity.

okłili, adv., obscurely.

okłili, v. n., to be dark, Matt. 6: 23; *oklieli*.

okłili, v. a. i., to darken; to be dark, Josh. 2: 5; *oklilit taha katimako chiaionokkili*, where did it darken on you? *oklieli*.

okłili, n., darkness, Matt. 6: 23; dark; an eclipse; gloom; melancholy; obscureness; opacity; a shadow.

okłili impa, n., supper.

okłili taloa, n., an evening song or hymn; an even song.

okłiliⁿka, n., darkness, Matt. 10: 27.

okłilinchi, v. a. i., to dawn; *onnat oklilinchi*, the day dawns; *onnat minti*, the day comes.

okłilinchi, n., the dawn of day.

okłołbi, okłulbi, okhubli, n., a rill.

okma, he whom, John 3: 34 [?]; conj., *miⁿko okma, ushi okma*, either the king or his son; *achafahosh miⁿko okma, atukla kąto ushi ąttok, Chihowa hokąt hatak okma, nanta hatokosh illahe keyushke; achikakokma, keyukmąt, tani cha nowa, achi kak okma*, Matt. 9: 5; *iⁿki okma, keyukmąt ishki okma*, "father or mother," Matt. 15: 4, 6; *chibbak okma, chiyi yokma*, Matt. 18: 8. Compounds: *okmak—okmaka—okmakano—okmakato—okmakhe—okmakheno—o k m a k h e t—okmako—okmakocha—okmakoka—okmakokano—okmakokąt—okmakokąto—o k makoke—okmakokia—okmakona—okmakosh—okmakot—okmano—o k mąno—okmąt—okmąto*.

okmąlli, see *okmoffi*.

okmilali, a., bald; having very short hair on the head.

okmilali, v. n., to be bald; *sheki ąt okmilali, fąkit ąt okmilali*.

okmilali, n., baldness.

okmilalichi, v. t., to make bald; to trim off the hair on the head quite short.

okmiląshli, a. pl., bald.

okmiląshli, v. n., to be bald.

okmiląshlichi, v. t., to make bald.

okmilołi, okmiloli, a. pl., bald; having the hair or ears cut short off.

okmilołi, v. n. pl., to be bald or to be cropped short; *shukhat okmiloli, isuba hąt okmiloli*.

okmilołichi, v. t. pl., to cut the hair of the head or the ears short; to crop close off.

okmilonli, a., bald.

okmisikali, v. a. i. pl., to raise or move the eyebrows; done by boys at play to entice others to play; *okmisakaⁿshli*, v. a. i. pl.

okmisli, v. a. i., to give a wink by raising the eyebrows.

okmocholi, v. a. i., to close the eyes; to have the eyes closed.

okmoffi, okmąlli, n., a rill or small branch.

okochi, v. t., to draw water.

okochi, n., a drawer of water.

okokaiilli, v. a. i., to drown.

okokaiilli, pp., drowned.

okokanowa, v. a. i., to wade; see *oka nowa*.

okokanowa, n., a wader.

okokąbi, v. t., to drown; to kill in the water.

okokko, int. of dissatisfaction or surprise.

okokkoahni, v. a. i., to marvel; to wonder.

okokkoahni, n., a marvel; a wonder.

okokkoahni, a., marvelous.

okokkoaiahni, v. a. i., to admire.

okokkoaiahnichi, v. t., to astonish; to amaze; to astound.

okomo, v. t., to dissolve in water, as sugar, salt, etc.; *ąlhkomo* pp.

okomuchi, v. t., to melt; to dissolve.

okomuchi, n., a melter.

okpalali, v. a. i., to float; to swim on the water; to drift; *iti ąt okpalali*.

okpalali, n., a float; a floating.

okpalalichi, v. t., to cause to swim.

okpalołi, v. a. i. pl., to float; to swim; also n. pl.

okpalołichi, v. t., to float; to swim; to cause to float.

okpąni, v. t., to destroy, Matt. 5: 17; Josh. 2: 10; to spoil; to abolish; to ruin; to injure; to mar; to scathe; to rend, Matt. 7: 6; to abuse; to blemish; to hurt; to consume; to contaminate; to corrupt; to damage; to damnify; to deface; to defile; to deprave; to depredate; to devastate; to devour, Matt. 15:11, 18, 20; to eat; to exterminate; to extinguish; to harm; to havoc; to infect; to lose; to misimprove; to misuse; to muddle; to mutilate; to overthrow; to palsy; to pervert; to profane; to raze; to ravage; to remove; to ruin; to slur; to trespass; to undo; to unmake; to vitiate; to vilify; to violate; to waste; *ilokpani*, to destroy himself; to abuse himself, etc.; *pisaokpani*, v. t., to disfigure; *itimokpani*, to destroy for each other; *imaiokpani*, v. t., to foil; *okpaiyani*, pro. form.

okpani, n., a spoiler; a destroyer; a hurter; a ravager; a ruiner; a perverter; a profaner; a violàtor; *ilokpani*, a self-destroyer; *aiokpani*, Matt. 6:19, 20.

okpanichi, v. t., to cause ruin, destruction; to make of none effect; to cumber or mar, Matt. 15: 6; *aiokpaninchi*, to cumber, Luke 13: 7.

okpanit tali, v. t., to consume; to destroy utterly; to raze.

okpata, okpatha, n., the shoulder-blade; the blade bone of man and beast.

okpata foni, n., the shoulder-blade.

okpeli, v. t., to skim off cream, froth, etc.; *okpiha*, pp.

okpicheli, v. a. i., to grow or spring up, as grass and weeds in the spring; to rise to the brim, like water.

okpichelichi, okpichechi, v. a. i., to grow or spring up, as grass.

okpiyanli, n., a word of reproach, a disgusting epithet.

okpolusbi, n., dark; dusk; twilight; vespers, 2 Kings 7: 5.

okpolusbichi, v. t., to render it dark.

okpolo, v. n., to be in a passion; to be dissatisfied, as *imokpolo*, he is dissatisfied or he is angry.

okpulo, a., bad, Matt. 13: 48; vile; wrong; wicked; absurd; arrant; base; baleful; angry, Luke 4: 28; dirty; corrupt; degenerate; unclean, Matt. 12: 43; deleterious; deplorable; difficult; dire; direful; dismal; evil; fatal; faulty; fearful; fell; felonious; fiendish; flagitious; flagrant; foul; gross; harsh; heinous; horrible; horrid; hurtful; ill; immoral; impetuous; impure; inclement; indecent; indirect; injurious; licentious; monstrous; nasty; naughty; noisome; noxious; obnoxious; obscene; odious; offensive; opprobrious; outrageous; pernicious; preposterous; profane; rough; ruinous; sanguinary; savage; sinful; sinister; sordid; terrible; terrific; ugly; vicious; vulgar; waste; wrong; *imokpulo*, displeased with him; harmed; hurt; *itimokpulo*, displeased with each other.

okpulo, v. n., to be bad, or vile; *okpunlo*, nasal form; *okpoyulo*, pro. form.

okpulo, v. a. i., to corrupt; to spoil; to damage; to fall; to perish, Matt. 5: 30.

okpulo, n., evil, Matt. 5: 11; badness; vileness; asperity; damage; destruction; depravity; devastation; an enormity; a fall; a hazard; harm; havoc; a hurt; impurity; meanness; an overthrow; pollution; rascality; ruin; sinfulness; turpitude; wickedness; wrong; *ikokpolo, ikokpulo*, a., unharmed; uninjured; unspoiled; unviolated; untainted.

okpulo, pp., ruined; destroyed; abolished; spoiled; spoilt; consumed; contaminated; corrupted; damaged; damnified; defaced; defiled; depraved; depredated; devastated; exterminated; extinguished; harmed; infected; injured; lost; misshapen; muddled; mutilated; perverted; polluted; razed; ravaged; undone; vitiated; violated; wasted; *imokpulo*, harmed.

okpulo, adv., badly; overmuch; rascally; vilely; *sabanna okpulo; umba okpulo*.

okpulo fehna, a., abominable; atrocious; nefarious; worse.

okpulo inshaht tali, a., worst.

okpulo isht inshat ia, a., worse; *ikokpulo*, a., inoffensive; unharmed.

okpulo keyu, a., incorrupt.

okpulochi, v. t., 1 Sam. 1: 6, to make her fret; to provoke; *okpulohonchi*, 1 Sam. 1: 7.

okpuloka, n., fall; ruin, Matt. 7: 27.

okpulosali, a., very inferior.

okpulot, adv., badly.

okpulot ia, okpulot isht ia, v. a. i., to degenerate.

okpulot iktaho, a., unconsumed.

okpulot taha, pp., razed; utterly destroyed.

okpulot taha, a., crazy; lost, Matt. 18:11; Luke 19: 10; perished; Matt. 18: 14.

oksuk, uksak (q. v.), n., a hickory nut.

oksakohchi, n., the high bush whortleberry.

oksanla, n., a mouse (a Six-towns word—Billy Thomas). It is a kind that eats sweet potatoes in the hill.

oksup, n., a long bead, sometimes 2 inches long, or a large, round bead; wampum. The long kind were once dear. *ikonla apakfopa achafakmat isuba iti illibekatok.*

oksup taptua, n., a joint snake.

okshachobi, n., twilight.

okshachobi, v. a. i., v. n., to become twilight; to be twilight.

okshachobichi, v. t., to cause twilight to appear.

okshahala, v. a. i., to be like the feces in diarrhea when streaked with blood.

okshakala, v. a. i., to rise, as water.

okshakla, n., high water; deep water.

okshalinchi, v. t., to make it coarse, sleazy.

okshammi, a., hoarse.

okshammi, v. n., to be hoarse; *siokshammi*, I am hoarse.

okshammi, n., hoarseness.

okshammichi, v. t., to cause hoarseness.

okshauanli, a., fair; clear; washed bright and clean; pp., bleached; whitened; *hatak okshauanli, ohoyo okshauanli, nafoka okshauanli.*

okshauanli, v. n., to be fair, clear, clean.

okshauanlichi, v. t., to cause it to be fair, clear, bright; to bleach; *na foka achefat ishokshauanlichi.*

okshauashli, a. pl., fair; clear; bright; clean.

okshauashli, v. n. pl., to be clear or fair; *okshauanshli*, n. f.

okshauashlichi, v. t., to make clear; to bleach.

okshauina, okshawilah, n., a sty; a small boil on the eyelid; *shawilah, hoshelah.*

okshauoha, a., shallow.

okshauoha, v. n., to be shallow.

okshauwi, see *okchauwi.*

okshawilah, see *okshauina.*

okshachinli, a., coarse, sleazy, like cotton baling; not woven tight; not knit tight.

okshachinli, v. n., to be coarse, sleazy.

okshash, n., acorn pudding; mush made of acorns.

okshianli, a., narrow, as a strip of land, or the forehead or face.

okshichanli, a., sleazy.

okshifeli, a., coarse, as corn after being beaten for *tanfula* before it is riddled and fanned.

okshifeli, v. n., to be coarse.

okshifeli, n., the rough appearance of corn in the above state.

okshikali, v. t., to sprinkle; *okshikanli*, nasal form.

okshikanshli, v. t. pl., to sprinkle.

okshilama, a., sloping; descending; gradually descending.

okshilama, v. n., to be sloping; *nani at okshilama.*

okshilama, n., a descent; down hill.

okshilammi, v. a. i., to go down hill.

okshilita, v. a. i., to shut.

okshillita, okshilita, pp., shut; closed; barred; fastened, *aboha yat okshillita; itonabi at okshillita; holisso hat okshillita; ikokshilito*, a., unshut; *okshillinta*, n. f. Luke 4:25.

okshilonli, oksholonli, a., having hollow eyes; hollow-eyed, or white.

okshilonli, v. n., to be hollow, as the eyes.

okshilonli, oksholonli, n., hollowness of the eyes, as the socket of the eye after it is taken out; *okshilonlichi, oksholonlichi*, v. t.

okshimmi, n., a mist; a drizzling.

okshimmichi, v. a. i., to drizzle; to mist; to sprinkle; *okshimmihinchi*, Deut. 32: 2.

okshinilli, v. a. i., to swim.

okshinilli, n., a swimmer.

okshinillichi, v. t., to swim; to cause to swim.

okshipanli, v. a. i., to appear as the socket of the eye after it is out.

okshiplichi, v. a. i., to mist.

okshita, okshitta, v. t. sing., to shut; to close; to bar; to fasten; to block up; to embar; *imokshita*, to fend; see *okshishta.*

okshita, n., one who shuts.

okshiyanli, a., long and narrow, as a strip of land.

okshochobi, n., dark; beginning of darkness; *okshochohbichi*, Ch. Sp. Book, pp. 93, 94.

okshohonli, v. a. i., to be speckled white and gray, the color of a cow's hair.

oksholonli, n., hollow eyes; see *okshilonli*.

okshonli, v. a. i., to ear; to head, as English grain; *tanch paⁿshi himo kuchakma okshonli*.

okshonli, pp., eared; headed.

okshonulli, v. a. i., to swim; *isuba hạt okshonulli*.

okshonulli, a., being deep enough to swim; being too deep to ford.

okshonulli, n., a swimmer.

okshonullichi, v. t., to swim; to cause to swim.

okshulba, v. i., to rise, as water on the bank of a stream.

[okshulba, n., the wild honeysuckle.— H. S. H.]

okshulbi, n., a rill.

okshunak talali, n., a sandbar.

oktababi, a., mixed like mush.

oktak, n., a prairie; a savanna; a field, Matt. 6: 30.

oktak ushi, n., a small prairie.

oktalonli, a., white-eyed; blue-eyed; gray-eyed; *oktalushli*, pl.

oktalonli, v. n., to be white-eyed; *oktalushli*, pl.; *nahollo kanimi kạt nishkin oktalonli chatuk*.

oktalonli, n., a white eye; a blue eye; a gray eye; *oktalushli*, n. pl., white eyes; blue eyes; gray eyes.

oktaneli, a., shining.

oktanelichi, v. t., to shine; to make a shining appearance, as the sun when coming out of a cloud.

oktạbi, v. t., to kill by frost.

oktạbi, a., frostbitten.

oktạblahe keyu, a., irresistible.

oktạbli, v. t., to hold; to prevent; to retard; to stifle; to dam; to stop water, breath, or air; to choke a creek, etc.; to clog; to bar; to arrest; to obstruct; to block up; to intercept; (to check is *imoktạbli*); *oka yaⁿ oktạbli; kinta aioktạbli*, a beaver dam; *isht fiopa yaⁿ oktạbli*, to stop the breath; *imoktạbli*, to check; to defend; to detain.

oktạbli, n., one who dams, stops, or obstructs; an obstructer; a stopper.

oktạbli, n., an obstruction.

oktạni, otạni, v. a. i., to appear in sight, but at a distance; to appear, Matt. 6: 16; 13: 26; to be revealed, Matt. 10: 26; *hạshi ạt oktạni; sheki ạt oktạni; luak ạt oktạni; isht otạni*, to be known by, Matt. 12: 33; *pạla ạt itoktạni; oktaiyani*, pro. form.

oktạni, otạni, n., an appearance; *isht otạni*, n., a testimony, Matt. 8: 4.

oktạnichi, otạnichi, v. t., to cause to appear, Matt. 6: 4, 18; to reveal, Matt. 11: 25, 27; 16: 17; to make known, Matt. 12: 16; to show, Matt. 7: 23; 12, 18; 16: 1; *otạnichit achili*, I profess; *aiisht ilotạnihinchishke*, show forth themselves in, Matt. 14: 2; to be given as a sign, Matt. 16: 4.

oktạpa, pp., stopped; dammed; obstructed; barred; fastened; choked; intercepted; prevented; *bok ạt oktạpa; peni koa yạt oktạpa*, the boat is calked; *oktạptua*, pl.

oktạpa, v. a. i., to choke.

oktạpa, n., an obstruction; a suppression; a dam; *oktạptua*, pl.

oktạptuli, v. t. pl., to dam; to stop.

oktạptuli, n. pl., those who make dams, etc.

okti, a., frosty; icy.

okti, v. n., to be frosty.

okti, n., frost; ice; an icicle.

okti chito, n., a great frost; much ice; iciness.

okti chuⁿli, n., frozen mud that has been trodden by horses, as in a prairie.

okti hạta, n., a white frost.

okti laua, a., icy.

okti pushi, n., fine snow.

okti tohbi, n., a white frost; a hoar frost.

oktiⁿk, n., a small speckled woodpecker.

oktimpi, n., still water in a river.

oktisheli, sing., *oktishishli*, pl. a., red, as the cheek; rosy.

oktoboha, v. a. i., to drizzle; to mist.

oktoboli, v. a. i., to drizzle; to mist.

oktobolichi v. a. i., to drizzle; to mist; diminutive of *oktoboli*.

oktohbi, n., a fog; a haze; a mist; humidity; vapor.

oktohbi, v. a. i., to vapor.

oktohbichi, oktohbi, a., foggy; hazy; humid; misty.

oktohbichi, v. n., to be foggy.

oktusha, n., a snow.

oktusha, v. a. i., to snow.

oktusha achąfa, n., a flake of snow.

oktushachi, v. t., to cause it to snow; to snow.

oktushshi, n., a green slimy, ropy matter, found in water ponds or in shallow water where there is soapstone.

okumba, oka umba, n., rainwater.

okwakli, n. pl., ridges.

okwalonli, a., white-eyed; nishkin okwalonli; okwalunshli pl.; shikąla okwalunshli.

okwalonli, v. n., to be white-eyed; okwalunshli, pl.

okwalonli, n., a white eye; okwalunshli, pl.

okwichinli, v. a. i., to scowl; to frown.

okwichinli, n., a scowl; a frown.

okwichinlit pisa, v. t., to frown; to look with a frown.

okwilonli; nishkin okwilonli, Gen. 29: 17.

okwotummi, v. i., to mist.

okwotummih, okwotummichih, okwatąmmi, okwatummi, v. a. i., to drizzle.

okyauinli, v. a. i., to pout; to scowl.

okyauinli, n., one who pouts.

okyauinlit pinsa, okinyauinlit pisa, v. a. i., v. t., to scowl upon.

okyifinli, n., the look of a lion.

okyohbi, a., moist; a little wet.

okyoŀi, v. a. i., to swim; shukha yat okyoŀi; shukątti ąt okyoŀi.

okyoŀi, n., a swimmer; a swimming.

okyoŀi, a., being deep enough to swim; being too deep to ford; bok ąt okyoŀi.

okyoŀi imponna, n., a swimmer.

okyoŀichi, v. t., to cause to swim.

ola, v. a. i., to sound; to ring; to blow, as a horn; to sing, as a bird; to caw, as a crow; to crow, as a cock; to gobble, as a turkey; to chink; to chirp; to chime; to coo; to croak; to jingle; to hoot; to intonate; to screech; to toll; to twang; okfochush ąt ola, to quack; ohunla, freq.; ikohonlo, Josh. 6: 10.

ola, n., a sound; a blast; a ringing; a sounding; a crowing; a chirp; a jingle; a kaw; a ring; a tone; a twang.

ola, pp., sounded; blown; rung.

ola achukma, n., melody.

ola imma, adv., in this direction; this way of it.

ola itilaui, v. a. i., to harmonize.

ola itilaui, n., harmony.

ola taklachi, v. t., to lighten; to reduce the price.

olabechi, v. t., to hinder; to prevent; to prevent fighting; ąllat itinnukoa hokma olabechi; see oląbbechi.

olachi, v. t., to sound; to ring; to wind; to blow; to chink; to intonate; to jingle; to play; to strike; to tinkle; to toll; to toot; to twang; ehąchimolachika, we have piped unto you, Matt. 6: 2; 11: 17; aiolachi, to sound there, or at; olanchi, nas. form; olahanchi, freq. form, Josh. 6: 4, 8, 9; ohunlahanchi.

olachi, n., one who sounds, blows, etc.; a player; one who performs on an instrument; a jingler; a minstrel; a ringer; a tooter, Matt. 9: 23.

olah, adv., this way; olah minti, come this way; bok an koi olah ąt intuklo, two miles on this side of the creek.

olah, v. n., to be on this side; to be this side.

olah intąnnąp, a., being on this side of it; on this side of, Josh. 1: 14, 15.

olah intąnnąp, v. n., to be on this side of it.

olanli, adv., nearby; not far; hina yąt olanli pit itonla.

olanli, v. n., to be close by.

olanlisi, adv., closely; very near—still nearer than olanli.

olanlisi, v. n., to be very close by; kąli ąt olanlisi.

olanlisichi, v. t., to cause to be very near by.

olanlusi, olanlosi, adv., very close by; at hand, Matt. 3: 2; 10: 7.

olanlusi, v. n., to be very close by.

olasi, adv., near by; near at hand.

olasi, v. n., to be near by.

oląbbechi, olabechi (q. v.), v. t., to rebuke; to prevent; to hinder.

oląbbi, v. t., similar in meaning to aląmmi; to choke, Matt. 13: 22; to hinder; to stop; to check; to cross; to forbid; to inhibit; to interpose; to refrain; to restrain; to scant; to stint; to thwart, Luke 4: 35; imoląbbi; la pibąnna tukkia pimoląbi; itimoląbbi, to contend; ikimolabo, a., unchecked; ilolabi, to hinder himself; to deny himself; to forbear; iloląbi, n., self-denial.

olạchi, olachi (q. v.), v. t., to sing.

olạllahe ạlhpesa, a., ridiculous.

olạlli, v. t., to laugh at; to deride; to mock; to ridicule; *sạlạlli*, he laughs at me; *olahanli*, freq.

olạlli, n., one who laughs at another; a derider.

olạlli, n., ridicule.

olbạl, a., behind.

olbạl, see *ulbạl*, Josh. 6: 9, 13; 10: 19; *olbạlaka*, Luke 2: 43.

olbạlhpila, adv., backward; to fall backward, 1 Sam. 4: 18.

olbochi, Ch. Sp. Book, p. 43.

olehma, olema, adv., this way; on this side; in this direction from it; from *ola* and *imma*.

olimma, adv., this way; on this side.

olitoma, olituma, adv., at a small distance on the hither side of another object that is some distance away; *chahe ạt iti kolofa yạmma olitoma yon itonla*.

olitomasi, adv., a little way on this side; a diminutive of *olitoma*.

ollochi, ollohchi, ullohchi, pp., drawn, as water from a spring; *ochi*, v. t.

ollupi, pp., stocked; hafted; handled; helved; *ohpi*, v. t.

olana, n., a horsefly.

olana atoba, n., the spawn of flies adhering to the stalks of grass and weeds, and looking like white foam or spittle.

olana chito, n., a big horsefly; an oxfly; a gadfly.

olana okchamali, n., the green horsefly most common on prairies.

onlipa, n., a lid; a cover; a roof.

om, um (q. v.), on; upon; sometimes written *on* and *on*, according to euphony; *omboli*, Josh. 8: 31.

oma, part., as *chashoma*.

omanili, ominili, v. t., to sit on; to back; to mount; to sit; to perch; (from *om* and *binili*, the letter *b* of *binili* being dropped).

omanili keyu, a., unbacked.

ombạla, ompạla, n., an opening in the woods where there are but few large trees.

ombinili, n., a ride.

ombinili, n., a rider; a seat; a throne, Matt. 23: 22.

ombitepa, umbitepa, v. t., to press on, Acts 8: 17, 18.

ome, int., well; indeed.

ome, yea, Matt. 5: 37.

ome ahni, v. a. i., to assent; to acquiesce; to be willing; to grant; to subscribe; to suffer; to take; to tolerate; to vouchsafe; *ome ishahnikma antalachin*.

ome imahni, v. t., to permit.

omiha, well, it may be; it is so; *omiha* and *anliha* have nearly the same meaning.

omikạto, well; so it is; so it is well enough; same meaning as *yuhmi mạli*.

ominili, see *omanili*.

omishke, well; give ear; it is so; a word used to call attention at the commencement of an address.

ompạla see *ombạla*.

ompoholmo, n., a covering, Ex. 26: 7.

ompoholmo, see *umpoholmo*, covered, Matt. 10: 26.

ompohomo, v. t., to cover, Josh. 2: 6; 7: 26; see *umpohomo*.

on, on; upon; as *ontalaia*, to sit on; to stand on; *onasha; onitula; onoktili; onumba;* see *on* and *om; onakmạt*, Matt. 12: 44; *imaiona mạt*, Matt. 13: 10; 14: 25.

ona, v. a. i., to go to; to reach; to amount to; to extend to; to attain; to gain; to go; to repair; to resort; to come to, Matt. 9: 1; 2: 13, 22, 23; *aiona*, Matt. 10: 6; Luke 3: 2; *isht imaiona*, they brought unto him, Matt. 4: 24; 8: 16; 15: 39; to arrive at, in going from the speaker, John 2: 6; *ohona* freq., *ona het*, Acts 7: 17; to lead to, Matt. 7: 13; 16: 13; to arrive, as time, John 4: 35; *tanchi ạt ikono; iti chanạlli laua kạt hạchimona keyu?; oyuna, aiona*, Luke 2: 21; *aiona*, to reach to the place, Matt. 10: 6; *itimona*, to come together; *ikitimono*, Matt. 1: 18; Luke 2: 27; *ikono*, a., defective; imperfect; incompetent; incorrect; ineffectual; insufficient; scant; short; unqualified; unreached; *ikono*, v. a. i., to lack; to want; *ikono*, n., a defect; a failing; a lack; a miscarriage; a scarcity; *onahe keyu*, a., inaccessible.

ona is placed after some numerals and words of multitude, as *achạfona*, to amount to one; *tuklona, tuklo ona*, to amount to two; *kanimona, kani ma ona; katimona*, etc., *hạch isht ohonahe*, "ye shall be brought."

ona, n., an arrival; a pass; a reach.

onachi, v. t., to cause to reach; to cause to go to; to attain, meaning in skill, as *anumpuli kat chikonacho*, neg. form, Josh. 3: 10; *itonachi, itunanchi*, to go there together, dual, Matt. 26: 60; *ikonancho*, n., a failing; *ikonancho*, v. a. i., to come short; to fail; *onanchi*, nas. f.

onafa, n., winter; the fall.

onafapi, n., autumn; fall.

onafash, n., last fall.

onahpi, n., first arrival.

onatula, see *onitula*, and *onutula*.

onchasanakli, v. t., v. a. i., to wag.

onchaba, n., a ridge; a hill; a summit.

onchaba, v. a. i., to be a ridge; *onchamba*, nasal form, being a ridge.

onchaba chaha, n., a mountain; a mount.

oncheli, v. t., to prime; to lay on.

onchuloli, see *unchololi*.

oni, n., name of a plant good for food; it grows in prairies.

onitola, n., a couch, Luke 5: 19.

onitula, onatula, v. a. i., to lie on, Luke 2: 14; to fall on, Josh. 2: 9; *onituyula*, *onatoyula*, pro. form; see *onutula*.

onna, n., daylight; morning light; day, Luke 4: 42; to-morrow, Josh. 7: 13; *onnat minti, onnat taiyaha; imonna*, the next day, or day following it, John 6: 22; *itimonnakalinchi*, every day; daily; to be every day, as a fever that returns daily.—Moses Dyer.

onna, v. a. i., to come, as daylight or morning light, as *onna, onnat taha*, daylight has arrived; Josh. 5: 11, 12; *ont onna; oyunna*.

onnaha, n., the morrow; to-morrow, Josh. 3: 5; morrow; *onnaha yahe an*, the morrow which shall be; *onnaha yokato*, the morrow (distinctly); Matt. 6: 30, 34.

onnahinli, n., the morning; before and soon after sunrise; the morn, Josh. 3: 1; *onnahinli yokma*, in the morning, Matt. 16: 3.

onnahinli, v. a. i. *onnahinlikma*, in the morning, Josh. 7: 14.

onnahinli aba inki imasilhha, n., matins; morning worship.

onnahinli fehna, n., the morning itself; very early in the morning, Josh. 3: 1; 7: 16.

onnahinli impa, n., breakfast.

onnahinli impa impa, v. t., to take breakfast; to breakfast.

onnakma, adv., to-morrow; on the morrow.

onnat isht inchi, v. a. i., to come, as the morning light; to dawn.

onnat isht inchi, n., the coming of morning light; aurora; the dawn.

onnat minti, v. a. i., to come, as the morning light; to dawn.

onnat minti, n., the morning light; the coming of morning light; the dawn; light; daybreak; daylight; the dawn of day; the break of day; the coming of daylight.

onnat oklilinchi, n., morning light; twilight in the morning.

onnat oklilinchi, v. a. i., to return, as morning light.

onnat oklinli, v. a. i., to return, as morning light.

onnat oklinli, n., the return of morning light.

onnat taha, onnat taiyaha, n., the full return of day.

onnat tohwikeli, n., "dawning of the day," Josh. 6: 15.

onochi, onnuchi, onuchi, v. t., to inflict; to oblige; to pass; to reproach; to rest; to set, as a price; to wreak; to send on, 2 Sam. 24: 15; to put on; to lay on, Josh. 2: 19; 4: 5; 8: 31; to impose; to apply; to throw on; to cast, Matt. 5: 25; to enact over, as laws; to charge; to enforce; to enjoin; to impute. This is the causative form; *itonnuchi*, v. t., to recriminate; to impose on each other; *anumpa onochi*, to condemn, Matt. 12: 41; *anumpa kallo onuchi*, v. t., to command; *isht ilonochi*, Josh. 1: 6; *isht ailonochi*, to lay on himself thereby, or therewith, Matt. 5: 33; *ilonuchi*, to engage himself; *isht imilonochi*, Josh. 5: 6; *ilonochichi*, had adjured, i. e., made them take on themselves, 1 Sam. 14: 24; *isht ilimonochi*, sware unto them, Josh. 9: 15; *onnuchi*, n., one who puts on; an inflicter; *onuchi*, n., an obligation.

ont, a "directive particle," indicating an action from the speaker, or the place of its origin; *ont oklieli hokma*, Matt. 6: 23; *ont isht chukowa*, Matt. 4: 5; *ont aiali*, n., end, Mark 13: 7; *ont lakofichilashke,* I will go and heal him, Matt. 8: 7; *ont binachi,* 2 Sam. 24: 5; *ont ia,* to go past; to go by; *ontalaka,* n., bank of a river, Josh. 12: 2; shore, Josh. 15: 2; *ont ali,* 2 Sam. 24: 2; *ont alichi,* 2 Sam. 24: 7; *ont ima,* v. t., to go and give; *ont ishi,* v. t., to go and take; *ont pisa,* v. t., to go and see; *ont onna,* Acts 10: 9. For other words, see *ont* as prefixed to them.

ont, adv., by; to go to, etc., from *ona* and *t,* contracted, as *ont atukla,* secondly, on to the second; *ont atuchina,* thirdly, on to the third, Matt. 17: 23; *ont aiushta,* fourthly; *ont isht talapi,* fifthly; *ont isht hanali,* sixthly; *ont isht untuklo,* seventhly; *ont isht untuchina, ont untuchina,* eighthly.

ontalaia, v. t., to sit on; to stand on; to rest on; to be on; to ride a horse; *shapo at itombi paknaka ontalaia.*

ontalaia, pp., founded; set on.

ontalaia, n., a rider; one who sits on; that which is on.

ontalaka, n., the shore; the brow; the edge of a hill, Josh. 15: 2; the brink, Josh. 3: 8.

ontalali, v. t., to sit on; to place on; to found; to establish; to strand.

ontaloha, n., riders; *ontalaia,* sing (q.v.).

ontaloha, v. t. pl., to ride.

ontala, sing., *ontalkachi,* pl.; *itontalkanchi,* to lie on each other, as stones, Mark 13: 2.

ontala, v. a. i., to strand; see *talali; ontala,* pp., stranded.

ontukafa, pp., shot, with a gun.

onuchi, see *onochi.*

onulhpohomo, n., a churn lid; *on* and *ulhpohomo.*

onush, n., wheat, Matt. 13: 30; rye, oats; English grain; small grain, corn, Matt. 12: 1; Josh. 5: 11; *isuba apa,* oats.

onush abasha, n., a stubble; the place where wheat was cut.

onush aiasha, n., a wheat barn; a granary.

onush aialmo, n., a stubble field; the field where wheat was cut; stubble.

onush amalichi, n., a wheat fan; a fanning mill, Luke 3: 17.

onush almo, n., wheat harvest, Josh. 3: 15.

onush alwasha, n., parched corn. Josh. 5: 11.

onush amo, v. t., to cradle; to cut wheat; to reap wheat.

onush api, n., the wheat stalk; straw.

onush api isht basha, n., a straw cutter.

onush api isht peli, n., a rake.

onush bashli, n., a scytheman; a reaper; a harvester; a harvestman.

onush bota, n., wheat flour; *bota tohbi,* white flour, or *taliko bota,* a Chickasaw equivalent.

onush chaha, onush lusa, n., rye.

onush haklupish, n., wheat chaff.

onush isuba apa, n., oats, a grain for horses.

onush isht almo, n., a sickle; a reaping hook; a cradle.

onush isht basha, n., a sickle; a cradle scythe; a scythe; a reaping hook.

onush isht basha api, n., a snath.

onush isht boli, n., a flail.

onush lakchi, n., rice.

onush lusa, see *onush chaha.*

onush pehna, n., seed wheat.

onush sita, n., a sheaf of wheat.

onush sita itanaha, n., a shock of wheat, or of English grain.

onush sita itannali, v. t., to shock wheat.

onutula, onatula, from *on* and *itula,* v. a. i., to fall on; to lie on, Mark 2: 4 (*onutula* is the correct form of the word.— Allen); to come upon, Matt. 1: 19; 10: 13; 11: 12; *onatoyula,* Josh. 2: 19; 7: 1.

onutula, onatula, pp., fallen on; lying on; accused; charged with; enforced; enjoined; imposed; imputed; inflicted; obligated; *isht onatula,* blamed for; *onochi,* v. t. (q. v.).

onutula, onatula, n., an obligation.

opa, n., an owl, of the large kind.

opahaksun, n., the petrified oyster shells found in prairies and other places.

opahaksun, n., the birch tree; it grows on the banks of rivers.

opi, hopi, oppi, v. t., to stock; to haft; to helve, as a plow or gun; *iskifa yan opi,* to helve the ax; *tanampo an opi,* to stock the gun; *hullohpi, aialhpi,* pass.

opia, v. a. i., to be evening; to become evening; *ikopia,* 1 Sam. 20: 5; *opiat taha ma,* when the evening was come, Matt. 8: 16; 14: 15, 23; *sionopia,* the evening is upon me; *opia*ⁿ*ka*, nasal form, when or while it is the evening.

opia, n., the evening, i. e., the latter part of the afternoon; even; eventide, Josh. 8: 29.

opiachi, v. t., to make it evening; *il-anumpuli kąt ilopiachitok*, we talked till evening.

opiaka, n., the evening; the time from about the middle of the afternoon until sundown, Matt. 16: 2; "even," Josh. 5: 10.

opiaka impa, n., supper; the evening meal.

opiaka impa Chisąs Klaist ąt apesatok, n., the Eucharist; the Lord's Supper.

opiakmaⁿya, v. a. i., to approach toward night; evening is approaching.

opiakmaⁿya, n., nightfall.

opitama, pp. sing., passed by; lapped.

opitamoa, pp. pl., passed by; lapped.

opitamoli, v. t. pl., to pass by; to lap.

opitąmmi, sing. (see *aiopitąmmi*), v. t., to pass by; to lap over, like shingles; *iti-opitąmmi*, to pass each other.

opoma, v. t., to mock, Gen. 39: 17.

oppi, see *opi*.

osapa, n., a lot; a field; a farm; a plantation; a cornfield, Luke 6: 1; an enclosure for cultivation, Matt. 12: 1; 13: 24, 44; a portion, 2 Kings 9: 21, 26; a plat of ground, 2 Kings 9: 26.

osapa atoni, n., a scarecrow; a field guard.

osapa chuka talaia, n., a farmhouse.

osapa isht ątta, n., a farmer; a husbandman; husbandry.

osapa pilesa, v. t., to cultivate a field; to farm.

osapa takkon aiasha, n., a peach orchard.

osapa toksąli, v. t., to work a field; to farm; to till a field.

osapa toksąli, n., a farmer; a planter; a tiller of the ground; a husbandman; husbandry.

osapushi, n., a small field; a garden; "a patch."

osapushi apesąchi, n., a gardener, John 20: 15.

osapushi toksąli, n., a gardener.

oⁿsini, n., a bumblebee; a humblebee.

oⁿsini bila, n., a bumblebee's honey.

oⁿsini hakshup, n., the comb of the bumblebee.

oⁿsini inchuka, n., the nest of the bumblebee.

[oskau, n., the white crane (Sixtowns dialect).—H. S. H.]

oski, uski, n., cane; *oski naki*, an arrow.

oskoba, n., small cane. [This word is worn down from *oski holba*, canelike, and is often used as a synonym of *kun-shak*, a reed, reedbrake. As a local name it still exists in the name of Scooba, Mississippi.—H. S. H.]

oskonush, n., old seed cane; *oski onush* is the word in full; *oskish*, small, low cane; *oski shifilli*, a small kind of cane.

oskula, n., a pipe; a flute; a fife, Matt. 11: 17; 9: 23.

oⁿssi, n., an eagle; applied to the gold coin called eagle.

oⁿssushi, n., an eaglet; an eagle's egg; a young eagle.

osh, an art. pro. in the nom. case. *Li-bias osh*, Lebbeus whose, Matt. 10: 3.

oshanichi, v. a. i., to have a redness or soreness of skin; slightly inflamed.

oshanichi, n., a redness and soreness of the skin.

oshawilah, n., a sty.

oshąn, n., the otter.

oshąto, n., the womb; *oshąto nana afoyuka keyu*, Luke 23: 29; *ishke imoshąto*, John 3: 4.

oshetik, ushetik, n. (from *ushi* and *tek*); a daughter, *ushetik hąchiama*, ye daughters, Luke 23: 28.

oⁿshichakmo, v. a. i., to be wet with the dew, as clothes, etc.

oshke, see *ishke*.

ot, an article pronoun.

oⁿtapa; *siaio*ⁿ*tapa*.

otąni, ottąni, oktąni (q. v.), to reveal, Matt. 1: 18; 10: 26; 17: 3; John 9: 3; Josh. 7: 15; *ikimotaiyano*, 1 Sam. 3: 7; *otąnichi*, causative; see *oktąnichi*.

otąpi, n., a chestnut tree.

oti, v. t., to make a fire; to kindle a fire; to strike up a fire; to kindle; to light; to ascend; *ulhti*, *olulhti*, pl. pp., kindled, etc.; *isht olulhti*, "kindling wood."

oti, n., a fire kindler.

oti, uti, n., a chestnut.

oti hakshup, n., a chestnut burr.

owa, n., a hunt; a long hunting expedition; when hunters are absent for weeks or months; *owa chito, owa ishto,* from whence is said to come *Washita,* a big hunting place. [This is certainly erroneous. The Washita was named from a tribe which probably spoke a language entirely distinct from Choctaw.—Eds.]

owatta, v. t. (from *owa* and *atta*), to hunt.

owatta, n., a hunter.

pachanli, v. a. i. sing., to crack; to chap; to open; *oti at pachanli, yakni at pachanli, ibbak at pachanli.*

pachanli, pp., cracked; chapped; opened.

pachanli, n., a crack; a chap.

pachanlichi, v. t. or caus., to cause to crack open.

pachaⁿsi, a., shallow.

pachalh, n., a mat made by weaving the bark of cane; a cane mat.

pachalhpali, pachalhpuli, n., a striped snake; the gartersnake.

pachashli, v. a. i., pl. of *pachanli,* to crack open; *pachashli,* pp.; *pachashlichi,* v. t. pl. or caus.

pachashli, n., cracks.

paⁿfa, pass. v., challenged.

paⁿfi, v. t., to challenge; to brave; to offer; to dare; to defy; to stump; to provoke; to fall on; *tiⁿkba sapaⁿfi,* he challenges me first; *itiⁿpaⁿfi,* to challenge each other; *paⁿffi,* nasal form.

paⁿfi, n., a challenge.

paⁿfi, nan paⁿfi, n., a challenger.

paⁿfichi, v. t., to cause to challenge; to cause a challenge.

pahshala, v. a. i., to be rough; *iti hakshup at pashala.*

pahshala, a., rough; husky.

pahshala, n., roughness; huskiness.

paieli, v. a. i., to wave, as water and standing grain or grass; *oka at paieli, mali hat mali na onush at paieli.*

paieli, n., a wave; a waving.

paielichi, v. t., to cause waves.

paiofa, v. a. i., to bend over, as the edge of a hoe or the leaf of a book; *chahe at paiofa; bashpo at paiofa.*

paiofa, pp., bent up; bent over.

paiofa, n., a bend or batter on a tool.

paioffi, v. t., to bend up; to batter; to dull a tool.

paioffi, n., one who bends.

paioha, pp. pl., bent up; bent over.

paiokachi, v. a. i., to wave; to swell and roll as water; to ride on the waves.

paiokachi, pp., waved; tossed on the waves; *okfochush at oka ka paiokachi,* the duck is tossed on the water.

paiolichi, v. t., to cause the waves to flow; to cause a tree to wave; to shake; *mali hat oka yaⁿ paiolichi; iti aⁿ paiolicheli.*

paioli, v. t. pl., to bend over; to bend up.

paiolichi, v. t., to cause to bend.

paⁿkachuⁿsi, paⁿkachaⁿshi, paⁿkuchashi, n., a small sour grape.

pakalichi, a.; *umba pakalichi;* v. i., to rain hard.

pakama, a., pp., deceived; fooled; imposed upon.

pakama, n., deceit.

pakamoa, pp. pl., deceived; fooled.

pakamoli, v. t. pl., to deceive; to impose upon.

pakanli, v. a. i., to blossom; to bloom; to flower; *isito api at pakahanli na bilia.*

pakanli, pp., blossomed; blown; bloomed; flowered.

pakanli, n., a blossom; a blow; a bloom; a flower.

pakanli laua, a., flowery; full of blossoms.

pakanlichi, v. t., to cause to blossom, etc.

pakammi, v. t., to deceive; to cheat; *isht pakammi,* to witch.

pakammi, n., a deceiver.

paⁿkapi, n., a grapevine; a vine.

paⁿkapi aholokchi, n., a vineyard.

paⁿki, paⁿkki, n., a grape; grapes, Matt. 7: 16.

paⁿki chito shila, n., a raisin.

paⁿki okchi, paⁿk okchi, n., wine; grape juice; the juice of the grape.

pakna, n., the top; the upper side; the surface; the face, Matt. 6: 10; *patalhpo pakna,* on a bed, Matt. 9: 2; *aboha pakna,* house top, Matt. 10: 27; 16: 19; Josh. 2: 11; *apakna,* an abundance; *paknali,* pl., the outside.

pakna, v. n., to be on the top; *itimpakna,* v. t., to compete; *kilitimpakna,* let us compete; to rival; to strive; *ikitimpakno,* not strive, Matt. 12: 19.

paknaka, n., the top; the surface; the brim; the peak; *yakni paknaka,* John

3: 12; *tali paknaka yo*ⁿ, upon a rock, Matt. 7: 25.

paknaⁿ**ka**, n., the summit; the outside, Matt. 2: 9; as *chu*ⁿ*kash paknaka*, the crown of a hat or hill, etc.; *yakni paknaka*, Matt. 17: 25; *paknakeka; paknakekachi*, v. t. caus.

paknaka, a., superficial; exterior; extrinsic; *paknali*, pl., Luke 6: 49[?].

paknaka, v. n., to be above.

paknaka, prep., over.

paknaka hikiąt pisa, v. t., to overlook.

paknaka ontalaia, n., the cap sheaf; that which lies on top.

paknakąchi, paknakachi, caus., Col. 3: 14.

paknanli, adv., Matt. 23: 28; to be outward and continue so.

paknąchi, v. t., to cause to go over; *paknąchit pila*, to bend over; *paknalichi*, pl.

pakota, pokota, v. a. i. sing., to break in two; to break off.

pakota, pp., broken; *tali ąt pakota*.

pakota, n., that which is broken.

pakti, n., a mushroom; a toadstool; a fungus.

pakti shobota, n., a puffball.

paⁿ**kuchąshi**, see *pa*ⁿ*kachu*ⁿ*si*.

pakulli, v. t., to break, but not to sever; to crack.

pakullichi, v. t., to cause to break.

palata, a., homesick; lovesick; longing for something; anxious; lonesome; solitary, as one alone in a great prairie or wilderness.

palata, v. n., to be homesick, 2 Sam. 13: 39; *impalata*, he is homesick.

palata, n., a homesickness; the feeling of that nature.

palatąchi, v. t., to cause to be homesick.

palammi, a., inexorable; mighty; oppressive; potent; powerful; rigorous; sharp; sore; stern; strict; terrible; tight; tremendous; tyrannical; violent; tedious; burdensome; cruel; austere; severe; arduous; strong; fearful; fell; grievous; hard; heavy.

palammi, v. a. i.; *na chi*ⁿ*palammi*, woe be to thee, Matt. 11: 21; *i*ⁿ*palammi*, woe unto it, Matt. 18: 7.

palammi, pp., embittered; *isht i*ⁿ*palammi*, Matt. 5: 10.

palammi, a., Almighty; n.; Almighty; used to describe one of the attributes of God.

palammi, v. n., to be almighty; *Chihowa hąt palammi hoke*.

palammi, n., a hardship; hardness; hardiness; power; rigor; severity; sharpness; strictness; woe, Matt. 23: 23; *kucha kapąssa kąt palammi fehna hoke; nana palammi*, wrath, Josh. 9: 20.

palammi, adv., sharply.

palammi atąpa, a., insufferable; insupportable; intolerable.

palammichi, v. t., to render tedious, severe, etc.; to embitter; *palamminchi*, n. f; *palammit*, con. form., severely.

palammichi, n., a tyrant.

palaska, v. a. i., to bake.

palaska, pp., a., baked; *ikpalasko*, a., unbaked; *paska*, v. t.

palaska, n., that which is baked; a loaf, etc., as *palaska achąfa; naki palaska, pishukchi palaska*.

palatha, n., the part of an earring that hangs loose at the lower end.

palsi, palisi, n., palsy. It is more natural to a Choctaw to say *palisi* than *palsi*.

palak, n. sing., a crack; a pop, and noise made when something splits.

palakachi, v. a. i. pl., to crack; lit., to say *palak*.

palali, v. a. i. pl., to split.

palali, pass., to be split.

palalichi, n., a splitter.

palalichi, v. t. pl., to split; to cause to split; to divide into several pieces.

palalak, n. pl., cracks.

palampoa, shaped like a four-sided bottle.

palanta, n., nasal form, anything split; a splitting; a piece split, as a board or shingle.

palata, v. a. i. sing., to split; to cleave; to divide.

palata, pass., split; cleft; *itapalata*, split apart, or in two; halved; divided.

palata, spalt; split; shaky.

palata, n., a side; a half; a piece split off; a cleft; a division.

palalli, v. t. sing., to split; to open; to halve; to divide; to cleave; to rend; see *pali; itapalalli*, to split apart, or asunder.

palalli, n., a splitter; an opener.

panaklo, ponaklo, v. a. i., v. t., to inquire after; to question; to ask; *nana ho*ⁿ *chimpanaklo sabąnna*.

panaklo, n., an inquirer.

panąla, a., crooked; winding, as a shingle.

panąshuk, n., linden; bass wood.

pancha, n., a flag called "cattail."

panti, n., cattail; the upper end of the stalk where the down grows.

pasalichi, see pąsalichi.

pashaⁿfa, pp., gashed; see chaⁿyąt pashaⁿfa.

paⁿshafoli, n., a green snake.

paⁿshahama, n., oil for the head; an oil bag, such as some animals have.

paⁿshaⁿsha, a., hairy; haired; having hair.

pashaya, v. n., to be slanting, not perpendicular or square, as in cutting off a tree.

pashąffi, v. t., to gash; see chaⁿyąt pashaⁿfa, gashed.

paⁿsh falakto, n., a fork-tailed hawk; a swallow-tailed hawk.

paⁿsh iksho, a., hairless; bald.

paⁿsh isht ahama, n., oil used in anointing the head, Luke 7: 46.

paⁿsh isht kashokąchi, n., a hairbrush.

paⁿsh isht kasholichi, n., a hairbrush.

paⁿsh isht talakchi, n., a fillet.

paⁿsh tohbi, n., white hair; gray hair.

paⁿsh tohbi, a., gray-headed.

paⁿsh umbąla, n., sorrel hair; isuba paⁿshumbąla.

paⁿsh yiⁿyiki, n., curled hair.

paⁿshi, n., hair; the long hair of the head, or simply the hair of the head; the head, Matt. 10: 30; hishi q. v. is the word for hair of other kinds.

paⁿshi chito, a., hairy; n., thick hair.

paⁿshi ialipa, n., a wig.

paⁿshi imahaiya, n., a cowlick.

paⁿshi isht hila, v. t., to dance round the scalp of an enemy.

paⁿshi isht hila, n., a war dance.

paⁿshi isht hila, n., a war dancer.

paⁿshi isht talakchi, n., a fillet.

paⁿshi luⁿfa, paⁿshi nushkobo luⁿfa, n., a scalp.

paⁿshi luⁿfa, paⁿshi nushkobo luⁿfa, pp., scalped.

paⁿshi luⁿfi, paⁿshi nushkobo luⁿfi, v. t., to scalp.

paⁿshi luⁿfi, n., a scalper.

paⁿshi sita, n., a hair ribbon; hair tied up, called a pig tail.

paⁿshi tąnna, n., sackcloth; hair cloth; na paⁿshi tąnna, Matt. 11: 21.

pashia, n., a rim of a hat or vial.

pashoha, pp., rubbed; stroked.

pasholi, posholi, pl. of potoli, v. t., to feel of; to rub; to stroke; to handle, as a horse; to palm.

paⁿshpoa, pp., swept, Matt. 12: 44; brushed.

paⁿshpuli, v. t., to sweep; to brush.

paⁿshpuli, n., a sweeper.

paⁿshtali, n., a cockleburr; the name of a weed.

patafa, v. a. i., to split open.

patafa, pp., split open; plowed; furrowed; tilled; ikpatafo, a., unplowed.

patafa, n., a split; a furrow.

patafa ąlhpesa, a., arable; suitable for plowing.

patafa hinla, a., arable.

patafa hinla, n., plow land.

patali, v. t., to spread; to spread out, as a blanket; to lay; to cover over; as iti shima patali, to strew; shukbo patali; see umpatali, etc., to spread on.

patali, n., a spreader.

patali, v. a. i. pl., to split; to come open.

patali, pp. pl., split open; cut open; furrowed.

patalichi, v. t., to split open; to cause to open; to rifle.

patalichi, n., a splitter.

patapo, n., a pallet; bed clothing; a blanket, skin, or bed spread to sleep on.

patasah, a., large, broad, and flat.

patasąchi, v. t. sing., to level; to make flat; to flat; to plain.

patasąchi, n., a leveler.

patasąchi, pąttasąchi, n., a level valley; a name applied to the Mississippi swamp; an interval; bottom land; a plain.

patasąchi, a., level; low; plain; as yakni patasąchi; pątąssąchi, pp., leveled.

patasąlli, v. t., to flatten; to make flat; to level; naki lumbo patasąlli; itilawichit patąssąli, to spread it even, like butter on bread or salve on a cloth.

pataspoa, pl., flat; iti pataspoa, flat pieces of wood; puncheons for a floor.

pataspoa, v. n., to be flat.

pataspoa, pp., made flat; flattened.

pataspuli, v. t. pl., to flatten; to make them flat; iti pąla pataspuli.

pataswa, pl., a flat.

pataswa, pataswa, pp., v. n., to be flat.

patashechi, v. t., to level.

patashua, pp., v. a. i., flattened.

patashuli, v. t. pl., to flatten.

pataffi, v. t. sing., to split open; to cut open; to plow; to furrow; to trench; yakni aⁿ pataffi; na foka yaⁿ pataffi; itapataffi, to till; patafa hinla, a., tillable.

pataffi, n., a splitter; a tiller.

patala, a., flat.

patala, v. n., to be flat.

patalhpo, pp., from palli, v. t., or patali, spread; strewed, Matt. 24: 26; aba patalhpo, a chamber.

patalhpo, n., a spread; a pallet; a couch, Luke 5: 24; Mark 2: 9; a bed, Matt. 9: 2, 6.

pataskachi, pp. pl., leveled; flattened.

pataspoa, a. pl., pataspoa (q. v.), flat.

patassa, a. sing., flat; level; smooth; small and flat; yakni patassa; pataspoa, pl.

patassa, n., flatness.

pataswa, see pataswa.

paⁿya, v. a. i., to cry; to halloo; to call; to bark; to whoop; to cry out, Luke 4: 33; iⁿpaⁿya, v. t., to exclaim; to roar; to shriek; to scream; to screech; to vociferate; to yell.

paⁿya, n., a cry; a whoop; a yell; a clamor; an exclamation; a war whoop.

paⁿya, n., a crier; one who halloos, whoops, yells; a recreant; one who cries for mercy in a contest; a roarer.

paⁿyachi, v. t., to cause him to cry; to make him whoop, etc.

pablikaⁿ, pablikan, n., a publican, Luke 3: 12; a collector of toll or tribute, Matt. 18: 17.

pachaiasha, n., a pigeon roost, or a resort for pigeons.

pachanusi, n., a pigeon roost.

pachalhpowa, pachalhpoba, n., a dove, John 2: 14.

pachi, n., a pigeon.

pachi yoshoba, pachi yoshuba, pach oshoba, n., a turtle dove, a dove, Luke 3: 22; Matt. 3: 16; 10: 16.

pachushi, n., a squab; a young pigeon; a pigeon egg.

pafachi, n., a puff, taken from English to puff, I presume.—C. B.

pafachi, v. a. i., to puff.

paffala, n., paffaloha, pl., a swelling; a bump, such as is made by a lash on the skin.

paffala alota, full of swellings.

pala, n., a candle; a lamp; a torch; a light; a taper, Matt. 5: 15; 6: 22; 25: 1, 7, 8; Luke 15: 8; pala isht ala, bring a candle.

pala, v. a. i., to shine, as a candle; pala hat pala, the candle shines.

pala, pp., lighted.

pala afoka, n., a candlestick; a sconce; a lantern.

pala aiakmo, n., a candle-mold.

pala aioⁿhikia, n., a candlestick, Matt. 5: 15; a candle-stand; a lamp-post.

pala inchuka, n., a lantern.

pala isht kalasha, n., snuffers; candle-snuffers.

pala isht kicheli, n., snuffers.

pala isht mosholichi, n., a candle-extinguisher.

pala isht taptuli, n., a candle-snuffer; snuffers.

pala ontalaia, n., a candlestick, Luke 8: 16.

pala ponola lua, n., candle snuff; burnt candlewick.

pala toba, n., candle stuff.

pala tohwikeli, n., candle light.

palali, v. t., to light a candle, torch, or lamp; to carry a light; to light, Matt. 5: 15; ninak palali, to make or carry a torchlight in the night.

palampa, n., a meteor.

palattokachi, v. a. i., to jar; iti at kinafama yakni at pallattokachi.

palhki, a., quick; hasty; soon; fast; rapid; spry; cursory; fleet; impetuous; swift.

palhki, v. n., to be quick; chipalhki fehna.

palhki, pp., quickened; hurried; hastened.

palhki, v. a. i., to dart; to move quickly.

palhki, n., quickness; activity; rapidity; velocity.

palhki, adv., quickly.

palhkichechi, v. t., to hasten; to accelerate.

palhkichi, v. t., to hasten; to hurry; to cause to move fast.

palhkit aⁿya, v. a. i., to skim; to go along fast; to fleet.

palhkit aⁿya, a., fleeting.

pạlhpakạchi, a. pl.; *nishkin pạlhpakạchi*, bright eyes.

pạli, a., short, as a vest.

pạli, n., a flying squirrel.

pạlli, a., hot; warm; sultry (a Chickasaw word).

pạlli, v. n., to be warm.

pạlli, n., summer.

pạlli, v. t. pl., *patali*, sing., to spread them, Matt. 21: 7; Mark 11: 7, 8.

pạlokạchi, v. a. i., to jar.

pạlokạchi, pp., jarred; *yakni winakạchi-mạt yakni ạt pạlokạchi.*

pạlokạchi, n., a jar; a shake.

pạła, v. a. i. pl., to split.

pạła, pp., split; *itapạla*, divided.

pạła, n. pl., that which is split.

pạłakạchi, v. t., to rebuke; to appease; *poakạchi*, Luke 8: 24.

pạłalichih, v. t. pl., Ps. 78: 15, to cleave (the rocks).

pạłi, v. t. pl., to split; to split them. See *pạlali, itakowa pạli*, to split firewood; *holihta pạli*, to split rails; *holihta toba pạli*, to split fence stuff; *itapạli*, to divide.

pạłi, n., a splitter; a divider.

pạna, v. a. i., to twist two or three strands together.

pạna, pp., a., twisted; braided; plaited; *aseta pạna*, John 2: 15; *ponola pạna; ita-pạna*, Ex. 26: 1.

pạna, n., a twist; a braid; that which is braided; a plait.

pạnni, v. t., to twist two or three strands together, as when a rope is made; to braid; to plait.

pạnni, n., a plaiter.

pạsa, pp., cut into thin slices or pieces, as meat is cut for drying in the sun; see *pạsli.*

pạsa, n., a thin piece; a slice; a side; as *shukha nipi pạsa; wak nipi pạsa.*

pạsaha, pạssaha, v. t. pl., to slap; to spank; to box; to cuff; to thwack, Mark 14: 65.

pạsaha, n., a slapping; one who slaps, boxes, etc.; a boxer.

pạsalichi, pasalichi, v. t. sing., to slap; to strike with the open hand; to spank; to buffet; to cuff; to pat; to thwack.

pạsalichi, n., a box; a slap; a blow with the open hand; a pat; one who smites with the open hand.

pạsk ạlwạsha, n., fried bread; a nut cake; a doughnut; a fritter.

pạsk ikbi, n., a baker.

pạska, v. t., to bake; *yạmmạskạt luak iksita onochit pạska*, Gen. 18: 6; *pạskali*, I bake bread.

pạska, n., bread, Matt. 7: 9; a loaf, Matt. 14: 17, 19, *pạska yash o^n*, the loaves, Matt. 14: 19; bread, Matt. 15: 2; *ạlla impạska*, children's bread, Matt. 15: 26; Josh. 5: 11.

pạska, n., a baker.

pạska alibishli, pạska libishli, n., a toasting iron.

pạska ayamạska, n., a kneading trough or tray; *tanch pushi ayamạska; onushbota ayamạska.*

pạska ạlhpusha, n., toast.

pạska bạnaha, n., the Choctaw bread which is rolled up in corn husks or leaves and then boiled; dumplings; a roll of bread.

pạska bạnahạchi, v. t., to make Choctaw bread, etc.

pạska champuli, n., cake; sweet bread.

pạska chạnaha, n., a loaf of bread; a wheel of bread.

pạska holitopa, n., showbread, Luke 6: 4; sacred bread.

pạska isht shatạmmi, n., leaven, Matt. 16: 6, 11.

pạska isht shatạmmichi, n., leaven; yeast.

pạska kạllo, n., a cracker; hard bread; biscuit.

pạska libishli, see *pạska alibishli.*

pạska otạni, n., the showbread, Matt. 12: 4.

pạska shatạmmi, n., leavened bread.

pạska shatạmmichi, v. t., to leaven bread.

pạska shatạmmichi, n., leaven, Matt. 13: 33.

Pạskokla, see *Bạshokla.*

pạsli, v. t., to cut meat into thin slices; to slice.

pạsli, n., one who cuts into thin slices.

pạssaha, see *pạsaha.*

passalohah, pl. of *pạssali*, warped up.

pạsha, n., a cracknel, 1 Kings 14: 3.

pạshanoha, v. a. i. pl., to warp.

pạta, v. a. i., to spread.

pạta, pp., spread; *pạlli*, v. t.; *pataya*, pro. form.

paṭakitta, n., a brave.

paṭha, a., wide; broad; capacious; large; ample; extensive, Matt. 7: 13; hopaṭka, pl.; ikpaṭho, a., narrow; scanty; pp., narrowed.

paṭha, v. n., to be wide, broad.

paṭha, n., width; breadth; latitude.

paṭha; pp., widened.

paṭha ạlhpiesa, a., ample; wide enough.

paṭhạchi, v. t., to widen; to make broad; ikpaṭhochi, v. t., to straiten; to narrow.

paṭkạchi, pp. pl. spread; paḷḷi, v. t.

paṭtasạchi, see patasạchi.

peh, adv., merely; simply; just; nothing; only, Josh. 1: 7; 2: 11; as peh makali, peh iali, nothing only I am going; peh iklạnna, just middling.

peh aⁿsha, a., neutral; merely sitting.

peh aⁿsha, v. n., to be neutral; merely to stay or sit.

peh ạlhpesa, a., ordinary.

pehna, pp., saved, as seed kept for planting.

pehna, n., seed for planting; seed corn.

pehnạchi, v. t., to save or lay up seed corn, or any seed for planting; ishpehnạchi ạlhpesa, you ought to save the seed.

pehta, n., a raft; a float.

peḷechi, n., a brood; a litter; peḷechi achạfa, one brood.

peḷi, v. t. pl., (pass., piha; sing., ishi), to take up; to take away dust, dirt, leaves, grass, to shovel up; to take up by means of an instrument; to rake; to scoop; to gather fish, Matt. 13: 47.

peḷi, n., one who takes up; a scooper.

peḷicheka, peḷecheka, n., a ruler; a chairman; a presiding officer; a moderator; a dominator; an earl; the executive; a governor; a head; a head man; an intendant; a leader; a president; a superintendent; master, Matt. 10: 25; peḷecheka ạliha, rulers.

peḷichi, v. t. pl., to manage; to order; to overrule; to oversee; to reign; to rule; to superintend; to sway; to govern more than one, Mark 11: 11; to conduct; to lead, Matt. 15: 14; to control; to convoy; to direct; to dominate; to domineer; to reign over, Luke 1: 33; to take, as a husband or father takes, Matt. 2: 20, 21; to guide; to head; to keep; to lord; to marshal; to preside,

Matt. 8: 9; 12: 45; peḷinchi, nasal form; peḷiechi, pro. form; peḷiet; peḷint, Luke 6: 17[?].

peḷichi, n., a reign; a rule.

peḷichi, n., a ruler; a leader; a governor; a chief; a controller; a guide; a lord; a manager; a marshal; a master; a president; a principal; a rector; a regent; a ringleader, Matt. 2: 4; 13: 52; 16: 21; John 3: 1; okla peḷichi, officers of the people, Josh. 1: 10.

peḷichi achạfa, n., a company.

peḷichika aiasha, n., a throne; a ruler's seat.

penafana, n., a helm; a steering oar.

penaḷopulli, n., a ferry.

peni, n., a boat; a trough; a barge; a yawl; a skiff; a canoe; peni oⁿ, a ship, Matt. 9: 1; peni chukowama, when he was entered into a ship, Matt. 8:23; peni ashoⁿ, the ship, Matt. 8: 24; a pirogue; a ship, Luke 5: 2, 3; Matt. 14: 13, 24, 32, 33; pehni ạt ạla, the boat has arrived; a ferry; peni ạto, the ship, Matt. 14: 24.

peni ahoponi, n., a caboose.

peni alota, n., a cargo; a shipload; a ship's cargo.

peni ataiya, n., a boat landing; a landing; a harbor; a port.

peni ataya, a., navigable.

peni chitataya, n., a ship harbor; a harbor; a haven.

peni chito, n., a ship; a brig; a vessel; a large boat; a sailer; peni hocheto, n., ships; shipping.

peni chito aiitibi, n., a sea fight; a naval action; a frigate.

peni chito fohki, v. t., to ship; to put on board of a ship; to embark.

peni chito fohkit pila, v. t., to ship.

peni chito foka, pp., shipped; embarked.

peni chito foka, v. a. i., to embark.

peni chito ibish, n., the bow of a boat.

peni chito ikbi, n., a shipbuilder; a shipwright.

peni chito iⁿkotah, n., the mast of a ship.

peni chito isht aⁿya, n., a shipmaster; a sailor.

peni chito kạpetạni, n., a shipmaster or a ship captain.

peni chito koa, n., a shipwreck.

peni chito koli, v. t., to shipwreck; to break a ship.

peni chito okpulo, pp., shipwrecked.

peni fohki, v. t., to put on board of a boat; to embark.

peni foka, pp., put on board of a boat; embarked.

peni foka, v. a. i., to go on board; to embark; to take ship, Matt. 15: 39.

peni hasimbish, n., the stem of a boat.

peni hochito, n., large ships; ships.

peni hochito kanomona, peni hochito laua, n., a navy.

peni ibish, n., the bow of a boat; the stem of a boat; the end of a boat; the prow.

peni inkapetani, n., a boat captain.

peni intalaia, n., a ferry.

peni inponola, n., a boat rope; a cable.

peni inshapo, n., a boat's cargo; a boatload.

peni isht afana, n., the helm of a boat.

peni isht anya, v. t., to navigate a boat; to navigate; to pilot.

peni isht anya, n., a sailor; a boatman; a pilot; a mariner; a navigator.

peni isht anya imalhtoba, n., pilotage.

peni isht atta, n., a ferryman; a boatman; a bargeman; a sailor; a waterman.

peni isht chanya, n., an adze; an addice.

peni isht fullolichi, n., a rudder; a helm.

peni isht moa, n., an oar.

peni isht munfa, n., a paddle.

peni isht talakchi, n., a boat rope; a cable; a painter.

peni koa kafolichi, v. t., to calk a cracked boat.

peni kucha, v. t., to disembark.

peni kucha alhtoba, n., ferriage.

peni kuchichi, v. t., to ferry.

peni kula, n., a canoe; a dug boat.

peni kula falaia, n., a long canoe; a pirogue.

peni luak, n., a steamboat; a steamer.

peni luak shali, n., a steamboat.

peni nushkobo, n., the bow of a boat.

peni patassa, n., a flatboat; a ferryboat; a pontoon; a scow.

peni patassa fohkit isht anya, v. t., to scow.

peni patha, n., a ferryboat; an ark; a large boat used on American rivers.

peni shohala, n., a batteau; a light boat.

penushi, n., a skiff; a yawl; a small boat; an ark, such as Moses lay in when found by Pharaoh's daughter, John 21: 8.

penushi palhki, n., a skiff; a fast-running skiff.

pi, per. pro., we; nom. case, 1st per. pl. of neuter verbs, as *pinusi*, we sleep; *pikallo*, we are strong; see *chi*. The vowel *i* is often dropped before another vowel, as *illi*, to die; *pilli*, we die.

pi, per. pro., we; nom. case, 1st per. pl. of passive verbs, as *pinala*, we are wounded.

pi, per. pro., us; obj. case, before active transitive verbs; *pipesa*, he sees us; *ishpitilelikma*, thou sendest us, Josh. 1: 16.

pi, pos. pro., our; nom. case, before nouns which are the names of the body and a few more, as *pihaknip*, our bodies.

pin, pos. pro., our; nom. case, 1st per. pl., as *pinholisso*, our book; *pinwak*, our cattle; *pin* is found before words that do not begin with a vowel, or the consonants *ch, l, t,* and *p*. (See *chi*.)

pin, per. pro., dative case and usually translated with a prep., as, of us, for us, from us, to us, etc., and found before words beginning as stated under *pin*; *ishpinmiha*, thou commandest us, Josh. 1: 16.

pin, pass. pro., 1st per. pl., us, our; removed from the noun in the nom. and placed before the verb, as *tali holisso pinhotina*, he has counted our money, or, he has counted the money for us.

pia, per. pro., 1st per. pl., we; *hatak api humma pia*, we red men.

piaichi, see *pialichi*.

piakachi, v. a. i., to wave; to swell and roll, as small waves; to ripple.

piakachi, pp., made to wave; rippled; moved; agitated, as water, John 4: 4[?].

pialichi, piaichi, v. t., to trouble water; to make water wave or ripple, John 4: 4[?].

pichali, n., a rat.

pichali isht illi, n., ratsbane; arsenic.

pichefa, v. a. i. sing., to break open and run out.

picheli, pl. of *pichefa*.

pichelichi, bichillichi, v. t., to burst them; to break them; to cause to ooze out.

pichi, pihchi, n., sorrel, name of a weed; see *hachukkashaha*.

pichiffi, v. t., to squeeze, so that something will run out.

pichilli, bichilli, v. a. i. pl., *pichefa*, sing., to ooze out; to leak out; to run out; to leak; to drip; *oka yąt sakti yaⁿ pichilli; itąlhfoa yąt bichilli*, the keg leaks.

piⁿfa, pp., brushed off; scraped away; scraped; *hituk ąt piⁿfa; piⁿfat itąnaha*, scraped together.

piⁿfi, v. t., to brush off; to scrape away; to scum; to sweep away, as water carries off leaves and the earth; *hituk aⁿ piⁿfi; piⁿfit itąnnali; hąshtąp aⁿ piⁿfi; bok aⁿ piⁿfi*.

piha, pp. (from *peti*), taken up; shoveled up; scooped; scummed; *hituk chubi ąt piha; ahe ąt piha; tanchi ąt piha*.

pihcha, pihchi, n., a loft; a chamber; a corn crib raised from the ground by long posts.

pihchi, see *pichi*.

pikalichi, v. t., to rinse, as a bucket or a cup when dirty.

pikayu, n., a groat; a half dime; half a bit.

piⁿki, n., our father.

Piⁿki ąba, Ąba piⁿki, n., our Heavenly Father; God.

Piⁿki chito, n., our great Father; the President of the United States.

Piⁿki chitokaka, n., our great Father; the President.

Piⁿki ishto, n., our Great Father; God; *Poⁿki ishto*, the Chickasaw equivalent.

Piⁿki ishtoka, n., our Great Father; the President of the United States; *Piⁿki ishtokaka ąba binili*, our Great Father who sits in Heaven.

pikofa, v. a. i., sing., to chafe, as, it chafes; to fret by rubbing; to fret; to gall.

pikofa, pp., chafed; heated; fretted by rubbing; excoriated; fretted; galled; *isuba nąli ąt pikofa; isuba haktampi ąt pikofa*.

pikoffi, v. t., to chafe; to fret and wear by rubbing; to excite inflammation by rubbing; to excoriate; to gall.

pikoffi, n., a chafer; one who chafes.

pikoffichi, v. t., to cause to chafe.

pikofichi, n., a chafer.

pikołi, pikoli, v. a. i. pl , to chafe; to fret by rubbing.

pikołi, pp., chafed; fretted; rubbed till sore.

pikołichi, v. t., to chafe; to fret; to rub.

piⁿkshi, n., a knag; a knot; as *tiak piⁿkshi*, a pine knot.

pila, v. t., to pitch; to project; to transmit; to send; to throw; to cast; to toss; to fling; to heave; to forward; to convey; to dispatch; to further; to launch; *holisso pila*, to convey a letter; *anumpa iⁿpiⁿla*, Josh. 2: 3; *holisso et pela*, to send a letter this way; *holisso pit pela*, to send a letter that way; *ilepila*, to cast himself down.

pila, n., a cast; a throw; a fling.

pila, n., a sender; a caster; a thrower.

pila, adv., toward and in a direction from the speaker; off; toward.

pilashash, yesterday, John 4: 52.

pilefa, v. a. i., to bend over, like the edge. of a hoe.

pilefa, pp., bent over.

pilefa, n., a bend.

pilesa, v. a. i., to work; to labor; to toil.

pilesa, n., a laborer.

pilesa, n., labor; work.

pilesąchi, v. t., to work; to cause to work; to labor; *ąmisuba haⁿ pilesąchi*.

piliffi, v. t., to pull up.

pilla, prep., at, to, from, or in a distant place or time; *pilla* refers to space and time both; off to; off there or at, as *faląmmi pilla*, to the north; at the north; *aiąli pilla*, Matt. 12: 42; *Chintail aiasha pilla*, the way of the Gentiles, Matt. 10: 5; toward, 2 Sam. 24: 5. This differs from *pila* (q. v.), meaning toward, in the direction of; *ilappa pilla*, away yonder; away this way.

pilla, adv., away; away off; remotely.

pilla, v. a. i., to be free; "freely," Gen. 2: 16; *pilla hoⁿ*, "freely," Matt. 10: 8.

pilla, adv., merely; nothing; a Chickasaw word having the force of *peh* in Choctaw.

piloa, v. a. i. pl., to bend over; *pilefa*, sing.

piloa, pp., bent over.

pilołi, v. t., to bend them over.

piłema, piłimha, v. t., to bend, as the leg; *iyi ąt pilimha*, to bend; *pilimkąchi*, pl.

piłuⁿka, v. a. i., to sneeze, as a horse. *shaⁿwa*, to snort, as a horse in play.

piłuⁿka, n., a sneezing.

piłuⁿkạchi, v. t., to cause to sneeze.

pim, pos. pro., our, 1st per. pl., before nouns beginning with a vowel, as *pimisuba*, our horse.

pim, pre. per. pro., 1st per. pl., in the dative case before active transitive verbs beginning with a vowel, and to be rendered generally with a prep.; as *pimanumpuli*, talk to us.

pim, per. pro., before some neuter verbs beginning with a vowel, and formed from an adjective, as *pimokpulo;* see *chim.*

pim, prefixed to neuter and other verbs instead of the noun, as *ạllat pimilli, ạllat pimạlla*, etc.

pimmi, adj. pro., our; ours.

pimmi, v. n., to be our.

pimmi toba, v. a. i., to become our.

pin, pre. pos. pro., our; 1st per. pl. nom. or other case before nouns beginning with *ch, l,* and *t,* as *pinchuka*, our house.

pin, pre. per. pro., in the dative case before verbs beginning with *ch, l,* and *t,* and usually translated with a prep., as of us, to us, for us, from us; *pinchumpa*, to buy of us.

pin, pos. pro., our; found before verbs beginning with *ch, l,* and *t,* where the pro. or sign of it has been removed from the noun and placed before the verb, as *pinak pintaha, tanchi ạt pintaha;* instead of *piⁿpinak ạt taha*, etc.

pinak, n., provisions for a journey; victuals prepared beforehand, Josh. 1: 11; 9:11; provisions for man, cooked or not; if cooked they are cold.

pinak imatałi, v. t., to victual.

pinak imatałi, n., a victualler.

pinak imạltaha, pp., victualled.

pinak toba, n., prepared provisions.

pinạsh, n., ropes of a vessel; rigging of a vessel; cordage for a vessel; oakum; tow.

pinti, n., a mouse.

pinti ahokli, n., a mouse trap.

pintukfi, n., a field rat; a field mouse.

pisa, v. t., v. a. i., to see; to find; to try; to attempt; to eye; to behold; to discern; to study; to detect; to discover; to look; to view; to examine; to search; to descry; to endeavor; to espy; to essay; to have, John 3: 15, 16; to read, Luke 6: 4; to receive, John 4: 36; to notice; to perceive; to pry into; to prove; to seek; to stare; to strive; to survey; to test; to view, Josh. 2: 1; to explore; to enjoy; to gain; to gape; to gaze; to inspect; to investigate; to ken; to notice; to reconnoiter; to regard; to remark; **to** view, Josh. 7: 2; to observe; to witness; Matt. 4: 1; 5: 1; 6: 4; 9: 9; 11: 8; 12: 44; Josh. 4: 12; John 1: 41, 45; *apisa*, Matt. 18: 10; *apiⁿsa*, to be seeing in or at, Matt. 6: 18; *ak apesoshke*, I have not seen in, Matt. 8: 10; *ilepisa*, to see himself; *ilapisa*, to look at or on himself; to consider himself; to pretend, John 19: 7; *pihiⁿsa*, to pore over; *piesa*, pro. form; *piⁿsa*, nas. form, *hoyoli kia akpeso*, though I seek I do not see; *ishkot pisa*, imp., try to drink; *ont pisa*, v. t., to visit; to go and see; *ikpeso*, a., unseen, unread, untried; *pitpisa*, Matt. 14: 26; *pist, piⁿst*, contractions.

pisa, n., a view; a vision; a visit; an aspect; a sight, as *pisa tuklo*; a description; the looks; appearance; a prospect; an enterprise; an essay; an examination; a gain; a gaze; an inspection; an investigation; a mien; a shape; a stare; a survey; a test; a trial.

pisa, n., one who sees; a student; a viewer; an examiner; an explorer; an eyer; a gainer; a gazer; an inspector; an investigator; a looker; an observer; a prier; a seer; a trier; a viewer; a witness.

piⁿsa, n., a notice.

piⁿsa, n., an observer.

piⁿsa, a., ocular.

pisa aiukli, v. a. i., to beautify; to become pleasant to the sight.

pisa aiukli, pp., beautified; adorned.

pisa aiukli, a., fair; handsome.

pisa aiukli keyu, a., homely; ugly.

pisa aiuklichi, v. t., to beautify; to adorn.

pisa fehna, v. t., to scan.

pisa hinla, a., visible; legible.

pisa ikachukmo, a., indecent; shapeless.

pisa inla, n., a prodigy.

pisa okpạni, v. t., to disfigure, or to spoil the looks; to deform.

pisa okpulo, pp., deformed; defaced, as to beauty.

pisa okpulo, a., grim; ghastly; hideous; ugly.

pisa shali, a., studious.

pisachi, v. t., to show; to exhibit; to teach; to instruct; to cause to see; *holisso han pisachi; iti an pisachi; yakni an pisachilachi; pisanchi*, making him see, Deut. 7: 10.

pisachi, n., a teacher; a shower; an exhibiter.

pisahe keyu, a., undistinguishable; illegible; unsearchable.

pisąt, from *pisa* and *t*, to see and.

pisąt lopulli, v. t., to perambulate.

pinsiksho, n., a slight.

pist anya, n., a spy, Gen. 42: 9.

pishaiyik, n., the name of a weed, the root of which is used in dyeing red.

pishankchi, n., an elder.

pinshali, n., our Master; our rabbi; see Luke 3: 12; John 3: 26; 4: 31; sir, Matt. 13: 27.

pishąnnuk, n., the basswood tree; the linden tree.

pishechi, v. t., to nurse; to suckle; to feed an infant at the breast or with a bottle, Luke 23: 29; *pishet*, con.

pishi, v. a. i., to draw the breast, as a child or the young of an animal.

pishi, v. t., to suck the mother, as an infant; to draw the milk from the teat with the mouth; to draw into the mouth.

pishi, n., suck.

pinshi, n., a suckling, 1 Sam. 15: 3.

pishi issa, v. a. i., to stop sucking, as children when weaned.

pishi issąchi, v. t., to wean.

pishik, ipinshik, n., a teat, Luke 23: 29.

pishilukchi, hishilukchi, n., bran; *tan-pishilukchi*, corn bran.

pishkak, n., name of a weed that grows along branches, used in coloring red; puccoon; blood root.

pishno, per. pro., 1st per. pl., nom. case, we, Matt. 6: 12.

pishno, per. pro., 1st per. pl., obj. case, us, Luke 3: 14; *pishno ąto*, we, in contrast with thee; i. e., the disciples and the Savior, John 4: 22; Matt. 17: 19.

pishno, pos. case, ours; our.

pishno akinli, ourselves.

pishno yoka, a., thine.

pishno yokąt, a., thine.

pishofa, pp. hulled, as corn in a mortar with a pestle; *tanchi ąt pishofa*, the corn is hulled.

pishpiki, v. a. i., to rise and inflame like a sore in the throat—*Ishmayąbi;* or like fungous flesh, called *nipi lobąfa*.

pishuffi, v. t., to hull; *tanchi pishuffi*.

pishuk, n., name of a weed used in dyeing red.

pishukchi, n., milk, Josh. 5: 6; I presume from *pishi*, to suck, and *okchi*.

pishukchi achibokąchi, pishukchi achibolichi, n., a churn.

pishukchi ahoiya, n., a milk strainer.

pishukchi aiasha, n., a buttery.

pishukchi aiąlbiha, n., a milk pan.

pishukchi aniachi, n., a churn.

pishukchi ansha, a., milky.

pishukchi ataloha, n., a dairy; milk shelves.

pishukchi bąnaha, n., a roll of butter.

pishukchi hauąshko, n., sour milk; bonnyclabber.

pishukchi holba, a., milky.

pishukchi homi, n., sour milk.

pishukchi kąskaha, n., sour milk; clabber.

pishukchi nia, n., butter; cream.

pishukchi nia aiąlhto, n., a cream pot; a cream bowl.

pishukchi nia isht chibolichi, n., a churn staff; a churn dasher.

pishukchi nia lapali, pp., buttered.

pishukchi nia lapalichi, v. t., to butter.

pishukchi nia okchi, n., buttermilk.

pishukchi nia paląska, n., cheese.

pishukchi niachi, v. t., to churn.

pishukchi okchi, n., whey.

pishukchi pakna, n., cream; the top of the milk.

pishukchi paląska, n., cheese.

pishukchi paląska kanchi, n., a cheese monger.

pishukchi sunkko, n., thick milk; sour milk.

pishukchi walasha, pishukchi walanto, n., bonnyclabber; coagulated milk.

pit (cont. of *pila*), a directive particle or adv., implying a motion from the speaker or object spoken of toward, onward, forward, forth, Josh. 1: 16;

pit imahni, v. t., to beckon to them; to wish them, Luke 5: 7; *pit okạchi,* v. t., to let down into water, Luke 5: 5; *pit takalechi,* v. t., to launch out, Luke 5: 4; *pit takanli,* Matt. 6: 21; *pit chumpa,* to send and buy; *pit anoli,* to send word; *pit ima,* to hand him; to send to him; *pit pisachi,* Matt. 4: 8; *ạba pit ish-anumpuli,* thou talkest toward heaven; *pit chukowa,* entered into, Matt. 9: 1; *pit tanạbli,* passed over, Matt. 9: 1; *pit weli,* he put forth, Matt 8: 3; *pit tileli,* he sent forth, Matt. 10: 5; *pit itula,* to fall in; *pit halạlli,* to lay hold on, Matt. 12: 11.

poa, n., a beast; a wild beast; vermin.

poa aiasha, n., a menagerie.

poa chito, n., a mammoth.

poa lạpish achạfa, n., a unicorn.

poa nipi, n., flesh; the flesh of animals.

poa nusi, n., a burrow; the nest of a wild beast.

poa okpulo, n., bad wild beasts.

poa ushi, n., vermin; young vermin.

poafa, a., unfortunate; unlucky.

poafa, v. n., to be unfortunate; to be un-lucky; *ampoafạshke,* I have bad luck.

poafạchi, poafichi, v. t., to cause mis-fortune; to make or cause bad luck.

poafạchi, n., the name of a weed that dyes black.

poakạchi, v. a. i., to wave high; to roll high, as great waves.

poakạchi, n., a high wave.

poakạchi, pp., made to run high, as waves.

poalichi, poyalichi, v. t., to cause the waves to roll high, or to move either in waves or with the tides; to shake water; as *isht ishko oka ạnit poalichit la-tạbli,* to rinse a cup.

pochuⁿhạtạpa, n., a whipsnake; *ipochi itimapa.*—Harris.

pochuko, v. a. i., to place the feet to-gether and sit on the heels as Choctaw women do; to sit with them placed sideways.

pochuko, n., one who sits on her heels, or with them sideways.

pohkui, fohkul (q. v.); n., a hornet.

pohokạchi, v. a. i., to fluctuate.

pohota, nam poheta (q. v.), n., a gown.

pokafa, v. t., to smite with the open hand or paw; to be dashed; to fall

against; *itapokạfa,* to dash against each other; *oka pokafa,* to dash water.

pokafa, n., a smiter.

pokaha, v. t., to smite with the open hand hollowed.

pokạffi, v. t., to strike sideways.

pokoli, n., a decade.

pokoli, a., ten; X; 10; *pokoli auahchạfa,* a., eleven; XI; 11, and so on to 19; *pokoli tuklo,* a., twenty; XX; 20; a score; *pokoli isht tuklo,* a., twentieth; 20th; or, *isht pokoli tuklo,* and so of other numbers above 20; *pokoli tuchina,* a., thirty; XXX; 30, Matt. 13: 8; *po-koli isht tuchina,* a., thirtieth; 30th; *po-koli ushta,* a., forty; XL; 40; two score; *pokoli isht ushta,* a., fortieth; 40th; or, *isht pokolushta; pokoli talapi,* a., fifty; L; 50; *pokoli isht talapi, isht pokoli ta-lapi; pokoli hanali,* a., sixty; LX; 60; three score, Matt. 13: 8; *pokoli untuklo,* a., seventy; LXX; 70; *pokoli untuchina,* a., eighty; LXXX; 80; four score; *po-koli isht untuchina,* eightieth; LXXX; 80th; *pokoli chakali,* a., ninety; XC; 90, Matt. 18: 12; *pokoli chakali akocha chak-kali,* ninety and nine, Matt. 18: 12, 13; *pukoli tukloha,* adv., twenty times; in the same way add *ha* to the other num-bers in order to express the same thing, i. e. as times; *pokoli tuklo bat tuchina,* three times 20, or three score.

pokoli, v. t., to plait; to pucker up; also pp. (see *pokulichi*).

pokospoa, n., clusters of grapes, Rev. 14: 18.

pokota, pakota (q. v.), v. a. i., to break.

pokota, pp., broken.

pokpo, n., cotton, name most common in the southern part of the old nation.

pokpokechi, v. t., to make suds, froth, or lather; to lather; to spume.

pokpoki, v. a. i., to foam; to froth.

pokpoki, n., suds; froth; lather; foam; scum; spume.

pokpoki, a., frothy.

poⁿkshi, poⁿkchi, n., a bulb; a knot on the side of a tree; a knob; a navel gall; a toadstool.

pokshia, v. a. i., snarly; tough, as a piece of wood; *itapokshia,* snarled to-gether, like tough timber which will not split.

pokta, v. a. i., to double; to grow together, as two peaches or potatoes.

pokta, pp., doubled; grown together.

pokulichi, v. t., to cause to pucker up; see *pokoli*.

pokuspali, pl. of *pokussali*.

pokuspoa, n. pl., skeins and clusters.

pokussa, n., a skein.

pokussali, v. t., to make a skein.

polaⁿka, adv., at last; at length; finally; *polaⁿka ishla*, ultimately.

[polhkash, n., chips, trash, rubbish.— H. S. H.]

polua, v. a. i., to wilt before a fire, like *bilakli polua*.

polukta, v. a. i., to double; *itapolukta*, to coalesce.

polukta, pp., doubled; a double; as *noti polukta*, a double tooth; *itapolukta*, pp., doubled together.

poluktachi, v. t., to double; to cause to double.

poluⁿsak, n., a black weed, used in coloring cotton; black or a dark shade.

pola, see *pula*.

pololi, v. a. i., to spark; to sparkle, as fire; *luak at pololi*.

pololi, n., sparks.

pololichi, v. t., to cause it to spark.

poloma, v. a. i., to bend, as the steel spring on a lock.

poloma, pp. sing., *pola*, (1 Kings 6: 34), *pula* pl., bent; doubled up; folded, as the arms, *shakba poloma;* shut, as a knife, *bashpo at poloma;* outside of the bend of a creek, etc.; *shokulbi*, the inside of the bend.

poloma, n., a bend; a fold; a bow; a rumple.

polomi, polummi, v. t., to bend; to double up; to fold up by turning up the side or end once; to shut, as a knife.

polomoa, v. a. i. pl., to bend; to turn up.

polomoa, a., elastic; having springs.

polomoa, v. n., to be elastic; v. a. i., to meander.

polomoa, pp., bent; doubled up; folded.

polomoa, n., folds; bends; bows.

polomoli, v. a. i., to meander.

polomoli, polomoli, v. t. pl., to bend; to double up; to fold; to ruffle.

polomolichi, v. t., to meander; to cause to bend and wind.

polota, v. a. i., to sparkle; to emit sparks, as fire.

polummi, see *polomi*.

pompokachi, v. t., to make rough, knotty, uneven.

pompoki, a., rough; uneven; knotty, like knots on a rope.

pompoki, v. n., to be rough.

ponaklo, n., an interrogation; a question.

ponaklo, panaklo (q. v.), v. a. i., v. t., to ask; to inquire; to seek after, Luke 2: 44; to demand; to interrogate; to query, Matt. 2: 4; 10: 11; 16: 13; *imponaklo*, to ask him, Matt. 12: 10; Josh. 4: 6; *ponaⁿhaⁿklo*, Matt. 2: 4; *itimponaklo*, to inquire of each other; to consult; *itimponaklot aⁿsha*, to be engaged in making inquiries of each other; *itimponaklot aⁿsha*, n., a consultation; *imponaklo*, v. t., to ask him; to question.

ponaklo, n., an inquirer; a demander.

ponobokanli, n., cotton pods, just breaking open.

ponohonulla, n., twine.

ponokallo, n., linen; holland; a rope; twine.

ponokallo ikbi, n., a rope maker.

ponokallokanchi, n., a draper; a linen draper.

ponokallopana, n., a rope; a cord.

ponol ashana, n., a spinning wheel.

ponol ashana chito, n., a jenny.

ponol lapushki, n., carded cotton.

ponola, n., cotton; cotton thread or yarn; a filament; linen ponola; linen yarn, 1 Kings 10: 28; a cord, Josh. 2: 15.

ponola ahotachi, n., warping bars for cotton.

ponola aialhto, n., a thread case; a thread box.

ponola anihelichi, ponola anihechi, n., a cotton gin; a gin.

ponola anihelichi chito, n., a large cotton gin.

ponola anihi, n., a cotton gin.

ponola ani, n., a cotton bale.

ponola fabassa achafa, n., a hank of thread; a skein.

ponola hulhtufa, n., a reel; warping bars.

ponola isht shiahchi, n., cotton cards.

ponola isht shiahchi chito, n., a carding machine.

ponola itapana, n., a skein of cotton; a hank of cotton.

ponola itapana achafa, n., one skein of cotton.

ponola łopullichi, v. t., to thread.

ponola nihechi, v. t., to gin cotton.

ponola nihi, n., cotton seed; ginned cotton, seeded.

ponola okshichanli, n., coarse cotton thread.

ponola pala atoba, n., a candle wick.

ponola pehna, n., cottonseed for planting.

ponola shana, n., spun cotton; cotton thread: cotton yarn.

ponola tali kucha, n., a broach of cotton.

ponola tanna, n., cotton cloth; woven cotton.

ponolapi, n., a cotton plant.

ponolushi, n., line of thread, Josh. 2: 18.

ponoshana, n., a line; twisted cotton.

ponoshiahchi, n., carded cotton.

posilhha, v. t., to reproach.

posilhha, n., one who reproaches.

posilhha shali, n., one who is addicted to using reproach.

posilhhachi, v. t., to reproach.

poshola, pp., wreathen, Ex. 28: 14.

posholi, v. t. pl., to feel; see pasholi.

poshukta, v. a. i., to ravel out; to become shreds; similar to shobobankachi.

pota, v. a. i., to borrow; to take; to transfer by way of borrowing or lending; imapota, to borrow of him, Matt. 5: 42; to hire, i. e., to engage or to hire out; impota, to lend him.

pota, n., a borrower.

pota, n., a loan.

pota alhtoba, n., rent.

potanno, a., grudging; jealous; envious.

potanno, v. n., to be grudging; to be jealous; to be envious; impotanno, v. t. to begrudge him; to envy him; itimpotanno, to be jealous of each other.

potanno, n., jealousy; envy.

potola hinla, a., palpable.

potoli, v. t., to handle; to feel of; to touch, Matt. 8: 3, 15; to take by the hand, Josh. 9: 19; akpotoli kia, let me touch; let it be, Matt. 9: 21; 14: 36; posholit hikikia, v. a. i., to grope; posholi, pl.

potoli, n., one who feels of, handles, etc.

potoli, n., a touch; ikpotolo, a., untouched.

potoni, v. t., to guard; to watch; to take care of.

potoni, n., a guard; a watch.

potunnuchi, v. t., to cause to be jealous; to make envious.

poyafo, a., unfortunate.

poyalichi, see poalichi.

punfa, v. t., to blow with the mouth; to spout, as a whale; to blow out any liquid from the mouth in a stream or in a scattering way, Josh. 6: 5; nani chito at oka yan punfat aba pila; allikchi at punfa.

punfa, n., a blower; a spouter.

punfachechi, v. t., to blow an instrument; to cause to blow; to squirt; luak isht punfa yan pufachechi.

punfachi, v. t., to blow with an instrument, as a pipe, a trumpet, a bellows, a blowpipe; to spurt.

punfachi, n., a blower.

pukussa, n., a bunch, as of hyssop, Ex. 12: 22; see pokussa.

pulhkachi, v. a. i. pl., to double up.

pulhkachi, pp., doubled up; shukbo at pulhkachi.

pulhkachi, n., rolls.

pulla, adv., surely; certainly; necessarily; ak atuk pulla makon, for, because of, Josh. 2: 9, 11, 24; hak atuk pulla makon, because of, Josh. 5: 1; akostinchi pulla, shall know, Matt. 7: 20; akpulla tokmakon, because of, Matt. 18: 7; pulla hatuk makon, Josh. 6: 1.

pulla, a., must be; necessary; poyulla.

pulla, v. n., to be necessary; that which must be; poyulla; isilapunla, proved; derived from pulla.

pullakako, pullamako, for the sake of; because of; for, John 4:39; pullamakona; pullahatukmakon, for the sake of; because of, Matt. 10: 18, 22.

pullasi, adv., nearly; almost; ilona pullasi; illi pullasi, he is about to die.

pulli, v. t. pl., to spread.

pulli, v. t. pl., to handle; potoli, sing.

puła, n., a roll; rolls.

puła, poła, v. a. i. pl., to double up; to roll up.

puła, poła, pp. folded; doubled up; plaited; shukbo at pula, holisso hat *pula;* applied to the leaves of a book turned down at the corners; *pulakąchi* pl.

puli, v. t. pl., to fold; to double over more than once; to roll up; to plait.

puli, n., a folder; one who folds, doubles, etc.; a plaiter.

puskus, n., a babe; a baby; an infant; a papoose (a familiar word).

puskusechi; *ilepuskusechi,* v. t., to render himself childish; a., childish; n., dotage.

pushahchih, v. a. i., like *potąnno,* jealous.

pushahollo, n., a heathen priest's sacred bag.

pushechi, v. t., to flour; to pulverize; to beat fine; to powder; to grind fine; to reduce to a powder; to convert into flour; to triturate.

pushechi, n., the one who flours.

pushi, pp., floured; pulverized; beaten fine; powdered fine; ground fine; triturated.

pushi, a., fine, as flour or sand; *lukfi pushi.*

pushi, n., flour; fineness; meal.

pushka, v. t., to scratch with the nails of the paw, or the nails of the hand; *kalaffi,* sing., to scratch.

pushka, n., a scratcher.

pushkąno, v. a. i., to crave flesh for food; to long for meat.

pushnayo, impushnayo (q. v.), n., the master of an animal; *ofi impushnayo,* Matt. 15: 27; *isuba impushnayo.*

puta, putta, a., all; every one; every, Luke 3: 5, and all of each kind, giving them all the plural number; *ilaiyuka puta,* every kind, Matt. 13: 47. It may be used for a collective and a distributive plural, *hatak putta ka,* men, Matt. 10: 17; *putta* is used to express the plural number; *iląppa puta ka,* these, Matt. 1: 20; *aheka puta,* debts, Matt. 6: 12; *hatak nowąt ańya puta kąt ilbąsha tok; hatak. ohoyo, ąlla puta moma hosh mintashke,* men, women, children, distributively, all do ye come; *hatak puta kąt,* men, Matt. 13: 25.

puta, v. n., to be all; *eputa hokąto,* we all the ones; *poyuta,* pro. form.

puta, putta, n., all, as *amputa,* my all, or all mine; *amputtah,* I have all or many; *aputa,* Matt. 8: 17.

putalechi, v. t., to extend to all; *putalechit ishi,* take all; *hatak, ohoyo, ąlla*

putalechit ińhollashke, he loves them all, i. e., the men, women, and children.

putali, a., all; the whole without exception.

putali, v. a. i., *tąmaha holihta putalit ańyąt,* city to city; all of them, 2 Chron. 30: 10.

putta, see *puta.*

sa, per. pro., 1st per. sing., I, before neuter verbs, as *sanusi,* I sleep; *salaksha,* I sweat; *sąlli,* I die.

sa, per. pro., obj. case, 1st per. sing., me, before active transitive verbs; *sapesa,* he sees me; *sachumpa,* he buys me.

sa, per. pro., 1st per. sing., I, before passive verbs; *sanąla,* I am wounded.

sa, pos. pro., 1st per. sing., my, prefixed to the names of the body and its members, and a few other words, as *sanushkobo,* my head; *sabaiyi,* my nephew; *sachuńkąsh,* my heart; *sa* is sometimes written *s, są, sai, si; saiyimmi; siachukma; sątekchi,* my wife, Luke 1: 18; *chiksaiyimmo,* Luke 1: 20; *saiyukpa* Matt. 17: 5.

san, pre. per. pro., before verbs in the neg. form, as *iksańhollo;* see *san, sam, sąm; a, am, an, ąm,* are found in the positive forms (q. v.); *issańkashofi,* Matt. 8: 2.

sachakla, n., inside ridge of the back bone near the shoulders.

sahnoyechi, a., old, protracted form of *asanochi.*

sak, n., the noise when striking a solid substance.

sakachi, n. sing., a thump.

sakaha, v. t. pl., to strike, as with an ax; to thump; to rap or tap anything hard or solid; to fillip.

sakaha, n., a thumping; a striking; the noise made by the blows of an ax or maul.

sakahanli, v. t., to hack.

sakakachi, pl., noise made with an ax or maul; *sakakahanchi,* freq. form.

sakalichi, v. t. sing., to thump; to rap; to strike; to make a noise by striking with a hammer, an ax, or the fist, etc.; *sakalihinchi,* freq.

sakalichi, n., a blow; one who strikes; a striker.

sakki, v. t., to overtake, Josh. 2: 5; to come up with; to overhaul; *echisakkikamo,* we overtook you.

sakki, n., one who overtakes.

sakkichi, v. t., to cause to overtake; *alla yaⁿ iⁿki aⁿ sakkichi.*

[**sakkin**, n., the guinea fowl (Sixtowns dialect).—H. S. H.]

sakli, n., a trout; the name of a fish; name of a serpent; Ch. Sp. Book, p. 91.

sakti, n., the bank of a stream; a bluff; a cliff, Josh. 4: 18.

sakti chaha, n., a steep place, Matt. 8: 32; a high bank; a steep bluff or bank; a precipice.

sakti foka, a., cliffy; clifty.

sakti humma, n., red banks; a red bank.

sakti ikbi, v. t., to bank; to make a dike, levee, or causeway; to imbank.

sakti ikbi, n., a bank; a dike.

sakti laⁿfa, n., a furrowed bank; a bluff marked with ridges or furrows made by water running down the sides; the name of the Chickasaw bluff on the Mississippi at Memphis.

sakti oka pit akinafa, n., a cataract.

sakti oka pit akinafa, v. a. i., to fall, as water over a bluff or bank.

sakti toba, n., a levee; an artificial bank.

salakha, n., the liver; the pluck.

saltili, n., a psaltery.

sam, sam (q. v.), pro., of me; used in the negative form of verbs before *p*, as *chiksampeso; isuba chiksampeso*, you have not seen any horses for me, or you have not seen my horses.

samahachi, samahachi (q. v.), v. a. i. pl., to ring, as a bell or bells; *himonna isuba nuchi at samahanchi na haⁿkloli.*

samahachi, n., the tinkling of a bell or bells; a jingle.

samak, n., the sound of a bell; a single sound of a bell.

samakachi, v. a. i., to ring.

samampa, n., the sharp sound of a bell.

samampa, a., having a sharp sound.

samanta, see *samanta.*

san, pro., of me; to me; also I; used with neg. verbs, as *iksanchukmo; iksanchumpo*, he did not buy of me or for me. See *saⁿ, sam, sam.*

sanahchi, sanichi, n., a wing; a fin; the skirt of a saddle.

sanahchi ikbi, v. t., to wing.

sanahchi takchi, v. t., to pinion.

sanali, *iⁿsanali*, n., his adversary, 1 Sam. 2: 10; *iⁿsanalali*, 1 Kings 11: 14, 23; *iⁿsanali*, to rebel against, Josh. 1: 18; *iliⁿsanali*, to go against himself, Matt. 12: 26; *sanali, asanali, iⁿsanali, itiⁿsanali, itasanali, itimasanali*, Matt. 5: 39; 12: 25; 14: 24; 2 Sam. 24: 1.

sa, my; me, Luke 1: 18; *sachukuh; sapesa*, to see me.

salaha, a., slow; dilatory; heavy; prolix; remiss; slack; tardy; tedious.

salaha, n., slowness; tardiness.

salaha, v. n., to be slow; *isamiⁿsalaha*, Matt. 18: 29.

salaha, v. a. i., to loiter; to slack.

salaha, n., a loiterer.

salahat, adv., slowly; moderately; gradually; heavily; leisurely.

salahachi, v. t., to cause to go slow; to impede; to retard.

salahat, adv., slackly.

salahat anumpuli, v. t., to drawl.

salahat aⁿya, v. a. i., to lag; to loiter; to move slowly; to jog on.

salahat aⁿya, n., a jogger.

salbash, n., a foot-log; a foot-bridge; a tree lying across a creek.

salbo, a., hardened, as the skin in the inside of the hand; hard; *salahbo*, v. a. i., to be "past feeling," Eph. 4: 19.

salbo, v. n., to be hard; v. a. i., to become hard.

salbo, n., a corn on the foot; the hard skin on the foot or hand of laboring people; a corn; a callous.

salbochi, v. t., to harden; to make a callous; to harden the flesh.

sam, per. pro. I, in neg. verbs, as *iksamiksho*, I have none; of me; for me; to me, Matt. 2: 8; see *sam.*

samahachechi, v. t., to jingle; to cause to ring; to tinkle.

samahachi, samahachi (q. v.), v. a. i., to jingle; to tinkle; *tali at samahachi, talikasa yat samahachi.*

samanta, n., peace.

samanta, samanta, imp., hush; silence; keep still (a Chickasaw word).

samanta, a., mum; still; peaceful.

sanali, v. a. i., to go against, Luke 2: 34.

saso, n., my son; my children, Matt. 17: 5.

saso tek, n., my daughter, Matt. 15: 22.

saso toba, n., my stepson.

satih, n., my mouth, Matt. 13: 35.

setąn, n., satan; lucifer; the devil.

si, a particle suffixed to form a diminutive; *olanli, olanlisi; chąbiha, chąbihasi.* It may be of Chickasaw origin, *yąppasi, yakosi.*

si, I; my, Luke 1: 19; *siąlhtoka, siokchulinchi,* Luke 1: 47; *sihaknip.*

sia, I; *Kebliel sia hosh,* Luke 1: 19. This pronoun is translated with the verb to be; *mihi yoⁿ sia hoke,* John 9: 9; *sia hoke,* I am, Matt. 8: 9; *Hatak ushi siaha,* I the Son of Man am, Matt. 16: 13.

sihiⁿka, sihiⁿkah, v. a. i., to neigh; to whinny; to bray.

sihiⁿka, n., a neigh; a whinnying; a bray.

sikkiliklik, see *shikkiliklik.*

siksiki, a., speckled; freckled; spangled spots; having small spots.

siksiki, v. n., to be speckled.

siksiki, n., freckles.

siksikichi, v. t., to speckle.

silhhi, v. t., to track; to course; to dog; to hunt; to trail; to act in order, Acts 11: 4.

silhhi, n., a tracker; a hunter.

silhhichi, v. t., to cause to track.

silik, n., silk.

silik, a., silken; silk.

simiⁿkahanchi, n., the sensation produced by a hot plaster on a sore.

simikli, a., severely painful.

simoa, a., striped; having small stripes.

simoa, v. n., to be striped.

simoachi, v. t., to make stripes.

sinakak, n., a synagogue, Luke 4: 16; the house appropriated to the religious worship of the Jews.

sinakak chuka, n., a synagogue; i. e., the building.

sini, n., a sycamore; a buttonwood tree.

sinimpa, v. n., to be sweet.

sint, n., a cent; the hundredth part of a dollar.

sinti, n., a snake; a serpent, Matt. 10: 16; *sinti yoⁿ,* Matt. 7: 10.

sinti basoa, n., the gartersnake; the striped snake.

sinti chilita, n., a viper, Matt. 12: 34.

sinti hakshup, n., a slough; a snake skin.

sinti kobali, n., a joint snake, called *oksup taptua.*

sinti kolokumpi, sinti kololumpi, n., the joint snake.

sinti kopoli, n., a snake bite.

sinti koyufa tohbi, n., the coachwhip snake; see *ipochi itimapa.*

sinti lapitta, n., a large horned snake.

sinti lusa, n., a blacksnake.

sinti lusluki, n., a large venomous serpent.

sinti okpulo, n., a viper, Luke 3: 7.

sinti pohkul, n., the king snake; a long snake, with small yellow spots.

sinti shaui, n., a large venomous serpent; a species of the rattlesnake.

sintulion, n., a centurion.

sintullo, n., a rattlesnake.

sintullo inchąsha, n., a rattlesnake's rattles.

sintushi, n., a young serpent; a serpent's egg.

sipąlka, n., a sepulcher, Matt. 23: 27; a tomb, Matt. 23: 29.

sipi, a., old; *shukha sipi,* an old hog.

sipi, v. n., to be old.

sipokni, a., pp., old; aged; stricken in years, Luke 1: 7; advanced in years; antique; out of date; worn out; inveterate; obsolete; trite; uncouth; veteran; antiquated.

sipokni, v. n., to be old; *ont achi sipokni,* John 21: 18; 1 Sam. 2: 22; Josh. 13: 1.

sipokni, n., old age; age; longevity; oldness; a veteran.

sipokni atąpa, a., superannuated.

sipokni inshąli, n., a senior; a., senior; older; superior.

sipokni kąt inshali, a., oldest; first in age; eldest.

sipokni kąt itilaui, a., coequal.

sipoknichi, v. t., to make old; to render aged.

Siptimba, n., September.

sita, pp., bound up; tied up, as a bundle of grain.

sita, n., a bundle; a sheaf.

sita, n., binding quality; wide ferret.

sita fataha, n., a ribbon.

sita lapushki, n., ribbon.

siteli, v. t., to bind; to tie up in a bundle; to sheaf.

sitlon, n., *iti sitlon,* thyine wood, Rev. 18: 12.

sitoha, pp. pl., bound up; tied up.

sitoha, n. pl., sheaves; bundles.

sitoli, v. t., to bind up; to tie up in bundles; to sheaf, Matt. 13: 30.

sitopa; *iksitopo,* a., decrepit, Luke 13: 12; n., a cripple; *iksitopuchi,* v. t., to cripple, Luke 13: 11.

sobonoa, v. n., to swell, as the flesh of a person.

sokbish, a. down, as a stream or a road.

sokbish, v. n., to be down.

sokbish, n., that end of a stream which lies toward the mouth; "nether," Josh. 15: 19; *ibetup,* the other part.

sokbish isht ashana, n., the breech of a gun.

sokbish pila, adv., toward the mouth; downstream.

sokbish pilla, at or quite to the mouth or end of the stream.

sokolichi, v. t. sing., to smite; to tap.

sokuⁿha, sokoⁿha, v. t., to smite; to tap; to rap; to strike with the knuckles, Luke 11: 9; to knock, Matt. 7: 7; Luke 13: 25, where it is used in the plural number.

sokuⁿha, n., a smiting.

sukko, v. a. i., to thicken.

sukko, pp., thickened; fulled.

sukko, n., a diameter, grossness.

sukko, a., thick; coarse; dense; gross; v. n. and n., thickness; diameter; *iksukko,* thin.

sukko, adv., thickly; *iksukko,* adv., thinly.

sukkochi, v. t., to thicken; to full, as cloth.

suko, n., a muscadine.

sukolichi, v. t., to tap; see *sokuⁿha.*

suⁿksowa, v. t., to kiss; to play with the lips; to make a whistling noise; *iⁿsuⁿksowa,* Luke 7: 38; see *iⁿpuⁿspoa.*

sh, and, used as a conjunction; derived from *cha* and pronounced *sh* for the sake of euphony, I should think, as *cha* is used for the other persons when *sh* is used with the first person; *chumpalish;* 2 Sam. 24: 21; *ialish,* Matt. 2: 8. It is used as a conjunction with *li* and *ki, lish* and *kish, ialish, akithanokish.*

sh suffixed to the article pronoun, *a, ha, ya, ka, ma,* forms the renewed or continued mention art. pro., thus: *ash, hash, yash, kash,* and *chash.*

shabahki, a., oval; long and round.

shabapa, v. a. i., to stand thick, as grain or corn in a hill.

shachaha, shạchaha, v. a. i., to rustle; to make a noise, as leaves.

shachaha, adv., course, as *shalintak shachaha.*

shachahạchi, v. t., to rustle, as dry leaves; *hạshtạp aⁿ shạchahạchi;* see *shạchahạchi.*

shachak, n., a noise made among dry leaves.

shachakachi, v. a. i., to make a single rustling noise.

shachạla, v. t., to bristle.

shachia, v. a. i., to bristle, as an angry hog, dog, etc.

shachuna, n., an onion; a name peculiar to some portions of the Choctaw, as the Sixtowns or Bay Indians.

shafa, n., that which is shaved; a shaving; *isht shaⁿfa,* a shave or drawing knife; a drawshave.

shaⁿfa, pp., shaved; planed; scraped; cut; *iti ạt shaⁿfa, shukha yạt shaⁿfa.*

shaⁿfi, v. t., to shave; to scrape; to plane; to cut; *ashaⁿfi,* n., place where shaving is done and the shaving or thin piece shaved off.

shaⁿfi, n., one who shaves; a shaver.

shaⁿfichechi, v. t., to cause one person to shave another, Judg. 16: 19.

shaⁿfit itiaiopitạmmi, pp., rabbeted.

shaⁿfit itiaiopitạmmichi, v. t., to rabbet; to shave and lap over.

shaha, pp., scraped; *hoshiⁿshi ạt shaha,* the quill is scraped.

shaⁿha, n., a kind of wild goose.

shaⁿha, n., a shell gorget; a gorget made of shell and worn on the neck.

shaⁿha toba, n., an oyster shell.

shahbi, a., pp., cleared; clear; *hina yạt shahbi,* exposed; open; vacant; void; uncovered, Gen. 9: 21; nakedness, Ex. 20: 26.

shahbi, n., openness; vacancy.

shahbichi, v. t., to clear; *hina shahbichi; yakni shahbichi,* to clear land; to expose.

shahbika, shahbeka, n., a clearing; an opening.

shahsholechi, v. t., *anumpa itiⁿshahsholechi,* to contend in conversation, Gal. 5:20.

shahsholi, shasholi, v. t. pl., to carry; used with *itiⁿ* prefixed; *itiⁿshasholi,* to exceed each other; to go backwards and forwards, or unequally; *iⁿshasholni,* pl. of *iⁿshali,* Acts 15: 22.

shaiksheli, v. a. i., to hobble; *shaiiksheli*, Gen. 30: 11, 31.

shaioksholi, v. a. i., to waddle, as a duck; to limp, as one with legs of unequal length.

shaiukli, v. a. i., to limp, as when the hip is out of joint.

shaiukli, n., a limper.

shakahạchi, v. a. i., to make a noise by grating the teeth; *shukha nuti ạt shakahạchi.*

shakahạchi, n., the grating of the teeth.

shakalạlli, v. a. i. sing., to slip, Deut. 32: 35; see *shalạlli.*

shakalạlli, n., a slip; one who slips.

shakalạllichi, v. t., to cause to slip.

shakali, v. a. i. sing., to make a noise by grating the teeth; *shakanli*, n. f.

shakampi, n., a projection like a promontory; as *yakni shakampi; shakanshubi*, pl.

shakanlichi, shakonlichi, v. t., to make a noise in eating.

shakanlichi, shukonlichi, n., the noise made by eating.

shakapa, v. a. i., to shout; to halloo; to make a loud noise; to ululate, 1 Sam. 4: 5; Josh. 6: 5, 10.

shakapa, n., a loud noise; a hallooing; a fuss; a hubbub; an uproar; a shout, 1 Sam. 4: 5, 6.

shakawa, n., a grating, harsh noise.

shakanwa, v. a. i., to make a grating noise, as horses do when they eat pumpkins.

shakạbli, v. t., to make a loud noise; to shout.

shakạbli, n., a shouter; a noisy person.

shakạblichi, v. t., to cause a noise.

shakba, n., the arm; a sleeve.

shakba achunli, v. t., to sleeve; to sew on a sleeve.

shakba afohomit ishi, v. t., to clasp.

shakba afoka, n., an armhole.

shakba alota, n., an armful.

shakba apoloma, n., a cuff.

shakba ạlhfạbeka, n., the left arm.

shakba ạlhfoa, n., arm bands. The Choctaw formerly wore large silver bands on the arms above and below the elbow.

shakba fohki, v. t., to embosom; to place in the arms; to sleeve.

shakba foka, pp., embosomed; placed in the arms.

shakba isht impaka, n., the right arm.

shakba isht inchanya, n., a spring lancet.

shakba isht lumpa, n., a lancet.

shakba inshunkạni, ibbak inshunkạni, n., the elbow; the point of the elbow.

shakba kạllo, n., a strong arm.

shakba lumpli, v. t., to bleed the arm; to let blood from the arm; to bleed.

shakba lumpli, n., veneration.

shakba poloma, n., the bosom; the bended or folded arms; the embrace of the arms.

shakba tạli haksi lapali, n., a sleeve button.

shakbatina, n., a wildcat.

shakbona, a., moldy; weevil-eaten; *tanchi shakbona*, brown; as *hishi shakbona* (P. F.); *wak shakbona*, a dusky or dun-colored cow.

shakbona, v. n., to be moldy.

shakbonạchi, v. t., to mold.

shakchi, n., a crawfish.

shakchi inchuka, n., the hole or house of a crawfish.

shakinlichi, shakanlichi, v. t., to grate; to scranch.

shakla, n., a riddle; a coarse sieve.

shakla, n., name of a fish; Ch. Sp. Book, p. 91.

shankolo, n., a cypress tree.

shankolo itibbi, n., a cypress knee; cypress knees.

shakonlichi, see *shakanlichi.*

shakshampi, n., a large black bug; a beetle.

shakulạp, n., a crabapple.

shala hinla, a., portable.

shalak, see *shelak.*

shalakli, v. a. i., sing., to slip (once).

shalankpa, a., rotten, as dry, rotten wood.

shalali, shalali, v. a. i. pl., to slip; to slide; to wallow, Mark 9: 20.

shalalichi, v. caus., to cause to slide.

shalạlli, v. a. i. sing., to slip; to slide; to drag.

shalạlli, n., a slip; one who slips.

shalạlli, pp., dragged.

shalạllichi, v. t., to cause to slip; to slide; to slip; to drag; to haul; to lug; to shuffle.

shali, a., heavy.

shali, v. t., sing.; *shawa*, pl., to carry; to haul; to convey; to bear; to drag; to carry young; *alla inshali*, Matt. 1: 18; to conceive, 1 Sam. 2: 21; *shat*, cont.; *shanli*, nasal form, *shahanli*, freq. form, as *shat anya*, to take along; to carry along; *shat anta*, to be now carrying; *shat ia*, to carry; *shat minti*, to bring; *shat ona*, to carry to; *shat ala*, to bring here; to fetch; *shat isht anya*, n., carriage; the loading; carrying.

shali, n., a carrier; a bearer; a bringer; a conveyer; a hauler.

shalichi, v. t., to cause to carry; to make a carriage ready, 2 Kings 9: 21.

shalichi, n., one who compels another to carry.

shalintak, hashintak, n., a comb; *shalintak inshinfi; shalintak inshilli.*

shalintak ikbi, n., a comb maker.

shalintak shachaha, n., a coarse comb.

shalintakoba, n., name of a weed.

shalontaki, shaluntaki, n., a cricket.

shali, a., addicted to any course or state; given to; habitual; excessive; *abeka shali, nukoa shali.*

shali, v. n., to be habitual, or addicted to.

shali, adv., habitually; excessively.

shalichi, v. t., to scrape; *hoshishi anshalichi.*

shamalli, v. a. i. sing., to stand in.

shamalli, pp., placed in; stuck in.

shamallichi, v. t., to place in; to stick in; to tuck; to wedge.

shamoli, v. a. i, pl., to stand in (a crack); to lie in; to stick in, as pins in a cushion.

shamoli, pp., stuck in.

shamolichi, v. t., to stick them in, as to place letters in cracks or pins in a cushion.

shanaia, v. a. i., to recline; to bend; to swerve; to tack; to turn, Matt. 5: 42.

shanaia, shanaiya, shanaia, a., pp., crooked; awry; askew; turned; diverted; perverse; slant; slanting; wry; wry necked; twisted; perverted.

shanaia, v. n., to be crooked.

shanaia, n., crookedness.

shanaia hinla, a., pliable; pliant.

shanaiachi, v. t., to turn, Deut. 13: 17.

shanaiahe keyu, a., immovable; immutable; unchangeable.

shanaiahe keyu, adv., immovably.

shanaiahe keyu, n., immutability.

shanaiachi, shanaiyachi, v. t. sing., to crook; to bend; to twist; to wrench; to divert; to pervert; to slant; to turn; to twirl.

shanaioa, a. pl., crooked; awry; inconstant; variable; mazy.

shanaioa, pp., bent; twisted.

shanaioa, v. n., to be crooked.

shanaioa, v. a. i., to fluctuate; to wabble.

shanaioa keyu, a., invariable.

shanaioli, v. t., to crook; to bend; to twist; to turn askew; to prevaricate.

shanaiya, see *shanaia.*

shanaiyachi, n., a diverter.

shanali, shanali, shanalichi, v. a. i., to turn.

shananchi, v. t., to turn; to twist.

shanakha, shinakha, n., the upper part of the back between the shoulders.

shaneli, v. t. sing., to turn; to twist.

shapo, shapoh, n., a pack; a load; a bundle; a burden; baggage; a package, Matt. 11: 28.

shapo, pp., loaded; packed.

shapoli, shapuli, pp., loaded; burdened; packed; laden.

shapoweki, n., luggage.

shapulechi, v. t., to pack; to load; to burden; to put into a bag; to load with bags; to load a horse, a boat, or a wagon; to lade; *atablit shapulechi*, v. t., to overload.

shapulechi, n., a loader.

shapuli, n., a lading.

shasholi, see *shahsholi.*

shataioa, a. pl., swollen in various places.

shataioa, v. n., to be swollen.

shataioli, v. a. i., to swell in various places.

shataiolichi, v. t., to produce swellings; to cause to swell.

shatali, v. a. i. sing., to swell, as flesh, a sore, etc., not as a stream or soaked grain, etc.; *shatoli*, pl.

shatali, shatali, pp., a., swollen; tumefied; turgid; *sashatali*, I have a swelling, or I am swollen, say with boils; *shatoli*, pl.

shatali, shatali, n., a swelling; a fistula; a swell; a whitlow; a windgall; *shatoli*, pl.

shatalichi, v. t., to cause to swell; to produce a swelling; to tumefy; *shatolichi*, pl.

shatapa, v. a. i., to swell.

shatapa, n., a swelling.

shatạbli, shitạbli, v. a. i., to swell; to bloat.

shatạbli, n., a swelling.

shatạbli, pp., swollen; bloated, as an animal; a., turgid.

shatạblichi, v. t., to cause to swell.

shatạblichi, a., swollen; bloated.

shatạmmi, shatummi, shitạmmi, v. a. i., to bloat; to swell up in the bowels; to cake up; to ferment.

shatạmmi, pp., swollen; swelled; caked; fermented; inflated; leavened, Matt. 13: 33; Josh. 5: 11.

shatạmmi, n., a hard swelling; a cancer; a botch.

shatạmmichi, v. t., to cause to swell; to ferment; to inflate.

shatạmmichi, a., swollen.

shatạnni, n., a tick; a wood tick.

shatạnnushi, n., a seed tick; a young tick.

shatohpa, v. a. i., to swell.

shatohpa, n., a swelling; a hard, dry swelling; a wen; a white swelling.

shatohpa, pp., swollen.

shatosholi, v. a. i. pl., to swell.

shatosholi, pp., swollen.

shatosholi, n., swellings.

shatosholichi, v. t., to produce swellings.

shatummi, see *shatạmmi*.

shauaha, a., wide apart, as the teeth of a rake.

shauaha, v. n., to be wide apart.

shauahạchi, v. t., to place them wide apart; to cause to be wide apart.

shaualoha, see *shauwaloha*.

shaualohạchi, see *shauwalohạchi*.

shauạla, see *shauola*.

shauạshko, n., name of a weed called boneset.

shaui, n., a raccoon.

shaui hatak, n., an ape; a monkey.

shaui hatak chito, n., a baboon.

shaui imanchaha, n., a pied moccasin snake; a moccasin.

shauiya, adv., having small specks, like some stained book covers; *shauiwinkachi*, pl.

shauola, shauạla, a., wide apart.

shauola, v. n., to be wide apart.

shauwa, n., brush; dead limbs of a tree; a shrub; underbrush.

shauwa takchi, v. t., to faggot; to tie brush.

shauwa talakchi, pp., faggotted.

shauwa talakchi, n., a faggot.

shauwaloha, shaualoha, a. pl., wide apart.

shauwaloha, v. n., to be wide apart; to grow with wide-spreading branches.

shauwalohạchi, shaualohạchi, v. t., to place them wide apart; to make grow with wide-spreading branches.

shawa, see *shali*.

shaⁿwa, v. a. i., to snort like a deer or a wild horse.

shaⁿwa, n., a snorting; a snorter.

shawila, n., a sty.

shaⁿya, pp., borne; carried; hauled; *shali*, v. t. (q. v.).

shạchaha, v. a. i., to be shrunk, as grains of corn on the cob.

shạchaⁿha, shạchaha v. a. i., to be coarse, like the teeth of a comb; *hashintak shạchaⁿha*, a coarse comb.

shạchahạchi, v. a. i., to rattle, like dried leaves when walked on; see *shachahạchi*.

shạchakạmo, a., moist; wet a little.

shạchakba, n., the spine of a hog.

shạcheha, v. a. i., to become tangled

shạcheha, pp., entangled.

shạchehạchi, v. t., to entangle.

shạchila, v. a. i., to be entangled, like uncombed hair; to be snarled up.

shạchoha, shochoha (q. v.), a., knurly.

shạchopa, v. a. i., to tangle.

shạchopa, pp., entangled.

shạchopạchi, v. t., to entangle.

shạfa, pp., scraped; scratched.

shạffi, v. t., to scrape; to scrabble; to scraffle; to scratch; to paw; to draw out, as to draw out ashes from a stove; *akaⁿka yạt yakni aⁿ shạffi; wak ạt yakni aⁿ shạffi*.

shạffichi, v. t., to cause to scrape.

shạlakli, v. a. i., to slip once, or to scrape the foot.

shạna, a., wry.

shạna, v. a. i., to twist; to turn; to kink; to writhe.

shạna, pp., twisted; spun; turned; kinked; screwed; wrested; wrenched; wringed; writhed.

shana, n., a kink; a twist.

shanachi, v. t., to twist; to turn; to divert, as *imanukfila shananchi; shananchi, shananchi* (q. v.), nasal form, to parry.

shanafila, chanafila, n., black haw; black hawthorn.

shanahe keyu, a., immovable.

shanaia, see *shanaia*.

shanakachi, v. a. i., to wind along, as a serpent; to writhe.

shanalichi, shanali, see *shanali*.

shanni, v. t., to spin; to screw; to turn; to wrench; to wrest; to wring.

shanni, n., a wrench.

shanni, n., a spinner; a wringer.

shannichi, v. t., to lock; to padlock.

shapha, n., a flag; a standard; a color; a banner; an ensign; a pendant; a pennant; a streamer.

shaphashali, n., an ensign.

shapo, n., a hat; a bonnet; a cap; borrowed from the French chapeau, a hat.

shapo anunkaka alata, n., a hat lining.

shapo haksobish, n., the brim of a hat.

shapo ikbi, shapikbi, n., a hatter.

shapo impahaia, shapo impahia, n., a hat brim; the brim of a hat.

shapo intalla, n., a hat crown.

shapo isht talakchi, n., a hat band.

shapo kallo, n., a headpiece; a helmet.

shapo nushkobo, n., a hat crown.

shapo paknaka, n., a hat crown.

shapoli, v. t., to put on a hat; to place a hat on one's own head; to wear a hat; to have a hat on.

shapolichi, v. t., to put a hat upon the head of another person.

shebli, shepli, v. t., to stretch; to draw out in length; to lengthen out; to extend; to draw; to sag; to wire draw; *nan tanna shebli; tali an shebli;* to draw out iron; to draw, as a bowstring, 2 Kings 9: 24.

shebli, n., one who stretches; a stretcher.

shebli, n., tension.

sheblichi, v. t., to cause to draw out.

shehkachi, see *shinfkachi*.

shekel, n., a shekel, 1 Kings 10: 29; 2 Sam. 24: 24; Josh. 7: 21.

sheki, n., a buzzard.

sheki chito, n., a vulture.

sheki kolofa, sheki tullo, sheki talhko, n., a short-tailed buzzard; a carrion crow.

shekonobli, v. t., to tie.

shekonopa, pp., tied; *itashekonopa*, tied together, Acts 10: 11.

shelak, shalak, n., the sound of a sudden slide.

sheli, v. t. pl., to unravel; to pull them out; to pick; to ravel; *ponola yan sheli; shinfi*, sing; shinli, v. t., to pick; shinli, n., a picker.

shelichi, v. t., to card wool, cotton, etc.

shelichi, n., a carder.

shema, v. t., to dress up one's self; to dress in fine clothes; to put on ornaments; to adorn; to apparel; to array; to attire; to accoutre; to ornament; to deck; to decorate; to habit; to prank; to prim; to rig; to trim; *ilakshema*, to deck himself.

shema, pp., dressed; apparelled; accoutred; adorned; ornamented; decorated; decked; embellished; garnished; graced; invested; trimmed, Matt. 12: 44; *ishit shema*, habited with; *isht ashema*, arrayed in, with, or by means of, Matt. 6: 29.

shema, n., a dresser; a rigger.

shemachechi, v. t., to embellish another.

shemachi, shemachi, v. t., to dress up another; to accoutre; to adorn; to ornament, Matt. 6: 30; 2 Sam. 1: 24; to array; to attire; to tire, 2 Kings 9: 30; to deck; to decorate; to garnish; to grace; to invest; to prank; to prim; to rig; to trim; (another in all instances).

shemachi, n., a dresser; a rigger.

shepa, n., tension.

shepa, v. a. i., to stretch; to draw out; to sag.

shepa, pp., stretched; drawn out; strained; wiredrawn.

shepa hinla, a., malleable.

shepkachi, pp. pl., stretched; drawn out.

shepkachi, v. a. i., to stretch; to draw out.

shepli, see *shebli*.

shepoa, v. a. i. pl., to stretch; to draw out; to extend.

shepoa, pp. pl., stretched.

shepolichi, v. t. caus., to cause to stretch; to stretch.

shepoḻi, v. t. pl., to stretch; to extend; to draw out.

shibafa, v. a. i. sing., to split; to splinter.

shibafa, pp., splintered.

shibafa, n., a splinter.

shibaḻi, v. a. i. pl., to split; to splinter.

shibaḻi, pp., splintered.

shibaḻi, n., splinters.

shibaḻichi, v. t., to splinter.

shibaffi, v. t. sing., to splinter.

shibaffi, n., one who splits or splinters.

shibbi, shimmi, v. t. pl., to split off, as the bark of cane for baskets (oskashiba, the cane from which the bark has been peeled off); to peel off or hull corn.

shinfa, v. a. i. sing.. to unravel; to draw out.

shinfa, pp., unraveled; drawn out.

shinfi, v. t. sing., to unravel; to draw out, as a lot; to trash; shoeli, pl.

shinfi, n., one who unravels.

shinfkachi, shehkachi, v. a. i. pl., to unravel; shifkanchi, shifkahanchi.

shifkachi, pp., unraveled.

shiha, v. a. i., to unravel; to come out; itashiha v. a. i., to tangle.

shiha, pp., unraveled; carded; raveled; teased; itasheha, tangled; snarled; see shochohah.

shihachi, pp., carded; unbraided; ponola yat shihachi, ponola isht shihachi, a cotton card; itashihachi, v. t., to tangle; itashihachichi, to snarl; to tangle.

shihtilema, shittilema (q. v.), v. t., to despise.

shinkachi, v. a. i., to whiz, as a musket ball.

shinkak, n., a small blackbird.

shikali, v. a. i., shikanli, n. f., to tingle the nose.

shikanli, n., a tingling; strong stinging, as red pepper when eaten.

shikanlichi, v. t., to tingle the nose; to strangle, as when mustard or pepper is taken in too large quantities.

shikanoachi; see ashekonoa; itashekanoachi, v. t., to snarl; to snarl up together.

shikaḻilli, n., a small white bead, such as are used in making belts, moccasins, etc.

shikaḻla, inshikaḻla, n., a bead; beads of the common kind; a necklace.

shikaḻla ikbi, n., a beadmaker.

shikaḻlak, n., name of a creek in the old Nation.

shikekli, v. a. i. pl., to stand tiptoe.

shikeli, v. a. i., to stand tiptoe.

shikiffi, v. a. i., to rattle in the throat; anukshikiffi.

shikiffi, n., an affection in the throat.

shikkiliklik, sikkiliklik, n., a sparrow hawk.

shikoa, see shikowa.

shikobli, v. t., to put on a plume; to plume one's self.

shikoblichi, v. t., to put a plume upon another.

shikofa, v. a. i., to wrinkle, as a man's face.

shikofa, pp., wrinkled; furrowed, as the face of the aged.

shikofa, n., a wrinkle.

shikoffi, v. t., to wrinkle; to contract, as the skin of the face.

shikoha, n., the creases on a screw.

shikoḻi, v. a. i. pl., to wrinkle; to tie up, as the ears of corn are tied up by the husks to dry—tanch shikoḻi.

shikoḻi, pp., wrinkled; tied up; creased.

shikoḻichi, v. t., to cause to wrinkle.

shikopa, n., a plume; a crest; a feather.

shikopa isht shema, v. t., to feather; to adorn with a plume.

shikowa, shikoa, v. a. i. pl., to wrinkle.

shikowa, pp., wrinkled; tied up, as ears of corn to dry for seed; a., rough; uneven, like the grains of sweet corn when dry.

shikowa, n., wrinkles; corn tied up.

shila, v. a. i., to dry; to bake, as the earth; to season, as wood; to cure; to contract; to wither; to evaporate.

shila, pp., dried; baked; cured; withered; contracted; evaporated; saved, as meat; seared; seasoned; shrunk; ikshelo, a., undried; unseasoned.

shila, a., dry; arid; husky; mealy; sere, Josh. 3: 17; 4: 22.

shila, n., dryness; huskiness; ashinla, a dry place.

shilachi, v. t., to dry.

shilaia, shillayah, v. a. i. pl., to toss up the hands and feet, as an infant when lying on its back.

shilaii, n., a species of frog.

shilaiyakachi, v. a. i. sing., to toss up the hands and feet.

shilaklak, n., a goose; a tame goose; *hankha*, a wild goose.

shilaklak nakni, n., a gander.

shilaklak tek, n., the female goose.

shilaklak ushi, n., a gosling; a goose egg.

shilachi, v. t., to dry.

shileli, v. t., to dry; to bake; to cure; to season; to save, as meat; to shrink; to dry up, Josh. 2: 10; 4: 23; 5: 1.

shileli, n., a drier; one who dries, etc.

shilla, pp., combed; curried; *panshi at shilla, isuba hat inshillat taha; ikshillo*, a., uncombed.

shillayah, see *shilaia*.

shilli, v. t., to comb; to curry an animal; to rub; to tease; *inshilli*, to curry him; *isuba inshilli*, to curry a horse.

shilli, n., a comber; one who curries.

shiloa, v. a. i., to ring; to rattle.

shilohachi, v. a. i., to whiz, as a minie ball, or one that is long.

shilombish, n., the shadow of a creature, an animal, or a man; the soul, Matt. 16: 26; the spirit; a ghost; a shade; a spectre; a sprite; *imishilombish*, his soul, Matt. 16: 26.

shilombish ahalaia, a., spiritual; *amishilombish on*, my spirit.

Shilombish chitokaka aba, n., Deity.

Shilombish holitopa, n., the Holy Spirit; the Holy Ghost; Deity; the Paraclete.

shilombish iksho, a., soulless.

shilombish isht aiatta, a., renewed by the spirit.

shilombish kania, v. a. i., to entrance.

shilombish okpulo, n., an unclean spirit; an evil spirit; the devil; satan; an unclean devil, Luke 4: 33; a demon; a fiend; hell, i. e., the infernal powers; an imp.

shilombish okpulo aiilbasha ansha, a., infernal; an infernal spirit.

shilombish okpulo holba, a., fiendlike.

shilunka, pp., a., weevil-eaten; eaten by weevils; *tanchi at shilunka, onush at shilunka*.

shilukafama, n., name of a weed.

shilunkachi, a., weevil-eaten; full of holes; *tanchi shilunkachi*.

shilukpa, shilupa, n., the lights; the lungs; the vitals; a lung; the pluck.

shilukpa lachowa, shilukpa shua, consumption; diseased vitals.

shilukwa, n., a toad; a wart.

shilukwa okpulo, n., a cancer.

shilukwushi, n., a young toad; the spawn of a toad.

shilup, n., a ghost; a spirit, Matt. 14: 26; a sprite; an apparition; a fantasm; the painting or picture of a man; manes; a phantom; a shade; a spectre.

shilup aiasha, v. a. i., v. t., to haunt.

shilup aiasha, pp., haunted.

shilupa, see *shilukpa*.

shima, v. a. i., to split; to rive; to scantle; to shatter.

shima, pp., split; riven; shattered.

shima, n., that which is split.

shimafa, v. a. i. sing., to split; to splinter; to cleave; to rift; to rive.

shimafa, pp., split; cleft; riven.

shimafa, n., a splinter.

shimali, v. a. i. pl., to split; to rive.

shimali, pp., split; riven.

shimalichi, v. t., to split into fine pieces; to rive; to splinter.

shimalichi, n., a splitter.

shimaffi, shimmaffi, v. t., to cleave; to split off one small piece; to rift.

shimimpa, shimipa, see *shinimpa*.

shimmi, shibbi, v. t., to split; to rive; to split into shingles; to shatter; to sliver. Capt. Miashambe used the second form See *shimnuffi*.

shimmi, n., a river; a boardmaker.

shimmoli, see *shimoli*.

shimnuffi, shinuffi, v. t., to split off one small piece; to splinter; *shibbi*, pl., in *oski an shibbi*, to peel off the thin outside bark of cane to make baskets.

shimoha, v. a. i., to have the nightmare; to sleep, as the limbs, arms, or legs; to have the jerks (*shimohat itula*); to swoon; to be insensible, as from drinking freely of ardent spirits.

shimoha, n., numbness of the limbs, as when asleep; the "jerks" or the exercise, such as some people exhibit at religious meetings; the nightmare; incubus; a swoon.

shimoha, a., numb; asleep, as the limbs.

shimoha, pp., benumbed; rendered torpid; paralyzed; intoxicated.

shimohąchi, v. t., to benumb; to bring on the nightmare, the jerks, etc.; to numb.

shimoli, shimmoli, v. a. i., to smart, as a flesh wound.

shimoli, shimmoli, n., smart.

shimoli, v. t., to benumb.

shimoli, pp., made to smart; benumbed.

shimolichi, v. t., to make the flesh smart.

shinąkha, shanąkha, n., the upper part of the back between the shoulders.

shinąkha umpątha, n., a cape.

shinąp, n., ash; white ash.

shinąsbi, shinisbi (q. v.), a., moist; sweaty; sticky.

shinąshbi, shinąshbo, a., thick; sticky, like honey or molasses.

shininfa, shiniffi, see nukshinifa, etc..

shinihąchi, v. a. i., to hum.

shinihąchi, n., a hum; a stir.

shinilli, v. a. i., to run out; to ooze out, as the juices of meat when roasted; to trickle, as perspiration.

shinillichi, v. t., to cause to run out, etc.

shinimpa, shimipa, shimimpa, a., swift; quick; rapid; hika kąt shinimpa, maleli kąt shinimpa.

shinimpa, v. n., to be swift, 2 Sam. 1: 23.

shinimpa, n., swiftness; celerity; quickness; rapidity; velocity.

shinimpąchi, v. t., to cause to go swiftly.

shinisbi, shinąsbi, a., moist, as the skin when sweaty; sweaty.

shinisbi, v. n., to be moist or sweaty.

shinisbi, n., moisture on the flesh.

shinisbichi, v. t., to make moist; to cause moisture.

shinli (from shilli, q. v.), v. t., to pick out from a hole or from between; to pick the teeth; noti inshinli, a toothpick; pass., shinyah like chanyah, from chanli.

shinli, n., a picker.

shinoa, v. a. i., to wrinkle.

shinoa, pp., wrinkled; nashuka yąt shinoat taha; tansh shinoa, name of sweet corn.

shinoa, n., wrinkles; a dimple.

shinofa, v. a. i., to wrinkle; talhko ąt shinofa.

shinofa, pp., wrinkled.

shinofa, n., a wrinkle.

shinoffi, v. t., to wrinkle; to draw up; to pucker up.

shinoli, v. a. i. pl., to wrinkle; to pucker; to contract.

shinoli, pp., wrinkled.

shinoli, n., wrinkles.

shinolichi, v. t., to wrinkle up; to cause to wrinkle.

shinonoa, v. a. i., to wrinkle.

shinonoa, pp., wrinkled.

shinonoa, n., wrinkles.

shinononkąchi, pp., wrinkled.

shinononkąchi, v. a. i., to wrinkle.

shinonolichi, v. t., to make wrinkles; to wrinkle.

shinuffi, see shimnuffi.

shinuk, n., sand; shinuk paknaka yon, the sand, Matt. 7: 26.

shinuk aiąlhto, n., a sand box.

shinuk foka, n., the desert; the sand barrens; a desert place; destruction; the sands.

shinuk haiemo, n., quicksand.

shinuk kaha, n., the dead; destruction; quicksand; sands; deserts; shinuk kaha ia, they have gone to the dead (not often used).

shinuk laua, a., sandy.

shinuk onlali, v. t., to sand.

shinuk onlaya, pp., sanded.

shinuktiłeli, n., wild balm; horsemint (a weed).

shinukyolulli, n., sarsaparilla.

shiota, v. a. i., to subside, as a swelling.

shipąchi, see shippąchi.

shippa, v. a. i., to dry, as a cow fails to give milk; to go dry.

shippa, v. a. i., to abate; to subside; to cool, as a fever; to go down; to ebb; to fall, as water in a stream; to evaporate; to lower; to remit.

shippa, pp., abated; subsided; cooled; assuaged; fallen; evaporated; ikshippo, a., unabated.

shippa, a., low.

shippąchechi, v. t., to abate; to cause to abate; to cool.

shippąchi, v. a. i., to cool; to abate; to subside; to remit; yąnha kąt shipąchitok, the fever left her.

shippąchi, shipąchi, a., pp., cooled; assuaged; abated.

shippąli, v. t., to cool; to assuage; to mitigate; to cause to fall or go down, ebb, etc.

shitąbli, see shatąbli.

shitąmmi, shatąmmi (q. v.), v. a. i., to swell up in the bowels.

shitibli, v. a. i., to swell, as grain when soaked.

shitibli, pp., swollen.

shitiblichi, v. t., to cause to swell; to swell.

shitimmi, a., puffy; v. n., to be puffy.

shitimmi, v. a. i., to puff; to swell.

shittilema, shihtilema, ishtilema (in old times), v. t., to despise; to scorn; to disdain; to contemn; to reject; to scout; to sneer; to spurn; to abhor, 1 Kings 11: 25; 1 Sam. 2: 17.

shittilema, n., one who scorns; a contemner; a scorner; a loather; scorn; a sneer.

shittilema, a., scornful; despicable; disdainful.

shittilemąchi, v. t., to render scornful; to cause to scorn.

shiⁿya, pp., picked; see sheli.

shiyuli, v. t., to fall on; to hold; see Gen. 45: 14, to fall on the neck, etc. (lipia is used in the last translation).

shke, see ishke.

shobi, see shohbi.

shobobuⁿkąchi, v. a. i., rent, like corn leaves by the hail.

shoboli, shobulli, v. a. i., to smoke; to ascend, as smoke, fog, steam, etc.; to fume; to reek, Josh. 8: 20; shobonli, reeking.

shoboli, shobulli, a., smoky; smoking. Matt. 12: 20; pp., smoked; oⁿshoboli.

shoboli, n., smoke; a current of smoke; a fume; steam.

shobolichi, v. t., to smoke; to fume; nipi aⁿ onshobolichi, to smoke meat; to fumigate; to smother; nipi aⁿ onshobullichi, to smoke on (oⁿ being on); oⁿshobullichi, n., a smoker.

shobota, v. a. i., to ascend, as ashes, dust, or sand; hitukchubi ąt shobota.

shobota, n., steam.

shobulli, see shoboli.

shochoha, a., pp., entangled; snarled; knurly; knurled; anumpa shochoha, iti shochoha.

shochoha, v. a. i., to tangle up; to become entangled; itashochoha.

shochoha, n., a snarl.

shocholi, v. t., to entangle; ponolayaⁿ ishshocholi na.

shoekąchi, v. a. i., to rip off, like the sole of a shoe; shulush ąt shoekąchi.

shoeli, shueli, v. t. pl., to divest; to unravel; to draw out; shiⁿfi, sing.

shofoha, v. a. i., to swell; pp., swollen.

shofoli, v. a. i., to swell; to rise, as flesh when it first begins to swell.

shofoli, pp., swollen.

shofoli, n., a swelling.

shofoli, a., sandy; yakni shofoli, sandy land.

shofolichi, v. t., to swell; to cause to swell.

shoha, pp., ground; sharpened; sholichi, v. t.

shohaląlli, v. a. i., to slip; to slide; sashohaląlli cha satula.

shohaląllichi, v. t., to cause to slip or slide.

shohala, shohhala, a., light; buoyant, Matt. 11: 30; tiak shohąla, dry pine, rotten through.

shohala, v. n., to be light; shohalaiya, pro. form.

shohala, pp., lightened.

shohala, n., levity; lightness; buoyancy.

shohalachi, v. t., to make light; to lighten.

shohbi, shobi, n., evening; the close of the day; all day; antali shohbi, I have stayed all day.

shohbi, v. a. i.; shobaⁿ hosi, Matt. 14: 15.

shohbichi, v. t., to continue at an employment till night; to make it night; to finish the day; to spend the day.

shohbikanli, n., evening.

shohbikanli, v. a. i., to become evening.

shohhalali, v. a. i. pl., to slip down.

shohhalalichi, v. t., to cause to slip.

shohhala, see shohala.

shohkalali, a., clear; bright; limpid; transparent; vivid; oką yąt shohkalali.

shohkalali, v. n., to be clear; apisa yąt shohkalali.

shohkalalichi, v. t., to clear; to make bright, etc.

shohkawali, n., pureness; clearness; transparency.

shohkawali, shohkauali, a., clear; limpid; transparent; lucid; pure, 1 Kings 7: 45; glittering, Deut. 32: 41.

shohkawali, shohkauali, v. n., to be clear or limpid.

shohkawalichi, v. t., to make clear, etc.

shohmakali, a., serene; calm; mild; pleasant; *kucha shohmakali achukma.*

shohmakali, v. n., to be serene.

shohmakali, n., sereneness; calmness.

shohmakalichi, v. t., to make serene; to calm.

shohmalali, n., glare; glory; brightness; irradiation; luster; a shining; splendor.

shohmalali, shohmilali, a., pp., bright; glittering; burnished; furbished; effulgent; shiny; irradiated.

shohmalali, shohmilali, v. n., to be bright; *hashi at shohmilali; tali hata at shohmilali.*

shohmalali, v. a. i., to shine; to glimmer; to dazzle; to glare; to glisten; to glitter; to reflect; *sanishkin a^n o^{n}shohmalali.*

shohmalalichi, v. t., to burnish; to brighten; to irradiate.

shohmalalichi, n., a burnisher.

shohmalashli, a. pl., bright; glistening.

shohmalashli, v. n., to be bright; v. a.i., to shine; *fichik at shohmalashli.*

shohpakali, v. a. i., to shine (but not bright, as on a cloudy day); see Matt. 17: 2.

shohwalashli, v. a. i., to be dainty, Rev. 18: 14.

sho^{n}kak, n., name of some bird.

shokatti, see *shukatti.*

shokula, n., sugar, a Chickasaw word, from sugar in English, I presume.

shokulbi, shukulbi, n., a nook; the inside corner of a field; the inside part of a bend; a fork; a bend; *bok shokulbi.*

shola hinla, a., portable.

sholi, v. t., to carry on the back or shoulder; to shoulder; to tote; to lift; *showa,* to take in the arms, Luke 2: 28; to hug; to take up, Mark 2: 9; Matt. 16, 24; to bear; to bring forth young, Luke 1: 13; Matt. 1: 23; *tanampo a^n sholi; iti a^n sholi; allosi a^n sholit hikikia; shoyuli,* pro. form, to bear, Josh. 3: 13, 14, 15; *shoyulit itanowa,* "bearing," Josh. 3: 3; *shot anta, shot a^{n}ya, shot ala, shot ia, shot minti, shot ona.*

sholi, n., a carrier; a bearer; a lifter.

sholi, n., parturition.

sholichi, v. t., to cause to carry.

sholi, v. t., to mash.

sholichi, v. t., to grind; to sharpen by grinding; to strop; to whet; to hone.

sholichi, n., one who sharpens; a whetter.

shonuya, n., a skein.

shonuyachi, v. t., to make a skein.

shotukli, v. a. i., to beat, as the pulse.

shua, a., rotten; foul; putrid; having a disagreeable smell; fulsome; fetid; loathsome; nasty; rank; *ikshuo,* uncorrupt.

shua, v. n., to be rotten or foul; *ahe at shuat taha; wishki at shua okpulo; nan illi at shua.*

shua, v. a. i., to smell disagreeably; to stink; to putrify; to rot; to corrupt.

shua, pp., tainted; made to smell bad; corrupted; putrified; rotted, as potatoes; *ikshuo,* a., untainted.

shua, n., stench; rottenness; filth; filthiness; rankness; rot; smell (of whisky).

shuachi, v. t., to rot; to cause to smell bad; to give an ill scent; to corrupt; to putrify.

shuachichi, v. t., to rot.

shuahchi, pp., ground; whetted; strapped; honed; sharpened.

shubbukli, v. a. i., to smoke up quickly, as burnt powder; to flash.

shuchapah, shuchopah, v. a. i., to soften; to give way; to grow easy, as pain.

shuekachi, v. a. i., to come off; to come out of the ground, like pea bushes and bean poles when pulled up.

shueli, shoeli, v. t. pl., to take them off; to divest; to doff; *na foka i^{n}shueli,* to take off his clothes; to denude; *shui^{n}li,* nasal form.

shu^{n}fa, pp. sing., taken off; stripped; uncovered; unstopped; *i^{n}shufa,* undressed; unfettered.

shu^{n}fa, v. a. i., to come off; to slip off or out of; *i^{n}shunfi,* to disengage.

shu^{n}fi, v. t., to take off, Josh. 5: 15; to loose a shoe; to take out; to strip off; to slip out; to draw out, Josh. 5: 13; to uncover; to ungird a belt; to unhinge; to unsheath; to unstring; *i^{n}shufi,* to unbridle; to unclothe; to uncouple; to undress; to unfasten; to unfetter; to unstop.

shufohachi, see *shaha,* scraped.

shuikachi, v. a. i., to scale off, as plastering.

shuiⁿkachi, pp. pl., taken off; or taken out, as a pin.

shuⁿka, v. t., to smoke a pipe; to suck and draw smoke into the mouth.

shuⁿka, n., a smoker.

shukafa, v. a. i., to peel off.

shukafa, pp., peeled off.

shukafa, n., that which is peeled off.

shukali, v. a. i. pl., to peel off; to chip; to come off, as chips.

shukali, pp., peeled off; chipped; *iti shukali.*

shukali, n., peelings; chips.

shukalichi, v. t., to cause to peel off.

shukanump ikbi, v. t., to fable.

shukanumpa anumpa, pp., fabled.

shukaffi, v. t. sing., to peel; to chip.

shuⁿkani, n., an ant; an emmet; a pismire; *ibbak iⁿshuⁿkani,* the elbow.

shuⁿkani inchuka, n., an ant-heap; an ant-hill.

shuⁿkani ushi, n., ant eggs.

shukata, n., an opossum.

shukatti, shokatti, n., a frog; a small frog; a young bullfrog.

shukattushi, n., the spawn of frogs.

shukbah, v. a. i., to be soft, as wet feathers dried.

shukbo, n., a blanket; a rug.

shukcha, n., a sack; a purse, Matt. 10: 9; a sheath; a scabbard; a bag; a case; a wallet; a scrip; a satchel; a pocket; a leather bottle, Matt. 9: 17; *iⁿshukcha shammallichi,* to purse; to case.

shukha, n., a hog; swine, Matt. 7: 6; 8: 30, 31, 32.

shukha aiasha, n., a range or resort for swine.

shukha aiimpa, n., a hog trough.

shukha anumpa, shukhanumpa, n., a fable; a tale; a romance; an idle story.

shukha ayupi, n., the place where swine wallow, whether in mud, sand, or water.

shukha bila, n., lard; hog's fat.

shukha chanla, n., a small hog, stunted and tough.

shukha chushak hishi, n., a bristle; bristles.

shukha himmita, n., a shote.

shukha hobak, n., a barrow; a male hog castrated.

shukha iⁿhoa, n., a word used in calling hogs.

shukha iⁿhollihta, shukiⁿhollihta, n., a hogpen; a pigpen; a hog yard; a swine lot; a sty.

shukha imilhpak, n., swill.

shukha inchuka, n., a hogsty; a hoghouse; a pigsty.

shukha iyubi shila, n., gammon.

shukha nakni, n., a boar; the male of swine not castrated.

shukha nia, n., lard; fat pork.

shukha nia shila, n., bacon.

shukha nipi, n., lean pork; the lean meat in a hog; pork.

shukha nipi shileli, v. t., to cure pork; to make bacon.

shukha pasa, n., the side pieces of a hog; the middling.

shukha pasa shila, n., bacon made of side pieces.

shukha tek, n., a sow.

shukha tek hobak ikbi, v. t., to spay.

shukha tek hobak toba, pp., spayed.

shukhanumpa, a., fabulous; see *shukha anumpa.*

shukhanumpikbi, v. t., to make a fable.

shukhushi, n., a pig; a shoot or shote.

shukhushi isht aiopi, n., a whinock.

shukhushi pelechi achafa, n., a farrow; a litter of pigs.

shukhushicheli, v. t., to pig; to farrow.

shukiⁿhollihta, see *shukha iⁿhollihta.*

shukli, v. t. pl., to score large logs and cut out large slabs or blocks; *shukali,* pass., scored; chipped.

shuⁿkoma, n., a red bug; a chigoe.

shukonlichi, see *shakanlichi.*

shukshi, n., a watermelon.

shukshi ikfuka, n., the core of a watermelon.

shukshi nipi, n., the core of a watermelon.

shukshi nipi pehna, n., watermelon seed.

shukshi okpulo, shukshukpulo, n., a gourd.

shukshua, v. a. i., to whisper, 2 Cor. 12: 20.

shukshubok, shukshihobak, n., a gourd.

shukto, v. a. i., to spread, as ink on poor paper.

shukulbi, see *shokulbi.*

shulaffi, v. t., to scratch.

shuli, v. t., to scratch, as a cat.

shulla, a., dry; withered; wasted; shrunk; lean; poor; *ibbak shulla*, a withered hand, Matt. 12: 10.

shulla, v. n., to be dry and decayed; *iti at shulla; nipi at shulla.*

shulla, n., dryness; the dry rot.

shullachi, v. t., to dry; to cause to decay, shrink, etc.

shulush, n., a moccasin; a sandal, a shoe, Matt. 10: 10; Josh. 5: 15.

shulush akalli, n., a cobbler.

shulush atoba, n., a last.

shulush chaha, shulush falaia, n., a boot.

shulush chaha atoba, n., a boot tree.

shulush hofaloha, n. pl., boots.

shulush ikbi, n., a shoemaker.

shulush imatali, v. t., to shoe; to furnish with shoes.

shulush imalhtaha, pp., furnished with shoes.

shulush isht akamassa, n., a shoe buckle.

shulush isht lusachi, n., shoe blacking; black ball.

shulush isht talakchi, n., a shoestring; a shoe latchet, John 1: 27; a latchet.

shulush itichapa, n., a pair of shoes.

shulush kamassa, n., an English shoe; a shoe with a hard sole.

shulush kallo, n., an English shoe; a shoe.

shulush kallo falaia, n., a boot.

shulush kallo falaia holo, v. t., to boot; to put on a boot.

shulush kallo falaia holo, pp., booted.

shulush shohala, n., light shoes; slippers; pumps.

shulush tapuski, n., slippers.

shumanta, v. a. i., to have rheumatic pains.

shumantabi, n., rheumatism; same as *nahishabi;* see *nahishi.*

shumatti, n., the arrow of a blowgun; *Ashumatti*, name of a woman.

shumatti, shumati, n., a thistle, Matt. 7: 16.

shumba, a., defective; rotten; dry, as a tooth or a hickory nut.

shumba, v. n., to be defective; to be rotten; *noti at shumba; oksak at shumba; tiak shumba*, a dead and decayed pine.

shumba, v. a. i., to rot.

shumbala, n., a cottonwood tree.

shummi, n., moisture; dampness; humidity.

shummi, a., moist; damp; dank; humid; muggy.

shummi, v. n., to be moist; to be damp; to be dank; *hatak at shummi; yakni at shummi; bota yat shummi.*

shummi, pp., moistened; dampened.

shummichi, v. t., to moisten; to dampen.

shumo, n., a thistle; thistle down.

shumo api, n., a thistle stalk.

shumo holutti, n., the arrow of a blowgun.

shumo laua, a., thistly.

shumo naki, n., an arrow; a bolt.

shumpalali, a., glimmering; light; bright.

shumpalali, v. n., to be light or bright; *luak at shumpalali; shutik at shumpalali.*

shumpalali, v. a. i., to shine.

shumpalalichi, v. t., to brighten; to cause to shine.

shunlulo, n., a lark.

shupik, n., the name of a fish called by some the mudfish.

shunshi, n., an insect; a bug; a fly; a worm; vermes; a moth, Matt. 6: 19, 20.

shunshi aiapa, a., wormeaten.

shunshi hakchuma, n., a tobacco worm.

shushi iskitini, n., a mite.

shunshi isuba acheli, n., a nitter.

shushi isht abeka a., wormy.

shunshi kalush apa, n., a cabbage worm.

shunshi laua, a., buggy; wormy.

shunshi nan tanna apa, n., a moth.

shunshi oka ansha, n., a water fly.

shunshi okchamali, n., a green fly.

shunshi okchamali isht wulhkuchi, n., Spanish flies; cantharides.

shunshi walana, shunshi olana, n., a horse fly; a biting fly.

shuti, n., an earthen pot used over the fire, and a kind made by the Choctaw; a *tanfula* pot, a boiler; a pot; a kettle.

shuti ansha, n., a kettle.

shuti asha atoba, n., a furnace.

shuti asha onlipa, n., a pot lid.

shuti boluktabi, n., erysipelas.

shuti chito, n., a caldron.

shuti fohki, v. t., to pot.

shuti iyasha, n., an iron kettle; a pot.

shuti iyasha akmuchi, n., a casting; castings.

shuti iyasha oⁿhpa, n., a pot lid.

shuti oka aialhto, n., a water-pot, John 2: 7.

shuti tana, n., a potter; one who makes *shuti.*

shutik, n., the sky; the heavens; heaven, Matt. 11: 23, 25; 16: 2.

shutik aba, n., the firmament.

shutik hata, n., daybreak; light in the sky.

shutik iklanna, n., midheaven.

shutik tabokaka, n., heaven; the circle or the convex of the sky; the heavens.

shutukshonli, v. a. i., to breathe quick and hard, as in speaking Choctaw loud and fast; to pant.

shutushi, n., a small earthen pot or vessel; lit., a son of the *shuti.*

t, sign of the nom. case or the art. the, placed at the end of nouns and adjectives. It has a definitive sense, as in *ilappa, ilappat, yamma, yammat;* in verbs, *toksalit ia,* for work he goes; *t* defines or marks out to work as an object, like *to* in English.

t, a conjunctive form of the article. It connects two verbs when both have the same nom., or where there is but one nom., as *chumpat ia, abit apa,* making a compound verb. The letter *t* suffixed to the particles *a, ha, ya, ka, ma,* gives them a connecting power, and *toka* and *oma,* a definite sense.

t, placed at the end of particles is a sign of the nom. case, as *kat, ot, at.*

t, when suffixed to a verb or adj. often gives it the force of an adverb, as *achukmat aⁿsha,* he sits well; he is well; *achukmat* is a word that qualifies *aⁿsha. t* has a definite as well as a connecting office, namely that of singling out and connecting two nominatives to different verbs. But see above.

ta, adv. of time, doubt, and surprise, as *ish lat ta?* have you been here some time, and I did not know it (recent past tense)? The word to which this is suffixed takes a *t,* as *ishla? ishlatta.* I think that *ta* is definite and *to* distinctive. *ishlatbatta?* def., *ishlatto?* dist.

tabakli, v. a. i., to gallop; to canter.

tabakli, n., one who canters; a gallop.

tabaklichi, v. t., to canter; to gallop; to cause to canter or gallop.

tabashi, tabashi, v. a. i., to mourn for the dead; to wear mourning clothes. When the old Choctaw mourn they put on old, filthy garments, and do not wash, shave, comb, or visit or attend any assembly of people. They also cry several times daily at the grave or at the poles set up for the dead, called mourning poles, 2 Sam. 14: 2.

tabashi, n., a mourning.

tabash, n., a mourning person, or in time of mourning; a nickname given to a poor fellow in Apehka, who died some years since; see *tabashi.*

tabeli, see *isht tabeli.*

tabikli, v. a. i., to limp; see *chahikli* and *haⁿchi.*

tabikli, n., a limper.

tabokaka, n., the top; an eminence; the summit; the vertex.

tabokoa, v. a. i., to reach the meridian. The sun, moon, or stars may *tabokoa.*

tabokoa, n., the meridian; noon; midday; the middle of the arch of heaven; the highest point.

tabokoa, a., vertical.

tabokoli, tabokonli, v. a. i., to reach the meridian; *tabokoli mat illitok,* when he reached noon, he died, 2 Kings 4: 20.

tabokoli, tabokuli, n., noon; midday; midheaven; meridian; noonday; midnight; zenith.

tabokoli foha, n., a nooning.

tabokoli foka, n., noontide; about noon.

tabokoli ikono, n., before noon.

tabokoli impa, n., dinner.

tabokoli impa ima, v. t., to give a dinner.

tabokoli impa impa, v. t., to dine.

tabokoli ont ia, n., afternoon; past noon.

tabokonli, see *tabokoli.*

tabokuli, see *tabokoli.*

tachammaha, n., a brass ring for the wrist, formerly worn by women.

taⁿchuka, n., sugar cane.

taⁿfula, n., Indian hominy; their drink.

taⁿfula hauashko, n., sour *tanfula.*

taⁿfula okchi, n., the liquid part of the Indian hominy.

tah may be a particle formed from the definite certain *a* and compounded with *t,* suffixed to the previous word.

tah, a particle in the remote past tense; *ishla tah?* did you come some time since?

tah, adv., assurance against doubt; *minti tah; okaiillit tahatok*, perished in the waters, Matt. 8: 32.

taha, v. a. i., to end; to be gone; to finish; to complete, Josh. 3: 17; 4: 23; 5: 1; Matt. 2: 9; *ont intaiyaha*, he had finished, Matt. 7: 28.

taha, pp., done; gone; finished; completed; exhausted; used; passed; *intaiyaha*, Matt. 11: 1; v. a. i., *alopullit taiyaha*, Josh. 4: 1, 11; *nitak at antahat iahashke*—Mikhobela's speech to his son; *taiyaha*, pro. form.

taha, a., complete; *iktaho*, a., undecayed.

taha, adv., completely; entirely; wholly; perfectly; quite; *holhtinat taha*, Matt. 10: 30; *tahashke*, Matt. 14: 15.

taha, n., the expiration; the end; *ont tahama*, at the end of, 2 Sam. 24: 8.

tahahe keyu, a., unfailing.

tahat ia, v. a. i., to fail; to wear out.

tahbi, v. a. i., to ululate, as a wolf.

tahchabana, n., a suspender; *tahchabankachi*, pl.

tahchi, n., the shoulder, Josh. 4: 5.

tahchi okpatha, tahchi foni, n., the shoulder blade.

tahchonchiya, n., an epaulet.

tahchukah, adv., a word expressing doubt, with an inquiry; see *chukah; tah* implies the recent past tense.

tahpala, v. a. i., to shout; to scream; to halloo; to call after; to exclaim; to shriek; to vociferate; to yell; *tahpalat okla mat*, they (2) cried out; to cry, Matt. 12: 19; 14: 26; 15: 22; *isht tahpala*, v. t.; *tapahanla*, freq.

tahpala, n., a shout; a shouter; an exclamation; an outcry; a shriek; a yell.

tahpali, tahpuli, v. t., to array; to dress, Luke 16: 19; used only with a pronoun, as *ilatapuli*, to dress himself.

tahpalichi, v. t., to array others; to dress another.

tahtua, pp., shaken; flirted.

tahtuli, v. t., to shake; to flirt; to shake off, Matt. 10: 14; *shukbo an tahtuli.*

tak, atak, (the *a* is a prefix particle), adv., usually; commonly; a colloquial word.

taka, pp., scooped; dipped.

takafa, pp., dipped up, as water in a cup.

takakanli, v. a. i., to incubate; to set.

takakanli, v. a. i., to circulate, as *anumpa hat takakanli;* to offer; to be tossed, Matt. 14: 24.

takalechi, takalichi, v. t., to hang; to hitch; to lodge, or cause to hang, as one tree on another; to put forth, Matt. 13: 24; to raise up, Luke 1: 69; to lift up, John 3: 14; to launch out (*pit takalechi*), Luke 5: 4; to enter; to lay on, as an account; to suspend, Josh. 8: 29; to offer, 2 Sam. 24: 12; *itatakalechi*, to concatenate; to link together; to connect; *iti intakalichi*, to clog him; to hang a piece of wood to him.

takali, v. a. i., to hang, Josh. 8: 29; to stand; to stick; to hitch; to lock; to be, Josh. 3: 4; Matt. 2: 9; 6: 21; *iktakalo kawa*, a double neg., Matt. 18: 7; *takant fahakachi*, to tangle.

takali, pp., a., hung; lifted; close; entered; hooked; suspended; *itatakali, itatakali*, pp., hung together; linked together; linked; concatenated; connected.

takali, n., a hanging; an entry; a lodge; a pendant.

takanli, a., imminent; pending.

takant, cont. from *takanlit*.

takant fahakachi, v. a. i., to dangle; to hang and swing.

takastua, a., having corners like a four-square bottle.

takat taha, pp. pl., dipped out.

takabli, takapli, v. a. i., to stop or suppress, like *anukbikeli*.

takaffi, v. t., to dip up; to dip out.

takaffi, n., one who dips.

takaffit kampila, v. t., to retail; to dip and sell.

takaffit kampila, n., a retailer.

takanha, v. a. i., to teeter; to palpitate at the pit of the stomach.

takassa, a., flat and thin, as a china-bean pod; *takaskoa*, pl.

takassa, v. n., to be flat and thin; *bala hakshup at takassa; takaskoa*, pl.

takassalli, v. t., to make flat and thin.

takashi, n., the milt; the spleen; *intakashi*, his milt.

takba, a., bitter; astringent; acrid; acerb; harsh—applied to the eyes.

takba, v. n., to be bitter, astringent, etc.; *uⁿkof ạt takba, bashukcha hishi ạt takba.*

takba, n., astringency.

takbạchi, a., bitterish; somewhat bitter, astringent, etc.

takbạchi, v. n., to be bitterish.

takbạchi, v. t., to render bitter or astringent; to embitter.

takchạka, n., the edge; the margin; the border; the list; *shukbo takchạka, yakni takchạka.*

takchạka ikbi, v. t., to border; to make a border; to margin.

takchạka ikbi, n., one who makes a border.

takchi, v. t., to tie; to bind, Matt. 12: 29; 14: 3; 16: 19; Josh. 2: 21; to enchain; to chain; to hobble; to confine; to lace; to lash; to leash; to restrain; to shackle; *iletakchi,* to tie himself; to thrum; to trammel; to truss; to constrain; to enchain; to fillet.

takchi, n., one who ties.

takchichi, v. t., to tie; *ititakchichi,* to tie together; to bunch; *atakchichi, ạtakchichi,* to tie to.

takchit ishi, v. t., to arrest; to take and bind.

takish intạshka chipota, n., a janizary; a soldier of the Turkish foot guards.

takkon, takon, n., a peach.

takkon aⁿli, n., a clingstone peach.

takkon ạpi, n., a peach tree.

takkon chito, n., an apple.

takkon fakopa, n., a freestone peach.

takkon foni, n., a peach stone.

takkon foni humma, n., a clingstone peach; a red peach stone.

takkon foni nipi, n., a peach meat.

takkon hakshup, n., a peach rind; a peach skin.

takkon hoshiko, n., peach fuzz.

takkon kạllo, n., a clingstone peach.

takkon masuⁿfa, takkon misuⁿfa, n., an apple.

takkon masuⁿfa ạpi, n., an apple tree.

takkon masuⁿfa honni, n., apple sauce.

takkonlạpi, n., a peach tree.

takkonlipun, n., an apple; heard among the Bay or Sixtowns Indians; *lipun* they borrowed from the French la pomme.

takkonlush ạpi, n., a plum tree.

takkonlushi, n., a plum; a wild plum.

takkonłitilli, n., peach-tree gum.

takla, a., being between.

takla, v. n., to be between; *itiⁿtakla,* to be between them; *hạchititakla,* between you, Josh. 4: 6; *itiⁿtakla,* Matt. 18: 2; into, Josh. 2: 19; *ititakla,* among, Josh. 7: 21; *aiitintakla,* through; by means of, Josh. 8: 9; *ițintakla atia,* n., a pass.

takla, taⁿkla, prep. adv., with; among, 1 Kings 11: 20, 21, 22; between; on this side; amid; amidst; till; until, Matt. 1: 23[?]; John 4: 40; *chitakla hikialahe,* 2 Sam. 18: 14.

takla, n., side; *itatakla,* this side of, and between this place and that; *bok itatakla,* between this place and the creek.

taⁿkla, n. f., during; while; along; being with; until; in the way, Matt. 5: 25; 9: 10; 13: 25; 14: 22; 15: 32.

taⁿkla, within, Josh. 1: 11.

taⁿkla aⁿsha, to sit with; to be present.

taⁿkla aⁿya, taklaya, v. a. i., to go along with; to accompany; to attend.

taⁿkla binili, v. a. i., to sit with; to intrude.

taⁿkla binili, n., an intruder; an intrusion.

taⁿkla binoli, v. a. i. pl., to sit with, Matt. 9: 10.

taⁿkla ia, to go with.

taⁿkla minti, v. a. i., to come with.

taklaya, see *taⁿkla aⁿya.*

taklạchi, v. t., to remove this way; to bring this way; *olataklạchi,* to reduce a price; *at, aklạchi,* n., "absence," Luke 20: 6[?]; but it is used here as a verb.

taklechi, v. t., to bring this way; as *olataklechi,* to reduce the price; to get it lower.

takli, v. t. pl., to dip up; to dip out; to ladle; to scoop; "to lap;" *oka taklit ishko, ofi yosh isunlạsh isht takli,* Judges 7: 5, 7.

takli, n., one who dips; a scooper.

takli, n., a dipper; dippers.

takoba, n., the belly; the abdomen; the paunch; the large stomach; the bowels; the maw.

takoba chito, n. and a., pot bellied.

takoba kashofa, pp., evacuated.

takoba kashoffi, v. t., to evacuate.

takoba kucha, pp., emboweled.

takoba kucha, v. a. i., to come out, as the bowels; for the bowels to come out.

takoba kuchi, v. t., to disembowel.

takofa, v. a. i. sing., to slip off; *shakba at takofa*, at the joint.

takofa, pp., slipped off; *takofi*, v. t.

takoinsha, takonwisha, tikoinsha, n., a willow; the common willow.

takoli, v. a. i. pl., to hang; *takohnli*, n. f., Luke 5: 2.

takoli, pp., hung; suspended (with *a* locative), Josh. 10: 26; *itatakoli*, linked together.

takolichi, v. t., to hang them (with *a* locative), Josh. 10: 26; *takoliechi*, pro. form; *takolinchi*, nas. form; *itatakolichi*, to link them together; *itatakolichi*, to link.

takonwisha, see *takoinsha*.

takonwisha naksish falaia, n., the weeping willow.

takshi, n., diffidence.

takshi, a., ashamed; bashful; afraid; timid; modest; abashed; diffident; sheepish.

takshi, v. n., to be ashamed, etc.

takshichi, v. t., to render bashful.

taksho, n., fragments of *tanfula* boilers.

Takshochiya, n., name of a place in the old Nation.

tanktaha, v. a. i., to cackle, as a fowl.

tanktaha, n., a cackling; a cackler.

taktaki, a., spotted; having a dirty color.

taktaki, pp., speckled.

taktaki, v. n., to be spotted; to have a dirty color.

taktakichi, taktakechi, v. t., to spot; to give a dirty color; to speckle.

tala, n., palmetto; also the name of a weed.

talaia, a., situated; stagnant.

talaia, v. a. i. sing., to stand; 2 Kings 9: 27; Matt. 12: 25; 2 Sam. 24: 5; to be, to lie, Matt. 8: 26; 11: 23, to remain; to stagnate, as water; to stand still, *ontalaia*, v. t., to ride; to sit on; to set on, Matt. 5: 14.

talaia, pp., placed; set; *ontalaia*, founded; *talanya*, n. f., standing in, as water or milk in some vessel.

talaia, n., a situation.

talaia, tallaia, n., that which stands, as a spot, a grove, one; a situation; a trail; *lusa talaia*, a black spot; *humma talaia*, a red spot; *bihi talaia; tiak talaia; okla talaia*, one people.

talakchi, pp., tied; bound, Matt. 16: 19; banded; enchained; chained; confined; constrained; corded; laced; lashed; packed; shackled; *ibbak at talakchi; iyi intalakchi; itatalakchi*, bound together; *iktalakcho*, a., unbound; unconfined.

talakchi, a., stiff; as *iyi talakchi; ibbak talakchi*.

talakchi, n., that which is tied; a bundle; a pack.

talali, v. t. sing., to set; to place; to set down; to set forth, John 2: 10; to put, Matt. 5: 15; *ontalali*, to set on; to found; to locate; to spread; *tali paknaka yon inchuka atalalitokan*, which built his house upon a rock, Matt. 7: 24; *shinuk paknaka yon atalalituk*, Matt. 7: 26; *hashi talali*, to change as, or to come out as the moon, i. e., the new moon.

talali, n., one who sets; one who sets on; a setter.

talhpa, n., soapstone; rotten limestone.

talimushi, n., high palmetto.

taliskachi, a. pl., numb, asleep, as a limb, hand, or foot.

taliskachi, v. n., to be numb.

taliskachi, n., numbness.

talissa, a. sing., numb; having the feeling of a limb that is asleep; asleep.

talissa, v. n., to be numb; to be asleep; *iyi at talissa, iyi at kapassat illi*, are expressions of one sense.

talissa, n., numbness.

taloa, talowa, talwa, talloa, v. a. i., to sing; to praise in song; to carol; to chant; to hymn; to tune; *intaloa*, v. t., to praise him; to sing to him; *isht taloa*, to pitch, as a tune; to sound; to warble; *ilhtalwa*, songs, Gen. 31: 27, *iktaloo*, a., unsung.

taloa, n., a ballad; a song; a ditty; music; a psalm, a tune; a warble; a note.

taloa, n., a singer; a chanter; a choir; a minstrel; a songster; a tuner; a warbler.

taloa abachi, n., psalmody.

taloa achukma, n., melody; good singing.

taloa afalamoa, v. a. i., to trill.

taloa aliha, n., a choir; a body of singers.

taloa ikbi, v. t., to make a song, a hymn, or tune; to harmonize.

taloa ikbi, n., a psalmist; a poet.

taloa ikhạnachi, n., a singing master; a music master.

taloa imponna, n., a skillful singer; a musician; a singing master.

taloa isht ia, v. t., to set a tune; to lead in singing.

taloa itilaui, v. t., to harmonize.

taloa tikba heka, n., a chorister.

taloa wạnnichi, v. a. i., to quaver.

taloat abạchi, v. a. i., to practice singing.

taloat takalichi, v. t., to tune.

taloha, v. a. i. pl., to stand; to lie; to be.

taloha, pp., placed; set, Matt. 14: 15; situated, Josh. 14: 1; *ampo hạt taloha.*

taloha, v. n. pl., to be; used to denote plurality, Luke 2: 37; 4: 31[?].

taloha, n., spots; as *lusa taloha, humma taloha.*

talohmaⁿya, v. a. i., to stand around, John 2: 6.

taloli, v. t. pl., to set; to place; to set down a vessel, a plate, a cup, a bucket, etc.

taloli, n., the one who sets, etc.

talot maya, v. a. i., to stand around.

talot maya, n. pl., the bystanders; those who stand around.

talowa, see *taloa.*

taluⁿshik, tạluⁿshik, n., gravel; a pebble.

talako, tạlaka, talakhạtta, n., the gray eagle.

talalaⁿka, talaklaⁿka, and **talalaⁿka,** either or both at once, 1 Kings 6: 31; 10: 19; Josh. 8: 33; Ex. 12: 7 (last best.—J. Edwards).

talapi, a., five; V; 5, Matt. 14: 17, 21; 16: 9; *talampi,* being five; all five; *talampit ia.*

talapiha, adv., five times.

talepa, n., a hundred; 100; C; *talepa tuchina,* John 12: 5.

talepa achạfa, n., one hundred; five score; 100; C; Matt. 13: 8; 18: 12.

talepa sipokni, n., a thousand; 1,000: M; mille; Matt. 14: 21; 15: 38; 16: 9, 10; Josh. 8: 3.

talepa sipokni achạfa, n., one thousand.

talepa sipokni pokoli, n., ten thousand; a myriad.

talepa sipokni talepa sipokni, talepa sipokni bat talepa sipokni, n., a thousand thousand; a million.

talepa sipokni tuklo, n., two thousand, Josh. 3: 4.

talepaha, adv., a hundred times.

tali (cont., *taht*), v. t., to finish (see *taha*); to consummate; to end; v. t., to complete; to exhaust; to make an end of; *ikbit tali; ishkot tali,* to drink and finish, or to drink ale; used as "had" in *itahobit tali,* had called, Matt. 10: 1; *taiyali,* pro. form; to finish, Matt. 13: 53; 17: 11; Josh. 2: 10; *taht kanchi,* to complete the sale or to sell off; to spend, Deut. 32: 23; *ilatali,* 2 Sam. 15: 1; Josh. 4: 23; 5: 1; *iktalo,* a., unexhausted; unspent; *ạbittali,* to kill all, Josh. 8: 21.

tali, n., a finisher.

taloⁿa, n., a sore; *taloⁿa ikhiⁿsh,* vaccine matter; *chilakwa ikhiⁿsh,* vaccine matter (a better name).

talofa, v. a. i., to get out of joint.

talofa, pp., dislocated; luxated; put out of joint; disjointed.

talofa, n., a dislocation; a luxation.

talofa naha, n., a strain.

talofa naha, pp., sprained; strained.

taloffi, a., a luxation.

taloffi, v. t., to dislocate; to luxate; to disjoint.

taloffi naha, v. t., to sprain.

taloha, pp. pl., dislocated; luxated.

taloli, v. t. pl., to dislocate; to luxate.

taluⁿwa, n., ivy; such as grows up and cleaves to oak trees on the side.—Alexander Traver [or Faver.]

tamạffi, see *tomạffi.*

tamampa, v. i., to sound.

tamoli, tạmoli, v. t., to scatter; *oka tamoli,* Ex. 10: 19.

tampki, a., dark; *oklili mạt tampki fehna.*

tanakbi, n., a crook; a hook; a bend; a curve.

tanakbi, a., hooked; crooked; bent; bow bent; curving; *tanantobih,* pl.

tanakbi, v. n., to be hooked, crooked, bow bent, etc.

tanakbi, pp., bended; incurvated.

tanakbichi, v. t., to bend, as a bow; to crook; to hook; to make hooked; to incurvate.

tanamp abeli, v. t., to charge a gun; to load a gun.

tanamp aiulhpi, tanampo aiulhpi, n., a gun stock.

tanamp chito, tanampo chito, n., a cannon; a big gun; a howitzer; a piece of ordnance or artillery; a field piece,

tanamp chito aiisht hunsa achafa, n., a gunshot.

tanamp chito innaki, n., a cannon ball; a cannon shot.

tanamp chito innaki pit akanchi alhpesa, n., a cannon shot; the range or distance which a cannon will throw a ball.

tanamp chito isht atta, n., a cannoneer.

tanamp fabassa, tanampo fabassa, n., a carbine; a musket; a smooth bore gun; a fowling piece.

tanamp fabassa iskitini, n., a fusee.

tanamp hochito, n. pl., cannon; big guns; ordnance; artillery.

tanamp hochito ontukalichi, v. t., to cannonade.

tanamp hoshintika, n., the guard on a gun.

tanamp ikbi, n., a gunsmith.

tanamp imatahshi, tanamp imatakashshi n., the breech of a gun; see tanamp sokbish.

tanamp isht kashokachi, tanampo isht kashokachi, n., a gun stick; a gun wiper; a rammer.

tanamp isht kasholichi, n., a gun stick; a gun wiper.

tanamp lapali, n., a gun lock.

tanamp nihi, n., a gun barrel; the caliber; the bore of a gun.

tanamp nihi chito, n., a large gun barrel; a blunderbuss.

tanamp patali, n., a rifle.

tanamp patali sholi, n., a rifleman.

tanamp puskus, n., a pistol.

tanamp puskus inshukcha, n., a holster.

tanamp sokbish, tanamp imatakashshi, n., the breech or butt end of a gun.

tanamp sokbish isht ashana, n., the screw of a gun at the breech.

tanamp shibata, n., a bow to shoot with.

tanamp shibata isht talakchi, n., a bowstring.

tanamp ushi, n., a pistol.

tanampi, a., hostile; in a state of war; imokla achafa itintanampi, n., an insurrection.

tanampi, v. i., to fight, Josh. 4: 13; 10: 5; tanampit ia, Josh. 8: 3.

tanampi, v. n., to be hostile; to be at war; itintanampi, to be at war with each other; to war; intanahampi, 1 Sam. 15: 18; Josh. 11: 23; itintanampi, n., hostility.

tanampo, n., a gun; a musket; firearms; a firelock.

tanampo ahalalli, n., the trigger of a gun.

tanampo aiulhpi, see tanamp aiulhpi.

tanampo anumpisa, tanampo aianumpisa, n., the sight of a gun.

tanampo anumpisachi, v. t., to take aim; to take sight.

tanampo albiha achafa, n., a charge; one load; a cartridge.

tanampo chito, see tanamp chito.

tanampo fabassa, see tanamp fabassa.

tanampo haksun chiluk, n., the touchhole of a gun.

tanampo isht kashokachi, see tanamp isht kashokachi.

tanampo ittopa, n., the muzzle of a gun; the caliber; the hole; ittopa is the outer hole of a gun barrel or bottle, or an auger hole; also the entrance of such a hole.

tanantobi, a. pl., crooked; bent.

tanantobi, v. n., to be crooked.

tanantobi, n. pl., crooks.

tanantobichi, v. t., to make crooked; to crook; to hook; to bend.

tanapa, pp. sing., put over; passed over; crossed over; wak at bok an tanapa.

tanapoa, pp., pl., put over; passed over; wak at hollihta yan tanapoa.

tanapolechi, v. t. pl., to drive them over; to put over; to cause to go over; to carry over; to ferry over; to get them over; alhpoyak an tanapolechit tali.

tanapoli, auanapoli, v. a. i. pl., to pass over; to cross over; to leap over; okhina yan tanapoli; oklat okhata chito tanapoli.

tanabli, auanabli, abanabli, v. a. i. sing., to pass over, Matt. 9: 1; to go over; to leap over; to get over; to cross over, whether a stream, a creek, a tree, a log, a bridge, a fence, etc., Josh. 2: 23; 3: 1, 6, 14; 4: 11, 12, 13.

tanabli, n., one who crosses over.

tanablichi, v. t., to drive over; to cause another to leap over; to take over; to ferry across, etc.; to bring over, Josh. 7: 7.

tanaffo, v. t., to plait; to braid; to plat; atanaffochi, to weave a basket with strands of different colors; like *apan-ąchi* and *ahokchichi*.

tanąffo, tąnąffo, n., a plaiter; a braider.

tanąllachi, tannąllachi, v. t., to bend; to make it crooked.

tanąllali, v. t., to bend.

tanąlloha, pp. pl., crooked; bent.

tanąlloli, v. t. pl., to bend; to crook.

tanch afotoha, n., a corn mill.

tanch ampi, n., an ear of corn; an ear.

tanch ąpi, n., a cob; a corncob.

tanchi, n., corn; maize; Indian corn, but not English grain or corn.

tanchi aholokchi, n., corn ground; a place where corn is planted.

tanchi ahoyo, n., a place where corn has been gathered.

tanchi apąta, tanchi apatąli, n., a corn sucker.

tanchi habali, n., a corn tassel just put out.

tanchi hakshup, n., a corn husk; a corn shuck.

tanchi hishi, taⁿsh hishi, n., corn leaves; corn fodder; a corn blade.

tanchi hishi sita, taⁿsh hishi sita, n., a bundle of corn fodder.

tanchi hoyo, v. t., to harvest corn; *tanchi ąt hoyot taha*, pp., harvested.

tanchi iⁿpashi, n., corn silk.

tanchi isht ąlhpisa, n., a corn measure; a half bushel, Matt. 5: 15.

tanchi isht pashpoa, tanchi isht bąshpoa, n., broom corn.

tanchi limimpa, n., flint corn; smooth and hard corn.

tanchi pąska, n., corn bread.

tanchi pąska atoba, n., bread corn.

tanchi pushi, n., corn meal, Matt. 13: 33.

tanchi shikoa, taⁿsh shikoa, n., sweet corn.

tani, v. a. i., to rise from a lying posture; to arise, Matt. 2: 13, 14; to rise up; to get up; to rise from the grave; *hatak illi moma kąt tanahioke; micha tanimąt*, and when he arose; *illituk ąt tani*, Matt. 11: 5; 17: 7; *tani cha nowa*, arise and walk, Matt. 9: 5; *tanit*, arise and; *tani cha inchuka iatok*, Matt. 9: 6, 7, Josh. 3: 1; 6: 12; 7: 10.

tani, n., a riser; a stirrer.

tani, n., a rising.

tanichi, v. t., to raise; to cause to rise; to raise to life or from the grave, Matt. 10: 8.

tanip (Eng.), n., a turnip.

tanlakchi, n., a pimple; a pustule; a tubercle, such as appears in the throat when sore, connected with bronchitis; a pimple on the face.

tanlubo, tanlubona. n., hominy.

tannąffo, tąnnąffo, pp., plaited; braided.

tannąffo, n., a plat.

tannąlla, pp., crooked; bent.

tannąllachi, see *tanąllachi*.

tapafakchi, n., prairie hawk; see *ibafakchi* and *hątabafakchi*.

tapąski, v. n., to be thin.

tapąskichi, v. t., to make thin; to thin.

tapena, n., a war club.

taⁿpi, a., very; a Sixtowns word, like *tokba*.

tapuski, tapąski, n., fineness.

tapuski, tapąski, a., thin, as cloth, paper, a board, glass, or the blade of a knife; fine; sleazy; subtle.

tapushiⁿk, n., a flat basket.

tasa, n., heavy lightning; the report of thunder.

tasaha, v. a. i. sing., to whoop; to shout; to scream; to halloo.

tasaha, n. pl., shouters; screamers.

tasaha, n. pl., a shouting; a whooping; a screaming; a yelling.

tasali, tasali, v. a. i. pl., to whoop; to scream; to yell; to shout; *nanta hosh tasali*, Acts 7: 57; *intasali* v. t., to whoop for him.

tasali, n., a shouter.

tasąlli, v. a. i., to be dull or blunt, as the point of a plow; to run down, as rain from a rubber coat.

tasąlli, v. t., to stir the surface of the ground; to plow shallow.

tasąnnuk, n., a flint.

tasembo, pp., crazed; distracted; infatuated; shattered.

tasembo, tasemmo, a., delirious; crazy; wild; besotted; ungovernable; fanatic; frantic; furious; giddy; insane; rabid; lunatic, Matt. 4: 24.

tasembo, tasemo, v. n., to be delirious.

tasembo, v. a. i., to faint; to rave.

tasembo, tasemo, n., craziness; alienation of mind; delirium; frenzy; a fury;

infatuation; insanity; lunacy; madness; mania; rabidness; a reverie; a trance.

tasembŏchi, tasemochi, v. t., to craze; to make anothei delirious; to distract; to infatuate; to render insane; to shatter; to stultify; to turn.

tasemmo, tasemo, see *tasembo.*

tasim holba, a., foolish.

tasimbo, n., a rake; a somnambulist.

tasuha, v. t., to snap with the thumb and finger.

tasup, n., a snap.

tasupachi, v. a. i., to snap; to sound, as when a person thus snaps.

tansh afotoha, n., a corn mill.

tansh akka pushli, n., corn suckers.

tansh apatulli, n., corn suckers.

tansh api, n., a cornstalk; a cob.

tansh api isht peli, n., a harrow.

tansh bokanli, n., pop corn.

tansh chilluka, n., shelled corn.

tansh fotoha, n., ground corn; corn meal.

tansh fotohli, n., a miller.

tansh haklupish, n., corn chaff.

tansh haksi, n., white corn; flour corn.

tansh hilonha, n., a roasting ear.

tansh hinak, n., a corn tassel.

tansh hishi, n., corn fodder; see *tanchi hishi,* and *tanchi hishi sita.*

tansh hoshunluk, tash hishunluk, corn bran.

tansh hoyo, n., corn harvest.

tansh isht alhpisa, n., a corn measure; a bushel of corn.

tansh kallo, n., flint corn.

tansh lakchi, n., corn grits; pimples on the face.

tansh lufa, n., shucked corn.

tansh nihi, n., a kernel of corn; a grain of corn.

tansh panshi, n., corn silk.

tansh panshi holusi, n., corn silk when dry and brown.

tansh pushi, n., beaten corn meal; flour.

tansh shikowa, n., corn tied up by the husks to dry; cf. *tanchi shikoa.*

tansh shila, n., dry corn; ripe corn.

tansh ushi, n., Canada corn; small corn; lit., baby corn.

tansh waya, n., ripe corn.

tansh yammaska, n., corn dough; dough.

tashaiyi, n., an island or isle; that which is surrounded by something, as land by water, as the wood of a handle in the eye of an ax, by the iron of the ax.

tashaya, a., slanting; applied to cutting off a tree when not cut square off.

tashke, particle of assertion of something in remote past tense.

tashukpa, n., spunk; tinder; touchwood.

tashukpa holba, n., a sponge.

tabashi, see *tabashi.*

tabbana, a., bent.

tabbana, v. n., to be bent; *uskilumpa yat tabbana,* the blowgun is bent.

tabbanachi, v. t., to bend; *isht abbanachituk,* you bent it.

tabbannohah, pl. of *tabbonah.*

tabi, n., a cane; a staff; a crutch; a walking stick or staff.

tabi, tambi, n., the termination of the names of many men.

tabi isht bakaha, v. t., to cane.

tabi isht isso, v. t., to cane.

tabikli, v. a. i., to limp.

tabikli, n., a limper.

tabli, tapli, v. t. sing.; *amo* and *taptuli,* pl.; to sever, Matt. 5: 30; to separate; to cut off, Matt. 14: 10; 1 Sam. 2: 31; Josh. 7: 9; to cut in two; to snap; to snip; to sunder; to top; to break in two; to clip; *himonna tabli,* to sever once; to disjoint; *tabli hosh isht anta,* clipping, employed in severing, etc.; to dissever; to dock; *hasimbish tabli.*

tabli, n., a breaker.

tablichi, taplichi, v. t., to cause to sever; to pluck, Luke 6: 1.

tala, v. a. i., to stand; to set; to fix; *ontala,* v. t., to ride; to sit on.

tala, pp., placed; set; *ampo at tala,* the bowl is set or placed.

tala achafa, n., one set; a set.

talaboa, n., an anvil.

talaboli, n., a blacksmith's shop; a forge.

talakabli, n., a stirrup.

talahabli isht talakchi, n., a stirrup strap or stirrup leather.

talashuahchi, tali ashuahchi, n., a grindstone.

talatakali, n., an iron hook; an iron hinge.

talalhpi, n., an iron spoon.

talbansa, n., petrifaction.

talbal, n., a double-wove basket made of the bark of cane.

talbasa, n., the name of a fish.

talhkachi, pl. of tashaiyi, an island; yakni tashayi, pl. yakni talhkachi (yakni, land).

talhko, n., dressed deerskin; buckskin; leather.

talhko ikbi, v. t., to make talhko.

talhko ikbi, n., a talhko maker; a leather dresser.

talhkochi, v. t., to dress skins; to dress a deerskin.

talhpakha, n., a prickly pear.

tali, n., a stone; a rock; iron; metal of all kinds; a mineral; lapis, Matt. 7: 24; 16: 18; tali yon, a stone, Matt. 7: 9; Josh. 4: 3.

tali abila, n., a furnace; an iron furnace; tali abila luak chinto hon, a furnace of fire, Matt. 13: 42.

tali afohoma, n., a ferrule.

tali aholhponi, n., a cooking stove.

tali aholissochi, n., a slate.

tali aiasha, n., a mine.

tali akula, n., a quarry.

tali ashuahchi, talashuahchi, n., a grindstone.

tali bacha, n., a reef; a stone ridge.

tali bashli, n., a stonecutter.

tali bita, n., a headpiece; a helmet.

tali boli, n., a blacksmith.

tali chanakbi, tali chinakbi, n., a hook; an iron hook.

tali chanakbi isht halalli, v. t., to hook.

tali chanli, n., a stonecutter.

tali chanaha, n., an iron ring.

tali chiluk, n., a cave in a rock; a cavern in a rock; a hole in a rock; a chasm, Josh. 10: 16; see hichukbi.

tali chiluk chito, n., a grot; a grotto.

tali chinakbi, tali chanakbi, n., an iron hook; a staple.

tali chishaiyi, n., a claw hammer.

tali chito, n., a rock; a large stone.

tali chito foka, n., rockiness; a rocky region.

tali chito isht talali, n., an anchor.

tali chosopa, n., an iron chain.

tali chufak, n., a pitchfork.

tali falakto, n., an iron fork.

tali fehna, n., cash; silver; coin; precious metals; the very metal.

tali fobassa, tali fabassa, n., an iron pin; an iron bolt; any slender round piece of iron; wire.

tali fobassa honula, n., an iron spindle belonging to a spinning wheel.

tali fobassa ikbi, v. t., to wiredraw.

tali fobassa isht akamassa, pp., bolted; fastened with a bolt.

tali fobassa isht akamassalli, v. t., to bolt; to fasten with a bolt.

tali fobassa isht attapachi, n., a rag bolt.

tali fobassa isht takchi, v. t., to wire.

tali fohoma, n., an iron band; an iron hoop.

tali foka, a., stony; rough; n., a stony region.

tali haksi, n., an iron button; a metal button.

tali haksi akamassa, n., a button hole.

tali haksi chiluk, n., a button hole.

tali haksi chufak, n., brass tacks.

tali haksi ikbi, n., a button maker.

tali haksi mitiffi, v. t., to unbutton.

tali haksi nishkin, n., a button eye.

tali halasbi, n., marble.

tali halupa ontala tabi, n., a spear, Josh. 8: 18.

tali hata, n., silver; white metal, Matt. 10: 9.

tali hata akkoli, v. t., to silver; to plate with silver.

tali hata alhkoha, pp., silvered; silver plated.

tali hata bita, n., a silver hatband.

tali hata chinakbi, n., a silver gorget in the shape of a half moon.

tali hata ikbi, n., a silversmith.

tali hata isht akamassa, n., a silver button.

tali hata isht akmi, n., borax, used in soldering silver.

tali hata isht impa, n., a silver spoon.

tali hatikbi, n., a silversmith.

tali hochito, n. pl., large stones; rocks.

tali hochito foka, n., a rocky region.

tali hochito kaha, n., a ledge of rocks.

tali holihta, n., a stone wall; a wall.

tali holihta ikbi, v. t., to wall.

tali holihta ikbi, n., a waller.

tali holihta isht apakfobli, v. t., to surround with a wall; to wall in.

tali holihta isht apakfopa, pp., walled.

tali holisso, n., coin; cash; money; silver money; a dollar, Matt. 17: 24, 25, 27; coinage; a bit; "iron writing" or "metal writing"; specie; funds; resource; resources; silver; stock in bank.

tạli holisso, pp., coined.

tạli holisso aboli, n., a treasury; a bank, Luke 19: 23.

tạli holisso ahnichi, a., covetous.

tạli holisso aiakmo, n., a mint.

tạli holisso aiakmo intạla, tạli holisso aiakmo apistikeli, n., a mint master.

tạli holisso aiạlhto, n., a coffer; a money purse, box, drawer, etc.

tạli holisso aiạlhtofoki, v. t., to coffer.

tạli holisso aiitahoba, n., receipt of custom, Matt. 9: 9.

tạli holisso aiitạnnali, n., a custom house; the receipt of custom.

tạli holisso aiitola, n., a treasury.

tạli holisso ạlhtoba, n., a disbursement in money.

tạli holisso ikbi, v. t., to make money; to coin money.

tạli holisso ikbi, n., one who makes money; a coiner.

tạli holisso imma, a., pecuniary; relating to money.

tạli holisso inlaua, a., moneyed.

tạli holisso ishi, n., a treasurer.

tạli holisso isht chumpa, n., purchase money.

tạli holisso isht ilawata, n., purse pride.

tạli holisso isht ilefehnạchi, n., a., purse-pride and purse-proud.

tạli holisso inshukcha, n., a money purse.

tạli holisso inshukcha foki, v. t., to purse; to put into a money purse.

tạli holisso itatoba, n., a money changer, John 2: 15; a broker; a banker.

tạli holisso itạnnali, v. t., to tax, Luke 2: 1.

tạli holisso itạnnali, n., a tax gatherer.

tạli holisso lakna, n., gold coin; gold; copper, Matt. 2: 11; 10: 9.

tạli holisso lakna, a., gold; golden.

tạli holisso lakna pilesa, n., a goldsmith.

tạli holisso lakna tạli holisso pokoli aiilli, n., an eagle; a gold coin of the value of ten dollars.

tạli holisso tapuski, n., a bank bill; paper money.

tạli holisso weki, n., a talent.

tạli holitompa, n., a pearl, Matt. 13: 45.

tạli holiya, tạli holuya, n., alum; borax.

tạli ,hollo, tạli hullo, n., a medal; a faced metal.

tạli humma, n., a ruby.

tạli ikbi, v. t., to petrify.

tạli inla fehna, n., the magnetic needle.

tạli inunchi, n., a medal.

tạli isuba kapali, n., bridle bits.

tạli isht afacha, n., a hasp.

tạli isht afinni, n., a crowbar.

tạli isht akamạssa, n., a metal button.

tạli isht ạtta, n., a smith.

tạli isht ạttapạchi, n., a button; a hasp.

tạli isht boa, n., an iron hammer; a hammer.

tạli isht boa, pp., stoned.

tạli isht boa chito, n., a sledge.

tạli isht boli, v. t., to stone, Josh. 7: 25.

tạli isht bot ạbi, v. t., to stone.

tạli isht fotoha, n., a drill.

tạli isht halạlli, n., a clevy or clevis.

tạli isht hokofa, n., a cold chisel.

tạli isht holihtạchi, v. t., to stone; to fence with stone; to wall.

tạli isht holisso, n., a printed book.

tạli isht holissochi, n., a pencil; a silver pen.

tạli isht kiseli, n., tongs; pincers; nippers.

tạli isht lumpa, n., a punch.

tạli isht minko, n., a medal for a chief.

tạli isht patạlhpo, pp., paved; spread with iron or stone.

tạli isht pạla, n., an iron wedge.

tạli isht talakchi, n., an iron button.

tạli isht tạna, n., a knitting needle.

tạli isht tạpa, n., a cold chisel; a chisel for cutting iron.

tali isht weki, n., a poise; a weight used with scales.

tạli itạchaka, tạli itạchakạlli, n., welded iron.

tạli itichạnaha apakfoa, n., a cart tire; a wagon tire; a tire for wheels.

tạli ititakạlli, n., an iron chain.

tạli iyạlhki, n., slag; dross.

tạli iyi isht ạlbi, n., fetters, Luke 8: 29.

tạli kạllo, n., steel; hard iron.

tạli kạllo atoba, a., steel; made of steel.

tạli kạllo ạchaka, pp., steeled.

tạli kạllo ạchukạlli, v. t., to steel.

tạli kạssa, n., thimbles worn as ornaments, so called from their tinkling.

tạli kolofa, n., a stump of iron; a plug or remnant of iron.

tạli kucha achạfa, n., a broach of yarn.

tạli lakna, n., brass; copper, Matt. 10: 9.

tạli lakna ikbi, n., a coppersmith.

tạli lakna isht ạlhkoha, pp., gilded or plated with brass.

tạli lakna isht ạlhkohachi, v. t., to gild; to plate with brass.

tạli lapali, pp., shod.

tạli lapalichi, v. t., to shoe, as a horse.

tạli laua, a., stony.

tạli luak, n., a steel used in striking fire from a flint.

tạli luak tikeli, n., an andiron.

tạli lumbo, n., a marble.

tạli lusa, n., a mole; a spot or mark, etc., on the human body.

tạli patali, v. t., to pave.

tạli patapo, tạli patạlhpo, n., a pavement.

tạli patạssa, n., a flatiron; a sad iron.

tạli pạta, n., a pavement.

tạli pilefa, n., a rivet.

tạli pilesa, n., a smith.

tạli połoma, n., a steel spring which is doubled up.

tạli połoma ushi, n., a small steel spring.

tạli shạna, n., an iron screw; twisted iron; a worm; the worm of a screw.

tạli shạna shuⁿfi, v. t., to unscrew.

tạli shiloha, tạli shilowa, n., small, round bells used as ornaments on shoes, etc., or garters.

tạli shiloha chito, n., a sleigh bell.

tạli shiluⁿhạchi, n., small, round bells.

tạli shochukshoa, n., stone formed from sand; sandstone.

tạli shuti, n., a stone pot, John 2: 6.

tạli tanakbi, n., an iron hook.

tạli tanch afotoha, tạli tanchi bołoli, n., a mill stone.

tạli tapạski, n., sheet iron; thin iron.

tạli toba, v. a. i., to petrify; to become stone.

tạli toba, pp., petrified.

tạli toba, n., a petrifaction.

tạli ulhtikeli, n., an andiron.

tạli uski, n., a poise; a weight.

tạliⁿ yạlhki, n., slag; the dross of metals.

tạliko, see *tiliko*.

tạlissa, n., numbness.

tạlissa, a., numb.

tạlissa, tạmissa, v. n., to be numb.

tạlissạchi, tạmissạchi, v. t., to numb; to render numb; to stun; *ibbak tạmissạchi*.

tạlkanchi; *itontạlkanchi*, to lie on, Matt. 24: 2; Luke 21: 6.

tạlli, v. n., to be scattered about, like grains of corn on an ear which is not full.

tạlli, a., scattered about, but standing.

tạlloa, see *taloa*.

tạlua, taloa (q. v.), v. t., v. a. i., to sing.

tạlukchi, n., a precious metal.

tạlukchi onchiya, tạluk onchiya, n., an epaulet.

tạlukchi tahchonchiya, n., an epaulet, the name in full.

tạlula, n., a bell (a word in use among the Sixtowns people).

tạluli, v. t., fixed; located.

tạluskula, n., a jewsharp.

tạlushik, tạluⁿshik, taluⁿshik, n., gravel; pebbles.

tạlushik patali, v. t., to gravel.

tạlushik patạlhpo, pp., graveled.

tạlwa, pp., sung; hymned; see *taloa*.

tạła, pp., whittled; pointed; hewed; *iti tila*, hewed timber; *tạlali*, hewn, as stone, Ex. 20: 25; *isht tạlachi*, a tool for hewing stone, Ex. 20: 25.

tạłaⁿhạta, n., name of a bird.

tạłaka, see *talako*.

tạłi, v. t., to hew; to whittle; to point.

tạłi, n., a hewer.

tạłichi, v. t., to sharpen.

tạmaha, n., a town; a village; a borough; a city; Matt. 8: 33, 34; 9: 1; 11: 1, 20; *ilap intạmaha*, his own city, Matt. 9: 1; *tạmaha hash osh momạt*, the whole town, Matt. 8: 34.

tạmaha chito, n., a great town; a city; a capital.

tạmaha hatak, n., a townsman.

tạmaha holihta, n., a city, 1 Sam. 1: 3; 2 Sam. 24: 5, 7; Josh. 6: 3, 11; 8: 1, 12, 19.

tạmaha wehpoa, pp., sacked.

tạmaha wehpulli, v. t., to sack a town.

tạmahichi, v. t., to benumb with cold.

tạmahushi, n., a small town or village; a hamlet; a villa, Matt. 14: 15.

tạmanchi, v. a. i., to buffet.

tạmissa, tạlissa, v. a. i., to be numb.

tạmissạchi, tạlissạchi, v. t., to benumb; to produce this sensation by a slight blow.

tammaha, v. t. pl., to strike with the part of the hand next the wrist.

tammalichi, v. t. sing., to strike once with the heel or the hand.

tammoli, pl. tr., to blind the eyes, 1 John 2: 11.

tamoa, v. a. i. pl., to wander; to go astray, Matt. 18: 13; to perish, as the eyes; to stray.

tamoa, pp., wandered; lost; gone astray, like sheep, Matt. 10: 6; 15: 24.

tamoli, see tamoli.

tana, v. t., to knit; to weave; to plait; to thrum; to wattle; atanachi, to weave with, i. e., to weave together, Judges 16: 13; where the locks of Samson's hair were to be woven with a web; see ahokchichi, Matt. 13: 25, where tares are sown with wheat.

tana, n., a knitter; a weaver.

tanaffo, tanaffo (q. v.), v. t., to plait.

tanap, n., an enemy, Matt. 5: 43, 44; a foe, Matt. 10: 36; 13: 25; Josh. 7: 8; an antagonist; an opponent; an army; intanap imilayak, booty; a fiend; intanap ala, to come over to the enemy; war; warfare; a warrior; a war, 1 Kings 22: 1; 1 Chron. 22: 8.

tanap ahalaia, a., martial.

tanap anumpuli, n., a secretary of war.

tanap anumpuli aiasha, n., a war office.

tanap anya, v. a. i., to go on a campaign, Josh. 5: 4.

tanap anya, n., a campaign; men of war, Josh. 5: 4; 8: 1.

tanap anya tikambi, a., war-beaten; warworn.

tanap holba, a., warlike.

tanap holihta, n., a barricade; a palisado.

tanap isht ashwanchi, v. t., to war.

tanap toba, v. a. i., to become an enemy; itintanap toba, to become enemies to each other.

tanna, pp., wove; woven; knit; plaited; knitted; wattled; linen tanna, 1 Sam. 2: 18.

tanna, n., that which is wove, knit, etc.; texture; a web; a weft.

tannaffo, tannaffo, pp., plaited.

tannap, n., the opposite side; one side; mishtannap, the other side, Josh. 2: 10; misha intannap, the other side of it,

Matt. 8: 18, 28; intannap, the other, Matt. 5: 39; sachunkash intannap at yukpa, sachunkash intannap at nukhanklo; intannap akinli hon chohmitok, like, as the other.

tapa, v. a. i., to sever; to come apart.

tapa, pp., severed; parted; broken in two; clipped; disjointed; dissevered; separated; topped; noshkobo tapa, beheaded; tabli, v. t.

tapa, n., a break; a separation.

tapahe keyu, a., irresistible.

tapak, n., a basket.

tapintapi, n., a break; name of a weed that grows in wet places.

tapishuk, tapishik, for tappakushi, a smaller basket than the tapak.

tapli, see tabli.

taplichi, see tablichi.

taptua, v. a. i. pl., to come apart; to separate; to sever.

taptua, pp., parted; severed; separated; cropped.

taptua, n., a separation.

taptuli, v. t. pl., to sever; to separate; to crop; to nip off, Josh. 5: 2, 3, 4.

tashiha, v. a. i., to have corners, or sharp edges, or ridges, as a rail, a hand iron, etc.

tashioha, pl. of above.

tashka, n., a warrior; a subject; a political dependent or adherent, male or female; a constituent; a yeoman.

tashka aliha, n., the yeomanry.

tashka chipota, n., a soldier; a regular; an army; a host; infantry; the military; militia; a private; hosts, 2 Sam. 24: 2, 4; soldiery; a train band; a troop; tashka chipota aleha, soldiers, Matt. 8: 9.

tashka chipota aheli, n , a post; a military post.

tashka chipota aiasha, n., a cantonment; a barrack; a garrison.

tashka chipota aiasha ashachi, v. t., to garrison.

tashka chipota holhtina, n., a regiment.

tashka chipota inchuka, n., a cantonment; a barrack; soldiers' quarters.

tashka chipota isht shema, n., regimentals; military ornaments; uniform.

tạshka chipota itạnnaha, n., pp., paraded.

tạshka chipota itạnnali, v. t., to muster; to parade.

tạshka chipota miⁿka, n., a fellow-soldier.

tạshka chipota peni aⁿsha, n., a marine; marines.

tạshka chipota tałepa hanali, n., a cohort.

tạshka chipota ushta, n., a quaternion; four soldiers.

tạshka chuka, tạshka chukka, n., a bone-house; an ossuary; a charnel house, used in ancient times to lay away boxes containing the bones of the dead.

tạshka paⁿya, v. a. i., to whoop at the grave when the poles are pulled to drive away ghosts, etc.

tạshka paⁿya, n., the death whoop.

tạshka sepokni, n., a veteran soldier; a veteran.

tạshki, v. a. i., to lie down; to recline, 1 Sam. 3: 3, 5, 6; Josh. 2: 8.

tạshki, a., recumbent.

tạshkichi, v. t., to lay down; to cause to lie down.

te, a nearly obsolete conj., used by old-fashioned speakers, the same as t; ai-ahnite, instead of aiahnit, etc.

tebli, tepli, tibli (q. v.), v. t., to touch, Matt. 17: 7; tepoa, pl.

teha, tiha, pp., plucked up; pulled up; tanchi ạt tiha, paⁿshi ạt tiha, onush ạt tiha; tihat taha, extirpated; rooted up, Matt. 15: 13.

teha, v. a. i., to come up by the roots.

tek, n., a female.

tek, a., female; she, as a she-bear (nita tek).

tekchi, n., a wife; a consort; a woman who is united to a man in the lawful bonds of matrimony, Matt. 5: 31; 8: 14; 14: 3.

tekchi, v. a. i., to be a wife; mihma ita-tuklot tekchit oklatok, 1 Sam. 25: 43; Gen. 34: 8.

tekchi iksho, n., a bachelor; a single man.

tekchi illi, n., a widower.

tekchi inlaua, n., polygamy.

tekhanto, n., a large wasp called a mud-dauber.

telihpa, n., a shield, 1 Kings 10: 16. See tilikpi (hymn 67, 4th verse).

teli, v. t. pl., to pull up; to pluck up; to extirpate.

teli, n., one who pulls up; a plucker.

tema, v. a. i., to strut, as a turkey cock.

tepa, sing., hotepa, pl., v. a. i., go ye ahead; start on.

tepli, see tebli.

tepoa, pp. pl., overhauled; tiapa, sing.

tepuli, v. t. pl., to overhaul; to take out, as itombi aⁿ tepuli, to look over the things in a trunk; tiạbli, sing.

tepuli, n., one who overhauls.

ti (Eng.), n., tea.

ti ahoni, n., a teapot.

ti aiạlhto, n., a tea canister.

ti isht ishko, n., a teacup.

tiak, n., pine; lightwood; pine wood; a turpentine tree.

tiak faⁿya, n., longleaf pine.

tiak foka, n., a piny region; piny.

tiak foka, a., piny.

tiak hobạk, n., yellow pine.

tiak iⁿpalạmmi, n., the name of a weed used by some Choctaw as a remedy for the bite of venomous serpents.

tiak iⁿsinti, n., the "diamond" rattlesnake.

tiak isht pạla, n., an iron wedge; any instrument used in splitting pine wood.

tiak isht shima, n., a frower used in splitting pine; where pine is the most common timber used in making shingles tiak isht shima is used.

tiak nia, n., tar; turpentine.

tiak nia ahama, pp., tarred.

tiak nia ahạmmi, v. t., to tar.

tiak nia atoba, n., a tar kiln.

tiak nia bano, a., tarry.

tiak nia kạllo, n., rosin; pitch; shoe maker's wax.

tiak nia lua, n., pitch.

tiak piⁿkshi, n., a pine knot.

tiak shima, n., a pine shingle; a pine board rived; riven pine.

tiak shoboli tułak, n., lampblack.

tiak shua, n., snake root.

tiak ushi, n., young pine.

tiapa, v. a. i., to scatter, Josh. 6: 5; to separate; to break down; to disperse; oklat tiapa, the people scatter; itatiapa, John 7: 53; tepia, pl.

tiapa, pp., broken down; scattered; over-hauled; razed; ruined; stirred; *oklat tiapa*, the people are dispersed, see 1 Sam. 3: 1, open; *mali fehna na chuka yat tiapat taha; tiabli*, v. t.

tiapa, n., a dispersion; a breaking down.

tiabli, v. t., to break down; to throw open; to scatter; to overhaul; to raze; to ruin; to unpack; to unroof; to open, Matt. 2: 11; *itatiabli*, to stir; to agitate; to divide; *aboha yaⁿ tiabli; na bonunta ishtiabli na; holihta yaⁿ tiabli; itiablit hoyo*, v. t., to rummage; pass. *tiapa*.

tiablit pisa, v. t., to ransack; to rummage.

tiapakachi, pp. pl., scattered; broken down; dispersed.

tibafa, v. a. i., to cave in, as *sakti at tibafa oka atibafah*.

tibafa, pp., caved in; *tibali*, pl.

tibaffi, v. t., to make the ground cave in; *tibalichi*, pl.

tiballi, v. a. i., to glance off; to hit and glance off; to hit and fly off sideways; *naki at tiballi, iskifa yat tiballi; iyi at tiballi*, to slip up or off.

tibikshi, a., round and large, applied to hard lumps formed in the flesh; see 1 Kings 7: 20, 41, 42 (where it is *kibiksht*).

tibikshi, n., a knob or knot.

tibikshi, see *kibikshi*.

tibiⁿllichi, v. t., to cause to hit and glance, or fly off sideways.

tibli, v. t., to touch; see *tebli*.

tiⁿfa, v. a. i. sing., to come up by the roots; *teha*, pl.

tiⁿfa, pp., pulled up; plucked up.

tiⁿfi, v. t., to pull out or up; to pluck, as *haiyukpulo aⁿ tiⁿfi; hoshinchi aⁿ tiⁿfi*.

tiha, see *teha*.

tikabi, v. a. i., to flag; to tire; to languish; *satikabi*, I am tired; *tikambi*, to fade; to faint; to wear.

tikabi, a., pp., tired; weary; exhausted; weakened, as by sickness; debilitated; enervated; faint; Matt. 15: 32; fatigued; harassed; faded; languid; overdone; tiresome; weakened; worried; *tikambi*, pp., *tikambi*, a., dull; enervate; feeble; frail; weak; weary; *iktikambo*, a., un-wearied; *tikambahe keyu*, a., untirable.

tikabi, v. n., to be tired, weary, etc.; debilitated; *tikambi*, to be dull.

tikabi, n., weariness; fatigue; languor; lassitude; *tikambi*, n., weakness; a weariness.

tikabichi, v. t., to tire; to weary; to jade; to spend; to worry; *iletikabichi*, to weary himself; *tikambichi*, v. t., to dull; to enervate; to fatigue; to harass; to macerate; to weaken; to wear, as an ax or millstone; to weary, Josh. 7: 3; *iskifa issantikambichi*, you have dulled my ax.

tikachi, v. a. i., to chick; to click.

tikafa, v. a. i., to shed the hair; to molt, as fowls.

tikaffi, v. t., to pick off the hair; see *tikafa*.

tikba, n., the van; an ancestor; *pintikba*, our fathers, John 4: 20; the face; the first begot; the foreside; the head; the original.

tikba, a., forward; precedent; primary; *itikba*, before; *shuka itikba*, Matt. 7: 6; Josh. 3: 6; in the sight of, Josh. 3: 7, 14.

tikba, adv., in front; ahead; first; forth; forward; prep., before; *tikba ayali*, I go along ahead; *itikba*, before the face of, Luke 2: 31; before him, her, or it; *intikba*, before him, Matt. 5: 12, and *chitikba, satikba; intikba hakshup*, his fore-skin.

tikba, v. n., to be ahead.

tiⁿkba, adv., prep., distinctive, first, Matt. 12: 29; John 1: 30, 41; formerly; anciently; before time; aforetime; before; former; heretofore, 1 Sam. 4: 7; Matt. 5: 24; first, Matt. 13: 30; 14: 22; 17: 10; Josh. 3: 4; 8: 33.

tiⁿkba, a., former; prior; antecedent; first; firstborn; fore; original; aboriginal; previous.

tiⁿkba, v. n., to be former; to be prior; to be hereafter, or first hereafter.

tikba anoli, v. t., to forbode; to foretell.

tikba apesa, v. t., to preconcert; to fore-judge.

tikba atali, v. t., to prefix.

tikba atokuli, v. t., to forechoose; to foreordain.

tikba aⁿya, tikbaⁿya, v. t., to perambulate; to precede.

tikba alhpisa, pp., preconcerted.

tikba alhtuka, pp., forechosen.

tikba annoa, pp., forewarned.

tikba atta, v. a. i., to be born the first.

tikba atta, n., the firstborn.

tikba chạfichi, v. a. i., v. t., to protrude.

tikba chumpạt aiishi, v. t., to forestall.

tikba fehna aⁿya, a., foremost.

tikba heka, v. a. i., to guide; to conduct; to lead.

tikba heka, n., a leader; a guide; a pilot; a conductor; a guider.

tikba hilechi, v. t., to prefix.

tikba holhtina, pp., forechosen.

tikba hotina, v. t., to forechoose.

tikba kaɫi, v. t., to put or place before, as in putting wood to the fire; *tikba kahpuli*, pl.

tiⁿkba okla, n., the aboriginal inhabitants; the aboriginal people.

tikba pisa, v. a. i., to scout; also n., a scout.

tikba pisa, v. t., to foresee; to forecast.

tikba tobli, v. t., to protrude.

tiⁿkbaha, adv., formerly; previously; at a previous time.

tikbaiachi, see *tikbiachi*.

tikbaɫi adv., beforehand; in advance; forward; *tikbaɫi fạllokạchi*, to go backward and forward in advance; *tikbaɫi aiowạtta*, to hunt beforehand, or in advance; *tikbanɫi*, n. form, being in advance; along before; a., early, Matt. 11: 10.

tikbaɫi, v. n., to be beforehand; "to prevent", Matt. 17: 25; *tikbaɫichi, tikbaɫint*, contraction of *tikbaɫinchit*.

tikbama, adv., heretofore.

tikbanɫi anoli n., a diviner; a prognosticator; a predictor; a prophesier; a soothsayer; *nana tikbanɫi anoli*, n., prophecy.

tikbanɫi anoli anumpa, n., a prediction; a prophecy.

tikbanɫi apesa, v. t., to predetermine; to predestinate.

tikbanɫi ikhana, n., prescience; foreknowledge.

tikbanɫi imanoli, v. t., to forewarn.

tikbanɫi imanukfila, n., a prejudgment; prejudice.

tikbanɫi iⁿmiha, v. t., to premonish; to precaution; to instruct before, Matt. 14: 8.

tikbanɫi ishi, v. t., to preoccupy; to prepossess.

tikbanɫit anoli, v. t., to divine; to foretell; to predict; to prognosticate; to prophesy.

tikbanɫit anukfilli, v. t., to prejudge; to premeditate.

tikbanɫit ithana, v. t., to foreknow.

tikbanɫit ithana, n., foreknowledge.

tikbanɫit pisa, v. t., to foresee.

tikbanɫit pisa, a., prospective.

tikbashalika, v. a. i., to be first and quickly; to get ready soon.

tikbaⁿya, tikba aⁿya, n., a harbinger; a forerunner; a precursor.

tikbaⁿya, a., headmost.

tikbaⁿya hinikbi, n., a pioneer.

tikbiachi, tikbaiachi, v. t., to impel; to cause to go forward.

tikbichi, v. t., to fix up a fire or to put the burnt sticks up together; *luak tikbichi*.

tikeɫi, v. a. i., to press; to press against; to reach or to touch, as the ends of a stick when lying in a horizontal position, as a round in a ladder; *tikinɫi*, nas. form, *pitikinɫi*, Luke 5: 8; *atikeɫi*, 2 Sam. 14: 30, 32; *tikoɫi*, pl., *itạttekiɫi*, to put endwise together for a fire, as the Choctaw do outdoors; *iti ititekiɫi*, pl., rafters, *iti ititikeɫi*, sing., a rafter.

tikeɫi, n., *tikoɫi*, pl., a prop; a buttress; a support; a brace used in the frame of a building; a wooden tenter; a shore; a slat; a stay; stays; a support; a supporter.

tikeɫi, pp., stretched, as a skin when hung up to dry; propped; racked; scotched; shored; *isi hakshup tikeɫi*, a deer skin stretched on cane and hung up; *tikoɫi*, pl.

tikeɫichi, v. t., to stretch; to hang on tenters; to prop; to rack; to scotch; to shore; *haksobish tikeɫichi hosh hạshhaklokạt* Matt. 10: 27; *itatikeɫichi*, to cause to touch each other, Gen. 50: 1; *tikoɫichi*, pl.

tikilbi, see *tiɫikpi*.

tiⁿkliha, v. i., to growl, as a cross dog.

tiⁿklish, n., the brisket of an ox.

tikoiⁿsha, takoiⁿsha, tokoiⁿsha, n., a willow.

tikoiⁿsha naksish falaia, n., a weeping willow.

tikpi, n., a bulb; a swell, as a cypress knee or bulb; a bend in a water course.

tikshạneɫi, n., a dictionary; a lexicon.

tiⁿkti, n., a large red-headed woodpecker.

tiⁿktiⁿkachi, v. a. i., to twang.

tiktikechi, v. t., to spot.

tiktiki, a., spotted; having small spots.

tiktiki, v. n., to be spotted with small spots.

tiliko, taliko, n., wheat (a Chickasaw word).

tiliko bota, n., wheat flour.

tiliko palaska, n., wheat bread.

tiliko palaska iskatini, n., a biscuit; a wheat cake.

tilikpi, a., blunt; dull (as an old ax).

tilikpi, tikilbi, telihpa, n., an ancient kind of shield, made of stiff hide of a cow, or of an alligator, and tied to the body; a target. This word was not generally known in 1854. See 1 Kings 10, 17; *telihpa* is the modern word, while *tilikpi* is the old word.

tilofa, a., pp., broken off; abridged; short; laconic; *anumpa tilofa*, a short talk or speech; *iti tilofa*, a stump.

tilofa, v. n., to be short.

tilofa, v. a. i., to break, 1 Sam. 4: 18.

tilofasi, a., shortish; short; brief; succinct; the diminutive of *tilofa; anumpa tilofasi kia chiaiokpachelachi hoke.*

tiloffi, v. t., to break short off; *bashpushi an tiloffi*, to break the blade of a penknife; *noti an tiloffi*, to break off a tooth; *noti an bolit tiloffi*, to strike and break off a tooth.

tiloha, a., pp., pl., short; broken off; abridged; *iti tiloha; anumpa tiloha; noti tiloha.*

tiloha, v. n., to be short.

tilokachi, a. pl., loose and standing up (not hanging down), and so as to bend or swing backwards and forwards, as at a joint or as the broken limb of a tree; *ibbak tilokachi*, the wrist joint.

tilokachi, v. n. pl., to be loose, so as to swing; *iti at tilokachi.*

tilokachi, n., a joint; *ibbak tilokachi*, wrist joint; *ibbak ushi tilokachi.*

tiloli, v. t., v. a. i., pl., to break off short; *noti at tiloli.*

tilolichi, v. t., to break them off, Matt. 12: 20, (reeds).

tilukachi, v. a. i., to say *tiluk*, the noise when anything hard is broken off, equal to saying *tilofa*, and used in speaking of a joint snake when broken in two.

tila, n., a mark.

tila, pp., marked; hewed; blazed, as a tree.

tilaya, v. a. i. dual and pl., to run; to flee; *tilahanya*, pl., 2 Sam. 15: 1, *falamat kehotilaya.*

tilaya, n., runners.

tilaya, pp., driven out.

tilayachi, v. t. to run.

tilefa, pp., squeezed; *hichi at tilefa.*

tileli, v. t. pl., to drive out, Matt. 14: 35; Josh. 3: 10; 13: 6, 13; to expel; to send, Matt. 2: 8; 10: 16; 11: 2; 13: 36; 14: 15, 35; Mark 11: 1; to make them run; to run; to drive, 2 Kings; 9: 21; to send, Josh. 7: 2, 22; 8: 3; *anshat tileli*, to send from, John 1: 19; *tilihinli*, freq.; *tilit*, contracted form.

tileli, n., driving, *tileli kat*, the driving, 2 K. 9: 20.

tilelichi, v. t., to cause to go, Gen. 45: 24.

tili, v. t., to blaze; to mark a tree; to hew; to whittle.

tili, n., a marker.

tilichi, v. t., to sharpen a stick by cutting; to bring to a point; to sharpen wood with an edge tool; to whittle.

tiliffi, v. t., to squeeze with the fingers; *hichi an tiliffi.*

tilit hobachit ikbi, v. t., to sculpture.

tiloa, pp., pl., squeezed.

tiloli, v. t. pl., to squeeze.

timihachi, v. a. i., to hum; to buzz, as bees; *foe bilishke at timihachi.*

timihachi, n., a buzzing; a stir.

timikachi, v. a. i., of the beating of a drum; to sound, as a drum; *alepa yat timikahanchi na haklot ayali*, I heard the beating of a drum as I came along.

timikli, v. a. i., to beat; to throb; to palpitate; *chunkash at timikli.*

timikmekli, timikmikli, v. a. i., to beat, as the heart.

timikmeli, timikteli, v. a. i., to beat quick; to throb; to pulsate; *sachunkash at timikteli*, my heart beats hard; *timiktinli*, n. f.

timikteli, pp., thumping, fluttering.

timpi, n., the shoulder or swell of a bottle near the neck.

tipelichi, v. t. sing., to strike; to smite with the hand, fist, or a stick, but to strike something soft, as a bed or the flesh; *ikkishi akon tipelichi, topa han ti-*

pelichi; when anything hard is struck say *sakalichi.*

tipiⁿha, v. t. pl., to strike any soft substance.

tipiⁿha, n., a striker.

Tisimba, n., December.

tisheli, v. a. i. pl., to scatter; to disperse; to retire; to rise, as a court; *oklat tisheli.*

tishelichi, v. t. pl., to send away, Matt. 14: 22; 15: 32, 39.

tishepa, a., v. n., scarlet; fiery red, Josh. 2: 18; n., scarlet.

tishi homi, hishi homi (q. v.), n., pepper.

tishi homi aialhto, n., a pepper box; a pepper bag.

tishi homi humma, n., red pepper; Guiana pepper; Cayenne pepper; capsicum.

tishi homi lusa, n., black pepper.

tishi humma, n., red paint; vermilion; rouge; *tishi humma isht ilanchali,* he paints himself with vermilion.

tishihachi, v. a. i., to sputter.

tiⁿshkila, n., a jay; a blue jay.

tishu, n., a waiter; a servant, Josh. 1: 1; a man servant; one who attends a chief to light his pipe, make his fire, etc.; *intishu,* an escort; a groom; a lackey; a page; a servitor; a valet; an eunuch; a chamberlain, 2 Kings, 9: 32; *antishu,* my servant, Matt. 8: 6, 8; 10: 25; 13: 27.

tiwa, tua, v. a. i., to open; to burst open.

tiwa, tua, pp., opened, Matt. 7: 7; unlocked; unfolded; unsealed; unstopped, Luke 3: 21; Matt. 3: 16; Josh. 8: 17; open, John 1: 51; *iktiwo,* a., unopened.

tiwakachi, int. pl., to stir, or to be in commotion.

tiwalichi, v. t., to stir up, as coffee while boiling, with a spoon.

tiwi, tuwi, v. t., to open; to unlock, Matt. 6: 19, 20.

tiwichi, tuwichi, v. t., to cause to open, Matt. 2: 11.

to, adv. in *amalla at amilli to!,* are my children dead? meaning that he had no knowledge of it, but, having heard so, makes the inquiry. This refers to a remote past time, and should not have a *t* suffixed to the verb it joins, as *illi to.*

toba, v. a. i., to make; to rise; to arise; *tobat kocha,* to form and come out, Matt. 8: 24; 13: 26; to be born, John 1: 13; to be made; to become, Matt. 13:32; to be, Matt. 5:32; to come; *tomba,* intensive; *na hollo ishtoba,* you have become or you are a white man; *tohumba* freq. form, John 1: 12;. *aba anumpuli toba,* to become a Christian; *achukma toba, kallo toba, nuna toba; atoba,* born of, Matt. 11: 11; to proceed out of, Matt. 15: 19.

toba, n., creation; a fabrication; a make; workmanship.

toba, a., step, as *ishke toba,* a stepmother.

toba, v. i., to be able; as *hikikia toba,* able to walk about; *ititoba,* to become each others, i. e., to exchange; *itatoba* (from *iti* reciprocal, *a* locative, and *toba*), v. t., to trade.

toba, pp., created; made; fabricated; formed; generated; raised; wrought; *iktobo,* a., unmade; *isht atoba,* by whom made, Matt. 18: 7.

tobachi, v. a. i., to ripen; *shukshi at tobachi,* the watermelon is getting ripe; *luak aⁿ ont tobachi,* go and make the fire blaze.

tobachi, v. t., to create; to make; to beget; *atobachi,* to beget of or by, Matt. 1: 2; *Tama yaⁿ atobachi,* Matt. 1: 3.

tobahchih, v. a. i., to make a noise by beating on a house.

tobaksakula, n., a fossil coal pit; a coal mine.

tobaksatoba, toboksi atoba, n., a coal pit.

tobaksi, n., a coal; a fire coal; coal.

tobaksi ikbi, v. t., to make coal; to coal.

tobaksi ikbi, n., a collier.

tobaksi inchuka, n., a coal house.

tobaksi kulli, n., a collier; a coal digger.

tobaksi lusa ohmi, n., coal-black.

tobaksi mosholi, n., charcoal.

tobbona, a., bent over; stooping; bowed down; curvated.

tobbona, v. n., to be bent over; *iti at tobbona,* the tree is bent over; *kato at tobbona,* the cat is humped up.

tobbona, n., a curve.

tobbonachi, v. t., to curve; to make crooked.

tobbonali, v. t., to bend; *uski aⁿ tobbonali.*

tobbonnoa, tobbonoha, v. n., to be crooked; *uski at tobbonoha; kato at tobbonoa*, curved, as an angry cat.

tobbonoa, tobbonoha, a. pl., crooked; bent.

tobbonoli, v. t. pl., to bend; *itipushi an tobbonoli*, to bend the saplings.

tobe hollo, n., a pea; peas.

tobe isht abela, n., a bean pole.

tobela, v. a. i., to be well on fire.

tobi, tubi, n., a bean; beans.

tobi abela, n., pole beans.

tobi hikint ani, n., bush beans; bunch beans.

tobi uski atuya, n., pole beans.

tobi uski oiya, n., pole beans.

tobli, v. t., to push; to press against; to hunch; to jog; to jostle; to propel; to resist; to shove; to thrust; *ititobli*, to push each other; *peni itintoblit isht anya*, they pushed the boat along together; *shunkani isht tobli*, to hunch; *tombli*, nas. form; *tohombli*, freq. form; *toyubli*, pro. form.

tobli, n., a pusher; a jogger; a thruster.

tobli, n., a push; a hunch; a jog; a shove; a thrust.

tobli aba isht ia, v. t., to boost.

toblichi, v. t., to cause to push; *iti chanalli toblichi*.

tobohachi, v. a. i., to roar.

tobokachi, v. a. i., to gurgle.

toboksi atoba, see *tobaksatoba*.

tobosinli, v. a. i., to close one eye.

toboshakchi, n., a log of wood.

tobunlli, v. a. i., to boil up, as water, in a spring; *tobohonli*, freq.

tobulli, pp., roiled.

tobulli, a., roily.

tobullichi, v. t., to cause water to boil up; to roil.

toffa, v. n., to be summer; *tonfa*, being still summer.

toffa, tofa, n., summer; the summer season.

toffa anta na lopulli, v. a. i., to summer.

toffah iklanna, n., midsummer.

toffahpi, n., spring; the first part of summer; the vernal season.

toffahpi, a., vernal.

toffokoli, a., faded; dim.

toffokoli, v. n., to be dim or faded.

toh, a particle in recent past tense; *ishla toh?* have you just come? See *to*, or rather *hatosh*, from *hat* and *osh*.

toh, n., the report of a gun.

toh, adverbial, *minkoh toh?* is he a chief and does so?

tohbi, a., white; light; hoar; hoary, Matt. 17: 2.

tohbi, v. n., to be white, or light; *tohmbi*, nas. form.

tohbi, n., whiteness; hoariness.

tohbi, pp., whitened; bleached; blanched; made white; *tohmbi*, nas. form.

tohbi chohmi, a., whitish.

tohbichi, v. t., to whiten; to bleach; to blanch; to paint white; to make white, Matt. 5: 36.

tohbichi, n., a whitener.

tohbit ia, v. a. i., to whiten.

tohbit taha, pp., whitened.

tohchalali, a., bright; clear.

tohchalali, v. n., to be bright or clear.

tohchalli, Ch. Sp. Book, p. 44.

tohchali, v. a. i., to scintillate.

tohe, n., cabbage.

tohkasakli, v. a. i., to shine dimly; to give a dim light, as a lightning bug; to flash.

tohkasakli, n., a flash; a glimmer; a glimmering.

tohkasali, a., bright.

tohkasali, v. n., to be bright.

tohkasalichi, v. t., to brighten; to make bright.

tohkasli, a., brilliant.

tohkasli, v. n., to be brilliant.

tohkaslichi, v. t., to render brilliant.

tohkil, n., the sensitive plant.

tohkilet pisa, v. a. i., to squint.

tohmali, v. a. i. pl., to shine with a feeble light; to shine quick; to flash.

tohmasakli, v. a. i., to shine dimly; to give a dim light, as a glow worm, or as fire that is seen at a distance in the woods.

tohmasaklichi, v. t., to cause to shine dimly.

tohmasali, v. a. i., to give a small bright light, as a candle when at a distance; to shine feebly; to glimmer.

tohmasalichi, v. t., to cause to shine feebly.

tohmasli, v. a. i., to flash, as lightning; to give a quick flash of light; *hashukmalli at tohmasli.*

tohmaslichi, v. t., to cause to flash.

tohno, tonho, v. t., to hire; to engage; to instigate; to incite; to send, Matt. 14: 35; John 4: 38; to employ; to fee; to procure by hiring; to warrant.

tohno, n., a hirer; an employer.

tohnochi, n., a stirrer.

tohnochi, tonhochi, v. t., to hire; to set on.

tohnochi, n., an instigator.

tohnot hochifo, v. t., to enlist.

tohpakali, a., dull.

tohpololi, n., a spark.

tohto, n., a red elm.

tohwali, n., an opening; the firmament; a glade.

tohwekikli, n., a flash of light; a glimpse.

tohwikekli, see *tohwikikli.*

tohwikeli, v. a. i., v. t., to shine; to give light; to gleam; to glimmer; to have light, Matt. 6: 22; to light; to lighten; to radiate; *luak at tohwikeli; pala yat tohwikeli.*

tohwikeli, pp., illuminated.

tohwikeli, a., lightsome, luminous; refulgent; shiny.

tohwikeli, n., light; a glimmering; a luminary; a shining, Matt. 5: 14; 6: 23.

tohwikeli, pp., enlightened; lighted.

tohwikelichi, n., an illuminator.

tohwikelichi, n., an illumination.

tohwikelichi, v. t., to cause daylight; to lighten; to give light; to enlighten; to illume; illumine; to illuminate; to radiate.

tohwiket minti, n., daybreak; daylight; aurora.

tohwikikli, tohwikekli, n. pl., flashes of light.

tohyuali, n., an opening or light seen in the woods through trees.

tohyualichi, v. t., to cause light.

tok, sign of the remote past tense; was; did; have; had; has been; *ikpesotok, ikhaklotok,* Matt. 13: 17; *Lewi atok,* 1 Kings 11: 13; *tokatok,* "had," Josh. 17: 10, *k* final has a demonstrative power in marking past time in *tok at, tok mat,* etc. Compounds: *toka, tukashkia,* Matt. 13: 12—*tokakinli — tokakkia—tok-*

akon — tokakocha — tokakokia — tokakono — tokakosh — tokakot — tokano—tokato — tokano — tokat — tokbe — tokheno — tokhet—tokheto—tokkia—tokma—tokmako — tokmakosh— tokmano — tokmat—tokmato — toko — tokocha — tokoka — tokokano — tokokat, tukokat, potoli tukokat, they who touched, Matt. 14: 36—*tokokato—tokoke—tokokia—tokokma—tokokmano — tokokmat — tokokmato — tokona—tokosh—tokot.*

tokali, tukali, pp. pl., fired off; discharged.

tokali, tukali, v. a. i. pl., to go off; to shoot; to fire.

tokalichi, tukalichi, v. t., to fire; to discharge; to cause to fire.

tokam, n., name of a tree used in making the pommel and forepart of saddles.

tokba, adv., very; very much; extremely; greatly; *sabanna tokba,* I want it very much; *okpulo tokba,* extremely bad.

tokofa, v. a. i., to fall, as the palate into the throat.

tokofi, v. a. i., to shed hair; *iletokufi,* he sheds his hair.

tokoinsha, see *tikoinsha.*

tokok, adv., probably; it may be; it might be; *kanima minti hatokok; tokoke; impa tokoke.*

tokomi, tukohmi, adv., improbably; unlikely.

[**toksakinla,** n., the snowbird (Sixtowns dialect).—H. S. H.]

toksalechi, v. t., to work; to cause to work; to employ in work; to employ; to exercise; to task; *wak an toksalechi, hatak an toksalechi.*

tonksalechi, n., a taskmaster.

toksali, v. a. i., to work; to labor, Matt. 6: 28; 11: 28; to hammer; to ply; to till; to toil; *na hollo intoksali,* he works for a white man; *iktoksalo,* not to work; to idle; a., idle; indolent; *toksanli,* n. f., *atoksali,* v. t., to cultivate; to work it, or there; *toksahanli,* freq. form; *ikatoksalo,* a., uncultivated; *ibatoksali,* to cooperate; to work with; *iktoksalo,* n., idleness; *intoksali,* to work for him; *itintoksali,* to work for each other.

toksali, n., a laborer; a worker; work; a domestic; a help; a helper; a jobber.

tonksali, n., work; exercise; fatigue; a job; labor; toil; working.

toksạli ạlhpisa, n., a task.
toksạli fehna, v. a. i., to drudge; to work hard.
toksạli fehna, a., laborious.
toksạli fehna, n., a drudge.
tonksạli imponna, n., an artisan; an artist; a workman; a wright.
tokumpa, a., large and round, like a hill.
tokumpa, a., being without a point, tail, or rump; akank tokumpa, a hen that has no tail.
tokumpa, v. n., to be without a point, tail, etc.
tola (see itula or itola), n., used with the dative pro., intola; okhissa intola, its foundation, 1 Sam. 5: 4, 5.
toli, v. t., to play ball; itibatoli, they play ball together; itintoli, they play ball against each other.
toli, n., a player; one who plays ball.
tolupli, tolubli, sing., tulli, pl., v. a. i., to leap; to bounce; to bound; to vault; to skip; to jump; to rebound; to spring; to dodge; to hop; ạlla yạt tolupli, isi ạt tolupli, towa yạt tolupli.
tolupli, n., a jumper; a leaper.
tolupli, a., salient; bounding.
tolupli, n., a bound; a leap; a jump; a hop; a skip; a spring.
toluplichi, v. t., to cause to leap, jump, bound, etc.
toluplit wakaya, v. a. i., to vault.
toluski, a. sing., short, thick, and round; shukha toluski, isuba toluski, sakti toluski.
toluski, v. n., to be short, thick, and round.
toluskichi, v. t., to make short, thick, and round.
tolusli, a. pl., short, thick, and round.
tolusli, v. n., to be short, thick, and round.
tomafa, pp., completed; the whole being taken; tomaffi, v. t.
tomalusi, tomalisi, adv., close by; very near but this way of it; chuka tomalisi, ola tomalusi.
tomaffi, v. t., to complete; to take the whole.
tomaffi, tamaffi, n., one who completes or takes all; pl. tomoli or tạmoli, see Gen. 9: 15, to destroy all.
tomba, adv., very; nowa tomba, he walks very well.

tombi, tomi, tommi, v. a. i., to shine, as the sun, not as a fire or a candle; to radiate; to reflect the rays of the sun; hạshi ạt siontomi, the sun shines on me; apisa yạt siontomi, the glass shines on me; ikatommi, let it there shine, Matt. 5: 16.
tombi, tomi, tommi, n., a ray of light; a sunbeam; sunshine; a ray, Matt. 17: 2.
tombi, a., radiant.
tombichechi, v. t., to cause to shine; Chihowa yạt tombichechi (or tombichi), Jehovah causes it to shine.
tombichi, tomichi, v. t., to cause to shine; to radiate.
tombushi, n., prickly heat; tombushi sạbi, I have the prickly heat.
tomi, tommi, see tombi.
tonho, tohno, v. t., to have; to employ; to engage.
tonhochi, tohnochi, v. t., to hire; to instigate; to set on.
toni, n., name of a small wild animal.
tonla, v. a. i., to lie; to lie down; intonla, to lie by him.
tonnik, tonnink, tonink, tonik, n., a post; a pillar, such as sustain the roof of a piazza; a stock, 1 Sam. 1: 9; 2: 8; 1 Kings 7: 3.
tonnoli, v. a. i. pl., to roll over, as a log; to tumble; to twirl.
tonnoli, pp., rolled over.
tonnolichi, v. t. pl., to roll them over, as a ball or a log; to tumble; to turn; to twirl.
tonokbi, tanakbi (q. v.), a., bent; crooked, as an oxbow; ititonokbi, an oxbow; ititonokbi katima ansha? where are the oxbows?
tonokbi, v. n., to be bent; to be crooked.
tonokbichi, v. t., to bend; to crook; to make crooked.
tononoli, a freq. v. a. i., to squirm; to wallow.
tonulli, v. a. i. sing., to roll over, as a log.
tonulli, pp., rolled over.
tonullichi, v. t. sing., to roll it over; to roll away, Josh. 5: 9; 10: 18.
topa, n., a bed; a bedstead; any frame on which beds, blankets, or skins are spread and where persons sleep; a couch; a lodging.
topa iskitini, n., a cot; a small bed.
topa isht talakchi, n., a bed cord.

topa iti kalaha atakali, n., a trundle bed.

topa iyi, n., a bedpost.

topa shuⁿshi, n., a bedbug.

topa umpatalhpo, n., a bed; a coverlet; *nan tanna topa umpatalhpo,* n., a sheet.

topoli, topulli, v. t., to push; pl. of *tobli.*

toshba hinla, a., perishable.

toshbahe keyu, a., imperishable.

toshbi, a., pp., rotten; corrupt; spoiled; perished; decayed; filthy; corrupted; ruined; *iktoshbo,* a., undecayed.

toshbi, v. n., to be rotten, etc.

toshbi, v. a. i., to rot; to perish; to decay; to corrupt; to ruin.

toshbi, n., rottenness; filthiness; rot.

toshbichechi, toshbichi, v. t., to rot; to cause to rot; to corrupt; to mildew.

toshbichi ammona, v. t., to mildew.

toshbit isht ia, v. a. i., to decay; to begin to rot.

toshboa, a., partially rotten, or injured.

toshboa, v. n., to be partially rotten; *alhpoyak at toshboa; ahe at toshboa.*

toshbulba, toshbi holba, a., somewhat decayed.

toshbulba, v. n., to be somewhat decayed.

toshke, tushkeh, adv. (from *toh,* sign of recent past tense, as in *ishlatoh*); particle of assertion, full form *hatoshke;* probably, John 2: 10; used by a person who is ignorant of the manner in which events took place. If a man in a drunken fit kills another, when his senses return he may say *abelitoshke.*

toshoa, toshowa, v. a. i., to remove, Josh. 3: 1, 3; 9: 17.

toshoa, pp., poured out; transferred; translated; construed; rendered; defined; explained; emptied; evacuated; expounded.

toshoa, n., an explanation; an explication; a translation; a version.

toshoa hinla, a., explainable; explicable.

toshoba, n., mildew (from *toshbi holba*).

tosholi, v. t., to pour out; to transfer, Josh. 8: 32; to translate; to construe; to explain; to render; to define words; to empty; to evacuate; to explicate; to expound; to gloss; to open; *anumpa toshole,* to translate; *atoshoyuli,* to pour from into, so as to cool, etc., as to pour

hot coffee from cup to saucer and back again.

tosholi, n., a translator; an explainer; an interpreter; an explicator; an expounder; an opener.

tosholi, n., a translation.

toshowa, see *toshoa.*

towa, n., a ball, used in sports.

towakali, n., the firmament, Gen. 1: 7.

towulhkachi, itowulhkachi, v. t., to blister by heat, Rev. 7: 16.

tuⁿ?; *mali tuⁿ?*

tua, a., open.

tua, tuwa, tiwa, pp., opened.

tua, v. a. i., to open; to come open.

tuakachi, pp., stirred while lying in a vessel.

tualichi, v. t., to stir; to move about, as to stir a liquid or grain which lies in a vessel or a bin, etc.; *tafala yaⁿ tualichi, tanchi aⁿ tualichi.*

tubbona, a., stooped, bent over.

tubi, see *tobi.*

tuchali, n., a piece; a slice.

tuchina, a., three; III; 3; *nitak tuchina,* three days; *ninak tuchina,* three nights; Matt. 12: 40; 15: 32; *tuchinakma,* Matt. 18: 16.

tuchina, v. n., to be three.

tuchina, v. a. i., to be three, or to make three, as *etuchina,* we three.

tuchinaha, adv., a third time.

tuchinanchi, v. t., to do the third time.

tuchinanchit, adv., thrice; *tuchinanchit anoli,* tell it thrice or tell of three things; *tuchinanchit abeli,* I have killed three.

tuchinna, all three; being three; *tuchinna hoshilhkoli,* all three have gone.

tufa, v. a. i., to spit; *ilontufa,* to spit on himself.

tufa, n., a spitter.

tuftua, v. a. i. pl., to spit; to keep spitting.

tuk, sign of the recent past tense; did; was; has; has been; have been; had, 1 Sam. 3: 8; Matt. 2: 13; used to describe just previous to another time whether the last time is recent or not, see John 4: 53; connected with the present; equal to was, and is in some connections; see *atok* for all the forms; *k* final is demonstrative; *tuk* is found in *tuk at, tukmat,* 1 Sam. 30:26, 27.

tukafa, tokafa, v. a. i., to discharge; to go off; to fire, as a gun; to shoot; to explode; to pop.

tukafa, pp., fired; discharged; shot; *ontukafa*, shot; fired on.

tukafa,n., an explosion; a shoot; *iktukafo*, a., unshot.

tukafa achąfa, n., a charge; a fire; a load.

tukakosh, because, Matt. 16: 8.

tukali, tokali, n., pl., to discharge.

tukali, pp., discharged.

tukali, n., a shooting; a discharge; a volley.

tukali, see *tokali*.

tukalichi, see *tokalichi*.

tukalichi, v. t., to discharge.

tukatok, had, Matt. 14:3; 16:5; 1 Kings 11:10; was, 2 Kings 9:15, 16; Josh. 2:6.

tukąffi, v. t. sing., to fire off; to fire; to discharge.

tukąffi, n., one who fires a gun.

tukbi, a., blunt; pp., blunted.

tukbi, v. n., to be blunt.

tukbichi, v. t., to make it blunt; to blunt.

tuklo, a., two; double, II; 2; n., a pair; a couple; a brace; a yoke, Matt. 11: 2; 14: 17.

tuklo, n., twain; a span; a deuce, a term used in gaming; *tuklokma*, Matt. 18: 16; *tuklokmąt,* when there are two.

tuklo, v. n., to be two; *ishtuklo; itatuklo*, to be two together, or both, Matt. 4: 21; 10: 29; *itatukloli*, I together with him, two; *itatuklo*, Matt. 17: 3; *ilitatuklo*, Matt. 17: 27; Josh. 9: 3; *toyuklo*, pro. form.

tuklo, v. a. i., to make two; to be two, as *etuklo*, we two; *itatuklo*, and, in *Chemis akosh nakfish Chan itatuklotok*, James and his brother John, Matt. 10: 2; Mark 11: 11.

tunklo, being two, or the two; both, Matt. 9: 17; 15: 14.

tuklochi, v. t., to do it twice, or to do two; to make two; *itatuklinchi*, to double; *tuklolichilahe keyu*, I can not do both things; to "two," literally, Matt. 6: 24; to take two, Matt. 10: 10.

tuklohila, n., a jig.

tuklohilahila, v. a. i., to jig.

tuklokia, even two.

tuklokia atampa, n., plurality; more than two.

tuklona, tuklo ona, v. a. i., to reach to two; to extend to two; even two; *tukok*, cont. for *tukokma; kaniona ishbolitukok*, perhaps you laid it somewhere.

tuklampuli, n., a cobweb; see *chuklampulli*.

tukma, written as one word in the definite form of recent past tense, sub. mood, obj. case, but after nouns should be written as two words, *tuk ma; tuk mat*, same in nom. case; *tuk okma; tuk okmat*.

tukohmi, see *tokomi*.

tuktua, v. a. i., to cluck.

tulhpakali, a., dim; obscure; hidden; applied to the eyesight, which, being dim, does not clearly behold objects.

tulhpakali, v. n., to be dim or obscure; *tanampo apisa pisalikma apisa yąt tulhpakali*.

tulli, pl., *tolupli*, sing., v. a. i., to frisk; to jump; to bound; to canter; to prance; to romp; to skip; to spring; to vault.

tulli, n., a frisker.

tullichi, v. t., to canter; to cause to leap, etc.

tullit fulokąchi, v. a. i., to caper.

tullit fulokąchi, n., a caper.

tulolichi, v. a. i., to walk with short steps like a duck-legged hen, or a child when it first begins to walk.

tulak, n., soot.

tulak chito, a., sooty.

tulak isht lusa, pp., sooted.

tulak isht lusachi, v. t., to soot.

tulak laua, a., sooty.

tulankoba, tulankobi, a., brown; orange red, like soot.

tuma, adv., probably; *yąmohmi tuma*.

tumashke; *hotumąshke*, Matt. 17, 26; *ihinma tumąshke*, Acts 11, 18; *chintuma, hetuma*, in the future.

tupashali, n., the long-legged spider, called "grand daddy long legs."

tunstubi, tunsubi, n., a fishhawk; a blue hawk.

tunsha, tusha; see *tushli*.

tushafa, v. a. i., to split off; *tali tushafat itula*, the stone split off and fell.

tushafa, pp., split off.

tushafa, n., a piece; a fraction; a part; a scrap; a slice, Matt. 17: 27; *paska tushafa sapeta*, give me a piece of bread.

tushaⁿfasi, n., a bit; a spark.

tushali, v. a. i. pl., to split off in pieces.

tushali, pp., split off; chipped; minced; nipped; sliced.

tushali, n., pieces cut off; fragments; shavings.

tushali ushtali, v. t., to quarter.

tushalichi, v. t., to cut in pieces; to break into pieces, Matt. 14: 19; to divide; to part; to shave; *paska yaⁿ tushalichi*, to break up the bread; to haggle; to mince; to nip; *itatushalichi*, to break in pieces; Luke 24: 30.

tushaffii, v. t. sing., to cut off a small piece; to break off a small piece; *paska yaⁿ tushaffi, nipi aⁿ tushaffi*.

tushkeh, see *toshke*.

tushli, v. t. pl., to cut in pieces; to cut off; to break in pieces; *paska yaⁿ tushli*.

tushpa, a., hasty; quick; spry; alert; active; agile; cursory; brisk; animated; expeditious; expert; forward; immature; instant; nimble; pert; posthaste; precipitous; ˙punctual; rapid; ready; speedy; sprightly; sudden; swift.

tushpa, n., expedition; haste; hastiness; precipitancy; quickness; rapidity; rashness; readiness; speed.

tushpa, v. n., to be spry, quick, alert.

tuⁿshpa, v. a. i., to go in haste; to act in haste; to bustle; to haste; to hie; to scramble; to fly; to precipitate; to speed, Matt. 5: 25; *etuⁿshpat ilaya*, we are going in haste.

tuⁿshpa, pp., hastened; hasted; precipitated.

tuⁿshpa, tushpat, adv., quickly; apace; immediately; rashly, readily.

tuⁿshpa achukma, a., prompt; ready.

tuⁿshpalechi, v. t., to hasten; to animate; to hurry; to expedite; to forward; to haste; to precipitate; to quicken; to speed.

tuⁿshpali, v. t., to hasten; to animate; to hurry; to haste; to huddle; *satuⁿshpali*, he hurries me.

tushpalit chafichi, v. t., to pack.

tuⁿshpat holitopa toba, n., an upstart.

tuⁿshpachi, v. t., to hasten; to hurry; to quicken another; to accelerate.

tuⁿshpat anumpuli, v. t., to sputter.

tuⁿshpat nowa, v. a. i., to walk fast; n., a tripper.

tushtua, v. a. i., to break in pieces; to crumble.

tushtua, pp., cut up; divided; broken; crumbled; dissected; sliced.

tushtua, n., pieces; fragments; crumbs.

tushtuli, v. t., to break off pieces; to carve; to cut off pieces; to dissect; to fritter; to slice; to break, Matt. 15: 36; *paska yaⁿ tushtuli, isi nipi tushtuli*.

tushtuli, n., a carver.

tuwa, see *tua*.

tuwi, tiwi, v. t., to open; to unlock; to broach; to unbar; to unbolt; to unclose; to unfasten; to unfold; to unroll; to unstop.

tuwi, n., an opener.

tuwichi, tiwichi, a., to cause to open; to open; to disclose.

ufka, hufka, v. t., to air; to dry; to sun; to expose to the sun; *tanchi aⁿ ufka, shukbo aⁿ ufka*, he suns the blanket; *holufka*, pp.

ufkaⁿya, okfaⁿya (q. v.) v. a. i., to snag the foot or flesh.

ufko, n., a fanner; a small hand fan; an instrument for winnowing grain, etc.

uha, a., all; see Hymn 148: 7; *nan uha*.

uha, v. n., to be all.

uhalichi, see Mark 12: 30.

uⁿhalinchi, v. t., to use all, Mark 12: 30.

uⁿkah, adv., yes; certainly (from *oⁿh* or *uⁿh* and *kah*, it is that).

ukbal, ulbal (q. v.), n., behind; the rear.

ukbal, adv., in the rear.

ukha, see *okha*.

ukhishta, okhishta (q. v.), v. t., to shut; to close a door, box, trunk, or gate, but not a knife, the eyes, or the hand.

uⁿkof, uⁿkaf, n., a persimmon.

uⁿkof api, n., a persimmon tree.

uksak, oksak, n., a hickory nut.

uksak alanta, n., hickory mush, an Indian dish.

uksak api, n., a hickory tree.

uksak api bisinli, n., a hickory withe.

uksak foni, n., a hickory-nut shell.

uksak hahe, n., a walnut.

uksak hata, n., a white hickory nut.

uksak nipi, n., hickory-nut meat; a kernel.

uksak ulhkomo, n., hickory milk, a dish of food.

ulbạl, ukbạl, a., behind; back; adv., in the rear.

ulbạl, v. n., to be behind.

ulbạl, n., the rear.

ulbạl isht ałopulli, n., a diarrhea.

ulbạl ont ia, v. a. i., to have a passage or stool.

ulbạl ont ia, n., a diarrhea; a stool; a passage; a dejection; a flux.

ulbạl ont iachi, n., a cathartic.

ulbạl ont iachi, v. t., to physic.

ulbạl pila, adv., backward.

ulbạl pilla, adv., away back.

ulbạlaka, a., hind, as to direction.

ulbạlakạchi, v. t., to cause it to go behind.

ulbạlhpela, adv., backwards.

ulbạlhpelạt ia, v. a. i., to go back; to go backwards; isuba hạt ulbạlhpelạt ia ikbạnno.

ulhchi, n., a drawer of water.

ulhkạchi, hulhkạchi, pp., soaked; steeped; tanchi ạt ulhkạchi.

ulhkạchi, v. a. i., to soften.

ulhkạchi, a., soggy.

ulhpi, n., a haft; a handle; a shaft.

ulhpi aⁿsha, pp., hafted; having a haft; shafted.

ulhpohomo, pp., covered.

ulhti, pp., enkindled; kindled.

ulhti, n., a fire; a council fire; a government; a state; a district; a domain; a dominion; a republic.

ulhti achạfa, n., a state; one council fire; a commonwealth.

ullohchi, pass. of ochi.

um, see om.

umba, uma (Sixtowns form), umma (Sixtowns form), umpa, v. a. i., to rain; to shower; ohumpa; onumba, to rain on; onumba, pp., showered.

umba, n., a rain; a shower; umba hatuk mạt, the rain, Matt. 7: 25, 27.

umba, a., rainy.

umba, v. n., to be rainy.

umba chito, n., a great rain.

umba chitoli, v. a. i., to rain hard.

umba laua, a., rainy.

umbạchechi, v. t., to engage one to make it rain.

umbạchi, umpạchi, umbachi, v. t., to make it rain; to rain; to shower.

umbi, n., a pawpaw; a custard apple.

umbitepa, ombitepa, v. t. sing., to press on with the hand, Matt. 9: 18; ilumbitepa, to smite himself with his hand, Luke 18: 13.

umbitka, v. t. pl., to press on with the hands.

umbokafa, n., an issue; issish umbokafa, Matt. 9: 20. See bokafa.

umma, umpa, see umba.

umpatali, v. t., to spread on; to put on; to saddle; ileumpatali, to spread on himself; ileumpatali, n., a shawl; a cape. See patali.

umpatạlhpo, n., a saddle; a carpet; a cushion.

umpatạlhpo, pp., covered; boarded; skinned.

umpạchi, see umbạchi.

umpạla, v. a. i., v. t., to shine on; to shed light upon.

umpạta, n., a cape; a cover.

umpạta, umpạtta, pp., spread on.

umpoholmo, v. a. i., to mantle; to skin.

umpoholmo, n., a covering; a lid; a cover; a tilt.

umpoholmo, pp., covered, Matt. 10: 26; boarded; hooded; topped; veiled; onulhpohomo.

umpohomi, v. t., to cover; to cover over; to board; to cover with boards; holisso haⁿ umpohomi.

umpohomo, ompohomo, v. t., to cover; to bury; to hood; to involve; to mantle; to skin; to smother; to tip; to tilt; to top; to veil; isht ompohomotok, was covered with, Matt. 8: 24.

umpohomot okpạni, v. t., to overwhelm.

unchạba, onchạba, n., a large hill.

unchạba chaha, n., a high hill; a mountain.

unchạba foka, a., hilly; n., a hilly region.

unchololi, onchuloli, v. a. i., to sprout at the root; to grow up again, as sprouts round a stump; to multiply; to increase; aiunchululi, Matt. 1: 17; itaiunchululi, generations.

unchololichi, v. t., to cause to sprout.

uncholulli, n., sprouts; the second growth; a generation; the descendants; the offspring; an offset.

unchululi, n., generation or descendants; isht aiunchululi, Matt. 12: 34.

untuchina, a., eight, VIII, 8.

untuchinaha, adv., eight times.

untuklo, a., seven, VII, 7, Matt. 12: 45; 15: 34, 36, 37; 16: 10.

untukloha, adv., seven times, Josh. 6: 4.

uskạp, n., a small white crane.

uski, oski, n., a cane.

Uski anunka, n., a., in the cane; among cane. The Choctaw name for Kentucky.

uski botona, n., cane bent and used for tongs.

uski chito, n., large cane; a thick cane brake.

uski chula, n., a slaie; a slay; a weaver's reed; a reed.

uski kapush, n., cane tongs.

uski kolofa, n., a cane spool.

uski kololi, n., pl., cane spools.

uski lumpa, n., a blowgun; an air gun made of cane; a wind gun.

uski naki, n., an arrow; a shaft; oski naki, 2 Kings 9: 24.

uski naki halupa, n., an arrow-head or -point.

uski pạta, n., a canebrake.

uski pạtak, n., a canebrake.

uski tạpa, n., a spool.

uski tạpa afoli, v. t., to spool.

uskula, n., a flute; a pipe, Matt. 11: 17.

uskula olachi, v. t., to flute; to play on a flute; to pipe.

uskula olachi, n., a piper.

uskulush olachi, n., a fifer; a whistler.

uskulushi, n., a whistle; a fife; a flageolet.

uskulushiolachi, v. t., to fife; to play on a fife.

ushahpi, n., firstborn; the first child.

ushạtto, n., a womb; a venter; a matrix.

ushelạbi, see hạshilạbi.

ushetik, see oshetik.

ushetik, oshetik, n., a daughter; his or her daughter; used in the third person only; Matt. 10: 35; 14: 6.

ushetik toba, n., a stepdaughter.

ushi, n., a son; a child, Josh. 1: 1; ushi yan, the Son, Matt. 11: 27; ilap ushi yon, a son of himself, Heb. 1: 2; offspring, Matt. 15: 22; a descendant, Luke 3: 23, 38; a brood; fruit; a litter; posterity; heirs; an egg; the young of any creature; not applied to infants (see Matt. 1: 21, 23; Luke 1: 13); sign of the diminutive, as chufak, chufak ushi; an imp, a word of reproach; issue; young; "a young

one;" ushi osh, his son, Matt. 7: 9; ushi is used only in the third person, and means his son, her son; son of; in the second and first person it is chiso, thy son, and sạsa, my son. See iso, a son.

ushi ahalaia, n., sonship.

ushi afoka, n., a womb.

ushi aiạlhto, n., a womb.

ushi cheli, v. t., to litter; to bring forth young.

ushi infohka, a., pregnant.

ushi infohka, v. n., to be pregnant.

ushi infohka, v. a. i., to conceive; to teem.

ushi infohka, n., pregnancy.

ushi iksho, ushiksho, a., barren; childless; issueless, Luke 1: 7.

ushi isht atiaka, n., seed.

ushi isht atoba, n., adoption.

ushi kaiya, v. a. i., to teem; to be with young.

ushi kaiya, a., pregnant.

ushi shali, v. t., to go with young.

ushi tek, ushetik, n., a daughter, 1 Sam. 1: 4; Matt. 15: 28; Josh. 17: 3. See oshetik.

ushi toba, n., a stepson; a stepchild.

ushi tobat taha, n., a fetus.

ushiksho, see ushi iksho.

ushta, a., four; IV; 4, Matt. 15: 38.

ushta, v. n., to be four; ushtali, I four; afạmmi ushtali, I four years; I am four years old.

ushta, v. a. i., to make four; as ilushta. ushtali.

unshta, all four.

ushtachi, to do it four times.

ushtaha, fourth time.

ushtali, v. t., to four; to make four (see to quarter), innafoka yatuk an isht itakạshkoa ushtali cha, took his garments and made four parts, John 19: 23.

uti, oti (q. v.), n., a chestnut.

wa, awa (q. v.); will not; shall not; can not, Luke 4: 4; John 3: 2.

wanhachi, v. a. i., to scream.

wahhaloha, v. a. i. pl., to spread; to branch out like vines on the ground.

wahhaloha, a. pl., pronged.

wahhaloha, v. a. i., to be pronged; isi lạpish ạt wahhaloha.

wahhạla, a. sing., pronged, as the horns of cattle and deer; wạhhạla, v. n.; wak lạpish ạt wahhạla.

wahwali, wahwuli, n., a whip-poor-will.

waiahpa, v. a. i. (from *waiya* and *ahpi*), to bow down; see John 8: 6.

waiaya*n*ya, waiayaya, motion of a horse in bending down his head to eat as he passes along.

waioha, n., bends.

waioha, v. a. i. pl., to bend; *iti at waioha.*

waioha, pp. pl., bent.

waiohachi, v. t., to bend.

waiya, n., a bend; a stoop.

waiya, v. a. i. sing., to bend; to impend; to lean; to recline; to swag; to sway.

waiya, pp., bent.

waiya, a., slant; slanting.

waiyakachi; *ito*ⁿ*waiyakachi*, to lean on each other, as fallen cane stalks; *tanchi at waiyakachi.*

waiyachi, v. t., to bend; to incurvate; to lean; to slant; to stoop; to sway.

wak, n., a cow; general name of the cow kind, and is of common gender and of both numbers; cattle; kine; neat; beef; beeves; black cattle. This word is probably an attempt to imitate the Spanish word vaca.

wak afammi, n., a yearling cow.

wak aiasha, n., a range for cattle; a place where cattle resort.

wak aiimpa, n., a manger; a rack; a cow trough; a cow range; a stall for cattle.

wak aiitanowa, n., a cow trail or path; a cow range.

wak apistikeli, n., a herdsman; a grazier; a neatherd.

wak abi, n., a butcher.

wak atampa, n., a yearling; one over a year old and under two years.

wak bila, n., the fat of beef; suet.

wak bishahchi, n., a milch cow.

wak hakshup, n., a cowhide.

wak hakshup ahumma, wak hakshup ahummachi, n., a tannery; a tanyard; a tan vat.

wak hakshup alallichi, n., a lapstone.

wak hakshup humma, n., sole leather; leather.

wak hakshup hummachi, n., a tanner; a leather dresser.

wak hakshup isht hummachi, n., ooze; tanner's bark.

wak hakshup lusa, n., upper leather.

wak hakshup lusachi, v. t., to curry.

wak hakshup shemachi, n., a currier.

wak hakshup shukcha, n., a portmanteau; saddle bags.

wak hobak, n., a steer; an ox; a bullock.

wak hobak toⁿksali, n., a working steer; a working ox.

wak iⁿholihta, n., a cowpen; a cow yard.

wak inlukfapa, n., a cowlick.

wak ishki, n., an old cow that has had calves.

wak isht fama, n., a cow whip.

wak isht inchuⁿwa, n., a cow brand.

wak itichapa, n., a yoke of cattle.

wak itihalalli, n., a yoke of oxen.

wak iⁿyalhki, n., cow dung; muck.

wak iⁿyalhki ont ashachi, pp., manured.

wak lapish, n., a cow's horn.

wak lapish iksho, n., a cow without horns.

wak nakni, n., a bull.

wak nakni nipi, n., bull beef.

wak nali tohbi, n., a line-back cow; a white-back cow.

wak nia, n., tallow.

wak nia ahama, pp., tallowed.

wak nia ahammi, v. t., to tallow.

wak nia pala, n., a tallow candle.

wak nipi, n., beef; the flesh of an ox or cow.

wak nipi albani, n., barbecued beef.

wak nipi apa, n., a beef-eater.

wak nipi shila, n., dried beef; cured beef.

wak pelichi, n., a herdsman; a grazier.

wak pishukchi, n., cow's milk.

wak pishukchi nia, n., butter of kine; butter.

wak pishukchi palaska, n., cheese.

wak tek, n., a cow; cows; kine.

wak tek himmeta, n., a young cow; a heifer; a young kine.

wak toksali, n., an ox; a working ox.

wak toksali abankachi, n. pl., ox yokes.

wak toⁿksali abanaya, n., an ox yoke.

wak toⁿksali hioli achafa, n., an ox team.

wak toⁿksali innuchi, n., an oxbow.

wak toⁿksali itapata, n., a yoke of oxen; a pair of oxen.

wak toksali itichapa, n., a yoke of working cattle.

wak ushi, n., a calf.

wak ushi cheli, v. t., to calve.

wak ushi hakshup, n., a calfskin.

wak ushi nakni, n., a bull calf.

wak ushi nipi, n., veal.

wak yushkoboli, n., a cow without horns.

wakalali, pl., wakla, sing., v. a. i., to crack.

wakalali, pp., cracked.

wakalali, n., cracks; crevices; interstices.

wakalalichi, v. t., to cause to crack.

wakama, v. a. i., to unfurl; to spread out; to open.

wakama, pp., opened; unfurled; holisso hat wakama, shaphat wakama, iti patalhpo at wakama, the floor is raised up entire so that one can look under it.

wakamoa, v. a. i. pl., to unfurl.

wakamoa, pp. pl., opened; unfurled.

wakamoli, v. t., to unfurl; to spread out; to open.

wakaya, n., a start.

wakaya, n., a starter.

wakaya, v. a. i., to rise from a seat, Matt. 9: 9; Luke 5: 28; to arise (from a sick bed), Matt. 8: 15; to get up; to rise up; to start; to start off on a journey, Josh. 1: 2; 8: 1; onwakayat hikia, to stand over, Luke 4: 39; nitak nantasho ishwakayatukon, on what day did you start?

wakayachi, v. t., to cause to get up; to cause to start; to start; to make him rise up, 2 Kings 9: 2.

wakayoha, v. a. i. pl., to rise up from a seat.

wakayohachi, v. t., to raise them up.

wakammi, v. t., to open, Luke 4: 17; Matt. 17: 27; holisso han wakammi, to open the book; nishkin wakammi; itombi wakammi; ikwakamo, a., unopened.

wakcha, a., forked; having two prongs or limbs straddled apart, as the two legs in one end of a bench.

wakcha, v. a. i., to straddle; onwakcha, v. t., to straddle on.

wakcha, v. n., to be forked; onwakcha, straddled over.

wakchala, v. a. i., to straddle.

wakchalali, v. a. i., to straddle.

wakchalalichi, v. t., to cause to straddle.

wakchalalit itonla, v. a. i., to sprawl.

wakchalachi, v. t., to make him straddle.

wakchalashli, a., forked; straddled.

wakchalashli, v. n., to be forked or straddled.

wakchalashlichi, v. t., to cause to straddle.

wakchali, n., a disease like the venereal disease.

wakchat hikia, v. a. i., to stand straddle.

wakchat nowa, v. a. i., to straddle; to straddle and walk.

wakeli, v. t., to lift up; to raise it up; iti an wakeli, to lift up a log.

wakkalih, v. a. i., to be low or just heard, as the human voice.

wakla, v. a. i. sing., to crack open; wakalali, pl.

wakla, pp., cracked open.

wakla, n., a crack; a crevice; an interstice; aboha wakla; iti patalhpo wakla; wakaloha, pl.

waklali, n., a fissure.

waklachi, v. t., to cause to crack.

wakoha, v. a. i., to open.

wakoha, pp., opened.

wakoli, v. t., to open.

wakolichi, v. t., to cause to open; to lift them up; to raise them up, i. e., anything flat; aboha isht holmo wakolichi, lift up the shingle on a roof.

wakshish, v. a. i., to stub; iyi wakshish, to stub the toe.—J. E.

walakshi, n., a dumpling; a Choctaw dumpling, made thus: cakes of corn meal are boiled in water gruel, with a mixture of dried peaches, and eaten in a bowl.

walanto, v. a. i., to be curdled, like milk; see walahachi.

walasha, a., tender or soft.

walasha, v. n., to be tender or soft.

walasha, pp., soaked till suppled; wak hakshup at walasha.

walabli, walapli, v. a. i., to go over; onwalapli, 1 Sam. 2: 1.

wali, v. t., to hold out to view; to hand to others; nushkobo an inwali, to beckon; tali holisso an inwali, to offer him money; paska yan inwali, to hand them the bread.

waloa, v. i., to grow, like a plant or a person; walwoki, pl.

walonchi, a., juicy; soft; applied to the part of pine-tree ball which squirrels eat.

waloha, a., tender; soft.

waloha, v. n., to be tender; *alla chuⁿkash at waloha, fuli at waloha; tanip holbi at waloha.*

walohachi, v. t., to make flexible.

walohbi, a. pl., flexible; limber; tender; soft; flimsy; supple; pliant.

walohbi, walonchi (Sixtowns word), v. n., to be flexible or tender; *nipi at walohbi; bashpo at walohbi; iti naksish at walohbi.*

walohbi, n., tenderness.

walohbi, v. a. i., to flag.

walohbi, pp., suppled.

walohbi keyu, a., unpliant.

walohbichi, v. t., to make limber or flexible; to supple.

waloli, v. t., to shake; to hold up to view.

walotachi, a. pl., tender, as the stalks of young vegetables.

walunchi, v. a. i., to be tender, like new grass; weak, as young animals; see *walohbi.*

walanta, v. a. i.; *oⁿwalanta*, to run over.

walalli, v. a. i., to boil, as hot water; to boil from the action of heat; to effervesce; to wallop; to seethe, 1 Sam. 2: 13.

walalli, pp., seethed.

walalli, a., boiling; fervent.

walalli, n., an ebullition; a ferment.

walalli ammona, v. a. i., to simmer.

walallichi, v. t., to cause to boil; to ferment; to seethe.

wananaha, v. a. i., to quiver.

wanananli, v. a. i., to quiver.

wanuksho, wanuksho, a., hairy.

wanuksho, n., short hair, as on a hog; fuzz.

wanuta, n., a door yard; a court; a yard.

washa, n., a locust, the large kind; *haⁿwa* is the small sort.

washahachi, washahachi, v. a. i., to sing, as locusts; to rattle, as the rattlesnake; to make a rustling or shrill noise; *washa yat washahachi; sintullo at washahachi.*

washalali, v. a. i., to extend.

washaloha, a., pronged; full of limbs or branches; having many limbs.

washaloha, v. n., to be pronged.

washana, v. a. i., to kick with the hind legs; *isuba hat washana.*

washala, a. sing., pronged; having two prongs or two tines.

washala, v. n., to be pronged.

washala, n., a prong; a tine.

washalahinchi, v. t., to strike with two feet.

washalachi, v. t., to make a prong.

washalwaⁿya, v. t., to strike with all the feet.

washlichi, n., a kind of locust.

washoha, v. a. i., to play with little things, as children; to play with toys; to game; to sport; to toy; to wanton.

washoha, n., playing with toys; one who plays with toys; a game; a pastime; a play; sport; *alla washoha*, a boy who plays.

washohachi, v. t., to cause to play with toys.

watali, v. t. pl., to unfold; to unfurl; *watanli*, nasal form.

watama, pp., unfolded; opened; v. a. i., to unfold; to open.

watalhpi, a., supine; *watalhpi.* v. n.

watalhpi, adv., supinely.

watalhpi, v. a. i., to lie on the back.

watammi, v. t., to unfold; to open; *na foka lumbo watammi; bashpo yoⁿ watammi; holisso haⁿ watammi.*

watammi, n., one who opens.

watammi, see *batammi.*

watonlak, watonla, n., a crane.

watonluk oshi, n., a white sand-hill crane.

waya, v. a. i., to bear; to bring fruit; to produce; to ripen; to grow; to yield; *ishtwaya*, Matt. 13: 23; to bring forth, Matt. 13: 26; *takkon api ilappat waya fehna; tanchi at waya; yakni ilappat ahe aⁿ awaya*, this land produces potatoes; Josh. 5: 11.

waya, n., produce.

waya, a., ripe; fruitful; *ikawayo*, unfertile; *ikwayo*, sterile; fruitless; unfruitful

waya achukma, a., rank.

waya fehna, v. a. i., to luxuriate.

waya fehna, a., luxuriant; prolific.

wayachi, v. t., to cause to bear; to produce; to yield; to grow; *ikwayayochi*, v. t., to sterilize.

walaha, v. a. i., to coagulate; to clot; to curdle; to congeal; *pishukchi at walaha; issish at walaha.*

waḷaha, pp., coagulated; curdled; congealed.

waḷaha, a., ropy.

waḷaha, n., coagulation and coagulum; a clot; ropiness; *pishukchi waḷaha; apish waḷaha.*

waḷahąchi, waḷakąchi, walanto, v. t., to coagulate; to congeal; to curdle.

waḷahąchi, n., a jelly.

waḷapolih, v. a. i., to lap over; *nitak itonwaḷapolih.*

waḷwa, n., a species of turtle; a softshelled turtle; *inwaḷwa,* the lower part of the breastbone.

waḷwąki, a. pl., *waloa,* sing., tender; soft; *chunkąsh waḷwąki.*

waḷwąki, v. n. pl., to be tender or soft; to grow, like a plant or a person.

waḷwąkichi, v. t., to make tender or soft.

waḷahąchi, v. a. i., to rattle, as dry leaves or dry sand, seeds, and powder, or as the throat with a cold.

wąnnichi, v. a. i., to shake, as with the ague; to quiver; to shudder; to tremble; *wąnnihinchi,* quivering.

wąnnichi, n., an ague fit; a shake; palsy; a quake; a waver; a shivering; a shudder; a trembling; tremor.

wąnnichi, a., tremulous.

wąnuksho, see *wanuksho.*

waslichi, n., see *wislichi.*

washkąli, v. a. i., to have the itch.

washko, n., the itch; the mange.

washkoli, washkuli, v. t., to cause the itch.

washlichi, v. a. i., to grit or chisel nuts like a squirrel.

watta, v. a. i., to be broad, like the horns of an ox; *waklapish watta.*

wattąchi, v. t. sing., *watali,* pl., to unclinch, as *ibbak wattąchi,* to open the mouth of a bag; to unfold or spread out the wings or open the hands; see *watta.*

weha, pp., ravaged; plundered.

wehkah, int. of mild displeasure, as don't; now don't.

wehpoa, pp. pl., robbed; plundered; depredated; deprived; despoiled; divested; extorted; rifled; stripped; *ikwehpoo,* a., unspoiled.

wehpoa, n., robbery; extortion; prey; prize; rapine; spoil, Josh. 7: 21; *na wehpoa,* spoils, Josh. 8: 2.

wehpuli, v. t., to rob; to plunder; to depredate; to deprive; to despoil; to divest; to extort; to pillage; to prey; to ravage; to rifle; to spoil, Matt. 12: 29.

wehpuli, n., a robber; a plunderer; a depredator; an extortioner; a ravager; a rifler.

wehpuli shaḷi, a., rapacious.

wehpuli shaḷi, n., rapacity.

wehput fullota, v. t., to scour; to pillage; to range about for pillage.

wehta, n., the lap of a legging.

weki, a., heavy; ponderous; weighty; burdensome; clumsy; dull, Matt. 11: 28; fat; firm (*chunkąsh weki,* a firm mind); slow (*hatak weki,* a slow man; a heavy man); flat; obtuse; onerous; oppressive; saturnine; unwieldy.

weki, v. n., to be heavy, etc.

weki, v. a. i., to weigh.

weki, pp., weighed; *ikweko,* a., unweighed.

weki, adv , heavily.

weki, n., a weight; a poise; the weight; a pound; gravity; heaviness; heft; luggage.

weki achąfa, n., one pound; a pound.

weki fehna, a., ponderous; very heavy.

weki inshaḷi, a., heaviest.

weki inshaḷi, v. n., to be the heaviest; v. a. i., to preponderate.

weki itilaui, v. a. i., to balance; to weigh against each other and alike.

weki itilaui, a., being of equal weight.

weki itilaui, pp., balanced; poised.

weki itilaui, n., an equilibrium.

weki itilauichi, v. t., to balance; to poise; to cause to weigh alike or to be of equal weight.

weki taḷepa achąfa, n., a kentle; a quintal.

weki taḷepa sipokni tuklo, n., a ton; 2,000 pounds.

wekichi, v. t., to weigh; to weigh up; to balance; to poise; to scale; *inwekichi,* to encumber him; *ikwikecho,* a., unweighed.

wekichi, n., a weigher.

weli, v. t. pl., *wali,* sing., to take out; to hold out to view; to stretch forth, Luke 6: 10; Matt. 12: 49; 14: 31; to offer, Luke 6: 29; to stretch out, 2 Sam. 24: 16; Josh. 8: 18; to show; to turn to, Matt. 5: 39; to put forth, Matt. 8: 3; *onweli,* to level, as a gun in shooting;

isht toksali isht weli, v. t., to ungear; *isht hallali isht weli,* v. t., to unharness.

weli, v. t., to rob; to despoil; to divest; to pillage; to plunder; to ravage; *shukha yaⁿ iⁿweli.*

weli, n., a plunderer.

[**wia,** n., a loft, a brush arbor. Wia Takali, Hanging Loft, was the name of a Choctaw town, so called from a large brush arbor erected there for public assemblies.—H. S. H.]

wichikli, v. a. i., pl., to move.

wiha, v. a. i. pl., to move; to remove; to change the place of residence; to swarm; *foe bilishki ạt wiha; oklat wiha; oklat wihạt aⁿya; kocha wiha,* to come forth, John 5: 28; *ilaweli, ilaueli,* to take along with himself.

wiha, n., movers; an emigrant.

wiha, n., a removal; a moving; a migration; a remove.

wihachi, v. t., to cause to move.

wihachi, v. a. i., to move and swarm, as flies, maggots, etc.

wihat aⁿya, v. a. i., to emigrate; to move along; to be on the way; to migrate.

wihat ạla, v. a. i., to immigrate; to move and arrive.

wihat ạla, n., an immigrant.

wihat binili, v. a. i., to move and settle.

wihat binili, n., a colony.

wik, n., a week, from the English word week.

wilaha, a., slimy.

wilaha, v. n., to be slimy.

wilaha, n., slime; sliminess.

wilahạchi, v. t., to cause to be slimy.

wilanli, v. a. i., to weep; *nishkin okchi ạt wilanli,* to drop, as tears.

wileli, v. t., to flap.

wiłali, v. a. i., to spread out (as the toes of some old women).

wimilichi, v. a. i., to roar, as a blazing fire, as a flame; *wimilihinchi,* freq.

winihạchi, winehạchi, v. a. i., to peal; to rumble, as thunder; to ring, 1 Sam. 4: 5.

winihạchi, n., a peal; a rumbling.

winnakạchi, v. a. i., to shake; to quake; *yakni ạt winnakạchi,* the earth shakes; *iti ạt winnakạchi,* the tree shakes; *winnakahanchi* freq. form.

winnakạchi, pp., shaken; jarred; joggled; jolted; jounced.

winnakạchi, n., a shake; a quake; a jolt.

winnali, v. a. i. pl., to shake.

winnali, pp. pl., shaken.

winnalichi, v. t., to shake; to cause to shake; to jar; to joggle; to jolt; to jounce.

winnalichi, n., a jolter.

winnattakachechi, v. t. sing., to shock; to cause a shock.

winnạttakạchi, v. i. sing., to shake.

winnạttakạchi, pp. sing., shaken.

winnạttakạchi, n. sing., a shake; a shock.

wisakạchi, v. a. i., to ripple; to wave; *wisakahanchi,* freq., rippling.

wisakạchi, n., water running in waves.

wisalichi, v. t., to ripple.

wisattakạchi, n., a ripple; a wave.

wislichi, wạslichi, n., a locust.

wishaha, v. a. i., to wave and bend like a plume; *shikopa wishaha.*

wishahchi, bishahchi, a., milch.

wishahchi, v. n., to be milch.

wishakchi, a., outmost; smallest; extreme; belonging to the tip end.

wishakchi, v. n., to be outmost; *wishakchechi,* caus. form.

wishakchi, n., the top; the tip; the point; the extremity; the apex; the summit; the end; the tip end; the peak; the pinnacle, Matt. 4: 5.

wishikachi, v. a. i., to spurt; to make a noise in spurting out, like a stream of blood from a vein.

wishilli, v. a. i., to spurt.

wishillichi, v. t., to spurt; to cause to spurt.

wishki, n., whisky.

wishlichi, v. t., to milk, as a cow, etc.; see *bishlichi.*

witekạchi, v. a. i. pl., to move, as insects.

witikli, v. a. i., to move, as an insect.

witikwinli, witạkwinli, v. a. i. sing., to move, as an insect.

woha, v. a. i., to bellow, as a bull; to bray, as an ass; to low, as a cow; to bark, as a dog; to howl, as a wolf; to waul.

woha, n., a bellowing; a howl.

wohola, v. a. i., to expand, like the lower skirts and garments.

woholachi, causative; *isht ilewoholachi*, a lady's hoop.

wohwah, wohwa, v. a. i., to bark; to howl; to yelp.

wohwoha, wohwoa, v. a. i., to bark; to howl; to yelp; *nashoba yat wohwoa*, the wolf barks.

wokkokli, v. t. sing., to throw up the earth, as a mole when rooting underground.

wokokoa, pp., ground turned or thrown up as by a mole.

wokokonli, pl. freq., to throw up the earth as moles when rooting.

wokokonlichi, pl., to root up, as a hog.

wokonlichi, v. t., to root up the earth, as a hog or mole; *awokonlichi*, n., the place rooted up.

wolichi, v. t., to bark at, as a dog; to yelp; to bay; *ofi at hatak an wolichi*.

wolobli, v. t. sing., to split, shiver, and break to pieces; *wuli*, pl.

wononunkachi, a., fuzzy; hairy.

wonuksho, v. a. i., to be hairy.

wonuksho, n., the inner or shorter hair of a hog and small feathers of a fowl.

woshoha, v. t., to root, as a hog.

woshoki, n., phlegm; spittle when a person has a cold; *hotilhko woshoki; woshokachi*, n., same.

woshulichi, v. t., to root, as a hog.

woshulli, see *wushulli*.

woshushuk, n., a noise heard in the inside of a living body, as the rumbling of the bowels.

woshushukachi, v. a. i., to make such a noise; to say *woshushuk*.

wowoha, wowoa, v. i., to bark; to howl; to yelp.

wuklo, v. a. i., to molt, or cast off the skin as a serpent does.

wulhko, v. a. i., to blister; to fester; *nipi at wulhko*.

wulhko, pp., blistered; vesicated; *towulhko*, Rev. 16: 9.

wulhko, n., a blister; a thin bladder on the skin containing water or blood; a blain; a vesicle.

wulhkochi, v. t., to blister; to cause to blister; to vesicate; *towulhkochi*, Rev. 16: 8.

wulhkuchi, n., a blister; a plaster applied to raise a blister or vesicle.

wula, v. i., to split; to shiver.

wula, pp., split; shivered; *uski at wula*.

wuli, v. t. pl., to split; to shiver anything that is hollow, as a cane or reed.

wulobli, wulubli, v. t., to split; to shiver; to sliver.

wulobli, n., shivering.

wulopa, v. a. i., to split; to shiver.

wulopa, sing., split; shivered; bruised to pieces.

wulubli, see *wulobli*.

wushohachi, v. a. i., to ferment; to work; n., working; fermentation.

wushulli, woshulli, v. a. i., to ferment; to form a froth on the surface; *woshohachi*, to ferment.

wushulli, n., a fermentation.

wushulli, pp., fermented.

wushullichi, v. t., to ferment; to cause fermentation.

wushwoki, a., slimy; thin, applied to stools of the sick.

ya, art., the; see *a* and *ha*, *Tama*, *yan*, *Thamar*, her; Matt. 1: 3.

yá, emphatic; see *okchanki yá*, 1 Sam. 2: 15; *chishno yá* "to thee," 2 Kings 9: 5.

ya, rel. pro., who; which; the one who, etc.; see *a* and *ha*.

yabata, yobota, a., flying, as clouds.

yaboboa, a., mellow, like ripe fruit.

yaboboa, v. n., to be mellow.

yabosha, a. pl., soft; mellow.

yabosha, v. n., to be soft or mellow.

yaboshachi, v. t., to make soft; to soften.

yabushki, v. n., to be mellow.

yabushli, a. sing., mellow; soft; spongy.

yabushli, v. n., to be mellow, soft, spongy.

yanfa, n., a large scar; a crease in the skin without a wound, as in the palm of the hand and finger joints.

yahapa, v. a. i., to scream; to shout; to racket; to make a racket; *isht yahapa*, v. t., to shout; *allat yahapa*.

yahapa, n., a screaming; a shouting; a racket; a riot; a shout; an uproar.

yahapa, n., a screamer; a shouter.

yahapa, a., rude; boisterous; noisy.

yahna, see *yanha*.

yahyachechi, v. t., to trot; to cause to trot; to make him trot.

yahyachi, v. a. i., to trot; *isuba hat yahyachi*.

yahyachi, n., a trotter.

yahyạchi, n., a trot.

yaiya, v. a. i., to cry; to weep; to moan; to howl; to wail; to lament; to beweep; to bewail; to bleat, as sheep, and to screak; to scream; to screech; to shriek; to snivel; to squall; to squeal; to wail; to whimper; *hạchiⁿyaiyaka*, we have mourned unto; *hạchikyaiyoshke*, ye have not lamented; *ayahaⁿya*, there crying, Matt. 8: 12; *yahaⁿya*, Matt. 13: 50; *isht yaiya*, v. t., to cry on account of or about; to lament; to moan; *isht ikyaiyo*, a., unwept; *itiⁿyaiya*, to cry for each other, as Joseph and Benjamin, Gen. 45: 14.

yaiya, n., obsequies; a funeral cry, etc.

yaiya, n., a weeper.

yaiya, n., a crying; a cry; one who cries; a mourner; a mourning; a shriek; a squall; a wail; a wailing, Matt. 13: 42.

yaiya, a., mournful.

yaiya shạli, n., a sniveler; one who is addicted to crying.

yak, art., the; see *ak* and *hak*, Matt. 17: 25; *yak oⁿ*, the, Matt. 14: 5, 10; *yak*, rel. pro., see *ak* and *hak*; *yak-banno*, Matt. 4: 4; *yako*, pro., this or thus; *yak aⁿsha*, they are here; *yakot*, thus; *yak ahaya*, he said this or thus; *yakaⁿshwa*, they are here; *yakahanchi*, Matt. 13: 24; *yakitonlalishke*, 1 Sam. 3: 4; *yak hikialishke*, 1 Sam. 3: 5; *yako hikia*, to stand thus or here.

yak, adv., thus; *yak achishke*, thus saith; 2 Kings 9: 3, 6; 2 Sam. 24: 12, here; *yak hinlishke*, *yak ashạshke*, 2 Sam. 24: 22.

yak, adv., here; *yakanta*, he is here; *yak maⁿya*, Matt. 4: 3.

yaki, yakeh, lo; look here; behold; see; come, John 4: 29; behold, Matt. 12: 2; Josh. 7: 21.

yaklạsh, yakolush, n., a jug; an earthen jug.

yakmichi, yakohmichi, v. a. i., to do thus.

yakni, n., the earth, Matt. 11: 25; Josh. 2: 11; the world; land; soil; ground; nation; coast, Matt. 15: 39; 16: 13; country; empire; kingdom; province; state; a continent; district; dust; the globe; territory; *yakni* is compounded with the name of a people to express the name of their country, as *Chu*

yakni, Judea, or the land of the Jews; *iⁿyakni*, home, his land, their coasts, Matt. 8: 34; *iⁿyakni aiạtta*, home born; *yakni achạfa*, one country.

yakni, a., temporal; worldly.

yakni achukma, n., good land; a good country; fertile land.

yakni ahalaia, n., secular; terrestrial.

yakni aiạli, n., the coast; the land's end.

yakni anuⁿka waya, n., ground peas; groundnuts; peanuts.

yakni anuⁿkaka, n., the inside of the earth, or under the ground.

yakni anuⁿkaka, a., subterraneous; underground.

yakni anuⁿkaka lua, n., a volcano; a burning underground.

yakni apisa ạli, n., a landscape.

yakni atoksạli, n., cultivated land; *yakni ikatoksalo*, n., wild land.

yakni ạlhpisa, n., a plot.

yakni ạlhpisa hikia, n., a landmark.

yakni ạli, n., the end of the land; the edge of the land; a frontier.

yakni bạla, n., ground peas; groundnuts.

yakni bạsha, n., plowed land.

yakni bạshli, v. t., to plow.

yakni bikeli, n., a tongue of land.

yakni bukli, n., a gopher, by some called *yumbak*, or *yakni bokli*.

yakni bunto, n., a round hill; a mound.

yakni chiluk, n., a cave; a cavern; a pit; a hole in the ground; a chasm; a fissure; a hole; a hollow.

yakni chuła, n., surveyed land; land surveyed and laid off in sections; sections of land; lots.

yakni chuli, v. t., to survey land; to lay off land in sections; to run off land.

yakni chumpa, n., a land speculator.

yakni foi, n., the yellow jacket's nest or comb; a yellow jacket; a small yellow wasp.

yakni foishke, n., a yellow jacket; a small yellow wasp.

yakni fullota, yakni fullota moma, n., all over the world; the circuit or circumference of the earth; a region.

yakni haiaka, n., a desert, Luke 1: 80; Matt. 4: 1; a wilderness, Luke 3: 2, Matt. 11: 7; 15: 33; Josh. 1: 4; 8: 15.

yakni haknip, n., a continent.

yakni hichukbi, n., a cave.

yakni hichukbi aiątta, v. a. i., to cave; to live in a cave; to den.

yakni hofobi, n., a ditch, Luke 6: 39.

yakni iⁿkaniohmi, n., coasts of, Matt. 15: 21.

yakni ikapatafo, n., a balk; a place not plowed.

yakni ikląna pilla, a., inland.

yakni ikląnna apakfoyupa, n., the equator.

yakni ikonlo, n., an isthmus.

yakni imafo, n., a black lizard, called "ground puppy."

yakni impota, v. t., to rent land; to let out land.

yakni impota, n., a renter; a lessor.

yakni isht ahalaia, a., earthly; earthy; pertaining to the earth.

yakni isht ąlhpisa, n., a land measure; a rod; a mile, etc.; a surveyor's chain.

yakni isht ąlhpisa holisso, n., a map.

yakni isht kula, n., a spade.

yakni isht patafa, n., a plow.

yakni isht patafa tąli, n., a plowshare.

yakni isht patafa tikbiⁿhika, n., a colter.

yakni kolukbi, n., a ditch; a drain; a gulf.

yakni kolukbichi, v. t., to ditch; to excavate; to dig a hollow.

yakni kula, v. a. i., to mine.

yakni kula, n., a ditch, Matt. 15:14; dug earth; a dug pit; a pit, Matt. 12: 11; a mine; a dike.

yakni kula ayanąlli, n., a trench; a drain.

yakni kula tąmaha apakfopa, n., a moat.

yakni kulli, v. t., to mine; to dig the earth; to spade.

yakni kullit tąmaha apakfobli, v. t., to moat.

yakni lapushkichi, v. t., to harrow land.

yakni lumbo, n., the round earth; the earth; the globe; the world; a ball of earth.

yakni luⁿsa, n., the world; the earth; the dark world, contrasted with heaven.

yakni łabeta, n., a marsh.

yakni matali, n., a plain; level ground, Luke 6: 17; Josh. 4: 13.

yakni moma, n., the world, John 4: 42; the whole earth, Josh. 3: 13.

yakni nąnih foka, n., a hill country, Luke 1: 39.

yakni niachi, v. t., to fertilize; to enrich land; to manure land.

yakni nushkobo, n., a peninsula.

yakni okhąta chito pit shamąli, n., a cape; land that extends into the sea.

yakni okpulo, n., bad land; a bad country.

yakni patafa, pp., furrowed land; fallowed land.

yakni patafa isht lapushkichi, n., a harrow.

yakni pataiya, n., flat land.

yakni patali, n., a plain; Josh. 3: 16; 12: 3.

yakni patąffi, v. t., to fallow; to furrow; to plow.

yakni patąffi, n., a plowman.

yakni patąssa, n., a flat; flat land.

yakni pattasąchi iskitini, n., a plat.

yakni patussąchi, n., a plain.

yakni pisąt aⁿya, v. t., to spy.

yakni pota, v. t., to take land by a lease.

yakni pota, n., a tenant; a lessee.

yakni pota, n., a lease.

yakni shila, n., the earth; the dry ground.

yakni winakąchi, n., an earthquake.

yakohmi, see yakomi.

yakohmi, a., being after this fashion, way, manner, or custom; being thus; this sort; these, Matt. 18: 6. Perhaps this word is compounded of yak and ohmi.

yakohmi, v. n., to be thus; to be so; to be on this wise; to come to pass; atukoⁿ yakohmitok, and it came to pass, Matt. 7: 28.

yakohmi, v. a. i., to do so; as eyakohmi, we do so; to come to pass, Josh. 1: 1; 2: 5; iląppa yakohmi na, Acts 16: 18; yakohoⁿmi, Josh. 6: 3.

yakohmi, pp., done so.

yakohmi, adv., thus; so; na yimmi chinto yakohmi ka akapesoshke, I have not seen so great faith in, pro. form, Matt. 8: 10.

yakohmichi, v. t., to do after this manner, Matt. 6: 9; 8: 9; to do it thus, Mark 2: 7; 11: 28; "so," Matt. 5: 12; yakohmiechi pro. form; yakomihinchi freq. form.

yakohmika, n., this way; this fashion; this place.

yakohmika koⁿ, "this is the cause," Josh. 5: 4..

yakoke, int., expressing thanks or pleasure, when spoken quickly.

yakoke, int. of regret, when spoken slowly.

yakoke ahni, v. a. i., to thank; to feel thankful; yakoke chimaiahnilishke, Matt. 11: 25.

yakolush, n., an earthen jug; same as lukfi kotoba; see yaklash.

yakomi, yakohmi, pro. pl., these; several; these here; hatak yakohmi, these men, Acts 16: 17; yakohmi kakoke, "are these," Matt. 10: 2; na yakohmi, these things, Matt. 11: 25.

yakosi, n., a short time.

yakosi, adv., instantly.

yakosi itintakla, adv., suddenly, Luke 2: 13.

yakosi ititakla, a., instantaneous; momentary; sudden.

yakosi ititakla, adv., anon; immediately; forthwith.

yakosi ititakla, yakosi itintakla, n., a moment of time, Luke 4: 5; an instant; a moment; a second.

yakot, see yak.

yalabli, v. t., to do this. ·

yalallaha, yalalloha, n., a quagmire; see lukchuk yalallaha.

yalatha, v. a. i., to tremble or quiver; as meat just after being killed, and while it is butchered.

yalatha, n., a spasm or quivering of the flesh; a local quivering or twitching of the flesh.

yalattakachi, v. a. i. pl., to quiver; to twitch.

yalattakachi, n. pl., spasms; quiverings.

yalubba, yaloba, n., a tadpole; a polliwog; a young frog.

yaluⁿs, haluⁿs, n., a leech; a bloodsucker; see yasunla.

yaluⁿs chito, n., the horse-leech.

yamaska, v. t., to knead; to work over mortar, clay, etc.

yamasli, v. t., to knead; to work over mortar, clay, etc.

yananta, v. n., to run along, as clouds or water.

yananta, n., a running; a flying.

yanalli, a., running; flowing; oka yanalli, running water; ikyanallo, a., stagnant.

yanalli, v. a. i., to run, as water; to flow; to glide; to pour; to go; to rill; to stream; to trickle; to trill; oka yat yanalli; yanahanli, freq. form.

yanalli, n., a current of water; a flux; a run; a stream; a tide.

yanallichi, v. t., to cause to run.

yanallit issa, v. a. i., to stagnate; to stop running.

yanha, yanha, v. a. i., to have a fever.

yanha, n., a fever.

yano, yano (see ano, hano), the, Matt. 13: 48.

yanusi, nan anusi (q. v.), a cry for the dead; obsequies.

yanushkichi, Ch. Sp. Book, p. 60.

yasinti, iasinti, n., an eel.

yasunla, n., a leech (Sixtowns dialect). [The best informed Sixtowns Indians have informed me that Hasunlawi, the Choctaw original from which the name of Sooenlovie creek has been corrupted, is itself a corruption of yasunlabi, meaning leech-killer. On d'Anville's map of 1732 the name Sonlahoue is applied to the Chickasahay river; later it was transferred or restricted to the present stream so called.—H. S. H.] See yaluⁿs.

yash, yashke (see ash and hash); ohoyo himita yash, the damsel; Matt. 14: 11; yasho; yashosh, Matt. 5: 25; leplosi yashosh, his said leprosy, Matt. 8: 3.

Yashu, n., name of a creek; perhaps from iahashoⁿ.

yatapa, v. a. i., to open wider, like a hole in the flesh; used by butchers in stretching up a carcass by the hamstrings, which open, etc.

yatabli, v. t., to widen.

yatosh, see hatosh.

yatoshba, see hatoshba.

yatotoa, a., mellow, like ripe fruit.

yatotoa, v. n., to be mellow.

yattotuⁿkachi, a., soft; yatokachi.

yattotuⁿkachi, v. n., to be soft.

yatuk (see atuk, hatuk); yatukokano, the, Matt. 8: 12; yatukaⁿ, Josh. 4: 18; yatukma, the, Matt. 13: 34; yatukmat, the; chuka yatukmat, the house, Matt. 10: 13.

yatush, adv., alias; otherwise; sinti, yatush Setan sinti holba ashosh, If aⁿ im-

anumpulit yakimachitok; see Scrip. Biog., Vol. I, p. 31; see *atush*.

yatushki, a., soft; mellow, like ripe peaches.

yatushki, v. n., to be soft; v. a. i., to mellow.

yatushkichi, v. t., to soften; to make mellow; to mellow.

yatushkoa, a. pl., soft; mellow.

yatushkoa, v. n., to be soft.

yatushkuli, v. t. pl., to soften; to mellow.

yau, adv., yes; yea; *yau, chitokaka ma,* Matt. 9: 28; 13: 51; some persons say *yoh,* but it is not in the best taste.

yauaha, a., wide apart, as rows of corn; coarse, as the teeth of a comb or rake.

yauaha, v. n., to be wide apart.

yauahachi, v. t., to place wide apart.

yauasha, see *yauashka*.

yaualli, a., partly dry, like the earth.

yaualli, v. n., to be partly dry; *yakni at yaualli, tanchi at yaualli, na foka yat yaualli.*

yauashka, yauaska, yauasha, n., the withers of a horse.

yauinyauf, v. a. i., to be dim sighted; *sanishkin at yauinyaui,* as though crooked hairs or kinked threads were played before the eye; to be misty, hardly visible.

yauolichi, v. a. i., to itch.

yauolichi, n., an itching, 2 Tim. 4: 3.

yanwa, v. a. i., to cry; to mew; to caterwaul, as a cat; to waul.

yanwa, n., a mewing.

yanya, n., a mourner; *hatak yanya,* a mourning man.

yafimpa, v. a. i., to be wrinkled or streaked, as the flesh; to be ribbed; *yaffihinya, yaffihinkachi,* and *yaffifonah,* pl., wrinkled; striped, as the flesh which has lain on hard objects.

yahmichi (not *yohmichi*), v. t., to cause it to be so.

yala, n., a grubworm; a large yellow dirt worm, short and thick.

yalhki, n., feces; dung, 2 Kings 9: 37; dross of metals; ordure; excrements; scoria; *inyalhki,* smut; rust, a disease of grain, as *tanchi inyalhki, onush inyalhki.*

yamichahe keyu, a., impracticable; incapable; *ikyamicho,* v. t., to omit; to neglect.

yamichi, n., a doer; a performer; *ikyammicho,* n., a neglecter; an omission; a neglect; negligence.

yamichi, n., a performance; *ayamihinchi,* Matt. 11: 20; *ilayamihchitok,* we have done, Matt. 7: 22; 8: 9.

yamihchi, yammichi, v. t., to do, Matt. 13: 54, 58; 17: 12; 2 Sam. 24: 10; Luke 4: 2; to fashion; to occasion; to perform; to perpetrate; to transact, Matt. 6: 30; Josh. 8: 8; *nana kia yammicha hinla,* able to do anything; *yammiht,* contracted form.

yamihchi, caus. form of *yohmi,* Matt. 13: 28; *aiyamihchi,* to do, Josh. 3: 5.

yamimma, see *yammimma*.

yamma, pro., that; those; them; these; they; it, Matt. 8: 10; his, Matt. 8: 14; him, Matt. 10: 4; them, Matt. 12: 27; pro., he, 2 Kings 25: 1; they, 2 Kings 25: 23; them, 2 Kings 25: 24; *nitak yamma,* that day, Matt. 7: 22; *yamma,* he, Matt. 11: 18; him, Matt. 14: 5; *yamma,* is a demonstrative of person, thing, and place; *yamma* refers to the most distant objects and *ilappa* to the nearest; *yamma,* "he," Josh. 8: 14; "it," Josh. 8: 18. This demonstrative often supplies the place of the def. article and of the pronouns he, she, it, they, them, their; *yamma haklo kat,* heard it, Matt. 8: 10; *yamma tekchi,* his wife, Matt. 8: 14; *yamma puttaka,* them, Matt. 10: 18.

yamma, v. n., to be that; to be those.

yamma, the; *yakni yamma,* the country, Josh. 7: 2.

yamma, there; yonder; that way; thereat; that place; yon; yond.

yamma, that is it; a word of approbation often used by Choctaw while they sit and hear others speak; like, well; indeed.

yamma achi, v. a. i., to assent; to approve.

yamma itintakla, adv., thenceforth.

yammak, they, Matt. 6: 2; a simple word like *ilappak, himak, himmak.*

yammak, there; then; that instant, Luke 2: 38.

yammak achi, to say, Luke 13: 17.

yammak ash, them, Matt. 4: 24; *chuka yammakash,* that house, Matt. 7: 25; him, Matt. 9: 10; 17: 3; that, Matt. 10: 27.

yąmmak ashoⁿ, thence, Matt. 9:9; him, Matt. 8: 34; 9: 9.

yąmmak ashosh, she, Matt. 8: 15; he, Matt. 12: 3.

yąmmak ashot, he, Matt. 8: 24.

yąmmak atuk aⁿ, thence, Matt. 5: 26.

yąmmak atuk aⁿ, thereof, Matt. 12: 36.

yąmmak atuk makoⁿ, n., sake; for the sake of that.

yąmmak beka, a., only; only that.

yąmmak foka, adv., thereabouts, as to time or place.

yąmmak fokalechi, v. a. i., to go or do at random, by hazard, or by chance; himak fokalechi (q. v.), to venture; yąmmak fokalechit anumpuli, he talks at random; yąmmak fokalechit ia, he goes without a path or guide; yąmmak fokalechit ia hosh apissant ona, he went straight there without path or guide.

yąmmak fokali, a., hazardous; venturesome.

yąmmak fokali, v. n., to be hazardous; yąmmak fokalit aⁿya, to go at random;

yąmmak haloka, a word of contempt or reproach; see makhaloka.

yąmmak iⁿ, same as; thus; so, John 3: 8.

yąmmak inli, a., the same, Luke 2: 8; themselves; even, Matt. 7: 17; "that same," Matt. 10: 19; 13: 1, 49; 15: 22.

yąmmak int, the same.

yąmmak kia, likewise; that too.

yąmmak ma, him also, 2 Kings 9: 27.

yąmmak o, at; therein; that; thereby; whereby; wherein; whereof.

yąmmak oⁿ? is it that? is it so? is it now (i. e., ready), etc.?

yąmmak oka, it, Matt. 7: 14; there, Matt. 8: 12; them, Matt. 10: 26; yąmmak okąto.

yąmmak okmąto, then, Matt. 12: 29.

yąmmak osh, that one; which, Matt. 10: 20.

yąmmąno, that, Luke 10: 31.

yąmmąska, pp., kneaded; mixed; worked, as mortar.

yąmmąska, n., dough.

yąmmąt, a., that.

yąmmąto, yąmmato, that one.

yąmmi, a., full.

yąmmi, pp., salted; sated; saturated; sweetened; impregnated; cloyed, Mark 9: 49; haknip ąt okahomi yąmmi; kąfi ąt

hapi champuli yąmmi; oka homi saiąmmi, I am full of whisky.

yąmmichi, v. t., to salt; to sweeten; to mix; to cloy; to saturate; to sate; to satiate; to impregnate; to preserve, as meat with salt; itiąmmichi, to blend; to mix.

yąmmichi, see yąmihchi.

yąmmimma, yąmimma, (from yąmma and imma), adv., that way, John 7: 32; Luke 19: 4.

yąmohma hinla, a., practicable; practical.

yąmohmahe ąlhpesa, a., necessary, or it must be so.

yąmohmahe ąlhpesąchi, v. t., to necessitate.

yąmohmahe ąlhpiesa, n., necessity.

yąmohmahe keyu, a., impracticable; yąmohmi, from yąmma and ohmi; chin-yąmohmahe keyu, shall not be unto thee, Matt. 16: 22.

yąmohmi, v. a. i., v. t., to do, Matt. 4: 1; 7: 12, 21; John 2: 18; 3: 2; Luke 4: 23; ayąmohmi, do there, Matt. 6: 2; to be, John 3: 9; to occur; to operate; to pass; to practice; to transpire; to come to pass; to take effect; to be done; Matt. 1: 23; yąmohomi, to work, Acts 10: 35; aiyąmohmi, Josh. 4: 8; 7: 20; yąmohmichatuk, accustomed to do so.

yąmohmi, adv., so as; so on; like that.

yąmohmi, n., an operator; a practicer.

yąmohmi, n., a fashion; a way; a mode; an event; a manner; an operation; a practice; the ton; the treatment.

yąmohmi ho, wherefore; whereupon.

yąmohmi hoka, therefore; whereas; whereat.

yąmohmi kako, thereupon.

yąmohmikia, but, Luke 4: 26.

yąmohmikma, and; moreover; furthermore.

yąmohmima, and so, Luke 4: 5.

yąnakąchi, v. a. i., to move, as a serpent.

yąnha, yanha, yahna, v. n., to have a fever; to be sick, Matt. 8: 14.

yąnha, n., a fever; a hectic; yąnha kąt, the fever, Matt. 8: 15.

yąnha chito, n., a high fever; a bilious fever.

yąnha chohmi, a., feverish.

yąnha fehna, n., a great fever, Luke 4: 38.

yạnha foka, n., an inflammation.

yạnha isht shipạchi ikhiⁿsh, n., a febrifuge.

yạnhạchi, v. t., to produce a fever; to cause a fever; to heat; to induce a fever; ayạnhạchi, to produce a fever thereby.

yạnnạsh, n., a buffalo; a bison.

yạnnạsh hakshup, n., a buffalo skin; a buffalo robe.

yạnnạsh iⁿlukfạpa, n., a buffalo lick.

yạnnạsh ushi, n., a buffalo calf; a young buffalo.

yạnnạsh ushi cheli, v. t., to calve; to bring forth a young buffalo.

yạno, see yano.

yạnoba, a., feverish.

yạnoba, v. n., to be feverish.

yạppạlli, to walk slowly and softly, not with a hard tread, 1 Sam. 15: 32.

yạslichi, v. t., to scratch, as a dog for an animal in the ground.

yạt, the; who, etc.; Hatak ushi yạt, "the Son of Man," iti achukma yạt, a good tree, Matt. 7: 18; ạni yạt okpulo yoⁿ, evil fruit, Matt. 7: 17.

yạto; inlaka yạto, others.

yichefa, pp., gripped; held by the hand or claws.

yicheli, yicholi, v. t. pl., to catch with the hands, fingers, or claws and have a strong hold.

yichiffi, v. t., to catch, seize, grip, or grasp, with the hand, claws, paws talons, etc., but not strongly; to grapple; to pounce; yichiffit isht kanchi, to catch away, Matt. 13: 19.

yichiffi, n., a catcher; a grasper.

yichiffichi, v. t., to cause to seize; to engrasp; to grapple; to grasp.

yichiffit ishi, v. t., to clinch; to seize and hold, or take; to clutch; to grab; to grip.

yichina, v. a. i., to stretch the limbs; to yawn; to exert; to flounce; to flounder; to strain; to struggle; to toil.

yichina, n., a strain; a struggle.

yichinachi, yichinạchi, v. a. i., to strain; to cause to exert all the powers.

yichinnikahchih, v. a. i., to make a sudden and strong effort.

yicholi, see yicheli.

yichowa, pp., seized; caught; grappled; held.

yihina, a., gaunt.

yihina, v. n., to be gaunt.

yikefa, pp., taken hold of and drawn off.

yikiffi, v. t., to catch hold of the skin and draw it up or off from the flesh, as when one pinches and pulls the cheeks, or the skin on a dog's back; ipạf aⁿ yikiffi.

yikila, pp., stitched.

yikila, n., selvage.

yikilạchi, v. t., to make a selvage.

yikili, v. t., to stitch.

yikili, n., a stitcher.

yikilichi, v. t., to stitch or to cause to stitch.

yikkowa, yikowa, yikyua, v. a. i. (pl. of yiⁿyiki), to wrinkle; yikyuachi, in paⁿshi aiena ka yikyuachi, 1 Tim. 2: 9.

yikkowa, pp., wrinkled.

yikkowa, n., a wrinkle; a line.

yikoa, v. a. i., to go to a bee or frolic; to collect together and work gratuitously for some person; yikoat ilia.

yikoa, n., a bee; a frolic.

yikofa, pp., wrinkled.

yikoffa, n., a gnat.

yikoha, pp., girdled or wrinkled.

yikokoa, yikokuⁿwa, pp., wrinkled; crisped; na foka yạt yikokuⁿwa.

yikokuⁿwa, n., wrinkles.

yikoli, v. t., to girdle a tree; to wrinkle; to make a ridge or wrinkle; to engirdle; to crisp.

yikolichi, v. t., to cause to wrinkle.

yikopa, see yokopa.

yikota, pp., crisped; wrinkled; puckered up; shriveled.

yikota, v. a. i., to wrinkle; to crisp; to shrink; to shrivel.

yikotạchi, v. t., to wrinkle; to cause to wrinkle; to crisp.

yikottakachi, n., a start; a crisp.

yikotua, v. a. i. pl., to wrinkle; to crisp.

yikotua, pp., wrinkled; crisped.

yikotua, n., wrinkles; crisps.

yikowa, yikkowa, yikyua; yikyuachi, to broider (hair), 1 Tim. 2: 9; to curl hair.

yikowạchi, v. t., to wrinkle.

yikulli, v. t., to wrinkle; to pucker up, as by putting fire on leather; to shrivel.

yikutkạchi, v. a. i. pl., to shrink; to crisp.

yikutkạchi, pp. pl., shrunk; crisped.

yikyua, see *yikkowa, yikowa.*

yiłeha, a., fallen, as trees. ·

yiłepa, n., a rout.

yiłepa, v. a. i. pl. (see *yiłibli,* transitive, Josh. 7: 22), to run; to move, or pass quickly, on the feet, on wheels, or on water; to course; to rush; to scamper; to flee, 1 Sam. 4: 10; *oⁿyilepa,* to storm; to run upon, Josh. 8: 20; *iⁿyilepa,* to flee from them, Josh. 7: 4; 8: 6, 20; *yiłepa fehnat,* ran violently, etc., Matt. 8: 32; *yiłepat,* fled, etc, i. e., together and not singly, Matt. 8: 33; *itiⁿyilepa,* to run from each other.

yiłepachi, v. t., to cause to run.

yiłepoa, pl., to run.

yiłepoachi, v. t., to cause to run.

yiłibli, v. t. pl., to run; to rout; to sail; to cause them to run or to sail; *peni yilibli; iti chanalli aⁿ yilibli; isuba haⁿ yilibli;* see *yiłepa,* v. a. i.

yiłishachi, v. a. i., to dodge; to be quick in motion, applied to the heart also; to start from a fright, or it may be an exclamation of surprise or fear.

yiliya, v. a. i., to start; to tremble; to struggle, like a dying beast.

yiminta, n., a sally.

yiminta, yimmita, yimita, a., pp., animated; strenuous; zealous; lively; earnest; engaged; aroused; spirited.

yiminta, v. n., to be animated.

yiminta, v. a. i., to cheer.

yiminta, n., animation; courage; excitement.

yiminta atapa, n., enthusiasm.

yiminta atapa, a., enthusiastic.

yiminta keyu, a., spiritless.

yimintachi, yimmitachi, v. t., to stimulate; to cheer; to encourage; to enliven; to rear; to hearten; to embolden; to inspirit; to invigorate; to refresh; to rouse; to spirit; to stimulate; to strengthen.

yimita, see *yiminta, yimmita.*

yimmahe alhpesa, a., credible; *iⁿyimmahe keyu,* a., incredible.

yimmi, iⁿyimmi, v. a. i., to believe, Matt. 11: 14; to have confidence; to confide; to credit; to receive; to rely; to repose; to trust; *ikyimmo, ikiyimmo,* v. t., to disbelieve; not to believe; to distrust; to be faithless; to misgive; to scruple; to unbelieve; a., faithless; in-

fidel; skeptical; *iliyimmi,* to believe in himself; *iliyimmi,* a., opinionated.

yimmi, v. n., to be convinced; *sayimmi,* I am convinced.

yimmi, pp., cheated; deceived; fooled; convinced; credited; deluded; gulled.

yimmi, a., confident; sanguine.

yimmi, n., belief; a believer; a fiduciary; *chiyimmi,* thy faith, Matt. 9: 22; *na yimmi,* a believer, Matt. 6: 30; *iⁿyimmi,* credit; reliance; trust; *ikyimmo,* unbelief; an unbeliever; a skeptic.

yimmi shali, a., credulous.

yimmichi, v. t., to cause to believe, whether true or false; to deceive; to befool; to cheat; to cog; to convince; to delude; to disappoint; to dupe; to fool; to gull; to mock; to sham; to wheedle.

yimmichi, n., a cheat; a cheater; a deceiver; a deluder.

yimmihechi, v. t., to cause to believe.

yimmita, yiminta, pp., stimulated; excited; enlivened; inspirited; invigorated; refreshed; vivified.

yiⁿyikechi, v. t., to crook; to twist; to cockle, as cloth; to curl; to furrow; to ruffle; to rumple; to wrinkle.

yiⁿyiki, yiyiⁿki, a., pp., crooked, curling, worming; zigzag; twisting; cockled; curled; furrowed; rumpled; ruffled; wrinkled; winding and crooked like the ridge of a hill.

yiⁿyiki, v. n., to be crooked, curling, winding, like a dividing ridge.

yiⁿyiki, v. a. i., to cockle, as cloth; to curl; to ruffle; to wrinkle.

yiⁿyiki, n., a furrow; a ruffle; a wrinkle.

yo, yoⁿ, art., the, see *o* and *ho; chuka yoⁿ,* "an house," Matt. 10: 12; *yó* is the form in the imperative, as *akaiyó,* "do let me go," making *yo* the helping verb do; *yo,* rel. pro., who, etc.; *ani okpulo yoⁿ,* Matt. 7: 18; *nanih chaha yoⁿ,* a mountain, Matt. 17: 1. Compounds: *yocha—yoka—yokaka—yokakano—yokakant—yokakanto—yokakat—yokakato—yokakhe—yokakheno—yokakhet—yokakheto—yokakkia—yokakoⁿ—yokakocha—yokakona—yokakosh—yokakot—yokano, yokano,* Matt. 11: 22; *inla yokano,* Matt. 15: 24; *yokat; ano yokat,* for I am, Matt. 8: 9, *yokato; iti okpulo yokato,* Matt. 7: 17; distinctive, as for the corrupt tree, in distinction from other trees; *ahopo-*

yuksa yokato, wisdom, Matt. 11: 19; 17: 26—*yoke—yokia, yjohkia—yokomo—yokono—yona—yosh—yot.*

yoba, perhaps; can, John 3: 27 [?]; lest; peradventure; perchance; *yoba hinla ká*, Mark 11: 13; Josh. 9: 7; *mintahe mak yoba tukosh*, Luke 10: 31.

yoba, v. n., it may be.

yobaheto, perhaps not.

yobakma, if it may be, Josh. 14: 12; *hiobakma*, if it shall, etc., Matt. 18: 13.

yobana, lest, Josh. 2: 16; 2 Tim. 2: 25.

yobota, v. a. i., to fly, as the clouds; see *yabata*.

yohabli, yuhabli, yuhapli, v. t., to slacken; to loosen; to relax.

yohablichi, v. t., to cause to slack; to loosen.

yohapa, yuhapa, v. a. i., to loosen; to slack; to slacken; to stretch.

yohapa, yuhapa, pp., a., loosened; slackened; lax; slack; stretched, as a rope.

yohapa, n., slackness.

yohapachi, v. a. i., to lope.

yohapat, adv., slackly.

yohapoa, v. a. i. pl., to loosen.

yohapoa, pp., loosened.

yohapoli, v. t., to slacken them.

yohbi, a., mild; serene; pleasant; fine; halcyon; lenient; meek; pacific; pure; urbane.

yohbi, v.n., to be mild, serene, or pleasant.

yohbi, v. a. i., to relent.

yohbi, n., mildness; lenity; pureness; purity; refinement; sanctity; serenity; stillness; suavity.

yohbi, pp., sanctified.

yohbi keyu, a., relentless.

yohbichi, yohbiechi, v. t., to make it mild; to render pleasant; to pacify; to refine; to sanctify.

yohbichi, n., a sanctifier; sanctification.

yohhuna, a., gaunt.

yohhuna, v. n., to be gaunt.

yohhunachi, v. t., to make gaunt.

yohma himma keyu, a., impossible.

yohma hinla, a., possible.

yohmahe ahoba keyu, a., improbable.

yohmahe keyu, a., incapable.

yohmi, v. t.; *nana achukma ka yohmi*, to do good things.

yohmi, yuhmi, a., so; this way; after such a way; such, Matt. 9: 8; such

power; *ikyuhmo*, unaccustomed; uncommon.

yohmi, adv., thus.

yohmi, v. n., to be so; *sayohmi chatuk*, to do so, Matt. 9: 19; *ikyuhmi ahni*, v. t., to concede; *yuhmikeyu achi*, v. t., to contradict; to deny that it is so.

yohmi, v. a. i., to do so, John 4: 28; Luke 6: 46; *ayohmi*, to do, Matt. 12: 2; *ayohmi*, to do so there or in, Matt. 6: 10; *aiyohmi*, Josh. 2: 21.

yohmi, n., a custom; a fashion; a manner; a way; *yohmi hohbeka*, Luke 4: 16.

yohmi aialhpesa, v. a. i., to become; to fit; to suit.

yohmi alhpesa, v. a. i., must.

yohmi chatuk keyu, a., unnatural; unwonted.

yohmi fehna keyu, a., unusual.

yohmi hoka, therefore, Matt. 7: 24; 12: 27; 13: 18.

yohmi hokmano, then, Matt. 20: 23[?].

yohmi hokmat, if so be, Matt. 18: 13.

yohmi ka, therefore, Luke 4: 7; for, Luke 4: 10.

yohmi kat, therefore.

yohmi kia, adv., notwithstanding, 2 Sam. 24: 4; although; although it is so; and; but, John 1: 33; howbeit; nevertheless; Matt. 10: 19; 13: 32; 2 Sam. 24: 3.

yohmi nana kia, notwithstanding, Matt. 11: 11.

yohmima, and; then; when it was so, Luke 3: 11, 12; therefore, John 4: 33; *yohmikma*, "and then;" and; Matt. 7: 23, 26; then, Matt. 13: 19.

yohmimat, and.

yohmit itintakla, n., an instant; while it was so.

yohmit pisa, v. t., to experiment; to try to do so.

yok, see *ok.* Compounds: *yoke; yakni haiakayoke*, Matt. 14: 15; *yokma; opiakayokma*, when it is evening, Matt. 16: 2; *yokmá; chuka yokmá*, or house; *inki yokmá*, or father; *ishki yokmá*, or mother, Matt. 10: 14; *ushi yokmá*, or son; *ushetik okmá*, or daughter, Matt. 10: 37—*yokmaka—yokmakano—yokmakato—yokmakhe—yokmakheno—yokmakheto—yokmako, yokmakoh; abeka yokmakoh chatuk oke*, they that are sick, Matt. 9: 12; *yokmakocha—yokmakoka—yokmakoka-*

*no — yokmakoke — yokmakokia — yokma-
kokat — yokmakokato — yokmakona — yok-
makosh — yokmakot — yokmano — yok-
mat — yokmato.*

yokbano, see *hokbano.*

yokopa, yikopa, n., a calm; a pause;
quietness; *yokopa aiaⁿlit talaia tok,*
there was a great calm, Matt. 8: 26.

yokopa, yikopa, v. a. i., to grow quiet;
to calm; to cease, Matt. 14: 32; to stop;
to halt; to pause; to relax; to relent;
to remit; to rest; to be stayed, 2 Sam.
24: 21, 25.

yokopa, pp., quieted; calmed; ceased;
stopped; assuaged; quelled; quenched;
relaxed.

yokopa, a., placid; quiet.

yokopa iksho, a., relentless.

yokopacha hinla, yikopacha hinla, a.,
quenchable.

yokopachi, yikopachi, v. t., to quiet; to
calm; to ease; to assuage; to quell; to
quench; to relax; to remit.

yokopuli, yikopali, v. t., to allay; to
appease; to quiet.

yolulli, see *yululli.*

yopisa, v. a. i., to witness a sport or
play; to juggle.

yopisa, n., a spectator of plays or sports;
a looker-on; a bystander.

yopisa, n., an exhibition.

yopisachi, v. t., to display; v. a. i., to
juggle; to show.

yopoma, Gen. 34: 17; *opoma,* to mock.

yopula, a., jocose; jocular; ludicrous.

yopula, v. a. i., to joke; to jest; to wanton; to revile, Matt. 5: 11; *isht yopula,*
v. t., to jeer; to joke, Matt. 9: 24; *yopula-
li,* I joke.

yopula, n., a jester; a joker.

yopula, n., irony; a jest; a joke.

yopula shali, a., facetious; jocular; jovial;
wanton.

yopula shali, n., a zany.

yopullachi, caus. form; *itayopullachi,* to
talk about committing sodomy.

yopunla; *yopunla keyu,* a., earnest; not
in a joke.

yosh, art., a, *lipsoli abi yosh,* a leper,
Matt. 8: 2; used with nouns, while *hosh*
is used with verbs chiefly.

yoshoba, yoshuba, a., lost; out of the
way; gone astray; sinful; evil; wicked;

guilty; ill; immoral; iniquitous; reprobate; vicious; wanton, Matt. 18: 12, 13.

yoshoba, v. n., to be lost; to be in the
wrong.

yoshoba, v. a. i., to go out of the way;
to sin; to deviate; to err; to fall; to lose
the right way; to miss; to stray; to
stumble; to swerve; to trespass.

yoshoba, n., a sin; an error; folly; guilt;
harm; illness; impiety; iniquity; sinfulness; a transgression; a trespass; uncleanness.

yoshoba, n., an offender; a sinner; a
wanderer; a straggler; a trespasser.

yoshoba, pp., lost; misled; misguided;
perverted.

yoshoba hinla, a., peccable.

yoshoba keyu, a., innocent.

yoshobatokkia nukhaⁿklo keyu, a.,
impenitent.

yoshobahe keyu, a., impeccable.

yoshobbi, yoshubi, v. t., to mislead; to
lead out of the way; to lead into sin;
to misguide; to offend; to pervert; to
stumble.

yoshobbi, n., one who misleads; a perverter; one who offends or leads
astray; *na yoshubi,* "that offends,"
Matt. 13: 41; *na yoshubli,* n., a deceiver, 2 John 1: 7.

yoshobiksho, a., sinless.

yoshobli, v. t., to lead out of the way;
to cause to err; to misguide, 1 Sam. 2:
24; to deceive, 2 John 1: 7.

yoshobli, n., one who misleads; a deceiver.

yoshoblichi, v. a. i., to deceive, Matt.
24: 4.

yuala, yuwala, n., disgust; contempt;
iⁿyuwala, contempt for it.

yuala, yuwala, a., nauseous; disgusting;
sickening to the stomach; hateful;
odious; fulsome; obscene; offensive.

yuala, pp., shocked.

yuala, yuwala, v. n., to be nauseous; to
have a sick stomach; to be sick at the
stomach.

yuala, v. a. i., to glut; to loathe; to
nauseate.

yuala, n., a loather.

yuala hinla, a., loathsome; loathful.

yuala shali, a., squeamish.

yualachi, v. t., to cause sickness at the
stomach; to render nauseous, disgust-

ing, etc.; to nauseate; *yuwalạchi*, n., an abomination; *nan ashạchi yuwalạchi*, 1 Kings 11: 5, 7.

yuha, v. a. i., to run through a sifter, riddle, etc.

yuha, pp., sifted; riddled; bolted; garbled.

yuhapa, a., boisterous; noisy; see *yahapa*.

yuhapa, v. n., to be boisterous; noisy, *yuhapoa; yuhapoli*.

yuhapa, n., a noise.

yuhạbli, yuhạpli, see *yohabli*.

yuhchashali, v. a. i., to stand up like the hair, or the feathers of a horned owl, or a plume.

yuhchonoli, v. a. i., to bow the head; to hold the head down; *yuhchonolimạt illitok*, he bowed his head and died.

yuhchunni, v. a. i. sing., to bow the head; to nod, John 13: 24; *yuhchunnolih*.

yuhchunukli, v. a. i., to bow the head once, a single sudden act; v. t., *iⁿyuchunukli*, to beckon to him, Luke 1: 22; *aka yuhchunuklimạt fiopissatok*, John 19: 30.

yuhe, n., a large hickory nut.

yuka, a., captivated; bond-bound, Josh. 9: 23; *ikyuko*, free.

yuka, pp., captured; enslaved; imprisoned; constrained; taken; enchained; subjected.

yuka, n., a captive; a prisoner; a slave; a bondman; a vassal.

yuka, n., confinement; custody; thrall; thraldom.

yuka ahalaia, a., slavish.

yuka anta, n., captivity; in bonds; in chains; in bondage.

yuka aⁿsha, n., servitude; bondage; vassalage.

yuka ạtta, a., slaveborn.

yuka chohmi, a., servile.

yuka hatak, n., a bondman.

yuka issa, n., a ransom; a release.

yuka issa, pp., freed; emancipated; liberated; enfranchised; manumitted; released.

yuka issachi, pp., liberated.

yuka issachi, v. t., to free; to emancipate; to liberate; to enfranchise; to manumit; to release; to unchain.

yuka issạchi, n., an emancipator; a liberator; a manumitter; an abolitionist.

yuka issạchi, n., emancipation; manumission.

yuka keyu, a., free; not bound.

yuka keyu, n., freedom; liberty.

yuka keyut ạtta, a., freeborn.

yuka kucha, pp., emancipated; liberated.

yuka miⁿka, n., a fellow-servant; fellow-servants.

yuka ohoyo, n., a bond woman; a bond maid.

yuka okla, n., an enslaved people; a tributary people.

yuka toⁿksạli, n., a bond servant.

yukabi, a., moistened; softened by being wet.

yukachi, v. t., to capture; to enslave; to imprison; to take captive; to take; to deprive of liberty; to hold as a prisoner; to constrain; to pen a wild creature or other animal and then catch him; to enchain; to subject; to subjugate; *yạnạsh, isuba, shukha nukshopa yukachi*.

yukachi, n., a captor; an enslaver.

yukachit halanli, yukachit iⁿshi, n., a hostage.

yukahbi, v. a. i., to soften; to become soft and pliable.

yukat aⁿsha, n., bondage.

yukbạbi, n., the venereal disease; the pox; see *luak shali*.

yukoma, yupoma, v. t., to waste; to squander; to spend; *nan isht yupoma*, to waste food about it, or him.

yukpa, v. a. i., to laugh; *yukpali, yukpachi; yokpa*, glad; *yokpạlli, yokpạchi* (some interpreters make these distinctions between *yokpa* and *yukpa*).

yukpa, a., glad; pleased; happy; joyful; gay; merry; pleasant; good-humored; good-natured; buxom; blithe; blessed; gratified; amused; halcyon; amiable; complacent; delighted; delightful; facetious; joyous; jocund; lightsome; lively; merry; well-natured; *yuppa*, Longtown form of this word; *ikyukpo*, uncheerful; unhappy; unpleased.

yukpa, v. n., to be glad, pleased, etc.; to be of good cheer, Matt. 9: 2; *chiyukpashke*.

yukpa, pp., refreshed; regaled; rejoiced; pleased, Matt. 3: 17; blessed, Matt. 11: 6; made happy; charmed; diverted;

elated; entertained; exhilarated; felicitated; gratified; joyed; recreated.

yukpa, n., joy; gladness; good nature; delight; a smile; laughter; complacency; exultation; glee; good humor; hilarity; a laugh; mirth; recreation; suavity.

yukpa, adv., fain; gladly.

yukpa, v. a. i., to smile; to laugh; to rejoice; to cheer; to chuckle; to delight; to snicker; to suit; to titter; to twitter; to exult; to giggle; to gladden; to glory; to gratify; to joy; to simper; to be pleased, Matt. 14: 6; ibaiyukpa, to rejoice with, Luke 1: 58; itibaiyukpa, to rejoice together with.

yukpa, n., a laugher.

yukpa atapa, pp., enraptured; enravished; a., rapturous.

yukpa hinla, a., placable; laughable; risible.

yukpa shali, n., a giggler.

yukpa shali, a., jolly; ticklish.

yukpahe keyu, a., difficult; he will not be pleased.

yukpalechi, v. t., to amuse; to make glad; to gratify; to beatify; to please; to gladden; to joy; ikyukpalecho, v. t., to disoblige.

yukpali, v. t., to gladden; to please; to give pleasure; to gratify; to beatify; to benefit; to amuse; to bless, 1 Sam. 2: 20; Josh. 8: 33; to make happy; to make glad; to charm; to cheer; to delight; to divert; to elate; to enrapture, to enravish; to entertain; to exalt; to exhilarate; to feast; to feed; to felicitate; to joy; to lighten; to oblige; to recreate; to refresh; to regale; to rejoin; to sport; to suit; to transport; ileyukpali, to please himself; ileyukpali, a., self-pleasing; yukpali, to gladden; yukpali, to make one laugh.

yukpali, n., a diverter; a pleaser.

yukpalit anumpuli, v. t., to bless, Josh. 14: 13.

yukpachi, v. t., to cause to laugh or smile; see yukpa; issiyukpachi, you make me laugh; ikyukpacho, neg. form.

yulhkun, n., a mole.

yulhkun chito, n., the elephant. A name given by some Choctaw. Others call the elephant hat~h lusa inyanash, the African buffalo.

yulhpokona, see holhpokunna.

yullichi, v. a. i., to twitch or start, as the nerves.

yululli, yolulli, v. a. i., to run under; to go through, as a hole; to run through; to run between; ofi at holihta itintakla yululli; hatak owatta yat Choctaw yakniyan yullit itanowa; hatak at uski an yullit anya; aiyululli, v. t., to over run.

yululli, pp., passed through; put through, as a thing is put through a long hole.

yulullichi, v. t., to cause to go through; to run through a hole, as to run a string through a hole; to drive through.

yulullit anya, v. a. i., to prowl; to worm round.

yulullit anya, n., a prowler.

yula, pp., demolished; scattered about; blown down, as a fence or the timbers of a building; chuka yat yula, 2 Cor. 5: 1.

yula, n., destruction.

yuli, v. t., to throw over; to blow down; to scatter; to demolish; yuli, Mark 12: 5; wak an yuli, holihta yan yuli.

yuli, n., a destroyer.

yuli, v. t., to sift; to bolt; to riddle; to garble.

yulichi, v. a. i., to tremble and start, like the flesh of a sick person.

yunlo, n., a whortleberry.

yumbak chito, n., a gopher.

yunna, pp., girdled.

yunni, v. t., to girdle.

yunushki, pp., girded.

yunushkichi, v. t., to girdle.

yunyuki, a., same as yinyiki, crooked.

yupechi, v. t., to bathe another; to cause another to bathe.

yupi, v. a. i., to bathe in water; to wash the body; to wallow in sand or mud; to lave; to roll in water, mud, or sand; to welter; allat yupi, shukha yat yupi, akanka yat yupi, kofi at yupi.

yupi, n., one who bathes.

yupoma, see yukoma.

yustimeli, see yushtimeli.

yustimmi, see yushtimmi.

yustololi, see yushtololi.

yushbokoli, a., having white hair; gray-haired; yushbokushli, pl.

yushbokoli, v. n., to be gray-headed.

yushbokoli, n., white hair; gray hair.

yushbokolichi, v. t., to cause the hair to be gray.

yushbonoli, n., a ringlet; a tress.

yushbonoli, pp., curled; frizzled.

yushbonuli, a., having curled hair; *yushbonushli*, pl.

yushbonuli, v. n., to be curly headed.

yushbonuli, v. a. i., to curl.

yushbonulichi, v. t., to curl the hair; to frizzle; *yushbonushlichi*, v. t. pl.

yushchunuli, v. a. i., to bow, Gen. 47: 31.

yushkabali, a., having the head shaved, trimmed, or clipped; *yushkabashli*, pl.

yushkabali, v. n., to be trimmed short or close, as hair.

yushkabalichi, v. t., to trim close; to clip the hair of the head; *yushkabashlichi*, pl.

yushkammi, v. a. i., to lust; to burn with carnal desires; *itaiyushkammi*, to rut; to lust for each other (applied to animals).

yushkammi, n., lust.

yushkilali, a., being partly bald, or having the hair cut close near the ears and a ridge left on top of the head; *yushkilashli*, pl.

yushkilali, v. n., to be partly bald.

yushkilalichi, v. t., to trim the hair close only in places; *yushkilashlichi*, pl.

yushkoboli, a., trimmed short and made round; rounded; *chufak yushkoboli*, a pin having a head; *yushkobushli*, pl.

yushkoboli, v. n., to be round-headed; to be trimmed and made round.

yushkobolichi, yushkobushlichi, v. t., to trim round; to make round-headed; to curtail.

yushkobolichi, to be bolled, as flax, Ex. 9: 31.

yushkololi, a., short, referring to things, not time or space; *iti yushkololi*, *shukha yushkololi; yushkolushli*, pl.

yushkololi, v. n., to be short.

yushkololi, pp., shortened.

yushkololichi, v. t., to make it short; to make them short; to shorten; *iti an yushkolushlichi*, cut the wood short; *yushkolushlichi*, pl.

yushkololichi, n., a shortener.

yushlatali, a., flat-headed.

yushlitalih, yushlitelih, a., round headed.

yushmilali, a., bald; having the hair very short; *yushmilashli*, pl.

yushmilali, pp., shorn.

yushmilali, v. n., to be bald.

yushmilali, n., baldness, in whole or in part.

yushmilalichi, v. t., to produce baldness; to make bald; *yushmilashlichi*, pl.

yushmitoli, a., short, as a frock or petticoat.

yushpakama, pp., bewitched, Rev. 18: 23; *yushpakamoa*, pl.

yushpakama, n., sorcery, Rev. 18: 23; *ikhinsh isht yushpakama*, witchcraft, Gal. 5: 20.

yushpakamoli, v. t. pl., to bewitch.

yushpakamolichi, v. t. pl. caus.

yushpakammi, v. t., to bewitch, Rev. 18: 23; 21: 8; to practice sorcery, Ex. 8: 7; *nan isht yushpakammi*, enchantments; *yushpakamoli* v. t. pl.; *yushpakamolichi*, v. t. pl. caus.

yushtimeli, yustimeli, a., dizzy; *yushtimashli*, pl.

yushtimeli, v. n., to be dizzy.

yushtimelichi, v. t., to make dizzy; *yushtimashlichi*, pl.

yushtimmi, yustimmi, a., dizzy.

yushtimmichi, v. t., to cause dizziness.

yushtololi, yustololi, a., short; brief; pp., shortened; *yushtolushli*, pl.

yushtololi, v. n., to be short.

yushtololi, pp., shortened.

yushtololichi, v. t., to shorten; to make brief; to contract; to scrimp; *yustolushlichi* pl.

yushwichali, a., brushy; having the hair spread out.

yushwichali, v. n., to be brushy.

yushwichalichi, v. t., to make brushy.

yushwiheli, a., brushy; having the hair spread out.

yushwiheli, v. n., to be brushy.

yushwihelichi, v. t., to render the hair brushy.

ENGLISH–CHOCTAW INDEX

ENGLISH—CHOCTAW INDEX

(NOTE.—This index does not give the Choctaw equivalent of the English word but shows where it may be found.)

a; *achạfa, ạt, ho, oⁿ, yoⁿ*
Abaddon, *nan isht ahollo okpulo*
abandon, to; *issa, issạchi*
abandon, to cause to; *aiissachechi*
abandoned, *aksho*
abandoned place, *aiissa*
abase, to; *akanlusechi*
abased, *akanlusi*
abash, to; *hofahyạchi, hofayali*
abashed; *hofahya, takshi*
abate, to; *habofa, haboffi, halata, hala-tali, halạtkạchi, shippa, shippạchechi, shippạchi*
abate, to cause to; *shippạchechi*
abate, to cause swellings to; *habolichi*
abated; *habofa, haboli, halata, halạtkạchi, shippa, shippạchi*
abated, entirely; *halatat taha*
abatement, *habofa*
abatement of swellings, *haboli*
abba, *iⁿki*
abdicate, to; *issa, kucha*
abdicated, *issa*
abdication, *issa*
abdomen; *iffuka, ikfuka, ilhfoka, takoba*
abet, to; *apela*
abettor, *apelachi*
abhor, to; *isht ikiⁿahno, nukkilli, shittilema*
abide, to; *anta, aⁿsha, ạtta, binili, binnili, maⁿya*
abject; *kalakshi, makali*
abjure, to; *anumpa kạllo ilonuchi cha ia*
able; *kanihmi, kạllo, laue, toba*
able-bodied; *aⁿli, nipi kạllo*
ablepsy, *lạpa*
abnegate, to; *haklo*
abode; *aianta, aiasha, aiạtta, chuka*
abolish, to; *akshuchi, issạchi, kobạffi, okpạni*
abolish, to cause to; *issạchechi*
abolished; *aksho, issa, kobafa, okpulo*
abolisher; *akshuchi, issạchi*
abolition, *akshuchi*

abolitionist, *yuka issạchi*
abominable; *haksi, okpulo fehna*
abominate, to; *isht ikiⁿahno*
abomination, *yualạchi*
aboriginal, *tiⁿkba*
aboriginal inhabitants, *tiⁿkba okla*
aboriginal people, *tiⁿkba okla*
abortion, *aiona*
abound, to; *apakna, laua*
about; *foka, fokali, imma, isht anumpa, pullasi*
about that time, *fokakash*
about then, *mih*
about this time, *himak foka*
about to have been, *chintok, chintuk*
above; *iⁿshali, paknaka*
abridged; *tilofa, tiloha*
abroad; *haiaka, imma, kucha, mishema fullota*
abscond, to; *luhmi*
absconder, *luhmi*
absence, *taklạchi*
absent, *iksho*
absolutely, to do anything; *ạmohmi*
absorbed at, *akạnia, ashippa*
abstain, to; *na hollochi, hullochi*
abstemious; *impa fena keyu, ishko fena keyu*
absurd, *okpulo*
abundance; *alotowa, apakna, laua, pakna*
abundance, to cause an; *apaknạchi*
abundance, to have an; *nan inlaua*
abundant; *apakna, laua*
abuse, to; *haksichi, hotupali, okpạni*
abused, *akkaona*
abyss, an; *ahofobi, aiokpuloka, kolokbi*
abyss, the; *ahofobika*
academy; *holisso aiithạna chito, holisso aiithạna chuka, holisso apisa chuka*
accelerate, to; *pạlhkichechi, tuⁿshpạchi*
accept, to; *aiokpạchi*
acceptable; *achukma, aiukli, imaⁿka*
access; *aiona, atia*
accident, *ishkanạpa*

accidental, *ishkanapa*
accommodate with, to; *ima*
accompany, to; *auataya, tankla anya*
accomplish, to; *aianlichi*
accomplished, *alhpesa*
accomplishment, *alhtaha*
accost, to; *aiokpachi*
account, *isht anumpa*
account, to; *hotina*
account book, *itatoba holisso*
accouple, to; *apotoli*
accoutre, to; *shema, shemachi*
accoutred, *shema*
accoutrements, *nan isht shema*
accumulate, to; *itannali*
accumulated, *itanaha*
accumulation, *itanaha*
accurate, *anli*
accursed, *isikkopa*
accursed thing, *nan inhullochi*
accusable, *anumpa onucha hinla*
accuse, to; *achokushpali, amihachi, anumpa onuchi, ikbi, nan alhpisa onuchi*
accuse falsely, to; *aholabechi*
accusation, *anumpa onutula*
accused; *achokushpa, anumpa onutula, onutula*
accuser, *anumpa onuchi*
accustom, to; *achayachi*
accustomed; *achaya, aiimomachi, yamohmi*
acerb, *takba*
acetous; *hauashko, homi, kaskaha*
ache, to; *hotupa, kommichi, mufka, nukhammi*
ache in the bones, to; *foni kommichi*
achieve, to; *loshummi, lushomi*
aching; *kommichi, nukhammi*
acid; *hauashko, kaskaha*
acid, to become; *hauashko*
acknowledge, to; *aiokpachi, anoli, ikhana*
acorn, *nusi*
acorn pudding, *okshash*
acquaint, to; *ikhana, ikhananchi*
acquaintance, *ikhana*
acquaintance, an; *hatak ikhana*
acquainted with, to be; *akostininchi*
acquiesce, to; *alhpesa ahni, ome ahni*
acquire, to; *ahauchi*
acquire knowledge, to; *anukfohki, ikhana*
acquire knowledge at, to; *aiithana*

acrid; *homi, takba*
acrid water, *oka homi*
acrimonious, to render; *nukhomechi*
across, *okhoata*
act, to; *akaniohmi*
act in order, to; *silhhi*
action; *akaniohmi, ilhkoli*
active; *ashwanchi, tushpa*
activity, *palhki*
actor; *isht atta, na, nan isht atta*
acute; *halupa, halupoa, kallo*
adage, *na miha*
add, to; *achakalechi, achakalechi, albilli, ibakali*
add on, to; *achakalechi*
add on at, to; *aiitachakalli*
add to, to; *achakali, ibafoki, ibani*
added together, *ibalhkaha*
adder; *hahta, hawash*
addice; *isht chanya, peni isht chanya*
addicted to, *shali*
addition; *achakaya, alhchakaya, ibalhkaha, itibalhkaha*
additional, *alhchakaya*
address, a short; *anumpa tilofa, anumpa tiloli*
address, a very short; *anumpa tilofasi*
address, an; *anumpa isht hika*
adept, an; *imponna*
adequate; *alauechi, alaui, laue*
adhere, to; *aialbo, alapali, anuksita, albo*
adhere, to cause to; *akmochi, aiakmochi, alapalechi*
adhered, *aialbo*
adherent, a political; *tashka*
adhesive, *niashmo*
adipose, *nia*
adjacent, *bilinka*
adjoin, to; *apotoli*
adjoining house; *chuka apanta, chuka apantali*
adjourn, to; *abanablichi*
adjudge, to; *apesa*
adjudicate, to; *apesa*
adjust, to; *aposkiachi*
adjusted rightly, *achukmat alhpisa*
administer, to; *ipeta*
administer medicine, to; *alikchi, ikhinsh ipeta*
administrator, *isht atta*
admire, to; *okokkoaiahni*
admit, to; *chukoa*
admonish, to; *miha*

adoption; *alla toba, ushi isht atoba*
adorn, to; *aiuklichi, atahpali, pisa aiuklichi, shema, shemachi*
adorn with a plume, to; *shikopa isht shema*
adorned; *pisa aiukli, shema*
adroit, *imponna*
adult, *asano*
adult, an; *asano*
adulterate, to; *ibani*
adulteress; *hatak i^{n}haklo, haui*
adulterous, *haui*
adultery, *hatak i^{n}haklo*
adultery, to commit; *hatak i^{n}haklo, haui itimalhpisa, luma^{n}ka*
advance, to; *achakali*
advance, to cause to; *achakachi*
advanced in years, *sipokni*
advantage, *isht ilaiyukpa*
adversary, *ichapa*
adversity; *isht aiilbasha, isht anukha^{n}klo, nan imokpulo*
advertiser, *anoli*
advice, *anumpa*
advise, to; *miha, nan i^{n}miha, nanuka, nanukachi*
adviser, *nan i^{n}miha*
advocate, to; *anumpuli*
advocate for, to; *apepoa*
advocates, *apepoa*
adz; *isht cha^{n}ya, peni isht cha^{n}ya*
affair, *nana*
affect, to; *haleli, kanihmi*
affect all, to; *mominchi*
affect the mouth, to; *itukwesoli, kaiolichi*
affections, the; *chu^{n}kash, chu^{n}kash imanukfila*
affirm, to; *a^{n}li achit anoli*
afflict, to; *ilbashachi, ilbashali, nukha^{n}klochi*
afflicted; *ilbasha, nukha^{n}klo*
affliction; *aiilbasha, ilbasha, isht nukha^{n}klo*
affluence, *nan inlaua*
affluent, *nan inlaua*
affluent, the; *nan inlaua*
affray, to; *nuklakanchichi*
affright, to; *nuklakanchichi*
affrighted, *nuklakancha*
affront, to; *chu^{n}kash hutupali, hotupali*
aforetime, *ti^{n}kba*
afraid; *anukwia, malali, nukshopa, nukwia, takshi*

afresh, *himona*
Africa, *hatak lusa i^{n}yakni*
African buffalo, *hatak lusa i^{n}yannash*
after; *ha, haya, himmak, i^{n}himmak, o^n*
after a while; *hopakikma, hopakikmako*
after the, *kma*
afternoon; *okataha, tabokoli ont ia*
afterward, *himmak*
aid, *anump imeshi*
aid, an; *apela, mi^{n}ko imanumpeshi, nan apela, nan apelachi*
aid-de-camp, *anumpeshi*
ail, to; *kanihmi*
ailment; *nan apa, nan i^{n}kanimi*
aim, to; *ahni, anompisachi, tanampo anumpisachi*
aimed at, the place; *abilepa*
air, the; *mali*
air, to; *hufka, ufka*
aired, *holufka*
again; *anoa, anonti, atuklant, falamat, inli, na*
against, the going; *asunanta*
against wind or tide, to go; *asonali*
age; *kasheho, sipokni*
age, old; *sipokni*
aged; *asahnoyechi, kamassa, kasheho, kauasha, sipokni*
aged, the; *asanonchi, asunonchi*
aged, to render; *sipoknichi*
aged man, *hatak kamassalli*
aged men, *hatak kamassalleka*
agent; *isht atta, na, na hollo holitopa, nan isht atta*
agent, a United States; *na hollo mi^{n}ko*
aggravate, to; *aiyabechi, atablichi, i^{n}shali*
aggrieved, *nukha^{n}klo*
agile, *tushpa*
agitate, to; *tiabli*
agitated; *anuktiboha, nukhobela, oka piakachi, piakachi*
agitation of the heart, an; *nukwimekachi*
ago, *fokakash*
agone, *fokakash*
agony, *nukhammi*
agony, to cause; *nukhammichi*
agree, to; *apesa, ibafoka, imanukfila achafa, imanukfila itibafoka*
agreeable; *alhpesa, chukma, hochukma*
agreed, *alhpesa*
agreeing, *alhpesa*
agreement; *apesa, anumpa alhpisa, nana alhpisa*

agriculturist, *hatak osapa to^nksạli*
aground, to run; *akkatạla*
ague; *ahochukwa, hochukwa*
ague fit, *wạnnichi*
aguish; *ahochukwa, hochukwa, hochuk-*
wạchi, hochukwoba
ah! *aiehnạ!, hiho, ikikki*
ah me! *huk*
ahead, *tikba*
aim, to; *anumpisachi*
Alabama, *Hạlbamo*
Alabama River, *Hạlbamo okhina*
alas! *aiehnạ!, hale!, hauk, huk, hush,*
ikikki
albumen; *aka^nk ushi i^nwạlaha, aka^nk*
ushi wạlakạchi
alcohol; *na homi, oka homi*
alert, *tushpa*
alias, *yatush*
alienate, to; *kanchi, i^nhollot issa*
alienated, *chu^nkạsh inla*
alienation; *kanchi, tasembo*
alight, to; *akkoa*
alike, *holba*
alike, made; *holbạt toba*
alike, to become; *holbạt toba*
alike in kind, *aiimmi bi^nka*
aliment; *ilhpak, nan ilimpa*
alive, *okcha^nya*
alive (as a tree), *okcha^nki*
all; *aiokluha, ạliha, bano, ilaiyuka, moma,*
momạt, nan uha, okluha, oklu^nha, puta,
putali, uha
all, one who takes; *tomạffi*
all about, *kanima moma*
all days, *nitak moma*
all men, *okluha*
all nature, *nana moma*
all over the world, *yakni fullota*
all people, *okla moma*
all round, *folota*
all things; *nan okluha, okluha, nana*
moma
all, to destroy; *tomạffi*
all, to use; *u^nhạlinchi*
allay, to; *chulosạchi, hopolạchi, nuktalali,*
nuktalalichi, yokopuli
allayed; *chulosa, hopola, nuktạla*
allege, to; *a^nli fehna achit miha*
allegory, *anumpa nan isht ạlhpisa*
alley; *anowa, atia, hina*
allies, *apepoa*
alligate, to; *atakchechi*
alligator, *hachunchubạ*

allot, to; *kạshkoli*
allotted, *kạshkoa*
allow, to; *apesa*
allowance, *afạmmikm̃a ilhpeta*
allure, to; *anukpạllichi, nukpạllichi*
ally; *apela, apelachi, itạpela, nan apela*
ally, to; *apoa*
almanac, *hạshi nitak isht ikhạna*
almighty, *palạmmi*
Almighty God, the; *Chihowa pạllạmmi*
almost; *a^nhe, a^nhesi, a^nhusi, he, naha,*
pullasi
alms, to do; *habenạchi*
almug tree, *almuk*
aloft; *ạba, chaha*
alone; *bano, beka, chanaia, ilap bano, ilap*
bieka
alone, to live; *ilap banot anta*
alone, to make; *banochi*
along; *abaiyạt, ta^nkla*
along before, *tikbali*
along the road, *hinanli*
along the side of, to be or lie; *abaiya*
along the side of, to go; *abaiyạchi*
along with; *awant, iba, itatuklo*
alongside of, *abaiyạt*
already; *mashko, ma^nshko*
also; *aiena, ak, hak, hokola, inli, kia*
altar; *ahoshmi, alta, ạba topa*
altar of incense; *na balama ahushmi,*
na balama alua
alter, to; *aiinla, aiinlạchi, hobạk ikbi,*
inla, inlạchi
altercate, to; *anumpa itinlauachi*
altercation, *anumpa itinlaua*
altercation, to have an; *anumpa*
itinlaua
altered; *aiinla, hobạk, inla*
although; *ik, kia, yohmi kia*
although it is so, *yohmi kia*
altitude, *chaha*
altogether, *bano*
alum, *tạli holiya*
alum salt, *hạpi lakchi*
always; *abilia, aiemoma, beka, bilia,*
chatok, chokạmo
always so; *aiimoma, atak, chatok*
amalgamated, *ibakaha*
amanuensis, *holissochi*
amass, to; *itahobi*
amassed, *itạnaha*
amaurosis, to have; *fichik ạsha*
amaze, to; *anuklakạshli, okokkoaiahnichi*
amazed; *anuklakancha, nuklakạnchạ*

amazement, *anuklakancha*

ambassador; *anumpa shali, inshali iman-umpeshi, minko imanumpeshi*

ambitious man, *hatak holitopa banna*

ambrosial, *balama*

ameliorate, to; *achchukmali, aiskia, aiskiachi*

ameliorated, *aiskia*

amended, *aiskia*

America; *Miliki, Milikl yakni*

American, *Miliki*

American, an; *Miliki hatak, Miliki okla*

amiable; *halhpansha, yukpa*

amid, *takla*

amidst; *iba, takla*

amiss, *ashachi*

amity, *kana*

ammunition; *isht hunsa, nan isht hunsa*

among; *aiititakla, iba, ibatankla, itin-takla, takla*

among themselves, *ilap binka*

amount, *moma*

amount to, to; *ona*

amount to several, to; *katohmona*

ample; *falaia alhpesa, laua alhpésa, patha, patha alhpiesa*

amplify, to; *lauachi*

amputate, to; *basht tapli*

amuse, to; *aiokpachechi, chukushpali, yukpalechi, yukpali*

amused, *yukpa*

an; *achafa, ho, on, yon*

ancestor; *hatak intinkba, hatak tinkba, tikba*

ancestors, his or her maternal; *intikba*

anchor, an; *tali chito isht talali*

ancient; *chanshpo, nitak tinkba*

ancient, an; *hatak tinkba*

ancient days, *nitak tinkba*

ancient man, *hatak chanshpo*

ancients, *hatak chanshpo*

anciently; *chanshpo, nitak tinkba, tinkba*

and; *aiena, akocha, akucha, amba, anonti, atuklonchi, aua, cha, ish, kesh, kish, mih, mikma, na, sh, yamohmikma, yohmi kia, yohmima, yohmimat*

and as, *mak*

and he, *atuk*

and so, *yamohmima*

and so forth, *chomi*

and so on, *chomi*

and the, *mih*

and then, *mih, na, yohmima*

and therefore, *mih*

andirons; *itakowa intula, tali luak tikeli, tali ulhtikeli*

angel; *aba hatak, aba shilombish, enchil*

anger; *aiinnukkilli, isht ittulá, nukhobela, nukkilli, nukoa*

anger, to; *nukhobelachi, nukoachi*

angle, to; *nan okweli, nani hokli*

angler; *nan okweli, nani hokli*

angry; *anukhobela, anukyiminta, chunkash halupa, hashanya, humma, nukhobela, nukoa, okpolo, okpulo*

angry, very; *nukoa shali*

anility, *kasheho*

animal, a certain small wild; *toni*

animate, *okchanya*

animate, to; *chiletalli, chilitachi, ilhfiopak, tunshpalechi, tunshpali*

animated; *aiyimita, chilita, tushpa, yiminta*

animation, *yiminta*

ankle; *imuksak, iyi imuksak*

ankle bone, *imuksak foni*

ankle joint; *iyi imuksak itachakalli, iyi tilokachi*

announce, to; *miha*

annoy, to; *anumpulechi*

annually; *afammaiyukali, afammikma*

annuity; *aiilhpeta, habena, nan ilhpita*

annul, to; *akshuchi, kobaffi*

annulled; *aksho, kobafa*

anodyne; *ikhinsh nusechi, nusilhhachi*

anoint, to; *ahammi, atokolit halalli, bilahammi, fohki*

anoint, to cause to; *ahammichi*

anoint another, to; *bilahammichi*

anointed; *ahama, bilahama*

anointed, the; *alhtoka*

anointing, *ahama*

anointing oil, *pansh isht ahama*

anon; *ashalinka, yakosi ititakla*

anonymous; *hochifo iksho, hochifo iktakalo*

another; *achafa, inla*

another clan, *iksa inla*

another man, *hatak inla*

another place, *kanon*

another's, *inla immi*

answer; *anumpa falama, anumpa falamoa*

answer, to; *achi, afalamichi, anumpa falamolichi, anumpa falammichi*

answer again, to; *falammichit anumpuli*

answered, *anumpa falama*

answering again; *ichapa, ichapoa*
ant, *shu^{n}kani*
ant eggs, *shu^{n}kani ushi*
ant-heap, *shu^{n}kani inchuka*
ant-hill, *shu^{n}kani inchuka*
antagonist, *ichapa, tanap*
antecedent, *ti^{n}kba*
antecessor, *hatak ti^{n}kba*
anthem, *ataloa*
anthropophagite, *hatak apa*
antiquated, *sipokni*
antique, *sipokni*
antiquity; *nitak ti^{n}kba, hatak ti^{n}kba*
antiquity, all; *hatak ti^{n}kba aliha*
antler; *lapish filamminchi, lapish i^{n}fil-
ammi*
anvil, *talaboa*
anxiety, *imanukfila komunta*
anxious; *imanukfila komunta, palata*
any; *kanima, kaniohmi, kia, nana kia*
any day; *nitak kaniohmi kia, nitak nana*
any more, *himmakma*
any other, *inla*
any time, *nitak kaniohmi kia*
anybody, *kana kia*
anyone; *kanima kia, kana, kana kia,
kanahosh, kata, nanta*
anyone whatever, *kanaho kia*
anything; *nana, nana hosh, nana kia,
nanta*
anywhere; *kanima kia, katima, kç̱ni*
apace, *tu^{n}shpa*
apartment, *aboha itatapa*
apathy, *hiahni iksho*
ape; *hatak shaui, shaui hatak*
ape, to; *hobachi*
aperture; *atiwa, itopa, okhisa*
apex, *wishakchi*
apiary, *foe bilishke inchuka i^{n}hoshontika*
apiece, *ayukali*
Apollyon, *nan isht ahollo okpulo*
apology, *nan isht amiha*
apostasy; *aba anumpa i^{n}filammi, iksa
issa*
apostate; *aba anumpa issa, aba anumpuli kobafa, iksa issa.*
apostatize, to; *aba anumpa issa, iksa
issa*
apostatize, to cause to; *iksa issachi*
apostle; *anumpeshi, aba anumpeshi,
Chisas Kilaist imanumpeshi*
apothecary, *ikhi^{n}sh kanchi*
appalled, *nukshopa*

apparel; *ilefoka, na fohka*
apparel, to; *na foka fokachechi, shema*
appareled; *na foka foka, shema*
apparently; *achini, chini*
apparition, *shilup*
appear, to; *achini, ahoba, aiahoba, auata,
haiaka, holba, kucha, oktani*
appear (as the new moon), to; *hashi
himo auata*
appear, to cause to; *haiakachi, oktanichi*
appear in sight, to; *oktani*
appear like, to cause to; *ahoballi*
appear so, to; *chini*
appearance; *ahoba, haiaka, holba, kaniohmi, oktani, pisa*
appeared, *haiaka*
appease, to; *chulosachi, hopolachi, nuktalali, palakachi, yokopuli*
appeased, *chulosa*
appetite, *na banna*
applaud, to; *ahnichi, aiokpanchi*
applause, *aiokpanchi*
apple; *na hollo intakkon, takkon chito,
takkon masu^{n}fa, takkonlipun*
apple, crab; *shakulap*
apple, custard; *umbi*
apple sauce, *takkon masu^{n}fa honni*
apple tree, *takkon masu^{n}fa api*
applicant, *nana silhha*
apply, to; *onochi*
apply the mind, to; *imanukfila onuchi*
appoint, to; *apesa, atokoli, hopena*
appoint for, to; *atali*
appointed; *aialhtokowa, alhpesa, alhtoka*
appointed days, *nitak alhpisa*
appointer, *hopena*
appointment, *alhtoka*
appraiser, *aiilli onuchi*
apprehend, to; *akostininchi, ishi*
approach, to; *akanali, atikkonofa, atukonofa, bili^{n}ka, minti*
approaching old age, *hatak kauashachi*
approbate, to; *aiokpanchi, alhpesa achi*
approve, to; *ahnichi, aiokpachi, alhpesa
achi, yamma achi*
approximate, to; *akanali, akanalichechi,
bili^{n}kachi*
April, *Eplil*
apron, *na foka intikba takali*
apt, *hepulla*
aqua vitae, *oka homi*
arable; *patafa alhpesa, patafa hinla*
arbiter, *nan apesa*

arbor; *chishakko, hoshontika, wia*
arch of heaven, the middle of the; *tabokoa*
archer, *iti tanampo isht aⁿya*
arctic, *falammi pilla*
ardent; *achunanchi, chilita, homi, lashpa*
ardent spirits; *oka homi, oka luak, oke homi, oke luak*
arduous, *palammi*
argil, *lukfi*
argue for, to; *apepoa*
arid, *shila*
arise, to; *oiya, tani, toba, wakaya*
arithmetic; *na holhtina, na holhtina holisso*
arithmetician, *hotina*
ark; *itombi holitopa, itombushi, peni patha, penushi*
Arkansas River, *Okahpa okhina*
arm; *ibbak, shakba*
arm, left; *shakba alhfabeka*
arm, right; *shakba isht impaka*
arm, strong; *shakba kallo*
arm, to; *na halupa ilatali, na halupa imatali*
arm bands, *shakba alhfoa*
arm bone, *ibbak foni*
arm of a lake, *okhata filomminchi*
arm of a tree, *iti naksish filamminchi*
arm of the sea, *okhata filomminchi*
armed, *na halupa imalhtaha*
armhole, *shakba afoka*
armor, *halupa*
armory, *na halupa aiasha*
armpit, *haktampi*
arms, *na halupa*
arms, the bended or folded; *shakba poloma*
army; *tanap, tashka chipota*
around, to be; *afopa, apakfokachi*
aroused; *okcha, yiminta*
arrange, to; *achukmat apesa, apoksiali*
arranged, *achukmat alhpisa*
arrant; *haksi, okpulo*
array, to; *fohkachechi, shema, shemachi, tahpali, tahpalichi*
arrayed by means of, *shema*
arrayed in, *shema*
arrayed with, *shema*
arrearage, *aheka takanli*
arrears, *aheka takanli*
arrest, to; *issachi, oktabli, takchit ishi*
arrival; *ala, ala, ona*
arrival, first; *onahpi*

arrive, to; *ala, anusi ona, ishla, ona*
arrive at, to; *ala, ona*
arrive at last, to; *aiyala*
arrive together, to; *alachi*
arrogant; *fehnachi, ilefehnachi*
arrow; *oski, shumo naki, uski naki*
arrow of a blowgun; *shumatti, shumo holutti*
arrow-head; *nakachosha, uski naki halupa*
arrow point, *uski naki halupa*
arsenic, *pichali isht illi*
artery; *akshish, hakshish, hakshish chito, issish akshish, issish iⁿhina*
article; *na, nana*
artificer, *nan isht apesa imponna*
artillery; *tanamp chito, tanamp hochito*
artisan; *nan isht apesa imponna, toⁿksali imponna*
artist, *toⁿksali imponna*
artless, *ikhana*
as, to be; *chohmi*
as, to do; *chohmichi*
as for me, *annonto*
as for the; *ato, ato, hano*
as for the one which, *ato*
as for the present time, *himak ano*
as much as one, *achafona*
as soon as, *mak*
ascend, to; *asonali, aba ia, abia, oiya, oti, shoboli, shobota*
ascend, to cause to; *oiyachi*
ascent, *oiya*
ascertain, to; *akostininchi*
ash, *shinap*
ash, white; *shinap*
ash-bin, *hituk chubi aialhto*
ash-box, *hituk chubi aialhto*
ash-house, *hituk chubi inchuka*
ash-tub, *hituk chubi aialhto*
ashamed; *hofahya, takshi*
ashes, *hituk chubi*
ashes, hot; *hituk yanha*
ashes, light white; *luak ipokni*
ask, to; *asilhha, asilhhachi, panaklo, ponaklo*
ask for, to; *hoyo*
askew, *shanaia*
asleep; *nusi, shimoha, taliskachi, talissa*
aspect; *pisa, nashuka*
asperity, *okpulo*
aspire to help, to; *ibawichi*
ass; *isuba haksobish falaia, isuba nashoba*
assassin, *haksinchit abi*

assassinate, to; *haksinchit ạbi*
assemble, to; *itahoba, itahobi, itahobli, itanali, itạnaha, itạnnali, itạnnalichi*
assemble, to cause to; *itạnahachi*
assemble at, to; *aiitahoba, aiitahobi, aiitạnaha, aiitạnnali*
assembled; *itahoba, itạnaha*
assembler; *itahobi, itahobli, itạnnali*
assembly; *hatak itahoba, hatak itạnaha, itahoba, itạnaha*
assent, to; *ataklamma, ạlhpesa miha, haklo, ome ahni, yạmma achi*
assert, to; *achi, aⁿli achit miha*
assigned, *aiạlhtokowa*
assimilate, to; *hobachi, hobachit ikbi*
assist, to; *apela, apepoa*
assistant; *apela, apelachi, nan apela*
associate, to; *ibafoka*
associated with, to be; *aiitạpiⁿha*
association, *itahoba*
assuage, to; *chulosa, halata, halatali, hopolạchi, nuktalali, shippạli, yokopạchi*
assuaged; *halata, halạtkạchi, hopola, shippa, shippạchi, yokopa*
assume, to; *ishi*
assurance against doubt, *tah*
assure, to; *aⁿlichi*
asthma; *fiopa imokpulo, nukshiniⁿfa*
astonish, to; *anuklakạshli, okokkoaiahnichi*
astonished, *anuklakancha, nuklakancha*
astound, to; *anuklakạshli, okokkoaiahnichi*
astray, gone; *yoshoba*
astray, to go; *ashạchi*
astray, to lead; *ashạchechi*
astringency, *takba*
astringent; *homi, itukwisli, takba, takbạchi*
astringent, to render; *takbạchi*
at; *a, ạ, ai, i, itoma, pilla, yạmmak o*
at a future time, *himmakma*
at a loss; *anuktuklo, imaiyokoma*
at all, *kạmomi*
at hand; *biliⁿka, mih, olanusi*
at last; *himmak, polaⁿka*
at length, *polaⁿka*
at once, *himonali*
at once, to do; *himonali*
at that time; *a, fokakash, fokali*
at the head, *ibetạp pilla*
at the same time, *himonna achạfa*
at this place, *ilạppak*
at this time; *himak, maⁿshko*

athletic; *kạllo, kilimpi, lampko, nipi kạllo*
athwart, *okhoata*
atmosphere, *mali*
atone, to; *atobbi*
atoned, *ạlhtoba*
atonement, *ạlhtoba*
atrocious, *okpulo fehna*
attach, to; *ishi*
attachment, *anuksita*
attack, to; *amokạfa*
attain, to; *ạla, ona, onachi*
attempt, *ilahobbi*
attempt, to; *ibawichi, ilahobbi, pisa*
attend, to; *atoni, haklo, haponaklo, taⁿkla aⁿya*
attend, to cause to; *haponaklochi*
attend to, to; *anta, hikikiⁿa*
attendant; *apạha, itạpiha*
attentive, *aiokpạchi*
attest, to; *aⁿlichi*
attested, *aⁿli*
attire; *isht shema, na fohka*
attire, to; *ilefoka foka, na foka foka, shema, shemạchi*
attorney; *anumpa nan ạlhpisa isht ạtta, isht ạtta, laya*
auburn, *lusbi*
auction, *kanchi*
audacious, *nukwia iksho*
audible, *haiaka*
audience, *haponaklo*
auditor; *haponaklo, na haklo*
auger; *isht fotoha, isht fotoha iskitini, iti isht fotoha, hopaii*
auger handle, *isht fotoha ulhpi*
August, *Akạs*
august; *chito, holitopa*
aunt; *ishki, ishki toba, iⁿhukni*
aurora; *onnat isht inchi, tohwiket minti*
austere, *palạmmi*
austere, to act as; *atạpa*
authentic, *aⁿli*
authenticate, to; *aⁿlichi*
authenticated, *aⁿli*
author; *ikbi, holisso ikbi*
authority; *ạlhtoka, nan isht aiạlhpesa*
authorize, to; *atohnuchi, atokoli, atonhuchi*
authorized, *ạlhtoka*
autocrat, *miⁿko*
autocrat of Russia, the; *Lạshe iⁿmiⁿko*
autumn; *ahpi, hạshtulahpi, onafapi*
auxiliary; *apela, apelachi, nan apela*

avail, to; *nan ihmi, nan ihmichi*
avail nothing, to; *nan ihmi keyu*
availing, *nan ihmi*
avails, *isht ahauchi*
avaricious; *hatak nan iⁿholitopa, nan iⁿholitopa*
avenge, to; *atobbi, okha*
avenged, *ạlhtoba*
avenger; *atobbi, okha*
avenue; *anowa, atia, hina*
averse, *bạnna*
avert, to; *falạmmichi*
avoid, to; *apakfokạchi*
avouch, to; *aⁿli achit miha*
await, to; *hoyo*
awake, *okcha*
awake, to; *okcha, okchạli*
awake, to cause to; *okchalechi*
awaken, to; *okchachi*
awakened, *okcha*
aware; *ahni, ikhana*
away; *bilia, pilla*
away here, *ilạppa pilla*
away off, *pilla*   .
awkward, *ikhana*
awl; *chufak, isht achunli*
awl-handle, *chufak ahokli*
awry; *shanaia, shanaioa*
ax; *iskifa, isht chaⁿya*
ax, a broad; *iskifa pạtha*
ax, a carpenter's; *iskifa pạtha*
ax, a sharp; *iskifa halupa*
ax, the bit of an; *iskifa wishakchi*
ax, the edge of an; *iskifa ahalupa*
ax, the eye of an; *iskifa chiluk, iskifa nishkin*
ax, the head of an; *iskifa chushak, iskifa nushkobo*
ax helve; *iskifa ulhpi, iskifapi*
axletree, *iti chanạlli achosha*
aye, *akạt*

baa (cry of a sheep), *baⁿhachi*
babble, to; *anumpuli ilahobi, himak fokalit anumpuli*
babbler, *anumpuli ilahobi*
babe; *ạlluⁿsi, chiⁿshka, puskus*
baboon, *shaui hatak chito*
baby; *ạlluⁿsi, chiⁿshka, puskus*
bacchanalian, *hatak okishko shali*
bachelor; *hatak ohoyo ikimiksho, tekchi iksho*
back, *ulbạl*
back, away; *ulbạl pilla*

back, small of the; *inchạshwa*
back, the; *nạli*
back, the upper part of the; *shinạkha*
back, to; *apela, falạmmichi, oiya, omanili*
back, to go; *ulbạlhpelạt ia*
back between the shoulders, the; *shanạkha*
back door, *aboha aⁿshaka okhissạ*
back of a horse, *isuba nạli*
back of the hand, *ibbak paknaka*
back of the head, *iachushak*
back of the neck, *iachuna*
back water; *oka bikeli, oka falama*
backbite, to; *achokushpali, anumpa chukushpali, aⁿshakachi, hatak nanumachi, na mihachi, nan iⁿmihachi*
backbiter; *achokushpali, aⁿshakachi, hatak nanumachi, na mihachi, nan iⁿmihachi*
backbiter, a great; *hatak nanumachi shali*
backbone; *nahchạba, nạli foni, sachakla*
backside, *aⁿshaka intạnnạp*
backslide, to; *afilema, ạba anumpa issạt falama, falama*
backslider; *ạba anumpa issạt falama, falama, falamoa.*
backward; *obạlhpela, okbạl, olbạlhpila, ulbạlhpela, ulbạl pila*
backward and forward, to go; *falamoa*
backward, to go; *ulbạlhpelạt ia*
backward, to move; *obạlh kanạli*
bacon; *shukha nia shila, shukha pạsa shila*
bacon, to make; *shukha nipi shileli*
bad; *achukma, aiokpulo, aknaⁿka, okpulo*
bad luck, to cause; *poafạchi*
badge, *isht ạlhpisa*
badly; *okpulo, okpulot*
badness, *okpulo*
bag; *bahta, hạchik, ipiⁿshik, shukcha*
bags, saddle; *wak hakshup shukcha*
baggage, *shapo*
baggage horse; *isuba shapo shali, isuba shapuli*
bail; *ahalạlli, isht halạlli, iyasha ahalạlli*
bait, *isht ạlbi*
bait, to; *hotoⁿsi, isht ạlbi intakalichi*
baiter for beaver, *hotoⁿsichi*
bake, to; *apushli, nuna, nunachi, palạska, pạska, shila, shileli*
bake, to cause to; *nunachechi*
baked; *nuna, palạska, shila*
baker; *pạsk ikbi, pạska*
bakery, *aboha apalạska*

baking place, *apalạska*
balance, *ạlhtampa*
balance, a; *nan isht weki, nan isht wekichi*
balance, the; *ạlhkucha*
balance, to; *weki itilaui, weki itilauichi, wekichi*
balanced; *weki itilaui*
balances, *isht wekichi*
bald; *okmilali, okmilạshli, okmiloti, okmilonli, paⁿsh iksho, yushmilali*
bald, to be partly; *yushkilali*
bald, to make; *okmilalichi, okmilạshlichi, yushmilalichi*
bald face, *ibakhatanli*
bald faces, *ibakhataⁿshli*
bald-faced; *ibakhatanli, ibakhataⁿshli*
baldness; *okmilali, yushmilali*
baldness, to produce; *yushmilalichi*
bale, *bahta chito*
bale, to; *bahta chito abeti*
baled, *bahta chito ạbiha*
baleful; *isht ạfekommi, okpulo*
balk, *yakni ikapatafo*
ball; *lumbo, towa*
ball (a dance), *hila*
ball, black; *shulush isht lusachi*
ball ground; *atoli, hitoka*
ball playground, a small; *isht aboli*
ball stick, *akkabata, kapucha*
ballad, *taloa*
ballroom, *ahila*
balm, *bam*
balm, wild; *shinuktiteli*
balmy, *balama*
balmy, to make it; *balamạchi*
bamboo brier, *bisakchakinna*
band; *afohoma, isht talakchi, nan isht talakchi*
band, a train; *tạshka chipota*
bandage; *ạlhfoa, isht apakfoa*
banded; *apakfoa, talakchi*
bane, *isht illi*
bang, to; *boli*
banish, to; *chạfichi*
banished, *chạfa*
bank; *bokko, sakti ikbi*
bank, a furrowed; *sakti laⁿfa*
bank, a high; *sakti chaha*
bank, a red; *sakti humma*
bank, a steep; *sakti chaha*
bank, an artificial; *sakti toba*
bank, to; *bokkuchi, sakti ikbi*
bank (for money), *tạli holisso aboti*

bank bill; *holisso lapushki, tạli holisso tapuski*
bank note, *holisso lapushki*
bank of a river, *ont*
bank of a stream, *sakti*
banked, *bokko*
banker, *tạli holisso itatoba*
bankrupt; *nan chumpa kobạfa, nan ittatoba kobạfa*
banks, red; *sakti humma*
banks of a river, *bok sakti*
banner; *na hạta, shạpha*
banquet; *chepulli, impa chito*
banquet, to make a; *chepulechi*
baptism; *baptismo, oka isht okissa*
baptist; *baptismochi, baptist*
baptize, to; *baptismochi, oka isht okissạchi*
baptized; *baptismo, oka isht okissa*
baptizer, *baptismochi*
bar, *holi*
bar, to; *okshita, oktabli*
bar holes in a post, *holihta okhisa aiachushkạchi*
barb, *isht ạtapạchi*
barb, to; *ạtapạchi, isht ạtapạchi ikbi*
barbecue, to; *abani*
barbecued beef; *wak nipi ạlbani*
barber, *hatak paⁿsh ạmo*
bard, *ataloa ikbi*
bare, *hishi iksho*
bareboned, *foni bano*
barebones, *hatak chunna*
barefaced, *nashuka bieka*
barefaced man; *hatak ạfikommi, hatak hofahya iksho*
barefoot; *bano, iyi bano, iyi beka*
bareheaded, *nushkobo beka*
barely, *illa*
barenecked, *ikonla bekạt aⁿya*
barenecked, to go; *ikonla bekạt aⁿya*
bargain, *anumpa itimapesa*
bargain, to; *anumpa itimapesa*
bargain away, to; *kanchi*
bargain for, to; *apobạchi*
bargained, *anumpa itimạlhpisa*
barge, *peni*
bargeman, *peni isht ạtta*
bark; *akchạlhpi, hakchạlhpi, hakchạlhpi shila, hakshup iti haklupish, iti hakshup*
bark, dry; *akchạlhpi, chạbli*
bark, to; *kaⁿwa, paⁿya, wowoha, woha, wohwah, wohwoha*
bark at, to; *wotichi*

barked, *loha*
barn, *kanchak*
barrack; *tashka chipota aiasha, tashka chipota inchuka*
barred; *alhkama, alhkomoa, okshillita, oktapa*
barrel, *italhfoa chito*
barrel, to; *italhfoa chito abeli, italhfoa chito fohki*
barreled; *italhfoa chito abeha, italhfoa chito foka*
barren; *ashabi, alla ikimiksho, ushi iksho*
barren, to render; *ashabichi*
barricade; *holihta, tanap holihta*
barrier; *isht okshilita, isht oktapa*
barrow (a hog), *skukha hobak*
barrow (a mound), *bunto*
barrow (a vehicle), *iti chanaha iskitini*
bars of a gate, *holihta okhisa achushkachi*
barter, to; *itatoba*
base; *makali, okpulo*
baseborn; *alla inki iksho, inki iksho*
base of a hill, *chakpatali*
baseness, *makali*
bashful, *takshi*
bashful, to render; *takshichi*
basin, *isht ishko patassa*
basin for a child, *alla aiimpa*
basin, pewter; *nakampo*
bask, to; *hashi inni*
bask in the sun, to; *hashi libisha*
basket; *kishi, kishi yancho, tapushink, talbal, tapak, tapishuk*
bass (in music), *chito*
bass drum, *alepa chito*
basswood, *panashuk*
basswood tree, *pishannuk*
bastard; *alla inki iksho, inki iksho.*
baste, to; *bakaha, bila onlali*
basted, *bila onlaha*
bastinade, to; *boli, iyi pata boli*
bat; *akkabata, halambisha*
bath; *aiyupi, ayupi*
bathe, to; *yupechi, yupi*
bathe, to cause to; *yupechi*
bathes, one who; *yupi*
bathing house, *aboha ayupi*
bathing place, *ayupi*
bathroom, *aboha ayupi*
bathing place for children, *alla ayupi*
batteau, *peni shohala*
batten, to; *niachi, niat isht ia*
batter, to; *boli, paioffi*
battering ram, *holihta kallo isht okpani*

battle, *itibbi*
battle ground, *aiitibbi*
bawdy house, *ohoyo haui aiasha*
bay; *filamminchi, okhata*
bay, a bright; *humma tishepa*
bay, to; *wolichi*
bay tree, *kolaha*
bayonet, *isht itibbi*
be, to; *anh, aiasha, ansha, h, hali, hikia, ho, hosh, itola, ma, manya, nanih, o, oh, takali, talaia, taloha, toba, yamohmi*
be in, to; *abeha, alhto, ibafoka*
be of, to; *aiahalaia*
be on, to; *ontalaia*
be there, to; *aiashwa, ashwa*
beach, *oka ont alaka*
bead; *innuchi, oksup, shikalilli, shikalla*
beadmaker, *shikalla ikbi*
beak, *ibishakni*
beam; *iti chito, iti bachoha*
bean; *bala, tobi*
bean pod, *bala hakshup*
bean pole, *tobe isht abela*
beans, *tobi*
beans, bunch; *tobi hikint ani*
beans, bush; *tobi hikint ani*
beans, pole; *tobi abela, tobi uski atuya, tobi uski oiya*
bear, *nita*
bear, a white; *nita tohbi*
bear, a young; *nitushi*
bear, to; *cheli, ieshi, shali, sholi, waya*
bear, to cause to; *chelichi, wayachi*
bear children, to; *alla eshi, ishi*
bear meat, *nita nipi*
bear on with the hands, to; *bitka*
bear testimony, to; *anumpa kallo ilonuchit anoli, atokolechi*
bear to, to; *ima*
bear up, to; *halalli*
beard, *nutakhish*
beard of grain, *hoshunka*
bearer; *na shali, na sholi, shali, sholi*
bear's fat, *nita nia*
bear's nest, *nita peli*
bear's oil, *nita bila*
bearskin, *nita hakshup*
beast; *na hopoa, nam poa, poa*
beat; *alepola, boa, isso*
beat, to; *aiisso, bakaha, boli, fahama, hussi, imaiyachi, isso, kabaha, kabalichi, lalli, lallichi, litinha, michikli, michikminli, michilhha, mitikli, mitikminli, motukli, nuktimekachi, shotukli, timikli, timikmekli*

beat, to make; *mitiklichi*
beat fine, to; *pushechi*
beat out, to; *łakoffichi*
beat quick, to; *timikmeli*
beat there, to; *ahosi*
beat up, to; *bali*
beat up meat in a mortar, to; *nipi bali*
beaten; *boa, boli, holussi, kobokạchi, pushi*
beaten down, *łohama*
beater; *bali, kạbaha*
beatify, to; *yukpalechi, yukpali*
beating; *mitikli, mitikminli*
beating of a drum, *timikạchi*
beautified; *aiukli, pisa aiukli*
beautiful; *aiukli, mismiki*
beautify, to; *aiuklichi, pisa aiukli, pisa aiuklichi*
beauty, *aiukli*
beaver, *kinta*
beaver, a young; *kintushi*
beaver bait, *kinta inkasoma*
beaver dam; *kinta oktạbli, oktạbli*
beaver fur, *kinta hishi*
beaver hat, *kinta hishi shạpo*
beaver trap, *kinta isht ạlbi*
becalm, to; *nuktalali*
becalmed; *chulosa, nuktạla*
because; *hakta, hatuk, ho, hokama, kama, kamba, na, tukakosh*
because of; *pulla, pullakako*
because of that, *mih*
beckon, to; *wali, yuhchunukli*
beckon to, to; *pit*
becloud, to; *hoshontichi, oklilechi*
become, to; *aholhtina, ạlhpesa, holhtina, toba, yohmi aiạlhpesa*
become, to cause to; *atobachi*
become each other, to; *toba*
become his, to; *immi toba*
become our, to; *pimmi toba*
bed; *aionusha, anusi, patapo, patạlhpo, topa, topa umpatạlhpo*
bed, grass; *hạshuk patạlhpo*
bed, small; *topa iskitini*
bed, straw; *hạshuk patạlhpo*
bed, trundle; *topa iti kạlaha atakali*
bed clothing, *patapo*
bed curtains, *isapuntak inchuka*
bedbug, *topa shunshi*
bedcord, *topa isht talakchi*
bedfellow; *ibanusi, itibanusi*
bedim, to; *oklilechi*

bedpost, *topa iyi*
bedroom; *aboha anusi, anusi*
bedstead, *topa*
bedtick, *bahta chito hoshinsh aiạlhto*
bedtime, *anusi ona*
beduck, to; *oklubbichi*
bee; *asananta, foishke, yikoa*
beebread; *foe akmo, foe inlakna*
beech, *hatombạlaha*
beechnut, *hatombạlaha ạni*
beef, *wak, wak nipi*
beef, cured or dried; *wak nipi shila*
beef eater, *wak nipi ạpa*
beehive, *foe bilishke inchuka*
beehouse, *foe bilishke inchuka inhoshontika*
beeswax; *foe akmo, foe hakmi*
beetle, *shakshampi*
beetle (for striking); *isht boa, iti isht boa, isht boa chito*
beeves, *wak*
befool, to; *haksichi, yimmichi*
before; *chanshpo, itikba, kinsha, tikba, tinkba.*
before next, *ha*
before time, *tinkba*
beforehand, *tikbali*
befriend, to; *kana*
beg, to; *asilhha, asilhhạchi*
beggar; *asilhha, asilhhạchi, habenạt anya, nana silhha*
beggar, to; *ilbạshali*
beggars' lice, *bissalunko*
beget, to; *ikbi, tobachi*
beget by, to; *tobachi*
beget of, to; *tobachi*
begetter, *nan tobachi*
begin, to; *hiket ia, ia, isht ia, nitak echi*
begin to heal, to; *ạttạt isht ia*
beginner, *isht ia*
beginning; *aiamona, aiisht ia, aiisht ia ạmmona, amona, atobahpi, ạmmona, isht ia, isht ia ạmmona*
beginning, place or time of; *aiahpi*
beginning of darkness, *okshochobi*
begird, to; *ạskufạchechi, ạskufạchi*
begirt, *ạskufa*
begot, the first; *tikba*
begotten, *nan toba*
begotten of, *atoba*
begrease, to; *litikfochi*
begrudge, to; *potạnno*
beguile, to; *haksichi*

behave well, to; *hopoksia*
behead, to; *nushkobo 'ṭabli*
beheaded; *nushkobo tạpa, tạpa*
behind; *aⁿshaka, obala, obạlaka, obạlh-pela, okbạl, olbạl, ukbạl, ulbạl*
behind, to cause to go; *ulbạlakạchi*
behold! *inta, yaki*
behold, to; *hopoⁿkoyo, pisa*
behold sideways, to; *afalapoa*
beholder, *na piⁿsa*
behoove, to; *ạlhpesa*
being, an invisible or supernatural; *nan isht ahollo*
being, human; *hatak*
being thus, *yakohmi*
being with, *taⁿkla*
belated; *achiba, atạpa*
belch, to; *akeluachi*
belie, to; *holabi, holabichi*
belied, *achokushpa*
belief, *yimmi*
believe, to; *anukfohki, yimmi*
believe, to cause to; *yimmichi, yimmi-hechi*
believe in, to; *ayimmi*
believe the gospel, to; *ạba anumpa yimmi*
believer; *na yimmi, yimmi*
believer in the gospel, *ạba anumpa yimmi*
bell; *tạli shiloha, tạli shiluⁿhạchi, tạlula*
bell collar, *isuba inuchi*
bell founder or maker, *isuba inuchi ikbi*
bellied, pot-; *takoba chito*
bellow, to; *fopa, woha*
bellowing, *woha*
bellows; *luak isht apuⁿfạchi, luak isht puⁿfa*
bellows, the mouth of a; *apuⁿfa*
belly; *iffuka, ikfuka, takoba*
belly, a fish's; *nạni intạli hạta*
bellyache, *ikfuka hotupa*
bellyband, *ikfuka isht talakchi*
bellyful, *kaiya*
belong to, to; *aiahalaia*
belonging to the public, *okla moma immi*
beloved; *haloka, holitopa*
beloved man, *hatak holitopa*
below; *nuta, nutaka*
below, the place; *akka*
below, the space; *nutaka*
belt, *isht ạskufạchi*
belted, *ạskufa*

bench; *aioⁿbinili falaia, aiomanili falaia*
bend; *apoloma, bikota, pilefa, poloma, shokulbi, tanakbi, tikpi, waiya*
bend, to; *bichokạchi, bicholi, bichota, bichulli, bichullichi, bikoha, bikokạchi, bikoli, bikota, bikulli, bitonoa, bitonoli, bokota, bokulli, chasạla, chasạlachi, chik-sanakli, kochofa, kochuffi, kusha, kush-kạchi, kushkoa, kushli, pilema, poloma, polomi, polomoa, polomoli, shanaia, shanaiạchi, shanaioli, tabbạnachi, tanak-bichi, tanantobichi, tanạllachi, tanạllali, tanạlloli, tobbonali, tobbonoli, tonok-bichi, waioha, waiohạchi, waiya, waiyạchi*
bend, to make; *bicholichi, bikolichi, bikullichi, paiolichi, polomolichi*
bend and break down, to; *akosha, akushlichi*
bend and turn up, to; *ibakchishinli, ibakchushli*
bend down, to; *akochofa, akochuffi, bi-kuttokạchi, kahạmmi, kocholi, kushkuli*
bend on a tool, a; *paiofa*
bend once, to; *bikotakạchi*
bend one's self, to; *chiksanạlli*
bend over, to; *apolomi, apolomolili, paiofa, paioli, paknạchi, pilefa, piloa, piloli*
bend up, to; *bokonoli, ibakchushlichi, paioffi, paioli*
bender; *bicholi, bichulli, bikoli, bikulli*
bends; *apolomoa, bikoha, chasaloha, polo-moa, waioha*
bends, one who; *paioffi*
beneath; *nuta, nutaka*
beneath, the place; *akka*
benediction, *aiokpanchi*
benefaction; *aiilhpeta, na hạlbina, nan ilhpita*
benefactor; *habenạchi, na habenạchi*
beneficiary, *na habena*
benefit; *aiisht ilapisa, na hạlbina*
benefit, to; *achchukmali, yukpali*
benevolent, *achukma*
benight one, to; *oklilechi*
benighted, *oklili*
bent; *bichokạchi, bichota, bikoha, biko-kạchi, bikota, bitonoa, bochusa, bokota, chasaloha, chasạla, chikisana, chikisanali, chiksanali, ibakchushli, kochofa, kofuna, kushkạchi, kushkoa, poloma, polomoa, shanaioa, tabbạna, tanakbi, tanantobi, tanạlloha, tannạlla, tobbonoa, tonokbi, waioha, waiya*

bent and broken down; *akosha, akushli*
bent and turned up, *ibakchishinli*
bent double, *apoloma, chunuli*
bent down; *akochofa, kocholi, kusha*
bent leg, *iyi tanakbi*
bent line, *auatali*
bent over; *paiofa, paioha, pilefa, piloa, tobbona*
bent up; *kobokshi, koshuna, manaia, paiofa, paioha*
benumb, to; *illichi, shimohąchi, shimoli, tąmahichi, tąmissąchi*
benumbed; *illi, shimoha, shimoli*
bereave, to; *ąlhtakląchi*
bereaved, *ąlhtakla*
bereavement, *ąlhtakla*
berry; *ąni, nan ąni*
beseech, to; *asilhha*
beside, *ichapaka*
beside, to stand; *apotoa*
besmear, to; *litehąchi, liteli, okashalayi*
besmeared, *liteha*
besotted; *haksi, tasembo*
bespeak, to; *apobąchi*
bespoken for, *ąlhpoa*
best, *achukma iⁿshaht tali*
bestir, to; *ilhkolechi*
bestow, to; *boli, ima, ipeta*
bestow in, to; *ashachi*
bet; *kaha, kali*
bet, to; *kali*
bet against, to; *aseta*
betake to, to; *aiona*
betray, to; *illiissa, ishit fohki*
betroth, to; *apoa, apobąchi*
betrother, *apoąchi*
better; *achukma iⁿshali, imachąnho, imaiya, iⁿshali, kanihmi*
better, to; *achchukmali, achukmalechi, aiskiachi, hochukmali*
better, to cause to get; *kanihmichi*
better, to get; *kanihmit ia*
bettered, *achukma*
between; *aiitintakla, ititakla, takla*
bewail, to; *nukhaⁿklo, yaiya*
beware of, to; *ahah ahni, ahah imahni, nuktąla*
beweep, to; *yaiya*
bewilder, to; *aiyokomichi, imaiyokomichi*
bewildered, *imaiyokoma*
bewitch, to; *haksichi, hatak yushpakąmmi, yushpakamoli, yushpakąmmi*
bewitched; *haksi, yushpakama*
bewitched man, *hatak yushpakama*

bewitcher, *hatak yushpakąmmi*
bewrap, to; *apakfoli*
beyond; *imma, misha, mishema, mishtąnnąp*
bibber; *hatak okishko, okishko, okishko shali*
Bible, the; *holisso, holisso holitopa*
bicker, to; *nukoa*
bid, to; *imissa, miha*
bidden, *anoa*
bier; *aionitola, hatak illi asholi*
big; *alota, chakali, chito, hocheto, ishto*
Big Black River, *luⁿsa chito*
bilbo, *bąshpo falaia*
bile; *basunląsh, lakna*
bilge of a cask, the; *itąlhfoa tikpi*
bilious; *lakna aⁿsha, lakna inchito*
bilk, to; *haksichi*
bill, *ibishakni*
billet of wood; *iti tąpa, iti tilofa, iti tiloli*
billow; *banątboa, banątha, oka banątha, oka banaⁿya*
billow, to; *banątboa, banątha*
billow, to make it; *banąthąchi*
bin; *aiąlhto, itombi*
bind, to; *anumpa kąllo ilonuchi, asitoli, ashelichi, hotti, ibbak takchi, katanlichi, siteli, sitoli, takchi*
binder, *isht ąlhfoa*
binding quality, *sita*
bins, *aiabiha*
biped, *iyi tuklo*
birch tree, *opahaksun*
bird, *hushi*
bird, a carnivorous; *okchąla chito*
bird, a certain; *biliⁿsbi, hąshuk hąta, hushlokussa, kaⁿshi, lanla, okchala chito, okchiloha, okchuⁿs, shoⁿkak, tąlaⁿhąta*
bird, a young; *hushushi*
bird cage; *hushi aiąlhpita, hushi inchuka*
bird snare, *hushi isht hokli*
bird trap, *hushi isht ąlbi*
birth, *ąttahpi*
birth, a; *ątta*
birthday; *aiąttatok nitak, ątta, nitak aiątta*
biscuit; *pąska kąllo, tiliko paląska iskątini*
bishop; *ąba anumpuli apistikeli, iksa apistikeli*
bishopric, *apelichika*
bison, *yąnnąsh*
bit; *chinifa, tushaⁿfasi*

bit (piece of money), *iskạli, iskạli achạfa, tạli holisso*
bit (of an auger), *isht fotoha wishakchi*
bit of a bridle, *isuba itikapali*
bit of paper, *holisso łilafa*
bitch; *nashoba tek, ofi tek*
bite; *impa iskitini, kopoli*
bite, one; *kopoli achạfa*
bite, to; *kiseli, kiselichi, kisli, kobli, kopoli*
biter; *kiselichi, kobli, kopoli*
bits, *boshulli*
bitter; *homi, takba*
bitter, to render; *takbạchi*
bitter heart, *chuⁿkạsh homi*
bitter thing, *na homi*
bitter water, *oka homi*
bitterish, *takbạchi*
bitterness, *homi*
bitterness of heart; *chuⁿkạsh-homi*
bitters, *ikhiⁿsh homi*
blab, to; *anoli*
blabber, *nan anoli shałi*
black; *alusa, lusa*
black, to; *lusachi*
black cravat, *inuchi lusa*
black dye, *isht lusachi*
black dyestuff, *nan isht lusachi*
black-eyed, *nishkin lusa*
black gum; *hush ạpa, iti ạni itạni*
black haw, *chạnafila*
black lead, *naki lusa*
black man, *hatak lusa*
black neckcloth, *inuchi lusa*
black place, *alusa*
black stock, *inunchi lusa*
blackberry, *bissa*
blackberry brier, *bissạpi*
blackbird, *okchạla*
blackbird, a large; *hałạn*
blackbird, a small; *shiⁿkak*
blacked, *lusa*
blacken, to; *alusachi, holuⁿsi, lusachi*
blackener, *lusachi*
blackguard; *chakapa, hatak chakapa*
blackguard, to; *chakapa*
blacking; *isht lusachi, nan lusachi*
blackjack, *chiskilik*
blackness, *lusa*
blacksmith, *boli, tạli boli*
bladder, *hoshuⁿ aiạlhto, imokạto*
blade; *api, bạshpo, hatak chilita, hatak ilakshema shałi, hishi*
blade (a youth), *nakni*

blade bone, *okpạta*
blain, *wulhko*
blame, *anumpa onutula*
blame, to; *anumpa onuchi*
blamed, *anumpa onutula*
blamed for, *onutula*
blanch, to; *kashoffichi, tohbichi*
blanched, *tohbi*
blandish, to; *anumpa achukmalit chukạshichi*
blank, a; *holisso ikaholisso*
blanket; *anchi, shukbo*
blanket another, to; *anchichechi, anchichi*
blanketing, blue; *nan okchako*
blanketing, red; *na humma*
blanketing, white; *nan tohbi*
blaspheme, to; *ahoba ạba isht ikahobalo*
blasphemer; *ạba isht ikahobalo, isht ikahobalo*
blast; *fiopa, mali achạfa, ola*
blast, to; *bạshechi, bạshi*
blasted, *bạshi*
blaze, *libbi*
blaze (a mark on a tree), *atiła*
blaze, to; *libbi*
blaze (or mark a tree), to; *tili, iti tiłi*
blaze, to cause it to; *libbichi*
blazed, *tiła*
blazed tree, *iti tiła*
bleach, to; *hatokbichi, kashoffichi, okshauanlichi, okshauạshlichi, tohbichi*
bleached; *okshauanli, tohbi*
blear eye, *nishkin oktalonli*
blear-eyed, *nishkin oktalonli*
bleat, to; *yaiya*
bled; *issish iⁿkucha, łumpa*
bleed, to; *issish iⁿhina łumpli, issish iⁿkuchi, issish kucha, issish minti, issish mitafa, issish mitạffi, łumpli, shakba łumpli*
bleed, to cause to; *issish mitạffi*
bleed, to make the nose; *ibikoạchi*
bleed at the nose, to; *ibikoa*
bleed the arm, to; *shakba łumpli*
bleeding, *issish mitafa*
blemish, *lusa*
blemish, to; *okpạni*
blend, to; *aiyuma, yạmmichi*
blended, *aiyuma*
bless, to; *aiokpạchi, holitobli, yukpali, yukpalit anumpuli*
blessed; *holitopa, na yukpa, yukpa*
blessing, *aiokpanchi nan isht aiyukpa*

blighted, *bashi*
blind; *lapa, nishkin lapa, nishkin tamoa*
blind, a; *isht ukhatapa*
blind, born; *lapa inmoma*
blind, entirely; *nishkin lapat kania*
blind, to; *lapa, nishkin lapachi, nishkin okpani*
blind eye, *nishkin lapa*
blind the eyes, to; *tammoli*
blind-eyed, *nishkin oktalonli*
blindfold, to; *nishkin luhmi*
blindfolded, *nishkin luma*
blindness; *lapa, lapa inmoma, nishkin lapa*
blister, *holhpa, wulhko*
blister, to; *itowulhkachi, itowulhko, wulhko, wulhkochi*
blister, to cause to; *wulhkochi*
blister by heat, to; *towulhkachi*
blistered; *itowulhko, wulhko*
blithe, *yukpa*
bloat, to; *shatabli, shatammi*
bloated; *shatabli, shatablichi*
block; *iti baka, iti tapa*
block, to; *bakati, bakatichi*
block out, to; *iti bakli*
block up, to; *atapachi, okshita, oktabli*
blocked, *bakati*
blocked up, *atapa*
blockhead, *hatak imanukfila iksho*
blood, *issish*
blood, sacred; *issish hanta*
blood, to vomit; *issish hoeta*
blood vessel; *issish akshish, issish inhina*
bloodroot, *pishkak*
bloodsucker; *haluns, lasun, yaluns*
bloody; *issish bano, issish bieka*
bloody, to; *issish bano*
bloody sweat, *issish laksha*
bloom; *nam pakanli, pakanli*
bloom, to; *pakanli*
bloomed, *pakanli*
blossom; *nam pakanli, pakanli*
blossom, to; *pakanli*
blossom, to cause to; *pakanlichi*
blossomed, *pakanli* ·
blot; *isht holissochi onlatapa, lusa, lusa talaia*
blot, to; *isht holissochi onlatabli, lusachi*
blot out, to; *kashoffichit kanchi*
blotted; *isht holissochi onlatapa, lusa*
blotted out, *kashofa*
blow; *aiisso, fahama, isso, kabak, kabuk, kobuk, sakalichi*

blow (flower); *nam pakanli, pakanli*
blow (wind), *mati*
blow, a slight; *chikinha*
blow (as a fly), to; *cheli*
blow (as a horn), to; *ola, olachi*
blow (as the wind), to; *apeli, apanukfila, mati, matichi*
blow (or pant), to; *fohukli*
blow (with the mouth), to; *apunfachi, punfa, punfachi*
blow, to cause to; *punfachechi*
blow an instrument, to; *punfachechi*
blow down, to; *yuli*
blow the nose, to; *linka*
blower; *punfa, punfachi*
blowgun, *uski lumpa*
blown; *alhpunfa, ola, pakanli*
blown about, *yula*
blown into, *alhpunfa*
blowpipe; *apunfachi, isht apunfachi*
blows; *kabakachi, kamakachi*
blows, one who; *olachi*
bludgeon; *atashi, itashi, iti tapena*
blue; *okchakalbi, okchako, okchamali*
blue, to; *okchakochi*
blue dyestuff; *nan isht okchakuchi, nan isht okchamalichi*
blue flag, *hashuk pancha*
bluebird, a small; *okchanlush*
blue-eyed, *oktalonli*
bluff, a; *sakti*
bluff, a high; *kunchonwaka*
bluff, a ridged; *sakti lanfa*
bluff, a steep; *sakti chaha*
blunder, *ashachi*
blunderbuss, *tanamp nihi chito*
blunderer, *ashachi*
blunderhead, *hatak nusilhha shali*
blunt; *ibaktokonli, ibaktokonshli, ibbak tokonli, tasalli tilikpi, tukbi, tukbichi*
blunt, to; *ibaktokonlichi, ibaktokoshlichi*
blunted; *ibaktokonli, tukbi*
blunt-faced, to be; *ibaklipinli*
blur, *lusa*
blur, to; *lusachi*
blurred, *lusa*
blush, to; *hummachi, nashuka hummat ont taha*
boar, *shukha nukni*
board (food); *ilhpak, impa*
board maker, *na shimmi*
board, to; *umpohomi*
board (give food), to; *ilhpak atali, impa*
boarded; *umpatalhpo, umpoholmo*

boarded (given food), *ilhpak imataha*
boarder, *aiimpa*
boast, *ilauata*
boast, to; *fehnachi, ilauata, ilefehnachi*
boaster; *hatak ilawata, ilauata*
boasting, an occasion of; *isht ilawata*
boat; *iti kula, peni*
boat, a flat; *peni patassa*
boat, a large; *peni chito*
boat, a light; *peni shohala*
boat, a small; *penushi*
boat captain, *peni inkapetani*
boat landing, *peni ataiya*
boat rope; *peni inponola, peni isht talakchi*
boatload, *peni inshapo*
boatman; *peni isht anya, peni isht atta*
bobtail, *hasimbish tapa*
bobtailed, *hasimbish tapa*
bodiless, *haknip iksho*
body; *apeliechi achafa, api, haknip*
body, a dead; *nan illi*
body, a strange; *haknip inla*
body, another; *haknip inla*
bog, *latimo*
boggy; *labeta, latimo*
boil, *hichi*
boil, to; *honi, labocha, laboshli, walalli*
boil, to cause to; *holbichi, laboshlichi, walallichi*
boil coffee, to; *kafi honi*
boil down, to; *ashepachechi*
boil in the kernel, to; *lubona, luboni*
boil potatoes, to; *ahe hobi*
boil up, to; *anuktobulli, tobunlli*
boil up, to cause to; *anuktobullichi, tobullichi*
boil whole, to; *hobi*
boiled; *holbi, honni, lubona, labocha, nuna*
boiled beans, *bala hobbi*
boiled coffee, *kafi honni*
boiled down, *ashepachi*
boiler; *alabocha, awalalli, honi, shuti*
boiler, a small; *awalalli iskitini*
boiling, *walalli*
boils, small; *hichushi*
boisterous; *kallo, yahapa, yuhapa*
bold; *aiyimita, nukwia iksho*
bold, to render; *naknichi*
bold man, a; *hatak chilita*
boldness; *aiyimita, chunkash nakni, nukwia iksho*
bolled, *yushkobolichi*
bolster, *alhpishi falaia*

bolt; *isht yuha, shumo naki*
bolt, a rag; *tali fobassa isht attapachi*
bolt, to; *iti bakli, tali fobassa isht akamassalli, yuli*
bolt of cloth, *nan tanna bonunta*
bolted; *tali fobassa isht akamassa, yuha*
bolter, *isht yuha*
bond; *isht itihalalli, isht talakchi, nan isht talakchi*
bondage; *yuka ansha, yukat ansha*
bondage, in; *yuka anta*
bond-bound, *yuka*
bondmaid; *ohoyo yuka, yuka ohoyo*
bondman; *hatak yuka, yuka, yuka hatak*
bonds, in; *yuka anta*
bondservant, *yuka tonksali*
bondwoman; *ohoyo yuka, yuka ohoyo*
bone, *foni, na foni*
bone-ache; *foni hotupa, foni kommichi*
boneless, *foni iksho*
boneset (a weed), *shauashko*
bonesetter, *foni falammint itifohki*
bonnet; *ialipa, ohoyo inshapo, shapo*
bonnyclabber; *pishukchi hauashko, pishukchi walasha*
bony; *foni bano, foni laua, kallo*
booby, *hatak nusilhha shali*
book; *holisso, tali isht holisso*
book, bad; *holisso okpulo*
book, to; *holisso takalichi*
book account, a; *itatoba holisso*
book cover; *holisso onlipa, holisso umpatha*
bookbinder, *holisso onlipa ikbi*
bookcase, *holisso aialhto*
booked, *holisso takali*
book-learned, *holisso pisa imponna*
bookmaking, *holisso ikbi*
bookmate, *holisso ibapisa*
bookseller, *holisso kanchi*
bookstore, *holisso aiitatoba*
bookworm; *holisso inshunshi, holisso pisa shali*
bookish, *holisso pisa shali*
boon; *habena, habenachi*
boost, to; *tobli aba isht ia*
boot; *shulush chaha, shulush kallo falaia, shulush hofaloha*
boot (something in addition), *alapanli*
boot, to; *shulush kallo falaia holo*
boot, to give; *alapalechi*
boot, to put on a; *shulush kallo falaia holo.*
booted, *shulush kallo falaia holo*

booth; *alhtipo, iti chishaⁿkko hosh ontika*
boot-tree, *shulush chaha atoba*
booty; *imilbik, na wehpoa, tanap*
booze, to; *ishko fena, nalli*
boozy; *haksi, haksi chohmi*
borax; *tali hata isht akmi, tali holiya*
border; *aiali, alaka, aposhokachi, ali,
· lapalika, takchaka*
border, one who makes a; *takchaka,
ikbi*
border, to; *fololichi, takchaka ikbi*
border of a dooryard, *akuchuli*
bore; *fotoha, nihi*
bore, to; *fotoli*
bore at, to; *afotoli*
bore of a gun, *tanamp nihi*
bore there, to; *afotoli*
Boreas, *falammi mali*
bored; *fotoha, lukali, luⁿkachi*
bored at, *afotoha*
bored through, *lukafa*
borer; *fotoli, isht fotoha, iti isht fotoha,
kitak, na fotoli*
born; *atta, toba*
born of, *toba*
born the first, to be; *tikba atta*
borne, *shaⁿya*
borough, *tamaha*
borrow, to; *pota*
borrower; *nam pota, pota*
bosom, *shakba poloma*
botch, to; *akkalli, alhkata, shatammi*
botched, *alhkata*
both; *aieninchi, biⁿka, iʰhapa, miⁿka,
· tuⁿklo*
both at once, *talalaⁿka*
both sides, on; *italaklaka*
both together, *itatuklo*
both ways at the same time, *italaⁿkla*
bothered, *imaiyokoma*
bottle; *kotoba, kotoba alota achafa*
bottle, a flat; *kotoba patassa*
bottle, a glass; *kotoba shohkalali*
bottle, a leather; *shukcha*
bottle, to; *kotoba abeli*
bottled; *kotoba abeha, kotoba alolua*
bottom, *akashtala, akka*
bottom land, *patasachi*
bottom of a chair, *aiomanili*
bough, *iti naksish*
bounce, to; *tolupli*
bound; *asheha, ashehachi, talakchi*
bound, a; *tolupli*

bound, to; *aiatichi, akallo, asitoha,
tolupli, tulli*
bound, to cause to; *toluplichi*
bound about, *afoli*
bound round; *apakfoa, alhfoa*
bound tight, *katanli*
bound up; *asehta, sita, sitoha*
boundary, *ali*
bounding, *tolupli*
bounds, *aiali*
bourne, *ali*
bow; *iti tanampo, poloma, polomoa,
tanamp shibata*
bow (an act of obeisance), *akkachunoli*
bow (for bass viol), *alepa chito isht olachi*
bow, to; *bikuttokachi, kushotah, yushchunuli*
bow bent, *tanakbi*
bow down, to; *waiahpa*
bow leg, a; *iyi tanakbi*
bow of a boat; *ibish, peni chito ibish,
peni ibish, peni nushkobo*
bow the head, to; *akashchunoli, akkachunni, akkachunoli, yuhchonoli, yuhchunni, yuhchunukli*
bowed, *chunuli*
bowed down; *chunuli, tobbona*
bowels, the; *anuⁿkaka, iffuka, ikfuka,
iskuna, nukhaⁿklo, takoba*
bower; *aboha anusi, hoshontika, iti
chishaⁿkko hosh ontika*
bowing, *mahaia*
bowl, *ampo*
bowl, a broken; *ampkoa*
bowl, a large; *ampo chito*
bowl, a small; *ampushi*
bowl, a small wooden; *itampushi*
bowl, a wooden; *itampo*
bowman, *iti tanampo isht aⁿya*
bowstring; *iti tanampo isht talakchi,
tanamp shibata isht talakchi*
box; *aialhto, itombi, itombi alota achafa,
pasalichi*
box, a small; *itombushi*
box, to; *pasaha*
box for oil, *kotoba*
box up, to; *itombi abeli, itombi fohki*
boxed; *itombi abeha, itombi fohka*
boxer; *hatak itishali, pasaha*
boxful, *itombi alota*
boy, *alla nakni*
brace; *isht tikili, tikeli, isht tikoli, obala
foka isht halalli*

brace (two); *ichapa, tuklo*
brace, to; *katanlichi, lampkuchi*
braced; *kallo, lampko*
brackish; *homi, kalancha*
brackishness, *kalancha*
brad; *chufak chipinta, chufak ushi*
brag; *hatak ilawata, hatak isht ilawata, ilauata*
brag, to; *ilauata*
braggadocio; *hatak ilawata, hatak isht ilawata*
braggart, *hatak isht ilawata*
braid, *pana*
braid, to; *panni, tanaffo*
braided; *alhtannafo, pana, tannaffo*
braider, *tanaffo*
brain; *imanukfila, lupi*
brainpan, *lupi aialhto*
brake, *aboli*
bramble; *bisakchakinna, bissapi, kantak api*
brambly; *bisakchakinna foka, bissapi foka*
bran; *haklopish, hoshunluk, pishilukchi*
branch; *felami, felamichi, filammi, filamminchi, iti naksish, naksish, naksish filamoli, naksish filamminchi naksish infilammi*
branch, a small; *okmoffi*
branch, to; *filamoli, filamminchi*
branch of a creek; *bok chulaffi, bok chuli, bok ushi*
branch of a horn, *lapish filamminchi*
branch off from, to cause to; *filammichi*
branch out, to; *wahhaloha*
branches, full of; *washaloha*
brand, *iti tapa lua*
brand, to; *inchunli*
brand (mark), *inchunwa*
brand iron; *isht inchunli, isht inchunwa*
brand new, *himmona*
brand of tobacco, *hakchuma palaska*
branded, *inchunwa*
branding instrument, *isht inchunli*
brandish, to; *fahfuli, fali*
brandished, *fahfoa*
brandisher, *fali*
brandy, *oka homi*
brangle, to; *achowa*
brass; *asonak lakna, tali lakna*
brass kettle, *asonak, asonak lakna*
brass pan, a large; *asonak lakna chito*
brass ring for the wrist, *tachammaha*
brass vessel, *asonak*

brassy, *asonak lakna chuhmi*
brat, *alla*
brave; *aiyimita, chilita, hichali, hoyopa, kamassa, kaninlau iksho, nakni, nukwia iksho*
brave, a; *nakni, patakitta*
brave man, *hatak nakni*
brave, to; *panfi*
brave, to render; *naknichi*
bravery; *aiyimita, chunkash nakni*
brawl, to; *nukoa*
brawny, *kallo*
bray, *sihinka*
bray, to; *hopunsi, hussi, sihinka, woha*
bray in, to; *ahosi*
brayed; *holhpusi, holussi*
braze, to; *asonak lakna isht akmichi*
brazed, *asonak lakna isht akmi*
brazen, *asonak lakna atoba*
brazier; *asonak lakna ikbi, asonak lakna isht akmichi*
breach, a; *akobafa, atiwa, kobafa, litafa, mitafa, mitali*
breach of the law, a; *anumpa kobafa*
bread; *banaha, ilhpak, paska*
breadth; *auata, hopatka, patha*
breadth of cloth, *okhoataka*
break; *akobafa, atiwa, mitafa, mitali, tapa*
break (a weed), *tapintapi*
break, to; *akalalli, akauwichi, apinnichi, bichillichi, kaloli, katapa, kauwa, kauwi, kauwichi, kawa, koa, kobafa, kobali, kobalichi, kobaffi, kochofa, kochuffi, kokoa, kokuli, koli, kostininchi, kushkachi, kushkoa, kushkuli, kushli, litafa, litali, litalichi, litaffi, pakulli, pichelichi, pokota, tilofa, tushalichi, tushli, tushtuli*
break, to cause to; *kobaffichi, pakullichi*
break a law, to; *anumpa kobaffi*
break a ship, to; *peni chito koli*
break and bend, to; *kusha*
break and bend, to cause to; *kushlichi*
break and bend down, to; *akauwi, akochuffi*
break and bend down, to cause to; *akochuffichi*
break at, to; *akobafa, ataptua, ataptuli*
break bushes, to; *okaloli*
break down, to; *akosha, akushlichi, kinafa, kinali, kinalichi, kinaffi, tiapa, tiabli*

break in pieces, to; *boshulli, boshullichi, kobulli, kobullichi, lishoa, tushtua, wolobli*

break in two, to; *kolofa, pakota, tạbli*

break of day, the; *onnat minti*

break off, to; *atạbli, kotafa, kotali, kotalichi, kotạffi, pakota, tiloffi, tilolichi, tushạffi*

break off pieces, to; *tushtuli*

break off short, to; *tiloli*

break open, to; *akalạlli, bokafa, bokakaⁿkạchi, bokalichi, bokạffi, kalali, mitafa, mitali, mitalichi, mitạffi, pichefa*

break through, to; *lukali*

break up, to; *tushalichi*

break wind, to; *huksoh*

breaker, a; *litạffi, kobạffi, kochuffi, kokuli, koli, tạbli*

breakfast, *onnahinli impa*

breakfast, to; *onnahĩnli impa impa*

breaking, a; *kạla*

breaking down, a; *tiapa*

breast, *ikkishi, imatananchi, ipiⁿshik, ohoyo ipiⁿshik*

breast, to; *beli*

breast of a fowl, the; *hạship*

breastbone; *ikkishi foni, imantạnanchi, imitaklish*

breastbone, the hole or notch in the; *imilhfitukhak*

breastbone, the lower part of the; *walwa, iⁿwalwa*

breastbone, the upper end of the; *ikfetạp, imikfetukhak*

breastpin; *isht alepulli, isht ạtopulli*

breastplate; *inuchi chinakbi*

breath; *fiopa, ilhfiopa, ilhfiopak*

breath, a consumptive person's; *likiⁿhạchi*

breath, to give; *fiopạchi*

breath of life, *ilhfiopa okchaya*

breath sundered, *fiopa tạpa*

breathe, to; *fiopa*

breathe, to cause to; *fiopạchi*

breathe hard, to; *kạllot fiopa, kạtanih*

breathe loud, to; *chitolit fiopa*

breathe quick and hard, to; *shutukshonli*

breathe with difficulty, to; *litiⁿka*

breathed in, *ạlhpuⁿfa*

breathless; *fiopa taha, nukbepa, nukbepoa*

breech, *obala*

breech of a gun, the; *sokbish isht ashana, tanamp imatạhshi, tanamp sokbish*

breeches, *obala foka*

breed, *isht atia*

breed, to; *cheli, ikhananchi*

breed, to cause to; *chelichi*

breeder; *cheli, hofạllichi*

breeze, *mali iskitini*

brethren; *itibapisa, itibapishi*

brew, to; *honi*

brewed, *honni*

bribe; *habenạchi, isht haksichi*

bribe, to; *chuⁿkash chumpa, haksichi*

briber, *isht haksichi*

brick, *lukfi nuna*

brickbat, *lukfi nuna tushafa*

bricklayer, *lukfi nuna boli*

brickmaker, *lukfi nuna ikbi*

bridge; *bok itipatạlhpo, iti patapo, iti patạlhpo*

bridge, to; *iti patạlhpo ikbi*

bridge maker, *iti patạlhpo ikbi*

bridle, *isuba kapali*

bridle a horse, to; *isuba kapali kapalichi*

bridle bit; *kapali, tạli isuba kapali*

bridle path, *isuba iⁿhina*

bridle reins; *isuba kapali isht talakchi, kapali isht talakchi*

brief; *tilofasi, yushtololi*

brief, a; *holisso*

brief, to make; *yushtololichi*

brier, a kind of; *kantak*

brier-root bread, *kantak pạska*

brig, a; *peni chito*

bright; *halaluⁿkạchi, hanta, malancha, malanta, malata, malmakạchi, okshauạshli, shohkalali, shohmalali, shohmalạshli, shumpalali, tohchalali, tohkasali*

bright, made; *halaluⁿkạchi*

bright, to make; *hantạchi, okshauanlichi, shohkalalichi, tohkasalichi*

brighten, to; *halaluⁿlichi, malantạchi, shohmalalichi, shumpalalichi, tohkasalichi*

brightened, *malantkạchi*

brightness; *halaluⁿkạchi, malancha, malạtha, shohmalali*

brilliant, *tohkasli*

brilliant, to render, *tohkaslichi*

brim, *paknaka*

brim of a hat; *impashia, shạpo haksobish*

brimful, *alotowa*

brimstone, *hituk lakna*

brinded; *bakoa, basoa*

brindled; *basasuⁿkạchi, basoa, chinisa*

brine; *hạpi okchi, oka hạpi*

brine spring, *kali hapi oka*
bring, to; *ala, isht ala, shali*
bring back, to; *falamichi, falammichi*
bring down, to; *akkachi*
bring forth, to; *cheli, ieshi, kuchi, waya*
bring forth a child, to; *alla eshi, alla sholi*
bring forth fruit, to; *anit wanya*
bring forth young, to; *sholi*
bring here, to; *shali*
bring in, to; *kuchi*
bring near, to; *akanalichechi, bilinkachi*
bring out, to; *kuchi*
bring out of, to; *akuchi*
bring over, to; *tanablichi*
bring this way, to; *auechi, taklachi, taklechi*
bring to, to; *isht ona*
bring to a point, to; *tilichi*
bring to nought, to; *ikshokechi*
bring together, to; *apeli, itannali*
bring up, to; *attat hofantichi, hofantichi, ikhananchi*
bring water, to; *ochi*
bringer; *isht ala, isht minti, shali*
brink, *ontalaka*
brink of a river, *okhina ontalaka*
brisk, *tushpa*
brisket; *bichunko, ikkishi*
brisket of an ox, *tinklish*
bristle; *chushak hishi kallo, nali hishi, shukha chushak hishi*
bristle, to; *shachala, shachia*
bristled, to become; *hashanya*
broach, *isht alopulli*
broach, to; *tuwi*
broach of cotton, *ponola tali kucha*
broach of yarn, *tali kucha achafa*
broad; *auata, hopatka, patha, patasah, watta*
broad, to make; *hopatkalli, pathachi*
broadcloth, coarse; *nana*
broadcloth, red; *nan tishepa*
broad-nosed, *ibaktabanli*
broadsword, *bashpo falaia patha*
broider, to; *yikowa*
broil; *achowa, itachoa, itachoa*
broil, to; *apushli*
broiled, *alhpusha*
broiled meat, *nipi alhpusha*
broken; *chilukoa, kalakshi, kauwa, kawa, kilhkiki, koa, kobafa, kobali, kochofa, kokoa, kostini, kusha, kushkachi, kushkoa, litafa, litali, pakota, pokota, tushtua*

broken and bent down, *akawa*
broken and split, *akala*
broken down; *akosha, akushli, kinafa, kinali, tiapa, tiapakachi*
broken in fragments, *boshulli*
broken in heart, *nukhanklo*
broken in two; *tapa*
broken off, *tilofa, tiloha*
broken open; *bokafa, bokali, bokokakachi*
broken pieces, *kobali*
broken there or at, *akobafa*
broken to pieces, *lishoa*
broken twigs, *fuli kaua*
broken up (as land), *okchaha*
broken wind; *fiopa kobafa, fiopat taha*
broken-winded, *fiopa taha*
broker, *tali holisso itatoba*
broom, *isht bashpoa*
broomstick, *isht boa api*
bronchitis, *chakwa*
brooch; *isht akamassa, isht alepulli*
brood; *akank ushi peliechi, pelchi, ushi*
brook; *bok, bok chulaffi, bok ushi*
broth, *okchi*
brothel, *ohoyo haui aiasha*
brother; *anakfi, amanni, imanni, innakfi, innakfish, itibapishi, itibapishi aliha, itibapishi fehna, nakfi, nakfish*
brotherhood, *itibapishi aliha*
brother-in-law; *amalak, amalak usi, amombalaha, imaiyopik, imalak, imalakusi, imombalaha*
brought out; *akucha, kucha*
brought up; *attat hofanti, hofanti*
brow; *imosana, ontalaka*
brow of a hill, *nanih aiali*
brown; *holunsi, homakbi, itolankabi, itolonkabi, lusakbi, shakbona, tulankoba*
brown, dark; *lusbi, lusluki*
brown, to; *haton laknachi, lusakbichi*
brown coffee, to; *kafi auashli*
brown color, *haton lakna*
bruise, *chilina*
bruise, to; *litoli*
bruised; *chilina, kushkoa, litoa*
bruised to pieces; *lishoa, wulopa*
brush; *isht kashokachi, isht kasholichi, nan isht kasholichi*
brush (bushes, etc.); *iti naksish tapa, shauwa*
brush, green; *bafalli*
brush, to; *kasholichi, panshpuli*
brush bower, *iti chishakko*
brushed; *kashokachi, panshpoa*

brush off, to; *monffi, pinfi*
brushed off, *pinfa*
brushed place, *apiha*
brushy; *yushwichali, yushwiheli*
brushy, to make; *yushwichalichi*
brushy, to render the hair; *yushwihe-lichi*
bubble, *nishkin toba*
bubble, to; *chobokachi, nishkin toba*
bubbling of water, *chobokachi*
buck; *chukfalhpowa nakni, chukfi nakni, chukfi pattakata nakni, isi kosoma nakni, isi nakni, lapitta*
buck, a spike; *isi chufakni*
bucket, *isht ochi*
buckeye; *atai, atai*
buckle; *isht akamassa, isht akamassachi, isht akamassalli*
buckle, to; *akamassali*
buckled, *akamassa*
buckshot, *nakunshi*
buckskin; *isi nakni hakshup, talhko*
bud; *bikobli, bokanli*
bud, to; *bikobli, bokanli, bokobli, bokupli*
bud, to cause to; *bikoblichi, bokanlichi*
budded; *bikobli, bokanli*
budge, to; *ilhkoli*
budget, *bahta*
buffalo, *yannash*
buffalo, a young; *yannash ushi*
buffalo calf, *yannash ushi*
buffalo lick, *yannash inlukfapa*
buffalo robe or skin; *yannash hakshup*
buffet, to; *pasalichi, tamanchi*
bug, *shunshi*
bug, a large black; *shakshampi*
bug, a red; *shunkoma*
bug, a water; *hasun*
bugbear, *nan lusa chito*
buggy, *shunshi laua*
bugle, *isht punfa*
build, to; *ikbi, talali*
build a fire, to; *tikbichi*
build a log house, to; *aboha itabanni*
builder (of a house), *aboha itabanni*
building; *aboha, aboha itabana, chuka*
bulb; *ponkshi, tikpi*
bulbous, *bambaki*
bull, *wak nakni*
bull beef, *wak nakni nipi*
bulldog, *na hollofi*
bullet, *naki lumbo*
bullet mold, *nakahakmo*

bullfrog, *halonlabi*
bullfrog, a young; *shukatti*
bullhead; *nakishtalali, nakishwana*
bullock, *wak hobak*
bulwark, *holihta kallo*
bumblebee; *imosini, onsini*
bump; *isso, paffala*
bump, to; *isso*
bunch, a; *fohopa kachombi, lukoli*
bunch, to; *lukolichi, takchichi*
bunch in the flesh, a hard; *kochombi*
bunch of hyssop, *pukussa*
bundle; *asehta, bonkachi, bonunta, buna, hulbona, na buna, na hobuna, sita, sitoha, shapo, talakchi*
bundle up, to; *bonulli*
bung, *italhfoa isht alhkama*
bung, to; *akammi, akamoli, kamali*
bunghole, *abicha*
bunt, to; *aboa, aiisso, bili, isso, komoha*
buoyancy, *shohala*
buoyant, *shohala*
bur, *hakshup*
burden; *na weki, shapo*
burden, to; *shapulechi*
burdened, *shapoli*
burdensome; *palammi, weki*
burial; *hatak hopi, hohpi*
buried, *hollopi*
burn, a; *alua, holhpa, holukmi, lua*
burn, to; *aluachi, anakshonffi, anakshoti, auashli, chunkash lua, holhpalli, hukmi, hushmi, hushpali, itobila, itot anya, itowulhko, kitaia, libbachih, libbi, lua, luachi, nipi lua*
burn a house, to; *chuka hukmi*
burn at, on, or there, to; *alua*
burn inwardly, to; *ituklua*
burn to coal, to; *akabunshli*
burned, *lua*
burner; *hushmi, luachi*
burning; *holushmi, hushmi, lashpa, lua*
burning glass, *apisahukmi*
burning in the stomach, *nukkiteli*
burnish, to; *shohmalalichi*
burnished, *shohmalali*
burnisher, *shohmalalichi*
burnt; *akabonsha, alohbi, anakshonfa, anakshua, holhpa, hollokmi, holushmi, hushpa, lua*
burnt, having the flesh; *nipi lua*
burnt place, *alua*
burrow, *poa nusi*

burst, *bokafa*
burst, to; *bichillichi, bokafa, bokalichi, kạlali, pichelichi*
burst, to cause to; *mitalichi*
burst open; *kaloha, kạla, mitafa, mitali*
burst open, to; *bokaka^nkạchi, fachanli, kaloli, kạla, mitafa, mitali, mitạffi*
burst open and spill, to; *kaloha*
burst through, to; *lukafa*
bursting open; *kạla, kaloha*
bury, to; *hohpi, hopi, umpohomo*
burying ground, *hatak aholopi*
bush; *bafaha, bafạlli, naksish*
bush, a certain; *akkasoli*
bush, to; *abili*
bush arbor, *iti chisha^nkko hosh ontika*
bushed; *abela, abila*
bushel; *bushul, isht ạlhpisa, ta^nsh isht ạlhpisa*
bushel, a half; *bushul iklạnna, tanchi isht ạlhpisa*
bushy; *bafạlli, bafạlli foka*
business; *isht ạtta, kaniohmi, nan isht anta, nan isht ạtta*
bustle, to; *tu^nshpa*
busy; *ashwanchi, ạshwanchi, nan isht ạtta imasha, nan isht ạtta inlaua*
busy about; *ạtta, anta*
busy with, *ạtta, isht anta*
but; *amba, he, illa,kama, kia, yạmohmikia, yohmi kia*
but if, *mih*
but the, *kak*
butcher; *nan ạbi, nipi bạshli, wak ạbi*
butcher, to; *ạbi*
butcher case (stars so called), *fichik issuba*
butler, *oka bicheli*
butt; *aiạli, akạshtạla, akishtạla, holisso lilafa, iti tila*
butt end of a gun, *tanamp sokbish*
butter, *wak pishukchi nia, pishukchi nia*
butter, to; *pishukchi nia lapalichi*
buttered, *pishukchi nia lapali*
butterfly; *hatapushik, hạtapushik*
buttermilk, *pishukchi nia okchi*
buttery, *pishukchi aiasha*
buttocks; *hapullo, obala*
button; *ahalạlli, atapạchi, isht akamạssa, isht akamạssachi, isht akamạssalli, isht ạtapạchi, tali isht ạttapạchi*
button, a metal; *tạli haksi, tạli isht akamạssa*

button, a sleeve; *shakba tạli haksi lapali*
button, an iron; *tạli haksi*
button, to; *akamạssạli, atapạchi*
button maker, *tạli haksi ikbi*
button to a door, *isht afacha*
buttoned, *akamạssa*
button eye, *tạli haksi nishkin*
buttonhole; *tạli haksi akamạssa, tạli haksi chiluk*
buttonwood tree, *sini*
buttress; *isuba iyakchush isht bạshli, tikeli*
buxom, *yukpa*
buy, to; *pit*
buy, to cause to; *chumpạchi*
buy with cash, to; *chumpa*
buyer, *chumpa, nan chumpa*
buyer on credit, *ahekạchi*
buzz, to; *timihạchi*
buzzard, *sheki*
buzzard, a short-tailed; *sheki kolofa*
buzzing, *timihạchi*
by; *a, apunta, lapali, ont*
by and by; *himmakma, hopakikma, hopakikmako*
by himself, *ilapissa*
by itself, *ila*
by means of; *ai, aiitintakla, isht, na, takla*
by reason of, *hatuk*
by surprise; *haksinchit, haksint*
by themselves; *ilap bi^nka, ilapissa*
by whom, *isht*
by-name, *hochifo okpulo*
by-place; *apotaka, naksika*
bystander; *yopisa, talot maya*

cabbage; *tohe, kalush*
cabbage worm, *kalushạpa*
cabin; *chuka, aboha iskitini*
cabin, an Indian; *hatak ạpi humma inchuka*
cabinetmaker, *itombi aiimpa chuhmi ikbi*
cable; *peni i^nponola, peni isht talakchi*
caboose, *peni ahoponi*
cabriolet, *iti chanạlli iskitini pạlhki*
cackle, to; *cha^nlchaha, ka^nlhkuha, ta^nktaha*
cackler; *ka^nlhkuha, ta^nktaha*
cackling, a; *ka^nlhkuha, ta^nktaha*
cadaverous, *hạta*
caddy, *itombushi*

cage, a lion's; *koi chito inchuka*
cage, to; *hushi inchuka fohki*
caged, *hushi inchuka fohka*
caitiff; *hatak haksi*
cajole, to; *haksichi*
cake, *paska champuli*
cake up, to; *shatammi*
caked; *kachombi, shatammi*
calamitous, *ilbasha*
calamity; *ilbasha, nan imokpulot ilbasha*
calash, *ohoyo inshapo*
calculate, to; *ahni, hotina*
calculation, *na holhtina*
calculator, *hotina*
caldron, *shuti chito*
calendar, *hashi nitak isht ikhana*
calf, *wak ushi*
calf, a bull; *wak ushi nakni*
calf of the leg; *hulhki, iyi hulhki, iyin shilukwa*
calfskin, *wak ushi hakshup*
caliber; *nihi, tanamp nihi, tanampo ittopa*
calico; *inchunwa, nantapaski*
calk a cracked boat, to; *peni koa kafolichi*
calked; *alhkama, alhkomoa*
call, to; *a, achi, maka*
call, to (to name); *hochifo*
call, to (to shout to); *inhoa, panya*
call after, to; *tahpala*
called; *hohchifo, hochifo*
called in, *hohchifo*
called to; *aianowa, apahyah*
caller; *inhoa, nan inhoa*
calling, *alhtayak*
callous; *kamassa, kallo*
callous, a; *salbo*
callous, to make; *salbochi*
calm; *chilosa, chulosa, kinint iksho, nuktala, shohmakali*
calm, a; *chilosa, nuktala, yokopa*
calm, to; *chilosachi, chulosa, nuktalachi, nuktalali, shohmakalichi, yokopa, yokopachi*
calm, to become; *chulosa*
calm, to make a; *chilosachi*
calmed; *chilosa, nuktala, yokopa*
calmer, *chulosachi*
calmness; *shohmakali*
calomel, *ikhinsh bota ishkot ikfia*
calumba, *akshish lakna chito*
calumet; *hakchuma ashunka, hakchuma shuti*

calumniate, to; *anumpa okpulo onuchi*
calumniated, *anumpa okpulo onutula*
calumniator, *anumpa okpulo onuchi*
calumny; *anumpa okpulo, anumpa okpulo onuchi*
calve, to; *cheli, wak ushi cheli, yannash ushi cheli*
camel, *kamil*
camel hair, *kamil hishi*
camp; *abina, aialbina, albina, bina*
camp, a deserted; *bina awiha*
camp, to; *abina, abinanchi, abinachi, atepuli, albinachi, binachi*
camp at, to; *aialbinanchi*
campaign, *tanap anya*
campaign, to go on a; *tanap anya*
camped, *bina ansha*
camper, *binachi*
camphor; *ikhinsh balam, nushkobo hotupa ahammi*
camping, a; *binanchi*
can; *ahinla, hinla, na, yoba*
can, a; *isht ochi, oka isht ochi*
can be, *hinla*
can have, *ahinlatok*
can not; *ahe keyu, aheto, awa, chinchint, hatoshba, he keyu, heto, hikbat, wa*
canal, *okhina ikbi*
cancel, to; *kashoffi, kashoffichit kanchi*
cancer; *kachombi, shatammi. shilukwa okpulo*
cancerous swelling, *kachombi*
candid man, *hatak imanukfila apissanli achukma*
candle, *pala*
candle extinguisher, *pala isht mosholichi*
candle mold, *pala aiakmo*
candle snuff, *pala ponola lua*
candle snuffer, *pala isht taptuli*
candle stand, *pala aionhikia*
candle stuff, *pala toba*
candlelight, *pala tohwikeli*
candlestick; *pala afoka, pala aionhikia, pala ontalaia*
candlewick, *ponola pala atoba*
candlewick, burnt; *pala ponola lua*
cane; *oski, uski, uski anunka*
cane (staff); *isht tabeli, tabi*
cane, a small; *oskoba*
cane, bent; *uski botona*
cane, large; *uski chito*
cane, young; *kuni*

cane, to; *bakaha, tǫbi isht bakaha, tǫbi isht isso*

cane mat, *pachǫlh*

cane spool; *uski kolofa, uski kololi*

cane tongs, *uski kapush*

canebrake; *uski pǫta, uski pǫtak*

canebrake, a thick; *uski chito*

canine, *ofi holba*

caning, *bakaha*

canister, *aiǫlhto*

canister of powder, *hituk aiǫlhto*

canker, to; *itǫkha litowa*

canker in the mouth, *itǫkha litowa*

cankered mouth, *itǫkha litowa*

cannibal, *hatak ǫpa*

cannon; *tanamp chito, tanamp hochito*

cannon ball, *tanamp chito i^{n}naki*

cannon shot; *tanamp chito i^{n}naki, tanamp chito i^{n}naki pit akanchi ǫlhpesa*

cannonade, to; *tanamp hochito ontukalichi*

cannoneer, *tanamp chito isht ǫtta*

canoe; *iti kula, iti kula peni, iti peni, peni, peni kula*

canoe, a long; *peni kula falaia*

canon, *anumpa kǫllo*

canopy, *hoshontika*

canteen; *kotoba bolukta, kotobushi bolukta*

canter, to; *hatulli, hatullichi, tabakli, tabaklichi, tulli, tullichi*

canter, to cause to; *tabaklichi*

canters, one who; *tabakli*

cantharides, *shu^{n}shi okchǫmali isht wulhkuchi*

canticle, *ataloa*

cantonment; *tǫshka chipota aiasha, tǫshka chipota inchuka*

canvas, *nan tǫnna na kǫllo*

cap; *iachuka, iatipa, shǫpo*

capable, *imponna*

capacious; *chito, pǫtha*

capacitate, to; *aiatali*

capacity, *aiahanta*

cape; *na foka ilumpatali, shinǫkha, umpatali, umpǫta, yakni okhǫta chito pit shamǫli*

caper, *tullit fulokǫchi*

caper, to; *tullit fulokǫchi*

capital, *tǫmaha chito*

capitation; *hatak hotina, nushkobo atobbi*

capitol, the; *chuka hanta*

capitulate, to; *ilissa*

capitulation, *ilissa*

capricious man, *hatak imanukfila shanaioa*

cap sheaf, the; *paknaka ontalaia*

capsicum; *hishi homi humma, tishi homi humma*

capsize, to; *filemǫt itola*

capsule; *haiyu^{n}kpulo nihi aiǫlhto, haiyu^{n}kpulo nihi hakshup*

captain; *hopaii, kǫpitǫni*

captain-general; *hopaii, mi^{n}ko*

captious, *nan isht amiha inlaua*

captivate, to; *chu^{n}kash ishi, imanukfila ishi, chu^{n}kǫsh yukachi*

captivated; *ǫffetipa, yuka*

captivating, *ishi*

captive; *hatak yuka, na yuka, yuka*

captive, a female; *ohoyo yuka*

captivity, *yuka anta*

captor; *na yukachi, yukachi*

capture, to; *yukachi*

captured, *yuka*

car, *iti chǫnaha*

caravan, *hatak lauǫt a^{n}ya*

carbine, *tanamp fabǫssa*

carbon, *luak tobaksi mosholi*

carcass, *nan illi*

card; *holisso isht bǫska, isht bǫska isht shiahchi*

card, to; *bǫska*

card cotton, to; *shelichi*

card wool, to; *shelichi*

carded; *shiha, shihachi*

carder, *shelichi*

carding machine, *ponola isht shiahchi chito*

care; *ahah ahni, isht ahalaia, nan isht ahalaia*

care, to; *ahalaia, ahni*

careful, *ahah ahni*

carefully, *ahah ahni*

careless; *ahah ahni, ahah ahni iksho*

carelessly, *himak fokalit*

caress, to; *hiahni*

cargo, *peni alota, peni i^{n}shapo*

caries, *foni toshbi*

carious, *foni toshbi*

carious, to render; *foni toshbichi*

carman, *iti chǫnaha isht a^{n}ya*

carnation, *homaiyi*

carnival, *impa chito*

carol, *ataloa*

carol, to; *taloa*

carousal, *okishko ma^{n}ya*

carouse, to; *okishko fehna*

carpenter; *chuka ikbi, iti shaⁿfi*
carpet; *iti patąlhpo umpatąlhpo, umpatąlhpo*
carriage, *shali*
carriage (freight), *ąlhtoba*
carriage, a; *iti chąnaha, iti chanąlli*
carried, *shaⁿya*
carrier; *isht aⁿya, isht aⁿya shali, na shali, na sholi, shali, sholi*
carrion; *nan illi, nipi shua*
carrion crow, *sheki kolofa*
carry, to; *aⁿya, ia, isht ia, shahsholi, shali*
carry, to cause to; *shalichi, sholichi*
carry along, to; *shali*
carry back, to; *faląmmint isht ia*
carry by, to; *ia*
carry in, to; *chukoa*
carry in a sling, to; *hannaweli*
carry on the back, to; *sholi*
carry on the head, to; *ia*
carry over, to; *tanapolechi*
carry through, to; *lopulli*
carry to, to; *isht ona, shali*
carry to heaven, to; *ąba isht ona*
carry up, to; *ąba isht ia*
carry young, to; *shali*
carrying, *shali*
cart; *iti chanąlli, iti chąnaha*
cart, to; *iti chanąlli ashali*
carter, *iti chąnaha isht aⁿya*
cartridge, *tanampo ąlbiha achąfa*
cartwright, *iti chąnaha ikbi*
carve, to; *tushtuli*
carved, *bąsha*
carver, *tushtuli*
cascade; *kihepa, oka chopa, oka pitafohopa, oka pitakinafa*
case; *afoha, afoka, itombi, itombushi, nana, shukcha*
case, to; *itombi abeli, itombi fohki, shukcha*
case knife, *bąshpo ibbak pishinli, bąshpo isht impa*
cased, *itombi abeha*
cash; *tąli fehna, tąli holisso*
cash, to; *itatobąt tąli holisso ishi*
cashier, *holisso lapushki ikbi*
cashier, to; *kalakshichi, kobąffi*
cashiered; *kalakshi, kobafa, kucha*
casing, *apolusli*
cask, *itąlhfoa chito*
casket, *itombushi*
cast, *hakmo*
cast, a; *pila*

cast, to; *ashachi, hakmuchi, onochi, pila*
cast away, to; *kampila, kanchi*
cast away, to be; *itokąnia*
cast back, to; *faląmmichit pila*
cast down, to; *akkakoli, akkapila*
cast headlong, to; *itihpilachi*
cast into, to; *aiashachi*
cast into the fire, to; *itąchi, itoashachi, itokaha*
cast into the sea, to; *okąchi*
cast lots, to; *na shoelichi*
cast off the skin, to; *wuklo*
cast out, to; *kohchi, kucha pila, kucha weli, kuchi*
cast up, to; *hotina*
caster; *hakmuchi, hotina, kanchi, kotobushi, pila*
castigate, to; *fąmmi*
castigator; *fąmmi, na fąmmi*
casting, *shuti iyasha akmuchi*
castle, *aboha kąllo*
castrate, to; *bąshli, hobąk ikbi*
castrated; *hobąk, hobąk toba*
castrato, *hatak hobąk*
casual, *ishkanąpa*
casualty, *ishkanąpa*
cat, a wild; *shakbatina*
catacomb, *hatak aholopi*
catamount, *koi*
cataplasm, *ashela*
cataract; *kihepa, sakti oka pit akinafa* (fall of water); *nishkin tanla, nishkin tąlhha* (disease of the eye)
catch, to; *ąlbonli, haląlli, haleli, hokli, kanapachi, lachąkat ishi, okhawi, yukachi*
catch, to cause to; *hoklichi*
catch away, to; *yichiffi*
catch fish, to; *nąni hokli*
catch sickness, to; *abeka haleli*
catch with the claws or fingers, to; *yicheli, yichiffi*
catcher; *hokli, na hokli, yichiffi*
catching, *abeka haleli*
caterpillar, a poisonous; *hatak holhpąlli*
caterpillar, a species of; *hatak holhpa, hatak holhpąlli holba*
caterwaul, to; *yaⁿwa*
catfish; *nakishtalali, nakishwana*
cathartic; *ikhiⁿsh ishkot ont iachi, ikhiⁿsh ishkot ikfia, ishkot ikfia, isht lopulli, ulbąl ont iachi*
cattail flag, *hąshuk pancha, panti*

cattle; ạlhpoa, wak
cattle, a pair of working; wak toksạli itichapa
cattle, a range for; wak aiasha
cattle, a stall for; wak aiimpa
cattle, a yoke of; wak itichapa
cattle, black; wak
caught; ashekonoa, halelili, yichowa
caul; inlapa, lapa
cause; nan ihmi, nana
cause, to; aiohmichi, chi, nan ihmichi
cause all, to; oklunhạchi
causeway, a wooden; iti patapo, iti patạlhpo
causeway, to make a; sakti ikbi
cauterize, to; luachi
cauterized, lua
caution, ahah ahni
caution, to; nan inmiha
cautioner, nan inmiha
cautious, ahah ahni
cavalry, isuba omanili tạshka ạliha
cave; hichukbi, hochukbi, tạli chiluk, yakni chiluk, yakni hichukbi
cave, to; yakni hichukbi aiạtta
cave, to live in a; yakni hichukbi aiạtta
cave in, to; oka hafeta, tibafa
cave in, to make; tibạffi
cave off, to; kitali
caved in, tibafa
cavern; hichukbi, hichukbi chito, hochukbi, tạli chiluk, yakni chiluk
cavil, nan isht amiha
cavity; chiluk, chuluk
caw, kakaachi
caw, to; kahkahachi, kakaachi, ola
cayenne pepper, hishi homi humma
cease, to; ahokofa, ahokoffi, auola, habofa, haboli, issa, issạchi, yokopa
cease, to cause to; auolạchi
cease to love, to; inhollot issa
ceased, yokopa
ceaseless, ahokofa
cedar, chuala
cede, to; ima, issa, kanchi
ceil, to; alatali
celebrate, to; aiokpanchi, holitoblichi, holitoblit isht anumpuli
celebrated, holitopạt isht anumpa
celebration, holitoblit isht anumpuli
celerity, shinimpa
celestial, ạba
celibacy, ikauayo (see auaya)
cellar, aboha anutaka kula

cement, to; aiạlbo, aiạlbuchi, akmochi
cemented; aiạlbo, akmo
cemetery, hatak aholopi
census; hatak holhtina, hatak puta holhtina, holhtina
cent, sint
center; aiiklạna, chunkạsh, iklạnna
center, to; iklạnnạchi
center of a tree, iti iskuna
centered, iklạnna
centipede, a large; nutachanha
centurion; kạpitạni, sintilion
century, afạmmi talepa achạfa
ceremony, nana kaniohmi
certain; anli, kanimi, kaniohmi
certain, a; achạfa
certainly; anli, ba, hatoshke, pulla, unkah
certainly so, to be; achini
certificate, holisso lilafa
certify, to; holissochit anoli
cessation, the; ahokofa, auola, foha, issa
cession; ima, kanchi
chafe, to; pikofa, pikoffi, pikoli, pikolichi
chafe, to cause to; pikoffichi
chafed; pikofa, pikoli
chafer; pikoffi, pikofichi
chaff; haklopish, hakshup
chagrin, to; nukoạchi
chagrined; hofahya, nukoa
chain; itatakạli, itạtakạli
chain, a surveyor's; yakni isht ạlhpisa
chain, an iron; tạli ititakạlli
chain, to; takchi
chain of cloth, ạpi
chained, talakchi
chains, in; yuka anta
chair; aionbinili, aiomanili, aionasha, iti chạnaha pạlhki
chair, elbow; aionasha aiataya ansha
chair leg, aionbinili ạpi, aiomanili ạpi, aiomanili iyi
chair post; aiomanili ạpi, aiomanili iyi
chairman, pelicheka
chaise; iti chạnaha pạlhki, iti chanạlli iskitini pạlhki
chalice, isht ishko
chalk, lukfi hạta
challenge, panfi
challenge, to; panfi
challenge, to cause to; panfichi
challenged, panfa
challenger, panfi
chamber, a; aboha anusi, ạba iti patạlhpo, patạlhpo, pihcha

chamber, an upper; aba patalho
chamber lye, hoshunwa
chamberlain, tishu
chameleon, fani imalakusi
chamois, isi kosoma
champ, to; hauansa, hoansa, hopansa, kapuli, kapulichi, kopolichi
champer, kapuli
chance, to do by; yammak fokalechi
chance, to go by; yammak fokalechi
change, inla
change, to; aiinla, aiinlachi, atobbichi, atobbit foka, inla, inlachi, talali, wiha
change (as the moon), to; hashi himmona talali, hashi himo auata, hashilli
change of the moon, hashilli
change the mind, to; chunkash inlachi
changeable; imanukfila laua, inla shali
changed; inla, inlat toba
changer, inlachi
changers of money, nan isht itatoba
channel; ayanalli, bok aiyanalli, oka aiyanalli
chant, to; taloa
chanter, taloa
chap; alla nakni, bitanli, kichanli, hatak himmita, pachanli
chap (on the hands), bisanlih
chap, the; nutakfa
chap, to; bitanli, bitanlichi, kichanli, kichanlichi, kichaya, mitali, mitalichi, pachanli
chapel, aianumpuli aboha hanta
chapiters, kibikshi
chaplain, aba anumpuli
chapped; kichanli, pachanli
chapped foot, iyi bitanli
char, to; akabunshli
character; alhtayak, hochifo, holisso
charcoal, luak tobaksi mosholi, tobaksi mosholi
charge (commission); aheka, anumpa
charge (for a gun); albiha, alhpintta, ilhpita achafa, tanampo albiha achafa, tukafa achafa
charge (price), alhtoba
charge, to; ahekachi, anumpa onuchi, onochi, miha
charge with a debt, to; aheka takalichi
charged; albiha, alhpitta, ilhpita
charged with, onutula
charger; amphata, hituk aialhpisa
chariot; iti chanalli, iti chanalli iskitini palhki, iti chanaha palhki

charity; chunkash imanukfila achukma, innukhanklo
charm, fappo
charm, to; chunkash ishi, fappo onuchi, fappuli, yukpali
charmed; fappo, yukpa
charmer, fappo onuchi
charnel house, hatak illi foni aiasha
charred, akabonsha '
chase, lioli
chase, to; iahinsht ia, lioa, lioli
chase with dogs, to; ofi isht lioli
chased away, chafa
chaser, lioli
chasm; chiluk, hichukbi, itamintafa, tali chiluk, yakni chiluk
chaste; hopoksia, kostini
chasten, to; fammi, isikkopali, kanichi
chastened, fama
chastener, fammi
chastise, to; fammi, isikkopali, kanichi
chastised, fama
chastiser; fammi, na fammi
chastity; hopoyuksa, kostini
chat, anumpa
chat, to; anumpuli
chattels, ilanyak
chatter, to; himak fokalechi, kasachi
chatterbox, anumpuli shali
chaw, hopansa
chaw, to; hauansa, hoansa, hopansa
cheap; ahoba, aiilli ikchito, aiilli iklauo, aiilli iskitini, alhchunna
cheapen, to; aiilli iskitinichi, alhchunnachi
cheat; haksichi, hatak haksichi, na haksi, yimmichi
cheat, to; haksichi, pakammi, yimmichi
cheated; haksi, yimmi
cheater; haksichi, yimmichi
check; bakoa, issachi
check, small; basosunkachi, chikichiki
check, to; atabli, hilechi, issachi, oktabli, olabbi
checked, bakokona
checked and tabby, to be; basoa
cheek, itisukpi
cheek bone, itisukpi foni
cheer, chunkash yukpa
cheer, to; aiokpachechi, aiyukpachi, okcha, yiminta, yimintachi, yukpa, yukpali
cheer, to be of; yukpa
cheerful; aiokpanchi achukma, nuktanla, nuktala

cheerless; *ilbasha, liposhi*
cheese; *pishukchi nia palaska, pishukchi palaska, wak pishukchi palaska*
cheesemonger, *pishukchi palaska kanchi*
chemise, *ohoyo i^nna foka lumbo*
cherish, to; *hofantichi, holitoblit hofantichi*
cherished; *hofanti, holitopat hofanti*
Cherokee, *Chalakki*
Cherokee man, *Chalakki hatak*
Cherokee Nation, *Chalakki okla*
Cherokee people, *Chalakki okla*
cherry, *italikchi ani*
cherry tree, *italikchi*
chest (box), *itombi*
chest (part of body), *haknip*
chest, to; *itombi fohki*
chestnut; *oti, uti*
chestnut (color), *lusbi*
chestnut, the dwarf; *hachofakti*
chestnut burr, *oti hakshup*
chew, to; *aua^nsa, haua^nsa, hoa^nsa, hopa^nsa*
chicane, *haksichi*
chick, *aka^nka*
chick, to; *offo, tikachi*
chicken; *aka^nk ushi, aka^nka*
chicken hawk; *biakak, biya^nkak*
chicken-hearted, *nukshopa*
chicken-pox, *'hashtap inchilakwa*
chide, to; *nukoat anumpuli*
chief; *hatak api humma i^nminko, mi^nko, pelichi*
chief man, *i^nshali hatak*
chieftainess, *mi^nko imohoyo*
chigoe, *shu^nkoma*
child; *alla, iso, ushi*
child, a white man's; *na hollo imalla*
child, the youngest; *alla isht aiopi*
child, to make himself a; *allachi, ilallachi*
childbearing, *alla eshi*
childhood, *alla tomba*
childish; *alla ilahobbi, ilallachi, puskusechi*
childless; *alla ikimiksho, ushi iksho*
childlike, *alla chuhmi*
children; *alla, saso*
children, young or small; *alla chipunta, chipota*
chill, a; *hochukwa*
chilliness; *ahochukwa, ahochukwachi, hochukwa*

chilly; *ahochukwa, ahochukwachi, hochukwa, hochukwachi*
chime, to; *ola*
chimney; *ashoboli, luak ashoboli*
chimney corner, *ashobolichukbi, ashobolinaksika*
chimney swallow, *chupilak*
chimney top, *ashobolipaknaka*
chin, *nutakfa*
chin, high; *itakwacholi*
chin bone, *nutakfa foni*
chine, *nali foni*
chine of a barrel, *italhfoa chito ibish*
chink, *chiluk*
chink, to; *chiluk toba, chusokachi, chusolichi, ola, olachi*
chinquapin, *hachofakti*
chinquapin tree, *hachofaktapi*
chip, *chobilhkan, chopilhkash, chupilkash, iti shukafa, iti shukali, iti tushafa, iti tushali, kobilhchap, koichup, polhkash, shukali*
chip, to; *iti chant tushalichi, shukali, shukaffi*
chipmunk, *chinisa*
chipped; *shukali, shukli, tushali*
chirographer, *holissochi*
chirp, *ola*
chirp, to; *ola*
chisel; *iti isht kula, nan isht kula*
chisel, a cold; *tali isht hokafa, tali isht tapa*
chisel nuts, to; *washlichi*
chit, *offo*
Choctaw, *Chahta*
Choctaw, a; *Chahta*
Choctaw blood, *Chahta isht ia*
Choctaw bread, *paska banaha*
Choctaw bread, to make; *paska banahachi*
Choctaw child, *Chahta alla*
Choctaw country, *Chahta yakni*
Choctaw descent, *Chahta isht ia*
Choctaw ground, *Chahta yakni*
Choctaw horse, *Chahta isuba*
Choctaw land, *Chahta yakni*
Choctaw language; *Chahta anumpa, Chahta imanumpa*
Choctaw man, *Chahta hatak*
Choctaw mile, *Chahta i^nkowi*
Choctaw Nation; *Chahta okla, Chahta yakni*
Choctaw origin, *Chahta isht ia*

Choctaw people, *Chahta okla*
Choctaw pony, *Chahta isuba*
Choctaw race, *Chahta isht ia*
Choctaw race, to be of the; *Chahta isht atia*
Choctaw soil, *Chahta yakni*
Choctaw tribe, *Chahta okla*
Choctaw woman, *Chahta ohoyo*
Choctaw, the, *Chahta okla*
choice; *achukma, aiyoba, holitopa*
choice, a; *atokoli*
choir; *taloa, taloa ąliha*
choke, to; *anuklamąlli, nuklamąlli, nuklamoli, nuklamolli, nuksiteli, nukshikanlichi, nukshiniffi, nuktakali, nuktakalichi, nuktilefa, nuktiliffi, oktąbli, oktąpa, oląbbi*
choke to death, to; *nuktakat illi*
choke up, to; *ląbli, ląblichi*
choked; *nuklamoli, nuklamolli, nuksakki, nuktakali, oktąpa, nuktilefa*
choked up, *ląbli*
choking, a; *nuktakali*
choler; *lakna, nukoa*
cholera, *abeka okpulo*
cholera morbus, *italaⁿkla ont ia*
choleric, *nukoa shali*
choose, to; *ahnit, aioa, apissali, atokolechi, atokoli, atokulit aiyua, atokulit ishi*
chooser, *atokoli*
chop, to; *chanli*
chop, to cause to; *chanlichi*
chop and fell, to; *chant akkąchi, chant kinąffi*
chop down, to; *kinąffi*
chopped, *chaⁿya*
chopper, *iti chanli*
chopping block, *achaⁿya*
chores, *nan toksąli chipinta*
chorister, *taloa tikba heka*
chosen, *aiyua*
Christ, *Kilaist*
christened, *okissąchi*
Christian, a; *ąba anumpuli*
Christian, a pretended; *ąba anumpuli ilahobbi*
Christian, a true; *ąba anumpuli aⁿli*
Christian, to become a; *ąba anumpuli toba*
Christianity; *ąba anumpa, ąba anumpa ikhana*
christianize, to; *ąba anumpuli ikbi*
Christians, *ąba anumpa ikhana*

Christmas, *nitak hollo chito*
chronometer, *hąshi isht ikhąna*
chuckle, to; *yukpa*
chunk, *iti tąpa*
chunk bottle, a common; *kotoba okchimali*
chunk of wood, *iti tilofa*
church, *aianumpuli aboha hanta, ąbai anumpuli chuka, ąba anumpuli iksa, chąch*
church, the; *ąba anumpuli ąliha*
church member, *ąba anumpuli iksa ibafoka*
church music, *ąba anumpa taloa*
churchyard, *hatak aholopi*
churl, *hatak nukoa shali*
churn; *pishukchi achibokąchi, pishukchi aniachi*
churn, to; *bohokąchi, pishukchi niachi*
churn dasher, *pishukchi nia isht chibolichi*
churn lid, *onulhpohomo*
churn staff, *pishukchi nia isht chibolichi*
cicatrix, *miⁿsa*
cicatrize, to; *ątta, ąttąchi*
cicatrized, *ątta*
cider, *oka hauąshko*
cigar, *hakchuma shąna*
cincture, *isht ąskufąchi*
cipher, to; *holhtina, hotina*
circle; *bolboki, bolkąchi, bolukta, chanąlli, chąnaha*
circle, to; *fullokąchi*
circled, *apakfopa*
circles, to make; *bolbokechi, bolkąchechi*
circuit; *afolota, chąnaha folota achąfa, folota, fullokąchi*
circuit, to; *apakfopa*
circuit of the earth, the; *yakni fullota*
circuitous, *folota*
circuits, to take; *folotoa*
circular; *bolboki, bolkąchi, bolukta*
circulate, to; *ilhkoli, ilhkolichi, takakanli*
circumcise, to; *hakshup tąbli*
circumcised; *hakshup tąpa, hakshup tąptua*
circumcision, *hakshup tąpa*
circumference, the; *apakfopa*
circumference of the earth, the; *yakni fullota*
circumspect, *ahah ahni*
circumstance, *akaniohmi*
cistern, *oka aiąlhto*

citadel, *aboha kạllo*
citation, *anoa*
citizens, *okla*
city; *tạmaha, tạmaha chito, tạmaha holihta*
civil; *hopoksia, kostini*
civil man, *hatak kostini*
civil war, *okla achạfa itibi*
civil war, to have a; *okla achạfa itibi*
civilize, to; *hopoksiachi, hopoyuksạlli, ikhananchi, kostininchi*
civilized, *kostini*
civilizer, *hopoyuksạlli*
clabber, *pishukchi kạskaha*
clad, *fohka*
clam, *fulush*
clam, fresh-water; *oka fulush*
clamp, *isht kiselichi*
clamshell;· *fulush hakshup, oka fulush hakshup*
clamor, *paⁿya*
clan, a; *iksa, isht atiaka*
clan, one; *iksa achạfa*
clandestine, *luma*
clangor, *chạmakạchi*
clank, *chạmakạchi*
clank, to; *chạmakạchi chạmalichi*
clap, to; *lobohạchi*
clap of thunder, *hiloha*
clapboards, *iti bạsha ahonạla*
clapper, *isuba inuchi anuⁿkaka takali*
clarified, *kashofa*
clarify, to; *kashoffi*
clash, *isso*
clash, to; *isso, issochi*
clashing, *itaiisso*
clasp, *atapạchi*
clasp, to; *akamạssạli, atapạchi, hokli, shakba afohomit ishi*
clasp knife, *bạshpo poloma*
clasped together, *akamạssa*
class; *apelichi, iksa, itibapisa*
classmate; *holisso ibapisa, itibapisa*
clatter, to; *kạlahạchechi, kạlahạchi*
clattering, *kạlahạchi*
claw, *iyakchush*
claw, bird's; *hushi iyakchush*
claw, to; *kạlli*
clay, *lukfi*
clay, white; *lukfi hạta*
clay cold, *kapạssa*
clean; *isht ahullochika, kashofa, okshauanli, okshauạshli*
clean, to; *kashoffi*
clean, to make; *kashoffichi*

cleaning, *lakoffi*
cleanly, *kashofa*
cleanness, *kashofa*
cleanse, to; *achefa, kashoffi, kashoffichi, lakoffichi*
cleansed, *kashofa*
cleanser, *kashoffi*
cleansing, *kashofa*
clear; *hanta, masheli, okshauanli, okshauạshli, shahbi, shohkalali, tohchalali*
clear, to; *shahbichi, shohkalalichi*
clear, to make; *hantạchi, okshauanlichi, okshauạshlichi, shohkawalichi*
clear away, to; *mashelichi*
clear land, to; *bạlli*
clear off, to; *masheli*
cleared; *kashofa, shahbi*
cleared off, *masheli*
clearing, *shahbika*
clearly; *haiaka, haiakạt*
clearness, *shohkawali*
cleave, to; *bakapa, chilaktochi, chulaktochi, pạlalichih, pạlata, pạlạlli, shimafa, shimạffi*
cleave to, to; *aiạlbo, alapali, anuksita, anuksitkạchi, asitia, ạsseta, halạlli*
cleft; *bakapa, pạlata, shimafa*
cleft, a; *bakapa, pạlata*
clemency, *chuⁿkạsh yohbi*
clement, *chuⁿkạsh yohbi*
clergy, *aba anumpa isht ạtta ạliha*
clergyman, *ạba anumpa isht ạtta*
clerk; *ạba anumpa isht ạtta, holissochi, na holissochi*
clever; *chuⁿkạsh yohbi, imponna*
clevis, *tạli isht halạlli*
clevy, *tạli isht halạlli*
click, to; *tikachi*
cliff, *sakti*
cliffy, *sakti foka*
clifty, *sakti foka*
climb, to; *iti oiya, oiyạ*
climb up, to; *apakchulli*
climber; *apakchulli, oiya*
clinch, to; *kiseli, yichiffit ishi*
cling, to; *apakchulli*
cling to, to; *apakshạna, halạlli*
clink, *chamak*
clink, to; *chamakachi*
clip, a single; *himonna tạpli*
clip, to; *ạmo, bạshli, tạbli, yushkabalichi*
clip off, to; *kạtelichi*
clip off once, to; *himonna tạpli*
clipped; *ạlmo, bạsha, tạpa, yushkabali*

clipping, *tabli*

clitoris, *imoksini*

cloak; *anchi, ilefoka chito, na foka chito*

cloak, to; *anchi, luhmi, na foka ·chito fohka*

cloak another, to; *anchichechi, anchichi*

clock, *hashi isht ithana chito*

clockmaker, *hashi isht ithana ikbi*

clod, *lukfi lumbo*

clog, to; *oktabli, takalechi*

close; *achunanchi, afacha, aⁿhollo, apoh-tukih, bilinka, iⁿhollo, itatoba kallo, katanli, luma, nan iⁿholitopa, nan iⁿhollo, takali*

close, the; *ataha, hokofa*

close, to; *akamali, akammi, akopulechi, hokofa, hokoli, isht aiopichi, itakopulechi, okhishta, okshita, ukhishta*

close, to make; *apohtukachi*

close and light, to be; *apohtuki*

close by; *bilinka, olanli, tomalusi*

close the eye, to; *mocholi, okhishta, okmocholi, tobosinli, ukhishta*

close the hand, to; *ukhishta*

close the lips tight, to; *itakkomulih*

close together; *chikihah, itakantali*

close together, to; *itakopuli*

close up, to; *akmochi*

closed; *hokofa, okhilishta, okshillita*

closed up; *akmo, labli*

closely, *olanlisi*

closet, *abohushi*

closet, to; *abohushi fohki, luhmi*

closeted, *abohushi fohka*

clot, *walaha*

clot, to; *walaha*

clot of blood, *issish walakachi*

cloth, *nan tanna*

cloth, black; *nan lusa*

cloth, checked; *nan tanna basoa, nan tanna holisso*

cloth, floor; *iti patalhpo umpatalhpo*

cloth, large checked; *nan tanna bakoa*

cloth, striped; *nan tanna basoa, nan tanna shauiya*

cloth, thick; *nan tanna sukko*

cloth, thin; *nantapaski*

cloth, white; *na hata, nan tanna tohbi*

cloth made of hair, *nam panshi tanna*

clothe, to; *askufa, askufachechi, asku-fachi, fohka, fohkachi, hanaweli, ilefoka, ilefoka foka, ilefoka fokachi, na foka foka, na foka fokachechi*

clothed; *abehkachi, fohka, ilefoka foka, na foka foka*

clothes; *anchi, ilefoka, na fohka*

clothesbrush; *ilefoka isht kashokachi, na foka isht kasholichi*

clothier; *chukfi hishi nan tanna aiskiachi, nan tanna*

clothing, *na fohka*

cloud; *ahoshonti, hoshonti, hoshontika, hoshontikilhkiki, okhapaioha*

cloud, to; *hoshonti, hoshontichi, oklilechi*

cloud up, to; *hoshonti toba*

cloud-capped, *hoshonti pit tikeli*

clouded; *hoshonti, hoshonti toba*

cloudy; *hoshonti, hoshontichi, okhapa-yabi*

clout; *apokshiama, alhkata, na lilafa*

clout, to; *akkalli, apokshiami, apok-shiamichi*

clouted; *apokshiama, apokshiammi, alh-kata*

cloven; *chilakto, chulakto*

cloven foot or hoof; *iyi chilakto, iyi falakto*

cloy, to; *fihobli, yammichi*

cloyed; *fihopa, yammi*

club; *atashi, itashi, iti nipa, iti tapa, iti taptua, tapena*

clubfoot, *iyi ponkshi*

clubfooted, *iyi ponkshi*

cluck, to; *kanlhkuha, tuktua*

clump, *bafalli talaia*

clump (of trees), *iti talaia*

clumsy, *weki*

cluster; *alokoli, lohto, lukoli, pokuspoa*

cluster, to; *lukoli, lukolichi*

cluster of grapes, *pokospoa*

cluster of little bushes, *bifisha*

clustered; *lohto, lukoli*

clutch, to; *yichiffit ishi*

clutches, *iyakchush*

clutter, *aiyokoma*

clutter, to; *aiyokomi*

cluttered, *aiyokoma*

coach, *iti chanaha holitopa*

coach box, *iti chanaha holitopa aiomanili*

coachmaker, *iti chanaha holitopa ikbi*

coadjutor; *apela, apelachi*

coagulate, to; *walaha, walahachi*

coagulated, *walaha*

coagulation, *walaha*

coagulum, *walaha*

coal, *tobaksi*

coal, fire; *tobaksi*

coal, to; *itobila, tobaksi ikbi*

coal, to make; *tobaksi ikbi*

coal-black, *tobaksi lusa ohmi*
coal digger, *tobaksi kulli*
coal house, *tobaksi inchuka*
coal mine, *tobaksakula*
coal of fire, *luak tobaksi*
coalpit, *tobaksatoba*
coalpit, a fossil; *tobaksakula*
coalesce, to; *apolukta, albo, polukta*
coalition, *fohka*
coarse; *lapushki, okshachinli, okshifeli, sukko, shachaⁿha, yauaha*
coarse, to make; *okshalinchi*
coarse-grained, *chichoⁿli*
coarseness, *okshifeli*
coast; *oka aialaka, aiali, alaka, oka alaka, oka ont alaka, yakni, yakni aiali*
coasts of, *yakni iⁿkaniohmi*
coat; *askufa tapa, hakshup, hishi, ilefoka, ilefoka lumbo, na fohka*
coat, a great; *na foka chito*
coat, a long; *na foka chashana*
coat, a short; *ilefoka kolofa, ilefoka kololi*
coat, a straight-bodied; *na foka chashana*
coax, to; *haksichi*
cob; *api, tanch api, taⁿsh api*
cobble, to; *akkalli*
cobbler, *shulush akalli*
cobweb; *chuklampulli, hachuklampuli, tuklampuli*
cock (faucet), *oka abicheli*
cock (rooster), *akaⁿk nakni*
cock, a brass; *isht bicheli, oka isht bicha, oka isht bicheli*
cock, to; *akachakali, hilechi*
cock of a gun lock, *luksi fulup*
cocked, *hika*
cockerel, *akaⁿk nakni himmita*
cockfight, *akaⁿk nakni itibbi*
cockle, to; *yiⁿyikechi, yiⁿyiki*
cocklebur, *paⁿshtali*
cockled, *yiⁿyiki*
cockroach; *bila chapka, nani chapka, nia chapka*
coequal, *itilaui, sipokni kat itilaui*
coffee, *kafi*
coffee, green; *kafi okchimali*
coffee, Java; *kafi tohbi*
coffee, strong; *kafi homi*
coffee, West India; *kafi okchimali*
coffee, white; *kafi tohbi*
coffee berry or seed, *kafi nihi*
coffee boiler, *kafahonni*

coffee cup, *kafaiishko*
coffee grounds, *kafi lakchi*
coffee mill, *kafafotoha*
coffee sack, bin, box, etc.; *kafaialhto*
coffee saucer, *kafaiishko*
coffeepot; *chakli, kafahonni, kafaialhto*
coffeepot spout, *kafabicha*
coffer; *itombi, tali holisso aialhto*
coffer, to; *tali holisso aialhtofoki*
coffer up, to; *itombi abeli*
coffered, *itombi abeha*
coffin, *itombi*
coffin, to; *itombi fohki*
coffin maker, *itombi ikbi*
cog; *achushoa, afashkachi*
cog, to; *yimmichi*
cogent; *kallo, kilimpi*
cogitate, to; *anukfilli*
cognate, *isht atiaka*
cognition, *ikhana*
cohabit, to; *anta, auaya, ibaianta*
cohere, to; *asitia, albo*
coherence, *itasitia*
cohort, *tashka chipota talepa hanali*
coif, *ialipa*
coif, to; *ialipeli*
coil, *chanaha*
coil, to; *chanaha, chanahachi*
coil of rope, *aseta chanaha*
coil up, to; *chanaha*
coiled up, *chanaha*
coin; *tali fehna, tali holisso*
coin, gold; *tali holisso lakna*
coinage, *tali holisso*
coined, *tali holisso*
coiner, *tali holisso ikbi*
cold; *ahochukwa, akmo, hochukwa, kapassa*
cold, a; *hochukwa, hotilhko, ibishano, kapassa*
cold, having a; *nukshammi*
cold, to have a; *ibishano*
cold climate, *akapassaka*
cold-hearted, *chuⁿkash kapassa*
cold region, *akapassaka*
coldness; *ahochukwa, ahochukwachi, kapassa*
colic; *iffuka hotupa, ikfuka hotupa, ikfuka katapa*
collander, *asonak aholuyachi*
collar; *iachunahika, ikonla afohoma, ikonla inuchi, inuchi*
collar, to; *ikonla afohoma ishi, inuchi foki*
collar bone, *imiskauata*
collard, *kalush*

collation, *impa iskitini*
colleague; *itapela, itapiha*
collect, to; *itahoba, itahobi, itahobli, itanali, itanaha, itannali, itannalichi, lukoli*
collect debts, to; *aheka*
collect hay, to; *hashuk itannali*
collected; *itahoba, itanaha, lukoli*
collection; *alokoli, fohopa, hatak itahoba, hatak itanaha, itahoba, itanaha*
collective; *itahoba, itanaha*
collector, *itannali*
collector of toll, *pablikan*
college; *holisso aiithana chito, holisso apisa chito*
collide, to; *isso*
collier; *tobaksi ikbi, tobaksi kulli*
colliquate, to; *bileli*
collision, *isso*
colloquy; *anumpuli, itimanumpuli*
colonel, *minko*
colonist, *abenili*
colonize, to; *abinolichi, kanallichit binilichi, binilichi, binolichi*
colonized, *binili*
colonizer, *binolichi*
colony; *abenili, binili, wihat binili*
color, *shapha*
color, a dirty; *taktaki*
color, to give a dirty; *taktakichi*
color, to have a dirty; *taktaki*
color blue, to; *okchamalichi*
color green, to; *okchamalichi*
colored green, *okchamali*
colt, *isubushi*
colt, to; *isubushi cheli*
colter, *yakni isht patafa tikbinhika*
columbo, *akshish lakna chito*
column; *anumpa bachaya, anumpa bachoha*
comb; *chaka, hakshup, hashintak, isht shilli, shalintak*
comb, a coarse; *hashintak yauaha, shalintak shachaha*
comb, a cock's; *impasha*
comb, a fine; *issap isht albi*
comb, an ivory; *issap isht albi*
comb, to; *shilli*
comb maker, *shalintak ikbi*
comb of a bumblebee, *onsini hakshup*
comb of a fowl, *inchaka*
comb of a turkey, *ibilatampa*
combat, *itibbi*
combat, to; *itibi*

combat, to cause to; *itibechi*
combatant, *itibi*
combed, *shilla*
comber, *shilli*
combination, *ibafoka*
combine, to; *fohki, ibafoki, ibafokichi*
combined; *fohka, ibafoka*
combustible, *nana lua hinla*
come! *inta, yaki*
come, to; *ant, atanya, anya, ala, ela, ilhkoli, ishla, manya, minti, onna, toba*
come, to begin to; *mintahpi*
come, to cause to; *mintichi*
come about, to; *filimmi*
come across, to; *afama*
come after, to; *iakaiya*
come again, to; *falamat ala*
come against, to; *insannih*
come along (as a verbal message) to; *anumpa kochanli*
come apart, to; *koyofa, lilafa, tapa, taptua*
come at last, to; *aiyala*
come away, to; *kanali*
come by, to; *ishi*
come down, to; *akkoa, attat akowa*
come forth, to; *kucha, wiha*
come from, to; *aminti, attat minti*
come in, to; *abehpa, chukoa*
come in two, to; *kolofa, litafa*
come near, to; *bilinka, bilinchi*
come off, a; *lakoffi*
come off, to; *alinfa, alikachi, fakoha, fakoli, fakopa, hokoli, issa, kolofa, kololi, lakoffi, lonfa, loha, shuekachi, shukali, shunfa*
come off at, to; *akolofa*
come open, to; *patali*
come out, to; *ansha kuchat, auata, haiaka, kucha, linfa, mokofa, shiha, takoba kucha*
come out, to cause to; *akuchechi*
come out of, to *akucha akuchawiha, kohcha*
come out of the ground, to; *shuekachi*
come over, to; *lopulli*
come round, to; *apakfopa*
come short, to; *onachi*
come through, to; *lopulli*
come to, to; *ala, falamat okcha, ona*
come to hand, to; *ibbak fohka*
come to pieces, to; *lishoa*
come to several, to; *katohmona*
come together, to; *itakopuli, itanaha*

come under, to; *nutaka ia*
come up, to; *afena, hokofa, offo*
come up by the roots, to; *teha, tinfa*
come up with, to; *sakki*
come upon, to; *onutula*
come with, to; *tankla minti*
comely; *aiukli, ạlhpesa*
comer, a; *ạla, minti*
comet; *fichik pọloli, fichik shobota*
comfort, *hopola*
comfort, to; *hopolạchi, hopolạlli, nukta-lachi*
comforted, *hopola*
comforter; *hopolạchi, hopolạlli, nan uktalali, nuktalali*
coming, *minti*
coming time, *himmak pila*
command, *anumpa kạllo*
command, to; *anumpa kạllo onuchi, apesa, miha*
commanded, *anumpa kạllo onutula*
commander; *isht boa chito, iti isht boa chito, minko*
commandment; *anumpa ạlhpisa, nan ạlhpisa, nana ạlhpisa*
commence, to; *ia*
commence from, to; *aiạli*
commencement; *ahpi, aiamona, aiisht ia ạmmona, aiisht ia, ạmmona, isht ia ạmmona*
commencement of the day, *nitak echi*
commensurate, *itilaui*
comment, to; *anumpuli*
commentary; *isht anumpa, isht anumpuli*
commentator, *isht anumpuli*
commerce, *itatoba*
commerce, to; *itatoba*
commingle, to; *aiyummi*
commingled, *aiyuma*
commiserate, to; *nukhanklo*
commission, to; *atokoli*
commissioned, *ạlhtokoa*
commissioner, *hatak ạlhtoka*
commissioner of the Government, *na hollo hochitoka*
commit, to; *ibbak fohki*
commit unto, to; *aianukcheto*
committed; *ibbak fohka, ibbak foka*
committee; *ạlhtoka, hatak nan apesa*
committeeman, *hatak ạlhtoka*
commix, to; *aiyummi*
commixed, *aiyuma*

commodious, *ạlhpesa*
commodity, *ạlhpoyak*
commonly; *atak, beka, chatok, chatuk, ke, tak*
commonwealth, *ulhti achạfa*
commotion, *tiwakạchi*
commune, to; *anumpuli, ạpa, oka panki*
communicant, *ibafoka*
communicate, to; *ima*
communicate by letter, to; *holisso-chit anoli*
communication; *anumpa, chukulbi*
community, *okla*
commutation, *itatoba*
commute, to; *atobachi, itatoba, itato-bạchi*
compact, to; *akamạssạli, ateli, atelichi*
compacted; *akamạssa, attia*
companion; *ahinna, apạha, ibachanfa, ibafoka, ibaianta, ibaiansha, ibaiishko, itahina, itibafoka*
companionship, *chukulbi*
company, *ahinna*
company, a; *anya achạfa, pelichi achạfa*
company, to; *ibafoka*
company of light horsemen, *isuba omanili tạshka ạliha*
company with, to go in; *apeha*
compare, to; *hobachi*
compared together, *holba*
comparison, *holba*
compass; *aiạli, apakfopa, falạm isht ikhạna, isht apesa, isht lanfi*
compass, to; *afolotạchi, apakfopa, ạlh-fullinchi*
compassion; *innukhanklo, nukhanklo*
compassion, to exercise; *nukhanklo*
compassionate, *nukhanklo*
compassionate, to; *nukhanklo*
compatible, *ạlhpesa*
compel, to; *atunshpalechi*
compensate, to; *atobbi*
compensated, *ạlhtoba*
compensation, *ạlhtoba*
compete, to; *apakna, pakna, imaiya*
competent, *ạlhpesa*
competition, *itimpakna*
competitor, *itimpakna*
complacency, *yukpa*
complacent, *yukpa*
complainer, *na miha shạli*
complaining, *na miha shạli*

complete; *aiạlhtaha, ạlhtaha, taha*
complete, to; *atali, loshummi, lushomi, taha, tali, tomạffi*
completed; *aiạlhtaha, ataha, ạlhtaha, bakạsto, lushoma, taha, tomafa*
completely; *bano, taha*
completes, one who; *tomạffi*
completion; *aiạlhtaha, ataha*
completion, to have a; *ataha*
compliment, *aiokpạchi*
comply, to; *ahni, aiaⁿlichi, ạlhpesa ahni, haklo*
compose, to; *holissochi, hopolạchi, nuktalali*
composed; *holisso, nuktạla*
composed, to be; *hopola*
composer, *holissochi*
composition, *holisso*
compound, to; *aiyummi*
compounded, *aiyuma*
comprehend, to; *akostininchi, nukfoka*
comprehension, *imanukfila kạllo*
compress, to; *atelichi*
compressed, *attia*
compression, *atelichi*
computation, *holhtina*
compute, to; *hotina*
computed, *holhtena*
computer, *hotina*
comrade; *itibafoka, onochi*
concatenate, to; *takalechi*
concatenated, *takali*
concatenation, *itatakạli*
concave; *kafakbi, kofussa*
concave, made; *kafakbi*
conceal, to; *aluhmi, luhmi, lumpuli*
concealed; *luma, lumboa*
concealment, *aluma*
concede, to; *yohmi*
conceit, *imanukfila*
conceit, to; *anukfilli*
conceive, to; *anukfilli, ạlla iⁿfoka, fohka, shali, ushi iⁿfohka*
conceived; *afohka, aiisht inchakali*
concern; *ahalaia, halaiya, ilaⁿyak, isht ahalaia, nana*
concern, object of; *nan isht ahalaia*
concern, to; *ahalaia*
concern, to have; *ahalaia*
concerned; *ahalaia, halaiya*
concerning; *imma, isht*
concert, *apesa*
concert together, to; *apesa*
concession; *anoli, ilanoli*
conciliate, to; *hopolạlli, nan aiyạchi*

conciliated; *hopola, nan aiya, nuktạla*
conclude, to; *ahokoffichi, apesa, atali*
concluded; *ahokofa, ataha, ạlhpesa*
conclusion; *aiạli, isht aiopi*
concord, *imanukfila achạfa*
concourse; *itahoba, itạnaha*
concubine; *aiina, itaiena*
concur, to; *imanukfila itibafoka*
concussion, *itaiisso*
condemn, to; *anumpa kạllo onuchi, anumpa onuchi, ilbạshali, onochi*
condemned; *anumpa kạllo onutula, anumpa onutula*
condescend, to; *akkachunoli*
condition, *aiahanta*
condole, to; *ibanukhaⁿklo*
conduct; *nana akaniohmi, nana kaniohmi*
conduct, to; *aⁿya, halạlli, ilaueli, ilauet aⁿya, pelichi, tikba heka*
conductor; *ilaueli, isht aⁿya, tikba heka*
conduit; *ataⁿya, oka abicheli*
confer, to; *ima*
conference; *anumpuli, itimanumpuli*
confess, to; *anoli, ilanoli*
confession; *anoli, ilanoli*
confessor; *anoli, ilanoli*
confide, to; *anukcheto, yimmi*
confidence; *aianukcheto, aiyimmika, anukcheto*
confidence, to have; *yimmi*
confident, *yimmi*
confiding, *anukcheto*
confine, *aiạli*
confine, to; *aboha kạllo foki, holihta fohki, takchi*
confined; *aboha kạllo foka, ạlla eshi, talakchi*
confinement, *yuka*
confirm, to; *kamạssạlli, kạllochi*
confirmed; *kamạssa, kạllo*
conflagration; *holukmi, holushmi, hushmi, lua, luak chito*
conflict, *itibbi*
conflict, to; *itibi, itishi, mokafa*
confluence, *aiitafama*
confluent, *ibạlhto*
conform, to; *antia, hobachi*
confound, to; *ibakali*
confound together, to; *kali*
confounded; *aiyokoma, ibakaha*
confounded together, *kaha*
confront, to; *asonali*
confuse, to; *haksubachi, ibakali*
confused, *haksuba*

confused together, *aiyokoma*
confusion; *aiyokoma, haksuba*
congeal, to; *akalapechi, akalapi, akmo, akmochi, hakmo, hakmuchi,walaha, walahachi*
congealed; *akalapi, akmo, hakmo, kalampi, walaha*
congelation, *hakmo*
congratulate, to; *aiokpachi*
congregate, to; *itahoba, itahobi, itahobli, itanaha, itanahachi, itannali*
congregated, *itanaha*
congregation, *hatak itahoba, hatak itanaha, itanaha*
Congress; *aboha hanta okla, Kankish, na hollo hochitoka*
conjecture, to; *ahoba, himak fokalit miha*
conjoin, to; *ibafoki*
conjoined, *ibafoka*
conjuration; *fappo, isht ahollo*
conjure, to; *isht ahollo ilahobi*
conjure (at the ball play), to; *apolumi*
conjurer, *hatak fappo*
conjurer at ball plays, *apoluma*
connect, to; *takalechi*
connected, *takali*
conquer, to; *ilissachi, imaiya, imaiyachi*
conqueror; *ilissachi, imaiya, imaiyachi*
conquest, *imaiya*
conscience; *chunkash, imanukfila, nan isht ilakostininchi*
conscientious; *anli, imanukfila anli achukma*
conscious, *ikhana*
consecrate, to; *holitoblichi*
consecrated, *holitopa*
consecrated object, *na holloka*
consent, to; *alhpesa ahni*
consequential; *fehnachi, ilefehnachi*
consequently, *chumba*
conserve, to; *okchalinchi*
consider, to; *akostininchi, anukfilli, pisa*
considerable, *laua chuhmi*
considerably, to do; *fehna*
considerate; *ahah ahni, hopoksia, nuktala*
consideration, *imanukfila*
considered, *anukfila*
considerer, *anukfilli*
consign, to; *ibbak fohki, ima*
consistent, *alhpesa*
consociate, to; *ibafoka, ibafoki*
consociated, *ibafoka*

consociation, *ibafoka*
consolation; *chunkash yukpa, nana isht ilaiyukpa*
console, to; *chunkash yukpali, hopolalli*
consolidate, to; *akamassali, kallochi*
consolidated, *akamassa, kallo*
consort; *hatak, itahina, tekchi*
consort together, to; *ahinna*
conspicuous; *haiaka, mabi*
conspire, to; *luhmit nana apesa*
constable; *hatak takchi, na hollo takchi*
constellation, *fichik lukoli*
constituent, *tashka*
constitute, to; *ikbi*
constitution, *anumpa alhpisa*
constrain, to; *miha, takchi, yukachi*
constrained; *talakchi, yuka*
construct, to; *ikbi*
construe, to; *anumpa tosholi, alhtosholi, tosholi*
construed; *alhtoshoa, toshoa*
consul; *anumpeshi, minko imanumpeshi*
consult, to; *ponaklo*
consultation, *ponaklo*
consume, to; *aluachi, apat tali, lua, okpani, okpanit tali*
consumed; *aiiksho, lua taha, okpulo*
consumer, *hukmi*
consummate, to; *tali*
consummated, *alhtaha*
consummation, *alhtaha*
consumption, *shilukpa lachowa*
consumption, a; *nukshulla*
contagion; *abeka haleli, haleli*
contagious, *abeka haleli*
contain, to; *alhto*
contaminate, to; *okpani*
contaminated, *okpulo*
contemn, to; *shittilema*
contemner, *shittilema*
contemplate, to; *ahni, anukfilli*
contemplation, *imanukfila*
contemplator, *anukfilli*
contempt; *makhaloka, isht ikinahno, yuala*
contempt, a word of; *yammak haloka*
contemptible; *isht ikinahno, makali*
contend, to; *achowa, afoa, itibi, olabbi*
contend in conversation, to; *shahsholechi*
contented; *alhpesa, alhpesa ahni, nuktala*
contention; *itachoa, itimafoa, itimolabbi, itinnukoa*

contentment, *nuktạla*
contest; *itibbi, itimafoa, itimanumpuli*
contest, to; *afoa, anumpuli*
contiguous; *apunta, bili^nka*
continent; *hopoksia, kostini*
continent, a; *yakni, yakni haknip*
continual, *bilia*
continual, to make; *biliachi*
continually, *bilia*
continuation; *achaka, chạkbi, moma*
continue, to; *achakalechi, achakạlechi, achakạli, achunanchi, a^nsha, bilia, ma^nya, moma*
continue at, to; *aiitachakạlli*
continue evermore, to; *bilia*
continued, *achaka*
contract; *apesa, itimapesa*
contract, to; *apesa, bạshi, bochupka, itatoba, shikoffi, shila, shinoli, yushtololichi*
contracted; *bạshi, shila*
contractor; *itatoba, nan chumpa, nan tohno*
contradict, to; *a^nli, ichapa, keyuachi, yohmi*
contrary, *inla*
contrary, a; *ichapa*
contribute, to; *ibafoki, itạnnali*
contributed, *itạnaha*
contribution; *ibafoka, ibakaha, itạnaha, itibafoka*
contributor, *ibafoki*
contrite; *ilbạsha, kobafa, litoa, nukha^nklo*
control, to; *pelichi*
controller, *pelichi*
controversy, *anumpa itinlaua*
controversy, to have a; *anumpa itinlaua*
contumacy; *afoa, ilafoa*
contuse, to; *kạlali, litoli*
contused; *kạla, litoa*
contusion; *kạla, litoa*
convalescent; *kanihmi, lakoffit isht ia*
covenant, to; *apesa*
convene, to; *itahoba, itahobi, itahobli, itạnaha, itạnnali*
convened; *itahoba, itạnaha*
convener; *itahobi, itahobli, itạnnali*
convenience, *ạlhpesa*
convenient, *ạlhpesa*
convention; *hatak itạnaha, itahoba, itạnaha*
conversation, *itimanumpuli*
converse together, to; *anumpuli*

conversion; *ạba anumpuli toba, inlat toba*
convert, *ạba anumpuli toba*
convert, to; *ạba anumpuli ikbi, hopoyuksạlli, inlạchi*
converted; *inla toba, inlat toba*
convex, *lumbo*
convey, to; *a^nya, ima, kanchi, pila, shali*
convey (news), to; *anoli*
conveyer; *isht ia, shali*
convince, to; *yimmichi*
convinced, *yimmi*
convocation, *itạnaha*
convoke, to; *itạnnali*
convoked, *itạnaha*
convoy, to; *pelichi*
convulse, to; *haiuchi, haiuchichi*
convulsed, *haiuchi*
convulsion, *haiuchi*
cony, *chukfi*
cony burrow, *chukfaluma*
coo, to; *ola*
cook; *honi, hoponi, laboshli, na hoponi*
cook, to; *honi, hoponi, laboshli, nuna, nunachi*
cook, to make; *honichi*
cook in the kernel, to; *luboni*
cook room; *aboha ahoponi, ahoponi*
cooked; *holhponi, honni, labocha, nuna*
cool; *kapạssạchi, nuktạla*
cool, to; *hakmo, hakmuchi, kapạssa, kapạssạchi, kapạssạlli, nuktalali, nuktạla, shippa, shippạchechi, shippạchi, shippạli*
cooled; *hakmo, kapạssa, nuktạla, shippa, shippạchi*
coolish, *ahochukwạchi*
coop, to; *chuka foki*
cooped, *chuka foka*
cooper; *itampikbi, itạlhfoa chito ikbi, itạlhfoa ikbi*
cooperate, to; *toksạli*
copartner, *apelachi*
copartnership, *itapelachi*
copied, *ạlbitạt holisso*
copier, *holissochi*
copious; *apakna, laua*
copper; *tạli holisso lakna, tạli lakna*
copperas, *nan isht laknạchi*
coppersmith, *tạli lakna ikbi*
copy, *ạlbitạt holisso*
copy, to; *ạlbitet holissochi, hobachit holissochi, hobachit ikbi*
copyist, *hobachit holissochi*
cord; *aseta, hakshish, ponokạllopạna*
cord, a large; *hakshish chito*

cord, to; *aseta*
cord maker, *asetikbi*
cordage for a vessel, *pinąsh*
corded, *talakchi*
cordial, *aⁿli*
cordial, a; *ikhiⁿsh chuⁿkąsh libishli*
core; *iffuka, iskuna, nihi*
core of a boil, *nishkin*
cork; *isht ąlhkąma, kotoba isht ąlhkąma, oka abicha isht ąlhkąma*
cork, to; *akamąli, akamoli*
corn; *onush, tanchi*
corn, a; *nihi, sąlbo*
corn, a grain or kernel of; *taⁿsh nihi*
corn, an ear of; *tanch ampi*
corn, bread; *tanchi pąska atoba*
corn, broom; *tanchi isht pashpoa*
corn, Canada; *taⁿsh ushi*
corn, dry; *taⁿsh shila*
corn, flint; *tanchi limimpa, taⁿsh kąllo*
corn, flour; *taⁿsh haksi*
corn, ground; *tanchi aholokchi, taⁿsh fotoha*
corn, Indian; *tanchi*
corn, parched; *onush ąlwąsha*
corn, pop; *taⁿsh bokanli*
corn, ripe; *taⁿsh shila, taⁿsh waya*
corn, shucked; *taⁿsh lufa*
corn, small; *taⁿsh ushi*
corn, sweet; *shinoa, tanchi shikoa*
corn, to; *hąpi yąmmichi*
corn, white; *taⁿsh haksi*
corn blade, *tanchi hishi*
corn bran; *pishilukchi, taⁿsh hoshunluk*
corn bread; *naksakawa, tanchi pąska*
corn chaff, *taⁿsh haklupish*
corn dough, *taⁿsh yammąska*
corn fodder; *tanchi hishi, taⁿsh hishi*
corn fodder, a bundle of; *tanchi hishi sita*
corn harvest, *taⁿsh hoyo*
corn house, *kanchąk*
corn husk, *tanchi hakshup*
corn leaves, *tanchi hishi*
corn loft, *kanchąk*
corn meal; *tanchi pushi, taⁿsh fotoha, taⁿsh pushi*
corn measure; *tanchi isht ąlhpisa, taⁿsh isht ąlhpisa*
corn mill; *tansh afotoha, taⁿsh afotoha*
corn on the foot, *sąlbo*
corn shuck, *tanchi hakshup*
corn silk; *tanchi iⁿpashi, taⁿsh paⁿshi*
corn silk when dry, *taⁿsh paⁿshi holusi*

corn sucker; *tanchi apąta, apulli, taⁿsh akka pushli, taⁿsh ąpatulli*
corn tassel; *hinak, okhinak, tanchi habali, taⁿsh hinak*
corn tied up, *taⁿsh shikowa*
corncob; *ąpi, tanch ąpi,*
corncrib; *kanchąk, pihcha*
corner; *achukbi, aiokhąnkąchi, aiyukhąna, naksika, naksiⁿka*
corner, inside; *chukbi, chukbika*
corner of a field, *shokulbi*
corner of the eye, *nishkin wishakchi*
corner of the eye, the flesh in the; *nishkin nukbilaⁿkchi*
corners, having; *takastua*
corners, to have; *tąshiha*
corners of streets, *itaiyukhąna*
cornfield, *osapa*
cornstalk; *ąpi, taⁿsh ąpi*
coronation; *miⁿko aiokpąchi, miⁿkochi*
coronet, *iachuka*
corpse; *hatak illi, nan illi*
corpulent, *nia*
correct; *aⁿli, ąlhpesa*
correct, to; *aiskiachi, ąlhpesąchi, fąmmi*
corrected; *aiskia, ąlhpesa*
corrected again, *atuklant aiskia*
correspond, to; *holissochi*
corroborate, to; *kąllochi, lampkuchi*
corrode (as copper), to; *okchamalichi*
corrupt; *okpulo, toshbi*
corrupt, to; *okpąni, okpulo, shua, shuachi, toshbi, toshbichechi*
corrupted; *okpulo, shua, toshbi*
corruption, *aninchichi*
corse, *hatak illi*
cost; *aiąlbi, aiilli, ąlbi*
cost, to; *aiilli*
cost free, *aiilli iksho*
costive, *alaka ikaiyu*
costly; *aiilli atąpa, aiilli chito*
cot; *aboha iskitini, abohushi, chukushi, ibbak ushi foka, topa iskitini*
cottage; *abohushi, chukushi*
cottager, *abohush ątta*
cotton; *pokpo, ponola*
cotton, carded; *ponol lapushki, ponoshiahchi*
cotton, ginned; *ponola nihi*
cotton, spun; *ponola shąna*
cotton, twisted; *ponoshąna*
cotton, woven; *ponola tąnna*
cotton bale, *ponola ąni*
cotton cards, *ponola isht shiahchi*

cotton cloth, *ponola tanna*
cotton gin; *ponola anihelichi, ponola anihi*
cotton gin, large; *ponola anihelichi chito*
cotton plant, *ponolapi*
cotton pods, *ponobokanli*
cotton thread; *ponola, ponola shana*
cotton thread, coarse; *ponola okshi chanli*
cotton yarn; *ponola, ponola shana*
cottonseed; *ponola nihi, ponola pehna*
cottonwood tree, *ashumbala*
couch; *anusi, onitola, patalhpo, topa*
couch, to; *boli, hachukbilhka, itola, luhmi*
cough, *hotilhko*
cough, to; *hotilhko*
could; *hinlatok, hinlatuk*
could have; *ahinlatok, ahinlatuk, hinlatok, hinlatuk*
council; *aianumpuli, hatak hochitoka itanaha, hatak itanaha, nan apesa aleha*
council fire, *aiulhti*
council ground; *aianumpulika, hatak aianumpuli*
council house; *aianumpuli chuka, chuka hanta, hatak aianumpuli chuka*
councilor; *hatak anumponli, nan i^nmiya*
counsel; *anumpa, imanukfila*
counsel, to; *anumpuli, nanukachi*
counselor; *anumpuli, hatak anumponli, miha*
count, *holhpena*
count, to; *hopena, hotina*
count upon, to; *ahni, anukfilli*
counted; *holhpena, holhtena*
countenance, *nashuka*
counter; *hopena, hotina, na hotina, nan tanna aiapesa*
counterfeit, *holabi*
counterfeit note, *holisso lapushki okpulo*
counterfeit paper money, to; *holisso lapushki okpulo ikbi*
country, *yakni*
country, a bad; *yakni okpulo*
country, a good; *yakni achukma*
country, one; *yakni*
countrymen, *okla chafa*
couple, a; *itauaya, tuklo*
couple, to; *apotoli, auaya, itauaya*
courage; *aiyimita, yiminta*
courage, to have; *amoshuli*
courageous; *nakni, nukwia iksho*

course; *apelichi, bachali, bachaya, bachoha, shachaha*
course, to; *hoyo, maleli, malelichi, silhhi, yilepa*
courser; *isuba, isuba shinimpa*
court; *hatak nan apesa, holihta, kasbi, wanuta*
courteous; *achukma, aiokpanchi*
courtesy, to; *bikuttokachi*
cousin; *a^nki, apokni, amafo, amoshi, imanni, impusnakni, itibapishi toba, nakfish*
covenant; *anumpa alhpisa, anumpa itimapesa, nan itimapesa, nana alhpisa*
covenant, to; *anumpa itimapesa*
covenanted, *anumpa itimalhpisa*
cover; *ialipa, o^nlipa, umpata, umpoholmo*
cover, to; *apohkochi, homo, ishi, luhmi, ohulmochi, ompohomo, umpohomi, umpohomo*
cover of a box, *itombi o^nlipa*
cover over, to; *patali, umpohomi*
cover with boards, to; *umpohomi*
covered; *apohko, holmo, alhpohomo, ialipa, luma, ohulmo, ompoholmo, ulhpohomo, umpatalhpo, umpoholmo*
covering; *alata, holmo, isht umpoholmo, ompoholmo, umpoholmo*
covering for a house, *chuka isht holmo*
covering of a camp, *alipo*
coverlet; *anchi, topa umpatalhpo*
covet, to; *anushkunna, banna fehna*
covetous; *banna fehna, tali holisso ahnichi*
cow; *wak, wak tek*
cow, dun-colored; *shakbona*
cow, line-back; *wak nali tohbi*
cow, milch; *wak bishahchi*
cow, old; *wak ishki*
cow, to; *nukshobli*
cow, white-back; *wak nali tohbi*
cow, yearling; *wak afammi*
cow, young; *wak tek inchunwa*
cow brand, *wak isht inchu^nwa*
cow dung, *wak i^nyalhki*
cow path, *wak aiitanowa*
cow range; *wak aiimpa, wak aiitanowa*
cow trail, *wak aiitanowa*
cow trough, *wak aiimpa*
cow whip, *wak isht fama*
cow without horns; *wak lapish iksho, wak yushkoboli*
cow yard; *holihta, wak i^nholihta*

coward; *hatak hobạk, hobạk, isht ilaueli*
cowardly; *hobạk, hobạk chohmi, isht ilaueli*
cowed, *nukshopa*
cower, to; *bikuttokạchi*
cowhide, *wak hakshup*
cowlick; *paⁿshi imahaiya, wak inlukfạpa*
cowpen, *wak iⁿholihta*
coxcomb; *hatak ilakshema shali, hatak shema shali*
coy; *hopoksia, nukshopa, nuktanla*
coyness, *nukshopa*
cozen, to; *haksichi*
cozened, *haksi*
cozener, *haksichi*
crab grass, *hạshuk pạta*
crack; *bisanlih, bitanli, bokạfa, fachanli, kichanli, kichaya, kisali, koa, pachanli, pachạshli, palak, wakalali, wakla*
crack, a large; *kitafa, kitanli*
crack, a small; *kisaⁿya*
crack, to; *basisakạchi, kaloli, kichali, kichanli, kichanlichi, kichaya, kichayạchi, kisaha, kisali, kisalichi, kisaⁿya, kisayạchi, kitanli, kitanlichi, kitạffi, koa, kokoa, kokuli, koli, lạllichi, pachanli, pakulli, palakachi, wakalali*
crack, to cause to; *kichanlichi, wakalalichi, waklạchi*
crack a whip, to; *lukatolachi*
crack open, to; *bitanli, bitanlichi, bitạtanya, bokalichi, fachanli, fạchanli, fichanli, kitafa, pachạshli, wakla*
crack open, to cause to; *pachanlichi*
cracked; *bokafa, kichanli, kichaya, kisali, kisaⁿya, kitafa, kitanli, koa, kokoa, litilakạchi, pachanli, wakalali*
cracked and curled up, *kusha*
cracked open; *bitanli, fichanli, wakla*
cracker, *pạska kạllo*
cracking open, *fichanli*
crackle, to; *libbachih*
cracknel, *pasha*
cracks; *palalak*
cradle; *ạlla anusi, onush isht ạlmo*
cradle, to; *ạlla anusi foki, onush ạmo*
cradle scythe, *onush isht bạsha*
craft, *imponna*
crafty, *imponna*
cram, to; *atelichi, isikopa*
cramp, *liⁿfa*
cramp, to; *liⁿfa*
cramp in the foot, *iyi liⁿfa*
cramp in the hand, *chukfi yoba*
cramped foot, *iyi liⁿfa*

crane (bird), *watonlak*
crane (for a kettle), *asonak atakali*
crane (of wood), *iti kusha yaiya*
crane, a small white; *uskạp*
crane, a white sand-hill; *watonluk oshi*
crane, the white; *oskan*
cranium, *nushkobo foni*
crank, *isht fali*
crash, to; *bimihạchi, bimimpa, kalali, litoli*
crater, *itopa*
cravat; *inuchi, nantapạski inuchi*
crave, to; *asilhha, bạnna*
crave meat, to; *pushkạno*
crawfish, *shakchi*
crawl, to; *balali*
crawler, *balali*
craze, to; *tasembochi*
crazed, *tasembo*
craziness, *tasembo*
crazy, *okpulot taha*
creak, *kạchakạchi*
creak, to; *kạchakạchi*
creak, to make; *kạchakạchechi*
creaking, *kạchakạchi*
cream; *ạlmochi, pishukchi nia, pishukchi pakna*
cream bowl, *pishukchi nia aiạlhto*
cream pot, *pishukchi nia aiạlhto*
crease, *laⁿfa*
crease, to; *laⁿfi*
crease in the skin, *yaⁿfa*
creased, *shikoli*
creases on a screw, *shikoha*
create, to; *ikbi, tobachi*
created, *toba*
creation, *toba*
creator, *ikbi*
creature, bad; *nan okpulo*
credible, *yimmahe ạlhpesa*
credit; *holitopa, yimmi*
credit, to; *ahekạchi, yimmi*
credited; *aheka, yimmi*
creditor; *aheka ishi, ahekạchi, nan ahekạchi*
credulous, *yimmi shali*
creek, *bok*
creek, a long; *bok falaia*
creep, to; *balali, balạlli*
creep after, to; *apali*
creeper; *balali, balạlli*
crest; *impạsha, shikopa*
crest of a turkey, *ibilatampa*
crevice; *bitanli, wakalali, wakla*

crew, *hatak kanomona*

crib; *alla anusi, isuba aiimpa peni, kanchak*

cricket; *aionasha, iti wanya, shalontaki*

crier; *hatak panya, nan anoli, nan inhoa, panya*

cries, one who; *yaiya*

crime, *anumpa kobaffi*

criminal; *anumpa kobaffi, na haksi*

crimson, *humma*

cripple; *hatak iksitopo, kinafkali, sitopa*

cripple, to; *sitopa*

crisp, a; *yikottakachi, yikotua*

crisp, to; *bokusa, yikoli, yikota, yikotachi, yikotua, yikutkachi*

crisped; *bokusa, yikokoa, yikota, yikotua, yikutkachi*

critical time, *aialhpesa*

croak, to; *ola*

crock, to; *lusachi*

crockery; *amphata, ampo*

crockery shelf, *ampo atala*

crook; *chasaloha, chawana, chinachubi, chinakbi, kofunoha, tanakbi, tanantobi*

crook, to; *chasalachi, shanaiachi, shanaioli, tanantobichi, tanakbichi, tanalloli, tonokbichi, yinyikechi*

crook, to make a; *chinakbichi*

crooked; *bokota, chanakbi, chasaloha, chasala, chawana, chikisanali, chinachubi, chinakbi, folota, folotoa, fulomoli, kofuna, kofunoha, koshuna, panala, shanaia, shanaioa, tanakbi, tanantobi, tanalloha, tannalla, tobbonoa, tonokbi, yinyiki, yunyuki*

crooked, to make; *chasalohachi, chinachubichi, chinakbichi, koshunachi, tanantobichi, tanallachi, tobbonachi, tonokbichi*

crooked, to stand, *auatali*

crooked leg; *iyi tanakbi, iyi tanalla*

crookedness, *shanaia*

crop; *awaya, hatip, na waya*

crop, to; *amo, kashoffichi, taptuli*

crop close off, to; *okmilolichi*

crop grass, *hashuk pata*

crop of a fowl, *impafakchi*

cropped; *almo, taptua*

cropped ears, *haksobish almo*

cropped short, to be; *okmiloli*

cropped tail, *hasimbish tapa*

cross (angry); *banshkiksho, hashanya, nukoa*

cross (intersecting lines); *aiyukhana, hashanya, ilepushpuli, itaiyukhana, iti taiyukhana, iyukhana, nan aiyukhana*

cross, to; *aiyukhana, aiyukhanni, apolomi, apolomolili, chukashaya, iyukhannali, lopulli, okhoatali, olabbi*

cross, to make one; *hashanyachi*

cross a row, to; *aiyukhaneli*

cross another road, to; *hina abanabli, hinakfoata*

cross-eyed; *nishkin itasunali, nishkin itiopitama, nishkin okhaiyanli, nishkin shanaiya, okhaiyanli.*

cross-legged, *iyi itabanali*

cross out, to; *kashoffi*

cross over, to; *tanapoli, tanabli*

cross over another road, to; *hina onhanabli*

cross the legs, to; *iyi itabanali*

crossbar, *okhoatkachi*

crossed, *iyukhanna*

crosses over, one who; *tanabli*

crossing, *alopulli*

crossing place, *akucha*

crosspiece; *okhoataka, okhoatkachi*

crossroad; *hina abanabli, hina onhanabli, hinakfoata*

crossway, *bok itipatalhpo*

crosswise; *afataiya, okhoata, okhoatakachi*

crotch, *falakto*

crotched, *falakto*

crouch, to; *akkachunoli, bikota*

croup, *hatip*

crow, *fala*

crow, to; *akank ola, ilauata, ilefehnachi, ola*

crow, young; *falushi*

crowbar; *isht tonolichi, tali isht afinni*

crowd; *hatak laua, laua*

crowd, to; *atelichi, atelifa, atelifichi, kantali*

crowded; *alota, atelifa*

crowing, *ola*

crowing, the time of cock; *akank ola*

crown; *aialipa, iachuka, minko imiachuka*

crown, to; *bitelichi, minko ikbi*

crown of a hat, *paknanka*

crown of a hill; *nanih paknaka, paknanka*

crown of the head, *nushkobo iyafunfo*

crowned; *minko, minko toba*

crucify, to; *iti taiyukhana ahonalichi*

crude; *imponna, nuna, okchaⁿki*
cruel; *halhpaⁿsha iksho, palammi*
crumble, to; *boshulli, boshullichi, lishoa, lisholili, tushtua*
crumble off, to; *liweli*
crumbled; *boshulli, tushtua*
crumbs; *boshulli, lishoa, tushtua*
crunch, to; *kapulhachi*
crupper, *hasimbish foka*
crush, to; *kalali, litoli*
crushed; *kala, litoa*
crust, *hakshup*
crust, to; *hakshup ikbi*
crutch; *isht ilaneli, isht tabeli, tabi*
crutches, *iti taptua isht nowa*
cry; *isht tahpala, nan nusi, paⁿya, yaiya*
cry, to; *akaⁿk ola, boluⁿkboa, liⁿsa, paⁿya, tahpala, yaiya, yaⁿwa*
cry, to cause to; *paⁿyachi*
cry about, to; *yaiya*
cry for each other, to; *yaiya*
cry for the dead; *nan anusi, yanusi*
cry on account of, to; *yaiya*
cry out, to; *paⁿya*
crying, *yaiya*
crying, one who is addicted to; *yaiya shali*
cub, *nitushi*
cub, fox; *chula ushi*
cub, to; *cheli*
cubit, *kubit*
cucumber; *na hollo imokchaⁿk, okchaⁿk holba*
cud, *hopaⁿsa*
cudgel; *atashi, itashi, iti tapena*
cuff; *ibbak tilokachi afohoma, ilefoka shakba afohoma, shakba apoloma*
cuff, to; *isso, pasaha, pasalichi*
cull, to; *aiyoa*
culled, *aiyua*
culprit; *anumpa kobaffi, hatak haksi*
cultivate, to; *toksali*
cultivate a field, to; *osapa pilesa*
cultivated fruits; *nan apoba, nan alhpoa*
cultivated plants, *nan alhpoa*
cultivated trees; *nan apoba, nan alhpoa*
cultivated vegetables, *nan apoba*
cumber, to; *ataklammi, okpanichi*
cumbered, *ataklama*
cumulate, to; *itannali*
cunning; *alalichi, haksi, imponna*
cup; *chakli, isht ishko*
cup, small; *isht ishkushi*

cup, tea; *isht ishkushi*
cup, tin; *isht ishko latassa*
cup, to; *lali*
cup with a horn, to; *lapish intakalichi*
cupboard, *kapbat*
cupidity, *holitopa banna*
cupped, *laha*
cupper, *lali*
cur, *ofi*
curable; *atta hinla, lakoffa hinla*
curator, *apesachi*
curb, to; *fololichi*
curb chain, *nutakfa isht atapachi*
curb strap, *nutakfa isht atapachi*
curdle, to; *hauashko, walaha, walahachi*
curdled; *walanto, walaha*
cure; *lakoffi, lakoⁿffi*
cure, to; *lakoffichi, masalichi, mominchi, na lakofichi, shila, shileli*
cure grass, to; *hashuk shileli*
cure over a fire, to; *abani, albani*
cured; *albani, atta, chanla, lakoffi, shila*
cured, a person; *na lakofi*
cureless, *lakoffahe keyu*
curer; *abani, allikchi, attachi, lakoffichi, na lakofichi*
curl, to; *bochusachi, bonunta, chanaha, yiⁿyikechi, yiⁿyiki, yushbonuli*
curl hair, to; *yikowa, yushbonulichi*
curl up, to; *bochusa, lasimo*
curled; *yiⁿyiki, yushbonoli*
curled hair, having; *yushbonuli*
curled up, *kusha*
curling; *yiⁿyiki*
curly headed, *yushbonuli*
current, *himak*
current of air, *mali*
current of water, *yanalli*
curried, *shilla*
currier, *wak hakshup shemachi*
curries, one who; *shilli*
curry, to; *shilli, wak hakshup lusachi*
currycomb, *isuba isht iⁿshilli*
curse; *anumpa kallo onutula, kalakshi, isht aiiⁿpalammi, na palammi, nam palammi*
curse, to; *anumpa kallo onuchi, ilbashali, isikkopali, kalakshichi, na mihachi*
cursed; *anumpa kallo onutula, ilbasha, isikkopa, kalakshi*
cursing, *isht aiiⁿpalammi*
cursory; *palhki, tushpa*
curtail, to; *yushkobolichi*
curtain, *nan tanna aba takali*

curvated, *tobbona*
curve, a; *mahaia, tanakbi, tobbona*
curve, to; *mahaia, tobbonachi*
curved; *mahaia, tobbonnoa*
curving, *tanakbi*
cushion; *aionasha umpataḷhpo, apataḷhpo, umpataḷhpo*
cushion, a pin; *chufak ushi ashamoli*
custody; *apistikeli, yuka*
custom; *aiimaḷhpesa, aiimomaka, imomachi, nan aḷhpisa, yohmi*
custom, receipt of; *tạli holisso aiitahoba, tạli holisso aiitạnnali*
customer, *itatoba*
customhouse, *tạli holisso aiitạnnali*
cut; *atila, aḷmo, basha, chaⁿya, chula, hobạk, shaⁿfa*
cut, a; *abasha, achaⁿya, basha, bạshli, kolofa, mitelichi*
cut, to; *abạshli, atilichi, ạmo, bạshli, chanli, hobạk ikbi, kacheli, shaⁿfi, tushalichi, tushli*
cut across, to; *lopulli*
cut and see, to; *bạsht pisa*
cut asunder, to; *ahokoffi*
cut down, to; *akkakoli, chant akkạchi, chant kinạffi*
cut in two, to; *tạbli*
cut into thin pieces, *pạsa*
cut off; *hokofa, hokoli, katapa, kolofa, kololi, nachofa, naha, nipafa*
cut off, piece; *ạhokuⁿfa*
cut off, to; *ạbit tali, bạsht tạpli, bạsht tushạffi, chant tạpli, chulạffi, hokoffi, hokolichi, katapoli, katiffi, katoli, kololichi, koluffi, koyoffi, nacholi, nachuffi, nalichi, nipalichi, tạbli, tushạffi tushli*
cut off at; *ahokofa, akolofa*
cut off at, to; *ahokoffi, akoluffi*
cut off pieces, to; *tushtuli*
cut open, *patali*
cut open, to; *patạffi*
cut open a blood vessel, to; *kitiffi*
cut out, to; *chuli, shukli*
cut the ears, to; *haksobish bạshli, okmiloli, okmilolichi*
cut the hair, to; *okmiloli, okmilolichi*
cut wheat, to; *onush ạmo*
cut with shears; *kachaⁿya, kalạsha*
cut with shears, to; *kalạshli, kạhchi*
cut up; *hokoli, katola, tushtua*
cut up (as grass); *okchaha*
cut up, to; *hokolichi*
cut up underbrush, to; *bạlli*

cuticle, *hakshup*
cutter; *bạshli, iti bạshli, iti chanli*
cutting block, *achaⁿya*
cutting-off place, *atoshafa*
cutworm, *haiyowạni*
cygnet, *okak ushi*
czar, *miⁿko*

dagger, *bạshpo falaia*
dagger, to; *bali*
daily; *nitak atukma, nitak moma, onna*
dainty, *shohwalạshli*
dairy, *pishukchi ataloha*
dairyman, *hatak pishukchikanchi*
dale, *okfa*
dam; *ishki, isht oktạpa, oktạpa*
dam, to; *oktạbli, oktạptuli*
damage, to; *okpạni, okpulo*
damaged, *okpulo*
damages, *ạlhtoba*
dame, *ohoyo*
dame, school; *ohoyo holisso pisachi*
dammed, *oktạpa*
damn, to; *aiokpuloka foki, anumpa kạllo miha, anumpa kạllo onuchi*
damnable, *ilbạshahe ạlhpesa*
damned; *aiokpuloka chukoa, aiokpulokạ foka*
damnified, *okpulo*
damnify, to; *okpạni*
damp; *hotokbi, lạcha, shummi*
damped; *hotokbi, kapạssa*
dampen, to; *hotokbichi, shummichi*
dampened, *shummi*
dampened (as to the feelings), *imanukfila akaⁿlusi*
dampness, *shummi*
dams, one who; *oktạbli*
damsel; *ohoyo himmita, yash*
dance; *chepulli, hila*
dance, a kind of; *nakni hila, nashoba hila*
dance, to; *chepulechi, chepulli, hila, paⁿshi isht hila*
dance, to cause to; *hilạchi*
dance at or on, to; *ahila*
dancer; *hila, na hila*
dandle, to; *ạlla sholi*
dandruff; *kotonli, isuba fochunli, nushkobo fochonli*
dandy, *hatak shema shali*
danger; *aleka, hepulla*
dangle, to; *fahakạchi, takant fahakạchi*
dank, *shummi*

dapple, *bakoa*
dapple, to; *bakoąchi*
dappled, *bakoa*
dare, to; *nukwia iksho, pa*^{n}*fi*
dark; *lusa, oklusbi, oklili, okpolusbi, okshochobi, tampi*
dark place, *oklileka*
dark, the; *aioklileka, oklileka*
. dark, to render it; *okpolusbichi*
dark-brown, *holu*^{n}*si*
dark-colored; *alusachi, lusluki*
darken, to; *lusachi, hoshontichi, oklilechi, oklili*
darkened, *oklili*
darkish, *oklusbi*
darkness; *aioklileka, aioklili, aioklili*^{n}*ka, aioklili*^{n}*kaka, oklileka, oklili, oklili*^{n}*ka*
darkness, night; *ninak oklili*
darkness, to produce; *oklilechi*
darling, *holitopa*
darn, to; *achunli*
dart; *isht hu*^{n}*sa, naki*
dart, to; *lipa, naki pila, pąlhki*
dash, to; *pokafa*
dash against, to; *pokafa*
dash to pieces, to; *kobullichi*
dash water, to; *oka pokafa*
dastard, *hobąk*
date, *nitak*
date, to; *nitak holhtina takalichi*
dated, *nitak holhtina takali*
daub, to; *apolusli*
daubed; *apolusa, ąlhpolosa*
dauber, *apolusli*
daubing; *apolusa, isht ąlhpolosa*
daughter; *iso tek, oshetik, sąso tek, ushetik, ushi tek*
daughter-in-law, *ippok.*
daunt, to; *chu*^{n}*kąsh akkalusechi, nukshobli*
daunted; *chu*^{n}*kąsh akka*^{n}*lusi, nukshopa*
dawn; *ąmmona, nitak tohwikeli, oklilinchi, onnat isht inchi, onnat minti, onnąt tohwikeli*
dawn, to; *oklilinchi, onnat isht inchi, onnat minti*
day; *nitak, nusi, onna*
day, all; *shohbi*
day, close of the; *shohbi*
day, next; *onna*
day, one; *nitak achąfa*
day, this; *himak nitak*
day after to-morrow, *misha*

day after to-morrow, on the; *mishshakma*
day before yesterday, *misha, mishakash, mishash*
day before yesterday, on the; *mishakasho*^{n}
daybreak; *onnat minti, shutik hąta, tohwiket minti*
daylight; *hashi tohwikeli, nitak tohwikeli, onna, onnat minti, tohwiket minti*
daylight, the coming of; *onnat minti*
daylight, to cause; *tohwikelichi*
daysman, *itinnan aiyąchechi*
daytime, *nitak*
dazzle, to; *botosha, illichi, shohmalali*
dazzling, *malancha*
deacon, *iksa asonunchi ąlhtoka*
dead; *fiopa tąpa, illi, kąnia, shumba*
dead, almost; *illa husi, illinaha*
dead, the; *ikląnna, illi, shinuk kaha*
dead man, *hatak illi*
dead-drunk, *haksit illi*
deaden, to; *illichi*
deadness, *illi*
deaf; *haklo, haksi, haponaklo*
deafen, to; *haksichi, haksubachi, haksulbachi*
deafened, *haksuba*
deafening, *haksuba*
deafness; *haksi, haksulba*
deal, to; *hopela, ima, itatoba, kanchi, kąshkoli*
deal together, to; *akaniohmi*
deal with, to; *anumpuli*
dealer; *itatoba, na kanchi, nan chumpa*
dealing, *akaniohmi*
dear; *haloka, holitopa, iąlli chito*
dear (not cheap), *aiilli atąpa, aiilli chito*
dear to, *a*^{n}*hollo*
dear to him; *i*^{n}*holitopa, i*^{n}*hollo*
dearness; *ąlhtoba chito, holitopa*
dearth, *iksho*
death; *aiilli, illi, illi atukla, nan illi*
death, cause of; *isht illi*
death song, *atąlwa*
deathbed, *aiilli*
deathblow, to give a; *aiyabechi*
deathless, *illahe keyu*
deathlike, *illuhmi*
debase, to; *kalakshichi*
debased, *kalakshi*
debate, *itimanumpuli*

debate, to; *achowa, anukfilli*
debated, *anumpa*
debater, *isht anumpuli*
debauch, to; *haksichi, haui ikbi*
debauched, *haksit okpulot taha*
debauchee, *hatak haksi*
debauchery, *isikopa*
debilitate, to; *kotachi*
debilitated; *kota, tikabi*
debility, *kota*
debit, to; *ahekachi*
debt; *aheka, ashachi*
debtor; *aheka*
debtor, a; *aheka imasha, nan aheka*
decade, *pokoli*
decalogue, the; *Chihowa imanumpa alhpisa pokoli*
decamp, to; *bina*
decanter, *kotoba shohkalali*
decapitate, to; *nushkobo tabli*
decapitated, *nushkobo tapa*
decay, to; *laue, toshbi, toshbit isht ia*
decay, to cause to; *shullachi*
decayed; *shulla, shumba, toshbi*
decayed, somewhat; *toshbulba*
decease, *illi*
decease, to; *illi*
deceased, *illi*
deceit; *haksi, pakama*
deceitful, *haksi*
deceive, to; *apakammi, apakamoli, haksichi, pakamoli, pakammi, yimmichi, yoshobli, yoshoblichi*
deceived; *apakama, apakamoa, haksi, pakama, pakamoa, yimmi*
deceiver; *apakammi, apakamoli, haksichi, pakammi, yimmichi, yoshobbi, yoshobli*
December, *Tisimba*
decency, *alhpesa*
decent; *achukma, alhpesa, kostini*
deception, *haksi*
decide, to; *ahokoffi, apesa, issachi*
decided; *ahokofa, alhpesa*
decider, *nan apesa*
decision; *ahokofa, anumpa alhpisa, alhpisa*
deck, to; *shema*
decked, *shema*
declaim, to; *anumpuli*
declaimer; *anumpa isht hika, anumpuli*
declamation, *anumpa*
declaration; *aiatokowa, anumpa, atokowa*
declare, to; *achi, anoli, atokoa*

declared; *anoa, anumpa*
declarer, *anoli*
decline, to; *akka ia, haklo*
declivity; *abaksacheka, okkattahakaia*
decoct, to; *honi*
decoction, *na honni okchi*
decollated, *nushkobo tapa*
decorate, to; *shema*
decorate another, to; *shemachi*
decorated, *shema*
decoration; *isht shema, nan isht shema*
decorous; *alhpesa, kostini*
decorum, *kostini*
decoy, to; *haksichi*
decrease, to; *laue, lauechi*
decreased, *laue*
decree, *anumpa alhpisa*
decree, to; *apesa*
decreed, *alhpesa*
decrepit, *sitopa*
decried, *kalakshi*
decry, to; *kalakshichi*
dedicate, to; *holitoblichi, imissa*
dedication, *ima*
deed; *akaniohmi, ayakohmi, nana kaniohmi*
deem, to; *anukfilli*
deem himself, to; *ilapisa*
deep; *hofobi, okshonulli, okyoli*
deep, the; *ahofobika, ahofombika, hofombika, okhata chito*
deep place; *ahofobi, ahofobika*
deepen, to; *hofobichi, hofobit ia*
deepened, *hofobi*
deepness, *hofobi*
deer, *isi*
deer, a forked-horn; *isi folaktuli*
deerskin, *isakshup*
deface, to; *kalakshichi, okpani*
defaced; *okpulo, pisa okpulo*
defamation, *nan umanchi*
defame, to; *hatak nanumachi, nan umachi*
defamer; *hatak nanumachi, nan umachi*
defeat, *imaiya*
defeat, to; *imaiya, imaiyachi, lakoffichi*
defect, *ona*
defection, *falama*
defective; *ona, shumba*
defend, to; *falammichi, itibi, oktabli*
defer, to; *abanablichi*
defile, to; *iakaiya, liteli, okpani*
defiled; *liteha, okpulo*
define, to; *atokoli*

define words, to; *tosholi*
defined, *toshoa*
definite, *atokoa*
deflower, to; *ohoyo himmita okpąni*
deform, to; *pisa okpąni*
deformed, *pisa okpulo*
deformed naturally, *imomokpulo*
deformity, *imomokpulo*
defraud, to; *haksichi*
defrauded, *haksi*
defrauder, *haksichi*
defray, to; *atobbi*
defrayed, *ąlhtoba*
defrayer, *atobbi*
defunct, *illi*
defy, to; *paⁿfi*
degenerate; *achukma, makali, okpulo*
degenerate, to; *makali, okpulot ia*
deglutition; *nanąbli, nąlli*
degrade, to; *kalakshichi, makalichi*
degraded; *ilbąsha, kalakshi, makali*
degree; *ahabli, ahika, isht ąlhpisa*
deify, to; *Chihowa hobachit ikbi*
deist, *ąba anumpa ikyimmo*
Deity; *Shilombish chitokaka ąba, Shilombish holitopa*
deject, to; *ilbąshachi, nukhaⁿklochi*
dejection, *ulbąl ont ia*
delay, to; *atakląmmi, ąbanąblichi, ąbanąpa, hopakichechi, hopakichi*
delayed; *atakląma, atakląmoa, ąbanąpa, mishema*
delegate, *ąlhtoka*
delegate, to; *atokoli*
delegated; *atokowa, ąlhtoka*
delegation, *hatak ąlhtoka*
deleterious, *okpulo*
deliberate, *ąlhpiesa*
deliberate, to; *anukfilli*
delicate, *achukma*
delicious, *achukma*
delight, *yukpa*
delight, to; *achukma, aiokpąchechi, yukpa, yukpali*
delighted, *yukpa*
delightful; *achukma, yukpa*
delineate, to; *laⁿfi*
delineated, *laⁿfa*
delirious, *tasembo*
delirious, to make; *tasembochi*
delirium, *tasembo*
deliver, to; *anumpuli, ibbak fohki, kanchi, łakoffichi, okchalinchi*
deliver to, to; *fohki, ima*

deliverance, *ąlakofi*
delivered; *anumpa, ibbak fohka, ibbak foka, łakoffi, okchaⁿya*
deliverer; *ąlakofichi, anumpuli, łakoffichi, nan okchalinchi, okchalinchi*
delude, to; *haksichi, imanukfila okpąni, yimmichi*
deluded; *haksi, yimmi*
deluder; *haksichi, yimmichi*
deluge; *oka bikeli, oka falama, okchito*
deluge, the; *oka falama chito* .
deluge, to; *oka bikelichi, okchitochi, okchitoli*
deluged; *oka bikeli, oka falama, okchito*
demand, to; *asilhha, hoyo, ponaklo*
demander; *asilhha, hoyo, ponaklo*
demiwolf, *nashoba ikląnna*
demolish, to; *akkąchi, kinąffi, yuli*
demolished; *akkama, kinafa, yula*
demolisher, *kinąffi*
demon, *shilombish okpulo*
demoniac, *isht ahollo*
demoralize, to; *chuⁿkąsh okpąni*
demoralized, *chuⁿkąsh okpulo*
den; *ąlhpichik, chuka, fichukbi, hichukbi, koi chito inchuka, nam poa inchuka*
den, to; *hichukbi foⁿka, yakni hichukbi aiątta*
denominate, to; *hochifo*
denominated, *hochifo*
denomination; *hochifo, iksa*
denomination, Christian; *ąba anumpuli iksa*
denominator, *hochifo*
denounce, to; *miha*
dense; *laua, sukko*
dent; *habefa, habifkąchi, hafakbi, isso, kafakbi, lanlaki*
dent, to; *afebli, habefoli, habiffi, habifli, kafakbichi*
dented; *habefa, kafakbi, habifkąchi*
denude, to; *shueli*
deny, to; *ahah achi, aⁿli, haklo, keyuachi, oląbbi, yohmi*
deny himself, to; *kanchi*
depart, to; *aⁿya, ąttąt ia, filąmmi, ia, ilhkoli, illi, issa, kanali, kucha*
departed; *illi, kąnia*
departure; *illi, issa, kanąlli, kąnia, kucha*
depend, to; *ąba takali*
depend upon, to; *anukcheto*
dependence, *aianukcheto*
dependent, *ąba takali*

dependent, a; *anukcheto*
dependent, a political; *tashka*
depict, to; *achukmat anoli, hobachi*
deplorable; *ilbasha, nukhaⁿklo, okpulo*
deplored, *nukhaⁿklo*
deplorer, *nukhaⁿklo*
depopulate, to; *chukillissachi*
depose, to; *anumpa kallo ilonuchit anoli, kobaffi*
deposed, *kobafa*
deposit, *aboli*
deposit, place of; *aboli*
deposit, to; *akkaboli, ashachi, boli*
deprave, to; *okpani*
depraved, *okpulo*
depravity, *okpulo*
depreciate, to; *kalakshichi*
depreciated, *kalakshi*
depredate, to; *huⁿkupa, okpani, wehpuli*
depredated; *okpulo, wehpoa*
depredation, *huⁿkupa*
depredator, *wehpuli*
depress, to; *akanlusechi, chuⁿkash akkalusechi, ilapissachi, ilbashachi, nukhaⁿklochi*
depress himself, to; *ilapissachi*
depressed; *chuⁿkash akkaⁿlusi, ilapissa, ilbasha*
deprive, to; *wehpuli*
deprive of hair, to; *hachunchubachi*
deprive of liberty, to; *yukachi*
deprive of sight, to; *nishkin okpani*
deprived, *wehpoa*
deprived of hair, *hachunchuba*
depth, *hofobi*
depth, the; *ahofobika, hofobika*
deputation, *hatak alhtoka*
depute, to; *atokoli*
deputed; *atokowa, alhtoka*
deputy, *alhtoba*
derange, to; *aiyokomichi*
deranged, *aiyokoma*
deride, to; *ahni, isht oklushi, isht uklakafa, olalli*
derider, *olalli*
descant, to; *anumpuli*
descend, to; *akka ia, akka itula, akkoa, minti, okataha, okatanowa, okkattaha*
descend from, to; *atia*
descend from heaven, to; *aba minti*
descendant; *ataya, uncholulli, unchululi, ushi*

descendants of man, the; *hatak isht unchololi*
descended from man, *hatak isht atia*
descending, *okshilama*
descent; *akkia, isht atia, okataha, okshilama*
descent of a hill, *nanih akkia*
describe, to; *anoli, laⁿfi*
described; *anoa, laⁿfa*
description; *isht anumpa, pisa*
descry, to; *pisa*
desert, *chukillissa*
desert, a; *chukushmi, kowi, shinuk foka, shinuk kaha, yakni haiaka*
desert, to; *aiissachi, chukillissa, issa, malelit kania*
desert a clan, to; *iksa issa*
desert place, *shinuk foka*
deserted; *aksho, issa*
deserted house, *chukillissa*
deserted place; *aiissa, awiha*
deserter, *malelit kania*
desertion; *issa, isht ilaweha*
deserve, to; *asitabi*
design, to; *ahni, laⁿfi*
designate, to; *anoli, laⁿfi*
designated, *anoa*
designed, *ahni*
desire, *na banna*
desire, a; *ahni*
desire, to; *ahni, anushkunna, banna, chuⁿkash ia*
desk; *aholissochi, aianumpuli, aioⁿholissochi*
desolate; *chukillissa, ilbasha*
desolate, to; *chukillissachi*
desolated; *chukillissa, okla iksho*
desolation, a; *aiokpuloka*
despicable, *shittilema*
despise, to; *ahnichi, ahoba, isht ikiⁿahno, isht ikiⁿyukpo, kanimachi, shihtilema, shittilema*
despised; *isht ikiⁿahno, kalakshi*
despite, *isht ikiⁿahno*
despite, to; *nukkilli*
despoil, to; *wehpuli, weli*
despoiled, *wehpoa*
despond, to; *chuⁿkash akkaⁿlusi*
destine, to; *ahni, ahokoffi, apesa*
destitute; *iksho, ilbasha*
destroy, to; *alechi, abi, abit tali, ikshokechi, ilbashali, issot kanchi, kobaffi, leli, mosholichi, nasholichi, nuklakashli, okpani*

destroy, to utterly; *okpanit tali*
destroy life, to; *fiopa tapli*
destroy the eye, to; *nishkin okpani*
destroyed, *okpulo*
destroyed, utterly; *okpulot taha*
destroyer; *chukillissachi, nan okpani, okpani, yuli*
destruction; *aiokpuloka, alechi, abi, illi, illi atukla, nan okpulo, nuklakancha, okpulo, shinuk foka, shinuk kaha, yula*
destruction, to cause; *okpanichi*
desuetude, *aksho*
detail, *anumpa*
detail, to; *anoli*
detailed, *anoa*
detain, to; *oktabli*
detained, *ataklama*
detect, to; *pisa*
determine himself, to; *ilap ahni, ilap anukfilli*
determined, *alhpesa*
dethrone, to; *minko kobaffi*
dethroned, *minko kobafa*
dethroned king, *minko kobafa*
detriment, *nan okpulo*
deuce, *tuklo*
devastate, to; *okpani*
devastated, *okpulo*
devastation, *okpulo*
develop, to; *haiakachi*
developed, *haiaka*
deviate, to; *apakfopa, ashachi, folota, yoshoba*
deviation, *ashachi*
devil, an unclean; *shilombish okpulo*
devil, the; *nan isht ahollo okpulo, setan, shilombish okpulo*
devil's shoestring, the; *imallunsak, isiminlusak*
devious, *fulomoli*
devise, to; *apesa, imissa*
devoid; *iksho, ilbasha*
devote, to; *apesa*
devour, to; *apa, apat tali, okpani*
devout, *aba anumpa nukfoka*
dew, *fichak*
dew, heavy; *fichak chito*
dew, honey; *fichak kashanha*
dew, to become; *fichak toba*
dewberry, *bissuntalali, haiyantalali*
dewdrops, *fichak*
dexterous, *imponna*
diabetes, *hoshunwa shali*
diadem, *minko imiachuka*

dial, *hashi isht ikhana*
dialect, *anumpa*
dialogue; *anumpuli, itimanumpuli*
diameter, *sukko*
diaper, *apokshiama*
diaphragm; *alaka, ilapa*
diarrhea; *chula isht abeka, ikfa, ulbal isht alopulli, ulbal ont ia*
dictate, *anumpa alhpisa*
dictate, to; *anumpa apesa, mihachi*
dictator, *anumpa apesa*
dictionary, *tikshaneli*
did; *hatuk, kamo, tok, tuk*
die, to; *illi, luak mosholi*
die in childbed, to; *alla isht illi*
diet; *ilhpak, impa, impachi*
differ, to; *achowa, chowa, holba, inla ikholbo*
differ, to cause to; *achowa*
different; *ilabinka, ilaiyuka, inla*
different and separate, *ilaminka*
different clan, *iksa inla*
different places, *kanon*
difficult; *ahchiba, okpulo, yukpahe keyu*
difficulty; *nan inkanimi, nan isht takalama*
difficulty, having some; *nan inkanimi*
diffidence; *nukwia, takshi*
diffident; *nukwia, takshi*
diffuse, to; *fimmi*
diffused, *fimimpa*
dig, to; *itakshish kulli, kulli*
dig a hollow, to; *yakni kolukbichi*
dig round, to; *kullit apakfobli*
dig the earth, to; *yakni kulli*
dig up, to; *okchali*
digest, to; *anukfilli, litoa*
digger, *kulli, na kulli*
digging, *kula*
dignify, to; *aiokpachi, holitoblichi*
dignity, *holitopa*
dike; *sakti ikbi, yakni kula*
dike, to make a; *sakti ikbi*
dilate, to; *chitoli*
dilatory, *salaha*
diligence, *aiokpachi*
diligent, *aiokpachi*
diligently, *achukmalit*
dilute, to; *homechi, kallochi*
diluted, *homi*
dim; *luma, toffokoli, tulhpakali*
dim, to; *oktilechi*
dime, a; *iskali*
diminish, to; *haboffi, iskitinichi, lauechi*

diminished, *iskitini*
diminutive, *iskitini, ushi*
dimly, to cause to shine; *tohmasaklichi*
dimly, to shine; *tohkasakli, tohmasakli*
dimness of eyesight, *nishkin tohbi*
dimple, *shinoa*
din; *chamakachi, kilihachi, kobohachi*
dine, to; *tabokoli impa impa*
dingy, *lusbi*
dining room, *aboha aiimpa*
dinner, *tabokoli impa*
dinner, to give a; *tabokoli impa ima*
dint; *kafakbi, likefa*
dint, to; *kafakbichi, likiffi*
dinted, *likefa*
diocese, *apelichika*
dip, to; *oklobushli, oklobushlichi, oklubbi, oklubbichi*
dip from, to; *atakli*
dip in, to; *atakli*
dip into, to; *atakli, chabbi*
dip out, to; *atakaffi, atakli, kaffi, takaffi, takli*
dip up, to; *takaffi, takli*
dip up water, to; *ochi*
dipped; *kafa, taka*
dipped out, *takat taha*
dipped up, *takafa*
dipper; *isht kafa, isht taka, isht takafa, isht takaffi, isht takli, lokush, takli*
dipper (one who dips), *atakaffi, takaffi, takli*
Dipper, The (stars so called); *fichik issuba*
dire, *okpulo*
direct; *apissali, apissanli*
direct, to; *afanali, anoli, apesa, apesachi, apissallechi, miha, pelichi*
direction, *oka imma*
directly, *apissanlit*
director; *anoli, apesa, apesachi*
directress, *ohoyo nan apesa*
direful, *okpulo*
dirk; *bashpo falaia, bashpo isht itibi*
dirk, to; *bali*
dirt; *liteha, lukfi*
dirtied, *liteha*
dirty; *boha, liteha, okpulo*
dirty, to; *litehachi, liteli*
dirty eye; *oklichanli, oklichoshli*
dirty man; *hatak litiha okpulo*
dirty nose, *ibaklatinli*
dirty-eyed, *oklichanli*
disadvantage, *isht ataklama*

disadvantageous, *ahchiba*
disaffect, to; *isht ikinahnochechi, nukkillichechi*
disagree, to; *achowa, imanukfila inla minka*
disagreeable, *alhpesa*
disallow, to; *apesa*
disannul, to; *akshuchi, kobaffi*
disappear, to; *hashi kania, kania, luma*
disappeared at, *akania*
disappoint, to; *yimmichi*
disaster, *ishkanapa*
disastrous, *achukma*
disbelieve, to; *yimmi*
disburden, to; *akkachi*
disburse, to; *atobbi*
disbursement, *alhtoba, tali holisso alhtoba*
discard, to; *kanchi*
discern, to; *akostininchi, ikhana, pisa*
discernible, *haiaka*
discernment, *imanukfila*
discharge; *bamppoa, tukali*
discharge, to; *asetili, hoeta, issachi, kuchi, tukafa, tukali, tukalichi, tukaffi*
discharge, to cause to; *okchushbachi*
discharge wind, to; *huksoh*
discharged; *hunssa, tokali, tukafa, tukali*
discharged from a blowgun, *bamppoa*
disciple; *aiithana, aiithana, anumpeshi, iakaiya, ikhana, nan aiithana, nan ikhana, nan ithana, nana aiithana, nana ithana*
discipline, to; *fammi, ikhananchi, ikhananchit pelichi, kostininchi*
disciplined, *kostini*
disclaim, to; *ammi keyu achi*
disclose, to; *anoli, haiakachi, tuwichi*
discommode, to; *ataklammi*
discompose, to; *aiyokomichi*
discomposed, *aiyokoma*
discontented, *komota*
discontinue, to; *ahokoffi, issa, issachi*
discourage, to; *akanlusechi*
discouraged, *imanukfila akanlusi*
discourse; *anumpa, aba isht anumpa*
discourse, to; *anumpuli*
discover, to; *ahauchi, haiakachi, pisa*
discovered, *haiaka*
discreet, *hopoksia*
discretion, *hopoksa*
discuss, to; *anumpuli*
disdain, to; *isht ikinahno, shittilema*
disdainful, *shittilema*

disease; *abeka, illilli, illilli okpulo, nan inkanimi*
disease, a certain; *wakcẖali*
disease, to; *abekạchi*
disease of grain, *yạlhki*
diseased, *abeka*
diseased, that were; *abeka yatuk*
disembark, to; *peni kucha*
disembodied, *haknip iksho*
disembogue, to; *asetili*
disembowel, to; *takoba kuchi*
disengage, to; *litoffi, shunfa*
disengaged, *litofa*
disentangle, to; *litoffi*
disentangled, *litofa*
disfigure, to; *ilapissachi, okpạni, pisa okpạni*
disfigured, *ilapissa*
disgrace, *kalakshi*
disgrace, to; *hofayali, kalakshichi*
disgraced; *ahoba, kalakshi*
disguise, to; *haksichi*
disguised; *haksi, luma*
disgust, *yuala*
disgust, to; *nukoạchi*
disgusting; *yuala, yualạchi*
dish; *aiimpa, ampmalaha, ampmạlha, atakafa*
dish, large; *ampo chito*
dishearten, to; *chunkạsh illichi*
disheartened, *chunkạsh illi*
dishonest, *anli*
dishonor, *hofahya*
dishonor, to; *haksichi, kalakshichi*
disinterested, *ahalaia*
disjoint, to; *taloffi, tạbli*
disjointed; *talofa, tạpa*
dislike, *aika*
dislike, to; *ahnichi, isht ikinahno, isht ikinyukpo*
disliked, *ahnichi*
dislocate, to; *kotalichi, kotạffi, taloffi, taloli*
dislocated; *kotafa, kotali, talofa, taloha*
dislocation; *kotafa, talofa*
dislodge, to; *kuchichi*
dislodged, *kucha*
dismal; *oklili, okpulo*
dismay, to; *nukshobli*
dismayed, *nukshopa*
dismember, to; *nibli*
dismembered, *nipa*
dismiss, to; *issạchi*
dismount, to; *akkoa*

disobedient, *antia*
disobey, to; *antia*
disoblige, to; *yukpalechi*
disorder; *abeka, aiyokoma*
disorder, to; *aiyokomi*
disordered; *abeka, aiyokoma*
disown, to; *ạmmi keyu achi, anoli*
disparage, to; *ahoba*
disparity, *itilaui*
dispassionate, *nuktanla*
dispatch, to; *ạbi, pila*
dispel, to; *fimibli*
dispelled, *fimimpa*
dispense, to; *hopela, kạshkoli*
dispensed; *holhpela, kạshkoa*
disperse, to; *fimibli, fimimpa, fimmi, kạshkoli, tiapa, tisheli*
dispersed; *fimimpa, tiapa, tiạpakạchi*
dispersion; *fimimpa, tiapa*
dispirited person, *chunkạsh iknakno*
displace, to; *kanạllichi*
display, to; *yopisachi*
displease, to; *nukoạchi*
displeased; *chowa, okpulo*
dispose, to; *achukmalit ashachi, ahni, apoksiachi, boli*
dispose of, to; *apesa, ima, kanchi*
disposed, *ahni*
disposition; *ahni, aiimạlhpesa, chunkạsh*
dispossess, to; *ishi*
disputant, *achowa*
dispute; *achowa, itachoa, itạchoa*
dispute, to; *achowa, anumpa itinlauachi, chowa*
disrelish, to; *kạshaha*
disrespectful, *ichapa*
disrupt, to; *habofạchi*
disruption, *mitafa*
dissatisfaction, *okokko*
dissatisfied; *ạlhpesa, okpolo*
dissatisfy, to; *ạlhpesa*
dissect, to; *nibli, tushtuli*
dissected; *nipa, tushtua*
dissemble, to; *ilahobbi*
disseminate, to; *fimmi*
disseminated, *fima*
disseminator, *fimmi*
dissent, to; *haklo, imanukfila achạfa*
dissertation; *holisso, isht anumpa*
dissever, to; *tạbli*
dissevered, *tạpa*
dissimilar; *holba, inla*
dissipate, to; *fima, fimibli, fimimpa, fimmi, ilanyak*

dissipated; *fima, fimimpa*
dissolution; *illi, kobafa*
dissolvable, *bila hinla*
dissolve, to; *ɑlhkomo, bila, bileli, ko-baffi, okomo, okomuchi*
dissolved; *ɑlhkomo, bila*
distance; *hopaki, tanamp chito innaki pit akanchi ɑlhpesa*
distance, at a small; *olitoma, olitomasi*
distant, *hopaki*
distemper; *abeka, illilli*
distemper, deadly; *illilli okpulo*
distemper, to; *abekɑchi*
distempered, *abeka*
distend, to; *chitoli*
distended, *chito*
distill, to; *holuya, honi*
distill spirits, to; *oka homi ikbi*
distilled; *holuya, honni*
distilled liquors, *oka homi*
distiller, *oka homi ikbi*
distillery; *oka homahonni, oka homatoba*
distinctive, *tinkba*
distract, to; *aiyokomichi, tasembochi*
distracted; *aiyokomi, tasembo*
distress; *aleka, ilbɑsha, isikkopa, komunta, nukhɑmmi*
distress, to; *ilbɑshachi, ilbɑshali, isikkopali, komuntɑchi, nukhɑmmichi*
distressed; *aleka, ilbɑsha, imaleka, imanukfila komunta, komota*
distresser, *ilbɑshachi*
distribute, to; *hopela*
distributed, *holhpela*
distributer, *hopela*
distribution, *holhpela*
district; *aiulhti, apelichika, ulhti, yakni*
distrust, to; *yimmi*
disturb, to; *anumpulechi, ataklɑmmi*
disturbance, *ataklɑma*
disturbed; *anuktiboha, ataklɑma*
disunite, to; *filɑmmichi*
disunited, *filama*
disuse, *aksho*
disuse, to; *aksho*
disused, *aksho*
ditch; *yakni hofobi, yakni kolukbi, yakni kula*
ditch, to; *yakni kolukbichi*
ditto, *mih*
ditty; *ɑlhtɑlwak, taloa*
diurnal, *nitak atukma*
dive, to; *oklobushli, oklubbi*
diver; *oklobushli, oklubbi*

divers; *ilaiyuka, ilaiyukali*
diversified, *ilaiyuka*
diversify, to; *ilaiyukalichechi*
diversion, *ilauɑlli*
diversity, *ilaiyuka*
diversity, to cause a; *ilaiyukachi*
divert, to; *shanaiɑchi, shɑnachi, yukpali*
diverted; *shanaia, yukpa*
diverter; *shanaiyɑchi, yukpali*
divest, to; *ishi, shoeli, shueli, wehpuli, weli*
divested, *wehpoa*
divide, to; *bakapa, bakastoa, hopela, kashapa, kashɑbli, kashkoa, katapa, katapoa, katɑbli, kɑshkoa, kɑshkoachi, kɑshkoli, kinɑffi, koyofa, palalichi, palata, palɑlli, pɑli, tiɑbli, tushalichi*
divide in the middle, to; *iklɑnnɑchi*
divided; *bakapa, holhpela, kashapa, kashkoa, katapa, katapoa, kɑshkoa, koyofa, palata, pɑla, tushtua*
divided in the middle, *iklɑnna*
divided into two, *bakastoa*
divider; *bakɑbli, filamolechi, hopela, pɑli*
divine, *ɑba*
divine, a; *ɑba anumpa isht ɑtta*
divine, to; *apuskiachi, tikbanlit anoli*
Divine Providence, *Ɑba pinki*
diviner, *tikbanli anoli*
Divinity, *Chihowa ɑbanumpa*
division; *holhpela, ilaiyukali, kashapa, kashkoa, katapa, kɑshkoa, palata*
divulge, to; *anoli, haiakɑchi*
divulged, *haiaka*
dizziness, *chukfoloha*
dizziness, to cause; *hanɑnukichi, yushtimmichi*
dizzy; *chukfoloha, chukfulli, hanɑnnunki, yushtimeli, yushtimmi*
dizzy, to make; *chukfulli, yushtimelichi*
do, *ishke*
do, to; *akaniohmi, atali, atokolit halɑlli, ayɑmihchi, ho, isht anta, kaniohmi, kaniohmichi, katiohmi, yɑmihchi, yɑmohmi, yohmi*
do, to cause to; *akaniohmichi, ikbichi*
do at random, to; *yɑmmak fokalechi*
do good things, to; *yohmi*
do not let, *na*
do something, to; *ayakohmichi*
do there, *yɑmohmi*
do thus, to; *yakmichi*
do with, to; *kanichi, katihchi*
do wrong, to; *ashɑchi*

dock, a; *hasimbish tapa*
dock, to; *hokoffi, tabli*
doctor; *alikchi, allikchi, hatak nan ikhana, ikhananchi*
doctor, to; *alikchi*
doctrine; *abachi, aiabachi, anumpa, nan isht aiithananchi*
dodge, to; *chiksanakli, kanakli, tolupli, yilishachi*
doe, *isi tek*
doer; *isht atta, yamichi*
does not, *keyushke*
doff, to; *shueli*
dog; *ipaf, ofi, ofi puta*
dog, English; *na holipafi, na hollofi*
dog, house; *ofi chuk atta*
dog, mad; *ofi holilabi, ofi tasembo*
dog, male; *ofi nakni*
dog, to; *iakaiya, silhhi*
dog like, *ofi holba*
dog tooth; *isht itibbi, noti isht itibi*
doggish, *ofi holba*
dogwood, *hakchupilhko*
dogwood berries, *hakchupilhko ani*
dogwood tree, *hakchupilhko api*
doleful, *nukhanklo*
dollar, *tali holisso*
dolor, *nukhanklo*
dolorous, *nukhanklo*
domain; *apelichika, ulhti*
dome; *aboha, chuka*
domestic, *chuka achafa ahalaia*
domestic, a; *ilhtohno, toksali*
domestic animals; *alhpoa, nan apoba, nan alhpoa*
domesticate, to; *apoa*
domesticated, *alhpoa*
domicile; *aboha, aiatta, chuka*
dominant, *inshali*
dominate, to; *inshalechichi, pelichi,*
dominator; *minko, pelicheka*
domineer, to; *pelichi*
dominion; *apelichika, minko apelichi, ulhti*
donation; *halbina, ilhpita, ima, na halbina*
done; *ataha, alhtaha, labocha, nuna, taha, yamohmi*
done so, *yakohmi*
donkey, *isuba haksobish falaia, isuba nashoba*
donor; *ilhpitachi, ima*
don't; *k, wehkah*
doom; *anumpa alhpisa, imaleka*

doom, to; *anumpa kallo onuchi, apesa*
doomsday, *nitak nana alhpisa*chito*
door; *aboha isht okhilishta, isht okshilita, okhisa, okhisa isht alhkama*
door bar, *okhisa imokhoata*
door hinge, *okhisa isht takali*
door latch; *okhisa aiafacha, okhisa isht afacha*
doorkeeper, *okhisa apistikeli*
doorscraper, *akasholichi*
dooryard; *chuka ituksita, kasbi*
dormant; *luma, nusi*
dormitory; *aboha anusi, anusi*
dose, *ishko achafa*
dose, to; *ishko achafa ikbit itakashkuli, ishkochechi*
dot; *lusa talaia, lusachikchiki*
dot, to; *lusachit talali*
dotage; *imanukfila iksho, puskusechi*
dotard, *imanukfila iksho*
dote upon, to; *hiahni*
dotted, *lusachikchiki*
double; *apokta, albita, inluhmi, mih, tuklo*
double, a; *apokta, polukta*
double, to; *apakfopa, apoktachi, albiteli, albitelichi, bonunta, mih, pokta, polukta, poluktachi, tuklochi*
double, to cause to; *poluktachi*
double and twist, to; *albitet shanni*
double over, to; *puli*
double up, to; *abunni, bonulli, bunni, polomi, polomoli, pulhkachi, pula*
double-dealer; *chunkash tuklo, haksichi*
double-edged; *halupa tuklo, italankla halupa*
double-faced; *haksi, nashuka tuklo*
double-hearted, *chunkash tuklo*
double-minded, *imanukfila tuklo*
double-tongued, *isunlash chulata, isunlash tuklo*
doubled; *apokta, hulbona, pokta, polukta*
doubled over, *afalapa*
doubled up; *bonkachi, bonunta, buna, bunni, poloma, polomoa, pulhkachi, pula*
doubles, one who; *puli*
doubletree, *iti ititakalli*
doubt; *atoma, ta, tahchukah*
doubt, to; *anuktuklo, aiyokoma, nukwia*
doubtful; *anukwia, chishba*
doubting, *anuktuklochi*
doubtless, *mali*
dough; *tansh yammaska, yammaska*

doughnut, *pask alwasha*
doughty; *aiyimita, chilita*
douse, to; *bohpuli, lobukachi, oka lobukachi*
dove; *pachalhpowa, pachi yoshoba*
down; *akka, hapukbo, kahat manya, sokbish*
down (fine feathers), *abukbo*
down hill; *okshilama*
down hill, to go; *okshilammi*
down this way, *akket*
downcast, *ilapissa*
downcast eye, to sit with a; *bilepa*
downfall, *kinafat itula*
downright, *apissanlit*
downstream, *sokbish pila*
downward; *akkapila, imma*
doze, to; *nusi, nusilhha*
dozen, *auah tuklo*
drab, *laknoba*
drachm, *iskali*
draft, *ishko*
draft, large; *ishko chito*
draft, one; *ishko achafa*
draft, to; *holissochi, ishi, lanfi*
draft horse; *isuba halalli, isuba toksali*
drag, to; *halalli, shalalli, shalallichi,
shali*
dragged, *shalalli*
draggle, to; *akkashalallichit liteli*
dragoon; *isuba omanili tashka, isuba ontala tashka*
drain; *yakni kolukbi, yakni kula ayanalli*
drain, to; *holuya, holuyachi*
drake, *okfochush nakni* .
dram; *ishko achafa, nanabli achafa, nalli,
oka homi nanabli achafa*
draper; *nan tanna kanchi, ponokallokanchi*
draper, a linen; *ponokallokanchi*
drapery, *nan tanna*
draught, *nanabli achafa*
draw, *halalli*
draw, small; *itombushi*
draw, to; *anoli, halali, halat isht anya,
halalli, ishi, kuchi, nukpallichi, shebli*
draw (on paper, etc.), to; *holissochi*
draw, to make; *halalichi, halallichi, sheblichi*
draw a line, to; *lanfi*
draw a liquid, to; *bicheli*
draw into, to; *oka foyuha*
draw into the mouth, to; *pishi*

draw liquor, to; *bicheli*
draw lots, to; *na shoeli*
draw near, to; *bilinkachi, bilinchi, isht
ala*
draw nigh, to; *bilinchi*
draw off liquid, to; *bichet tali*
draw on, to; *holo*
draw out, to; *achibali, chisbichi, kuchichi, mampli, shaffi, shepa, shepkachi,
shepoa, shepoli, shinfa, shinfi, shoeli,
shunfi*
draw out in length, to; *shebli*
draw the breast as in nursing, to;
pishi
draw through a noose, to; *anuklinffi,
anukliffichi, anuklilelichi*
draw tight, to; *katanlichi*
draw up, to; *bokusa, shinoffi*
draw water, to; *ochi, okochi*
drawer (one who draws); *bicheli, halalli*
drawer (in a table, etc.); *itombi, itombi
onlipa, itombushi*
drawer of water; *ochi, okochi, ulhchi*
drawers, *obala foka*
drawing, *halali*
drawing knife; *isht shanfa, iti isht shanfa*
drawl, to; *salahat anumpuli*
drawn, *falaia*
drawn (as water), *ollochi*
drawn (from a cask), *bicha*
drawn off, *bichataha*
drawn on, *hollo*
drawn out; *linfa, shepa, shepkachi, shinfa*
drawn through; *anuklinfa, anukliha*
drawn tight, *katanli*
drawn up, *bokusa*
drawshave; *isht shanfa, iti isht shanfa,
shafa*
dray, *iti chanalli*
dread; *komunta, nukshopa*
dread, to; *akomuta, anukwia, komunta*
dream; *aholhpokunna, holhpokunna*
dream, to; *aholhpokunna, holhpokunna*
dream, to cause to; *holhpokunnachi*
dream, to make one; *auahsholichi, auasholechi*
dreamer; *hatak holhkunna, holhpokunna,
nuseka*
dregs, *lakchi*
drench, *ishko achafa*
drench, to; *ikfiachi, ishkochechi, lachali,
nanablichi, nallichi*
drenched, *lacha*

drencher, *nanąblichi*
dress; *ąlhkuna, fohka, ilefoka, ilefoka isht shema, isht ilakshema, isht shema*
dress, to; *aiskiachi, apissąllechi, atahpąli, atahpąlichi, fohka, fohkachechi, fohkąchi, ilakshema, ilefoka foka, ilefoka fokąchi, na foka foka, na foka fokąchechi, shemąchi, tahpąli, tahpąlichi*
dress a deerskin, to; *tąlhkochi*
dress in fine clothes, to; *shema*
dress skins, to; *tąlhkochi*
dress up, to; *ilakhąta, shema*
dressed; *apissa, fohka, ilefoka foka, labocha, na foka foka, shema*
dressed deerskin, *tąlhko*
dresser; *fokąchi, shema, shemąchi*
dressy, *isht ilakshema shali*
dribble, to; *holuya*
dried; *chakowa, chilakbi, holufka, shila*
dried away, *ashepąchi*
dried up at, *ashippa*
drier, *shileli*
drift; *ahchihpo, akchihpo, hąshtąp mali shali*
drift, to; *okpalali*
driftwood; *akchihpo, hakchihpo*
drill; *isht lumpa, tąli isht fotoha*
drill, to; *ikhananchi, ilauąllichi*
drill (to bore), to; *isht fotolit lumbli*
drink; *ishko, nan ishko*
drink, a certain; *tąⁿfula, tąⁿfula hauąshko*
drink, to; *ishko, tali*
drink, to give; *ishkochechi*
drink, to try to; *ishkot pisa*
drink a little, to; *lumąt ishko*
drink and finish, to; *tali*
drink ardent spirits, to; *okishko*
drink at, to; *aiishko*
drink deeply, to; *ishko fena*
drink from or out of, to; *aiishko*
drink largely, to; *chitot ishko*
drink up or off, to; *ishkot tali*
drink with, to; *ibaiishko*
drinker; *hatak okishko, ishko, nan ishko*
drinker, great; *ishko shali*
drinker, hard; *hatak okishko shali, ishko fena*
drinking, *ishko*
drinking place, *aiishko*
drinking vessel, *aiishko*
drip, to; *bichilli, chuloli, hoiya, holuya, pichilli*
dripping, *holuya*

drive, to; *aⁿya, nukoa, tileli*
drive forward, to; *amohsholechi*
drive off, to; *chąfichi*
drive out, to; *tileli*
drive over, to; *tanapolechi, tanąblichi*
drive through, to; *yulullichi*
drivel, to; *itaklaląshli*
driven out, *tilaya*
driver; *chąfichi, isht aⁿya, nan chufichi, nan tileli*
driving, *tileli*
drizzle, fine; *butummi*
drizzle, to; *okshimmichi, oktoboha, oktoboli, oktobolichi, okwotummih*
drizzling, *okshimmi*
drones, *foe bilishke iⁿpokni*
drool, to; *itukholaya, ituklipaya, ituklikali, luwali*
droop, to; *bilakli*
drop; *hoiya, latapa*
drop, to; *chilofa*
drop as tears, to; *wilanli*
drop fast, to; *lotohąchi*
drop off, to; *fakoha, fakopa, liweli*
dropped off, *fakoha*
dropping, *liweli*
dross, *tali iyąlhki*
dross of lead, *naki yąlhki* ·
dross of metals; *taliⁿyąlhki, yąlhki*
drought; *chahto, itukshila*
drought, to cause a; *chahtochi*
droughty; *chahto, itukshila*
drove, *lukoli*
drover, *nan tileli*
drown, to; *oka aiąbi, oka aiilli, oka illi, oka kąnia, okokaiilli, okokąbi*
drowned; *nuksakki, okokaiilli*
drowse, to; *nusi, nusilhha, nusilhhąchi*
drowsiness, *nusilhha*
drowsy, *nusilhha*
drub, to; *kąbaha*
drubbed, *boa*
drudge, *toksąli fehna*
drudge, to; *toksąli fehna*
drug, *ikhiⁿsh*
drug, to; *ikhiⁿsh ipeta*
druggist, *ikhiⁿsh kanchi*
drum; *alepa, alepa chito*
drum, to; *alepa boli, alepa chito boli, alepa olachi, koboha, kobohąchi*
drummer; *alepa boli, alepa chito boli*
drumstick, *alepa chito isht boli*
drunk; *chukfoloha, chukfulli, haksi, oka haksi*

drunk, partly; *haksi chohmi*
drunk, to get; *haksi*
drunk, to make or get; *haksichi*
drunkard, *okishko*
drunkard, a great; *hatak okishko shali, okishko shali*
drunkard, an habitual; *okishko shali*
drunken; *haksi, hatak okishko atapa, oka haksi*
drunken frolic, *okishko manya*
drunken man, *hatak haksi*
drunkenness; *haksi, oka haksi, okishko*
dry; *chahto, chanla, chilakbi, itukshila, nukshila, shila, shulla, shumba*
dry, partly; *yaualli*
dry, to; *abani, ashepachechi, chilakbichi, hufka, shila, shilachi, shilachi, shileli, shippa, shullachi, ufka*
dry, to go; *shippa*
dry and stiff, *chilakbi*
dry place; *ashinla, shila, ashippa*
dry away, to; *ashepachi*
dry up, to; *shileli*
dry rot, *shulla*
dry timber, *iti shila*
dry wood, *iti shila*
dryad, *konwi anunkasha*
dryness; *chahto, shila, shulla*
dual, *onachi*
dubious; *aianli ikithano, kaniohmi*
duck; *hankhobak, nan tanna sukko, okfochush*
duck, female; *okfochush tek*
duck, large green-headed; *inlachi*
duck, to; *oklobushli, oklobushlichi, oklubbi, oklubbichi*
duck, wood; *hinluk*
duck, young; *okfochushushi*
ducked; *oklobushli, oklubbi*
duck-legged, *akkatalla*
dudgeon, *nukoa*
due; *aheka, aheka takanli, apissali, alhpesa*
due, a; *aheka, aheka takanli*
duel, *itibbi*
duelist, *itibi*
duffel, *nan tanna shukbo*
dug; *kula, kulha*
dug, the; *ipinshik*
dug around, *kula*
dug boat, *peni kula*
dug earth, *yakni kula*
dug pit, *yakni kula*
duke, *minko*

dukedom, *apelichika*
dulcet; *champuli, kashaha*
dull; *halupa, ibbak tokonli, ilapissa, intakobi, lusa, nukhanklo, nusilhha, tasalli, tikabi, tilikpi, tohpakali, weki*
dull, to; *paioffi, tikabichi*
dumb, *anumpuli*
dumb person; *anumpuli, hatak anumpuli*
dump, *nukhanklo*
dumpling, *paska banaha, walakshi*
dumpling, Choctaw; *walakshi*
dun, *lusakbi*
dun, to; *aheka*
dunce; *hatak imanukfila iksho, hatak nusilhha shali*
dung; *chopilhkash, yalhki*
dungeon, *aboha kallo*
dunghill, *chopilhkash*
dupe, to; *haksichi, yimmichi*
duped, *haksi*
dure, to; *imoma*
during; *aiitintakla, tankla*
dusk; *oklusbi, okpolusbi*
dust; *botulli, hituk bofota, hituk chubi, hituk tohbi, lukfi, lopish, yakni*
dust, flying; *hituk tohbi, hituk shibota*
dust, to; *kasholichi*
dust of wood, *iti botulli*
dutiful, *imantia*
duty; *aialhtoka, imantia*
duty, a; *aheka*
dwarf, a; *hatak inmoma, imoma*
dwell, to; *aiasha, aiatta, anta, atta, hichukbi fonka*
dwell at, to; *achuka*
dwell with, to; *ibaianta, ibaiansha*
dwelling; *aboha, chuka*
dwelling, royal; *minko inchuka*
dwelling place of Jehovah, *Chihowa aiasha*
dwindle, to; *kania*
dyed green, *okchamali*
dyer, *na hummachi*
dysentery, *issish ikfia*

each; *aiyuka, aiyukali, ayuka, aliha, bat, binka, ilaiyuka, minka*
each one; *achafa yuka, ayukali*
each other; *it, iti*
each other, from or to; *itin, itim, itin*
eager; *achillita, aiyimita*
eagerness; *achillita, aiyimita*
eagle *onssi*

eagle (a gold coin), *ţali holisso lakna ţali holisso pokoli aiilli*

eagle, gray; *taɫako*

eagle, small; *haṇaṇ*

eagle, young; *onssushi*

eagle-eyed; *imanukfila tunshpa, nishkin halup*

eaglet, *onssushi*

ear; *haksobish, tanch ampi*

ear (of corn), *ampi*

ear, cut or cropped; *haksobish başha, haksobish hokofa, haksobish hokoli, haksobish ţapa, haksobish ţaptua*

ear, forked; *haksobish itakchulali, haksobish itakchulanshli*

ear, foxed; *haksobish ibakchufanli, haksobish ibakchufanshli*

ear, roasting; *tansh hilonha*

ear, slit; *haksobish chulafa, haksobish chula, haksobish chulali*

ear, to; *okshonli*

ear band, *isuba imbita*

earache, *haksobish hotupa*

eared, *okshonli*

earless, *haksobish iksho*

earlock; *haksun hishi, haksun tapaiyi hishi*

earmark, *haksobish başha*

earmark, to; *haksobish başhli*

earring; *haksobish awiachi, haksobish takali, haksobish takoli*

ears of a pot, *iyasha ahalaḷli*

earwax, *haksobish litilli*

earl, *pelicheka*

early, *tikbali*

early morning, *akank ola*

earn, to; *asitạbi*

earner, *asitạbi*

earnest; *yiminta, yopunla*

earth, *lukfi*

earth, a ball of; *yakni lumbo*

earth, dug; *yakni kula*

earth, the; *yakni, yakni lumbo, yakni lunsa, yakni shila*

earth, the round; *yakni lumbo*

earth, the whole; *yakni moma*

earthen, *lukfi atoba*

earthen jug, *yaklạsh*

earthenware, *ampo*

earthly; *akka, yakni isht ahalaia*

earthquake, *yakni winakachi*

earthworm, *lapchu*

earthy; *akka, yakni isht ahalaia*

ease; *foha, nan isht takalamiksho*

ease, to; *foha, fohachi, nuktalali, yokopạchi*

easily; *luma, lumasi, nan imahombiksho*

east; *hashi akochaka, hashi akuchaka, hashi kuchaka*

east, at, to, or in the; *hashi akuchaka pilla*

easterly, *hashi akuchaka imma*

eastern people, *hashi akuchaka okla*

eastward; *hashi akuchaka imma, hashi akuchapila*

easy; *lumasi, miha, nuktaiyala*

eat, to; *ampa, apa, ạpa, epa, ḷabbi, hopohka, hopohkạchi, ilimpa, impa, ishpa, okpạni*

eat, to cause to; *impachi*

eat at, to; *aiimpa*

eat holes, to; *lunkạchi*

eat noisily, to; *shakanlichi*

eat on, to; *aiimpa*

eat there, to; *aiimpa*

eat together, to; *aiimpa*

eat with, to; *ibaiimpa*

eatable; *ilhpa, nan ạpa*

eater; *ạpa, impa, nan impa*

eating, to be; *ampa*

eating house, *aboha aiimpa*

eave trough, *iti oka aiyanạlli*

eaves; *aboha isht holmoạli, chuka isht holmo ạli, chuka isht holmo ibitahaka*

ebb, to; *oka bikeli, shippa, shippạli*

ebriety, *oka haksi*

ebullition, *waɫạlli*

echo, *hobachi*

echo, to; *hobachi*

eclat, *aiokpạchi*

eclipse; *hashi kạnia, oklili*

eclipse the sun, to; *hashi luhmi*

eclipsed, *hashi luma*

economical, *ilatomba*

economist, *ilatomba*

economize, to; *ilatomba*

economy, *ilatomba*

ecstasy, *chunkạsh yukpa atạpa*

eddy, *oka foyulli*

edge; *ahalupa, aiạli, alaka, alakali, ạli, halupa, lapalika, takchạka*

edge, feather; *ahalupa anukpilefa*

edge, to; *fololi, haluppạchi*

edge of a dooryard, *akachuli*

edge of a fireplace, *ituksita*

edge of a hill; *nạnih aiạli, ontalaka*

edge of the water, *oka sita*

edge tool, *halupa*

edged, *folota*
edged, feather; *ahalupa anukpilefa*
edges of a field, etc.; *alakchakali*
edges, to have sharp; *tashiha*
edging, *folota*
edging of lace, *infolota*
edict, *anumpa alhpisa*
edification, *ikhana*
edifice, *chuka*
edify, to; *ikhananchi*
editor, *holisso ikbi*
educate, to; *attat hofantichi, ikhananchi, nan ikhananchi*
educated; *attat hofanti, holisso ikhana, nan ikhana*
education, *nan ikhana*
eel; *iasinti, yasinti*
e'er, *bilia*
efface, to; *kashoffi*
effaced, *kashofa*
effect, to; *fehna, kanihmi*
effect, to make of none; *okpanichi*
effect, to take; *yamohmi*
effect much, to; *fehnachi*
effected, *alhpesa*
effectual; *anli, nan ihmi*
effectual, to render; *nan ihmichi*
effeminate, *ohoyo holba*
effervesce, to; *walalli*
effigy, *hatak hobachi*
effort, to make a sudden and strong; *yichinnikahchih*
effulgent, *shohmalali*
effusion; *fohopa, latapa*
egg, *ushi*
egg, a crow's; *falushi*
egg, a duck's; *okfochushushi*
egg, a hen's; *akank ushi, akank ushi lobunchi*
egg, a nest; *akank ushi achafa bonli*
egg, a rotten; *akank ushi lobunchi shua*
egg, a swan's; *okak ushi*
egg, an eagle's; *onssushi*
eggshell, *akank ushi hakshup*
egotism, *isht ileanumpuli shali*
egotist, *isht ileanumpuli shali*
egregious, *chito*
Egyptian darkness, *kamak at kania*
eh!, *cho*
eight, *untuchina*
eight times; *untuchinaha*
eighteen, *auah huntuchina*
eighth, *isht untuchina*
eighth time, *isht untuchinaha*

eightieth; *isht pokoli, pokoli*
eighty, *pokoli*
eightfold, *inluhmi*
either; *kanima, kanimampo kia, talalanka*
eject, to; *kanchi, kuchi*
ejected, *kucha*
eke, to; *ibani*
elastic; *falamoa, polomoa*
elate, to; *yukpali*
elated, *yukpa*
elbow; *ibbak inshunkani, shakba inshunkani, shunkani*
elder; *akni, bashankchi*
elder, an; *asanochika, asanonchi, asunonchi, asunonchika, hatak asahnonchi, hatak hochitoka itanaha, hatak sipokni, hatak tinkba, iksa asonunchi alhtoka, pishankchi*
elder (in a church), an; *asanochi*
elderly man, *hatak asahnonchi*
eldest; *akni, sipokni kat inshali*
elect, *alhtoka*
elect, an; *nan alhtoka*
elect, to; *atokoli*
elected, *alhtoka*
elector, *atokoli*
electricity, *hashuk malli*
elegant, *achukma*
elephant; *elefant, hatak lusa inyannash, yulhkun chito*
elevate, to; *chahachi, chitoli, ilefehnachechi*
elevated; *chaha, chashaiyi, chishinto, ilefehnachi*
eleven; *auah achafa, pokoli*
eleventh, *isht auahchafa*
eligible, *alhpesa*
elixir, *ikhinsh balam*
elk, *isi chito*
elm, red; *tohto*
elocution, *anumpa*
elongate, to; *falaiachi*
elongated, *falaia*
elope, to; *kania*
eloquent, *anumpu imponna*
else, *inla*
elsewhere, *kanima inla kia*
elucidate, to; *haiakachi*
elucidated, *haiaka*
elude, to; *lakoffi*
emaciate, to; *chunna, liposhi*
emaciated; *chunna, liposhi*
emanate, to; *kucha*
emancipate, to; *yuka issachi*
emancipated; *yuka issa, yuka kucha*

emancipation, *yuka issạchi*
emancipator, *yuka issạchi*
emasculate, to; *bạshli*
embar, to; *okshita*
embark, to; *peni chito fohki, peni chito foka, peni fohki, peni foka*
embarked; *peni chito foka, peni foka*
embarrass, to; *anuktuklichi, anuktuklochechi, anuktuklochi, anumpulechi, apistikeli*
embarrassed, *anuktuklo*
embassage, *inshali imanumpa*
embassy, *inshali imanumpa*
embellish, to; *aiuklichechi*
embellish another, to; *shemạchechi*
embellished; *aiukli, shema*
embellishment; *aiukleka, isht aiukli*
embers, *hituk yạnha*
embitter, to; *homechi, palạmmichi, takbạchi*
embitter the heart, to; *chunkạsh hominchi*
embittered; *homi, palạmmi*
emblem, *isht ạlhpisa*
embodied, *itạnaha*
embody, to; *haknip ikbi, itạnaha, itạnnali*
embolden, to; *aiyimitachi, yimintạchi*
embosom, to; *shakba fohki*
embosomed, *shakba foka*
embottle, to; *kotoba abeli*
embottled, *kotoba abeha*
embowel, to; *iffuka kuchi, iskuna kuchi*
emboweled; *iffuka kucha, iskuna kucha, takoba kucha*
embower, to; *hoshontika ashachi*
embrace, to; *anukfohki, ikhạna, ishi, nukfoka*
embrace of the arms, *shakba poloma*
embrocate, to; *ahạmmi*
embroider, to; *inchunli*
embrown, to; *lusbichi, oklilechi*
emerge, to; *kucha*
emetic; *hoetạchi, ishkot hoeta*
emetic, vegetable; *haiyunkpulo ishkot hoita*
emigrant, *wiha*
emigrate, to; *wihat anya*
eminence, *holitompa*
eminence, an; *chaha inshali nạnih, nạnih, tabokaka*
eminent; *chaha, ikhana achukma*
emit, to; *kucha, kucha pila*
emit sparks, to; *polota*

emmet, *shunkạni*
empale, to; *holihtạchi*
emperor, *minko*
emphatic, *yá*
empire; *apelichika, minko apelechika afullota, minko apelichi, yakni*
empiric, an; *alikchi ilahobi*
employ, *nana isht ạtta*
employ, to; *atohno, ạtta, tohno, toksalechi, tonho*
employed; *ashwanchi, ạlhtohno, ilhtohno, manya*
employed about, to be; *isht anta*
employer; *atohnuchi, tohno*
employment; *ashwanchi, atoksạli, isht anta, isht ạtta, nana isht anta, nana isht ạtta, nan toksạli*
empoison, to; *isht illi fohki, isht illi ipeta, isht illi yạmmichi*
emporium, *aiitatoba*
empower, to; *atonhuchi, atokoli*
empress; *minko imohoyo, ohoyo minko*
emptied, *toshoa*
emptiness, *nana ạlhto keyu*
empty; *chukillissa, nana ạlhto keyu*
empty, to; *asetili, asetoli, tosholi*
empty house, *chukillissa*
empurple, to; *homaiyichi*
emulate, to; *inshali bạnna*
emulator, *inshali bạnna*
emulous, *inshali bạnna*
enable, to; *atali*
enact, to; *apesa*
enact a law, to; *anumpa ạlhpisa ikbi*
enact over, to; *onochi*
enacted, *ạlhpesa*
enactor, *apesa*
encamp, to; *ạlbinachi, binachi, binili*
encampment; *abinachi, aiạlbina, ạlbina, bina*
enchain, to; *takchi, yukachi*
enchained; *talakchi, yuka*
enchant, to; *afetibli, afetipoli, ạffetạbli, ạffetipoli*
enchanted; *afetipa, afetipoa, ạffetipa, ạffetipoa*
enchanter; *afetibli, afetipoli, afetipoa, fappo onuchi, hatak hulloka*
enchantment; *afetipa, fappo, yushpakạmmi*
encircle, to; *afobli, afolubli, afoluplichi, apakfobli, apakfokạchi, apakfopa*
encircled; *afolupa, apakfokạchi, apakfopa*
enclosure for cultivation, *osapa*

encomium, *isht anumpuli*
encounter, to; *afama*
encourage, to; *yimintachi*
encourage by shouts, to; *apanlichi*
encumber, to; *wekichi*
end; *ahokofa, aiali, asetilli, ataha, ali, hokofa, ibiali, ibish, illi, ont, taha, wishakchi*
end, at the; *alipilla*
end, being the; *anli*
end, the lower; *akashtala, akishtala, api isht ala*
end, the tip; *wishakchi*
end, to; *ahokofa, ahokoffichi, aiissachechi, alhtaha, ali, alichi, hokofa, hokoffi, hokoli, illichi, issa, taha, tali*
end, to have an; *ataha*
end, to make an; *isht aiopichi, tali*
end, toward the; *alipila*
end, what can have an; *ataha hinla*
end at, to; *aiali*
end of, at the; *taha*
end of a boat, *peni ibish*
end of a house log, *oklafashli*
endeavor, to; *pisa*
ended; *ahokofa, aiissachi, hokofa, hokoli*
endless; *ahokofa, ataha iksho, atahahe iksho*
endure, to; *achunanchi, lopulli*
enemy, *tanap*
enemy, to become an; *tanap toba*
enemy, to come over to the; *tanap*
energetic, *kallo*
energy, *kallo*
enervate; *kallo, tikabi*
enervate, to; *kallochi, kotachi, tikabichi*
enervated; *kallo, kota, tikabi*
enfeebled, *botosha*
enforced; *kallo, kallochi, onochi, onutula*
enforcer, *kallochi*
enfranchise, to; *kuchichi, yuka issachi*
enfranchised, *yuka issa*
engage, to; *apesa, atohno, atonho, atohnuchi, itibi, atonhuchi, onochi, pota, tohno, tonho*
engage in, to; *ponaklo*
engaged; *achillita, alhtohno, ilhtohno, nukpalli*
engaged, *yiminta*
engaged about, *ashwanchi*
engaged in some employment, *ashwanchi*
engagement, *itibbi*
engaging, *ishi*

engender, to; *ikbi*
engirdle, to; *yikoli*
English; *Inklisha, Minkilish*
English, the; *Inkilish okla*
English language, the; *Inkilish imanumpa, Minkilish imanumpa, na hollo imanumpa*
English Nation, the; *Inkilish okla*
Englishman, *Minkilish hatak*
Englishmen, *Inkilish okla*
englut, to; *kaiya, nanabli*
engorge, to; *nanabli*
engrasp, to; *kallot ishi, yichiffichi*
engrave, to; *bashlit holissochi*
engraved; *bashat holisso, holisso*
engraver, *bashlit holissochi*
engraving, *bashat holisso*
engross, to; *hochitolit holissochi, mominchi*
engrossed, *hochitot holisso*
enhance, to; *chahachi, chitolichi, inshalechichi*
enjoin, to; *miha, onochi*
enjoined, *onutula*
enjoy, to; *pisa*
enjoy again, to; *atuklant isht ilaiyukpa*
enjoyment, *aiisht ilaiyukpa*
enkindle, to; *luachi, nuklibeshachi, nuklibishachi*
enkindled; *lua, nuklibisha, ulhti*
enlarge, to; *aiakachi, chitochi, chitoli, chitolichi, chitot ia, hochetoli, inshaht ia*
enlarged, *chito*
enlarger; *hochetochi, hochetoli*
enlargement, *chito*
enlighten, to; *anukfohkichi, ikhananchi, tohwikelichi*
enlightened; *anukfohka, ikhana, tohwikeli*
enlightener; *anukfokichi, ikhananchi*
enlist, to; *holisso lapalichi, hotina, ibafokat hochifot takalichi, tohnot*
enliven, to; *okchalechi, yimintachi*
enlivened; *okcha, yinmita*
enmity, *nukkilli*
ennoble, to; *chahachi, holitoblichi*
ennobled, *holitopa*
enormity, *okpulo*
enormous, *chito*
enough, *alhpesa*
enrage, to; *anukbatachi, anukhobelachi, nukhobelachi, nukoachi*
enraged; *anukhobela, nukhobela, nukoa*
enrapture, to; *yukpali*

enraptured, *yukpa atąpa*
enravish, to; *yukpali*
enravished, *yukpa atąpa*
enrich, to; *holitoblichi, nan inlauachi*
enrich land, to; *yakni niachi*
enriched, *holitopa*
enripen, to; *nunachi*
enroll, to; *hochifo holisso takalichi*
enrolled, *hochifo holisso takali*
ensign; *isht ąlhpisa, shąpha, shąphashali*
enslave, to; *yukachi*
enslaved, *yuka*
enslaved people, *yuka okla*
enslaver, *yukachi*
ensnare, to; *afetibli, afetipoli, ąffetąbli, ąffetipoli, hokli*
ensnared, *ąffetipoa*
ensnarer, *afetibli*
entangle, to; *shąchehąchi, shąchopąchi, shocholi*
entangled; *shącheha, shąchila, shąchopa, shochoha*
entangled, to become; *shochoha*
enter, to; *abeha, abehpa, chukoa, fohka, holisso takalichi, ibachukoa, ibafoki, pit, takalechi*
enter a debt, to; *aheka takalichi*
enter a house, to; *chuka chukoa*
enter the name, to; *hochifo takalichi*
entered; *ąnsha, holisso, holisso takali, takali*
enterer, *chukoa*
enterprise, *pisa*
entertain, to; *aboha anusechi, ahni, anukfilli, impachi, ishi, yukpali*
entertained, *yukpa*
entertainment; *ilhpak, impa, nan isht ilaiyukpa*
enthrone, to; *aiasha holitopa ombini-lichi, miⁿkochi*
enthroned; *aiasha holitopa ombinili, miⁿko*
enthusiasm, *yiminta atąpa*
enthusiastic, *yiminta atąpa*
entice, to; *nukpąllichechi, nukpąllichi*
enticed; *anukpąlli, nukpąlli*
enticement, *isht nukpąllichi*
enticer, *nukpąllichechi*
entire; *bano, moma*
entire, to make it; *banochi*
entirely; *bano, kąnia, moma, taha*
entirely, to do anything; *ąmohmi*
entitle, to; *hochifo, immi ikbi*
entitled; *hochifo, immi toba*

entomb, to; *ahollopi boli, hohpi, hollohpi*
entombed; *hollohpi, hollopi*
entrails, *iskuna*
entrance; *achukoa, atua, chukoa, okhisa, shilombish kąnia*
entrap, to; *hokli*
entreat, to; *asilhha, asilhhąchi*
entreated, *asilhha*
entreater; *asilhha, asilhhąchi*
entrench, to; *kullit apakfobli*
entrenched, *kula, kulat apakfopa*
entry; *aboha ititakla, achukoa, okhisa, takali*
enumerate, to; *hopena, hotina*
enumerated; *holhpena, holhtena*
enumeration; *holhpena, holhtina*
enunciate, to; *anoli, anumpuli*
enunciated; *anoa, anumpa*
enunciation, *anumpa*
envelop, to; *luhmi*
envelope, *afoachi*
enveloped, *luma*
envenom, to; *chuⁿkąsh hominchi, isht illi ipeta*
envious; *anukchaha, nukkilli, potąnno*
envious, to make; *potunnuchi*
environ, to; *afolubli, apakfobli*
environed, *apakfopa*
envoy, *iⁿshali imanumpeshi*
envy; *anukchaha, potąnno*
envy, to; *nukkilli, potąnno*
envy, to cause; *anukchahąchi*
epaulet; *tahchonchiya, tąlukchi onchiya, tąlukchi tahchonchiya* ˈ
epicure; *hatak impashali, hatak isikopa*
epilepsy, *haiuchi*
epistle, *anumpa holisso nowąt aⁿya*
epithet, a disgusting; *okpiyanli*
Epsom salts, *ikhiⁿsh hąpi holba*
equable, *mih*
equal; *aiitilaui, alaui, alauechi, ąmiffi, ibachaⁿfa, itilaui, laue*
equal, not; *isht ikalauo*
equal, to; *itilauichi, lauechi*
equal, to make; *itilauichi*
equality; *aiitilaui, itilaui*
equality, an; *itihoba*
equator, *yakni ikląnna apakfoyupa*
equilibrium, *weki itilaui*
equip, to; *na halupa ilatali, na hadupa imatali*
equipped, *na halupa imąlhtaha*
equitable, *aⁿli*
equity, *aⁿli*

equivalent, *itilaui*
equivocate, to; *anumpa afolotowąchi*
equivocation, *anumpa afolotowa*
eradicate, to; *lobąffi*
eradicated; *lobafa, lobali*
erase, to; *kashoffi, kashoffichi, kashoffichit kanchi, kobąffi*
erased, *kashofa*
erasure, *akashofa*
erect; *apissanli, apissąt hikia*
erect, placed; *haioli*
erect, to; *hielichi, haiolichi, ikbi*
erected; *hikia, hioli*
erecter, *haiolichi*
err, to; *ashąchi, yoshoba*
err, to cause to; *ashąchechi, yoshobli*
err at, to; *aiashąchi*
errand, *anumpa*
erring, *ashąchi*
erroneous; *aⁿli, ąlhpesa*
error; *aiashąchi, aiyoshoba, ashąchi, yoshoba*
erudite, *nan ikhana*
erudition, *ikhana*
eruption; *bokafa, kucha, kula, mitafa*
erysipelas, *shuti boluktąbi*
escape; *łakoffi, na łakofi*
escape, to; *kąnia, łakoffi*
escape at, to; *ałakofi*
escape disease, to; *łakoffi*
escape from, to; *ałakofi*
escaped, *łakoffi*
escaping, *łakoⁿffi*
eschalot, *hatoⁿfalaha*
eschalot, large; *hatoⁿfalaha chito*
escort; *ahinna, tishu*
esculent, *ilhpak*
especially, *atuk*
especially that, *ak*
espouse, to; *apoa, asilhha*
espoused, *ąlhpoa*
espy, to; *pisa*
essay; *holisso, pisa*
essay, to; *pisa*
essential, *nana yuhmahe ąlhpesa*
establish, to; *abenilichi, aⁿlichi, apesa, binilichi, hilechi, kąllochi, ontalali*
establish at a place, to; *abinolichi*
established; *aⁿli, ąlhpesa, hikia, kąllo*
establishment; *ahilechi, aiapesa, akąllo*
estate; *ahikia, imilayak*
esteem, to; *ahnichi, hiahni, holitoblichi*
esteemed; *achukma, holitopa*
esteemer, *aiokpanchi*

estimable, *holitopa*
estimate; *aiilli, ąlhpisa*
estimate, to; *apesa, hotina*
estimated; *ąlhpesa, holhtena*
estimation, *holhtina*
estimator, *apesa*
estuate, to; *fopa*
etc., *chomi*
eternal; *ataha iksho, ąmmona, bilia*
eternally, *bilia*
eternity, *ąmmona*
eternity, to; *bilia*
Eucharist, the; *opiaka impa Chisąs Klaist ąt apesatok*
eulogize, to; *holitoblichit isht anumpuli*
eulogized, *holitopąt isht anumpa*
eulogy, *holitoblit isht anumpa*
eunuch; *hobąk, tishu*
evacuate, to; *kuchichi, takoba kashoffi, tosholi*
evacuate the bowels, to; *iffuka kashoffi, ikfiachi*
evacuated; *iffuka kashofa, kucha, takoba kashofa, toshoa*
evade, to; *anumpa apakfokąchi, łakoffi*
evangelist; *ąba anumpa isht ątta, ąba anumpa tosholi, Chisąs Kilaist isht anumpuli, holisso holitopa holissochi*
evangelize, to; *ąba anumpa ithananchi, ąba anumpa nukfokichi*
evaporate, to; *shila, shippa*
evaporated; *shila, shippa*
evasion, *anumpa apakfopa*
even; *ak, kia, yąmmak inli*
even (evening), *opia*
even (level), *itilaui*
even, to; *itilauichi*
even as, *ak*
even one, *achąfona*
even so, *ąlhpesashke*
even that one, *ash*
even the, *ak*
even two, *tuklokia*
evened, *itilaui*
evener, *iti ititakąlli*
evening; *okłilahpi, okłilampi, opia, opiaka, shohbi, shohbikanli*
evening, to become; *shohbikanli*
evening, to make it; *opiachi*
evening hymn or song, *okłili taloa*
evenly, *itilauit*
evenness, *itilaui*
event; *nana, nana kanihmi, yąmohmi*
eventide, *opia*

eventuate, to; *alhpesa, ali*
ever; *bilia, chatok, nitak moma*
evergreen, *okchamali bilia*
evergreen tree, *iti okchako*
everlasting; *ataha iksho, bilia*
every; *ilaiyuka, moma, puta*
every day; *nitak moma; onna*
every kind; *ilaiyuka, puta*
every one; *achafa yuka, aiyuka, moma, puta*
every place, *kanima moma*
everyone; *nan uha, okluha*
everything, *nana moma*
everywhere, *kanima moma*
evidence; *isht aianli, nana pinsa*
evidence, to; *anlichi*
evident, *haiaka*
evidently, *hatuma*
evil; *achukma, aialhpesa, aiokpulo, aiok-puloka, alhpesa, haksi, nan ikaialhpeso, nan okpulo, okpulo, yoshoba*
evil eye, *nishkin tamp*
evil-minded, *imanukfila okpulo*
evil speaking, *anumpa chukushpa*
evil thing, *nana ikachukmo*
evil worker, *hatak haksi*
evildoer, *hatak haksi*
evince, to; *anlichi*
eviscerate, to; *iffuka kuchi, iskuna kuchi*
eviscerated; *iffuka kucha, iskuna kucha*
ewe; *chukfalhpowa tek, chukfi tek*
exact, *alhpiesa*
exact, to; *atobbichi*
exactor, *atobbichi*
exaggerate, to; *atabli*
exaggerated, *atapa*
exaggeration, *atapa*
exalt, to; *chahachi, holitoblichi, ilefehna-chechi, yukpali*
exaltation, *holitopa*
exalted; *chaha, holitopa*
examination, *pisa*
examine, to; *pisa*
examiner, *pisa*
exasperate, to; *nukoachi*
exasperated, *nukoa*
excavate, to; *kafakbichi, kofussachi, ko-lokbichi, kulli, yakni kolukbichi*
excavated; *kafakbi, kolokbi*
excavation, *kofussa*
exceed, to; *atabli, ia, imaiya, imaiyachi, inshali, ishalichi*
exceed, to cause to; *inshalechichi*
exceeding; *affekomi, fehna*

excel, to; *chito, imaiyachi, imponna, ishalichi*
excellence; *achukma, hochukma*
excellency; *achukma, chitokaka*
excellent; *achukma, aiyoba, hochukma, holitopa*
excess; *atapa, imaiya*
excess, to go to; *anuktapli, anuktap-tuli, asilballi*
excess, to lead another into; *asilbal-lichi*
excessive; *atapa, fehna, shali*
excessively, *shali*
exchange, *itatoba*
exchange, to; *apunta, atobbichi, alhto-boa, itatoba, toba*
exchanged, *alhtoba*
exchanger; *itatoba, nan isht itatoba, nan ittatoba*
excision, *basht tapli*
excitable, *ilhkola hinla*
excite, to; *aianukpallichi, anukpallichi, ilhkolechi, nukpallichi, okchali, okchali*
excite inflammation, to; *pikoffi*
excited; *anukpalli, nukhobela, nukpalli, okcha, yimmita*
excitement; *nukhobela, nukpalli, yi-minta*
exclaim, to; *panya, tahpala*
exclamation; *panya, tahpala*
exclude, to; *hotina, kuchichi*
excluded; *holhtena, kucha*
excommunicate, to; *aba anumpuli iksa kuchi*
excommunicated, *aba anumpuli iksa kucha*
excommunicated person, *aba anum-puli kucha*
excoriate, to; *pikoffi*
excoriated, *pikofa*
excrement, *yalhki*
excursion, *folota*
excusable, *anumpa onutulahe keyu*
excuse; *ahaksi, isht amiha, nan isht amiha*
excuse, to; *ahaksichi, miha, mihachi*
excused, *ahaksi*
excuses, to have; *nan isht amiha inlaua*
except; *keyuhokmat, keyukmat*
execrate, to; *ahni, anumpa kallo onuchi*
execute, to; *anlichi, atali*
execute by hanging, to; *anuksiteli*
executed, *alhpesa*
execution; *anli, alhpesa*
executioner, *hatak nuksiteli*

executive, the; *miⁿko, pelicheka*
exempt, to; *hotina*
exempted, *holhtena*
exercise; *abachi, toⁿksali*
exercise, to; *abachi, imomachi, toksalechi*
exert, to; *kilimpi, yichina*
exert all the powers, to cause to; *yichinachi*
exhaust, to; *kotachi, tali*
exhaust the breath, to; *fiopa tali*
exhausted; *akania, kota, taha, tikabi*
exhibit, to; *haiakachi, pisachi*
exhibit by argument, to; *okfali*
exhibited, *haiaka*
exhibiter, *pisachi*
exhibition, *yopisa*
exhilarate, to; *yukpali*
exhilarated, *yukpa*
exhort, to; *anumpuli*
exigency, *komunta*
exile; *chafa, hatak kania*
exile, to; *chafichi*
exiled; *chafa, kania*
exit; *atia, kucha*
exorbitant, *atapa, fehna*
exotic, *alhpoba*
expand, to; *auata, auatachi, wohola*
expanded, *auata*
expatriate, to; *chafichi*
expect, to; *ahni, hoyo*
expectant; *ahni, hoyo*
expectation, *ahni*
expecter; *ahni, hoyo*
expectorate, to; *hotilhkot tofa*
expedient, *aialhpesa*
expedite, to; *tuⁿshpalechi*
expedition; *itanowa, tushpa*
expeditious, *tushpa*
expel, to; *chafichi, kuchi, tileli*
expelled; *chafa, kucha*
expended, *kania*
expense; *alhtoba, kania*
expensive, *aiilli chito*
experience; *ikhana, imomaka*
experiment, *imomaka*
experiment, to; *albachi, imomakachi, yohmit pisa*
expert; *alhtaha, ikhana, imponna, tushpa*
expiable, *alhtoba hinla*
expiate, to; *atobbi*
expiated, *alhtoba*
expiatory; *alhtoba, alhtoba hinla*
expirable; *illa hinla, issa hinla*

expiration; *fiopa, taha*
expire, to; *illi, issa, mosholi, nitak taha*
expire (breathe out), to; *apuⁿfachi, fiopa, fiopa isht aiopi*
explain, to; *tosholi*
explainable, *toshoa hinla*
explained; *anumpa toshoa, alhtoshoa, toshoa*
explainer, *tosholi*
explanation; *anumpa toshoa, toshoa*
explicable, *toshoa hinla*
explicate, to; *tosholi*
explication, *toshoa*
explicator, *tosholi*
explicit, *apissanli*
explode, to; *akshuchi, basali, bokafa, kalakshichi, tukafa*
exploded; *aksho, kalakshi*
exploder, *kalakshichi*
explore, to; *pisa*
explorer, *pisa*
explosion, *tukafa*
expose, to; *haiakachi, shahbichi*
expose to the sun, to; *ufka*
exposed; *apohko, haiaka, shahbi*
exposer, *haiakachi*
expositor, *anumpa tosholi*
expostulate, to; *anumpuli*
exposure, *haiaka*
expound, to; *tosholi*
expounded, *toshoa*
expounder, *tosholi*
express, *apissanli*
express, an; *hatak anumpa isht aⁿya, iⁿshali imanumpa isht aⁿya*
express, to; *anumpuli, bushli, holissochi*
expressed; *anumpa, busha, haiaka, holisso*
expressible; *busha hinla, holissa hinla*
expunge, to; *kashoffi, kashoffichi*
expunged, *kashofa*
expurgate, to; *kashoffi, kashoffichi*
expurgated, *kashofa*
exquisite; *achukma, imponna*
extant, *aⁿsha*
extemporize, to; *hehkat anumpuli*
extemporizer, *hehkat anumpuli*
extend, to; *ashatapoli, ashatabli, ashatablichi, auata, auatachi, auatalli, chisbi, chisbichi, chisemochi, lapa, lapuchi, mabli, mampa, mampli, shebli, shepoa, shepoli, washalali*
extend to, to; *ona*

extend to all, to; *okluhanchi, putalechi*
extend to two, to; *tuklona*
extended; *ashatapa, ashatapoa, asha-*
tạpa, ashatạpoa, auata, chisbi, chisemoa,
lapa, mampa, mampoa
extended, to cause to be; *ashatạpo-*
lichi
extension, *lapa*
extensive; *chito, pạtha*
extent; *aiạli, auata, ạli, chito*
extenuate, to; *iskitinichi*
extenuated, *iskitini*
exterior; *kucha, paknaka*
exterminate, to; *lubbi, okpạni*
exterminated; *lopa, luba, okpulo*
external, *kucha*
extinct; *aksho, issa, mosholl*
extinction, *mosholi*
extinguish, to; *ahokoffichi, okpạni*
extinguish fire, to; *luak mosholichi,*
mosholichi
extinguishable, *mosholicha hinla*
extinguished; *ahokofa, mosholi, okpulo*
extinguished fire, *luak mosholi*
extirpate, to; *lubbit tali, teha, teli*
extirpated, *luba*
extol, to; *afehnichi, holitoblichit isht*
anumpuli
extort, to; *wehpuli*
extorted, *wehpoa*
extortion, *wehpoa*
extortioner, *wehpuli*
extract, *akucha*
extract, to; *bushli, honi, kuchi*
extract from, to; *akuchi*
extracted; *akucha, busha, honni, kucha*
extraction, *isht atia*
extravagant, *imilayak isht yopomo*
extreme; *aiinshali, inshali, isht aiopi,*
wishakchi
extreme, the; *aiạli, aiisht aiopi*
extreme distress, *ilbạsha*
extremely; *fehna, tokba*
extremity; *aiạli, aiinshali, ilbạsha, wi-*
shakchi
extricable, *lakoffa hinla*
extricate, to; *kuchichi*
extricated; *kucha, lakoffi*
extrication; *kucha, lakoffi*
extrinsic; *kucha, paknaka*
exuberant, *apakna*
exude, to; *litilli*
exude, to cause to; *litilli*
exult, to; *yukpa*

exultation, *yukpa*
eye; *chiluk, nishkin*
eye, bad; *nishkin okpulo*
eye, black; *nishkin lusa*
eye blue; *oktalonli*
eye, corner of the; *nishkin ạli*
eye, dim; *nishkin tohbi*
eye, edges of the; *nishkin ạli*
eye, gazing; *okchilali*
eye, gray; *oktalonli*
eye, large; *okchilali*
eye, light-colored; *nishkin hạta*
eye, perished; *nishkin shamba*
eye, ruined; *nishkin okpulo*
eye, sockets of the; *nishkin aheli chiluk*
eye, to; *apistikeli, atokot pisa, pisa*
eye, white; *oktalonli*
eye of a needle, *chufak nishkin*
eye of the mind, *imanukfila*
eye salve, *nishkin imikhinsh*
eyeball, *nishkin*
eyebrow; *imosana, imosana hishi*
eyed, one-; *nishkin achafa*
eyelash, *nishkin shilinhchi*
eyelid; *nishkin hakshup, nishkin shilinh-*
chi hakshup
eyer; *apistikeli, pisa*
eyes, bright; *pạlhpakạchi*
eyes, goggled; *okchilunli*
eyes, large; *okchilunli, okchilanshli*
eyes, rolling; *okchilanshli*
eyes, sharp; *okchilunli*
eyesight; *holhponayo, hoponkoyo, isht*
hopunkoyo, isht hopunayo, nishkin nihi
eyesight, to give; *holhponayochi*
eyetooth; *isht itibbi, noti isht itibi*
eyewater, *nishkin imikhinsh*
eyewitness; *na pinsa, nana pinsa*

fable; *holabi, shukha anumpa*
fable, to; *holabi, shukanump ikbi, shuk-*
hanumpikbi
fabled, *shukanumpa anumpa*
fabric; *aboha, nan tạnna, nana toba*
fabricate, to; *ikbi*
fabricated, *toba*
fabrication; *holabi, toba*
fabricator, *ikbi*
fabulous, *shukhanumpa*
face; *apaknali, kaniohmi, muyaha, na-*
shuka, pakna, tikba
face, red; *nashuka humma*
face, to; *alatali, asạnni, asonali*
face, to cause to; *asanalichi*

faced; *folota, alata*
facetious; *yopula shali, yukpa*
facile, *miha*
facing, *alata*
fact; *aⁿli, kaniohmi, nana*
factor, *isht atta*
factory; *aiitatoba, aiitatoba chuka*
faculties, *imanukfila*
faculty; *imanukfila, imponna*
fade, to; *bashi, kashofa, kashoffi, tikabi*
faded; *bashi, kashofa, vikabi, toffokoli*
faggot, *shauwa talakchi*
faggot, to; *shauwa takchi*
faggoted, *shauwa talakchi*
fail, to; *akshuchi, ashachi, hokofa, illi, issa, laua, onachi, tahat ia*
failing; *ona, onachi*
fain, *yukpa*
faint; *hoyabli, kallo, kota, tikabi*
faint, to; *bila, illi, kota, tasembo, tikabi*
faint-hearted, *hobak toba*
faintness, *kota*
fair (clear); *masheli, okshauanli, okshauashli*
fair (handsome), *pisa aiukli*
fair (just); *achukma, aⁿli, apissanli, alhpesa*
fair, a; *aiitatoba chito*
fair, to cause to be; *okshauanlichi*
fair man, *hatak alhpesa*
fair weather, *masheli*
fair weather, entirely; *kamak at kania*
fairly, *alhpesa*
fairness; *achukma, aⁿli, apissanli, alhpesa, kashofa*
fairy, *koⁿwi anuⁿkasha*
fairy, female; *kushikanchak*
fairy, male; *abitampa*
faith; *aiyimmika, aba anumpa, na yimmi, yimmi*
faithful, *aⁿli*
faithfully, *aⁿli*
faithfulness, *aⁿli*
faithless, *aⁿli, na yimmi, yimmi*
fall (autumn), *ahvi, hashtulahpi, onafa, onafapi*
fall (ruin), *okpuloka*
fall, a; *akkitula, itola, liweli, kaha, kinafa, oka fohopa, okattula, okpulo*
fall, last; *onafash*
fall, liable to; *kinafa hinla*
fall, to; *akakoha, akama, akkama, chilofa, itihpila, itola, ittula, kaha, kihepa, kinafa, kinali, kobafa, liweli, oka pita-*

fohopa, oka pitakinifa, okpulo, sakti oka pit akinafa, shippa, tokofa, yoshoba
fall, to be suffered to; *latapa*
fall, to cause to; *akakolichi, chilofachi, liwelichi, shippali*
fall against, to; *aboa, pokafa*
fall as dew, to; *fichak toba*
fall back, to; *falama*
fall backward, to; *olbalhpila*
fall down, to; *akka itula, akkakaha, akkakoha, akkama, akkitola, fohopa, kaha, lipiat itola, lipkachi*
fall into, to; *fohki*
fall into the water, to; *lobukachi, okatula, okattula*
fall on, to; *onitula, onutula, paⁿfi, shiyuli*
fall on the face, to; *lepa, lipia*
fall out, to; *achowa*
fall over, to; *filemat itola*
fallacious, *aⁿli*
fallacy, *haksichi*
fallen; *akkakoha, akkitula, chilofa, kinafa, kinali, shippa, yileha*
fallen down; *akkakoha, akkama, kaha, luhama*
fallen man, *hatak yoshoba*
fallen on, *onutula*
fallible; *haksa hinla, haksicha hinla*
falling, *chilofa*
fallow, *homaiyi*
fallow, a; *aholokchi*
fallow, to; *yakni pataffi*
fallow ground, *aholokchi*
false; *aⁿli, holabi, isunlash chulata, isunlash tuklo*
false accuser or swearer; *aholabechi, aholabi*
false witness, to bear; *aholabi*
falsehood; *aⁿli, holabi, lushka*
falsely; *aⁿli, holabi*
falsifier, *holabi*
falsify, to; *holabi, holabichi*
falsity, *holabi*
falter, to; *anukchito*
fame; *aianoyuwa, anoa, anowa, annoa*
famed, *anoa*
familiar; *chuⁿkash yohbi, ikhana*
familiarize, to; *ikhananchi*
family; *chuka achafa, chukachafa, hatak chuka achafa, oklushi*
famine, *hopoa*
famous, *anoa*
fan; *amashlichi, alhpatak, almachi, isht amalichi, isht ilamalichi*

fan, small hand; *ufko*
fan, to; *amatichi, amashtichi*
fan pride, to; *ilefehnachechi*
fanatic, *tasembó*
fanciful, *imanukfila laua*
fancy, *anushkunna*
fancy, a; *inholitopa, imanukfila*
fancy, to; *anushkunna, inhollo*
fane, *aboha hanta*
fang; *isht itibbi, iyakchush, noti isht itibi*
fanged; *isht itibbi ansha, iyakchush ansha*
fanned, *mashahchi*
fanning mill, *onush amatichi*
fanner; *amashtichi, ufko*
fantasm, *shilup*
far; *atapa, fehna, hopaki*
far up, *aba pilla*
fare; *aiilli, ilhpak*
fare, to; *anya, apa, manya*
farewell, *anya*
farish, *hopahki*
farm, *osapa*
farm, to; *impota, osapa pilesa, osapa toksali*
farmer; *hatak osapa tonksali, osapa isht atta, osapa toksali*
farmhouse, *osapa chuka talaia*
farrier; *isuba imalikchi, isuba iyi tali iyi lapalichi*
farrow, *shukhushi pelechi achafa*
farrow, to; *shukhushicheli*
farther; *hopaki inchali, mishapilla, mishema*
farther side of a creek, *bok mishtannap*
farther up, *abehma*
farthest; *hopaki fehna, hopaki inchali*
fascinate, to; *chunkash ishi, chunkash yukachi, haksichi*
fashion; *akanimi, kaniohmi, yakohmika, yamohmi, yohmi*
fashion, to; *ikbi, yamihchi*
fast (swift); *chali, palhki*
fast (tight); *afacha, alhkama*
fast, a; *okissa*
fast, to; *hullochi, impa, na hollochi, na hullochi, nan hullochi, nukhanklot nan-hullochi, okissa*
fast asleep; *illi, nusit illi*
fast day, *okissa nitak*
fast walker, *chali*
fasten, to; *afacha, afachali, afashli, aka-massali, atakalichi, atapachi, atapachi, attapachi, hokli, okshita*

fasten with a bolt, to; *tali fobassa isht akamassalli*
fastened; *afacha, afachali, afashkachi, akamassa, ashana, atokowa, alhfasha, okshillita, oktapa*
fastened up, *alhkama*
fastened with a bolt; *tali fobassa isht akamassa*
fastener; *isht afacha, isht akamassalli*
fastener (one who fastens); *afachali, atapachi*
faster, *na hollochi*
fastness, *holihta kallo*
fat; *bila, na bila, nia, weki*
fat, a; *iti honni aialhto, iti isht honni aialhto*
fat, hog's, *shukha bila*
fat, to; *nia, niachi, niat isht ia*
fat of beef, *wak bila*
fatal; *isht illa hinla, okpulo*
fatal sickness, *abeka okpulo*
fatality, *aiyamohmahe alhpesa*
father; *anki, chinke, ikbi, inki, pinki, tikba*
Father, our Great; *Pinki ishto, Pinki chito, Pinki chitokaka*
Father, our Heavenly; *Pinki aba*
father, to; *inki ilikbi*
Father in Heaven, his; *Inki aba*
father-in-law; *amafo, haloka, imafo, imafo, ipochi, ipochi halloka*
fathered, *inki toba*
fatherhood; *inki, inki chohmi*
fatherless, *inki iksho*
fathers, the; *asanonchi, asunonchi*
fathom; *ashatapa, ashatapoa, isht alhpisa tuklo*
fathomless; *akka iksho, akkahoyo, ikhana*
fatigue; *tikabi, tonksali*
fatigue, to; *tikabichi*
fatigued, *tikabi*
fatness, *nia*
fatten, to; *niachi, niat isht ia*
fattened, *nia*
fattener, *niachi*
fatty, *nia*
faucet; *abicha, isht bicheli, oka abicha, oka isht bicheli*
fault; *aiashachi, ashachi*
faulty, *okpulo*
favor, *aiahninchi*
favor, to; *apela, apelachi*
favored, *imola*

favorer, *apelachi*
favorite; *i^{n}holitopa, i^{n}hollo*
fawn; *isi ushi, isushi*
fawn, to; *ahpạlli, aiokpạchi, isi ushi cheli*
fay, to; *ạlhpiesa*
fear, *nukshopa*
fear, exclamation of; *yilishachi*
fear, to; *ahni, anuklakancha, holitobli, nukshopa*
fear, to produce; *nukwiachi*
fearful; *anukwia, nukshopa, nukwia, okpulo, palạmmi*
fearless, *nukshopa*
fearlessly, *nukshompiksho*
feast; *chepulli, impa chito, impạchi, nan ipetạchi, nan isht ilaiyukpa*
feast, to; *chepulechi, chepulli, chu^{n}kạsh yukpali, impa, impachi, yukpali*
feast, to attend a; *chepullit a^{n}sha*
feast, to make a; *chepulechi*
feaster; *impa, impachi*
feasting, *nan isht ilaiyukpa*
feat, *na fehna*
feather; *abukbo, aka^{n}k hishi, hapukbo, hishi, hoshi^{n}shi, hushi hishi, shikopa, wonuksho*
feather, to; *shikopa isht shema*
feather bed; *hoshi^{n}shi patạlhpo, hoshi^{n}shi patạlhpo topa, hoshi^{n}shi topa*
feathered, *hishi toba*
feathered entirely, *hishi tobat taha*
febrifuge, *yạnha isht shipạchi ikhi^{n}sh*
February, *Fibueli*
feces; *lakchi, okshahala, yạlhki*
fed, *ilhpita*
fee, *ạlhtoba*
fee, to; *atobbi, tohno*
feeble; *botosha, kota, tikabi*
feeble-minded, *hatak imanukfila ikkạllo*
feebleness; *haknip kota, kạllo*
feed; *impa, isuba imilhpak*
feed, to; *ạpa, impa, impachi, impạchi, ipeta, niachi, yukpali*
feed an infant, to; *pishechi*
feeder; *impachi, ipeta*
feel, to; *anukfilli, hushshiho, ikhana, posholi*
feel of, to; *pasholi, potoli*
feeling; *chu^{n}kạsh, ikhana, imanukfila*
fees, *ạlhtoba*
feet, naked; *iyi beka .*
feign, to; *ilahobbi*
feint, *ilahobbi*

felicitate, to; *yukpali*
felicitated, *yukpa*
fell; *hiahni iksho, okpulo, palạmmi*
fell, to; *akakoli, akkạchi, kinalichi, kinạffi*
felled, *akka*
feller, *kinạffi*
fellow; *apạha, bi^{n}ka, ibabinili, ibafoka, ibaianta, ichapa, ichapoa, itichapa*
fellow, to; *ichapa*
fellow-citizen, *okla chạfa*
fellow-laborer, *ibato^{n}ksạli*
fellow-mortal, *illi bi^{n}ka*
fellow-scholar, *holisso itibapisa*
fellow-servant, *yuka mi^{n}ka*
fellow-soldier, *tạshka chipota mi^{n}ka*
fellow-student; *holisso ibapisa, holisso itibapisa*
fellow-traveler; *ibaia^{n}ya, itiachi, itibanowa*
fellowship, *itibafoka*
felly, *chạnaha*
felon, *hu^{n}kupa*
felonious; *haski, hu^{n}kupa, okpulo*
felt, *chukfi hishi shạpo*
female; *hatak ohoyo, ohoyo, tek*
female, aged; *ohoyo kasheho*
female fox, *chula tek*
female sex, *ohoyo pisa aiukli*
feminine, *ohoyohmi*
fen; *lu^{n}sa, okla^{n}shko*
fence, *holihta*
fence, crooked; *holihta yi^{n}yiki*
fence, picket; *holihta halupa*
fence, to; *holihtạchi, itibi*
fence, Virginia; *holihta yi^{n}yiki*
fence, worm; *holihta yi^{n}yiki*
fence side, *holihta apotaka*
fence with stone, to; *tạli isht holihtạchi*
fenced, *holihta*
fenceless, *holihta iksho*
fencer, *itibi*
fencing stuff, *holihta pạla*
fend, to; *katạbli, okhatạbli, okshita*
fenny, *okla^{n}shko*
ferment, *walạlli*
ferment, to; *chibokạchi, shatạmmi, shatạmmichi, walạllichi, wushohạchi, wushulli, wushullichi*
fermented; *shatạmmi, wushulli*
fermentation; *wushohạchi, wushulli*
fermentation, to cause; *wushullichi*
ferret, to; *kuchichi*
ferret, wide; *sita*

ferreted, *kucha*
ferriage; *ạlhtoba, peni kucha ạlhtoba*
ferrule, *tạli afohoma*
ferry; *akucha, ałopulli, isuba iⁿpeni, penałopulli, peni, peni intalaia, peni patạssa, peni pạtha*
ferryman, *peni isht ạtta*
ferry, to; *peni kuchichi, tanapolechi, tanạblichi*
fertile; *awaya achukma, imanukfila laua*
fertility, *awaya achukma*
fertilize, to; *yakni niachi*
ferule, a; *iti shimafa shaⁿfa*
fervent; *chuⁿkạsh homi, lạshpa, walạlli*
fervid, *lua*
fervor, *lạshpa*
fester, to; *aninchichi, wulhko*
festival, *impa chito*
festival, to make a; *chepúlechi*
fetch, *lushka*
fetch, to; *aiilli, ạla, shali*
fetch near, to; *biliⁿkạchi*
fetid; *bitema, kosoma, kotoma, shua*
fetid smell, *kosoma*
fetid smell, to cause a; *kosomạchi*
fetlock, *isuba iyi hishi*
fetor, *kotoma*
fetor, to cause; *kotomạchi*
fetter; *iyi isht intalakchi, tạli iyi isht ạlbi*
fetter, horse; *isuba iyi isht talakchi*
fetter, to; *iyi intakchi, iyintakchi*
fettered; *isht intalakchi, iyi isht intalakchi, iyintalakchi*
fetus, *ushi tobat taha*
feud, *achowa*
fever; *nan abeka, nipi lua, yanha, yạnha*
fever, bilious; *yạnha chito*
fever, great; *yạnha fehna*
fever, high; *yạnha chito*
fever, to cause a; *yạnhạchi*
fever, to have a; *yanha, yạnha*
fever, to induce a; *yạnhạchi*
fever and ague, *hochukwa yạnha*
feverish; *imanukfila shanaioa, libbikạchi, mạfkạchi, yạnha chohmi, yạnoba*
few; *achafoha, chạbiha, chạbihasi, chukachạfa abinili, laua*
few, to cause a; *ạchafoachi*
few, to select or take a; *ạchafoachi, ạchafolechi, ạchafoli*
few, very; *chạbihasi, kanomusi*
few and scattering; *achafoa, ạchafoa*
fiat, *anumpa ạlhpisa*
fib; *anumpa holabi, holabi*

fib, to; *holabi*
fibber, *holabi*
fiber, *akshish*
fickle; *imanukfila laua, imanukfila shanaioa*
fiddle, *ałepa*
fiddle, to; *ałepa olachi, ałepushi olachi*
fiddle bow, *ałepushi isht olachi*
fiddle maker, *ałepush ikbi*
fiddler; *ałepolachi, ałepush olachi*
fiddlestick, *ałepushi isht olachi*
fiddle-string, *ałepushi isht talakchi*
fiddling, *ałepush olachi*
fiducial, *iyimmi*
fiduciary, *iyimmi*
fiduciary, a; *yimmi*
field; *aiitibbi, atoksạli, oktak*
field, large; *ạffekoma*
field, small; *osapushi*
field guard, *osapa atoni*
field of battle, *aiitibbi*
fieldpiece, *tanamp chito*
fiend; *shilombish okpulo, tạnạp*
fiendish, *okpulo*
fiendlike, *shilombish okpulo holba*
fierce; *achillita, anukshomunta, chilita, nukoa*
fierce, rendered; *achillita*
fierce, to make; *achiletạli, achillitạchi*
fierce-minded, *chuⁿkạsh yiminta*
fierceness, *nukoa*
fiery; *chuⁿkạsh homi, homi, hushmi, lạshpa, lua, nukoa*
fife; *oskula, uskulushi*
fife, to; *uskulushiolachi*
fifer, *uskulush olachi*
fifteen, *auah tałapi*
fifth, *isht tałapi*
fifthly, *isht tałapi*
fiftieth, *isht pokoli*
fifty, *pokoli*
fig; *bihi chito, fik*
fig leaf, *bihi chito hishi*
fight, *itibbi*
fight, to; *boli, fehna, itibi, itoti, tanampi*
fight, to cause to; *itibechi*
fight for, to; *apepoa*
fighter, *itibi*
figurative, *isht ạlhpisa*
figure; *holba, holhtina, holisso, isht ạlhpisa*
figure, to; *hobachi, ikbi, imahoba*
filament, *ponola*
filch, to; *huⁿkupa*

filcher, *huⁿkupa*
file (for arranging things); *aholhtapi, holhtampi*
file (rank), *itiakaya*
file (tool), *isht milofa*
file, large; *isht milofa chito*
file, to; *haluppachi, miloffi, miloha, milohachi, milolichi*
file (to arrange), to; *hotampi*
file, to advance in; *baiallit maⁿya*
filed; *halupa, milofa, milohachi, miloli*
filed (arranged), *holhtapi*
filed place, *amilofa*
filed there, *amilofa*
filer, *miloffi*
files, to stand in; *baialli, baiilli*
filing, *hotampi*
filings, *botulli*
fill, *alota*
fill, to; *alotoli, alulli, alachaya, hilechi, kaiyachi*
fill a place, to; *atobachi*
fill bottles, to; *kotoba aloli*
fill up, to; *alolua, alota, alotowa, alacha, alachkachi, asheli, ashinli, labli*
fill with water, to; *oka kaiya, oka kaiyachi*
filled; *alolua, alota, alhpesa, kaiya, kotoba alolua*
filled up; *aialota, alotowa, ashiⁿya*
filled with, *isht anukfokat alota*
filled with water, *oka kaiya*
fillet; *iachuka, paⁿsh isht talakchi, paⁿshi isht talakchi*
fillet, royal; *miⁿko imiachuka*
fillet, to; *takchi*
filling, *ahaya*
filling, the; *isht tanna*
fillip, *ibbak ushi olachi*
fillip, to; *sakaha*
filly, *isuba tek himmita*
film, *hakshup*
filter; *ahoiya, aholuya*
filter, to; *hoiya, hoiyachi, holuya*
filtered; *hoiya, holuya*
filth; *na shua, shua*
filthiness; *shua, toshbi*
filthy; *chakapa, likokoa, toshbi*
filthy, to render; *likokoachi*
filtrate, to; *holuya, holuyachi*
filtrated, *holuya*
fin; *isht okyoli, iyi, naniyi, sanahchi*
final, *isht aiopi*
finally; *isht aiopi, polaⁿka*

find, to; *ahauchi, ahayu, atali, ikhana, pisa*
find fault, to; *na miha shali*
find out, to; *akostininchi*
finder, *ahauchi*
fine (good); *achukma, aiukli, imponna, lisepa, mismiki, yohbi*
fine (small and soft); *chipinta, halupa, lapushki, lipihbi, lipiⁿka, pushi, tapuski*
fine, a; *alhtoba*
fine (in music), *iskitini*
fine, to; *anumpa alhpisa onuchi, kashoffi*
fine, to make; *lihpibichi, mismikichi*
fine and soft; *lipeha, lipemo, lipinto, lipisto*
fine and soft, to make; *lipehachi, lipemochi, lipistochi*
fine and soft, very; *lisisiⁿkachi*
fine clothes, *isht shema*
fine snow, *okti pushi*
fined; *anumpa alhpisa onutula, kashofa*
finely; *achukma, lapushki*
fineness; *aiukli, kashofa, pushi, tapuski*
finery, *isht shema*
finger, *ibbak ushi*
finger, little; *ibbak ush ali*
finger, to; *ibbak ushi isht pasholi*
finger end, *ibbak ushi wishakchi*
finger joint, *ibbak ushi itachakalli*
finger nail, *ibbak chush*
finger ring; *ibbak ushi foka, ibbak ushi abiha*
finical, *achukma*
finis, *isht aiopi*
finish, to; *ahokoffichi, atali, alhtaha, bakastuli, loshummi, lushomi, taha, tali*
finish off at, to; *aloshummi*
finish the day, to; *shohbichi*
finished; *ataha, alhtaha, bakasto, loshuma, lushoma, taha*
finished off at, *aloshuma*
finisher; *bakastuli, tali*
finite, *aiali*
fire; *chuⁿkash homi, ito, luak, nukoa, nukhobela, tukafa achafa, ulhti*
fire, council; *ulhti*
fire, everlasting; *luak ataha iksho*
fire, great; *luak chito*
fire, night; *ninak luak, ninak palali*
fire, one council; *ulhti achafa*
fire, to; *hukmi, hushmi, lua, luachi, nukhobelachi, nukoachi, tokali, tokalichi, tufaka, tukaffi*
fire, to be well on; *tobela*

fire, to cause to; *tokalichi*
fire, to kindle a; *oti*
fire off, to; *tukaffi*
fire kindler, *oti*
fire pan, *luak apala*
fire poker, *luak isht chilichi*
fire water, *oka luak*
firearms, *tanampo*
fired; *hollokmi, holushmi, lua, tukafa*
fired off, *tokali*
fired on, *tukafa*
firedogs, *itakowa intula*
firelock, *tanampo*
fireman; *luak ikbi, luak mosholichi*
fireplace; *aiulhti, luak ashoboli, luak atoba, luak iksita, luak ituksita*
firer, *hukmi*
fires a gun, one who; *tukaffi*
firewood; *itakowa, iti ulhti*
firm; *apissanli, kamassa, kallo, weki*
firm, a; *itapelachi*
firm man; *hatak kamassa, hatak kamas-salli*
firmament; *atohwakali, auataya, shutik aba, tohwali, towakali*
firmness; *kamassa, kallo*
first; *ahpi, amona, ammona, tikba, tiⁿkba, tikbashalika*
first child, *ushahpi*
first darkness, *oklilahpi*
first hereafter; *tiⁿkba*
first one, to be the; *achafahpi*
first rate, *achukma iⁿshaht tali*
firstborn; *akni, attahpi, iⁿki ichapa, ishahpi, tiⁿkba, tikba atta, ushahpi*
firstling, *chelahpi*
fish, *nani*
fish, a great; *nani chito*
fish, a red; *nani humma*
fish, a species of; *kaⁿshka lusa, kashka, sakli, shakla, talbasa*
fish, to; *nan okweli*
fish, young; *nan ushi*
fish basket, *nani isht hokli*
fish eater, *nanapa*
fish net, *nani isht hokli*
fish pot, *nani isht hokli*
fish trap; *nanalbi, nani isht hokli* ·
fisher; *nan okweli, nanabi*
fisherman; *nan okweli, nanabi, nani hokli*
fishery; *nan aiokweli, nan okweli*
fish hawk, *chuⁿkcho*

fishhook; *nan isht albi, nan isht okwia, nani isht hokli*
fishing place, *nan aiokweli*
fishy, smelling; *nakshobi*
fishy smell, *nakshobi*
fissure; *waklali, yakni chiluk*
fissures, large; *kitanli*
fist, *ibbak bonunta*
fist, to; *ibbak bonuht isht isso*
fistula, *shatali*
fit, *alhpesa*
fit, a; *haiuchi, haiuchichi, haiyichichi*
fit, to; *aiskiachi, atali, yohmi aialhpesa*
fit in, to; *alacha, alachaya, alachkachi*
fit together, to; *itabana*
fitness, *alhpesa*
fitted, *alhtaha*
five, *talapi*
five score, *talepa achafa*
five times; *talapiha*
fivefold, *inluhmi*
fix, to; *aiiskia, aiiskiachi, aiskiachi, akallochi, apesa, hilechi, iksiachi, kallochit hilechi, tala*
fix up a fire, to; *tikbichi*
fixed; *aiiska, aiskachi, aiskia, kallo, taluli*
flaccid, *bilakli*
flag; *hashuk pancha, na hata, shapha*
flag (called "cat-tail"), *pancha*
flag of truce, *na hata*
flag, to; *bashi, kota, tikabi, walohbi*
flageolet, *uskulushi*
flagitious; *haksi, okpulo*
flagon, *isht ochi*
flagrant; *humma, okpulo*
flagstaff, *kohta*
flail; *isht boli, onush isht boli*
flake of snow, *oktusha achafa*
flame; *libbi, libbika*
flame, to; *libbi, libbichi*
flank, *ikfichukbi*
flannel; *chukfi hishi nan tanna, chukfi hishi tanna*
flap, *apokshiama*
flap, to; *wileli*
flare, to; *lipkachi, lipli*
flare, to cause to; *liplichi*
flash; *malkachi, tohkasakli, tohwekikli, tohwikikli*
flash, to; *hashuk malli, mallahtakachi, shubbukli, tohkasakli, tohmali, tohmasli*
flash, to cause to; *tohmaslichi*

flash of lightning; *hashuk malli, mallahtakachi*
flask, *kotoba patassa*
flask, powder; *hituk aialhto*
flat; *kallo, latasa, latastua, lataswa, latassa, malaspoa, malaswa, malassa, patasah, pataspoa, patala, pataspoa, patassa, takassa, weki*
flat, a; *pataswa, yakni patassa*
flat, to; *patasachi*
flat, to make; *patasachi, patasalli*
flat and smooth, *malassa*
flat and thin, to make; *takassa*
flat land, *yakni patassa*
flat-nosed; *ibichilu patassa, ibishakni patassa*
flat ones, *malaswa*
flatfish, *nani patassa*
flatiron, *ilefoka halushkichi*
flatness; *latasa, patassa*
flatten, to; *latasalli, latastuli, latassachi,
malaspoachi, malaswachi, malassachi,
patasalli, pataspuli, patashuli*
flattened; *lataswa, latassa, pataspoa,
patashua, pataskachi*
flatter, to; *anumpa achukmalit chukashichi*
flatulency, *akeluachi*
flatulency, to cause; *akeluachechi*
flatulent, *akeluachi*
flavor, *balama*
flaw; *bitanli, mali*
flaw, to; *bitanlichi, koli*
flawed, *koa*
flax, *nuchi*
flay, to; *lonffi, loli*
flayed; *lonfa, loha*
flayer, *lonffi*
flea, *kashti*
fleabite; *kashti akobli, kashti akopoli*
fleam; *issish isht kuchi, isht lumpa*
fled; *chafa, yilepa*
fledge, to; *hishi toba*
fledged, *hishi toba*
fledglings, *aliktichi*
flee, to; *chafa, lakoffi, maleli, tilaya, yilepa*
fleece; *chukfi hishi almo, hishi*
fleece, to; *chukfi hishi amo*
fleeced, *chukfi hishi almo*
fleer, to; *isht yopula*
fleet, *palhki*
fleet, to; *palhkit anya*
fleeting, *palhkit anya*
flesh; *nipi, poa nipi*

flesh, dead; *nipi illi*
flesh, dry or dried; *nipi shila, nipi
shulla*
flesh, perished; *nipi shulla*
flesh, putrid; *nipi shua*
flesh, withered; *nipi shulla*
flesh of animals, *poa nipi*
fleshed, *nia*
fleshhook; *bili, okhawi*
fleshy, *nia*
flexible; *bikota hinla, walohbi*
flexible, to make; *walohachi, walohbichi*
flier; *chafa, heli, hika, maleli, na hika*
flight, *chafa*
flight of stairs, *atuya*
flimsy; *kallo, walohbi*
flinch, to; *issa*
fling, *pila*
fling, to; *kanchi, pila*
flint, *tasannuk*
flint-hearted, *chunkash kallo*
flippant, *anumpuli shali*
flirt, to; *fali, tahtuli*
flirt the tail, to; *hasimbish fali*
flirted, *tahtua*
flit, to; *chachachi, hika*
float; *ahchihpo, okpalali, pehta*
float, to; *mahaiyat anya, okpalali, okpalalichi, okpaloli, okpalolichi*
float, to cause to; *okpalolichi*
floated, *okchito*
floating, a; *okpalali*
flock; *anya, anya achafa, lukoli*
flock, to; *ibakaha, itanaha, lukoli*
flog, to; *fammi, mitinha*
flogged, *fama*
flood; *laua, oka falama, okchito*
flood, to; *okchitochi*
flood, to become a; *okchito*
flood, to make a; *okchitochi, okchitoli*
flooded, *okchito*
floor; *aboha itipatalhpo, iti patapo, iti
patalhpo*
floor, to; *iti patali*
floor, upper; *aba patalhpo*
flop, to; *lopohachi*
florid, *humma*
flounce, *apohota*
flounce, to; *yichina*
flounder, to; *yichina*
flour; *bota, bota lashpa, pushi, tansh
pushi*
flour, cold; *bota kapassa*
flour, corn; *bota tanshpa*

flour, to; *pushechi*
flour, to become; *bota*
flour, wheat; *bota ḥata, bota tohbi*
flour of sulphur or of brimstone; *hituk lakna bota*
floured, *pushi*
flout, to; *isht yopula*
flow, to; *mati, nishkin okchiyanạlli, oka bikeli, okchitochi, okchitoli, yanạlli*
flow, to cause to; *paiolichi*
flow in, to cause to; *oka bikelichi*
flow in or over, to; *bikeli*
flow out, to; *asetili*
flower; *himmita, himmithoa, nam pakanli, pakanli*
flower, to; *pakanli*
flowered, *pakanli*
flowery, *pakanli laua*
flowing, *yanạlli*
fluctuate, to; *bạnakạchi, pohokạchi, shanaioa*
fluctuate, to cause to; *bạnakạchechi*
fluctuating, *imanukfila laua*
flue; *ashoboli, luak ashoboli*
fluency, *anump inkucha achukma*
fluent, *anumpuli imponna*
flurry, *mati*
flush, *okcha*
flush, to; *humma*
flute; *oskula, uskula*
flute, to play on a; *uskula olachi*
flutter, *aiitaiyokoma*
flutter, to; *topohạchi, mitihạchi, nukkitekạchi*
flutterer, *mitihạchi*
fluttering, *timikteli*
flux; *ulbạl ont ia, yanạlli*
fly; *chukani, shunshi*
fly, biting; *shunshi watana*
fly, green; *shunshi okchạmali*
fly, horse; *shunshi watana*
fly, Spanish; *shunshi okchạmali isht wulhkuchi*
fly, to; *apakfopa, anya, fichamoa, fitelichi, heli, hika, maleli, tunshpa, yobota*
fly (as a spark), to; *chulotah*
fly, to cause to; *helichi, hikachi*
fly, water; *shunshi oka ansha*
fly against, to; *asonali*
fly into a passion, to; *nuklibishlikạchi*
fly off sideways, to; *tibạlli*
fly off sideways, to cause to; *tibinllichi*

fly open, to; *fichama*
flyblow, *chukanushi*
flyblow, to; *chukanicheli*
flyblown, *chukanushi ansha*
flying; *heli, hika, yabota*
flying, a; *yananta*
flying clouds, *hoshonti yabata*
flying stars, *fichik heli*
foal, *isubushi*
foal, to; *cheli, isubushi cheli*
foam; *oka pokpoki, pokpoki*
foam, to; *oka pokpoki, pokpoki*
foam, to cause to; *oka pokpokechi*
fob, *hạshi isht ikhạna inshukcha*
fodder, *ạlhpoa imilhpak*
fodder, to; *ạlhpoa ipeta*
foddered, *ạlhpoa ilhpita*
foe, *tạnạp*
fog, *oktohbi*
foggy, *oktohbichi*
foil, to; *okpạni*
fold, *inluhmi*
fold, a; *potoma, potomoa*
fold, to; · *apotomichi, bunni, holihtạni, itakomoli, kochofa, potomi, potomoli, puti*
fold up in, to; *abonulli*
folded; *bonkạchi, holihtạlhto, potoma, potomoa, puta*
folder; *holihtạni, puti*
folks; *hatak, okla*
follow, to; *atioa, atia, iakaiya, iakaiyachit pisa, iakaiyoha, ibafoka, ibafokat anya, isht ạtta, tioa*
follow, to cause to; *iakaiyachi, iakaiyohachi*
follow by scent, to; *ahchishi*
follow in haste, to; *iahinsht ia*
follower; *iakaiya, iakaiyoha, ibafoka*
following; *achanka, himmak*
folly; *aiạlhpesa, haksulba, yoshoba*
foment, to; *hobi*
fond of; *ahinnia, anushkunna*
fondle, to; *ahpạlli, akomuta*
fondler, *ahpạlli*
font, *kạli*
food; *ạpa, honni, ilhpa, ilhpak, ilimpa, impa, na holhponi, nan ạpa, nan ilhpak, nan ilimpa, nan impa, uksak ulhkomo*
food, boiled; *tabocha, tobocha*
fool; *hatak imanukfila iksho, imanukfila iksho*
fool, to; *haksichi, isht yopula, yimmichi*

fooled; *haksi, pakama, pakamoa, yimmi*
foolish; *haksulba, imanukfila iksho, tasim holba*
foolish man, *hatak hopoyuksa*
foolishness, *haksulba*
foot, *iyi*
foot, naked; *iyi bano*
foot, to; *habli, hotina*
foot joint, *iyi tilokachi*
foot log; *achaba, asilhchap, hahchabah, salbash*
foot of a hill; *chakpatali, chakpatalika, okkattahaka*
foot of a tree, *iti akishtala*
footbridge; *achaba, asalbash, asechip, alhchaba, salbash*
footing, *ahikia*
footman, *hinka*
footpad; *akkahunkupa, hunkupa akka nowa*
footstep; *anowa, iyi*
fop; *hatak ilakshema shali, hatak shema shali*
for; *atuk, hatok, hatuk, he, isht, pulla, pullakako*
for a long time or way, *hopaki*
for a season, *kanima*
for a time, *naha*
for the sake of; *hatuk, pullakako*
for us, *pin*
forage, *alhpoa imilhpak*
forage, to; *alhpoa imilhpak itannali*
forbear, to; *nukchinto, olabbi*
forbid, to; *alammi, alammichi, olabbi*
forbidden, *alama*
forbode, to; *tikba anoli*
force; *kallo, kilimpi, lampko*
force, to; *afoa, hoklit aiissa*
forcible; *kallo, kilimpi*
ford; *akucha, alopoli, alopulli, hina kucha, okhina, okhina akucha*
ford a river, to; *okhina akka nowat lopulli*
fore, *tinkba*
fore horse, *isuba tikba heli*
forearm, *italhpali*
forecast, to; *tikba pisa*
forechoose, to; *tikba atokuli, tikba hotina*
forechosen; *tikba alhtuka, tikba holhtina*
forefather, *hatak tinkba*
forefinger, *ibbak ushi tikba*
forefoot, *iyi tikba*
forefront of a rock, *asanali*
forego, to; *issa*
forehanded, *nan inlaua*
forehead; *ibitakla, imosana*

foreign; *inla, oklush inla*
foreign man, *oklush inla hatak*
foreign nation, *oklush inla*
foreign people, *okla inla*
foreign tribe, *oklush inla*
foreigner; *hatak inla, okla inla, oklush inla, oklush inla hatak*
forejudge, to; *tikba apesa*
foreknow, to; *tikbanlit ithana*
foreknowledge; *tikbanli ikhana, tikbanlit ithana*
foremost, *tikba fehna anya*
foreordain, to; *tikba atokuli*
fore part of the day, *nitak echi*
forerunner, *tikbanya*
foresee, to; *tikba pisa, tikbanlit pisa*
foreside, *tikba*
foreskin; *itikba hakshup, tikba*
forest; *iti anunka, konwi chito, konwi hochito*
forestall, to; *tikba chumpat aiishi*
foretell, to; *na tikbanli anoli, tikba anoli, tikbanlit anoli*
foretooth; *noti ibish, noti tikba*
foretop; *ibishachi, ibitakla panshi, imosana hishi*
forever, *bilia*
forewarn, to; *tikbanli imanoli*
forewarned, *tikba annoa*
forge; *apunfa, talaboli*
forge, to; *boli*
forget, to; *ahaksi, alhkania, imahaksi, imahaksichi, imihaksi*
forgetful; *ahaksichi shali, imahaksi*
forgetfulness, *imahaksi*
forgetter, *na imahaksi*
forgive, to; *ahaksichi, imahaksi, kashoffi, kashoffichit kanchi*
forgiven, *kashofa*
forgiven, to cause to be; *imahaksichi*
forgiveness, *imahaksichi*
forgiver, *ahaksichi*
forgotten; *ahaksi, alhkania, imahaksi*
forgotten, to cause to be; *imahaksichi*
fork; *afolakto, afolaktua, chufak, chufak falakto, chukulbi, falakto, fichapa, fichapoa, filamminchi, shokulbi*
fork, iron; *tali falakto*
fork, table; *chufak isht bili*
fork, to; *chulaktochi, falakto, falaktuli, fichapa, fichapoa, fichapoli, fichabli, itakchulalichi*
fork, to cause to; *afolaktochi, afolaktuli, falaktuchi, fichapolichi*
fork in the road, *hina falakto*
fork of a creek, *bok falakto*

fork them, to; *itakchulashlichi*
forked; *afolakto, afolaktua, chilakto, chulakto, falakto, fichapa, fichapoa, itakchulakto, itakchulali, itakchulashli, wakcha, wakchalashli*
forked, to make; *chilaktochi*
forked at, to be; *afolakto*
forked foot, *iyi falakto*
forked nail, *chufak falakto*
forlorn, *alhtakla*
form; *aiomanili falaia, aiukli, holba*
form, to; *ikbi*
form and come out, to; *toba*
form as skin, to; *hakshup toba*
form thin clouds, to; *okhapaioli*
formed, *toba*
former; *chanshpo, tinkba*
formerly; *chanshpo, tinkba, tinkbaha*
formidable, *nukshobba hinla*
fornicate, to; *lumanka*
fornication; *haui toba, itinlumanka*
fornication, a; *hatak inhaklo*
fornication, to commit; *lumanka*
fornicatress; *hatak inhaklo, haui*
forsake, to; *issa, kanchi*
forsaken; *aksho, issa*
forsaken, a place; *aiissa*
forsaker, *issa*
fort, *holihta kallo*
forth; *kucha, pit, tikba*
forthwith; *chekusi, himonali, himonanli, yakosi ititakla*
fortieth; *isht pokoli, pokoli*
fortification, *holihta kallo*
fortify, to; *holihta kallo ikbi*
fortnight, *nitak hollo tuklo*
fortress; *aboha kallo, holihta kallo*
fortunate; *imala, imola*
fortune, *nan inlaua*
fortune-teller, *nuseka*
forty, *pokoli*
forward; *alhtaha, isht afekommi, pit, tikba, tikbali, tushpa*
forward, to; *pila, tunshpalechi*
forward man, *hatak chilita*
foster, to; *hofantichi, impachi, ipeta*
foul; *okpulo, shua*
foul, to; *litehachi, liteli*
foul smell, to cause a; *ashuwachi*
foul smelling, *ashua*
found; *ahauchi, haiaka*
found, to; *akmochi, hakmuchi, ia, ikbi, ontalali, talali*

found again, *atuklant haiaka*
foundation; *aiisht awechi, intolahpi, intula*
foundation of a house; *aboha intula, chuka aiitola, chuka aiontala*
founded; *ontalaia, talaia*
founded upon, *abana*
founder; *akmochi, hakmuchi, ikbi, isht ia*
foundered, *iyi isht abeka*
foundry, *aiakmo*
fount, *kali*
fountain; *aminti, ataiyuli, ateli, bok wishahchi, ibetap, kali*
four, *ushta*
four, all; *unshta*
four, to; *ushtali*
four, to make; *ushta, ushtali*
four times, to do it; *ushtachi*
fourfold, *inluhmi*
four-sided; *palampoa*
foursquare, *iti tapokachi*
fourteen, *auah hushta*
fourth; *aiushta, isht aiushta*
fourth time; *aiushtaha, ushtaha*
fourthly, *aiushta*
fowl, *hushi*
fowl, to; *hush abi*
fowler, *hush abi*
fowling piece, *tanamp fabassa*
fox, *chula*
fox, barking; *kanwa*
fox, mad; *chula holilabi, chula tasembo*
fox, male; *chula nakni*
fox, young; *chula ushi*
fox fur, *chula hishi*
fox hair, *chula hishi*
fox hunter, *chulabi*
fox trap, *chula aiabi*
fracas, *itinnukoa*
fraction, *tushafa*
fracture; *koa, kobafa*
fracture, to; *kobaffi, kokuli, koli*
fractured; *koa, kobafa, kokoa*
fragile, *kanliksho*
fragments; *boshulli, kobulli, kokoa, tushali, tushtua*
fragments of boilers, *taksho*
fragments of wood, *iti boshulli*
fragrant, *balama*
fragrant, to make it; *balamachi*
fragrant thing, *na balama*
frail; *kota, liposhi, tikabi*
frame, *haknip*

frame, to; *fohki, ikbi*
frame for head deformation, *atalhpi*
framed, *fohki*
framed house, *chuka limishki*
framer, *ikbi*
France, *Filanchi yakni*
frank, *anli, haiaka*
frank, a; *holisso alhtoba iksho*
frankincense, *filankinsin*
frankness; *anumpa lumiksho, apissanli*
frantic; *nukoa, tasembo*
fraternal, *itibapishi on*
fraternity, *itibapishi aliha*
fraternity, a; *itibapishi*
fraud, *haksichi*
fraudulent, *haksi*
fraught; *abeha, alota*
fray, *itibbi*
freckle; *chikchiki, siksiki*
freckled; *chikchiki, siksiki*
free; *ahalaia, ilap ali hikia, kucha, pilla, yuka, yuka keyu*
free, to; *issachi, kashoffi, lakoffichi, litoffi, yuka issachi*
free-born, *yuka keyut atta*
freed; *kashofa, kucha, lakoffi, litofa, yuka issa*
freedom, *yuka keyu*
freely; *apakna, fehna, ilap aiahni, laua, pilla*
freeman, *hatak yuka keyu*
freeze, to; *akalapechi, akalapi, hochukwa, kalampi, kalampichi*
freight, *alhtoba*
French, *Filanchi*
French country, *Filanchi yakni*
French language, *Filanchi anumpa*
French Nation, *Filanchi okla*
French people, *Filanchi okla*
Frenchman, *Filanchi hatak*
frenzy; *holilabi, nukoa, tasembo*
frequently, to be; *himonnan*
fresh; *hapi yammi, himmita, himmona, humma, kapassa, okchanki*
freshet, *okchito*
fret, to; *hashanyachi, nukoachi, pikofa, pikoffi, pikolichi*
fret, to make her; *okpulochi*
fret by rubbing, to; *pikoli*
fretful, *hashanya*
fretful, to make one; *hashanyachi*
fretfulness, *nukoa*
fretfulness, the cause or occasion of; *isht hashanya*

fretted; *nukoa, pikofa, pikoli*
fricassee, *nipi alwasha*
fricassee, to; *nipauashli*
fried, *alwasha*
fried bread, *pask alwasha*
fried meat, *nipi alwasha*
friend; *hatak ikhana, hatak itinkana, inholitopaka, itibapishi, kana*
friendly; *banshka achukma, ilhpansh, itinkana, kana*
friendship; *itinhollo, kana*
friends, mutual; *itinhollo, itinkana*
frigate, *peni chito aiitibi*
fright, *anuklakancha*
fright, a; *nuklakancha, nukshopa*
fright, to take; *anuklakancha*
frighten, to; *anuklakashli, anukwiachi, malalichi, nuklakashli, nukshobli, nukshoblichi*
frightened; *anuklakancha, malali, malata, nuklakancha, nukshopa*
frightener, *nukshobli*
frigid, *kapassa*
frigidity, *kapassa*
frill, *awalakachi*
fringe; *apohota, awalakachi, imposhota*
fringe, to; *imposhot infullolichi*
frisk, to; *tulli*
frisker, *tulli*
fritter, *pask alwasha*
fritter, to; *tushtuli*
frizzle, to; *lasimo, yushbonulichi*
frizzled, *yushbonoli*
frock; *alhkuna falaia, na foka lumbo falaia, nam piheta*
frog, *shukatti*
frog, a small; *kalanska, kiba, shukatti*
frog, horned; *halanchilanwa chito*
frog, species of; *shilaii*
frog, young; *yalubba*
frolic; *chepulli, hila, ilaualli, yikoa*
frolic, to; *chepulli, hila, ilaualli*
frolicker; *hila, ilaualli*
from; *a, ai, aiali, hikiat ia, minti, pilla*
from above, *akket*
from the fountain, *ibetap pilla*
from us, *pin*
front, *ibitakla panshi*
front, to; *asanni, asonali*
frontal, *bita*
frontier, *yakni ali*
frontlet, *bita*
frost; *akalapi, hotonti, okti*
frost, great; *okti chito*

frost, hoar; *okti tohbi*
frost, to cause a; *hotontichi*
frost, to kill by; *oktąbi*
frost, white; *okti hąta, okti tohbi*
frostbitten; *kalampi, oktąbi*
frosty; *hotonti, kapąssa, okti*
froth; *itukpokpoki, pokpoki*
froth, to; *itukpokpoki, pokpoki*
froth, to make; *pokpokechi, wushulli*
frothy, *pokpoki*
frower, *tiak isht shima*
frown, *okwichinli*
frown, to; *okwichinli, okwichinlit pisa*
frowsy; *hauąshko, homechi*
frozen; *akaląpi, kalampi*
frozen mud, *okti chuⁿli*
frozen up, *akaląpit taha*
frugal, *ilatomba*
fruit; *ąni, isht atiaka, na waya, nan ąni,*
nana waya, ushi
fruit, evil; *yąt*
fruit, to bear or yield; *ąni*
fruit, to bring; *waya*
fruit trees, *ąlhpoa*
fruitful; *awaya fehna, waya*
fruitless; *nan ihmake keyu, waya*
frustrate, to; *kobąffi*
frustrated, *kobafa*
fry, to; *auąshli, ąlwąsha*
fry meat, to; *nipauąshli*
frying pan; *aiąlwąsha, apąla*
fuddle, to; *haksichi*
fuddled, *haksi*
fuel; *lua, luak toba*
fugitive; *kąnia, maleli*
fulfill, to; *aiaⁿlichi, aiąlhpiesa*
fulfill a promise, to; *aⁿlichi*
fulfilled; *aiaⁿli, aiąlhpiesa, aⁿli, ąlhpesa*
fulfillment; *aiaⁿli, ąlhpisa*
full; *abeha, aiąlhtaha, alolua, alota, haia-*
ka, ikląnna, kaiya, laua, moma, nia,
yąmmi
full, a; *moma*
full, to; *sukkochi*
full (as the moon), to; *hąshi bolukta*
full banks, *alotoli*
full cloth, to; *kashoffichi, nan tąnna*
sukkuchi
full of blossoms, *pakanli laua*
full of swellings, *pąffąla alota*
full return of day, *onnat taha*
fulled; *kashofa, nan tąnna sukko, sukko*
fulled cloth, *nan tąnna sukko*
fuller of cloth, *nan tąnna sukkuchi*

fulling mill, *nan tąnna akashofichi*
fullness; *aialota, aiąlhtaha, alolua, alota,*
alotowa, apakna, ąlhtaha, chito, nan
inlaua
fullness of the blood vessels, *michila*
fulminate, to; *anumpa apesa, hiloha*
fulsome; *shua, yuala*
fume, *shoboli*
fume, to; *shoboli, shobolichi*
fumigate, to; *shobolichi*
fun, *ilauąlli*
function, *isht ątta*
functionary, *isht ątta*
fundament, *obala*
funds; *isht chumpa, tąli holisso*
funeral, *hatak hopi*
funeral cry, *yaiya*
fungus; *oktushshi, pakti*
funnel; *aiąni, ashoboli, isht bicheli, oka*
abicha, oka isht bicheli
fur, *hishi*
fur hat, *kinta hishi shąpo*
furbished, *shohmalali*
furious; *anukhobela, kąllo, nukhobela,*
nukoa, tasembo
furl, to; *afolichi*
furled, *ąffoa*
furnace; *aiokpuloka, asonak atoba, shuti*
asha atoba, tąli abila
furnace, iron; *tąli abila*
furnace of fire, *tąli abila*
furnish, to; *ahauchi, aiatali, atali, ipeta*
furnished, *ąlhtaha*
furniture; *aboha nan chukushpa, chuka*
na chokushpa
furrow; *bachali, hina, patafa, yiⁿyiki*
furrow, to; *hina ikbi, patąffi, yakni pa-*
tąffi, yiⁿyikechi
furrow, to make a; *bachali*
furrow, water; *oka iⁿhina*
furrowed; *patafa, patali, shikofa, yiⁿyiki*
further; *anonti, misha, mishapilla, mi-*
shema
further, to; *apela, apelachi, pila*
furthermore; *himmakma, yąmohmikma*
fury; *anukhobela, nukoa, tasembo*
fuse, to; *bila, bileli, itobila*
fused; *bila, itobila*
fusee, *tanamp fabąssa iskitini*
fusible, *bila hinla*
fusion, *itobila*
fuss, a; *shakapa*
future; *chaⁿshpo, himmak, himmak pilla,*
nitak tiⁿkba minti

future, in the; *chetoma, tumąshke*
futurity, *nitak himmak pilla ma*
fuzz; *hishi ląpishta, hishi wanuksho, wa-nuksho*
fuzzy, *wononuⁿkąchi*

gab, to; *anumpuli*
gabble, to; *anumpuli*
gad about, to; *chuka abaiyąt nowa*
gadabout, *chuka abaiyąt nowa*
gadder, *chuka abaiyąt nowa*
gadfly, *olana chito*
gag, *itąkha isht ąlhkąma*
gag, to; *hoeta bąnna, hoetąt pisa, itąkha akkąmi*
gage; *isht apesa, isht laⁿfi*
gaged, *ąlhpesa*
gagged, *itąkha ąlhkąma*
gain, *pisa*
gain, to; *ahauchi, asitąbi, ishi, ona, pisa*
gain the affections, to; *chuⁿkash ishi*
gainer; *ahauchi, pisa*
gainsay, to; *aⁿli*
gait, *nowa*
galaxy, the; *ofi hasimbish iⁿhina, ofi hąta kolofa*
gale; *mali, mali chito, mali kąllo*
gall, the; *basunląsh, basunląsh okchi, chuⁿkąsh homi, nukoa*
gall bladder, *basunląsh aiątto*
gall, to; *iti loli, pikofa, pikoffi*
galled, *pikofa*
gallery; *aboha hoshontika, hoshontika*
galley (on shipboard), *aboha ahoponi*
gallon; *isht ąlhpisa, kaląn, koat ushta, oka isht ąlhpisa, okisht ąlhpisa*
gallop, *tabakli*
gallop, to; *hątapakli, hątapaklichi, ta-bakli, tabaklichi*
gallop, to cause to; *tabaklichi*
gallows; *anuksiteli, anuksita, hatak anuk-sita, hatak anuksitkąchi*
gamble, to; *bąska*
gambler; *bąska, hatak bąska*
gambling room, *aboha abąska*
gambol, to; *hila*
gambrel; *atakali, atakoli, iyukbąl*
game, *nam poa*
game, a; *isht yopula, washoha*
game, a certain; *achąpi*
game, to; *bąska, washoha*
gamester, *hatak bąska*
gaming house, *aboha abąska*
gammon, *shukha iyubi shila*

gander, *shilaklak nakni*
gang, *hatak kanomona*
gangrene; *nipi illi, nipi shua*
gap; *ahokofa, atiwa, atua, lilafa*
gap, a mountain; *kolofa*
gap in a fence, *holihta atiwa*
gape, to; *bąnna, hawa, itakpąshpąli, pisa*
gape, to cause to; *hawąchi*
gaper, *hawa*
gaping, *itakpąshpąli*
garb, *isht shema*
garble, to; *aiyoa, yuli*
garbled; *aiyua, yuha*
garden, *osapushi*
gardener, *osapushi apesąchi, osapushi toksąli*
garfish, *nąni kąllo*
gargle, to; *itukwąlahąchi, itukwąlichi, itukwololichi*
garland, *ialipa hąshtąp toba*
garment; *anchi, fohka, ilefoka, na fohka*
garment, lady's; *ohoyo iⁿna foka*
garment, large; *na foka chito*
garner, *kanchąk*
garnish, to; *aiuklichi, shemąchi*
garnished; *aiukli, shema*
garniture; *isht aiukli, isht shema*
garrison; *holihta kąllo, tąshka chivota aiasha*
garrison, to; *tąshka chipota aiasha ashachi*
garter; *isht ąlhfoa, iyafoa, iyąlhfoa, iyubi huski isht ąlhfoa, iyubiha isht ąlhfoa*
garter, to; *iyafoli*
gash; *abąsha, achaⁿya, bąsha, chaⁿya, chaⁿyąt pashaⁿfa*
gash, to; *bąshli, chanli, pashąffi*
gashed; *bąsha, chaⁿya, pashaⁿfa, pashąffi*
gasp, *itakpashakli*
gasp, to; *itakpashakli, itąkpashakli*
gate; *holihta isht ąlhkąma, holihta okhisa, isht okshilita, okhisa*
gather, to; *ąmo, itahoba, itahobi, ita-hobli, itąnnali*
gather at, to; *aiitahoba*
gather fish, to; *peli*
gather from or of, to; *aiąmo*
gather fruits, to; *hoyo*
gather into, to; *ashachi*
gather up, to; *apoyua, ąlbąlli*
gathered; *aiyua, itahoba, itąnaha*
gatherer; *ąmo, hoyo, itahobi, itahobli, itąnnali*

gathering; *hatak itahoba, itahoba, ita-naha*
gathers, *awalakachi*
gauge, *isht alhpisa*
gauge, to; *apesa*
gauged; *alhpesa, lanfa*
gaunt; *yihina, yohhuna*
gaunt, to make; *yohhunachi*
gay, *yukpa*
gaze, *pisa*
gaze, to; *pisa*
gaze about, to; *okchilanli, okchilanshli*
gaze at, to; *aiokchipelih, okchilanli, okchilunli*
gazer, *pisa*
gazette, *holisso*
gear of a horse; *isuba isht halalli, isuba isht toksali*
gear, to; *isuba isht halalli fohki*
gears, *nan isht halalli*
geld, to; *bashli, hobak ikbi*
gelded; *basha, hobak, hobak toba*
gelding; *hobak, isuba hobak*
gelid, *kapassa*
general, *moma chuhmi*
general, a; *chanal, hopaii*
generality, *moma chuhmi*
generally, *moma chuhmi*
generate, to; *ikbi*
generated, *toba*
generation; *aiitishali, aiunchululli, isht atiaka, isht aiunchululli, itaiunchululi, itashali, uncholulli, unchululi*
generation, to form a; *aiunchululi*
generator, *ikbi*
generous, *achukma*
genius, *imanukfila kallo*
Gentile; *Chintail, Chintail hatak, Chintail okla, okla nan ikithano, oklushi abanumpa ikithano*
gentle; *imoklaya, kostini*
gentle disposition, *banshka*
gentleman; *hatak alhpesa, hatak holitompa, hatak holitopa*
gentleness, *honayo*
genuine; *achukma, anli, apissanli*
germ; *aiisht ia, aminti, atoba, bikobli*
germinate, to; *abasali, bisali, offo*
gesticulate, to; *ibbak fahfulli*
get, to; *hikia, ikbi, ikhana, ishi*
get all, to; *bakastuli*
get among, to; *ibalhto*
get away, to; *haili, ia*

get down, to; *akkoa*
get here, to; *ala*
get it lower, to; *taklechi*
get on, to; *oiya*
get out of joint, to; *kotafa, kotali*
get out of the way, *kanali*
get over, to; *abanabli, tanapolechi, tanabli*
get ready soon, to; *tikbashalika*
get satisfaction, to; *okha*
get the affections, to; *chunkash ishi*
get there, to; *ala*
get through, to; *alhtaha*
get to, to; *ala*
get up, to; *tani, wakaya*
get up, to cause to; *wakayachi*
get well, to; *lakoffi, masali*
ghastly, *pisa okpulo*
ghost; *shilombish, shilup*
Ghost, the Holy; *Shilombish holitopa*
giant, *hatak chito*
gibbet; *anuksita, anuksiteli*
gibe, to; *isht yopula*
giddiness, *chukfoloha*
giddy; *chukfoloha, hannanuki, tasembo*
gift; *afammikma ilhpeta, aiokpachi, aba isht aiokpachi, habena, habenachi, halbina, ilhpita, ima, isht aiokpachi, na halbina, nan isht aiokpachi*
gifted, *imponna*
gig, *iti chanalli iskitini palhki*
gigantic, *chito*
giggle, to; *yukpa*
giggler, *yukpa shali*
gild, to; *tali lakna isht alhkohachi*
gilded, *tali lakna isht alhkoha*
gilding, *isht alhkoha*
gills; *chaka, itakha, nani itakha*
gills of a fowl; *impakti, impasha, inchaka*
gimlet; *isht fotoha iskitini, isht fotohushi, iti isht fotohushi*
gin, *oka homi*
gin, a; *ahokli, ponola anihelichi*
gin, to; *hokli, niheli*
gin cotton, to; *ponola nihechi*
ginned; *niha, nihi*
gird, to; *atali, askufachechi, askufachi, fohkachechi, katali*
girded; *askufa, askufachi, fohka, katanli, yunushki*
girding, *katanli*
girdle, *isht askufachi*
girdle, to; *fohkachechi, yunni, yunushkichi*

girdle a tree, to; *iti chant, ạbi, yikoli*
girdled; *yikoha, yunna*
girl; *ạlla tek, ohoyo himmita*
girl, a young; *ohoyo himmitasi*
girth; *ikfukạ isht talakchi, ikfukasita*
give!, *echi*
give, to; *atobbi, ạma, boli, ema, habenạchi, ibbak fohki, ilhpitachi, ima, imissa, ipeta, ipetạchi, issa, lạcha*
give alms, to; *hopela*
give away, to; *shuchapap*
give back, to; *falạmmichi*
give charge over, to; *miha*
give ear!, *omishke*
give ear, to; *haponaklo*
give himself, to; *kanchi*
give himself up, to; *ilapissa*
give knowledge, to; *anukfohkichi*
give up, to; *ilissa*
give up to death, to; *illiissa*
given; *ibbak fohka, ilhpita*
given to, *shali*
giver; *ilhpitachi, ima, ipeta*
giving, *ibbak fohki*
gizzard, *chakiffa*
glad; *aiyukpa, yukpa*
glad, to; *yukpali*
gladden, to; *aiokpạchechi, aiyukpali, yukpa, yukpalechi, yukpali*
glade, *tohwali*
gladly, *yukpa*
gladness, *yukpa*
glair, *akaⁿk ushi wạlakạchi*
glance, to; *anaktibafa, anaktibaloa, anaktibạffi, anaktiboa*
glance, to make or cause to; *anaktibaloli, anaktibạffi, anaktibạlli, anaktibạllichi*
glance off, to; *chasạlli, chasạllichi, tibạlli*
glanced; *anaktibafa, anaktibaloa, anaktiboa*
glare, *shohmalali*
glare, to; *shohmalali*
glass, *apisa*
Glauber salts, *ikhiⁿsh hạpi holba*
gleam, to; *tohwikeli*
glean, to; *ạlbạlli*
gleaned, *ạlbạla*
gleaner, *ạlbạlli*
gleaning, *ạlbạlli*
glee, *yukpa*
gleet, *hạta*
glen, *okfa*

glib; *halạsbi, halushki*
glib, to; *halạsbichi, halushkichi*
glide, to; *yanạlli*
glimmer, *tohkasakli*
glimmer, to; *shohmalali, tohmasali, tohwikeli*
glimmering, *shumpalali*
glimmering, a; *tohkasakli, tohwikeli*
glimpse, *tohwekikli*
glisten, to; *chạlhchakạchi, mạlkạchi, shohmalali*
glistening; *malạtha, mạlkạchi, shohmalạshli*
glitter, to; *shohmalali*
glittering, *shohmalali*
globe, *lumbo*
globe, the; *yakni, yakni lumbo*
globe, wooden; *iti lumbo*
globular; *lobuhbo, lumbo*
gloom; *imanukfila ilbạsha, nukhaⁿklo, oklili*
gloomy, *oklili*
gloomy thoughts, *imanukfila ilbạsha*
glorified, *holitopa*
glorify, to; *aiokpạchi, holitoblichi, holitoblit aiokpạchi, holitopạchi*
glorious, *holitopa*
glory; *aholitopaka, aholitopaⁿka, aialika, ạba yakni aholitopa, holitopa, holitopạt annoa, nan isht aholitopa, shohmalali*
glory, the; *isht aholitopa*
glory, to; *yukpa*
gloss, to; *tosholi*
glossy; *malancha, malanta*
glossy, made; *malantkạchi*
glossy, to make; *malantạchi*
glove; *ibbak abeha, ibbak foka*
glow, to; *humma, lạshpa, malantạchi, nuklibisha*
glowworm, *hạlba*
glue, *kauehto*
glue, to; *aiạlbuchi, ạlbochi*
glued; *aiạlbo, ạlbo*
glut; *isht pạla, iti isht pạla, nanạbli*
glut, to; *nanạbli, yuala*
glutinous, *holishki*
glutton; *hatak isikopa, isikopa*
glutton, a great; *isikopa shali*
gluttonize, to; *isikopa*
gluttonous; *atibạlli, holillạbi, isikopa*
gluttonous to excess, *isikopa shali*
gnarled, *nukshiah*
gnash, to; *ạpa, kiseli, kiselichi*
gnash the teeth, to; *noti itikiselichi*

gnat, *yikoffa*
gnaw, to; *kili, kiselichi, kisli*
gnawed, *kila*
gnawer, *kili*
go, to; *aia, ataⁿya, aⁿya, hashi kania, hikia, ia, ilhkoli, illi, kanali, maⁿya, nowa, ona, yanalli*
go, to cause to; *tilelichi*
go across, to; *topulli*
go after water, to; *ochi*
go against, to; *sanali*
go ahead; *hotepa, mia, tepa*
go along, to; *aiya*
go along fast, to; *palhkit aⁿya*
go along with, to; *taⁿkla aⁿya*
go and give, to; *ont*
go and make the fire blaze, *tobachi*
go and see, to; *ont*
go and take, to; *ont*
go around, to cause to; *afoblichi*
go astray, to; *tamoa*
go at random, to; *himak fokalit aⁿya, yammak fokalechi*
go away, to; *itokania, kanali, kania, kucha*
go back, to; *falamat ia*
go backward, to; *tikbali*
go beneath, to; *nutaka ia*
go by, to; *ia, ont*
go down, to; *akka ia, akkaona, akkoa, habofa, haboli, okatula, okkattaha, shippa*
go down, to cause to; *shippali*
go far off, to cause to; *hopakichechi*
go first, *hotepa*
go forth, to; *kucha*
go forward, to; *maiya*
go forward, to cause to; *tikbiachi*
go from, to; *akanalli, attat ia, itot ia*
go in, to; *chukoa*
go in, to cause to; *afohkachi, fokichi*
go in at, to; *afohka*
go in haste, to; *heli*
go in quest of a favor, to; *habenat aⁿya*
go in there, to; *afohka*
go into, to; *fohka*
go into, to cause to; *afohkechi*
go off!, *kanima*
go off, to; *tukafa, tokali*
go on!, *hotepa*
go on board, to; *peni foka*
go on foot, to; *akkaya*
go openly, to; *kucha*
go out, to; *kucha, kuchat ia, kuchat, luak mosholi, mosholi*

go out, to cause to; *kuchichi*
go over, to; *auanapoli, abanabli, abano-poli, topulli, tanabli, walabli*
go over, to cause to; *auanapolichi, abanablichi, paknachi, tanapolechi*
go past, to; *ont*
go round, to; *afobli, fullokachi*
go round at, to; *afolota*
go slow, to cause to; *salahachi*
go there together, to; *itonachi*
go through, to; *lipulli, lopotoli, topulli, yululli*
go through, to cause to; *lopolichi, yulullichi*
go to, to; *aiona, ona, ont*
go to, to cause to; *onachi*
go to a frolic, to; *yikoa*
go to all, to; *mominchi*
go to heaven, to; *aba ia*
go under, to cause to; *nutakachi*
go under water, to; *oklobushli, oklo-bushlichi*
go up, to; *atia, aba ia, oiya*
go with, to; *aiena, ibaiaⁿya, itatuklo, taⁿkla ia*
goat, *isi kosoma*
goat, he; *isi kosoma nakni*
goat, she; *isi kosoma tek*
gobble, to; *nanabli, ola*
gobbler, *fakit homatti*
God; *Aba iⁿki, Aba piⁿki, Chitokaka, Hashtali, Iⁿki aba, Piⁿki aba, piⁿki ishto*
God Jehovah, *Iⁿki Chihowa*
godly; *aba anumpuli aiaⁿli, Aba iⁿki imantia*
goer, *ia*
goggle-eyed, *nishkin itasunali*
going; *aia, aⁿya, ia*
gold, *tali holisso lakna*
golden, *tali holisso lakna*
goldsmith, *tali holisso lakna pilesa*
gone; *alhkania, iksho, kania, kaniachi, taha*
gone astray, *tamoa*
gone by; *chamo, chikki*
gone down, *habofa*
gone off, *itamoa*
gone out, *mosholi*
gone over or by, *auanapa, auanapoa*
gone through, *lukafa*
good; *achukma, aiachuⁿkma, aiyoba, aⁿli, apoksia, chukma, hochukma, holitopa, hopoksia, nitaⁿki*
good, made; *achukma*

good, the; *achukma*
good, to do; *achukma, hochukma*
good, to make; *achchukmali, achukma-lechi, aiyobachi, hopoksiachi*
good deal, a; *laua chuhmi*
good fortune; *imilbik, imola*
good humor, *yukpa*
good-humored, *yukpa*
good-looking, *ilafaya*
good luck, *imola*
good nature, *yukpa*
good nature, a; *ba*ⁿ*shka*
good-natured; *ba*ⁿ*shka, hopola, yukpa*
good-natured, to become; *hopola*
good place; *aiachukma, aiyoba*ⁿ*ka*
good place, the; *aiachukmaka*
good to, to do; *aiyobachi*
goodness; *achukma, achukma*ⁿ*ka, aiachukmaka, hochukma*
goods; *alhpoyak, ila*ⁿ*yak, imilayak, nan alhpoyak, nana imila*ⁿ*yak*
goose; *ha*ⁿ*kha, sha*ⁿ*ha, shilaklak, shilaklak tek*
goose egg, *shilaklak ushi*
gopher; *luksi konih, yakni bukli, yumbak chito*
gore, *issish*
gore, a; *kafanli*
gore, to; *bahaffi, bali*
gore, to make; *balichi*
gored; *baha, bahafa*
gorer, *bahaffi*
gorge, the; *i*ⁿ*nalapi, nalapi*
gorge, to; *nanabli*
gorget, *inuchi chinakbi*
gorget, shell; *sha*ⁿ*ha*
gormandize, to; *asilballi*
gormandizer, *asilballi*
gosling, *shilaklak ushi*
gospel, the; *aba anumpa*
gospel path, the; *hina hanta*
gospel, to; *aba anumpa ithananchi*
gospel, to desire the; *aba anumpa ahni*
gossip, to; *anumpa chukushpashali*
gossiper; *anumpa chukushpali, anumpa chukushpashali*
gouge, *iti isht kula kofusa*
gouge, to; *fulli, kulli, nishkin kuchi*
gouge out, to cause to; *fullichi*
gouged, *nishkin kucha*
gourd; *isht kafa, shukshi okpulo, shukshubok*
gourd, water; *lokush*

govern, to; *a*ⁿ*ya, ilaueli, ilauet a*ⁿ*ya, pelichi*
govern there, to; *apelichi*
government; *aiulhti, anumpa alhpisa, apelichika, ulhti*
governor; *mi*ⁿ*ko, na pelichi, nam pelichi, pelicheka, pelichi*
gown; *alhkuna, nam poheta, pohota*
gown, lady's; *nam piheta*
gown, long; *alhkuna falaia*
grab, to; *ishi, yichiffit ishi*
grace; *achukma, aiahninchi, aiukli, chu*ⁿ*kash achukma, kana*
grace, to; *holitoblichi, shemachi*
graced; *holitopa, shema*
graceful, *amakali*
graceful, to render; *amakalichi*
gracious, *achukma*
gradually; *kanallit a*ⁿ*ya, salahat*
grain, *nan apawaya*
grain, a; *chu*ⁿ*kash, nihi*
grain, English; *onush*
grain, small; *onush*
grains, *lakchi*
granary; *kanchak, onush aiasha*
grand; *chaha, chito*
grandchild, *ippok*
granddam; *appokni, ippokni*
granddaughter, *ippok tek*
grandees, *hatak pelichika*
grandeur; *chaha, chito, holitopa*
grandfather; *amafo, imafo*
grandmother; *apokni, appokni, ipokni, ippokni*
grandsire, *imafo*
grandson, *ippok nakni*
grant, to; *ibbak fohki, ima, kanchi, ome ahni*
grape; *pa*ⁿ*ki, pa*ⁿ*kachu*ⁿ*si*
grape juice, *pa*ⁿ*ki okchi*
grape water, *oka pa*ⁿ*ki*
grapevine, *pa*ⁿ*kapi*
grapple, to; *halalli, yichiffi, yichiffichi*
grappled, *yichowa*
grasp, *ishi*
grasp, to; *ishi, yichiffi, yichiffichi*
grasper, *yichiffi*
grass, *hashuk*
grass, great; *hashuk chito*
grass, stout; *hashuk chito*
grass, thick and heavy; *hashuk chito*
grass, tough; *nita i*ⁿ*pisa*
grass, wild; *nakshilup, hashuk ba*ⁿ*si*

grasshopper; *chashạp, chishaiyi, habin-shak, hataffo, hauachikchik, hạshuk chanshlichi, hionshakeli, iachikchik*
grassy, *hạshuk foka*
grate, to; *kanshkạchi, shakinlichi*
grate the teeth, to; *noti itikiselichi*
grateful, *aiokpanchi*
gratification, *fihopa*
gratified; *fihopa, yukpa*
gratify, to; *fihobli, yukpa, yukpalechi, yukpali*
grating, *kanshkạchi*
grating of the teeth, *shakahạchi*
gratitude; *aiokpanchi, aiokpạchi*
gratuitous, *aiilli iksho*
gratuity, *hạlbina*
gratulate, to; *aiokpạchi*
grave, *nuktanla*
grave (in music); *akanlusi, chito*
grave, a; *ahollohpi, hollohpi*
grave, to; *kullit holissochi*
graved; *bạshạt holisso, kulat holisso*
gravedigger; *ahollopi kạlli, hohpi*
gravel; *talunshik, tạlushik*
gravel, to; *tạlushik patali*
graveled, *tạlushik patạlhpo*
grave-minded, *chunkạsh weki*
graver, *kullit holissochi*
gravestone, *ahollopi tạli hikia*
graveyard; *ahollohpi, hatak aholopi*
gravid, *chakali*
gravity; *chunkạsh weki, weki*
gravy; *bila, na bila*
gray, *okchamali*
graybeard, *hatak sipokni*
gray-eyed, *oktalonli*
grayheaded, *pansh tohbi*
graze, to; *halelili, hạshuk impạchi, hạshuk ipeta, hopohka, hopohkạchi*
graze, to cause to; *ạmishoffi*
grazier; *wak apistikeli, wak pelichi*
grease; *bila, liteha, litikfo, na bila*
grease, to; *ahạmmi, fohki, litehạchi, litikfochi*
greased; *ahama, liteha, litikfo*
greasy; *bila, liteha, litikfo*
great; *aiyaka, anli, chakali, chito, hocheto, ishto*
great coat, *ilefoka chito*
Great Father, our; *Pinki ishtoka*
great-grandfather, *imafo*
great-grandmother; *apokni, ipokni*
great man; *hatak chito, hatak chitokaka, hatak hochitoka*

great one; *chitokaka, ishtokaka*
Great Spirit, *Hạshtali*
greater, *inshali*
greatest; *inshaht tati, moma inshali*
greatest, made; *inshaht taha*
greatly; *chitot, tokba*
greatness; *chito, hocheto*
greedy; *amosholi, anuktạpa, anuktạp-tua, atibạlli, bạnna fehna, holillạbi*
green; *himmitasi, kilinkoba, okchamali*
green (as newly cut wood), *okchanki*
green, to turn; *okchamali*
green dyestuff, *nan isht okchamalichi*
greenish; *okchakạlbi, okchakkuchi*
greenness, *okchamali*
greet, to; *aiokpạchi*
greet, to cause to; *aiokpạchechi*
greeter, *aiokpạchi*
greeting, *aiokpanchi*
greyhound, *ofi pạlhki*
griddle; *ampmahaia, ampmahaia apalạska*
gridiron, *nipaiạlhpusha*
grief; *nan isht anukhanklo, nukhanklo*
grieve, to; *ạlhpesạchi, nukhanklochi*
grieved, *nukhanklo*
grievous; *chito, elli, ilbạsha, illechi, nuk-hanklo, palạmmi*
grievously, *fehna*
grim, *pisa okpulo*
grimace, *nashuka okpulo*
grin, to; *itakyuinli*
grind, to; *fotoha, fotoli, hopansa, il-bạshali, shołichi*
grind at, to; *afotoli*
grind fine, to; *pushechi*
grind the teeth, to; *noti itikiselichi*
grind there, to; *afotoli*
grinder; *fotoli, na fotoli*
grinder (tooth); *noti, noti chukbi, noti isht impa, noti pokta*
grinding, *fotoha*
grindstone; *ashuahchi, chashampik, tạla-shuahchi, tạli ashuahchi*
grip, to; *apakshạna, yichiffi, yichiffit ishi*
gripe, *halạlli*
gripe, to; *ikfuka hotupali, ilbạshali*
gripped, *yichefa*
grit nuts, to; *wạshlichi*
grits, corn; *tansh lakchi*
gritted, *chichonli*
groan; *hinha, kifaha*
groan, to; *hinha, kifaha, kifanli*
groat, *pikayu*
grocery, *oka aiishko*

grog, *oka homi oka ibąlhto*
groggy, *haksi*
groom; *hatak himona ohoyo itauaya, tishu*
groove, *kula*
groove, to; *kulli*
grooved, *kula*
grope, to; *potoli*
gross; *achukma, chito, nia, okpulo, sukko*
gross, a; *auah tuklo bat auah tuklo*
grossness; *nia, sukko*
grot, *tąli chiluk chito*
grotto, *tąli chiluk chito*
ground; *aiisht ia ąmmona, akka, lukfi, yakni*
ground (sharpened); *fotoha, shoha, shuahchi*
ground, dry; *yakni shila*
ground, to; *akkaboli, akkatąla, hilechi*
ground, under the; *yakni anunkaka*
ground at, *afotoha*
ground fine, *pushi*
ground floor, *akka itipatąlhpo*
ground peas; *yakni anunka waya, yakni bąla*
ground thrown up, *wokokoa*
ground turned up, *wokokoa*
groundless; *anli, isht amiha iksho*
groundnuts; *yakni anunka waya, yakni bąla*
grounds, *lakchi*
group, *lukoli*
group, to; *lukolichi*
grouped, *lukoli*
grove; *iti lukoli, talaia*
grovel, to; *balali, makali*
groveler; *balali, hatak makali*
grow, to; *achoshunni, alikti, bafaha, bafąlli, hishi toba, hofąlli, ia, ikbi, inshaht ia, kunti, offo, okpicheli, okpichelichi, waloa, waya, wayąchi, wąlwąki*
grow, to cause to; *aliktichi, offochi*
grow at the side, to; *apatąli*
grow easy, to; *shuchapah*
grow long, to; *falaiat ia*
grow mean, to; *makali*
grow together, to; *pokta*
grow up, to; *asąno, hofanti*
grow up again, to; *unchololi*
growing, the; *offo*
growing up now, to be; *himona hofanti*
growl, *kileha*
growl, to; *kileha, tinkliha*
growler, *kileha*
grown; *asąno, hofanti, hofąlli*

grown person, *asąno*
grown together; *apokta, pokta*
grown up; *alikti, hofantit taha*
growth; *chaha, chito*
growth, a; *hofanti, hofąlli, offo*
growth, the; *alikti*
growth, the second; *uncholulli*
grub, *itakshish*
grub, to; *itakshish kulli, kulli*
grub ax, *itakshish isht chanya*
grubbed, *kula*
grubber, *itakshish kulli*
grubbing hoe, *itakshish isht chanya*
grubworm, *yąla*
grudge, *nukoa*
grudge, to; *haklo*
grudging, *potąnno*
gruel, water; *ashelokchi*
grumble, to; *nukoąt anumpuli*
grumbler, *nukoąt anumpuli*
grunt, to; *kifaha, kifanli, łunka, łunklua*
grunter; *łunka, łunklua*
grunting; *łunka, łunklua*
guard; *apistikeli, atoni, nam potoni, nan aiapistikeli, nan apistikeli, potoni*
guard, to; *ahinna, apistikeli, atoni, potoni*
guard a prison, to; *aboha kąllo apistikeli*
guard on a gun, *tanamp hoshintika*
guarded, *imaląma*
guarder, *apistikeli*
guardian, *apistikeli*
guess, *imahoba*
guess, to; *himak fokalit miha, imahoba*
guest, *nowąt anya*
guide; *ilaueli, na pelichi, pelichi, tikba heka*
guide, to; *afanali, ashummi, fololichi, ilaueli, pelichi, tikba heka*
guider; *ilaueli, tikba heka*
guile; *apakama, haksi*
guileful, *haksi*
guileless, *haksi keyu*
guilt; *aiokpulo, yoshoba*
guiltless; *ashąchi keyu, haksi keyu*
guilty; *haksi, yoshoba*
guilty man, *hatak hofahya*
guinea fowl, *sakkin*
guinea hen; *akank kofi, kofi chito*
guise, *isht shema*
gulf; *kolokbi, kolokobi, okhąta, yakni kolukbi*
gull, *haksi*
gull, to; *haksichi, yimmichi*

gulled; *haksi, yimmi*
gullet, *iⁿnalapi*
gully, *kolokbi*
gulp, to; *balakachi, hoeta, kalakachi, nalli*
gum; *hika nia, iti litilli, litilli, na litilli*
gum, to; *ahammi*
gum of the teeth; *noti itabalakchi, noti italbakchi, noti nukbalaⁿkchi, nutakbalaⁿkchi*
gum tree, *hika*
gun, *tanampo*
gun, air; *uski lumpa*
gun, big; *tanamp chito*
gun, to charge or load a; *tanamp abeli*
gun barrel, *tanamp nihi*
gun barrel, large; *tanamp nihi chito*
gun wiper; *tanamp isht kashokachi, tanamp isht kasholichi*
gunlock, *tanamp lapali*
gunner, *na huⁿssa*
gunpowder, *hituk*
guns, big; *tanamp hochito*
gunshot; *ahuⁿsa achafa, tanamp chito aiisht huⁿsa achafa*
gunsmith, *tanamp ikbi*
gunstick; *tanamp isht kashokachi, tanamp isht kasholichi*
gunstock, *tanamp aiulhpi*
gurgle, to; *tobokachi*
gush, to; *mitafa, mitaffi*
gust, *mali*
guts, *iskuna*
gutted, *iskuna kucha*
guzzle, to; *nalli*

habiliment; *isht shema, na fohka*
habit, *aiimalhpesa*
habit, a; *aiimomaka, aiimomachi, aiyamohmi, na fohka*
habit, to; *na foka foka, shema*
habitable, *aiokla hinla*
habitant, *aiokla achafa*
habitation; *aboha, aiasha, aiatta, chuka*
habited, *na foka foka*
habited with, *shema*
habitual; *aiimomaka, aiimomachi, shali*
habitually, *shali*
habituate, to; *achayachi, aiimomachi*
habituated, *aiimomachi*
hack; *chanaha holitopa, iti chanaha holitopa, iti chanaha palhki, lakofa*
hack, to; *chant tushtuli, iti chant tushalichi, sakahanli*

hackney, *isuba toksali*
had; *atok, atuk, hatuk, tali, tok, tuk, tukatok*
had been; *atuk, hatuk*
haft; *ahokli, aieshi, aiishi, aiulhpi, api, ulhpi*
haft, to; *hopi, opi*
hafted; *holopi, ollupi, ulhpi aⁿsha*
hag, *ohoyo isht ahollo*
haggle, to; *tushalichi*
hail, *hataⁿfo*
hail, to; *hataⁿfo, hatafottula, iⁿhoa*
hail, to cause to; *hataⁿfochi*
hailstone, *hataⁿfo*
hair; *hishi, hishi lapishta, paⁿshi*
hair, curled; *paⁿsh yiⁿyiki*
hair, gray; *paⁿsh tohbi, yushbokoli*
hair, having white; *yushbokoli*
hair, short; *wanuksho*
hair, short fine; *hishi wanuksho*
hair, sorrel; *paⁿsh umbala*
hair, thick; *paⁿshi chito*
hair, white; *paⁿsh tohbi, yushbokoli*
hair of a hog, *wonuksho*
hair of the head, *paⁿshi*
hair of the tail, *hasimbish hishi*
hair ribbon, *panshi sita*
hair tied up, *paⁿshi sita*
hairbrush; *paⁿsh isht kasholichi, paⁿsh isht kashokachi*
haircloth, *paⁿshi tanna*
haired; *hish aⁿsha, paⁿshaⁿsha*
hairless; *fomosa, paⁿsh iksho*
hairless being, *hachunchuba*
hairy; *hish aⁿsha, hishi chito, paⁿshaⁿsha, paⁿshi chito, wanuksho, wonuksho, wononuⁿkachi*
halcyon; *yohbi, yukpa*
hale; *hatak nipi achukma, nipi achukma*
hale, to; *halalli*
half; *aiiklanna, aiiklannaⁿka, bakapa, bakastoa, iklanna, kashapa, koyofa, palata*
half a bit, *pikayu*
half a day, *nitak iklanna*
half dead; *illa husi, illinaha*
half dime, *pikayu*
half-blood; *issish iklanna, itibapishi toba*
halfway; *aiiklana, iklanna*
halfway up, *abema*
hall; *aboha chito, aboha itintakla, aboha ititakla, aiapesa*
halloo, *ale*

halloo, to; *apahyạchi, apanlichi, atohni-chi, iⁿhoa, paⁿya, shakapa, tahpạla, tasaha*

hallooing, *shakapa*

hallow, to; *holitoblichi*

hallowed, *holitopa*

halo; *akonoli, hạshi akonoli*

halt; *hanali, imomokpulo*

halt, to; *issa, yokopa*

halter, *ibichilu foka*

halter, long; *isuba imponolo*

halter, to; *ibichilu foka foka*

halve, to; *bakastuli, bakạbli, kashạbli, koyoffi, palạlli*

halved; *bakapa, kashapa, koyofa, palata*

ham; *iyubi, obi*

hame; *ikonla inuchi, iti isht halạlli*

hamlet, *tạmahushi*

hammer; *chufak isht ahonạla, isht boa, tạli isht boa*

hammer, claw; *tạli chishaiyi*

hammer, iron; *tạli isht boa*

hammer, to; *anukfilli, boli, kạbaha, toksạli*

hammer, wooden; *iti isht boa*

hammered, *boa*

hammerer; *boli, kạbaha*

hamper; *isht talakchi, kishi*

hamper, to; *anuktuklichi*

hamstring, *iyiⁿ kalaⁿkshish*

hand, *ibbak*

hand!, *echi*

hand, to; *halạlli, ima, wali*

hand bone, *ibbak foni*

hand iron, *tạshiha*

handcuff, *ibbak isht talakchi*

handcuffed, *ibbak talakchi*

handful; *ibabukbo, ibbak alota, ibbak ạlhto*

handful, double; *ibbabukbo, ibbabukbo achạfa, ibbapukko*

handiness, *imponna*

handkerchief; *iachuka, nantapạski*

handle; *ahalạlli, ahokli, aiạlhpi, aieshi, aiïshi, aiulhpi, ạpi, ulhpi*

handle, to; *anumpuli, pasholi, potoli, pulli*

handled, *ollupi*

handmaid, *ohoyo*

hand-organ, *alepushi*

handsome; *achukma, aiukli, chito, ila-faya, ilafia, pisa aiukli*

handspike; *isht afana, isht tonolichi, iti isht tonolichi*

handwriting; *holisso, holissochi*

handy; *ạlhtaha hinla, imponna*

hang, to; *atakali hilechi, atakalichi, nuk-sita, nuksiteli, nuksitiffi, nuksitoha, nuksitoli, nukshiⁿfi, nukshinifa, taka-lechi, takali, takant fahakạchi, takoli, takolichi, tikelichi*

hang, to cause to; *takalechi*

hang a man, to; *hatak anuksiteli*

hang by or to, to; *atakali*

hang by the neck, to; *anuksiteli, nuk-shiniffi*

hang in the throat, to; *anukbikeli*

hang on, to; *atakoli, atakolichi, halạlli*

hang over, to cause to; *chashạnạchi*

hang over and down, to; *chashạna*

hang to, to; *achuⁿsha, anuksita, anuksit-kạchi, asitia, atakoli*

hang up, to; *ạba takali, ạba takalichi*

hanged, *nuksita*

hanger; *atakali, nuksiteli*

hanging, *takali*

hanging in, *achuⁿsha*

hanging over and down, *chashạna*

hanging to, *anuksitkạchi*

hangman; *hatak anuksiteli, hatak nuksi-teli, nuksiteli*

haniger, *nạni kạllo*

hank of cotton, *ponola itapạna*

hank of thread, *ponola fabạssa achạfa*

hank of yarn, *chukfi hishi itapana achạfa*

hanker, to; *bạnna fehna*

hapless, *imaleka shali*

happen, to; *ishkanạpa*

happiness; *isht ilaiyukpa, nana yukpa*

happiness, place of; *aiyukpa*

happy; *imanukfila ikkạllo, imponna, itiⁿkana, yukpa*

happy, to make; *yukpali*

happy place, *aiyukpa*

harangue, *anumpa isht hika*

harangue, to; *anumpa isht hika, anum-puli*

haranguer; *anump isht ika, anumpa isht hika*

harass, to; *intakobichi, tikabichi*

harassed; *intakobi, tikabi*

harbinger, *tikbaⁿya*

harbor; *afoha, anusi, peni ataiya, peni chitataya*

harbor, to; *anta, atukko, foha, fohachi, ishi*

hard; *achiba, chilakbi, chitoli, chitolit, hauạshko, homi, itatoba kạllo, kachombi,*

kamąssa, kapąssa fehna, kąllo, limimpa,
paląmmi, sąlbo
hard bread, pąska kąllo
hard-fisted man, hatak nan iⁿholitopa
hard-hearted; chuⁿkąsh kąllo, imanukfila kąllo, nukhaⁿklo iksho
hard-hearted man, hatak chuⁿkąsh kąllo
hard potato, ahe kamąssa
harden, to; akamąssa, akąllo, akmo,
akmochi, chilakbichi, hakmo, hakmuchi,
kamąssalli, kąllo, kąllochi, sąlbochi
harden by pounding, to; aląllichi
hardened; akmo, hakmo, kamąssa, kąllo,
sąlbo
hardener; kamąssalli, kąllochi
hardihood; chuⁿkąsh nakni, nukwia iksho
hardiness; nukwia iksho, paląmmi
hardly; chohmi, naha
hardness; kamąssa, kąllo, limimpa
hardness of heart, chuⁿkąsh kąllo
hardship, paląmmi
hardy; kąllo, kilimpi, nipi achukma, nukwia iksho
hare, chukfi pąttakita
hare, male; chukfi pąttakata nakni
hark! ah, mah!
hark, to; haponaklo
harlot; haui, ohoyo haui
harlot, to act the; haui, haui tobąt nowa
harlot, to become a; haui toba
harm; ashąchi, nan imokpulo, okpulo,
yoshoba
harm, to; hotupali, okpąni
harmed; hotupa, okpulo
harmful, nan okpąna hinla
harmless; nan okpąnahe keyu, nuktąla
harmonious; itiⁿkana, itilaui achąfa, itilaui fulota
harmonize, to; holba, itilauichi, kana,
ola itilaui, taloa ikbi, taloa itilaui
harmony; holba, itilaui, itilaui achąfa,
kana, ola itilaui
harness; isuba isht pilesa, isuba isht toksąli, isht haląlli, nan isht haląlli
harness, wagon; iti chąnaha isht haląlli
harp; alepa, hap
harp, to; alepa olachi
harper, alepolachi
harrow; taⁿsh api isht peli, yakni patafa
isht lapushkichi
harrow land, to; yakni lapushkichi
harsh; haksuba, homechi, kąllo, okpulo,
takba
harshness; imanukfila kąllo, kąllo
hart, isi chito nakni

hart leaf (the name of a plant), fakit
salakoba
harvest; abąsha, ahoyo, hoyo, na hoyo,
nan ahoyo, nan ąpawaya ahoyo
harvest, to; hoyo, kanchąk fohki, na waya
hoyo, na waya kanchąkfoki
harvest corn, to; tanchi hoyo
harvest ground, hoyo
harvested; kanchąk foka, tanchi hoyo
harvester; na waya hoyo, onush bąshli
harvestman; na waya hoyo, onush bąshli
has; atok, atuk, hatuk, tuk
has been; atuk, hatuk, tok, tuk
hasp; afacha, aiąlhpi, atapąchi, isht afacha,
isht ątapąchi, tąli isht afacha, tąli isht ąt-
tapąchi
hasp, to; afachali, ątapąchi, attapąchi
haste, tushpa
haste, to; tuⁿshpa, tuⁿshpalechi, tuⁿshpali
haste, to act in; tuⁿshpa
haste, to be in; anukwaⁿya
haste, to go in; tuⁿshpa
hasted, tuⁿshpa
hasten, to; anukwaⁿyąchi, ashaliⁿkąchi,
atuⁿshpa, atushpąchi, pąlhkichechi, pąlh-
kichi, tuⁿshpalechi, tuⁿshpali, tuⁿshpąchi
hastened; atuⁿshpa, pąlhki, tuⁿshpa
hastily, ashaliⁿka
hastiness, tushpa
hasty; anukwaⁿya, pąlhki, tushpa
hasty pudding, ashela
hat, a; shąpo
hat, to put on or wear a; shąpoli,
shąpolichi
hat brim, shąpo impahaia
hat crown; shąpo intąlla, shąpo nushkobo,
shąpo paknaka
hat lining, shąpo anuⁿkaka alata
hatband, shąpo isht talakchi
hatch, hofąlli
hatch, to; ahofąllechi, hofąlli, hofąllichi
hatched; ahofąlli, hofąlli
hatchet, iskifushi
hate, to; ahni, anukkilli, isht ikiⁿahno,
isht ikiⁿyukpo, nukkilli
hate, to cause to; isht ikiⁿahnochechi,
isht ikiⁿahnochi, nukkillichechi, nukkillichi
hateful, yuala
hater; isht ikiⁿahno, isht ikiⁿyukpo, nukkilli
hatred; anukkilli, nukkilli
hatter, shąpo ikbi
haughtiness, ilapunla

haughty; *ilapakpuⁿa, ilapakpunla, ila-*
puⁿa, ilapunla, ilefehnạchi
haul, *halạlli*
haul, to; *halạlli, shalạllichi, shali*
hauled, *shaⁿya*
hauler; *halạlli, shali*
haunt, to; *aiona, shilup aiasha*
haunted, *shilup aiasha*
hauteur, *ilefehnạchi*
have; *hatuk, tok*
have, to; *ahauchi, ahoba, ahumba, aⁿsha,*
halạlli, hikia, hokli, imaⁿsha, intola,
ishi, iⁿshi, itola, nukfoka, pisa, tonho
have been, *tuk*
haven; *atukko, peni chitataya*
havoc, *okpulo*
havoc, to; *okpạni*
haw, *chạnafila*
haw, black; *shạnafila*
hawk; *aiyichifichi, biakak, biyaⁿkak, hạnạn*
hawk, blue; *tuⁿstubi*
hawk, fish; *tuⁿstubi*
hawk, fork-tailed; *paⁿsh falakto*
hawk, hen; *aiyichifichi, akaⁿk ạbi, hatak-*
lipush
hawk, large red-tailed; *hasimbish*
humma
hawk, night; *luksupa foli*
hawk, pigeon; *aiyichifichi*
hawk, prairie; *hatapofokchi, hạtapofuk-*
chi, tapafakchi
hawk, sparrow; *shikkiliklik*
hawk, swallow-tailed; *paⁿsh falakto*
hawk, to; *kila*
hawthorn, black; *shạnafila*
hay; *hạshuk bạsha shila, hạshuk shila*
hay, to; *hạshuk shileli*
haycock, *hạshuk itạnaha*
haymaker, *hạshuk shileli*
hazard, *okpulo*
hazard, to go or act at; *himak fokali,*
yạmmak fokalechi
hazard, to run a; *himak fokalechi*
hazard, with; *himak fokalit*
hazardous; *himak fokalechi, yạmmak*
fokali
haze, *oktohbi*
hazy; *okhapayạbi, oktohbichi*
he; *atuk, ạt, ạto, ilap, ilapạt, ilaposh,*
ilạppa, in, mih, yạmma, yạmmak ashosh,
yạmmak ashot
he that; *kạnaho, kạnahosh*
he whom, *okma*

head; *anumpa nushkobo, ibetạp, nashuka,*
nushkobo, nushkoboka, paⁿshi, pelicheka,
tikba
head, to; *katapoli, nushkobo ikbi, nush-*
kobo tạbli, pelichi
head (as grain), to; *okshonli*
head, to cause to; *katạblichi*
headband; *bita, isuba imbita, nushkobo*
isht talakchi
head first; *hachowanạshi, himak fokalit*
head man, *pelicheka*
head of, *noshkoboka*
head of a cask, *ibish isht ạlhkạma*
head of a creek or stream; *ateli, bok*
wishahchi, ibetạp iⁿbok
headache, *nushkobo hotupa*
headdress; *iachuka, nushkobo isht shema*
headdress, king's; *miⁿko imiachuka*
headed; *katapa, okshonli*
headed, flat; *yushlatali*
headed, gray; *yushbokoli*
headed, round; *yushlitalih*
header, *nushkobo ikbi*
headlong; *hachowanạshi, himak fokalit*
headman; *hatak pelichi, hatak pelichika*
headmost, *tikbaⁿya*
headpiece; *shapo kạllo, tali bita*
headquarters, *anumpa aiạlhpisa*
headstall; *kapali isht talakchi nushkobo*
foka, nushkobo foka
headstrong; *chuⁿkạsh kạllo, halata kạllo,*
ilafoa
heady; *ahah ahni iksho, ilapunla*
heal, to; *alakofi, alakofichi, ạtta, ạttạchi,*
hopolạlli, lakoffi, lakoffichi, lakofolichi,
masalichi
heal the heart, to; *nuktalachi*
healable; *ạtta hinla, lakoffa hinla*
healed; *aiaⁿli, alakofi, ạtta, hopola,*
lakoffi, lakofoạt taha, lakofoht taha,
masali
healer; *ạttạchi, lakoffichi, na lakofichi*
health, *haknip achukma*
healthful; *achukma, haknip achukma*
healthy; *achukma, chukma, haknip achuk-*
ma, hatak nipi achukma, nipi achukma
healthy man, *hatak nipi achukma*
heap, to; *apullichi, ạlhpoachi, itạnahachi,*
itạnnali, itạnnalichi
heaped, *itạnaha*
heaper, *itạnnali*
hear, to; *haklo, haponaklo, ikhạna, nuk-*
foka

hear, to cause to; *haklochi, haponaklochi*
hear all, to; *oklunhalinchi*
heard, *haponaklo*
heard, just; *wakkalih*
hearer; *haklo, haponaklo, na haklo*
hearing; *ahaklo, haklo, haponaklo*
hearing, mutual; *itihaklo*
hearken, to; *haklo, haponaklo*
hearkener, *haponaklo*
hearsay, *anumpa chukushpa*
hearse, *hatak illi ashali*
heart; *chunkash, iklanna, imanukfila, iskuna*
heart, bad; *chunkash okpulo*
heart of a tree, the; *iti iskuna*
heart rising, *nuklibekachi*
heartache, *ilbasha*
heartbreak, *nukhanklo atopa*
heartburn; *akeluachi, chunkash lua, nuklibekachi*
heartburn, to cause the; *akeluachechi*
hearten, to; *yimintachi*
hearth; *iksita, luak aiulhti, luak ashoboli, luak iksita, luak ituksita*
heartily; *aiokluha, anli, fehna*
hearty; *chunkash yiminta, kamassa, kallo, nipi achukma*
heat; *alohbi, lashpa, maleli achafa, nukoa*
heat, mild; *lashpa ammona*
heat, prickly; *tombushi*
heat, to; *alohbichi, lahbachi, lashpachi, lashpali, libishli, yanhachi*
heated; *alohbi, lahba, lashpa, libisha, nuklibisha, nuklibishakachi, pikofa*
heater; *ilefoka halushkichi, lashpali, libishli*
heathen; *aba anumpa ikithano, hatak nan ikithano, okla nan ikithano, oklushi nan ikithano*
heathen nation, *oklushi abanumpa ikithano*
heathenism, *aba anumpa ikithano*
heave, *banatha*
heave, to; *aba pila, aba takalichi, banatha, chitot fiopa, hoetat pisa, kallot fiopa, pila*
heaven; *aba, aba aiachukmaka, aba shutik, aba yakni, shutik, shutik tabokaka*
heaven, in; *aba pilla*
heaven, to; *aba pilla*
heaven above, *aba aholitopa*
heavenly, *aba*
Heavenly Father, our; *Inki aba*

heavenly king, *aba minko*
heavens, the; *shutik, shutik tabokaka*
heavenward; *aba pilla, aba yakni pila*
heaver, *aba pila*
heaviest, *weki inshali*
heavily; *salahat, weki*
heaviness, *weki*
heavy; *chito, ilbasha, kallo, lukchuk chito, nukhanklo, nuna, palammi, salaha, shali, weki*
heavy, very; *weki fehna*
heavy thing, *na weki*
Hebrew, *Chu hatak*
hectic, *yanha*
hector, *hatak itakhapuli shali*
hector, to; *anumpulechi*
hectorer, *anumpulechi*
hedge, *aboli*
heed; *ahah ahni, haklo*
heed, to; *ahah ahni, anukfilli, haklo, imantia*
heedful; *aiokpanchi, haponaklo achukma*
heedless, *ahah ahni*
heedlessness, *ahah ahni iksho*
heel, *iyin kotoba*
heeler, *itakhapuli*
heels over head, to fall; *hachowanashi, hachowani*
heels over head, to throw; *hachowanashichi, hachowanichi*
heft, *weki*
heifer; *chelahpi, wak tek himmeta*
heigh !, *eha*
heigh ho !, *eha*
height; *chaha, falaia, nanih*
heighten, to; *achukmalechi, aiyabechi, chahachi*
heightened; *aiyabbi, chaha*
heinous, *okpulo*
heir; *immi, ushi*
held; *yichefa, yichowa*
hell; *aiilbasha, aiilbashaka, aiokpuloka, aiokpulunka, hatak illi shilombish aiasha, luak chito, shilombish okpulo*
hell fire, *aiokpuloka luak*
hellish, *aiilbasha imma*
helm; *penafana, peni isht afana, peni isht fullolichi*
helmet; *shapo kallo, tali bita*
helmsman, *afanata*
help; *apela, apelachi, ibawichi, ilhtohno, itapela, nan apela, nan apelachi, toksali*
help, to; *apela, apelachi, apepoa*
helper; *apela, apelachi, apepoa, itapela, nan apela, toksali*

helpless, *apela*
helve, *ąpi*
helve, to; *hopi, opi*
helved; *holopi, ollupi*
hem; *afohoma, apołoma, apołomoa, aposhokąchi, na foka afohoma*
hem, to; *afohommi, apołomąchi, apołomi, apołomolili, na foka afohomi*
hem of a garment, *apołomachi*
hemmed; *afohoma, apołoma, apołomachi, apołomoa*
hemmer, *apołomi*
hemorrhage, *issish mitafa*
hemp cloth; *na kąllo, nan tąnna kąllo*
hen; *akaⁿk tek, akaⁿka*
hen, old; *akaⁿk ishke*
hence, *kanima*
henceforth, *himmak pila*
henceforth, from; *himmak pillama*
henceforward; *himmak pila, himmak pillama*
hencoop, *akaⁿk inchuka*
henhouse, *akaⁿk inchuka*
henpecked, *hatak tekchi imantia*
henpecked husband, *hatak tekchi imantia*
her; *aⁿ, ilap, im, immi, in*
her own, *ilap immi*
herald; *anumpuli, nan anoli, nan apesa*
herb; *ąlba, haiyuⁿkpulo*
herbage; *haiyuⁿkpulo, hąshuk*
herculean, *chito*
herd; *aⁿya, aⁿya achąfa, lukoli*
herd, neat; *wak apistikeli*
herd, to; *itąnaha, itąnnali*
herdman; *ąlhpoa apistikeli, wak pełichi, wak apistikeli*
here; *iląppa, iląppak, iląppasi, yak*
here and there, *kanoⁿ*
herabout, *iląppa foka*
hereafter; *himmak, himmak foka, himmak pila, himmak pillama, himmakma, nitak tiⁿkbahe*
herein, *iląppa*
heretofore; *tiⁿkba, tikbama*
hermit; *hatak haiaka keyu, ilap biekąt kanima ątta*
heron, American green; *okataktak*
herpes, *hąllampa*
hers; *ilap, immi*
herself; *ilap, ilap akinli, ilapinli*
hesitate, to; *anukchito, anuktuklo, anukwia*
hesitation; *anuktuklo*
heterodox, *ąba anumpa yimmi keyu*

hew, to; *apąlichi, atushali, atilichi, chanli, kulli, tąli, tili*
hewed; *atila, tąla, tila*
hewed, place; *atila*
hewed on both sides, *ateląchi*
hewed timber, *tąla*
hewer; *apąlichi, atilichi, chanli, kulli, nan tili, tąli*
hewer of wood, *iti chanli*
hewn, *tąla*
hewn down, *akakoha*
hiccough; *chukfikoa, itukfikowa, nukfichoa, nukficholi*
hiccough, to; *chukfikoa, itukfikowa*
hiccough, to make one; *chukfikoli, chukfikolichi*
hickory, white; *uksak hąta*
hickory bark, *baluhchi*
hickory milk, *uksak ulhkomo*
hickory mush, *uksak alanta*
hickory nut; *oksuk, uksak*
hickory nut, large; *kapko, yuhe*
hickory-nut meat, *uksak nipi*
hickory-nut shell, *uksak foni*
hickory tree, *uksak ąpi*
hickory withe, *uksak ąpi bisinli*
hickup; *nukfichoa, nukficholi*
hickup, to; *nukfichoa, nukficholi*
hickup, to cause one to; *nukficholichi*
hid, *lumboa*
hid at, *aluma*
hidden; *luma, lumboa, lumaⁿka, tulhpakali*
hidden at; *aluma, alumpoa*
hide, to; *luhmi, luhminchi, lumpuli*
hide, *hakshup*
hide, to; *aluhmi*
hide at or in, to; *aluhmi, fohki*
hideous, *pisa okpulo*
hider, *luhmi*
hiding place; *aluma, alumpoa*
hie, to; *tuⁿshpa*
high; *aiilli chito, alota, ąba, ąba imma, chaha, kąllo*
high (as a price), *chito*
high (as to sound), *iskitini*
high and open, *mabi*
high price; *ąlhtoba chito, aiilli chaha*
high priest; *na hollochi iksa pełichi*
high rank, *holitompa*
higher, *chaha iⁿshali*
higher up; *abehma, abema*
highest; *chaha iⁿshaht tąli, chaha moma iⁿshali, iⁿshaht tąli, moma iⁿshali, nana moma iⁿshali*

high-hearted, *chuⁿkash chaha*
highland, *nanih foka*
high-minded; *chuⁿkash chaha, ilapunla, ilefehnachi, imanukfila chaha*
highness; *alhtoba chito, holitopa*
high-tempered, *chuⁿkash halupa*
high-water mark, *okchito aiali*
highway; *aiitanowa, hina chito, hina patha*
highwayman, *hina takla kahat huⁿkupa*
hilarity, *yukpa*
hill; *bokko, bunto, ibish, nanih, nanih foka, onchaba*
hill, high; *nanih chaha, unchaba chaha*
hill, large; *unchaba*
hill, made into a; *bunto*
hill, round; *nanih bunto, okfichoha, yakni bunto*
hill, small; *okfichoha*
hill, small round and long; *bilaⁿkti*
hill, to; *ibish ikbi*
hill corn, to; *apolichi, hopochi*
hill country, *yakni nanih foka*
hill up, to; *apullichi, buntochi*
hillock, *bokko*
hillock, small; *bokkushi*
hillside, *nanih chakpaka*
hilly, being; *bokko, kilhkiki, nanih foka, unchaba foka*
hilly region, *unchaba foka*
hilt; *ahalalli, ahokli, aiulhpi, bashpo falaia aiulhpi*
him; *aⁿ, iⁿ, ilap, ilapoma, im, in, yamma, yammak ash, yammak ashoⁿ*
him also, *yammak ma*
himself; *ilap, ilap akinli, ilap fena, ilapat, ilapinli, ilapo, ilaposh, ilappak*
himself, to; *ila*
hind; *okbal, ulbalaka*
hind, a; *isi humma tek*
hind legs, *obala*
hinder, *okbal*
hinder, to; *ataklammi, ataklammichi, ataklamoli, ataklokami, atapachi, imalami, olabechi, olabbechi, olabbi*
hinder, to cause to; *imalammichi*
hindered; *ataklama, ataklamoa*
hinderer; *ataklammi, ataklammichi, ataklamoli, ataklamolichi, hatak nan olabechi*
hindmost, *isht aiopi*
hindrance; *ataklama, ataklammi, isht ataklama, nan isht takalama*
hindrances, to cause; *ataklamolichi*
hindward, *aka*

hinge; *atakali, isht takali, isht takoli*
hinge, to; *atakali hilechi*
hip; *iyubbachosha, iyubi achoshoa, iyubi achoshuli*
hip joint; *iyubi achoshoa, iyubi achoshuli, obachoshuli*
hipped, *iyi kinafa*
hipped leg; *iyi kinafa, iyi kinali*
hire, *alhtoba*
hire, to; *atohno, atonho, tohno, tohnochi, tonhochi*
hire out, to; *pota*
hired; *alhtohno, ilhtohno*
hireling; *alhtohno, hatak na pilesa, hatak toⁿksali, ilhtohno, nam pilesa*
hirer; *atohno, atonho, nam pota, nan tohno, tohno*
his; *aiimmi, iⁿ, ilap, ilapo, im, imi, immi, in, yamma*
his excellency, *miⁿko*
his honor, *miⁿko*
his kind, *aiimmi*
his own; *ilap immi, ilap in, immi*
hit, *isso*
hit, to; *abolichi, bali, boli, isso*
hit and glance, to cause to; *tibiⁿllichi*
hit off, to; *tiballi*
hitch, to; *atakchechi, isso, kanali, takalechi, takali*
hitched, *atalakchi*
hitched to, *atakali*
hither; *ilappa, ilappak*
hitherto, *beka*
hive bees, to; *foe bilishke inchuka fohki*
hived, *foe bilishke inchuka foka*
hoar, *tohbi*
hoard, to; *achukmat boli*
hoariness, *tohbi*
hoarse; *itakha chinto, itukshila, kalanchah, nukshammi, nukshikiffi, nukshila, okshammi*
hoarseness; *nukshikiffi, okshammi*
hoarseness, to cause; *nukshammichi, nukshilachi, okshammichi*
hoary, *tohbi*
hoax, *lushka*
hobble; *isuba iyi isht talakchi, iyi isht intalakchi*
hobble, to; *iyintakchi, shaiksheli, takchi*
hobbled, *iyintalakchi*
hobby; *aiasittia, isuba*
hobgoblin; *abitampa, chuka ishi kanchak*
hobnail, *chufak nushkobo chito*

hock; *iyin kalankshish, iyinchampko foni iyubi*

hock, to; *iyin kalankshish tabli*

hod, *asholi*

hoe, *chahe*

hoe, to; *leli, okchali*

hoe corn, to; *hopochi*

hoe handle, *chahapi*

hoe up, to; *apelichi*

hoed; *lia, okchaha*

hoer, *okchali*

hog; *koshu, shukha*

hog, small; *shukha chanla*

hog, the side pieces of a; *shukha pasa*

hog house, *shukha inchuka*

hog sty, *shukha inchuka*

hog trough, *shukha aiimpa*

hog yard, *shukha inhollihta*

hogpen, *shukha inhollihta*

hogshead, *italhfoa chito*

hoist, to; *aba isht ia*

hold; *halanli, ishi*

hold!, *kia*

hold, to; *anli, asinta, alhto, eshi, halali, halalli, hikia, ishi, inshi, oktabli, shiyuli*

hold, to have a strong; *yicheli*

hold as a prisoner, to; *yukachi*

hold fast, to; *bochubli*

hold in the mouth, to; *kapali*

hold once, to; *halakli*

hold out, to; *achebachi*

hold out to view, to; *wali, weli*

hold the ears forward, to; *akkashaloli*

hold the head down, to; *yuhchonoli*

hold under the arm, to; *kifanali*

hold up, to; *auola*

hold up to view, to; *waloli*

holder; *halanli, halalli, ishi, isht ishi*

holding, *ishi*

holding up, *auola*

hole; *chiluk, chilukoa, chuluk, fichukbi, hichukbi, hochukbi, itopa, kolokbi, luna, lukafa, lukali, lunkachi, lumpa, tanampo ittopa, yakni chiluk*

hole, auger; *afotoha*

hole, to; *chiluk chukoa, chiluk ikbi, lukalichi, lukaffi*

hole, to enter a ; *chiluk chukoa*

hole, to make a; *chiluk ikbi*

hole of the ear, *haksobish chiluk*

hole in a rock, *tali chiluk*

hole in the ground, *yakni chiluk*

hole or house of a crawfish, *shakchi inchuka*

holes, full of; *shilunkachi*

holland, *ponokallo*

hollow; *chiluk, chilukoa, haksi, kofusa*

hollow, a; *chiluk, kofussa, kolokbi, yakni chiluk*

hollow, to; *kolokbichi*

hollowed; *kofusa, kofussa, kolokobi*

hollow-eyed; *okshilonli, oksholoni*

hollowhearted, *anli*

hollowness; *anli, chiluk, haksi, kolokbi*

hollowness of the eyes, *okshilonli*

holly tree, *iti hishi halupa*

hollyhock, *haiyunkpulo*

holster, *tanamp puskus inshukcha*

holy; *aianli achukma, aiyoshoba iksho, chunkash yohbi, holitopa*

holy; *aiyoshoba iksho, holitompa, holitopa*

holy day; *nitak hollo, nitak ilaualli*

holy-minded man, *hatak imanukfila holitopa*

holy one, *aba holitopa*

holy seat, *aionbinili holitopa*

homage, to; *aiokpachi, holitoblit aiokpachi*

home; *aiilli, chuka, inchuka, yakni*

home, to be or sit at; *chuka ansha*

home-born, *yakni*

home-bred, *chunka ansha*

homely; *aiukli keyu, pisa aiukli keyu*

homemade, *chuka akinli atoba*

homesick; *chuka impalata, palata*

homesick, to cause to be; *palatachi*

homesickness; *chuka impalata, palata*

homespun, *chuka akinli ashana*

homestead, *chuka osapa*

homeward; *chuka pila, chukimma*

homicide, *hatak abi*

homily, *aba anumpa isht ika*

hominy; *tanfula, tanlubo*

hominy salt, *hapi lakchi*

hone; *isht halupalli, isht shuahchi*

hone, razor; *nutakhisht shanfa ahalapuchi, nutakhisht shanfa ashuahchi*

hone, to; *sholichi*

honed, *shuahchi*

honest; *achukma, anli, apissanli, alhpesa, kostini*

honest heart, *chunkash anli*

honey; *champuli, foe, foe bila*

honey, bumblebee's; *onsini bila*

honey, to; *champulachi*

honey, wild; *foe bila iti ansha*

honeybee, *foe bilishke*

honeycomb; *foe bila hakshup, foe nia*

honeydew, *fichak champuli*
honeysuckle, wild; *okshulba*
honor; *aholitopa, chitokaka, holitopa*
honor, to; *aiokpachi, holitobli*
honorable, *holitopa*
honored, *holitopa*
honorer, *holitobli*
honorless, *holitopa*
hood; *hoshontika, ialipa*
hood, to; *ialipeli, ialipelichi, umpohomo*
hooded; *ialipa, umpoholmo*
hoof; *iyakchush, iyi*
hoof of a horse, *isuba iyakchush*
hook; *atakali, atakoli, chawana, chinachubi, chinakbi, hashuk isht bashli, tanakbi, tali chanakbi*
hook, iron; *tali chanakbi*
hook, to; *atakchechi, chinakbichi, tanakbichi, tanantobichi, tali chanakbi isht halalli*
hook, to make a; *chinakbichi*
hook and jab, to; *bali*
hook up, to; *okhawi*
hooked; *chinachubi, chinakbi, takali, tanakbi*
hooked, to make; *tanakbichi*
hoop; *italhfoa isht talakchi, iti poloma*
hoop, lady's; *woholachi*
hoop, to; *italhfoa takchi*
hooped; *alhfoa, italhfoa talakchi*
hooper; *italhfoa ikbi, italhfoa takchi*
hoot, to; *ola*
hop; *atonli, hanahchi, tolupli*
hop, to; *atonli, atulli, hanahchi, hila, tolupli*
hop and flit, to; *chachachi*
hope, to; *ahni*
hopper; *atonli, hanahchi*
horizon, *apisaka ali*
horn; *isht punfa, lapish*
horn, cow's; *wak lapish*
horner, *isht punfolachi*
hornet; *fohkul, pohkul*
horrible, *okpulo*
horrid, *okpulo*
horror; *nipi wannichi, nukshopat illi*
horse, *isuba*
horse, handsome; *isuba ilafia*
horse, roan; *isuba bokboki*
horse, small; *isuba iskitini*
horse bell, *isuba inuchi*
horse breaker, *isuba kostininchi*
horse collar, *isuba inuchi*
horse dealer, *isuba kanchi*

horse ford, *isuba akucha, isuba alopulli*
horse hobble, *isuba iyi isht talakchi*
horse mill, *isuba tanchi fotoli*
horse pass; *isuba akucha, isuba alopulli*
horse pasture, *isuba aiimpa*
horse race, *isuba itintimia*
horse range; *isuba aiimpa, isuba aiitanowa*
horse team, *isuba hioli achafa*
horse thief, *isuba hunkupa*
horse trader, *isuba itatoba*
horse trough, *isuba aiimpa peni*
horseback; *isuba nali, isuba omanili*
horsefly, *olana*
horsefly, big; *olana chito*
horsefly, green; *olana okchamali*
horsehair, *isuba hishi*
horseleech, *yaluns chito*
horseload, *isuba shali achafa*
horseman, *isuba omanili*
horsemint, *shinuktileli*
horseshoe; *isuba inshulush, isuba iyi tali lapali*
horseshoer, *isuba iyi tali iyi lapalichi*
horseway, *isuba inhina*
horsewhip, *isuba isht fama*
hose; *iyubi huski, obala foka*
hosier, *iyubi huski kanchi*
hosiery, *iyubi huski*
hospitable man, *hatak inkana achukma*
host; *albina, bina, chuka afoha hatak, laua, tashka chipota*
hostage, *yukachit halanli*
hostess, *chukafoha ohoyo*
hostile, *tanampi*
hostility; *itintanampi, tanampi*
hosts, *tashka chipota*
hot; *alohbi, alohbi, lashpa, nuklibisha, nukshikanli, palli*
hot, scalding; *lashpa fehna*
hot, to cause to be; *alolichi*
hot-brained man, *hatak nukoa shali*
hotel; *chuka afoha, chuka anusi*
hothouse; *alaksha, anunka lashpa*
hotness, *lashpa*
hotspur, *hatak nukoa shali*
hound, *ofi haksobish falaia*
hound, to; *ofi isht lioli*
hour; *hashi kanalli, hashi kanalli alhpisa, hashi kanalli isht alhpisa*
house; *aboha, aboha mismiki, chuka, chuka achafa, chukachafa, hatak chuka achafa, inchuka, isht atiaka*
house, bone; *tashka chuka*

house, charnel; *tashka chuka*
house, Indian; *hatak api humma inchuka*
house, king's; *miⁿko inchuka*
house, old-fashioned; *chukapishia*
house, single; *apelichika*
house, small; *chukushi*
house, to; *chuka, chuka chukoa, chuka foki, homo*
house door, *chukokhisa*
house field, *chuka osapa*
house lock, *chukashana*
house raising, *chuka itabanni*
housed; *chuka foka, holmo*
household; *chuka achafa, chukachafa, hatak chuka achafa*
household stuff, *aboha nan chukushpa*
householder; *chukachafa pelicheka, chukachafa pelichi*
housekeeper; *chukachafa pelicheka, chukachafa pelichi, itinchuka*
housewife, *ohoyo chuka pelichi*
housewright, *chukikbi*
housing; *aboha, chuka*
housing (for a horse), *isuba umpatalhpo oⁿlipa nan tanna*
hover, to; *awiachi, lopohachi*
how; *hacha, katimichi, katiohmi, katiohmi hoⁿ*
how is it?; *katiohmi, nantihmi*
how many?; *kanohmi, katohmi*
howbeit, *yohmi kia*
however; *amba, kaniohmi kia*
howitzer, *tanamp chito*
howl, *woha*
howl, to; *itabi, woha, wohwoha, wohwah, wowoha, yaiya*
howsoever, *kanohmi kia*
hubbub, *shakapa*
huckster, *nan chokushpa itatoba*
huddle; *itanaha, itapaiyata, lokussa*
huddle, to; *itahoba, itanaha, itapaiyali, lokussa, lokussalli, lukoli, tuⁿshpali*
huddled; *lokussa, lukoli*
huddler, *itapaiyali*
huffy; *nukoa*
hug, to; *sholi*
huge; *chito, hocheto, ishto*
hull, *hakshup*
hull, to; *pishuffi*
hull corn, to; *shibbi*
hulled, *pishofa*
hulloa, *ale*
hum; *kinihachi, kininiachi, shinihachi*

hum, to; *kinihachi, komohachi, lohmat taloa, lumat taloa, shinihachi, timihachi*
human, *hatak isht ahalaia*
human race or species, *hatak isht atia*
humane; *kana, nukhaⁿklo*
humanity; *hatak iⁿkana, hatak okla*
humble; *akaⁿlusi, akanli, hopoksia, ilbasha, nukhaⁿklo*
humble, to; *akanli, akanlusechi, chuⁿkash akkalusechi, hofayali, imaiyachi, kobaffi, kostininchi, nukhaⁿklochi*
humblebee, *imosini*
humbled; *akaⁿlusi, chuⁿkash akkaⁿlusi, ilbasha, kostini, nukhaⁿklo*
humbler; *akanlusichi, kobaffi*
humid; *oktohbichi, shummi*
humidity; *oktohbi, shummi*
humility, *chuⁿkash akkalusi*
hummingbird, *likuⁿklo*
hummock, *bokko*
humor, *aiimalhpesa*
humor, a; *lachowa*
humor, to; *alhpesachi*
humorist, *hatak yopula*
hump; *kobuna, kobunoa, kofuna, kofunoha*
humpback, *kofuna*
humpbacked; *kobuna, kofuna, koshuna*
humped; *kofuna, kofunoha, tobbona*
"humph," to say; *humpah*
hunch; *kofuna, tobli*
hunch, to; *tobli*
hundred, *talepa*
hundred, one; *talepa achafa*
hundred times, *talepaha*
hundredth, *isht talepa*
hung; *nuksita, nuksitiⁿfa, nuksitoha, takali, takoli*
hung by the neck, *nukshiniⁿfa*
hung up; *atakali, atakoli, aba takali, tikeli*
hunger; *hochaffo, hopoa*
hunger, to; *hochaffo, hopoa*
hungry; *hochaffo, hopoa*
hunks, *hatak nan iⁿholitopa*
hunt; *aiowa, hoyo, owa*
hunt, to; *aiowa, hoyo, ilhpapa, owatta, silhhi*
hunt beforehand, to; *tikbali*
hunter; *hatak illi achopa, hoyo, ilhpapa, isi abi, na hoyo, owatta, silhhi*
hunting expedition, *owa*
hunting frock, *ilefoka patafa*

hunting ground, *aiowạta*
huntress, *ohoyo owạtta*
huntsman, *hatak owạtta*
hurl, to; *fahạmmi, kanchi*
hurler, *fahạmmi*
hurricane, *apeli*
hurried; *anukwaⁿya, atuⁿshpa, pạlhki*
hurry, to; *anukwaⁿya, anukwaⁿyạchi, ashaliⁿkạchi, atuⁿshpa, atushpạchi, chekichi, pạlhkichi, tuⁿshpalechi, tuⁿshpali, tuⁿshpạchi*
hurt; *afetạpa, biła, fahama, hotupa, okpulo*
hurt, a; *hotupa, okpulo*
hurt, to; *bạshli, biłi, chanli, hotupachi, hotupali, ibatepa, okpạni*
hurter; *hotupali, okpạni*
hurtful, *okpulo*
husband; *achuka, aⁿhạtạk, hatak, iⁿhatak, ilauet aⁿya, itinchukali, ohoyo iⁿhatak*
husband, to; *ilatomba*
husbandman; *osapa isht ạtta, osapa toksạli*
husbandry; *osapa isht ạtta, osapa toksạli*
hush; *chulosa, issa, lumat aⁿsha, sạmanta*
hush, to; *chulosạchi, issa*
hush money, *isht haksichi*
hushed, *chulosa*
husk; *hakshup, lufa*
husk, to; *luffi, luli*
husked; *lufa, luha*
husker, *luffi*
huskiness; *pahshạla, shila*
husky; *pahshạla, shila*
hussar, *isuba omanili tạshka*
hussy, *ohoyo haksi*
hut; *aboha iskitini, abohushi, chukushi*
hut, to; *chukushi abeli*
hydrophobia, *holilạbi*
hymn; *ataloa, ạba taloa, ạlhtaloa, ạlhtạlwak*
hymn, to; *taloa*
hymn, to make a; *taloa ikbi*
hymn book, *holisso ataloa*
hymned, *tạlwa*
hypochondriac; *chuⁿkạsh iknakno, nakni*
hypocrisy; *ilahobbi, nan ilahobbi*
hypocrite; *ạba anumpuli ilahobbi, ilahobbi, nan ilahobbi*

I; *am, ạm, an, ạno, la, le, li, liⁿ, lin, lint, lish, lishke, sa, san, sạm, si, sia*
ibex, *isi kosoma nukshopa*

ice, *okti*
icicle; *okchanawisha, okti*
iciness; *kapạssa, okti chito*
icy; *kapạssa, okti, okti laua*
idea, *imanukfila*
ideal, *imanukfila*
identical, *mih*
identified, *atokowa*
identify, to; *atokoli, ibafoki*
idiocy, *imanukfila iksho*
idiot; *imanukfila iksho, imanukfila iksho aiimoma*
idiotic, *imanukfila iksho*
idle; *ahoba, ạlhpesa, intakobi, toksạli*
idle, to; *toksạli*
idle talk, *atukłakafa*
idleness; *intakobi, toksạli*
idler, *hatak intakobi*
idol, *Chihowa hobachi*
idolater, *Chihowa hobachit ikbit aiokpạchi*
if; *hokma, ikma, kma, ok*
if haply, *mak*
if it is not so, *keyuhokmạt*
if it may be, *yobakma*
if it shall; *hokma, yobakma*
if not, *keyukma*
if so be, *yohmi hokmạt*
ignis fatuus, *luak palali*
ignite, to; *lua, luachi*
ignited, *lua*
ignition; *lua, luachi*
ignoble, *makali*
ignominious, *makali*
ignoramus; *imanukfila iksho, nan ikhana, nan ikithano*
ignorance, *ikhana*
ignorant; *ikhana, imanukfila iksho, nan ikithano*
ignorant man, *hatak nan ikithano*
ignorantly, *ikithano*
ill; *abeka, achukma, ạlhpesa, nukoa, okpulo, yoshoba*
ill, an; *ishkanạpa*
ill-bred, *hopoksia*
ill-breeding, *hopoyuksa*
ill-nature; *anukchaha, hạlbaⁿsha iksho, nukoa*
ill-nature, to cause; *anukchahạchi*
ill-natured; *anukchaha, hạlhpaⁿsha iksho, nukoa*
ill-will; *hạlbaⁿsha iksho, nukkilli, nukoa*
illegal, *ạlhpesa*
illegible, *pisahe keyu*
illegitimate; *ạlla iⁿki iksho, iⁿki iksho*

illegitimate, an; *alla inki iksho*
illiberal, *inhollo*
illicit, *alhpesa*
illiterate, *holisso ithana*
illness; *abeka, ilbasha, yoshoba*
illume, to; *imanukfila tohwikelichi, toh-wikelichi*
illuminate, to; *imanukfila tohwikelichi, tohwikelichi*
illuminated, *tohwikeli*
illumination, *tohwikelichi*
illuminator, *tohwikelichi*
illumine, to; *imanukfila tohwikelichi, toh-wikelichi*
illusion, *ahoba*
illustrate, to; *haiakachi, holitoblichi*
illustrated; *haiaka, holitopa*
illustrious; *anoa, holitopa*
image; *aholba, holba*
image, to; *anukfillit hobachi*
image of a man, *hatak holba*
imagination, *imanukfila*
imagine, to; *anukfilli, anukfillit hobachi*
imbank, to; *sakti ikbi*
imbecile; *kota, liposhi*
imbibe, to; *ishi, ishko, nukfoka*
imbrue, to; *lachali*
imbrued, *lacha*
imitate, to; *ahobachi, hobachi, holbachi*
imitated, *holba*
imitation; *hobachi, holba, na holba*
imitator; *hobachi, hobachit ikbi*
immaculate; *anli, kashofa*
immaterial; *na fehna keyu, nana fehna keyu*
immature; *aiona, nuna, tushpa*
immeasurable; *ataha iksho, alhpesa*
immediate, *chekusi*
immediately; *ashalinka, cheki; chekusi, himonasi, mih, tunshpa, yakosi ititakla*
immemorial, *aiithanaka misha*
immense; *ataha iksho, chito, hocheto, ishto*
immensity, *ataha iksho*
immerge, to; *oklobushlichi*
immerse, to; *oklobushlichi, oklubbichi*
immersed; *oklobushli, oklubbi*
immersion; *oklobushli, oklobushlichi*
immigrant, *wihat ala*
immigrate, to; *wihat ala*
imminent; *bilinka, takanli*
immoderate, *atapa*
immoderately, *atapa*
immodest; *hofah iksho, kostini*

immolate, to; *Chihowa aiokpachi*
immoral; *haksi, okpulo, yoshoba*
immortal; *ataha iksho, illahe keyu*
immortalize, to; *illahe keyu ikbi, issahe keyu ikbi*
immovable; *kanallahe keyu, kanallichahe keyu, shanaiahe keyu, shanahe keyu*
immovably, *shanaiahe keyu*
immure, to; *aboha kallo foki, holihtachi*
immured, *aboha kallo foka*
immutability, *shanaiahe keyu*
immutable; *kanallahe keyu, kanallichahe keyu, shanaiahe keyu*
imp; *shilombish okpulo, ushi*
impair, to; *aiyabechi*
impaired, *aiyabbi*
impalpable, *lapushki*
imparity, *itilaui*
impart, to; *ima, ipeta*
impart knowledge, to; *anukfohkichi*
impartial, *kanimachi*
impartiality, *kanimachi*
impassable, *lopullahe keyu*
impassionate, *nuklibishakachi*
impassioned, *nuklibishakachi*
impatience, *nuktala*
impatient; *afekommi, affekomi, nuktanla iksho, nuktala*
impeach, to; *anumpa onuchi*
impeachable, *anumpa onucha hinla*
impeached, *anumpa onutula*
impeachment; *anumpa onuchi, anumpa onutula*
impeccable, *yoshobahe keyu*
impede, to; *ataklammi, salahachi*
impediment; *anuktuklo, ataklama, ataklammi, nan isht takalama*
impel, to; *iachi, tikbiachi*
impend, to; *waiya*
impenetrable, *chukowahe keyu*
impenitent, *yoshobatokkia nukhanklo keyu*
(imperative), *ashke*
imperfect; *alhtaha, ona*
imperishable, *toshbahe keyu*
impertinent; *ahalaia, inla immi kia ahalaia*
impetuous; *okpulo, palhki*
impiety; *Chihowa ikimantio, Chihowa inyimmi keyu, yoshoba*
impious, *Chihowa ikimantio*
implacable; *kostinahe keyu, nuktalahe keyu*
implement, *isht tonksali*

implore, to; *asilhha, asilhhachi*
implorer; *asilhha, asilhhachi*
impolite, *hopoksia*
impolitic, *hopoksia*
import, to; *miha*
importance, *nana fehna*
important, *nana fehna*
importune, to; *asilhha, ilbasha*
impose, to; *haksichi, onochi, pakamoli*
imposed; *apakama, onutula, pakama*
imposition, *ibbak onuchi*
impossible; *heto, nan ihma heto, nantih maheto, yohma himma keyu*
impostor, *hatak haksichi*
impotency; *hopoa, ilbasha, imomokpulo*
impoverish, to; *ilbashachi, ilbashalechi*
impoverished, *ilbasha*
impracticable; *yamichahe keyu, yamohmahe keyu*
imprecate, to; *ahni*
impregnate, to; *yammichi*
impregnated, *yammi*
impress, *inchunwa*
impress, to; *inchunli*
impression; *imanukfila, inchunwa*
impressive, *chunkash ishahinla*
imprint, to; *inchunli*
imprison, to; *aboha kallo foki, yukachi*
imprisoned; *aboha kallo foka, yuka*
imprisoner, *aboha kallo foki*
imprisonment, *aboha kallo foka*
improbable, *yomahe ahoba keyu*
improbably, *tokomi*
improper, *alhpesa*
impropriety, *alhpesa*
improve, to; *achchukmali, achukmalechi, achukmat inshaht isht ia, aiskia, aiskiachi, hochukmali, ikhana, kanihmi*
improve opportunity, to; *kaniohmichi*
improved; *achukma, imponna*
improver, *achukmali*
improvement; *ikhana, imponna*
imprudence, *hopoyuksa*
imprudent, *hopoksia*
impudent; *hofah iksho, ichapa, ichapoa, isht afekommi*
impudent man, *hatak afikommi*
impure; *haksi, kashofa, liteha, okpulo*
impurity; *kashofa, liteha, okpulo*
impute, to; *onochi*
imputed, *onutula*
in; *a, a, ai, aialhto, anunka, foka, i, pilla*
in a moment, *himonali*

in a short time; *ashalint, hopakikma, hopakikmako*
in advance *tikbali*
in company with, *iba*
in doubt, *anuktuklo*
in front, *tikba*
in haste, *ashalinka*
in particular, *ak*
in person, *ilap fena*
in season, *nitanki*
in some degree, *chohmi*
in that place, *a*
in that time, *fokakash*
in the least degree, *kamomi*
in the meanwhile, *aiitintakla*
in the rear, *anshaka*
in the sight of, *tikba*
in the smallest amount, *kamomi*
in the way, *tankla*
in them, *okla ilappakon*
in this direction; *ilappa pila, olehma*
in this place, *ilappak*
in time, *nitanki*
in truth, *anlit*
in vain, *keyut*
in whom, *ilappak*
inability; *isht ikono, kallo keyu, lauechi kat ikono*
inaccessible, *ona*
inaccurate; *anli, ashachi*
inaction, *ilhkoli keyu*
inadequate, *lauechi*
inadmissible; *alhpesa, ishahe keyu*
inanimate, *nan okchaya keyu*
inattentive, *aiokpanchi keyu*
inaugurate, to; *hilechi*
incalculable, *holhtinahe keyu*
incapable; *yamichahe keyu, yohmahe keyu*
incarcerate, to; *aboha kallo foki*
incarcerated, *aboha kallo foka*
incarceration, *aboha kallo foka*
incarnate, *haknip toba*
incarnation, *haknip toba*
incase, to; *itombi fohki*
incased, *itombi fohka*
incautious, *ahah ahni*
incendiary, an; *chuka hukmi, hukmi*
incendiary (one who inflames the minds of people), an; *achowa*
incense; *balama, na balama*
incense, to; *nukoachi*
incense (scatter incense on), to; *balamachechi*

incensed, *nukoa*
incessant, *bilia*
inch, *ibbak ishki pątta achąfa*
incipient, *ąmmona*
incision; *bąsha, bąshli*
incite, to; *okchąli, tohno*
incited; *nukpąlli, okcha*
incitement, *nan isht nukpąllichi*
inclement, *okpulo*
inclination, *ahni*
incline, to; *ahni, chiksanąlli, imanukfila shananchi*
inclined to one side, *chiksanali*
inclose, to; *apakfobli, fohki, holihtąchi*
inclosed; *apakfopa, fohka, holihta*
inclosure; *aholihta, holihta*
include, to; *aieninchi, ishi*
incombustible, *luahe keyu*
income, *ibafoka*
incommode, to; *anumpulechi, atakląmmi*
incompetent, *ona*
incomplete, *ąlhtaha*
incomprehensible, *ikhąnahe keyu*
inconsiderate, *ahah ahni*
inconstant, *shanaioa*
incorporeal, *haknip iksho*
incorrect; *aⁿli, ąlhpesa, ona*
incorrigible, *kostinahe keyu*
incorrupt, *okpulo keyu*
increase, *ibafoka*
increase, to; *atoba, chitoli, hochetoli, ia, iⁿshaht ia, iⁿshaht isht ia, iⁿshali, laua, lauachi, nan inlauachi, unchololi*
increased, *iⁿshali*
incredible, *yimmahe ąlhpesa*
incrust, to; *hakshup ikbi*
incubate, to; *alata, binili, takakanli*
incubus, *shimoha*
incurable; *alakofahe keyu; ąttahe keyu, lakoffahe keyu*
incurvate, to; *bikulli, tanakbichi, waiyąchi*
incurvated, *tanakbi*
indebted, *aheka intakanli*
indecent; *chakapa, okpulo, pisa ikachukmo*
indecisive, *imanukfila laua*
indeed; *akąt, aume, chukah, hato, mąli, ome, yąmma*
indemnify, to; *aiskiachi*
indent, to; *lakolichi, lanlakechi*
indented; *lakofa, lakoli, lanlaki*
indents, *lakoli*
independence, *ilapunla*

independent; *ilapunla, inla anukcheto keyu*
india rubber, *holisso isht kashoffi*
Indian; *hatak, hatak ąpi humma*
Indian agent, *na hollo holitopa*
indicate, to; *haiakąchi*
indict, to; *anumpa kąllo onuchi, anumpa onuchi*
indicted, *anumpa onutula*
indifferent, *ahni*
indigence, *ilbąsha*
indigent, *ilbąsha*
indignant; *isht ikiⁿahno, nukkilli, nukoa*
indignation; *nukkilli, nukoa*
indigo; *nan isht okchakuchi, nan isht okchamalichi*
indirect; *aⁿli, apissali, okpulo*
indiscreet, *hopoksia*
indispose, to; *abekąchi*
indisposed; *abeka, ahni*
indisposition; *abeka, ahni*
indissoluble, *bilahe keyu*
indite, to; *holissochi*
indited, *holisso*
individual; *achąfa, hatak achąfa, hatak lumbo, nan achąfa*
individually, *achąfalit*
indocile, *nan ikhąnahe keyu*
indoctrinate, to; *ikhananchi, imabąchi*
indoctrinated, *ikhana*
indolence, *intakobi*
indolent; *intakobi, toksąli*
indoors, *aboha*
indue, to; *fohkąchi*
indurate, to; *kąllo, kąllochi*
indurated, *kąllo*
industrious, *aiokpąchi*
industry, *aiokpąchi*
inebriate, to; *haksi, haksichi*
inebriated; *haksi, oka haksi*
inebriation; *haksi, oka haksi*
inebriety, *haksi*
ineffable, *anoa tąpa*
ineffectual; *aⁿli, nan ihmi keyu, ona*
inefficient, *ahoba*
inequality, *itilaui*
inestimable; *holhtinahe keyu, holitopa atąpa*
inevitable; *alakofahe keyu, apakfopahe keyu*
inexcusable; *mosholahe keyu, nan isht amihahe iksho*
inexorable, *paląmmi*

inexperience; *ikhana, imomakat pisa keyu*
inexperienced; *ikhana, imponna*
inexpert, *imponna*
inextinguishable, *mosholahe keyu*
infallible, *ashachahe keyu*
infamous, *nan okpulo anno*
infancy, *atta ammona*
infant; *allunsi, atta ammona, puskus*
infant boy, *chinshka keyu*
infant girl, *chinshka*
infanticide, *allonsabi*
infantry, *tashka chipota*
infatuate, to; *tasembochi*
infatuated, *tasembo*
infatuation, *tasembo*
infect, to; *abekachi, isht abekachi, okpani*
infected; *abeka, okpulo*
infection; *abeka, abeka haleli, isht abeka, nana haleli*
infection, to take; *albonli*
infectious, *abeka haleli*
inferior, *laue*
inferior, very; *okpulosali*
infernal; *aiilbasha imma, shilombish okpulo aiilbasha ansha*
infernal powers, *shilombish okpulo*
infernal spirit, *shilombish okpulo aiilbasha ansha*
infest, to; *apistikeli*
infidel; *aba anumpa ikyimmo, aba anumpa yimmi, yimmi*
infidelity, *aba anumpa ikyimmo*
infinite; *aiali iksho, ataha iksho*
infinity, *ataha iksho*
infirm; *kallo, liposhi*
infirmity; *iksitopa, liposhi*
inflame, to; *chiletalli, chilitachi, libbichi, luachi, nukoa, nukoachi*
inflamed; *chilita, humma, lashpa, libbi, lua, nukoa, oshanichi, pishpiki*
inflamed with passion, *chunkash lua*
inflammation; *oshanichi, yanha foka*
inflammation of the kidneys, *haiyinhchi hotupa*
inflate, to; *shatammichi*
inflated, *shatammi*
inflexible, *bikotahe keyu*
inflict, to; *onochi*
inflicted, *onutula*
inflicter, *onochi*
infold, to; *abonulli*
infolded, *abunkachi*

inform, to; *anoli, haklochi, ikhananchi, imabachi*
informant; *anoli, haklochi, nan anoli*
information; *anoa, ikhana*
informed; *anoa, ikhana*
informer; *anoli, anumpa onuchi, hatak nan anoli, nan anoli*
infringe, to; *kobaffi*
infringed, *kobafa*
infuriate, *nukoa*
infuriate, to; *nukhobelachi, nukoachi*
infuriated, *nukhobela*
infuse, to; *ani*
ingenious, *imponna*
ingenuity, *imponna*
ingenuous, *lumiksho*
ingratitude, *aiokpachi*
inhabit, to; *aiatta, aiokla, anta, atta*
inhabitable, *aiokla hinla*
inhabitant; *aiasha, aiatta, aiokla achafa, hatak, okla*
inhabitant, male; *nakni tashka*
inhabited, *aiokla*
inhale, to; *fiopa*
inherit, to; *ishi*
inheritance, *immi*
inhibit, to; *olabbi*
inhume, to; *hohpi*
inimical, *kana*
inimitable, *hobachahe keyu*
iniquitous, *yoshoba*
iniquity; *nan ikalhpeso, yoshoba*
inject, to; *bohpuli, fohki*
injudicious, *hopoksia*
injunction, *anumpa alhpisa*
injure, to; *hotupachi, hotupali, ibatepa, okpani*
injure the feelings, to; *bili*
injure the heart, to; *chunkash okpani*
injured; *hotupa, okpulo*
injured, partially; *toshboa*
injurious; *achukma, okpulo*
injury; *imokpulo, kanapa, nan okpulo*
injury, accidental; *afetapa*
injustice, *alhpesa*
ink, *isht holissochi*
ink, black; *isht holissochi lusa*
ink, red; *isht holissochi humma*
ink bottle, *isht holissochi aialhto*
ink maker, *isht holissochi ikbi*
inkhorn, *isht holissochi aialhto*
inkstand, *isht holissochi aialhto*
inland, *yakni iklana pilla*

inmate, *ibaiątta*
inmost, *anuⁿkaka fehna*
inn; *aboha afoha, aboha aiimpa, anusi, chuka afoha, chuka anusi*
inner; *aṇuⁿka, anukaⁿka ikląnna*
innkeeper; *chuka afoha hatak, chuka afoha iⁿhikia*
innocence, *aiokpulo iksho*
innocency, *aiokpulo iksho*
innocent; *aⁿli, ashąchi keyu, yoshoba keyu*
innovate, to; *inląchi*
innovation, *inla*
innovator, *inląchi*
innumerable; *aholhtina iksho, holhtinahe keyu*
inoculate, to; *ibbak iⁿlumplit ikhiⁿsh foki*
inoculated, *ibbak iⁿlumpąt ikhiⁿsh foka*
inoffensive, *okpulo isht iⁿshat ia*
inordinate, *atąpa*
inquire, to; *aponaklo, ponaklo*
inquire after, to; *hoyo, panaklo*
inquirer; *aponaklo, hoyo, nam ponaklo, panaklo, ponaklo*
inquiry, *aponaklo*
inquiry, mutual; *itimponaklot aⁿsha*
inquisitive, *aponaklo shali*
insane, *tasembo*
insane, to render; *tasembochi*
insanity, *tasembo*
insatiable; *anuktąpa, anuktąptua, fihopahe keyu*
insatiate, *fihopahe keyu*
inscribe, to; *holissochi*
inscribed, *holisso*
inscription; *holisso, oⁿholisso*
inscrutable; *akostininchahe keyu, ikhąnahe keyu*
insect, *shuⁿshi*
insect, a kind of; *lanla*
insecure, *atukko*
insensibility, *imanukfila kapąssa*
insensible; *chuⁿkąsh kapąssa, ikhana, imanukfila kapąssa, shimoha*
insert, to; *achoshuli, ibafoki*
inserted; *achushkąchi, achushoa*
inside; *aiąlhto, anuⁿka*
inside, the; *anuⁿka, anuⁿkaka*
inside of the bend; *potoma*
inside of the earth, *yakni anuⁿkaka*
inside out, to turn; *anukfilema, anuk-filemoa, anukfilemoli, anukfilimmi, anukpiliffi, anukpiloli*

inside out, turned; *anukfilema, anuk-filemoa, anukpilefa, anukpiloa*
insidious, *haksi*
insight, *anuⁿkaka pisa*
insignia, *isht ąlhpisa*
insignificant; *ahoba, makali*
insincere, *aⁿli*
insipid, *ahoba*
insolent; *ilapunla, ilefehnąchi*
insolvent, *aheka*
inspect, to; *pisa*
inspection, *pisa*
inspector, *pisa*
inspiration; *ilafiopa, nukfokichi*
inspire, to; *fiopa, nukfokechi, nukfoki*
inspired; *ąlhpuⁿfa, nukfoka*
inspirit, to; *okchąli, yimintąchi*
inspirited; *okcha, yimmita*
inspissate, to; *ashelachi*
inspissated, *ashela*
install, to; *binilichi, hilechi*
installation, *hilechi*
installed, *hikia*
instance; *himonna, nana yąmohⁿni*
instant; *himak, tushpa*
instant, an; *yakosi ititakla, yohmit itintakla*
instantaneous, *yakosi ititakla*
instantly; *himonali, himonasi, yakosi*
instate, to; *hilechi*
instead, *ąlhtoba*
instep; *iyi paknaka, iyi pąta paknaka*
instigate, to; *itohnichi, tohno, tonhochi*
instigated, *ilhtohno*
instigation, *itohnichi*
instigator; *itohnichi, nan tohno, ann tohnochi, tohnochi*
instinct, *aiimąlhpesa*
institute, to; *hilechi, ia*
institution; *anumpa ąlhpisa, ąlhpisa, holisso aiithąna*
institutor; *hilechi, holisso ithąnanchi, nan apesa*
instruct, to; *ahobąchi, anukfohkachechi, apesa, ikhananchi, ikhąnanchi, imabąchi, imponnąchi, miha, nukfokąchi, pisachi*
instruct before, to; *tikbanli iⁿmiha*
instructed; *ąlbąchi, ikhana, nan ikhana, nukfoka*
instruction; *anumpa, ikhana, ikhananchi*
instructions, to receive; *anump imeshi*
instructor, an; *anukfokichi, hatak imabąchi, holisso ithąnanchi, holisso pisachi, ikhananchi, nan ikhananchi, nan imabąchi, nana imabąchi*

instructress, *ohoyo holisso ithananchi*
instrument; *holisso, isht toⁿksạli, isht yạmmichi*
instrument for winnowing grain, *ufko*
insufferable; *atạpa fehna, palạmmi atạpa*
insufficient; *laua, ona*
insulate, to; *naksika binilichi*
insulated, *naksika binili*
insult, to; *chuⁿkạsh hutupali, hotupali*
insulted, *chuⁿkạsh hutupa*
insupportable, *palạmmi atạpa*
insurrection; *okla achạfa itibi, tanampi*
integrity; *aⁿli, apissanli*
integument, *hakshup*
intellect, *imanukfila*
intellectual, *imanukfila aiimma*
intelligence; *anumpa, ikhana*
intelligent, *ikhana*
intelligible, *ikhạna hinla*
intemperance, *okishko*
intemperate; *atạpa, hatak okishko atạpa*
intend, to; *ahni, imanukfila*
intendant, *pelicheka*
intense; *atạpa, fehna*
intensely, to do; *fehna*
intensity, *kallo*
intent; *ahni, chilita, imanukfila*
inter, to; *hohpi*
intercede, to; *anumpuli*
intercept, to; *katapoli, katạbli, oktạbli*
intercept, to cause to; *katạblichi*
intercepted; *katapa, oktạpa*
intercession; *isht anumpa, isht anumpuli*
intercessor, *isht anumpuli*
interchange, *itatoba*
interchange, to; *itatoba*
intercourse; *ahalaia, itimahalaia*
interdict, *anumpa ạlhpisa*
interest; *ahalaia, alapanli, halaiya, isht ahalaia*
interest, object of; *nan isht ahalaia*
interest, to; *ahalaia, anukpạllichi, nukpạllichi*
interest, to cause to bring; *chelichi*
interest, to feel; *anukpạlli*
interest, to give or charge; *alapalechi*
interest, to have an; *ahalaia*
interest the mind, to; *imanukfila ishi*
interested; *afetipa, ahalaia, anukpạlli, ạffetipa, halaiya, nukpạlli*
interested in, to be; *aiahalaia, halaia*

interfere, to; *ataklạmmi, isso*
interior; *anuⁿka, anuⁿkaka, iklạnna*
interment; *hatak hopi, hohpi*
intermingle, to; *aiyummi*
intermission, *foha*
intermit, to; *issạchi*
intermix, to; *aiyummi*
intermixed, *aiyuma*
internal, *anuⁿkaka*
interpose, to; *apela, olạbbi*
interpret, to; *anumpa tosholi, ạlhtosholi*
interpretation, *anumpa toshoa*
interpreted; *anumpa toshoa, ạlhtoshoa*
interpreter; *anumpa tosholi, tosholi*
interred, *hollopi*
interrogate, to; *ponaklo*
interrogation; *atoma, cho, ponaklo*
interrupt, to; *ataklạmmi*
interrupted, *ataklạma*
interruption; *ataklạma, ataklạmmi*
intersect, to; *aiyukhạna, aiyukhạnni*
intersperse, to; *fimmi*
interspersed, *fimimpa*
interstice; *wakalali, wakla*
interval; *ititakla, patasạchi*
intervene, to; *itintakla*
intervention, *itintakla*
interview, *itipesa*
intestine, *anuⁿkaka*
intestines, the; *iskuna*
intimate, *fehna*
intimate, an; *kana*
intimidate, to; *nukshobli*
intimidated, *nukshopa*
into, *takla*
intolerable; *atạpa, palạmmi atạpa*
intolerant, *atạpa*
intonate, to; *hiloha, ola, olachi*
intoxicate, to; *haksichi*
intoxicated; *haksi, oka haksi, shimoha*
intoxication; *haksi, oka haksi*
intrepid, *nukwia iksho*
intrigue, *haksichi*
intrinsic; *aⁿli, anuⁿkaka, fehna*
intrinsical, *anuⁿkaka*
introduce, to; *ikhananchi*
introducer, *isht ạla*
introduction, *isht ạla*
intrude, to; *binili, taⁿkla binili*
intruder; *binili, taⁿkla binili*
intrusion, *binili, taⁿkla binili*
intrust, to; *ibbak fohki*
intrusted, *ibbak fohka*

intwine, to; *apakshạnni*
intwined, *apakshạna*
inundate, to; *okchitochi, okchitoli*
inundated, *okchito*
inundation; *oka bikeli, okchito*
inure, to; *imomạchi*
inured, *imoma*
invade, to; *chukoa, ibachukoa*
invaded, *ibachukoa*
invader, *ibachukoa*
invalid, *aksho*
invalid, an; *abeka shali, liposhi*
invalidate, to; *kobạffi*
invalidated, *kobafa*
invaluable, *holitopa atạpa*
invariable; *apissanli, shanaioa keyu*
invasion, *ibachukoa*
invective, *anumpa okpulo*
inveigh, to; *chakapa*
invent, to; *anukfilli*
inventory, *ạlhpoyak holisso*
invert, to; *atobbichi, lipeli*
inverted; *lipa, lipia*
invest, to; *fohkạchi, hilechi, ima*
invest another, to; *shemạchi*
invested; *fohka, shema*
investigate, to; *pisa*
investigation, *pisa*
investigator, *pisa*
inveterate; *kamạssa, kạllo, sipokni*
invidious, *nukkilli*
invigorate, to; *kạllochi, nukoa, yimin-
    tạchi*
invigorated; *kạllo, yimmita*
invincible, *imaiyahe keyu*
invitation, *asilhha*
invite, to; *asilhha, hoyo, nukpạllichi*
invited, *aianowa*
invocate, to; *asilhha*
invocation, *asilhha*
invoke, to; *asilhha*
involuntary, *ilap ahni keyu*
involve, to; *afoli, ibafoki, umpohomo*
inward, *anuⁿkaka*
inwards, the; *iffuka, iskuna*
inwrap, to; *abonulli, afoli*
inwrapped, *abuⁿkachi*
ipecacuanha, *haiyuⁿkpulo ishkot hoita*
irascible, *nukoa shali*
ire, *nukoa*
Ireland, *Ailish yakni*
iris, *hinak bitepuli*
Irish, *Ailish*
Irish people, *Ailish okla*

Irish potato, *ahe lumbo*
Irishman, *Ailish hatak*
irksome, *ahchiba*
irksomeness, *ahchiba*
iron, flat; *tali patạssa*
iron, hard; *tali kạllo*
iron, plug of; *tali kolofa*
iron, remnant of; *tali kolofa*
iron, sad; *tali patạssa*
iron, sheet; *tali tapạski*
iron, slender round piece of; *tali fo-
    bạssa*
iron, stump of; *tali kolofa*
iron, thin; *tali tapạski*
iron, to; *ahạmmi*
iron, twisted; *tali shạna*
iron, welded; *tali itạchaka*
iron band, *tali fohoma*
iron bolt, *tali fobạssa*
iron button, *tali isht talakchi*
iron chain, *tali chosopa*
iron hinge, *tạlatakali*
iron hook; *tạlatakali, tali chinakbi, tali
    tanakbi*
iron hoop, *tali fohoma*
iron pin, *tali fobạssa*
iron pot, *iyasha*
iron ring, *tali chạnaha*
iron screw, *tali shạna*
iron spindle, *tali fobạssa honula*
iron spoon, *tạlạlhpi*
iron wedge, *tali isht pạla*
ironsmith, *boli*
ironwood; *itukawiloha, iyanạbi*
irony, *yopula*
irradiate, to; *shohmalalichi*
irradiated, *shohmalali*
irradiation, *shohmalali*
irrational, *imanukfila iksho*
irreconcilable; *ạlhpesa, hopolahe keyu,
    itilauahe keyu, nan aiya*
irrecoverable, *falama*
irredeemable; *chumpahe keyu, lakoffahe
    keyu*
irregular, *itilaui iksho*
irreligious, *ạba anumpa yimmi keyu*
irreparable, *aiskiahe keyu*
irreproachable, *anumpa onutulahe keyu*
irresistible; *oktạblahe keyu, tạpahe keyu*
irrigate, to; *lạchali*
irrigated, *lạcha*
irritable; *baⁿshkiksho, nukoa hinla, nu-
    koa shali*
irritate, to; *nukhobelạchi, nukoạchi*

irritated, *nukhobela*
irruption, *ibachukoa*
is it now?, *yammak oⁿ?*
is it so?, *yammak oⁿ?*
is it that?, *yammak oⁿ?*
island; *nanih tashaiyi, tashaiyi, talhkachi*
isle, *tashaiyi*
isolate, to; *naksika hilechi, naksikachi*
Israelite, *Chu hatak*
issue, *ushi*
issue, an; *kucha, umbokafa*
issue, to; *fimmi, kucha, kuchi*
issueless, *ushi iksho*
isthmus, *yakni ikonlo*
it; *aⁿ, ak, hoh, iⁿ, ilappa, im, in, mih, yamma, yammak oka*
it is, *oke*
it is so; *omiha, omishke*
it is the, *oke*
it may be; *hota, tokok, yoba*
it might be, *tokok*
it must be so, *yamohmahe alhpesa*
it seems so, *hota*
itch, the; *washko*
itch, to; *yauolichi*
itch, to cause the; *washkoli*
itch, to have the; *washkali*
itching, *yauolichi*
iterate, to; *albiteli*
iteration, *albiteli*
itinerant, *nowat fullokahanchi*
itinerate, to; *nowat fullokahanchi*
its; *ilap, immi, in*
itself; *ilap, ilap akinli, ilapo inli, ilappak*
itself, to; *ila*
ivory; *aifoli, hatak lusa iⁿyannash noti isht itibbi*
ivy, *taluⁿwa*

jab, *baha*
jab, to; *bahaffi, bali*
jabbed; *baha, bahafa*
jabber, *labaha*
jabber, to; *labahachi*
jabberer, *labaha*
jabbering, to keep; *labahahanchi*
jackass; *isuba haksobish falaia nakni, isuba nashoba nakni*
jacket; *ilefoka yushkololi, na foka kolukshi*
jade; *isuba liposhi, ohoyo makali*
jade, to; *liposhichi, tikabichi*
jaded, *liposhi*
jag, to; *lakoli*
jagged, *lakowa*

jags, *lakoⁿwa*
jaguar, *koi*
jail, *aboha kallo*
jail, to; *aboha kallo foki*
jailor, *aboha kallo apistikeli*
jamb, *asanali*
jamb, to; *ateblichi*
jangle, *itachoa*
jangle, to; *achowa*
janitor, *okhisa apistikeli*
janizary, *takish intashka chipota*
January, *Chanueli*
jar; *akolas, lukfi kotoba, palokachi*
jar, to; *palattokachi, palokachi, winnalichi*
jarred; *palokachi, winnakachi*
jaundice, *abeka lakna*
jaunt; *nowat falama, nowat fullota*
jaunt, to; *nowat aⁿya, nowat fullota*
javelin, *isht itibbi*
jaw, *nutakfa*
jaw, to; *nukoa*
jawbone, *nutakfa foni*
jay, *tiⁿshkila*
jealous; *nuktala, potanno, pushahchih*
jealous, to cause to be; *potunnuchi*
jealousy; *nuktala, potanno*
jealousy, to excite; *nuktalali*
jeer, to; *hobachi, isht yopula, yopula*
Jehovah, *Chihowa*
Jehovah Father, *Iⁿki Chihowa*
jejune, *ahoba*
jelly, *walahachi*
jenny, *ponol ashana chito*
jeopard, to; *ishkanapachi*
jerk, *halali*
jerk, to; *halakli, halali, halalli*
jerker, *halali*
jerkin, *na foka kolukshi*
jerks, the; *shimoha*
jerks, to bring on the; *shimohachi*
jerks, to have the; *shimoha*
Jerusalem; *Chelusalim, Chilusalim*
Jerusalem people, *Chilusalim okla*
Jerusalemite, *Chilusalim hatak*
jest, *yopula*
jest, to; *atuklakafa, isht uklakafa, lushka, yopula*
jester; *hatak yopula, yopula*
Jesus, *Chisas*
Jesus Christ; *alhtoka, Chisas Kilaist*
jet, *lusa*
Jew; *Chu, Chu hatak*
jewel, *haksobish takali*

jeweler, *haksobish takalikbi*
jewelry, *haksobish takali*
Jewess, *Chu ohoyo*
Jewish, *Chu*
Jewish nation or people, *Chu okla*
Jewish synagogue, *Chu okla imabohahanta*
Jewish temple, *Chu okla imabohahanta*
jewsharp, *taluskula*
jig, *tuklohila*
jig, to; *tuklohilahila*
jingle; *ola, samahachi*
jingle, to; *ola, olachi, samahachechi, samahachi*
jingler, *olachi*
job, *tonksali*
jobber, *toksali*
jockey, *isuba itatoba*
jocose; *atuklakafa, ituklakafa, yopula*
jocular; *yopula, yopula shali*
jocund, *yukpa*
jog, a; *chikinha, tobli*
jog, to; *chikinha, tobli*
jog on, to; *salahat anya*
jogger; *salahat anya, tobli*
joggle, to; *winnalichi*
joggled, *winnakachi*
join, to cause one to; *ibafokichi*
join together, to; *achanka, achakalechi, achakali, afama, apeha, asitia, auaya, auayachi, aba anumpuli ibafoka, aba anumpuli ibafoki, halalli, halallichi, ibafoka, ibafoki, ibalhkaha*
joined; *achaka, halalli, ibafoka*
joiner; *chukikbi, iti shanfi*
joiner's bench, *iti ashanfa*
joiner's horse, *iti ashanfa*
joint; *achakli, aiitachaka, ibafoka, itachaka, itachakachi, naksish, tilokachi*
joint, at the; *takofa*
joint, to; *nibli, nipaffi*
joint, to get out of; *talofa*
jointed; *nipa, nipali*
joist; *bachali, iti bachoha*
joke; *atuklakafa, lushka, yopula*
joke, to; *atuklakafa, isht oklushi, ituklakafa, lushka, lushkachi, yopula*
joker; *hatak yopula, isht yopula, ituklakafa, lushka, nan lushka, yopula*
joker, a great; *hatak yopula shali*
joking, *ituklakafa*
jolly, *yukpa shali*
jolt, *winnakachi*
jolt, to; *winnalichi*

jolted, *winnakachi*
jolter, *winnalichi*
jostle, to; *isso, tobli*
jot, *iskitinisi*
jounce, to; *winnalichi*
jounced, *winnakachi*
journal, *nitak moma holisso*
journey; *nowa, nowat anya*
journey, to; *akkahikat anya, ibaianya, nowa, nowat anya*
jovial, *yopula shali*
jowl, *nutakfa*
joy; *aiyukpa, ayukpa, na yukpa, na yukpali, yukpa*
joy, to; *yukpa, yukpalechi, yukpali*
joyed, *yukpa*
joyful, *yukpa*
joyful heart, *chunkash yukpa*
joyful man, *na yukpa*
joyous, *yukpa*
Judea, *Chu yakni*
judge; *apesa, hatak nan apesa, nan apesa*
judge, to; *anukfilli, apesa, mihachi*
judged; *alhpesa, alhpisa*
judgment; *anumpa alhpisa, alhpisa, imanukfila, nan alhpisa, nan alhpisa chinto*
judgment, day of; *nan alhpisa nitak, nitak nana alhpisa chito*
judgment, place of; *aiapesa*
judgment seat, *abinilit nan apesa*
judicious, *hopoksia*
jug; *akuhish, lukfi kotoba, yaklash*
jug, earthen; *yakolush*
juggle, to; *isht ahollo ilahobi, haksichi, yopisa, yopisachi*
juggler; *haksichi, isht ahollo ilahobi*
jugular vein, *issish inhina chito ikonla bachaya*
juice, *okchi*
juicy; *okchilaua, walonchi*
July, *Chulai*
jumble, to; *aiyokomi*
jumbled, *aiyokoma*
jump; *malli, tolupli*
jump, to; *abanabli, hatonchi, hatonli, hatulli, malli, tolupli, tulli*
jump, to cause to; *hatullichi, toluplichi*
jump over, to; *atanapoa, atanapoli*
jump over, to cause to; *atanapolechi*
jumper; *hatonchi, hatonli, hatulli, malli, tolupli*
junction; *aiitafama, aiitibafoka, aiitisetali, itibafoka*

junction of creeks or streams; *aseti-lechi, bok aiitisetili, bok itahnoli*
June, *Chuni*
junior; *inhimmak, nakfish*
just; *aianli, anli, alhpesa, ba, bilinka, himona, peh*
just, the; *hopoyuksa*
just grown, *himona hofanti*
just now, *himonasi*
just raised, *himona hofanti*
justice, *aianli*
justifiable, *alhpesa*
justification; *alhpisa, kashofa*
justified; *aialhpiesa, alhpesa, kashofa*
justifier; *apepoa, alhpesachi, kashoffi*
justify, to; *achchukmali, alhpesachi, kashoffi*
justly, *alhpesa*
jut, to; *kucha takanli*

kaw, *ola*
keen; *achunanchi, chilita, halupa, halupoa*
keen eye, *nishkin halupa*
keenness; *chilita, halupa*
keep, to; *halalli, holitobli, ilhpitachi, imansha, ishi, inshi, pelichi*
keep a jail, to; *aboha kallo apistikeli*
keep back, to; *ishi*
keep company, to; *ahinna*
keep holy, to; *holitobli*
keep house at, to; *achuka*
keep on, to; *manya*
keep still; *lumat ansha, samanta*
keeper; *aboha kallo apistikeli, apesachi, inhikia, imansha*
keg; *italhfoa, italhfoushi*
keg of powder, *hituk aialhto*
ken, *apisali*
ken, to; *pisa*
kennel; *nam poa inchuka, ofanusi, ofi inchuka*
kennel, to; *ansha, nusi*
kentle, *weki talepa achafa*
Kentucky, *Uski anunka*
kept, *imalama*
kerchief, *nantapaski ialipa*
kernel; *nihi, nipi, uksak nipi*
kernel, coffee; *kafi nihi*
kettle; *asonak, iyashushi, mahaia, shuti, shuti ansha*
kettle, iron; *shuti iyasha*
kettle bail, *asonak atakali*
key, *isht tiwa*

keyhole, *isht tiwa chiluk*
kick, *habli*
kick, to; *habli, hali, washana*
kicked, *hala*
kicker, *habli*
kid, *isi kosomushi*
kid, to; *cheli, isi kosomushicheli*
kidnap, to; *hatak hunkupa*
kidnaper, *hatak hunkupa*
kidney meat, *haiyinhchi nipi*
kidneys, *haiyinhchi*
kill, to; *abi, abi, abit tali, ebi, hatak abit tali, illichi, ishbi, tali*
kill birds, to; *hush abi*
kill by lightning, to; *hiloha abi*
kill in water, to; *okokabi*
kill timber, to; *iti chant abi*
kill with rust, to; *alaknabi*
killdee, *okchuns*
killed by lightning, *hiloha abi*
killer; *abi, nan abi*
killing, *abi*
kiln, *aionshobolichi*
kiln, board; *iti basha ashila*
kiln, brick; *lukfanuna*
kin, *itinkanomi*
kind; *achukma, halhpansha, imoklaya, kana*
kind, a; *aiachafa, kaniohmi*
kind-hearted, *itinkana*
kindle, to; *lua, oti*
kindled; *libbi, lua, oti, ulhti*
kindling wood, *oti*
kindness; *hatak inkana, halhpansha, kana*
kindred; *hatak inkanohmi, holba, itinkanomi, kanomi*
kine; *wak, wak tek*
kine, young; *wak tek himmeta*
king, *minko*
king of heaven, *aba minko*
kingdom; *apelichi, apelichika, minko apelechika afullota, minko apelichi, minko apeliechika, pelichika, yakni*
kingdom of heaven, *aba apelichika*
kingdom of Jehovah, *Chihowa apiliechika*
kingless, *minko ikimiksho*
kingly; *minko, ahalaia, minko chohmi*
king's evil, *chilanli*
king's evil, to cause the; *chilanlichi*
kink, *shana*
kink, to; *shana*
kinked, *shana*
kinsfolk; *itinkanomi, kanomi*
kinsman, *aiisht atiaka*

kiss, to; *impunsa, impunspoa, insunksowa, sunksowa*
kitchen; *aboha ahoponi, ahoponi*
kitchen maid, *ohoyo hoponi*
knab, to; *kobli*
knack, *imponna*
knag; *filamminchi, pinkshi*
knapsack, *bahta*
knave, *hatak haksi*
knavery, *haksichi*
knavish; *haksa hinla, haksichi shali*
knead, to; *yamaska, yamasli*
knead in, to; *ayamasli*
kneaded, *yammaska*
kneading tray or trough; *ayamaska, paska ayamaska*
knee, *iyin kalaha*
knee, cypress; *shankolo itibbi*
knee deep, *iyin kalaha ali*
kneecap, *iyin kalaha wishakchi*
knee-high, *iyin kalaha ali*
knee-joint, *iyin kalaha itachakalli*
kneepan; *iyin kalaha, iyin kalaha wishakchi*
kneel, to; *hachukbilhka, hachukbilepa, hachumbilhka*
kneel, to make; *hachukbilhkachi*
kneeler, *hachukbilepa*
knife, *bashpo*
knife, chopping; *nipi isht chanya*
knife, drawing; *shafa*
knife blade, *bashpo*
knife-handle, *bashpapi*
knit, *tanna*
knit, to; *tana*
knitted, *tanna*
knitter; *nan tanna, tana*
knob; *ahalalli, ponkshi, tibikshi*
knock; *kabak, kabakachi, kabuk, kamakachi, kobak, kobokachi, kobuk, komokachi*
knock, to; *aboa, isso, kobolichi, komoha, komolichi, sokunha*
knock off, to; *mokafa*
knocked, *kobokachi*
knocker, *isso*
knoll, *bokko*
knop; *bikbina, lohboachi*
knot; *ashekonoa, ashekonopa, atalakchi, itashekonompa, itasheponopa, itashekonowa, iti naksish, naksish, pinkshi, tibikshi*
knot, large round; *iti tikbi*
knot, to; *ashekonoachi, ashekonobli*

knot on the side of a tree, *ponkshi*
knotted, *nukshiah*
knotty; *naksish laua, pompokachi, pompoki*
know, to; *akostininchi, anukfohka, chishba, ikhana*
know about, to; *aiakostininchi*
know nothing, to; *imanukfila iksho*
knower, *ikhana*
knowing, *ikhana*
knowledge; *aiikhana, aiithana, anukfohka, ikhana, nan ithana*
knowledge, to give; *nukfokechi, nukfoki*
knowledge of, having; *anukfohka*
known; *anoa, ikhana, ikhana*
known by, *oktani*
knuckle, *ibbak ushi itachakalli*
knuckle, to; *issa*
knurled; *naksish laua, shochoha*
knurly; *shachoha, shochoha*
Kunshaws, *Kunsha*

label, *hochifo*
label, to; *hochifo takalichi*
labeled; *hochifo, hochifo takali*
labor; *nan toksali, pilesa, tonksali*
labor, a day's; *nitak holhtina tonksali*
labor, to; *alla eshachin inpalammi, pilesa, pilesachi, toksali*
labor with, to; *ibatonksali*
laborer; *hatak na pilesa, hatak tonksali, na hollo tonksali, nam pilesa, pilesa, toksali*
laborious; *achiba, ahchiba, toksali fehna*
lace; *folota, infolota*
lace, a; *isht talakchi*
lace, to; *infolota ikbi, takchi*
lace the chest, to; *chunuko takchi*
laced; *infolota, talakchi*
lacerate, to; *lilaffi*
lacerated, *lilafa*
laceration; *lilafa, lilaffi*
lack, *ona*
lack, to; *ikimiksho, laua, ona*
lackey, *tishu*
laconic, *tilofa*
lad; *alla nakni, hatak himmita*
ladder, *atuya*
lade, to; *fohki, shapulechi*
laded, *fohka*
laden, *shapoli*
lading; *alhto, fohka, shapuli*
ladle; *isht kafa, lokush, nakabila*

ladle, to; *takli*
lady, *ohoyo*
lady, old; *ohoyo sipokni*
lag, to; *salahat aⁿya*
laid across; *abankachi, abanni, abana, albana, okhoata*
laid at the side; *apata, aputkachi*
laid down; *akkakaha, akkalipia, alhkaha, kaha*
laid in a line; *bachaya, bachoha*
laid in rows, *bashkachi*
laid off; *bachaya, chula*
laid on, *alhpohomo*
laid up in a crack, *kafoli*
lair, *nam poa anusi*
lake; *haiyip, hohtak, okhata*
lamb; *chukfalhpoyushi, chukfushi*
lamb, to; *chukfushicheli*
Lamb of God, *Chihowa inchukfalhpo yushi*
lamblike, *chukfushi holba*
lame; *chushukli, hanali, imomokpulo, iyi hotupa, kinafha, kinafkali*
lame, the; *imomokpulo*
lame, to; *iyi hotupali*
lamely, *iyi hotupa chohmi*
lameness, *iyi hotupa*
lameness, a; *imokpulo*
lament, to; *nukhaⁿklo, yaiya*
lament with, to; *ibanukhaⁿklo*
lamentable, *nukhaⁿklo*
lamentation; *ayaiya, nan illcsha, nukhaⁿklo*
lamenter; *isht nukhaⁿklo, isht yaiya*
lamenting, *isht yaiya*
lamp; *bila pala, pala*
lampas; *noti italbakchi chito, nutakbalaⁿkchi offo*
lampblack, *tiak shoboli tulak*
lamp-post, *pala aioⁿhikia*
lance, *na halupa*
lance, to; *lumpli*
lanced, *lumpa*
lancet; *issish isht kuchi, isht lumpa, shakba isht lumpa*
lancet, spring; *shakba isht inchaⁿya*
land, *yakni*
land, a tongue of; *yakni bikeli*
land, bad; *yakni okpulo*
land, bottom; *okfa pattasachi*
land, cultivated; *yakni atoksali*
land, fallowed; *yakni patafa*
land, fertile; *yakni achukma*
land, flat; *okfa pattasachi, yakni pataiya*

land, furrowed; *yakni patafa*
land, good; *yakni achukma*
land, his; *yakni*
land, low; *okfa pattasachi*
land, plowed; *yakni basha*
land, sections of; *yakni chula*
land, surveyed; *yakni chula*
land, the edge of the; *yakni ali*
land, the end of the; *yakni ali*
land, to; *ataioha, ataiya, kucha, kuchichi*
land, to bring to; *ataiohali, ataiyali*
land, to let out; *yakni impota*
land, to rent; *yakni impota*
land, to run off; *yakni chuli*
land, to survey; *yakni chuli*
land, wild; *yakni atoksali*
land flood; *okchito*
land in sections, to lay off; *yakni chuli*
land laid off; *yakni chula*
land speculator, *yakni chumpa*
land that extends into the sea, *yakni okhata chito pit shamali*
landed; *ataiya, kucha*
landing; *aiataia, ayataia, akucha, ataioha, ataiya, peni ataiya*
landing, brought to the; *ataioha*
landmark, *yakni alhpisa hikia*
land's end, *yakni aiali*
landscape, *yakni apisa ali*
lane, *hina ikpatho*
lane between stakes, *holihta itintckla*
language, *anumpa*
language, bad; *anumpa okpulo*
language of white men, *na hollo imanumpa*
languid; *intakobi, kota, liposhi, tikabi*
languidness; *intakobi, kota*
languish, to; *bashi, tikabi*
languish, to make; *liposhichi*
languisher; *bashi, kota*
languor; *kota, liposhi, tikabi*
lank, *lapushki*
lantern; *pala afoka, pala inchuka*
lap, *iyubi pakna*
lap, to; *alatali, apolomi, oklabbi, opitamoli, takli*
lap of a legging, *wehta*
lap over, to; *aiopitama, halapoli, opitammi, walapolih*
lapis, *tali*
lapped; *opitama, opitamoa*
lapper, *oklabbi*
lapping, *oklabbi*
lapse, *ashachi*

lapstone; *alạllichi, wak hakshup alạllichi*
larceny, *hunkupa*
lard; *shukha bila, shukha nia*
lard, to; *niachi*
larded, *nia*
larder, *aboha inpaiasha*
large; *aiaka, ạffekomi, chito, chitoli, hocheto, ishto, laua, patasah, pạtha*
large, to cause to be; *hochetochi*
large and round, *tokumpa*
large when others are small, *achinto*
largely, *chito*
largeness, *chito*
larger, a little; *inshalakli*
largess, *ima*
largest, *inshaht tali*
lark, *shunlulo*
lascivious; *haksi, haui*
lash; *fahama, isht fạma, isht lukata*
lash, to; *fạmmi, lukaha, lukalichi, takchi*
lash on, to; *atakchichi*
lashed; *fạma, talakchi*
lasher; *fạmmi, lukalichi*
lashing, *lukaha*
lass; *ạlla tek, ohoyo himmita*
lassitude; *kota, tikabi*
last; *aiạli, aiisht aiopi, isht aiopi, kash*
last, a; *shulush atoba*
last, to; *anta*
last among men, *hatak wishakchi*
last one, *isht aiopi*
lasting, *bilia*
latch; *afacha, isht afacha, isht akamạssạchi*
latch, to; *afachali, afạshli*
latched; *afacha, afachali, afạshkachi, ạlhfạsha*
latchet, *shulush isht talakchi*
late; *achiba, atạpa fehna, atạpa ont ia,
chash, cheki, hopaki, kash*
lately; *chekikash, kash*
lateness, *atạpa*
latent; *haiaka, luma*
later, *inhimmak*
lateral, *lapali*
lath; *abasa, ạlbạsa, ạlbạska*
lath, to; *abạsli*
lathed, *ạlbạska*
lather, *pokpoki*
lather, to; *pokpokechi*
lather, to make; *pokpokechi*
lather box, *isht ahchifa apokpokechi*
lather for shaving, *isht ahchifa nashuka
ahạmmi*
lathing, *iti ạlbạsa*

latitude, *pạtha*
latter, *inhimmak*
latterly, *chekusikash*
laud, to; *afehnichi, aiokpanchi*
laudable, *aiokpancha hinla*
laudanum; *ikhinsh ishkot nusechi, ikhinsh
nusechi*
lauder, *isht anumpuli*
laugh, *yukpa*
laugh, to; *yukpa*
laugh, to cause to; *yukpali, yukpạchi*
laugh at, to; *olạlli*
laughable, *yukpa hinla*
laughing, to be half; *ibaklalanli*
laughter, *yukpa*
launch, *oka tobli*
launch, to; *oka tobli, pila*
launch out, to; *pit, takalechi*
launderer; *hatak nan achefa, nan achefa*
laundress; *nan achefa, nan achefa ohoyo,
ohoyo nan achefa*
laundry, *aboha nan aiachefa*
laundryman, *hatak nan achefa*
laurel tree, *iti chinisa*
lave, to; *ahchifa, yupi*
laver; *aiokami, aiyupi*
lavish, *isht yopomo shali*
lavish, to; *isht yopomo*
lavished, *isht yopomo*
lavisher, *isht yopomo*
law; *anumpa, anumpa ạlhpisa, anumpa
kạllo*
law, to become a; *anumpa ạlhpisa toba*
law, written; *anumpa ạlhpisa holisso*
law book; *anumpa ạlhpisa holisso, nan
ạlhpisa holisso*
lawbreaker, *anumpa kobạffi*
lawful, *ạlhpesa*
lawgiver, *anumpa apesa*
lawless; *anumpa ạlhpisa iksho, anumpa
ạlhpisa keyu*
lawmaker; *anumpa apesa, anumpa kạllo
ikbi*
lawyer; *anumpa nan ạlhpisa isht ạtta,
laya*
lax, *yohapa*
lax, a; *ikfia, ikfihechi*
laxative; *ikfiachi, ikfihechi*
laxity, *ikfihechi*
laxness, *ikfihechi*
lay, a; *ataloa, kaha, kali*
lay, to; *boli, cheli, hokchi, isso, kali, nuktalalichi, patali*
lay a plan, to; *apesa*

lay across, to; *abanali, abanni, okhoatali, okhoalli*
lay aside, to; *naksika boli*
lay at, to; *aiashachi*
lay back to the fire, to; *alahkichi*
lay crosswise, to; *okhoatali*
lay down, to; *akkaboli, akkakali, akkalipeli, ashachi, kahpuli, kali, tashkichi*
lay hold on, to; *pit*
lay in a row or line, to; *bachali, bacholi*
lay laths, to; *abasli*
lay low, to; *akkachi*
lay off, to; *chuli*
lay on, to; *aiashachi, abanali, boli, oncheli, onochi, takalechi*
lay on a stratum, to; *atanabli*
lay on the face, to; *lipoli*
lay on the hands, to; *bitepa*
lay on the neck or shoulder, to; *abanali, iabannali, iabannalichi*
lay out a road, to; *hina apesa*
lay over, to; *abanali*
lay the ribs of a roof, to; *abasli*
lay there, to; *aiashachi*
lay up, to; *achukmat boli, atali*
lay up seed corn, to; *pehnachi*
lazaretto, *imomokpulo aiasha*
lazily, *intakobi*
laziness, *intakobi*
lazy; *asanata, intakobi*
lazy, to make; *intakobichi*
lazy man, *hatak intakobi*
leach, *hituk chubi aholuya*
leach, ash; *hituk chubi ahoiya, hituk chubi aholuya*
leach, lye, *hituk chubi ahoiya*
leach, to; *holuyachi*
leach tub, *aholuya*
lead, *naki*
lead, sheet; *naki tapuski*
lead, to; *a^nya, halalli, ilaueli, ilauet a^nya, isht ia, pelichi, tikba heka*
lead along, to; *ilaueli*
lead astray, to; *haksichi, kaniachi*
lead into sin, to; *yoshobbi*
lead off from, to; *filammichi*
lead out of the way, to; *yoshobli*
lead round, to; *afolotowachi*
lead to, to; *ona*
leader; *hatak pelichi, ilaueli, ilauet a^nya, pelicheka, pelichi, tikba heka*
leader, military; *hopaii*
leading line, *isuba isht fullota*
leads astray, one who; *yoshobbi*

leaf; *hishi, iti hishi*
leaf, dead; *hashtap*
leaf, fallen; *hashtap*
leaf, to; *hishi toba*
leafed, *hishi toba*
leafed out, *hishi tobat taha*
leafy; *hishi chito, hishi laua*
league; *anumpa kallo, apesa, itimapesa*
league, to; *apesa*
leagued, *ibafoka*
leak; *chiluk, hoiya*
leak, to; *bichilli, hoiya, holuya, pichilli*
lean; *chunna, ilbasha, kofanto, kopipia, nipi, shulla*
lean, to; *ataiyachi, ataya, waiya, waiyachi*
lean, to make; *chunnachi*
lean against, to; *ataiya, ataiyali*
lean on, to; *ataiya, waiyakachi*
leanness; *chunna, nipi*
leap; *malli, tolupli*
leap, to; *abanabli, hatonchi, ilhkoli, malli, tolupli*
leap, to cause to; *toluplichi, tullichi*
leap over, to; *abanabli, tanapoli, tanabli*
leap over, to cause to; *tanablichi*
leap up, to; *balakli*
leaper; *hatonchi, malli, tolupli*
learn, to; *holisso ithana, ithana*
learn, to cause to; *ikhananchi*
learn at, to; *aiithana*
learn by practice, to; *abachi*
learned; *holisso ithana, ikhana*
learned man; *hatak imponna, hatak nan ithana*
learner; *aiithana, holisso ithana, ikhana, nan aiithana, nan ikhana*
learning, *ikhana*
learning, the means of; *isht ikhana*
lease, *yakni pota*
lease, to; *impota*
leash, *isht talakchi*
leash, to; *takchi*
least; *isht aiopi, kamomi, laue, moma, moma iklauo*
leather; *na hakshup, talhko, wak hakshup humma*
leather, sole; *wak hakshup humma*
leather, to; *fammi*
leather, to make; *talhko ikbi*
leather, upper; *wak hakshup lusa*
leather dresser; *talhko ikbi, wak hakshup hummachi*
leave, to; *ashachi, filammi, ibbak fohki, ima, issa, kanchi, kania, kucha*

leave a church, to; ǫba anumpuli iksa kucha
leave off, to; aiissǫchi
leaved, hishi toba
leaven; pǫska isht shatǫmmi, pǫska isht shatǫmmichi, pǫska shatǫmmichi
leaven bread, to; pǫska shatǫmmichi
leavened, shatǫmmi
leavened bread, pǫska shatǫmmi
leaver, issa
leavings, atampa
lecherous, aiyushkǫmi
lecture; anumpa, ǫba isht anumpa
lecture, to; anumpuli
lecturer, anumpuli
led horse, isuba shapuli
ledger, holisso
lee, chukbi
leech; haluⁿs, lasun, yaluⁿs, yasunla
leech, horse; haluⁿs chito
leek, hatoⁿfalaha
leer, to; akamaloli, akamalushli, nukoa
lees, lakchi
left; afabi, ǫlhfǫbeka
left, a part; akolofa
left, a place; aiissa
left hand; afǫbeka, ibbak ǫlhfǫbeka
left hand, on or to the; afǫbekimma
left hand, toward the; ibbak ǫlhfǫbek imma
left-handed; afabi, afǫbekimma
left-handed person, afabi
leg; ǫpi, iyǫpi, iyi ǫpi
leg bone; hulhki foni, iyulhki foni
leg of a stool, aiomanili iyi
legacy, ima
legal, ǫlhpesa
legalize, to; apesa
legate, anumpeshi
legation, hatak ǫlhtoka
leggings; iyabiha, iyubiha
legible; haiaka, pisa hinla
legibly, haiaka
legion, laua
legislate, to; anumpa ǫlhpisa ikbi
legislated, anumpa ǫlhpisa
legislator; anumpa ǫlhpisa ikbi, anumpa kǫllo ikbi
legitimate; aⁿli, iⁿki aⁿsha
leisure; aⁿshakba, nan isht ǫtta ikimiksho
leisurely, sǫlahat
lend, to; impota, pota
lend an ear, to; haponaklo
lendable, impota hinla

lender; impota, nan impota
lending, impota
length; ahekǫchi, ahheka, ahhekǫchi, falaia, hofaloha
length of time, hopaki
lengthen, to; aiakǫchi, falaiachi, falaiat ia, hofalohǫchi, shebli
lengthened, falaia
lengthwise; abaiyǫchi, ahekǫchi
lengthy; falaia, hofaloha
lenient, yohbi
lenity; nukhaⁿklo, yohbi
leopard, koi chikchiki
leper; illilli okpulo, leplosi ǫbi, liahpo ǫbi isht illi, liplosi ǫbi, yosh
leprosy; illilli okpulo, leplosi, liahpo ǫbi isht illi, liplosi
lessee, yakni pota
lessen, to; iskǫtanichi, iskitinichi, laue, lauechi
lessened, iskitini
lesson; apisa, imaiǫlechi
lessor, yakni impota
lest; keyukma, na, yoba, yobana
let; ashke, kia, kil
let, a; ataklǫma
let, to; iⁿna, impota
let blood, to; issish iⁿkuchi
let into the water, to; okǫchi, pit
let go, to; ia
let me; ak, lashke
let one have, to; ima
let us all, kiloh
let us all not, kiloh
lethargic, nusilhha
lethargy, nusi fehna
letter, holisso
letter, small; holisso iskitini
letter, to; holissochi
letter bag; holisso aiǫlhto, holisso iⁿshuk-cha
lettered, holisso
levee; nowǫt itǫnaha, sakti toba
levee, to make a; sakti ikbi
level; itilaui, matali, patasǫchi, patǫssa
level, to; anumpisachi, anompisachi, ma-talichi, patasǫchi, patasǫlli, patashechi, weli
level, to make; itilauichi
level ground, yakni matali
leveled; itilaui, matali, patasǫchi, pa-tǫskǫchi
leveler; itilauichi, patasǫchi
lever; isht afana, isht afinni, isht tono-lichi, isht wakeli, iti isht tonolichi

levied, itạnaha
levity, shohạla
levy, itạnaha
levy, to; itạnnali
lewd; haksi, haui
lewdness; haksi, haui, lumaⁿka
lexicon, a; tikshạneli
liable; hepulla, hinla
liar; aholạbi, holabi, lushka
libel, anumpa chukushpa
libel, to; anumpa chukushpali
libeler, anumpa chokushpikbi
liberate, to; yuka issạchi
liberated; yuka issa, yuka issachi, yuka
    kucha
liberator, yuka issạchi
liberty, yuka keyu
library, holisso aiasha
lice, issạp
license, imạlhpisa
license, to; apesa
licentious; haksi, okpulo
lick; fahama, isso, lukfạpa
lick, to; fạmmi, holakshi
licker, holakshi
lid; iạtipa, isht iⁿkạma, oⁿtipa, umpoholmo
lid of a box, itombi oⁿtipa
lie; holabi, lushka
lie, to; aholạbi, akka itula, chiya, holabi,
    itola, itula, itunla, lushka, talaia, taloha,
    tonla
lie, to cause to; lushkạchi
lie about, to; kahat maⁿya
lie across, to; ạbana, ạlbạna, okhoata
lie across, to cause it to; okhoatạchi
lie at the side, to; apata, apota, apotali
lie back to the fire, to; alahki
lie by, to; tonla
lie crosswise, to; okhoatakachi
lie down, to; akkakaha, akkakahat aiasha,
    akkakahạt maⁿya, akkatipia, akkatipkạ-
    chi, kaha, tạshki, tonla
lie down, to cause to; tạshkichi
lie face down, to; tipia
lie hard in the stomach, to; anukbikeli
lie hard on the stomach, to cause to;
    anukbikelichi
lie in, to; shamoli
lie in a retired place, to; apotaka itola
lie in ambush, to; aiihchi
lie in courses, to; bachoha
lie in rows or lines, to; bachohạt maⁿya
lie in wait for, to; aiihchi
lie in water, to; oka kaha

lie low, to; bilepa, tipkạchi
lie on, to; onitula, ontạla, onutula, tạl-
    kanchi
lie on fire, to; itotonla
lie on the back, to; watạlhpi
lie on the face, to; atipa, bilepa, lepa,
    tipkạchi
lie on the side, to; alatkạchi, naksi
lie together, to; itạtonla
lien, ạlhtoba
lieutenant; imanumpeshi, kạpitạni ima-
    numpeshi
life; aiokchaⁿya, ilhfiopak, nana okchaⁿya,
    nana yukpa, okchaⁿya
lifeblood, issish isht okchaya
lifeless, illi
lifetime, okchaⁿya takla
lift, to; ạba isht ia, ilefehnạchechi, sholi
lift the head, to; akạshchukali
lift up, to; akachakali, akachakalichi, ạba
    chakali, ạba takalichi, takalechi, wakeli,
    wakotichi
lifted, takali
lifted up, ạba takali
lifter, sholi
ligament, isht talakchi
ligature, ạlhfoa
light; anitaⁿki, apisa, atohwikeli, atohwi-
    kinli, ạba anumpa, hạshi, hạshninak
    aⁿya, ikhana, malạtha, nitak, nitaⁿki,
    okhisa, onna, onnat minti, pạla, shum-
    palali, tohbi, tohwikeli
light, the place of; atohwikạliⁿka
light, to; binili, oti, pạlali
light, to carry a; pạlali
light, to cause; tohyualichi
light, to give; tohwikeli, tohwikelichi
light, to have; tohwikeli
light, to make; shohạlachi
light color, hạtachi
light horse, isuba omanili tạshka
light-horseman; isuba omanili tạshka,
    isuba ontạla tạshka
light in the sky, shutik hạta
light in weight, shohạla
light-minded, imanukfila shanaioa
light off, to; akkoa
light upon, to shed; umpạla
lighted; pạla, tohwikeli
lighten, to; hạshuk mạlli, ikhananchi, ola
    taklạchi, tohwikeli, tohwikelichi, yukpali
lighten in weight, to; shohạlachi
lightened, shohạla
lightly, loma

lightness in temperament, *imanuk-fila shanaioa*
lightness in weight, *shohąla*
lightning; *hąshuk mąlli, malątha*
lightning, heavy; *tasa*
lightning bug, *hąlba*
lights, *shilukpa*
lightsome; *tohwikeli, yukpa*
lightwood, *tiak*
ligneous, *iti osh toba*
like, *bⁿka, chohmi, chomi, holba, laue, mⁿka, ohmi, yąmma*
like, to; *ahni, ahnichi, aiahninchi, anushkunna*
like, to act or do; *chohmi*
like, to make it; *chohmichi*
like-minded; *imanukfila achąfa, imanukfila itiholba*
like that, *yąmohmi*
like the other, *hokoła*
likely; *achini, chechik, chiishke, chik, hinla*
liken, to; *apesa, hobachi*
likened; *ąlhpiesa, holba*
likened to, *ąlhpesa*
likeness; *holba, ohmi*
likeness, to make a; *ohmichi*
likewise; *aiena, ak, hak, yąmmak kia*
liking, *anushkunna*
lily, *lilli*
limb; *feląmi, feląmichi, iti naksish, naksish, naksish filamoli, naksish filąmminchi*
limb, to; *nibli*
limb cut off, *nipąfa*
limb of the body, *hanali*
limber, *walohbi*
limber, to make; *walohbichi*
limbs, full of; *washaloha*
limbs, the four; *hanalushta*
limestone, rotten; *talhpa*
limit; *aiąli, ąli*
limit, to; *aiąlichi*
limitation, *aiąli*
limited, *aiąli*
limn, to; *holissochi*
limp, to; *chahikcheli, chahikli, chilukli, iachushukli, kinakkali, kinakli, kinąfha, kinąfkali, shaioksholi, shaiukli, tabikli, tąbikli*
limper; *chahikcheli, chahikli, kinakkali, kinakli, kinąfkali, shaiukli, tabikli, tąbikli*
limpid, *shohkalali*
linchpin; *achuⁿsha, iti chąnaha afacha*

linden; *balup, panąshuk, pishąnnuk*
line; *aioⁿholissochi, alaⁿfa, ąli, bachaya, hika, holisso iskitini, iti tiła bachaya, laⁿfa, ponoshąna, yikkowa*
line, to; *afohommi, alatali*
line of thread, *ponolushi*
lineage; *chukachąfa isht atia, isht atiaka*
lined; *afohoma, alata, alątkąchi*
linen; *na foka lumbo, na kąllo, nan tąnna kąllo, ponokąllo, ponola*
linen yarn, *ponola*
linguist; *anumpa tosholi, anumpuli imponna*
lining; *alata, anuⁿka alata*
lining, to put on a; *alatali*
link; *itatakąli, itątakąli*
link together, to; *takalechi, takołichi*
linked; *takali, takoli*
lion, *koi chito*
lioness, *koi chito tek*
lip, *itiąlbi*
lips, thick; *itukshibeli*
lips closed tight or firm, having the; *itakmofoli*
lips open a little, *itakhauali*
liquefied, *bila*
liquefy, to; *bileli*
liquid, *oka*
liquidate, to; *atobbi, chilofa, hotina*
liquidated; *ąlhchilofa, ąlhtoba, holhtena*
liquor; *na homi, oka, oka homi*
lisp, to; *isunląsh illi*
list, *takchąka*
list, to; *achunli, hochifo ishi, hochifo takali*
listed, *hochifo takali*
listen!; *ah, mah!*
listen, to; *afaląpa, haklo, hąponaklo*
listener; *haklo, hąponaklo, na haklo*
listless, *haklo*
literate, *ikhana*
litter, *fimimpa*
litter (brood); *pelechi, ushi, shukhushi pelechi achąfa*
litter (to ride on), *iti ąlbąsto*
litter, to; *ushi cheli*
littered, *fimimpa*
little; *chipunta, fehna keyu, iskitini, kitinisi*
little, very; *kanomusi*
little ones, *chipota*
littleness, *iskitini*
live; *okchaⁿki, okchaⁿya*

live, to; *anta, 'atta, chuka, okcha*nki,
   *okcha*nya
live, to cause to; *okcha*nyachi
live by, to; *aiokcha*nya
live stock, *alhpoa*
livelong, *falaia*
lively; *yiminta, yukpa*
liver, *salakha*
living, *okcha*nya
living creature; *nan okchaya, nana okcha*nya
living God, *okcha*nya
living thing, *nana okcha*nya
lizard; *chila*nwa, halanchila*nwa, kalaki
lizard, black; *yakni imafo*
lizard, small; *hashtap yuloli*
lo, *yaki*
load; *albiha, alhpitta, shapo, tukafa achafa*
load (for a gun), *ilhpita achafa*
load, one; *tanampo albiha achafa*
load, to; *fohki, shapulechi*
load a horse, to; *isuba shapulechi*
loaded; *alhpitta, fohka, shapo, shapoli*
loader; *nan apitta, shapulechi*
loading, *shali*
loaf; *palaska, paska*
loaf of bread, *paska chanaha*
loan; *impota, pota*
loan, to; *impota*
loath, *banna*
loathe, to; *chukyiweta, yuala*
loathed, *ahnichi*
loather; *shittilema, yuala*
loathful, *yuala hinla*
loathsome; *chukyiweta, shua, yuala hinla*
lobe of the ear, *haksobish walobi*
locate, to; *binilichi, talali*
located; *binili, taluli*
lock; *isht ashana, luksi*
lock, to; *afacha, ashannichi, shannichi,
   takali*   ,
locked; *ashana, ashana, ashakachi*
locust; *ha*nwa, wislichi, washa, washlichi
locust, honey; *kati*
lodge; *aboha iskitini, alhtipo, takali*
lodge, to; *anta, anukfohka, binoli, fohki,
   kinali, takalechi*
lodge in a room, to; *aboha anusechi*
lodged; *fohka, kinali*
lodger; *aiatta, hatak nowat a*nya
lodging; *aboha, aiatta, anusi, topa*
lodging out of doors, *abina*
lodging place, *bina*
lodging room, *aboha anusi*

loft; *pihcha, wia*
loftily, *ilefehnachi*
loftiness; *chaha, ilefehnachi*
lofty; *chaha, ilefehnachi*
log, *iti chito tapa*
log house; *aboha itabana, chuka itabana*
log of wood, *toboshakchi*
loin; *chashwa nipi, inchashwa nipi*
loiter, to; *salaha, salahat a*nya
loiterer, *salaha*
loll, to; *hahka, hakha*
loll, to cause to; *hahkachi*
lone, *ilap bano*
lonely, *ilap bano*
lonesome; *ashabi, palata*
lonesome, to render; *ashabichi*
long; *aiaka, falaia, hofaloha, hopaki, na,
   okshiyanli*
long, to; *banna*
long, to make; *hofaloli*
long ago, *hopaki kash*
long and slender; *fabaspoa, fabasfoa,
   fabassa, fabassoa, fahko*
long and slender, to make; *fabassachi,
   fahkochi*
long enough, *falaia, alhpesa*
long way or time, *hopaki*
longer, *falaia i*nshali
longer (as to time), *hopaki i*nchali
longest, *falaia i*nshat tali
longevity, *sipokni*
longing, *banna*
longitude, *falaia*
long-lived, *nitak i*nfalaia
look, to; *ahah ahni, ahoba, anukfilli, apistikeli, hikia, hopo*nkoyo, pisa
look about, to; *hopumpoyo, hopunayo*
look after, to; *hoyo*
look after, to cause to; *hoyochi*
look for, to; *hoyo*
look here, *yaki*
look on himself, to; *ilapisa*
look out for, to; *ahah imahni*
look over, to; *tepuli*
look sidelong, to; *afalapoa*
look sideways, to; *afalapoli*
look through, to; *afananchi, lopulli*
looker; *nam pisa, pisa*
looker on; *hatak yopisa, yopisa*
looking-glass, *apisa*
lookout, *hopo*nkoyo
looks; *nashuka, pisa*
loom; *atana, nana tanna*
loon, *okchala chito*

loop, *atakali*

loose; *litoa, miteli, mokofa, tilokachi*

loose and standing up, *tilokachi*

loose, to; *hotofi, litoffi, shunfi*

loose, to get; *miteli*

loosed; *litoa, litofa, litofkachi*

loosely; *ahah ahni iksho, kallo keyu*

loosen, to; *litofa, litoffi, litofkachi, yohabli, yohablichi, yohapa, yohapoa*

loosened; *litofa, yohapa, yohapoa*

looseness, *ikfia*

looseness of the bowels, *chula isht abeka*

lop, to; *nacholi, nalichi*

lope, to; *yohapachi*

lopped; *nachofa, nachoha*

lopper; *nacholichi, nachuffi, nalichi*

loquacious, *anumpuli shali*

lord; *anshali, chitokaka, hatak, hatak chitokaka, hatak hochitoka, inhatak, inshali, ishtokaka, pelichi*

lord, to; *pelichi*

Lord Jehovah, *Chihowa chitokaka*

lord of, *immi*

lordly; *ilapunla, ilefehnachi*

Lord's Supper, the; *opiaka impa Chisas Klaist at apesatok*

lore, *ikhana*

lose, to; *illi, lakoffi, kania, okpani*

loser; *inkania, illi, imilli, kania*

loss; *inkania, imilli, imokpulo, kania*

lost; *illi, itamoa, kania, kaniachi, okpulo, okpulot taha, tamoa, yoshoba*

lost man, *hatak yoshoba*

lot (drawn); *na fuli halali, na shoeli, na shoelit ishi*

lot (office), *aialhtoka*

lot (piece of ground); *holihta, osapa, yakni chula*

lot, small; *holihtushi*

lot, to; *hopela, kashkoli*

lotion, *isht ahchifa*

loud, *chitoli*

loudly, *chitolit*

loudness, *chito*

lounge, to; *intakobi*

lounger, *intakobi*

louse, *issap*

louse trap, *issap isht albi*

lousy; *issap laua, issap likeli*

love; *holitobli, holitopa*

love, to; *achukma, ahnichi, anhollo, anushkunna, asitia, asseta, hiahni, holitobli, inholitopa, inhollo, kashaha*

love, without; *hiahni iksho*

loved, thing; *nan inholitopa, nan inhollo*

loved by him; *inholitopa, inhollo*

lover; *anushkunna, hiahni, holitobli, inhollo*

lovers, mutual; *itinhollo*

lovesick, *palata*

low; *akanlusi, akanli, akanlusi, akkanlusi, alhchunna, chakapa, halatat taha, ilbasha, liposhi, makali, patasachi, shippa, wakkalih*

low (in music); *akanlusi, chito*

low, to; *woha*

low, very; *akanlusi*

low-down, *akanlusi*

low-spirited; *imilhlah, liposhi*

lower, to; *akanli, akanlusechi, akka ia, akkachi, alhchunnachi, lotama, shippa*

lower floor, *akka itipatalhpo*

lowest; *akkafehna, moma*

lowly, *chunkash akkanlusi*

lowness; *akanlusi, makali*

loyal, *aianli*

loyally, *aianlit*

lubricate, to; *halasbichi*

lubricated, *halushki*

lubricity, *halushki*

lucid, *haiaka*

Lucifer; *fichik, chito, Setan*

luck, *imaiyamohmi*

lucky, *imola*

lucre, *nan ilahanchi*

ludicrous, *yopula*

lug, to; *shalallichi*

luggage; *shapoweki, weki*

lukewarm, *lahba*

lukewarm, to make; *lahbachi*

lull, to; *chulosa, chulosachi, nuktalali, nuktala*

lulled; *chulosa, nuktala*

luller, *chulosachi*

lumber, *iti basha*

lumber, to; *aiyokomi*

lumber house, *aboha nana aiasha*

lumber room; *aboha nana aiasha, nana aiasha*

luminary; *hashi, hashninak anya, tohwikeli*

luminous, *tohwikeli*

lump, *lumbo*

lump, to; *itannali*

lump of clay, *lukfi lumbo*

lumped, *itanaha*

lunacy, *tasembo*
lunar measurement, *hashninak aⁿya isht alhpisa*
lunatic, *tasembo*
lunatic, a; *hatak tasembo, lunatik*
lunatic asylum, *hatak tasembo aiasha*
lunch, *impa iskitini*
luncheon, *impa iskitini*
lung, *shilukpa*
lure; *haksichi, nukpallichi*
lure, to; *haksichi, nukpallichi*
lurk, to; *apali, luma*
lurking place, *aluma*
luscious, *champuli*
lust; *aiyushkammi, nan nukpalli, yushkammi*
lust, to; *aiyushkammi, nukpalli, yushkammi*
luster; *shohmalali*
lusty; *chito, kallo, kilimpi, lampko*
luxate, to; *taloffi, taloli*
luxated; *talofa, taloha*
luxation; *talofa, taloffi*
luxuriant, *waya fehna*
luxuriate, to; *waya fehna*
lyceum; *holisso aiithana, holisso apisa*
lye; *hituk chubi holuya, hituk hoiya*
lying, *holabi*
lying at the side, *aputkachi*
lying crosswise, *abankachi*
lying down; *akkabilepa, kinali*
lying in a row, *bachaya, bashkachi*
lying on, *onutula*
lying on the face, *lipkachi*
lyre, *alepa*

maccaboy, *habishkuchi*
macerate, to; *liposhichi, tikabichi*
macerated, *liposhi*
machinate, to; *apesa*
"mackerel clouds", *hoshontikilhkiki*
mad; *anukbata, anukhobela, chukachi, hacho, holilabi, nukhobela, nukoa*
mad, to get; *hashaⁿya*
mad, to make; *hashaⁿyachi, nukhobelachi*
madcap; *hatak nukoa shali, nukoa shali*
madden, to; *anukhobelachi, nukoa, nukoachi*
maddened, *nukoa*
madder, *nan isht hummachi*
made, *toba*
made, by whom; *toba*
made alive, *okchaⁿya*

made his, *immi toba*
madhouse, *hatak tasembo aiasha*
madman; *nukoa, nukoa shali*
madness; *anukbata, anukhobela, nukoa, tasembo*
magazine; *holisso, na halupa aiasha*
maggot, *chukanushi*
maggoty, *chukanushi laua*
magi, *hatak hopoyuksa*
magic; *fahpo, fappo*
magician; *fappuli, hatak fappo, hatak fappoli*
magisterial, *ilefehnachi*
magistrate, *nan apesa*
magnanimity, *imanukfila chito*
magnanimous; *imanukfila chaha, imanukfila chito, imanukfila hopoyuksa*
magnate, *hatak chitokaka*
magnetic needle, *tali inla fehna*
magnificent; *holitopa, isht ahollo*
magnifier, *holitobli*
magnify, to; *aiokpanchi, chitolichi, holitobli, holitoblichi*
magnitude; *chito, holitopa*
magnolia, *kolaha*
maid, *ohoyo himmita*
maid, serving; *ohoyo toⁿksali*
maid, waiting; *ohoyo nan iⁿhoyo*
maiden, *ohoyo himmita*
mail, *holisso aialhto*
mail, to; *holisso shali fohki*
mail a letter, to; *holisso bahta chito fohki*
mail coach, *iti chanaha holisso shali*
mailed, *holisso shali foka*
maim, to; *imalechi*
maimed; *imaleka, imomokpulo*
main; *iⁿshali, laua iⁿshali*
main body, *iⁿshali*
mainly; *iⁿshali, moma chuhmi*
maintain, to; *imatali, ishi*
maintained, *imalhtaha*
maintainer; *imatali, ishi*
maintenance, *aiimalhtaha*
maize, *tanchi*
majestic; *chito, isht ahollo*
majesty; *chito, chitokaka, holitopa*
major, *iⁿshali*
major, a; *miⁿko iakaiya*
major general, *hopaii*
majority; *iklanna atampa, iⁿshali*
make; *ikbi, toba*
make, to; *atobachi, ikbi, ilapisa, ishi, lapisa, toba, tobachi*

make (as money), to; *ahauchi*
make, to cause to; *ikbichi*
make a canal, to; *okhina ikbi*
make all, to; *oklunhachi*
make bank bills, to; *holisso lapushki ikbi*
make fun of, to; *isht oklushi*
make known, to; *oktanichi*
make mortar in, to; *ayamasli*
make much of, to; *fehnachi*
make of or from, to; *atoba*
make ready, to; *atali*
make run, to; *tileli*
make something, to; *na fehnachi*
make very much, to; *oklunhali*
make water, to; *hoshunwa*
maker; *ikbi, nan ikbi, nan tobachi*
making, *ikbi*
malady; *abeka, illilli*
male; *hatak nakni, nakni*
malefactor, *hatak yoshoba*
malevolence, *imanukfila okpulo*
malevolent, *imanukfila okpulo*
malice; *nukkilli, nukoa*
malice, to bear; *anukkilli*
malicious; *nukkilli, nukoa*
malign; *nukkilli, nukoa*
malignant; *nukkilli, nukoa*
maligner, *isht yopula*
malignity, *imanukfila okpulo*
mall; *anowa, iti isht boa*
mallard, *hankhobak*
malleable, *shepa hinla*
malleate, to; *bot shebli* .
malleated, *bot shepa*
mallet; *isht boa, iti isht boa iskitini, iti isht boa ushi*
mamma, *hashki*
mammon, *imilayak*
mammoth; *nan isht ahollo, poa chito*
man; *hatak, hatak at, hatak nakni, nakni*
man, a single; *tekchi iksho*
man, bad; *hatak haksi*
man, my; *anhatak*
man, one; *hatak achafa*
man, to; *hatak hilechi*
man-hater, *hatak innukkilli*
man-killer, *hatak abit tali*
man of mind, *hatak imanukfila ansha*
man pleaser, *hatak yukpali*
manacle, *ibbak isht talakchi*
manacle, to; *ibbak takchi*
manacled, *ibbak talakchi*
manage, to; *apesa, apesachi, apistikeli, kostininchi, nana kanihchi, pelichi*

manager; *apesa, apesachi, apistikeli, isht atta, nan apesa, pelichi*
manager of a funeral; *hatak inminko, hatak itinmiko*
mandate; *anumpa, inmiha* .
mandrake; *fala imisito, fala intanchi*
mane, *chushak hishi*
maned, *chushak hishi ansha*
manes, *shilup*
maneuver, to; *apesa*
manful, *nakni*
mange, *washko*
manger; *aiilhpeta, aiimpa, isuba aiimpa peni, iti peni, wak aiimpa*
mangle, to; *kisli, lilalichi, lilechi*
mangled; *lilafa, lilali*
mangler, *lilalichi*
manhood; *hatak ona, hatak toba*
mania; *nukoa, tasembo*
maniac, *hatak tasembo*
manifest, *haiaka*
manifest, to; *haiakachi*
manifested, *haiaka*
manifestly, *haiakat*
manifold; *ilaiyukali laua, laua*
mankind; *hatak, hatak okla*
mankind, all; *hatak moma*
manlike, *nakni*
manlike, to render; *naknichi*
manliness, *nakni*
manly, *nakni*
manner; *aiyamohmi, akanimi, kaniohmi, katiohmi, yamohmi, yohmi*
manner, to do after this; *yakohmichi*
mansion; *aboha, aiasha, aiatta, chuka*
manslaughter, *hatak abi*
mansuetude; *honayo, kostini*
mantelpiece, *aba tala*
mantle, *anchi*
mantle, to; *anchichechi, anchichi, umpoholmo, umpohomo*
mantua, *ohoyo inna foka*
mantua maker, *ohoyo inna foka ikbi*
manual; *holisso iskitini, ibbak isht tonksali*
manufactory, *nana atoba*
manufacture, to; *ikbi*
manufactured, *alhpoyak toba*
manufacturer; *alhpoyak ikbi, ikbi, nan ikbi*
manufactures, *alhpoyak*
manumission, *yuka issachi*
manumit, to; *yuka issachi*
manumitted, *yuka issa*

manumitter, *yuka issachi*
manure land, to; *yakni niachi*
manured, *wak iⁿyalhki ont ashachi*
manuscript, *holisso*
many; *aiyaka, akaieta, ayaka, kanomona, laua, okla chito*
many, as; *laua kat kaniohmi*
many, to do; *lauachi*
many times, *laua fehna*
map, *yakni isht alhpisa holisso*
maple, hard; *chukchu chito*
maple, soft; *chukchu*
maple sugar, *chukchu hapi champuli*
mar, to; *okpani, okpanichi*
maraud, to; *huⁿkupat itanowa*
marble, *tali halasbi*
marble, a; *isht basto, tali lumbo*
March, *Macha*
march; *alepola, baiillit nowa, nowa*
march, to; *baiillichi*
mare, *isuba tek*
mare, breeding; *isuba ishke*
mare, old; *isuba ishke*
margin; *alaka, alapali, ali, takchaka*
margin of a river, *okhina takchaka*
margin, to; *takchaka ikbi*
marine, *okhata aialhtaha*
marine, a; *tashka chipota peni aⁿsha*
mariner, *peni isht aⁿya*
maritime; *okhata aiahalaia, okhata imma*
mark; *aialbi, alaⁿfa, basosuⁿkachi, basha, iti tila, laⁿfa, laha, lahkachi, na lafa, tila*
mark, to; *ahni, bashli, haklo, holissochi, laⁿfi, lali, lalichi, tili*
mark on the human body, *tali lusa*
marked; *basha, chula, holisso, kalafa, laⁿfa, lahkachi, tila*
marked tree, *iti tila*
marker; *bashli, holissochi, laⁿfi, na laⁿfi, tili*
marker of trees, *nan tili*
market; *achumpa, aiitatoba, ilhpak akanchi, nana aiitatoba*
market, to; *itatoba*
market house, *aiitatoba chuka*
marksman, *huⁿssa imponna*
marriage; *itauaya, ohoyo ipetachi*
marriage, to celebrate a; *ohoyo ipetachi*
marriage state, *auaya*
marriageable; *auaya, auaya alhpesa, auaya ona*
married, *auaya*

married man; *hatak awaya, itauaya*
marrow; *foni lupi, lupi*
marrowbone, *iyinchampko*
marry, to; *aiina, auaya, auayachi, halallichi, ipetachi, itatuklo, itauaya, okoyo ipetachi*
Mars, *fichik homma*
marsh, *yakni labeta*
marshal; *nan apesa, pelichi*
marshal, to; *apesa, pelichi*
marshy; *labeta, labeta foka*
martial; *nakni, tanap ahalaia*
martin (a bird), *choⁿki*
martingale, *isuba ikonla isht talakchi*
martyr, *apepoa*
martyr, to; *abi*
martyrdom; *apepoa, aba anumpa apiha at illi*
marvel, *okokkoahni*
marvel, to; *anuklakancha, okokkoahni*
marveled, *nuklakancha*
marvelous; *inla, inla fehna, okokkoahni*
masculine; *chilita, kallo, nakni*
mash, to; *boshullichi, lisholili, lisholichi, litoli, sholi*
mashed; *boshulli, lishoa, litoa*
mason; *lukfi nuna isht atta, lukfi nuna pilesa*
mass; *hatak laua itanaha, itahoba, itanaha, laua*
massacre, *isikkopalit abi*
massacre, to; *chuka patali, isikkopalit abi*
massive, *chito*
mast; *na waya, nusi*
mast, a; *kohta*
mast of a ship, *peni chito iⁿkotah*
master; *aⁿshali, iⁿshali, na hollo, nan ithanachi, nan ithanarchi, pelicheka, pelichi*
Master, our; *piⁿshali*
master, to; *imaiya, imaiyachi, ishalichi*
master hand, *imponna*
master of an animal; *impushnayo, pushnayo*
masterly, *imponnat*
masticate, to; *hoaⁿsa, hopaⁿsa*
mastiff, *na holipafi*
match; *auaya, ichapa, itibbi, itishi, luak isht ikbi*
match, to; *holba, ichabli, ichapa, ichapoli, itilauichi*
matched; *auaya, ichapa, ichapoa, itilaui*

mate; *ibaianta, ichapa, itichabli*
mate, to; *auaya, ichabli, ichapa, ichapoa, ichapoli*
mated; *auaya, ichapa, ichapoa*
material; *na fehna, nana*
maternal, *ishki ahalaia*
mates; *ichapoa, itichapa*
mathematics; *na holhtina, nana holhtina*
matins, *onnahinli aba inki imasilhha*
matricide, *ishki abi*
matrimony, *auaya*
matrix, *ushatto*
matron, *ohoyo asanonchi*
matter; *akaniohmi, aninchichi, kaniohmi*
matter, a; *nana*
matter, to; *aninchichi, na fehna*
mattock; *chahe iskifa, itakshish isht chanya*
mattress, *apatalhpo*
maturate, to; *aninchichi*
maturate, to cause to; *aninchichechi*
mature; *aninchichi, asano, kamassa, nuna*
matured; *alhtaha, nuna*
maturely, *fehna*
maturity; *asano, alhtaha, nuna*
maul; *isht boa, iti isht boa, nan isht boa*
maul, large; *isht boa chito, iti isht boa chito*
maul, to; *bakaha, boli*
maw, *takoba*
maxim; *achi, amiha, na miha*
May, *Me*
may; *ahinla, hinla, na*
may apple, *fala imisito*
may be, *fo*
may have, *ahinlatok*
mayor, *hatak tamaha pelichi*
maze, *imanukfila laua*
maze, to; *imaiyokomichi*
mazy, *shanaioa*
me; *an, am, an, am, ano, la, sa, sam, san, sa, sam*
meadow; *hashuk aiamo, hashuk abasha, okfa pattasachi*
meager; *chunna, ilbasha, liposhi*
meal, *pushi*
meal, a; *impa*
meal, coarse; *bota lakchansha*
meal, the evening; *opiaka impa*
mealtime, *aiimpa ona*
mealy, *shila*
mean; *ahoba, iklanna, makali*
mean, the; *iklannaka*
mean, to; *ahni, miha*
mean, to render; *makalichi*

meander, to; *polomoa, polomoli, polomolichi*
meaning, *miha*
meanly, *makali*
meanness, *okpulo*
means, *akanimi*
meantime, in the; *ataklachi*
measles, *chiliswa*
measles, to be sick with the; *chiliswa abi*
measurably, *chohmi*
measure; *alhpisa, isht alhpisa, nan isht apesa, oka isht alhpisa*
measure (regulation), *kaniohmi*
measure, a land; *yakni isht alhpisa*
measure, a liquid; *oka isht alhpisa*
measure, a quart; *isht ishko chupak*
measure, to; *apesa*
measure with, to; *isht apesa*
measured; *alhpesa, alhpisa*
measurement, *apesa*
measurer, *apesa*
meat; *ilhpak, ilhpita, ilimpa, nan apa, nan ilhpak, nipi*
meat, a piece of; *nipi tushafa*
meat, boiled; *nipi honni, nipi labocha*
meat, cooked; *nipi honni*
meat, cured or dried; *nipi shila*
meat, fresh; *nipi okchanki*
meat, rotten; *nipi shua*
meat, slices of; *nipi tushali*
meat, slices of fresh; *nipi okchanki tushali*
meat, stewed; *nipi honni*
meat ax, *nipi isht chanya*
meat barrel, *nipi aialhto*
meat beaten up in a mortar, *nipi baha*
meat bench, *nipi abashli*
meat bin, *nipi aialhto*
meat cured and dried, *chohpa*
meat house, *nipinchuka*
meat market, *nipi aiittatoba*
meat trough, *nipi aialhto*
mechanic, *nan ikbi*
medal; *tali hollo, tali inunchi*
medal, a faced; *tali hollo*
medal for a chief, *tali isht minko*
meddle, to; *ahalaia*
meddler, *ahalaia*
meddlesome, *ahalaia*
mediate, to; *apesa, nan aiyachi*
mediator; *hatak nan olabechi, itinnan aiyachechi, nan aiyachi*
medicament, *ikhinsh*

medicine; *ikhi^nsh, ishki^nsh*
medicine, a powdered; *ikhi^nsh bota*
medicine-man, *alikchi*
meditate, to; *anukfilli*
meditation; *anukfilli, imanukfila*
meditative, *imanukfila fehna*
medium, *aiisht itintakla*
meed, *alhtoba*
meek; *anukhobela iksho, chu^nkash yohbi, yohbi*
meekness; *chu^nkash yohbi, imanukfila yohbi*
meet, *alhpesa*
meet, to; *afama, ahauchi, mokafa*
meet at, to; *aiitafama*
meet in battle, to; *amokafa*
meet with, to; *i^nsannih*
meeter, *afama*
meeting; *abenili, aiitafama*
meetinghouse; *aianumpuli aboha hanta, aba anumpa aiisht atta, abai anumpuli chuka*
meeting place, *aiitanaha*
melancholy; *chu^nkash akkalusi, imanukfila nukha^nklo, nukha^nklo, oktili*
mellow; *haiyi^nko, haksi, lapushki, nuna, yaboboa, yabosha, yabushki, yabushli, yatotoa, yatushki, yatushkoa*
mellow, to; *haiyi^nko, haiyi^nkuchi, nuna, nunachi, yatushki, yatushkichi, yatushkuli*
mellow, to make; *yatushkichi*
mellowed, *lapushki*
mellowness, *lapushki*
melody; *ola achukma, taloa achukma*
melt, his; *intakashi*
melt, to; *abila, alhkomo, bila, bileli, bilelichi, itobila, nukha^nklochi, okomuchi*
melted; *bila, itobila, nukha^nklo*
melter; *bileli, okomuchi*
melting, *itobila*
member; *hanali, ibafoka*
membership, *ibafoka*
memoir, *isht anumpulit holissochi*
memorable; *ikhana alhpesa, ikhana fehna*
memorial, *isht ikhana*
memory; *aiithana ali, imanukfila, isht ikhana*
men; *hatak ashosh, okla*
men, all; *hatak hikia puta*
men of war, *hatak tanap a^nya*
menace, *miha*
menace, to; *miha*
menagerie, *poa aiasha*

mend, to; *achukmalechi, aiiskiali, aiskiachi, akalli, apoksia, kanihmi, kanihmit ia*
mended; *achukma, aiskachi, aiskia, apoksia, alhkata, kanihmi, kanihmit taha*
mender; *aiskiachi, akalli*
menses; *hashi alhpisa, hollo*
menstruate, to; *hollo*
mensuration, *apesa*
mental; *imanukfila, imanukfila ahalaia*
mention, *anumpa*
mention, to; *anoli, anumpuli*
mentioned; *anoa, anumpa*
mercenary, *ilhtohno*
merchandise; *alhpoyak, ila^nyak, imilayak, itatoba, nan alhpoyak*
merchant; *hatak nan chumpa, itatoba, na kanchi, nan chumpa*
mercies, *nukha^nklo*
merciful; *hiahni, nukha^nklo*
merciless, *nukha^nklo iksho*
mercy; *imanukfila nukha^nklo, i^nnukha^nklo, nan i^nnukha^nklo*
mere; *bano, beka, bieka*
merely; *ba, bano, beka, bieka, illa, peh, pilla*
merely sitting, *peh a^nsha*
merge, to; *oklobushlichi*
meridian; *tabokoa, tabokoli*
meridian, to reach the; *tabokoa, tabokoli*
merit; *alhtoba, holitopa*
merit, to; *asitabi*
merry, *yukpa*
mess, *ilhpak tola achafa*
mess, to; *impa*
message; *anumpa, anumpa a^nya*
message, a verbal; *anumpa kochanli*
message, to carry a; *anumpa isht a^nya, anumpa shali*
message, to hear a; *anump imeshi*
messenger; *anumpa isht a^nya, anumpa shali, anumpeshi, hatak anumpa isht a^nya*
Messiah, *alhtoka*
messmate; *ibaiimpa, impa, itibaiimpa*
metal, *tali*
metal, precious; *tali fehna, talukchi*
metal, white; *tali hata*
metaphor, *isht alhpisa*
mete, *ali*
mete, to; *apesa*
meteor; *fichik heli, fichik hika, palampa*
method, *aiyamohmi*
methodize, to; *apesa*

mettle, *imanukfila*
mew, to; *ya^{n}wa*
mewing, *ya^{n}wa*
mid, *ikląnna*
midday; *nitak ikląnna, tabokoa, tabokoli*
middle; *aiikląna, aiikląnaka, ikląnna, ikląnnaka*
middle age, near to; *kauashąchi*
middle-aged, *kauasha*
middle place, *aiikląnna^{n}ka*
middling, *ikląnna*
middling, the; *shukha pąsa*
middling old, *chikki*
midheaven; *shutik ikląnna, tabokoli*
midnight; *ninak ikląnna, tabokoli*
midriff; *ataka, itapa, imataka, i^{n}wąlwa*
midst; *ikląnna, ikląnnaka*
midst of days, *nitak chakpa*
midsummer, *toffah ikląnna*
midway, *ikląnna*
midwife, *ohoyo ąlla eshi apistikeli*
midwinter, *hąshtula ikląna*
mien, *pisa*
might (potential); *ahinlatok, ahinlatuk, hinlatuk*
might (power); *aia^{n}li, kąllo, kilimpi*
might have been, *he*
mightily, *fehna*
mighty; *aia^{n}lika, chito, fehna, kąllo, kilimpi, lampko, paląmmi*
mighty work, *na fehna*
migrate, to; *wihat a^{n}ya*
migration, *wiha*
milch; *bishahchi, wishahchi*
mild; *nita^{n}ki, shohmakali, yohbi*
mild, to make; *yohbichi*
mildew; *fichak champuli, fichak kasha^{n}ha, toshoba*
mildew, to; *toshbichechi, toshbichi ąmmona*
mildness, *yohbi*
mile; *isht ąlhpisa, koi, yakni isht ąlhpisa*
mile, English; *na hollo i^{n}kowi*
milepost, *koi isht ikhąna*
milestone, *koi isht ikhąna*
militant, *itibbi*
military, *tąshka chipota*
military ornaments, *tąshka chipota isht shema*
militia, *tąshka chipota*
milk, *pishukchi*
milk, coagulated; *pishukchi walasha*
milk, cow's; *wak pishukchi*

milk, sour; *pishukchi hauąshko, pishukchi homi, pishukchi kąskaha, pishukchi su^{n}kko*
milk, thick; *pishukchi su^{n}kko*
milk, to; *bislichi, bishlichi, wishlichi*
milk pail, *abishlichi*
milk pan, *pishukchi aiąlbiha*
milk shelves, *pishukchi ataloha*
milk strainer, *pishukchi ahoiya*
milked, *bishahchi*
milker, *bishlichi*
milkmaid, *ohoyo bishlichi*
milkman, *hatak pishukchikanchi*
milkweed, *nuchi*
milky; *pishukchi a^{n}sha, pishukchi holba*
milky way, the; *ofi hasimbish i^{n}hina, ofi hąta kolofa, ofi tohbi i^{n}hina*
mill; *abąsha, afotoha*
mill, grist; *afotoha*
mill, to; *fotoli*
mill horse, *isuba ta^{n}sh fotoli*
mille, *talepa sipokni*
millennium, the; *afąmmi talepa sipokni achąfa*
miller; *fotoli, na fotoli, ta^{n}sh fotohli*
milliner, *ohoyo i^{n}shapo ikbit kanchi*
million, *talepa sipokni talepa sipokni*
milt; *itapa, takąshi*
mimic, a; *hobachi*
mimic, to; *hobachi, hobachit anumpuli*
mimicker, *hobachit anumpuli*
mince, to; *tushalichi*
minced, *tushali*
mind; *anukfila, imanukfila*
mind, to; *haklo, imantia*
mind of man, *hatak imanukfila*
minded; *ahni, anukfila, bąnna*
mindful; *ahah ahni, haklo, ikhana*
mindless; *anukfilli, haklo, imahaksi*
mine; *ąmmi, ąno*
mine, a; *tąli aiasha, yakni kula*
mine, to; *yakni kula, yakni kulli*
mine, to become; *ąmmi toba*
mineral, *tąli*
mingle, to; *aiyuma, aiyummi, ashuma, ashummi, ibąlhto*
mingled; *aiyuma, ashuma*
mingler, *ashummi*
minister; *ąba anumpuli, imanumpeshi, i^{n}shali nan isht imątta, nan ąlhtoka*
minister, to; *ątta, imatali, ipeta*
ministered, *imąlhtaha*
minor, *laua*

minor, a; asano
minstrel; olachi, taloa
mint, tali holisso aiakmo
mintmaster, tali holisso aiakmo intala
minuet, hila
minute; holisso, hopaki achafa
minute, one; himonasi achafa
minuted, holisso
miracle; aiisht ahollo, isht ahollo
miracle, to perform a; aiisht ahollochi,
    isht ahollo
mire; haiyinko, lukchuk, labeta, labishko,
    lafeha, lafeta, latinko, latimo
mire, to; lukchuk okakania, oka kania,
    oka kaniachi
mire, to make; haiyinkuchi
mirror, apisa
mirth, yukpa
miry; haiemo, haiyinko, lukchuk chito, la-
    beta, labishko, lachopa, lafeha, lafeta,
    latinko, latimo, oklachanko, oklachinko,
    oklanshko
miry, being; labinta
miry, made; haiyinko
miry, to make; haiemuchi, labetachi, la-
    fetachi, latinkuchi, latimuchi, oklansh-
    kochi
misbehave, to; hopoksia
miscarriage, ona
miscarry, to; aiona
mischief, isht afekommi
mischief, to cause; isht akanohmechi
mischievous; acheba, afekommi, affekomi,
    isht akanohmi, isht afekommi
mischievous, to make; afekommichi
miscount, to; ashachi
miser, hatak nan inhollo
miserable; ilbasha, isikkopa
miserably, ilbasha
misery; aiilbasha, aleka, ilbasha, isik-
    kopa, kommichi, nukhammi
misfortune, imaleka
misfortune, to cause; poafachi
misgive, to; nukwia, yimmi
misguide, to; yoshobbi, yoshobli
misguided, yoshoba
misimprove, to; okpani
misinterpret, to; anumpa tosholi asha-
    chi, ashachit tosholi
misjudge, to; ashachit anukfilli, ashachit
    apesa
mislay, to; ashachit boli
mislead, to; haksichi, yoshobbi
misleads, one who; yoshobbi, yoshobli

misled, yoshoba
mismanage, to; ashachit isht attamisname, to; ashachit hochifo
misremember, to; imahaksi
misrepresent, to; ashachit anoli, holabit
    anoli
miss, ashachi
miss, to; ahaksichi, ashachi, imahaksi, la-
    koffi, yoshoba
missed, lakoffi
misshapen; imomokpulo, okpulo
missing; ashachi, iksho, lakoffi
missionary, aba anumpuli
mist; okshimmi, oktohbi
mist, to; okshimmichi, okshiplichi, okto-
    boha, oktoboli, oktobolichi, okwotummi
mistake; aiashachi, aiashachika, ashachi,
    nan ashacheka
mistake, to; ashachi, ashachit anukfilli,
    ashachit ishi
mistake, to make a; aiashachi
mistaken; ashachi, chikimba
mistaker, ashachi
mistletoe, fani shapha
mistranslate, to; anumpa tosholi asha-
    chi
mistress, ohoyo chuka pelichi
mistress, school; ohoyo holisso pisachi
mistrust; ahah ikahno, nukwia
mistrust, to; nuktala, nukwia
misty; oktohbichi, yauinyaui
misuse, to; okpani
mite; nana iskitinusi, shushi iskitini
miter, minko imiachuka
mitigate, to; nuktalali, shippali
mitigated, nuktala
mitigation, nuktala
mitten; ibbak abeha, ibbak foka
mix, to; aiyobali, aiyuma, aiyummi, ala-
    tali, ashuma, ashummi, ayamasli, iba-
    foki, ibakaha, ibakali, ibani, ibalhkaha,
    kali, yammichi
mixed; aiyuma, alanta, ashuma, alhto,
    ibafoka, ibakaha, ibalhto, ibalhkaha, ok-
    tababi, yammaska
mixed, to cause to be; ibakahachi
mixer; ashummi, ibafoki, ibakali, ibani,
    itaiyumi
mixture; ashuma, ibakaha, ibalhto, ita-
    biha, itaiyuma, itashuma, itibafoka, iti-
    balhkaha, itibalhto, nana itaiyuma
moan, to; kifaha, nukhanklo, yaiya
moat, yakni kula tamaha apakfopa
moat, to; yakni kullit tamaha apakfobli

mob, *hatak laua itąnaha*
moccasin; *shaui imanchaha, shulush*
moccasin snake, *chunasha*
moccasin snake, pied; *shaui imanchaha*
mock, *hobachi*
mock, to; *ahoba, hobachi, hobachit anum-puli, isht uklakafa, oląlli, opoma, yim-michi, yopoma*
mocker, *hobachit anumpuli*
mockery, *hobachi*
mocking bird, *hushi bąlbaha*
mode; *aiyąmohmi, yąmohmi*
model; *aiakmi, isht ąlhpisa*
model, to; *apesa*
moderate, *ąlhpesa*
moderate, to; *chulosa, chulosąchi, nuk-talali, nuktąla*
moderated; *chulosa, nuktąla*
moderately; *chohmi, sąlahat*
moderation; *chulosa, nuktąla*
moderator; *hatak itąnaha pelichika, nuk-talali, pelicheka*
modern, *himak*
moderns, the; *hatak himaka*
modest; *kostini, nuktanla, takshi*
modesty, *imanukfila nuktanla*
modified, *inlat toba*
modify, to; *inląchi, nuktalali*
moiety, *ikląnna*
moist; *anukyohbi, hokulbi, hotokbi, lącha, okyohbi, shąchakąmo, shinąsbi, shinisbi, shummi*
moist, to make; *shinisbichi*
moist in the mouth, to be; *itaklaląshli*
moisten, to; *anukyohbichi, hokulbichi, hotokbichi, ląchali, shummichi*
moistened; *anukyohbi, lącha, shummi, yukabi*
moisture, *shummi*
moisture, to cause; *shinisbichi*
moisture on the flesh, *shinisbi*
molasses, *hąpi champuli okchi*
mold, *hakbona*
mold, to; *akkoli, hakbonąchi, shakbonąchi*
mold anew, to; *atuklant akmichi*
molded; *ąlhkoha, hakmo*
molded anew, *atuklant akmi*
moldy; *bokboki, hakbona, shakbona*
mole; *tąli lusa, yulhkun*
molest, to; *anumpulechi, apistikeli*
mollify, to; *nuktalali*
molt, to; *boyafa, boyąffi, loⁿffi, tikafa, wuklo*
molted, *boyafa*

moment, *yakosi ititakla*
momentary, *yakosi ititakla*
monarch, *miⁿko*
monarchy, *apelichika*
Monday, *nitak hollotuk onna*
money, *tąli holisso*
money, paper; *tąli holisso tapuski*
money, purchase; *tąli holisso isht chumpa*
money, silver; *tąli holisso*
money, to coin; *tąli holisso ikbi*
money box, *tąli holisso aiąlhto*
money changer, *tąli holisso itatoba*
money drawer, *tąli holisso aiąlhto*
money purse, *tąli holisso aiąlhto*
money purse, to put into a; *tąli ho-lisso iⁿshukcha foki*
moneyed, *tąli holisso inlaua*
mongrel, *ikląnna*
monitor; *iⁿmiha, miha*
monkey; *hatak shaui, shaui hatak*
monster; *haknip inla, hatak okpulo, im-omokpulo*
monstrous; *inla fehna, okpulo*
month, *hąshi*
month, one; *hąshi achąfa*
month, this; *himak hąshi*
monthly; *hąshi achąfakma, hąshi moma*
monument, *nan isht ikhana*
monumental record, *isht ikhana*
moon; *hąshi, hąshi ninak aⁿya, hąshninak aⁿya*
moon, one; *hąshi achąfa*
moon, the full; *hąshi bolukta*
moon, the new; *hąshi himmona, hąshi himmona talali, hąshi himo auata, hąshi talali*
moon, the old of the; *hąshi loshuma*
moonlight; *hąshninak aⁿya tohwikeli, ni-tak omi*
moonshine; *hąshninak aⁿya tohwikeli, nitak omi*
moor; *kuⁿshak aⁿsha, oklaⁿshko*
mop, *nan isht kasholichi*
mop, to; *kasholichi*
moral; *hopoksia, kostini*
moral man; *hatak ąlhpesa, hatak kostini*
morality, *hopoksa*
moralize, to; *hopoksiachi*
morbid, *liposhi*
more; *akucha, atampa, himakma, iⁿshali, moma*
more, being a little; *iⁿshalakli*
more than one, *achąfa atampa*

moreover; *himakma, yạmohmikma*
morn, *onnahinli*
morning; *onna, onnahinli, onnahinli fehna*
morning light; *onnat minti, onnat oklilinchi*
morning light, the coming of; *onnat minti*
morning light, the return of; *onnat oklinli*
morning worship, *onnahinli ạba inki imasilhha*
morose; *banshkiksho, nukoa*
moroseness, *nukoa*
morrow, *onnaha*
morsel; *ạpa kitinisi, kitinisi*
mortal; *illa hinla, illahe imma, isht illa hinla*
mortal, a; *hatak*
mortal sickness, *abeka okpulo*
mortar; *chuka isht ạlhpolosa, isht ạlhpolosa, lukfi yạmmạska*
mortar, a; *ahosi, kitti*
mortar, meat; *abaha*
mortar, to make; *lukfi yamạska*
mortar, wooden; *abaha*
mortification; *hofahya, nip illit shua, nipi shua*
mortified; *hofahya, kostini, nip illit shua, nipi shua*
mortify, to; *hofahyạchi, kostininchi, nip illit shua, nip illit shuachi*
mosquito; *chunkạsh ạpa, hatak chunkạsh ạpa, isapuntak*
mosquito bars, *isapuntak inchuka*
mosquito hawk, *haksobish anli*
moss, tree; *iti shumo*
mossy, *iti shumo laua*
most; *anhusi, fehna, laua inshali*
most distant, *intạnnạp*
Most High, The; *nana moma inshali*
mote; *hoshunluk, iskạtinosi, nana iskitinusi*
moth; *shunshi, shunshi nan tạnna ạpa*
mother; *chishke, hạshki, ishki*
mother (in vinegar), *likaha*
mother-in-law; *ippokni, ipochi ohoyo, ipokni, ohoyo haloka*
mother tongue, *ishki imanumpa*
motion; *anya, ilhkoli, michik*
motion, to be quick in; *yilishachi*
motive, *ahni*
mound; *bokko, bunto, nạnih, nạnih bunto, yakni bunto*

mount; *bokko, nạnih, nạnih bunto, nạnih chaha, onchạba chaha*
mount, to; *ạba isht ia, ạbia, oiya, omanili*
mountain; *chaha inshali nạnih, nạnih, nạnih chaha, onchạba chaha, unchạba chaha*
mountain, a burning; *nạnih lua*
mountain side; *abaksacheka, abaksileka*
mounter, *oiya*
mourn, to; *ilbạsha, na nukhanklo, nukhanklo, tabashi*
mourn with, to; *ibanukhanklo*
mourned unto, *yaiya*
mourner; *yaiya, yanya*
mournful; *ashabi, yaiya*
mournful, to render; *ashabichi*
mourning; *nan lusa isht tabashi, tabashi, yaiya*
mourning, in time of; *tabạsh*
mourning clothes, to wear; *tabashi*
mourning for the dead, *nan anusi*
mourning person, *tabạsh*
mourning pole, *iti humma*
mouse; *oksanla, pinti*
mouse, field; *pintukfi*
mousetrap, *pinti ahokli*
mouth; *itạkha, iti, sạtih*
mouth, to; *ạpa*
mouth, toward the; *sokbish pila*
mouth of a crater or bottle, *itopa*
mouth of a creek, *bok asetili*
mouth of a jug, *kotoba ittopa*
mouth of a stream; *asetili, sokbish*
mouth of a stream, at the; *sokbish pila*
mouthful; *itạkha achafa, kopoli achafa*
movable, *kanạlla hinla*
move, *kanali*
move, to; *chanạlli, fotoha, ia, ilhkolechi, ilhkoli, ilhkolichi, kanali, kanalichi, kanạllichi, mali, nowa, nukoạchi, wichikli, wiha, witekạchi, witikli, witikwinli, yạnakạchi*
move, to cause to; *poalichi, wihachi*
move about, to; *bininili, fahfoa, fahfuli, fullokạchi, tualichi*
move along, to; *akanalichi, anya, kanạllit anya, wihat anya*
move and arrive, to; *wihat ạla*
move and settle, to; *kanạllit binili, wihat binili*
move and swarm, to; *wihachi*
move away, to; *kanakli*
move camp, to; *bina awiha*

move from, to; *akanạlli*
move out, to; *kucha weheli, kucha wiha*
move quickly, to; *kạnnakli, pạlhki, yilepa*
move slowly on, to; *sạlahạt a^nya*
move suddenly, to; *lipa*
move the eyebrows, to; *okmisikali*
move the head and neck, to; *konamisli*
move to do or say, to; *nukfoki*
moved; *kanali, piakạchi*
moved out, *kucha wiha*
movement, *ilhkoli*
mover; *a^nya, ilhkoli, kanali, kanạlli, wiha*
moving; *kanali, kanạlli, wiha*
moving about, to be; *kananant a^nya*
moving about, to keep; *kananali, kạnanali*
mow, *hạshuk itạnaha*
mow, to; *ạmo, bạshli, hạshuk ashachi, hạshuk bạshli*
mowed; *bạsha, hạshuk bạsha*
mowed, place; *hạshuk abạsha*
mower; *bạshli, hạshuk bạshli*
mown; *ạlmo, bạsha, hạshuk bạsha*
much; *aiaka, fehna, laua*
much, to do; *lauachi*
much, very; *lauachit*
much ice, *okti chito*
muck, *wak i^nyạlhki*
mud; *haiyi^nko, lukchuk, łabeta, lachi^nko, łafeha, łafeta*
mud, deep; *lukchuk chito*
mud, to; *liteli*
mud dauber, *tekhanto*
muddied, *lukchuk bano*
muddle, to; *haksichi, okpạni*
muddled; *haksi, okpulo*
muddy; *boha, liteha, lukchuk a^nsha, lukchuk bano, łabeta, łacha^nko, lachi^nko, łafeha, łafeta, łati^nko, okłacha^nko, okłachi^nko*
muddy, to; *liteli, lukchuk banuchi, łabetạchi, lachi^nkochi, łafehạchi, okłacha^nkochi, okłachi^nkochi*
muddy, very; *lukchuk chito*
mudfish, *shupik*
muff, *ibbak alibishli*
mug; *isht ishko, isht ishko chaha*
mug, small; *isht ishkushi*
muggy, *shummi*
mulatto; *hatak lakna, hatak lusa iklạnna, hatak lusa lakna, hatak lusa nipi humma, nipi humma*

mulberry, *bihi*
mulberry grove, *bihi talaia*
mulberry tree, *bihi ạpi*
mule; *isuba haksobish falaia, isuba nashoba*
mullein, *hakchuma holba*
multiplied, *ibakaha*
multiply, to; *ahofạllechi, lauachi, unchololi*
multitude; *hatak itạnaha, hatak laua, laua, okla, okla chito, okla laua*
multitude of travelers, *hatak lauạt a^nya*
mum; *anumpuli keyu, chulosa, sạmanta*
mumble, to; *bimihạchi*
mumps, *ikonla shatali*
munition, *isht itibbi*
murder, *hatak ạbi*
murder, to; *ạbi, hatak ạbi, hatak illichi*
murder all, to; *hatak ạbit tali*
murdered, *hatak ạbi*
murderer; *ạbi, hatak ạbi, hatak ạbit tali, hatak bi^nka ạbi, hatak illichi, nan ạbi*
murderous; *hatak ạbi, ilbạshali, ilbạshalit ạbi*
murmur, *anoli*
murmur, to; *bimihạchi, fo^nhka, fopa, lumanamihachi, nan isht miha*
murmurer, *nan isht miha*
muscadine, *suko*
muscles near the groin, *i^nnasobaksobish*
muse, to; *anukfilli*
mush, *ashela*
mush, to make; *ashelikbi*
mush made of acorns, *okshạsh*
mushlike, *moạshki*
mushroom; *chulahtu^nsh, lu^nslo, pakti*
mushy; *moạshki, moyaya^nkạchi*
music, *taloa*
music book, *ataloa*
music master, *taloa ikhạnachi*
music of the drum, *alepola*
musician, *taloa imponna*
musket; *tanamp fabạssa, tanampo*
muskmelon; *okcha^nk, okcha^nk balama*
must; *kalama, yohmi ạlhpesa*
must be, *pulla*
must not; *ahe keyu, n, na*
mustard, *mạstạt*
mustard seed, *mạstạt nihi*
mustard stalk, *mạstạt ạpi*
muster, to; *itạnnali, tạshka chipota itạnnali*
musty, *kalama*
mutable, *inla hinla*

mute; *anumpuli, anumpuli keyu*
mute, a; *anumpuli, hatak anumpuli*
mutilate, to; *basht tapli, okpani*
mutilated, *okpulo*
mutton, *chukfalhpowa nipi*
mutual friends, *kana*
mutual helps, *itapela*
mutual interest, *ahalaia*
mutual relations, *kanomi*
mutually strengthened, *kallo*
muzzle; *ibishakni foka, itopa*
muzzle of a bottle, *kotoba ittopa*
muzzle of a gun, *tanampo ittopa*
muzzle, to; *itihtakchi*
my; *a^n, an, ann, ammi, sa, sa, si*
myriad; *laua, talepa sipokni pokoli*
myrrh, *mali*
myself, *ano*
mystery; *nan inla, nan luma*

nab, to; *kopoli*
nag; *isuba, isuba iskitini*
nail; *atakali, atakoli, chufak*
nail, short; *chufak yushkololi*
nail, small; *chufak chipinta, chufak ushi*
nail, toe; *iyakchush*
nail, to; *ahonali, ahonalichi, anali, ana-
    lichi, honalichi*
nailed; *ahonala, anala, honala*
nailer, *chufak ikbi*
naked; *bano, fomosa, haiaka, haknip
    bano, hishi iksho, luma, na foka iksho,
    nipi bano*
nakedness; *haiaka, shahbi*
name; *hochifo, hohchifo*
name, to; *hochifo, hochifochi*
named; *hochifo, hochifo takali, hohchifo*
nameless, *hochifo iksho*
namer; *hochifo, na hochifo*
nap, *nusi iskitini*
nap, to; *nusi iskitini*
nape; *iachuna, iachushak*
napkin, *ibbak isht kasholichi*
narrate, to; *anoli, holissochi*
narrated; *anoa, holisso*
narration; *anoa, anoli*
narrative; *anoli, isht anumpa*
narrator, *anoli*
narrow; *atikkonofa, libanta, okshianli,
    okshiyanli, patha*
narrow, to; *iskitinichi, pathachi*
narrow way, *hina ikpatho*
narrowed, *patha*
narrows, *itintakla atia*

nasty; *okpulo, shua*
Natchez, *Nahchi*
Natchez trace, the; *hina*
nation; *okla, oklushi, yakni*
national; *okla, ahalaia, oklushi ahalaia*
native; *aiatta, hatak*
native place, *aiatta*
natural; *aiimoma, ima^nka*
natural, a; *imanukfila iksho*
natural fool, *imanukfila iksho aiimoma*
naturally, *aiimomachi*
naturally small; *aiimoma, imoma*
nature; *aiimalhpesa, alhtayak, nana moma*
naught, to set at; *keyukechi*
naughty; *haksi, okpulo*
nausea, *hoeta banna*
nausea, to feel; *nukpoalli*
nauseate, to; *anukpoali, yuala, yualachi*
nauseous; *nukpaualli, yuala*
nauseous, to render; *yualachi*
naval action, *peni chito aiitibi*
nave of a wheel, *iti chanaha iklanna*
navel, *hatambish*
navel gall, *po^nkshi*
navel string; *haiombish, hatambish*
navigable, *peni ataya*
navigate, to; *peni isht a^nya*
navigator, *peni isht a^nya*
navy, *peni hochito kanomona*
nay; *aha^nh, keyu, okho*
nay, a; *keyu*
neap, *isunlash*
near; *a^nhusi, apunta, bili^nka, bilinchi,
    cheki, holitopa, itoma*
near, quite; *bili^nkasi*
near, to; *bili^nka, bilinchi*
near, to be very; *bili^nkasi*
near, to make; *bilinchi*
near, very; *bili^nkasi, itomasi, tomalusi*
near at hand, *olasi*
near by; *olanli, olasi*
near to, *atikkonofa*
nearest, *bilinchi kat i^nshaht tali*
nearly; *a^nhesi, a^nhusi, bilinchi, he, naha,
    pullasi*
nearness; *bili^nka, itoma*
nearsighted, *bili^nka*
neat, *kashofa*
neat (of cattle), *wak*
neatly, *kashofat*
neb; *ibichilu, ibishakni*
necessarily, *pulla*
necessary; *alhpesa, pulla, yamohmahe
    alhpesa*

necessitate, to; *yamohmahe alhpesachi*
necessitous, *ilbasha*
necessity; *ilbasha, yamohmahe alhpiesa*
neck, *ikonla*
neck, the back side of the; *chushak*
neck, the joint of the; *i^{n}nosishboya*
neck of a junk bottle, *chu^{n}sa*
neckcloth; *innuchi, inuchi*
necklace; *innuchi, inuchi, shikalla*
necromancer, *hatak holhkunna*
need; *aialhpiesa, banna, ilbasha*
need, to; *banna*
needle; *chufak nan isht achunli, chufak nishkin a^{n}sha, chufak ushi, isht achunli*
needle, knitting; *tali isht tana*
needle maker, *chufak ush ikbi*
needleful, *chufak nishkin lopulli achafa*
needy; *ilbasha, na banna*
ne'er; *chatuk, himma keyu*
nefarious, *okpulo fehna*
negation; *aha^{n}h, keyu*
negative; *aha^{n}h, keyu*
negative, to; *ahah achi, keyuachi*
neglect; *aksho, yamichi*
neglect, to; *ahaksi, ahaksichi, aksho, ya-michahe keyu*
neglected; *ahaksi, aksho*
neglecter, *yamichi*
negligence, *yamichi*
negotiate, to; *anumpuli, chumpa*
negotiator; *na kanchi, nan chumpa*
negress, *hatak lusa ohoyo*
negro, *hatak lusa*
neigh, *sihi^{n}ka*
neigh, to; *sihi^{n}ka*
neighbor; *bili^{n}katta, chuka abili^{n}ka, chuka apanta, chuka apantali, chuka apalli, chukapanta*
neighborhood; *bili^{n}ka, chuka lukonli, itibili^{n}ka a^{n}sha*
neither; *achafahpi, aiena, kanimampo keyu, kesh*
nephew, *ibaiyi*
nerve, *kallo*
nerve, a; *akshish*
nervous; *halali, kallo*
nervous, to make; *halalichi*
nest; *alhpichik, chuka*
nest, bird's; *hushi imalhpichik*
nest, hornet's; *fohkul inchuka*
nest, to; *alhpichik ikbi*
nest maker, *apeli*
nest of a wild beast, *poa nusi*
nest of the bumblebee, *o^{n}sini inchuka*

nestle, to; *alata, binili*
nestling, *hushushi*
net; *isht albi, isht hokli*
nether; *nutaka, sokbish*
nethermost, *akkafehna*
nettle, *hatak holhpa*
nettle, bull; *hashtapola, hatapusha*
nettle, to; *hatak holhpalli, holhpalli*
nettled; *hatak holhpa, holhpa*
neuter, *kanimampo keyu*
neutral; *ahalaia, kanimampo keyu, peh a^{n}sha*
never; *chahtoshba, chatok, chatuk, himma, himma keyu, himmona, nitak nana, nitak nanta*
never can, *hatoshba*
never mind, *kia*
nevertheless; *kia, yohmi kia*
new; *himmona, inla*
new heart, *chu^{n}kash himmona*
New Orleans, *Balbancha*
newish, *himmona chuhmi*
newly, *cheki*
newness, *himmona*
news; *anumpa kaniohmi, nana kaniohmi*
newsman; *hatak nan anoli, nan anoli*
newsmonger, *nan anoli*
newspaper, *holisso nowat a^{n}ya*
next; *acha^{n}ka, atukla, himmakma*
nibble, to; *chinoli, kili*
nibbler, *kili*
nice; *achukma, a^{n}li, alhpiesa, kashaha*
nicely, *a^{n}li*
nick, to; *bashli*
nick of time, *aialhpesa*
nickname; *himak fokalit hohchifo, hochifo okpulo, tabash*
nickname, to; *himak fokalit hochefo*
niece, *ibitek*
niggard, *hatak nan i^{n}hollo*
niggardly, *makali*
nigh; *bili^{n}ka, itoma, naha*
night, *ninak*
night, birth; *ninak aiatta*
night, this; *himak ninak*
night, to work till; *shohbichi*
night craziness, *ninak tasembo*
nightcap, *ninak ialipa*
nightfall, *opiakma^{n}ya*
nightmare, *shimoha*
nightmare, to bring on the; *shimo-hachi*
nightmare, to have the; *shimoha*
nightshade, *ofi inhoshuwa*

nightwalker, *ninak tasembo*
nihility, *na fehna keyu*
nimble, *tushpa*
nine, *chakali*
nine, to make; *chakali*
nine times, *chakaliha*
ninefold, *inluhmi*
ninepence; *iskali, iskali achafa*
nineteen; *abichakali, ahbichakali*
nineteen, to make; *ahbichakali*
nineteen times; *abichakaliha, ahbicha-*
kaliha
nineteenth, *isht ahbichakali*
nineteenth time, *isht ahbichakaliha*
ninetieth, *isht pokoli*
ninety, *pokoli*
ninth, *isht chakali*
ninth time, *isht chakaliha*
nip, to; *kobli, tushalichi*
nip off, to; *taptuli*
nipped, *tushali*
nippers, *tali isht kiseli*
nipple; *ibish, ipinshik*
nit; *issap nihi, nihi*
niter, *hapi kapassa*
nitter, *shunshi isuba acheli*
no; *ahanh, chikimba, han, iksho, keyoh,*
keyu, kia
no, to cause; *keyuchi*
no, to say; *ahah achi*
no one; *kana keyu, kata*
noble, *chito*
noble, a; *hatak chitokaka, holitompa*
nobleman, *hatak holitompa*
nobly, *chitot*
nobody, *kana keyu*
nocturnal, *ninak foka*
nod, *inmiha*
nod, to; *faiokachi, yuhchunni*
noggin, *iti isht ishko*
noise; *chamakachi, kas, kilihachi, kini-*
hachi, kitik, kolak, komok, komuk, ko-
taha, lachak, michik, mishuk, palak, sak,
sakaha, sakakachi, shachak, shakanlichi,
shakapa, shakawa, tilukachi, yuhapa
noise, to; *anoli*
noise, to make a; *kabakachi, kilihachi,*
lobukachi, mishukachi, nutikahchi, saka-
lichi, shachaha, shachakachi, shakahachi,
shakapa, shakanwa, shakabli, shakablichi,
tobahchih, washahachi
noised; *anoa, annoa*
noisome, *okpulo*
noisy; *yahapa, yuhapa*
nominal, *hochifo bieka*

nominate, to; *atokoli*
nominated; *atokowa, alhtoka*
none; *amohmi, iksamiksho, iksho, kanima*
none, to have; *iksho*
none there, to be; *iiksho*
nonesuch, *mih*
nonplus, *aiyokoma*
nonplus, to; *aiyokomichi*
nonsense; *anumpa kaniohmi keyu,*
anumpa keyu
nook, *shokulbi*
noon; *tabokoa, tabokoli*
noon, about; *tabokoli foka*
noon, before; *tabokoli ikono*
noon, past; *tabokoli ont ia*
noonday, *tabokoli*
nooning, *tabokoli foha*
noontide, *tabokoli foka*
noose, *ashekonopa*
noose, to; *hokli*
nor, *kia*
north, *falammi*
north star, *falammi fichik*
north wind, *falammi mali*
northeast, *chukfikpelo*
northerly; *falammi chohmi, falammi im-*
ma, falammi pila
northern; *falammi chohmi, falammi im-*
ma, falammi minti, falammi pilla
northward; *falammi imma, falammi pila*
northwest, *falammi hashi aiokatula itin-*
takla
nose; *ibichilu, ibishakni*
nosebleed, *ibikoa*
nostril, a; *ibishakni chiluk*
nostrils, the; *ibichilu*
nostrum, *ikhinsh luma*
not; *ak, atoshba, atuko, atukosh, chikimba,*
chint, hatosh, hatuko, hatukosh, ik, kahe,
kahinla, kahioke, katimi, ke, keho, keyu,
kil, kiloh, n, na
not, shall; *wa*
not, will; *kashke, wa*
not any; *iksho, keyu*
not bound, *yuka keyu*
not far, *olanli*
not so; *ahanh, han, hatosh*
not yet; *kin, kinsha*
notable; *anoa, ikhana alhpesa, na fehna*
notch, to; *chakoffi, chakoli, chakolichi, ka-*
lowa, lakoffi, lakoli, lakolichi, lanpli
notch deep, to; *lakabli*
notched; *chakoa, chakofa, kalowa, lakapa,*
lakofa, lakowa, lampa
notched stick, *iti chauana*

notcher, *chakoffi*

notches; *chakoa, chakofa, kalowa, kolofa, lakofa, lakoli, lako*ⁿ*wa, lanlaki*

note; *holisso, holisso iskitini, isht alhpisa, taloa*

note in music; *ataloa, ilhtalowak*

note, to; *holissochi, ikhana*

noted; *anoa, holisso, ikhana, ikhana achukma*

nothing; *ba, na fehna keyu, nan ikahobo, nana keyu, nana kia, peh, pilla*

notice; *aiokpanchi, ikhana, pi*ⁿ*sa*

notice, to; *ahni, aiokpachi, haklo, pisa*

notified, *anoa*

notifier; *hatak nan anoli, nan anoli*

notify, to; *anoli, haklochi*

notion, *imanukfila*

notional, *imanukfila laua*

notorious; *haiaka, ikhana*

notwithstanding; *kia, yohmi kia, yohmi nana kia*

nourish, to; *hofantichi, hopolalli, ikhananchi, ipeta*

nourished; *hofanti, ilhpita*

nourisher; *hofantichi, ipeta*

nourishment; *ahofanti, anumpa, ilimpa*

novel, *himmona*

novelty; *himmona, na himmonna*

November, *Nofimba*

novice; *himmona isht atta, himonna isht atta*

now; *himak, himak nitak, himaka, himo, himona, himonasi, inta, ma*ⁿ*shko*

now don't, *wehkah*

noway, *kanima kia keyu*

nowhere; *kanima kia, kanima kia keyu*

noxious, *okpulo*

nuisance, *ataklama*

null; *aksho, kashofa, kobafa*

null, to; *akshuchi, kashoffi, kobaffi*

nullification, *akshuchi*

nullified, *kobafa*

nullifier, *kobaffi*

nullify, to; *akshuchi, kobaffi*

nullity, *kobafa*

numb; *illi, shimoha, taliskachi, talissa, talissa, tamissa*

numb, to; *illichi, shimohachi, talissachi*

number; *aholhtina, holhpena, holhtina, kanomona, laua*

number, a small; *kanomusi*

number, to; *hopena, hotina*

numbered; *aholhtina, holhpena, holhtena*

numbered, men; *hatak holhtina*

numberless, *aholhtina iksho*

numbness; *chilina, illi, shimoha, taliskachi, talissa, talissa*

numbness, great; *chilinoha*

numerable, *holhtina hinla*

numerate, to; *hopena*

numeration; *hopena, hotina*

numerator; *hopena, hotina*

numerous; *kanomona, laua*

nuptial, *auaya*

nuptials; *auaya, ohoyo ipetachi*

nurse; *abeka apistikeli, alla apistikeli, alla sholi*

nurse, to; *abeka apistikeli, alla apistikeli, pishechi*

nurture; *ahofanti, ilhpak, ilimpa*

nurture, to; *hofantichi, ipeta*

nut, *ani*

nut cake, *pask alwasha*

nutriment; *ahofanti, ilhpak, ilimpa, nan apa*

nutshell, *foni*

nymph, *ko*ⁿ*wi anu*ⁿ*kasha*

O!; *aume, ikikki, kbano, ma*

O dear; *aiehna!, huk*

oak, a species of; *bishkoni, bushto, nusapi*

oak, blackjack; *chiskilik*

oak, overcup; *bashto*

oak, post; *chisha*

oak, Spanish; *chilhpatha*

oak, white; *baii*

oaken, *baii toba*

oakum, *pinash*

oar; *isht mofi, peni isht moa*

oar, long; *isht halalli*

oar, to; *mo*ⁿ*ffi, mo*ⁿ*ffit isht ia*

oath, *anumpa kallo*

oats; *isuba apa, onush, onush isuba apa*

obdurate, *kallo*

obedience, *imantia*

obedient, *imantia*

obeisance, *akkachunoli*

obey, to; *antia, atia, imantia*

obeyer, *imantia*

obituary, *hatak illi isht anumpa*

object; *na kanimi, nana*

object, to; *haklo, imalami*

objections, to cause; *imalammichi*

objector, *imalammi*

oblation, *isht aiokpachi*

obligated, *onutula*

obligation; *aheka, onochi, onutula*

obligation, to assume an; *anumpa ilo-nuchi*

obligations, to lay oneself under; *anumpa kąllo ilonuchi*

oblige, to; *anumpa ilonuchi, onochi, yukpali*

obliquity, *filąmmi*

obliterate, to; *kashoffi, kashoffichi*

obliterated, *kashofa*

oblivion, *ahaksit kąnia*

oblong; *akaⁿk ushi holba, falaiakąt auataka iⁿshali*

obloquy, *mihachi*

obnoxious; *hepulla, hinla, okpulo*

obscene; *okpulo, yuala*

obscenity, *nana yuwala*

obscure; *oklili, tulhpakali*

obscure (applied to language), *afaląpa*

obscure, to; *oklilechi*

obscurely; *luma, lumasi, oklili*

obscureness; *aioklileka, aluma, oklili*

obscurity; *aioklileka, aluma*

obsequies; *hohpi, yaiya, yanusi*

obsequious, *imantia achukma*

observance; *aiokpanchi, imantia*

observation; *anumpa, imantia*

observe, to; *ahni, ahnit, anumpuli, apistikeli, holitobli, ikhana, imantia, pisa*

observer; *ikhana, pisa, piⁿsa*

obsolete; *aksho, akshot taha, sipokni*

obstacle, *atakląma*

obstinacy; *chuⁿkash kąllo, isht ąfekommi*

obstinate; *chuⁿkash kąllo, haksi, ilafoa*

obstruct, to; *atapąchi, ląblichi, okhatapa, oktąbli*

obstructed, *oktąpa*

obstructer, *oktąbli*

obstruction; *anukbikeli, isht okshilita, isht oktąpa, nan isht takaląma, oktąbli, oktąpa*

obtain, to; *ishi*

obtain, to endeavor to; *iakaiyąchit pisa*

obtain a favor, to; *habena*

obtain food as a present, to; *chukalahąchi*

obtained as a present, *habena*

obtainer, *ishi*

obtrude, to; *chukoa, ibachukoa, ibafoka, ibafoki*

obtund, to; *illichi*

obtuse; *halupa, weki*

obviate, to; *bąshpuli, kanąllichi, naksika boli*

obviated, *kąnia*

obvious, *haiaka*

occasion; *heąlhpesa, kaniohmi, nan ihmi*

occasion, to; *yąmihchi*

occasion of death, *aiisht illi*

occasional, *kaniohmika*

occidental; *hąshi aiokatula, hąshi aiokatula imma, hąshi aiokatula pila*

occult; *luma, lumpoa*

occupant, *ątta*

occupation; *ishi, isht anta, isht ątta, nan isht anta*

occupier; *haląlli, iⁿshi*

occupy, to; *aiasha, anta, ątta, haląlli, iⁿshi*

occur, to; *haiaka, ikhana, nukfoka, yąmohmi*

occurrence; *kaniohmi, nana kanihmi*

ocean, *okhąta chito*

October, *Aktoba*

ocular, *piⁿsa*

oculist, *nishkin imalikchi*

odd; *atampa, illa, inla, itilaui keyu*

odd one, *ąlhkucha*

oddity, *inla*

oddly; *illa, inla*

odds; *holba, itilaui keyu, itinnukoa*

ode, *ataloa*

odious; *okpulo, yuala*

odium, *isht yuwala*

odor; *balama, na balama*

odoriferous, *balama*

odorous, *balama*

of; *a, imma*

of any kind, *kaniohmi kia*

of old, *nitak tiⁿkba*

of us, *pin*

off; *bilia, intąnnąp, misha, pila, pilla*

offal; *atampa, na shua*

offence; *nan isht aiibitąbli, nana aiibetąbli*

offend, to; *ashąchi, chuⁿkash hutupali, chuⁿkash nąli, ibetąblichi, nukoąchi, yoshobbi*

offended; *ąlhpiesa, chowa, chuⁿkash hutupa, chuⁿkash nąla, ibetąbli, nukoa*

offended spirit, *chuⁿkash hutupa*

offender; *anumpa kobąffi, chuⁿkash hutupali, nukoąchi, yoshoba*

offends, one who; *yoshobbi*

offense; *aiibetąbli, ashąchi, atakląmmichi, hąshcha, hotupa, nukoa*

offensive; *achukma, nukoa, okpulo, yuala*

offer, to; *boli, ima, imissa, paⁿfi, takakanli, takalechi, wali, weli*

offer to death, to; *illiissa*
offerer; *boli, imissa*
offering; *imissa, isht aiokpachi*
office; *aiapoksia, aialhtoka, aiyamohmahe alhpesa, isht atta*
officer; *afisa, anumpeshi, hatak alhtoka, hatak hullo, nan alhtoka, okla pelichi, pelichi*
officer, to; *anumpeshi atokulli*
official, *nan alhtoka*
officiate, to; *apuskiachi*
officious; *aiokpanchi, ataklama, kana*
offset; *isht kashofa, kashoffi, kania, uncholulli*
offspring; *iso, isht atiaka, uncholulli, ushi*
oft, *fehna*
often; *fehna, himonnan*
ogle, to; *afalapoli*
oh! *ah, aiehnal, alleh, hale!, huk, hush, ikbano, ikbato, ikikki, ohhoh*
oh dear! *akshuki!, akshupi!, ali, alleh, eha, hauk*
oh that; *hokbano, ikbano, ikbato, kbano, kbato*
oil; *ahama, bila, na bila*
oil, to; *ahammi*
oil bag, *panshahama*
oil for the head, *panshahama*
oiled; *ahama, bilahama, litikfo*
oily, *bila bieka*
oint, to; *ahammi*
ointed, *ahama*
ointment; *ahama, ikhinsh, isht ahama*
old; *asahnoyechi, chikki, hopaki, imomachi, kasheho, lipa, sipi, sipokni*
old, to make; *chikkichi, sipoknichi*
old man, *hatak sipokni*
old woman, *kasheho*
older; *akni, sipokni inshali*
oldest, *sipokni kat inshali*
oldest son, *inki ichapa*
oldness, *sipokni*
omen, *isht alhpisa*
omission, *yamichi*
omit, to; *ahaksi, ahaksichi, imahaksi, yamichahe keyu*
on; *a, ai, on, on, um*
on account of, *isht*
on high; *aba, aba pilla, chaha*
on the left hand, *alhfabek imma*
on the morrow, *onnakma*
on this side; *olah intannap, olehma, olimma, takla*

once; *himmona, himonna, himonna achafanli, himonnaha*
once more; *anoa, anonti*
one; *achafa, ak, amih achafa*
one, to; *chafali*
one, to do; *achafa, achafali, chafali*
one, to give; *achafali*
one, to make; *achafa, achafonachi, chafali*
one, to single or select out; *achafali, achafalichi, achafonachi*
one accord, *imanukfila achafa*
one nation, *okla talaia*
one people, *okla chafa, okla talaia*
one time, to be at; *himonna achafa*
one to another, *itim*
one who reproaches, *posilhha shali*
one with; *aiena, aiibachanfa, ibachafa*
oneness, *achafa*
onerous, *weki*
onion; *hatonfalaha, shachuna*
onion, large; *hatonfalaha chito*
only; *bano, bat, beka, bieka, hokbano, hokbato, illa, peh, yammak beka*
only that, *yammak beka*
only the, *ak*
onset, *amoshuli*
onward, *pit*
ooze; *okchi, wak hakshup isht hummachi*
ooze, to; *bichilli, bishbeli, okchushba, pichilli, shinilli*
ooze out, to cause to; *bichillichi, pichelichi*
opacity, *oklili*
opaque, *oklili*
open; *aianli, akamassa, anli, chilafa, fatema, haiaka, itakmofoli, itakpashali, itakpofonli, mabi, shahbi, tiapa, tiwa, tua*
open, to; *anoli, amiffi, bokafa, fachanli, fatummi, fichanli, kalali, kala, kalali, lumpli, mitaffi, pachanli, palalli, tiabli, tiwa, tiwi, tosholi, tua, tuwi, tuwichi, wakama, wakamoli, wakammi, wakoha, wakoli, watama, watammi, wattachi*
open, to burst; *tiwa*
open, to cause to; *fatummichi, tiwichi, tuwichi, patalichi, wakolichi, yatapa*
open and form a fissure, to; *chiluk toba*
opened; *fatoma, fichanli, kala, mitafa, pachanli, tiwa, tua, wakama, wakamoa, wakoha, watama*
opener; *fatummi, fatummichi, palalli, tosholi, tuwi*

opening; *atiwa, atohwali, atua, haiaka,
  shahbika, tohwali, tohyuali*
opening in a fence, *holihta atiwa*
opening in the woods, *ombạla*
openly, *haiakạt*
openness; *aⁿli, shahbi*
opens, one who; *watạmmi*
operate, to; *yạmohmi*
operation, *yạmohmi*
operator, *yạmohmi*
opiate; *ikhiⁿsh nusechi, ishkot nusi*
opiate administered, *ishkochechit nusechi*
opinion, *imanukfila*
opinionated, *yimmi*
opium; *ikhiⁿsh nusechi, nalit illi ạpạt nusi*
opodeldoc, *ikhiⁿsh ahama*
opossum, *shukạta*
opponent, *tạnạp*
opportune, *aiạlhpesa*
opportunity, *aiạlhpiesa*
oppose, to; *ataklạmmi, ichapa, imalạmi*
opposer, *ataklạmmi*
opposite; *ichapa, ichapaka*
opposite directions at once, in; *italaⁿkla*
opposite side of a creek, *bok intạnnạp*
oppress, to; *ilbạshachi, ilbạshalechi, ilbạshali*
oppressed, *ilbạsha*
oppression; *ilbạsha, ilbạshali*
oppressive; *palạmmi, weki*
oppressor; *ilbạshachi, ilbạshali*
opprobrious, *okpulo*
option, *ahni*
optional, *ahni*
opulence, *nan inlaua*
opulent, *nan inlaua*
or; *kia, yok*
or else, *keyukmạt*
oral, *anumpa*
orally, *anumpa*
orange, *hạta lakna*
orange red, *tulaⁿkoba*
oration; *anumpa, anumpa isht hika*
orator, *anumpa isht hika*
oratory, *anumpa isht hika*
oratory, an; *aianumpuli aboha hanta*
orb; *na bolukta, nan chạnaha, nan lumbo*
orbed; *bolukta, chạnaha, lumbo*
orbit, *atia*
orbit of a planet, *fichik atia*
orchard, peach; *osapa takkon aiasha*
ordain, to; *atokoli, hilechi*

ordained; *atokowa, ạlhtoka*
order; *aiyạmohmi, anumpa ạlhpisa, itilaui achạfa*
order, to; *anumpa kạllo onuchi, apesa,
  miha, pelichi*
ordered; *anumpa kạllo onutula, ạlhpesa*
orderly; *achukmat, itilauit*
ordinance; *anumpa ạlhpisa, anumpa kạllo, ạlhpisa*
ordinary; *aiạlhpesa, na fehna keyu, peh
  ạlhpesa*
ordination; *atokoli, ạlhtoka*
ordnance; *tanamp chito, tanamp hochito*
ordure, *yạlhki*
organ, *alepa*
orient, *hạshi akuchaka*
oriental, *hạshi akuchaka*
orientals, the; *hạshi akuchaka okla*
orifice, *chiluk*
origin; *aiisht awechi, aiisht ia ạmmona,
  aminti*
origin, place of; *atoba*
original, *tiⁿkba*
original, the; *tikba*
originate, to; *ia, ikbi*
originate at, to; *minti*
ornament; *aiukleka, isht aiukli, isht
  ilakshema, isht shema, nan isht shema*
ornament, to; *fohka, fohkạchi, shema,
  shemạchi*
ornament with, to; *isht aiuklichi*
ornamented, *shema*
orphan; *ạlhtakla, ạlla ạlhtakla*
orphanage, *ạlhtakla*
orthodox, *ạba anumpa yimmi*
orts; *atampa, lishoa*
oscillate, to; *fahata, falamoa*
ossify, to; *foni ikbi, foni toba*
ossuary; *hatak illi foni aiasha, tạshka
  chuka*
ostensible, *haiaka*
ostentation, *haiaka*
ostentatious, *ilefehnạchi*
other; *achạfa, inla, intạnnạp, tạnnạp,
  yạto*
other side, *mishtạnnạp*
other side of a creek, *bok mishtạnnạp*
otherwise; *keyukma, yatush*
otter, *oshạn*
ought; *he, hetuk*
ounce, *auⁿs*
our; *hạpi, hạpiⁿ, hạpim, hạpimmi, hạpin,
  hạpishno, hạpimmi, pi, piⁿ, pim, pimmi,
  pin, pishno*

our, to become; *hapimmi toba*
ours; *hapimmi, pimmi, pishno*
ourselves, *pishno akinli*
oust, to; *akuchi, kuchichi*
ousted, *kucha*
out; *akuncha, haiaka, kochanli, kucha*
out, to; *akuchi, kuchichi*
out of; *akucha, kucha*
out of date; *aksho, sipokni*
out of the way, *yoshoba*
outcast, *kucha*
outcry; *komuntat panya, tahpala*
outdo, to; *imaiya, imaiyachi, ishatichi*
outer, *kucha fehna*
outgo, to; *ia, imaiya*
outgrow, to; *imaiya*
outlast, to; *imaiya*
outlive, to; *imaiya*
outmost; *alipilla, wishakchi*
outrage, to; *hotupali*
outrageous; *nukoa, okpulo*
outside; *anaksika, kucha, pakna, pak-nanka*
outside of the bend, *poloma*
outwalk, to; *imaiya*
outward; *kucha, kuchimma, paknanli*
oval; *akank ushi holba, lumbo, shabahki*
ovation, *isht ika*
oven; *aiapushli, aialhpusha, apalaska*
over; *akucha, mishtannap, paknaka*
over again, *na*
over all, *moma inshali*
overalls, *obala foka*
overcharge; *aiilli atapa, albiha atapa*
overcharge, to; *aiilli atabli, atablit abeli*
overcharged, *aiilli atapa*
overcome, to; *aiimaiyachi, chunkash ishi, imaiya, imaiyachi*
overdo, to; *atabli, atablit tikambichi*
overdone; *atapa, nuna atapa, tikabi*
overflow, to; *atabli, abanabli, oka banapa, oka bikelichi, okchitochi*
overflow, to cause an; *atablichi*
overflowed; *oka banapa, oka bikeli, oka falama*
overgladness of heart, *chunkash yukpa atapa*
overgo, to; *atapa, abanabli, imaiya*
overhaul, to; *sakki, tepuli, tiabli*
overhauled; *tepoa, tiapa*
overhauls, one who; *tepuli*
overload, *albiha atapa*
overload, to; *atablit abeli, atablit shapulechi, shapulechi*

overlook, to; *ahaksichi, aiashachi, ima-haksi, paknaka hikiat pisa*
overlooked, *ahaksi*
overmuch; *atapa fehna, laua fehna, okpulo*
overpack, to; *atablit shapulechi*
overplus; *atampa, atapa, alhtampa, chakbi*
overplus, to cause an; *atablichi*
overpower, to; *imaiya, imaiyachi*
overreach, to; *abanabli, abanablichi, haksichi, issochi*
overreached, *haksi*
overrule, to; *petichi*
overrun, to; *abanabli, lohummichi, yululli*
oversee, to; *apesachi, apistikeli, petichi*
overseer; *apesachi, apistikeli, nan apesachi*
overset, to; *kinafa, kinaffi*
overshadow, to; *akapoa, akopoa, hoshontikachi*
oversight, *aiashachi*
overstock, to; *atabli*
overstocked, *atapa*
overt, *haiaka*
overtake, to; *sakki*
overtake, to cause to; *sakkichi*
overthrow; *kinafa, okpulo*
overthrow, to; *imaiya, imaiyachi, kinaffi, tipeli, okpani*
overthrown; *kinafa, tipia*
overtire, to; *atablit tikambichi*
overtop, to; *imaiya*
overvalued, *aiilli atapa*
overwhelm, to; *kinaffi, umpohomot okpani*
owe, to; *aheka, aheka intakanli*
owed, *aheka*
owl, horned; *ishkitini*
owl, large; *opa*
owl, screech; *ofunlo*
own; *fehna, ilap*
own, to; *anoli, halalli, immi, inshi*
owner; *immi, inshi*
ox; *wak hobak, wak toksali*
ox team, *wak tonksali hioti achafa*
ox yoke; *wak toksali abankachi, wak tonksali abanaya*
ox, working; *wak hobak tonksali, wak toksali*
oxbow; *wak tonksali innuchi, tonokbi*
oxen, a yoke of; *wak itihalalli, wak tonksali itapata*
oxfly, *otana chito*

oyster, *chakla*
oyster shells, petrified; *opahaksun*

pabulum; *ahofanti, ilhpak, ilimpa*
pace; *ahabli, aⁿya, habli, kaialli, nowa*
pace, to; *aⁿya, ilhkoli, kaiilli, nowa*
pace, to make; *kaialli*
pacer, *kaialli*
pacific; *nuktala, yohbi*
pacified, *nuktala*
pacifier, *nuktalali*
pacify, to; *hopolachi, hopolalli, nukta-lali, yohbichi*
pack; *bahta, bonunta, shapo, talakchi*
pack, to; *boli, shapulechi, tushpalit cha-fichi*
pack (as meat), to; *alalli*
pack a horse, to; *isuba shapulechi*
pack horse; *isuba shapo shali, isuba sha-puli*
pack of cards; *isht baska*
package, *shapo*
packed; *itallat akkachit kaha, shapo, sha-poli, talakchi*
packet, *lumbo*
packsaddle, *isuba umpatalhpo falakto*
pact; *itimanumpa, itimalhpisa*
pad; *akkahuⁿkupa, huⁿkupa*
paddle; *isht mofi, peni isht muⁿfa*
paddle, short; *isht moeli*
paddle, to; *moⁿffi, mofi, moeli, moli*
paddled, *moⁿfa*
paddler, *moⁿffi*
padlock, *luksi*
padlock, house; *aboha inluksi*
padlock, to; *shannichi*
pagans, *oklushi abanumpa ikithano*
page; *holisso intannap achafa, holisso pata achafa*
page (attendant), *tishu*
paid; *atobbi, alhchilofa, alhtoba, chilofa*
pail; *isht ochi, itampo*
pailful, *isht ochi alota*
pain; *anukhammi, hotupa, kinoha, kom-michi, na hotupa, nan ukhamachi, nuk-hama, nukhammi*
pain, great; *chilinoha*
pain, to; *hotupali, kommichechi, kommi-chi, mufkachi*
pain, to cause; *anukhammi, imalekache-chi, imalekachi, kommichechi, nukha-machi, nukhammichi*
pain, to suffer; *aleka*
pain on both sides, *italaⁿkla hotupa*

pained, *imaleka*
painful; *anukhammi, hotupa, kommichi, mufka, nukhammi*
painful, severely; *simikli*
paint, *isht anchaha*
paint, to; *anchali, anchalichi*
painted, *anchaha*
painter, *anchali*
painter (of a boat), *peni isht talakchi*
painting of a man, *shilup*
pair; *hollo, ichapa, ichapoa, itichabli, iti-chapa, tuklo*
pair, to; *ichabli*
paired, *ichapa*
palace; *aboha holitopa, miⁿko inchuka*
palatable, *kashaha*
palate, *isunlash ushi*
pale; *hanta, hatokbi, hata, okhatali*
pale, a; *iti shima halupa*
pale, to; *holihta halupa ikbi*
pale, to become; *hatachi*
pale, to make; *hatokbichi*
pale, very; *hatat kania*
paled, *holihta halupa*
pale-faced; *ibakhatanli, nashuka hata*
paleness, *hata*
Palestine, *Chu yakni*
paling, *holihta halupa*
palisade; *holihta halupa, holihta kallo*
palisade, to; *holihta halupa ikbi*
palisado, *holihta kallo*
pall, *anchi holitopa*
pallet; *hashiⁿka, patapo, patalhpo*
palliate, to; *lauechi, mihachi*
pallid, *hata*
palm, to; *haksichi, pasholi*
palm of the hand, *ibbak pata*
palmetto, *tala*
palmetto, high; *talimushi*
palpable; *haiaka, potola hinla*
palpitate, to; *mitikli, mitikminli, nuk-bimikachi, nukbimimkachi, nukkitekachi, nuktimichi, nukwimekachi, takanha, ti-mikli*
palpitation; *mitikminli, nukbimikachi, nukkitekachi, nukwimekachi*
palsied, *haknip illi*
palsy; *haknip illi abi, palsi, wannichi*
palsy, to; *haknip illichi, illichi, kotachi, okpani*
paltry; *iskitini, makali*
pamphlet; *holisso, holisso hakshup iksho*
pan; *amphata, ampo, ampo mahaia, nush-kobo tabokaka*

pan, tin; *malha*
pander, to; *haui pelichit nowa*
pane of glass, *apisa achafa*
panegyric, *holitoblit isht anumpa*
panegyrize, to; *holitoblit isht anumpuli*
pang, *hotupa*
pant, to; *banna, bufboli, fiopat taha, fohukli, fotukfunli, hahka, shutukshonli*
pantaloon, *obala foka*
panther, *koi*
pap; *ipinshik, ohoyo ipinshik*
papa, *inki*
paper, *aholisso*
paper, a; *holisso*
paper, to; *holisso alapalachi*
paper maker, *holisso ikbi*
paper mill; *holisso aiikbi, holisso atoba*
paper money, *holisso lapushki*
papered, *holisso alapali*
papoose; *alla, allunsi, puskus*
papulæ, *lakchi*
par, *itilaui*
parable; *anumpa isht alhpisa, anumpa nan isht alhpisa, nana isht apesa*
paraclete; *apelachi, Shilombish holitopa*
parade, to; *ilaualli, ilauallichi, itanaha, itannali, tashka chipota itannali*
paraded, *tashka chipota itannaha*
paragraph, *anumpa achafa*
paralyze, to; *illichi*
paralyzed, *shimoha*
paramount, *inshali bano*
parapet, *holihta kallo*
parasol, *ohoyo imisht ilonhoshontikachi*
parboil, to; *honammona*
parboiled, *hononammona*
parcel; *bonunta, kanomona, na buna*
parch, to; *anakshonfa, anakshonffi, anaksholi, anakshua, auashli, alwasha*
parch coffee, to; *kafi auashli*
parched; *anakshonfa, anakshua, alwasha*
pardon; *kashofa, nana kashofa*
pardon, to; *imahaksi, imahaksichi, kashoffi*
pardonable; *ahaksa hinla, imahaksicha hinla, kashofa hinla*
pardoned; *ahaksi, imahaksi, kashofa*
pardoner; *ahaksichi, na imahaksi, na kashofichi, nana ahaksichi*
pare, to; *luffi, luli*
pared; *lufa, luha*
parents, *inki ishki itatuklo*
parer; *isht luli, luffi, luli*
paring, *hakshup lufa*

parlance, *anumpa*
parley; *anumpa, anumpuli*
parley, to; *anumpuli*
parrakeet, *kilinkki*
parricide, *inki ishki abi*
parrot, a species of; *kilinkki*
parson, *aba anumpuli pelicheka alhtoka*
part; *folota, kaniohmi, kashapa, kashkoa, tushafa*
part, to; *filamolechi, filamoli, filammi, fullottokachi, issa, kashabli, kashkoli, tushalichi*
part of an earring, *palatha*
part way, *chakpa*
part with, to; *kanchi*
partake, to; *ishi, ishko*
partake with, to; *ibatankla*
partaker; *ibafoka, ibatankla, ishi, ishko*
parted; *filama, kashapa, kashkoa, tapa, taptua*
partial, *kanimachi*
partially, *chohmi*
particle; *chipintasi, iskitinisi, kaniohmusi*
particular; *achafa, fehna*
particularize, to; *atokoli*
particularly, *atuk*
partition; *itintakla, kashkoa*
partly, *chohmi*
partly worn, *chikki*
partner; *apela, itapela, itauaya, itapela, itichapa*
partnership; *itauaya, itibafoka, itichapa*
partridge; *kofi, kofi chito*
parts of, *kaniohmi*
parturition; *cheli, eshi, sholi*
party, *okla*
Pascagoula, *Bashokla*
pasha, *minko*
pass; *akucha, alopoli, alopulli, ala, hina, hina kucha, holisso, itintakla atia, ona, takla*
pass, to; *anya, abanabli, ia, illi, imahaksi, kanchi, kania, lopotoli, mosholi, onochi, yamohmi*
pass, to come to; *yakohmi, yamohmi*
pass around, to; *afobli*
pass away, to; *masheli*
pass by, to; *aiopitama, aiopitammi, opitamoli, opitammi*
pass forth from, to; *attat ia*
pass over, to; *auanapoli, auanabli, abanapoli, abanabli, pit, tanapoli, tanabli*
pass over, to cause to; *abanapolechi*

pass quickly, to; *yilepa*
pass through, to; *alopoli, alopulli, anaklopulli, tipulli, lopoli, lopulli*
passable; *aⁿya hinla, alhpesa, lopulla hinla*
passage; *aboha ititakla, aiaya, anumpa, atia, aⁿya, fohka, fohkat aⁿya, ulbal ont ia*
passage into, *achukoa*
passed; *aiopitama, alhpesa, lopulli, taha*
passed by; *opitama, opitamoa*
passed over; *abanapoa, auanapa, auanapoa, abanapa, tanapa, tanapoa*
passed through; *lopoli, yululli*
passenger; *aⁿya, fohkat aⁿya, nowat aⁿya*
passing; *aⁿya, fehna*
passion; *anushkunna, nuklibishlikachi, nukoa*
passion, to be in a; *okpolo*
passionate; *nukhobela, nukoa shali*
passive, *kachi*
Passover, the; *abanablit ont ia, nan abanablit ont ia, Chu chepuli chito*
passport, *holisso*
past; *chamo, chikki*
"past feeling," *salbo*
past time, *kamo*
paste, *isht akamassa*
paste, to; *kamassalli*
pastime; *ilaualli, washoha*
. pastor; *aba anumpuli apistikeli, alhpoa apistikeli*
pasture; *alhpoa aiimpa, holihta alhpoa albiha*
pasture, to; *hashuk impa, hashuk impachi*
pat, *alhpiesa*
pat, a; *pasalichi*
pat, to; *pasalichi*
patch; *akataiya, akalli, alhkata, isht alhkata, osapushi*
patch, to; *akatali, akkalli*
patched; *akataiya, alhkata*
patched together, a thing; *nan italhkatta*
patcher, *akkalli*
patchwork, *italhkatta*
pate; *nushkobo, nushkobo hakshup, nushkobo tabokaka*
patella, *iyiⁿ kalaha wishakchi*
paternal ancestors, *iⁿki aiokla*
path; *anowa, hina*
path, bright; *hina hanta*
path, large; *hina chito*
path, to; *hina ikbi*
pathway; *atia, hina*
patience; *na mihiksho, nuktanla, nuktala*

patient; *nuktanla, nuktala*
patient, a; *hatak abeka*
patriarch, *intikba*
patriotic, *okla*
patron, *apelachi*
patronize, to; *apelachi*
patter, to; *kasahachi, kassahachi*
pattern, *isht ahobachi*
pattern, to; *hobachi*
paunch, *takoba*
pauper, *hatak ilbasha inla anukcheto*
pause, *yokopa*
pause, to; *issa, nuktala, yokopa*
pave, to; *lukfi nuna patali, tali patali*
paved, *tali isht patalhpo*
pavement; *tali patapo, tali pata*
pavilion; *alhtipo, na hata alhtipo*
pavilion, to; *attepuli*
paw; *ibbak, iyi*
paw, to; *shaffi*
pawn, *boli*
pawn, to; *ahinnachi, atobbichi hilechi, boli, hilechi*
pawned; *ahinna, hika*
pawner; *boli, hilechi, inuchi*
pawpaw, *umbi*
pay, *alhtoba*
pay, to; *atobbi, chilofa, chiloffi*
pay, to cause to; *chilofachi*
pay attention, to; *nowa*
pay day, *nitak aialhtoba*
payer, *atobbi*
paymaster, *atobbi*
payment; *atobbi, alhtoba, chilofa, isht alhtoba*
pea, *tobe hollo*
peace; *achukma, aiachukmaka, chulosa, hanta, halhpaⁿsha, itiⁿkana, itinnan aiya, kana, na yukpa, nan aiya, nuktanla, samanta*
peace, to act for; *nan aiya*
peace, to make; *achukmalechi, nan aiyachi*
peaceable; *hanta, halhpaⁿsha, hopola, kana, nuktanla*
peaceably, *halhpaⁿshi*
peacebreaker; *anumpa chukushpashali, hatak itachowachi*
peaceful; *chulosa, halhpaⁿsha, hopola, nan aiya, samanta*
peaceful, to become; *nuktala*
peacemaker; *hatak itiⁿnanaiyachi, hatak nan olabechi, itinnan aiyachechi, nan aiyachi*
peach, *takkon*

peach, clingstone; *takkon aⁿli, takkon foni humma, takkon kallo*
peach, freestone; *takkon fakopa*
peach fuzz, *takkon hoshiko*
peach meat, *takkon foni nipi*
peach rind, *takkon hakshup*
peach skin, *takkon hakshup*
peach stone, *takkon foni*
peach stone, red; *takkon foni humma*
peach tree; *takkon api, takkonlapi*
peach-tree gum, *takkonlitilli*
peacock, *okchanlush chito*
peacock feather, *okchanlush chito hoshiⁿshi*
peak; *paknaka, wishakchi*
peaked; *ibakchufanli, ibakchufaⁿshli*
peal; *bimihachi, winihachi*
peal, to; *bimihachi, winihachi*
peal of thunder, *hiloha*
peal of thunder, sharp; *hiloha tassa*
peanuts, *yakni anuⁿka waya*
pear, prickly; *talhpakha*
pearl; *holitopa, tali holitompa*
Pearl River, *hacha*
pearlash; *hituk, hituk tohbi*
peas, *tobe hollo*
pebble; *taluⁿshik, talushik*
pecan, *fala*
peccable, *yoshoba hinla*
peck; *bushul iklanna iklanna, kalan tuklo*
peck, to; *chanli, chikiⁿha, lunlichi*
pecked, *chaⁿya*
pecker; *chanli, hushi iti chanli, iti chanli*
peculate, to; *huⁿkupa*
peculiar, *fehna*
pecuniary, *tali holisso imma*
pedant; *hatak nan ithana ilahobbi, holisso pisachi, nan ikhana ilahobbi, nan ithana ilahobbi*
peddle, to; *itatobat aⁿya*
peddler; *alhpoyak shali, itatobat aⁿya, na shali*
pedestrian; *akkahikat aⁿya, akkanowa*
pedigree, *isht atiaka*
pedo-baptism, *alla oka isht imokissa*
peek, to; *afananchi*
peel; *hakshup, hituk chubi isht peli falaia*
peel, to; *chilafa, fachanli, fakoha, fakoli, fakopa, fakopli, falla, falli, iti loli, luffi, luli, loⁿfa, loⁿffi, loha, loli, moli, moⁿfa, moⁿffi, shibbi, shimnuffi, shukafa, shukaffi, shukali*
peel, to cause to; *fachanlichi, fakoplichi, lolichi, shukalichi*

peel off in strips, to; *anukbiaffi*
peeled; *anukbiafe, fakoha, fakoli, fakopa, fakowa, lufa, luha, loⁿfa, loha, moⁿfa, moⁿfkachi, moha, shukafa, shukali*
peeler; *fakolichi, fakopli, loⁿffi, loli*
peeling; *fakoha, fakoli, fakopa, hakshup, shukali*
peeling, the act of; *fachanli*
peelings from intestines, *anuⁿklupatka*
peep, *haiaka*
peep, to; *afananchi, haiaka*
peer; *aiitibafoka, itilaui*
peevish; *anukshomota, anukshomunta, chuⁿshkiksho, isht afekommi*
peevishness, *anukshomunta*
peg; *atakali, atakoli, iti achushkachi, iti isht ahonala*
peg, wooden; *iti chakbi, itichakbi*
pelican, *chilantakoba*
pelt, *hakshup hish aⁿsha*
pelt, to; *boli, isso*
pelter; *boli, isso*
peltry; *na hakshup, nam poa hakshup*
pen; *holihta, isht holissochi*
pen, silver; *tali isht holissochi*
pen, small; *holihtushi*
pen, to; *holihta fohki, holihtani, holissochi, yukachi*
pen maker, *isht holissochi ikbi*
pencil, to; *holissochi, isht holissochi, nan isht laⁿfi, tali isht holissochi*
pencil maker, *isht holissochi ikbi*
pendant; *haksobish takali, haksobish takoli, na hata, shapha, takali*
pending; *aiaⁿli, takanli*
penetrable, *chukowa hinla*
penetrate, to; *ibachukoa, lopulli, lopullichi, lumpa, lumpli*
penetrated, *lumpa*
peninsula, *yakni nushkobo*
penitent, *hatak nana yoshoba isht nukhaⁿklo*
penitentiary, *hatak yuka atoksali*
penknife, *bashpushi*
penman; *hatak holissochi imponna, holissochi*
pennant; *na hata, shapha*
penned; *holihta fohka, holihtalhto, holisso*
penner, *holissochi*
penny, *iskali*
pension, *afammikma ilhpeta*
pension, to; *afammikma ilhpitachi*

pensive, *ilapissa*
pent, *holihta ạlbiha*
penurious, *ilatomba atạpa*
penury, *ilbạsha*
people, *okla*
people, great; *okla chito*
people, one; *talaia*
people, small; *oklushi*
peopled, *abinili*
pepper; *hishi homi, tishi homi*
pepper, black; *tishi homi lusa*
pepper, Cayenne; *tishi homi humma*
pepper, Guiana; *tishi homi humma*
pepper, red; *hishi homi humma, tishi homi humma*
pepper bag, *tishi homi aiạlhto*
pepperbox, *tishi homi aiạlhto*
peppercorn, *hishi homi ạni*
per capita, *nushkobo chumpa*
peradventure, *yoba*
perambulate, to; *pisạt lopulli, tikba aⁿya*
perceive, to; *akostininchi, pisa, ikhana*
perceptible; *akostinincha hinla, ikhana hinla*
perch; *iti fabạssa, iti tạpa ahabbi talapi*
perch (a fish), *nạni bạsa*
perch, to; *binili, hikia, omanili*
perchance; *fo, yoba*
percolate, to; *bichilli, hoiyạchi, holuya, holuyạchi*
percolated, *holuya*
perdition; *aiokpuloka, aiokpuluⁿka*
peremptory, *aiaⁿli*
perennial; *ataha iksho, bilia*
perfect; *achukma, aiaⁿli, imponna taha*
perfect, to; *atali*
perfection, *aiạlhtaha*
perfectly; *bano, taha*
perfidious, *aⁿli*
perfidy, *anumpa kobafa*
perforate, to; *lopolichi, luⁿa, lukalichi, lukạffi, lumpli, lunli, lunlichi*
perforate at, to; *bili*
perforated; *bila, lopulli, luⁿa, lukafa, lukali, lumpa*
perforated at, *alukali*
perforation; *alukafa, alukali, alumpa, luⁿkạchi, lumpli*
perforator; *isht lukạffi, isht lumpli*
perform, to; *aiaⁿlichi, atali, yạmihchi*
performance; *nana kaniohmi, yạmichi*
performer, *yạmichi*
perfume, *na balama*

perfume, to; *balamạchechi*
perfumed, *balama*
perhaps; *chalik, chechik, chishba, fokahota, fota, hacha, hah, yoba*
perhaps not, *yobaheto*
perhaps one, *achạfona*
peril; *isht imaiokpulo, nan aiisht imaleka, nana aiisht imaleka*
period; *aiạli, folota, nitak ạlhpisa*
perish, to; *bạshi, illi, okpulo, tạmoa, toshbi*
perishable; *bạsha hinla, illa hinla, toshba hinla*
perishables, *nan toshbi*
perished; *okpulot taha, toshbi*
perjure, to; *aholạbi, holabit anumpa kạllo ilonuchi*
perjurer; *aholạbi, holabit anumpa kạllo ilonuchi*
permanent; *bilia, kamạssa*
permit, *holisso*
permit, to; *ome imahni*
permit to go, to; *ia*
pernicious, *okpulo*
perpendicular, *apissanli*
perpetrate, to; *yạmihchi*
perpetual, *bilia*
perpetual, to make; *biliachi*
perpetually, *bilia*
perpetuate, to; *biliachechi*
perpetuity, *ataha iksho*
perplex, to; *aiyokomi, ataklạmmi*
perplexed; *ataklạma, imaiyokoma*
perplexity, to cause; *imaiyokomichi*
persecute, to; *hotupali, ilbạshachi, ilbạshali, isikkopali*
persecuted; *hotupa, ilbạsha*
persecution; *hofayali, hotupa, hotupali, ilbạsha, ilbạshali*
persecutor; *hotupali, ilbạshali*
perseverance, *achunanchi*
persevere, to; *achunanchi, amoshuli, asitopa*
persevering, *achunanchi*
persimmon, *uⁿkof*
persimmon tree, *uⁿkof ạpi*
persist, to; *achunanchi*
person; *hatak, kạna, okla*
person, noisy; *shakạbli*
personal, *hatak ahalaia*
personally, *ilap fena*
personate, to; *inla ilahobbi*
perspicuous, *haiaka*
perspiration, *laksha*

perspire, to; *laksha*

persuade, to; *anukfohkachechi, anumpulit chunkqsh ishi, imanukfila shananchi*

pert, *tushpa*

pertain, to; *ahalaia, aiachafa*

pertinacious, *achunanchi*

perturbation, *imanukfila laua*

pervade, to; *lopulli*

perverse; *banshkiksho, na shanaiya, nukoa shali, shanaia*

pervert, to; *okpqni, shanaiqchi, yoshobbi*

pervert the heart, to; *chunkqsh shanaiqchi*

pervert the mind, to; *imanukfila shananchi*

perverted; *okpulo, shanaia, yoshoba*

perverted in opinion, *imanukfila shanaia*

perverter; *okpqni, yoshobbi*

pest; *abeka okpulo, nan okpulo*

pester, to; *anumpulechi, apistikeli*

pestilence; *abeka okpulo, ililli, illilli*

pestilent, *isht qfekommi*

pestle; *kitqpi, kitush*

pestle handle, *kitush qpi*

pet; *qlhpoa, nukoa*

pet, to; *apobqchi*

petition; *anumpa asilhha, asilhha, holisso asilhha*

petition, to; *asilhha, asilhhqchi*

petitioner; *asilhha, nana silhha*

petrifaction; *italbansa, tqlbansa, tali toba*

petrified, *tqli toba*

petrify, to; *tqli ikbi, tqli toba*

petticoat; *qlhkuna kolofa, qskufa, qskufa tqpa*

petty, *iskitini*

petulant, *isht qfekommi*

pew, *abinili*

pewter, *naki kqllo*

pewter plate, *naki kqllo aiimpa*

phantasm; *imanukfila, iti boli*

phantom; *imanukfila, shilup*

Pharisee, *Falisi*

phial, *kotobushi*

philosopher, *nan ikhana*

phlegm; *ibilhkqn, kalanfa, woshoki*

phlegmatic; *ibilhkqn chito, kapqssa*

phrase, *anumpa*

phrase, to; *anumpuli*

phthisis, *nukshininfa*

physic; *ikfiachi, ikhinsh*

physic, to; *ulbql ont iachi*

physician; *alikchi, qllikchi*

piazza; *aboha apishia, aboha hoshontika, apashia, qpishia, chukimpqta, hoshontika*

piazza post, *hoshontikiyi*

pick, *isht kula*

pick, to; *atokulit ishi, qmo, qpa, bau, chanli, chiniffi, chinoli, emo, ishmo, kili, nalichi, sheli*

pick off the hair, to; *tikqffi*

pick out, to; *atokulit aiyua, foeli, fulli, shinli*

pick out, to cause to; *fullichi*

pick out seed, to; *niheli*

pick the teeth, to; *shinli*

pick up, to; *aioa, aiyoa, apoyua*

pickax; *isht chanli, isht kula*

picked; *qlmo, shinya*

picked off, *naha*

picked up; *aioa, aiyua*

picker; *qmo, hopohka, nan qmo, sheli, shinli*

picket, *holihta halupa*

picket, to; *holihta halupa ikbi*

pickle, *oka hqpi yqmmi*

pickle, to; *oka hqpi yqmmi fohki*

picture; *holba, na holba, isht qlhpisa*

picture, to; *lanfit hobachi*

picture of a man; *hatak holba, shilup*

piece; *ataptua, holisso, kobulli, lishoa, tuchali, tushafa, tushali, tushtua*

piece, small; *chinifa*

piece, thin; *pqsa*

piece, to; *achakqli*

piece split, *palanta*

pied; *bakoa, bakokona*

pied, to make; *bakoqchi*

pierce, to; *bahqffi, bali, honqli, lifelichi, lifinha, lopolichi, luna, lukafa, lumpa, lumpli*

pierced; *baha, honala, lopoli, lukafa, lukali, lumpa*

piercer; *isht baha, lumpli*

pig, *shukhushi*

pig, to; *cheli, shukhushicheli*

pig of lead; *naki fabqssa, naki palqlka*

pigeon, *pqchi*

pigeon egg, *pqchushi*

pigeon roost; *pqchaiasha, pqchanusi*

pigeon shot, *nakunshi*

piggin; *isht ochi, oka anlhto, oka isht ochi*

pigmy, *hatak inmoma*

pigpen, *shukha inhollihta*

pigsty, *shukha inchuka*

pike (a fish), *bqsa*

pike (a weapon), *na halupa*

piked, *halupa*
pile; *fohopa, itanaha, itanahachi, nakacho-sha*
pile, to; *itannali, itannalichi*
pile of corn, *alhpinkachi*
piled, *itanaha*
pilfer, to; *hunkupa, nan chokushpa hunkupa*
pilferer, *nan chokushpa hunkupa*
pilgrim, *hatak nowat anya*
pilgrimage, *nowat anya*
pill; *ikhinsh lumbo, ikhinsh lumboa*
pillage, *na wehpoa*
pillage, to; *wehpuli, wehput fullota, weli*
pillar; *hika, inhika, tonnik*
pillion, *ohoyo aiomanili*
pillow, *alhpishi*
pillow, to; *alhpishi*
pillow, to prepare a; *alhpishechichi*
pillowcase; *alhpishi afoka, alhpishi inshukcha*
pilot; *hatak peni isht anya, intikba heka, peni isht anya, tikba heka*
pilot, to; *peni isht anya*
pilotage; *alhtoba, peni isht anya imalhtoba*
pimple; *lakchi, tanlakchi, tansh lakchi*
pin; *atakali, atakoli, chufak ushi, chufak yushkoboli, iti chufak, iti isht ahonala, na halupa*
pin, headed; *yushkoboli*
pin, wooden; *iti tala, itichakbi*
pin, to; *kamassalli*
pin maker, *chufak ush ikbi*
pincers; *isht kiselichi, tali isht kiseli*
pinch, *chiniffi*
pinch, to; *chinoli, ilbashali, katali, katanlichi, kopoli, yikiffi*
pinch with the fingers, to; *chiniffi*
pinched; *chininffa, chinowa*
pincher, *chiniffi*
.pinchers, *isht kiselichi*
pinching, *chinowa*
pine, *tiak*
pine, dry; *shohala*
pine, longleaf; *tiak fanya*
pine, riven; *tiak shima*
pine, to; *liposhichi*
pine, yellow; *tiak hobak*
pine, young; *tiak ushi*
pine away, to; *liposhi*
pine knot; *pinkshi, tiak pinkshi*
pine shingle, *tiak shima*
pine wood, *tiak*

pined away, *liposhi*
pinfeather; *aliktichi, hishi alikti*
pinion, to; *ibbak takchi, sanahchi takchi*
pinioned, *ibbak talakchi*
pink, a; *haiyunkpulo pakanli humma*
pink, the Carolina; *haiyunkpulo pakanli humma*
pinnacle, *wishakchi*
pinned, *kamassa*
pinner, *itakamassalli*
pint; *isht ishko latassa achafa, koat iklanna*
pintado; *akank kofi, kofi chito*
piny, *tiak foka*
piny region, *tiak foka*
pioneer, *tikbanya hinikbi*
pious; *aba anumpa nukfoka aianli, aba anumpa yimmi aiali*
pipe; *ayanalli, hakchuma ashunka, hakchuma shuti, isht punfa, italhfoa chito, oskula, uskula*
pipe, to; *uskula olachi*
piper, *uskula olachi*
pique, *nukoa*
pique, to; *chunkash bili, chunkash nali, nukoachi*
piqued; *chunkash bila, chunkash nala, nukoa*
pirogue; *iti kula peni, peni, peni kula falaia*
pismire, *shunkani*
pistol; *tanamp puskus, tanamp ushi*
pit; *chiluk, chilukoa, chuluk, hichukbi, lachowa, yakni chiluk, yakni kula*
pit, natural; *hochukbi*
pit, tan; *ahummachi*
pit of the stomach, *inwalwa*
pitch; *tiak nia kallo, tiak nia lua*
pitch, the; *aiali*
pitch, to; *akka ia, pila*
pitch (a tune), to; *taloa*
pitch (cover with pitch), to; *apolusli*
pitch a camp, to; *albinachi, bina hilechi*
pitch down, to; *lotama*
pitch down, to give a; *lotammi*
pitch of a hill, *nanih akkia*
pitch too high, to; *iskitinichi*
pitched; *apolusa, alhpolosa, hika, hikia*
pitcher; *isht ishko chaha, oka aialhto*
pitchfork, *tali chufak*
piteous, *ilbasha*
pith; *iskuna, kallo*
pithy; *iskuna laua, kallo*
pitiable, *nukhanklo*
pitiful, *nukhanklo*

pittance, *kanomusi*
pity, *nukhaⁿklo*
pity, to; *nukhaⁿklo*
pivot, *aiontalạt fulokachi*
placable, *yukpa hinla*
place; a, *aiasha, foka*
place, steep; *sakti chaha*
place, that; *yạmma*
place, this; *takla, yakohmika*
place, to; *hilechi, talali, taloti*
place before, to; *tikba kali*
place in, to; *shamạllichi*
place in the arms, to; *shakba fohki*
place not plowed, *yakni ikapatafo*
place of another, to be in the; *ạlhtoba*
place on, to; *atalali, ontalali*
place ruled; *apelichi, apelichika*
place shaved, *shaⁿfi*
place wide apart, to; *shauahạchi*
placed; *hieli, hika, hikia, talaia, taloha,*
tạla
placed in; *achushkạchi, shamạlli*
placed in, being; *achushkanchi*
placed in the arms, *shakba foka*
placed in the hand, *ibbak foka*
placed in there, *afohka*
placed on; *atalaia, ataloha*
placenta, *haiombish*
placer, *hilechi*
placid; *nuktanla, yokopa*
plague; *abeka okpulo, ataklạma, ataklạ-*
moti
plague, to; *anumpulechi, apistikeli*
plaguy, *isht ạfekommi*
plain (evident); *aiaⁿli, haiaka, lumiksho*
plain (level), *patasạchi*
plain, a; *yakni matali, yakni patali, pa-*
tasạchi, yakni patussạchi
plain, to; *patasạchi*
plain, to make; *haiakachechi*
plainly; *achukmat, apissanlit, haiakạt*
plaint; *ilbạsha, nukhaⁿklo*
plaintive, *nukhaⁿklo*
plait; *awalakachi, pạna*
plait, to; *awalakachechi, pạnni, pokoti,*
puli, tanạffo, tạna, tạnạffo
plaited; *awalakachi, ạlhtạnnafo, pạna,*
pula, tannạffo, tạnna, tạnnạffo
plaiter; *awalakachechi, pạnni, puli, ta-*
nạffo
plan; *ahni, apesa, isht ạlhpisa*
plan secretly, to; *luhmit nana apesa*
plane; *isht shaⁿfi, iti isht shaⁿfiⁿ, iti isht*
shaⁿfit haluskichi

plane, to; *halushkichi, shaⁿfi*
planed; *halushki, shaⁿfa*
planed board, *iti shaⁿfa*
planer, *iti shaⁿfi*
planet; *fichik, fichik chito*
plank; *iti bạsha, iti bạsha sukko*
plank, to; *iti bạsha patali*
plant; *ạlba, haiyuⁿkpulo, haiyuⁿkpulo ho-*
lokchi, holokchi, na holokchi
plant, a certain; *akunti, hashiⁿko, kifạsh,*
oni
plant, sensitive; *tohkil*
plant, to; *hokchi*
plant at, to; *ahokchi*
plant with something, to; *ahokchichi*
plantation; *apelichika, osapa*
planted, *holokchi*
planted, ground; *aholokchi*
planter; *hatak osapa toⁿksạli, hokchi, na*
hokchi, osapa toksạli
plaster, *isht ạlhpolosa*
plaster, to; *apolusli*
plastered; *ạlhpolosa, apolusa*
plasterer, *apolusli*
plastering, *apolusli*
plat; *osapa, tannạffo, yakni pattasạchi*
iskitini
plat, to; *tanạffo*
plate; *aiimpa, amphạta, ampmalaspoa,*
ampmalaswa, ampmalạssa
plate, large; *amppatạssa*
plate over, to; *akkoti*
plate with brass, to; *tạli lakna isht ạlh-*
kohachi
plate with silver, to; *tạli hạta akkoli*
plated; *akkoti, ạlhkoha, lapali*
plated with brass, *tạli lakna isht ạlhkoha*
platform, *iti patạlhpo*
platter; *amphạta chito, ampmalaspoa*
play; *aiitauạlli, itauạlli, washoha*
play, to; *bạska, ibaiitauạlli, itauạlli, ola-*
chi, suⁿksowa, washoha
play, to make; *ilauạllichi, washohạchi*
play ball, to; *toli*
playday, *nitak itauạlli*
player; *ilauạlli, olachi, toli, washoha*
playfellow, *ibaiitauạlli*
playground; *aiitauạlli, awashoha*
playhouse, *aiitauạlli chuka*
playmate, *ibaiitauạlli*
plaything, *isht washoha*
plead, to; *anumpuli, apepoa*
pleader, *hatak anumpuli*
pleasant; *achukma, hochukma, nitaⁿki,*
shohmakali, yohbi, yukpa

pleasant, to render; *yohbichi*
pleasant to the sight, to become; *pisa aiukli*
pleasant to the taste; *akomachi, kashaha*
please, to; *alhpesa, yukpalechi, yukpali*
pleased; *ayukpa, halhpanshi, yukpa*
pleaser, *yukpali*
pleasing, *aiukli*
pleasure; *na yukpa, nana aiisht ilaiyukpa*
pleasure, expressing; *yakoke*
pleasure, to give; *yukpali*
pledge; *ahinna, boli*
pledge, to; *ahinnachi, boli, hilechi*
pledged, *ahinna*
pleiades, the; *fichik watalhpi*
plenary, *aialhtaha*
plenitude; *aialhtaha, alota*
plenteous; *apakna, laua*
plentiful, *laua*
plenty; *apakna, laua*
plenty, to make a; *apaknachi*
plethora; *issish inchito, issish inlaua*
plethoric; *issish inchito, issish inlaua, michila*
pleura, the; *chunuko*
pleurisy; *abi, chunukabi, illilli*
pliable; *hokulbi, lapushki, shanaia hinla*
pliant; *shanaia hinla, walohbi*
plod, to; *achunanchi*
plot; *alhpisa, yakni alhpisa*
plover, the whistling; *isi nia pichelichi*
plow; *isuba inchahe, yakni isht patafa*
plow, to; *aleli, leli, pataffi, tasalli, yakni bashli, yakni pataffi*
plow boy, *alla yakni pataffi*
plowed; *basha, patafa*
plowed place, *apatafa*
plowland, *patafa hinla*
plowman, *yakni pataffi*
plowshare, *yakni isht patafa tali*
pluck; *chunkash, salakha, shilukpa*
pluck, to; *leli, naffi, tablichi, tinfi*
pluck ears of corn, to; *nalichi*
pluck out, to; *chukali, chukaffi, chukli*
pluck up, to; *lobaffi, lobbi, lubbi, teli*
plucked out; *chukafa, chukali*
plucked up; *lobafa, lopa, teha, tinfa*
plucker; *chukaffi, chukli, teli*
plug, *isht alhkama*
plug, to; *kamali, kammi*
plum, *takkonlushi*
plum, wild; *isi intakkonlushi, takkonlushi*

plum tree, *takkonlush api*
plume, *shikopa*
plume oneself, to; *shikobli*
plump; *loboa, lobobumkachi, lampko, lobboa, loboboa*
plunder; *na wehpoa, nana wehpoa*
plunder, to; *hunkupa, wehpuli, weli*
plundered; *weha, wehpoa*
plunderer; *na wehpuli, wehpuli, weli*
plunge, *okattula*
plunge, to; *okattula, oklobushli, oklobushlichi, oklubbi*
plunged, *oklobushli*
plunger, *oklobushli*
plurality, *tuklokia atampa*
ply, to; *anta, toksali*
poach, to; *auashli*
poached, *alwasha*
poacher, *akank hunkupa*
pock; *chilakwa, lachowa*
pocket; *afoha, ilefoka shukcha, shukcha*
pocketbook; *holisso aialbiha shukcha, holisso inshukcha*
pocketknife, *bashpo poloma*
pod; *haiyunkpulo nihi hakshup, hakshup*
pod, to; *hakshup toba*
poet; *ataloa ikbi, taloa ikbi*
poignant; *halupa, homi*
point; *aiahni, halupa, wishakchi*
point, highest; *tabokoa*
point, to; *haluppachi, tali*
point, to be without a; *tokumpa*
point at, to; *abitibli, bili, bitibli*
point of a knife, *bashpo wishakchi*
point of a needle, *chufak wishakchi*
point of an auger, *isht fotoha wishakchi*
point of the elbow, *shakba inshunkani*
point out, to; *atokoli, bilibli*
pointed; *chunsa, halupa, ibakchufanli, ibakchufanshli, ibakpishanli, ibakpishanshli, tala*
pointed at, *abila*
pointed at, the place; *abilepa*
pointed out; *atokowa, alhtoka, alhtokoa*
pointer; *bilibli, na bili*
pointers (stars), *fichik issuba*
poise; *isht weki, tali isht weki, tali uski, weki*
poise, to; *weki itilauichi, wekichi*
poised, *weki itilaui*
poison, *isht illi*
poison, to; *isht illi fohki, isht illi ipeta*
poison of serpents, *lakna*
poisoned, *isht illi foka*

pokeweed, *koshiba*
polar, *falammi pilla*
polar star, *falammi fichik*
pole; *iti fabassa, iti fabassoa, kohta*
pole, to; *abili*
pole of a cart, *isunlash*
polecat, *koni*
poled; *abela, abila, abeta*
polish, *millinta*
polish, to; *millinta, millintachi*
polished, *millinta*
polisher, *millintachi*
poll, *nushkobo*
poll, to; *naksish nalichi, naksish taptuli*
poll tax; *nushkobo atobbi, nushkobo chumpa*
pollard; *lapish kobafa, naksish naha*
polliwog, *yalubba*
pollute, to; *liteli*
polluted; *liteha, okpulo*
pollution; *liteha, okpulo*
poltroon; *hatak hobak, hobak*
polyandry, *hatak inlaua*
polygamy, *tekchi inlaua*
pommel; *ibish, isuba umpatalhpo nush-kobo, nushkobo*
pommel, to; *litoli*
pommeled, *litoa*
pomp; *ilefehnachi, isht ilawata*
pompion, *isito*
pompous, *ilefehnachi*
pond; *haiyip, hohtak, okhatushi*
pond, large; *okhata*
pond, small; *hohtak ushi*
pond, to; *haiyip ikbi*
ponder, to; *anukfilli*
ponderous; *weki, weki fehna*
poniard, *isht itibbi*
pontoon, *peni patassa*
pony; *isuba, isuba iskitini*
pool, *oka atalaia*
poor; *chunna, ilbasha, kopipia, makali, shulla*
poor, to make; *chunnachi*
poor man, *hatak ilbasha*
poorly, *abeka chuhmi*
poorness, *chunna*
pop; *basaha, basak, lukalichi, palak*
pop, to; *basaha, basahkachi, basakachi, basali, basisakachi, tukafa*
pop, to cause to; *basahachi*
popping; *basahkachi, basali, basasunkachi*
popping, to cause a; *basalichi*
populate, to; *aioklachechi*

population, *okla*
populous; *okla chito, okla laua*
porch; *aboha hoshontika, apashia, chuka-pishia, hoshontika*
pore, *laksha akucha*
pore over, to; *pisa*
pork, *shukha nipi*
pork, fat; *shukha nia*
pork, lean; *shukha nipi*
pork, to cure; *shukha nipi shileli*
porridge, bean; *bala okchi*
porringer, *alla aiimpa*
port, *peni ataiya*
portable; *shala hinla, shola hinla*
porter, *okhisa apistikeli*
portico; *aboha hoshontika, apashia*
portion; *holhpela, kashkoa, osapa*
portmanteau, *wak hakshup shukcha*
positive, *aianli*
possess, to; *immi*
possessed, *fohka*
possession, *ishi*
possessor; *inhikia, imansha*
possible; *chalek, chali, na fehna, yohma hinla*
possibly; *chalik, chalin, chishba*
post; *ahika, iti hika, iyi, tonnik*
post, military; *tashka chipota aheli*
post, to; *anoachi*
postage; *alhtoba, holisso alhtoba, holisso nowat anya alhtoba*
posted, *anoa*
posterity; *isht ataya, ushi*
posthaste, *tushpa*
postman, *holisso shali*
postmaster, *holisso nowat anya ishi*
post office; *holisso nowat anya inchuka, holisso shali inchuka*
postpone, to; *abanablichi, mishemanchit apesa*
postponed; *abanapa, mishemat alhpisa*
pot; *alabocha, shuti, shuti iyasha*
pot, large; *iyasha chito*
pot, small; *iyashushi, shutushi*
pot, to; *shuti fohki*
pot, water; *shuti oka aialhto*
pot lid; *iyasha onlipa, shuti asha onlipa, shuti iyasha onlipa*
potable, *ishko hinla*
potash; *hituk, hituk tohbi*
potation, *ishko*
potato, *ahe*
potato, boiled; *ahe holbi*
potato, Irish; *na hollo imahe*

potato, rotten; *ahe shua*
potato, wild; *ahe kamąssa, ahsakti, kuⁿshak ahe*
Potato-eating people, *ahe pąta okla*
potato hill; *ahe bunto, ahe ibish*
potato hills, to make; *ahe buntuchi*
potato house, *ahe inchuka*
potato patch, *ahe aholokchi*
potato vine; *ahąpi, ahe ąpi*
potency, *kąllo*
potent; *kąllo, kilimpi, paląmmi*
potentate; *hatak paląmmi, miⁿko*
pother, *atakląma*
pother, to; *aiyokomichi, atakląmmi*
pothook; *asonak atakali, asonak isht talakchi, iyasha isht talakchi*
potion, *ishko achąfa*
potsherd, *ampkoa*
pottage, *łabocha*
potter; *ampo ikbi, shuti tąna*
pottery; *amphąta, ampo*
pottery, a; *ampatoba*
pouch; *atohchi, bahtushi*
poultice, *ashela*
poultice, to; *ashela lapalechi*
poultry, *akaⁿka*
pounce, *hushi iyakchush*
pounce, to; *yichiffi*
pound; *weki, weki achąfa*
pound, one; *weki achąfa*
pound, to; *boli, hopuⁿsi, hussi, isso, kąbaha*
pound fine, to; *botoli*
pound there, to; *ahosi*
pounded; *boa, bota, holhpusi, holussi*
pounder; *ilefoka isht boa, kitush, nan isht
boa*
pounds, 2,000; *weki tałepa sipokni tuklo*
pour, to; *folichi, lali, łatapa, łatąbli,
yanąlli*
pour, to cause to; *łalichi*
pour from, to; *tosholi*
pour in, to; *ani*
pour in with, to; *ibani*
pour into, to; *ąni, tosholi*
pour out, to; *akkałaya, fohobli, fohopa,
tosholi*
pour out and scatter, to; *akkałatapa*
poured down, *akkałatapa*
poured in; *ąlhto, ibąlhto*
poured out; *fohopa, toshoa*
pourer, *lali*
pout, to; *hąshaⁿya, ibaksukuⁿlichi, okyauinli*

pouter, *okyauinli*
poverty; *aiilbąsha, ilbąsha*
powder; *bota, botulli, hituk*
powder, to; *botolichi, pushechi*
powder charger, *hituk isht ąlhpisa*
powder with wheat flour, to; *bota
tohbi isht oⁿfimmi*
powdered; *bota, bota oⁿfima*
powdered fine, *pushi*
powderhorn; *hituk aiąlhto, łapish hituk
aiąlhto*
powdermill; *hituk aiikbi, hituk atoba*
power; *aiaⁿli, aialika, aiąlhpesa, isht
shima, iti isht shima, kąllo, kilimpi,
miⁿko, na kąllo, nan isht aiaⁿli, paląmmi*
powerful; *kąllo, kilimpi, paląmmi*
powerless, *kąllo keyu*
pox, *yukbąbi*
practicable, *yąmohma hinla*
practical, *yąmohma hinla*
practice; *abąchi, yąmohmi*
practice, to; *abąchechi, abąchi, ąlbąchi,
yąmohmi*
practice (as a physician), to; *alikchi*
practiced upon with tricks, *fappo
onuttula*
practicer; *abąchi, isht atta, yąmohmi*
practitioner, *isht atta*
prairie, *oktak*
prairie, small; *oktak ushi*
praise, *isht anumpa*
praise, to; *afehnichi, anumpuli, holitoblit isht anumpuli, taloa*
praise in song, to; *taloa*
praiser, *isht anumpuli*
prance, to; *hattaui, tulli*
prance, to cause to; *hattauichi*
prancer, *hattauichi*
prank, *ilauata*
prank, to; *shema, shemąchi*
prate, to; *anukchilafa, anukchilali, anumpuli shali, himak fokalit anumpuli*
prater; *anukchilafa, anᴜkchilali, anumpuli shali*
prattle, to; *bąlbaha*
pray, to; *anumpuli, asilhha, ąba anumpuli, ąba pit anumpuli*
pray for, to; *ąba isht anumpuli*
pray to, to; *ilbąsha*
prayer, *anumpa asilhha*
prayer book, *anumpa asilhha holisso*
prayerful, *Ąba iⁿki imasilhha shali*
prayerless, *asilhha keyu*

preach, to; *anoli, anumpuli, aba anumpa isht anumpuli, aba anumpa isht atta, aba anumpuli, aba isht anumpuli*
preach in the open air, to; *kucha aianumpuli*
preached, *anumpa*
preacher; *aba anumpa isht anumpuli, aba anumpa isht atta, aba anumpuli, aba isht anumpuli*
preacher, field; *kucha aianumpuli*
preaching, *anumpuli*
precaution, to; *tikbanli inmiha*
precede, to; *tikba anya*
precedent, *tikba*
precept, *anumpa alhpisa*
preceptor; *ikhananchi, nan ikhananchi*
precinct, *apelichika fullota*
precious; *achafoa, holitopa*
precipice, *sakti chaha*
precipitancy; *amoshuli, tushpa*
precipitate, to; *akka itula, amohsholechi, amoshuli, tunshpa, tunshpalechi*
precipitated, *tunshpa*
precipitous; *amosholi, apissanlit, alhpiesa, tushpa*
preclude, to; *kamali, katabli*
precluded; *katapa, kama*
preconcert, to; *tikba apesa*
preconcerted, *tikba alhpisa*
precursor, *tikbanya*
predestinate, to; *tikbanli apesa*
predetermine, to; *tikbanli apesa*
predicate, to; *anoli*
predict, to; *tikbanlit anoli*
prediction, *tikbanli anoli anumpa*
predictor, *tikbanli anoli*
predominant, *inshali*
predominate, to; *ishalichi*
preemption, *apoa*
preengage, to; *apobachi*
prefer, to; *holitoblichi, inshali*
preferable, *achukma inshali*
prefix, to; *tikba atali, tikba hilechi*
pregnancy; *chakali, ushi infohka*
pregnant; *aiisht inchakali, chakali, chakali, kaiya, ushi infohka, ushi kaiya*
pregnant, to become; *alla infoka*
prejudge, to; *tikbanlit anukfilli*
prejudgment, *tikbanli imanukfila*
prejudice, *tikbanli imanukfila*
prejudice, to; *imanukfila shananchi*
prejudiced, *nuktala*
premeditate, to; *tikbanlit anukfilli*
premium, *alhtoba*

premonish, to; *tikbanli inmiha*
preoccupy, to; *tikbanli ishi*
preparation; *aialhpesa, alhtaha*
prepare, to; *apoksia, apoksiachi, atali, alhtaha*
prepared; *alhtaha, imalhtaha*
prepared victuals, *pinak*
preparer, *atali*
preponderate, to; *weki inshali*
prepossess, to; *imanukfila shananchi, tikbanli ishi*
preposterous; *achukma, okpulo*
presbyter; *asanonchi, aba anumpuli iksa nana isht imatta, hatak asahnonchi*
Presbytery, *aba anumpuli iksa nana ishi imashwa aliha*
prescience, *tikbanli ikhana*
prescribe, to; *apesa*
prescribe medicine, to; *ikhinsh apesa*
presence, *itintakla*
present, *himak, himmona, tankla ansha*
present, a; *chukalaha, habena, halbina, na halbina, nan ilhpita, nan isht aiokpachi*
present, to; *habenachi, haiakachi, hilechi, ima, ipeta*
present day, *himak nitak*
present generation, *himona hofanti*
present time; *himak nitak, himaka*
presented; *habena, haiaka, halbina*
preserve, to; *achebachi, halalli, ilatomba, ishi, okchalinchi, yammichi*
preserver, *apoba*
preserver of life, *okchanyachi*
preside, to; *pelichi*
preside in, to; *apelichi*
president; *minko, pelicheka, pelichi*
President of the United States, the; *Pinki chito, Pinki chitokaka, Pinki ishtoka*
presiding officer; *anumpeshi, pelicheka*
press; *akantalichi, na foka abohushi*
press, to; *akantalechi, akantali, ateblichi, atelifa, atunshpalechi, bushli, kantali, tikeli*
press against, to; *bikeli, tikeli, tobli*
press down, to; *alhtekachi*
press in the throat, to; *anukbikeli*
press on, to; *atebli, ateblichi, bitepa, ombitepa*
press on with the hand, to; *umbitepa, umbitka*
press together, to; *akantalechi, akmochi, akopulechi, itakopulechi, kamassalli*

press up, to; *bokonoli*
pressed; *akanta, atelifa*
pressed against, *bokonnoa*
pressed down in, *attia*
pressed on both sides, *atukonofa*
pressed together, *kamąssa*
presser, *ateblichi*
pressure in the throat, to cause; *anukbikelichi*
presume, to; *ahni, imahoba*
presumption, *imahoba*
presumptuous; *himak fokalechi, ilapunla*
pretend, to; *ahobi, ilahobbi, pisa*
pretended, *ilahobbi*
pretender; *ilahobbi, nan ilahobbi*
pretense, *ilahobbi*
pretext, *nan isht amiha*
pretor, *nan apesa*
pretty; *achukma, aiukli, chohmi*
prevail, to; *imaiya, iⁿshali*
prevail against, to; *imaiyachi*
prevalent; *aiaⁿli fehna, iⁿshali*
prevaricate, to; *anumpa shanaioa, shanaioli*
prevarication, *anumpa shanaioa*
prevaricator, *anumpa shanaioa*
prevent, to; *aląmmi, aląmmichi, atakląmmi, atakląmoli, oktąbli, olabechi, oląbbechi*
prevented; *alama, atakląma, atakląmoa, oktąpa*
previous, *tiⁿkba*
previous time, at a; *tiⁿkbaha*
previously, *tiⁿkbaha*
prey; *imilbik, na wehpoa, wehpoa*
prey, to; *ąbit ąpa, huⁿkupa, wehpuli*
price; *aiąlbi, aiąlli, aiilli, ąlbi, ąlhtoba, iąlli, itiąlbi, itiąlli*
price, to; *aiąlbichi, aiilli onuchi, aiillichi, ąlbichi, iąllichi*
price high, to; *aiili chitoli*
priced, *aiilli onitula*
priced high; *aiilli chito*
priceless, *aiilli iksho*
prick, to; *bali, bili, bilibli, hauąshko, homi*
pricked; *baha, bila*
pricket, *isi nakni ląpish falaktuchi*
prickle, to; *hushshiho*
prickly ash, *ikhiⁿsh patąssa*
prickly heat, *itomushi*
pride; *fehnąchi, ilefehnąchi*
pride, to; *ilefehnąchi*
pried; *afena, afiⁿkąchi*
prier, *pisa*

priest; *ąba anumpa isht ątta, hatak hullo, holitompa, hopaii, na holitompa isht aⁿsha, na holitompa isht ątta, na hollochi, na hollochi iksa, nan apuskiachi*
priesthood, *ąba anumpa isht ątta imąlhtayak*
prig; *hatak isht ąfekommi, huⁿkupa*
prim, to; *shema, shemąchi*
primary, *tikba*
prime, *achukma aiąli*
prime, to; *cheli, haksun oncheli, oncheli, haksun onchiya*
priming, *hituk haksun onchiya*
priming pan; *haksun, haksun aionchiya, hituk aionchiya*
priming wire, *haksun chiluk isht shinli*
primitive, *nitak tiⁿkba*
primogenital, *ątta ąmmona*
primogeniture; *ątta ąmmona, ąttahpi*
prince; *chitokaka, holitompa, miⁿko*
prince of darkness, *nan isht ahollo okpulo*
princess, *ohoyo miⁿko*
principal, *iⁿshali*
principal, a; *iⁿshali hatak, pelichi*
principle, *aiyąmohmi*
principle, to; *nukfokechi*
principled, *nukfoka*
prink, to; *ilefehnąchi*
print, *holisso*
print, to; *holisso ikbi, holissochi*
printed; *holisso, inchuⁿwa*
printer; *holisso ikbi, holissochi*
printing office, *holisso aiikbi*
prior, *tiⁿkba*
prison; *aboha kąllo, nan aiapistikeli*
prison, to; *aboha kąllo foki*
prisoned, *aboha kąllo foka*
prisoner; *aboha kąllo ąlhpinta, aboha kąllo foka, aiashąchi, hatak yuka, yuka*
prisoner, female; *ohoyo yuka*
private; *ilap immi, nana luma*
private, a; *tąshka chipota*
privateer, *hatak huⁿkupa peni fokąt aⁿya*
privation; *iksho, ilbąsha*
privily, *luma*
privity, *lumat ikhana*
privy, *luma*
prize; *ąlhtoba, wehpoa*
prizer, *aiilli onuchi*
probable; *chechik, chiishke, chiⁿshki, hepulla*
probably, *achike, achini, atoshke, chalin, chechik, chechike, chik, chiⁿshki, hota, hotukohmi, hotukok, tokok, tuma*

probity; *apissanli, kostini*
proboscis, *ibishakni*
proceed, to; *ia, kucha, manya*
proceed out of, to; *akucha, toba*
proceeding, *ia*
proceeds, *isht ilahauchi*
process, *manya*
procession; *itakaiyat ia, itichapat ia*
proclaim, to; *anoachi, anoli*
proclaimed, *anoa*
proclaimer, *anoachi*
proclamation, *anumpa*
procrastinate, to; *abanablichi, abanapa*
procreate, to; *ikbi*
procreator; *ikbi, inki*
procure, to; *ahauchi, ishi*
procure by hiring, to; *tohno*
procurer, *ahauchi*
prodigal, *isht yopula*
prodigally, *isht yopulat*
prodigious, *chito*
prodigy, *pisa inla*
produce; *alhpoa, waya*
produce, to; *ikbi, waya, wayachi*
produce pods, to; *hakshup toba*
product, *awaya*
productive, *awaya fehna*
profane; *isht yopula, okpulo*
profane, to; *kobaffi, okpani*
profaned, *kobafa*
profanely, *isht yopulat*
profaneness, *chakapa*
profaner; *kobaffi, okpani*
profess, to; *ilahobbi, miha*
profess religion, to; *aba anumpuli iba-foka*
professed, *ilahobbi*
profession; *alhtayak, miha*
professor; *holisso ithananchi, ilahobbi*
professor of the Gospel, *aba anumpa yimmi*
proffer, *imissa*
proffer, to; *imissa*
profferer, *imissa*
proficient, *hatak imponna*
profit; *aiisht ilahauchi, isht ahauchi*
profitable; *aiisht ilahauchi, aiisht ilapisa, alhpesa*
profited; *ahauchi, aiyukpa*
profligate, *haksi*
profligate, a; *hatak haksi, hatak okpulo*
profound; *hofobi, kallo*
profound, the; *okhata chito*

profuse, *chito*
profusely; *chito, laua*
progenitor, *aiisht atiaka*
progeny; *ataya, atia, hatak isht uncholo/i, isht atiaka*
prognosticate, to; *tikbanlit anoli*
prognosticator; *nan ithana, tikbanli anoli*
progress, to; *inshali, manya*
progression, *manya*
project; *aiahni, imanukfila*
project, to; *anoli, apesa, kucha pit hikia, kucha takanli, lanfi, pila*
projection; *chakbi, shakampi*
prolific; *cheli imponna, waya fehna*
prolix; *falaia, salaha*
prolong, to; *falaiachi*
prolonged, *falaia*
prominent; *chito, haiaka, kucha hikia*
promise; *anumpa, miha*
promise, to; *anumpa ilonuchi, imissa, miha*
promiser, *miha*
promontory, *shakampi*
promote, to; *apelachi*
promoter, *apelachi*
prompt, *tunshpa achukma*
prompt, to; *aiyimitachi, atohnuchi, okchalechi*
prompter, *atohnuchi*
promulgate, to; *anoachi, anoli*
promulgator; *anoachi, anoli*
promulge, to; *anoachi, anoli*
prone; *banna, lipia*
proneness, *lipia*
prong; *filamminchi, washala*
prong, to make a; *washalachi*
pronged; *wahhaloha, wahhala, wakcha, washaloha, washala*
pronounce, to; *anumpuli*
pronounced, *anumpa*
pronunciation, *anumpuli*
prop; *isht ilaneli, isht tikili, isht tikoli, tikeli*
prop, to; *tikelichi*
propagate, to; *cheli, lauachi*
propagator, *anumpa fimmi*
propel, to; *tobli*
proper; *anli, alhpesa, ilap immi, imanka*
property, *imilayak*
property in, *immi*
prophecy; *anumpa tikbanli anoli, tikbanli anoli, tikbanli anoli anumpa*

prophesier, *tikbanli anoli*
prophesy, to; *na tikbanli anoli, tikbanlit anoli*
prophet; *hopaii, hopaii puta, nan ikhana, nan ithana*
propinquity; *aiitinbilinka, bilinka*
propitiate, to; *hopoḷachi, hopoḷalli, nuktalali*
propitiator, *hopoḷachi*
propitious; *kana, nukhanklo*
proportion, *kashapa*
proportion, to; *kashkoli*
proposal, *imissa*
propound, to; *imissa*
propounder, *imissa*
propped, *tikeli*
proprietary, *ilap immi*
prorogue, to; *aḅanaḅlichi*
proscribe, to; *illiissa*
proscription, *illiissa anumpa*
prosecute, to; *aianlichi, anumpa kạllo onuchi, anumpa onuchi, atali*
prosecuted, *anumpa kạllo onutula*
prosecution, *anumpa kạllo onutula*
prosecutor; *anumpa kạllo onuchi, anumpa onuchi*
proselyte, *nan inla yimmi*
proselyte, to; *nana inla yimmihechi*
prospect; *ahoba, apinsa, apisaka, pisa*
prospective, *tikbanlit pisa*
prosper, to; *aianli, aiokpạchi*
prospered, *aianli*
prostitute, *ohoyo haui*
prostitute, to; *haui toba*
prostrate; *fabạssạt itonla, kinafa*
prostrate, to; *akkạchi, kinalichi*
prostrated; *akkama, kinali*
prostration; *itola, lipia*
protect, to; *apohkochi, atukko, atukkuchi, hofantichi, okchalinchi*
protected; *apohko, hofanti, okchanya*
protection; *apohko, atukko*
protector, *aiatokko*
protest, to; *miha*
protract, to; *achibali, falaiachi*
protracted, *falaia*
protrude, to; *tikba chạfichi, tikba tobli*
protuberant, *chito*
proud; *auata, fehnạchi, ilạlechia, ilefehnạchi*
proud, to make; *fehnạchi*
prove, to; *akostininchi, anli, anlichi, pisa*
proved; *atokowa, pulla*
proverb, *anumpa*

provide, to; *ahauchi, atali, inshi*
provided, *ataha*
providence; *akaniohmi, atali, ilahtali*
Providence (the Deity), *Ạba pinki*
provider; *atali, ilhpak atali*
province; *apelichika, yakni*
provision, *atali*
provisions; *ilhpa, ilhpak, pinak, pinak toba*
provocation; *nukoạchi, nukpạllichi*
provoke, to; *aiyimitachi, anukchahạchi, chililli, chilitạchi, nukhobelạchi, nukoạchi, okpulochi, panfi*
provoked; *chilita, nukoa*
provoker, *nukoạchi*
prow; *ibish, peni ibish*
prowess, *amoshuli*
prowl, to; *yulullit anya*
prowler, *yulullit anya*
proximate, *bilinka*
proxy, *ạlhtoba*
prudence, *ilatomba*
prudent; *hopoksia, ilatomba, nan ithana*
prune, to; *naksish nalichi*
pruned, *naksish nahachit taha*
pruner, *naksish nalichi*
pry; *isht afana, isht wakeli*
pry, wooden; *iti isht tonolichi*
pry, to; *afinni, afinnit ạbishtia, hoyo*
pry into, to; *pisa*
pry up, to; *afenali*
psalm; *ataloa, ạba taloa, taloa*
psalm book, *holisso ataloa*
psalmist, *taloa ikbi*
psalmody, *taloa abạchi*
psaltery, *saltili*
pshaw; *hin, oe*
puberty, *asạno*
public, *okla moma*
publican, *pạblikạn*
publication, *anoli*
publish, to; *anoli, haiakạchi, holisso ikbi*
published, *anoa*
publisher, *nan anoli*
puccoon, *pishkak*
pucker; *akkapushli, awalakachi*
pucker, to; *awalakachechi, nuktakba, pokoli, shinoffi, shinoli, yikulli*
pucker, to cause to; *itukwislichi, pokulichi*
puckered; *awalakachi, yikota*
pudding; *ashela, bahpo*
puddle; *haiyip, oka talaia*
pudenda mulieris, *imoksini*

pudgy, *nia*
puerile; *ạlla chuhmi, ạlla ilahobbi*
puff, *pạfachi*
puff, to; *apu^nfạchi, chitot fiopa, fohukli, pạfachi, shitimmi*
puffball, *pakti shobota*
puffed; *ạlhpu^nfa, ilefehnạchi*
puffy; *ạlhpu^nfa chuhmi, shitimmi*
pugilist, *ibbak isht itibbi*
pugnacious, *nukoa shali*
puke; *hoeta, hoetạchi, hohoeta, ikhi^nsh ishkot hoita*
puke, to; *hoeta, hohoetạchi*
puke, to cause to; *hoetạchi*
puke continually, to; *hohoeta*
puking and purging, *itala^nkla ont ia*
pule, to; *kifaha*
pull, *halạlli*
pull, to; *ạmo, halạlli*
pull down, to; *halat akkạchi*
pull off, to; *liffi*
pull out, to; *chukali, chukalichi, chukạffi, chukli, halat kuchi, kohchi, kuchi, sheli, ti^nfi*
pull out, to make; *chukalichi*
pull up, to; *piliffi, teli, ti^nfi*
pulled, *ạlmo*
pulled out; *chukafa, chukali, li^nfa*
pulled up; *teha, ti^nfa*
puller, *halạlli*
pullet, *aka^nk tek himmita*
pulmonary disease, *nukshulla*
pulp; *lupi, nipi*
pulpit; *ahikiạt anumpuli, aianumpuli, ạba aianumpuli .*
pulsate, to; *mitikminli, mitilhmiya, motukli, nuktimekạchi, timikmeli*
pulsation; *mitikli, mitilhmiya, nukkitekạchi, nuktimekạchi*
pulse, the; *michilhha, mitikminli, mitilhmiya*
pulverize, to; *botoli, botolichi, pushechi*
pulverized; *bota, pushi*
pump, to; *halali*
pumpkin, *isito*
pumpkin, cooked or stewed; *isito honni*
pumpkin, yellow or hard-shelled; *isito sạla*
pumpkin, yellow or ripe; *isito lakna*
pumpkin color, *likowa*
pumpkin stem, *isht takali*
pumpkin vine, *isito ạpi*
punch; *isht lumpa, tạli isht lumpa*
punch, to; *lukalichi, lukạffi*

punched; *lukafa, lukali*
puncheon; *itạlhfoa chito, iti pạla patạlhpo, pataspoa*
puncher; *isht lumpa, lunlichi*
punctual, *tushpa*
puncture; *alumpa, lumpli*
puncture, to; *lumpli*
punctured; *lukafa, lumpa*
pungency; *homi, nukhomi*
pungent; *homi, nukhomi*
pungent, to render; *nukhomechi*
punish, to; *fạmmi, isikkopali, nana kanihchi*
punished; *fạma, isikkopa, nana kaniohmi*
punishment, *ilbạsha*
puny; *hashonti, iskitini*
pup, to; *ofu^nsikcheli*
pupil; *ạlla holisso pisa, holisso pisa, nan ikhạna, nana aiithạna*
pupil of the eye, *nishkin nihi*
pupilage, *ạlla holisso pisa*
puppet, *hatak holba isht washoha*
puppy; *ofu^nsik, ofushi*
puppy, to; *ofu^nsikcheli*
purblind, *nishkin lạpa ạmmona*
purchasable, *chumpa hinla*
purchase, *chumpa*
purchase, to; *chumpa*
purchase money, *isht chumpa*
purchaser; *chumpa, nan chumpa*
pure; *aia^nli, a^nli, kashofa, yohbi*
pure heart, *chu^nkash a^nli*
pureness; *achukma, shohkawali, yohbi*
purgated, *kashofa*
purgation; *kashofa, kashoffi*
purgative, *ikfiachi*
purge, to; *ikfia, ikfiachi, kashoffi*
purged, *ikfia*
purging; *ikfiachi, itala^nkla ont ia*
purification; *kashofa, kashoffi*
purification, ceremonious; *okissa*
purification day, *okissa nitak*
purification of oneself, *nan ilachifa*
purified, *kashofa*
purify, to; *achefa, kashoffi, kashoffichi, okissạchi*
purify, to cause to; *okissạchi*
purify ceremoniously, to; *okissa*
purity; *achukma, kostini, yohbi*
purl, to; *chusohạchi*
purloin, to; *hu^nkupa*
purloiner, *hu^nkupa*
purple; *homaiyi, homakbi, okchakạlbi*
purple, to; *homaiyichi, homakbichi*

purport, *ahni*
purport, to; *ahni*
purpose, *ahni*
purpose, to; *ahni, anukfilli, apesa*
purposely, *ahnit*
purr, *kileha*
purr, to; *kileha*
purse; *shukcha, tali holisso iⁿshukcha*
purse, to; *shukcha, tali holisso iⁿshukcha foki*
purslane, *lobuna*
purse-proud; *tali holisso isht ilawata, tali holisso isht ilefehnachi*
pursue, to; *atioa, atioli, aliyuha, iakaiya, lioa, lioli*
pursuer; *iakaiya, lioli*
pursuit; *iakaiya, lioli*
purvey, to; *atali*
purveyance, *atali*
purveyor, *atali*
pus, *aninchichi*
pus, to gather; *aninchichi*
push; *bali, tobli*
push, to; *bali, tobli, topoli*
push, to cause to; *toblichi*
push each other, to; *tobli*
push in, to; *atelichi*
push into the water, to; *oka tobli*
push up, to; *apelichi*
pusher, *tobli*
pushing pole, *isht tobli*
pusillanimity; *nukshopa, nukwia*
pusillanimous; *nukshopa, nukwia*
pusley, *lobuna*
pustule, *tanlakchi*
put, to; *boli, fohki, talali*
put a neckcloth on, to; *inuchechi, inuchi*
put a plume upon another, to; *shikoblichi*
put among, to; *ibafoki*
put an end to at, to; *ahokoffi*
put away, to; *kahpuli, kanchi*
put before, to; *tikba kali*
put beneath, to; *nutakachi*
put down, to; *akkaboli, ashachi*
put endwise together, to; *tikeli*
put farther off, to; *mishemachi*
put forth, to; *takalechi, weli*
put in; *abeha, afoka, albihkachi, alhpitta, alhto, ilhpita*
put in, to; *abeli, afohka, afohkachi, afohki, apitta, fohki, fohka, fokichi, maiachi*
put in with, to; *ibafoki, ibani*

put into a bag, to; *shapulechi*
put into a crack; *kafali, kafoli, kafalichi*
put into the hand, *ibbak fohka*
put into the hand, to; *ibbak fohki*
put into the mouth, to; *kapali, kapalichi*
put off, *isht amiha*
put on; *abeha, albihkachi, fohka, hollo*
put on, to; *abeli, abanali, fohka, fohobli, holo, holochi, ialipeli, ialipelichi, na foka foka, onochi, umpatali*
put on a plume, to; *shikobli*
put on board, to; *peni chito fohki, peni fohki, peni foka*
put on ornaments, to; *ilakhata, shema*
put out, *kucha*
put out fire, to; *luak mosholichi*
put out of joint, *kotali*
put out of joint, to; *kotalichi, kotaffi*
put over; *auanapa, auanapoa, abanapoa, abanapa, tanapa, tanapoa*
put over, to; *auanapolichi, auanablichi, abanapolechi, abanablichi, tanapolechi*
put round; *folota, folotoa*
put the hands on, to; *bitepa*
put the log out too far, to; *oklafashlichi*
put through; *lopoli, yululli*
put through, to; *lopolichi, lopullichi*
put to shame, to; *hofayalichi*
put together, *kaha*
put together, to; *apelichi, ibakali, ichabli, itabana, itabani*
put together with, to; *aieninchi*
put up, to; *hilechi, hiolichi*
put up a house, to; *aboha itabanni*
put up in a crack, to; *kafolichi*
put up to, to; *atohnuchi*
put with, to; *aieninchi, kali*
putrid, *shua*
putrified, *shua*
putrify, to; *shua, shuachi*
puts on, one who; *onochi*
putty; *apisa isht alhpolosa, isht akamassa*
putty, to; *albochi, albokachi*
puzzle; *aiitaiyokoma, itaiyokoma*
puzzle, to; *aiyokoma, aiyokomi, aiyokomichi*
puzzled, *aiyokoma*
puzzler, *itaiyokommi*

quack; *alikchi ilahobi, nan ikhana ilahobbi, nan ithana ilahobbi*
quack, to; *hiⁿlhhiⁿlhachi, ola*
quadrangle, *bolukta*

quadrangular, *bolukta*
quadroon, *na hollushi*
quadruped, *iyi ushta*
quaff, to; *chitot nanạbli*
quaffer, *chitot nanạbli*
quagmire; *lukchuk yalạllaha, yalạllaha*
quail, *kofi*
quail, to; *hauạshko, nutaka ia*
quail, young; *kofushi*
quail's egg, *kofushi*
quaint, *inla*
quake; *wạnnichi, winnakạchi*
quake, to; *nukshopat wạnnichi, winnakạchi*
qualified; *aiataha, ạlhtaha*
qualify, to; *aiatali, atali*
qualm, *hoeta bạnna*
qualmish, *hoeta bạnna*
quantity, *kanomona*
quantity, small; *kanomusi*
Quapaw (a certain tribe), *Okahpa*
quarrel, *itạchoa*
quarrel, to; *achowa, nukoa*
quarreler; *itạchoa, itinnukoa*
quarrelsome; *itạchoa shali, itinnukoa shali, nukoa*
quarry, *tạli akula*
quart; *isht ishko patạla tuklo, koat*
quarter; *hanali, iklạnnaka iklạnna*
quarter, to; *tushali ushtali*
quarterly, *hạshi tuchinakma*
quarters, *koyofa*
quarters, the four; *hanalushta*
quash, to; *akshuchi, kashoffi, litoli*
quashed; *aksho, kashofa, litoa*
quaternion, *tạshka chipota ushta*
quaver, to; *taloa wạnnichi*
queasy, *hoeta bạnna*
queen; *miⁿko imohoyo, miⁿko tekchi, ohoyo miⁿko*
queen bee, *foe bilishke iⁿmiⁿko*
queer, *inla*
quell, to; *yokopạchi*
quelled, *yokopa*
quench, to; *mosholichi, yokopạchi*
quenchable; *mosholicha hinla, yokopạcha hinla*
quenched; *mosholi, yokopa*
querl, to; *chạnaha*
querulous, *na miha shali*
query, to; *aⁿonaklo, ponaklo*
quest, *hoyo*
quest, to; *hoyo*
question; *cho, ponaklo, to*

question, to; *panaklo, ponaklo*
quibble, to; *himak fokalit anumpuli*
quibbler, *himak fokalit anumpuli*
quick; *cheki, pạlhki, shinimpa, tushpa*
quick, to; *okchaⁿya*
quick-minded, *imanukfila tuⁿshpa*
quick motion, *nuklibekạchi*
quick-sighted, *nishkin halup*
quicken, to; *ashalinchi, okchaⁿya, okchaⁿyạchi, tuⁿshpalechi, tuⁿshpạchi*
quickened; *okchaⁿya, pạlhki*
quickener, *okchaⁿyạchi*
quickly; *ashaliⁿka, cheki, chekusi, chekusi fehna, pạlhki, tuⁿshpa*
quickness; *pạlhki, shinimpa, tushpa*
quicksand; *shinuk haiemo, shinuk kaha*
quiescent; *chulosa, luma*
quiet; *chilosa, chulosa, hopola, illi, nuktaiyala, nuktạla, yokopa*
quiet, to; *chilosạchi, chulosạchi, hopolạchi, hopolạlli, nuktalachi, nuktalali, nuktaloli, yokopạchi, yokopuli*
quiet, to become; *chulosa, hopola, nuktạla*
quiet, to grow; *yokopa*
quieted; *chulosa, hopola, nuktạla, yokopa*
quieter; *chulosạchi, nuktalali*
quietly, *lumasi*
quietness; *chulosa, luma, nuktạla, yokopa*
quietness, to cause; *nuktalalichi, nuktalolichi*
quill, *hoshiⁿshi*
quilt, *nan itạlhkạtta*
quilt, to; *nan itạlhkạtta ikbi*
quinsy, *ikonla shatali*
quintal, *weki talepa achạfa*
quit, *issa*
quit, to; *atobbi, issa*
quit, to cause to; *aiissạchi, issạchi*
quit of, *mokofa*
quite; *fehna, kiⁿsha, taha*
quite enough, *laua ạlhpesa*
quitting, *issa*
quiver, to; *wananaha, wanananli, wạnnichi, yalạtha, yalạttakạchi*
quivering; *wạnnichi, yalạtha, yalạttakạchi*
quoth, *achi*

rabbet, to; *shaⁿfit itiaiopitạmmichi*
rabbeted, *shaⁿfit itiaiopitạmmi*
rabbi; *aⁿshali, iⁿshali, piⁿshali*
rabbit; *chukfi, chukfi luma*

rabbit, domesticated; *chukfạlhpoba*
rabbit, small; *kuchasha*
rabbit, young; *chukfushi*
rabble, *hatak yahapa laua*
rabid; *holilạbi, nukoa, tasembo*
rabid fox; *chula holilạbi, chula tasembo*
rabidness; *nukoa, tasembo*
raccoon, a; *shaui*
race; *aiunchululli, imaiya, isht atia, itim-pakna, itintimiya*
race, to; *isuba itintimia, itintimiya*
race ground, *isuba aiitintimiya*
race horse, *isuba intintimia*
racer, *imaiya*
rack; *atikeli, ạlhpoa foni, wak aiimpạ*
rack (for eating), *aiimpa*
rack, to; *bichet tali, isikkopali, kaiilli, tikelichi*
racked; *bichạtaha, ilbạsha, isikkopa, tikeli*
racket, *yahapa*
racket, to make a; *yahapa*
racking pace, *kaiạlli*
racy, *homi*
radiant, *tombi*
radiate, to; *tohwikeli, tohwikelichi, tombi, tombichi*
radicate, to; *hofobichit hilechi*
raft, *pehta*
rafter; *aboha aionholmo itiitikoli, hoshontikiyi, iti itikeli, iti ititekili, tikeli*
rag, *na lilafa*
rag, white; *na hạta lilafa*
rage; *anukbạta, anukshomunta, nukoa*
rage, to; *anukbạta, anukshomota, chitoli, kạllo, lua, nukoa*
ragged, *lilalankạchi*
raging; *anukbạta, anukshomunta*
rags; *lilalankạchi, na lilali*
rail; *holihta pạla, innukoa, iti pạla*
rail, to; *holihtạchi, nanukachi, nukoa*
rail stuff, *iti pạla*
raiment; *anchi, na fohka*
rain, *umba*
rain, fine; *butummi*
rain, great; *umba chito*
rain, to; *umba, umbạchi*
rain, to engage one to make it; *umbạchechi*
rain, to make it; *umbạchi*
rain hard, to; *pakalichi, umba chitoli*
rain on; to; *umba*
rain water; *oka umba, okumba*
rainbow, *hinak bitepuli*
rainy; *umba, umba laua*

raise, to; *akachakali, akachakalichi, apoa, apoạchi, ạba isht ia, atobachi, ạttạt hofantichi, bokonoli, chahạchi, hilechi, hiolichi, hofantichi, hofạllichi, ikbi, itạnnali, takalechi, tanichi, wakayohạchi, wakeli, wakolichi*
raise (as from the dead), to; *okchanyạchi*
raise a log house, to; *abạnni, aboha itabạnni*
raise the eyebrows, to; *okmisikali*
raise the price, to; *aiilli chahạchi*
raised; *ạbaona, ạlhpoa, ạttạt hofanti, chaha, hofanti, hofạlli, toba*
raiser; *chahạchi, hofantichi, ikbi*
raisin, *panki chito shila*
raising; *chahạchi, itabạnni, okchanyạchi*
rake; *chupilhkạsh isht piha, hạshuk isht itạnnali, onush ạpi isht peli*
rake (person); *hatak tasembo, tasimbo*
rake, to; *itạnnali, peli*
rake an open fire, to; *kinni*
rake hay, to; *hạshuk itạnnali*
rake up, to; *apeli*
raked, *itạnaha*
raked place, *apiha*
raker, *apeli*
rally, *itạnnali*
rally, to; *atuklant itạnnali, itạnaha*
ram; *chukfạlhpowa nakni, chukfi nakni*
ram, to; *atelichi*
ramble, *nowa*
ramble, to; *fullokạchit anya*
ramble in speaking, to; *fullokạchit anumpuli*
rambler, *nowa shali*
ramify, to; *iti naksish laua toba*
rammed in, *abeha*
rammer, *tanamp isht kashokạchi*
rampart, *holihta kạllo*
rancid; *hauạshko, kalancha, kalama, kosoma, kotoma*
rancid, to make it; *kalamạchi*
rancidity; *kalancha, kalama*
rancor, *nukoa atạpa*
rancorous, *nukoa atạpa*
random, *himak fokali*
random, to act at; *himak fokalechi, himak fokali*
random, to do at; *yạmmak fokalechi*
random, to go at; *himak fokali, yạmmak fokalechi, yạmmak fokali*
range; *afolota, tanamp chito innaki pit akanchi ạlhpesa*

range, to; *abaiyạchi, itilauit hika, itilauit hilechi*
range about for pillage, to; *wehput fullota*
range (for eating), *aiimpa*
range for swine, *shukha aiasha*
ranged, *itilauit hika*
ranges, placed in; *baiilli*
rank (foul), *shua*
rank (luxuriant), *waya achukma*
rank, single; *itiakaya*
rank, to; *baiilli*
ranked, *baiilli*
rankle, to; *aninchichi, kạllot ishi ia, nu-koa*
rankness; *asạno, chaha, shua*
ranks, *bachoha*
ranks, to cause to follow in; *baiillichi*
ranks, to march in single; *baiillit nowa*
ranks, to move in; *baiet bịⁿya*
ranks, to stand in; *baiạllit heli*
ransack, to; *tiạblit pisa*
ransom; *isht ạlhtoba, yuka issa*
ransom, to; *chumpa, lakoffichi*
ransomed, *lakoffi*
ransomer, *lakoffichi*
rant, *anumpa nukoa*
rant, to; *chitot anumpuli, nukoạt anum-puli*
ranter, *chitot anumpuli*
rap; *kabuk, kạmakạchi, kobak, kobokạchi, komokạchi*
rap, to; *chuⁿkạsh ishi, komoha, komolichi, sakaha, sakalichi, sokuⁿha*
rap on a bell, *komak*
rapacious; *ạbit ạpa shali, wehpuli shali*
rapacity, *wehpuli shali*
rape; *hoklit aiissa, ohoyo hokli*
rape, to; *aiissa, hoklit aiissa*
rapid; *pạlhki, shinimpa, tushpa*
rapid, a; *fopa, oka yanạllipạlhki*
rapidity; *pạlhki, shinimpa, tushpa*
rapidly, *fehna*
rapids, *oka yanạllipạlhki*
rapier; *bạshpo falaia, bạshpo isht itibi*
rapine, *wehpoa*
rapper, *kobolichi*
rapture, *chuⁿkạsh ishi*
rapturous, *yukpa atạpa*
rare; *achafoa, achukma fehna, keyuchohmi, okchaⁿki*
rascal; *haksichi, hatak haksi*
rascality; *haksipi, okpulo*
rascally; *haksi, okpulo*

rase, to; *kashoffichi*
rash, *ilapunla*
rasher; *nipi tushafa, nipi tushafa pạsa*
rashly, *tuⁿshpa*
rashly, to act; *himak fokalechi*
rashness; *ahah ahni keyu, tushpa*
rasp; *isht milofa, isht milofa chito, iti isht milofa*
rasp, to; *miloffi, miloha milolichi*
raspberry, *na hollo iⁿbissa*
rasped; *milohạchi, miloli, milofa*
rasure, *kashoffi*
rat, *pichali*
rat, field; *pintukfi*
rate, *foka*
rate, to; *aiilli onuchi, hotina, iạllichi, miha, nukoa*
rated, *aiilli onitula*
rater, *aiilli onuchi*
rather, *keyukmạt*
ratified; *aiaⁿli, kạllo, lopulli*
ratifier, *kạllochi*
ratify, to; *aiaⁿlichi, aⁿlichi, kạllochi*
ration; *ilhpita, imạlhpisa, impa*
rational, *imanukfila aⁿsha*
ratsbane, *pichali isht illi*
rattle (the instrument); *chasha, chạsha, inchạsha, lạbahahanchi*
rattle (the noise), *kinihahanohi*
rattle, to; *chaⁿsha, chashahạchi, chashli-chi, chạlakạchi, chạmakạchi, chisoha, chi-sohạchi, chusoha, chusohạchi, chusopa, kạlahachechi, kạlahạchi, kinihạchi, kitihạ-chi, kolahachechi, kolahạchi, shạchahạchi, shiloa, washahạchi, wạlahạchi*
rattle, to make; *chashahạchechi, chuso-pạchi*
rattle in the throat, to; *shikiffi*
rattler, *chisohạchi*
rattlesnake, *sintullo*
rattlesnake, a species of; *sinti shaui*
rattlesnake, ground; *chukfitchtololi*
rattlesnake, the "diamond;" *tiak iⁿsinti*
rattlesnake's rattles, *sintullo inchạsha*
rattling; *chashak, chashakạchi, chisoha, chạlakchi, chusoha, chusopa, kạlahạchi, kinihahanohi, kolaha, kolahạchi, lạbaha-hanchi*
rattling noise, *kitihạchi*
ravage, to; *okpạni, wehpuli, weli*
ravage by fire, to; *itot aⁿya*
ravaged; *okpulo, weha*
ravager; *okpạni, wehpuli*

rave, to; *anukbata, tasembo*
ravel, to; *li*ⁿ*fa, poshukta, sheli*
raveled; *li*ⁿ*fa, shiha*
raveling, *li*ⁿ*fa*
raven, *fala chito*
raven, to; *isikopali*
ravenous, *isikopali*
ravine; *kolokbi, okfa*
ravines, deep; *kolhkobeka*
raving fox, *chula tasembo*
ravish, to; *aiissa, hoklit aiissa*
ravisher, *hoklit aiissa*
raw; *foni bano, humma, imponna, ka-pạssa, lofa, okcha*ⁿ*ki*
raw bones, *foni bano*
rawboned; *chunna, foni bano*
rawhide, *hakshup hish a*ⁿ*sha*
rawhide, twisted; *aseta pạna*
rawness; *ikhana, okcha*ⁿ*ki*
ray, *tombi*
ray of light, *tombi*
rayless, *oklili*
raze, to; *akkạchi, kashoffichi, okpạni, ok-pạnit tali, tiạbli*
raze a house, to; *aboha kinạffi*
razed; *kashofa, okpulo, okpulot taha, tiapa*
razor, *nutakhish isht shafa*
reach; *aiạli, ona*
reach, to; *aiạli, bikeli, bikelichi, haksichi, lopullit ona, ona, tikeli*
reach, to cause to; *onachi*
reach forward, to; *mampoa*
reach round, to; *apakfoa*
reach the clouds, to; *hoshonti pit tikeli*
reach to all, to cause to; *oklu*ⁿ*halinchi*
reach to or there, to; *aiona*
reach to two, to; *tuklona*
react, to; *atuklant yạmmichi, falama*
read, to; *akostininchi, anumpuli, holisso aiitimanumpuli, holisso imanumpuli, holisso itimanumpuli, holisso pisa, pisa*
reader; *anumpuli, holisso imanumpuli, holisso itimanumpuli*
readily; *aiokpạchi achukma, tu*ⁿ*shpa*
readiness; *aiokpanchi achukma, ạlhtaha, tushpa*
reading, *itimanumpuli*
ready; *ạlhtaha, tushpa, tu*ⁿ*shpa achukma*
ready, nearly; *ahikma*
ready-minded man, *hatak imanukfila tu*ⁿ*shpa*
real; *aia*ⁿ*li, a*ⁿ*li, fehna*
real thing, *na fehna*

reality; *aia*ⁿ*li, na fehna, nana aia*ⁿ*li, nana fehna*
realize, to; *akostininchi*
really; *a*ⁿ*li, mạli*
realm; *mi*ⁿ*ko apelechika afullota, mi*ⁿ*ko apelichi*
ream of paper; *holisso pụla pokoli tuklo akucha ushta, holisso talakchi achạfa*
reanimate, to; *okchalechi*
reannex, to; *achakạlechi*
reannexed, *achaka*
reap, to; *ạmo, bạshli*
reap wheat, to; *onush ạmo*
reaped; *ạlmo, bạsha*
reaper; *bạshli, na bạshli, nan ạmo, onush bạshli*
reaping hook; *isht ạlmo, onush isht ạlmo, onush isht bạsha*
reappear, to; *atuklant haiaka*
reappoint, to; *atuklant atokoli*
rear; *a*ⁿ*shaka intạnnạp, imashaka, isht aiopi, okbạl, ukbạl, ulbạl*
rear, in the; *okbạl, ukbạl, ulbạl*
rear, to; *ạba isht ia, hilechi, yimintạchi*
rear (bring up), to; *hofantichi, ikhanan-chi*
rear, to be in the; *a*ⁿ*shaka*
rear, to place in the; *a*ⁿ*shakachi*
rear up, to; *hilechi*
reared, *hofanti*
rearward; *aka, isht aiopi a*ⁿ*ya, okbạl*
reascend, to; *atuklant oia*
reason; *ạlhpesa, imanukfila, isht miha, nan ihmi*
reason, to; *aiimomạchi, anukfilli, anum-puli, imanukfila*
reason for death, *aiisht illi*
reasonable; *ạlhpesa, imanukfila a*ⁿ*sha*
reassemble, to; *atuklant itạnnaha, atuk-lant itạnnali*
reassembled, *atuklant itạnnaha*
reassume, to; *atuklant ishi*
reassure, to; *atuklant a*ⁿ*lichi*
reattempt, to; *atuklant yạmmiht pisa*
rebel, *anumpa kobạffi*
rebound, to; *issot falama, tolupli*
rebuild, to; *atuklant ikbi*
rebuke, to; *alạmmi, alạmmichi, anum-puli, hokoffi, olạbbechi, pạlakạchi*
recall, to; *atuklant apesa, atuklant hoyo, falạmmichi*
recant, to; *issa, kanchi*
recapitulate, to; *ạlbitet anoli*
recapture, to; *falạmmichit ishi, okha*

recast, *atuklant akmi*
recast, to; *atuklant akmichi, atuklant pila*
recede, to; *falama*
re-cede, to; *falammint inkanchi*
recede, to cause to; *falammichi*
receipt; *holisso, ishi*
receipt of custom, *aiitahoba*
receive, to; *ahnichi, habena, haklo, ishi, nukfoka, pisa, yimmi*
receive as a gift, to; *ilhpita*
receive well, to; *aiokpanchi, aiokpachi*
received; *ibbak foka, nukfoka*
received as a present, *habena*
receiver, *ishi*
recent; *cheki, himmona*
recently; *cheki, chekusikash*
receptacle; *aiabiha, aiashachi, aialhto*
reception; *aiokpanchi, ishi*
recess; *aluma, anunkaka, falama*
rechoose, to; *atuklant atokoli*
rechosen, *atuklant alhtuka*
reciprocate, to; *alhtoboa*
recital, *anoli*
recite, to; *anoli*
reckless, *ahah ahni*
reckon, to; *ahni, ahnichi, anukfilli, hotina, imahoba*
reckoned, *holhtena*
reckoned in, *holhtina*
reckoning, *hotina*
reclaim, to; *falammichechi, falammint hoyo, hopoyuksalechi, kostininchi*
reclaimed; *hopoyuksa, kostini*
recline, to; *ataiya, shanaia, tashki, waiya*
recluse; *hatak haiaka keyu, hatak luma, luma*
recoil, *falamakachi*
recoil, to; *falama, falamakachi, falamakachi, hehka*
recoiling, *falamakachi*
re-collect, to; *atuklant itannali*
recollect, to; *akostininchi, ikhana*
recollection, *ikhana*
recommence, to; *atuklant isht ia*
recommend, to; *aiokpanchit anoli*
recompense; *alhtoba, ilaiukha*
recompense, to; *atobbi, chiloffi, falammichi, okha*
recompensed, *alhtoba*
reconcile, to; *aiiskiachi, apesa, apoksiachi*
reconciled; *apoksia, alhpesa, nan aiya*
reconciliation; *itimalhpisa, itinnan aiya*
recondite, *luma*

reconnoiter, to; *pisa*
reconquer, to; *imaiyat falammint ishi*
reconsider, to; *atuklant anukfilli*
reconvey, to; *falammint inkanchi*
reconvey, to; *falammint isht ona*
record; *holisso, holisso atakali, isht anoli*
record, to; *holisso lapalichi, holisso takalichi*
recorded; *holisso, holisso takali*
recorder; *holisso takalichi, holissochi*
recount, to; *anoli*
recover, to; *falammint ishi, lakoffi, lakoffichi*
recover from, to; *alakofi*
recover, to begin to; *lakoffit isht ia*
recovered; *kanihmit taha, lakoffi, masali*
recovery; *falama, falammint ishi, lakoffi, lakonffi*
recreant; *hobak, holabi, panya*
re-create, to; *okchali*
recreate, to; *fohachi, yukpali*
recreated, *yukpa*
recreation; *foha, okcha, yukpa*
recriminate, to; *onochi*
recruit, to; *atali, atuklant imatali, foha*
recruited, *atuklant imalhtaha*
rectified, *achukma*
rectify, to; *achchukmali*
rectitude, *hopoksa*
rector, *pelichi*
rectum, *kobish*
recumbent; *ataiya, itola, tashki*
recur, to; *ikhana*
red; *homaiyi, humma*
red (as the cheek), *oktisheli*
red, fiery; *tishepa*
red, to color; *homaiyichi, hummachi*
red dye; *isht hummachi, nan isht hummachi*
red lead, *naki humma*
red man; *hatak, hatak api humma*
red paint; *lukfi humma, na humma, tishi humma*
red pole, *iti humma*
Red river, *oka humma*
red spot; *humma talaia, humma taloha*
red warrior, *na humma*
red water, *oka humma*
redbird; *bishkumak, hushi humma*
redden, to; *humma, hummachi*
reddened; *humma, hummachi, kichanli*
reddish; *homaiyi, homakbi, hummaiyi, hummalhha*

reddish, to make; *homaiyichi*
redeem, to; *chumpa, falamat chumpa, falammint chumpa, lakoffichi*
redeemable, *falammint chumpa hinla*
redeemed, *lakoffi*
redeemer; *chumpa, falammint chumpa, lakoffichi*
redeliver, to; *falammint ima*
redemption; *aiokchalinka, falammint chumpa, lakoffichi*
redhot, *lashpat humma, luat humma*
red-hot, to heat; *lashpat hummachi, luat hummachi*
redly, *humma*
redness, *humma*
redolent, *balama*
redouble, to; *atuklant polomi, albitet yammichi*
redoubled, *atuklant poloma*
redress, to; *achukmalechi, aiskiachi, apoksiachi, atobbi, lakoffichi*
redressed; *achukma, aiskia, apoksia, lakoffi*
reduce, to; *ala, falammichi, haboffi, haksichi, homechi, iskitinichi, kalakshichi*
reduce the price, to; *ola taklachi, taklachi, taklechi*
reduced; *falama, homi, ilbasha, iskitini, kalakshi*
redundant; *atapa fehna, laua fehna*
reecho, to; *atuklant hobachi*
reed; *kunshak, uski chula*
reed, large; *kunshak chito*
reed, low; *kunshak patakchi*
reed, weaver's; *uski chula*
re-edify, to; *atuklant ikbi*
reedy, *kunshak chito*
reef, *tali bacha*
reek, to; *shoboli*
reeking, *shoboli*
reel; *aholhtufa, ponola hulhtufa*
reel, to; *afoli, chukfoloha, faiokachi, faiunkli*
reel, to cause to; *chukfulli, faioli*
reelect, to; *atuklant atokoli*
reeled, *alhfoa*
reeling, *faiokachi*
reenjoy, to; *atuklant isht ilaiyukpa*
reenter, to; *atuklant chukoa*
reestablish, to; *atuklant hilechi*
reexamine, to; *atuklant pisa*
refectory, *aboha aiimpa*
refine, to; *achukmalechi, kashoffichi, yohbichi*

refined; *achukma, kashofa*
refinement; *kashofa, kashoffi, yohbi*
refiner, *kashoffichi*
refit, to; *aiskiachi*
refitted, *aiskia*
reflect, to; *anukfilli, falammichi, shohmalali, tombi*
reflect light, to; *malattakachi*
reflection, *imanukfila*
reflection of light, *malattakachi*
reform, *kostini*
reform, to; *aiskiachi, apoksiachi, kostini, kostininchi*
reformer; *apoksiachi, hopoksiachi, kostininchi*
refractory; *isht afekommi, nukoa shali*
refrain, to; *auola, olabbi*
refresh, to; *kapassachi, kapassalli, okchali, yimintachi, yukpali*
refreshed; *kapassa, okcha, yimmita, yukpa*
refreshment; *nusi, okcha*
refrigerate, to; *kapassachi, kapassalli*
refuge; *aiatokko, alakofi*
refugee; *alakofi*
refulgent, *tohwikeli*
refund, to; *falammichi, falammint atobbi*
refunded; *alhtoba, falama, falamat alhtoba*
refusal; *apoa, haklo*
refuse; *ahoba, ahopoka, atampa*
refuse, to; *ahah achi, aiokpachi, haklo, ilafoa, inshi, keyuachi*
refused, *aiokpachi*
refute, to; *imaiya*
regain, to; *atuklant ishi*
regal, *minko ahalaia*
regale, to; *impa, yukpali*
regaled, *yukpa*
regard, *ikhana*
regard, to; *ahnichi, aiokpachi, anukfilli, holitobli, pisa*
regarded, *ikhana*
regenerate, *chunkash himmona*
regenerate, a; *atuklant toba*
regenerate, to; *chunkash himmonachi, atuklant ikbi*
regenerated; *atuklant toba, chunkash himmona*
regeneration; *atuklant ikbi, chunkash himmona*
regent, *pelichi*
regimen, *ahah ahnit impa*
regiment, *tashka chipota holhtina*
regimentals, *tashka chipota isht shema*

region; *folota, okla, yakni fullota*
register, *holisso anumpa atakali*
registered, *holisso takalichi*
regorge, to; *falammint nanabli, hoeta*
regress, *falama*
regret; *nukhaⁿklo, okko, yakoke*
regret, to; *nukhaⁿklo*
regular, *apissanli*
regular, a; *tashka chipota*
regularly; *apissanli, bilia*
regulate, to; *achchukmali, aiiskia, aiskiachi, apesa, apoksiachi*
regulated; *achukma, aiiska, aiskia, apoksia, alhpesa*
regulator, *aiiskia*
rehear, to; *atuklant haklo*
rehearse, to; *achi, anoli, atuklant miha, hobachit miha*
rehearser; *achi, anoli, miha*
reign, *pelichi*
reign, to; *amiⁿko, miⁿko, miⁿko toba, pelichi*
reign over, to; *pelichi*
reimburse, to; *falammint atobbi*
rein, *kapali isht talakchi*
rein, to; *fololichi, nukoa*
reins, the; *chuⁿkash, haiyiⁿhchi*
reinstate, to; *falammint fohki, falammint heliche*
reiterate, to; *anoli*
reject, to; *issa, kampila, kanchi, shittilema*
rejecter, *kanchi*
rejection, *kanchi*
rejoice, to; *na yukpa, yukpa*
rejoice the heart, to; *chuⁿkash yukpali*
rejoice with, to; *yukpa*
rejoiced, *yukpa*
rejoicing, *na yukpa*
rejoin, to; *yukpali*
rejuvenate, to; *himmitachi*
rekindle, to; *atuklant oti*
rekindled, *atuklant ulhti*
relapse; *afalama, afilema, afilemoa, falama*
relapse, to; *afalama, afilema, afilimmi, falamat abeka*
relapse, to cause a; *afilimmichi*
relate, to; *anoli*
related; *anoa, kanomi*
relation (story); *anoa, anoli*
relation (relative); *hatak iⁿkanohmi, itiⁿkanomi, kanomi*
relative, *itiⁿkanomi*
relator, *anoli*

relax, *ikfia*
relax, to; *ikfia, ikfiachi, kota, nuktala, yohabli, yokopa, yokopachi*
relaxed; *ikfia, kota, nuktala, yokopa*
release; *issa, kucha, lakoⁿffi, yuka issa*
release, to; *issa, lakoffichi, yuka issachi* •
released; *kucha, lakoffi, yuka issa*
relent, to; *lacha, yohbi, yokopa*
relentless; *yohbi keyu, yokopa iksho*
reliance, *yimmi*
relics; *hatak illi, nan illi*
relief; *nuktala, nuktallachi*
relieve, to; *aiskiachi, apelachi, lakoffichi*
relieved; *aiskia, lakoffi*
religion; *aba anumpa, nana aiyimmika*
religious; *aba anumpa nukfoka, aba anumpa yimmi*
religiously clean, *isht ahullochika*
relinquish, to; *issa*
relish, *kashaha*
relish, to; *ahinnia, kashaha, kashahachi*
relish, to cause to; *kashahachi*
re-live, to; *atuklant okchaya*
reluctant; *anukwia, banna, haklo*
rely, to; *anukcheto*
remain, to; *aiasha, anta, itola, talaia*
remainder; *atampa, alhkucha, alhtampa*
remains; *atampa, hatak illi, nan illi*
remake, to; *atuklant ikbi*
remark; *amiha, holisso*
remark, to; *ahni, anukfilli, pisa*
remarkable, *na fehna*
remarried, *atuklant itauaya*
remarry, to; *atuklant itauaya, atuklant itauayachi*
remedied; *apoksia, atta, lakoffi, masali*
remediless, *lakoffahe keyu*
remedy; *alakofi, apelachi, isht lakoffi*
remedy, to; *aiskiachi, lakoffichi*
remember, to; *ahnit, akostininchi, anukfohka, ikhana, ikhana*
remembrance; *ikhana, isht ikhana*
remembrancer; *ikhananchi, isht ikhana*
remind, to; *ikhananchi*
remiss; *ahaksichi shali, salaha*
remission; *imahaksi, issa, isht akashofa*
remit, to; *falammichi, halata, imahaksi, issa, laua, shippa, shippachi, yokopa, yokopachi*
remitted, *kashofa*
remnant, *atampa*
remnants of men, *hatak wishakchi*
remonstrate, to; *ahnichi*
remorse, *nukhaⁿklo*

remote, *hopaki*
remotely; *hopaki, pilla*
removal; *kobaffi, wiha*
remove; *hopaki, wiha*
remove, to; *akanalichi, akanallechi, aka-nalli, aⁿsha, alhtosholi, bashpuli, ha-boffi, kanali, kanalichi, kanallichi, kana-lichi, kania, kobaffi, mishemachi, okpani, taklachi, toshoa, wiha*
remove swellings, to; *habolichi*
removed; *alhtoshoa, hopaki, kanalli, ka-nia, kobafa, mishema*
remunerate, to; *atobbi*
remunerated, *alhtoba*
remuneration; *atobbi, alhtoba*
rencounter, *itibbi*
rencounter, to; *itibi*
rend, to; *liabli, litoli, lilalichi, lilaffi, lilechi, lilli, nipa, okpani, palalli*
rend from, to; *mokofi*
render; *alhtoba, falama, ima, lilaffi, lile-chi*
render, to; *anoli, falammichi, falammint ima, ima, tosholi*
render childish, to; *puskusechi*
render into, to; *alhtosholi*
render proud, to; *ilefehnachechi*
rendered, *toshoa*
rendered into, *alhtoshoa*
rendezvous, *aiitanaha*
rendezvous, to; *aiitanaha*
rendor, *issa*
renegade, *hatak haksi okpulo*
renew, to; *atuklant ikbi, atuklant isht ia, albitet ikbi, himmitachi, himonachi*
renew the heart, to; *chuⁿkash himmo-nachi*
renewable, *himmonacha hinla*
renewed; *atuklant toba, himmona*
renewed by the spirit, *shilombish isht aiatta*
renewed heart, *chuⁿkash himmona*
rennet; *bakna, imbakna*
renounce, to; *issa, kanchi*
rencvate, to; *aiskiachi, himonachi*
renovated; *aiskia, himmona, himmona toba*
renown, *anoa*
rent; *litoa, lilafa, lilalaⁿkachi, lilali, lilli*
rent (payment for something), *pota alhtoba*
rent, to; *impota, shobobuⁿkachi*
rent and worn out, to be; *bihkachi*
renter; *impota, yakni impota*

reorganize, to; *atuklant ikbi*
repaid; *falamat alhtoba. falammint alh-toba*
repair, to; *achchukmali, achukmalechi, aiiskia, aiiskiachi, aiiskiali, aiskiachi, apoksia, apoksiachi, hochukmalechi, ho-chukmali, iksiachi, ona*
repaired; *aiskachi, aiskia, apoksia*
repairer; *achukmalechi, achukmali, aiis-kia, aiiskiachi, aiskiachi, apoksiachi, ho-chukmalechi, hochukmali*
reparable; *aiskia hinla, aiskiacha hinla*
repass, to; *atuklant lopuli*
repast, *impa*
repay, to; *atobbi, falammint atobbi*
repayment, *falamat alhtoba*
repeal, to; *akshuchi, kashoffichi*
repealed, *aksho*
repeat, to; *anoli, atuklanchi, atuklant achi, atuklant anoli, atuklant miha, al-behkachi, albilli, albiteli, albitet anoli, miha*
repeat three times, to; *atuchinanchi*
repeated; *atuⁿkla, albita, albitkachi*
repeatedly, *himonnaⁿ*
repel, to; *falammichi*
repent, to; *akostininchi, kostininchi, nuk-haⁿklo*
repentance, *aiilekostininchi*
repentant; *nana yoshoba isht nukhaklo, nukhaⁿklo*
repeople, to; *himmona aioklachi*
repetition; *atuklanchi, albita*
repine, to; *alhpesa*
repiner; *alhpesa, nana isht miha shali*
replace, to; *atobbichi, falammichi, falam-mint boli*
replace bones, to; *foni falammint iti-fohki*
replaced, *foni falammint itifohka*
replant, to; *albitet hokchi*
replanted, *albitat holokchi*
replenish, to; *alotoli*
replete, *alota*
reply; *anumpa falama, anumpa falamoa*
reply, to; *afalamichi, anumpa falamo-lichi, anumpa falammichi, yimmi*
report; *aianoyuwa, anoa, anumpa, anum-pa chukushpa, kobak*
report, to; *anoli*
report of a gun; *humpah, toh*
reported, *anoa*
reporter; *anoli, nan anoli*
repose, *nusi*

repose, to; *anukcheto, foha, fohachi, nusi, yimmi*
reprehend, to; *anumpuli*
represent, to; *ahobachi, ahoballi, anoli, haiakachi*
representative; *anoli, anumpeshi*
repress, to; *imaiya*
reprieve, to; *abanablichi*
reprieved, *abanapa*
reprimand, to; *anumpuli, miha*
reproach; *ahofahya, hofahya, isht ahofahya*
reproach, a word of; *okpiyanli, ushi, yammak haloka*
reproach, to; *miha, onochi, posilhha, posilhhachi*
reproachful, *chakapa*
reprobate, *yoshoba*
reproof, *inmiha*
reprove, to; *fappuli, miha*
republic; *okla moma, ulhti*
repudiate, to; *kanchi*
repugnant, *ichapa*
repulse, to; *falammichi*
repulsive; *aiokpachi, kapassa*
repurchase, *falammint chumpa*
repurchase, to; *falammint chumpa*
repurchaser, *falammint chumpa*
reputable; *achukma, holitompa*
reputation, *holitopa*
repute, *holitopa*
repute, to; *anukfilli*
request; *anumpa asilhha, asilhha*
request, to; *asilhha, asilhhachi*
required, *aialhtokowa*
requite, to; *atobbi*
rescue, to; *alakofichi, lakoffichi, okchalinchi*
rescued, *alakofi*
re-search, to; *hoyo fehna*
reseize, to; *atuklant hokli*
resemblance; *holba, itihoba, itiholba, na holba*
resemblance of a man, *hatak holba*
resemble, to; *aholba, holbachi*
resemble, to cause it to; *chohmichi, ohmichi*
resembled, *holba*
resembling; *binka, holba, ohmi*
resend, to; *atuklant pila*
resent, to; *nukoa*
resentful, *nukoa banna*
resentment, *chunkash imanukfila nukoa*
reservation, *inshi*

reserve; *ilatomba, inshi*
reserve, to; *ilatomba, inshi*
reserved; *anumpa ilatomba, ilatomba*
reserved person, *na miha iksho*
reservoir, *oka atalaia*
reside, to; *aianta, anta, ansha, atta, itola*
reside at, to; *achuka, aiatta*
reside near, to; *bilinkatta*
residence; *aboha, aiatta, chuka, foka*
resident; *aiasha, anumpeshi, atta*
residue, *atampa*
resign, to; *akkachunoli, anukcheto, ibbak fohki, ima, issa, kucha*
resignation; *ibbak fohki, issa, kucha*
resin, *litilli*
resinous substance, *na litilli*
resist, to; *afoa, ichapa, tobli*
resistless, *kallo*
resolute; *achillita, amosholi, chilita, kamassa, nakni, nukwia iksho*
resolute, made; *achillita*
resolution; *achunanchi, anumpa alhpisa, chilita, imanukfila achafa*
resolve, *imanukfila achafa*
resolve, to; *anukfilli, apesa, bila, bileli*
resolved; *alhpesa, bila*
resort, *aiitanaha*
resort, to; *ia, ona*
resort for swine, *shukha aiasha*
resound, to; *hobachi*
resource; *aianukcheto, tali holisso*
resow, to; *atuklant fimmi*
respect, *aiokpanchi*
respect, to; *ahnichi, aiahninchi, aiokpachi, aninchi, holitobli*
respectable; *achukma, alhpiesa*
respected, *holitopa*
respected man, *hatak holitopa*
respiration, *fiopa*
respire, to; *fiopa, foha, kucha fiopa*
respite; *abanapa, foha*
respite, to; *abanablichi*
respited, *abanapa*
respond, to; *anumpuli italhpesa, atobbi, alhpesa, falammichit miha*
responding, *alhpesa*
responsible; *atobba hinla, isht ahalaia*
rest; *afoha, aionitola, foha, illi, inla, nusi*
rest (remainder), *atapa*
rest, to; *anta, ataiya, foha, hokofa, illi, issa, itola, nusi, onochi, yokopa*
rest, to give; *fohachi*
rest against, to; *ataiyali*
rest against, to make; *ataiyachi*

rest another, to; *fohachi*
rest at, on, in, or there, to; *afoha*
rest at, on, in, or there, to give; *afohachi*
rest in, to; *hika*
rest on, to; *ontalaia*
rest upon, to; *bitepa*
resting place, *ayataia*
restitution, *falammichi*
restive, *isht afekommi*
restless; *komota, nowa shali, nusi*
restoration, *lakoffi*
restore, to; *falama, falamichi, falammichi, falammint ima, lakoffichi, masalichi*
restored, *lakoffi*
restorer; *falammichi, lakoffichi, na lakofichi*
restrain, to; *halalli, inshi, olabbi, takchi*
restraint; *halanli, isht ataklama*
restrict, to; *apesa*
resume, to; *atuklant isht ia, falammint ishi*
resurrection, *illit okosh falamat tani*
resuscitate, to; *okchanyachi*
resuscitated; *falamat okchanya, okchanya*
retail, to; *kashkolit kampila, takaffit kampila*
retailer; *kashkolit kampila, takaffit kampila*
retain, to; *halalli, inshi*
retake, to; *atuklant ishi, falammichit ishi, falammint ishi*
retaliate, to; *atobbi, falammichi, okha*
retaliation, *ilaiukha*
retard, to; *oktabli, salahachi*
retch, to; *hoeta banna, hoetat pisa*
retire, to; *anta, binili, kucha, naksika binili, tisheli*
retired; *anta, luma*
retirement; *binili, kucha*
retort, *anumpa chunkushnali*
retort, to; *falammichit anumpuli, falammichit pila*
retreat; *atukko, binili, luma*
retreat, to; *kucha*
retreat, to cause to; *falammichi*
retrench, to; *iskatanichi*
retribute, to; *atobbi, falammichi*
retrograde, *falamat ia*
retrograde, to; *falamat ia*
return; *afalama, afalamaka, falama, falamaka, falamat anya, falammichi, falammichit pila*

return, to; *afalama, anoli, atobbi, falama, falamichi, falamoa, falamat ala, falamat ia falamat ona, falammichi*
return (as morning light), to; *onnat oklilinchi, onnat oklinli*
return, to cause to; *falamolichi*
return along, to; *falamat anya*
return from, to; *attat falama*
returned; *falama, falamoa*
returner; *falamat anya, falamolichi, falammichi*
returns; *falamoa, falamoaka*
reveal, to; *anoli, haiakachi, oktanichi, otani*
revealed; *anoa, haiaka, oktani*
revel, to; *ilaualli*
revelation; *aba anumpa, Chihowa abanumpa*
reveler, *ilaualli*
revenge, to; *atobbi, itialbi abi, okha*
revenged, *alhtoba*
revenger; *atobbi, ilaiukha, itialbi abi*
reverberate, to; *hobachi*
revere, to; *aiokpachi, holitobli*
revered, *holitopa*
reverence, *aiokpanchi*
reverence, to; *aiokpachi, holitobli, holitopa*
reverend, *holitopa*
reverie; *imanukfila chito, tasembo*
reverse; *ichapa, intannap*
reverse, to; *atobbichi, lipeli*
reversed, *lipia*
revert, to; *falama, falammichi*
reverted, *falama*
review, to; *albitet pisa*
revile, to; *chakapa, mihachi, yopula*
reviler; *chakapa, mihachi*
reviling, *chakapa*
revise, to; *atuklant aiskiachi, atuklant pisa*
revised, *atuklant aiskia*
revival, *falamat okchanya*
revive, to; *falamat okcha, falamat okchanya, okchanyachi*
revived, *falamat okchanya*
revoke, to; *atuklant apesa*
revolt, to; *anumpa kobaffi, imaiya, issa*
revolution; *folotat ala, nana inkaniohmi chito*
revolve, to; *falama*
reward; *aialbi, aialhtoba, alhtoba*
reward, to; *atobbi*

rewardable; *atobba hinla, ạlhtoba hinla*
rewarded, *ạlhtoba*
rewarder, *atobbi*
rewritten, *ạlbitạt holisso*
rheum; *ibilhkạn, itukholaya, ituklipaya*
rheumatic pains; *nahishi, shumanta*
rheumatism; *foni hotupa, shumantạbi*
rib; *isht ukfoata, naksi*
rib bone; *naksi foni, okhoata foni*
rib pole, *iti ana*
ribbed, *yạfimpa*
ribbed (as a roof), *ạlbạska*
ribbing, *iti ạlbạsa*
ribbon; *fataha, sita fataha, sita lapushki*
ribs of a house, *chukạlbạska*
ribs of a roof, *abasa*
rice, *onush lakchi*
rich; *awaya achukma, holitopa, nan inlaua*
rich man; *hatak holitompa, hatak holi-*
  topa, hatak nan inlaua
riches; *holitopa, ila^{n}yak, nan inlaua*
richly; *a^{n}li, fehna*
richness; *awaya achukma, laua*
rick of hay, *hạshuk itạnaha*
rid, to; *ạmo, chạfichi*
riddle; *isht okchila, okchila, shakla*
riddle, to; *yuha, yuli*
riddled, *yuha*
ride, *ombinili*
ride, to; *binili, ontaloha, talaia, tạla*
ride double, to; *aiitisholi*
ride on, to; *ontalaia*
ride on the waves, to; *paiokạchi*
ride ostentatiously, to; *hattauichi*
ride treble, to; *aiitishali*
rider; *isuba omanili, ombinili, ontalaia,*
  ontaloha
ridge; *bạhcha, bạnaiya, bạnaiyạchi, okwakli,*
  onchạba
ridge, straight; *bạhcha pissa*
ridge, to; *bạhcha ikbi, bạnaiyạchechi*
ridge, to make a; *yikoli*
ridge top, *bạhcha tabokaka*
ridges, to have; *tạshiha*
ridicule, *olạlli*
ridicule, to; *isht yopulạt isht anumpuli,*
  olạlli
ridiculous, *olạllahe ạlhpisa*
rifle, *tanamp patali*
rifle, to; *patalichi, wehpuli*
rifled, *wehpoa*
rifleman, *tanamp patali sholi*
rifler, *wehpuli*
rift, to; *shimafa, shimạffi*

rig, *isht shema*
rig, to; *shema, shemạchi*
rigger; *shema, shemạchi*
rigging; *isht shema, pinạsh*
right; *aiisht ahalaia, a^{n}li, apissanli, apis-*
  sanlit, ạlhpesa, immi
right, the; *isht impaka*
right, to; *ạlhpesạchi*
right, toward the; *isht impak imma*
right against, *ichapaka*
right hand, the; *ibbak isht impak imma,*
  ibbak isht impaka, isht impak imma ibbak
right hand, to the; *ibbak isht impak*
  imma
right here, *ilạppak*
right side of, the; *isht impak imma*
righteous; *achukma, aiạlhpiesa, hopok-*
  sia, hopo^{n}ksia, hopoyuksa
righteous before him, *nan imaia^{n}li*
righteousness; *ahopoyuksaka, aiạlhpie-*
  sa, chu^{n}kash yohbi, hanta
rightful; *ahalaia, aiạlhpesa*
rightly; *a^{n}li, ạlhpesa*
rigid; *kamạssa, kạllo*
rigidity; *kamạssa, kạllo*
rigidly; *kamạssa, kạllo*
rigor; *kamạssa, palạmmi*
rigorous; *ilbạsha, kapạssa, palạmmi*
rill; *bok ushi, oklotbi, okmoffi, okshulbi*
rill, to; *yanạlli*
rim, *afohoma*
rim, to; *afohommi, afoli*
rim of a basket; *ạlhtanafo, kishi afohoma*
rim of a hat, *pashia*
rim of a vial, *pashia*
rimmed, *afohoma*
rind, *hakshup*
ring; *chạnaha, ola*
ring, to; *abeli, chạmakạchi, kabakạchi,*
  kabukachi, kạmakạchi, kạsahạchi, kạssa,
  kạssaha, kobohạchi, kobokạchi, komaka-
  chi, komokachi, komokạchi, mishukachi,
  ola, olachi, samahạchi, samakachi, shiloa
ring, to cause to; *sạmahạchechi*
ringer, *olachi*
ringing; *chạmakạchi, kobohạchi, ola*
ringleader, *pelichi*
ringlet, *yushbonoli*
ringworm; *halampa, hạllampạ*
ringworm, to have a; *hạllampạbi*
rinse, to; *ahchifa, chobolichi, itukwạlichi,*
  itukwololichi, pikalichi
riot, *yahapa*
riot, to; *itakhapuli shali*

rioter, *hatak itakhapuli shali*
riotous, *itakhapuli shali*
rip;, *mitefa, miteli*
rip, to; *mitelichi*
rip off, to; *shoekachi*
ripe; *alakna, aninchichi, hanta, hatachi, imponna, lakna, nuna, waya*
ripe, to become; *aninchichi*
ripe in years; *kamassa, kamassalli*
ripen, to; *aiskiachi, alakna, alaknachi, atali, alhtaha, hatachi, hatachi, nuna, nunachi, tobachi, waya*
ripen, to begin to; *alaknat ia, halabushli*
ripen, to cause to; *nunachechi*
ripened; *alakna, alhtaha, laknabi*
ripeness; *alhtaha, hatachi, nuna*
ripped; *mitefa, miteli*
ripple, *wisattakachi*
ripple, to; *banakachi, chobohachi, piakachi, wisakachi, wisalichi*
ripple, to cause to; *banakachechi*
rippled, *piakachi*
rippling, *wisakachi*
rise; *aiisht ia ammona, ateli, ibish, oiya*
rise, to; *afena, amokafi, anuktobulli, aba ia, abana, ammona isht ia, attat isht ia, chitot ia, inshaht ia, kucha, offo, oiya, okchito, okpicheli, okshakala, okshulba, pishpiki, shofoli, tani, tisheli, toba, wakaya*
rise, to cause to; *tanichi, wakayachi*
rise again, to; *falamat tani*
rise from, to; *atia*
rise from a seat, to; *wakaya, wakayoha*
rise from the dead, to; *falamat okchanya, illit akosh falamat tani*
risen, *kucha*
riser, *tani*
risible, *yukpa hinla*
rising; *oiya, tani*
rite; *aiyamohmi, okissa*
rival; *imaiya, itimpakna*
rival, to; *imaiya, pakna*
rive, to; *chulafa, chuli, shima, shimafa, shimali, shimalichi, shimmi*
rived, *chulata*
riven; *bakapa, chula, chulafa, chulata, shima, shimafa, shimali*
river; *bok, chuli, hacha, okhina*
river (splitter); *na shimmi, shimmi*
river's side, *okhina takchaka*
river water, *okhina oka*
rivet, *tali pilefa*
rivet, to; *boat pilefa, bot apelifichi, bot apiliffi*

riveted, *boat pilefa*
rivulet; *bok chulaffi, bok ushi*
road; *aiitanowa, atia, hina*
road, broad; *hina patha*
road, large; *hina chito*
road, old deserted; *hinakshu*
road, to make a; *hina ikbi*
road, unused; *hinakshu*
road maker, *hina ikbi*
roam, to; *abaiyachi, fullokachi*
roamer; *abaiyachi, fullokachi*
roan, *bokboki*
roar; *bimihachi, fopa, kileha*
roar, to; *bimihachi, bimimpa, chobohachi, chopa, fapa, fonhka, fomohachi, fopa, kileha, kofoha, kofohachi, oka pitafohopa, panya, tobohachi, wimilichi*
roar, to cause to; *fopachi*
roarer; *kileha, panya*
roaring; *bim, bimihachi, fonhka, fomohachi, fopa*
roaring, to make a; *bimihachechi*
roaring of water, *chobohachi*
roaring of wind, *kofohachi*
roast, *alhpusha*
roast, to; *apushli*
roasted; *alhpusha, nuna*
roasted meat, *nipi alhpusha*
roasted potato, *ahe alhpusha*
roaster, *apushli*
roasting, a vessel used for; *aialhpusha*
roasting ear, *nipasha*
roasting ear, to become a; *nipashi*
rob, to; *bakastuli, hunkupa, wehpuli, weli*
robbed; *holhta, wehpoa*
robber; *na wehpuli, wehpuli*
robbery, *wehpoa*
robe, *anchi*
robe, to; *anchi, anchichechi, anchichi*
robe, turkey-feather; *kasmo*
robed, *anchi*
robin, *bishkoko*
robust; *kallo, kilimpi, lampko*
rock; *tali, tali chito, tali hochito*
rock, to; *faiokachi, faiolichi*
rock salt, *hapi lakchi chito*
rocked, *faiokachi*
rocker; *aionfaiokachi, faiolichi*
rockiness, *tali chito foka*
rocks, a ledge of; *tali hochito kaha*
rocky region; *tali chito foka, tali hochito foka*
rod; *fuli, yakni isht alhpisa*
rogue; *haksichi, hatak haksi, na haksi, na haksichi*

roguery, *haksi*
roguish, *haksi*
roil, to; *tobullichi*
roiled; *anuktiboha, tobulli*
roily; *boha, tobulli*
roll; *banaha, bonkachi, bonuha, bonunta, buna, holisso, hulbona, iti kalaha, iti lumbo, lumbo, na buna, pulhkachi, pula*
roll, to; *atonoli, banatha, banakachi, bonunta, chanalli, chanallichi, chanichi, chanaha, chanahachi, channichi, faiokachi, lumbochi, piakachi, yupi*
roll, to make it; *banathachi*
roll away, to; *tonullichi*
roll high, to; *poakachi*
roll high, to cause to; *poalichi*
roll of bread, *paska banaha*
roll of butter, *pishukchi banaha*
roll of cloth, *nan tanna bonunta*
roll over, to; *chanahachi, chanalli, chanaha, tonnoli, tonnolichi, tonulli, tonullichi*
roll round, to; *afoli*
roll up, to; *abunni, alelichi, bonkachi, bonuha, bonulli, buna, bunni, pula, puli*
roll up in, to; *abonulli*
rolled; *chanaha, lumbo*
rolled over; *tonnoli, tonulli*
rolled up; *abonunta, abunkachi, bonkachi, hulbona, bonna, bonuha, bonunta, buna*
roller; *iti chanaha, iti kalaha, iti tapa tonoli*
rolling; *bambaki, banatha*
Roman nose, to have a; *okkohonlih*
romance, *shukha anumpa*
romp, *alla tek haksi*
romp, to; *ilaualli, tulli*
roof; *aboha isht holmo, aboha pakna, alipo, chuka isht holmo, holmo, isht holmo, onlipa*
roof, to; *homo*
roofed, *holmo*
room; *aboha, aiatta, aionasha, ansha, alhtoba*
room, adjoining; *aboha atampa*
room, separate; *aboha atampa*
room, single; *aboha achafa*
room, spare; *aboha atampa*
roost, *akank anusi*
roost, to; *nusi*
rooster, *akank nakni*
root; *akashtala, akishtala, akshish, hakshish, itakshish, iti akishtala*
root, a certain; *hichuk, hehio*

root, to; *akshish toba, awokokonlichi, hofobichit hokchi, lubbi, wokkokli, wokonlichi, wokonlichi, woshoha, wosholichi*
rooted; *akshish toba, kallot hika*
rooted up, *teha*
rooted up, place; *awokokonlichi, wokonlichi*
roots turned up, *lobafa*
rope; *aseta, ponokallo, ponokallopana*
rope, long; *aseta falaia*
rope, plaited hide; *aseta tanaffo*
ropemaker; *asetikbi, ponokallo ikbi*
ropes of a vessel, *pinash*
ropiness; *likaha, walaha*
ropy; *likaha, likansha, likashbi, likoa, walaha*
ropy, to render; *likahachi*
rose, wild; *kati ancho*
roseate, *humma*
rosin, *tiak nia kallo*
ross bark; *akchalhpi, hakchalhpi shila, haklopish, iti haklupish*
rosy, *oktisheli*
rot; *shua, toshbi*
rot (a disease among sheep), *chukfi isht abeka*
rot, to; *hatakwa, shua, shuachi, shuachichi, shumba, toshbi, toshbichechi*
rot, to begin to; *toshbit isht ia*
rot, to cause the bone to; *foni toshbichi*
rot, to cause to; *toshbichechi*
rotation; *alhtoboa, chanalli, italhtoboa*
rotted, *shua*
rotten; *ashua, shalankpa, shua, shumba, toshbi, toshboa*
rotten bone, *foni toshbi*
rotten things, *nan toshbi*
rottenness; *shua, toshbi*
rottenness, to cause; *ashuwachi*
rotund; *chanaha, lumbo*
rouge; *humma, lukfi humma, na humma, tishi humma*
rouge, to; *anchali, anchalichi*
rough; *bambaki, banakachi, bombaki, halupa, kallo, okpulo, pahshala, pompoki, shikowa, tali foka*
rough, to make; *pompokachi*
rough-edged, *kachoa*
roughness; *halupa, pahshala*
round; *apakfoa, apakfopa, bokko, bolukta, chashaiyi, chanaha, folota, kalaha, loboa, lobuhbo, lumbo, lobboa, loboboa, lobonto, lobukta, okhoatkachi, toluski, tolusli*

round, to; *boluktachi, chanaha, chanaha-chi, lumbochi, lobboachi*
round, to go; *apakfoa, apakfobli, apakfo-kachi, apakfopa, boluktali, fololi, folota, folotoa*
round, to make; *lobuhbochi, toluskichi*
round, to put; *folotolichi*
round, to take; *boluktali, fololi*
round, to trim; *yushkobolichi*
round and elevated, *chishinto*
round and large, *tibikshi*
round and pointed; *ibakpishanli, ibak-pisha*ⁿ*shli*
round and pointed, to make; *ibakpi-shanlichi, ibakpisha*ⁿ*shlichi*
round lead, *naki lumbo*
round potato, *ahe lumbo*
round thing, *nan chanaha*
roundabout; *afolupa, folota, folumpa*
roundabout, a; *ilefoka kolofa, ilefoka ko-loli, kolokshi, na foka kolukshi*
rounded; *bolukta, lumbo, yushkoboli*
round-headed, *yushkoboli*
round-headed, to make; *yushkobolichi*
roundness; *bolukta, chanaha, lumbo*
rounds; *folota, fullokachi*
rouse, to; *chafichi, okcha, okchali, yimin-tachi*
roused, *okcha*
rout; *hatak laua yahapa shali, yilepa*
rout, to; *yilibli*
route; *aiaya, hina*
rove, to; *fullokachi, fullokachit a*ⁿ*ya*
rover; *fullokachi, hu*ⁿ*kupa*
row; *atia, bachali, bachaya, bachoha, ba-choli, baieta, bashkachi, hina, okishko ma*ⁿ*ya*
row, to; *moeli, mo*ⁿ*ffi, mofi, okishko laua*
row, to arrive in a; *baiallit ala*
row, to begin to; *mo*ⁿ*ffit isht ia*
row, to come in a; *baiallit minti*
row, to make a; *hina ikbi*
row, to stand in a; *baiallit hika*
row, to stand or go in a; *baieta*
row of blazed trees, *iti tila bachaya*
rowdy, *hatak itakhapuli shali*
rowed, *mo*ⁿ*fa*
rowel, *chufak*
rower, *mo*ⁿ*ffi*
rowlock, *isht mo*ⁿ*fa atapachi*
rows, laid or lying in; *bashkachi, baiilli*
rows, to lie in; *bashkachi*
rows, to make; *bacholi*
rows, to stand in; *baiilli*

royal; *achukma, holitopa, mi*ⁿ*ko ahalaia, mi*ⁿ*ko imma*
rub, *amishokachi*
rub, to; *amisholichi, bili, kasholichi, mi-sholi, mo*ⁿ*fa, pasholi, pikolichi, shilli*
rub, to make; *misholichi*
rub against, to; *amishoffi, amishohachi, ami*ⁿ*shokachi, amishoa, amisholichi, ka-shokachi, mo*ⁿ*fkachi*
rub against, to cause to; *amishoffi*
rub fine, to; *botolichi*
rub gently, to; *ahammi, hammi*
rub in the hands, to; *koyoli, linli*
rub off, to; *mishofa, mo*ⁿ*ffi*
rub on or against, to; *amisho*ⁿ*fa*
rub the hair off, to; *boyalichi, boyaffi*
rub to pieces, to; *lishoa, lisholili*
rub to pieces, to cause to; *koyolichi*
rubbed; *amisho*ⁿ*fa, amishoha, amishofa, hama, kashokachi, mishoha, mishokachi, misholi, mo*ⁿ*fkachi, pashoka*
rubbed in pieces, *koyoha*
rubbed off; *amishokachi, boyafa, boyali, laha, mishofa, mishokachi, mo*ⁿ*fa*
rubbed till sore, *pikoli*
rubbed to pieces, *lishoa*
rubber, *holisso isht kashoffi*
rubber; *amisholichi, isht milofa, isht mi-sholichi, isht shuahchi*
rubbing, *mishokachi*
rubbish; *aboha toshbi, chiffoko, nan tosh-bi, polhkash*
rubstone; *asholichi, isht shuahchi*
ruby; *humma, tali humma*
rudder, *peni isht fullolichi*
ruddy, *humma*
rude; *chilita, halupa, imponna, kostini, yahapa*
rude girl, a; *alla tek haksi*
rudely; *kostini, kostinit*
rueful; *ilbasha, nukha*ⁿ*klo*
ruff, *ikonla awalakachi*
ruffian, *hatak haksi atapa*
ruffle; *awalakachi, ikonla awalakachi, yi*ⁿ*yiki*
ruffle, to; *awalakachechi, banaiyachechi, banakachi, nukoachi, polomoli, yi*ⁿ*yike-chi, yi*ⁿ*yiki*
ruffle of a shirt, *ilefoka awalakachi*
ruffled; *awalakachi, banakachi, nukoa, yi*ⁿ*yiki*
ruffled shirt, *ilefoka walaha*
rug, *shukbo*
rugged; *ba*ⁿ*shkiksho, halupa, itilaui iksho*

ruin; *aiissa, kinafa, okpulo, okpuloka*
ruin, to; *hushmi, ilbasha, ilbashali, ok-*
pani, tiabli, toshbi
ruin, to cause; *okpanichi*
ruined; *aiokpuloka, chunkash okpulo, il-*
basha, kalakshi, okpulo, tiapa, toshbi
ruiner, *okpani*
ruinous, *okpulo*
rule; *anumpa alhpisa, anumpa kallo, isht*
alhpisa, nan isht apesa, nana isht apesa,
pelichi
rule, to; *apesa, apesachi, ilaueli, ilauet*
anya, lanfi, lali, minko, pelichi
rule at, to; *apelichi*
ruled, *lanfa*
ruler (commander); *hatak chitokaka,*
hatak hochitoka, hatak pelichi, hatak peli-
chika, ilauet anya, ishtokaka, na pelichi,
nam pelichi, nan apesa, pelichekia, pelichi
ruler (for making lines); *holisso isht*
lanfa, isht lanfa
ruler of a house, *chukachafa pelicheka*
rum, *oka homi*
rum bud, *oka homi bikobli*
rumble, to; *chulhah, kabahachi, kofoka-*
chi, winihachi
rumbling; *kilihachi, kofokachi, winihachi,*
woshushuk
rumbling in the bowels, to make a;
woshushukachi
ruminate, to; *anukfilli, hopansa*
rummage, to; *tiabli, tiablit pisa*
rumor; *anoa, anumpa anya*
rumor, to; *anoli*
rumored, *anoa*
rump; *hapullo, hatip*
rump, to be without a; *tokumpa*
rumple, *poloma*
rumple, to; *yinyikechi*
rumpled, *yinyiki*
run; *hakmo, maleli, yanalli*
run, to; *akmochi, anukfilli, anya, balalli,*
baleli, bileli, chanalli, chafa, chafichi, ia,
imaiya, lopulli, maleli, tilaya, tilayachi,
tileli, yanalli, yilepa, yilepoa, yilibli
run (as a mill), to; *fotoha*
run (as an old sore), to; *okchushba*
run, to cause the nose to; *ibaklatin-*
lichi
run, to make; *malelichi, yanallichi, yile-*
pachi, yilepoachi, yilibli
run a piece of wood into one's flesh,
to; *okfanya*
run a road, to; *hina apesa*
run after, to; *achafa, iahinsht ia*

run against, to; *apokofa*
run along, to; *yananta*
run around, to cause to; *chanichi*
run at the nose, to; *ibaklatinli, ibaklo-*
loli
run away, to; *malelit kania*
run between, to; *yululli*
run crosswise, to; *okhoatakachi*
run down, to; *achafa, tasalli*
run from each other, to; *yilepa*
run high, to; *poakachi*
run in debt, to; *ahekachi*
run in large waves, to; *oka poakachi*
run in waves, to; *oka piakachi*
run on, to; *amoshuli*
run out, to; *bichilli, okchushba, pichefa,*
pichilli, shinilli
run out, to cause to; *shinillichi*
run over, to; *abanabli, walanta*
run through, to; *anukliha, lopolichi,*
yululli, yulullichi
run through a noose, to; *anuklinfa*
run under, to; *yululli*
run up, to; *oiya*
run upon, to; *amokafa, yilepa*
runaway; *hatak baleli, hatak chafa, male-*
lit kania
rundle; *atuya, kalaha*
rung, *ola*
runner; *anumpa isht anya, anumpa shali,*
baleli, chafa, iti shalalli, maleli, maleli-
chi, na maleli, tilaya
runnet, *bakna*
running; *yananta, yanalli*
running, to stop; *yanallit issa*
running at the nose, *ibaklatinli*
runt, *imoma*
ruption, *mitafa*
rupture; *iskuna kucha, kobafa, kobaffi*
rupture, to; *iskuna kuchi, kitiffi, kobaffl,*
mitafa, mitali, mitalichi, mitaffi
ruptured; *iskuna kucha, kobafa, mitafa*
rush, *amoshuli*
rush, to; *amoshuli, yilepa*
russet, *lakna*
Russia, *Lashe*
Russian Empire, *Lashe yakni*
rust; *lakna, na lakna, yalhki*
rust, to; *alakna, alaknabi, alaknachi,*
lakna, laknabi, okchamali
rusted; *alakna, lakna*
rustle, to; *chashahachi, chashakachi, cha-*
shlichi, kalahachi, kolahachi, shachaha,
shachahachi
rustling; *chashak, chashakachi, kalahachi*

rustling, to cause a; *kalahạchechi, wa-shahạchi*
rusty; *alakna, lakna aⁿsha, laknạbi, lak-noba*
rut, *iti chạnaha anowa*
rut, to; *lioli, yushkạmmi*
ruthless, *nukhaⁿklo iksho*
rye; *onush, onush chaha*

Sabbath breaker, *nitak hollo kobạffi*
Sabbath day; *nitak hollo, nitak hollo ni-tak*
Sabbathless, *nitak hollo ikimiksho*
sable, *lusa*
saccharine, *champuli*
sachem; *hatak ạpi humma iⁿminko, minko*
sack; *ạlbehpo, shukcha*
sack a town, to; *tạmaha wehpulli*
sackcloth; *nam paⁿshi tạnna, paⁿshi tạnna*
sacked, *tạmaha wehpoa*
sacrament, *Chisạs Kilaist inanisht ạlh-pisa*
sacred; *haloka, holitopa*
sacred, to keep; *na hollochi*
sacred bag, a priest's; *hopulbona, pu-shahollo*
sacred book, *holisso holitopa*
sacred bread, *pạska holitopa*
sacred man, *hatak hullo*
sacred music, *ạba anumpa taloa*
sacred seat, *aioⁿbinili hanta*
sacred thing; *aholloka, hulloka, na ho-litopa, na holloka*
sacred writer, *holisso holitopa holissochi*
sacredly, *holitopạt*
sacrifice; *ạba isht aiokpạchi, isht aiokpạ-chi*
sad; *ilapissa, ilạpissa, imanukfela, nuk-haⁿklo, nukwiloha*
sadden, to; *imanukfelạchi, nukhaⁿklochi*
saddened, *ilapissa*
saddle; *isuba umpatạlhpo, umpatạlhpo*
saddle, to; *isuba umpatạlhpo patali, um-patali*
saddle maker, *isuba umpatạlhpo ikbi*
saddle pad, *isuba umpatạlhpo alata*
saddle skirt, *isuba umpatạlhpo haksobish*
saddlebow, *ibish*
saddler, *isuba umpatạlhpo ikbi*
sadiron, *ilefoka halushkichi*
sadly, *ilapissa*
safe; *imalekahe keyu, na kaniohmi keyu*
safe, a; *ataloha*

safe-conduct, *holisso*
safely, *na kaniohmi keyu*
safety; *achukma, imalekahe keyu*
saffron, *lakna*
saffron, to; *laknạchi*
sag, to; *bikota, bikulli, shebli, shepa*
sagacious; *achishi imponna, imponna, kostini*
sagamore; *hatak ạpi humma iⁿminko, minko*
sage; *hopoksia, kostini*
sage, a; *hatak hopoyuksa*
said, the; *chash, chokạmo, chokạsh*
sail, *na hạta*
sail, to; *aⁿya, ia, mahaiyat aⁿya, yilibli*
sail, to cause to; *yilibli*
sail against, to; *asonali*
sail slowly in curves, to; *mahaiyakachi*
sailer, *peni chito*
sailing; *aⁿya, mahaiyạt aⁿya*
sailing in airy circles, *mahaiyakachi*
sailmaker, *na hạta ikbi*
sailor; *peni chito isht aⁿya, peni isht aⁿya, peni isht ạtta*
saint; *hatak imanukfila holitopa, holitopa, iⁿholitopa*
sainted, *holitopa*
sake, *yạmmak atuk makoⁿ*
sake of that, for the; *yạmmak atuk makoⁿ*
salable, *kancha hinla*
salad, *nan ạpa okchaki*
salamander, *hạshtạp yuloli*
salary, *ạlhtoba*
sale; *ima, kanchi*
salesman, *nana itatoba*
salient, *tolupli*
saline, *hạpi holba*
saline, a; *hạpi atoba, hạpi kạli, kạli hạpi oka, lukfạpa*
saliva; *itukchi, ituklipaya*
saliva, thick; *itukpilawa*
saliva, to discharge; *itukpilawa, lupaha*
salivate, to; *itukchi ikbi*
salivation, *itukchi ikbi*
sallow, *hạta*
sally; *kucha, yiminta*
sally forth, to; *kucha*
salt, *hạpi*
salt, blown; *hạpi pushi*
salt, coarse; *hạpi lakchi*
salt, fine; *hạpi pushi*
salt, to; *hạpi yạmmichi, yạmmichi*
salt basin, *hạpi aiạlhto*

salt bin, *hapi aialhto*
salt sea, *hapi okhata*
salt spring; *hapi kali, kali hapi oka*
salt water; *hapi oka, oka hapi*
salt with or in, to; *aiyammichi*
salt work; *hapi aiikbi, hapi atoba*
saltcellar, *hapi aialhto*
salted; *aiyammi, hapi yammi, yammi*
salted with, *aiyammi*
salter; *hapi kanchi, hapi yammichi*
saltpeter, *hapi kapassa*
salts; *hapi holba, ikhinsh hapi holba*
salubrious; *abeka, aiabeka*
salutary, *achukma*
salute, *isht aiokpachi*
salute, to; *aiokpachi*
saluter; *aiokpanchi, aiokpachi*
saluting, *aiokpanchi*
salvable, *okchanya hinla*
salvage, *alhtoba*
salvation; *aiokchanya, aiokchanya alhpisa, alakofi, lakoffi, nan aiokchaya, okchalinka, okchalinchi*
salve; *ikhinsh, ikhinsh akmo, lachowa imikhinsh*
salver; *kafaiishko aiontala, kafaiontala*
same, that; *yammak inli*
same, the; *ak, amih achafa, chash, mih, miya, yammak inli, yammak int*
same as, *yammak in*
sameness, *mih*
samp, *holhponi*
sample, *isht alhpisa*
sampler, *aioholissochit achunli*
Samson's post, *atuya*
sanable, *lakoffa hinla*
sanative, *isht attacha hinla*
sanctification, *yohbichi*
sanctified; *holitopa, yohbi*
sanctified mind, *chunkash yohbi*
sanctfier; *holitoblichi, yohbichi*
sanctify, to; *chunkash yohbichi, holitoblichi, hullochi, yohbichi*
sanction, to; *aianlichi, aiokpachi, apesa*
sanctity; *holitopa, yohbi*
sanctuary; *aholitopa, chuka aholitopa*
sand; *shinuk, shinuk foka, shinuk kaha*
sand, to; *shinuk onlali*
sand bar, *okshunak talali*
sand barrens, *shinuk foka*
sand box, *shinuk aialhto*
sandbag, *bahta shinuk aialhto*
sandal, *shulush*

sanded, *shinuk onlaya*
sandish, *chukushmi*
sandstone, *tali shochukshoa*
sandy; *chukushmi, shinuk laua, shofoli*
sandy land, *shofoli*
sane; *achukma, kostini*
sang-froid; *chunkash kallo, nan ikahno*
sanguinary; *humma, issish bano, issish laua, okpulo*
sanguine; *issish laua, libesha, yimmi*
sanity, *kostini*
sap; *iti iskuna paknaka, iti okchi, itichunkash paknaka, okchi*
sap, to; *akishtala kullit kinaffi*
sapience, *hopoksa*
sapling, *iti pushi*
sappy; *himmita, okchilaua*
sapsucker, *biskinak*
sarcasm, *anumpa chunkushnali*
sarsaparilla, *shinukyolulli*
sash; *aboha apisa aialbiha, isht askufachi*
sassafras; *iti kafi, kafi*
Satan; *nan isht ahollo okpulo, Setan, shilombish okpulo*
satchel; *bahtushi, hachik, holisso aialhto, shukcha*
sate, to; *yammichi*
sated, *yammi*
satiate, to; *yammichi*
satiety, *fihopa*
satisfaction; *alhtoba, fihopa, okha*
satisfactory, *fihobli*
satisfied; *fihopa, imalhtaha*
satisfied, to make; *fihoblichi*
satisfier; *fihobli, fihoblichi*
satisfy, to; *atali, atobbi, fihobli, imatali, nukshitilimmi*
satisfy the mind, to; *fihoblichi*
saturate, to; *yammichi*
saturated; *aiyammi, yammi*
Saturday, *nitak hollo nakfish*
Saturn, *fichik chito*
saturnine, *weki*
satyr, *konwi anunkasha*
sauce, *haiyunkpulo ilhpak*
saucepan; *awalalli iskitini, haiyunkpulo awalalli*
saucy, *haksi*
saunter, to; *chuka pallit anya, intakobi*
saunterer, *chuka pulalit anya*
sausage meat, *nipi baha shila*
savage; *nukhanklo iksho, okpulo*
savage, a; *hatak nan ikithano*

savanna, *oktak*

save, to; *alakofichi, atobbi, fiopachi, inhollo, ilatomba, lakoffichi, okchalinchi, shileli*

save up seed corn, to; *pehnachi*

saved; *aiokchanya, alakofi, alhpoa, lakoffi, okchanya, pehna, shila*

saved alive, *okchanya*

saver; *apoba, ilatomba, lakoffichi, okchalinchi*

saving, *ilatomba*

Savior; *hatak moma okchalinchi, lakoffichi, na lakofichi, nan okchalinchi, okchalinchi*

savor; *balama, kashaha*

savor, to; *ahnichi, holba, holbachi, kashaha*

saw; *isht basha, iti isht basha*

saw, crosscut; *isht basha chito*

saw, pit; *iti isht basha chito*

saw, sawmill; *iti isht basha chito*

saw, to; *bashli*

sawdust, *iti botulli*

saw-edged, *kachoa*

sawmill; *abasha, iti abasha*

sawn, *basha*

sawpit; *abasha, iti abasha*

saw-tooth border, having a; *kalaskachi*

sawyer; *bashli, iti bashli, kitak*

say, to; *a, achi, anoli, anumpuli, maka, miha, nanak, nantukachi, nanuka, nanukachi, yammak achi*

say that, to; *maka, makachi*

saying; *achi, amiha, anumpa, na miha*

scab; *liahpo hakshup, lachowa hakshup*

scabbard; *bashpo chito, bashpo falaia inshukcha, shukcha*

scabbard, to; *bashpo falaia inshukcha fohki*

scabbed; *lachowa chito, makali*

scabbed off, *fichonli*

scabby, *lachowa chito*

scaffold, *aba tala*

scaffold, to; *aba tala boli* (to put on a scaffold), *aba tala ikbi* (to make a scaffold)

scaffolding, *aba tala*

scald; *alua, holhpa*

scald, to; *hukmi, luachi, oka lashpa*

scald head, *nushkobo lachowa*

scalded; *holhpa, hollokmi, lua, oka lashpa*

scalding hot, *hukma hinla*

scale; *atuya, isht alhpisa, nan isht weki, nan isht wekichi*

scale, fish; *nani hakshup*

scale, to; *apesa, fachanli, fachanlichi, loli, oiya, wekichi*

scale off, to; *fakoha, fakoli, fakopa, fakopli, falli, fichonli, fichonlichi, shuikachi*

scale off, to cause to; *fichonlichi*

scaled; *hakshup ansha, loha*

scaled off; *fakoha, fakowa, fala, fichonli*

scales; *haklopish, hakshup, isht wekichi*

scales of a fish, *hakshup fachowa*

scalings, *fakoha*

scalp; *hatak panshi, panshi lunfa*

scalp, to; *panshi lunfi*

scalped, *panshi lunfa*

scalper, *panshi lunfi*

scaly; *fachonwa, hakshup laua*

scamper, to; *maleli, yilepa*

scan, to; *hoyo, pisa fehna*

scandal; *anumpa okpulo, hofahya, makali, nukoa*

scandal, to; *isht yopula*

scandalize, to; *isht yopula, nukoachi*

scandalized, *nukoa*

scandalous; *hofahya, makali*

scant; *chito, ona*

scant, to; *olabbi*

scantle, to; *chulata, shima*

scantling, *iti basha*

scanty; *iskitini, laua, patha*

scar; *basosunkachi, lansa, minsa, misisunkachi*

scar, large; *yanfa*

scar, to; *lanfi*

scarce; *chabiha, laua*

scarce, to render; *chabihachi*

scarcely; *chohmi, naha*

scarcity; *chabiha, ona*

scare, to; *malalichi, malalli, nuklakashli, nukshobli, nukshoblichi*

scare away, to; *helichi, hikachi*

scarecrow; *fala atoni, isht nukshobli, osapa atoni*

scared; *malali, malata, nuklakancha, nukshopa*

scarf, *anchi*

scarf, to; *achakali*

scarfskin, *hakshup*

scarification, *laha*

scarified; *lanfa, laha*

scarifier, *lali*

scarify, to; *lanfi, lali, lalichi*

scarlet; *humma, humma tishepa, tishepa*

scarred; *basasunkachi, minsa, misisunkachi*

scathe, to; *okpạni*

scatter, to; *fima, fimibli, fimiblichi, fimimpa, fimmi, fimmichi, fimpkạchi, habofạchi, ḷali, ḷeli, tamoli, tiapa, tiạbli, tisheli, yuli*

scatter swellings, to; *habolichi*

scattered; *fima, fimimpa, laⁿya, ḷia, tiapa, tiạpakạchi, yula*

scattered about, to be; *tạlli*

scatterer; *fimibli, ḷali, ḷeli, nafimmi, fimmi, fimmichi*

scattering, *achafoa*

scavenger, *hina bạshpuli*

scene; *aiiḷaualli, aiiḷaualli chito, aiyopisa, awashoha*

scenery, *apisa*

scent; *ahchishi, balama, na balama, na shua, nana huⁿwa*

scent, to; *achishi, ahchishi, balamạchi, huⁿwa*

scepter, *miⁿko intạbi*

scepticism, *ạba anumpa yimmi*

schedule, *holisso*

schedule, to; *holisso atakalichi*

scheme, to; *anukfilli, apesa, ạlhpisa*

schemer, *nan apesa*

schism; *aiiⁿfalạmmi, itatiapa*

scholar; *aiithạna, holisso ikhana, holisso imponna, holisso ithạna, holisso pisa, nan ikhạna, nana aiithạna*

scholarship, *holisso ikhana*

school; *aiikhạna, aiikhạnanchi, aiithạna, holisso aiithạna, holisso apisa, nana aiikhạna*

school, to; *anumpuli, holisso ithạnanchi*

school day, *nitak holisso pisa*

schoolboy, *ạlla holisso pisa*

schoolhouse; *aiithạna chuka, holisso aiithạna chuka, holisso apisa, holisso apisa chuka*

schooling; *holisso ithạnanchi, holisso pisa ạlhtoba*

schoolmaid, *ạlla tek holisso pisa*

schoolmaster, *holisso pisachi*

schoolmate, *holisso ibapisa*

science, *ikhana*

scientific; *ikhana, imponna*

scimitar; *bạshpo falaia, na halupa*

scintillate, to; *chạlhchakạchi, tohchali*

scion, *offo*

scirrhus, *kachombi*

scissors; *isht kachaya, isht kachayushi, isht kalashushi*

scoff, to; *isht yopula*

scoffer, *isht yopula*

scold; *iⁿhiyạchi, ohoyo nukoa*

scold, to; *iⁿhiyạchi, mihachi, nukoa*

scolded, *iⁿhiya*

scolder; *iⁿhiyạchi, nukoa*

sconce; *imanukfila chito, pạla afoka*

scoop; *isht piha, nan isht piha, oka isht taka*

scoop, to; *kofussạchi, peli, takli*

scooped; *kofussa, piha, taka*

scooper; *peli, takli*

scope, *chito*

scorch, to; *anakshoⁿfa, anakshua, luachi*

scorched; *anakshoⁿfa, anakshua, itowulhko, lua*

score; *aheka, lakofa, pokoli*

score, to; *aheka takalichi, baklichi, chant lakot bakli, lakoffi, lakoli, ḷaⁿfi, shukli*

scored; *lakofa, lakowa, ḷaⁿfa, shukli*

scorer (meaning one who splits wood), *abaklichi*

scores, *lakoⁿwa*

scoria, *yạlhki*

scorn, *shittilema*

scorn, to; *shittilema*

scorn, to cause to; *shittilemạchi*

scorner, *shittilema*

scornful, *shittilema*

scornful, to render; *shittilemạchi*

scorpion, *halambia*

scotch, to; *tikelichi*

scotched; *ạtapa, tikeli*

scoundrel, *hatak haksi*

scour, to; *ikfia, ikfiachi, kasholichi, wehput fullota*

scour cloth, to; *kashoffichi*

scoured, *kashokạchi*

scourer, *kasholichi*

scourge, *isht fạma*

scourge, to; *fahạmmi, fạmmi, ḷukaha*

scourged, *fạma*

scourger; *fạmmi, ḷukaha*

scourging, *ḷukaha*

scout, *tikba pisa*

scout, to; *shittilema, tikba pisa*

scow, *peni patạssa*

scow, to; *peni patạssa fohkit isht aⁿya*

scowl, *okwichinli*

scowl, to; *okwichinli, okyauinli, okyauinlit piⁿsa*

scrabble, to; *shạffi*

scraggy, *lanlaki*

scramble, to; *balạlli, tuⁿshpa*

scrambler, *balạlli*

scranch, to; *shakinlichi*
scrap, *tushafa*
scrape, to; *apeli, monffi, pinfi, shanfi, shalichi, shaffi, shalakli*
scrape, to cause to; *shaffichi*
scraped; *pinfa, shanfa, shaha, shafa*
scraper; *akkashalachi, isht shaffi*
scratch; *kalafa, kalli*
scratch, to; *kalaffi, kalli, pushka, shaffi, shulaffi, shuli, yaslichi*
scratch with the nails, to; *pushka*
scratched; *kalafa, kala, shafa*
scratcher; *kalaffi, pushka*
scratches, the; *lachowa*
scratches, to have the; *kichali*
scrawl, *holisso okpulo*
scrawl, to; *himak fokalit holissochi, holissochi*
scrawler, *himak fokalit holissochi*
scream; *chalanka, chilank*
scream, to; *chalanka, chilankachi, panya, tahpala, tasaha, tasali, wanhachi, yahapa, yaiya*
screamer; *hushi, tasaha, yahapa*
screaming; *tasaha, yahapa*
screech, to; *ola, panya, yaiya*
screen; *atukkuchi, isht hoshintikachi*
screen, to; *atukkochechi, hoshontikachi*
screw, *isht ashana*
screw, to; *ateblichi, ilbashachi, shanni*
screw, wooden; *iti shana*
screw of a gun at the breech, *tanamp sokbish isht ashana*
screwed; *atepa, ilbasha, shana*
scribble, to; *holissochi*
scribe; *anumpa alhpisa isht atta, hatak holissochi, holissochi, na holissochi, nan inholissochi*
scrimp, *hatak nan inholitopa*
scrimp, to; *iskitinichi, yushtololichi*
scrip; *bahta, bahtushi, shukcha*
scriptural, *holisso holitopa takali*
Scripture; *aba anumpa, holisso, holisso holitopa*
scrivener, *holissochi*
scrofula, *chilanli*
scroll, *holisso pula*
scrub, *hatak makali*
scrub, to; *kasholichi*
scruple, *nukwia*
scruple, to; *nukwia, yimmi*
scrupulous; *ahah ahni, alhpesa*
scrutinize, to; *achukmalit pisa*
scud, *hoshontoba*

scud, to; *maleli*
scuffle, *itishi*
scuffle, to; *afoa, aleli, haieli, itishi*
scuffler; *aleli, haieli, itishi*
scull, to; *moeli, monffi*
scullion, *hatonfalaha*
sculpture, to; *tilit hobachit ikbi*
scum; *almochi, pokpoki*
scum, to; *pinfi*
scummed, *piha*
scurrility, *anumpa makali*
scurrilous, *makali*
scythe; *isht almo, onush isht basha*
scytheman, *onush bashli*
sea; *banakachi, okhata, okhata chito*
sea, concerning the; *okhata imma*
sea, great; *okhata chito*
sea bank, *okhata ont alaka*
seaboard *okhata ont alaka*
seacoast; *okhata chito lapalika, okhata lapalika, okhata ont alaka*
sea fight, *peni chito aiitibi*
seashore, *okhata ont alaka*
seaside, *okhata chito lapalika*
sea water, *okhata oka*
seal (mark); *inchunwa, isht akamassa, isht inchunli, isht inchunwa*
seal, to; *akamassali, akallochi, inchunli*
sealed; *akamassa, akallo, inchunwa, kamassa*
sealing wax; *holisso isht akamassa, holisso isht akallo, holisso isht ashana, isht akamassa*
seam; *aiachunwa, aialhchunwa*
seaman, *okhata anya*
seamed, *achunwa*
seamster, *nan achunli*
seamstress; *achunli, nan achunli, ohoyo nan achunli*
sear, to; *kallochi*
search, *hoyo*
search, to; *afanalechi, ahoyo, hikikia, hoyo, ibakoli, pisa*
searcher, *hoyo*
seared; *kallo, shila*
seasick, *okhata aiabeka*
seasickness, *okhata aiabeka*
season; *aiona, aialhpesa, nitak*
season, to; *homechi, kallochi, kashahachi, shila, shileli*
season, vernal; *toffahpi*
seasonable, *nitanki*
seasoned; *kashaha, shila*
seasoned wood, *iti shila*

seat; *abinili, aiasha, aionbinili, aiomanili, aionasha, apatalhpo, binoli, chuka,
chukachafa abinili, hapullo, iti wanya,
ombinili*
seat, to; *abinolichi, binilichi, binolichi,
hilechi*
seat mate, *ibabinili*
seat of learning, *aiikhana*
seat with, to; *ibabinilichi*
seated; *binili, binoli, chiya*
seated round; *abilepa, binoht aiasha*
seated with, *ibabinili*
secede, to; *issa*
seclude, to; *kuchichi*
secluded, *kucha*
second; *atukla, hitukla, hotukla, iakaiya*
second, a; *apela, yakosi ititakla*
second, to; *apela, iakaiya*
second, to make the; *itatuklo*
second time; *anonti, atuklant, hituklaha*
second time, to do it a; *hituklanchi*
secondly, *atukla*
secrecy, *lumanka*
secret; *alumanka, haiaka, luma, lumasi,
na luma, nan luma*
secret, in; *lumanka*
secret place; *alumanka, alumpoa*
secretary; *anump imeshi, anumpeshi,
hatak holissochi, holissochi*
secretary, king's; *minko imanumpeshi*
secrete, to; *aluhmi, luhmi, lumpuli*
secreted; *luma, lumboa*
secretly; *luma, lumasi, lumasit, lumat*
sect, *iksa*
sect, Christian; *aba anumpuli iksa*
secular, *yakni ahalaia*
securely, *achukmat*
security, *ahinna*
sedate, *nuktala*
sedateness, *nuktala*
sedentary, *binili*
sediment, *lakchi*
sedition; *anukfohkachechi, okla anumpa
kobaffi*
seduce, to; *isht akanohmechi, nukpallichechi*
seduced, *haksi*
seducer, *haksichi*
sedulous, *achunanchi*
see, *yaki*
see, to; *ahah ahni, ahni, akostininchi,
holhponayo, hoponkoyo, hopumpoyo, hopunayo, ikhana, nowa, pisa*
see, to cause to; *holhponayochi, pisachi*

see all, to; *mominchi*
see and, to; *pisat*
see into, to; *afanalechi*
seed; *atia, haiyunkpulo nihi, na nihi, nan
nihi, nihi, ushi isht atiaka*
seed, to; *nihi chitofa, nihi fimmi, nihi
toba*
seed cane, *oskonush*
seed corn, *pehna*
seed potatoes, *ahe pehna*
seed wheat, *onush pehna*
seeded, *ponola nihi*
seedtime; *nihi aholokchi aiona, nitak*
seedy, *nihi laua*
seek, to; *ahni, banna, hoyo, pisa, ponaklo*
seeker; *hoyo, na hoyo*
seem, to; *ahoba*
seem, to cause to; *ahoba*
seem so, to; *achini, chini*
seemer, *ilahobbi*
seeming, *holba*
seemingly; *achini, chini*
seemly, *alhpesa*
seer; *hopaii, na pinsa, nan ikhana, pisa*
seesaw, to; *fahakachi*
seethe, to; *honi, laboshli, walalli, walallichi*
seethed; *honni, labocha, walalli*
seine; *nan isht okwia, nani isht hokli*
seize, to; *asinta, hokli, ishi, yichiffi*
seize, to cause to; *yichiffichi*
seize and hold, to; *yichiffit ishi*
seize the heart, to; *chunkash ishi*
seize the mind, to; *imanukfila ishi*
seize there or at, to; *aiishi*
seized, *yichowa*
seizer; *hokli, ishi, na hokli*
seizure, *hokli*
seldom, *fehna keyu*
select, *aiyoba*
select, to; *achafoachi, achafolechi, achafoli, atokoa, atokolechi, atokulit ishi*
selected; *aiyoba, alhtoka*
self; *ak, fehna, hak, ilap, ilap akinli, ile,
inli*
self-abased, *ilbasha*
self-abuse, *ilokpani*
self-conceit, *ilefehnachi*
self-conceited, *ilapakpuna*
self-confidence, *ileyimmi*
self-deceived, *ilehaksi*
self-dedication, *imissa*
self-denial; *ilolabbi, olabbi*
self-destroyer, *okpani*

self-determination; *ilap ahni, ilap anukfilli*
self-devoted, *ilap ahni ilekanchi*
self-esteem; *ahnichi, holitobli, ilahninchi*
self-evident, *lumiksho*
self-examination; *anukfillit pisa, ilanukfillit pisa*
self-homicide, *ilebi*
self-important, *fehnachi*
self-interest, *nan isht ilaiyukpa*
self-knowledge, *ikhana*
self-love, *ileholitobli*
self-murder; *abi, ilebi*
self-pleasing; *ileyukpali, yukpali*
self-praise, *isht ilanumpuli*
self-respect, *holitobli*
self-sufficient, *ilefehnachi*
self-torment, *isikkopali*
self-tormentor; *ileissikkopali, isikkopali*
self-will, *ilap aiahni*
self-willed; *ilapakpu^na, ilapu^na*
selfish; *ilapakpu^na, ilapakpunla, ilapu^na, ilapunla*
selfish, to make; *ilapakpuachi*
selfishness, *ilapunla*
selfsame, *mih*
sell, to; *ima, kanchi, takaffit kampila*
sell, to cause to; *kanchichi*
sell a book, to; *holisso kanchi*
sell back, to; *falammint i^nkanchi*
sell off, to; *tali*
seller; *kanchi, kinalichi, na kanchi*
seller on credit, *ahekachi*
selvage, *yikila*
selvage, to make a; *yikilachi*
semblance, *holba*
semi, *iklanna*
semiannual, *afammi iklanna*
semiannually, *afammi iklannakma*
semicircle, *chanaha iklanna*
seminary, *aiithana*
seminate, to; *fimmi, ikbi*
sempiternal, *atahahe iksho*
senate, *hatak hochitoka itanaha*
senate house; *aboha hanta, anu^nka hanta, chuka hanta*
senator; *hatak hochitoka, hatak nan apesa*
send, to; *apesa, atohno, atokoli, bohpuli, boli, iachi, ima, kampila, pila, pit, tileli, tohno*
send after, to; *iakaiyachi*
send away, to; *tishelichi*

send back, to; *falamichi*
send for, to; *i^nhoa*
send from, to; *tileli*
send in, to; *kuchi*
send off, to; *chafichi*
send on, to; *onochi*
send this way, to; *auechi*
send to, to; *pit*
sender; *bohpuli, chafichi, isht auechi, nan chufichi, pila*
senior, *sipokni i^nshali*
sensation, a painful; *simi^nkahanchi*
sense; *imanukfila, isht akostininchi, kostini*
senseless, *imanukfila iksho*
sensible; *imanukfila a^nsha, kostini*
sensible man, *hatak kostini*
sent; *atokowa, alhtoka, boppoa*
sentence; *anumpa, anumpa achafa, anumpa alhpisa, anumpa kallo onutula*
sentence, to; *anumpa apesa, anumpa kallo onuchi, anumpa onuchi*
sentenced; *anumpa onutula, anumpa kallo onutula*
sentiment; *aiahni, imanukfila*
sentinel; *atoni, atoni hikia, atoni hioli*
separate; *ilabi^nka, ilami^nka*
separate, to; *atabli, ataptua, ataptuli, filamolechi, filammichi, hota, kashabli, kashkoa, katapa, katabli, kashkoli, kinaffi, kotafa, tabli, taptua, taptuli, tiapa*
separated; *atapa, filama, filamoli, holhta, kashapa, kashkoa, tapa, taptua*
separately; *ilabi^nka, ilap bi^nka, itakashkulit*
separation; *itakashkoa, itakashkuli, ititapa, tapa, taptua*
separator; *filamolechi, itakashkuli*
September, *Siptimba*
septennial, *afammi untuklo*
septennially, *afammi untuklokma*
sepulcher; *ahollohpi, hatak aholopi, sipalka*
sepulcher, to; *ahollopi boli, hohpi, hopi*
sequel, *iakaiya*
seraph, *aba hatak*
sere, *shila*
serene; *masheli, shohmakali, yohbi*
serene, to make; *shohmakalichi*
serene heart, *chu^nkash yohbi*
sereneness, *shohmakali*
serenity; *masheli, yohbi*
serious; *aba anumpa nukfoka, nuktanla*

serious person, ạba anumpa ahni
sermon; anumpa, ạba anumpa anumpa,
  ạba isht anumpa, fulumi
sermonize, to; ạba anumpa isht anumpuli
sermonizer, ạba anumpa isht anumpuli
serous matter, okchushba
serpent, sinti
serpent, a certain; sakli, sinti lusluki,
  sinti shaui
serpent, a young; sintushi
serpent's egg, sintushi
serpentine, fullokạchi
serrate, lakowa
serrated, lakowa
servant; anumpeshi, inshali nan isht
  imạtta, ilhtohno, nan ạlhtoka, tishu
servant, man; tishu
serve, to; anukcheto, atia, holitobli, holitoblit aianlichi, imantia, ipeta
service, intoksạli
serviceable, achukma
servile, yuka chohmi
servitor, tishu
servitude, yuka ansha
session, anumpulit ansha
set; ạlhtokoa, haioli, hika, kạllo, talaia,
  taloha, tạla
set (of bones), foni falạmmint itifohka
set, a; tạla achafa
set, to; ahokoffi, alata, apesa, binilichi,
  fohki, hilechi, hokchi, ia, kahpuli, okatula, okạttula, onochi, takakanli, talali,
  taloli, tạla
set apart, ạlhtoka
set apart, to; holitoblichi, hullochi
set back, to cause to; oka bikelichi
set bones, to; foni falạmmint itifohki
set deep, to; hofobichit hilechi
set down, to; talali, taloli
set down into water, to; okkạchi
set forth, to; talali
set in, to; alachahạchi, alachali
set in endwise, to; abili, achoshuli
set on; atalaia, ataloha, ontalaia
set on, to; atohnichi, talaia, talali, tohnochi, tonhochi
set on edge, to; kaiolichi
set on fire, to; hukmi, luachi
set up; hieli, hikia, hioli
set up, to; haiolichi, hielichi, hilechi, hiolichi
sets, one who; talali, taloli

setter; binili, talali
setter up, hilechi
setting pole, isht tobli
settle, aiomanili falaia
settle, to; abenilichi, abinolichi, aioklạ-
  chi, aiskiachi, akamạssa, apesa, atali,
  auaya, binili, binilichi, binoli, binolichi,
  hilechi, hotina, kamạssa, oka tạla, okatula
settle a liquid, to; oka talaia
settle at, to; abenili, abinili, aiokla
settle with, to; ibabinili
settle with, to cause to; ibabinilichi
settled; aiokla, ạlhpesa, binili, binoli,
  oka tạla
settled with, ibabinili
settlement; abinili, abinoli, aiokla,
  auaya, chuka lukonli
settler; abenili, abinili, abinoli
seven, untuklo
seven nights, nitak untuklo
seven stars, the; fichik watạlhpi
seven times, untukloha
sevenfold, inluhmi
seventeen, auah huntuklo
seventh, isht untuklo
seventh time, isht untukloha
seventieth, isht pokoli
seventy, pokoli
sever, to; hokolichi, kololichi, koluffi, litafa, litạffi, lilạffi, tạbli, tạpa, tạptua,
  tạptuli
sever, to cause to; tạblichi
sever from, to; filemolechi
several; ilaiyuka, kanohmi, kanomona,
  katohmona, yakomi
severe; kạllo, nukhạmmi, palạmmi
severe, to render; palạmmichi
severed; akolofa, hokoli, kolofa, kololi,
  litafa, tạpa, tạptua
severely; kạllot, palạmmichi
severity; kạllo, palạmmi
sew, to; achunli
sew on a sleeve, to; shakba achunli
sewed; achunwa, ạlhchunwa
sewer (one who sews), achunli
sewing, achunli
sewn, ạlhchunwa
sexennial; afạmmi hannali, afạmmi hannalikma
sexton; ahollopi kạlli, hohpi
shabby; lititunkạchi, lilalankạchi
shackle, isht talakchi
shackle, to; takchi

shackled, *talakchi*
shade; *ahoshontika, aioklilinka, hoshonti-ka, isht hoshintikachi, hoshonti, shilombish, shilup*
shade, dark; *polunsak*
shade, to; *hoshontika, hoshontikachi, kapassachi*
shade of inanimate objects, *hoshontika*
shade tree, *iti alhpoa*
shaded; *hoshontika, oklili*
shadow; *ahoshontika, hoshonti, oklili, shilombish*
shadow, to; *kapassachi, oklilechi*
shadowy; *haiaka, oklili*
shady; *hoshontika, hoshontika laua*
shaft; *ahalalli, ulhpi, uski naki*
shafted, *ulhpi ansha*
shag, *hishi chito*
shag lock, *hishi chito*
shagbark hickory; *fala, kapun api*
shagbark hickory nut, *kapun*
shagged, *hishi chito ansha*
shaggy, *hishi chito*
shake; *palokachi, wannichi, winnakachi, winnattakachi*
shake, to; *cholobichi, fahalichi, faiokachi, faioli, faiolichi, faiotlakachi, fattahachi, fotokachi, haiuchi, ilhkolichi, nukwimekachi, paiolichi, poalichi, tahtuli, waloli, winnakachi, winnali, winnalichi, winnattakachi*
shake, to cause to; *haiuchichi, winnalichi*
shake hands, to; *aiokpachi*
shake loosely, to; *fatokachi*
shake off, to; *liwelichi, tahtuli*
shake the purpose, to; *chunkash inlachi*
shake with the ague, to; *wannichi*
shaken; *boli, fahali, faiokachi, tahtua, winnakachi, winnali, winnattakachi*
shaky, *palata*
shall; *a, an, achin, achik, ahe, ahinla, ashke, chin, chuk, hachin, he, het, hi, hinla, hokma, lashke*
shall hereafter, *himma*
shall not; *ahe keyu, aheto, awa, he keyu, heto*
shall toward, *himma*
shallow; *hofobi, okshauoha, pachansi*
shallow, a; *ahofobi*
shallow-brained, *imanukfila iksho*
shallowness; *hofobi, imanukfila iksho*
sham, *holabi*

sham, to; *yimmichi*
shaman, *alikchi*
shambles, *nipi aiittatoba*
shame; *ahofahya, hofahya, isht hofahya*
shame, to; *hofayali, hofahyachi*
shamed man, *hatak hofahya*
shameful, *hofahya*
shamefully; *hofahyqt, hofayalit*
shameless, *hofah iksho*
shameless man, *hatak hofahya iksho*
shamer; *hofahyachi, hofayali*
shank, *iyinchampko*
shape; *holba, pisa*
shape, to; *akkoli, apoksiachi, hobachi, ikbi*
shape of a man, *hatak holba*
shaped, *alhkoha*
shapeless, *pisa ikachukmo*
share, *kashapa*
share, to; *kashapa ishi, kashablit ishi, kashkoli*
share with, to; *ibatankla ishi*
shared, *kashkoa*
sharer, *ibatankla ishi*
shark, *nani chito*
shark, to; *hunkupa*
sharp; *chilita, halupa, halupoa, homi, nukhammi, palammi*
sharp, to; *haksichi*
sharp eye, *nishkin halupa*
sharp-sighted; *isht hopunkoyo imachukma, nishkin halupa*
sharp sound; *haksobish chansa, samampa*
sharpen, to; *achakali, haluppachi, haluppalli, ibakchufanlichi, ibakchufanshlichi, sholichi, talichi, tilichi*
sharpened; *halupa, halupoa, shoha, shuahchi*
sharpener, *nan isht tali*
sharpens, one who; *sholichi*
sharper; *haksichi, hatak haksichi*
sharply; *halupa, palammi*
sharpness; *halupa, homi, palammi*
sharpshooter, *hunssa imponna*
shatter, to; *fimibli, litoa, shima, shimmi, tasembochi*
shattered; *litoa, shima, tasembo*
shatters, *litoa*
shave, to; *ilbashachi, shanfi, tushalichi*
shave, to cause to; *shanfichechi*
shave and lap over, to; *shanfit itiaiopitammichi*
shaved, *shanfa*
shaved, having the head; *yushkabali*

shaved board, *iti shaⁿfa*
shaver; *ạlla nakni, hatak himmita, ita-toba kạllo, shaⁿfi*
shaving; *ashaⁿfi, shafa, shaⁿfi, iti ashaⁿfa botulli, tushali*
shawl; *anchi, iachuka, inuchi, nantapạski anchi, nantapạski chito, umpatali*
shawl, turkey-feather; *kasmo*
she; *ilạppa, in, yạmma, yạmmak ashosh*
she-bear, *tek*
sheaf; *asehta, sita, sitoha*
sheaf, to; *siteli, sitoli*
sheaf of wheat, *onush sita*
shear, to; *ạmo, bạshli, chukfi hishi ạmo*
sheared; *ạlmo, bạsha*
shearer; *ạmo, bạshli, chukfi hishi ạmo, kacheli*
shears; *isht kachaya, isht kalasha, kalasha*
shears, large; *isht kachaya chito*
sheath; *bạshpo chito, shukcha*
sheathe, to; *alatali*
shed; *aboha apishia, hoshontika*
shed, to; *katạbli, latạbli, moⁿfa*
shed forth, to; *fohobli*
shed hair, to; *boyafa, boyali, luehạchi, tikafa, tokofi*
shed light upon, to; *umpạla*
shed tears, to; *nishkin okchi*
shedding of the hair; *boyafa, boyali*
sheep; *chukfạlhpoba, chukfi*
sheepfold; *chukfạlhpowa iⁿhollihta, chukfi aiasha*
sheepish; *chukfoba, hofahya, takshi*
sheepskin, *chukfi hakshup*
sheer, *aⁿli*
sheet, *topa umpatạlhpo*
sheet of paper, *holisso pula*
sheeting, *nan tạnna tohbi*
shekel, *shekel*
shelf; *atalaia, atạla, ạba tạla*
shelf, a book; *holisso ahikia, holisso aiasha, holisso akaha, holisso atalaia, holisso ataloha*
shelf, milk; *pishukchi ataloha*
shell, *hakshup*
shell of a nut, *foni*
shell, oyster; *shaⁿha toba*
shell, to; *chilukka, fakopa, hakshup akuchichi, hanchi, hanlichi, luffi, luli, loha*
shelled; *chilukka, fakopa, hanla, haⁿya, lufa, luha, loha, nihi*
shelled corn, *taⁿsh chilluka*
shelter, *aiatokko*
shelter, to; *atukko, atukkochechi, atukkuchi*

sheltered, *ohulmo*
shelves; *ataloha, atalohmaya*
shepherd; *apesạchi, chukfạlhpowa apistikeli, chukfi apesạchi, chukfi apistikeli*
sheriff; *hatak takchi, na hollo takchi*
shield; *telihpa, tilikpi*
shield, to; *atukkuchi, lakoffichi*
shielded, *lakoffi*
shift; *haksi, kanạlli, ohoyo iⁿna foka lumbo*
shift, to; *ilaiyuka, inlạchi, kanali, kanchi*
shift a garment, to; *atobbit foka*
shift about, to; *fitiha*
shifter, *kanạllichi*
shin; *champko, chibaⁿko, chumaⁿko, iyinchampko*
shin bone; *iyạpi champko, iyinchampko foni*
shine, to; *chạlhchakạchi, halaluⁿkạchi, malancha, malantkạchi, mạlmakạchi, oktanelichi, pạla, shohmalali, shohpakali, shumpalali, tohwikeli, tombi*
shine, to cause to; *chạlhchakạchechi, malanchạchi, shumpalalichi, tombichechi, tombichi*
shine dimly, to; *chukpalali, tohkasakli, tohmasakli, tohmasali*
shine dimly, to cause to; *tohmasaklichi*
shine feebly, to; *tohmasali*
shine feebly, to cause to; *tohmasalichi*
shine on, to; *umpạla*
shine quick, to; *tohmali*
shine with a feeble light, to; *tohmali*
shingle; *aboha isht holmo, chuka isht holmo, isht holmo, iti shima*
shingle, to; *homo*
shingled, *holmo*
shining; *chạlhchakạchi, halạsbi, limishko, malancha, malạtha, mạlmakạchi, oktaneli, shohmalali, tohwikeli*
shining appearance, to make a; *oktanelichi*
shiny; *shohmalali, tohwikeli*
ship; *peni, peni chito, peni hochito*
ship, to; *peni chito fohki, peni chito fohkit pila*
ship, to take; *peni foka*
shipbuilder, *peni chito ikbi*
ship captain, *peni chito kạpetạni*
shipload, *peni alota*
shipmaster; *peni chito isht aⁿya, peni chito kạpetạni*
shipped, *peni chito foka*
shipping, *peni chito*
shipwreck, *peni chito koa*

shipwreck, to; *peni chito koli*
shipwrecked, *peni chito okpulo*
shipwright, *peni chito ikbi*
shirt; *fohka, ilefoka lumbo, na fohka, na foka lumbo*
shirt, hunting; *na foka patafa*
shirt, to; *na foka lumbo foka, na foka lumbo fokạchi*
shirted, *na foka lumbo foka*
shirting, *nan tạnna tohbi*
shitepoke, *okataktak*
shiver, *chulafa*
shiver, to; *chula, chulali, wolobli, wula, wuli, wulobli, wulopa*
shivered; *chula, wula, wulopa*
shivering; *chuli, hochukwoba, wạnnichi, wulobli*
shoal; *hofobi, itahoba, itạnaha, laua, okchapạssi, okchawaha*
shoal, to; *itahoba, itạnaha*
shock; *itaiisso, winnạttakạchi*
shock, to; *nuklakạshli, winnattakachechi*
shock, to cause to; *winnattakachechi*
shock of English grain, *onush sita itạnaha*
shock of wheat, *onush sita itạnaha*
shock wheat, to; *onush sita itạnnali*
shocked; *nuklakancha, yuala*
shod, *tạli lapali*
shoe; *shulush, shulush kạllo*
shoe, English; *shulush kamạssa, shulush kạllo*
shoe, to; *isuba iyi tạli lapalichi, shulush imatali, tạli lapalichi*
shoe blacking, *shulush isht lusachi*
shoe buckle, *shulush isht akamạssa*
shoe latchet, *shulush isht talakchi*
shoe string, *shulush isht talakchi*
shoe with a hard sole, *shulush kamạssa*
shoemaker, *shulush ikbi*
shoes, a pair of; *shulush itichapa*
shoes, furnished with; *shulush imạlhtaha*
shoes, light; *shulush shohạla*
shoes, to furnish with; *shulush imatali*
shoot; *bamppoa, offo, tukafa*
shoot, to; *aⁿya, bikobli, huⁿssa, nạli, offo, tokali, tukafa*
shoot forth, to; *bisali*
shoot of a plant, the; *bikobli*
shoot with a blowgun, to; *bamppulli*
shoot with a witch ball, to; *isht ạlbi nạli*
shooter, *huⁿssa*

shooter with a blowgun, *bamppulli*
shooting; *huⁿssa, tukali*
shooting star; *fichik heli, fichik hika*
shop; *aiitatoba, atoksạli*
shop, blacksmith's; *tạlaboli*
shop, slop; *na foka aiitatoba*
shop, to; *aiitạtobanowa, chumpa, itatoba*
shopkeeper, *na kanchi*
shore; *alaka, oka aialaka, oka alaka, oka ạli, oka ont alaka, ont, ontalaka, tikeli*
shore, to; *tikelichi*
shored, *tikeli*
shorn; *ạlmo, bạsha, yushmilali*
short; *falaia, kolhkoki, kolokshi, laua, motohki, ona, pạli, tilofa, tilofasi, tiloha, toluski, tolusli, yushkololi, yushmitoli, yushtololi*
short, to make; *kolokshichi, toluskichi, yushkololichi*
short and round, *lobukta*
short and round, to render; *lobuktạchi*
short and thick, *lotuski*
short and thick, to make; *lotuskichi*
short breath; *fiopa kobafa, fiopat taha*
short hair, to have; *okmilali*
short speech, *tilofa*
short talk, *tilofa*
short time, in a; *chekusikma*
short-breathed; *fiopa ikfalaio, fiopa kobafa, fiopa taha*
shorten, to; *hokolichi, yushkololichi, yushtololichi*
shortened; *yushkololi, yushtololi*
shortener, *yushkololichi*
short-faced; *ibaklipinli, ibaktokonli*
shortish, *tilofasi*
short-lived, *nitak ikiⁿfalaio*
shortly; *ashaliⁿka, chekusi*
shorts, *haklopish*
short-sighted, *nishkin ikhalupo*
short-winded; *fiopa kobafa, ilhfiopak*
shot (noun), *nakuⁿshi*
shot (participle); *huⁿssa, nạla, ontukafa, tukafa*
shot bag, *atohchi*
shot from a blowgun, *bamppoa*
shot pouch, *atohchi*
shot with a witch ball, *isht ạlbi nạla*
shote; *shukha himmita, shukhushi*
should; *hinlatuk, hotuk*
should be, *chintok*
should have; *ahetok, ahetuk, he*
should have been; *chintok, chintnk, he*

should have to be; *achintok, achintuk*
shoulder; *fulup, tahchi*
shoulder, to; *ilabannali, sholi*
shoulder-blade; *fulup foni, okpata foni, tahchi okpatha*
shoulder of a bottle, *timpi*
shout; *shakapa, tahpala, yahapa*
shout, to; *shakapa, shakabli, tahpala, tasaha, tasali, yahapa*
shout at, to; *apahyachi*
shouted at, *apahyah*
shouter; *apahyachi, shakabli, tahpala, tasaha, tasali, yahapa*
shouting; *tasaha, yahapa*
shove, *tobli*
shove, to; *tobli*
shovel; *isht piha, lukfi isht piha, nan isht piha*
shovel, ash; *hituk chubi isht piha*
shovel, fire; *hituk chubi isht piha, luak isht shafa, luak isht shaffi*
shovel, large fire; *hituk chubi isht peli falaia*
shovel up, to; *peli*
shoveled up, *piha*
show, to; *anoli, haiaka, haiakachi, imabachi, oktanichi, pisachi, weli, yopisachi*
show bread; *paska holitopa, paska otani*
show by argument, to; *okfali*
shower; *pisachi, umba*
shower, to; *lali, umba, umbachi*
showered, *umba*
shown by argument, *okfaha*
shred, *chulata*
shred, to; *chulalli, chuli*
shreds, to become; *poshukta*
shrew; *ohoyo isht ahollo, ohoyo nukoa*
shrewd, *imponna*
shrewdly, *imponnat*
shriek; *tahpala, yaiya*
shriek, to; *chansa, panya, tahpala, yaiya*
shrill; *chansa, halupa*
shrill, to; *chansa*
shrill noise, to make a; *washahachi*
shrine; *itombi, na holitopa aialhto*
shrink, to; *bashechi, nukshopa, nukwia, shileli, yikota, yikutkachi*
shrink, to cause to; *shullachi*
shrinker, *nukwia*
shrivel, to; *yikota, yikulli*
shriveled, *yikota*
shroud, *hatak illi isht afoli*
shroud, to; *hatak illi isht afoli, isht afoli*

shrub, *shauwa*
shrubby, *bafalli*
shrunk, *shachaha, shila, shulla, yikutkachi*
shucked, *hanya*
shudder, *wannichi*
shudder, to; *nukshopa, wannichi*
shuffle, to; *aiyummi, fullokachi, shalallichi*
shuffled, *aiyuma*
shuffler, *fullokachi*
shun, to; *apakfopa, nukwaya*
shunned, *apakfopa*
shut; *fohka, hokofa, luma, okhilishta, okshillita, poloma*
shut, to; *afacha, akammi, fohki, hokoffi, luhmi, okhishta, okhitta, okshilita, okshita, polomi, ukhishta*
shut in, *apohtuka*
shut in, to; *apohtukachi, holihta fohki*
shut the mouth, to; *itakommuchi*
shut up; *aiokshilinta, akama, alhkama*
shut up, to; *akammi*
shutter; *isht okshilita, isht oktapa, isht ukhatapa*
shutter, window; *apisa isht alhkama*
shuttle; *isht tana, nan isht tana*
shy; *honayo, nukshopa, nukwia*
shy, to; *nukshopa*
shyness; *honayo, nukshopa*
sick; *abeka, abi, chukyiweta, yanha*
sick at the stomach; *anukpoali, itukchabachi, itukchuba*
sick in the feet, *iyi isht abeka*
sick man, *hatak abeka*
sick with, *isht abeka*
sick with the pleurisy, *chunukabi*
sicken, to; *abeka, abekachi*
sickish, *hoetachi banna*
sickle; *isht almo, onush isht almo, onush isht basha*
sickliness, *abeka shali*
sickly; *abeka, abeka chuhmi, abeka shali, abekoma*
sickness; *abeka, nan abeka*
side; *abaiya, alapalika, anaksi, anaksika, apota, apotaka, chakpaka, chunuko, ikfeksa, ikfichukbi, isht ukfoata, lapali, lapalika, naksi, naksika, okhoataka, palata, pasa, takla*
side, being on the; *lapali*
side, one; *tannap*
side, situated at the; *apanta*
side, the opposite; *tannap*
side, the upper; *pakna*

side, to; *apela, ataiya*
side, to be at the; *apota, apotoa*
side, to go to the; *anaksika*
side, to place on the; *lapalichi*
side, to put to one; *anaksikachi*
side, to stay on the; *lapali*
side, to turn the; *anaksi*
side by side, to lie or stand; *apalli, aputkachi*
side hill, *abaksacheka*
side of (a swamp or creek), *abaiyaka*
side of, this; *takla*
side of, to place by the; *apotoli*
side of a boat, *alaka*
side of a creek, *bok intannap*
side of a fence, *holihta okhowataka*
side of a hill; *nanih chakpataka, nanih chakpatalika, okkattahaka*
side of a house; *chuka itabana, chuka naksika*
side of a tree, *iti chakpa*
side saddle, *isuba umpatalhpo falakto*
sided, *alata*
sidepiece of a fireplace, *asanali*
sideways, *okhoata*
sidewise, to lie; *apota*
sieve, *isht yuha*
sieve, coarse; *shakla*
sift, to; *yuli*
sifted, *yuha*
sifter, *isht yuha*
sifter, to run through a; *yuha*
sigh, *chitolit fiopa*
sigh, to; *chitolit fiopa, chitot fiopa, nukhanklo*
sigher, *chitolit fiopa*
sight; *apisaka, hoponkoyo, isht pisa, nishkin, pisa*
sight, to take; *tanampo anumpisachi*
sight of a gun; *aianompisa, tanampo anumpisa*
sight of the eye, *nishkin nihi*
sightless, *nishkin kania*
sign; *aiisht ahollo, isht aialhpisa, isht atokowa, isht alhpisa, nan isht atokowa*
sign, to; *hochifo takalichi, holissochi*
signal, *chito*
signature, *hochifo takali*
signed, *hochifo takali*
signer, *hochifo holisso takalichi*
signify, to; *anoli, haklochi,*
silence; *chulosa, na mihiksho, samanta*
silence, to; *ahokoffi, alammichi, chulosachi, hokoffi, hopotalli, nuktalali*

silence, to keep; *nukchinto*
silenced, *alama*
silent; *anumpa inlaua, anumpuli, kinint iksho, nukchinto*
silent, to become; *chulosa*
silent man, *hatak luma*
silent person, *na miha iksho*
silently, *lumat*
silk, *silik*
silken; *lapushki, silik*
sill, *aboha intula*
silly, *imanukfila iksho*
silver; *tali fehna, tali hata, tali holisso*
silver, to; *tali hata akkoli*
silver button, *tali hata isht akamassa*
silver gorget, *tali hata chinakbi*
silver hatband, *tali hata bita*
silver plated, *tali hata alhkoha*
silver spoon, *tali hata isht impa*
silvered, *tali hata alhkoha*
silversmith; *tali hata ikbi, tali hatikbi*
similar; *chohmi, holba,*
similarity, *itiholba*
simile, *isht alhpisa*
similitude, *holba*
simmer, to; *walalli ammona*
simper, to; *yukpa*
simple; *achafa, anli, bano, haksulba, imanukfila iksho*
simpleton, *imanukfila iksho*
simplicity; *anli, apissanli*
simplify, to; *haiakachechi*
simply; *bano, beka, haiakat, peh*
simulate, to; *hobachi*
simultaneous, *mih*
sin; *aiashachi, aiashachika, aiyoshoba, ashachi, na yoshoba, nan aiashacheka, nan ashacheka, nan ashachi, yoshoba*
sin, to; *ashachi, yoshoba*
sin about, to; *aiashachi*
sinapism, *ashela*
since; *ho, itintakla*
sincere, *anli*
sincere heart, *chunkash anli*
sincerely, *anli*
sincerity; *anli, chunkash anli*
sinew; *akshish, kallo*
sinewed; *akshish ansha, kallo*
sinews; *hakshish, inchashwa*
sinews of the loins, *chashwa*
sinewy; *akshish, kallo*
sinful; *achukma, ashachi, haksi, okpulo, yoshoba*
sinful man, *hatak yoshoba*

sinfulness; *okpulo, yoshoba*
sing, to; *hehi, kanwa, ola, olachi, taloa, talua*
sing as locusts, to; *washahachi*
singe, to; *anakshonffi, anaksholi*
singed; *anakshonfa, anakshua*
singer; *hehi, taloa*
singer (one who singes); *anaksholi*
singer, a skillful; *taloa imponna*
singers, a body of; *taloa aliha*
singing, good; *taloa achukma*
singing, to lead in; *taloa isht ia*
singing, to practice; *taloat abachi*
singing book, *ataloa*
singing master; *taloa ikhanachi, taloa imponna*
single; *achafa, anli, auaya, ilap bano*
single file, to move in a; *baiallit anya*
single file, to stand in a; *baiallit hika*
single haul, *himonna achafa halalli*
single man, *hatak ohoyo ikimiksho*
single out, to; *achafolechi, achafolechi*
single time, *himonna*
single word, *illa*
singled out, *achafoa*
singleness; *achafa, anli*
singly; *ilap achafa, ilap bano*
singular; *illa, inla*
sinister; *afabekimma, okpulo*
sink, to; *akka ia, alhchunnachi, hafikbi, oka kania, okatula, okbilhha, oklobushli, oklobushlichi*
sink, to cause to; *oka talali*
sinless; *ashachi, yoshobiksho*   •
sinner; *ashachi, hatak yoshoba, nan ashachi, yoshoba*
sinuate, to; *fullokachi*
sip, to; *lumat ishko*
sir; *chitokaka, inshali*
sire; *anki, inki*
sirloin, *nali nipi*
sirocco, *mali lashpa*
sirup (of sugar), *hapi champuli okchi*
sister; *antek, amanni, imanni, innakfish, intek, itibapishi, nakfish*
sisterhood, *intek aliha*
sister-in-law; *amalak usi ohoyo, inhaiya, imalakusi ohoyo, impusnakni, ipo*
sit, to; *aiasha, alata, ansha, ashwa, binili, binnili, binoli, chiya, hikia, omanili*
sit, to cause to; *binnilechi*
sit apart, to; *naksika binili*
sit around, to; *binoht aiasha, hioht ansha*
sit at, to; *abinili*

sit by, to; *binoht maya*
sit down, to; *abenili, akkabinoli*
sit here and there, to; *bininili*
sit in secret, to; *lumat chinya*
sit on, to; *abinili, omanili, ontalaia, ontalali, talaia, tala*
sit on the heels, to; *pochuko*
sit out, to; *kucha ansha*
sit round, to; *abinot manya, ataloht maya, binoht maya*
sit sideways, to; *naksi*
sit with, to; *ibabinili, ibaiansha, tankla ansha, tankla binili, tankla binoli*
site, *aiontalaia*
site of a house, *chuka aiitola*
sitter; *binili, binoli*
sitting; *abenili, alata, anumpulit ansha, ansha, binili, bininli*
sitting round, *binohmaya*
situated; *talaia, taloha*
situation, *talaia*
six, *hannali*
six, to make; *hannalichi*
sixfold, *inluhmi*
sixteen, *auah hannali*
sixth, *isht hanali*
sixth time, *isht hanaliha*
sixtieth, *isht pokoli*
sixty, *pokoli*
size; *chito, kauehto*
size thread, to; *chilakbichi*
sizy; *likaha, okchauabi*
sizy, to render; *likahachi*
skein; *pokuspoa, pokussa, ponola fabassa achafa, shonuya*
skein, to make a; *pokussali, shonuyachi*
skein of cotton; *ponola itapana, ponola itapana achafa*
skeleton; *alhpoa foni, hatak chunna, na foni*
skeptic, *yimmi*
skeptical, *yimmi*
skiff; *peni, penushi, penushi palhki*
skill, *imponna*
skilled, *imponna*
skillet, *oka alibisha*
skillful, *imponna*
skillful magician, *fappuli imponna*
skillful person, *imponna*
skillful writer, *hatak holissochi imponna*
skim, to; *mahaiyat anya, moeli, moli, okpeli, palhkit anya*
skimmed; *moa, moha*
skimmer; *isht moeli, isht mofi, isht okpeha*

skin, *hakshup*
skin, to; *luffi, lonffi, loli, monfa, um-poholmo, umpohomo*
skinned; *lonfa, loha, monfa, umpatalhpo*
skinner; *lonffi, loli, na hakshup kanchi*
skip, *tolupli*
skip, to; *tolupli, tulli*
skirmish, *itibbi*
skirmish, to; *itibi*
skirt; *haksobish, hasimbish*
skirt, to; *fololichi*
skirt of a saddle, *sanahchi*
skirted, *folota*
skittish, *nukshopa*
skulk, to; *luhmi*
skull, *nushkobo foni*
skunk, *koni*
sky, *shutik*
sky, fair; *masheli*
sky, the convex of the; *shutik tabokaka*
slab; *banspoah, iti basha*
slab, to; *bakali, bakalichi*
slabbed, *bakali*
slack; *salaha, yohapa*
slack, to; *mokoffi, salaha, yohapa*
slack, to cause to; *yohablichi*
slacken, to; *yahapoli, yohabli, yohapa*
slackened, *yohapa*
slackly; *salahat, yohapat*
slackness, *yohapa*
slag; *tali iyalhki, talin yalhki*
slaie, *uski chula*
slake, to; *fihobli*
slam; *aiisso, isso*
slander, *anumpa okpulo onuchi*
slander, to; *achokushpalechi, achokush-pali, anumpa chukushpali, anumpa okpulo onuchi, na mihachi, nan umachi, nan umanchi*
slandered; *achokushpa, achokushpachi*
slandered, to cause to be; *achokushpa-chechi*
slanderer; *achokushpalechi achokushpali, anumpa chukushpali, anumpa chukush-pashali, na mihachi, nan umachi*
slanderer, noted; *na mihachi shali*
slanderous; *achokushpa, chukushpa, nan umachi*
slant; *shanaia, waiya*
slant, to; *naksikachi, shanaiachi, waiyachi*
slanting; *pashaya, shanaia, tashaya, waiya*
slap, *pasalichi*

slap, to; *lasaha, lasalichi, pasaha, pasa-lichi*
slapping, *pasaha*
slaps, one who; *pasaha*
slash, to; *bashli, chanli*
slat; *banspoah, okhoatkachi, tikeli*
slate; *aholissochi, tali aholissochi*
slate, to; *holisso takalichi*
slated, *holisso takali*
slattern, *ohoyo litiha*
slaughter, *abi*
slaughter, to; *abi*
slave, *yuka*
slave-born, *yuka atta*
slaver, *itukchi*
slaver, to; *itukholaya*
slavish, *yuka ahalaia*
slay, *uski chula*
slay, to; *akkakoli, abi, illichi*
slayer; *abi, nan abi*
sleazy; *hoyapa, okshachinli, okshalinchi, okshichanli, tapuski*
sled, *iti shalalli*
sled, to; *iti shalalli isht anya*
sledge, *tali isht boa chito*
sleek; *halushki, limimpa, limishko*
sleek, to; *halushkichi, limimpachi, limish-kuchi*
sleeked, *halushki*
sleekness; *halushki, limimpa*
sleep, *nusi*
sleep, to; *nusi*
sleep (as the limbs), to; *shimoha*
sleep, to cause; *nusechi*
sleep, wanting to; *nusachaya*
sleep at, in, on, there; to: *anusi*
sleep with, to; *ibanusi*
sleeper; *iti bachoha, nusi*
sleepily, *nusolba*
sleepy; *nusachaya, nusi, nusilhha, nusolba*
sleepy fellow, *hatak nusilhha shali*
sleet, *bachalusha*
sleet, to; *bachalusha*
sleet, to cause; *bachalushachi*
sleeve, *shakba*
sleeve, to; *shakba achunli, shakbc fohki*
sleigh, *iti shalalli*
sleigh bell, *tali shiloha chito*
sleight, *haksi*
slender; *chauala, fabaspoa, fabasfoa, fahko, fomosa, kota*
slice; *pasa, tuchali, tushafa*
slice, to; *basht tushaffi, pasli, tushtuli*

sliced; *tushali, tushtua*
slicing-off place, *atoshafa*
slide, to; *shalali, shalalli, shalallichi, shohalalli*
slide, to cause to; *shalalichi, shohalal-lichi*
slight, *lumasi*
slight, a; *aiokpachi, pinsiksho*
slightly, *lapali*
slim; *chauala, fabasfoa, fabassa, fabassoa, fomosa*
slime, *wilaha*
sliminess; *likancha, likanli, likoa, wilaha*
slimy; *likaha, likancha, likanli, likashbi, likoa, wilaha, wushwoki*
slimy, to render; *likanchachi, likanlichi, likohichi, wilahachi*
sling; *hannaweli, isht bopuli, nan isht fahammi, nan isht pila*
sling, wooden; *nan isht fakuli*
sling, to; *bohpuli, fahammi*
slink, to; *akkamololi*
slip; *alhkuna falaia, chulata, fuli, shaka-lalli, shalalli*
slip, to; *ashachi, amo, lakoffi, shakalalli, shalakli, shalali, shalalli, shalallichi, shohalalli*
slip, to cause to; *shakalallichi, shalalli-chi, shohalallichi, shohhalalichi*
slip down, to; *shohhalali*
slip in, to; *lumat fohki*
slip of paper, *holisso lilafa*
slip off, to; *shunfa, takofa*
slip once, to; *shalakli*
slip out, to; *mokofa, mokoffi, shunfa, shunfi*
slip through a noose, to; *anuklinfa*
slipknot, *anuklinfa*
slipknot, to make a; *anuklinffi*
slipped off; *takofa*
slippers; *shulush shohala, shulush tapuski*
slippery; *halasbi, likanli*
slippery, to make; *halasbichi*
slippery elm, *balup*
slipping through, *anuklinfa*
slips, one who; *shakalalli, shalalli*
slit; *chula, chulata*
slit, a; *chulafa, chulata*
slit, to; *chulalli, chuli*
slitter, *chuli*
sliver; *iti shibafa, iti shimafa, iti shimali*
sliver, to; *shimmi, wulobli*
slobber, *itukholaya*
slobber, to; *itukchuba, itukholaya*

slobberer, *itukchuba*
slop, *oka lanya*
slope, *okkattahaka*
slope, to; *okkattahakachi*
sloping, *okshilama*
slosh, *oka lanya*
sloshy, *oka laua*
sloth, *intakobi*
slothful, *intakobi*
slothfulness, *intakobi*
slough; *lukchuk chito, sinti hakshup*
slough, to; *fakoli*
sloven, *hatak litiha okpulo*
slow; *achiba, ahchiba, alhchiba, salaha, weki*
slow, to cause to be; *achibachi*
slowly, *salahat*
slowness, *salaha*
sluggard, *hatak intakobi*
sluice, *oka ayanalli*
slumber, *nusi*
slumber, to; *nusi*
slumberer, *nusi*
slung, *bohpoa*
slur, to; *kalakshichi, lusachi, okpani*
slush; *lukchuk, labeta*
slut; *ofi tek, ohoyo litiha*
sly; *alalichi, imponna*
slyly, *luma*
small; *chimpoa, chipinta, chipintasi, chipota, chipunta, chukushpa, iskatani, iskitini, iskitinisi, patassa*
small, to render; *chipintachi, imomachi, iskatanichi, iskitinichi*
small, very; *chipinta, iskatanusi, kitinisi*
smallest, *wishakchi*
smallest amount, in the; *kamomi*
smallish; *iskatinosi, iskitinisi, iskitini chohmi*
smallness, *iskitini*
smallpox, *chilakwa*
smallpox, to have the; *chilakwa abi*
smart (able), *imponna*
smart (bitter), *homi*
smart (painful), *hotupa, shimoli*
smart, made to; *shimoli*
smart, to; *ilbasha, imaleka, shimoli*
smart, to make the flesh; *shimolichi*
smart in the throat, to; *nukshikanli*
smash, to; *litoli*
smear, to; *apolusli*
smear with grease, to; *ahammi*
smeared; *alhpolosa, liteha*
smell; *balama, nana hunwa*

smell, bad; *kosoma*
smell, to; *achishi, hu*n*wa, ibakchishinli, ishwa*
smell bad, to cause to; *shuachi*
smell disagreeably, to; *shua*
smell fishy, to; *nakshobi*
smell fishy, to cause to; *nakshobichi*
smell of, to; *aiishwa*
smell of whisky, *shua*
smell strong, to; *kosoma*
smell the track, to; *ahchishi*
smilax, *kantak*
smile, *yukpa*
smile, to; *yukpa*
smile, to cause to; *yukpachi*
smite, to; *akkakolichi, abi, abichi, boli, fahama, isso, nali, nukbepuli, pokafa, pokaha, sokolichi, soku*n*ha, tipelichi, umbitepa*
smite at, there, or on; to: *aiisso*
smiter; *isso, nan isso, pasalichi, pokafa*
smith; *tali isht atta, tali pilesa*
smiting, *soku*n*ha*
smitten, *akkakoha*
smoke, *shoboli*
smoke, current of; *shoboli*
smoke, to; *hoponti, shoboli, shobolichi*
smoke a pipe, to; *shu*n*ka*
smoke of powder, *hituk shibota*
smoke on, to; *shobolichi*
smoke tobacco, to; *hakchuma shu*n*ka*
smoke up quickly, to; *shubbukli*
smoked, *shoboli*
smoker; *shobolichi, shu*n*ka*
smoking, *shoboli*
smoky, *shoboli*
smooth; *halalua, halasbi, halushki, itilaui, limimpa, limishko, malancha, malassa, patassa*
smooth, to; *halushkichi, itilauichi*
smooth-bore gun, *tanamp fabassa*
smoothed; *halushki, itilaui*
smoothness, *limimpa*
smother, to; *shobolichi, umpohomo*
smut; *liteha, lusa, yalhki*
smut, to; *lusachi*
smutty; *lusa, likokoa*
snack; *impa iskitini, kashapa*
snag, *itakshish*
snag, to; *ufka*n*ya*
snail, *hatak yoshubli*
snake, *sinti*
snake, a species of; *hala, sinti pohkul*

snake, black; *sinti lusa*
snake, chicken; *abaksha*
snake, coachwhip; *ipochi itimapa, sinti koyufa tohbi*
snake, copperhead; *chilakwa, chalakwa*
snake, garter; *pachalhpali, sinti basoa*
snake, green; *pa*n*shafoli*
snake, joint; *oksup taptua, sinti kobali, sinti kolokumpi*
snake, king; *sinti pohkul*
snake, large horned; *sinti lapitta*
snake, striped; *pachalhpali, sinti basoa*
snake, water; *nanapa*
snake bite, *sinti kopoli*
snake skin, *sinti hakshup*
snakeroot, *tiak shua*
snap; *basaha, basak, chalak, tasup*
snap, to; *basaha, basahkachi, basakachi, basali, basisakachi, chalakachi, kobafa, kobaffi, kopoli banna, litafa, litalichi, litaffi, lukatola, tasupachi, tabli*
snap, to cause to; *basahachi*
snap a whip, to; *lukalichi, lukatolachi*
snap of a rope, *litak*
snap the fingers, to; *tasuha*
snapper, *lukata wishakchi*
snapping; *basahkachi, basali, basasu*n*kachi*
snapping, to cause a; *basalichi*
snapping of a whip, *lukatola*
snappish; *kopoli banna, nukoa*
snare, *isht albi*
snare, to; *isht albi isht hokli*
snarl; *itashiha, shochoha*
snarl, to; *ashekonoachi, kileha, shihachi, shikanoachi*
snarl up together, to; *shikanoachi*
snarled; *pokshia, shachila, shiha, shochoha*
snarly, *pokshia*
snatch, to; *haili, lachakat ishi*
snath, *onush isht basha api*
sneak off, to; *lumat kania*
sneer, *shittilema*
sneer, to; *ahoba, shittilema*
sneeze, *habishko*
sneeze, to; *habishko, habishko, pilu*n*ka*
sneeze, to make; *habishkuchi, pilu*n*kachi*
sneezing, *pilu*n*ka*
snicker, to; *yukpa*
sniff, to; *lotu*n*ka*
snip, to; *tabli*
snivel, to; *ibilhkan kucha, yaiya*

sniveler, *yaiya shali*
snore, to; *laba^nka*
snorer, *laba^nka*
snoring, *laba^nka*
snort, to; *lotu^nka, pilu^nka, sha^nwa*
snorter; *lotu^nka, sha^nwa*
snorting; *lotu^nka, sha^nwa*
snout, *ibishakni*
snow, *oktusha*
snow, to; *oktusha, oktushachi*
snow, to cause to; *oktushachi*
snowbird; *lafintini, toksakinla*
snuff; *hakchuma bota, habishkuchi*
snuff, to; *fiopa, hu^nwa*
snuffbox, *hakchuma bota aialhto*
snuffers, *pala isht kicheli, pala isht kalasha*
snug, *bili^nka*
snug, to make; *apota*
so; *achuhmi, aiohmi, chohmi, chumba, moma, yakohmi, yammak i^n, yohmi*
so, to do; *aiyakohmi, aiyakohmichi, aiyohmi, yakohmi, yohmi*
so, to make it; *aiohmichi, yahmichi*
so as, *yamohmi*
so it is, *omikato*
so it is well enough, *omikato*
so long as, *ititakla*
so much as, *ak*
so on, *yamohmi*
so that, *na*
soak, to; *okishko, okkachi*
soaked; *okachi, ulhkachi, walasha*
soaker; *okishko shali, okkachi*
soap; *isht ahchifa, isht alhchefa*
soap, bar; *isht ahchifa kallo*
soap, castile; *isht ahchifa balama*
soap, hard; *isht ahchifa kallo*
soap, scented; *isht ahchifa balama*
soap, to; *isht ahchifa o^nlali*
soapstone, *talhpa*
soapsuds, *isht ahchifa pokpoki*
soar, to; *hika, hikat a^nya*
sober; *kostini, nuktanla, nuktala*
sober, to; *kostininchi, nuktalali*
sober, to become; *nuktala*
sobered; *kostini, nuktala*
sobriety; *kostini, nuktanla*
society, *iksa*
sock; *iyubi huski kolofa, iyubi huski kololi*
socket of the eye; *nishkin ahika chiluk, okshilonli*
sodden; *honni, labocha*
sodomy; *ayofanichih, yopullachi*

soft; *anukyohbi, haiemo, kallo, lapushki, lipeha, lipemo, lipisto, lipi^nka, lipinto, lisisi^nkachi, lachopa, latimo, likanli, lopushki, shukbah, walasha, walo^nchi, waloha, walohbi, walwaki, yabosha, yabushli, yattotu^nkachi, yatushki, yatushkoa*
soft and pliable, to become; *yukahbi*
soften, to; *anukyohbi, anukyohbichi, hokulbi, kostini, kostininchi, lapushki, lapushkichi, lachopachi, lopushkichi, nuktala, okkachi, shuchapah, ulhkachi, walwakichi, yaboshachi, yatushkichi, yatushkuli, yukahbi*
soften with water, to; *oka kaiyachi*
softened; *anukyohbi, kallo, kostini, lapushki, lopushki, yukabi*
softened by water, *oka kaiya*
softly; *loma, luma, lumasi*
softness; *lapushki, nuktala*
soggy; *lacha, ulhkachi*
soil; *lukfi, lusa, yakni*
soil, to; *lukchuk banuchi, lusachi*
soiled; *liteha, lusa*
sojourn, to; *anta*
sojourner, *a^nya*
solace, *hopola*
solace, to; *hopolalli, nuktalali*
solaced; *hopola, nuktala*
solar, *hashi ahalaia*
sold, *alhtoba*
solder, *isht akmo*
solder, to; *aiakmochi, aialbuchi, akmochi, albochi, albokachi*
solder with brass, to; *asonak lakna isht akmichi*
soldered; *akmo, albo*
soldered with brass, *asonak lakna isht akmi*
soldier, *tashka chipota*
soldier, Turkish; *takish intashka chipota*
soldier, veteran; *tashka sepokni*
soldiers' quarters; *tashka chipota inchuka*
soldiery, *tashka chipota*
sole, *achafa*
sole, a; *iyi*
sole of the foot, *iyi pata*
solemn, *holitopa*
solemnize, to; *holitoblichi*
solemnize a marriage, to; *itauayachi*
solemnly, *holitopat*
solicit, to; *asilhha*

solicitor, *asilhha*
solicitous, *ahah ahni*
solid; *aⁿli, kamạssa, kạllo*
solidity; *kamạssa, kạllo*
solitary; *ilap bieka, naksika, palata*
solitary, to make; *banochi*
solitude, *chukillissa*
solve, to; *haiakạchi*
solvent, *aheka*
sombre, *oklili*
some; *chạbiha, kanima, kanimi, kaniohmi, kanohmi, kanomona, kạto*
some manner, in; *akanimi, katiohmi*
some other, *inla*
some sort, of; *kaniohmi*
some time, *kanima*
some way, in; *kaniohmi, katimichi, katiohmi*
some way, to do it in; *katiohmichi*
somebody; *kanimi, kạna kia*
somehow; *akanimi, kaniohmi kia, kaniohmiho*
somehow, to cause to be; *kaniohmichi*
somehow, to do; *kanimichi, kaniohmi*
somerset; *hachowanạshi, hachowani*
something; *na fehna, nana, nana kia*
sometime, *aka*
sometimes; *kanimash inli, kaniohmikma*
somewhat, *chohmi*
somewhere; *kanima, kanima kia, kạni*
somnambulist, *tasimbo*
somnolent; *nusi bạnna, nusilhha*
son; *ạlla nakni, chiso, iso, iso nakni, sạso, ushi*
Son of God, *Chihowa ushi*
Son of Man; *Hatak Ushi, yạt*
song; *ataloa, atạlwa, atạlwạchi, ạlhtaloa, ạlhtaloak, ạlhtạlwak, ilhtalowak, taloa*
song, death; *hoyopa taloa*
song, sacred; *ạba taloa*
song, to make a; *taloa ikbi*
songster, *taloa*
son-in-law; *haloka, ippok, iyup*
sonorous, *chitot ola*
sonship, *ushi ahalaia*
soon; *cheki, chekusi, pạlhki*
soon, to cause it to be; *chekichi*
soon, very; *chekusi*
soot, *tulak*
soot, to; *tulak isht lusachi*
sooted, *tulak isht luak*
soothe, to; *hopolạchi, nuktalali, nuktalalichi*
soothed; *hopola, nuktạla*

soother; *nuktalali, nuktalalichi*
soothsayer; *hatak fappo, tikbanli anoli*
sooty; *tulak chito, tulak laua*
sop, *lạbbi*
sop, to; *lạbbi*
soporific; *nusechi, nusilhhạchi*
sorcerer, *isht ahollo*
sorcery, *yushpakama*
sorcery, to practice; *yushpakạmmi*
sordid; *liteha, makali, okpulo*
sore; *hotupa, litoa, liwạli, luwali, lachowa, palạmmi*
sore, a; *hotupa, liahpo, lachowa, taloⁿa*
sore, a running; *okchushba*
sore, to become; *itạkha litowa, lachowa*
sore, to make; *litoli, lacholi*
sore eyes, *hạlbạbi*
sore mouth, *itạkha litowa*
sore throat, *chakwa*
sore throat, to have; *chakwạbi*
soreness, *lachowa*
sorrel, *hachukkashasa*
sorrel (a weed), *pichi*
sorrel, a; *isi nakni afạmmi tuchina*
sorrow; *nukhaⁿklo, okko*
sorrow, cause of; *isht nukhaⁿklo, nan isht anukhaⁿklo*
sorrow, occasion of; *anukhaⁿklo*
sorrow, man of; *nan nukhaⁿklo*
sorrow, overmuch; *nukhaⁿklo atopa*
sorrow, place of; *anukhaⁿklo*
sorrow, to; *nukhaⁿklo*
sorrowful; *imanukfela, nukhaⁿklo, nukwiloha*
sorry, *nukhaⁿklo*
sort, *kaniohmi*
sort, to; *aiyoa*
sort with, to; *ibafoka*
sot; *hatak okishko, imanukfila iksho, okishko shali*
sottish; *imanukfila iksho, okishko*
soul, *shilombish*
soulless, *shilombish iksho*
sound; *achukma, aⁿli, na kanimi keyu*
sound, a; *fopa, ola*
sound, to; *akkahoyo, kabakạchi, kạsachi, kitikachi, kobakuchi, komakachi, komokachi, komokạchi, ola, olachi, taloa, tamampa, tasupachi, timikạchi*
sound of a bell; *chubuk, samak, samampa*
sound of a sudden slide, *shelak*
sounded, *ola*
sounding; *kobohạchi, ola*
soundly, *achukma*

soundness; *achukma, aiokpuloka iksho*
sounds, one who; *olachi*
sour; *hauashko, homechi, homi, kalama, kaskaha*
sour, to; *hauashkochi, homechi, homi, kaskaha, kaskahachi*
sour water, *oka hauashko*
sour wood, *iti kosoma*
source; *akshish, aminti, ataiyuli, ateli, ibetap, ikbi*
soured, *hauashko*
sourish; *homechi, homi chohmi, homilhha*
sourness; *hauashko, kaskaha*
souse, to; *oklubbichi, oklobushlichi*
soused, *homi·*
south, *oka mali*
south, at or in the; *oka mali pilla*
southeast, *oka mali hashi akuchaka itintakla*
southerly; *oka mali imma, oka mali pila*
southern, *oka mali pila*
southward; *oka mali imma, oka mali pila*
southwest, *oka mali hashi aiokatula itintakla*
sovereign, *inshali*
sovereign, a; *minko*
sow, *shukha tek*
sow, to; *fimibli, fimmi, hokchi, na hokchi*
sowed; *fima, fimimpa, fimpkachi*
sower; *fimibli, fimmi, hokchi, na hokchi, nafimmi*
sown; *fima, fimimpa, holokchi*
space; *aboha itintakla, aboha ititakla*
spade; *lukfi isht kula, nan isht kula, yakni isht kula*
spade, to; *yakni kulli*
Spain; *Ishpani, Ishpani yakni*
spalt, *palata*
span; *ibbak umbitepa achafa, ichapa, ichapoa, tuklo*
span of horses, *isuba itichapa*
span, to; *apesa, holba*
spangled spots, *siksiki*
Spaniard; *Ishpani hatak, Ishpani okla*
spaniel, *ofi*
Spanish, *Ishpani*
Spanish moss, *iti shumo*
spank, to; *lasaha, lasalichi, pasaha, pasalichi*
spanking, *lasaha*
spare; *atampa, chunna, kofanto*
spare, to; *apoa, inhollo, ilatoba, ilatomba, nukhanklo*

spare rib, *naksi foni*
spark; *basaboa, basacha, chalhchaki, hatak ilakshema shali, kitinisi, pololi, tohpololi, tushanfasi*
spark, to; *pololi*
sparkle, to; *chalhchakachi, chalhchaki, pololi, polota*
sparkle, to make; *chalhchakachechi, chilichi, pololichi*
sparkling, *chalhchaki*
sparks, to make; *basahachi*
sparrow; *chinsa, chunsa, hushi chipunta*
sparse, *fimimpa*
spasm; *haiuchichi, haiyichichi, yalatha, yalattakachi*
spatter, to; *fimmi*
spatterdashes, *iyubiha*
spattered, *fimimpa*
spawn; *ashela, nan ushi, olana atoba, shukattushi*
spawn, to; *cheli*
spay, to; *shukha tek hobak ikbi*
spayed, *shukha tek hobak toba*
speak, to; *achi, anoli, anopoli, anumpuli, nanuka*
speak again, to; *atuklant achi*
speak for, to; *apobachi*
speakable, *anumpa hinla*
speaker; *anumpa isht hika, anumpuli, hatak anumponli*
spear; *api, isht baha, na halupa, tali halupa ontala tabi*
spear, to; *na halupa isht bali*
specie, *tali holisso*
specify, to; *anoli, hochifo*
specimen, *isht alhpisa*
specious, *achukma ahoba*
speck, *shauiya*
speck, to; *lusachi*
speckle, to; *siksikichi, taktakichi*
speckled; *chikchiki, okshohonli, siksiki, taktaki*
speckled, to make; *chikchikechi*
spectacle, *nam pisa*
spectacled, *nishkin alata ansha*
spectacles; *alata, nishkin alata*
spectator; *hatak yopisa, na yopisa, nam pisa, yopisa*
spectre; *shilombish, shilup*
speculate, to; *anukfilli, itatoba*
speculation; *imanukfila, itatoba*
speculator; *anukfilli, nam pisa, nan ittatoba*

speculum, *apisa*
speech; *anumpa, anumpa isht hika, anumpa kololi, anumpa tiloli*
speech, a short; *anumpa ikaiako, anumpa kolunfa, anumpa tilofa*
speech, the last; *hekano*
speech, to make a; *anump ikbi, anumpa isht hika*
speechless; *anump iksho, anumpuli keyu*
speechmaker; *anump ikbi, anumpuli*
speed, *tushpa*
speed, to; *tunshpa, tunshpalechi*
speedy; *cheki, tushpa*
spell; *chunkash ishi, hopaki*
spell, to; *holisso hochifot itimanumpuli, holisso itimanumpuli*
spencer: *ilefoka kolofa, ilefoka kololi, na foka kolukshi shakba ansha*
spend, to; *isht yopomo, kanchi, kania, tali, tikabichi, yukoma*
spend the day, to; *shohbichi*
spendthrift, *isht yupomo*
spew, to; *hoeta*
sphere; *apelichika, nan chanaha, nan lumbo*
spherical, *lumbo*
spicery, *na balama*
spices, *na balama*
spider, *chulhkan*
spider, long-legged; *tupashali*
spider's nest, *chulhkan inchuka*
spider's web; *chuklampulli, chulhkan inchuka, hachuklampuli*
spigot; *abicheli isht akamassa, oka abicha isht alhkama*
spike; *chufak, chufak chito*
spike, to; *akammi, chufak chito isht ahonalichi*
spiked, *chufak chito isht ahonala*
spile; *abicheli isht akamassa, oka abicha isht alhkama*
spill, to; *akkafohobli, akkalali, akkalatapa, akkalatabli, akkalaya, fohobli, kaloha, latapa, latabli*
spilled; *fohopa, latapa*
spiller, *latabli*
spilt; *akkafohopa, akkalatapa, akkalaya, latapa, lanya*
spilt water, *oka lanya*
spin, to; *hachuklampulechi, shanni*
spin on, to; *ashanni*
spin on, to cause to; *ashannichi*
spin out, to; *falaiachi*

spinal marrow, *nali foni lupi*
spindle; *ashanatali fabassa, haksobish anli*
spine, *nali foni*
spine of a hog; *shachakba*
spinner; *ashannichi, hachuklampulechi, na shanni, shanni*
spinning wheel; *ahonola, ashana, ponol ashana*
spinning wheel, small; *ahonolushi*
spiral, *apakfopa*
spire; *ashana, api, hishi*
spire, to; *offo*
spirit; *chunkash, imanukfila*
spirit (liquor), *oka homi*
spirit, a; *na shilombish, nan isht ahollo, shilombish, shilup*
spirit, an evil; *shilombish okpulo*
spirit, an unclean; *shilombish okpulo*
Spirit, Holy; *Shilombish holitopa*
spirit, to; *yimintachi*
spirit of heaven, *aba shilombish*
spirited; *chilita, yiminta*
spiritless, *yiminta keyu*
spirits, ardent; *na homi, oka, oka homi*
spirits, the; *chunkash*
spiritual; *imanukfila ahalaia, shilombish ahalaia*
spirituous, *oka homi ahalaia*
spit, *itukchi*
spit, to; *tufa, tuftua*
spite; *hichali, nukkilli, nukoa*
spite, to; *nukkilli, nukoa*
spiteful; *hichali, nukkilli, nukoa*
spitter, *tufa*
spitting, to keep; *tuftua*
spittle; *itukchi, woshoki*
splash; *chibak, lali*
splash, to; *chibakachi, lali*
splash on, to; *fimmi*
spashed on, *lali*
spleen; *ilapa, nukoa, takashi*
spleeny; *nukhanklo, nukoa*
splendid; *chito, holitopa*
splendor; *chito, holitopa, shohmalali*
splice, to; *achakali, achakli*
splice at or with, to; *aiitachakalli, aiitachakli*
spliced; *achaka, alhchaka, alhchakoa*
spliced at; *achakaya, aiitachaka*
splint, *iti shimafa*
splinter; *chulafa, iti shibafa, iti shibali, iti shimafa, iti shimali, shibafa, shibali, shimafa*

splinter, to; *chulali, chulaffi, shibafa, shibali, shibalichi, shibaffi, shimafa, shimalichi, shimnuffi*
splintered; *shibafa, shibali*
splinters, one who; *shibaffi*
split; *abakli, bakali, chilakto, chula, chulafa, chulata, palali, palata, pala, shima, shimafa, shimali, wula, wulopa*
split, a; *abakli, itamintafa, patafa*
split, to; *abakli, abaklichi, bakali, bakalichi, bakapa, bakli, chilaktochi, chula, chulata, iti bakli, palali, palalichi, palata, palalli, patali, pala, pali,* · *shibafa, shibali, shima, shimafa, shimali, shimmi, wolobli, wula, wuli, wulobli, wulopa*
split, to cause to; *palalichi*
split boards, *iti palanta*
split in two, *bakastoa*
split in two, to; *bakastoa, bakastuli, bakabli*
split into fine pieces, to; *shimalichi*
split into shingles, to; *shimmi*
split off; *bakafa, tushafa, tushali*
split off, to; *bakafa, chulafa, chulaffi, chulalli, shibbi, shimaffi, shimnuffi, tushafa, tushali*
split open; *patafa, patali*
split open, to; *patafa, patalichi, pataffi*
split wood; *iti palanta, iti pala, iti shima*
splitter; *abaklichi, bakalichi, bakabli, chulaffi, chulalli, chuli, palalichi, palalli, patalichi, pataffi, pali, shibaffi, shimalichi*
splitting, *palanta*
spoil; *na yuka, wehpoa*
spoil, to; *okpani, okpulo, wehpuli*
spoiled; *okpulo, toshbi*
spoiler, *okpani*
spoils, *wehpoa*
spoilt, *okpulo*
spoke, a; *achushoa*
spoken, *anumpa*
sponge, *tashukpa holba*
sponge, to; *akania, haksichi*
spongy, *yabushli*
spontaneous, *ilap ahni yamohmi*
spool; *iti kalaha, uski tapa*
spool, to; *uski tapa afoli*
spoon; *isht abahchakli, isht impa*
spoon, horn; *alhpi, lapish isht impa*
spoon, pewter; *alhpi*
spoon, shell; *fulush isht impa*
spoon, small; *isht impushi*
spoon, tea; *isht impushi*
spoon, wooden; *alhpi*

spoonful, *isht impa alota*
sport; *ilaualli, washoha*
sport, to; *ilaualli, washoha, yukpali*
sportsman, *na hunssa* .
spot; *bakokoa, bakokunkachi, basoa, chikchiki, misisunkachi, talaia, taloha, tali lusa, tiktiki*
spot, black; *lusa talaia, lusa taloha, talaia*
spot, red; *talaia*
spot, to; *lusachi, taktakichi, tiktikechi*
spotted; *bakoa, bakokona, bakokunkachi, bakokunkachi, chikchiki, chukchuki, misisunkachi, siksiki, taktaki, tiktiki*
spotted, to make; *bakoachi, chikchikechi*
spouse; *itauaya, itinchuka*
spout; *abicha, isht bicheli, oka abicha, oka isht bicheli*
spout, to; *bicha, punfa*
spouter, *punfa*
sprain, to; *taloffi naha*
sprained, *talofa naha*
sprawl, to; *wakchalalit itonla*
spread; *ashatapa, ashatapoa, lapa, pata, patkachi*
spread, a; *apatalhpo, patalhpo*
spread, the wings; *ashatapa*
spread, to; *apatalechi, ashatapoli, ashatabli, auata, auataya, auatachi, fimibli, lapa, lapuchi, patali, palli, pata, pulli, shukto, talali, wahhaloha*
spread down, to; *akkalipeli*
spread evenly, to; *patasalli*
spread on, *umpata*
spread on, to; *umpatali*
spread out, to; *patali, wakama, wakamoli, wattachi, wilali*
spread paper, *holisso pata*
spread the nose, to; *ibakshulanli*
spread with iron or stone; *tali isht patalhpo*
spreader; *fimibli, patali*
spreading; *fimibli, lapa*
sprig, *fuli*
sprightly, *tushpa*
spring; *ahpi, aiisht ia, aminti; toffahpi*
spring, a; *apoloma, kali, tolupli*
spring, deep; *kali hofobi*
spring, dug; *kali kula*
spring, to; *bichokachi, bichota, bichotakachi, bichulli, fichama, fichamoli, chafichi, tolupli, tulli*
spring, wooden; *iti poloma*
spring and fly, to; *fichamoa*

spring and throw, to; *fichammi*
spring open, to; *fichama, fichammi*
spring up, to; *alikti, offo, okpicheli, okpichelichi*
spring water, *kali oka*
springe, *isht albi*
springing, *offo*
springs, to have; *polomoa*
sprinkle, to; *fimmi, fimmichi, fimpkachi, foechi, lali, lali, lalinchi, okshikali, okshikanshli, okshimmichi*
sprinkled; *fima, fimimpa, fimpkachi*
sprite; *shilombish, shilup*
sprout; *abasali, aiunchululli, apatali, apushi, bisali, bisanli, iti pushi, iti unchuloli, offo, uncholulli*
sprout, to; *abasali, bisali, bisanlichi, offo*
sprout, to cause to; *abasalichi, unchololichi*
sprout at the root, to; *unchololi*
sprouted, *bisali*
sprung; *bichokachi, bichota*
sprung open; *fichama, fichamoa*
spry; *palhki, tushpa*
spume, *pokpoki*
spume, to; *pokpokechi*
spun, *shana*
spunk; *chilita, nukoa, tashukpa*
spur; *chufak iyalhfoa, inchahe*
spur, to; *bali, bili*
spurious, *anli*
spurn, to; *habli, kali, shittilema*
spurt, to; *punfachi, wishikachi, wishilli, wishillichi*
spurt, to cause to; *wishillichi*
spurting out, to make a noise in; *wishikachi*
spurway; *isuba aiomanili itanowa, isuba inhina*
sputter, to; *fimiblichi, tishihachi, tunshpat anumpuli*
spy; *apistikeli, ibatankla, na hopunkoyo, pist anya*
spy, to; *na pisat anya, yakni pisat anya*
spy glass, *apisa isht hoponkoyo*
squab; *nia, pachushi*
squabble, *itishi*
squabble, to; *itishi*
squalid, *liteha*
squall; *mali, yaiya*
squall, to; *yaiya*
squally, *mali shali*
squander, to; *isht yopomo, yukoma*

square; *bolboki, bolkachi, bolukta, chanaha folota achafa, isht alhpisa*
square, to; *apesa*
square, to make a; *boluktachi*
square off, to; *kololi*
square with, to; *itilaui*
squared, *bolukta*
squares, to make; *bolbokechi, bolkachechi*
squash; *isito, isito holba*
squash, to; *litoli*
squat, to; *bikuttokachi*
squeak, *kachakachi*
squeak, to; *kanshkachi, kachakachi*
squeak, to cause to; *kachakachechi*
squeaking, *kanshkachi*
squeal, to; *chinka, yaiya*
squealer, *chinka*
squeamish, *yuala shali*
squeeze, to; *ateblichi, atelichi, bichubli, bocholi, bochubli, katanlichi, pichiffi, tiloli*
squeeze out, to; *bushli*
squeeze up, to; *bochunoli*
squeezed; *atelichi, bichupa, bochokachi, bochopa, bochunoa, busha, kataya, tilefa, tiliffi, tiloa*
squint, to; *tohkilet pisa*
squint-eyed, *nishkin shanaiya*
squirm, to; *tononoli*
squirrel, *fani*
squirrel, a large yellow; *falankna*
squirrel, a young; *fani ushi*
squirrel, black; *fani lusa*
squirrel, flying; *pali*
squirrel, fox; *fanakla*
squirrel, gray; *fani okchako, fanitasho*
squirrel, ground; *chinisa*
squirrel shot, *nakunshi*
squirt, to; *punfachechi*
stab; *baha, bali*
stab, to; *bahaffi, bali, lifelichi, lifinha*
stab, to make; *balichi*
stabbed; *baha, bahafa*
stabber; *bahaffi, bali, lifelichi, lifinha*
stable; *anli, isuba inchuka, kamassa, kallo*
stable, to; *isuba inchuka fohki*
stable-minded, *imanukfila apissanli*
stack, *itanaha*
stack, to; *itannali*
stacked, *itanaha*
staddle; *apushi, itapushi*
staff; *api, isht tabeli, tabi*

staff, king's; *miⁿko intabi*
stag; *isi lahpitta, isi nakni humma, lapish kobafa, lapitta*
stage; *aiilaualli, iti chanaha palhki, iti patalhpo*
stagger, to; *chukfoloha, chukfulli, faiokachi, faiuⁿkli, nukwia, nukwiachi*
staggers, the; *chukfoloha*
stagnant; *talaia, yanalli*
stagnate, to; *talaia, yanallit issa*
stain, *liteha*
stain, to; *liteli*
stained, *liteha*
stair, *atuya*
stake; *apushi hika, iti hika, kali*
stake, to; *boli, kali*
stake a fence, to; *holihta itafenali*
stake out, to; *aiimpa foki*
staked; *afana, holihta itafena, kaha*
staked fence, *holihta itafena*
stale; *ahoba, kallo*
stalk, *api*
stalk, to; *fehnachi, fihopa, ilefehnachit nowa, nowa*
stall; *aiilhpeta, isuba aiimpa*
stall, to; *aiimpa foki, isuba aiimpa foki, lukchuk okakania*
stallion, *isuba nakni*
stammer, to; *anuktuklo, anumpuli anuktuklo*
stamp, *isht inchuⁿwa*
stamp, to; *habli, hali, inchunli*
stamped, *inchuⁿwa*
stanch, to; *hokofa, hokoffi, issa, issachi*
stanched; *hokofa, issa*
stand, a; *ahika, aianumpuli, aiimpa iskitini, hika, hikia*
stand, to; *akkahika, atelifa, hieli, hikia, hioht aⁿsha, hioli, isso, lopulli, takali, talaia, taloha, tala*
stand, to be able to; *hikia toba*
stand around, to; *hikikiⁿa, hiohmaⁿya, hioht maⁿya, talohmaⁿya, talot maya*
stand at, to; *ahika*
stand erect, to; *akashchukali*
stand in, to; *achuⁿsha, achushoa, ahika, alacha, alachaya, alhto, shamalli, shamoli*
stand near each other, to; *itakonofa*
stand on, to; *hika, ontalaia*
stand on end, to; *achushkaⁿchi*
stand out, to; *kucha, okbileli*
stand over, to; *wakaya*
stand still, to; *talaia*
stand there, to; *ahika*

stand thick, to; *shabapa*
stand tiptoe, to; *shikekli, shikeli*
stand up, to; *haioli, lochussa, yuhchashali*
stand up for, to; *apepoa*
standard, *alhpisa, shapha*
standers, *haioli*
standing; *hika, hinli*
standing in, *talaia*
standing on, *ataloha*
standing over against, *ichapaka*
standing round, *hiohmaⁿya*
staple, *alhpesa*
staple, a; *aiafacha, tali chinakbi*
star, *fichik*
star, blazing; *fichik luak, fichik pololi*
star, large; *fichik chito*
star in the forehead; *ibaktasanli, ibaktasaⁿshli*
starch, to; *chilakbichi*
starched, *chilakbi*
stare, *pisa*
stare, to; *pisa*
stare at, to; *okchilanli, okchilaⁿshli, okchilunli*
stark; *bano, beka*
starlight, *fichik tohwikeli*
starry; *fichik aⁿsha, fichik laua*
stars, the ell; *fichik isi nala silhhi*
stars, the yard; *fichik baieta, fichik isi nala silhhi*
start; *aiisht ia, fullottokachi, wakaya, yikottakachi*
start, to; *anuklakancha, hehka, hiket ia, ia, ilhkolichi, minti, nuklakanchichi, nukshichaiakachi, nukshoblichi, wakaya, wakayachi, yilishachi, yiliya, yullichi*
start, to cause to; *wakayachi*
start back, to; *falamakachi, falamakachi, falamat minti*
start from, to; *aiali, aiisht ia, attat ia*
start of a horn, *lapish filamminchi*
start off !, *hotepa*
start off, to; *ilhkoli, mia, mintichi, wakaya*
start on !, *tepa*
start quick, to; *nuklibekachi*
start with, to; *ia*
starter; *hehka, nukwia, wakaya*
startle, to; *hehka, hehkachi, nuklakanchichi, nuklakashli, nukshoblichi*
startled, *nukshopa*
starvation, *hopoa*
starve, to; *hochaffo, hochaffochi, hochaffochit abi, hochaffot illi, hopoa*

starved, *hochaffo*
starved to death, *hochaffot illi*
state; *aiahanta, yakni*
state, a; *aiulhti, ulhti, ulhti achafa*
state, to; *anoli, atokoli*
state of, *atuk*
state prison, *hatak yuka atoksali*
stated, *anoa*
statehouse; *aboha hanta, anunka hanta, chuka hanta*
stately, *chaha*
statement, *anumpa*
statesman, *hatak nan ithana*
station; *ahika, ahikia*
station, to; *hilechi*
stationary; *kanallahe keyu, kobafahe keyu*
stationer, *holisso kanchi*
statue; *hatak holba, na holba*
stature, *chaha*
statute, *anumpa alhpisa*
stave, *iti shima*
stave, to; *koli*
stay; *anta, halanli, tikeli*
stay, to; *anta, anukcheto, ashwa, atta, halalli, issachi*
stay at, to; *aianta*
stay there, to; *aiashwa*
stay with, to; *ahinna, anta, ibaianta*
stayed; *nuktala, yokopa*
stays, *tikeli*
stead, *alhtoba*
stead of another, to be in the; *alhtoba*
steadfast; *kamassa, kallo*
steadiness; *kamassa, kallo*
steady, *kallo*
steady, to; *halalli, inshi*
steak, *nipi okchanki tushali*
steal, to; *hunkupa*
steal the affections, to; *chunkash ishi*
stealer, *hunkupa*
stealth, *hunkupa*
steam; *kifeta, kifilli, kofkokachi, kofota, kofulli, shoboli, shobota*
steam, to; *hobechi, kifeta, kifetachi, kifilli, kofkokachi, kofkoli, kofota, kofulli, kofullichi*
steam, to cause to; *kifillichi*
steamboat; *peni luak, peni luak shali*
steamed; *kifeta, kofota*
steamed potato, *ahe holbi*
steamer, *peni luak*
steaming, *hobechi*

steed, *isuba*
steel; *tali kallo, tali kallo atoba*
steel, to; *tali kallo achukalli*
steel spring, *tali poloma*
steel spring, small; *tali poloma ushi*
steel used in striking fire, *tali luak*
steeled, *tali kallo achaka*
steelyards; *isht wekichi, nan isht weki, nan isht wekichi*
steep, *chaha*
steep, to; *okkachi*
steeped, *ulhkachi*
steeper, *aiulhkachi*
steepness, *chaha*
steer, *wak hobak*
steer, working; *wak hobak tonksali*
steering oar, *penafana*
stem; *atakali, atakoli, isht takali, isht takoli*
stem, to; *asanni, asonali*
stem of a boat; *peni hasimbish, peni ibish*
stemmed, *katapa*
stench; *kosoma, kotoma, na shua, shua*
stench, to cause; *kotomachi*
stentorian, *chitoli*
step; *ahabli, habli, toba*
step, to; *habli, hali*
step aside, to; *kanali*
stepbrother, *itibapishi toba*
stepchild, *ushi toba*
stepdame, *ishki toba*
stepdaughter, *ushetik toba*
stepfather, *inki toba*
stepmother; *ishki toba, toba*
stepping place, *ahabli*
stepping-stone, *atuya*
steps; *atuya, hali*
stepsister, *intek toba*
stepson; *saso toba, ushi toba*
sterile, *waya*
sterling; *achukma, aianli*
sterilize, to; *ilbashachi, wayachi*
stern; *palammi, kallo*
stern of a boat, *ibish*
sternum, *ikkishi foni*
stew, *honni*
stew, to; *honi*
steward, *chukachafa nan isht atta*
stewed, *honni*
stewed dry, *ashippa*
stick; *iti tapa, iti taptua*
stick, to; *abili, albo, albochi, bchaffi, bali, hilechi, takali*

stick in, to; *okfanya, shamallichi, shamoli, shamolichi*
stick on, to; *aialbo*
stick to, to; *alapali*
stickle, to; *apela*
stickler; *itachoa, itishi*
sticky; *aialbo, shinasbi, shinashbi*
stiff; *chilakbi, kamassa, kallo, talakchi*
stiff leg, *iyi kallo*
stiff-necked, *ilapunla*
stiffen, to; *akmo, chilakbi, chilakbichi, ilapunla, kamassa, kamassalli, kallo, kallochi*
stiffened; *chilakbi, kamassa*
stiffening, *isht kallochi*
stiffly; *kamassa, kallo*
stiffness; *chilakbi, ilapunla, kamassa, kallo*
stifle, to; *issachi, luhmi, mosholichi, nukbikili, oktabli*
stifled, *mosholi*
stigma, *inchunwa*
stigmatize, to; *hofayali, inchunli*
stiletto, *bashpo isht itibi*
still; *chilosa, chulosa, moma, samanta*
still, to; *chulosachi, issachi, nuktalali, oka homi ikbi*
still, to become; *chulosa*
still and without wind, *alohbi*
still water, *oktimpi*
stillborn, *illicha atta*
stilled; *chulosa, nuktala*
stillness; *nuktala, yohbi*
stilly, *lumasi*
stimulant; *ikhinsh okchalechi, okchalechi*
stimulate, to; *okchalechi, yimintachi*
stimulated; *okcha, yimmita*
stimulus, *nan isht okchalechi*
sting; *innaki, isht nali, isht pila, naki, nali*
sting, to; *honali, nali*
stinginess, *inhollo*
stinging, strong; *shikanli*
stinging worm, *hatak holhpa*
stingy; *inholitopa, inhollo, nan inholitopa, nan inhollo*
stink, to; *bitema, nakshobi, shua*
stinking, *kotoma*
stint; *alhpisa, imaialechi*
stint, to; *olabbi*
stipend, *alhtoba*
stipulated, *alhpesa*
stipulation, *alhpisa*
stir; *shinihachi, timihachi*

stir, to; *afulli, anya, ia, ilhkolechi, ilhkoli, ilhkolichi, okchalechi, tasalli, tiabli, tiwakachi, tualichi*
stir, to make or cause to; *afullichi*
stir up, to; *tiwalichi*
stirred; *affula, alhfula, tiapa, tuakachi*
stirrer; *anya, iachi, ilhkolichi, tani, tohnochi*
stirrup; *ahabli, talahabli*
stirrup leather, *talahabli isht talakchi*
stirrup strap, *talahabli isht talakchi*
stitch, *aialhchunwa*
stitch, to; *achunli, yikili, yikilichi*
stitch, to cause to; *yikilichi*
stitched; *alhchunwa, yikila*
stitcher, *yikili*
stitching, *achunli*
stock; *alhpoa, nan alhpoa*
stock, a; *api, inuchi, isht atia, isht atiaka, nan ithana, tonnik*
stock, to; *boli, hopi, nan alhpoba imatali, opi*
stock in bank, *tali holisso*
stock lock, *isht ashana*
stockade, *holihta kallo*
stocked; *holopi, ollupi*
stocking, *iyubi huski*
stocky, *chito*
stole; *akkapushli, anchi*
stolen; *hunkupa, hulhkupa*
stomach; *bakna, chunkash, nukoa*
stomach, the large; *takoba*
stomach, to; *nukoa*
stone, *tali*
stone (of fruit), *foni*
stone, large; *tali chito, tali hochito*
stone, mill; *tali tanch afotoha*
stone, to; *tali isht boli, tali isht bot abi, tali isht holihtachi*
stone, to become; *tali toba*
stone blind, *nishkin lapat kania*
stone bruise, *chukfi nishkin*
stone horse, *isuba nakni*
stone pot, *tali shuti*
stone ridge, *tali bacha*
stone wall, *tali holihta*
stonecutter; *tali bashli, tali chanli*
stoned, *tali isht boa*
stony; *kilhkiki, tali foka, tali laua*
stony region, *tali foka*
stool; *aiomanili, iti wanya, ulbal ont ia*
stool, to have a; *ulbal ont ia*
stoop; *aboha hoshontika, waiya*
stoop, to; *akka ia, waiyachi*

stooped, *tubbona*
stooping, *tobbona*
stop, *issa*
stop, to; *atabli, atapachi, auola, hikia, issa, issachi, kamali, katabii, oktabli, oktaptuli, olabbi, takabli, yokopa*
stop sucking, to; *pishi issa*
stop the mouth, to; *itakha akkami*
stop up, to; *akamali, akamolechi, akamoli, akammi, asheli, kammi, lablichi*
stop water, to; *oktabli*
stoppage; *anukbikeli, atapa, atapoa*
stoppage in the throat, to cause; *anukbikelichi*
stopped; *akama, akkama, kama, oktapa, yokopa*
stopped up; *alhkama, alhkomoa, labli*
stopper; *akammi, issachi, isht oktapa, oktabli*
stopple; *isht akama, isht alhkama, isht okshilita, oka abicha isht alhkama*
store; *aiitatoba, alhpoyak aiasha*
store, to; *ashachi, boli, imatali*
stored, *imalhtaha*
'storehouse; *aiitatoba chuka, alhpoyak aiasha, nana aiitatoba*
storekeeper; *nan chumpa, nan ittatoba*
storeroom, *alhpoyak aiasha*
stories, to make; *anumpa chukushpa ikbi*
storm; *itibbi, mali chito*
storm, to; *apeli, mali chito, nukoa, yilepa*
stormy, *mali chito laua*
story; *anumpa nan anoli, holisso nan anoli*
story, an idle; *shukha anumpa*
story, to; *anoli*
story book, *holisso nan anoli*
story in a building, *chuka itontala*
story-teller; *anoli, anumpa ikbi*
stout; *chito, kallo, kilimpi, lampko*
stout, to render; *naknichi*
stove, cooking; *tali aholhponi*
stow, to; *boli*
straddle, to; *wakcha, wakchala, wakchalali, wakchat nowa*
straddle, to make; *wakchalalichi, wakchalachi, wakchalashlichi*
straddle, to stand; *wakchat hikia*
straddle and walk, to; *wakchat nowa*
straddle on, to; *wakcha*
straddled, *wakchalashli*
straddled over, *wakcha*
straggle, to; *folota*

straggle away, to; *fimimpa*
straggler; *hatak kania, yoshoba*
straight; *anli, apissa, apissali, apissanli, ashalinka, alhpesa, chekusi*
straight, to make; *apissallechi*
straight and tapering, *ibakshakanli*
straighten, to; *apissallechi, apissalli, katanlichi, kallochi*
straightened, *apissa*
straightlaced, *kallo*
straightway; *ashalinka, chekusi, mih*
strain; *talofa naha, yichina*
strain, to; *hoiya, hoiyachi, holuyachi, linfa, yichina, yichinachi*
strained; *hoiya, holuya, shepa, talofa naha*
strainer, *ahoiya*
straining, *hoiyachi*
strait; *aiatikonofa, ilbasha*
strait-laced; *chunuko talakchi, kamassa*
straiten, to; *ilbashachi, pathachi*
straitly, *kallo*
strand; *chula, chulata, oka ont alaka*
strand, red; *na humma*
strand, the; *okhata ont alaka*
strand, to; *ontalali, ontala*
stranded, *ontala*
strange; *inla, ma*
strange thing, *nan inla*
strangely, *inlat*
strangeness; *inla, kapassa*
stranger; *hatak inla, oklush inla*
strangle, to; *akamolechi, akomolechi, anuklamalli, anuklamallichi, nuklamoli, nuklamolichi, nuklamolli, nuklamollichi, nukshikanlichi, nuktakali, nuktakalichi, shikanlichi*
strangle, to cause to; *nuklamolichi*
strangled; *anuklamalli, nuklamoli, nuklamolli, nuksakki, nukshikanli, nukshikanshli, nuktakali*
strangler, *anuklamallichi*
strangulation, *anuklamallichi*
strap; *aseta, inuchi, isht ahabli, isht halupalli*
strap, to; *aseta isht fammi*
strapped, *shuahchi*
stratagem, *haksichi*
straw, *onush api*
straw, a; *api*
straw cutter, *onush api isht basha*
strawberry, *biunko*
strawberry vine, *biunko api*
stray, *kania*

stray, to; *folota, hopakichi, kạnia, tạmoa, yoshoba*
strayed, *kạnia*
streak; *basoa, laⁿfa*
streak, to; *basoachi, laⁿfi, maleli*
streaked; *basoa, laⁿfa, yạfimpa*
stream; *bok, okhina, yanạlli*
stream, to; *yanạlli*
streamer, *shạpha*
street; *aiitạnowa, hina, hina pạtha*
strength; *imanukfila chito, isht alampko, kamạssa, kạllo, kilimpi, lampko, na kạllo*
strengthen, to; *aⁿlichi, apela, kamạssạlli, kạllochi, kạllot ia, kilimpichi, lampkuchi, yimintạchi*
strengthened; *akamạssa, kamạssa, kạllo, lampko*
strengthener; *kamạssạlli, kạllochi, lampkuchi*
strenuous; *chilita, yiminta*
stress; *kạllo, nana fehna*
stretch, to; *chisbi, chisbichi, chisemo, chisemoa, chisemochi, chisemoli, chitoli, mabli, mampoa, mampoli, shebli, shepa, shepkạchi, shepoa, shepolichi, shepoli, tikelichi, yichina, yohapa*
stretch, to cause to; *shepolichi*
stretch forth, to; *weli*
stretch in length, to; *mampa*
stretch out, to; *mampli, weli*
stretched; *ashatapa, ashatapoa, auataya, chisbi, chisemo, chisemoa, lapa, lohama, mampa, mampoa, shepa, shepkạchi, shepoa, tikeli, yohapa*
stretcher; *mampli, shebli*
strew, to; *fimibli, patali*
strewed; *fima, patạlhpo*
strewn, *fimimpa*
stricken in years, *sipokni*
strict; *aⁿli, ạlhpiesa, katanli, kạllo, palạmmi*
strictly, *aⁿli*
strictness; *katanli, kạllo, palạmmi*
stride, to; *chali, hopakichit habli*
strife; *itạchoa, itishi*
strike, to; *abolichi, aiisso, aⁿya, bakaha, boli, chanli, fahama, isso, kasali, kạbalichi, lạsaha, lạsalichi, litelichi, litiⁿha, mạssalichi, mitihạchi, nukbepli, olachi, pạsalichi, pokạffi, sakaha, sakalichi, sokuⁿha, tạmmaha, tạmmalichi, tipelichi, tipiⁿha, washạlahinchi, washạlwaⁿya*
strike, to cause to; *issochi*
strike against, to; *ạboa, bikelichi*

strike and knock off, to; *mokafa*
strike at or on, to; *afahama*
strike with lightning, to; *hiloha ạbi*
striker; *boli, isso, lạsaha, litiⁿha, na boli, nan isso, sakalichi, tipiⁿha*
striking, *sakaha*
string; *aholhtạpi, aseta, holhtampi, isht talakchi, libata, nan isht talakchi*
string, to; *chakoli, hotampi, hotạpi*
stringiness; *likaha, likaⁿsha*
stringy; *akshish laua, likaha, likaⁿsha*
strip, a; *falaia*
strip, to; *ilbạshachi, luffi, liffi*
strip, to cause to; *fakoplichi, liffichi*
strip naked, to; *nipi banuchi*
strip off, to; *aliⁿffi, aliⁿkạchechi, fakoli, fakopli, leli, lili, loⁿffi, loli, nacholi, nacholichi, nipalichi, shuⁿfi*
stripe; *basoa, basoli, fahama, ilbạsha, lukalichi, miⁿsa, misisuⁿkạchi*
stripe, to; *basoachi, basoli, oklauinlichi, simoachi*
striped; *basasuⁿkạchi, basoa, chinisa, misisuⁿkạchi, oklauinli, simoa, yạfimpa*
striped work, to make; *basolichi*
stripes, small; *basosuⁿkạchi, simoa*
stripling, *ạlla himmita*
stripped; *ashabi, fakowa, ilbạsha, lufa, liⁿfa, loⁿfa, loha, shuⁿfa, wehpoa*
stripped of limbs, *nipafa*
stripped off; *alifa, aliⁿkạchi, liha, loha, nipali*
stripped off, to cause to be; *fakolichi*
stripper; *fakolichi, fakopli, liffi*
stripping; *fakoli, fakopa*
strive, to; *achowa, achunanchi, apakshạna, bạnna, ichapa, itishi, pakna, pisa*
striver; *itimpakna, itishi*
stroke, *isso*
stroke, a single; *mitelichi*
stroke, to; *hạmmi, pasholi*
stroked; *hạma, pashoha*
stroker, *hạmmi*
stroll, to; *folota*
stroller, *folota*
strong; *akạllo, homi, kalama, kamạssa, kamạssạlli, kạllo, kilimpi, lampko, palạmmi, nan inlaua*
strong, not; *hoyapa*
strong, to make; *akạllochi, nukhomechi*
strong enough, *kạllo ạlhpesa*
strong man, *hatak kamạssa*
stronger, *kạllo iⁿshali*
strongest, *kạllo iⁿshaht tali*

stronghold, *holihta kallo*
strongly, *kallot*
strop, razor; *nutakhisht shaⁿfa ahala-*
puchi
strop, to; *sholichi*
stroud, *nana*
stroud, black; *nan lusa*
stroud, blue; *nan okchako*
stroud, red; *na humma chulata, nan*
tishepa
stroud, white; *nan tohbi*
structure, *chuka*
struggle; *itishi, yichina,*
struggle, to; *ilafoa, komunta, nukhammi,*
yichina, yiliya
struma, *chilanli*
strumpet; *hatak lusa haui, haui, ohoyo*
haui
strung; *holhtapi, honala*
strung up and dried, *chakowa*
strut, to; *fehnachi, ilefehnachit nowa,*
tema
stub, *iti kolofa*
stub, to; *ibetabli, itakshish kulli, wak-*
shish
stubbed, *kitikshi*
stubble; *onush abasha, onush aialmo*
stubble field, *onush aialmo*
stubborn; *haksi, ilapunla, kallo*
stuck in; *shamalli, shamoli*
stud, *iti atikoa*
student; *holisso ithana, holisso pisa, pisa*
studhorse, *isuba nakni*
studious; *achunanchit pisa, pisa shali*
study; *anukfilli, apiⁿsa, holisso apisa*
study, to; *anukfilli, holisso pisa, pisa*
study together, to; *holisso itibapisa*
stuff; *alhpoyak, nan tanna, nana*
stuff, to; *abeli, alotoli*
stuffed; *alota, albiha*
stuffing, *isht albiha*
stultify, to; *tasembochi*
stumble, *ibetabli*
stumble, to; *anaktibaffi, anaktiballi, ash-*
achi, ibetabli, yoshoba, yoshobbi
stumble, to make; *ibetablichi*
stumbler; *ashachi, ibetabli*
stump; *ahokofa, akolofa, iti kolofa, tilofa*
stump, to; *ibetabli, paⁿfi*
stun, to; *haksichi, haksubachi, nukbepli,*
nukbepuli, talissachi
stun, to cause to; *nukbeplichi*
stung, *nala*
stunned; *haksi, nukbepa, nukbepoa*

stunt, to; *liposhichi*
stunted, *liposhi*
stupefy, to; *kotachi*
stupendous; *hocheto, na fehna*
stupid, *imanukfila iksho*
stupor; *imanukfila iksho, kostinit kania,*
nusilhha
sturdy, *kallo*
stutter, to; *anumpuli anuktuklo, isun-*
lash illi
stutterer, *isunlash illi*
sty (for swine), *shukha iⁿhollihta*
sty (on the eyelid), *hashi labi, hoshila,*
isht aniwilali, okshauina, oshawilah,
shawila
sty, to have a; *hoshilabi*
style (designation), *hochifo*
style (manner), *aiimalhpesa, aiyamohmi,*
anumpa
style (to cross a fence), *atuya*
style, to; *hochifo*
styled, *hochifo*
suavity; *yohbi, yukpa*
subacid, *hauashko chohmi*
subdivide, to; *chuti*
subdue, to; *imaiyachi, ishalichi, kostinin-*
chi
subdue the heart, to; *chuⁿkash yohbichi*
subdued; *imaiya, kostini, nuktala*
subdued heart, *chuⁿkash yohbi*
subduer; *imaiyachi, kostininchi*
subject; *hatak, hepulla, nakni tashka,*
nana, nutaka aⁿsha, tashka
subject, to; *imaiyachi, yukachi*
subject-matter of a speech, *anumpa*
nushkobo
subjected, *yuka*
subjection; *imaiya, imaiyachi, nutaka,*
nutaka ia
subjoin, to; *achakali*
subjugate, to; *yukachi*
sublimate, to; *chahachi*
sublime; *chaha, chito, holitopa*
sublime, to; *chahachi, holitoblichi*
sublimity; *chaha, chito, holitopa*
submerge, to; *oklobushli, oklobushlichi,*
oklubbi, oklubbichi
submerged, *oklobushli*
submission, *nutaka ia*
submissive; *ilbasha, imantia*
submit, to; *nutaka ia*
suborn, to; *holabichi*
suborner, *holabichi*
subscribe, to; *hochifo takalichi, ome ahni*

subscriber, *hochifo takalichi*
subsequent; *himmak, iakaiya*
subserve, to; *apela*
subservient, *apela*
subside, to; *chulosa, habofa, haboli, halata, hopola, nuktala, oka tala, shiota, shippa, shippachi*
subsided; *habofa, haboli, shippa*
subsidiary, *apela*
subsist, to; *ilhpak atali, okchaⁿya*
subsistence, *ilhpak*
substance; *imilayak, nana*
substantial; *achukma, aiaⁿli, kallo*
substantiate, to; *achchukmali, aiaⁿlichi*
substitute, *alhtoba*
subterraneous, *yakni anuⁿkaka*
subtle; *haksi, kostini, tapuski*
subtract, to; *akuchaweli, kashabli*
subtracted; *akuchawiha, kashapa*
subtraction, *akuchaweli*
suburb, *biliⁿka*
subvert, to; *kinalichi, kinaffi*
subverted; *kinafa, kinali*
subverter, *kinaffi*
succeed, to; *aiaⁿli, alhtoba*
succeeder; *alhtoba, iakaiya*
succeeding, *achaⁿka*
success, *aiaⁿli*
successful, *aiaⁿli*
successor; *alhtoba, iakaiya*
succinct, *tilofasi*
succor, *apelachi*
succor, to; *apela, apelachi*
succorer, *apelachi*
succulent, *hokulbi*
succumb, to; *nutaka ia*
such; *chohmi, chomi, yohmi*
suck, *pishi*
suck, to; *okfulli, pishi*
suck in, to; *oka foyuha*
sucked (by the doctors), *laha*
sucker; *chalabakko, apatali*
suckle, to; *pishechi*
suckle a child, to; *alla pishechi*
suckling; *alluⁿsi, piⁿshi*
sudden; *tushpa, yakosi ititakla*
sudden motion, *lip*
suddenly; *ashaliⁿka, haksint, yakosi ititakla*
sudorific, *ikhiⁿsh lakshachi*
suds; *isht ahchifa pokpoki, pokpoki*
suds, to make; *pokpokechi*
sue, to; *anumpa kallo onuchi*
sued, *anumpa kallo onutula*

suet; *haiyiⁿhchi nia, wak bila*
suffer, to; *ahni, halalli, ilbasha, imaleka, issikkopa, ome ahni*
sufferer, *ilbasha*
suffering, *ilbasha*
suffice, to; *fihobli, laua*
sufficed, *fihopa*
sufficiency; *alhpesa, laua*
sufficient; *alhpesa, laua*
sufficient number, *katohmona*
suffocate, to; *nuklamalli, nukliⁿfa, nukliⁿffi, nuksiteli*
suffocated; *nukliⁿfa, nuksita*
suffocating, *nukshikanli*
suffrage, *holisso*
sugar; *hapi champuli, shokula*
sugar, loaf; *hapi champuli tohbi*
sugar, lump; *hapi champuli tohbi*
sugar, to; *hapi champuli yammichi*
sugar, white; *hapi champuli tohbi*
sugar barrel, *hapi champuli aialhto*
sugar bowl, *hapi champuli aialhto*
sugar box, *hapi champuli aialhto*
sugar cane; *hapi champuli api, taⁿchuka*
suggest, to; *achi, anoli*
suicide; *abi, ilebi*
suicide, to commit; *abi*
suit, *asilhha*
suit, to; *alhpesa, yohmi aialhpesa, yukpa, yukpali*
suit exactly, to; *alhpiesa*
suit of clothes, *fohka*
suitable; *aialhpesa, alhpesa, imaⁿka*
suited, *alhpesa*
suitor; *anumpa alhpisa onuchi, asilhha*
sulky; *hashaⁿya, nukoa*
sulky, a; *iti chanalli iskitini palhki, iti chanaha palhki*
sullen; *baⁿshkiksho, nukoa*
sullied, *liteha*
sully, to; *liteli, lusachi*
sulphate of magnesia, *ikhiⁿsh hapi holba*
sulphate of soda, *ikhiⁿsh hapi holba*
sulphur, *hituk lakna*
sultriness, *alohbi*
sultry; *alohbi, lashpa, palli*
sultry, to cause to be; *alolichi*
sum, *moma*
sum total, *aiali*
sumac; *bashukcha, bati*
sumless, *aholhtina iksho*
summary; *anumpa nushkobo, anumpa tikba*
summed, *holhtena*

summed up, *kaha*
summer; *palli, toffa*
summer, the first part of; *toffahpi*
summer, to; *toffa anta na topulli*
summit; *onchaba, paknanka, tabokaka, wishakchi*
summon, to; *anoli, hoyo*
summoner, *na hoyo*
sumpter; *isuba shapo shali, isuba shapuli*
sumptuous, *holitopa*
sun, *hashi*
sun, to; *hashontombichi, hufka, ufka*
sunbeam; *hashtomi, tombi*
sunburnt, *hashi lua*
sunlike, *hashi holba*
Sunday, *nitak hollo*
sunder, to; *hokoffi, kashabli, litaffi, tabli*
sunder at, to; *atabli, ataptuli*
sunder once, to; *himonna tapli*
sundered; *hokofa, kashapa, litafa*
sundown, *hashi okatula*
sundry; *ilaiyuka, kanomona*
sunflower, *hashi*
sung; *alhtalwa, talwa*
sunned, *holufka*
sunrise, *hashi kucha*
sunset, *hashi okatula*
sunshine; *hashi atomi, hashtomi, tombi*
sup, to; *ishko, nanabli, ninak impa impa*
superabound, to; *atapa, abanabli, laua*
superabound, to cause to; *atablichi*
superabounding, *affekomi* .
superadd, to; *atabli*
superannuated, *sipokni atapa*
superb; *chito, na fehna*
supercilious; *ilapunla, ilefehnachi*
supereminent; *achukma atapa, achukma inshali, inshali*
superficial; *apaknali, paknaka*
superfine, *achukma inshali*
superfluous, *atapa fehna*
superintend, to; *apistikeli, pelichi*
superintendent; *nan apesachi, pelicheka*
superior; *imaiya, inshali, sipokni inshali*
superlative, *inshaht tali*
supernatural being, *na hollo*
supervise, to; *apistikeli*
supervisor, *apistikeli*
supine; *ahah ahni ikshc, intakobi, watalhpi*
supinely, *watalhpi*
supper; *ninak impa, oktili impa, opiaka impa*
supplant, to; *alhtoba hosh ishi, fahammi*

supple; *lapushki, walohbi*
supple, to; *lapushkichi, walohbichi*
suppled; *walasha, walohbi*
suppliant; *asilhha, nana silhha*
supplicant, *nana silhha*
supplicate, to; *asilhha, ilbasha*
supplied, *imalhtaha*
supply; *laua, laua alhpesa*
supply, to; *imatali*
supply a place, to; *atobachi*
support; *aiokchanya, bikeli, halalli, tikeli*
support, to; *aiantichi, apela, atali, halalli*
supporter; *bikeli, halalli, imatali, kamassalli, tikeli*
suppose, to; *imahoba*
supposition, *imahoba*
suppress, to; *akkachi, imaiyachi, issachi, luhmi, nuktalali, takabli*
suppressed, *luma*
suppression, *oktapa*
suppurate, to; *aninchichi*
suppurate, to cause to; *aninchichechi*
suppuration, *aninchichi*
suppuration, to promote; *aninchichechi*
supremely, *inshati*
surcharge, to; *atablit abeli*
surcingle; *ikfuka isht talakchi, ikfukasita, isuba foka sita*
surcingled, *iffuka sita*
surd, *haponaklo*
sure; *akallo, akat, anli*
surely; *anli, anlit, ba, chatik, hepulla, kaheto, pulla*
surety; *ahinna, aianli*
surf, *oka pokpoki*
surface; *apaknali, pakna, paknaka*
surfeit, *impa atabli*
surfeit, to; *atablit apa, ipeta atabli*
surge; *banatha, oka banatha, oka bananya*
surge, to; *oka banathat anya*
surly; *hashanya, nukoa*
surmise, *imahoba*
surmise, to; *imahoba*
surmount, to; *abanabli, imaiya, imaiyachi*
surname, *apunta*
surpass, to; *imaiya, imaiyachi, ishalichi*
surpassing; *imaiya, inshali*
surplus; *atapa, alhtampa*
surprise; *ata, haksint ishi, okko, okokko, ta, yitishachi*
surprise, to; *anuktakashli, haksichi, haksint ishi*

surprise, to feel; *anuklamampa*
surprised; *anuklakancha, nuklakancha*
surrender, *ilissa*
surrender, to; *ilissa, na halupa boli, nutaka ia*
surrender, to cause to; *ilissąchi*
surround, to; *aboluktoli, afololichi, afolubli, afoluplichi, apakfobli, apakfoli*
surrounded; *apakfokąchi, apakfopa*
surtout; *ilefoka chito, na foka chashąna falaia*
survey, *pisa*
survey, to; *apesa, chuli, pisa*
surveyed; *ąlhpesa, chula*
surveyor, *apistikeli*
suspect, to; *ahni, imahoba*
suspend, to; *atakalichi, takalechi*
suspended; *ąba takali, takali, takoli*
suspender, *tahchabana*
suspenders; *hąnawia, hąnnaweli, obala foka isht haląlli*
suspense, *anuktuklo*
suspicious, *nuktąla*
sustain, to; *haląlli*
sustained; *imąlhtaha*
sustenance; *aiokchaⁿya, ilhpak, nan ilimpa*
suture; *aiitąchakilli, nushkobo foni aiitąchakąlli*
swab, to; *kasholichi*
swaddle, to; *na foka afoli*
swaddled, *na foka ąlhfoa*
swag, to; *waiya*
swagger, to; *ilefehnąchi*
swaggerer, *ilefehnąchi*
swain, *hatak himmita*
swallow; *isht nanąbli, isht nąlli, kolumpi, nanąbli,, nąląp, nąlli,*
swallow (bird), *chopilak*
swallow, a single; *nanąbli achafa*
swallow, half a; *nanąbli ikląnna*
swallow, to; *bąlakachi, nanąbli, nąlli*
swallow, to cause to; *nanąblichi, nąllichi*
swallow largely, to; *chitot ishko*
swallow loudly, to; *kolakachi*
swallowing, the act of; *nanąbli*
swamp; *bok anuⁿka, luⁿsa, patasąchi*
swamp, a large; *luⁿsa chito*
swamp, a large round; *luⁿsa tikpi*
swamp, an open; *luⁿsa shahbi*
swamp, the edge, end, or limits of a; *luⁿsa aiąli*
swampy; *bok anuⁿka, luⁿsa foka*

swan, *okak*
swan, a young; *okak ushi*
swap, *itatoba*
swap, to; *faląmmichi, itatoba*
swapper, *itatoba*
sward, *hąshuk*
swarm; *awiachi, laua*
swarm, to; *awiachi, wiha*
swarthy, *lusa*
swath, *hąshuk itąnaha*
swathe, to; *afoli*
sway, to; *bikota, pelichi, waiya, waiyąchi*
swear, to; *anumpa kąllo ilonuchi, anumpa kąllo isht anumpuli*
swear by, to; *miha*
sweat, *laksha*
sweat, a profuse; *laksha chito*
sweat, to; *hobechi, laksha, lakshąchi*
sweat blood, to; *issish laksha*
sweaty; *laksha, shinąsbi, shinisbi*
sweep, to; *aⁿya, bąshpuli, fali, paⁿshpuli, piⁿfi*
sweep the whole, to; *mominchi*
sweep together, to; *apeli*
sweeper; *bąshpuli, paⁿshpuli*
sweepings, *chupilhkąsh*
sweet; *akomachi, balama, champuli, kąshaha, sinimpa*
sweet, to make; *balamąchi*
sweet bread, *pąska champuli*
sweet gum, *hika*
sweet potato, *ahe*
sweeten, to; *champuląchi, yąmmichi*
sweeten with, to; *aiyąmmichi*
sweeten with sugar, to; *hąpi champuli yąmmichi*
sweetened; *aiyammi, champuli, yąmmi*
sweetened with, *aiyąmmi*
sweetened with sugar, *hąpi champuli yąmmi*
sweetness, *champuli*
swell; *bokko, ibish, oka banątha, shatali, tikpi*
swell, to; *chitoli, ilefehnąchi, iⁿshaht isht ia, kachombi toba, mitibli, mitiblichi, piakąchi, sobonoa, shataioli, shatali, shatapa, shatąbli, shatohpa, shatosholi, shitąmmi, shitibli, shitiblichi, shitimmi, shofoha, shofoli, shofolichi*
swell, to cause to; *shataiolichi, shatalichi, shatąblichi, shatąmmichi, shitiblichi, shofolichi*
swell, to make the cords; *chilinanchi*
swell and roll as water, to; *paiokąchi*

swell the lips, to; *itukshibeli*
swelled; *kachombi, mitibli, shatammi*
swelled neck or throat, *ikonla shatali*
swelling; *paffala, shatali, shatapa, sha-tabli, shatohpa, shatosholi, shofoli*
swelling, a hard; *kachombi, kochombi, shatammi*
swelling, a white; *shatohpa*
swellings, to produce; *shatosholichi*
swept; *abashpoa, panshpoa*
swept place, *abashpoa*
swerve, to; *shanaia, yoshoba*
swift; *chali, lipko, palhki, shinimpa, tushpa*
swiftly, to cause to go; *shinimpachi*
swiftness, *shinimpa*
swig, *ishko chito*
swig, to; *chitot ishko*
swill, *shukha imilhpak*
swim, to; *hachonmalhmokki, mulhmakki, okpalali, okshinilli, okshinillichi, oksho-nulli, okshonullichi, okpaloli, okpaloli-chi, okyoli*
swim (the head), to; *chukfoloha, folota*
swim, to cause to; *chukfulli, okbillichi, okpalalichi, okshinillichi, okshonullichi, okyolichi*
swimmer; *isht pinfi, okshinilli, oksho-nulli, okyoli, okyoli imponna*
swimming, *okyoli*
swindle, to; *haksichi*
swindled, *haksi*
swindler, *haksichi*
swine, *shukha*
swine lot, *shukha inhollihta*
swing; *afahata, afataha, fahattakachi*
swing, to; *fahakachechi, fahali, fahalichi, fahata, fahatachi, fahattakachi, fatali, fattahachi, takant fahakachi, tilokachi*
swing, to cause to; *fatalichi*
swing around, to; *fatohachi*
swing in, on, or at, to; *afahata*
swing slowly and heavily, to; *fahaka-chi*
swinger, *fahalichi*
swinging; *fahata, fahattakachi*
swingle, to; *fahakachi*
swingletree; *isuba ahalalli, iti isht halalli, iti ititakalli*
switch; *fuli, itapushi*
switch, to; *fuli isht fammi, mitelichi, mitinha*
switched, *fuli isht fama*
switching, *fuli isht fama*

swollen; *shataioa, shatali, shatabli, sha-tablichi, shatammi, shatammichi, sha-tohpa, shatosholi, shitibli, shofoha, shofoli*
swollen in the bowels, *ikfelichi*
swoon, *shimoha*
swoon, to; *shimoha*
sword, *bashpo falaia*
sword belt, *bashpo falaia atakali askufachi*
sword blade, *bashpo falaia halupa*
swung; *fahakachi, fahali, fahata*
sycamore; *bihi holba, fanikoyo, sini*
sycophant, *anumpa chukushpashali*
sylvan, *iti anunka*
symbol, *isht alhpisa*
sympathetic, *nukhanklo*
sympathize, to; *nukhanklo*
sympathize with, to; *ibanukhanklo*
sympathizer, *ibanukhanklo*
sympathy, *nukhanklo*
symptom, *isht alhpisa*
synagogue; *aba isht aianumpa chuka, sinakak, sinakak chuka*
synonymous, *mih*
syphilis, *luak shali*
syringe, *ikhinsh isht apunfachi*

tabby; *bakoa, basoa*
tabernacle; *aba anumpa isht aianum-puli, alhtipo, bina*
tabernacle, to; *anta*
table; *aiimpa, holisso, ilimpa*
table, to; *holissochi*
table cloth; *aiimpa onlipa, aiimpa um-patalhpo*
table knife; *bashpo ibbak pishinli, bashpo isht impa*
table leg, *aiimpa iyi*
tabor, *alepa*
tache, *isht akamassa*
tacit, *luma*
tack; *chufak chipinta, chufak ushi, chufak yushkololi*
tack, brass; *tali haksi chufak*
tack, to; *achunli, ahonalichi, honalichi, shanaia*
tackling, *iti chanaha isht halalli*
tadpole, *yalubba*
tail, *hasimbish*
tailed, to be long; *chashanoha*
tailless; *motohki, tokumpa*
tailor; *na foka ikbi, nan achunli*
tailor, to; *na foka ikbi*
tailoress; *nan achunli, ohoyo na foka ikbi, ohoyo nan achunli*
taint, to; *ashuwachi*

tainted, *shua*
take, to; *eshi, hokli, holissochi, ia, ikhana,*
  ilaueli, imaiyachi, ishi, ishko, isht, ishwa,
  nanabli, ome ahni, pelichi, pota, yichiffit
  ishi, yukachi
take, to cause to; *eshichi*
take a census, to; *hotina*
take a few, to; *achafoa*
take a start, to; *attat isht ia*
take ahead, to; *ma^nya*
take all, to; *aiokluhali, aiokluhanchi,*
  bakastuli, mominchi
take along, to; *a^nya, shali, wiha*
take along with, to; *aueli*
take also, to; *aiokluhanchi*
take and bind, to; *takchit ishi*
take and put in, to; *ishit fohki*
take and spill, to; *fohobli*
take away, to; *hota, ishi, kanallichi,*
  kanchi, kuchi, peli
take back, to; *okha*
take by the hand, to; *potoli*
take captive, to; *yukachi*
take care, to; *ahah ahni*
take care of, to; *potoni*
take down, to; *akkachi*
take ease, to; *foha*
take food, to; *impa*
take from, to; *alammi*
take heed, to; *ahah ahni, ahah imahni*
take hold of, at, or there, to; *ahalalli,*
  aieshi, aiishi
take in, to; *chukoa*
take in the arms, to; *sholi*
take it!, *maki*
take land by a lease, to; *yakni pota*
take leave, to; *ilhkoli*
take off, to; *ashueli, ashu^nffi, ishi, nipa-*
  lichi, nipaffi, shueli, shu^nfi
take on high, to; *aba isht ona*
take out, to; *akuchi, atokoa, foeli, fohobli,*
  fulli, kohchi, kucha weheli, kuchi, shu^nfi,
  tepuli, weli
take out, to cause to; *fohoblichi*
take out from, to; *akuchaweli, akuche-*
  chi, atokoli
take out of the way, to; *kanalichi*
take over, to; *tanablichi*
take part away, to; *koyoffi*
take part with, to; *apehachi*
take pay, to; *okha*
take place at, to; *ayakohmi*
take refuge, to; *atukko*

take round, to; *afolotowachi, foloto-*
  wachi
take the place of, to; *alhtoboa*
take the whole, to; *mominchi, okluhan-*
  tishi
take through, to; *alopolichi, alopullichi,*
  lopulli
take together with, to; *aiokluhanchi*
take turns with, to; *alhtoboa*
take up, to; *hilechi, oiya, peli, sholi*
taken; *alhtoka, imaiya, yuka*
taken away, *kania*
taken from; *akucha, akuchawiha*
taken hold of and drawn off; *yikefa*
taken off; *ashu^nfa, shui^nkachi, shu^nfa,*
  nipali
taken off, the place where; *ashueli,*
  ashu^nfa
taken out; *holhta, kucha, kucha wiha,*
  shui^nkachi
taken round; *folota, folotoa, fullokachi*
taken together, to cause all to be;
  aiokluhalinchi
taken up, *piha*
taker; *hokli, ishi*
takes all, one who; *tomaffi*
taking, *ishi*
tale; *anumpa, holhtina, shukha anumpa*
tale bearer; *anumpa chukushpa ikbi,*
  anumpa chukushpashali, hatak nan anoli,
  nan anoli
talent, *tali holisso weki*
talented, *imponna*
tales, to make; *anumpa chukushpa ikbi*
talk, *anumpa*
talk, a very short; *anumpa kolu^nfasi*
talk, to; *anopoli, anumpuli, aba anum-*
  puli, balbaha, kebibi, kehepa, mihachi
talk about a book, etc., to; *holisso isht*
  anumpuli
talk at random, to; *himak fokalit anum-*
  puli
talk impertinently, to; *anukchilafa*
talkative; *anumpa inlaua, anumpuli*
  shali
talked, *anumpa*
talker; *anumpuli, anumpuli shali, miha-*
  chi
tall; *chaha, falaia, hofaloha*
tallness; *falaia, hofaloha*
tallow; *isi nia, wak nia*
tallow, to; *niachi, wak nia ahammi*
tallow candle, *wak nia pala*

tallowed; *ahama, nia, wak nia ahama*
tally, to; *itilaui, itilauichi, itilauichit takolichi*
talon; *hushi iyakchush, iyakchush*
tamable, *alhpoba hinla*
tame; *alhpoba, honayo, kostini*
tame, to; *apoa*
tamed, *alhpoa*
tamely, *nan mihiksho*
tameness, *honayo*
tan, *isht hummachi*
tan, to; *hummachi*
tan vat, *wak hakshup ahumma*
tan yard, *wak hakshup ahumma*
tangle, *itashiha*
tangle, to; *shachopa, shiha, shihachi, shochoha, takali*
tangled, *shiha*
tangled, to become; *shacheha*
tank, *oka aialhto chito*
tankard, *isht ishko*
tanned, *itolankabi*
tanned red, *humma*
tanner; *na hummachi, wak hakshup hummachi*
tanner's bark, *wak hakshup isht hummachi*
tannery, *wak hakshup ahumma*
tansy, wild; *fani hasimbish holba*
tantalize, to; *haksichi*
tantamount, *itilaui*
tap; *isht alhkama, isht bicheli, oka abicha isht alhkama, oka abicha isht shana, oka isht bicha*
tap, to; *lumpli, sakaha, sokolichi, sokunha, sukolichi*
tap hole; *abicha, abichkachi, oka abicha, oka isht bicheli*
tap house, *oka akanchi*
tap root, *akshish*
taper, *ibakchufanshli*
taper, a; *pala*
taper, to; *ibakchufanli, ibakchufanlichi, ibakchufanshli, ibakchufanshlichi*
tapered, *ibakchufanli*
tapering; *chunsa, ibakchufanli, ibakshakanli*
tapster; *bicheli, oka bicheli*
tar, *tiak nia*
tar, to; *tiak nia ahammi*
tar kiln, *tiak nia atoba*
tardiness; *haklo, salaha*
tardy, *salaha*
tare, *haiyunkpulo*

target; *holisso, iti tila, tilikpi*
tarnish, to; *lusachi*
tarnished, *lusa*
tarred, *tiak nia ahama*
tarry, *tiak nia bano*
tarry, to; *aiasha, anta*
tart; *hauashko, homi, kaskaha*
tartar emetic, *ikhinsh bota ishkot hoita*
tartness, *homi*
task; *ahchiba, toksali alhpisa*
task, to; *toksalechi*
taskmaster, *tonksalechi*
tassel, *habali*
tassel, ready to; *habani*
tassel, to; *habali, hinak toba, okhinak*
tassel, to cause to; *habalichi*
tasseled, *habali*
tasseling of corn, *hinak kucha*
tasselled, *hinak toba*
taste, to; *apat pisa, ishkot pisa*
tattered, *tilalankachi*
tattle, *anumpa*
tattle, to; *achokushpalechi, achokushpali, anoli, anumpuli*
tattler; *achokushpalechi, nan anoli*
tattoo, *inchunwa*
tattoo, to; *inchunli*
tattooed, *inchunwa*
taught; *holisso ithana, ikhana, imponna*
tavern; *aboha aiimpa, chuka afoha, hatak afoha*
taverner, *chuka afoha inhikia*
tawdry, *isht ilakshema shali*
tawny, *humma*
tax, *nushkobo atobbi*
tax, to; *nushkobo atobbi onuchi, tali holisso itannali*
tax gatherer, *tali holisso itannali*
tea, *ti*
tea canister, *ti aialhto*
teach, to; *abachechi, abachi, holisso ithananchi, holisso pisachi, ikhananchi, ikhana, ikhananchi, imabachi, imponnachi, kostininchi, pisachi*
teachable; *ikhana hinla, ikhanahe pulla*
teacher; *hatak ikhananchi, hatak imabachi, holisso ithananchi, holisso pisachi, ikhananchi, ikhananchi, imabachi, imponnachi, kostininchi, nan ikhananchi, nan imabachi, nan ithananchi, nan ithananchi, nana imabachi, nukfoki, nukfokichi, pisachi*
teaching, the means of; *isht ikhananchi*

teacup, *ti isht ishko*
team, to; *hiolichi*
teamster; *hiolichi, isht a^nya, iti chąnaha isht a^nya*
teapot, *ti ahoni*
tear, *nishkin okchi*
tear, to; *fakopli, haiochichechi, liąbli, lunlichi, nukoa, lilafa, lilalichi, liląffi, lilechi, lilli*
tearer; *lilalichi, liląffi, lilechi*
tease with, to; *afekommi*
teased, *shiha*
teaser, *nukoa*
teat; *ibish, ipi^nshik, pishik*
tedder, *aseta falaia*
tedder, to; *aseta falaia isht takchi*
tedious; *achiba, ahchiba, ąlhchiba, komota, paląmmi, sąlaha*
tedious, to cause to be; *achibachi, achibali, paląmmichi*
tediousness, *ahchiba*
teem, to; *cheli, kaiya, ushi i^nfohka, ushi kaiya*
teeter, to; *takąnha*
teeth, *noti*
teethe, to; *noti offo*
tegument, *hakshup*
teil tree, *balup*
telescope, *apisa isht hopo^nkoyo*
tell, to; *a, anoachi, anoli, haiakąchi, hotina, ikhananchi*
teller; *anoli, hotina*
telltale; *nan anoli, nan anoli shali*
temerity, *nukwia iksho*
temper; *chu^nkąsh, imanukfila, itiąmmi, nuklibisha*
temper, to; *aiyuma, kąllochi, nuktalali*
temperance, *nuktanla*
tempered; *kąllo, nuktanla*
tempest; *apeli, ąbai anumpuli chuka, mali chito, mali kąllo*
temple; *aboha holitopa, chuka hanta*
temple (in anatomy), *haksun tapaiyi*
temporal; *nitak, yakni*
tempt, to; *anukpąllichi, imomaka pisa, nukpąllichi*
tempt with, to; *aianukpąllichi*
temptation; *aianukpąlli, aianukpąllika, anukpąllika, nan nukpąlli, nukpąllichi*
temptation, to feel a; *anukpąlli*
tempted; *anukpąlli, nukpąlli, ashuchoha*
tempter; *aianukpąllichi, anukpąllichi, imomaka pisa, nukpąllichi*
ten, *pokoli*

Ten Commandments, *nan ąlhpisa*
tenacious; *haląlli, kąllot ishi*
tenant, *yakni pota*
tend, to; *ahinna, ahni, apesąchi, apistikeli, a^nya*
tend the sick, to; *abeka apistikeli*
tender; *kanliksho, kostini, nukha^nklo, nuktanla, walasha, waloha, walohbi, walotąchi, walunchi, wąlwąki*
tender, a; *apesąchi*
tender, to; *imissa*
tender, to make; *lachopąchi, wąlwąkichi*
tender-footed, *iyi taha*
tender-hearted, *chu^nkash wąlwaki*
tenderloin; *anukba^nkchi, chąshwa nipi*
tenderness; *i^nhollo, kanliksho, nukha^nklo, walohbi*
tenement, *chuka*
tenet, *imanukfila*
tenfold, *inluhmi*
tenor, *miha*
tense, *kąllo*
tension; *shebli, shepa*
tent; *atepa, ąlhtipo, bina, na hąta ąlhtipo*
tent, to; *atepuli, ąttepuli, bina talali*
tented; *ąlhtipo, bina a^nsha*
tenter, wooden; *tikeli*
tenters, *isht tikoli*
tenth, *isht pokoli*
tepid; *lahba, libesha*
terce, *itąlhfoa chito*
term; *aiąli, anumpa, apelichi, nitak, tuklo*
term, to; *hochifo*
termagant, *ohoyo nukoa*
termed, *hochifo*
terminate, to; *aiąlichi, ąli, hokofa, hokoffi*
terminated, *hokofa*
termination; *ahokofa, aiąli, ataha*
terms; *anumpa, hąshi ąlhpisa*
terrapin, *luksi*
terrestrial, *yakni ahalaia*
terrible; *okpulo, paląmmi*
terribly, *fehna*
terrific, *okpulo*
terrified; *nuklakancha, nukshopa*
terrify, to; *nuklakąshli, nukshobli*
territory; *apelichi fullota, yakni*
terror; *komunta, nuklakancha, nukshopa*
tertian, *misha*
test; *isht ąlhpisa, pisa*

test, to; *apesa, pisa*
testament, *imissa*
Testament, the; *holisso holitopa*
testator, *imissa*
testatrix, *ohoyo imissa*
testifier, *atokoli*
testify, to; *aⁿli achit anoli, anumpa kạllo onuchit anoli, atokoa*
testimony; *aiatokowa, anumpa, anumpa kạllo, nan ạlhtokowa, nan isht atokowa, nan isht ạlhtokowa, oktạni*
testimony, to bear; *aiatokowali*
tether; *isht talakchi, nan isht talakchi,*
tetter; *halampa, hạllampa*
tetter, to have a; *hạllampạbi*
text; *anumpa, anumpa nushkobo*
texture, *tạnna*
thank, to; *aiokpanchi, aiokpạchi, yakoke ahni*
thankful; *aiokpanchi, yakoke ahni*
thankfulness, *aiokpanchi*
thanks, expressing; *yakoke*
that; *ak, ash, ho, hoh, hokma, ilạppak, kak, mak, mạt, na, nana hoⁿ, oⁿ, yạmma, yạmmak ash, yạmmak o, yạmmạno, yạm-mạt*
that again; *ak, inli*
that also, *inli*
that instant, *yạmmak*
that one; *yạmmak osh, yạmmạto*
that only; *ak, hak*
that same; *mih*
that too, *yạmmak kia*
that way; *imma, yạmmimma*
that which, *aⁿ, ano, chash, ka, kash, kato, kạno, kạt, kạto, kosh, ma, nana hạt*
that which is on, *ontalaia*
thatch; *hạshuk isht holmo, hạshuk um-poholmo*
thatch, to; *hạshuk isht homo, hạshuk umpohomo*
thatched, *hạshuk umpoholmo*
thaw, to; *abila, bila, bileli*
thawed, *bila*
the; *aⁿ, ak, amo, ash, at, ạt, haⁿ, hatuk, hạt, heno, het, heto, ho, ilạppa, ilạppak, k, kak, kano, kanoha, kato, kạt, kosh, ma, mak, mạno, mạt, mạto, ok, t, ya, yak, yano, yatuk, yạmma, yạt, yoⁿ*
the also; *ma, mạt*
the one; *ash, ato, ạt, ạto, kạto, mạto*
the one also, *ash*
the one which; *amo, ano, ash, haⁿ, ka*

the one which also, *ash*
the one which or who, *ato*
the one who; *at, ạt, ạto*
the present time, moment, or instant; *himak*
the present year, *himak afạmmi*
the said; *amo, ash, chash, hash, kash, mih*
the said one, *chashoⁿ*
the sake of, *hatok*
the same; *ash, hash, mih*
the same also which was, *chash*
the same that, *kash*
the same that was, *chash*
the same which; *chash, chashoⁿ*
the which; *ano, ạt, haⁿ, ka, kano, kanoha, kạno, kosh*
theater, *aiilauạlli chuka*
thee; *chi, chiⁿ, chia, chim, chin, chishno*
theft, *huⁿkupa*
their; *iⁿ, ilap, im, immi, in, yạmma*
their own, *ilap im*
their thoughts, *okla imanukfila*
theirs; *ilap, immi*
them; *aⁿ, im, nana, yạmma, yạmmak ash, yạmmak oka*
themselves, *yạmmak inli*
then; *atuk, himmakma, hokma, mạno, mih, yạmmak, yạmmak okmạto, yohmi hokmạno, yohmima*
thence; *ilạppa, itintakla, yạmmak ashoⁿ, yạmmak atuk aⁿ*
thenceforth, *yạmma*
theologian, *ạba anumpa ithana*
theology; *ạba anumpa, Chihowa ạba-numpa*
theory; *anumpa, imanukfila*
there; *a, ai, i, yạmma, yạmmak, yạmmak oka*
thereabouts, *yạmmak foka*
thereat; *isht, yạmma*
thereby; *isht, yạmmak o*
therefore; *akta, hakta, mih, yạmohmi hoka, yohmi hoka, yohmi ka, yohmi kạt, yohmima*
therein; *isht, yạmmak o*
thereof, *yạmmak atuk aⁿ*
thereupon; *chekusi, yạmohmi kako*
therewith, *isht*
thermometer, *lạshpa isht akostininchi*
these; *ilạppa, ka, yakohmi, yakomi, yạmma*
these here, *yakomi*
they; *ilạppa, okla, yạmma, yạmmak*

thick; *chito, hofobi, holishki, lotuski, okchalabi, sukko, shinashbi, toluski, tolusli*

thick, to make; *toluskichi*

thick, to make short and; *lotuskichi*

thick and close together, *chikihah*

thicken, to; *afulli, ashela, ashelachi, sukko, sukkochi*

thickened; *ashela, affula, holashki, sukko*

thicket; *aboti, bafaha, bafalli, kohchi*

thicket, a small; *bafalli talaia*

thickly; *chito, hofobi, sukko*

thickness, *hofobi*

thickset, *bilinka*

thief; *hatak hunkupa, hunkupa, na hunkupa*

thieve, to; *hunkupa*

thievish, *hunkupa shali*

thigh; *iyubi, obi*

thill, *ahalalli*

thimble; *ibbak ushi foka, tali kassa*

thin; *fahko, laua, moaha, sukko, takassa, tapaski, tapuski, wushwoki*

thin, to; *tapaskichi*

thin lips, *itakmacheli*

thine; *chin, chin, chishno, chishno yokan, chishno yokat, ish, pishno yoka, pishno yokat*

thine, to become; *chimmitoba*

thing; *na, nam, nan, nana, nana ka, nana kia, nanta*

thing, bad; *nan okpulo*

thing, one; *nan achafa*

thing, the very; *nana fehna*

thing, this; *na yakohmi*

things prepared, *nan alhtaha*

think, to; *ahni, ahoba, anukfilli, imanukfila*

think about, to; *aiahni*

think himself, to; *ilap anukfilli*

think much of, to; *fehnachi*

think of, to; *aiahni, anukfilli*

thinker, *anukfilli*

thinking, *anukfilli*

thinly, *fimimpa*

third; *atuchina, hituchina*

third time, *tuchinaha*

third time, to do the; *hituchinanchi, tuchinanchi*

thirdly, *atuchina*

thirst; *itukshila, nukshila*

thirst, to; *itukshila*

thirst, to cause; *nukshilachi*

thirsty; *itukshila, nukshila*

thirsty, to be very; *ituklua*

thirteen, *auah tuchina*

thirteenth, *isht auahchafa*

thirtieth; *isht pokoli, pokoli*

thirty, *pokoli*

this; *himak, ilap, ilappa, ilappak, ilappat, mih, yak*

this, to do; *yalabli*

this is the cause, *yakohmika kon*

this is the one; *ilappak osh, ilappano*

this is the one which; *ilappak okat, ilappato*

this moment, *himonasi*

this side, *olah*

this side of the creek, *bok ola intannap*

this sort, *yakohmi*

this the one which, *ilappak oka*

this way; *auet, et, ilappimma, imma, olah, olehma, olimma*

this year, *himak afammi*

thistle; *shumatti, shumo*

thistle down, *shumo*

thistle stalk, *shumo api*

thistly, *shumo laua*

thitherward, *ilappimma pilla*

thole; *atakali, api aiishi*

thong; *aseta, libata*

thorax; *haknip, haknip foni*

thorn; *bissukchanaki, kati, kati holba*

thorny; *bisakchakinna foka, kati chito, kati laua*

thorough, *alhtaha*

thoroughwort, *haiyunkpulo*

those, *yamma*

those which were, *hatuk*

thou; *chi, chia, chik, chim, chishno, is, ish*

thou-me; *issan, issi*

though, *kia*

thought; *anukfila, imanukfila*

thoughtful; *anukfilli, imanukfila, imanukfila fehna*

thoughtless, *imanukfila iksho*

thoughts of man, *hatak imanukfila*

thoughts of the heart, *chunkash imanukfila*

thousand, *talepa sipokni*

thousand, one; *talepa sipokni achafa*

thousand, ten; *talepa sipokni pokoli*

thousand, thousand; *talepa sipokni talepa sipokni*

thousand, two; *talepa sipokni tuklo*

thousandth, *isht talepa sipokni*

thraldom, *yuka*

thrall, *yuka*

thrash, to; *boli, niheli*
thrashed; *niha, nihi*
thrasher; *boli, nihelichi*
thread, to; *ponola łopullichi*
thread box, *ponola aiąlhto*
thread case, *ponola aiąhlto*
threadbare, *lipa*
threat, *miha*
threaten, to; *miha*
threatener, *mihachi*
three, *tuchina*
three, all; *tuchinna*
three, being; *tuchinna*
three, to make; *tuchina*
three-cornered, *hanaiya*
three times; *atuchinaha, hituchinaha*
three times, to do; *hituchinanchi*
threefold, *inluhmi*
thresh, to; *niheli*
threshing floor, *anihechi*
threshing place, *anihechi*
threshold, *okhisa*
thrice; *atuchinaha, hituchinaha, tuchinanchit*
thrift, *aiaⁿli*
thrifty, *aiaⁿli*
thrill, to; *łumpli, nukshąchaiyakachi*
thrive, to; *chitot ia, iⁿshali, laua*
throat; *iⁿkolumpi, ikonla, iⁿnaląpi, kolombish, naląpi*
throat affection, *shikiffi*
throatlatch; *isuba ikonla isht talakchi, nutakfa isht talakchi*
throb, to; *lipkąchi, michikli, mitikli, mitikmiⁿkli, mitikminli, mototuⁿkli, motukli, timikli, timikmeli*
throb, to cause to; *mitiklichi, mitikminlichi*
throbbing; *mitikli, mitikminli, mototuⁿkli*
throe; *hotupa, nukhąmmi*
throe, to; *hotupa, nukhąmmi*
throne; *aiasha, aiasha holitopa, aioⁿbinili holitopa, ombinili, pelichika aiasha*
throne of Jehovah, *Chihowa aiasha*
throng; *itąnaha, laua*
throng, to; *atelifichi, itąnaha laua*
throttle, to; *nuktakali*
through; *aiąli, aiitintakla, łopulli, takla*
throughout; *moma, mominchit*
throw; *akkąchi, kanchi, pila*
throw, to; *akkąchi, bohpuli, fichąmmi, kampila, naki pila, pila*
throw away, to; *kanchi*

throw by springing a stick, to; *fachachi, fachamoli, fachąmmi, fichamoli*
throw down, to; *akkaboli, akkapila, kinalichi, kinąffi, łuhąmmi*
throw into the fire, to; *itokanchi*
throw mud with a stick, to; *faⁿkulli*
throw on, to; *onochi*
throw on a fire, to; *itąchi, itopihinla*
throw open, to; *tiąbli*
throw out, to; *kucha*
throw over, to; *auanapolichi, yuli*
throw sideways, to; *fahąmmi*
throw up, to; *ąba pila*
throw up the earth, to; *wokkokli, wokokonli*
thrower; *bohpuli, kanchi, pila*
thrown, *bohpoa*
thrown by a stick; *fachama, fachamoa*
thrown down, *kinali*
thrum, to; *takchi, tąna*
thrush, *itąkha litowa*
thrust; *bąli, tobli*
thrust, to; *bali, chukoa, fahąmmi, tobli*
thrust against, to; *apokofa*
thrust in, to; *maia, maiachi*
thrust into a corner, to; *anaksikachi*
thrust out the tongue, to; *okchilabi, okchilaklali*
thrust upward, to; *bahąffi*
thruster; *bali, tobli*
thumb, *ibbak ishki*
thumb, to; *lusachi*
thump, *sakachi*
thump, to; *kasolichi, kasuha, ląsaha, ląsalichi, sakaha, sakalichi*
thumper, *ląsalichi*
thumping; *sakaha, timikteli*
thunder; *hiloha, tasa*
thunder, to; *hiloha*
thunder, to cause to; *hilohąchi*
thunder clap, *hiloha*
thunder cloud, *hiloha hoshintika*
thunder shower, *hiloha umba chito*
thunder strike, to; *hiloha ąbi*
thunderbolt; *hąshuk mąlli, maląttakąchi*
thunderer, *hilohąchi*
thus; *achuhmi, aiyohmi, yak, yakohmi, yąmmak iⁿ, yohmi*
thus, to do; *aiyakohmichi, imoma, maⁿya, yakohmichi*
thus always, to be; *aiimoma*
thwack, to; *pąsaha, pąsalichi*
thwart, to; *asonali, okhoatali, oląbbi*

thy; *chi, chin, chim, chimmi, chin, chishno, ish*

thyine wood, *sitlon*

thyself, *chishno akinli*

tick; *bahta chito hoshinsh aialhto, shatanni*

tick, seed; *shatannushi*

tick, wood; *shatanni*

tick, young; *shatannushi*

ticket, *holisso lilafa*

ticking, *nan tanna bahta atoba*

tickle, to; *chukchulli*

tickled, *chukchua*

tickler, *chukchulli*

tickling; *chukchua*

ticklish; *kinafa hinla, nukoa shali, yukpa shali*

tide; *okhata bikeli, yanalli*

tidewater, *oka bikeli*

tidiness, *kashofa*

tidings; *anoa, anumpa, anumpa annoa, anumpa himona*

tidy, *kashofa*

tie, *ashekonopa*

tie, to; *ashekonobli, itashekonopli, shekonobli, takchi, takchichi*

tie, to make; *asetilechi*

tie a noose, to; *alinfachi*

tie at, on, to, or up, to; *asitilli, asitoli ashelichi, atakchechi, atakchi, atakchichechi, atakchichi, shikoli, takchichi*

tie brush, to; *shauwa takchi*

tie together, to; *takchichi*

tie up in a bundle, to; *siteli, sitoli*

tie with a noose, to; *alinfichi*

tied; *ashekonoa, ashekonopa, atalakchi, shekonopa, talakchi*

tied round, *apakfoa*

tied up; *asehta, asitoha, asheha, ashehachi, sita, sitoha, shikoli, shikowa*

tierce, *italhfoa chito*

ties, one who; *takchi*

tiger; *koi, koi nakni*

tight; *afacha, apohtukih, chiluk iksho, inhollo, katanli, kallo, nan inholitopa, nan inhollo, palammi*

tighten, to; *katanlichi*

tightly, *katanli*

tigress, *koi tek*

till; *kinsha, na, takla*

till, to; *osapa toksali, pataffi, toksali*

tillable; *atoksala hinla, pataffi*

tilled, *patafa*

tiller, *pataffi*

tiller of the ground, *osapa toksali*

tilt; *alhtipo, umpoholmo*

tilt, to; *umpohomo*

timber; *iti, iti basha, iti bashkachi*

timbered, *iti ansha*

time; *aiona, nitak, okchanya, ta*

time, a short; *yakosi*

time, to; *apesa*

timekeeper, *hashi isht ikhana*

timely; *alhpesa, nitanki*

timepiece, *hashi isht ikhana*

times; *bat, ha*

timid; *anukwia, imala, nukshopa, nukwia, takshi*

timid, to render; *anukwiachi, nukwiachi*

timorous; *nukshopa, nukwia*

tin, *asonak toba*

tin kettle, *asonak hata*

tin pail, *asonak hata*

tin pan; *asonak hata maiha, asonak malha*

tinder, *tashukpa*

tine, *chufak wushala, washala*

tingle, *chansa*

tingle, to; *chansa, nukshikanli*

tingle the nose, to; *shikali, shikanlichi*

tingling, *shikanli*

tinker, *asonak isht atta*

tinkle, to; *kamahachi, kassa, kassaha, kassahachi, olachi, samahachechi, samahachi*

tinkle, to cause to; *kamahachechi*

tinkling; *kamahachi, kassahachi*

tinkling of a bell, *samahachi*

tip, *wishakchi*

tip, to; *haluppachi, umpohomo*

tip end, *wishakchi*

tip end, belonging to the; *wishakchi*

tip-end men, *hatak wishakchi*

tipple, to; *okishko*

tippled, *haksi*

tippler; *hatak okishko, okishko, okishko shali*

tippling house, *oka aiishko*

tipsy, *haksi*

tiptoe, *iyushi wishakchi*

tire; *bita, iti chanaha isht talakchi, tali itichanaha apakfoa*

tire, to; *hoyablichi, intakobichi, tikabi, tikabichi*

tire another, to; *shemachi*

tire with, to; *aiintakobichi*

tired; *ataha, intakobi, tikabi*

tired out with, *aiintakobi*

tiresome; *ahchiba, alhchiba, komota, tikabi*

tithe, *isht pokoli*
title; *hochifo, holisso, immi*
title, to; *ima*
titter, to; *yukpa*
to; *a, pilla*
to some extent, *chohmi*
to the end that, *na*
toad, *shilukwa*
toad, spawn of a; *shilukwushi*
toad, tree; *chukpalantak, hachukpalan-tak*
toad, young; *shilukwushi*
toadstool; *pakti, ponkshi*
toast, *paska alhpusha*
toast, to; *anakshonffi, anakshoti, auashli*
toasted; *anakshua, alhpusha, alwasha*
toasting iron, *paska alibishli*
tobacco, *hakchuma*
tobacco, roll of; *hakchuma alhfoa*
tobacco leaf, *hakchuma hishi*
tobacco pipe, *hakchuma shuti*
tobacco worm, *hakchuma inshunshi*
today, *himak nitak*
toe, great; *iyishke*
toe, little; *iyush ali, iyushi*
toe, the long; *iyush tikba*
together; *aiena, iba, it, itatuklo*
together, to cause to be or go; *apehachi*
together with; *aiena, apiha, iba*
toil, *tonksali*
toil, to; *pilesa, toksali, yichina*
token; *isht alhpisa, nan isht ikhana*
token of respect, *nan isht aiokpachi*
told; *aianowa, anoa*
tolerable; *alhpesa, chohmi*
tolerably, *chohmi*
tolerate, to; *apesa, ome ahni*
toll, *alhtoba*
toll, to; *atobbi, ola, olachi*
toll bridge, *iti patalhpo alhtoba ahoyo*
toll gate, *okhisa alhtoba ahoyo*
tomahawk, *iskifushi*
tomahawk, to; *iskifushi*
tomb; *ahollohpi, hatak aholopi, hatak illi aiasha, sipalka*
tomboy, *alla haksi*
tombstone, *ahollopi tali hikia*
tome, *holisso*
tomorrow; *onna, onnaha, onnakma*
tomorrow, after; *mishshakma*
tomtit, *biskantak*
ton; *weki talepa sipokni tuklo, yamohmi*
tone, *ola*

tongs; *botona, tali isht kiseli, uski botona*
tongs, cane; *kapash*
tongs, fire; *luak isht kiseli*
tongs, flesh; *nipi isht kapash, nipi isht kafa*
tongue (language); *anumpa, okla*
tongue (organ of speech), *isunlash*
tongue-tied, *isunlash illi*
tonic; *ikhinsh nipi kallochi, ikhinsh okcha-lechi*
tonight, *himak ninak*
too; *ak, atapa*
tool; *isht tonksali, nan isht tonksali*
tool for hewing stone, *tala*
toot, to; *olachi*
tooter, *olachi*
tooth, *noti*
tooth, cheek; *noti isht itibi*
tooth, corner; *noti chukbi*
tooth, double; *noti bolukta, noti pokta, noti polukta*
tooth, front; *noti ibish, noti tikba*
tooth edge, *noti shakaya*
toothache, *noti hotupa*
toothbrush, *noti isht kasholichi*
toothpick; *noti isht shinli, shinli*
top; *apaknanka, nushkobo, pakna, paknaka, tabokaka, wishakchi*
top (for spinning), *na hila*
top, to; *ishalichi, tabli, umpohomo*
top of a hill, *nanih paknaka*
top of a side, *bok wiheka*
top of a tree, *iti wishakchi*
top of the foot, *iyi paknaka*
top of the head; *bokko, iyatoboka, nush-kobo tabokaka*
top of the milk, *pishukchi pakna*
toper, *okishko shati*
tophet, *aiokpuloka*
topic; *anumpa, anumpa nushkobo, nana*
topped; *tapa, umpoholmo*
topple, to; *kinafa*
torch, *pala*
torch pan, *luak apala*
torch-holder, *apala*
torchlight, to make a; *palali*
torment; *ilbasha, isikkopa, isikkopali*
torment, to; *ilbashachi, isikkopalechi, isikkopali*
tormented; *ilbasha, ilbashachi, isikkopa, isikkopalechi, isikkopali, issikkopa*
torn; *lilafa, lilalankachi, lilali*
torn up, *fakowa*
tornado, *mali chito*

torpid; *illi, nusilhha, shimoha*
torpor; *illi, nusilhha*
torrent, *oka yanallipalhki*
torrid; *lashpa, lua*
tortoise; *hachotakni, luksi, luksi chito*
torture; *hotupa, nukhammi*
torture, to; *hotupali, nukhammichi*
toss, *aba pila*
toss, to; *aba pila, pila*
toss the hands and feet, to; *shilaia, shilaiyakachi*
toss the head, to; *kanaktakli*
tossed, *takakanli*
tossed on the waves, *paiokachi*
total, *moma*
totality, *moma*
totally; *bano, beka*
tote, to; *ia, sholi*
totter, to; *faiokachi*
touch; *isso, ishi, potoli*
touch, to; *anoli, ala, ataiya, bikeli, haleli, ia, isso, ishi, nukhanklochi, potoli, tebli, tibli, tikeli*
touch each other, to cause to; *tikelichi*
touch the feelings, to; *chunkash ishi*
touch with the tongue, to; *labbi*
touchhole; *haksun chiluk, tanampo haksun chiluk*
touchiness, *nukoa okpulo*
touchwood; *iti toshbi, tashukpa*
touchy, *nukoa shali*
tough; *kamassa, kallo, pokshia*
tough meat of the neck, *ikistap*
toughen, to; *kamassalli, kallochi, kallot ia*
tour, *nowat fullota*
tourist, *nowat fullota*
touse, to; *halali*
tow, *pinash*
tow, to; *halat isht anya*
toward; *imma, pila, pilla, pit*
toward the head, *ibetap pilla*
toward the left, *alhfabek imma*
toward the speaker; *auet, et*
toward this place, *ilappa pila*
towel, *nashuka isht kasholichi*
tower; *aboha chaha, aboha kallo chaha, chuka chaha*
tower, to; *chaha*
town; *apelichika, tamaha*
town, a certain Choctaw; *Wia Takali*
town, a great; *tamaha chito*
town, a small; *tamahushi*

townsman, *tamaha hatak*
toy; *hatak holba isht washoha, isht washoha, na hila*
toy, to; *ilaualli, washoha*
trace, *atanfa*
trace (part of harness); *isuba isht shali, isht halalli*
trace (trail); *anowa, hina*
trace, to; *iakaiya, lanfi*
traced, *lanfa*
track; *anowa, atia, hina, iyi*
track, deer's; *isi anowa*
track, to; *silhhi*
track, to cause to; *silhhichi*
tracker, *silhhi*
tract, *anumpa*
tractable; *kostina hinla, kostini*
trade; *aiyamohmi, itatoba*
trade, to; *itatoba*
trader; *itatoba, na kanchi, nan chumpa, nan isht itatoba, nan ittatoba*
trading house; *aiitatoba chuka, nana aiitatoba*
trading place, *aiitatoba*
tradition; *anumpa isht auehinchi, anumpa kochanli, nana alhpisa*
traduce, to; *isht yopula*
traffic, *itatoba*
traffic, to; *itatoba*
trafficker, *itatoba*
tragical; *hatak abi, ilbashahe alhpesa, nukhanklo*
trail; *kahama, lohama, talaia*
trail, to; *silhhi*
trail the grass, to; *hashuk lohammichi*
trailed, *lohama*
train; *iakaiya, isht haksichi*
train, to; *ikhananchi, kostininchi*
train of powder, *hituk laya bachanya*
trained, *kostini*
traitor; *issi okla issa, kanchi*
trammel, *asonak atakali*
trammel, to; *hokli, katabli, takchi*
tramp, to; *nowa*
tramping of horses, *litetuk*
trample, to; *ahabli, ahali, habli, hali, halichi, kahammi*
trample down, to cause to; *kahammichi*
trampled, *ahala*
trampler; *ahalichi, kahammi*
trance, *tasembo*
tranquil; *hopola, nuktanla*
tranquil, to become; *hopola*

tranquilize, to; *hopolạchi, hopolạlli, nuktalali*
tranquilly, *nuktanlạt*
transact, to; *apesa, apistikeli, yạmihchi*
transaction, *nan isht ạtta*
transactor, *nan isht ạtta*
transcend, to; *ạbanạbli, ia, ımaiya*
transcendent, *achukma iⁿshati*
transcribe, to; *ạlbitet holissochi*
transcript, *holisso*
tranfer, *kanchi*
transfer, to; *ạlhtosholi, ia, ima, kanạllichi, kanchi, pota, tosholi*
transferred, *toshoa*
transfigured, *inlat toba*
transform, to; *inla ikbi*
transgress, to; *anumpa kobạffi, ạbanạbli, kobạffi*
transgression; *anumpa kobafa, anumpa kobạffi, yoshoba*
trangressor; *aiashạchi, anumpa kobạffi*
transient, *chekusi ont ia*
transitory, *chekusi kạnia*
translate, to; *anumpa tosholi, ạlhtosholi, kanạllichi, tosholi*
translate slightly, to; *lapalit tosholi*
translated; *anumpa toshoa, ạlhtoshoa, illi, kạnia, toshoa*
translation; *anumpa toshoa, toshoa, tosholi*
translator; *anumpa tosholi, ạlhtosholi, tosholi*
transmit, to; *pila*
transmit toward, to; *auechi*
transparency; *shohkawali*
transparent, *shohkalali*
transpire, to; *haiaka, yạmohmi*
transpire at, to; *ayakohmi*
transport, to; *ia, yukpali*
transpose, to; *ạlhtoboa*
trap; *isht hokli, isht ạlbi*
trap, to; *hokli, isht ạlbi talali*
trash; *chopilhkạsh, chupilhkạsh, polhkash*
trash, to; *shiⁿfi*
travail, *hotupa*
travail, to; *ạlla eshachiⁿ iⁿpalạmmi, eshichi, hotupa, ishi, nowa*
travel, to; *akka itạnowa, akkahika, akkahikạt aⁿya, akkanowa, akkaya, atia, aⁿya, itanowa, nowa, nowạt aⁿya, nowạt fullota*
travel with, to; *ibanowa*
traveled, *anowa*
traveler; *aⁿya, hatak nowạt aⁿya, itanowa, na hollo itanowa, nowa, nowạt aⁿya*

traveling companion, *ibanowa*
traverse, to; *lopulli*
tray; *itampo, iti kula*
treacherous, *aⁿli*
treachery; *aiaⁿli, aⁿli, haksichi*
tread; *habli, nowa*
tread, to; *habli, hạli, kahạmmi, lohạmmi, luhạmmi, nowa*
tread down, to cause to; *lohummichi*
tread into, to; *ahablichi*
tread into the ground, to; *ahạlichi*
tread on, to; *ahabli, ahạli, hika*
tread on, to make; *ahablichi, ahạlichi, hablichi, hạlichi*
tread there, to; *ahabli*
tread under foot, to; *ahạlichi*
treader; *ahablichi, ahạlichi, habli, hạli*
treadle (belonging to a loom), *ahabli*
treasure; *ilaⁿyak, na holitompa, na holitopa, nan ilayak, nana imilaⁿyak*
treasurer, *tạli holisso ishi*
treasury; *tạli holisso aboli, tạli holisso aiitola*
treat, to; *aiokpạchi, anumpuli, aⁿya, halạlli, ipeta, nana kanihchi*
treater; *isht aiokpạchi, isht anumpuli*
treatise; *anumpa, holisso*
treatment, *yạmohmi*
treaty; *anumpa, holisso holitopa*
treble, *inluhmi*
treble, to; *inluhmi*
tree; *ạpi, iti*
tree, a certain; *tokạm*
tree, chestnut; *otạpi*
tree, cottonwood; *shumbạla*
tree, cypress; *shaⁿkolo*
tree, dead; *iti illi*
tree, domesticated; *iti ạlhpoa*
tree, dry; *iti shila*
tree, fallen; *iti kinafa, iti kinali, iti yileha*
tree, good; *yạt*
tree, large; *iti chito*
tree, leaning; *iti waiya*
tree, slender; *iti fabạssa*
tree, standing; *iti hikia*
tree, to; *oiyạchi*
tree, turpentine; *tiak*
tree lying across a creek, *sạlbạsh*
tree turned up by the roots, *itakchulakto*
tree without limbs, *fako*
tremble, to; *nukshichaiakạchi, nukwạnnichi, nukwimekạchi, wạnnichi, yalạtha, yiliya, yulichi*

trembling; *ilapissa, nukwannichi, wan-nichi*
tremendous; *chito, palammi*
tremor, *wannichi*
tremulous, *wannichi*
trench, *yakni kula ayanalli*
trench, to; *kulli, pataffi*
trencher; *itampo, iti kula aiimpa*
trespass, *yoshoba*
trespass, to; *ashachi, okpani, yoshoba*
trespasser, *yoshoba*
tress, *yushbonoli*
trial; *momaka pisa, pisa*
trial, to make a; *imomaka pisa*
triangle, *hanaiya*
triangle, to make a; *hanaiyachi*
triangular, *hanaiya*
tribe; *aiunchululli, apelichi, apelichika, aiunchololi, isht aiunchululli, isht atiaka, okla*
tribe, a single; *okla chafa*
tribe, a small; *oklushi*
tribulation, *isikkopali*
tribunal, *nan apesa abinili*
tributary people, *yuka okla*
tribute; *aba isht aiokpachi, nushkobo atobbi, nushkobo chumpa, nushkobo isht chumpa*
tribute, to put to; *nushkobo atobbichi*
trick; *fappo, haksichi, isht haksichi*
trick, to; *haksichi*
tricked, *haksi*
trickle, to; *lotohachi, shinilli, yanalli*
tricky, *haksichi shali*
triennial, *afammi tuchinakma*
trier; *momaka pisa, pisa*
trifle, *nana iskitinusi*
trifle, to; *ilaualli, isht yopula*
trifler, *isht yopula*
trigger; *ahalalli, tanampo ahalalli*
trill, to; *taloa afalamoa, yanalli*
trim, to; *aiskiachi, amo, emo, imanukfila tuklo, nalichi, nolichi, okmilalichi, shema, shemachi, yushkabalichi, yushkilalichi*
trimmed; *aiskia, almo, naha, naksish naha, shema, yushkabali, yushkoboli*
trimmer, *anumpa intuklo*
Trinity, the; *Chihowa*
trinket, *isht washoha*
trip; *isso, lasalichi*
trip, to; *apakchiloffi, batammi, ibetabli, lasalichit akkachi, nowa palhki*
tripe, *iskuna*
triple, *inluhmi*

tripped up, *apakchilofa*
tripper, *tunshpat nowa*
trite; *lipa, sipokni*
triturate, to; *lapushkichi, pushechi*
triturated; *lapushki, pushi*
triumph, *imaiya*
triumph, to; *hila, imaiya*
triumphant, *imaiya*
troat, to; *linsa*
trochings, *isi lapish filamminchi*
trodden; *anowa, hala*
trodden down; *ahala, kahama, lohama, luhama, lukama*
trodden on; *ahabli, ahala*
trodden soft, *litoa*
trollop, *fullokachi*
troop, *tashka chipota*
troop, to; *itanowa, itanaha*
trooper, *isuba omanili tashka*
trophy, *na wehpoa*
trot, *yahyachi*
trot, to; *yahyachechi, yahyachi*
trot, to make; *yahyachechi*
trotter, *yahyachi*
trouble; *ataklama, ilbasha, nan inkanimi*
trouble, to; *ahchibali, anuktuklochi, anumpulechi, apistikeli, ataklammi, ataklamoli, ilbashali, kanihmi, nukoachi*
trouble water, to; *pialichi*
troubled; *ataklama, ilbasha, komunta*
troubler; *anumpulechi, apistikeli, ataklamoli, ataklamolichi*
troublesome; *acheba, ahchiba, apistikeli, isht afekommi, itakhapuli, komota*
troublesome, to cause to be; *achibachi, itakhapulichi*
troublous; *achukma, isht afekommi*
trough; *aiilhpeta, iti kula, iti peni, peni*
trough, long; *iti kula falaia*
trough, water; *oka aialhto*
trousers, *obala foka*
trout; *nani shupik, sakli*
trowel, *lukfi isht patasalli*
truant, *intakobi*
truck; *itatoba, iti kalaha*
truck, to; *itatoba*
truckle, to; *nutaka ia*
true; *aianli, aianlishke, anli, apissanli, alhpesali, nan imaianli*
true, to make; *anlichi*
true heart, *chunkash anli*
trueness; *aianli, anli*
truly; *anli, anlit, hatoshke, mali*
truly, to act; *anli*

truly, to speak; aⁿlit achi
trump, isht puⁿfa
trump, to; itannali
trumpery, nan chokushpa
trumpet; isht puⁿfa, lapish
trumpeter, isht puⁿfolachi
truncate, to; koluffi
truncated, kolofa
trunk (body), haknip
trunk (for clothing), itombi
trunk (tree, etc.), api
trunk maker, itombi ikbi
trunk of an elephant, ibishakni
truss, to; takchi
trust; aianukcheto, yimmi
trust, to; ahekachi, aianukcheto, anukcheto, yimmi
trusted, aheka
trustee, hatak nan apistikeli alhtuka
truster, nan ahekachi
trusting, anukcheto
trusty; aⁿli, anukcheta hinla, kallo
truth; aiaⁿli, aⁿli
truth, to establish the; aⁿlichi
truthless, aiaⁿli keyu
try, to; kashoffichi, momaka pisa, pisa
try to do, to; ibawichi
try to do so, to; yohmit pisa
tub; itampo chito, oka aialhto
tube, ayanalli
tubercle; hichi, hichushi, tanlakchi
tuck, to; fohki, shamallichi
tucker, inuchi
Tuesday, nitak hollotuk iⁿmisha
tuft; bafalli talaia, lukoli
tug; halalli, isht halalli
tug, to; halat isht aⁿya, halalli
tuition, ikhananchi
tumble, to; aiyuma, kinafa, tonnoli, tonnolichi
tumbled; aiyokoma, aiyuma
tumbler, ilaualli
tumbler, glass; kobli
tumefied, shatali
tumefy, to; shatalichi
tumor, kachombi
tumult, kitihachi
tun, italhfoa chito
tune, taloa
tune, to; taloa, taloat takalichi
tune, to make a; taloa ikbi
tune, to set a; taloa isht ia
tuner, taloa
tunic, ilefoka

tunnel; aiani, isht bicheli, oka abicha, oka
isht bicheli
turban; aialipa, bita, iachuka, ialipa,
nantapaski ialipa
turban, king's; miⁿko imiachuka
turban, to; biteli, bitelichi, iachuka,
iachukolechi, iachukoli, ialipeli, ialipelichi
turbaned; bita, iachuka, ialipa
turbid, liteha
turbulent, haksi
turf, isuba aiitintimiya
turgid; shatali, shatabli
turkey; akaⁿk chaha, fakit
turkey, a hen; fakit ishke, fakit tek
turkey, a male; fakit nakni
turkey, a very young; biliⁿsbili
turkey, a young; fakit ushi
turkey, a young male; fakit kuchaⁿkak
turkey cock; fakit homatti, fakit nakni
turkey's egg, fakit ushi
turkey's spur, fakit inchahe
turn; fotoha, fotoli
turn, to; afinni, afolichi, anukpiliffi,
anukpiloli, ashana, ashannichi, chanalli,
chasallichi, chanaha, fahattakachi, fahfuli,
falama, filema, filemachi, filimmikachi,
fololichi, fotoli, shanaia, shanaiachi, shanaiachi, shanali, shananchi, shaneli, shana,
shanachi, shanni, tasembochi, tonnolichi
turn about or around, to; afololichi,
chanahachi, chanichi
turn askew, to; shanaioli
turn at, to; afalama
turn away, to; filamolechi, filamoli,
filammi, filimmi
turn away, to cause to; filemolechi
turn away from, to cause to; filammichi
turn back, to; afilimmi
turn back and forth, to; filehkachi
turn back at, to; afalama
turn back or about, to; falama
turn backwards and forwards, to;
filemoa
turn noses and lips, to; ibakpishinli
turn off, to; fichapoli, fichabli
turn off, to cause to; fichablichi
turn out, to; kuchichi
turn out of doors, to; aboha kuchichi
turn over, to; afilimmi, chanallichi,
filemat itola, filemoli, filimmi, fitilimmi,
lipeli, lipoli
turn over, to cause to; filimmichi

turn over and over, to; *filemoa*
turn over back, to; *afilema*
turn over on the face, to; *lipkachi*
turn round, to; *chanaha, hannanuki*
turn round, to cause to; *filimmichi, fololichi, folotolichi*
turn sideways, to; *naksi*
turn sour, to; *hauashkochi*
turn suddenly, to; *filetakachi*
turn there, on, or over, to; *amali*
turn to, to; *weli*
turn up, to; *apelulichi, bokusa, ibakchushlichi, lobbi, polomoa*
turn up, to cause to; *ibakchishinlichi*
turn up by the roots, to; *lobafa, lobaffi, lobali, lopa* ·
turn up the edge, to; *ahalupa anukpilifi*
turncoat; *falama, filammi, issa*
turned; *anukpilefa, anukpiloa, ashana, ashakachi, homi, shanaia, shana*
turned away; *filama, filamoa*
turned back; *falama, falamoa, filema*
turned down, *pula*
turned from, *filamoa*
turned over; *filemoa, fitilema, lipia, lipkachi*
turned round, *filema*
turned up; *apelua, ibakchushli*
turned up by the roots; *lobafa, lobali*
turner, *fotoli*
turning, *filekachi*
turning back; *falama, falamaka, falamoa*
turning back, to cause a; *afilimmichi*
turnip, *tanip*
turnip, wild; *hichi*
turnkey, *ashannichi*
turpentine, *tiak nia*
turpitude, *okpulo*
turtle, a species of; *walwa*
turtle, loggerhead; *hachotakni*
turtle, sea; *hachotakni okhata a^nsha*
turtle, soft-shelled; *halwa, walwa*
turtle, striped-headed; *luksi bashka*
turtle dove, *pachi yoshoba*
tusk; *isht itibbi, noti, noti isht itibi*
tusk of an elephant, *hatak lusa i^nyannash noti isht itibbi*
tutor; *hatak ikhananchi, nan ikhananchi*
tutoress, *ohoyo ikhananchi*
twain, *tuklo*
twang, *ola*
twang, to; *ola, olachi, ti^nkti^nkachi*
twelfth, *isht auahchafa*

twelve, *auah tuklo*
twentieth; *isht pokoli, pokoli*
twenty; *pokoli*
twenty times, *pokoli*
twice; *atuklaha, hituklaha*
twice, to do; *hituklanchi, tuklochi*
twig; *bisali, fuli*
twilight; *okpolusbi, okshachobi*
twilight, to become; *okshachobi*
twilight, to cause; *okshachobichi*
twin, *haiyup*
twin-born; *haiyup atta, ibaiatta*
twine; *ponohonulla, ponokallo*
twine, to; *afoli, ishi*
twinge, to; *hotupa, hotupali*
twinkle, to; *chalhchakachi*
twinkle, to cause to; *chalhchakachechi*
twinkling, *chalhchakachi*
twins, *haiyup*
twirl, to; *shanaiachi, tonnoli, tonnolichi*
twist; *honula, pana, shana*
twist, to; *apinni, ashana, bochusa, bochusachi, honola, honula, okaloli, shanaiachi, shanaioli, shananchi, shaneli, shana, shanachi, yi^nyikechi*
twist of tobacco, *hakchuma shana*
twist on or at, to; *ashanni*
twist on, to cause to; *ashannichi*
twist round, to; *apakshanni*
twist together, to; *pana, panni*
twisted; *apakshana, ashana, ashakachi, bochusa, chikisana, chikisanali, honula, pana, shanaia, shanaioa, shana*
twister, *honola*
twisting, *yi^nyiki*
twit, to; *miha*
twitch, *halali*
twitch, to; *fullottokachi, halali, lachakat ishi, yalattakachi, yullichi*
twitching, *yalatha*
twitter, to; *yukpa*
two; *tuklo, tu^nklo*
two, even; *tuklona*
two to do; *tuklochi*
two, to extend to; *tuklona*
two, to make; *tuklo, tuklochi*
two, to reach to; *tuklona*
two, to take; *tuklochi*
two-edged; *halupa tuklo, itala^nkla halupa*
two-edged knife, *bashpo itala^nkla halupa*
two to go together, *itiachi*
two together; *itatuklo, itachanaia*
two-tongued, *isunlash tuklo*

twofold, *inluhmi*
type; *holisso atoba, isht ạlhpisa, isht inchuⁿwa*
tyrannical; *kạllo, palạmmi*
tyrannize, to; *isikkopalit peɫichi*
tyrant, *palạmmichi*

ubiquity, *himona achạfanlit kanima anta*
udder, *ipiⁿshik*
ugly; *aiukli, okpulo, pisa aiukli keyu, pisa okpulo*
ulcer; *ạtta, chukfi nishkin, liahpo, ɫachowa*
ulcer, an old; *okchushba*
ulcer in the throat, *chakwa*
ulcerate, to; *lachowa, lachowạchi*
ulcerated, *lachowa*
ulcerated bone, *foni toshbi*
ulcerous, *ɫachowa lạua*
ulterior, *misha*
ultimate; *isht aiopi, mishapilla*
ultimately; *isht aiopi, polaⁿka*
ululate, to; *shakapa, tahbi*
umbilicus, *hatambish*
umbrage, *hoshontika*
umbrageous; *hoshontika, okɫili*
umbrella, *isht ilehoshontikachi*
unabated, *shippa*
unable, *lauechi*
unacceptable, *achukma*
unaccepted; *iⁿshi, kanchi*
unaccustomed, *yohmi*
unacquainted, *ikhana*
unadvisable; *achukma keyu, ạlhpesa*
unaffected, *aⁿli*
unaided, *apela*
unallowed, *ạlhpesa*
unalterable, *inlahe keyu*
unanimated, *aiyimita*
unanimity, *imanukfila*
unanimous, *imanukfila achạfa*
unappalled, *nukshopa*
unapproved, *ạlhpesa*
unapt; *achukma, ạlhpesa, ikhạnahe keyu*
unasked, *asilhha*
unassisted, *apela*
unattainable, *ishahe keyu*
unattended; *ilap achạfa, ilap bano*
unawaked, *okcha*
unaware, *ahni*
unbacked, *omanili keyu*
unbaked, *palạska*
unbar, to; *tuwi*
unbecoming, *ạlhpesa*
unbegotten; *bilia, ikbi*
unbelief; *na yimmi, yimmi*

unbeliever, *yimmi*
unbend, to; *apissạlli*
unbent; *apissa, chasạla*
unbiased, *kanimachi*
unbidden, *anoa*
unbind, to; *hotofi, hotoɫichi, litoffi, litoɫi*
unblemished; *aiokpuloka iksho, lusa iksho*
unblushing, *hofah iksho*
unboiled, *honni*
unbolt, to; *tuwi*
unborn; *ạtta, himmak*
unbosom, to; *haiakạt anoli*
unbought, *chumpa*
unbound; *hotoɫi, talakchi*
unbounded, *ataha iksho*
unbraided, *shihachi*
unbridle, to; *shuⁿfi*
unbroken; *kobafa, kostini, litoa*
unbuckle, to; *litoffi*
unburden, to; *fohachi*
unburied, *hollopi*
unburnt; *hollokmi, lua*
unbutton, to; *tạli haksi mitiffi*
uncalled; *ano, iⁿhoa*
uncandid, *anli*
unceasing, *bilia*
unceded, *kanchi keyu*
uncertain; *aiaⁿli ikakostinincho, akostininchi, chishba, kaniohmi chishba*
unchain, to; *yuka issạchi*
unchangeable; *inlahe keyu, shanaiahe keyu*
unchastised, *fạma*
unchecked, *olạbbi*
uncheerful, *yukpa*
unchopped, *chaⁿya*
unchristian, *ạba anumpa ahalaia keyu*
unchurch, to; *ạba anumpuli iksa kuchi*
uncivil, *hopoyuksa keyu*
uncivilized, *hopoksia*
uncle; *aⁿki, ạmoshi, hatak tiⁿkba, imoshi*
unclean; *kashofa, okpulo*
uncleanness, *yoshoba*
uncleansed, *kashofa*
unclinch, to; *ibbak wạttạchi, wạttạchi*
unclog, to; *aiskiachi*
unclose, to; *fatummi, tuwi*
unclothe, to; *shuⁿfi*
unclouded, *masheli*
uncloudy, *hoshontika*
uncocked, *hika*
uncoiled, *chạnaha*
uncollected; *iⁿshi, itạnaho*

uncombed, *shilla*
uncomely, *achukma*
uncomfortable, *achukma*
uncommanded; *ano, ạlhpesa*
uncommon, *yohmi*
uncomplaining, *nan ikmiho*
uncompounded, *ibafoka*
unconcern; *ahoba, nan ikimahobo*
uncondemned, *anumpa onutula*
unconfined, *talakchi*
uncongealed, *kalampi*
unconnected, *achaka*
unconquerable, *imaiya*
unconquered, *imaiya*
unconscious; *akostininchi, ikhana*
unconsoled, *hopola*
unconstant; *achunanchi, aiokpạchi*
unconsumed, *okpulot iktaho*
uncontrollable, *nutaka iahe keyu*
unconverted, *inlat toba*
uncork, to; *kạma*
uncorrected, *aiskia*
uncorrupt, *shua*
uncounted, *holhtena*
uncouple, to; *shuⁿfi*
uncouth; *inla, sipokni*
uncover, to; *shuⁿfi*
uncovered; *shahbi, shuⁿfa*
unction; *ahama, ahạmmi, isht ahama*
unctuous; *bila, nia*
uncultivated; *atoksạli, toksạli*
uncured, *lakoffi*
undam, to; *kinạffi*
undaunted; *nukshompiksho, nukwia ik-sho*
undecayed; *taha, toshbi*
undeceive, to; *haiakạchi*
undeceived, *haiaka*
undecided, *akostininchi*
undemolished, *kinafa*
undeniable, *aⁿli, lushka*
under; *nuta, nutaka*
under a hill, *okkạttahaka*
under foot; *iyinuta, lohama, nutaka*
under side, *nutaka*
underbrush; *ạtanạbli, shauwa*
undergarment; *ilefoka, na foka lumbo*
undergird, to; *akkasiteli*
undergo, to; *ilbạsha, lopulli*
underground, *yakni anuⁿkaka*
underground, a burning; *yakni anuⁿkaka lua*
undergrowth, *ạtanạbli*
underhand; *luma, makali*

underlay, to; *nutaka boli*
undermine, to; *akishtạla kullit kinạffi, nutaka yakni kulli*
undermost, *nutaka fehna*
underneath, *nutaka*
underpin, to; *intula boli*
underpinning; *chuka aiontạla, intula*
underrate, to; *aiilli onanchi*
understand, to; *akostininchi, anuk-fohka, ikhana, ikhạna, imponna, nukfoka*
understand, to cause to; *nukfokạchi*
understand a book, to; *holisso ithana*
understanding; *aiikhana, anukfohka, ikhana, imanukfila, imponna, kostini*
understanding of man, *hatak imanukfila*
undertake, to; *ia*
undertaker; *hatak halạlli, hatak iⁿminⁿko, ilhtohno*
undervalue, to; *aiilli onanchi*
undersigned, *ahni*
undesirable; *ahni, aⁿli*
undetected, *haiaka*
undetermined; *achi, akostininchi, apesa*
undignified, *ạlhpesa*
undirected, *ano*
undisciplined, *kostini*
undisguised, *luma*
undissembled; *haiaka, luma keyu*
undissembling, *haiaka*
undissolved; *abila, ạlhkomo, bila*
undistinguishable; *akostininchahe keyu, pisahe keyu*
undisturbed, *atakalam iksho*
undivided; *achafa, kashapa*
undo, to; *akshuchi, litoffi, okpạni*
undone; *ạlhtaha, okpulo*
undoubted, *aⁿli*
undress, to; *shuⁿfi*
undressed, *shuⁿfa*
undried, *shila*
undue; *aiạlhtoba ikono kiⁿsha, ạlhpesa*
undulate, to; *bạnakạchi, fahakạchi*
unduly; *atạpa, ạlhpesa*
unduteous, *antia*
undutiful, *antia*
unearned, *asitạbi*
uneasiness; *komunta, nukhạmmi*
uneasy; *komota, komunta*
uneasy, to render; *komuntạchi*
uneasy in mind, *imanukfila komunta*
uneducated, *holisso ikithano*
unembarrassed; *anuktuklo, atakalam iksho, nukwia iksho*
unengaged; *ạlhtuka keyu, ilhtohno keyu*

unenvied, *nukkilli keyu*
unequal; *itilaui, itilaui iksho, laue, lauechi*
unequally, *itilaui*
unequivocal; *apissanli, haiaka*
uneven; *bamboki, bombąki, chukashaya, itilaui, pompokachi, pompoki, shikowa*
uneven, to make; *bambąkichi*
unexecuted, *ąlhtaha*
unexhausted, *tali*
unexpected, *haksinchi*
unexpectedly, *haksint*
unexpectedly, to arrive; *haksint ąla*
unexpert, *imponna*
unexposed; *haiaka, luma*
unfaded, *kashofa*
unfading, *kashofahe keyu*
unfailing, *tahahe keyu*
unfair; *a^nli, haksi*
unfaithful, *a^nli*
unfashionable, *aiyąmohmi keyu*
unfasten, to; *shu^nfi, tuwi*
unfavorable, *achukma*
unfeared, *nukshopa*
unfeeling; *anukfilli, imanukfila kąllo*
unfeigned, *a^nli*
unfence, to; *holihta okpąni*
unfenced, *holihta*
unfertile, *waya*
unfetter, to; *litoffi, shu^nfi*
unfettered; *litofa, shu^nfa*
unfinished, *ąlhtaha*
unfirm; *kąllo, liposhi*
unfit, *ąlhpesa*
unfixed, *aiątta ikithano*
unflinching, *achillita*
unfold, to; *anoli, haiakąchi, tuwi, watali, watama, watąmmi, wątląchi*
unfolded; *haiaka, tiwa, watama*
unfortunate; *imaleka, poafa, poyafo*
unfound, *haiaka*
unfriended, *kana*
unfriendly, *kana*
unfruitful, *waya*
unfurl, to; *wakama, wakamoa, wakamoli, watali*
unfurled; *wakama, wakamoa*
unfurnish, to; *ishi*
unfurnished, *ikimiksho*
ungear, to; *weli*
ungenerous; *aiokpanchi keyu, nan i^nholitopa*
ungenial, *achukma*
ungenteel, *ąlhpesa*

ungentle, *kostini*
ungird, to; *mitiffi, shu^nfi*
ungodliness, *Chihowa ikimantio*
ungodly, *Chihowa ikimantio*
ungovernable; *imantiahe keyu, kostinahe keyu, tasembo*
ungoverned, *kostini*
ungranted; *ima keyu, kanchi keyu*
ungrateful; *aiokpanchi, imahaksi*
unguarded, *ahah ahni*
unguent, *isht ahama*
unhallowed, *holitopa*
unhandsome; *aiukli, a^nli*
unhandy, *imponna*
unhappily, *ilbąsha*
unhappy; *ilbąshahe ąlhpesa, komota, komunta, yukpa*
unhardened; *kamąssa, kąllo*
unharmed; *nana kaniohmi iksho, okpulo, okpulo isht i^nshat ia*
unharness, to; *weli*
unhatched, *hofąlli*
unhealthy; *achukma, aiabeka*
unheard, *haklo*
unhelped, *apela*
unhesitating, *anuktuklo iksho*
unhinge, to; *ishi, shu^nfi*
unholy; *achukma, holitopa*
unhonored, *holitopa*
unhorse, to; *akkapila*
unhouse, to; *aboha kuchichi*
unhumbled, *chu^nkąsh akkalusi keyu*
unhurt, *hotupa*
unicorn, *poa ląpish achafa*
uniform, *mih*
uniform (dress), *tąshka chipota isht shema*
unimpaired, *achukma moma*
unimportant, *na fehna keyu*
unindebted, *aheka iksho*
uninformed; *akostininchi, ikhana*
uninhabitable, *hatak aiąttahe keyu*
uninhabited, *aiokla*
uninjured, *okpulo*
uninterested, *ahalaia*
unintermitted, *bilia*
uninterrupted, *atakalam iksho*
uninvited, *ano*
union; *ibafoka, ibąlhkaha*
unit, *achąfa*
unite, to; *achakąli, fohki, ibafoka, ibafoki, itatuklo*
unite, to cause one to; *ibafokichi*
unite with a class, clan, or denomination, to; *iksa ibafoka*

united, *achaka, chukulbi, ibafoka*
United States; *Miliki, Miliki yakni, na hollo yakni*
united to the church, *aba anumpuli ibafoka*
unity; *achafa, ibafoka*
universal; *moma, okluha*
universalist, *okchanya*
universe, *nana toba puta*
unjoint, to; *ahokoffi, hokoffi*
unjointed; *ahokofa, hokofa*
unjust; *achukma, anli*
unkind; *halhpansha iksho, kana*
unkindness, *kana*
unknown; *chishba, ikhana*
unlaid, *boli*
unlawful, *achukma*
unlearn, to; *imahaksi*
unlearned; *holisso ithana, imahaksi, nan ikithano*
unless; *amba, keyukma*
unlike, *holba*
unlikely, *tokomi*
unlimited, *aiali iksho*
unlink, to; *litoli*
unliquidated, *chilofa*
unload, to; *fohobli, kuchi*
unloaded; *fohopa, kucha*
unloader, *fohobli*
unlock, to; *tiwi, tuwi*
unlocked, *tiwa*
unloose, to; *litoffi, litoli, mitefa, mitelichi, mitiffi*
unloosed; *litofa, litofkachi*
unlovely; *achukma, hollohe keyu*
unlucky; *imaleka, poafa*
unmade, *toba*
unmake, to; *okpani*
unman, to; *hobak tobachi, ishi*
unmanageable, *kostinahe keyu*
unmanaged; *ikhana, kostini*
unmanly; *hobak toba, makali*
unmannerly, *hopoyuksa keyu*
unmarked; *ahni, basha, lanfa*
unmarried, *auaya*
unmarried man, *hatak ohoyo ikimiksho*
unmask, to; *haiakachi*
unmeasured; *alhpesa, laua*
unmeditated, *anukfilli*
unmelted; *alhkomo, bila*
unmerciful, *nukhanklo iksho*
unmerited, *asitabi*
unmilked, *bishahchi*
unmindful; *ahah ahni, imahaksi*

unmingled; *aiyuma, anli, ibakaha*
unmixed, *ibakaha*
unmolested, *atakalam iksho*
unmoved, *kanalli*
unnamed, *hochifo iksho*
unnatural; *imanka, yohmi chatuk keyu*
unnerve, to; *kotachi*
unnerved, *kota*
unnoticed, *aiokpachi*
unnumbered; *aholhtina iksho, holhtena, holhtina atapa*
unoffended; *chunkash ikhotopo, nukoa*
unopened; *fatoma, tiwa, wakammi*
unowned; *immi, impushnayo iksho*
unpack, to; *tiabli*
unpaid; *alhchilofa, alhtoba, chilofa*
unpalatable, *kashaha*
unpardonable; *imahaksahe keyu, kashofahe keyu*
unpardoned; *imahaksi, kashofa*
unpassable, *lopullahe keyu*
unpeaceable; *banshkiksho, nukoa*
unperceived; *ahni, ikhana*
unperforated; *lukafa, lukali, lumpa*
unpin, to; *chufak ushi shueli*
unpinned, *chufak ushi shuekachi*
unpitied, *nukhanklo*
unpleasant, *achukma*
unpleased, *yukpa*
unpliant; *kamassa, walohbi keyu*
unplowed, *patafa*
unpopular, *anonowa achukma keyu*
unpracticed; *ikhana, imponna*
unprejudiced; *imanukfila alhpesa, nuktala keyu*
unpremeditated; *ahni, anukfillituk keyu*
unprepared; *alhtaha, imalhpisa*
unprincipled; *haksi, imanukfila achafa keyu*
unprofitable; *achukma, aiisht ilapisahe keyu*
unprovided, *imalhpisa*
unprovoked, *nukoa*
unpublished; *anoa, haiaka*
unpunished, *fama*
unqualified; *imalhpisa, ona*
unquenchable, *mosholahe keyu*
unransomed, *lakoffi*
unravel, to; *haiakachi, linfa, mitelichi, sheli, shinfa, shinfi, shinfkachi, shiha, shoeli*
unraveled; *linfa, shinfa, shifkachi, shiha*
unravels, one who; *shinfi*
unreached, *ona*

unread; *holisso ikithano, pisa*
unreadiness, *imalhtaha*
unready; *alhtaha, imalhpisa*
unreasonable, *alhpesa*
unreceived, *inshi*
unreconciled, *hopola*
unrecoverable; *ishit fohki, lakoffahe keyu*
unrecovered, *lakoffi*
unredeemed, *lakoffi*
unreformed; *hopoyuksa, kostini*
unregarded, *aiokpachi*
unregenerate, *himmona iktobo*
unrelated; *iksa keyu, isht atiaka keyu*
unrelenting; *kallo, nukhanklo iksho*
unrelieved; *lakoffi, nuktala*
unremembered; *ikhana, imahaksi*
unremitted; *bilia, kashofa*
unremoved, *kanalli*
unrenewed, *himmona iktobo*
unrepaid; *alhtoba, falammint alhtoba*
unrepealed, *kashofa*
unrepentant, *nukhanklo*
unreserved; *ilatoba, luhmi keyu, mo-minchi*
unresisted, *atakalam iksho*
unrespected, *aiokpachi*
unrewarded, *alhtoba*
unrighteous, *achukma*
unripe; *lakna, nuna, okchanki*
unroll, to; *tuwi*
unroof, to; *tiabli*
unruffled; *chulosa, nuktala*
unruly; *haksi, isht afekommi*
unsaddle, to; *ishi*
unsaddled, *isuba umpatalhpo akama*
unsafe, *imaleka hinla*
unsaid, *achi*
unsalted, *hapi yammi*
unsatisfied, *fihopa*
unscattered, *fimimpa*
unschooled, *holisso ikithano*
unscorched; *anakshonfa, anakshua*
unscrew, to; *tali shana shunfi*
unseal, to; *mitelichi, mitiffi*
unsealed; *kamassa, tiwa*
unsearchable; *luma, pisahe keyu*
unseasonable, *alhpesa*
unseasoned; *hapi yammi, kallo, kashaha, shila*
unseated, *binili*
unseemly, *alhpesa*
unseen; *luma, pisa*
unsettle, to; *kinaffi, kanallichi*
unsettled; *anta, binili*

unshackle, to; *litoffi*
unshaded, *hoshontika*
unshaken; *ilhkoli, kamassa, kallo*
unshamed, *hofah iksho*
unsheath, to; *shunfi*
unshed; *boyafa, latapa*
unship, to; *kuchi*
unshot; *nala, okshillita, tukafa*
unskilled, *imponna*
unsmooth, *itilaui*
unsocial, *anumpuli*
unsoiled, *lusa*
unsold, *kanchi keyu*
unsolicited, *asilhha*
unsolid, *kallo*
unsought, *hoyo*
unsound; *abeka, anli, kallo*
unsowed, *fima*
unsown, *fima*
unsparing; *ilatomba keyu, nukhanklo iksho*
unspent, *tali*
unspilt, *latapa*
unspoiled; *okpulo, wehpoa*
unspotted; *kashofa, lusa*
unstable; *anli, imanukfila apissanli keyu, kallo*
unstaid, *imanukfila achafa keyu*
unsteady; *ilaiyuka takoli shali, inla shali*
unstop, to; *shunfi, tuwi*
unstopped; *shunfa, tiwa*
unstored, *boli*
unstrained; *holuya, lumasi*
unstring, to; *litoffi, mitiffi, shunfi*
unstudied, *anukfilli*
unsubdued; *imaiya, kostini*
unsuccessful, *aianli*
unsuitable; *alhpesa, imanka*
unsuited, *alhpesa*
unsullied, *lusa*
unsung; *alhtalwa, taloa*
unsunned, *holufka*
unsupplied; *alhtaha, imalhpisa*
unsupported, *apela*
unsuspected, *ahni*
untainted; *okpulo, shua*
untaken; *hokli, inshi*
untamable; *hopoyuksahe keyu, kostinahe keyu*
untamed; *honayo, hopoyuksa*
untasted; *apa, ishkot ikpeso*
untaught; *holisso ithana, ikhana*
unteachable, *ikhanahe keyu*
unthankful; *aiokpanchi, aiokpanchi keyu*

unthawed, *bila*
unthinking; *ahni, anukfilli*
untie, to; *hotofi, hotolichi, litoa, litofa, litoffi, litofkachi, litoli, mitefa, mitelichi, mitiffi*
untie, to cause to; *litoffichi, litolichi*
untied; *hotoli, litofa, litofkachi, litoha, mitefa, miteli*
until; *aiali, takla, taⁿkla*
untimely, *aiona*
untirable, *tikabi*
unto, *aiali* ·
untold, *anoa*
untouched, *potoli*
untoward, *kostini*
untraveled; *anowa, nowa*
untried; *momaka ikpeso, pisa*
untrodden, *anowa*
untroubled, *atakalam iksho*
untrue; *aⁿli, holabi*
untruly; *aⁿli, holabi*
untruth; *aⁿli, holabi*
untwine, to; *fatummi*
unusual, *yohmi fehna keyu*
unutterable, *anoli*
unvalued; *aiilli atapa, holitobli keyu, holitopa atapa*
unviolated; *kobafa, okpulo*
unwarped; *chasaloha, chasala*
unwary, *ahah ahni*
unwashed, *kashofa*
unwashen, *achefa*
unwealthy; *holitopa, imilayak iklauo*
unwearied; *achunanchi, tikabi*
unweighed; *weki, wekichi*
unwelcome, *aiokpanchi*
unwell; *abeka, nipi ikinchukmo*
unwept, *yaiya*
unwholesome, *achukma*
unwieldy; *chito, weki*
unwilling; *ahni, banna, haklo, ilafoa*
unwind, to; *hotofi, litofa, litoffi, litoha, litoli*
unwise; *hopoyuksa, kostini*
unwittingly, *ikithano*
unwomanly, *ohoyo keyu chohmi*
unwonted; *achaya, inla, yohmi chatuk keyu*
unworthy; *achukma, ahoba*
unwound; *litofa, litofkachi*
unwounded; *basha, chaⁿya, chuⁿkash ikhotopo, nala*
unwritten; *holisso, laⁿfa*
unyielding; *bikota keyu, ilafoa, nutaka iahe keyu*

unyoke, to; *ikonlabana imaiishi*
up, *aba*
upbraid, to; *miha, mihachi*
uphold, to; *halalli*
upholder, *halalli*
upland, *nanih foka*
uplift, to; *aba takalichi*
upon; *oⁿ, on, um*
upper, *chaha iⁿshali*
uppermost, *chaha iⁿshaht tali*
upright; *aⁿli, apissanli*
uprightly, *apissanlit*
uproar; *shakapa, yahapa*
upset, to; *filimmi, kinaffi*
upshot; *aiali, isht aiopi*
upstart, *tuⁿshpat holitopa toba*
upstream, *ibetap*
upward; *aba imma, aba pila, aba pilla, imma*
urbane; *nuktanla, yohbi*
urchin, *alla haksi*
urethra, *hoshuⁿwa aminti*
urgent, *chilita*
urinate, to; *hoshuⁿwa*
urine, *hoshuⁿwa*
us; *hapi, hapiⁿ, hapim, hapin, hapishno, ke, keho, kil, kiloh, pi, piⁿ, pim, pin, pishno*
use, *isht atta*
use, to; *atta, nana kanihchi*
used; *lipa, taha*
useful, *achukma*
useless, *ahoba*
usher, *holisso pisachi*
usual; *atak, chokamo*
usually; *atak, beka, chatok, chatuk, chokamo, ke, tak*
usually so, *chatok*
utensil, *isht toⁿksali*
utmost; *aiali, isht aiopi*
utter, *misha*
utter, to; *achi, anoli, anumpuli, miha*
utterable, *anumpa hinla*
utterance, *anumpa*
uttered, *anumpa*
utterly; *amohmi, bano, momint*
uttermost; *isht aiopi, momint*
uttermost, to do the; *kanchi*
uttermost part of, *asetilli*

vacancy, *shahbi*
vacant; *chukillissa, iksho, kana iksho, nana iksho, shahbi*
vacant house, *chukillissa*
vacate, to; *akshuchi, issa, kashoffichi*

vacated; *aksho, issa, kashofa*
vacation; *akshuchi, foha, holisso apisa akucha*
vaccinate, to; *ikhiⁿsh shakba fohki*
vaccinated, *ikhiⁿsh shakba fohka*
vaccine matter, *taloⁿa*
vacillate, to; *faiokạchi, fali, imanukfila ilaiyuka*
vacillation, *faiokạchi*
vagabond; *aiạtta iksho, chuka abaiya, chuka pulalit aⁿya, chukbaiyạchi*
vagabond, to act the; *chukbaiyạchi*
vagrant; *aiạtta iksho, chuka abaiya, chukbaiyạchi, nana silhha*
vagrant, to act as a; *chuka abaiyạchi*
vague; *apissali, haiaka*
vain; *ahoba, aⁿli, fehnạchi, ilefehnạchi*
vainly, *ilahobbi*
vale; *kolokbi, okfa*
valediction; *aiokpạchi, isht aiopi aiokpachi*
valet, *tishu*
valiant; *aiyimita, kạllo, nakni, nukwia iksho*
valid; *achukma, aⁿli, kạllo, lampko*
valley, *okfa*
valley, a deep; *kolokbi, kolokobi*
valley, a level; *patasạchi*
valley, a wide; *okfa maiha*
valor; *kạllo, nukwia iksho*
valorous, *nukwia iksho*
valuable, *holitopa*
value; *aiilli, ạlhtoba, holitopa, iạlli*
value, to; *aiilli onuchi, aiillichi, ạlbichi, holissochi, hotina, iⁿhollo*
valued; *aiilli, ạlbi, holhtena, holitopa*
van; *itikba, tikba*
vandyke, *ikonla umpạtta, na foka ilumpatali, na foka umpạtta*
vane, *mali isht ikhạna*
vanish, to; *kạnia, mosholi*
vanity; *aⁿli, fehnạchi, ilefehnạchi, nana keyu*
vanquish, to; *imaiyạchi*
vanquisher, *imaiyạchi*
vantage, *imaiya*
vapid; *ikhomoki taha, illi*
vapor, *oktohbi*
vapor, to; *ilauata, kifilli, oktohbi*
vaporer, *ilauata*
variable; *ilaiyuka takoli shali, inla hinla, shanaioa*
variance; *inla toba, itachoa*
variation, *inla toba*

variegated, *bạkokuⁿkachi*
variety; *ilaiyuka, nan isht aiyukpahe keyu*
various; *ilabiⁿka, ilaiyuka, ilaiyukali, kanohmi*
various, to make; *ilaiyukachi*
varnish, to; *mạlmakạchechi*
varnishing, *isht ạlhkoha*
vary, to; *achowa, ilaiyukachi, inla, inlạchi*
vassal, *yuka*
vassalage, *yuka aⁿsha*
vast; *chito, hocheto*
vastness, *chito*
vat; *aiạlhto, iti honni aiạlhto, iti isht honni aiạlhto, itombi aiạlhto, oka aiạlhto*
vat, tan; *ahumma, ahummạchi*
vault, *ahollohpi*
vault, to; *tolupli, toluplit wakaya, tulli*
vaunt, to; *ilauata*
vaunter, *ilauata*
veal, *wak ushi nipi*
veer, to; *filema, filemạchi, filemoa, fitekạchi, fitiha, fititekạchi*
vegetable; *haiyuⁿkpulo, na holokchi*
vegetate, to; *offo*
vegetation; *ạlba, nan offo*
vehicle, *ashali*
veil; *na hạta, nashuka isht umpoholmo*
veil, to; *luhmi, umpohomo*
veiled, *umpoholmo*
vein; *akshish, bachaya, hakshish, issish akshish, issish iⁿhina*
vein, a big; *hakshish chito*
velocity; *pạlhki, shinimpa*
venal; *chumpa hinla, haksi*
vend, to; *kanchi*
vender, *kanchi*
vendible, *kancha hinla*
vendue, *kanchi*
venerable, *holitopa*
venerate, to; *holissochi*
venerated, *holitopa*
veneration, *shakba lumpli*
venereal disease; *luak shali, yukbạbi*
venesection; *issish iⁿhina lumpli, issish iⁿkuchi*
vengeance; *nukoa, okha*
vengeance, to take; *okha*
venial, *kashofa hinla*
venison, *isi nipi*
venison, dried; *chohpa*
venom, *isht illi*
venom, to; *isht illi ipeta*

venomous temper, *chunkash homi*
vent; *chiluk, kanchi, kucha*
vent, to; *anoli, kuchi*
vent of firearms, *haksun chiluk*
venter, *ushatto*
ventilate, to; *malichi*
venture, to; *amoshuli, kali, nukwia iksho, yammak fokalechi*
venturesome, *yammak fokali*
Venus, *fichik chito*
veracity, *ianli*
veranda; *aboha apishia, aboha hoshontika*
verbal, *anumpa*
verbally, *anumpa*
verbose, *anumpa laua*
verdant, *okchamali*
verdigris, *okchamali*
verdure, *okchamali*
verge, *ali*
verge, to; *mahaia, manya*
verified, *anli*
verify, to; *aianlichi, anlichi*
verily; *anli, anli hon, anli makon*
verity, *anli*
vermes, *shunshi*
vermifuge; *ikhinsh shunsh isht abi, lapchu abi*
vermilion; *lukfi humma, na humma, tishi humma*
vermin; *poa, poa ushi*
vernal, *toffahpi*
versatile, *ilaiyuka hinla*
verse; *anumpa, anumpa atatoa*
versed, *imponna*
version, *toshoa*
vertebra; *innosishboya, nali foni aiitachaka*
vertex; *nushkobo, tabokaka*
vertical, *tabokoa*
vertigo, *chukfoloha*
very; *afehna, fehna, filinka, tanpi, tokba, tomba*
very, that; *fehnakma*
very close by; *olanlisi, olanusi*
very much, *tokba*
very near; *chekusi, olanlisi*
very near, to cause to be; *olanlisichi*
vesicate, to; *wulhkochi*
vesicated, *wulhko*
vesicle, *wulhko*
Vesper, *fichik chito*
vespers; *oklilahpi, okpolusbi*
vessel; *aialbiha, aialhto, ampo, peni chito*
vessel, a small earthen; *shutushi*

vessel for boiling, *alabocha*
vessel used for cooking meat, *nipi ahoni*
vest; *ilefoka yushkololi, kolokshi, na foka kolukshi*
vest, to; *fohkachi, ilakshema, ishi*
vestal, *kostini*
vested, *fohka*
vestibule, *okhisa*
vestige; *aionhikia, iyi*
vestment, *na fohka*
vesture, *na fohka*
veteran; *aiimomachi, sipokni, tashka sepokni*
vex, to; *nukoa, nukoachi*
vexation; *isht nukoa, nukoa, nukoachi*
vexatious; *isht atakalama chito, komota*
vexed; *aiokpuloka, hashanya, nukoa, komota*
vial, *kotobushi*
viand; *ilhpak, ilimpa*
vibrate, to; *fahakachechi, fahakachi, fahali, fahalichi, fahata, fahatachi*
vibrated; *fahakachi, fahali, fahata*
vibration; *fahakachi, fahata*
vicarious, *alhtoba*
vice, *nana achukma*
vice-agent, *imanumpeshi*
vicegerent; *alhtobat atta, kapitani iakaiya*
vicinage, *bilinka*
vicinity, *bilinka*
vicious; *haksi, okpulo, yoshoba*
victor, *imaiya*
victorious, *imaiya*
victory, *imaiya*
victual, to; *pinak imatali*
victualled, *pinak imaltaha*
victualler, *pinak imatali*
victuals; *holhponi, honni, ilhpak, ilimpa, impa, labocha, na holhponi, nan ilhpak, nan ilimpa*
vie, to; *imaiya*
view; *apisaka, apisali, imanukfila, nishkin, pisa*
view, to; *anukfilli, hoponkoyo, pisa*
viewer, *pisa*
vigil; *apistikeli, ninak aba pit anumpuli*
vigilance; *apistikeli, okcha*
vigilant; *ahah ahni, apistikeli, okcha*
vigor; *kallo, kilimpi*
vigorous; *kamassa, kallo*
vile; *aknanka, chakapa, haksi, okpulo*
vile language; *anumpa okpulo, chakapa*

vilely, *okpulo*
vilely, to act; *haksi*
vileness, *okpulo*
vilify, to; *chakapa, isht yopula, okpạni*
villa, *tạmahushi*
village; *lukoli, tạmaha*
village, small; *tạmahushi*
villain; *haksichi, hatak haksi, na haksi*
villainous, *haksi*
vincible, *imaiya hinla*
vindicate, to; *anumpuli*
vindictive; *nukoa, nukoa shali*
vine, a; *ạpi, balạlli, paⁿkạpi*
vine, a species of; *chukfi imaseta, kauehto*
vinegar, *oka hauạshko*
vineyard, *paⁿkạpi aholokchi*
viol, *alepa chito*
violate, to; *hoklit aiissa, kobạffi, okpạni*
violated, *okpulo*
violator; *hoklit aiissa, kobạffi, okpạni*
violence; *kạllo, nan okpulo*
violent; *kạllo, palạmmi*
viper; *chukfitohtoloti, sinti chilita, sinti okpulo*
virago, *ohoyo chito*
virgin; *aⁿti, himmona, kostini*
virgin, a; *ohoyo hatak ikhalelo, ohoyo himmita*
virtue; *achukma, aiaⁿti, aⁿti, kạllo, lampko*
virtuous; *achukma, ạlhpesali, kostini*
virulent; *homi fehna, isht illi okpulo*
virus; *isht illi, okchushba*
visage, *nashuka*
viscera, *iskuna*
viscerate, to; *iskuna kuchi*
viscid, *likaha*
vise, *isht kiselichi*
visible; *haiaka, kucha, pisa hinla*
visible, hardly; *yauiⁿyaui*
vision; *apisaka, nan inla, pisa*
visit; *iⁿnowa, nowa, pisa*
visit, to; *aⁿya, iⁿnowa, nowa, pisa*
visitor, *iⁿnowa*
vital, *aiokchaⁿya*
vitality, *aiokchaⁿya*
vitals; *aiisht aiokchaya, shilukpa*
vitals, diseased; *shilukpa lachowa*
vitiate, to; *okpạni*
vitiated, *okpulo*
vivacious, *okcha*
vivacity, *okcha*
vivid; *okcha, shohkalali*

vivificate, to; *okchalechi*
vivified, *yimmita*
vivify, to; *okchalechi*
vocal, *itạkha*
vocation, *imạlhtayak*
vociferate, to; *paⁿya, tahpạla*
voice; *anumpa, anumpuli, imanukfila, itạkha*
void; *iksho, shahbi*
void, to; *issa, kuchi*
voidable, *akshucha hinla*
voided, *kucha*
vogue, *aiyạmohmi*
volant; *heli, hika*
volatile; *hika, okcha*
volcano, *yakni anuⁿkaka lua*
volition, *ahni*
volley, *tukali*
voluble, *anumpuli shali*
volume, *holisso*
voluntary; *ilap ahni, ilap ahni yạmohmi*
volunteer, to; *ilap ahni*
voluptuary, *isikopa shali*
vomit; *hoeta, hoetạchi, ikhiⁿsh ishkot hoita*
vomit, to; *hoeta, hohoetạchi, okissa*
vomit, to cause to; *hoetạchi*
vomit continually, to; *hohoeta*
vomiting; *hoeta, hohoeta*
voracious; *impa aiyimita, impa fena*
vortex, *oka foyulli*
vote; *anumpa, atokoli, holisso*
voted, *ạlhtoka*
voter, *atokoli*
vouch, to; *anumpa kạllo ilonuchi cha ia*
vouchsafe, to; *ome ahni*
vow, *anumpa kạllo onutula*
vow, to; *anumpa kạllo ilonuchi cha ia*
vow of revenge, *ilaiukha*
voyage at sea, *okhạta chito aⁿya*
voyager, *okhạta chito aⁿya*
vulgar; *chakapa, makali, okpulo*
vulgar, the; *okla makali*
vulgarity; *aiyạmohmi makali, makali*
vulnerable, *nạla hinla*
vulture, *sheki chito*

wabble, to; *shanaioa*
wad; *isht ạlhkạma, isht oktạpa*
wadding; *ạlhpitta, isht impạtta, naki impạtalhpo*
waddle, to; *kaiakạchi, shaioksholi*
wade, to; *anowa, okokanowa*
wade a river, to; *okhina akka nowạt lopulli*

wade in the water, to; *oka nowa*
wader, *okokcnowa*
wading, *oka nowa*
wafer; *holisso isht akamassa, holisso isht akallo, holisso isht ashana, holisso isht alhkama*
waft, to; *anya, aba anya, aba isht anya*
wag, *hatak yopula*
wag, to; *kania, onchasanakli*
wag the head, to; *akkachunni, akkachunochunli*
wage, to; *anta, kali*
wager; *boli, kaha, kali*
wager, to; *kali*
wager, to accept a; *aseta*
wagered, *kaha*
wages; *alhtoba, nan alhtoba*
waggish, *itakhapuli shali*
wagon; *iti chanalli, iti chanaha*
wagon, to; *iti chanalli ashali, iti chanaha isht anya, iti chanaha isht shali*
wagon, hand; *iti chanallushi*
wagon, small; *iti chanallushi, iti chanaha iskitini, iti chanaha ushi*
wagon body; *iti chanalli haknip*
wagon cover, *iti chanaha umpoholmo*
wagon load, *iti chanaha alota*
wagon maker, *iti chanaha ikbi*
wagon road; *hina chito, hina patha, iti chanalli inhina, iti chanaha inhina*
wagoner, *iti chanaha isht anya*
wagonful, *iti chanaha alota*
wail, *yaiya*
wail, to; *nukhanklo, yaiya*
wailing, *yaiya*
waist, *iffuka*
waistband, *iffuka apakfopa*
waistcoat; *ilefoka yushkololi, na foka kolukshi*
wait, to; *anta, anukcheto, hoyo, hoyot anta, nan inhoyat anya*
wait in secret, to; *lumat chinya*
waiter; *kafaiishko ataloha, kafaiontala, tishu*
waive, to; *issa*
wake, to; *okcha, okchali*
wakeful, *okcha*
wakefulness, *okcha*
waken, to; *okchali*
wakened, *okcha*
wakener, *okchali*
waker, *okchali*
walk; *anowa, hina, nowa*
walk, to; *akkanowa, nowa, nowachi*

walk, to be able to; *hikia toba*
walk about, to; *hikikina*
walk fast, to; *chali, tunshpat nowa*
walk fast, to cause to; *chalichi*
walk in the water, to; *oka nowa*
walk like another, to; *hobachit nowa*
walk over, to; *abanopoli*
walk proudly, to; *fehnachi*
walk slowly and softly, to; *yappalli*
walk through, to; *lopulli*
walk with, to; *ibanowa*
walk with, to cause to; *ibanowachi*
walk with short steps, to; *tulolichi*
walker; *hikikina, nowa*
walking, *nowa*
walking stick, *tabi*
wall, *tali holihta*
wall, to; *tali holihta ikbi, tali holihta isht apakfobli, tali isht holihtachi*
wall-eyed; *nishkin oktalonli, nishkin okwalonli*
walled, *tali holihta isht apakfopa*
waller, *tali holihta ikbi*
wallet; *bahta, bahtushi, shukcha*
wallop, to; *walalli*
wallow, to; *okashalayi, shalali, tononoli, yupi*
wallowing place, *ayupi*
walnut; *hahe, uksak hahe*
walnut tree, *hahe api*
wampum, *oksup*
wan, *hanta*
wand, *fuli*
wander, to; *chuka abaiya, fullokachi, himak fokalechit anya, himak fokalit anya, itamoa, naksikaia, tamoa*
wandered, *tamoa*
wanderer; *folota, yoshoba*
wandering; *aiyoshoba, folota, himak fokalechi*
wane, to; *kanchi, laua*
wanness, *hanta*
want, to; *baiyana, banna, iksho, laua, ona*
wantage, *iksho*
wanting; *banna, iksho*
wanton; *haksi, haui, haui anukfoyuka, yopula shali, yoshoba*
wanton, to; *folota, haksi, ilaualli, washoha, yopula*
war; *itoti, tanampi, tanap*
war, secretary of; *tanap anumpuli*
war, to; *tanampi, tanap isht ashwanchi*
war chief, *hopaii*

war club, *iti tapena*
war dance, *paⁿshi isht hila*
war dancer, *paⁿshi isht hila*
war office, *tanap anumpuli aiasha*
war prophet, *hopaii*
war song, *atalwachi*
war whoop; *hopatuloa, kohuⁿachi, paⁿya*
war worn, *tanap aⁿya tikambi*
war-beaten, *tanap aⁿya tikambi*
warble, *taloa*
warble, to; *taloa*
warbler, *taloa*
ward; *aboha kallo, apistikeli, holihta kallo*
ward, to; *apistikeli*
warden, *apistikeli*
warder, *apistikeli*
wardrobe; *na fohka, na foka aiasha*
wares; *alhpoyak, ilaⁿyak, imilayak, nan alhpoyak*
warfare, *tanap*
warily, *ahah ahni*
warlike; *hoyopa, tanap holba*
warm; *alohbi, atohbi, lahba, lashpa, libesha, palli*
warm, to; *atohbichi, lashpachi, lashpali, libisha, libishli, lahbachi, likema, likemachi, likimmi, nuklibisha, nuklibishli*
warm, to cause to be; *alotichi*
warm by the sun, to; *hashi inni, hashi libisha*
warm climate, *alashpaka*
warm over, to; *hokbali*
warmed; *alohbi, lahba, lashpa, libisha, nuklibisha*
warmth; *alohbi, lahba, lashpa, libesha, nuklibisha*
warn, to; *anoli, atohno, miha*
warned; *anoa, anumpa*
warp, to; *bochusa, bochusachi, bokusa, chasalohachi, chasala, chasalachi, pashanoha*
warp, to cause to; *bokusachi*
warp of cloth, *api*
warped; *bochusa, bokusa, chasaloha, chasala*
warped up, *passalohah*
warping bars; *ahotachi, ponola ahotachi, ponola hulhtufa*
warrant, *holisso*
warrant, to; *aiokpachi, aⁿlichi, atokoli, tohno*
warrior; *nakni, nakni tashka, tanap, tashka*
warrioress, *ohoyo tashka*

wart; *chilakchawa, shilukwa*
wary, *ahah ahni*
was; *atok, atuk, hatuk, hok, kamo, tok, tuk, tukatok*
was about to be, *chintok, chintuk*
was to be; *achintok, achintuk*
wash, *ahchifa*
wash, to; *achefa, ahchifa, aieli, aielichi, aiokami, kashoffi, okami, okamichi, yupi*
wash bowl; *aiokami, ampo aiachefa*
wash place, *aiachefa*
wash room, *aboha nan aiachefa*
wash the hands, to; *ibachifa, ibbak achefa*
washed; *achefa, aieha, alhchefa, alhchifa*
washed bright, *okshauanli*
washed clean, *okshauanli*
washtub; *aiachefa, nan aiachefa*
washwoman; *nan achefa, nan achefa ohoyo, ohoyo nan achefa*
wasp, a large; *tekhanto*
wasp, a large yellow; *chanashik*
wasp, a small yellow; *yakni foi, yakni foishke*
wasp, a yellow-striped; *koafabi*
waspish, *nukoa shali*
waste; *ahoba, chukillissa, isht yupomo, okpulo*
waste, to; *chunnat ia, isht yopomo, kanchi, okpani, yukoma*
waste paper, *holisso okpulo*
waste time, to; *nitak isht yopomo*
wasted; *isht yopomo, okpulo, shulla*
wasteful; *isht yopomo shali, isht yopula*
waster; *isht yopomo, isht yupomo*
watch; *apistikeli, atoni, nam potoni, nusi, okcha, potoni*
watch (timepiece), *hashi isht ikhana*
watch, to; *ahinna, aiihchi, apistikeli, atohni, atoni, hopoⁿkoyo, hoyo, okcha, potoni*
watch, to cause to; *apistikelichi*
watch crows, to; *fala atoni*
watch maker, *hashi isht ithana ikbi*
watch of the night, *isht alhpisa*
watch pocket, *hashi isht ikhana iⁿshukcha*
watch the sick, to; *abeka apistikeli*
watcher; *abeka apistikeli, ahinna, apistikeli*
watchful; *ahah ahni, apistikeli, hopoⁿkoyo shali*
watchhouse, *apistikeli ahikia*

water; *fichak, oka, okchi, okchushba, okhata*
water, astringent; *oka takba*
water, bitter; *oka takba*
water, cold; *oka kapassa*
water, cool; *oka kapassa*
water, deep; *okshakla*
water, fresh; *oka kapassa*
water, high; *okchito, okshakla*
water, hot; *oka lashpa*
water, lukewarm; *oka lahba*
water, tepid; *oka lahba*
water, to; *banna, lachali, oka ipeta, oka toba, okachi*
water, to be in; *oka hinka*
water, warm; *oka libesha*
water bucket, *oka isht ochi*
water edge; *oka ati, oka ont alaka, oka sita*
water flood, *okchito*
water mill, *oka tanch afótoha*
water pail, *isht ochi*
water trough, *iti oka aiyanalli*
water vessel, *oka alhto*
water wheel, *iti chanaha*
watercourse, *okhina*
waterfall; *kihepa, oka pitafohopa, oka pitakinafa*
water-furrow, *oka ayanalli*
waterfowl, *oka hushi*
watering place, *aiishko*
water-man, *peni isht atta*
watermelon, *shukshi*
watermelon, the core of a; *shukshi ikfuka, shukshi nipi*
watermelon seed, *shukshi nipi pehna*
waterpot; *isht ochi, oka alhto, oka isht ochi*
waterproof, *bichillahe keyu*
waterside, *oka lapalika*
watery; *oka holba, oka toba, okchauwi, okchawaha*
wattle, *fuli*
wattle, to; *tana*
wattled, *tanna*
wattles of a hen; *akank chaka, akank impasha*
waul, to; *woha, yanwa*
wave; *banatha, banakachi, banatboa, oka banatha, oka bananya, paieli, wisattakachi*
wave, a high; *poakachi*
wave, made to; *piakachi*

wave, to; *banatboa, banatha, fahakachi, fahali, fahalichi, faiokachi, fali, fatali, oka banathat anya, oka piakachi, oka poakachi, paieli, paiokachi, piakachi, wisakachi*
wave, to cause the water to; *banatbohachi, banathachi, faioli, fatalichi, paiolichi*
wave and bend, to; *wishaha*
wave backward and forward, to cause to; *folotowachi*
wave high, to; *poakachi*
wave in small waves, to; *oka wisakachi*
wave the hand, to; *fali*
wave the head, to; *akkachunni, akkachunochunli*
waved; *faha, fahakachi, fahali, paiokachi*
waver, *wannichi*
wavering, *imanukfila achafa keyu*
waves, to cause; *paielichi*
waving; *faiokachi, paieli*
waving in the wind, *fataha*
wax; *foe hakmi, foe inlakna, litilli*
wax, shoemaker's; *tiak nia kallo*
wax, to; *inshaht ia, inshali*
wax of the ear, *haksobish litilli*
wax tree, *hika*
way; *aiimalhpesa, aiyamohmi, atanya, atia, hina, katiohmi, yamohmi, yohmi*
way, a broad; *hina chito*
way, after such a; *yohmi*
way, out of the; *yoshoba*
way, that; *yamma*
way, this; *yakohmika, yohmi*
way, to be on the; *wihat anya*
way maker, *hina ikbi*
way mark, *iti tila*
way of peace, *hina hanta*
way to, *imma*
wayfarer, *hatak nowat anya*
wayfaring, *nowat anya*
wayward, *ilapunla*
we, *e, eho, hapi, hapia hapishno, il, ilo, ke, keho, kil, pi, pia, pishno*
weak; *homi, kallo, kota, tikabi, walunchi*
weak, to render; *kotachi*
weak and trembling, *ilapissa*
weaken, to; *homechi, kallochi, kotachi, tikabichi*
weakened; *kota, tikabi*
weakly, *kallo*
weakness; *kallo, kota, tikabi*

weal, *achukma*
wealth, *nan inlaua*
wealthy; *imilayak chito, nan inlaua*
wean, to; *pishi issąchi*
wean the affections, to; *chuⁿkąsh shanaiąchi*
weaned, *iṅahaksi*
weapon; *isht itibbi, na halupa, nan isht itibbi*
wear, *isht oktąpa*
wear, to; *lipli, pikoffi, tikabi, tikabichi*
wear a turban, to; *ialipa*
wear out, to; *lipachi, liposhichi, tahat ia*
wearied; *ataha, hoyąbli, intakobi, komota, komunta*
wearied with, *aiintakobi*
weariness; *komunta, tikabi*
wearisome, *ahchiba*
weary; *hoyąbli, tikabi*
weary, to; *ahchibali, fomoli, hoyąblichi, intakobichi, tikabichi*
weary with, to; *aiintakobichi*
weather; *kocha, kucha*
weather, to; *achunanchi, lopulli*
weathercock, *mali isht ikhąna*
weatherwise, *kuchapisa imponna*
weave, to; *tanąffo, tąna*
weaver; *nan tąnna, tąna*
web; *nan tąnna, tąnna*
wed, to; *auaya*
wedded, *auaya*
wedding; *ohoyo ipetąchi, ohoyo itihaląllichi*
wedding day, *auaya, nitak aiitauaya*
wedding feast, *auaya*
wedge; *holi, isht pąla*
wedge, a wooden; *iti isht pąla*
wedge, an iron; *tiak isht pąla*
wedge, to; *iti isht pąla, shamąllichi*
wedlock, *auaya*
weed; *ąlba, haiyuⁿkpulo, nan lusa isht tabashi*
weed, a black; *poluⁿsak*
weed, a certain; *bisakchula, hakonlo, kanumpa, paⁿshtali, shalintakoba, shilukafama, tala, tąpintąpi, tiak iⁿpaląmmi*
weed, to; *aleli, leli*
weed that dyes black, *poafąchi*
weed used in dyeing red, *pishaiyik, pishkak, pishuk*
weeded; *alia, lia*
weeder; *aleli, leli*
week; *nitak hollo, wik*
week day, *nitak inla*

weekly, *nitak hollo achąfakma*
weep, to; *nishkin okchi, nishkin okchi minti, nukhaⁿklo, wilanli, yaiya*
weeper, *yaiya*
weeping, *nishkin okchiyanąlli*
weevil, *hapąlak*
weevil-eaten; *shakbona, shiluⁿka, shiluⁿkąchi*
weft, *tąnna*
weigh, to; *anukfilli, ąba isht ia, weki, weki itilaui, wekichi*
weigh alike, to cause to; *weki itilauichi*
weighed, *weki*
weigher, *wekichi*
weight; *na weki, tąli isht weki, tąli uski, weki*
weight, being of equal; *weki itilaui*
weight, to be of equal; *weki itilauichi*
weighty, *weki*
welcome, *aiokpanchi*
welcome, to; *aiokpąchi*
weld, to; *achakąli, aiitachakąlli*
welded; *achaka, ąlhchąka, ąlhchąkoa*
welfare, *achukma aⁿsha*
well; *achukma, achukma aⁿsha, achukmaⁿka, achukmat, ąlhpesa, chukma, fehna, hochukmat, imponna, yąmma*
well! (excl.); *aume, inta, okinta, ome, omikąto, omishke*
well, a; *kąli, kąli hofobi*
well, it may be; *omiha*
well, to do; *achukma, hochukma*
well, to look; *ilafia*
well curb, *kąli aholihta*
well done, *ąlhpesa*
well rope, *aseta isht ochi*
well water, *kąli oka*
well-disposed, *hopoksia*
well-fed, *kaiya*
well known; *anoa, ikhana achukma*
well-natured, *yukpa*
well-nigh; *he, naha*
welt, *afohoma*
welt, to; *afohommi*
welted, *afohoma*
welter, to; *okatonoli, yupi*
wen, *shatohpa*
wench; *hatak lusa haui, ohoyo haui*
west; *hąshi aiitolaka, hąsih aiokatula, hąshi aiokatula, hąshi aopiaka*
west, to or at the; *hąshi aiokatula pilla*
western; *hąshi aiokatula, hąshi aiokatula pilla*

westward; *hashi aiokatula, hashi aiokatula imma, hashi aiokatula pila*
wet; *hokulbi, lacha, oka, oklanshko*
wet, a little; *okyohbi*
wet, to; *lachali, okkachi, oklanshkochi*
wet weather, *kucha umba*
wet with the dew, *onshichakmo*
wetness, *lacha*
wetted, *lacha* .
whale, *nani chito*
whaling, *afama*
what; *hacha, katih, katimakakosh, katiohmi, kat, kata, nana, nanta, nantami,
nantihmi*
what for; *na katimi, nantami*
what is the matter, *na katimiho*
what is the reason, *na katimiho*
what kind, of; *katiohmi*
what manner, in; *katiohmi*
what number, *katohmi*
what time, about; *katiohmi*
whatever, *nana kia*
whatsoever; *nana hon, nana kia*
wheat; *onush, tiliko*
wheat barn, *onush aiasha*
wheat bread, *tiliko palaska*
wheat cake, *tiliko palaska iskatini*
wheat chaff, *onush haklupish*
wheat fan, *onush amalichi*
wheat flour; *onush bota, tiliko bota*
wheat harvest, *onush almo*
wheat stalk, *onush api*
wheedle, to; *yimmichi*
wheel; *chanalli, chanaha, iti chanaha, iti
kalaha, kalaha*
wheel, a truck; *iti kalaha chanalli*
wheel, to; *chanallichi, chanaha, folota*
wheel band, *ahonola isht talakchi*
wheelbarrow; *iti chanallushi, iti chanaha
iskitini, iti chanaha ushi*
wheelwright, *iti chanaha ikbi*
wheeze, to; *chitot fiopa*
whelm, to; *oklobushlichi, oklubbichi*
whelmed; *oklobushli, oklubbi*
whelp; *nashobushi, ofunsik, ofushi*
whelp, to; *cheli*
when; *hokma, ikma, kaniohmi foka hon
kaniohmi kash, katiohmi, kma, ma, mano,
mano, mat, mih, yok*
when he, *atuk*
when it was so, *yohmima*
whence; *katima, katimakon, katiohmi*
whencesoever, *kanima kia*
whenever, *kanimash inli kia*

where; *i, kanima, katima, katimaho,
katimahosh, katimakon, mato*
whereabout, *katimafoka*
whereas, *yamohmi hoka*
whereat, *yamohmi hoka*
whereby, *yammak o*
wherefore; *katiohmi, na katimi, na
katimiho, na katiohmi, nanta, nantimiho,
yamohmi ho*
wherein, *yammak o*
whereof, *yammak o*
wheresoever, *kanima kia*
whereunto, *nanta*
whereupon, *yamohmi ho*
wherever, *kanima kia*
wherewith, *nanta*
whet, to; *haluppachi, sholichi*
whether; *katimakakosh, katimampo, katimampo kakosh, ok*
whetstone; *ashuahchi, isht halupalli,
isht shuahchi*
whetted; *halupa, shuahchi*
whetter, *haluppachi, sholichi*
whey, *pishukchi okchi*
which; *an, ho, kak, katima, katimaho,
katimahosh, katimaian, katimakon, katimampo ho, katimampo ka, katimampo
kakon, katimampo kakosh, kat, 'ma, mak,
mano, mat, mato, nanta, on, ya, yammak
osh*
which, the one; *an*
which having been, *atuk*
which of all, *katimampo aiyukali kakosh*
which of two, *katimampo*
whichever, *nana*
whichsoever; *kanimampo, katimampo*
whiff, *fiopa* .
whiff, to; *fiopa*
whiffle, to; *imanukfila shanaioa*
whiffletree; *isuba ahalalli, iti ahulalli,
iti isht halalli*
whiffling, *imanukfila shanaioa*
while; *itintakla, ititakla, tankla*
while, a; *hopaki, itintakla, kanima*
while, to; *anta, nitak isht yopomo*
while it was so; *yohmit itintakla*
whilst, *itintakla*
whimper, to; *yaiya*
whimsical, *imanukfila ilaiyuka*
whine, *binkbia*
whine, to; *binka, binkbia, kifaha*
whiner, *binkbia*
whinny, to; *kileha, sihinka*
whinnying, *sihinka*

whinock, *shukhushi isht aiopi*

whip; *isht fama, lukata*

whip, to; *fammi, massaha, massalichi*

whip handle, *lukatapi*

whiplash; *isht lukata, lukata wishakchi*

whipped, *fama*

whipper; *fammi, fuli isht fammi, na fammi*

whipping; *fama, fammi, fuli isht fama*

whipping post, *afama*

whippletree, *isuba ahalalli*

whip-poor-will; *chukkilakbila, hachukbilankbila, wahwali*

whipsaw, *iti isht basha falaia*

whipsnake, *pochunhatapa*

whipstock, *lukatapi*

whirl, *fali*

whirl, to; *afolichi, fahfoa, fali, fitekachi, fitiha, fitihachi, fititekachi, oka foyuha, oka foyulli*

whirl bone, *iyin kalaha wishakchi*

whirl quickly, to; *fitelichi*

whirled; *fahakachi, fitekachi, fititekachi*

whirled about, *fahfoa*

whirler, *fali*

whirling; *fahakachi, fitekachi*

whirlpool; *oka foyuha, oka foyulli*

whirlwind; *apanukfila, apeli, apanukfila*

whisk, *isht pashpoa iskitini*

whisk, to; *fali, hasimbish fali*

whisker, *nutakhish*

whisky; *na homi, oka, oka homi, wishki*

whisper, *lumat anumpa*

whisper, to; *lumat anumpuli, shukshua*

whisperer; *lumat anumpuli, na mihachi shali*

whistle, *uskulushi*

whistle, to; *kunta, sunksowa*

whistler; *kunta, uskulush olachi*

whistling, *kunta*

whit, *iskitinisi*

white; *hanta, hatachi, hata, hatakbi, tohbi*

white, made; *tohbi*

white, to grow; *hatachi*

white, to make; *hantachi, tohbichi*

white, to paint; *tohbichi*

white, to turn; *hatachi*

white-faced and -footed, *ibakshulanli, ibakshulanshli*

white face and feet, to have; *ibakshulanli*

white flour, *onush bota*

white man; *hatak nipi tohbi, hatak nipi tohbika, na hollo*

white of an egg, *akank ushi walakachi*

white paper, *holisso tohbi*

white people, *na hollo*

white-eyed; *okshilonli, oktalonli, okwalonli*

whiten, to; *hatokbichi, tohbichi, tohbit ia*

whitened; *okshauanli, tohbi, tohbit taha*

whitener, *tohbichi*

whiteness, *tohbi*

whites, the; *hata ont ia*

whitewash, *lukfanta*

whitewood, *iti hata*

whither; *kanima, katima*

whitish; *hatokbi, tohbi chohmi*

whitlow, *shatali*

whittle, to; *tali, tili, tilichi*

whittled, *tala*

whiz, to; *shinkachi, shilohachi*

who; *at, anankosh, at, ho, kato, kanahosh, kata, ket, nanta, ya, yat, yon*

who, the one; *ya*

who is, *atuk*

who so, *kanaho*

whoever, *kana kia*

whole; *achukma, aliha, lakoffi, moma, okluha, putali*

whole, to take the; *tomaffi*

wholesome, *achukma*

wholly; *bano, mominchi, taha*

whom; *katimampo ho, kata, on*

whom, to; *kanaho*

whomsoever, *kana kia*

whoop; *kohunachi, panya*

whoop, the death; *tashka panya*

whoop, to; *humpah, kumpachi, panya, tasaha, tasali*

whoop, to make; *panyachi*

whoop at the grave, to; *tashka panya*

whooping, *tasaha*

whooping cough, *hotilhko finka*

whoops, one who; *panya*

woodpecker, a small, speckled; *oktink*

whore; *haui, ohoyo haui*

whoredom, *haui*

whoredom, to commit; *alia*

whoremaster, *haui ikbi*

whoremonger, *ohoyo imalia*

whoremonger, to act the; *haui petichit nowa*

whortleberry, *yunlo*

whortleberry, high bush; *oksakohchi*

whose; *kata, osh*

whoso, *kanahosh*

whosoever; *kana kia, kanahosh*

why; *katihmi, katiohmi, katiohmi hoⁿ, na katimi, na katimiho, na katiohmi, nanta, nantami*
wick of a candle, *honula*
wicked; *alhpesa, haksi, okpulo, yoshoba*
wicked, the; *hatak haksi*
wicked one, *nan tasembo*
wickedness, *okpulo*
wicker, *fuli atoba*
wide; *auata, hopalhka, hopatka, hopaki, maiha, patha*
wide apart; *shauaha, shauola, shauwaloha, yauaha*
wide apart, to cause to be; *shauahachi*
wide apart, to make grow; *shauwalohachi*
wide apart, to place; *shauwalohachi, yauahachi*
wide enough, *patha alhpiesa*
wide foot, *iyi patha*
widely; *hopaki, hopakichit, kostinit, łapat*
widen, to; *pathachi, yatabli*
widened, *patha*
widow; *alhtakla, iⁿhatak illi, ohoyo iⁿhatak illi*
widower, *tekchi illi*
width; *auata, hopatka, patha*
width of the foot, *iyi patha*
wife; *achuka, amohoyo, itaiena, kasheho, ohoyo, tekchi*
wife, old; *ohoyo kasheho*
wife, white man's; *na hollo imohoyo, na hollo tekchi*
wig, *paⁿshi iałipa*
wiggle, to; *fatokachi*
wiggletails; *chuⁿkash apa, hatak chuⁿkash apa*
wigwam, *hatak api humma inchuka*
wild; *aiokla, honayo, hopoyuksa, imała, iti anuⁿkaka, kostini, nukshopa, tasembo*
wild beasts, *nan nukshopa*
wild beasts, bad; *poa okpulo*
wild creatures, *nan nukshopa*
wilderness; *iti anuⁿka, koⁿwi anuⁿka, koⁿwi chito, koⁿwi haiaka, koⁿwi shabi, yakni haiaka*
wildly, *nukshopa*
wildness; *honayo, hopoyuksa, kostini*
wile, *isht haksichi*
wilily, to act; *kostini*
will; *a, aⁿ, achiⁿ, achik, ahe, ashke, chiⁿ, chike, chuk, hachiⁿ, he, het, hi, himma, hinla, hokma, kachiⁿ, lashke*
will (a document), *imissa*

will, his; *ilap ahni*
will, the; *ahni, aiahni, imanukfila, nan aiahni*
will, to; *ahni, aiahni, apesa, anukfilli, banna, imissa*
will be, *chiⁿshki*
will be, probably; *achike*
will not; *ahe keyu, aheto, awa, chiⁿchint, he keyu, heto*
willful, *ilap ahni bieka*
willing; *ahni, alhpesa ahni, ome ahni*
willow; *takoiⁿsha, tikoiⁿsha*
willow, weeping; *takoⁿwisha naksish falaia, tikoiⁿsha naksish falaia*
wilt, to; *balakłi, balakłichi, bashechi, bashi, bilakłi, bilakłichi*
wilt before a fire, to; *polua*
wilted; *balakłi, bashi, bilakłi*
wily, *haksi*
win, to; *abi, imaiya, iⁿshi*
win back, to; *okha*
wince, to; *hehka*
wincer, *hehka*
winch; *isht fotoli, isht shanni*
winch, to; *habli*
wind; *fiopa, ilhfiopak, mali*
wind, bad or dangerous; *mali okpulo*
wind, great; *mali chito*
wind, hot; *mali lashpa*
wind, south; *oka mali mali*
wind, strong; *mali kallo*
wind (or track), to; *ahchishi*
wind (turn), to; *afoli, aiskiachi, fotoli, olachi*
wind, to make; *afolichi, polomolichi*
wind, violent; *mali kallo*
wind, water; *oka mali*
wind along, to; *shanakachi*
wind around, to cause to; *afoblichi*
wind feathers on an arrow, to; *hotti*
wind its way, to; *abaiyachi*
wind round, to; *afoli, apakchulli, apakfoa, apakfoblichi, apakfoli, apakfopa, affoa*
windfall, *ani chilofa*
windgall, *shatali*
winding; *panala, yiⁿyiki*
winding and crooked, *yiⁿyiki*
windmill, *mali tanch afotoha*
window; *aboha apisa, apisa, apisa isht alhkama, okhisushi*
window blind, *okhisushi isht alhkama*
window shutter, *okhisushi isht alhkama*
windpipe; *isht fiopa, kolumpi*

windpipe of a fowl, *kalonshi*
windward, *mali pila*
windy, very; *mali shali*
wine; *oka hauashko, oka homi, oka panki, panki okchi*
wine, claret; *oka panki humma*
wine, port; *oka panki humma*
wine, red; *oka panki humma*
wine bibber, *oka panki ishko shali*
wine cask, *oka panki aialhto*
wine glass, *oka panki aiishko*
wine merchant, *oka panki kanchi*
winefat, *aialbiha*
wing; *ali, sanahchi*
wing, to; *hika, sanahchi ikbi*
wink; *mocholi achafa, mochukli*
wink, to; *mocholi, mochukli, mushli, mushmushli, okmisli*
wink at, to; *amochonli*
winker, *mushli*
winking of the eye, *nishkin mochukli*
winner; *imaiya, ishi*
winning; *imaiya, ishi*
winnow, to; *amalichi, mashlichi*
winnowed; *mashahchi, mishahchi*
winnowing floor, *amalichi*
winter; *hashtula, onafa*
winter, the early part of; *hashtulam- mona*
winter, to; *hashtula anta na lopulli*
winter house, *anunka lashpa*
winter quarters for an army, *hashtula tashka chipota aiasha*
wintry; *hashtula chohmi, kapassa*
wipe, to; *kasholichi*
wipe out, to; *kashoffichit kanchi*
wiped; *kashofa, kashokachi*
wiper; *isht kashokachi, isht kasholichi, kasholichi, nan isht kasholichi*
wire, *tali fobassa*
wire, to; *tali fobassa isht takchi*
wiredraw, to; *shebli, tali fobassa ikbi*
wiredrawn, *shepa*
wisdom; *ahopoksinka, ahopoyuksa, ho- poksa, hopoyuksa, nan ithana*
wise; *ahopoksa, ahopoksia, ahopoyuksa, apoksia, hopoksa, hopoksia, kostini*
wise, the; *na kostini*
wise, to be on this; *yakohmi*
wise, to make; *hopoksiachi*
wise man; *hatak hopoksia, hatak hopo- yuksa, hatak kostini*
wisely, *hopoyuksa*
wish; *ahni, banna*

wish, his; *ilap ahni*
wish, to; *ahni, aiahni, anukfilli, asilhha, banna, pit*
wish for, to; *chunkash banna, chunkash ia*
wish for more, to; *anukshumpa*
wish intently, to; *banna fehna*
wish to go, to; *ia*
wisher; *ahni, banna*
wishful; *anukfilli, banna*
wit; *ikhana, imanukfila, imponna*
wit, a; *hatak imanukfila tunshpa*
wit, to; *ikhana*
witch; *chuka ishi kanchak, hatak holhkun- na, hatak yushpakammi, holhkunna, isht ahollo, nan apoluma, nan isht ahollo, ohoyo isht ahollo*
witch, a ball-play; *apoluma*
witch, a great; *hatukchaya*
witch, to; *apolumi, isht ahollo, pakammi*
witch ball, *isht albi*
witch-hazel, *iyanabi*
witchcraft; *fappo, holhkunna, isht ahollo, yushpakama*
witchcraft, to pretend to; *isht ahollo ilahobi*
with; *aiena, aieninchi, aiitapinha, apeha, apiha, atakla, aua, awant, hiket anya, iba, ibafokat, isht, takla*
with, to go; *ibafokat anya*
with all, *akaieta*
with haste, *ashalinka*
with truth, *anlit*
withal, *aiena*
withdraw, to; *kucha, mokofa*
withe, a hickory; *bisali*
wither, to; *bashechi, bashi, bilakli, bilak- lichi, chunnat ia, shila*
withered; *bashi, bilakli, shila, shulla*
withers; *iachuna, ikkishi, inkoi, yauashka*
withheld, *katapa*
withhold, to; *halalli, katabli*
within; *anunka, anunkaka, tankla*
without; *iiksho, iksho, keyukma, kucha*
without inhabitants, *okla iksho*
withstand, to; *asonali*
witling, *imanukfila iksho*
witness; *aiatokowa, nan anoli, nan ato- kowa anoli, nana pinsa, pisa*
witness; an ear; *haklotokosh anoli*
witness, to; *anoli, ikhana, pisa, yopisa*
witty; *hopoksia, imanukfila tunshpa*
wizard; *hatak holhkunna, hatak isht ahollo*
woe; *ilbasha, na palammi, palammi*

woful; *ilbạshahe ạlhpesa, nukhaⁿklo chito*
wolf, *nashoba*
wolf, he; *nashoba nakni*
wolf, she; *nashoba tek*
wolf, young; *nashobushi*
wolf dog, *nashoba iklạnna*
wolf trap, *nashoba inchuka*
woman; *hatak ohoyo, ohoyo*
woman, aged; *ohoyo kasheho*
woman, despised; *ohoyo makali*
woman, fair; *ohoyo pisa aiukli*
woman, laboring; *ohoyo toⁿksạli*
woman, large; *ohoyo chito*
woman, mad; *ohoyo nukoa*
woman, married; *tekchi*
woman, very young; *ohoyo himmitasi, ohoyo himmitushi*
woman, white; *na hollo ohoyo*
woman, young; *ohoyo himmita*
womanish, *ohoyo holba*
womankind, *ohoyo isht atiaka*
woman's seat, *ohoyo aiomanili*
womb; *imoshạtto, oshạto, ushạtto, ushi afoka, ushi aiạlhto*
women, young; *ohoyo himmithoa*
wonder; *aiisht ahollo, okokkoahni*
wonder, to; *okokkoahni, nanta*
wondered, *nuklakancha*
wonderful, *na fehna*
wonderful work, *na fehna*
wonders, *na fehna*
wonders, to perform; *aiisht ahollochi*
wondrous, *na fehna*
wont; *achaya, chokạmo*
wont, to; *achayạchi*
woo, to; *asilhha*
wood, *iti*
wood, burnt; *iti alua*
wood, green; *iti okchaⁿki, iti okchako, iti okchamali*
wood, to; *iti hoyo, iti ishi*
wood ashes, *hituk chubi*
wood-shaver, *iti ashaⁿfi*
woodcock, the yellow; *fitukhak*
wooden; *iti atoba, iti osh toba*
wooden wheel, *iti chạnaha*
woodland deity, *koⁿwi anuⁿkasha*
woodpecker; *biskinak, fitukhak, hushi iti chanli*
woodpecker, a large, red-headed; *tiⁿkti*
woodpecker, a red-headed; *bakbak, chạkchạk*

woodpecker, a small, red-headed; *chilantak*
woods; *iti anuⁿka, kowi*
woods, being in the; *koⁿwi anuⁿka*
woody; *iti anuⁿka, iti laua*
woof, *isht tạnna*
wool; *chukfạlhpowa hishi, chukfi hishi, hishi*
wool hat, *chukfi hishi shạpo*
woolen, *hishi atoba*
woolen cloth; *chukfi hishi nan tạnna, chukfi hishi tạnna*
woolen yarn, *chukfi hishi shạna*
woolsack, *hishi aiạlhto*
word, *anumpa*
word, short; *anumpa kololi, anumpa koluⁿfa*
Word, the; *ạba anumpa*
word, to; *anumpuli*
word of life, *anumpa isht okchaya*
worded, *anumpa*
wordy, *anumpa laua*
work; *atoksạli, holisso, ikbi, nan toksạli, pilesa, toksạli, toⁿksạli*
work, a day's; *nitak achạfa toⁿksạli*
work, not to; *toksạli*
work, to; *bili, ikbi, ilhkolichi, pilesa, pilesạchi, toksalechi, toksạli, wushohạchi, yamạska, yamạsli, yạmohmi*
work (as a liquid), to; *chibokạchi*
work, to cause to; *pilesạchi, toksalechi*
work, to employ in; *toksalechi*
work a field, to; *osapa toksạli*
work hard, to; *toksạli fehna*
work in the corn, to; *apolichi*
work through, to; *lukali*
work with, to; *ibatoksạlechi, ibatoⁿksạli*
worked, *yạmmạska*
worker, *toksạli*
workhouse, *atoksạli chuka*
working; *toⁿksạli, wushohạchi*
working day, *nitak toⁿksạli*
workingman, *hatak na pilesa*
workman; *hatak toⁿksạli, nam pilesa, toⁿksạli imponna*
workmanship; *imponna, toba*
workshop, *atoksạli chuka*
world; *hatak moma, yakni, yakni lumbo, yakni luⁿsa, yakni moma*
world, the dark; *yakni luⁿsa*
worldly, *yakni*
worm; *hạshwish, lạpchu, shuⁿshi, tạli shạna*

worm, cabbage; *shunshi kalush apa*
worm, large yellow dirt; *yala*
worm, tobacco; *shunshi hakchuma*
worm around, to; *yulullit anya*
worm of a screw, *tali shana*
worm-eaten; *lunkachi, shunshi aiapa*
worming, *yinyiki*
wormy; *shushi isht abeka, shunshi laua*
worn, *lipa*
worn in, to have a place; *lampa*
worn out; *ataha, lipa, sipokni*
worn through, *lukafa*
worried, *tikabi*
worry, to; *afekommi, anumpulechi, tika-bichi*
worse; *aiyabbi, okpulo fehna, okpulo isht inshat ia*
worse, to be made; *inshalit okpulo*
worship, *holitopa*
worship, to; *aholitobli, aiokpachi, aba isht aholitobli, holitobli, holitoblit aiokpachi*
worship Jehovah, to; *Chihowa aiokpachi*
worship of Jehovah, *Chihowa aiokpachi*
worshiper; *aiokpachi, aba isht holitobli, holitobli, isht holitabli, lipiat itola, lipkachi*
worshiper of Jehovah, *Chihowa aiokpachi*
worshipful, *aiokpachi alhpesa*
worst, *okpulo inshaht tali*
worth; *aiilli, holitopa, ialli*
worthily, *holitopat*
worthiness, *holitopa*
worthless; *ahoba, aknanka, makali, nanka*
worthless, to render; *makalichi*
worthless man, *hatak keyu*
worthy; *ahoba, alhpesa, alhpiesa, holitopa*
worthy man, *hatak holitopa*
wot, to; *ikhana*
would; *hinla, hinlatok, hinlatuk, okbano*
would have; *ahetok, ahetuk*
wound, *holoti*
wound, a; *abasha, achanya, ahotupa, anala*
wound, to; *anali, bili, hotupachi, hotupali, mitaffi, nali, nalichi*
wound, to cause to be; *afolichi*
wound round; *afoa, afoyua, apakfoa, apakfopa, affoa, alhfoa*
wound the feelings, to; *hotupali*
wounded; *achanya, bila, hotupa, nala*

wounded heart; *chunkash hutupa, chunkash nala*
wounder; *bili, hotupali, nali*
wounding, *hotupali*
wove, *tanna*
woven; *alhtannafo, tanna*
woven wool, *chukfi hishi tanna*
wrangle, *itachoa*
wrangle, to; *achowa*
wrangler, *itachoa*
wranglesome, *itachoa shali*
wrap round, to; *afoli, apakfobli, apakfoblichi, apakfoli*
wrap round with, to; *isht afoli*
wrap up, to; *abonullichi, bonulli*
wrapped round, *apakfopa*
wrapped up; *abonunta, bonkachi*
wrapper; *abonunta, afoachi, bonulli*
wrath; *aiisikkopa, isht nukhobela, nukhobela, nukkilli, nukoa, palammi*
wrathful, *nukoa shali*
wrathless, *nukoa keyu*
wreak, to; *onochi*
wreath; *aialipa, ialipa hashtap toba*
wreathe, to; *ialipeli*
wreathed, *ialipa*
wreathen, *poshola*
wreck, *aiokpulunka*
wren; *chikchik, chiloha, okchiloha*
wrench, *shanni*
wrench, to; *shanaiachi, shanni*
wrenched, *shana*
wrest, to; *ishi, shanni*
wrested, *shana*
wrestle, to; *ishi, itishi*
wrestler; *itishi, itishi imponna*
wrestling, *itishi*
wretch; *hatak makali, hatak okpulo, hatak yoshoba*
wretched; *ilbasha, ilbashahe alhpesa*
wretchedness; *aiilbasha, ilbasha*
wright, *tonksali imponna*
wring, to; *bushli, ilbashachi, okbushli, shanni*
wringed, *shana*
wringer; *bushli, shanni*
wrinkle; *shikofa, shikowa, shinoa, shinofa, shinoli, shinonoa, yikkowa, yikokunwa, yikotua, yinyiki*
wrinkle, to; *shikofa, shikoffi, shikoli, shikowa, shinoa, shinofa, shinoffi, shinoli, shinonoa, shinononkachi, shinonolichi, yikkowa, yikoli, yikota, yikotachi, yikotua, yikowachi, yikulli, yinyikechi, yinyiki*

wrinkle, to cause to; *shikolichi, shino-lichi, yikoli, yikolichi, yikotachi.*

wrinkled; *shikofa, shikoli, shikowa, shi-noa, shinofa, shinoli, shinonoa, shino-noⁿkachi, yafimpa, yikkowa, yikofa, yikoha, yikokoa, yikota, yikotua, yiⁿyiki*

wrist, *ibbak aska*

wrist-bands; *ibbak tilokachi abiha, ibbak tilokachi afohoma, ilefoka shakba afohoma*

wrist joint; *ibbak itachakalli, ibbak tilo-kachi*

writ, *holisso kallo*

write, to; *holisso ikbi, holissochi, laⁿfi*

writer; *hatak holissochi, holissochi, laⁿfi, na holissochi*

writhe, to; *shana, shanakachi*

writhed, *shana*

writing, *holisso*

writing master, *holissochi ikhananchi*

writing paper, *holisso tohbi*

writing table; *aholissochi, aioⁿholissochi*

writing tablet, *aholissochi*

written; *holisso, laⁿfa*

written on, *holisso*

wrong; *alhpesa, inla, okpulo, yoshoba*

wrong, to; *ilbashachi*

wrong side out; *anukfilema, anukfile-moa, anukpilefa*

wrongdoer, *ilbashachi*

wronged, *ilbasha*

wronger, *ilbashachi*

wrongful; *alhpesa, ilbashahe alhpesa*

wroth; *anukhobela, nukoa fehna*

wrought, *toba*

wrung out; *busha, okbusha*

wry; *shanaia, shana*

wry mouth, *itiboshali*

wry-necked, *shanaia*

yacht, royal; *miⁿko iⁿpeni*

yam; *ahe, ahe kashaha*

Yankee, *Miliki hatak*

yard; *holihta, isht alhpisa, nan isht apesa, wanuta*

yard, door; *wanuta*

yardstick; *iti isht alhpisa, nan tanna isht alhpisa*

yarrow, *fani hasimbish holba*

yawl; *peni, penushi*

yawn, to; *chisemo, hawa, yichina*

ye; *hachi, hachia, hachik, hachim, ha-chishno, has, hash, ho*

yea; *ome, yau*

year, *afammi*

year, one; *afammi achafa*

yearling; *afammi, atampa, wak atampa, atanapa*

yearly; *afammikma, afammaiyukali*

yearn, to; *nukhaⁿklo*

yeast; *nan isht shatammichi, paska isht shatammichi*

yell; *paⁿya, tahpala*

yell, to; *paⁿya, tahpala, tasali*

yelling, *tasaha*

yellow; *alakna, lakna*

yellow, to; *alakna, laknachi*

yellow dye, *isht laknachi*

yellow dyestuff, *nan isht laknachi*

yellow fever, *abeka lakna*

yellow hammer, *fitukhak*

yellow jacket; *yakni foi, yakni foishke*

yellow jacket's nest, *yakni foi*

yellow man, *hatak lakna*

yellow negro, *hatak lusa lakna*

yellow woodcock, *fitukhak*

yellowish, *laknoba*

yells, one who; *paⁿya*

yelp, to; *biⁿka, biⁿkbia, wohwoha, wohwah, wolichi, wowoha*

yeoman, *tashka*

yeomanry, *tashka aliha*

yes; *aⁿh, akat, iⁿ, uⁿkah, yau*

yesterday, *pilashash*

yesternight, *ninak ash*

yet; *kiⁿ, moma*

yield, to; *haklo, issa, kinafa, nutaka ia, waya, wayachi*

yielded, *issa*

yoke; *ichapoa, ikonlabana, tuklo*

yoke, to; *ichabli, ikonlabanali*

yoked, *ikonlabana*

yokefellow, *ichapa*

yolk; *akaⁿk ushilakna, lakna*

yon, *yamma*

yond, *yamma*

yonder, *yamma*

you; *chim, hachi, hachiⁿ, hachia, hachik, hachim, hachin, hachishno, has, hash, is, ish, oh*

young; *himmita, himmitasi, himmita-cheka, himmithoa, himmitushi, himmona, ushi*

young, to be with; *ushi kaiya*

young, to bring forth; *ushi cheli*

young, to go with; *ushi shali*

young, to make; *himmitachi*

young man; *hatak himmita, hatak himmi-taiyachi, hatak himmⁱtacheka, hatak him-mithoa*

young ones; *himmithoa, ushi*
younger; *himmak, laua*
youngest, *isht aiopi*
youngish, *himmita chohmi*
youngster, *himmita*
your; *chim, chin, hachi, hachi^n, hachim, hachimmi, hachin, hachishno*
your, to become; *hachimmi toba*
your own, *hachishno*
yourself; *chishno akinli, hachishno*
youth, *himmita*
youth, a; *hatak himmita*
youth, the; *himmita aliha, himmithoa*
youthful, *himmita*

zambo; *hatak lusa isht atiaka, hatak lusa ushi*
zany; *itakhapuli shali, yopula shali*
zeal, *aiyimita*
zealot, *hatak aiyimita*
zealous; *achillita, chilita, chu^{n}kash yiminta, yiminta*
zealous, to make; *chilitachi*
zebra, *isuba basoa*
zenith, *tabokoli*
zephyr, *hashi aiokatula mali*
zest, *kashaha*
zest, to; *kashahachi*
zigzag, *yi^{n}yiki*
zone; *apakfopa, folota*

CPSIA information can be obtained at www.ICGtesting.com
Printed in the USA
LVOW012307151212

311834LV00004B/715/P